DATE DUE

DE 1 98			
NO 27 00			
DE 20 00			
FE 17 03			
AP 21 '03			
MY 12 03			
AG 6 03			
NO 11 08			

DEMCO 38-296

The North and South Korean Political Systems

A Comparative Analysis

The North and South Korean Political Systems

A Comparative Analysis

Sung Chul Yang

Westview Press • Seoul Press

The North and South Korean Political Systems

Published in the U.S. in 1994 and distributed exclusively throughout
the world, except in Japan and Korea by
Westview Press, Inc.
5500 Central Avenue
Boulder, CO 80301-2877
U.S.A.
Phone: (303)444-3541 Fax: (303)449-3356

ISBN: 0-8133-8862-7 9000
Library of Congress Catalog Card Number: 94-4443

Published in Korea in 1994 by
Seoul Press
Jin Wang Kim, Publisher
C.P.O. Box 8850
Seoul 100, Korea
Phone: (02)275-6566 Fax: (02)278-2551

ISBN: 89-7225-021-X 93350

Copyright © 1994 by Sung Chul Yang

Printed in the Republic of Korea by Seoul Press

PREFACE

For nearly five decades Korean people in the both halves of the country have been living under two diametrically different political and economic systems with little or no mutual contacts and communications.
Still, the cultural homogeneity and national affinity of the Korean people continue to be overwhelming. Unfortunately, however, this rather
untenable situation of political and economic experiments imposed upon
the culturally homogenous people is likely to remain so in the foreseeable future. The two states in the Korean Peninsula cannot be easily
united into one statehood as did the former West Germany and East
Germany. An attempt to emulate German unification by Korea will be
near suicidal. Until and unless the two political and economic systems
presently persisting on both sides of the Korean Peninsula become more
comparable and compatible, it is not only inconceivable but unwise for
government policy-planners or others to hasten a genuine and bloodless
unification.

The two systems and two states presently existing in the Korean
Peninsula are like the two bowls molded out of the same clay. The main
focus of this study has been to find North and South Korea's *differences*
of recent origins rather than their basic *sameness* of long standing. To
pursue the clay-bowl analogy further, the primary interest has been to
examine these two new bowls, their respective shapes (political structures and economic models), usages (political process and economic
policy), primary users (political elites and masses) and things (political
outputs and economic performance).

For a long time, I have been advocating that the two Koreas are the
best living laboratories for comparativists, be they political scientists,
sociologists, economists or other social scientists. To compare two
Koreas' political processes and economic performance is, for example,

different from studying the same topics of two states. For one thing, if enormous differences exist in political processes and economic performance in the both halves today, an explanation must necessarily lie in the two entirely different political and economic systems they adopted in 1948. In analyzing both Koreas' diametrically opposed political and economic realities, cultural and other non-politico-economic factors are mostly *given* or irrelevant, and they cannot be the main explanatory variables.

The first draft of this study was completed around 1986 in the United States, the year that I repatriated to Korea. I felt then that it was incomplete for publication. Thus, I have been doing continuous research to revise and update the information for nearly seven years while readjusting to the life in my native land. In the summer of 1992, I finally undertook the revamping and revising of this manuscript.

Between 1986 and 1993 not only North Korea and South Korea but the whole world had undergone a cataclysmic metamorphoses. The seismic political and economic transformations at home and abroad had to be incorporated into this text. During this period North Korea has become further isolated from the rest of the world, and it is now an economic basket case as well as an international test case for nuclear nonproliferation. South Korea in the meantime has successfully moved away from a prolonged praetorian authoritarianism to a working democracy. The former Communist Soviet Union and Eastern Europe have also been erased from the world map and are still struggling to create new political and economic identities, let alone some agreeable political boundaries.

This book is the first comprehensive analysis of North and South Korean political systems and processes in a systematic and comparative perspective. It examines the evolution and development of the two systems from 1945 to the present. It consists of six parts. In Parts One and Two both the Korean political heritage and the contemporary political background for the emergence of the two separate regimes on the Korean Peninsula are explicated in detail as a way of preliminary introduction. In Parts Three and Four the North Korean political system as a totalitarian political order and the South Korean political system as a democratizing political order are scrutinized in a greater detail, respectively. In Part Five, the differences in both Korea's economic systems, economic strategies and policies and their actual economic performance for the last five decades are studied on the basis of available economic data. Finally, Part Six focuses on four critical and chronic issues which two Koreas have confronted over the years and require resolution. They include the problem of political succession in particular and of democratization and liberalization in general, the continuing arms race and twin fortifications, and two models of education and of reunification.

The summer in Seoul is unbearably hot and humid. During the summer of 1992, my wife, who helped in the final editing of the manuscript, and I suffered through the heat to complete the manuscript in the present form. I am sure, we will remember the ordeal for a long time to come. Besides my wife, I owe the completion of this work to many people who rendered assistance over the many years it took to complete. Just a few who have given direct assistance are acknowledged here. Mr. Jin Wang Kim, the President of Seoul Press, generously and enthusiastically supported the manuscript project by typesetting the work which already looks like a published work. Professors Young Whan Kihl of Iowa State University, Chin Park and Reinhard Drifte of the University of New Castle upon Tyne in England have been helpful in locating a prospective publisher. My big Mahalo goes to Mrs. Myungjin Chung who almost magically transformed my numerous unreadable chicken-scratches into a legible printout. My appreciation is also extended to Ms. Susan McEachern, Senior editor of Westview Press, who corresponded with me for more them a year in the process of having this book published.

Last but not least, I dedicate this book to my wife, Daisy Chung Chin Lee, and my children, Eugene and Susan, with whom I share the joy of living and loving. This book, I hope, will finally put to rest my children's constant inquiries, "What happened to your book, Dad?"

Seoul, Korea, 1994

CONTENTS

CONCLUSION

APPENDICES

LIST OF MAPS

PART I

THE KOREAN POLITICAL HERITAGE

CHAPTER 1

A HISTORICAL OVERVIEW

History, which undertakes to record the transactions of the past, for the instruction of future ages, would ill serve that honorable office if she condescended to plead the cause of tyrants, or to justify the maxims of persecution....

Edward Gibbon[1]

If all human beings are in certain respects like all other human beings, like some other human beings, and like no other human beings,[2] so are nations. Korea as a nation is no exception in this regard. It shares some universal political qualities with other nations, and possesses at the same time unique political qualities and paradoxes as well.

The history of Korea dates back to the Paleolithic period. Paleolithic remains and sites have been found in virtually every part of the Korean Peninsula. It is generally estimated that Paleolithic man began to inhabit the Korean Peninsula some 40,000 or 50,000 years ago, although the Korean people of today may or may not have descended from these Paleolithic inhabitants in the Peninsula.[3]

Around the second century B.C. with the advent of the use of the bronze implements, the walled-town states with articulated political structures emerged in the Korean Peninsula. In the northern region, the walled-town states such as Puyŏ in the Sungari River basin, Yemaek along the middle reaches of the Aprok (Yalu) River, Old Chosŏn in the Liao and Taedong River basins, Imdun in the Hamhŭng plain on the northeast seacoast and Chinbŏn in the Hwanghae area were notable.

3

To the south of the Han River, the state of Chin was the typical walled-town state. The most advanced among these was Old Chosŏn whose existence was known to and recorded in China.[4]

The Korean *nation* has existed for millennia, if a nation stands for an aggregation of people sharing basically the same culture, language, history, religion and ethnic origin (or some combination of these) in a particular territory.[5] Ethnically, like the origins of other national groups, the Korean people probably descended from the various confluent ethnic groups in surrounding regions—Chinese, Mongols, Manchurians and Japanese. Yemaek people, according to one study, constitute the core ethnic element which has developed into the people known as Koreans today.[6] Be it as it may, the Korean people have evolved from a slow and tedious process. More than fifty thousands years have elapsed in the evolution of people known as Koreans.[7]

Korea was founded by its legendary primogenitor, *Tankun*, some 2,333 years before Christ. The recorded history of the Korean state(s), as a ruling organization that monopolized the legitimate use of physical force, began during the era of the Three Kingdoms (57 B.C.-661 A.D.), if not earlier.[8]

The first united Korean nation-state was established in 676 by the Silla Dynasty (57 B.C.-935 A.D.). With the help of China's T'ang Dynasty (618-907 A.D.), Silla unified Korea by defeating two other indigenous Korean kingdoms, Koguryŏ (37 B.C.-668 A.D.) and Paekche (18 B.C.-661 A.D.).

Silla's unification of Korea in 676 can be interpreted in three ways. First, Silla's alliance with T'ang resulted in involvement of foreigners into Korean politics.[9] Silla with the help of T'ang's military forces defeated the indigenous coalition forces of Koguryŏ and Paekche.

Second, the vast territorial loss deprived Korea of its status as a tripartite power in East Asia along with China and Japan. Silla's unification paid a dear price—the loss of Manchuria, which had been a part of the Koguryŏ Kingdom. Several attempts by Silla to regain the lost territories in Manchuria have been unsuccessful.[10]

Third, the Kingdom of Parhae(698-926), which was founded by Taejoyŏng, a former Koguryŏ general, with his fellow expatriates of the fallen Koguryŏ, soon controlled most of the former Koguryŏ territory north of Taedog River. In that sense, the Silla's unification of the Three Kingdoms was a misnomer. Silla incorporated Paekche, but most of the former Koguryŏ territory was under Parhae's control.

Silla's unification, then, produced a divided Korea—Silla and Parhae which fell to the Khitans in 926. The united Silla (676-935) survived for more than 200 years before mass rebellions erupted around 888, which divided the Korean Peninsula into three new kingdoms; the Later Koguryŏ (901-917), the Later Paeckche (900-936), and the United Silla (676-935). Koryŏ, an outgrowth of the Later Koguryŏ, established the second united nation-state on the Korean Peninsula in 936 by absorbing the other two. The Koryŏ unification, then, was the first bona fide united Korean state, which occupied most of the present Korean Peninsula south of Ch'ŏngch'ŏn River. The United Koryŏ lasted five hundred years before it fell to the Yi Dynasty.

The Yi Dynasty (1393-1910) was created by Yi Sŏng-kye, a commanding general of Koryŏ, who successfully staged a military coup in 1388. During the reign of Sejong the Great (r. 1418-50), the present Korean national boundary in the north, marked by Aprok (Yalu) and Tuman (Tumen) rivers, was formalized, and it has remained ever since. The Yi Dynasty ruled Korea for over five hundred years until it fell a victim to the Japanese colonial rule in 1910.

The Japanese rule, the first outright foreign colonization of the entire Korean Peninsula, ended in 1945 when Japan was defeated in World War II. The price of Korean liberation from Japan in 1945 was, however, arbitrary and artificial partition of the country by the United States with the tacit agreement of the former Soviet Union. The physical partition of the country, the human separation and the political and ideological rivalry between the two halves have persisted ever since.

MAP 1-1. Designless Pottery Sites in Korea
(Bronze Age, ca. 800-300 B.C.)

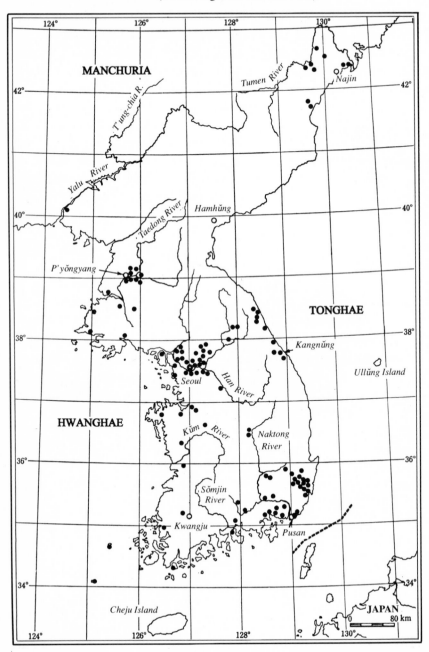

MAP 1-2. Korea in the Confederated Kingdoms Period
(ca. 1st-3rd Centuries A.D.)

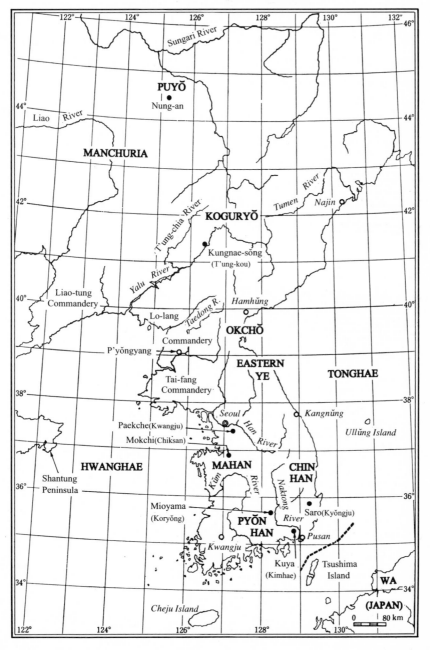

MAP 1-3. The Early Three Kingdoms (5th Century)

MAP 1-4. The Early Three Kingdoms (7th Century)

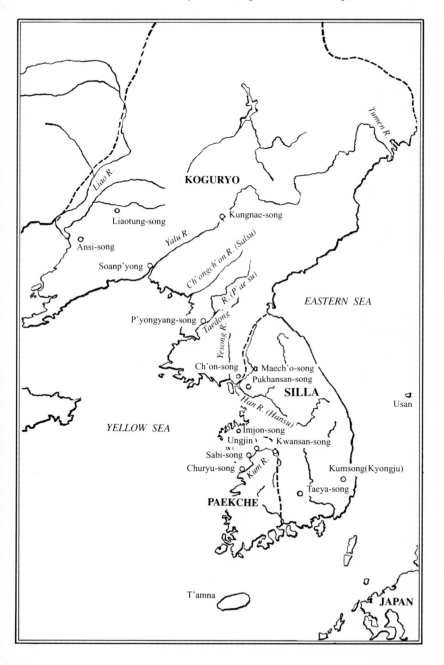

Notes:

1. Edward Gibbon, *The Decline and Fall of the Roman Empire*, 3 vols. (New York: Modern Library, 1980), 1: 453-54.
2. Clyde Kluckhohn and Henry A. Murray, "Personality Formation: The Determinants," in Clyde Kluckhohn and Henry A. Murray eds., *Personality in Nature, Society and Culture* (New York: Knopf, 1953), p. 53.
3. For details, see Pyŏng-do Lee, *Kuksa Daekwan* [Outline of Korean National History] (Seoul: Pomunkak, 1957), pp. 15-21 and his *Hankuk Kodaesa Yonku* [The Study of Korean Ancient History] (Seoul: Pakyŏng-sa, 1976), especially chapters one and two, pp. 27-64; Woo-keun Han, *The History of Korea*, trans. Kyung-shik Lee and Grafton K. Mintz (Honolulu: East-West Center Press, 1970), pp. 3-8; William E. Henthorn, *A History of Korea* (New York: The Free Press, 1971), pp. 6-17; Ki-baik Lee, *A New History of Korea*, trans. Edward W. Wagner (Seoul: Iljokak, 1984), pp. 1-2. T'ae-wŏn Kwŏn, *Hankuk Sahoe P'ungsoksa Yŏnku* [A Study of Korean Cultural History] (Seoul: Kyŏngin Munhwa-sa, 1980), pp. 12-67. A critical view on the origins of Korean people, which differs from the writers of twenty-eight-volume *Hankuk-sa*, published by South Korea's National History Publications Committee (Kuksap'yŏnch'anwiwŏnhoe), is found in Byŏng-sik Han, "The Problems of National Origin Seen in *Hankuk-sa*" in *Hanyang* (January-February and March-April, 1984), pp. 118-126 and pp. 122-132, respectively.
4. For details, see Pyŏng-do Lee, *Hankuk Kodaesa Yŏnku*, especially, pp. 44-96.
5. The term "nation" generally stands for a large group of people who share common traditions and culture and usually a common language. Haas, for instance, defined nation as "a socially mobilized body of individuals, believing themselves to be united by some set of characteristics that differentiate them (in their own minds) from "outsiders," and striving to create or maintain their own state." See Ernst B. Haas, *Beyond the Nation-state: Functionalism and International Organization* (Stanford: Stanford University Press, 1968), p. 465. The term, "state," generally consists of a permanent population with a defined territory and a government which is capable of both enlisting people's habitual obedience and entering into relations with other states. In Europe, with the emergence of the nation-state in the fifteenth and sixteenth centuries, the nation has been equated with the state. Despite these distinctions, the confusion surrounding the terms, nation, state and nation-state has not dissipated. A source of confusion stems from its misuse, e.g., in the United States, the *states* such as Kentucky and California are only constituent part of the American state; "nations" in the United Nations mean "states," not "nations." The political reality also contributes to such confusion, e.g., the former Soviet

Union was a state consisting of many nations; Korea (and Germany was) is "one nation with two states" or "two regimes in one state." For a discussion of this confusion, see, for instance, Cecil V. Crabb, Jr., *Nations in a Multipolar World* (New York: Harper and Row, 1968), pp. 2-4 and pp. 50-68; Karl W. Deutsch, *Nationalism and Social Communication* (Cambridge: The M.I.T. Press, 1953, 1966), *passim.* A good survey of the concepts such as nation, nationality, and nation-state is found in Dankwart A. Rustow, *A World of Nations: Problems of Political Modernization* (Washington, D.C.: The Brookings Institution, 1967), especially, pp. 1-134. For a discussion of the meaning of (nation) in the Korean context, see Ki-pyŏk Ch'a, "Resistant Nationalism in Foreign Relations" (in Korea) Il-ch'ŏl Shin, "Resistant Nationalism in Internal Settings;" and also, Yong-hee Lee, "The Concept of Nationalism," in Chae-bong No, ed., *Hankuk Minjok chui wa Kukjechŏngch'i* [Korean Nationalism and International Politics] (Seoul: Minum-sa, 1983), pp. 13-32, pp. 69-86 and pp. 211-239. For an analysis of the concept of nation in North and South Korea, see Sang-yong Choi, "A Comparative Study on the Concepts of Nation in South and North Korea" (in Korean), *Unification Policy Quarterly* (Winter 1978), pp. 12-44.

6. Pyŏng-do Lee, *Kuksa Daekwan,* pp. 11-15; T'ae-wŏn Kim, *Op. Cit.,* pp. 12-70.

7. Ki-baik Lee, *A New History of Korea,* pp. 1-8.

8. For a detailed analysis of Korea's ancient historical developments, see Pyŏng-do Lee, *Hankuk Kodaesa Yŏnku* [A Study of Ancient Korean History] (Seoul: Pakyŏng-sa, 1976); Henthorn, *Op. Cit.,* pp. 18-32. For a study of the evolution of the Silla state, see Chong-uk Lee, *Silla Kuka Hyŏngsŏngsa Yŏnku* [A Study of Silla's Development as a State] (Seoul: Iljokak, 1982), especially, pp. 12-73.

9. The earliest recorded history of foreign invasion in the Korean Peninsula occurred between 108 and 109 B.C. when the Emperor Wu Ti of China's Han Dynasty created four colonies or commanderies: Nangnang (Lo-lang in Chinese), Chinbŏn (Chen-fan), Imdun (Lin-t'un) and Hyŏnt'o (Hsuant'u) in today's northwestern Korea. For details, see Pyŏng-do Lee, *Hankuk Kodaesa Yŏnku,* pp. 97-112; Woo-keun Han, *Op. Cit.,* pp. 12-22; Ki-baik Lee, *Op. Cit.,* pp. 19-21.

10. After the collapse of Koguryŏ, Parhae Kingdom (698-926) was created by the people of Koguryŏ in the Manchurian area. When it fell in 926 to the indigenous Malgal people, Manchuria ceased to serve as a stage for the unfolding drama of Korean history. For details, see Ki-baek Lee, *Op. Cit.,* pp. 88-91; Woo-keun Han, *Op. Cit.,* pp. 86-89.

CHAPTER 2

POLITICAL CULTURE
AND TRADITIONS

*It would be absurd to cut every culture down to the Procrustean bed
of some catchword characterization.*

Ruth Benedict[1]

*It may be said of Korea that there is no country of comparable signifi-
cance concerning which so many people are ignorant.*

Cornelius Osgood[2]

If the present political scene in the Korean Peninsula is partially, if
not entirely, the mirror image of the country's political past, an understanding of its political culture and traditions, however perfunctory, is in
order. For, the Korean political culture, shaped by its people's common
historical and political experiences, continues to influence the political
behavior of both its rulers and people.

Like cultures of other traditional societies which can be divide into
"high" and "low," "great" and "little," or "elite" and "mass" cultures,
the traditional Korean political culture is by and large bifurcated, one
rooted in the ruling elite, and the other in the masses.[3] Although these
two cultures are, in reality, meshed together in a seamless whole, they
are divided here into two "boxes" for the sake of analysis.

Authoritarian political order, class-based socio-political structure,
centralized bureaucratism and political longevity, factionalism and civil-

13

military rivalry, land-based power dynamics, state religion, and external linkages and pacifism represent Korea's "elite political culture," whereas armed revolts, peasant rebellions, nativistic resilience and nationalism, its "mass political culture."[4]

As it will become clear in the following chapters, some fragments of these "two cultures" survive even in contemporary political culture of the two Korean regimes. Traditions, including political ones, are indeed diehard. Revolutions attempt to reshape traditions but, in the long run, they accommodate traditions, not the reverse.

Elite Political Culture

Authoritarianism

In the political history of all nations, an authoritarian order has been a rule. Even in our world of some 180 nations, an autocratic or authoritarian order is the rule, not an exception. Traditional authoritarianism,[5] characterized by a centralized bureaucratic monarchy, may indeed be one of the most enduring political traditions in Korea.

Authoritarianism exists if, among other things, the ruler or the ruling elites of a given political system perceive the law as a device for controlling the subject rather than as a principle regulating relations between themselves and their people.

Korea has had its share of authoritarian traditions. The government office or department which administered law in the Koryŏ and Yi dynasties, for example, was called respectively *hyŏngbu* [the Department of Punishment] and *hyŏngjo* [the Ministry of Punishment]. *Hyŏng* literally means "punishment."[6] The Korean conception of law was akin to that of the Chinese Legalist School of the third century B.C. The law was "a tool of absolutism to aid in administrative unification." It was "an arm of the state."[7]

The law in Korean, Chinese and Japanese life was not developed to protect either the individual's political rights or his or her economic position. Nor did it represent an accumulation of collective experiences of the society.[8] The notion that a process of law is essential for the protection of life, liberty and property was simply not "Oriental." In the Korean political tradition, law was "an instrument of chastising the vicious and the depraved." Further, Pyŏng-choon Hahm wrote:

> It [law] was an unpleasant necessity prescribed by the failure of reason in politics. Law as a political norm always meant the positive law. It was something that had been legislated by the ruler. It was sharply distinguished from custom. It always signified a norm with physical force as sanction behind it. It was therefore synonymous with punishment, no more no less.[9]

The role of the Korean equivalent of the Western ministry of "law" or "justice" (*ius, droit* or *recht*) was to "punish" subjects who failed to comply with the government orders, rules and laws than to administer law, to uphold justice or to adjudicate disputes. To put it another way, the department of punishment existed in the Koryŏ and the Yi dynasties, not the department of law or justice.

The concept of kingly authority evolved gradually in Korea. During the period of Wiman Chosŏn (194 B.C.?-106 B.C.), the farming population in the villages was ruled by the elites in the walled-town states. In Puyŏ and Koguryŏ, the two northern Korean kingdoms, for instance, their kings were chosen by some form of elective process in their early formative periods, and they were held accountable for poor harvests and were often either replaced or even killed for such "failures." Noteworthy also is that as early as in 49 A.D., the Puyŏ ruler adopted the use of the term, *wang*, the Chinese appellation for "king."[10] It was around the second or the third century in Puyŏ and Koguryŏ, respectively, that a loosely organized confederated kingdom gradually transformed itself into a centralized state with kingly authority.

In Koguryŏ the right to the throne was permanently secured by the Ko house of the Kyeru lineage in the time of King T'aejo (r. 53-146?). During the reign of Kogukch'ŏn (r. 179-196), the idea of kingly authority in a centralized state began to take root. Under his reign the pattern of succession to the throne changed from brother-brother to father-son. In Paekche a centralized aristocratic state came into being during the reign of Kŭn Ch'ogo (r. 346-375). In Silla the father-son succession pattern was established during the reign of Nulchi (r. 417-458), and an incipient centralized aristocratic state emerged in the reign of Pŏphŭng (r. 514-540).[11]

The political traditions of father-son hereditary succession and a centralized monarchical authoritarian order made further entrenchment in the subsequent Korean kingdoms—the Unified Silla (676-935), Koryŏ (918-1392) and Yi Chosŏn (1392-1910). The authoritarian political order continued under the Japanese colonial rule (1910-1945) after the demise of the Yi Dynasty. Nor has this tradition shown a sign of decline in the post-World War Korean politics of division.

The Korean political tradition of an authoritarian order under a centralized bureaucracy has existed throughout 2,200 years of its recorded history. In other words, Korea lacks democratic and liberal political traditions embodied in concepts such as law and justice, civil liberties and civil rights, local autonomy, decentralization and political pluralism.[12] It is true that as a backdrop of this prevailing authoritarian political tradition, there have been numerous governmental institutions which were rudimentarily, at least, democratic. The historical records, for instance, indicate that in the formative period of ancient Silla the leaders were elected by lineage group assembly.[13] In Koguryŏ *Taedaero* [the Chief Minister] was elected by a council of aristocrats. Paekche had *Chŏngsa-am*, the "rock." A name of three or four possible candidates were put under it, and some time later the person whose name had the special sign or signature was chosen as chief minister.

The gradual evolution of Silla's political institution from *Kongch'ŏng* [the Village Council], *Chŏngsa-tang* [the Political Affairs Council] to Nam-tang, the government headquarters for a council of the king and his ministers, and to *Hwan-baek* [the Council of Nobles] is another example. *Hwabaek* was an assembly of Silla nobility which reached its decisions by consensus on the most important matters of state, such as succession to the throne, the declaration of war and the adoption of state religion.[14] The Koryŏ Dynasty's *Todang* [Top'yŏng' uisasa] [the Privy Council] and the Yi Dynasty's *Uijŏngbu* [the State Council] were similarly structured.[15]

This evidence suggests that kingly authority in traditional Korea was not always autocratic, i.e., monarchs often shared power with their ministers and nobles. Still, the mass remained their subjects, who could not participate in the political process. In that sense, the Korean monarchies, be they the Three Kingdoms, the Koryŏ or the Yi dynasties, were far from being *democratic.* To use Almond-Powell's typology, traditional Korean political culture was a prototype of "subject political culture."[16] The Korean mass publics were subjects who passively obeyed government authorities and laws, but they seldom participated in political processes.

In brief, the authoritarian tradition in Korean politics is indeed long, while the democratic experiment is rather short and is largely of recent Western origin. Most surveys on the South Korean people's political belief system, for instance, have shown weak commitment to and respect for, fundamental democratic values and beliefs such as political competition, majority rule and minority rights, political accountability and assertive self-role perception. Conversely, their influence from authoritarian values remains strong and persistent.[17]

Although no comparable surveys on the North Korean people are available, their traditional political belief system may not have been drastically altered even under the present communist system. Or, more accurately, the current North Korean regime has effectively utilized the authoritarian tradition to its maximum advantage. As Stephen White pointed out, political-cultural variables are not the only and may not even be the main ones that explain a contemporary political system, but even in communist states which claim to have broken decisively with their traditional inheritance, there seem "good grounds for regarding pre-revolutionary patterns of political belief and behavior as at least an important contributory factor in any adequate explanation of their contemporary politics.[18] In a nutshell, both North Korea's present communist totalitarian rule and South Korea's authoritarian and currently democratizing politics, albeit their fundamental dissimilarities, have a common authoritarian root, deeply imbedded in the Korean historical and cultural psyche.

Class Society

As noted previously, it was around the second century in ancient Korea when the division occurred between the peasants living in the farming villages and the ruling elites residing in the walled towns. The majority of the farming population at that time were free peasants, and below them were some slaves and tenant farmers or *yuin* [wanderers]. The ruling elites also maintained a large retinue of household slaves.

In the sixth century the *kolp'um* [bone-rank] system was introduced in Silla as its ruling class system. Under this system social status was determined by heredity, and kinship and marriage systems were strictly controlled. At the top of the society were two classes called *sŏnggol* [sacred blood or hallowed-bone] and *chingol* [true blood or true-bone]. They were made up exclusively of the royal family. Below them were six grades called *tup'um* [head ranks], where head-rank six was the highest and head-rank one, the lowest. [19]

In the final years of Silla, the powerful local gentry, *sŏngju* [castle lord], appeared with its private army and military garrison, as Silla's local maritime trade with T'ang China and Japan flourished. But the local gentry, largely defiant of the central royal authority, was short-lived. The local gentry class gave in to Koryŏ, the new centralized monarchy, which reunified the country after the fall of Silla.

In Koryŏ a much more sophisticated *ban* [class or orders] was created. The population segments in each class were assigned certain rights and obligations, in principle at least, on a hereditary basis. *Munban* [civil official order] filled civil offices, *muban* [military official order], military offices, *namban* [court functionary order], palace service offices and *kunban* [the soldiering order], filled the ranks of the military units. Below these orders were local and central minor bureaucrats, artisans and the like. The bottom rungs of the society were made up of *paekchŏng* [butchers] and *ch'ŏnin* [low-born] or slaves, both of whom were not eligible to hold a government office.[20]

The introduction of *kwakŏ* [a civil service examination system] and *Nobiankŏmbŏp* [The Slave Review Act] had an impact on the Korean class structure. A rudimentary form of a state examination system for the selection of government officials was introduced in 788 A.D. in Silla, but it was Koryŏ's Kwangjong (r. 949-75) who, with the help of Shuang Chi, a Chinese embassy member from the state of the Later Chou, institutionalized a civil service examination system in Korea in 958 as the principal avenue through which a person can enter the government bureaucracy. Two years earlier Kwangjong enacted the Slave Review Act to reduce the number of bloated slave population. Both moves by Kwangjong were calculated to strengthen his centralized monarchical power.

The civil service examination limited the number of civil and military officials recruited from the hereditary ranks (mostly from the late Silla royal families and /or the descendants of the Koryŏ's founding fathers). Technically, any *yangin* [a free-born] except *ch'ŏnmin* [low-born] was eligible to take the civil service examination, but in reality it was impossible for the general peasant population, free or low-born, to take the examination, let alone pass it.[21] Likewise, the Slave Review Act was enacted to control the power of the local gentry who held a large number of slaves, their main source of economic and military strength. The king restored "slaves," who were originally commoners, to free status, thereby, mitigating the power base of the local gentry.[22]

The Yi Dynasty also enforced a rigid ruling class system, although it was much more broadly based than Silla's true-bone royal aristocracy or Koryŏ's class-based hereditary aristocracy. Yi's new ruling class, *yangban* [two classes or two orders], literally meant both the civil and military officials. However, it generally referred to the civil officials, the literati, because the military officials were considered socially and politically inferior. *Yangban* virtually monopolized the Yi dynasty's bureaucracy by a variety of control mechanisms by: (1) maintaining a clan exogamous and class endogamous marriage system; (ii) banning children from second marriages of *yangban* class and their illegitimate children from key government posts; (iii) segregating *yangban*'s residence from the rest of the populace; (iv) discriminating against people from regions such as Pyŏngan and Hamgyŏng provinces; and (v) managing the educational institutions and, thereby, controlling the state examination system.[23]

The Yi Dynasty's socio-political class system was divided broadly into four strata. At the top were *yangban,* the ruling elites who virtually monopolized both power and wealth (land).[24] *Yangban* occupied the top class, *sa* [literati or gentry] of *sa-nong-gong-sang,* the so-called four social class division—literati, farmers, artisans and merchants.

Next were *chungin* [middle class people], who were medical officers, translator-interpreters, technicians in the astronomy and meteorology office, accountants, law clerks, scribes and artists. Included also in this class were *sŏri* [petty clerks], *ajŏn* [local civil functionaries] and *kun'gyo* [military cadre members].

To the third class, *yangin* or *sangin* [good people or common people], belonged the majority of the people who were engaged in farming, industry and trade. *Ch'ŏnin* [lowly class people or slaves] were at the bottom rung of the class system. Ch'ŏnin were divided into *kongch'ŏn* [public or government-owned slaves] and *sach'ŏn* [private slaves]. The slave status was hereditary in that the owners claimed descendants of their slaves as property and could use them as public tribute or sell them to other owners. Besides slaves, *paekjŏng* [butchers], *kisaengs* [actors, actress and singers] and *mudang* [female shamans] belonged to *ch'ŏnin* class. Slavery was formally abolished in 1801, but the traditional class structure proved to be rigid; it persisted well into the modern era.

Doubtless, class distinction or social distancing among people is a universal phenomenon. One society differs from another only in its criteria for such distinction and distancing, scope and magnitude. The criteria range from birth or blood (heredity), marriage or kinship ties, race, ethnicity, religion, region, wealth, education to occupation. The criteria may be ascriptive or achievement-based. What distinguishes the traditional Korean class system from others is its high degree of rigid bifurcation of the ruling elites and the ruled; immobility; closed inter-locking systems of marriage among powerful family clans; regional favoritism; and the virtual monopoly of power and wealth by the ruling elite.

Y.M. Kim, in his study[25] of the Yi Dynasty's top political elites (a total of 4,693 top bureaucrats of *chŏngsamp'um* [rank three] or above in the period of Kojong [r. 1864-1907] and Sunjong [r.1907-10]), identified the salience of civil character, blood ties, family and clan networks and regional favoritism:

1. The top bureaucrats were recruited predominantly from those passing the civil examination: 60.7% from those who passed *munkwa* [civil exam]; 13.6% from *mukwa* [military exam]; 8.4% from *munum* [recruitment through parental connections]; and the rest from unknown or other channels.
2. These elites were mostly from well-known family clans, e.g., 10.6% from Yi clan of Chŏnju; 5.9% from Min clan of Yŏhŭng; 5.2% from Kim clan of Andong; 3.4% from Cho clan of Pungyang; 3.5% from Sŏ clan of Taegu; 3.4% from Kim clan of Kwangsan; 2.5% from Hong clan of Namyang; 2.2% from Han clan of Ch'ŏngju; and 2.1% from Pak clan of Bŏnam. These powerful family clans were interlocked through the maintenance of the closed marriage practices among themselves.
3. They were mostly from the capital. Among those recruited through *munkwa,* Seoulites represented 72.4%, Kyŏnggi Province, 5.9%, Ch'ungch'ŏng, 7.6%, Kyŏngsang, 3.7%, Chŏlla, 1.8%, Kangwŏn, 1.3%, Pyŏngan, 1.3% and Hamgyŏng, 0.3%.
4. These ruling elites represented only 1.1% of the total Korean household. They belonged mostly to the top bureaucratic group or the rich local landed gentry. A high degree of Yi bureaucracy's hereditary characteristic was evident in the fact that the fathers (more than two thirds) of these ruling elites were top bureaucrats.

In short, merits and capabilities were necessary but never sufficient conditions for a person to become a member of the ruling elites in the Yi Dynasty, and for that matter, in Koryŏ as well.[26] The elite recruitment practices of applying extra criteria such as the interlocking family clan and marriage links, school and regional ties and corresponding political favoritism have not been eliminated either from North Korea's communist party and its state bureaucracy or from South Korea's political officialdom. The essence of this legacy still lingers on in the both halves of the Peninsula. The father-son succession scheme and conspicuous nepotism in North Korea, similar nepotistic practices under the Park, the Chun and even the Roh regimes in South Korea, not to mention the serious Yŏng-Honam regional rivalry and rift are the contemporary manifestations.

Centralized Bureaucratism and Political Longevity

Another salient feature of Korean political tradition is characterized by the longevity of the dynastic rule under a centralized bureaucracy. In a way, the longevity and stability of the dynastic rule and a centralized bureaucracy had been mutually reinforcing. The physical setting of Korea—a peninsula of relatively small size—had also been a contributing factor to the rise and durability of strong centralized bureaucratic governing apparatus.

In the Three Kingdoms, for instance, Koguryŏ lasted 705 years, Paekche, 679 years and Silla, nearly a millennium (992 years) of which Korea was unified for some 260 years. Of the next two dynasties, Koryŏ survived nearly half a millennium (479 years) and Yi Chosŏn, over half a millennium (518 years).

In addition to this dynastic longevity and stability, the history of territorial unity of Korean kingdoms was one of the longest in the world. From the period of the unified Silla (though not the entire area of the Korean peninsula) to the present, the duration of Korea's territorial unity amounted to nearly thirteen hundred (1,284) years, while the territorial division lasted less than one hundred years, including the years of partition since 1945.

Like other political developments, the evolution of a centralized bureaucracy in traditional Korea had been piecemeal and gradual. As noted earlier, the kingly authority took root around the second century B.C. in Puyŏ and Koguryŏ. The more elaborate aristocratic centralized governing structure took shape in Silla with the introduction of the "bone-rank" system, although all three kingdoms had somewhat similar type of officialdom.

Koguryo had twelve office ranks, Paeckche, sixteen ranks and Silla, seventeen ranks. In Paekche and Silla, each rank within the government was assigned an official robe of specific color. In Paekche 16 ranks were divided into three tiers—purple denoting the top six ranks, scarlet, the next five ranks and blue robes, the bottom five ranks. In Silla, official robes had four colors—purple for the top five ranks, scarlet for the next four ranks, blue for the two low ranks, and yellow for the lowest six ranks.[27]

Besides the aforesaid official rank system, the councillor bodies, composed primarily of leaders of the royal and aristocratic families, such as Koguryŏ's council of high aristocracy, Paekche's *chŏngsa-am* and Silla's *hwabaek* played a significant role in political decision making. Administratively, the three kingdoms were separated into several local districts. The local administrative units were called *kun* [county or district]. The head of each district is called *ch'ŏryŏngunji* (or *tosa*) in Koguryŏ, *kunjang*, in Paekche and *kunt'aesu* in Silla. These local administrative units were combined to form five larger provinces called *pu* (north, south, east, west and inner) in Koguryŏ, *pang* (center, north, south, east and west) in Paekche and *chu* (upper, lower, new, etc.) in Silla. The governors of *pu, pang* and *chu* were called *yŏksal, pangnyŏng* and *kunju,* respectively.

In Silla each province established its own military garrison, *chong,* which was commanded by the generals of the "true-bone" origin. And *hwarang* [flower of youth or youth military cadet] was created as the institution where elite military officers were trained for the garrison (Koguryŏ was known to have had a similar organization called *kyŏngfang*).[28] Noteworthy also is that in 651 *Chipsabu* [the Chancellery or the Executive Council] was founded and its head acted as prime minister to supervise the various ministries such as the military affairs, disbursements, rites, tax collections, official surveillance and justice (punishment).[29]

Under the Unified Silla a number of government apparatus was restructured to further strengthen its centralized bureaucratic control. In 685 soon after its unification, Silla established nine *chu* [province] which was headed by *ch'ŏnggwa* (later called *todŏk*). Each province was divided into *kun* [prefecture], headed by *t'aesu,* who controlled several *hyŏn* [small town or counties], headed by *yŏng. Hyŏn* was subdivided into villages (*ch'on*) and settlements for people of unfree status (e.g., prisoners of war, rebels) known as *hyang, so* and *pugok.*[30]

During the Koryŏ Dynasty a centralized bureaucratic system reached its maturity. Its governing apparatus began to take shape in 983 in the reign of *Sŏngjong* (r. 981-97) and was completed in 1076 under

Munjong (r. 1046-83). The central governing apparatus, *Top'yŏngmasa* [Cabinet or State Council] consisted of *Samsŏng* [Three Chancelleries], *Yukbu* [Six Ministries], *Chungch'uwŏn* (later called *Ch'umilwŏn* [Royal Secretariat]), *Osadae* (later *Sahŏnbu* [the Censorate] and *Samsa* [Treasury]).

The first two chancelleries merged into a single organ called *Chung-sŏmunhasŏng* or *Chaebu* (the Chancellery for State Affairs or the Directorate of Chancellors) which consisted of directors holding rank two or above who made policy decisions and those with rank three or below who were entrusted with the functions of proposing policy and acting as policy critic or censors.

The third chancellery, the Secretariat for State Affairs, was responsible for carrying out policy through the six ministries: Personnel, Military Affairs, Taxation, Punishment (justice), Rites and Public Works. The Royal Secretariat transmitted royal commands and handled urgent military matters. The Censorate reviewed administrative performance and censured official misconducts. The Treasury originally collected taxes and administered official salaries, but its function was reduced to auditing (For details, see Table 2-1).[31]

The local government divided its administrative units into *kyŏng* [capitals], *tohobu* [regional military commands] and *mok* [cities]. These districts were further divided into smaller local units called *kun* [counties], *hyŏn* [towns] and *chin* [garrisons] (See Table 2-1). In 1018, *Hyŏnjong* (r. 1009-31), for instance, divided the country into *kyŏngki* [capital region], *to* [large circuits] and *kye* [border regions].

The centralized governing apparatus underwent further systematization and refinement during the Yi Dynasty. The bureaucracy consisted of *munkwan* (or *tongban* [civil officials]) and *mukwan* (or *sŏban* [military officials]). They were divided into central and local government officials. Two ranking systems—regular and auxiliary—existed. Each had nine ranks and the highest was *chŏngilpum* [regular rank one], and the lowest, *chŏngkupum* [auxiliary rank nine].

The highest governing organ under the king was *Uijŏngbu* [the State Council]. It supervised *yukjo* [six ministries] which consisted of the Personnel, Taxation, Rites, Military Affairs, Punishments (justice) and

Public Works. Several governing organs, independent of the State Council, were directly responsible to the monarch. *Sŭngjŏngwŏn* [the Royal Secretariat] transmitted documents to and from the king. There were also *Sahŏnbu* [the Inspectorate] and *Saganwŏn* [the Censorate]. In addition, there were three special advisory organs —*Hongmun'gwan* [the Office of Special Counselors], *Yemun'gwan* [the Office for Drafting Memorials] and *Ch'unch'ugwan* [the Office of Historiography] (See Table 2-2).[32]

In the reign of T'aejo in 1413 the local government of the Yi Dynasty was divided into a total of 334 units, from *to* [provinces] to *hyŏn* [townships] (For details, see Table 2-2). Two special cities—Hanyang and Kaesŏng—were placed under the direct control of the central government. Central government officials were appointed for a period of 3 years to serve at all local posts except for the provincial governor, who received an annual appointment. And the local magistrates were prohibited by law from serving in the area of their own ancestral home. This appointment rule, similar to the Chinese practices, was instituted to preempt the rise of local power, which may be dangerous to the central authority.

Three points warrant attention here. First, in both the Koryŏ and the Yi dynasties the affairs of government were run by the same six ministries. In Koryŏ, *pyŏngbu* [the Ministry of Military Affairs] ranked second among six ministries, whereas in Yi Chosŏn it occupied the fourth. The position of *pyŏngjo* in the Yi Dynasty was indicative of the rise of the civil officials over the military officials and further civilianization of Korean politics.

Second, feudalism comparable to that of medieval Europe or Japan had never existed in Korea. To that extent, traditional Korean society resembles traditional Chinese society.[33] A system of rights and duties based on land tenure and personal relationships (in which land is held in fief by vassals from lords to whom they owe specific services and with whom they are bound by personal loyalty) did not develop fully in Korea under the rule of powerful centralized bureaucratic state. The system of land tenure with the landowners and tenant farmers did exist in Korea, but the central monarchical bureaucracy had rarely become fragmented and decentralized. Hence, local landlords seldom exercised over the tenants and serfs a wide variety of policing, judicial, fiscal and other rights, independent of the central authority or of the central authority-appointed local and provincial magistrates. One conspicuous exception in this connection was the short-lived "castle lords" in the final years of Silla, which may be regarded as a rudimentary form of feudalism.[34]

Three, as in other countries, a long tradition of centralized bureaucracy in Korea was Janus-faced—both positive and negative. It meant both stability and stagnation, hierarchy and inequality, efficiency and red tape, conservatism and rigidity, expertise and arrogance and procedural due process and formalism. The dualistic tradition of centralized bureaucratic culture in Korea was indeed long. Such tradition had lasted more than a thousand years since the Koryŏ period. It had not broken down even during the Japanese colonial rule. It is continuing in the present two regimes in Korea. The root is deep and still growing.[35]

Factionalism and Civil-Military Rivalry

If politics is a conflict among contending groups for power, factionalism is a universal phenomenon. What distinguished factionalism in Korea was its degree of intensity, tenacity and duration. The Korean factional struggles were rendered more acute and fierce by the scarcity of the governmental positions even for those small ruling elites and their followers.

Factionalism has two meanings in traditional Korean politics. Broadly defined, it is a phenomenon where two or more elite groups are engaged in power struggle for hegemony in court politics. Such political rivalry existed among royal clans, between central aristocrats and local gentry, between civilian and military officials or within military leaders. Narrowly defined, it refers to political rivalry among literati class or *tangjaeng* [factional strife] which began during the reign of Sŏnjo (r. 1567-1608) in the Yi Dynasty.[36]

As noted earlier, the schism between the sacred-bone royal clans in Silla, especially during the reign of Hyegong (r. 765-80) and the struggle for the throne between the central royal clan and the local gentry in the later Silla during the reign of Huigang (r. 836-37) in 836 were notable. But the most potent form of factionalism was manifested in the political rivalry between the civilian and military officials.

In the era of the Three Kingdoms, the monarch was technically the commander-in-chief of the military forces, and he or she, appointed *sŏngju* [castle lords or regional military commanders]. In Silla, the county was divided into six military garrisons, which were run by the regional garrison commanders. In rare instances as the case of Chang Po-go, the commander of the Ch'ŏnghae Garrison, which was established in 828, the powerful castle lord not only challenged the kingly authority but struggled for the throne itself.[37]

Koryŏ's military forces were divided into two garrisons and six divisions. These were, in turn, composed of forty-five regiments, each with 1,000 soldiers. Initially, the military officials who took part in the founding of Koryŏ were influential in the court politics. A series of measures were enacted to curb the influence of these old military officials. Among them were the Slave Review Act of 956, the Civil Service Examination of 958 and the *Chŏnsikwa* [Stipend Land Law] of 976. Consequently, the civil officials dominated the Korean court in the early years of Koryŏ. The military officials ranked below the civil officials politically and had a lower socio-economic status. To counter the predominance of civilian officials, the top military officials organized a deliberative body called *Chungbang* [the Council of Generals], but it could not match its civilian counterpart, *Todang* [the Privy Council], in power and prestige.[38]

The practice of civilian supremacy in Koryŏ eventually led many disgruntled military officers to resort to a violent showdown. One such attempt was the military coup d'etat, staged by two military officials, Kim Hun and Ch'oe Chil in 1014. As a result, military officers took precedence over civilian officials in government stipends and land grants. This favorable changes notwithstanding, civilian officials continued to mistreat military officers.

A major military-civilian confrontation erupted in a bizarre incident in 1170. Kim Ton-jung, the son of Kim Pu-sik (1075-1151), a leading Koryŏ politician and historian, reportedly burned General Chŏng

Chung-bu's beard with a candle. Having suffered indignities from this and other incidents at the hands of civil officials, military officers under the command of Generals Chŏng Chung-bu, Yi Ui-bang and Yi Ko revolted with the slogan: "Death to all who wear the civil official head-dress!" The coup was swift and successful. These three military strong men deposed Uijong (r. 1146-70) and placed his younger brother Myŏngjong (r. 1170-1197) on the throne. The military troika made the king a titular head and controlled the power. This opened a new era of Koryŏ's military politics through *Chungbang* [the Council of Generals], replacing the Privy Council, its civilian counterpart. The pendulum of power now swung in the direction favorable to military officials. Thenceforth for almost a century, military leaders fought for power amongst themselves.[39]

The original military triumvirate of Chŏng Chung-bu, Yi Ui-bang and Yi Ko ended in tragedy. Yi Ui-bang murdered Yi Ko in their first year of rule, but the former was, in turn, assassinated by Chŏng Kyun, the son of Chŏng Chung-bu. Gen. Chŏng Chung-bu, thus, emerged for a short time as the one-man military dictator, but he, too, was slain by his young associate, General Kyŏng Tae-sung, in 1179. Kyŏng himself died of illness in less than four years after taking power. After Kyŏng's death, his military rival, Yi Ui-min, seized power, but in due course he, too, was assassinated in 1196 by the Ch'oe brothers—Ch'ung-hŏn and Ch'ung-su. The Ch'oe brothers ended some three decades of military internecine power struggles and opened an era of the Ch'oe clan military rule (For details, see Table 2-3).

Unlike his military predecessors, Ch'oe Ch'ung-hŏn succeeded in consolidating his power by eliminating his own brother and erstwhile co-conspirator, Ch'oe Ch'ung-su. Thereby, he paved the way for his own family to exert political domination for four decades. Ch'oe Ch'ung-hŏn deposed three monarchs and placed the fourth on the throne. In the process he controlled the affairs of state through *Chungbang*. In 1225, his son, Ch'oe U created a civilian council called *Chŏngbang* and conducted the state affairs through this organization.[40]

The decline of the Ch'oe clan rule coincided with the Mongol invasion of Koryo. The Mongols (later China's Yuan Dynasty) invaded six times, beginning in 1231 and lasting for thirty years. The Ch'oe clan domination ended when Ch'oe Ui was assassinated by the civilian official Yu Kyŏng and the military official Kim Chun in 1258. Kim Chun then seized the power and ruled for a decade before falling a victim to General Im Yŏn in 1268. When Im Yŏn died of illness in less than two years of his rule, his son, Im Yu-mu, succeeded him but Yu-mu, too, was slain in 1270. So a hundred years of military rule in Koryŏ ended with the surrender to the Mongol invaders.[41]

With the conclusion of peace compact with the Mongols in 1271, Koryŏ was *de facto* under the Mongol domination, which in effect ended the Koryŏ Dynasty. The Koryŏ Dynasty continued as a tributary power of the Yuan Empire (1279-1368) until its demise in 1389.

The immediate cause for the downfall of Koryŏ was the dynamics created by external politics and internal rivalry among military leaders. The disputes between the rising Ming (1368-1644) and the declining Yuan over Koryŏ led, in turn, to the power struggles within Koryŏ's pro-Ming and pro-Yuan civil and military officials. At first, General Ch'oe Yŏng and General Yi Sŏng-kye collaborated in ousting Yi In-min and his pro-Yuan military faction. When Ming attempted to create a Ch'ŏllyŏng Commandary in 1388 in Korea's northeastern territory, a former Yuan Ssangyŏng Commandary, General Ch'oe Yŏng, Koryŏ's new military commander-in-chief, dispatched a military expedition under the command of his deputy, Yi Sŏng-kye, to counter the Ming forces. Although he had grave reservations about the military venture, Yi initially advanced his troops into the Korean-Manchurian border; but short of invading the Liao-tung region of Manchuria, Gen. Yi marched his army back from Wiwha Island in the mouth of Aprok River. Upon returning to Kaesŏng, Koryŏ's capital, he staged a military coup d'etat and removed the king, Gen. Ch'oe Yŏng and other anti-Ming civil and military officials, and created his own Yi Chŏson.[42]

In the early years of Chosŏn, *kaeguk kongsin* [meritorious subjects who helped found the Yi Dynasty], mostly of literati background, became the ruling elite. To boost the dwindling *kaeguk kongsin, yangban* were recruited into the ruling elites of the Yi Dynasty. While *yangban* literally refers to both civil and military officials, it actually signifies the literati class, which predominated the Yi's ruling hierarchy. Thus, factional strife was confined to the literati during the Yi dynasty. One of the earliest factional divisions among the ruling elites of the Yi Dynasty appeared when Sejo (r. 1455-68) usurped power in 1455. Sejo deposed the rightful boy-king Tanjong (r. 1452-55), his own nephew, and ascended the throne. Sejo's usurpation of power sharply divided the ruling elites into two camps—those loyal to the deposed king and those supportive of the usurper. This schism in literati class for power struggle was, however, only the beginning.[43]

The seedbeds of literati factionalism in the Yi Dynasty were *sŏwŏn* [private Confucian academies], founded by the literati on their estates. The first *sŏwŏn* was established in 1543 by Chu Se-bung, a county magistrate in Kyŏngsang Province. During the reign of Sŏnjo (r. 1567-1606), there were more than one hundred *sŏwŏn* mostly in southern provinces.[44] *Sŏwŏn* functioned as a power base and a training ground for the factional power struggles among the literati.

In 1575, during the early years of Sŏnjo, a conflict flared up between the two factions—*Tongin* [the Easterners] led by Kim Hyo-wŏn (1532-1590) and *Sŏin* [the Westerners] led by Sim Ui-gyŏm (1535-1587)—over their disagreement of a government personnel appointment. The two factions clashed again over the investiture of the crown prince in 1591. Sŏnjo had no sons by his wives, but he had thirteen sons by his concubines. The Westerners backed one of these sons for the crown prince. A new split occurred among the Easterners over this issue which gave rise to *Namin* [the Southerners], who took a conciliatory position, and *Pukin* [the Northerners], who strongly opposed it. *Pukin* was later splintered into *Sopuk* [the Lesser Northerners] and *Taepuk* [the Greater Northerners]. *Sopuk* was further subdivided into *T'ak* [the Muddy] and *Ch'ŏng* [the Clean].

Meanwhile, the Westerners successfully put Injo (r. 1623-1649) on the throne and eliminated both the Greater and Lesser Northerner factions by a bloody purge. The Westerners themselves, then, subdivided into two factions: *Hun* [the Merit] and Ch'ŏng [Clean]. *Hun* was further divided into *No* [the Old Doctrine] and *So* [the New or Young Doctrine]. At a first glance, as Table 2-3 illustrates, factional division and subdivision were virtually interminable. But in reality factional fracturing simply reflected the unceasing power struggle among the literati; each faction resorted to employing whatever means necessary to curry favor from the reigning monarch and to eliminate the opposing factions from the royal court. In Edward Wagner's words, Yi Dynasty factionalism was "no more than a naked struggle for political power, motivated by desires for economic affluence and social prestige."[45] Factions grew like a cancer cell, sapping in the process the vitality of the government. Factional struggles were myopic since each faction was far more concerned about its own power and position than the general interest of the nation. Prolonged factional struggles were partly responsible for the eventual collapse of the Yi Dynasty.[46]

Even in the political arenas in both halves today, the myopia of political factionalism still lingers. Neither the naked struggle for political power motivated primarily by desires for economic affluence and social prestige nor the military intervention in politics has completely disappeared in Korean politics. To the contrary, one of the 23 syndromes in the South Korean politics has been its factional myopia within and between parties.

The *politicizations* of the South Korean military, at least since 1961 up to 1993, had also been a significant factor in South Korean politics. In North Korea, the political myopia and the naked nature of power struggles have been visible only within the ruling party since Kim Il Sung and his Workers' Party of Korea (WPK) proscribe the very notion of party competition itself. The North Korean military has been functioning as the political military in that it serves as the WPK's military instrument (For a detailed analysis of the differences between the North Korean political military and the South Korean politicized military, see Chapter 18).

Land-based Power Dynamics

The emergence of centralized bureaucratic states during the Three Kingdoms era coincided with the development of the *concept* that all land belonged to the king and everyone was his subject. In reality, private ownership of land had not disappeared because the monarch had no technological and bureaucratic means to control all the subjects directly. The concept simply meant that the monarch had the authority to dispense with any land and to mobilize the subjects at any time. Thus, the monarchs often granted lands and prisoners of war to his or her victorious commanders and meritorious court officials. The masses, free peasants and tenants alike, could be mobilized by the monarch as soldiers or as corvee laborers to construct fortifications and irrigation works.

The monarch's land policy played five important functions in traditional Korean politics: (i) land was utilized as a key weapon to control the ruling elites by rewarding it to those who were loyal and withholding it from those who were disloyal; (ii) land was the power base for both the monarch and the ruling elites through which the subjects were controlled and "squeezed"; (iii) the concept of state (monarch's) ownership of land necessitated a centralized bureaucratic monarchy in the Korean Peninsula, thereby preventing feudalism from taking root; (iv) the success and failure of the monarch's land policy were directly related to the strength and weakness of his or her monarchical rule; and (v) the monarch granted land as a material compensation to the public officials for their services, at least, until it was replaced by the salary system.

In Silla, for instance, the ruling elites were awarded appanages which included everything and everyone on the land. Two kinds of land grants were made to deserving civil and military officials: *sajŏn* was a permanent grant which became the hereditary property of the family of the grantee; *sigŭp* was the assignment of the tax revenue from a given tract of land to the grantee during his lifetime, after which it reverted to the royal ownership. Silla also had a system of *nogŭp* [salary appanages] and *kwallyojŏn* [stipend appanages], which were developed to support the expenses of government officials. In 689 *nogŭp* was abolished and *chikjŏn* [office-land] was allocated from which officials were permitted to receive only the grain tax.[47]

In Koryŏ, the concept that all land in the country belong to the king became firmly entrenched. The so-called *yŏkpunjŏn* system was first introduced in 940. Under this system land was mostly distributed to those civil and military officials who helped found the new dynasty.[48]

In 976 during the first year of Kyŏngjong (r. 975-81) a more comprehensive land law called *chonsikwa* [stipend land] system was established. It granted land to four classes of officials in eighteen stipend grades.[49] It was revised in 998 during the reign of Mokjong (r. 997-1009). The revised system allocated land according to official ranks ranging from first *kwa*, the highest rank, receiving 170 *kyŏl* (a unit of land measurement) to the eighteenth *kwa*, the lowest rank, receiving 38 *kyŏl*. The classification of Koryŏ's land systems ran as follows:

> *yangbanjŏn:* land for incumbent civil and military officials;
> *yangban kongumjŏnsikwa:* land for top officials (rank five and above);
> *haninjŏn:* land for officials (rank six and below);
> *kupunjŏn:* land for local officials;
> *kuninjŏn:* land for soldiers;
> *kungwŏnjŏn:* land for palace needs;
> *sawŏnjŏn:* land for Buddhist temples;
> *t'uhwajŏn:* land for foreigners who were naturalized;
> *sajŏn:* land granted to officials as "gifts" by the king;
> *sigŭp:* practice modeled after Silla (tax villages);
> *minjŏn:* a part of kongjŏn (public land);
> *naepaengjŏn:* land directly controlled by the royal court;
> *konghaejŏn:* land for the central and local governments;
> *tunjŏn:* land for military supplies;
> *hakjŏn:* school land;
> *chokjŏn:* land set aside for the monarch's ritual worship of heaven.[50]

Beginning with the Yi Dynasty, the new land law called *Kwajŏnpŏp* [the Rank Land Law] was promulgated in 1391. It allowed both the former officials and the incumbents to receive allocation of land based on the government's eighteen office rank structure. The land available to this allocation was, however, limited to Kyŏnggi Province where the capital was located, in order to check the rise of *yangban* bureaucrats' regional power base. The Rank Land Law mandated that the peasant farmers pay one-tenth of their harvest to the government. In addition, the new land system permitted a number of special lands:

> *susinjŏn:* land for an official's widow who did not remarry;
> *hyuryangjŏn:* land for upbringing of orphans;

kongumjŏn: land for merit subjects who helped found the Yi Dynasty;
kunjŏn: land for junior military officers;
naesusajŏn: land for palace needs;
konghaejŏn: land for public agency;
nŭmjŏn: land for local government support;
hakjŏn: school land;
sawŏnjŏn: temple land (Buddhist temples);
kuktunjŏn: garrison land[51]

In 1444 Sejong the Great (r. 1418-50) introduced *Kongpŏp* [the Tribute Tax Law] which required the peasant farmers to pay one-twentieth of their harvest as a land tax. In addition, the peasants were obligated to pay *t'ogong* [the tribute tax] or products indigenous to a particular locale such as utensils, fabrics, paper, woven mats, marine products, furs, fruits and lumber. All able-bodied male peasants and commoners were also subject to military and corvee labor service.

In 1466 Sejo (r. 1455-1468) replaced *Kwajŏnpŏp* with *Chikchŏnpŏp* [the Office Land Law]. Under it land was allocated only to the incumbent office-holders, and former officials were excluded. It was abandoned in 1556, due primarily to the shortages of land for distribution, and from thence, the officials were paid salaries, and they no longer received land. In 1708 during the reign of Sukjong (r. 1674-1720), *Taedongpŏp* [the Uniform Land Tax] was enforced throughout the country. This new law required the peasants to pay twelve *tu* of rice (only about one percent of the harvest) from each *kyŏl* of land, and the tax could be paid in cotton cloth or in coin. *Kyunyŏkpŏp* [the Equalized Tax Law] in 1750 was another attempt to ostensibly reduce the peasant farmer's cloth tax burden (the cloth tax was reduced from two bolts to one, and the loss in revenue could be made up by taxes on fish traps, salt production and a grain surtax), but in reality it did not bring much improvement because yangban class was still exempt from paying such a tax.[52]

A final point needs to be made here. Several terms, *kongjŏn* [public land], *sajŏn* [private land] and *minjŏn* [people's land], need to be clarified. As in Koryŏ, the monarch in the Yi Dynasty theoretically owned all the land, but in reality, private ownership of land had increased steadily because, among other things, land was constantly awarded to public officials. *Kongjŏn* was not the land owned by the state, but a designated land from whom the state collected "rent" initially set at ten percent of the harvest. *Sajŏn* was the land distributed to the office-holders from which they collected the rent, although many of their heirs inherited those pieces of land as if they were their "private pieces of land." *Minjŏn* was private land belonging to the people whose ownership rights were recognized by the state.[53]

Because Korea is relatively small in size but has a large population, land has been one of the most prized elements among the elites and the masses alike. To the elites, it represented not only the tangible booty of their successful power struggle but also the means through which the masses were controlled and even exploited. To that extent, like the traditional Chinese government, the traditional Korean government was, to borrow Fairbank's phrase, an "organized corruption."[54] Since 1945, North Korea abolished private lands except for allowing small garden plots, thereby putting a stop to the old practice of the ruling elites' expropriation of the land as their personal booty. Still, North Korea's ruling elites are using it as their *political* control mechanism of the masses. In South Korea the tradition of land grabbing (now in the form of real estate scandals) as the prized spoils by the ruling elites, or as their political control mechanism of the masses has not completely died away.

State Religion as Political Control Mechanism

Long before Confucianism and Buddhism played the role of giving legitimacy to the Korean dynasties, the shamanistic founding myths abounded in Ancient Chosŏn, Koguryŏ, Paekche and Silla. *Tan'gun-wanggŏm,* the mythical progenitor of the Korean people was reputed to be the son of *Ung'nyŏ* [a female bear] and *Hwan'wung,* the son of Hwanin, a sun god. Lady *Yuhwa* supposedly conceived *Chumong,* the founder of Koguryŏ, from an egg when the sun rays touched her body. Onjo, the founder of Paekche, was *Chumong's* adopted son, whose lineage was also linked to *Haemosu* [the son of heaven]. Likewise, *Pak Hyŏkkŏse,* the legendary founder of Silla, came into being from an egg.[55]

Beyond the foundation myths, religion in Korean kingdoms has played manifold functions. As in other countries, religion in Korea has been: (i) the source of other-worldly hope and solace; (ii) the medium for celebration and mourning; and (iii) the escape from this-worldly economic, social and political oppression.

Specifically, for the monarch and the ruling elites, religion served several political functions. It provided: (i) the rationale and justification for political rule[56]; (ii) the purposes and the governing principles of the state; (iii) the harmony and unity of the state and the people; (iv) the educational means through which the ruling elites and their children became literate and learned; and (v) the pretext through which competing elites vied for political power. From this standpoint, religion and state in traditional Korea were *intermixed,* and the concept of separation of the two was rather alien.

All three kingdoms laid great stress on inculcating the Confucian ethos as a means of maintaining their aristocratic social and political order. Similarly, Buddhism and its various sects began to influence the court politics of the Three Kingdoms. Buddhism was introduced to Koguryŏ in 372 by the monk Sundo via the Earlier Ch'in state in northeastern China and to Paekche from the Eastern Ch'in state in 384.[57]

Buddhism was introduced to Silla some time during the mid-fifth century (417-458). At first, it met with local hostility, especially from the ruling aristocracy. But by 527 near the end of Pŏphung's reign (r. 514-539), it was officially recognized. The concept of a single body of believers devoted spiritually to observing the way of the Buddha, together with the notion of the people serving the king, played a major role as a force shaping unity and cohesion in these early Korean states. It was accepted as a system of thought particularly suited to the needs of a centralized aristocratic state headed by a king.

The concept of Buddhism as the protector of the state and as the unity of belief and discipline was especially attractive to the monarchs and the ruling elites as their governing principles. It was no accident, therefore, that many monks emerged as the powerful political advisers to kings in Silla. The three great Buddhist monks, among others, are Chajang, Wŏngwang and Uisang. Chajang's Vinaya sect was popular for its doctrine of the unity of belief and discipline. Vinaya doctrine became the governing principles of the ruling elites in Silla. By synthesizing the Confucian virtues of loyalty and filial piety and the Buddhist injunctions against killing, Wŏngwang (?–630) formulated *Sesok Ogye* [Five Secular Commandments] in 602 as the governing ethos of the *hwarang*, the warrior youth corps. They were to: (i) serve the King with loyalty; (ii) take care of the parents with filial piety; (iii) keep trust with friends; (iv) never retreat in battle; and (v) never kill indiscriminately.[58] Likewise, Uisang's Hwaŏm sect was popular due to its doctrine of all encompassing harmony: "the one contains the multitude and yet the multitude is one." The concept of embracing myriad of sentient beings within the single Buddhistic mind was well suited to a state with a centralized power structure.[59]

Confucianism[60] played a pivotal role in the Three Kingdoms as the provider of the social ethos and the governing formula for the aristocratic ruling elites and as the educational medium through which the ruling elites learned the Chinese classics and its political, legal and other institutions. The establishment of *T'aehak* [National Confucian Academy] by Koguryŏ in 372 during the reign of Sosurim (r. 371-384) and the founding of *Kukhak,* the first Confucian National Academy in 682, which was renamed *T'aehakkam,* the Great Learning Institute, around 750 in Silla were noteworthy in this regard.

Both Buddhism and Confucianism thrived together for half a millennium in the late Silla period. The latter's this-worldly social ethos complemented the former's other-worldly teachings. Confucianism preached such virtues as benevolence, righteousness, propriety, wisdom and sincerity. It provided the basic ideals of government, centered on the conduct of men in their relationship to each other. *Samgang Olyun* [Three Bonds and Five Principles] delineated: bonds between parents and children, between king and subjects and between husband and wife; and principles of love between parents and children, righteousness between king and subjects, distinction between husband and wife, order between old and young and trust between friends.

In short, Buddhism supplying answers to questions in the spiritual realm dealing with individual's relationship to the universe and his future, and Confucianism defining men's relationships with each other and with the governing authority in secular realm had maintained a remarkable symbiosis.

In the early Koryŏ period, the mutually complementary functions of Buddhism and Confucianism, the former ministering to people's spiritual needs, while the latter dominating their social ethics, education and relations to government, continued. Buddhism flourished during the Koryŏ Dynasty because the royal family and the old landed aristocrats continued to find not only their spiritual solace from its teachings but the very legitimacy of their rule. For example, in the first of his *Sip hŭnyo* [Ten Injunctions] Koryŏ's founding father, Wang Kŏn, instructed that "the success of every great undertaking of our state depends upon the favor and protection of Buddha...."[61] In short, Buddhism became Koryŏ's *de facto* state religion.

In the meantime Confucianism played a vital role as a link between the government and the people. Through Confucianism, the Chinese political, legal and administrative institutions and its governing principles were introduced to Koryŏ's centralized bureaucratic rule.

The coexistence of Buddhism and Confucianism ended, however, with the rise of neo-Confucianism in the late Koryŏ.[62] Religion found its new political dimension in Korean politics. Thenceforth, it became the mechanism through which both the old and the new political elites vied for political power. The so-called rational school of neo-Confucianism developed by the Sung China's Chu Hsi (1130-1200) was introduced into Koryŏ by a Korean scholar An Yu (1243-1306). The neo-Confucianists in the late Koryŏ period openly attributed all the social and political ills to Buddhism. They were sharply critical of the great expenses incurred by the state in sponsoring Buddhist festivals and temple construction. In a sense, neo-Confucianism furnished the ideological weapon through which the new literati and scholar-bureaucrats waged their power struggle against the old Buddhist establishment of the Koryŏ Dynasty. From the standpoint of political power struggle, the downfall of Koryŏ and the rise of Yi Chosŏn meant the triumph of neo-Confucian elites over the old establishment of Koryŏ's Buddhist ruling oligarchs.[63]

During the Yi Dynasty, Buddhism retreated from the political ruling circles. The suppression of Buddhism started from the beginning. T'aejo (r. 1392-98), the founder of the Yi Dynasty, banned the construction of temples, and imposed the monk registration system to control the monk population. His son T'aejong (r. 1400-18) suppressed the monks even more harshly. In 1406 he reduced the number of temples in the country to 242 and confiscated their lands and slaves. During the reign of Sejong the Great (r. 1418-50) and Sejo (r. 1455-68), the government relaxed its suppression a little but under Sŏnjong (r. 1469-94) Buddhism was again the main target of political suppression. Sŏnjong abolished the monk registration system and imposed a total ban on those entering the Buddhist priesthood. In 1507 Chungjong (r. 1506-44) abolished the examination process by which monks hitherto had been selected for positions in the administrative hierarchy of the Buddhist establishment. Thus, the formal ties between the state and Buddhism were finally severed. The examination system for the monks was briefly reinstituted in 1552 but Sŏnjo (r. 1567-1608) abolished it totally.

With Buddhism taking the back seat in the political arena, Confucianism (and neo-Confucianism) rose as the *de facto* state religion of the Yi Dynasty. Through its civil and military service examination which was based on the Chinese *Four Books* and *Five Classics,* the *yangban* literati found the avenue to enter the government service. In the absence of other competing religion, the elites waged their power struggles over the "interpretation" of Confucianism and neo-Confucianism. During the Yi Dynasty, the power struggle among elites was, in short, within religion —the disputes among literati over interpretations of Confucianism and neo-Confucianism—rather than between religions—the rivalry between Buddhist and Confucian adherents. The factional struggles during the Sŏnjo period were the prime example. Ironically, one of the major reasons for the decline and fall of the Yi Dynasty, which originally rose as a Confucian state, was the power struggle among Confucian literati elites in and out of government over their claims of orthodoxy. Their competing claims often appeared trivial, but the triviality was only the guise under which they waged deadly quarrels for political power. The introduction of Christianity into Korea in the seventeenth century further complicated the religious dimension of Korean politics.

In brief, a parallel can be drawn between the lack of religious toleration among the power elites in the Koryŏ and Yi dynasties and that of
ideological toleration among the political elites today in North and
South Korea. The continuing hostile relations between North Korea's
communist ruling elites and South Korea's anti-communist political
elites and the disputes between South Korea's ruling and opposition
elites over the *correct* meaning and process of democratic rule (e.g., the
cabinet-responsible system vs. the presidential system) resemble the
past conflicts between the Buddhist and Confucian ruling elites and the
Confucian literati's fatal arguments over the *proper* interpretation and
practice of Confucian and Neo-Confucian rites.[64]

Above all, North Korean ban on religious practices except for token
religious organizations on paper, and the South Korean political link
with various religious organizations, especially the relations between
political opposition forces and Catholics, in post-liberation politics can
be seen as a contemporary manifestation of long tradition of politico-
religious symbiosis as well as rivalry.

One final observation is in order. As the idea of religious toleration
extends to all religion, so must the concept of ideological toleration
embrace all ideologies, be they communism, capitalism, nationalism or
any other blend of political and/or economic blueprints. Religious toleration emanated originally from the idea that no individual has a monopoly
on wisdom and knowledge to be able to dictate the form of religion for
another; that each individual is ultimately responsible for his actions
before God; that no compulsion, contrary to the will of the individual,
can secure more than an outward conformity; and that there is an unend-
ing vicious circle of wars between the persecutor and the persecuted.

Similarly, ideological toleration stems from the realization that no
nation has a monopoly on the best form of government to impose it on
other nations; that each nation is ultimately responsible for its own form
of government; that no coercion by the external powers can ensure more
than a superficial emulation by the coerced; and that an unceasing conflict exists between the coercer and the coerced nation. As the idea of
religious toleration was to end the vicious circle of religious wars

among different sects, the concept of ideological toleration may be the answer to terminating the continuing ideological conflicts between North and South Korea. Fortunately, with the demise of Communist regimes in the former Soviet Union and Eastern Europe, the ideological rivalry between the two superpowers has now virtually ended and a new world order is in the making. Ideally at least, the two pillars emerging in the aftermath of the demise of Communism and dismantling of the U.S.-Soviet nuclear rivalry are the human rights and the green rights. The pillar of the human rights was symbolically represented by the 1975 Helsinki Final Acts and the success of the Conference in Security and Cooperation in Europe (CSCE). The edifice of the green rights is now being built. The UN-sponsored Earth Summit in Rio de Janeiro in June 1992 graphically signaled the coming of the new age. From this perspective, the two Koreas, the last remaining "lone island of the cold war" cannot, will not and should not be the torch-bearers of post-war ideological rivalry forever.

External Linkages and Pacifism

Excessive foreign linkages and pacifism mark another Korean political traditions. The first foreign attempt to subjugate Korea occurred in 109 B.C. when Emperor Wu Ti of China's Han Empire (206 B.C.-222 A.D.) invaded Wiman Chosŏn (194 B.C.?-108 B.C.), reportedly with an army of sixty thousand and a navy of seven thousand men. The Korean forces fought back but a year later Wiman Chosŏn fell to the Han China. The northern part of present Korea was, thus, divided into four Chinese colonies. Of the four, Korea regained three colonies—Chinbŏn and Imdun in 82 B.C. and Hyŏnt'o in 75 B.C. But the Nangnang colony lasted beyond the demise of the Han until 313 A.D. Then, Koguryŏ, one of the Korean tribal states in northern Korea, began to emerge as a new contender of power in the region.[65]

Under King Mich'ŏn (r. 300-31), Koguryŏ succeeded in conquering Nangnang (Lo-lang in Chinese), and ended nearly four centuries of Chinese colonial rule in northern Korea. During the reign of Kwang-gaet'o the Great (r. 391-412), Koguryŏ expanded its territory into the

Liaotung area by defeating the Hsiao Sin. In the end he created a vast kingdom, extending over two-thirds of the Korean Peninsula and much of Manchuria. In retrospect, the military conquest of Kwanggaet'o the Great was one of the first and last offensive moves by Korea in its history.[66]

When China's Sui Dynasty (589-618) unified the empire in 589 after the prolonged division of the Northern and Southern Dynasties, the new balance-of-power alliances emerged in Northeast Asia. The north-south alignment forces represented by T'uueh (Turks), a new rising power in the steppe region of north-central Asia, Koguryŏ and Paekche against the east-west alliance of forces formed by Sui, Silla and Japan were notable. Koguryŏ first launched its attack against Liao-hsi across Liao River in 598. Wen Ti, the Sui emperor, invaded Koguryŏ but was repulsed. Again in 612 Yang Ti, the next Sui emperor, invaded Koguryŏ with over a million men but in the end had to withdraw his forces. Sui attempted two more invasions in 613 and 614, but again without success. When the Sui fell, primarily due to the cost of the Korean expeditions, T'ang (618-907) emerged.

The first T'ang offensive against Koguryŏ began in 645, but it was repulsed by the Koguryŏ forces. T'ang forces invaded again from 658 to 659, but it too ended in failure. In concert with Silla, T'ang attempted to conquer both Koguryŏ and Paekche in 660. T'ang's army under General So Chŏng-bang (Su Ting-fang in Chinese), fresh from victories over the Turks in 657, crossed the Yellow Sea to invade Paekche by landing at the mouth of Kŭm River. Paekche fell but Koguryŏ once more resisted the T'ang and Silla assault. Seven years later in 667, the T'ang and Silla forces successfully launched offensives against Koguryŏ, which fell in the winter a year later.

The collapse of Koguryŏ and Paekche had two significant political implications and consequences. In the short run, it paved the road for Silla's unification of Korea (the first groundwork for the Korean people as a united nation), although the price for such unity was the permanent loss of the vast territory in Manchuria. With the fall of Koguryŏ and Paekche, T'ang swiftly established its administrative control over the areas of the two fallen kingdoms and attempted to subjugate Silla as well. The T'ang-Silla alliance, as a result, was severed which brought about the eventual military confrontation between the two. Silla's military campaign against the T'ang forces in the Peninsula was successful, and Silla recovered all the Paekche and Koguryŏ's territories up to the Taedong River area. T'ang, meanwhile, retreated, and its military governor's headquarters were moved to Manchuria.

Meanwhile in 698, the kingdom of Parhae (P'o-hai in Chinese, 698-927) was established by the former Koguryŏ general and other Korean expatriates in Manchuria. When it collapsed in 926 by the Khitan invasion, many Parhae refugees migrated southward into the Korean Peninsula and thereby, Korean link with Manchuria suffered a permanent schism. Minor territorial adjustments occurred during the Koryŏ and the Yi dynasties, but Manchuria was never recovered.

In the long run, the defeat of the two indigenous alliances of Paekche and Koguryŏ by Silla with the help of T'ang further undermined the stature of Korea as an independent state to withstand foreign pressures, especially the impact of political changes in the continental China. To put it differently, Korea had ceased to become a contender in the power struggles for hegemony in the northeast Asia. It, instead, became vulnerable to the rising powers in the continental China, including the Khitans, the Jurchens, the Mongols and the Manchus in the north and northwest and later to Japan in the east as well. It had to make political adjustments and accommodations according to the incessant rise and fall of the neighboring powers.

One of the end products of Korea's weaker and minor political and military status vis-a-vis the powers in the continental China and the maritime Japan was the development of a syndrome called *mohwa sasang* [emulating China] in particular and *sadae* [serving the great] in general in the mindset of the ruling elites in the subsequent Korean kingdoms and beyond.[67] *Mohwa* and *sadae* extended beyond the mental orientation of the Korean elites and literati to revere and emulate the "superior" Chinese culture and to serve the interest of the great powers such as China. They also served as a political stratagem to the Korean ruling elites, who developed an ability to swiftly align with forces in power in China (later, other powers in the area as well) and to sustain and strengthen their own political powers (or, to challenge the existing ruling elites) through alliance with, and support from, such big powers.

Koryŏ reunified Korea after the fall of Silla but it soon confronted the Khitan (Liao) in the north, which overthrew the Parhae. During the reign of its founder T'aejo (r. 918-943), Koryŏ launched a series of minor northward military expeditions and succeeded in recovering its northern boundary beyond the Daedong River and up to the Ch'ŏng-ch'ŏn River area. The northern boundary stopped there owing to the presence of the Khitan. An uneasy balance had been sustained between Koryŏ and Khitan along this new border until the latter invaded the former in 993. A consummate diplomatic maneuvering by Koryŏ's Sŏ Hui persuaded the Khitan invading forces not only to withdraw volun-tarily but to concede the areas south of the Aprok (Yalu) River to Koryŏ. The Khitan, then, in war with the Sung China (907-1127) gave in to the demands of the Koryŏ chief delegate Sŏ Hui, who contended that Koryŏ, as the successor to Koguryŏ, had a claim to the Koguryŏ's former Manchurian territories. He promised Koryŏ's cooperation with the Khitan if the areas south of the Aprok were returned to Koryŏ. Thus, Koryŏ not only averted the war with the Khitan but expanded its territory to the Aprok.[68]

The Khitan soon launched invasions against Koryŏ in 1010 and again in 1018, but both ended in failure. Another Manchurian tribe, the Jurchen, founded the Ch'in state in 1115. In 1125 the Ch'in overran the Khitan Liao (907-1127) and put pressure on Koryŏ. In the end, Koryŏ yielded to Ch'in's demand for a suzerain-subject relationship.

A nomadic tribe in the north, the Mongols, emerged as a new con-tender of power in northeastern Asia by 1202. Chingis (Genghis) Khan and his Mongol army subjugated the Ch'in in 1215 and controlled all the territories north of the Yellow River and Manchuria. Ogodei Khan, the successor to Chingis Khan, destroyed the last remnants of the Ch'in in 1231. He also dispatched Gen. Sartai's army to Koryŏ. Koryŏ put up resistance but the Mongols seized part of the kingdom north of the Han River by December 1232. The Mongols repeated attacks in 1235, 1253 and in 1257. A scattered resistance was put up by the remnants of the Koryŏ forces until the fall of Cheju Island in 1273. By then, the Mongol dominion over Korea was complete. Koryŏ continued to function until 1389 as a tributary state to the Mongol Empire (Yuan). (The conquest of China by the Mongols was accomplished by 1279, and Khubilai, the grandson of Chingis Khan became "Emperor," the Son of Heaven). The Mongols with the help of Korea embarked on a conquest of Japan in 1274 and again in 1281, but both expeditions ended in failure.[69]

In its final years, Koryŏ faced two persistent invaders—*Hong'gŏn-chŏk* [the Red Turbans], a powerful Chinese brigand force from across the Aprok River, and *waegu* [the Japanese marauders] in Korean coastal regions. The Red Turbans ravaged the northern regions of Koryŏ in 1359 and in 1361. As early as the reign of Kojong (r. 1213-1259), the seaborne Japanese marauders pillaged the Korean coastal regions. The Japanese marauding became rampant after 1350.

As the Yuan declined and the Ming Dynasty rose in China, Koryŏ felt more than a political ripple effect. Koryŏ began to shed the Mongol dominion but had to accommodate the wishes of the new Ming (1368-1644). The ruling elites in the Korean court were bifurcated into the pro-Ming or pro-Yuan factions. More accurately, they were torn between the external pressures from the declining Mongol force and the rising Ming power. It was no accident, therefore, that the downfall of the Koryŏ kingdom was carried out by the military coup of a pro-Ming general Yi Sŏng-gye in 1388.[70]

From the outset, the Yi dynasty founder, T'aejo (General Yi Sŏnggye), began to recoup its northeastern territories previously held by the Jurchen and the northwestern areas controlled by the Mongols. During the reign of Sejong the Great (1418-50), the northern military expeditions succeeded in establishing the Aprok (Yalu) and the Tuman (Tumen) rivers as Korea's new northern boundaries, which remain Korea's northern borders today. Sejong the Great sent General Yi Chŏng-mu to attack the Tsushima Island in 1419 to prevent the Japanese marauders from using it as their launching base of piracy. In 1443, the Yi Korea and Japan reached a trade agreement, which was revised in 1510.

The first Japanese invasion of Korea was launched in 1592 during the reign of Sŏnjo (r. 1567-1608). At first, the Japanese forces swiftly overran Korea. The war dragged on, as Admiral Yi Sun-sin's brilliant strategy and his newly invented iron-clad battle ship *kŏbuksŏn* [the turtle ship] scored a series of naval victories, and the scattered armed resistance and guerrilla attacks were waged by numerous Korean compatriots. Meanwhile, a Ming Chinese army of 50,000 strong under the command of Gen. Li Ju-sung recaptured Pyongyang and pursued the Japanese southward. At this point, Japan agreed to negotiate peace with Korea but the negotiation halted when Japan demanded the cession of some portion of Korea. When the negotiation failed, Japan launched its second invasion in 1597 but Korea was better prepared, and the Ming relief army came quickly to the defense of Korea. In mid-1598, when the Japanese ruler Hideyoshi died, the Japanese forces withdrew completely from the Peninsula. Thus, the seven-year struggle ended and the new peaceful relations were restored between Japan and Korea by 1606, but the war devastated Korea's economy, not to mention the invaders' pillaging and mass slaughter.[71]

The Manchus (later Ch'ing) in the north, meanwhile, invaded Korea in 1627 and again in 1636. As before, the Korean ruling elites in the Yi Dynasty were split into the waning pro-Ming and the rising pro-Ch'ing factions, although the latter group soon dominated the Korean court by accepting Ch'ing's suzerainty. This new Korea-Ch'ing relationship survived well into the late 19th century, until the Ch'ing dynasty (1644-1912) began to decline and Japan emerged as the new rising power in the region. Externally, Japan clashed, first, with the Ch'ing China and next, with Russia over Korea. After her two victorious military showdowns—the Sino-Japanese War of 1894-95 and the Russo-Japanese War of 1904-05—Japan was able to claim Korea under her dominion. Japan made Korea her protectorate in 1905 and its outright colony five years later in 1910. Japan's colonial rule in Korea lasted until 1945.

Internally, the factional constellations of the ruling elites in the Korean court in the final days of the Yi Dynasty were more complex. Unlike the two-way patterns of their predecessors, their factional divisions were, at least, tripartite—pro-Ch'ing, pro-Russian and pro-Japanese. The old establishment groups sided with the ailing Ch'ing and later, with Russia, while the reformist groups allied with the modernizing Japan. It is true that the political leaders in the Korean court, traditionalists and reformists alike, were too blinded by their own political ambitions to ward off foreign aggression in Korea. In the end, it was the foreign powers, especially Japan, which took advantage of these internal political disarray among Korean ruling elites and realized her aggressive and imperialistic design on Korea.

From this cursory historical survey of foreign inroads into the Korean Peninsula, one general observation may be drawn. As noted above, the emergence of a united Korea under Silla after the collapse of Koguryŏ and Paekche meant that Korea lost the clout in becoming the power contender in the northeast Asia as an independent political partner. To be sure, Korea continued to play a role in the correlation of forces in the region. Thenceforth, however, Korea simply accommodated the emergent hegemonic power in the region, be it T'ang, Sung, Yuan, Ming, Ch'ing, Russia or Japan. The rise, decline and the fall of the hegemonic power in the region adversely affected the fate of the Korean kingdoms. The suzerain-vassal arrangements typified Korea's posturing toward the external hegemonic power as much as the *mohwa* and *sadae* characterized the Korean ruling elites' mental orientations. North and South Korea's post-War political and military linkages vis-a-vis the United States, the former Soviet Union, China and Japan in the region can also be seen and analyzed from the standpoint of this long-standing historical tradition and mental orientations of the ruling strata in the two halves.

To put it another way, after the collapse of Koguryŏ and Paekche alliance, Korea had become the target of external aggression and interference, not the aggressor. Korea had become defensive and pacifistic; it lost both the initiative and the capacity to invade other countries. It had been repeatedly overrun by the rising powers in China, Manchuria and Japan, which colonized it in 1910. In short, from the time when the current Korean boundary was secured under Sejong the Great (1418-50), the Korean pacifism, i.e., the absence of external incursion or invasion, lasted nearly 500 years, or over 1200 years from the time of united Korea in 661. It is indeed remarkable that Korea has been able to successfully maintain its identity, not withstanding all the foreign invasions, interference, colonization, and, now artificial division as well.

Mass Political Culture

Peasant Rebellion and Mass Uprising

Throughout its history, Korea has experienced a variety of internal conflicts and armed violence, ranging from regicide, palace coups and conspiracy, military coup d'etat, peasant rebellions and brigandage, armed internal conflict to revolution. In exploring the generality and peculiarity of the Korean tradition of internal violence, two caveats need to be spelled out at the outset. One, it is extremely difficult, if not impossible, to differentiate the cause(s) from the symptom(s) of violence. More often than not, the cause and the symptom are chain of events. The causal chain(s) may be of internal origin such as a palace coup or of external source such as a foreign invasion. These various forms and types of internal violence are often *intertwined* in that one leads to the other, which, in turn, ignites a bigger and wider internal conflict, even involving foreign powers.

Two, as noted earlier, the bifurcation of political culture and traditions in Korea into elite and mass (or mass-peasant distinction, for that matter) is only for an *analytic* purpose, for in reality the two are inseparable. Traditional Korea, like other traditional societies, had been predominantly agrarian. Hence, any mass movement without a sizable participation of the peasants is unimaginable. Thus, separating the typical peasant uprisings from other mass movements presents difficulty. Interestingly, the elites usually led both the peasant and mass movements. The leaders of these movements were seldom from their own strata. The peasant uprising led by the peasant or the mass movement by the mass is indeed rare in history. Their leaders seldom came from their own ranks. Their leaders were *with* them, but rarely *from* them. These rebel leaders felt either hopeful about regaining their erstwhile power (fallen *yangban*) or hopeless about gaining it through the existing political, economic and social frameworks. Thus, they resorted to the mass movement or other political and military intrigues.

Bearing these two caveats in mind, the culture and tradition of Korean internal violence are divided into four prototypes, again, for the purpose of analysis, although they are usually inextricable in reality: (1) palace conspiracies and military coups; (2) rebellions against the central government and its legitimacy; (3) peasant and mass uprising against the central and/or local governments' abuses of power and corruption; and (4) resistance against foreign invasions and domination.

(1) Palace Coups and Military Conspiracies

Unlike the other three, the palace conspiracies and military coups[72] belong to the elite political culture than to that of the mass. They are included here along with more typical mass political cultural tradition, because they, too, are often linked to the mass, as their spillover. The ultimate aim of both the palace conspiracies and military coups is to seize power. Hence, their plot is invariably secretive, their operation, speedy, their size, small, and their scope is limited to palaces or to the capital city where the central machinery of government is located. Palace conspiracies and military coups frequently erupt either at the end or at the beginning of a dynasty because in both instances the central power or the central machinery of government is relatively weak. The central power is weak in the former because of its decline and disintegration and in the latter because of its lack of established rules and governing framework, let alone legitimacy.

One of the earliest examples of a palace coup in Korea was the power struggle in Koguryŏ among General Yŏn Kaesomun's younger brother and three sons. In the final years of Koguryŏ, General Yŏn Kaesomun emerged as a military strong man and in 642 appointed himself the *Taemakniji*, the position equivalent to a military dictator or a generalissimo. When he died in 665, his younger brother Yŏn Chŏng-t'o and his three sons—Nam-saeng, Nam-gŏn and Nam-san—fought over his position. Briefly, Nam-saeng, the eldest son, took his father's position, but he was ousted by Nam-gŏn, the second son and Nam-san, the third son. Nam-gŏn then removed Nam-san and rose, temporarily at least, as the new dictator.

In the meantime, Yŏn Chŏng-t'o sought political asylum in Silla and Nam-saeng fled to Kungnae-sŏng, Koguryŏ's old capital, and surrendered to T'ang. This internecine power struggle expedited a coordinated military offensive against the rapidly disintegrating Koguryŏ by T'ang from the north and Silla from the south in 667. For a year Koguryŏ withstood the siege of its capital by the T'ang-Silla forces, but it surrendered to the invading forces in the winter of 668. Thus, the Korean state, which successfully resisted seventy years of intermittent massive Chinese invasions, fell rather haplessly in the end.[73]

A century later in the Unified Silla a series of palace conspiracies, assassinations and civil wars erupted. Beginning in 768 the power struggles ensued between the two royal clans—the Naemul and the Muyŏl—over the succession to the throne. The succession struggle lasted off and on for the next 150 years, until the collapse of the Silla. It involved some twenty kings in the process and hastened the breakdown of the central authority of the government and the rise of local and regional power centers.

Specifically, in 768 a group of royal clans, fearful of the threat to their power posed by the newly adopted Chinese system of government, revolted, but they were soon suppressed. In 774 Kim Yang-sang, a descendant of Naemul clan, seized power and made the king titular head. Kim Ung-go and others countered Kim Yang-sang and tried to restore the authority to the throne. This attempt failed and Kim Yang-sang assassinated Hyegong (r. 765-779) and ascended the throne himself (posthumously titled, Sŏndŏk r. 780-785). In 822 Kim Hŏn-Ch'ang, the leader of another royal clan, the Muyŏl, led a large-scale insurrection against the central authority of the Unified Silla.[74]

Upon the death of Hŭngdŏk (r. 826-835), his cousin, Kim Kyun-jong, was first put forward as king, but he was immediately slain by the supporters of his nephew, Kim Che-ryong, who became Huigang (r. 836-837). In less than a year, Huigang took his own life, and his second cousin, Kim Myŏng, acceded the throne as Minae (r. 838). Against this move, Kim U-jing, the son of Kim Kyun-jong, with the support of Chang Po-go, the Commissioner of Ch'ŏnghae Garrison Command, attacked the capital and dethroned King Minae. He acceded the throne as Sinmu (r. 839). Thenceforth, Silla lasted another century, but its central authority was irreparably damaged to control the rising local powers throughout the country.

The collapse of Later Paekche (892-936) was the result of a typical fratricidal palace intrigue among royal members over the succession question. Kyŏnhwŏn, its founder, had several dozen children from his wives and court ladies. The trouble began when he designated his fourth son, Kŭm-gang, as the Crown Prince, instead of his eldest son, Sin-gŏm. Resentful of his father's act, Sin-gŏm in 936 assembled a following and murdered his brother Kŭm-gang and vanished his father, Kyŏnhwŏn, to a Buddhist temple (Kŭmsan-sa) in Kimche, Chŏlla Province. Enraged by his eldest son's bloody palace coup, Kyŏnhwŏn, in turn, fled to Koryŏ's T'aejo for help in less than three months of his forced exile. Koryŏ welcomed Kyŏnhwŏn and treated him royally. Meanwhile, Sin-gŏm ascended the throne and called himself *taewang* [Great King] but the Later Paekche soon collapsed and was annexed by Koryŏ.[75]

Upon the death of the founder of Koryŏ, T'aejo (r. 918-43), in 943, the succession struggle ensued. The succession strifes broke out despite the fact that T'aejo specified the formula for royal succession in the third article of his famous "Ten Injunctions."[76] Three factions fought for the throne. Pak Sur-hui factions supported Prince Mu, T'aejo's eldest son; Wang Sing-nyŏm faction pushed Prince Yo, T'aejo's son by another wife, and Wang Kyu faction backed Prince Kwangju, T'aejo's son by his sixteenth wife (Wang Kyu was a royal-in-law, who gave two daughters to T'aejo as his fifteenth and sixteenth queens). In accordance with T'aejo's will, Prince Mu succeeded to the throne (posthumously Hyejong, r. 943-45). Wang Kyu plotted to eliminate both Mu and Yo in order to bring Prince Kwangju to the throne. Prince Mu died two years later, most likely as a result of Wang Kyu's scheme, but when Yo (King Chŏngjong r. 945-49) succeeded to the throne, he quickly removed the Wang Kyu forces from the royal court.

Yi Cha-gyŏm's conspiracy represents an attempt at regency.[77] Yi had given a daughter as queen to Yejong (r. 1105-22), and he successfully conspired to put his grandson, Injong (r. 1122-46), on the throne. To strengthen his own power Yi gave two of his daughters to Injong. Through this in-law connections and machination, Yi emerged as the strong man and the king became a figurehead. He even plotted to win the throne himself. To forestall Yi's political ambition, Injong developed a plot to oust Yi, but his plan was foiled by Yi and his military associate, Ch'ŏk Chungyŏng in 1126. A year later, Ch'ŏk removed Yi from power and exiled him. Thus, Yi's attempt at regency ended in tragedy.

Another fratricidal succession struggle transpired among princes at the beginning of the Yi Dynasty. It erupted partly because Yi Sŏng-gye, the founder of the Yi Dynasty, did not even bother to lay down the rule for the succession to his throne. When he took the throne in 1392, he was fifty-nine. He had two principal wives. His first wife from the Han clan bore him six children before her death. From his second wife, of the Kang clan, he had two sons. He selected Prince Pang-sok (d. 1398), the son of Queen Kang, as the crown prince. Angered by this rumor, Prince Pang-wŏn, the son of Queen Han, who had helped his father in founding the dynasty, countered this move by assassinating his two brothers, Pang-sŏk and Pang-bŏn, and their two powerful supporters, Chŏng To-jŏn and Nam Ŭn. When T'aejo (Yi Sŏng-gye) abdicated his throne in September 1398, the strong man Pang-wŏn allowed his brother, Pang-gwa (Chŏngjong r. 1398-1400) to take the helm. Meanwhile, Pang-wŏn removed his other brother, Pang-gan, from contention. Two years later, when all of his actual and potential foes were removed, Pang-won forced Chŏngjong to step down and he himself took the throne (T'ae-jong, r. 1400-1418).

Along with these succession struggles among the royal clans,[78] high-ranking military officials staged numerous coups throughout Korean history to control the government. Although the primary aims of both palace conspiracies and military coups were to seize power, the former dealt primarily with the issue of the succession to the throne, while the latter aimed at the control of power. Hence, as discussed earlier, the military strong men like Yŏn Kaesomun of Koguryŏ, Chŏng Chung-bu and the Ch'oe Clan during Koryŏ wielded power by making their monarchs a titular head, instead of outrightly deposing them and confiscating the throne itself. In that sense, Yi Sŏng-kye's military coup in 1388 was different. He not only seized power but created his own dynasty by overthrowing Koryŏ. Yi's coup, then, somewhat resembles the military coup d'etat of May 16, 1961, and the military putsch of December 12, 1979. In both instances, not only were the existing governments overthrown but new regimes were established. Park's military government and his Yushin regime and Chun's rule are the cases in point.

Whether the coup leaders emerged as strong men while making kings titular heads or as the founder of a new dynasty or a regime, one common denominator has been the power struggle among these leaders immediately after their successful seizure of power until the strong man arose from within these power seekers. Such power struggle has often been bloody and merciless. Above all, as these strong men catapulted themselves to power by force, they were often doomed to perish by force.

Setting aside the accomplishments and/or the failures of a military regime for the moment, and examining from the standpoint of the ruling elites' contest for power, the political power plays of the military regime may consist of several acts. But whether such power plays end in one or six acts, they invariably have been tragedies. Chŏng Chung-bu's military coup for one, represented one of the prototypes. It consisted of three acts: the military power play—the seizure of power by General Chŏng Chung-bu and his two associates, Yi Ui-bang and Yi Ko (Act one); Chŏng's elimination of his associates after the successful power seizure (Act two); and his death at the hand of his new young associate, General Kyŏng Tae-sung (Act three), whose rule spanned nearly a ten-year period from 1170 to 1179 in Koryŏ Dynasty.

The military power play was repeated in less than four years. Upon Kyŏng's death in 1183, his military rival, Yi Ui-min, seized power (Act one), but he, too, was assassinated by the three Ch'oe brothers in 1196 (Act two). Ch'ung-hŏn, one of the Ch'oe brothers, in turn, eliminated his two brothers immediately (Act three), and he ruled for nearly 24 years (Act four) until his own son, Ch'oe Ŭi succeeded him in 1218 (Act five). The Ch'oe clan rule, thus, continued for another 40 years until Ch'oe Ui, the last of Ch'oe clan ruler was assassinated by two conspirators (Kim Chun and Yu Kyŏng) in 1258 (Act six).

Although the military power play is nearly eight hundred years apart, the resemblance in scenario between Gen. Chŏng Chung-bu and the

Ch'oe clans and Gen. Park Chung Hee and Gen. Chun Doo Hwan in South Korea is unmistakable. Again, grossly oversimplified, Gen. Park Chung Hee seized power by staging the military coup in May 16, 1961, with the direct and indirect help of two of his senior military associates, Gen. Chang Do-young, then army chief of staff and Gen. Song Yo-ch'an, ex-Army Chief of Staff (Act one). On July 3, Park arrested Chang, who served as the chairman of the military junta (the Supreme Council of National Reconstruction) from May 16 until his (Chang's) arrest; next, in October 1963 during the presidential election, he imprisoned Song, who served as the head of the cabinet under Park's military junta from July 3, 1961, to June 16, 1962 (Act two). Park emerged as president of the new regime in January 1964 (Act three); Park revised the constitution on October 17, 1969, to permit his third presidential term, and he revised it again on October 27, 1972, in order to continue his presidency indefinitely. He emerged as the president-dictator of the new Yushin system in December 27, 1972 (Act four); and his 18 years of rule, however, abruptly ended when he was assassinated by his own right hand man, Kim Chae-kyu, the Director of the CIA on October 26, 1979 (Act five).[79]

The Chun Doo Hwan government had gone through a similar political power play. After murdering President Park Chung Hee, Kim Chae-kyu, the Director of the South Korean CIA, attempted to collaborate with the two generals, Kim Kye-wŏn, then, Park's chief of the Presidential Secretariat, and Chŏng Sŏng-hwa, Army Chief-of-Staff. Kim was arrested by Gen. Chŏng immediately, and, for a while, Gen. Chŏng (like his predecessor Gen. Chang Do-young during the 1961 coup) impressed the public as the man in charge; but the Kim Chae-kyu–Chŏng Sŏng-hwa Kim–Kye-wŏn power play turned out to be abortive, or, at best, a prelude to the real power play by another military trio—General Chun Doo Hwan, then, the Commander of Defense Security Command, and two South Korea's field army commanders, Generals Roh Tae-Woo and Chŏng Ho-yŏng.

Through a swift military putsch on December 12, 1979, General Chun and his two collaboraters, Roh Tae-woo and Chŏng Ho-yŏng (they belong to the eleventh class of the South Korean Military Academy), arrested Generals Chŏng Sŏng-Hwa and Kim Gye-wŏn. First, the new military trio executed Kim Chae-kyu and imprisoned two generals— Chŏng Sŏng-hwa and Kim Gye-wŏn (Act one); next, the constitution was again overhauled in October 27, 1980, to make room for Chun and his associates, and under this new constitution Gen. Chun was elected as the 12th president of the new regime on February 25, 1981 (Act two).

Chun stepped down from the presidency in February 25, 1988, and one of the trio, Roh Tae Woo, became the 13th president and set the precedence for the peaceful transfer of power, albeit *within* the ruling party (Act three). Ironically, Roh ordered Chun to political banishment or internal political exile in a remote Buddhist temple called *Paekdam-sa* in Kangwŏn Province and forced the third trio, Chŏng Ho-yŏng, to temporary political exile (Act four). This new trio's political power play is in its fifth act now. The Roh regime ended in February 25, 1993, and Kim Young Sam, the first civilian politician since 1961, took the presidency. The final outcome of this trio is still uncertain. But if the Korean history is any guide, it may not be a happy ending. Chun, the first of this trio, however, kept, at least, one promise. During his presidency, he repeatedly assured the public at home and abroad that he will step down.[80] He kept his promise by stepping down when his presidential term expired on February 25, 1988, thereby establishing a new tradition of peaceful transfer of political power. The succeeding Roh administration had continued the newly launched liberalization and democratization process further. This new phase of Korean political process has largely eliminated the tradition of military power play. The new Kim Young Sam presidency will further accelerate not only liberalization and democratization, but also civilianization of the South Korean political process.

(2) Armed Revolts

The primary objective of an armed revolt is not to seize power but to challenge the central governments' legitimacy, usurpation of power, and/or discrimination against certain regions and/or people. Unlike palace coups and military conspiracies, an armed revolt usually erupts at the periphery of power, not at its center. Coup leaders and military conspirators launch frontal attack at the strongest locus of the governmental power, while rebels usually stage their struggle in the rear against the weakest link of the central government machinery.

The rebel leaders often win the peasant support in their struggle. An armed revolt and a peasant rebellion may take place hand-in-hand as a united front against the central government machinery but the primary aim of the armed revolt differs from that of a typical peasant rebellion. The former challenges the legitimacy of the central government, but the latter simply reacts against its abuses and excesses. To that extent, peasant rebellions are alike in traditional Korea and China. As Franz Michael pinpointed, peasant rebellions in traditional China (and traditional Korea as well) were "directed against oppression but did not aim at a change of the system itself."[81]

A series of armed revolts broke out during the final years of the Unified Silla. Beginning in 889, armed revolts and peasant rebellions erupted and spread virtually to every corner of Silla. Yanggil at Pukwŏn (now Wŏnju), Kihwŏn at Chuksan and Kyŏnhwŏn at Chŏnju were most notable. Kungye, a fallen Silla prince, first sided with Kihwŏn in 891 and later became the key lieutenant of Yanggil. In 901 Kungye murdered Yanggil and founded the state of Later Koguryŏ as the successor to the former Koguryŏ kingdom and made Songak (now Kaesŏng) its capital. Kungye, in turn, was removed by Wang Kŏn, who emerged as the founder of Koryŏ in 918. Meanwhile, Kyonhwŏn appeared at Mujinju (now Kwangju) in South Chŏlla Province as the leader of an armed revolt in 892. In 900 he captured Wansanju (now Chŏnju) and created a kingdom, Later Paekche. The Korean Peninsula was once again divided into "three later kingdoms"—Later Koguryŏ, Later Paekche and Silla—until Wang Kŏn reunified the country under Koryŏ by incorporating Silla in 935 and Later Paekche in 936.

The Myoch'ong Revolt of 1135 was a typical armed revolt. It erupted during the time of acute crisis. Internally, the Yi Cha-gyŏm's domination in the Koryŏ court just ended; externally, the rising Jurchen Ch'in of Manchuria menaced Koryŏ. Myoch'ŏng, a Buddhist monk, and his followers, Chŏng Chi-sang, Yu Am and Cho Kwang, contended that the

Koryŏ monarch should be called an "emperor" (the title then used by the Sung, Ch'in and Japanese rulers) rather than "king." They urged the relocation of Koryŏ's capital from Kaesŏng to Pyongyang. They also proposed an alliance with the Sung China to wage a joint military campaign against the Jurchen Ch'in of Manchuria.

Based on a mixture of animism-shamanism, Buddhism, Taoism and geomancy, Mych'ŏng and his followers claimed that Kaesŏng lost its geomantic virtue, while Pyongyang was geomantically a favored location for the seat of power. But their advocacy was ignored and ridiculed by the ruling Confucian group, notably Kim Pu-sik. Failing to persuade Injong (r. 1122-46), Mych'ŏng and his followers resorted to an armed revolt. He raised an army and proclaimed a new kingdom Taewi in 1135. His revolt was short-lived, however. His forces in Pyongyang fell in February of 1136 to the royal army led by Kim Pu-sik. The Myoch'ŏng revolt was a typical regional challenge against a central government. It also represented a power struggle between the Pyongyang-based Buddhist "fallen" elites and the Kaesŏng-based Confucian ruling elites.[82]

The Yi Chir.g-ok Revolt of 1453 epitomized the case of a regional challenge against the central government's usurpation of power. Yi Ching-ok, the military commander in Hamgyŏng Province, formed an alliance with the Jurchen when Sejo (r. 1455-68) dispatched Pak Ho-mun to replace Yi. His anger against the King was deep-seated. Yi was a protege of Gen. Kim Chong-sŏ, a famed general, who led a successful northern expedition during the reign of Sejong the Great (r. 1418-50). With the backing from the disgruntled elements among the literati, Sejo deposed his nephew Tanjong (r. 1452-55) "subsequently putting him to death" and ascended the throne. In the process, he disposed of a great many elder statesmen, including Hwang Bo-in, Kim Chong-sŏ, his younger brother, the Prince of Anpyŏng and the "six martyred ministers."[83] In brief, Sejo's threat to Yi's personal career triggered him to revolt but the chief underlying cause was the former's usurpation of power. The Yi Ching-ok Revolt was soon quelled by the central government forces, but it exhibited a prevailing public wrath of the time against Sejo's naked abuse of power.

The Yi Si-ae Revolt of 1467, again, in Hamgyŏng Province demonstrated the conflict between the local elite and the central power. Yi Si-ae, the leader of a powerful local clan in Kilju and the former chief magistrate of Hoeryŏng, was angered by the central government's practice of sending the local officials from the capital instead of recruiting them from the local influentials. The interests of the established local influentials clashed with those of Sejo's policy of government centralization. For a while, Yi Si-ae succeeded in gaining support from the increasingly squeezed peasants, but his rebel forces, too, was soon put down by Sejo's royal army.

The Chŏng Yŏ-ŭp armed conspiracy of 1589 in Chŏnju, Chŏlla Province, though aborted, during the reign of Sŏnjo (r. 1567-1608) and the Yi In-jwa Revolt of 1728 in Kyŏngsang Province during the reign of Yŏngjo (r. 1724-76) characterized the case of the "fallen" elites' rebellion against the central government. The Revolt of Yi Kwal in 1624, meanwhile, occurred because he felt that he deserved a better political reward than what he received. Yi Kwal, a military leader of the Westerner faction, helped Injo (r. 1623-49) ascend the throne. Feeling that he was not sufficiently rewarded for his services, Yi and his troops rose against the central government. For a while he even threatened Hanyang (Seoul), but his forces were defeated by the government troops. Some of his rebel forces who fled to Manchuria, apparently urged the Manchus to invade Korea to redress the unjust removal of Kwanghaegun (r. 1608-1623) from the throne. Under the pretext of righting this wrong the Manchus launched their first invasion of Korea in 1627 (*Chŏngmyo horan*).

All three revolts—the Chŏng Yŏ-ŭp, the Yi In-jwa and the Yi Kwal —had several things in common. They took place during the period of intense factional power struggle in the central government. The leaders of these revolts were composed either of the fallen or disgruntled members of the factional struggle. They challenged the central power weakened by factional strifes from their local power bases, but all failed in the end. Although the faction-ridden central government was weak, the local rebel forces were not strong enough to overpower it. More recent incidences such as the Cheju Island Revolt of 1948 and the Yŏsu-

Sunch'ŏn Revolt of 1948 and the Kwangju Uprising of 1980 may be seen from the same perspective.[84]

(3) Peasant Rebellions and Mass Uprising

As noted in the above, many of the aforesaid armed revolts were either supported by the peasants or coincided with peasant rebellions and mass uprisings. Unlike the aims of the palace coup and armed revolts, peasant rebellion and mass uprisings are rarely staged to seize power or to challenge it. Both erupt when plunderings and abuses of power by the government and/or by the invading foreign forces, often coupled with natural calamities such as flood, drought, and accompanying famine, are too oppressive and severe for the peasants and the masses to endure. The peasants and the masses are, thus, usually driven to react to the abuses of power.

A series of peasant uprisings begun in 889 in the Korean Peninsula, which ultimately led to the downfall of the Unified Silla, was one of the early cases. Peasant rebellions of 1172 in Pyŏngan Province, the revolt of Mangi and Mangsoi in 1176 in Kongju, Ch'ungch'ŏng Province, the insurrections of Kim Sami and Hyosim in 1193 in Kyŏngsang Province and the peasant rebellion in 1199 in Myŏngju (Kangnung), Kangwŏn Province were notable during the Koryŏ Dynasty.[85]

During the Yi Dynasty the central government's squeezing of the peasants became more systematic. During the reign of Sejo, the government issued *hop'ae* [identification tag] law in order to prevent the peasants from leaving their farmlands. The able-bodied peasant farmer was required to wear an identification tag at all times on which the registrant's name, date of birth, class status and county of residence were recorded. Sejo, also, enacted *Oga chakt'ongpŏp* under which farm households were organized into units of five, and neighbors were made mutually responsible for their members' whereabouts in each unit. In return for having land to cultivate, the peasant farmer had to pay a land tax. And all able-bodied male commoners were subject to military and/or corvee labor service.[86]

During the era of *sedo chŏngch'i* [in-law politics] which began in

1800 upon the death of Chŏngjo (r. 1776-1800), the government corruption and abuses of power exercised by the few royal in-law family clan members were rampant and soon reached the crisis level, which was typified by the so-called "disarray in the three administrations—the land tax, the military tax and the grain loan system." The central government-appointed county magistrates and *hyangni* [local intermediaries] who extorted the already downtrodden peasant farmers to the hilt through the three administrations.

These local officials and functionaries exploited the peasants in the following ways: (1) in the administration of *chŏngjŏng* [land tax], the local officials and their minions extorted by imposing taxes on the waste land (*chingyŏl*), on unregistered land (*ungyŏl*) and by levying higher tax rates than officially permitted (*togyŏl*); (2) in the administration of *kunchŏng* [military tax], they collected fines from the relatives of soldiers who died or deserted (*chokjing*), from the villagers of such soldiers (*tongjing*), from those who were younger than sixty whom they exempted from military draft (*hangnyŏnch'ae*) and from those who were discharged from the military service (*magamch'ae*); and (3) in the administration of *hwan'gŏk* [the grain loan system], the local magistrates and their local functionaries pocketed the grains by falsely recording and reporting the loan transactions (*panjak*), by loaning the grains which were supposed to be on reserve (*kapun*), by reporting the non-existent grains (*holyu*), by loaning money in anticipation of price hike due to poor harvest (*ipbŏn*), by selling grains at a higher price than the official price (*cheung'ko*), by mixing grains with husks (half and half) (*panpaek*) and by doubling the amount of grain by adding husks (*punsŏk*).[87]

Abuses in the three administrations made the lives of the peasantry wretched in the extreme. Many turned to a life of wandering and brigandage. The brigandage led by Im Kkŏk-chŏng was notable. *Im*, a Korean Robinhood, was active for three years, between 1559-1562, in Hwanghae Province. The peasants, often led by the fallen *yangban* rebelled against the extreme hardships imposed upon them. The Hong Kyŏng-nae Rebellion of 1811, the Chinju Uprising of 1862 and the Tonghak Rebellion of 1894-95 were the most notable.

Hong Kyŏng-nae, a fallen *yangban* from Pyŏngan Province, was frustrated by his inability to pass the civil service examinations to enter an official career. Blaming his failure on the central government's policy of discrimination against the people from Pyŏngan Province, U Kun-ch'ik, Kim Sa-yong and he staged open rebellion. Due to a severe famine in the region, many peasants and landless wanderers joined Hong's rebellion, which spread quickly to the region north of Ch'ŏng-ch'ŏn River. The Hong rebellion was repressed by the government forces within a year, but it set the precedent for a series of peasant rebellions and mass uprisings, such as the Cheju Island Uprising in 1813, the Chinju Uprising in the spring of 1862 and finally culminating in the Tonghak Rebellion of 1894-95, which will be examined in detail under the section on Korean nationalism.

(4) Resistance Against Foreign Invasions and Domination

The Korean people's resistance against foreign invasions and domination has been another proud political tradition. An anti-foreign resistance in premodern period has already been discussed under the section on excessive external linkages and pacifism of Korean political tradition. An anti-foreign resistance in modern period along with Korean nationalism will be explored fully in the next chapter.

MAP 2-1. Silla Under King Chinhŭng (540-576)
(ﾛ: sites of four monument stones)

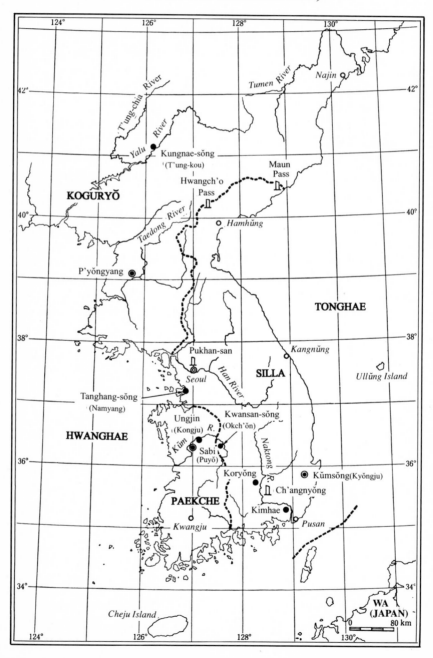

MAP 2-2. The Unification Struggle Among the Three Kingdoms
(7th Century)

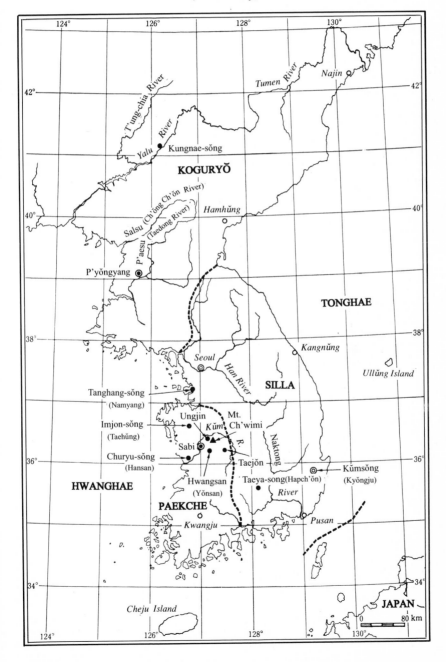

MAP 2-3. Silla and Parhae (Administrative Divisions)

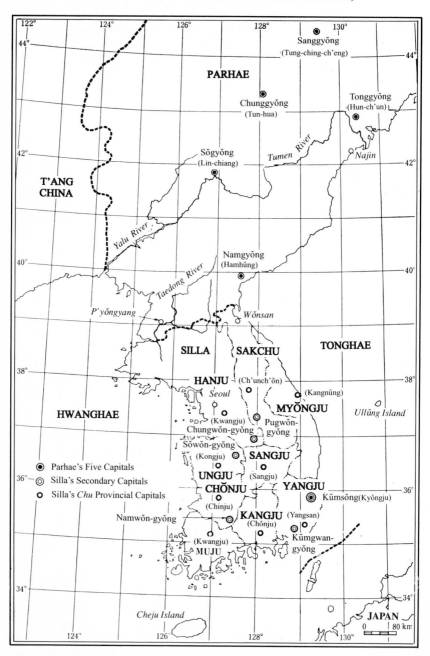

MAP 2-4. Koryo Dynasty Administration Divisions
(11-14th Century)

KHITAN

⊙ Capital

● tohobu

○ mok

JUCHEN

PUK-KYE

Anbuk-pu

SOGYONG

Anbyon-bu

EASTERN SEA

Hwangju-mok

Kyoju-mok

SOHAE

KYOJU

Anso-bu

KYONGGI

TONG-GYE

KAEGYONG

Myongju-mok

NAMGYONG

Kwangju-mok

Ullung Is.

Ch'ungju-mok

YANGGWANG

YELLOW SEA

Ch'ongju-mok

Andong-bu

Sangju-mok

KYONGSANG

Chonju-mok

Annam-bu

TONGGYONG

CHOLLA

Chinju-mok

Naju-mok

T'AMNA

JAPAN

MAP 2-5. *The Five Circuits and Two Border Regions
of Koryŏ (11th Century)*

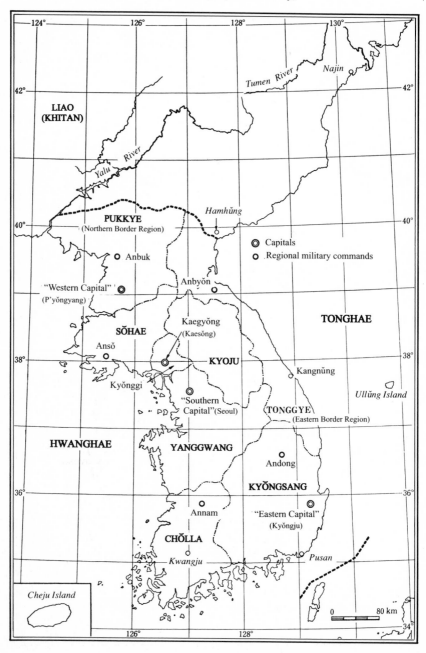

MAP 2-6. The Eight Provinces of the Yi Dynasty
(14th-19th Century)

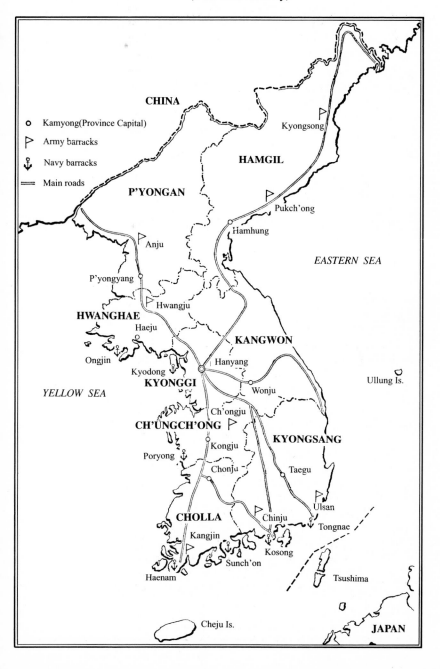

MAP 2-7. Chosŏn's Eight Provinces and Regional Military Commands (15th Century)

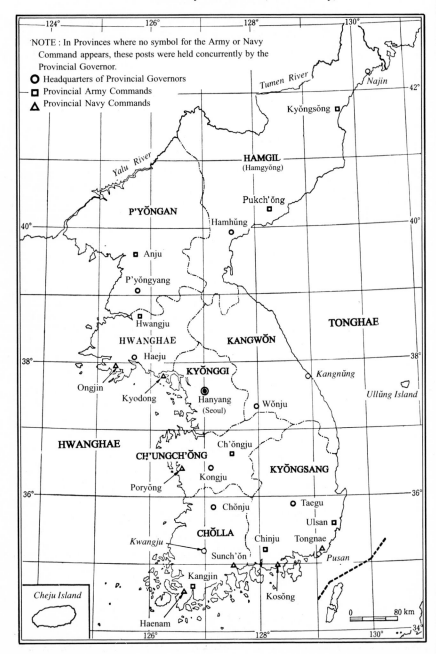

NOTE : In Provinces where no symbol for the Army or Navy
Command appears, these posts were held concurrently by the
Provincial Governor.

O Headquarters of Provincial Governors
◻ Provincial Army Commands
△ Provincial Navy Commands

MAP 2-8. Korea in the Later Three Kingdoms Period
(Late 9th-Early 10th Centuries)

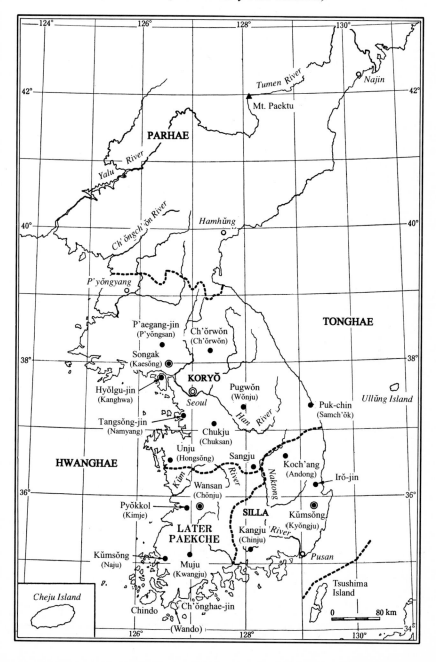

MAP 2-9. Koryŏ and the Mongols (13th Century)

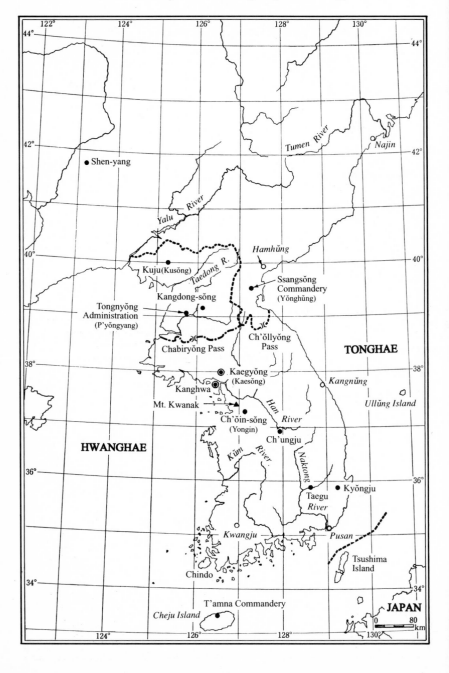

MAP 2-10. *Koryŏ's Northern Frontier Region*
(Late 10th to Early 12th Centuries)

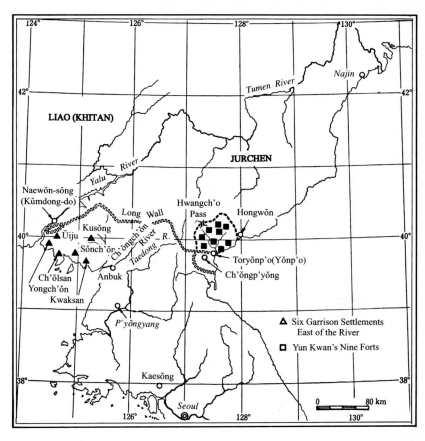

MAP 2-11. The Hideyoshi Invasion (1592-1598)

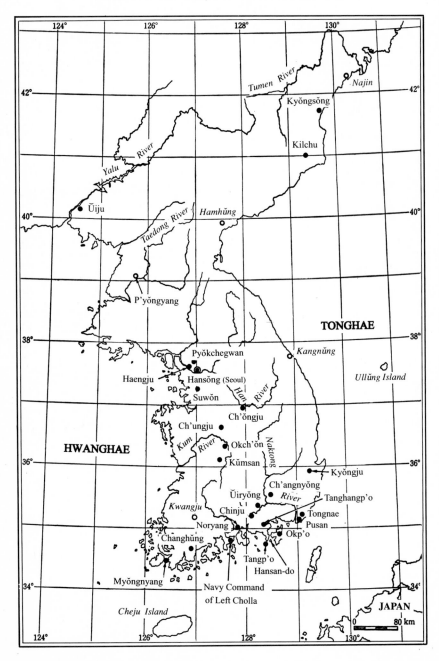

MAP 2-12. The Six Garrison Forts and Four Yalu Outposts (ca. 1450)

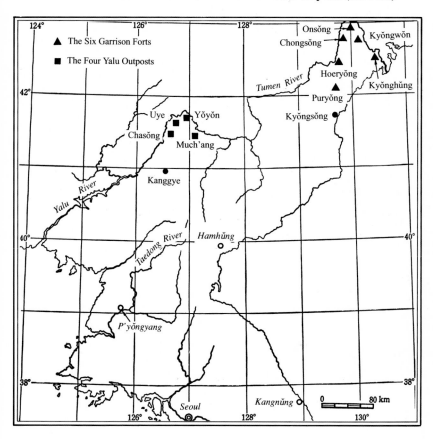

74   The Korean Political Heritage

Table 2-1. Koryŏ Dynasty's Governing Apparatus

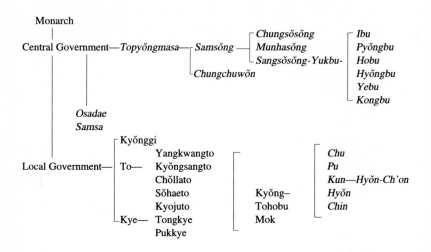

Source: Adapted from T'aesŏp Byŏn, *Koryŏ chŏngch'i jedŏsa yŏnku*, pp. 18-83 and Woon-tae Kim, *Hankuk chŏngch'iron*, pp. 104-115.

Table 2-2. *Yi Dynasty's Governing Apparatus*

Monarch
|
Central Government
|
                                              Ijo
  ┌─ Ŭijŏngbu ──────── Yukjo ──── Hojo
  │ ─ Saganwŏn   Yejo
  │ ─ Sahŏnbu   Pyŏngjo
  │ ─ Hongmun'gwan   Hyŏngjo
  │ ─ Yemun'gwan   Kongjo
  └─ Ch'unch'u'gwan

Local Government

Unit	No.	Administrators (Ranks)
To┌[Provinces]	8	Kwanch'alsa (Aux. 2)
│ Kyŏngki		
│ Ch'ungch'ŏng		
│ Kyŏngsang		
└ Chŏlla		
│ Hwanghae		
│ Kangwŏn		
│ Hamgil (Hamgyŏng)		
└Pyŏngan		
Yudobu	1	
Pu	6	Puyun (Aux. 2)
Taedohobu	5	Taedohobusa (Reg. 3)
Mok	20	Moksa (Reg. 3)
Tohobu	74	Tohobusa (Aux. 4)
Kun	73	Kunsu (Aux. 5)
Hyŏn	154	Hyŏllyŏng (Aux. 5)
		Hyon'gam (Aux. 6)

Sources: Adapted from Woontae Kim, *Chŏson Wangjohaengjŏng-sa*, pp. 79-146;
           William Henthorn, *Op. Cit.*, pp. 158-161.

The Korean Political Heritage

Table 2-3. Koryŏ Military Rulers

Generals	Years of rule
Chŏng Chung-bu	1170-1179
Kyŏng Tae-sung	1179-1183
Yi Uimin	1183-1196
Ch'oe Clan	1196-1258
(Ch'oe Ch'ung-hŏn)	(1196-1218)
(Ch'oe U)	(1218-1249)
(Ch'oe Hang)	(1249-1256)
(Ch'oe Ui)	(1256-1258)
Kim Chun	1258-1268
Im Clan	1268-1270
(Im Yŏn)	(1268-1270)
(Im Yu-mu)	(1270)

Table 2-4. Yi Dynasty's Factional Pedigree

Reign	Factions	Leaders
Sejo (1455-68)-	Hunku [Conservatives]	Chŏng In-ji
Sŏngjong (1469-94)		Ch'oe Hang
		Sin Suk-ju
	Chŏlui [Loyalists]	Kim Si-sup
		Nam Hyo-on
		Wŏn Ho
	Salim [Literati]	Kim Koeng-p'il
		Chŏng Yo-ch'ang
		Cho Wi
	Ch'ongdam [Up-right]	Nam Hyo-on
		Hong Yu-son
		Yi Chŏng-eun
Yŏnsan (1494-1506)		
1498 (Muo sawha)	Purge of Scholars	Salim factions purged
1504 (Kapcha sawha)	Purge of Scholars	Yun P'il-sang
		Han Ch'i-hyŏng
		Yi Kuk-kyun
		purged
Chŏngjong (1506-44)		
1519 (Kimyo sawha)	Purge of Scholars	Cho Kwang-jo
		Kim Sik
		Kim An-kuk
		purged
Myŏngjong (1545-67)		
1545 (Ulsa sawha)	Purge of Scholars	Yun Im
		Yu Kwan
		Yu In-suk
		purged
Sŏnjo (1567-1608)		
1575	Tongin [Easterners]	Kim Hyo-wŏn
		Yi Hwang
		Cho Sik
	Sŏin [Westerners]	Sim Ui-gyŏm
		Yi I
		Song Hŏn

Table 2-4.   Continued

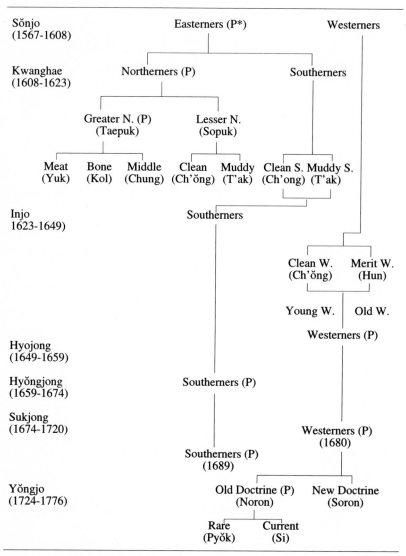

Source: A simplified version by the Author, based primarily on Pyong-do Lee, *Kuksa Taek-wan*, especially, pp. 381-400. *: (P) means in power. See also, Edward Willet Wagner, *The Literati Purges: Political Conflict in Early Yi Korea* (Cambridge: Harvard East Asian Monographs, 58, 1974).

Notes

1. Ruth Benedict, *Patterns of Culture* (Boston: Houghton Mifflin Co., 1934, 1959), p. 228.
2. Cornelius Osgood, *The Koreans and Their Culture* (New York: The Ronald Press, 1951), p. v.
3. Dividing people in a given country into the ruler (the ruling elites) and the ruled (the mass people) is a gross oversimplification. The ruling elite-mass distinction in this study is no exception. Lasswell and Kaplan, for instance, define elites as those with most power in a group, the mid-elite with less power and the mass, with the least power. Further, they define the rulers as "the most active members of the elite." For details, see Harold D. Lasswell and Abraham Kaplan, *Power and Society: A Framework for Political Inquiry* (New Haven: Yale University Press, 1950, 1963), pp. 200-203; see also, William A. Welsh, *Leaders and Elites* (New York: Holt, Rinehart and Winston, 1979), pp. 1-21. By the same token, the dichotomy of the elite-mass, high-low, or great-little culture is arbitary and useful only for analytic purposes. For example, human culture may be divided into "high culture" and "low culture." The high culture is to be found in the schools, temples and palaces of the cities, and the low culture, in the villages. The high culture was passed on to posterity in writing by philosophers, theologians and literary men; the low culture was transmitted by word of mouth among illiterate peasants. Redfield stated, "for every such great culture there are two traditions, the Little Traditions of the village and the common people and the Great Tradition of the reflective few." For details, see Margaret P. Redfield, ed., *Human Nature and the Study of Society: The Papers of Robert Redfield* (Chicago: University of Chicago Press, 1962-63), p. 57. Peacock and Kirsch, on the other hand, distinguished the urban-centered "great traditions" from the rural-centered "little traditions of the peasant masses." See James L. Peacock and A. Thomas Kirsch, *The Human Direction: An Evolutionary Approach to Social and Cultural Anthropology* (New York: Appleton-Century-Crofts, 1970), p. 190.
4. In his survey of studies on contemporary Korean political culture, Chi-hun Yi identified some 39 components of Korean political culture. Among these, he pinpointed seven key elements. They are: 1) authoritarianism; 2) citizenship; 3) community consciousness; 4) alienation; 5) factionalism; 6) resistance; and 7) national self-reliance. For details, see "The Basic Elements of Korean Political Culture" (in Korean) in *Hankukchŏngch'ihakbo* 16 (1982), quoted in Hakjoon Kim, *Hankuk Chŏngch'ilon* [On Korean Politics] (Seoul: Hankil-sa, 1985), pp. 189-190. See, also, Kim's survey of studies dealing with Korean political culture, especially, on pp. 175-190. Kang, for instance, identified the

Korean culture as the *nunch'i* culture and contended that the basic concept for understanding social actions in Korea is *nunch'i*. The word as a noun denotes "a social sense," "an eye for social situations," "tact" or "savoir faire." The word as a verb means "to try to read one's mind," "to study one's face," "to grasp a situation," "to espy one's motivation" or "to see how the wind blows." The word *nunch'i* also is used to describe "a deceitful tact" of the weak (subordinates) toward the strong (superiors). For details, see Shin-pyo Kang, "Toward a New Understanding of the Culture of the East Asians: Chinese, Korean and Japanese," *Journal of East and West Studies* 3 (1975): 40-41. Also, his *The East Asian Culture and Its Transformation in the West: A Cognitive Approach to Changing Worldview Among East Asian Americans in Hawaii*, (Seoul National University American Studies Institute Monograph Series No. 3) (Seoul: Seoul National University Press): 64-66 and his "Principles of Structure of Korean Traditional Culture: An Essay for a New Understanding of East Asian Culture—China, Korea, and Japan," (in Korean), *A Study of Korean Society* (Seoul: Minum-sa, 1980). Quoted in Mahn-kee Kim, "Administrative Culture of Korea: A Comparison with China and Japan," *Korean Social Science Journal* 10 (1983): 122. A good survey of the traditional Korean culture and transformation is found in Sang-bok Han, "The Korean Culture: Tradition and Change," paper delivered at the Conference for American Textbook Authors and Editors, Seoul, Korea, 15-17 October 1982. Also, Cornelius Osgood, *Op. Cit.*, especially Parts Four and Five. For a detailed survey of the definitions of culture and political culture, see Sung Chul Yang, "The Study of Divided Nations: Problems and Prospects," paper delivered at the 1983 Joint Conference of the Korean Political Science Association and the Association of Korean Political Scientists in North America, Seoul, Korea, 6-9 August 1983.

5. Recently, Perlmutter made a distinction between modern and early notions of authoritarianism. The early version, according to him, was "rule by the few in the name of the few; modern authoritarianism is rule by the few in the name of the many." The authoritarian regimes are characterized by "repression, intolerace, encroachment on the private rights and freedom of citizens, and limited autonomy for nonstatist interest groups." Further, he stated that the function of the authoritarian state or regime is "to politicize and bureaucratize society at the expense of cultural, social, and intellectual resources. It seeks both vertical and horizontal domination. The major preoccupation of the officials of the authoritarian system is to establish institutions that provide or facilitate intelligence gathering, domination and control of politics, instruments and practices that inhibit autonomous social action, politicizing controlled social action, bureaucratization of society and political structures, creation of administrative and punitive instruments, regulation and supervision of culture, and control

over its own instruments of repression." For details, see Amos Perlmutter, *Modern Authoritarianism: A Comparative Institutional Analysis* (New Haven: Yale University Press, 1981), p. 2 and pp. 7-8.

6. The earliest punitive law recorded in Korean history was the Ancient Chosŏn's *P'aljo Pŏpkŭm* [Eight Prohibitory Articles or Criminal Code]. Only three of the eight articles remain on record, e.g., article one stipulates that "the murderer shall be executed immediately." This criminal code was later expanded to include over sixty articles during the Han Chinese colonial period. For details, see Pyŏng-do Lee, *Kuksa Daekwan*, pp. 34-37. Also, his, *Hankuk Kodaesa Yŏnku*, pp. 62-64. During the early Silla, the criminal code was reportedly expanded from eight to sixty. See, for instance, Chŏng-uk Lee, *Silla Kukka-Hyŏngsŏng-sa Yŏnku*, pp. 79-81. During the reign of Munmu (r. 661-80), the Unified Silla adopted a fully developed bureaucratic government (a modified version of the Chinese administrative model) including *Ibangbu* [the Ministry of Justice or Punishment]. For details, see Woo-keun Han, *Op. Cit.*, pp. 91-92. An extensive study of Yi Korea's judicial system is found in Byŏng-hwa Kim, *Hankook Sabŏp-sa* [The History of Korean Judiciary] (Seoul: Iljogak, 1982), Vols. 1, 2 and 3. A caricature of the criminal justice (punishment) system in the late Yi Dynasty is found in Kyut'ae Lee, *Kaehwa Paekyŏng* [The Kaleidoscopic Scenes of Korea's Opening to the World] (Seoul: Sint'aeyang-sa, 1969), pp. 197-322.

7. John King Fairbank, *The United States and China,* 4th ed. (Cambridge: Harvard University Press, 1979), p. 117 and p. 123.

8. Fairbank pointed out that the "law" in China was "an arm of the state and something to avoid—a very different from that which has nourished political leadership, guided legislation, trained statesmen, served corporations, and protected individual rights among the legal-minded and litigious American people." See *Ibid.*, p. 123. Similarly, Hideo Tanaka wrote a typical Japanese view of law:

   All society's troubles are of the law's own making; the less we are bothered by the law, the better off we are; they therefore crane their necks to see the day when they will be freed from the encumbrance of the law and believe that if they persist in their wish, a law-free society will arrive some day. Implicit in this kind of emotional attitude is not just a reasoned denial of the significance of law but also an instinctive abhorrence of the very idea of law....The Japanese feel that they are better off when not bothered by law. If they can do without law, so much the better. Law is something to be shunned.

   For details, see Hideo Tanaka, ed., *The Japanese Legal System: Introductory Cases and Materials* (Tokyo: University of Tokyo Press, 1976), pp. 302-303.

9. Pyŏng-Choon Hahm, *The Korean Political Tradition and Law* (Seoul: Hollym Corporation, 1967), p. 19 and p. 210. In the book, he also distinghuished the

ethical or *alegalistic* Eastern political tradition from the legalistic Western political tradition. See *Ibid.*, p. 6. Byŏng-ho Park also wrote that the Korean law was nothing more than the government's "administrative law" which prescribes and proscribes the people's activities. See his, *Hankuk Bŏpchaesa-kyo* [A Study of Korean Legal System] (Seoul: Bŏpmun-sa, 1983), p. 407. See also, Bong-dŏk Chŏn, *Hankuk Kundae Bŏpsasang-sa* [History of Modern Korean Legal Philosophy] (Seoul: Pakyŏng-sa, 1981), pp. 32-56; Chŏngko Choi, *Hankuk ue Sŏyangbŏp Suyong-sa* [History of Korea's Reception of European Laws] (Seoul: Pakyŏng-sa, 1983), pp. 16-18, pp. 30-34 and pp. 330-336. Byong-hwa Kim, *Hankuk Sabŏp-sa* [History of Korean Judicial Law] (Seoul: Iljogak, 1982), Vol. I, pp. 3-9 and pp. 147-151. See also, Dae-Kyu Yoon, *Law and Political Authority in South Korea* (Seoul: Westview Press and Kyungnam University Press, 1990), pp. 5-37.

10. For a detailed study of Puyŏ kingdom, see Pyong-do Lee, *Hankuk Kodaesa Yŏnku*, pp. 213-227; Ki-baik Lee, *Op. Cit.*, p. 21.

11. After carefully examining pertinent historical records, Lee speculates that *namtang*, the government headquarters of Silla, which appeared sometime during the reign of King Nisakŭm (310-356 A.D.), symbolized the emergence of a centralized monarchical state. For details, see Pyŏng-Do Lee, *Hankuk Kodaesa Yŏnku*, p. 630. Another noted Korean historian, Ki-baik Lee, pinpointed that Silla's *Chipsabu* [Chancellery Office], created in 651 during the reign of Queen Chindŏk (r. 647-53) and fully developed in 685 in the reign of Sinmun (681-91), was one of the first central administrative apparatus. For details, see Lee, *Silla Chŏngch'i Sahoesa Yŏnku* [A Study of Silla's Political and Social History] (Seoul: Iljogak, 1984), pp. 134-194.

12. For a survey of the history of Korean accommodation of European and American legal systems and philosophy of law, see Chŏngko Choi, *Op. Cit.*, pp. 402-428. Also, Pyŏng-Choon Hahm, *Op. Cit.*, pp. 205-217.

13. Leaders or chiefs of family clans called, *kunjang* or *ch'onjang*, were chosen, according to *Samkuk Yusa* (a semi-legendary account of Korean history written during the Koryŏ dynasty) by an assembly of each family clan. The same record indicates that Pak Hyŏkkŏse, the legendary founder of Silla was elected by the assembly of six family clan chiefs. In ancient Korea, an assembly of villagers called, *kongch'ŏng* or *toch'ŏng*, similar to India's Manjhi Than or Liberia's Palaver house, also existed. For details, see Pyŏng-do Lee, *Hankuk Kodaesa Yŏnku*, pp. 595-642; Woont'ae Kim and others, *Hankuk Chŏngch'i-ron* [On Korean Politics] (Seoul: Pakyŏng-sa, 1982), pp. 83-86.

14. The evolutionary transformation of a native governmental consultative body from *kongch'ŏng* to *namtang* and to *hwabaek* is discussed by Pyŏng-do Lee in *Hankuk Kodaesa Yŏnku*, pp. 595-642. See also, Chŏng-uk Lee, *Silla Kukka Hyŏngsŏngsa Yŏnku*, pp. 12-73 and Ki-baek Lee, *Silla Chŏngch'i Sahoesa*

Yŏnku, passim.

15. The political institutions of Koryŏ are discussed by T'aesop Byŏn in *Koryŏ Chŏngch'i Chaedosa Yŏnku* [A Study of Koryŏ's Political Institutional History] (Seoul: Iljogak, 1984), especially, pp. 3-115. Woont'ae Kim gives a succinct account of the Yi Dynasty's political institutions in *Chosŏn Wangcho Haengjŏngsa*, pp. 104-146.

16. The three models of political culture—participant, parochial and subject—are found in Gabriel A. Almond and G. Bingham Powell, Jr., *Comparative Politics: A Developmental Approach* (Boston: Little, Brown, 1966), pp. 23-24; Gabriel A. Almond and Sidney Verba, *The Civic Culture: Political Attitudes and Democracy in Five Nations* (Princeton: Princeton University Press, 1963), pp. 3-42; Gabriel A. Almond, ed., *Comparative Politics Today: A World View* (Boston: Little, Brown, 1974), pp. 50-56. In his study of political participation in Korea in the period from the opening of Korea in 1876 to the Japanese annexation in 1910, Palais concluded that in absolute terms the numbers of politically conscious and participating individuals remained small, but in relative terms there was a significant increase over previous decades. For details, see James B. Palais, "Political Participation in Traditional Korea, 1876-1910," *The Journal of Korean Studies* (1979): 73-122. Brandt, in his article "Sociocultural Aspects of Political Participation in Rural Korea," in the same Journal, pointed out that "no matter how political participation is defined, there is relatively little of it in rural Korea" (p. 222).

17. See, for instance, Nam Young Lee, "The Structure of Democratic Belief System: An Analysis of Political Culture in Korea," *Korea and World Affairs* (Winter, 1983), pp. 629-655. Also, Dong-suh Bark and Chae-jin Lee, "Bureaucratic Elite and Development Orientations," Dae-sook Suh and Chae-jin Lee, eds., *Political Leadership in Korea* (Seattle: University of Washington Press, 1976), pp. 91-133; Joong-gun Chung and Sung-moun Pae, "Orientation of the Korean Bureaucrats Toward Democracy: A Study of Background and Institutional Characteristics," *Korea and World Affairs* (Summer, 1977), pp. 219-236; Chŏng Lim Kim and Byŏng-kyu Woo, "Legislative Leadership and Democratic Development," in Suh and Lee, *Op. Cit.,* pp. 41-66. Chŏng Lim Kim, ed., *Political Participation in Korea* (Santa Barbara: Clio Books, 1980), pp. 119-141.

18. Stephen White, "Political Culture in Communist States: Some Problems of Theory and Method," *Comparative Politics* (April 1984): 351-365, especially, p. 363. On the basis of interviews with recent Soviet emigres, DiFranceisco and Gitelman concluded that Soviet political culture is neither a "subject" nor a "subject-participant" one. The Soviet citizens participate illegally and covertly in policy implementation process. They identified three modes of participation in the Soviet political system: formal-ritualistic participation;

citizen-initiated contacts with official persons and institutions; and contacts with the policy-implementers. For details, see Wayne DiFranceisco and Zvi Gitelman, "Soviet Political Culture and Covert Participation in Policy Implementation," *American Political Science Review* (September 1984): 603-621.

19. A discussion of Silla's "head-rank" system is found in Chŏng-uk Lee, *Op. Cit.*, pp. 175-195 and in Ki-baek Lee, *Silla Chŏngch'i Sahoesa Yŏnku*, pp. 34-65. See also, Ki-dong Yi, "Shilla's Kolp'um System and Japan's Kabane System," *Korean Social Science Journal* 11 (1984): 7-24.

20. Koryŏ's social and class system is detailed in Hŭng-shik Hŏ's *Koryŏ Sahoesa Yŏnku* [Study of Koryŏ Social History] (Seoul: Asea Munwha-sa, 1981), especially, pp. 17-22. An extensive study of Koryŏ's slavery system is found in Seung-ki Hong, *Koryŏ Kwijok Sahoe wa Nobi* [Koryŏ's Artistocratic Society and Slaves] (Seoul: Iljogak, 1983). See also, Ki-baik Lee, *A New History of Korea*, pp. 110-113 and T'ae-sŏp Pyŏn, *Koryŏ Chŏngch'ijedosa Yŏnku* [A Study of Korea's Political System] (Seoul: Iljogak, 1984).

21. T'ae-sŏp Pyŏn, *Koryŏ Chŏngch'i Chaedosa Yŏnku*, pp. 454-459.

22. Ki-baik Lee, *A New History of Korea*, pp. 180-182.

23. Wagner, for instance, observed that "a process of continuous reconcentration of examination success within ever narrowing lineage segments and subsegment is apparent" in Yi Korea's state examination system. For details, see Edward W. Wagner, "The Korean Chokpo as a Historical Source," and June-ho Song, "The Government Examination Rosters of the Yi Dynasty," both in Spencer J. Palmer, ed., *Studies in Asian Genealogy* (Provo: Brigham Young University Press, 1972), pp. 141-152 and pp. 153-176, respectively. An extensive study of Koryŏ's civil service examination system is found in Hŭng-sik Hŏ, *Koryŏ Kwakŏ Chedosa Yŏnku* [A Study of Koryŏ's Civil Service Examination System] (Seoul: Iljogak, 1984). It should be noted that except for the children of *yangban*, others had little or no access to education during the Yi Dynasty. The typical education of *yangban* class boys was as follows: at age seven or eight the *yangban* boy entered a *sŏtang* or elementary school, where he learned the rudiments of Chinese language and literature. After eight years of schooling at *sŏtang*, he entered one of the four *haktang* or secondary schools at age fifteen or sixteen, if he lived in Seoul. If he lived outside Seoul, he entered *hyangkyo* in each district. The graduates of *haktang* or *hyangkyo* were entitled to sit for the lower civil service examination. Among the graduates, two hundred students (later reduced to one hundred twenty-six) annually entered *Sŏnggyun'gwan*, the national university in Seoul, and they were eligible to take the higher civil service examination. For a comprehensive history of Korean educational institutions, see Ki-un Han, *Hankuk Kyoyuk-sa* [History of Korean Education] (Seoul: Pakyŏng-sa, 1983), especially, pp. 63-71 and pp. 102-156. For a detailed analysis of Yi Dynasty's class system, see

Woon-t'ae Kim, *Chosŏn Wangjo Haengjŏngsa* [History of Chosŏn Dynasty's Administration] (Seoul: Pakyŏng-sa, 1981), pp. 34-42.

24. *Yangban* is quite similar, if not identical, to the traditional Chinese gentry. Fairbank, for instance, defined the Ch'ing Chinese gentry as an office-holder, land-holder, or both office and land-holder. For details, *Op. Cit.*, pp. 32-39. For a detailed study of *Yangban* in early Yi Dynasty, see Song-mu Lee, *Chosŏn Ch'oki Yangban Yŏnku* [A Study of Yangban in Early Yi Chosŏn] (Seoul: Iljogak, 1985). Also, Edward Willett Wagner, *The Literati Purges: Political Conflict in Early Yi Korea*, pp. 11-12.

25. Yŏng-mo Kim, *Chosŏn Chibaech'ung Yŏnku* [The Study of Chosŏn Ruling Class] (Seoul: Iljogak, 1977), pp. 16-28.

26. *Ibid.*, pp. 184-187. Note a social mobility study on Ming-Ch'ing China in this regard. Ho, for instance, finds some fundamental differences in social mobility between Ming-Ch'ing China and the modern West. He concludes that while in industrial societies the continual technological revolution and economic dynamism, on balance, brought about a steady upward mobility trend in terms of income and occupation, in Ming-Ch'ing China the multiplication of population and technological and institutional stagnation made a long-range downward mobility trend inevitable. For details, see Ping-ti Ho, *The Ladder of Success in Imperial China: Aspects of Social Mobility, 1368-1911* (New York: Columbia University Press, 1962, 1967), especially, pp. 255-266.

27. For details, see Ki-baik Lee, *A New History of Korea*, pp. 48-54.

28. *Ibid.*, pp. 53-54.

29. *Ibid.*, pp. 75-77. See also, Ki-baik Lee, *Silla Chŏngch'i Sahoesa Yŏnku*, pp. 149-174.

30. Ki-baik Lee, *A New History of Korea*, pp. 75-77.

31. T'aesŏp Pyŏn, *Koryŏ Chŏngch'i Chaedosa Yŏnku*, pp. 18-83; also, Woon-t'ae Kim, *Hankuk Chŏngch'iron*, pp. 104-115.

32. A discussion of *Sahŏnbu* and its ten-point guide for the first monarch of the Yi Dynasty is found in Pyŏng-Choon Hahm, *Op. Cit.*, pp. 54-62. See also, Byŏng-hwa Kim, *Op. Cit.*, pp. 4-6. A well-documented study of Yi Dynasty's central and local administration is found in Woont'ae Kim, *Chosŏn Wangjo Haengjŏngsa*, especially, pp. 61-146.

33. See, for instance, John King Fairbank, *Op. Cit.*, pp. 32-39. Fairbank wrote that the medieval serf was bound to the land and could not leave or dispose of it, whereas the Chinese peasant both in law and in fact has been free to sell and, if he had the means, to purchase land. His bondage has resulted from a press of many circumstances but not from a legal institution similar to European feudalism. Nor has it been maintained by the domination of a professional warrior caste like the Japanese *daimyo*.

34. Chin-ch'ŏl Kang examined Koryŏ's land tenure system in *Koryŏ T'ochichae-*

88 The Korean Political Heritage

53. See, for instance, Chin-ch'ŏl Kang, Op. Cit.

54. John King Fairbank, Op. Cit., pp. 115-117.

55. Pyŏng-do Yi's study of Tan'gun legend is found in his Hankuk Kodaesa Yŏnku, pp. 27-43. The legends of Chumong and Pak Hyŏkkŏse are found in Ki-baik Lee, A New History of Korea, pp. 7-8. Chŏng-uk Lee also examined Pak Hyŏkkŏse's pedigree. See his Silla Kukga Hyŏngsŏngsa Yŏnku, pp. 133-143. See also, Hyŏn-yong Kim, Hankuk Kosŏlhwalon [On Korea's Old Legendary Stories] (Seoul: Saemunsa, 1984), pp. 9-77; Yŏl-kyu Kim, Hankuk ui Sinhwa [Korean Mythology] (Seoul: Iljogak, 1985), pp. 9-27.

56. A survey of legitimacy in Korean history is found in Hyoun-jong Lee, "Legitimacy in Korean history," East Asian Review (Spring, 1976), pp. 58-72.

57. Woo-keun Han, Op. Cit., pp. 48-49. See also, Myŏng-jong Yu, Hankuk Ch'ŏlhak-sa [History of Korean Philosophy] (Seoul: Ilsin-sa, 1982), pp. 17-21.

58. Pyŏng-do Lee, Kuksa Daekwan, p. 126.

59. For details, see Myŏng-jong Yu, Op. Cit., pp. 37-56.

60. Yu examined the introduction of Confucianism in the Three Kingdoms in his Hankuk Ch'ŏlhak-sa, pp. 16-17. A succinct summary of Confucianism is found in W. Richard Comstock and others, Religion and Man: An Introduction (New York: Harper and Row, 1971), pp. 271-295. Arthur Wright, for instance, identified thirteen "approved attitudes and behavior patterns of what he called 'Confucian personality'"; submissiveness to authority—parents, elders and superiors; submissiveness to the mores and norms (li); reverence for the past and respect for history; love of traditional learning; esteem for the force of example; primacy of broad moral cultivation over specialized competence; preference for non-violent moral reform in state and society; prudence, caution, and preference for a middle course; non-competitiveness; courage and sense of responsbility for a great tradition; self-respect (with some permissible self-pity) in adversity; exclusiveness and fastidiousness on moral and cultural grounds; and punctiliousness in treatment of others." For details, see Arthur F. Wright, "Values, Roles and Personalities," in A. F. Wright and Denis Twitchett, eds., Confucian Personalities (Stanford: Stanford University Press, 1962), p. 8. See also, W. Theodore de Bary, ed. Sources of Chinese Tradition (New York: Columbia University Press, 1960), especially, Chapters 5 and 18.

61. The English translation of Wang Kŏn's Ten Injunctions is found in Pyŏng-Choon Hahm, Op. Cit., pp. 46-54.

62. In China, after the Buddhist interlude which extended from the end of Han to the end of the T'ang Dynasty, Confucianism reasserted through the Neo-Confucian movement led by such scholarly figures as Han Yu (768-824) and Li Ao (c. 789). It was critical of the religious practices of Taoism and Buddhism. It was also more metaphysical and systematic in that it synthesized all major

thought streams which had developed in China up to that time. Usually, the neo-Confucian movement in China can be divided into two periods—the Rational school of the Sung era (960-1279), which culminated in the thought of Chu Hsi (1130-1200), and the Mind school of the Ming dynasty (1368-1644), represented in the thought of Wang Yang-ming (1472-1529). A detailed analysis of neo-Confucianism in the Yi Dynasty is found in Yŏng-wu Han, "Chosŏn Chŏnki Sŏnglihak ui Sahoekyŏngchaesasang" [Socio-Economic Thought of neo-Confucianism during the Early Period of Chosŏn] in *Hankuk Sasang Daekye* [Outline of Korean Thought] (Seoul: Sŏnggyunkwan University Press, 1976), Volume II, pp. 51-204. See also, Myŏng-jong Yu, *Op. Cit.,* pp. 119-258.

63. For details, Woo-keun Han, *Op. Cit.,* pp. 203-228.

64. As Wagner aptly pointed out, one of the striking features of factional conflict in Yi Korea was the control between the depth of the factional division in the society and the shallowness of the issues under contention. Major disputes centered around questions such as the designation of an heir-apparent or the proper period of mourning for a deceased queen. For details, see Edward Wagner, *The Literati Purges, passim.*

65. A study of Koguryŏ's expansionist policy, particularly during the reign of Kwanggaet'o the Great is found in Pyŏng-do Lee, *Hankuk Kodaesa Yŏnku,* pp. 374-390 and pp. 423-454.

66. *Ibid.*

67. Yŏng-u Han, for instance, differentiates several schools of *sadae* thought, although all agree on one fundamental premise, i.e., Korea is small and needs, therefore, a good neighborly alliance with, and/or aid from China. The *sadae* thought by Chŏng To-jŏn (1337?-1398) was derived from more strategic consideration. That is, making alliance with the Ming China would lead to the attack of the Khitans and ultimately to the recovery of the Koguryŏ's lost territory in Manchuria. The *sadae* thought of Pyŏn Kyae-ryang, a neo-Confucian scholar, during the reign of T'aejong (r. 1400-18) and Sejong (r. 1418-50) had two main features. He rejected the revanchist advocacy voiced by Chŏng To-jŏn and other scholars. He, also, contended that the Korean king's sovereignty was not derived from the Chinese Emperor's blessing, but from *Tangun*, the legendary father of Korea. Yang Sŏng-ji's *sadae* was more nationalistic in that he stressed *inter alia*: (i) Korea's self-determination and national independence; (ii) its geographical peculiarity; (iii) its historical uniqueness; (iv) its cultural superiority and originality; (v) its victorious legacy of anti-foreign resistance; and (vi) its political and cultural prosperity. Finally, *sadae* thought by Yi Hwang (1501-1570) and Yi I (1536-1584) were far less nationalistic. Under the maxim that "Heaven has no two days and People have no two kings," Yi Hwang acknowledged that China was the sole source of Korean

king's sovereignty. Yi I also stressed the cultural affinity of China and Korea as if they were senior and junior members of the same cultural family. For details, see Yŏng-u Han, *Op. Cit.*, pp. 75-91. See also, Woon-t'ae Kim, *Chosŏn Wangcho Haengjŏngsa*, pp. 53-56.

68. According to T'ae-sŏp Pyŏn, Sŏ Hi was a civil official (*munban*), not a military general (*muban*), who negotiated with the Khitan as the representative of the Koryŏ army. For details, see his *Koryŏ Chŏngch'i Chaedosa Yŏnku*, pp. 282-288.

69. For details, see Pyŏng-do Lee, *Kuksa Daekwan*, pp. 258-261.

70. *Ibid.*, pp. 279-295.

71. For details, see William E. Henthorn, *A History of Korea*, pp. 178-185.

72. Ted Gurr, for instance, distinguishes three major forms of political violence— turmoil, conspiracy and internal war. In his typology, the military coup d'etat belongs to the "conspiracy" dimension. For details, see his *Why Men Rebel* (Princeton: Princeton University Press, 1970), pp. 7-15. Also, James F. Short, Jr. and Marvin E. Wolfgang, eds., *Collective Violence* (Chicago: Aldine, 1972), pp. 3-46; Eric A. Nordlinger, S*oldiers in Politics: Military Coups and Governments* (Englewood-Cliffs: Prentice-Hall, 1977).

73. A detailed account of Koguryŏ's resistance against China's Sui and T'ang forces and its ultimate downfall is found in Pyŏng-do Lee, *Hankuk Kodaesa Yŏnku*, pp. 423-454.

74. See Ki-baik Lee, *Silla Chŏngch'i Sahoe Yŏnku*, pp. 255-278.

75. Pyŏng-do Lee, *Kuksa Daekwan*, pp. 163-165.

76. The third article of Wang Kon's Ten Injunctions laid out the succession formula as follows: In the matters of royal succession by the eldest legitimate royal issue [son] should be the rule. Yao of ancient China allowed Shun to succeed him because his own son was unworthy. This was indeed putting the interests of the state ahead of one's personal feelings. Therefore, if the eldest son is unfit to rule, let the second eldest succeed to the throne. If the second eldest, too, is unworthy, choose one among the brothers considered the best qualified for the throne. The complete English translation of the Ten Injunctions is found in Pyŏng-Choon Halm, *Op. Cit.*, pp. 47-51.

77. Pyŏng-do Lee, *Kuksa Daekwan*, pp. 232-235.

78. A discussion of the rule of royal succession during the Yi Dynasty is found in Pyŏng-Choon Hahm, *Op. Cit.*, pp. 85-107.

79. For details, see Sung Chul Yang, *Korea and Two Regimes* (Cambridge: Schenkman Publishing Co., 1981), pp. 221-277.

80. For instance, Chun remarked: "I will be in the office not a single day more or less than the term guaranteed by the Constitution." *The Korea Herald*, 4 May 1985.

81. Franz Michael, *The Taiping Rebellion: History and Document* (Seattle:

University of Washington Press, 1966), Volume I, p. 192.

82. Pyŏng-do Lee, *Kuksa Daekwan*, pp. 235-238.

83. They were Sŏng Sam-mun, Pak P'aeng-nyŏn, Ha Wi-ji, Yi Kae, Yu Ung-bu and Yu Sŏng-wŏn. For details, see Ki-baik Lee, *A New History of Korea*, pp. 172-173.

84. An account of the Yŏsu-Sunch'on Revolt is found in Sung Chul Yang, *Korea and Two Regimes*, pp. 107-108.

85. Ki-baik Lee, *A New History of Korea*, pp. 142-144.

86. Woon-t'ae Kim, *Chosŏn Wangjo Haengjŏngsa*, pp. 194-195.

87. Pyong-do Lee, *Kuksa Daekwan*, pp. 493-495.

CHAPTER 3

NATIVISTIC RESILIENCE, NATIONALISM AND BEYOND

The sentiment of ethnic solidarity does not itself make a "nation."

Max Weber[1]

If the first reaction of the peoples on whom the West imposed itself was generally a xenophobic defense of the existing order, the next phase was likely to be a swing in the direction of an uncritical self-humiliation and acceptance of alien superiority. The third phase...was a nationalist synthesis in which there was an assertion or reassertion of a community with pride in itself and its past but still looking at least as far as its leaders were concerned, in the direction of Westernization and modernization. Those leaders were, almost without exception, men who had achieved substantial acquaintance with the West.

Rupert Emerson[2]

Even at a cursory examination of Korean political traditions and culture, one can easily see a remarkable historical feat of the Korean people. That Korea has survived as a nation and has maintained its independent political entity, national identity and high degree of cultural homogeneity despite incessant foreign invasions and domination by the Chinese, Khitans, Jurchens, Mongols, Manchus and Japanese is indeed extraordinary. Its artificial division in 1945 notwithstanding, the same unifying historical and cultural tradition persists against the strong currents of divisive ideological and political forces in the both halves of the Korean Peninsula today.

Two explanations are readily available for this historical legacy. One is here called the Korean people's nativistic resilience.[3] It is the spirit of the people to cling to its own indigenous cultural heritage amid prevailing foreign political and cultural influences, be they Sinicization, Mongolization, Japanization, Americanization or Russianization. Noteworthy, also, is that throughout Korean history the "ignorant" multitudes have often been the guardians of its culture and national identity, not the few "clever" ruling elites and the educated—the literati, well-versed in Chinese classics, or the intelligentsia educated under the Japanese rule or the intellectuals of today.

As the Russian elites were divided between the Slavophils and the Westerners[4] in the nineteenth century, a similar bifurcation existed (and still do, to a certain degree) among the Korean elites—the one mainly obsessed with preserving Korea's indigenous native traditions, and the other, primarily concerned with adopting more developed life of foreign countries like China and Japan or the West. But the Korean bifurcation has been more between the elites and the masses rather than between the elites themselves, that is, elites diligently emulated and adapted to new and alien culture of the day, while the masses, resiliently adhered to and transmitted old and native culture to the next generation.[5]

It is no accident, therefore, that during the Yi Dynasty, the Korean masses preferred traditional Korean clothes—*chima, chŏgori, baji* and *durumagi*—to Chinese, Japanese or Western apparels; that they preferred *han'gŭl,* the Korean alphabet, to Chinese and/or other foreign languages; and that they continued to observe native Shamanistic practices–*mudang gut*–along with Buddhist, Confucian, or Christian rites and ceremonies. They also appreciated other uniquely Korean ethnic arts, sports, plays and songs.[6] The Yi Dynasty's ruling elites and literati often despised, ridiculed and even suppressed the "ignorant" masses for such preferences and practices. In the end, however, the masses' unflinching nativistic resilience had preserved the Korean national and ethnic identity.

Closely intermingled with the aforesaid nativistic resilience is Korean nationalism. They are the two sides of the same coin. If Korean nationalism gives expression to politics, the nativistic resilience, their culture, and the former, a response to foreign political and military influences and dominations, and the latter, a retention of native traditions and cultures amidst foreign cultural infiltrations.

The Korean nationalistic responses at home and abroad against foreign aggressors and colonizers manifested itself in various forms—from diplomatic and political maneuverings, terrorism, armed resistance, guerrilla warfare, mass uprising and to literary and educational enlightenment movements. In human terms, the presence of foreign invaders and colonizers divided Koreans into complicated yet familiar camps, ranging from undaunted patriots to unscrupulous quislings, from radicals to moderates and from ideologues to pragmatists.

Like nationalism of other countries, Korean nationalism displays both uniquely Korean features and universally common elements. Before a more detailed examination of Korean nationalism is undertaken, a discussion of the genesis, the meaning and the typology of nationalism *per se* is warranted here.

Nationalism

Genesis

Broadly, the views on the origins of nationalism may be divided into two schools—the Europocentrist and the universalist. The Europocentrists believe that nationalism is uniquely of European origin—a political phenomenon which emerged in a specific period of history in Europe. Although they generally agree that (modern) nationalism originated in Europe, they differ from each other as to when and how it surfaced, let alone in what shape. Hans Kohn, for one, asserted that three essential traits of modern nationalism originated with the Hebrews. These traits are the idea of the chosen people, the emphasis on a common stock of memories of the past and of hopes for the future and national messianism.[7]

Elie Kedourie, on the other hand, stated that nationalism is a doctrine "invented in Europe at the beginning of the nineteenth century." He differentiated nationalism from both patriotism–affection for one's group, loyalty to its institutions and zeal for defense–and xenophobia or tribalism–dislike of the stranger, the outsider and reluctance to admit him into one's group. He contended that sentiment neither depends on a particular anthropology nor on a particular doctrine of the state or of the individual's relation to it. Nationalism, according to him, does both. Nationalism is "a comprehensive doctrine which leads to a distinctive style of politics. Far from being a universal phenomenon, nationalism is "a product of European thought in the last 150 years."[8]

Marvin Perry is even more specific than Kedourie when he pinpoints that the essential components of modern nationalism emerged at the time of the French Revolution. The French Revolution affirmed the principle of popular sovereignty, the idea that man's highest loyalty should be directed to the nation as a whole rather than to a province, an estate, a lord, the person of the King or a universal church.[9] It should be noted here that the Europocentrists designate the Middle East and/or Europe as the locus of modern nationalism. In so doing, they implicitly, at least, assumed that they focused only on a particular set of idea (of nationalism) associated with a specific historic period in Europe and the Middle East.

The universalists, on the other hand, view nationalism as a universal cultural trait, irrespective of time and place. If, for instance, nationalism is a modern political variant of ethnocentrism, it has existed nearly everywhere. William Graham Sumner defined ethnocentrism as the view of things in which "one's own group is the center of everything, and all others are scaled and rated with reference to it."[10] He further wrote:

> ...each group nourishes its own pride and vanity, boasts itself superior, exalts its own divinities, and looks with contempt upon outsiders. Each group thinks its own folkways are the only right ones, and if it observes that other groups have other folkways, these excite scorn.[11]

In a similar vein, Harold R. Isaacs described what he called "basic group identity."[12] Basic group identity consists of the ready-made set of endowments and identifications which every individual shares with others from the moment of birth by the chance of the family into which he is born at that given time in that given place. First, there is the new baby's body itself, all the shared physical characteristics of the group acquired through the long process of selection. Next, even as the new infant draws his or her first breath, hears the first sound, feels the first touch, he or she begins to acquire everything the family offers. He wrote:

> The baby acquires a *name,* an individual name, a family name, a group name. He acquires the *history and origins* of the group into which he is born. The group's cultural past automatically endows him, among other things, with his *nationality* or other condition of national, regional, or tribal affiliation, his *language, religion,* and *value system*—the inherited clusters of mores, ethics, aesthetics, and the attributes that come out of the *geography* or *topography* of his birthplace itself, all shaping the outlook and way of life upon which the new individual enters from his first day.[13]

John Fairbank credits the emergence of modern nationalism with the nation-state. The nation-state had many roots such as the self-consciousness and the kingship institution of the Germanic tribes, the economic needs of new enterprises growing beyond the limits of the city-state type of economy and the growth of representative institutions as a means of bringing people into larger political groupings.[14] But, his view of Chinese nationalism extends beyond the typical Europocentrism. He contends that "the idea of One China or the unity of the Chinese realm goes back to the beginning of Chinese history. It cannot be expunged from the Chinese language or from the minds of Chinese people."[15] Further, he wrote:

> This (the idea of One China) is not only an idea but a sentiment, a basic feeling habituated by millennia of conduct. It attaches the highest importance to Chinese civilization, which consists of all those people who live in the Chinese way. This is expressed in the ancient phrases, "all within the four seas" or "all under heaven"... China's unity, in short,

is an attribute of Chineseness itself. It springs from a sense of culturalism, something a good deal stronger than mere Western-style nationalism. [16]

In the end, the origin (s) of nationalism, modern or ancient, Occidental or Oriental, depends on how one perceives its meaning (s). It can be specified if one views it as a historic event; it cannot be specified if one sees it as a cultural phenomenon. To put it another way, the definition of "nationalism" ("nation," or "nation-state," for that matter) *precedes* its origin. What nationalism *is,* determines when, how and where it originated.

Meanings

Generally, the term "nationalism" denotes either a psychological state, a political doctrine, a historical movement or a various mix of these three. In other words, nationalism consists of, at least, three dimensions: emotive, cognitive and historical. On an emotive dimension, it is defined as a psychological state of an aggregate of people in a nation, e.g., "anti-feeling" (S. Nehru), "national consciousness" (Lasswell-Kaplan), "sentiment unifying a group of people" (B.C. Shafer), "a state of mind" (H. Kohn), "a sense of nationhood" (R. Dahl), "an assertion of a people's right" (D.A. Wilson), "transcending collective ambition" (K. Davis), "a sentiment for the preservation of collective (ethnic) solidarity and cultural and political autarchy" (A.D. Smith), "collective will to justify my country's political, economic and cultural development" (Y.H. Lee), "new ferments of national feeling" (G. Smith), "outgroup antipathies and ingroup attachments" (R. Gibbins), "an awareness shared by a group of people" (M. Perry) and "the awareness of being drawn together by a common history, including both common cultural achievements and common horrors and sufferings" (R. Lowenthal). [17]

On a cognitive dimension, nationalism may stand for a political doctrine or an ideology, e.g., "the doctrine that the only legitimate type of government is national self-government" (E. Kedourie), "the political religion of modernization" (A.D. Smith), "anti-colonialism" (A.D. Smith), "the body of beliefs held by those people as legitimating their search for uniqueness and autonomy" (E. Haas), "the myth of the successful nation," (E. Haas), "the doctrine stemming from the idea of the nation or nationhood" (C.V. Crabb), "the ideology of the nation-state" (L.P. Baradat), "the action ideology of the nationalists," (Y.H. Lee), "the ideology and movement to realize the nation's unity, independence, and development" (K.P. Ch'a), "the right of a given nationality to form a state" (R. Macridis) and "the infusion of the political with cultural content" (F.M. Barnard).[18] In a similar vein, Roger Gibbins identified four minimal characteristics of nationalism as a political ideology: intergroup relations within national political boundaries; ingroup attachments and outgroup antipathies; a politicization; and a social construct.[19]

Nationalism as a historical event, movement, or phenomenon, defies a cogent definition due to its diversity. In Louis Snyder's words, nationalism may mean "whatever a given people, on the basis of their own historical experience, decide it to mean;" "it is what the nationalists have made it;" "it is not a neat, fixed concept but a varying combination of beliefs and conditions."[20] Similarly, Rupert Emerson wrote that "to assign to nationalism any particular political coloration is presumably impossible since it has been associated with almost every conceivable regime and attitude."[21] Hans Kohn is even more categorical on this point: "nationalism is in itself neither good nor bad."[22] Historically, nationalism or a nationalist movement is associated with liberalism, romanticism, volkish thoughts, anti-Semitism, fascism, Nazism, communism, independent and local autonomy movements and others. It is tied to an ethnic and national identity, such as pan-Hellenic, pan-Germanic, pan-Slavic and pan-Arabic appeals, as well as Chinese, French, Korean or Japanese nationalist movements. It may accentuate a geographic area of some historical or cultural affinity such as Asian, African, European or Latin-American nationalism.

Depending upon one's view or analysis, nationalism as a historical event or phenomenon may be subdivided into different categories. Karl Deutsch discerned "the destructive and the constructive aspects of national development, consciousness and will.[23] Likewise, Richard Preston dichotomized nationalism into positive and negative ones. By positive nationalism, he meant a constructive urge for internal cohesion accompanied by a striving for democratic autonomy and freedom and by resistance to oppression. Negative nationalism is a destructive force, which is inclined toward aggression and expansion; it is often stimulated by undue fear of political and cultural domination, and it is suspicious of international cooperation.[24] Gordenker identified what he called "new nationalism," doctrines and politics which give overwhelming importance to the development of legally existing states, rather than to any cosmopolitan or transnational movement or institution. "New nationalism" also tends to restrict or control foreign influences as a means of "fostering national development. It emphasizes the point that the welfare of groups and individuals finds its fullest expression in cohesion, loyalty and cooperativeness within state boundaries.[25] Philip Thayer pointed out the "dual nature" of nationalism–one type focused on the nation and the achievement of national freedom as the stepping stone toward a peaceful and collaborative world order, and the other propelled the nation forward as the summation of all human values to which the interests of the remainder of mankind may legitimately be sacrificed if what appears to be the national interest is thereby advanced.On the basis of this dual nature, he further portrayed the "two faces" of nationalism—the one angry and distorted, with the desire of trampling on all other nations for the greatness of his own, and the other face smiling and kindly, with the intention of leading his nation to live in peace with others.[26] Recently, Selig Harrison described his version of the "two faces" of nationalism —one was turned inward on the task of marshaling national strength, another looked vigilantly outward. Both aspects are "part of the same historical continuum, inseparably linked in a close cyclical interaction."

In the final analysis, nationalism is only a label for the idea (s) of how a nation as a collective political and cultural entity in a given territory should live. The idea (s), in turn, stems from the sentiment of a group of people who share such ingredients of nationalism as language, history, culture, religion, traditions, myths, legends, economic interests and the like. The nationalistic ideas and sentiments are open-ended in that they can be either good, constructive, positive, peaceful or exhilarating, or they can be bad, destructive, negative, warlike, suffocating or a mix of the two. Throughout history, nationalism has been associated more with negative ideas and sentiments such as fascism, Nazism and anti-Semitism than with positive ideas and sentiments such as pacifism, internationalism or individualism. As Kohn warned, communism uses anti-imperialism and nationalism as two of its strongest ideological weapons in the war against freedom.[28]

Although nationalism is in itself neither good nor bad until and unless it incorporates certain political ideologies, it has an inherent limitation as a concept, if, as Leo Strauss pointed out, the natural political community is not the nation but the city, that is, if the nation is only a half-way house between the polis and the cosmopolis.[29] In other words, if a human community progresses from family to village, to polis and to cosmopolis, or from band to tribe, to kingdom, to empire, to nation-state and to the world community, nationalism is intrinsically transient and regressive, if not anachronistic, no matter what its positive and constructive intent may be.

In Erik Erikson's words, nationalism is another "pseudo-species":

> ...mankind...has been divided into...pseudo-species; national, ideological, or religious bodies that consider their own kind the model image of mankind as fully intended in their version of creation and history, for the survival of which they are ready to kill as well as to die.[30]

In a similar vein, Yong-Hee Lee rejects the idea of "nationalism in one country," and stresses what he called "denationalism" (t'almin-jokchui)—the idea of each nation living together by removing the unnecessary national barriers—as the ultimate goal of a nation.[31]

In the ultimate unfolding of human history, the nation may be a half-way house or a pseudo-species. Still, it is the prevailing human association. The cosmopolis and world state are in the realm of a national consciousness, national sovereignty, national boundaries, and even national spirit. The world is still divided into no fewer than 180 nation-states. Although science, technology and commerce have considerably narrowed the gap among human communities on the globe, national politics persists and the ultimate cosmopolis or the world state remains unrealized.

Beyond Nationalism: Theory A and Theory B Phenomena

It appears that at a first glance the post-Communist, post-nuclear and post-Cold War world today manifests itself as the seemingly contradictory cross-currents. On the one hand, the march continues toward the establishment of a bigger, better and more harmonious economic and political entity with decreasing identity of, and attachment to, the old-fashioned national, ethnic and other parochial proclivity. On the other hand, the revival of nationalism, revanchism, let alone the militant religious fetishism such as Islam, seems to gain currency in certain areas and regions.

At a closer look, however, the two ostensibly conflicting global phenomena today are pointing toward and progressing in the same direction. The first trend—integration, unification, union, consolidation —may be called here "Theory A phenomenon." It is a nation or a group of nations' centripetal propensity to break away from its rigid national/ political boundary and to move toward a more integrated, less-bounded larger political-economic entity. The second trend, "Theory B phenomenon"—disintegration, division, disunion, fragmentation—is some ethnic and/or national groups' centrifugal proclivity to regain their lost civil rights and liberties and their ethnic and/or national identities and self-rule. If the first trend leads to political amalgamation, the second, to political fragmentation. These two trends are, however, not fundamentally contradictory to each other because Theory B phenomenon is an inevitable transitional process before Theory A phenomenon can be realized.

Concretely, the European Community's accelerating integration process set by the Maastricht Treaty of December 1991 is the prime example of Theory A phenomenon. Conversely, the dissolution of the former Soviet Union, the internal war in Yugoslavia and the partition of Czechoslovakia exemplify Theory B phenomenon. Noteworthy here is the fact that the countries currently undergoing Theory A trend are characterized by a set of common features. All twelve European Community (EC) member states, for example, have joined the community voluntarily, usually via the consent of their citizens. All these states respect their citizens' fundamental civil rights and liberties. EC started out as the European Community for Coal and Steel (ECSC) with six countries in 1951. The market force, be it trade, travel or transportation, has been the principal locomotive of the first stage of integration. EC's integration process has also been gradual and piecemeal. Through trials and errors, ECSC has evolved into European Economic Community (EEC) in 1957, which is now set for the birth of European Union by creating the Economic and Monetary Union with the adoption of a single currency by 1997 or 1999 at the latest and by establishing the European Political Union with the development of a common foreign and security policy.

By contrast, the countries presently confronting Theory B phenomenon also share many similar characteristics. The citizens of the Baltic states, Yugoslavia or Czechoslovakia, for example, have all lost their national independence and/or ethnic self-rule forcibly against their free will. Their annexation or consolidation, let alone ideological solidarity, was usually imposed upon by the foreign military occupation forces, i.e., the Soviet Red Army. The military force, be it in the name of ideological solidarity or socialist fraternity, had been the chief means for such forcible annexation and consolidation. Worse still, during the communist rule citizens in these countries were largely deprived of their basic civil rights and freedom. Hence, to these nations and/or ethnic groups regaining their national independence and self-rule and restoring their civil liberties and rights should be the first and foremost task to be realized before and above all else.

In the long run, however, like the citizens and the states which are currently experiencing Theory A change, the people and the nations, which are now suffering from Theory B phenomenon, will eventually follow Theory A course after they, too, have regained their national sovereignty and their citizens' civil liberties and rights.

From this standpoint, Korea, still as a divided nation, has also been suffering from the persistence of Theory B phenomenon. For both Koreas, the realization of national unification is in fact the first step toward Theory A change, not to mention their full restoration of people's political rights and civil liberties.

Korean Nationalism: Origins and Peculiarities

Late Silla's Spirit of Territorial Integration

To determine when and how Korean nationalism originated is subjective and arbitrary. If nationalism represents an idea of a nation or nation-building, a rudimentary form of Korean nationalism might have developed as early as the middle of the seventh century, if not earlier, when the first united nation-state under the Silla Dynasty emerged in the Korean peninsula. Culturally, *idu*, the writing system using Chinese characters phonetically to record Korean songs and poems (*hyangch'al*, a more sophisticated writing system was later developed), may be considered one of the earliest manifestations of Korean nationalistic elan. Sŏl Ch'ong (mid-eighth century), a Buddhist scholar and the son of famous monk Wŏnhyo (617-698), is credited with its invention. But Sŏl Ch'ong's claim to inventing *idu* may be in error since *hyangch'al* was in use at least two centuries before his birth.[32] A number of works on Silla history and geography by Kim Tae-mun, a scholar who flourished in the earlier years of the eighth century, may also be considered an incipient expression of Korean nationalism. Unfortunately, his deep concern for native Silla traditions recorded in his works, *Kyerim chapchŏn* [Tales of Silla], *Kosŭng chŏn* [Biographies of Eminent Monks], *Hwarang segi* [Chronicles of the Hwarang], *Ak pon* [Book of Music] and *Hansan ki* [Record of Hansan] to counter the impact of Chinese Confucian learning did not survive —the remnants of his works are found in Kim Pu-sik's *Samguk sagi* [History of the Three Kingdoms] published in 1145 and Iryŏn's *Samguk Yusa* [Memorabilia of the Three Kingdoms] published in 1279.[33]

Silla's *Paekwa Kanghoe* [Assemblies for Sutra Recitation by one Hundred Monks] and *P'algwanhoe* [Festival of the Eight Vows] in particular, though Buddhistic in origin, portrayed the early form of national ceremonies, which pray for the well-being and protection of the state.[34] Likewise, *Ch'ŏmsŏngdae*, the world's oldest astronomical observatory constructed sometime between 632 and 647, typified the Korean people's creative achievements.

Politically, Koguryŏ's famed military commander, Ulchi Mundŏk, who defeated the invading forces of Sui's Yang Ti in 612 at *Salsu* [Ch'ŏng ch'ŏn River], Yŏn Kaesomun, who repulsed the military might of T'ang's T'ai Tsung at An-sih Fortress (now Ying-ch'eng-tzu) in 645, and Paeckche's military commander, Kyeback, who defended, though unsuccessfully, his kingdom against the combined forces of the T'ang and Silla at Sabi Fortress, may be considered Korea's early national heroes. Besides them, there have been numerous political and military national heroes. According to one Korean historian, three great Korean military heroes are: Ulchi Mundŏk who repulsed Sui China's invading forces in 612; Ch'oe Yŏng who unsuccessfully attempted to invade the Liao-tung region of Manchuria in 1388; and Yi Sun-sin who led successful naval battles against the Japanese in 1592.[35]

Hwarang [flower of youth], composed of the sons of Silla ruling elites and their spirit manifested in military valor, may also be regarded as one of the earliest rudiments of Korean nationalism. Such spirit was also evident in the political and military leadership of many *hwarang* members, notably Kim Yu-sin and Kim Ch'un-ch'u, who unified the Peninsula in 660. It was the same spirit which enabled Silla to drive out the forces of T'ang China from the Korean Peninsula in 676.

Early Koryŏ's Revanchist Dream

From the very beginning, the Koryŏ Dynasty had shown some rudiments of nationalistic spirit. The spirit moved Koryŏ to declare itself the rightful heir of Koguryŏ, the erstwhile powerful Korean state during the Three Kingdom period, which ruled most of the present North Korea and Manchuria. Implicit and explicit in this spirit was the Korean version of revanchism—the ultimate goal or dream to recover Koguryŏ's vast lost territory in Manchuria. This spirit was captured in the name of Koryŏ Dynasty, which was derived from the Later Koguryŏ (901-918). Kungye, the founder of the Later Koguryŏ proclaimed that he was the successor to the former Koguryŏ Kingdom. Likewise, Wang Kŏn, the founder of Koryŏ (T'aijo, r. 918-43), considered himself the successor to the mantle of Koguryŏ.

The same spirit was reflected in the Wang Kŏn's *Sip hunyo* [Ten Injunctions]. In its fifth article he urged that "the Western Capital (Pyongyang, capital of Koguryŏ) has the elements of water in its favor and is the source of the terrestrial force of our country. It is thus the veritable center of dynastic enterprises for ten thousand generations. Therefore, make a royal visit to the Western Capital four times a year— in the second, fifth, eighth and eleventh months—and reside there a total of a hundred days. By this means secure peace and prosperity."[36]

It is no accident that Koryŏ chose its new capital, *Songhak* [Kae-sŏng], located in the northwestern part of the Korean Peninsula, closer to the old Koguryŏ capital, Pyongyang, and farther away from Silla's capital. When the Korean state of Parhae in Koguryŏ's old Manchurian territory collapsed under the Khitans in 927, Wang Kŏn welcomed many of the Parhae aristocrats who fled to Koryŏ and assimilated them into his ruling strata. The plan by Chŏngjong (r. 945-49) to move the capital to Pyongyang, and various northward military push by Kwang-jong (r. 948-75) were triggered by the same spirit. In the end Koryŏ's northern expansionist policy clashed with the then rising power of the Khitans. As noted earlier, Sŏ Hui's diplomatic maneuvers in 993 to reclaim the Manchurian territories formerly under Koguryŏ's dominion from the Khitan were notable. To a certain extent, the afore-mentioned Myoch'ŏng Revolt in 1135 in Pyongyang may also be seen in the con-text of the northern expansionist spirit.

Culturally, T'aijo (Wang kŏn) instructed in the first of his Ten Injunc-tions that "the success of every great undertaking of our state depends upon the favor and protection of Buddha." Buddhism, though foreign in origin, had become *de facto* state religion and many Buddhist festivals such as *yŏndunghoe,* on the fifteenth of the first month and *p'algwan-hoe,* on the fifteenth of the eleventh month, have become a part of Korean national cultural heritage.[37]

It is particularly significant that T'aijo was conscious of his people, though his conception of them was by no means an open and liberal one. For instance, in the fourth of Ten Injunctions he declared:

> In the past we have always had a deep attachment for the ways of

T'ang [China] and all of *our institutions* have been modeled upon those of T'ang. But *our country* occupies a different geographical location and the character of *our people* is different from that of Chinese. Hence, there is no reason to strain ourselves unreasonably to copy the Chinese way. Khitan is a nation of savage beasts and its language and custom are also different. Its dresses and institutions should never be copied.[38]

His use of the terms such as "our institutions," "our country" and "our people" were extremely meaningful because he created an awareness for "we-they" feeling. But he viewed the Khitan people rather harshly. Above all, his eighth Injunction concerning the people of former Paek-che area was outright prejudicial as the passage below indicates. He wrote:

> The topographic features of the territory south of Kongju and beyond the Kongju River are all treacherous and disharmonious, and its inhabitants are also treacherous and disharmonious. For that reason, if they are allowed to participate in the affairs of state, to intermarry with the royal family, aristocracy, and royal relatives and to take the power of the state, they might imperil the state or injure the royal safety—grudging the loss of their own state (Paeckche) and being resentful of the unification. Those who have been slaves or engaged in dishonorable trades will surrender themselves to the powerful in order to evade prescribed services. And some of them will surely seek to offer their services to the noble families, to the palaces or to the temples. They then will cause confusion and disorder in government and engage in treason through crafty words and treacherous machinations. They should never be allowed in the government service, though they may no longer be slaves and outcasts. [39]

In short, while Wang Kŏn was conscious of national identity, he was not free from parochial prejudices and/or racial and regional biases.

Koryŏ's Resistance against Northern Invaders

Koryŏ's revanchist hope was soon buried under the increasing military threats and invasions of the rising powers in Manchuria, the Khitans, the Jurchen (Chin) and the Mongols. Koryŏ's dream of recovering Koguryŏ's lost territory was replaced by its defense against the northern invaders. Koryŏ's resistance against the Khitan (Liao) invasions in 1010, 1018 and 1019 and its military campaigns against the Jurchen (Chin) in 1107 led by Koryŏ General Yun Kwan are remarkable. Above all, Koryŏ's struggle against the Mongol invasions, which began in the autumn of 1231 and lasted off and on for some thirty years, devastated the country but did not crush the Korean people's anti-foreign national-istic spirit. Along with the government forces, the Korean anti-Mongol resistance was carried out largely by the peasants and commoners. They were organized into local querrilla forces which attacked the invaders by ambush and hit-and-run tactics. Koryŏ eventually surrendered to the Mongols in 1258, but some anti-Mongol remnant forces such as *sam-byŏlch'o* continued their resistance for another 15 years until 1273.

Most importantly, the Koryŏ Tripitaka embodied the lasting achieve-ment of the Korean people's nationalistic anti-foreign resistance spirit. The carving of wooden blocks to print the Buddhist scriptures began during the early years of Hyŏnjong (r. 1009-31) as a kind of prayer to bring a halt to the Khitan invaders. It was completed around 1087. Much of the early editions were destroyed by the Mongol invaders, but the new edition was completed in 1251 while the Korean Court sought exile at Kanghwa Island from the Mongol invasions.[40]

Sejong the Great and the Creation of the Korean Writing System

Among all the nationalistic traditions and treasures of the Yi Chosŏn, the invention of an indigenous Korean alphabet, *han'gul,* in 1446 would undoubtedly be the most significant. Sejong the Great (r. 1418-50), who masterminded the creation of this system, called it *hunmin chŏngŭm,* "correct sounds for instructing the people." Sejong's preface to the *hun-min chŏngŭm* not only sets forth the reasons behind this new creation but reveals new dimension of Korean nationalistic traditions:

> The sounds of *our language* differ from those of China and they do not accord with written Chinese. Therefore, many *common people* who have something to express, are unable to convey their feelings. In sym-pathy with them, I have newly invented twenty-eight letters, which *people* can easily learn and use for everyday communication.[41]

If language is one of the most enduring ingredients of nationalism,[42] the invention of the Korean writing system in the middle of the fifteenth century indeed provided the new catalyst. It was no accident that the Sejong the Great in his preface employed the phrases such as "our language" (national language) and "people" or "common people." Despite the availability of this new Korean alphabet, the Yi dynasty's ruling elites and Confucian literati continued to use Chinese as their primary written medium. But *han'gul* became popular among the common people, especially among women of both high and low social strata.

In addition to *han'gul*, Sejong the Great's northern expeditions, which extended the frontier to the natural defense line formed by the two rivers, Aprok and Tumen, stood out as another of his many illustrious nationalistic achievements. For these expeditions he dispatched General Kim Chong-sŏ to the Tuman (*Tumen*) River regions and Generals Ch'oe Yun-dŏk and Yi Ch'ŏn to the Aprok (Yalu) River area to consolidate the regions under the Korean domain, which has remained Korea's northern boundary to this day.

If the invention of *han'gul* symbolized the Yi Dynasty's positive nationalistic traditions, the Korean resistance against the Japanese and Manchu invaders represented its long standing anti-foreign political traditions.

The Japanese invasion of 1592 (*Imjin waeran*) and the Manchus invasion of 1627 (*Chŏngmyo horan*) and in 1636 (*Pyŏngja horan*) were the representative cases. During the Japanese invasion, the Korean masses, mostly peasants, took up arms in defense of their homeland. Interestingly enough, these peasant farmers and slaves were led by the local *yangban* leaders, most of whom were neo-Confucian literati, who launched a guerrilla-type war against the Japanese intruders. Ch'oe Hŏn in Ch'ungch'ŏng Province, Kwak Chae-u in Kyŏngsang Province, and Ko Kyŏngmyong in Chŏlla Province, Kim Ch'ŏn-il in Kyŏnggi Province and Chŏng Mun-bu in Hamgyŏng Province were the prime leaders. Above all, Admiral Yi Sun-sin's naval victory and his invention of *kŏbuksŏn*, an iron-clad turtleship, exemplified the Korean people's resolve to fight against the foreign invading forces.[43]

The Korean Response to Western Powers

The Korean responses to the Western inroads and Japanese encroachments in the middle and late 19th century may also be seen in the context of nationalism. Except for her long standing relations with China
(and other continental Asian powers—the Khitans, the Jurchens, the
Mongols and the Manchus) and Japan—Korea had remained largely a
"Hermit Kingdom" until the 19th century. Since then, however, Korea
had to come to grips with all three principal Western agents—the missionaries, the merchants and the military forces. Korea's early contacts
with the West were incidental and indirect. Its initial response was a
matter of intellectual curiosity among a few progressive scholars and
officials, especially among *Sirhak* [Practical Learning] scholars and
Namin [Southerners] political faction.[44] The Korean government perceived the Western presence in Korea at first with mixed feelings of
curiosity and annoyance and later with increasing fear and suspicion.
The high officials in the Korean court identified the Western influences
as menaces, and they became rather xenophobic.

By the early 18th century, Catholicism had spread among the masses
with followers becoming increasingly numerous, particularly in the
Hwanghae and Kangwŏn provinces. In response, Yŏngjo (r. 1724-76)
proclaimed Catholicism as an alien and evil practice and banned it in
1758. In 1786 Chŏngjo (r. 1776-1800) denounced Catholicism as *Sahak*
[Evil Learning] and persecuted a number of Korean Catholic leaders.
The government persecuted Korean Catholic leaders mostly associated
with "the Southerners" in 1795 and 1800. In 1841 the government executed about thirty Korean Catholics and three French priests. During the
reign of Ch'ŏljong (r. 1849-64), the number of Catholic adherents numbered some 17,000. However, the religious toleration was short-lived.
With the demise of Ch'ŏljong, another wave of massive Catholic perse-
cutions swept the country. Between 1860 and 1872, some 8,000 Korean
Catholics and nine of the twelve French priests were executed.[45]

Meanwhile beginning with the voyage of the British ship *Providence*
in 1797, British, French and Russian ships had sporadically reconnoi-
tered the Korean coast. British ships alone had made four such trips in

1797, 1816, 1840 and 1845. For two years, 1846 and 1847, French war-ships appeared on the west coast to protest the Korean government's persecution of three French Catholic priests in 1841, but their presence accomplished little. Again, in 1865 three French warships sailed up to Yanghwajin on the Han River. A month later, nine French warships attacked Kanghwa Island, but the Korean troops' counterattack forced them to retreat .

It was during the latter half of the nineteenth century that the Western interests intensified in the Korean Peninsula. Ironically, Regent Taewŏn-gun, the chief architect of the seclusion policy, was at the helm of the Korean Court during this period. In July 1866, *General Sherman*, an American merchant vessel, sailed up the Taedong River in defiance of the Korean officials in Pyongyang and demanded commercial trade relations. On August 27 when the *Sherman*'s crew abducted Yi Hyŏn-ik, the deputy commander of the Pyongyang Military Garrison, the Korean troops and civilians retaliated by sinking the ship with its entire crew. The United States sent the warship *Wachusett* to Korea early in 1867 to protest against the Korean government for this incident, but the envoys on the ship made no headway. A year later, the *USS Shenandoah* was sent to Korea with the same mission, but it too met with similar results. In 1871 the United States government commissioned five war-ships, under the command of Admiral John Rodgers of the *Asian Fleet*, to invade Korea. The U.S. troops assaulted three fortresses on Kanghwa Island—Kwangsŏngjin, Ch'ojijin and Kapkŏji—but after a series of clashes with the Korean troops, they, too, retreated without success.[46]

The Tonghak Rebellion and Japan's Colonization of Korea

Japan had not been an idle bystander during these turbulent years. In 1875 the Japanese government dispatched three warships including *Unyo,* which sailed into Pusan and the Bay of Yŏnghung on the pretext of surveying the sea routes. The ships invaded Kanghwa Island in September of that year, ostensibly to fetch drinking water but actually to scrutinize the island's fortresses. When Korean guards on the island fired at them, they withdrew. The ships then reappeared at Yŏngjongjin near Inch'ŏn and ransacked the area. In January of the following year, the Japanese envoy landed at Kanghwa Island with six naval vessels. He blamed the Korean government for the *Unyo* incident of the previous year and demanded new trade relations.

The Korean Court was then in an acute political crisis. Regent Tae-wŏngun's uncompromising seclusion policy had spurred the formation of political opposition, led by the Min clan members within the Court. At the same time, mass unrest caused by Taewŏngun's heavy tax (used primarily to reconstruct the Kyŏngbok Palace) intensified. By 1874, a year before the *Unyo* incident, the strongman, Taewŏngun, had already been forced out of power. He had been impeached by the coalition of political forces led by Ch'oe Ik-hyŏn, including Queen Min (Taewŏngun's daughter-in-law), and her brother, Min Sung-ho, Yi Chae-ŭng (Taewŏngun's brother) and the key members of the Kim clan of Andong. These disparate political coalition forces argued that Kojong (r. 1864-1907), then twenty-two years old, was mature enough to rule and a regent was no longer necessary. In actuality, the political turnover did not restore Kojong's power but merely replaced Regent Taewŏngun's power with that of Queen Min and the Min clan forces. Moreover, it meant an irrevocable setback to Taewŏngun's seclusion policy.

Under such delicate and unstable political circumstances, the Korean government was unable to withstand the Japanese pressures, and yielded to her demands and signed the Kanghwa Treaty of 1876. The door of the Hermit Kingdom was, thus, forced to open, not by the Western powers which tried repeatedly earlier and failed but by the neighboring Japan, which sought it at an opportune political time and succeeded. Heeding Chinese advice, the Korean government belatedly attempted to offset the inordinate Japanese influence by concluding treaties with a number of Western nations in rapid succession—the United States in 1882, England and Germany in 1883, Italy and Russia in 1884 and France in 1886. Korea's door was now opened wide but too late to pre-empt or prevent the ultimate Japanese colonization.

A closer scrutiny of political arenas following the opening of Korea evinced both classic complicity and dilemma for the political actors—Korean political leaders and foreign participants as well. On the one hand, the principal Korean political leaders during these turbulent periods were hopelessly entangled in a political dilemma—the pursuit of their own *personal* political ambitions commingled with their *patriotic* desires to save the nation from falling prey to foreign powers. The foreign powers, on the other hand, were deeply entrenched in Korean affairs and Korea became the object of their conflicts. Their *common* goal to control Korea led them on a collision course. The Korean political leaders sought alignment with foreign powers—Chinese, Japanese, Russian or American—to fulfill either their own *personal* ambitions, or reformist goals or both. Conversely, the foreign participants in Korea during this period sought collaboration with the Korean political leaders to fulfill their ultimate aim of controlling Korea.

In the process, two layers of political constellations came into play. On the palatial level, an intense political rivalry among the Korean leaders bred factionalism and gave impetus to frequent shifting of political allegiances within and alignment without. Internally, political intrigues among the various factions (such as the Taewŏngun adherents, the Queen Min faction, the Independents and the Progressives and their pro-Chinese, pro-Japanese and pro-Russian alignments) instigated a series of coups and revolts. The abortive coup of 1881, the Army Revolt of 1882 (*Imo kullan*) and the Kapsin Coup of 1884 (*Kapsin chŏngbyŏn*) were notable.[47] Externally, this sorry state of political affairs in the Korean Court invited foreign intervention, which ultimately triggered the outbreak of the Sino-Japanese and Russo-Japanese wars.

At the grass-roots level, the *Tonghak* Rebellion of 1894 sparked mass unrests, rooted in long-standing peasant grievances. Drought, famine, incessant political intrigues in the Korean court, corrupt and tyrannical local officials and foreign, particularly Japanese, exploitation of Korean grains and other farm products gave ample ammunition to fuel this uprising, the Korean equivalent of the Taiping Rebellion of 1850.[48]

Unlike the Army Revolt of 1882 and the Kapsin Coup of 1884, the *Tonghak* Rebellion of 1894 was a mass uprising initiated by the oppressed segment of the Korean populace. It was a variant of the peasant war; its immediate causes were official abuse and plunder of the disintegrating grain-loan, taxation system and the need for land reform.

While many leaders of the *Tonghak* came from the politically disenfran-chised and economically impoverished *yangban* class, the rebels were mostly recruited from the rural farms and villages. The *Tonghak* Rebel-lion had a xenophobic religious undercurrent in direct opposition to *Sŏhak* [Western Learning] or Catholicism.

Tonghak [Eastern Learning] as a religious sect was founded in 1860 by Ch'oe Che-u (1824-1864), who was executed in 1864 by the Korean government authorities for practicing "evil" religious ideas. *Tonghak* contained eclectic ideas and doctrines extracted from Confucianism, Buddhism, native shamanism and Christianity. Ch'oe's preachings were egalitarian, anti-Western, anti-foreign and anti-Christian. He attacked the privileged classes and directed his religion toward the peasantry and the underprivileged masses.[49]

After Ch'oe's death, his successor, Ch'oe Si-hyŏng, continued the movement. In 1892 widespread *Tonghak* demonstrations erupted in Chŏlla and Ch'ungch'ŏng provinces demanding religious toleration and a posthumous pardon for its founder, Ch'oe Che-u.[50] In April 1893, forty *Tonghak* leaders went to Seoul, knelt down in front of the king's palace gate, and presented petitions similar to those of the previous year; they were dispersed by the Royal Korean troops. In May, over twenty thousand *Tonghak* followers assembled at Poun, Ch'ungch'ŏng Province, and demanded, among other things, domestic reforms and the expulsion of Westerners and Japanese; they, too, were disbanded by the government troops.

In 1894 the *Tonghak* peasant war started in Kobu, Chŏlla Province. The precipitant was the district magistrate's blatant abuse of power. Cho Pyŏng-gap, the district magistrate, under the pretext of constructing a reservoir, exploited the local farm laborers, levied heavy irrigation taxes, and blackmailed the local well-to-do with false criminal accusa-tions. Local peasants appealed without success to Cho's superiors and to the provincial governor that something be done about Cho's usurpation of power. In February of that year, Chŏn Pong-jun, the local *Tonghak* leader, realized that their appeal was futile; under his leadership, a thou-sand angry farmers destroyed the newly constructed reservoir, attacked the government office, broke into the government armory and took weapons, seized the government grain stores and distributed grain to the poor and needy. In addition, the *Tonghak* rebels demanded a twelve-point program:

1. recognize the *Tonghak* adherents;
2. punish all corrupt officials, including the governor of Chŏlla Province and Cho Pyŏng-gap, the chief magistrate of Kobu;
3. punish men of wealth who owe their fortunes to high-handed extortionate practices;
4. discipline those *yangban* in or out of office whose conduct is improper;
5. abolish all forms of slavery and destroy the slave registers;
6. rectify the treatment of "low" and "mean" people (*sangmin* and *ch'ŏnin*);
7. grant widows the right to remarry;
8. ban arbitrary and unstatutory taxes;
9. recruit government officials on the basis of merit and competence rather than family background;
10. punish Koreans who collaborate with the Japanese;
11. cancel all outstanding debts, whether owed to government agencies or to private individuals; and
12. distribute land equitably for cultivation to owner-farmers.[51]

The rebels gained immediate support from the local peasantry, and by May 31 they had captured Chŏnju, the capital of Chŏlla Province. King Kojong, alarmed by the news of the rebellion, appealed to China for help. China responded quickly by dispatching some 2,000 Chinese forces which landed at Asan Bay on June 8 in Ch'ungch'ŏng Province. With the arrival of the Chinese, the *Tonghak* rebels lost their momentum, and the government troops recaptured Chŏnju on June 11. Meanwhile, Japanese troops arrived at Inch'ŏn on June 10 ignoring the Korean government's protest that the *Tonghak* peasant uprising had been quelled and foreign troops were no longer necessary. Deaf to the Korean government's request, both Chinese and Japanese troops showed no sign of withdrawal. China, which had the upper hand in the conduct of Korean affairs, proposed to Japan a simultaneous troops withdrawal from Korea. Japan responded that her troops would remain in Korea in order to "reform the Korean government."

At midnight on July 23, 1894, the Japanese troops under the direction
of Otori Keisuke, the Japanese Minister in Korea, seized the Korean
royal palace. They pressured Kojong to recall Regent Taewŏngun from
his political exile in Peking and to expel the pro-Chinese Min faction
from the cabinet. Two days later, the Sino-Japanese War officially
began when Chinese ships in the Yellow Sea near Asan Bay were
attacked by the Japanese naval forces. With a series of swift and sweeping victories, Japan defeated China and drove the latter out of Korea.
The Treaty of Shimonoseki of 1895,[52] which officially ended the Sino-
Japanese War, signaled the beginning of Japanese domination in Northeast Asia and her further dismemberment of Ch'ing China.

Following the Chinese withdrawal, Korea was virtually at the mercy
of Japan. Japan obtained rights to build railroads and telegraph systems
in Korea. All ports in Chŏlla Province were opened to Japan. These new
developments spurred the *Tonghak* rebels to regroup in October 1894,
and they rose once again in Chŏlla, Ch'ungch'ŏng and other provinces.
They attacked the Japanese supply bases and clashed with the Japanese
troops. The *Tonghak* forces could not match the superior Japanese military. In the end, the *Tonghak* rebels lost their battles, and their leader,
Chŏn Pong-jun, was captured. Chŏn and several other leaders were
taken to Seoul and publicly beheaded in December 1894.

The *Tonghak* Rebellion ended after numerous bloody confrontations,
including several massacres of *Tonghak* adherents by the Japanese
troops. The few remaining forces continued their struggle until January
1895, but for all practical purposes the rebellion ended with Chŏn's
execution at the close of 1894. In retrospect, it was a political irony
par excellence that the *Tonghak* rebels who rose to expel foreigners,
especially the Japanese, from Korea, provided Japan the perfect opportunity and pretext for further entrenchment in Korea (For details, see
Map 3-1).

To a great extent, the political fate of Regent Taewŏngun symbolized
the last phase of the Yi Dynasty. Taewŏngun was impeached by the
internal political forces, i.e., the Min faction, in 1874, but returned
briefly to power during the Army Revolt in 1882. In less than a month,
he was again deposed and taken to Peking by the Chinese troops as a

political hostage. Despite strong opposition from the Min faction, he returned to Korea in the fall of 1885. Japan placed him in power and created the pro-Japanese Kim Hong-jip cabinet in July 1894, during the *Tonghak* Rebellion. Less than three months later, in October 1894, Taewŏngun once again lost his titular power when a plot to put his grandson, Yi Chun-yong, on the throne was allegedly uncovered.[53]

Meanwhile, the Min faction, in a coalition with pro-Russian groups, ousted the pro-Japanese groups and established a pro-Russian cabinet in July 1895. Japan reacted promptly to this pro-Russian move. In August, under the aegis of Miura Goro, the Japanese Minister in Korea, Japanese assassins stormed into Kojong's Kyŏngbok Palace and fatally stabbed Queen Min, leader of the Min faction. Ignoring the outrage at home and abroad against this hideous crime, Japan immediately created another pro-Japanese cabinet headed by Prime Minister Kim Hong-jip (1842-96).

Russia plotted its own version of a bizarre act against Japan. In February 1896, pro-Russian groups led by Yi Pŏm-jin, with the close cooperation of Alexander de Speyer, the Russian Minister in Korea, abducted Kojong and the Crown Prince from the Kyŏngbok Palace and detained them in the Russian legation in Seoul. During the course of this incident, the ministers of the pro-Japanese cabinet, including Prime Minister Kim Hong-jip, were murdered and the second pro-Russian cabinet, headed by Park Chŏng-yang, was installed. The rivalry between Japan and Russia over their respective interests in Korea (as well as Manchuria and China) continued to escalate, leading them to a final military showdown in 1904. As was the case in the Sino-Japanese War, Japan emerged the victor and was thus able "to drive the Russians out of Korea." By 1905, with China and Russia out of the way, and England and the United States on her side, Japan had virtually fulfilled her dream of incorporating Korea as "an integral part of the Japanese Empire."[54]

In hindsight, the demise of the Yi Korea was the result of both intense political factionalism and aggressive foreign intervention. An undue emphasis on the internal political factionalism and the short-sighted seclusion policy of Regent Taewŏngun as the major causes of the Yi Dynasty's fall, is, however, unwarranted. It is true that the political leaders in the Korean Court, traditionalists and reformists alike, were too blinded by their political ambitions to ward off foreign aggression in Korea. Still, it was the foreign powers, especially Japan, which wontonly disregarded Korean sovereignty to realize her own aggressive and imperialistic design on Korea.

Korean Independence Movement

Even before the Japanese absorption of Korea, a few enlightened and reform-minded Koreans desperately attempted to preserve Korea's independence. Sŏ Chae-p'il's *Tongnip Hyŏphoe* [Independence Club] of 1896 was a case in point. *So Chae-p'il* (Dr. Philip Jaison), a founding member of the *Kaehwa-dang* [Progressive Party], fled to the United States via Japan after the abortive Kapsin Coup of 1884. When he returned to Korea from his self-imposed political exile in 1896, he founded the Independence Club and the *Tongnip Sinmun* [the Independence News]. Particularly noteworthy is the fact that "the Independence News" was published only in *hangŭl;* its first issue was published on April 7, 1896, a few days before the founding of the Independence Club. The paper provided impartial news reports to the mass public and tried to educate their rights as citizens while fighting to preserve the nation's independence from foreign powers, especially Japan. For similar purposes, Namgung Ok founded the *Hwangsŏng Sinmun* [the Capital News] in 1898. Unlike the vernacular *Tongnip Sinmun,* "the Capital News" was published in a mixed Chinese-*han'gŭl* script, thereby appealing to the readers from the middle and upper classes who were proficient in classical Chinese. Both newspapers were in the forefront of the resistance against the Japanese aggression.[55] The editorial response of Chang Chi-yŏn, editor of the *Hwangsŏng Sinmun,* to the signing of the Protectorate Treaty of 1905 was memorable:

> Alas! What sorrow! O now enslaved twenty million countrymen of mine! Are we to live or are we to die? Our Korean *nationhood,* nurtured for over four thousand years since Tan'gun and Kija—is it thus in a single night to be abruptly extinguished, forever? What sorrow, oh my countrymen![56]

(1) Diplomatic and Political Maneuverings

When the 1905 Protocol was signed, which for all practical purposes deprived Korea of sovereignty, the Korean people launched their anti-Japanese independence movement in earnest. Through several feeble but frantic diplomatic jugglings, Korean diplomats at home and abroad and foreign residents in Korea attempted to rescue Korean sovereignty. Korean residents in Hawaii dispatched Yi Sung-man (Syngman Rhee) and Rev. Yun Pyŏng-ku to the Portsmouth Conference, but they failed to enlist the sympathy of the U.S. President Theodore Roosevelt for the Korean cause. Homer B. Hulbert, an American missionary and a friend at the Korean Court, sought an appointment with President Roosevelt for the same purpose, but he, too, failed. In December 1905, a month after the Protectorate Treaty was signed, Min Yŏng-ch'an, Korean Minister to France, made a futile plea through the United States Secretary of State Elihu Root to annul the Treaty. E. T. Bethell, an Englishman who founded the *Taehan Maeil Sinbo* [the Korean Daily News] with Yang Ki-t'ak in July 1904, printed a letter from Emperor Kojong on 20 January 1906. In the letter, the Emperor declared the 1905 Treaty null and void on the grounds that he neither agreed to nor signed it. Intimidated by the Japanese, however, Kojong immediately denied the authenticity of the letter. In June 1907, Kojong secretly dispatched three Korean delegates, Yi Sang-sŏl, Yi Chun and Yi Wi-jong, to the Second International Peace Conference at the Hague to solicit international support for the Korean cause; these efforts were blocked by the Japanese delegates at the conference.

Under such helpless circumstances, some Koreans resorted to either self-destruction or terrorism. Immediately following the 1905 Treaty, Min Yŏng-hwan, the chief aide-de-camp to Emperor Kojong, and Cho Pyŏng-se, an ex-Premier, took their own lives in protest. Other lesser Korean officials—Yi Han-ŭng, Hong Man-sik, Yi Sang-ch'ŏl, Song Pyŏng-sŏn and Chŏn Pong-hak—also committed suicide. Yi Chun, one of the Korean delegates at the Hague International Peace Conference, died in anguish when his mission failed to materialize. Noteworthy is the testament left by Min Yŏng-hwan before he committed suicide. In it he appealed emotionally to the "twenty million people of the Korean Empire" for their "national awakening" by using such phrases as "our country," "our nation," "our compatriots" and "the restoration of freedom and independence."[57]

(2) Terrorist Acts

Anti-Japanese terrorists were in abundant supply at that time. The house of Yi Wan-yong, the Minister of Education and a signer of the Treaty, was set on fire by the protestors. In December 1909, Yi, then, Prime Minister, was attacked and fatally wounded by an enraged young Korean. Another signer, Yi Kŭn-t'aek, the Defense Minister, was stabbed by a Korean youngster. In San Francisco, in March 1908, two Korean youths, Chang In-hwan and Chŏn Myong-ŭn, assassinated Durham W. Stevens, a pro-Japanese American, who had been a counselor to the Japanese-run Korean government from 1905 to 1908. He was on his way to Washington on a furlough. On October 26, 1909, Ito Hirobumi, the first Japanese Resident-General in Korea and the chief architect of Japan's Korean colonization plan, was shot to death in Harbin, Manchuria, by a young Korean patriot, An Chung-kŭn. In Seoul on September 2, 1919, Kang Wu-kyu threw a bomb at the newly arrived Japanese Governor-General, Saito Makoto. Makoto narrowly escaped the explosion, but several dozen Japanese and pro-Japanese Korean dignitaries were killed or wounded.

Anti-Japanese terrorism in the 1920s and 1930s was better organized and more closely coordinated by the Korean independence organizations. In addition to earlier terrorist organizations such as *Kisa-tan* [the Knights Corps] and *Amsal-tan* [the Assassination Corps], *Ŭiyŏl-tan* [the Righteous Corps] was organized by Kim Wŏn-bong in Kirin, Manchuria, in November 1919. In the spring of 1930, Kim Ku founded *Aeguk-tan* [the Patriotic Corps] in Shanghai as a terrorist arm of the Korean independence movement. *Aeguk-tan* was responsible for the bombing of the Pusan Police Station in 1921 as well as the Milyang Police Station and the Korean Government-General Building in Seoul. Na Sŏk-ju (1892-1926), who bombed the Japanese-run Oriental Development Company

Building in Seoul in July 1926, was a member of *Aeguk-tan*. On January 8, 1932, Yi Pong-ch'ang (1900-32), a member of *Aeguk-tan*, threw a hand grenade at the Japanese Emperor during a state procession outside the Sakurada Gate of the Imperial Palace in Tokyo. The Emperor barely escaped Yi's explosives, but several high-ranking Japanese officials were killed or severely wounded. Yun Pong-gil (1908-32), another member of *Aeguk-tan,* threw a bomb and killed several Japanese military commanders and diplomats who were standing on the dais during a Japanese military parade in Hungku Park in Shanghai in April 1932.[58]

(3) Quislings and Collaborators

Korean quislings were abundant during this period. Many Koreans swiftly rode the Japanese tide and fanned the flames of Japanization of Korea for the sake of their own personal and political gains. Song Pyŏng-jun and Yun Si-byŏng's *Yusin-hoe* [Renovation Association] and Yi Yong-gu's *Chinbo-hoe* [Progress Association], both of which later merged under the name *Ilchin-hoe* [United Progress Association], were typical. *Hŏnjŏng Yŏnguhoe* [Constitutional Government Study Association], led by Yi Chun and Yang Han-muk, emerged to take a stand against *Ilchin-hoe* and condemned it for betraying of the nation.[59]

There were also Korean cabinet members such as Yi Wan-yong, Pak Che-sun, Yi Kŭn-t'aek, Kwŏn Chung-hyŏn and Yi Ha-yong, who signed the 1905 Protectorate Treaty. Han Kyu-sŏl, the Prime Minister and a former Independence Club member, who firmly opposed the Treaty, was dragged out from the chamber by the Japanese gendarmes. The members of the Yi Wan-yong cabinet, which signed the 1910 Annexation Treaty, were Yim Sŏn-jun, Yi Pyŏng-mu, Yi Che-kon, Ko Yong-hi, Cho Chung-ŭng and Song Pyŏng-jun.[60]

(4) The Righteous Army's Resistance

Following the signing of the 1905 Protocol, the Korean armed resistance began. *Ŭlbyŏng* [Righteous Army], loyal remnant troops of the Yi Dynasty who were forced to disband by the Japanese in 1907, staged a stiff resistance against the Japanese troops in Korea. Some notable leaders of the Righteous Army units were: Min Chong-sik, an ex-official of the Yi Dynasty in South Ch'ungch'ŏng Province; Ch'oe Ik-hyŏn, a noted Confucian scholar in North Chŏlla Province; Sin Tol-sŏk in North Kyŏngsang Province; and Yi Un-ch'ang in Kangwŏn Province. A Japanese source estimated that the Righteous Army during the 1907-1911 period numbered over 141,000. During this time it waged over 2,800 battles against the Japanese troops and 23,000 of its soldiers were either killed, wounded and/or captured. Its strength began to diminish after 1909, and by 1911, according to the same Japanese source, its resistance ended although some other sources indicated that it continued to fight until 1915.[61]

(5) Mass Uprisings and Protests

Anti-Japanese mass uprisings and unarmed protests were not uncommon during the Japanese rule. Some notable instances were: The March First Movement of 1919, sparked by the death of Kojong (r. 1864-1907); the June Tenth Incident of 1926 at the death of Sunjong (r. 1907-10), the last Korean monarch; and the Kwangju Student Uprising of November 1929, begun by a fight between the Japanese and Korean students in a commuter train from Songjŏng-ri to Kwangju, capital of South Chŏlla Province. The Kwangju Student Uprising, for instance, quickly spread nationwide as a national anti-Japanese student protest, involving some 194 schools and 54,000 students.[62]

Of all the anti-Japanese mass resistance demonstrations, the March First Uprising was monumental in magnitude and significance. It was one of the largest anti-colonial mass protests in the annals of the struggle for national independence in the world. It began formally with the Declaration of Korean Independence, which was signed by thirty-three prominent Korean nationalist leaders at the Pagoda Park in Seoul on March 1, 1919. One to two million Koreans of all ages, occupations and social strata participated in this nation-wide mass upheaval. Although substantial differences still exist over the statistics of this event, some 7,000 Koreans were killed by the Japanese military and police forces and over 52,000 Koreans were jailed.[63]

(6) The Korean Provisional Government

Immediately following the March First Movement, the Korean Provisional Government (KPG) was established as a political united front in Vladivostok on March 21, in Shanghai on April 11 and in Seoul on April 21, 1919. From then on, the two-pronged anti-Japanese liberation movement—political struggle and armed resistance, especially in Manchuria, China and Soviet Siberia—was launched. From the outset, however, the Korean independence movement at home and abroad was marred by ideological differences and factional struggles among the leaders. To avert such disunity, united front movements like the KPG were often organized. The KPG itself was barely able to maintain a facade of unity under its broad umbrella. The Association for Promotion of the United Korean Independence Party was organized in March 1927 by Yi Dong-yŏng, Kim Tu-bong, Kim Ku and Cho So-ang in Shanghai, and *Singanhoe* [New Korea Society] was organized in February 1927 by Yi Sang-jae and Kwŏn Tong-ji in Seoul. More often than not, the intense struggle between the Communists and the nationalists within these united front organizations and factional feuds within each camp did not cease completely.[64]

Long before the March First Movement of 1919, various anti-Japanese independence organizations existed at home and abroad. Among the more notable ones were: *Sinmin-hoe* [New People's Association], organized by An Ch'ang-ho, Yi Kap and Yi Tong-hwi in Pyongyang in 1906; *Kukmin-hoe* [National Association] organized by students of the Sungsil School in Pyongyang in 1917; *Kukmin-hoe* organized in Los Angeles by An Ch'ang-ho; and *Tongji-hoe* [Comrades Association], organized by Yi Sung-man in Honolulu, Hawaii.[65]

Meanwhile, the KPG moved its headquarters from Shanghai to Nanking in 1932 and to Chinkiang in 1935. In 1940, it moved to Chungking via Changsha as the Nationalist Chinese government retreated west to escape Japan's advancing army. Still, the KPG survived under the leadership of Kim Ku, albeit nominally, during the trying years of Japan's military march into China proper. The KPG, in fact, outlived the Japanese imperialism which fell in 1945. With the unconditional surrender of Japan, the former Soviet Union and the United States occupied the northern half and the southern half of Korea, respectively. The 38th parallel had been established as the demarcation line by the General Order No. 1 issued by General MacArthur, Supreme Commander of the Allied Forces in the Pacific. Ironically, the United States occupation forces and the military government in South Korea refused to recognize the legitimacy of the twenty-six year old KPG in exile. The KPG leaders, after a long, bitter and tenuous struggle against the Japanese colonialism in foreign lands, were allowed to return to their fatherland only after they disclaimed their official association with the KPG at the adamant insistence of the United States occupation forces. Most of these leaders thus returned as private citizens.[66]

(7) Ideological Bifurcation

The Korean independence movement, from the March First Movement of 1919 until the Japanese surrender in 1945, may be divided into two broad political and ideological strands, the communists and their sympathizers and the nationalists with their adherents. The formal origin of the Korean communist movement can be traced back to June 26, 1918, when Yi Tong-hwi (1873-1935) and Kim Rip founded *Hanin Sahoe-tang* [Korean People's Socialist Party] in Khabarovsk, Soviet Siberia.[67] Earlier, Yi Tong-hwi along with Yi Sang-sŏl, established *Tae-han Kwangbokkun Chŏngbu* [the Government of the Korean Restoration Army] in the Russian maritime province in 1914. After the March First Movement, Yi Tong-hwi was named the first Premier of the KPG in Shanghai on August 30, 1919. His Korean People's Socialist Party also moved to Shanghai via Vladivostok. Earlier, on January 22, 1918, a Korean section of the Russian Communist Party in Irkutsk was founded under the leadership of Nam Man-ch'ŏn. From the outset, therefore, the Korean communist movements had two foreign origins, the Irkutsk group and the Khabarovsk-Shanghai group. These two groups vied for the hegemony of the Korean communist movement and for the official recognition and support of the Communist International.

In the 1920s, numerous communist and communist-leaning organizations and study groups appeared in Korea. Kim Yak-su's *Ilwŏl-hoe* [January Society], Kim Chae-bong and Cho Pong-am's *Hwayo-hoe* [Tuesday Society] and Yi Yŏng's Seoul Youth Association were noteworthy. The January Society was the offshoot of the earlier *Hukto-hoe* [Black Wave Society], which had been organized in Tokyo by the leftist Korean students in November 1921. When the Black Wave Society moved its base from Tokyo to Seoul in November 1924, its official name was changed to *Puksŏng-hoe* [North Star Society] and finally to *Ilwŏl-hoe* in January 1925.

Likewise, the Tuesday Society, the outgrowth of the earlier *T'oyo-hoe* [Saturday Society], was organized by Kim Chae-bong and Cho Pong-am on May 20, 1923. The Saturday Society changed its name to *Sinsasang Yŏnku-hoe* [New Thought Study Association] on July 7, 1923, and again to *Hwayo-hoe* on November 19, 1924.

The Seoul Youth Association, led by Yi Yŏng, Pak Hŏn-yŏng and Kim Sa-guk, was the leftist offshoot of a larger pan-national youth organization, *Choson Ch'ŏngnyŏnyŏnhap-hoe* [Federation of Korean Youth], which was created under the leadership of Chang Tŏk-su on December 20, 1920. The Seoul Youth Association kept close relations with such communist-leaning organizations as *Musanja Tongji-hoe* [Proletariat Comrade Society] which was founded in January 1922 and later became *Musanja Tongmaeng-hoe* [Proletariat League] on March 31, 1922.

In terms of the Korean communist lineage, the original Irkutsk group had an organizational link with the Tuesday Society in Korea while the Khabarovsk-Shanghai group had a close affiliation with the Seoul Youth Association. On April 17, 1925, these three major communist groups in Korea agreed to merge and immediately convened their first United Congress of the Korean Communist Party (KCP) in Seoul under the leadership of Kim Chae-bong, who was elected its first secretary.

The close Japanese surveillance and constant crackdowns on Korean communist leaders severely hampered the growth of the Korean communist movement at home. When Kim Chae-bong, the first KCP chairman, was arrested by the Japanese authorities in February 1926, Kang Tal-yong, another KCP leader, succeeded him as chairman at the second

KCP Congress in March. Kang, too, was captured by the Japanese authorities on July 17, 1926, and the KCP remained for a while without a leader. The Third KCP Party Congress was controlled by the leaders of the executive committee of the Congress, often called the Marxist-Leninist group. They were a coalition of three groups within the KCP: the Seoul group led by Yi Chong-yun; the Shanghai group led by Kim Ch'ŏl-su; and the January Society led by An Kwang-ch'ŏn. On February 27, 1928, the Fourth KCP Congress was convened under the leadership of Ch'a Kŭm-bong, but Ch'a and the key leaders of the KCP were arrested by the Japanese authorities. Two more attempts were made to reactivate the KCP, first by Kim Ch'ŏl-su, who organized the KCP's Reestablishment Preparation Association in June 1929, and again by Kwŏn Tae-hyŏng, who created the KCP's Reestablishment Council in February 1931. Both attempts failed without making much headway. The KCP remained inactive from 1931 to the end of the Japanese rule in Korea in August 1945.[68]

Paralleling the anti-Japanese movements formed by the Korean communist organizations were the anti-Japanese movements of the non-communist (and often anti-communist) nationalist Korean organizations. Among the prominent nationalist leaders were An Ch'ang-ho, Pak Yong-man, Kim Ku, Kim Kyu-sik, Yi Sung-man and Yŏ Un-hyŏng. Within these nationalist camps, the strategies for national liberation and independence varied considerably. An Ch'ang-ho, the founder of the *Sinmin-hoe* and later *Hungsa-tan* [Knight Development Corps], for instance, advocated a gradual and long-term struggle for Korean independence.[69] Kim Ku, the founder of the Korean Independence Party and *Aeguk-tan* and a long-time head of the KPG, often resorted to radical and violent means in his struggle against the alien Japanese rule; he later organized *Kwangbok-gun* [Korean Independence Army] in 1940 as the KPG's military arm.[70]

Between these two poles—evolutionary and revolutionary strategies for Korean independence—lay many moderate and less obdurate leaders. Yŏ Un-hyŏng, for instance, who founded *Sinhan Ch'ŏngnyŏn-tang* [New Korea Youth Party] in Shanghai in 1933, was less doctrinaire than many nationalist leaders, although he did lean toward the communist line of the Korean independence movement.[71] Similarly, Kim Kyu-sik, who headed *Hanguk Taeil Chosŏnt'ongil-tongmaeng* [Anti-Japanese Korean Independence League] founded in 1932 in Shanghai, represented moderate, middle-of-the-road, nationalist groups. Still others, like Yi Sŭng-man, played an important role in American and international diplomatic circles for the attainment of Korean national liberation.[72]

Armed Struggles

In conjunction with political independence movements, tenacious anti-Japanese armed struggles and guerrilla warfares were staged by Koreans abroad, especially in Manchuria. After the failure of earlier anti-Japanese armed resistance within Korea by the Korean Righteous Army, the preparation for the armed struggle was launched overseas by the Korean exiles. The Korean military training schools established by Pak Yong-man in Nebraska in 1910-1912 and in Hawaii in 1912-1916 were part of these pioneering attempts. Later, Korean military training schools were established at Ninganhsin in Manchuria in June 1919 by Kim Chwa-jin and at Mishan in Manchuria near the Russian border in 1921 by Yi Tong-hwi.[73]

Sporadic anti-Japanese Korean armed clashes occurred off and on in Manchuria while the Korean military training schools were being established. Hong Pŏm-do in the Nikolsk-Ussurisk area, Mun Ch'ang-bŏm in Vladivostok, Sŏ Il and Yi Pŏm-yun in the Wangching and Chientao areas, were notable in these early armed conflicts. In the late 1920s, various Korean anti-Japanese guerrilla forces in the North Chientao region were united as the Greater Korean Independence Army at Mishan under the leadership of Sŏ Il.[74] Two of the widely acclaimed early victories in the history of the Korean armed struggles against the Japanese were the *Pong-o-tong* (Feng-wu-tung in Chinese) and the *Ch'ŏngsan-li* (Ch'ing-shan-li) battles in 1920. In the former instance, the Korean independence Army led by Hong Pŏm-do and Ch'oe Tong-jin surrounded a Japanese army contingent and inflicted casualties of over 160 killed and more than 300 wounded. The Ch'ŏngsan-li battle was fought against a

Japanese force by Generals Kim Chwa-jin and Yi Pŏm-sok of the North Route Army in North Chientao in October 1920. In this battle the Japanese lost over 1,000 soldiers despite their superiority in number and arms.[75]

In the early 1930s, as Japan forcibly created the puppet government, Manchukuo, in Manchuria, Korean liberation movement gained a new momentum. Many Chinese-Korean allied forces were formed to resist the Japanese. As Korean independence movements divided sharply along ideological lines in the 1930s, so did the Korean armed struggles. Among the nationalist groups, Kim Ku's *Hanguk Tongnipt'ukmu-dae* [Korean Independence Special Corps] founded in 1934 and the Korean Independence Liberation Front] founded in 1939 in Linchou, Kwangsi Province in China, which was renamed *Hanguk Kwangbok-gun* [Korean Restoration Army] in 1940, were most notable.[76]

The communist-led anti-Japanese armed struggles, especially in Manchuria, had been much more active and widespread. The early communist-led Korean armed struggle was carried out, for instance, by *Chosŏn Hyŏkmyŏng-gun* [Korean Revolutionary Army] founded in 1931. It was the military arm of *Chŏsonhyŏkmyŏng-tang* [Korean Revolutionary Party], the successor to the earlier *Kukmin-bu* [National Headquarters], which was established in Kuentien and Chian in April 1919 as a prominent Korean independence organization.[77] In the 1930s in Manchuria, from the Russian border in the north and the east to the Korean border in the south, existed at one time or another some eleven "people's revolutionary armies" and "allied armies" of Chinese and Korean communists fighting against the Japanese forces in the region.[78] From mid-1930 on, Kim Il Sung's anti-Japanese guerrilla forces in Manchuria, a part of the Northeast Anti-Japanese United Army, played a significant role in the history of the Korean armed struggles against the Japanese forces.[79]

In June 1938, two communist Korean youth groups, led by Ch'oe Ch'ang-sŏk and Kim Wŏn-bong merged and were renamed the Korean Youth Vanguard League; it was later renamed the Korean Volunteers Corps in October 1938 in Hankow, China, under the leadership of Kim Wŏn-bong.[80] In January 1941, Mu Chŏng, a high ranking Korean officer

of the Chinese People's Liberation Army and a Long Marcher, organized *Hwabuk Chosŏn Ch'ŏngnyŏn Yŏnhap-hoe* [North China Korean
Youth Federation] in Tungko, Lo Prefecture, in Shansi Province. A year
later, Mu Chŏng renamed it the North China Independence League.[81]
The Korean Volunteers Corps in North China was also reactivated by
the League leadership during this time. The core members of the North
China Independence League and the Korean Volunteers Corps later
became known as the Yanan Group in post-liberation North Korean
political arenas.

In conclusion, the Korean liberation movement did not cease until
Japan was driven out of Korea in 1945. Diplomatic maneuverings, economic boycotts, political pressures, unarmed mass protests and numerous armed guerrilla struggles had occurred, beginning with Japan's
forcible attempt to absorb Korea in 1905. Underground societies and
open organizations with either gradualist and moderate objectives or
with radical and violent methods had tried to remove the Japanese rule
in Korea. Ironically, despite the tenacious struggles for liberation staged
by the Korean nationalists and communists, the end of the Japanese rule
came, not by the triumph of the Korean liberation movement per se but
by the defeat of Japan in World War II. The unfolding of the tangled
mystery of post-war Korean politics and the semi-permanent partition of
Korea lie in this historical irony. Like the Gordian knot, the Korean
problem will be untangled only when this irony is fully understood by
those in power in the both halves of Korea today.

Korean Nationalism: An Overview

It is clear from the foregoing that Korean nationalism did not occur
overnight. Korean nationalism represents the cumulative common
achievements of the Korean people for five millennia. Koguyrŏ's
defense against the Sui and the T'ang China's invasions; Late Silla's
hwarang spirit, which led to the first territorial integration of the Korean
people; early Koryŏ's revanchist dream of recovering Koguryŏ's lost
territory in Manchuria; Koryŏ's gallant struggle against the invading

Khitans, Jurchens and the Mongols; Sejong the Great's invention of the indigenous Korean alphabet, *han'gŭl*; the Korean resistance against the Japanese invasion and Admiral Yi Sun-sin's naval victory and, later, the Korean resistance against the Manchus; and, above all, the Korean people's anti-Japanese independence struggles, typified by the March First Movement of 1919, during the period of Japanese colonization are some of the ingredients which molded and forged Korean nationalism. Some of these events are the sources of the Korean people's pride; others, bring back the memory of horrors and sufferings; and still others serve as the reminder of shame and remorse. Regardless, all of them make up the national identity of being a Korean.

Setting aside the long and cumulative nature of Korean nationalism for the moment, even on the question of origins, nature and periodization of modern Korean nationalism, scholar's views vary widely.[82] Still, a number of general observations on this question can be made.

One, a series of intrusions and invasions by the Western merchant marines and warships, beginning in the latter half of the nineteenth century gave rise to modern Korean nationalism. The Korean resistance against these foreign encroachments manifested itself in Taewŏngun's anti-foreign (primarily anti-Western) seclusion policy. To that extent, modern Korean nationalism contained a high degree of negativism— anti-foreign, anti-Western, anti-Japanese, anti-Christian and anti-colonial. Korea's anti-foreign negativism was characterized by its reactive urge to restore the traditional order and to expel foreigners from the native soil. The persecution of the French and native Catholic priests and their adherents by the Korean government authorities; the sinking of *General Sherman*, a U.S. merchant marine, at the Taedong River in 1866; the subsequent military skirmishes between the Korean royal troops and the French naval forces which landed on the Kanghwa Island in 1866 (*Pyŏngin Yangyo*) and between Korean troops and the U.S. naval contingents on the same island in 1871 (*Sinmi Yangyo*) typified such mood and sentiment of the Korean court. Even later incidents such as the Korean Army Revolt of 1882 (*Imo Kullan*) the *Tonghak* Rebellion of 1894 and a protracted Righteous Army Resistance, beginning in 1905, were motivated primarily by such anti-foreign negativism.

Two, although most of these historic events were marked, on the surface at least, by anti-foreign negativism, it would be too simplistic and superficial for anyone to characterize the nature of modern Korean nationalism as being totally negative. On the contrary, the positive character of modern Korean nationalism was as strong as, if not stronger than, its negative features. The ideas and ideals of the *Sirhak* [True or Practical Learning] school of the mid-seventeenth century, of *Kaehwa* [Enlightenment] and *Tongnip* [Independence] movements in the late nineteenth century embody positive nature of Korean nationalism.

The current of history was overwhelmingly tipped against the positive responses to the Western and Japanese challenges by some progressive forces in Korea. Still, the positive, progressive and reformist ideas and ideals took root, even though they had failed to blossom during this turbulent period of Western and Japanese encroachments in Korea. From this standpoint, the early phase of modern Korean nationalism, beginning in 1850 to 1910, was more or less an admixture of positive and negative ideas and sentiments. Its early stage was characterized by a combination of national reaction against the Western and Japanese intrusions and invasions, an awareness of the technological and scientific superiority of the West, the need for rapid modernization and reform, an awakening of national consciousness and identity, an exhibition of xenophobia and a revival of Eastern and Western religious syncretism.

Three, a full-fledged Korean nationalist movement was activated by the Japanese annexation of Korea in 1910. The Japanese colonization spawned an entirely different dimension of Korean nationalism and nationalist movement. After annexation, Japan became the undisputed common "enemy" against whom the Korean people rallied regardless of their social backgrounds and ideological proclivities. The forcible loss of the Korean statehood reawakened a new sense of identity and solidarity among the Korean people, and regaining an independent Korean nation-state became their urgent and paramount obsession and objective.

The 1919 March First Movement epitomized this new dimension of Korean nationalism. It also provided the necessary catalyst for beginning an organized mass anti-Japanese Korean independence struggle. The Korean Provisional Government started with the March First Move-

ment and the two-pronged anti-Japanese Korean liberation movement—
political struggle and armed resistance—began in earnest. During this
nation-wide mass upheaval, some two million people of all ages, occupations, and social strata participated. Thus, began the era of the mass
phase of Korean nationalism. If the *Tonghak* Rebellion was *nativistic*
mass upheaval, the March First Movement was *nationalistic* mass movement. The former *reacted* to the oppressive authorities, foreign and/or
domestic, and the latter, rose to *regain* the Korean national sovereignty.

Four, the Korean independence movement was often plagued by
factional strifes and ideological conflicts among its leaders. During the
Japanese colonial period, the ideological differences among the Korean
leaders took a political back-seat. With the exit of Japan in 1945, the
ideological splits among the Korean leaders of liberation movement surfaced and intensified as a result of Korea's territorial partition into the
two halves with the former Soviet Union occupying the North and the
United States, the South. Initially, under the aegis of the Soviet occupation forces, the leftists found their political haven in the North, as the
rightists found their own staging area in the South under the protection
of the American occupation administration. The ideological split, compounded by Korea's persistent territorial division, still continues, and
ironically, nationalism has now taken a political back-seat.

Five, unlike other Asian, African and Latin American nations,
the Korean nationalist movement was not triggered by the Western or
American colonialists but by the Japanese. Until 1945, the Korean
nationalists did not identify the West with colonialism, imperialism or
repression. To the contrary, they perceived the West as a source of progressive ideas and anti-colonialism, viz., a significant number of Korean
nationalists had been in close contact with the Christian missionaries in
Korea, especially those from the United States; many Korean nationalists had embraced not only Christian ideas and ideals but liberal Western political thought through such associations; and many had received
their education in the West, especially in America which became one of
the staging grounds for their anti-Japanese independence movement.[83]

Six, the physical partition of the country since 1945 and the corresponding human separation added extra dimensions to the present Korean

nationalism. First is the concurrent existence of both genuine advocates and pseudo-advocates of Korean unification question. The Korean people's desire for reunification, whether they reside in the North, the South or abroad, is genuine. By contrast, the motives of the ruling elites in advocating reunification in the two halves are often questionable. More often than not, the ruling elites on both sides exploit the people's genuine desire for reunification for their own political gains. To put it differently, the ruling elites, who can make a difference in negotiating a reunited fatherland, pay lip service, while the people, who are sincerely interested in realizing such a dream, are usually devoid of power. Thus, a reunited fatherland remains a dream, while the unification rhetoric continues.

The existence of the two political regimes in Korea since 1948 raises various legalistic questions: are the DPRK and ROK two states in one nation? Are they two states and two nations? Do they constitute one lawful and one unlawful governments? Or are they two governments in one state and one nation? There is no question that there are two sets of government in the Korean Peninsula today. But are they also two "states"? If the standard prerequisites of a state are a permanent population, a defined territory and a government to which the population renders habitual obedience and a capacity to enter into relations with other states, both North and South Korea can easily qualify as two states. Each has its own national anthem, flag, capital and other separate national symbols, let alone two heads of states under two separate governments. What is more, both have now joined the United Nations, let alone most of the UN specialized agencies. Both have established diplomatic relations with foreign countries. Both participate in various international meetings, conferences and events, be they political, economic, military, cultural or athletic, as two separate independent entities, although some athletic events have taken place under a single unified team. Hence, their claims and disclaimers notwithstanding, the DPRK and the ROK are *de facto* and *de jure* two states.

Closely related to the controversy surrounding the nature and status of two regimes in Korean Peninsula is the dispute over the proper name for Korea and its people. Since the Korean partition, North Korea is called

Chosŏn, an abbreviation of *Chosŏn Inmin Minjujui Konghwakuk* [the Democratic People's Republic of Korea] or the DPRK and South Korea, *Hankuk,* an abbreviation of *Daehan Minkuk* [the Republic of Korea] or the ROK. Korea and Korean people are, for instance, called *Chosŏn* and *Chosŏnin,* respectively in the former Soviet Union and China, while they are called *Hankuk* and *Hankukin* in the United States, South Korea's principal ally. Interestingly enough, in Japan where the Korean residents are divided into pro-North Korean and pro-South Korean groups, they are called both *Chosŏn* and *Chosŏnin* and *Hankuk* and *Hankukin.*

The origin of the term *Chosŏn* dates back to one of the earliest Korean state, Old Chosŏn (2333 B.C.-?), and it reappeared in Kija *Chosŏn* (1193 B.C.?-1122 B.C.?), Wiman *Chosŏn* and recently the Yi *Chosŏn* (1392-1910). Likewise, the genesis of the term *Han* may have been derived from the names of the three tribal *Han* states—Chinhan, Pyŏnhan and Mahan—in the southern region of the Korean Peninsula, some time around the second or the third century B.C. More recently, *Taehan Cheguk* [the Korean Empire], 1897-1910, and *Taehan Minguk Imsi-chŏngbu* [the Korean Provisional Government], 1919-1945, were notable.

Both *Chosŏn* and *Taehan* were interchangeably used during the Japanese rule. For example, 33 patriots who signed the Declaration of Korean Independence during the March First Movement of 1919 were called *Chosŏn Minjok Taep'yo,* [the representatives of *Chosŏn* people], but the Korean Provisional Government (KPG) which was formed immediately after the March First Movement was named *Taehan Minguk Imsi Chŏngbu* [the provisional government of the great *Han* people's state]. Likewise, Yi Tong-Hwi, a leading anti-Japanese figure and the first President of the KPG, created the first Korean Communist Party in February of 1918 in Khabarovsk, Soviet Siberia, which was named, ironically, not *Chosŏn* but *Hanin Kongsandang* [the communist party of *Han* people].[84] Those who wrote Korean language texts during the Japanese rule, too, freely and interchangeably used both *Chosŏn* and *Taehan.*[85]

According to Pyŏng-do Lee, the term *Han* denotes "big" and *Han* as a family name, was one of the oldest in Korea. Most importantly, in the legendary kingdom of Kija *Chosŏn*, its royal family name reportedly was *Han*, and *Han* was apparently the most numerous family name in that state.[86]

Several implications of *Chosŏn* and *Han* are worth examining here. Both terms are inseparably connected with each other from the outset of the formation of a Korean state: *Chosŏn* was the name of the state, and *Han* was a family name. *Chosŏn* refers primarily to the governing body, while *Han* stands mainly for the people. The oldest *Chosŏn* state originated in the northern regions in the Korean Peninsula, while the oldest *Han* state(s) emerged from its southern region. In that sense, calling North Korea *Chosŏn* and South Korea, *Hankuk* is apropos, perhaps, with a historical significance.

Seven, the views on nationalism differ rather diametrically in North and South Korea. North Korea, officially at least, rejects the so-called "bourgeois nationalism" and upholds "proletarian internationalism." But in reality, Kim Il Sung's *Juche* idea, the core fetish of Kim Il Sungism or the Kim Il Sung revolutionary thought may be seen as a variant of extreme nationalism. It is a closed, fanatical and inward-looking fetishism which has led, among other things, to the Kim Il Sung cult. The official rejection of the concept "nationalism" and the reverence for the idea of *Juche* are the typical example of North Korea and other socialist countries' Orwellian Newspeak.

Meanwhile, South Korea embraces nationalism, which was initially an ideology to fight against the Japanese imperialism and colonialism in Korea, and, now, it can serve as an ideal through which the unification of the nation can be accomplished and the separated family members can be reunited. Furthermore, the rights of its citizen can be fully realized through the spirit of nationalism. For example, while Ch'a identified independence, modernization and national territorial integration, Sohn listed unification, modernization and democratization as the major task of the present Korean nationalism.[87]

Finally, with the emergence of the two mutually irreconcilable regimes in the Peninsula, intense contests have been undergoing between North and South Korea. The race between the two is not confined to political, economic or military arenas. It embraces practically all aspects of human endeavors—ideological rivalry, political animosity, arms race, economic competition, diplomatic maneuvering, socio-cultural show-off, athletic show-down and even moral wrangling. Some competitions such as ideological and political intransigence and arms race have been destructive, although others such as economic development efforts and athletic promotions have been, by and large, constructive. In the final analysis, as long as the destructive race continues between the two, the peaceful realization of a reunited statehood is nearly unattainable. Hopefully, the currently on-going dialogue between the North and the South will lead to a new road toward the realization of a united Korea. Still, if the German unification can be any guide, it is clear that the realization of genuine unification—political, social and economic unity as well as mental and human unity—will be a protracted, painful and costly process. The present Korean nationalism is, in fine, unfinished as long as Korea remains divided. And the territorial division and human separation will continue to flame the present Korean nationalism.

MAP 3-1. Lines of March of the Tonghak Peasant Army

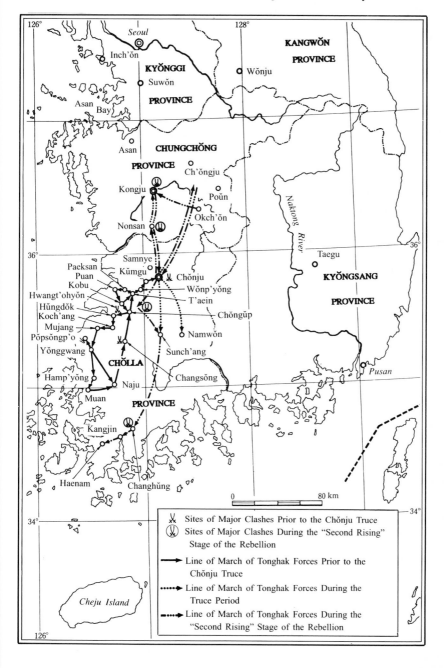

Baradat, *Political Ideologies: Their Origins and Impact* (Englewood Cliffs: Prentice-Hall, 1979), p. 37; Yong-Hee Lee, "The Concept of Nationalism" (in Korean), in Jae-Bong Noh, *Hankuk Minjokjui wa Kukjechŏngch'i* [Korean Nationalism and International Politics] (Seoul: *Minum-sa*, 1983), p. 212; Ki-pyŏk Ch'a, "The Problem of Resistant Nationalism" (in Korean), in Jae-Bong Noh, *Op. Cit.*, p. 14; Roy Macridis, *Contemporary Political Ideologies: Movement and Regimes* (Boston: Little, Brown, 1983), p. 252; and F. M. Barnard, "National Culture and Political Legitimacy: Herder and Rousseau," *Journal of the History of Ideas* 44 (1983): 252.

19. Roger Gibbins, *Op. Cit.*, pp. 341-389.
20. Louis Snyder, *The Meaning of Nationalism* (New York: Rutgers University Press, 1954), p. 11.
21. Rupert Emerson, "Nationalism and Political Development," *The Journal of Politics* 22 (1960): 18.
22. Hans Kohn, "A New Look at Nationalism," *The Virginia Quarterly Review* 32 (1956): 321.
23. Karl Deutsch, *Nationalism and Social Communication* (Cambridge: M.I.T. Press, 1953, 1966), p. 189.
24. Richard A. Preston, "Nationalism in the Atomic Age," *International Quarterly* 11 (1956): 178.
25. Léon Gordenker, "The New Nationalism and International Organizations," *International Studies Quarterly* 13 (1969): 31-45.
26. Philip W. Thayer, *Nationalism and Progress in Free Asia* (Baltimore: the Johns Hopkins University Press, 1956), pp. 81-82.
27. Selig S. Harrison, *The Widening Gulf: Asian Nationalism and American Policy* (New York: the Free Press, 1978), p. 31.
28. Hans Kohn, "A New Look at Nationalism," pp. 321-332.
29. Leo Strauss, "Plato" in Leo Strauss and Joseph Cropsey, eds., *History of Political Philosophy* (Chicago: Rand McNally, 1963), pp. 7-63; Also, William Mathie, "Political Community and the Canadian Experience: Reflections on Nationalism, Federalism, and Unity," *Canadian Journal of Political Science* 12 (March 1979): 3-20. In a similar vein, Hans Kohn wrote that it was the Greeks (e.g., Plato) who developed the concept of supreme loyalty to the political community called polis. But at the end of the fourth century B.C., Alexander's dream of a world empire, un-Greek in its origin, helped to transform the sharp division between Greeks and Barbarians into a new and universal attitude, surpassing all ethnic frontiers and distinctions. Under the influence of Alexander's aspiration, the Greek Stoic philosophers taught mankind to consider that their fatherland was the whole inhabited earth, the cosmopolis, and that man was a citizen not of a nation but of mankind. For details, see his *Nationalism*, p. 12.

30. Erik H. Erikson, "Reflections on Dr. Borg's Life Cycle," *Daedalus* (Spring, 1976), p. 16.
31. Yong-Hee Lee, "The Concept of Nationalism," p. 238.
32. Chu-dong Yang's painstaking life-long collection, translation, and interpretations of Silla poems and songs are found in his, *Koga Yŏnku* [Study of Old Songs] (Seoul: Iljokak, 1965, 1983). The questions about Sŏl Ch'ong's invention of *idu* is raised by William Henthorn, *A History of Korea*, p. 73. Also, Pyŏng-do Lee, *Kuksa Daekwan*, p. 143.
33. Pyong-do Lee, *Kuksa Daekwan*, pp. 143-144. Ki-baik Lee, *A New History of Korea*, p. 60.
34. Both *yŏndŭnghoe* and *p'algwanhoe* began during the reign of T'aejo but then were discontinued during the reign of Sŏng-jong (r. 981-97). They were revived under Hyŏnjong (r. 1009-31). Both ceremonies were held once a year; Since Uijong (r. 1146-70), *yŏndung* was reportedly held on January 15th, and *p'algwan* during the month of November. For details, see *Ibid.*, p. 132 and Pyŏng-Do Lee, *Kuksa Daekwan*, p. 191.
35. See Pyŏng-do Lee, *Kuksa Daekwan*, pp. 203-256.
36. An English translation of Wang Kŏn's Ten Injunctions are found in Pyŏng-Choon Hahm, *The Korean Political Tradition and Law* (Seoul: Hollym, 1967), pp. 46-51.
37. *Ibid.*
38. *Ibid.*
39. *Ibid.*
40. For details, see Woo-keun Han, *The History of Korea*, pp. 165-176.
41. Pyŏng-do Lee, *Kuksa Daekwan*, p. 322.
42. Kedourie, for instance, asserts that people who speak an original language are nations, and that nations must speak an original language. Further, he states that "to speak an original language is to be true to one's character, to maintain one's identity...." See his *Nationalism*, p. 67.
43. Pyŏng-do Lee, *Kuksa Daekwan*, pp. 404-428.
44. For a detailed anaysis of *Sirhak* social and economic theory, see Ki-jun Cho, "An Analysis of *Sirhak* and Its Socio-economic Understanding," and Yong-dŏk Kim, "Social-Economic Thought of *Sirhak* School." Both studies are found in *Hankuk Sasang Daekye* [Outline of Korean Thought] (Seoul: Sungkyungwan University Press, 1976), Volume 2, pp. 205-258 and pp. 259-336. See also, Myŏng-jong Yoo, *Hankuk Ch'ŏlhaksa*, pp. 276-353.
45. For an excellent study of Catholicism in Korea, see Hong-ryeol Ryu, *Hankuk Sahoesasangsa Ronkyo* [Studies on the History of Korean Social Thought], pp. 160-325.
46. One of the earliest accounts of the *Sherman* Incident by an American historian is found in William Elliot Griffis, *Corea: The Hermit Nation* (New York:

Charles Scribner's Sons, 1889), pp. 388-395. Griffis' two points are note-worthy here. First, he quoted a Korean who said that "the murder of the *Sherman*'s crew was entirely the work of the people and farmers, and not of the magistrates or soldiery." Second, he concluded that "few of the unpreju-diced will believe that the General *Sherman*'s crew were murdered without cause." See also *Hankuksa* [Korean History] (Seoul: Kuksap'yŏnch'anuiwŏn-hoe, 1975), Vol. 16, pp. 13-94. Also, for the North and South Korean versions of the Incident, see Sung Chul Yang, *Korea and Two Regimes* (Cambridge: Schenkman, 1981), pp. 29-32.

47. *Hankuksa*, pp. 392-444 and pp. 500-550.

48. A study of the Taiping Rebellion in English is found in Franz Michael, *The Taiping Rebellion: History and Documents* (Seattle: University of Washington Press, 1966).

49. For a discussion of the history of the *Tonghak* movement in Korea. See Chi-yong O, *Tonghaksa* [History of *Tonghak*], trans. Kyu-t'ae Lee (Seoul: Munsonkak, 1973). See also Yu-han Wŏn and Pyŏng-sŏk Yun, *Hankuksa Daekye* [Outline of Korean History] (Seoul: Samchin-sa, 1973), Volume 7, pp. 69-80.

50. Ch'oe Che-u's *Tonghak* philosophy is found in Myŏng-Jong Yoo, *Op. Cit.*, pp. 370-371.

51. Yu-han Wŏn and Pyŏng-sŏk Yun, *Hankuksa Daekye*, pp. 76-77.

52. For a discussion of the 1895 Shimonoseki Treaty, see Roy Hidemichi Akagi, *Japan's Foreign Relations, 1542-1936, A Short History* (Tokyo: the Hokusei-do Press, 1936), p. 160.

53. For a detailed analysis of *Taewŏngun* in English, see Ching Young Choe, *The Rule of Taewŏngun: 1864-1873; Restoration of Yi Korea* (Cambridge: Har-vard University Press, 1972); Martina Deuchler, *Confucian Gentlemen and Barbarian Envoys: The Opening of Korea, 1875-1885* (Seattle: University of Washington Press, 1977).

54. Akagi, *Japan's Foreign Relations*, pp. 241-261.

55. Yu-han Wŏn and Pyŏng-sŏk Yun, *Hankuksa Daekye*, Vol. 8, pp. 291-307 and pp. 314-325.

56. A full text of Chang's editorial in Korean is found in Pyŏng-do Lee, *Hankuk-sa*, p. 557.

57. A full text of Min's suicide note in Korean is found in Pyŏng-do Lee, *Ibid.*

58. A full survey of anti-Japanese Korean patriots, martyrs and heroes is found in *Uisa wa Yŏlsa dŭl* [Korean Martyrs and Heroes] (Seoul: Minjokmunhwa mungo kanhaenghoe, 1982), Vol. 5.

59. Sŏn-kun Lee, *Taehan Kuksa* (Seoul: Sint'aeyangsa, 1977), Vol. 9, pp. 287-288.

60. The full members of Yi Wan-yong Cabinet is found in Pyŏng-do Lee, *Kuksa*

Daekwan, p. 564.

61. Chosen Chusatsugun Shireibu, *Chosen Boto Tabatsu Shi* [Records on the Subjugation of Korean Rebels] (Ryusa, 1913). Quoted in C. I. Kim and Han-kyo Kim, *Korea and the Politics of Imperialism*, 1876-1910 (Berkeley: University of California Press, 1968), p. 231. F. A. McKenzie, the only foreigner who visited and met the Righteous Army soldiers in the battle fields, wrote that the Korean armed resistance continued until 1915. See F. A. McKenzie, *Korea's Fight for Freedom* (London: Fleming H. Revell, 1920), pp. 132-170. A full account of the Righeous Army's anti-Japanese armed struggle is found in *Ŭibyong tului Hangchaeng* [The Righteous Army's (anti-Japanese) Resistance] (Seoul: Minjokmunhwa mungo kanhaenghoe, 1982), Vol. 1.

62. A few studies are available on the Kwangju Student Uprising of 1929. Dongju Yang, *Hangil Haksengsa* [History of Anti-Japanese Student Movement] (Kwangju, 1956); Chun-ch'e Park, "The Kwangju Student Movement" (in Korean) in Pyŏng-sŏk Yun et al, *Hankuk Kundaesalon* (Seoul: Chisiksanŏpsa, 1977), Vol. 3, pp. 34-61.

63. A recent account of the March First Movement is found in *Samil Undong* (Seoul: Minjokmunhwa mungo kanhaenghoe, 1982), Vol. 2. See also Volume 9 of the same publisher's *Taejung Undong* [Mass "anti-Japanese" Movements], and Vol. 8, *Haksaeng Undong* [Student (anti-Japanese) Movements]. See also, Chong-ki Paek, *Hankuk Kundaesa Yŏnku* [A Study of Modern Korean History] (Seoul: Pakyŏng-sa, 1981), pp. 390-430 and Pyŏng-sŏk Yun et al, *Op. Cit.*, Vol. 2. For a discussion of varying data and statistics see, Sung Chul Yang, *Korea and Two Regimes*, pp. 61-64 and p. 71 footnote 7.

64. For an account of dissension within the Korean Provisional Government, particularly between Yi Sung-Man and Yi Tong-hwi, see *Chongch'i Oekyo T'uchaeng* [Anti-Japanese Political and Diplomatic Struggles] (Seoul: Minjokmunhwa mungo kanhaenghoe, 1982), pp. 117-126.

65. *Ibid.*

66. Sung Chul Yang, *Korea and Two Regimes*, pp. 65-66 and p. 72 footnote 11.

67. The founding date of Yi Tong-hwi's *Hanin Sahoe-tang varies:* (i) June 26, 1918, in *Chongch'i Oekyo T'uchaeng*, p. 92; and (ii) February 1918 in Robert A. Scalapino and Chong-sik Lee, *Communism in Korea, Part one: The Movement* (Berkeley: University of California Press, 1972), p. 6. However, June 26 appears to be the correct founding date.

68. A detailed account of various communist societies and their activities in English is found in Scalapino and Chong-sik Lee, *Comunism in Korea*, especially, pp. 3-136. Also, Dae-sook Suh, *The Korean Communist Movement, 1918-1948* (Princeton: Princeton University Press, 1967). For a concise pedigree of Korean communist societies and parties, see Sung Chul Yang, *Korea and Two Regimes*, pp. 408-413.

69. An Ch'ang Ho's brief biography and his activities are found in *Taejung Undong*, pp. 192-198 and pp. 507-509.

70. Kim Ku's activities are found in his autobiography, *Paekpŏm Ilchi, Kim Ku Chasŏjŏn* [Memoirs of Paekpŏm, the Autobiography of Kim Ku] (Seoul: Paekpŏm Ilchi Ch'ulp'an Samuso, 1947).

71. Yŏ Un-hyŏng's biography was written by his own younger brother, Yŏ Un-hong, *Mongyang Yŏ Un-hyŏng* (Seoul: Ch'ŏnghagak, 1967).

72. See Yi Sung Man's biography in English, e.g., Robert T. Oliver, *Syngman Rhee, the Man behind the Myth* (New York: Dodd Mead, 1960); and Richard C. Allen, *Korea's Syngman Rhee: An Unauthorized Portrait* (New York: Rutland, Charles E. Tuttle, 1960).

73. For details, see *Tongripkun u Chŏnt'u* [The Struggles of (Korean) Independence Army] (Seoul: Minjokmunhwa mungo kanhaenghoe, 1982), Vol. 4.

74. *Ibid.*, pp. 67-70 and pp. 416-418.

75. *Ibid.*, pp. 100-106 and pp. 107-146.

76. *Ibid.*

77. *Ibid.*, pp. 243-279.

78. *Ibid.*, pp. 184-185.

79. See Chong-sik Lee, *Korean Worker's Party: A Short History* (Stanford: Hoover Institution Press, 1978), pp. 58-72.

80. For an extensive discussion of Kim Il Sung's anti-Japanese guerrilla activities, see Sung Chul Yang, *Korea and Two Regimes*, pp. 75-96.

81. *Ibid.*, pp. 70-71.

82. For example, Wŏn-sŏn Lee and Sŏn-kŭn Lee identified the last half of the nineteenth century as the beginning of modern nationalism in Korea. Chŏng-sik Lee contended that the period of the *Tonghak* Rebellion (1894-1896) and the Righteous Army Uprisings in the Protectorate Treaty of 1905 were the beginning of modern Korean nationalism. Woo-keun Han saw the March First Movement of 1919 as the origin of modern Korean nationalism. Samuel Kim, meanwhile, believed that the 36 years (1910-1945) of Japanese colonial rule in Korea were the period of modern Korean nationalism. For details, see Wŏn-sŏn Lee and Sŏn-kŭn Lee, "*Kaehang i chŏn u Kuknaewoesachŏng*" [Situations at Home and Abroad before the Opening of Korea] in *Hankuksa* [History of Korea] (Seoul: Kuksa P'yŏnch'anwiwŏnhoe), Vol. 16, pp. 1-14; Chong-sik Lee, *The Politics of Korean Nationalism* (Berkeley: University of California Press, 1965), pp. 51-53; Woo-keun Han, *The History of Korea*, trans. Kyung-sik Lee and ed., Grafton K. Mintz (Honolulu: East-West Center Press, 1971), p. 477; Samuel S. Kim, "The Developmental Problems of Korean Nationalism," in Sejin Kim and Chang-hyun Cho, eds., *Korea: A Divided Nation* (Silver Springs: The Research Institute on Korean Affairs, 1976), pp. 10-37.

83. For an account of Christian influences on Korean nationalism, see, for

instance, Kenneth M. Wells, "Yun Ch'i-ho and the Quest for National Integrity: The Formation of a Christian Approach to Korean Nationalism at the End of the *Chosŏn* Dynasty," *Korea Journal* (January 1982), pp. 42-59.

84. For an account of Yi's party and its evolution, see Sung Chul Yang, *Korea and Two Regimes*, Appendix IV.

85. For example, Kil-jun Yoo's *Chosŏn Munjŏn* and *Taehan Munjŏn;* Kwang-ok Ch'oe's *Taehan Munjŏn*; Si-kyŏng Chu's *Taehan Kukŏ Munbŏp;* Kyu-sik Kim's *Taehan Munbŏp* and *Chosŏn Munbŏp.* For details, see the hundred-volume, *Yŏkdae Hankuk Munbŏpdaekye* [Great Outline of Korean Language Grammar Works] (Seoul: T'ap Ch'ulp'ansa, 1985).

86. See Pyŏng-do Lee, *Hankuk Kodaesa Yŏnku*, p. 54. A study of the developments of the three Han states is found in Tae-wŏn Kwŏn, *Hankuk Sahoe P'ungsok-sa*, pp. 12-59. Hyŏn-yong Kim, for one, contends that a meaning of *Chosŏn* [the land of morning calm] is identical to that of Asadal, the mountain near Pyongyang. See his *Hankuk Kosŏlhwalon* [On Korea's Old Legends] (Seoul: *Saemun-sa*, 1984), pp. 14-19. From this standpoint, it is quite evident that while *Chosŏn* refers to locale, Han mostly stands for a clan name.

87. Ch'a and Sohn's concepts are found in Chae-bong Noh, ed., *Op. Cit.*, pp. 13-32 and pp. 113-135. For a comparative analysis of North and South Korean conceptions of nationalism, see Sang-yong Choi, "A Comparative Study on the Concepts of the Nation in South and North Korea" (in Korean) *Unification Policy Quarterly* (Winter 1978), pp. 12-26.

PART II

CONTEMPORARY POLITICAL SETTINGS

CHAPTER 4

POLITICS OF PARTITION

The history of the Far East for the last fifty years proves that no lasting peace is possible in that part of the world as long as Korea is used as a pawn by rival powers in international politics.

Cho, So-ang [1]

No division of a nation in the wake of World War II is so arbitrary, abnormal and artificial as the division of Korea. Korea was arbitrarily divided by the external powers against the wishes of her people. As Henderson pointed out, no division is "so unrelated to conditions or sentiment within the nation itself at the time the division was effected" as the division of Korea. There is no division for which "the U.S. government bears so heavy a share of the responsibility as it bears for the division of Korea."[2] Koreans had no input in this fateful and tragic decision.

The Korean division was not merely a physical partition of the Peninsula, but it also led to separation of families. This division spurred the North-South political, ideological, economic, military, diplomatic and other competitions. A high degree of homogeneity in Korean culture, history, language and other socio-economic heritages which bind them together as a nation is undermined by this unnatural partition. Still, the present military demarcation line (DMZ), a slightly modified version of the original 38th parallel drawn in the wake of the Korean War, continues. A delicate political and strategic rivalry among the United States,

Russia, China and Japan surrounding the Korean Peninsula and East Asia and the balancing acts staged by the North and South Korean political leaders amidst shifting external power balance among these four powers persist. The external and internal political and strategic *dynamics* in the *static* Korean partition represent the bare essence of the present Korean politics.

At the end of the 19th century, a weak and secluded Korean kingdom became a prey to power rivalry among neighboring giants and Western powers. The Japanese Prince Yamagata proposed the Korean division at the 38th parallel to the Russians in 1896. In 1899 and again in 1903, Russia suggested the division of Korea at the 39th parallel to Japan.[3] In the meantime, Japan forced Korea to open its doors in 1876. In 1905, via the Sino-Japanese War of 1894-1895 and the Russo-Japanese War of 1904-1905, Japan claimed Korea as her protectorate, and, five years later, as her outright colony. Thus, for 35 years Korea had been under the Japanese colonial rule until the Allied Powers defeated Japan in World War II.

In August 1945 the exit of Japan from Korea as the colonial power was synchronized by the entry of the United States and the former Soviet Union as the occupation forces. It reportedly took the United States only five days to artificially slice Korea into two halves at the 38th parallel.[4] The North was placed under the occupation forces of the former Soviet Union[5] and the South, under the U.S. occupation authorities.

In accordance with the Korean provisions in the Cairo Declaration of December 1, 1943, the Potsdam Conference of July-August, 1945, and, more specifically, within the guidelines of the Moscow Three Ministerial Conference of December 27, 1945, which called for a four-power trusteeship in Korea, the efforts to create a united Korea began. Amidst futile bickering and countercharges between the U.S. and Russian representatives, three years elapsed with no visible results on the Korean question.[6]

In hindsight, three political and ideological incongruities worked against the realization of a united Korea from the outset.

First, Korean *liberation* in 1945 did not result directly from the anti-Japanese liberation struggle of the Koreans. It was a by-product of the

Allied Powers' victory over the Axis Powers in World War II. Hence, Korean *liberation* meant that the Koreans were "liberated" from the Japanese but not from the "liberators." The North was immediately placed under the Soviet occupation authorities as the South were under the supervision of the American military government.

Even before the realization of this dubious liberation, some key decisions such as the Korean provisions in the Cairo Declaration, the 38th Parallel Decision, and a Four-Power Trusteeship Decision of the Moscow Three Ministerial Conference, which largely determined and shaped the fate of post-War Korea, were made without the participation of and/or input from the Koreans. Not only were the Koreans left out of such crucial decision-making process, but the United States government refused to recognize the legitimacy of the Korean Provisional Government (KPG) in exile which had survived for over a quarter of a century. Since its formation in 1919 in the wake of the March First Anti-Japanese mass upheaval, the KPG sustained its activities, if nominally, even during the trying years of Japan's military march into China proper, and in fact, outlived the Japanese colonial administration which fell in 1945. The KPG moved its headquarters from Shanghai to Nanking in 1932 and to Chungking in 1935. In 1940, it moved to Chungking via Changsha as the Nationalist Chinese Government retreated west to escape Japan's advancing army.[7]

Soon after Japan unconditionally surrendered to the Allied Powers in August 1945, the KPG tried to return to Korea. Ironically, the United States occupation forces and military government in the South refused to recognize the legitimacy of the twenty-six year old KPG. The KPG leaders, after a long, bitter and tenuous struggle against Japanese colonialism in Korea, were allowed by the U.S. occupation authorities to return to their fatherland only after they disclaimed their official association with the organization.[8] Most of these leaders, thus, returned home as private citizens. The U.S. authorities' refusal in the South to recognize KPG as the *official* body and to admit its leaders into their homeland as its *officials* closely paralleled the Soviet authorities' denial of entry to the so-called Yanan Koreans (Korean Volunteer Corps) into the North with their arms and weapons.[9] It is not difficult to surmise that the

U.S. decision might have been based on the long term political-strategic considerations stemming from the KPG ties with the Chiang Kai-shek Nationalist Government, as the Soviet decision might have been influenced by the Yanan faction's association with the Mao Zedong Communist forces. The United States occupation authorities' denial of the existence of the Korean People's Republic established by Yŏ Wun-yŏng (1895-1947) on September 1945 may be seen in the same light.[10] In essence, Korean *liberation* denoted that one foreign power exited, and two entered in its place.

Second, the Koreans had to adjust to the ideological and political incongruity of the two occupation forces. The rivalry between the two "liberators"—the United States and the former Soviet Union—was in the offing long before the end of World War II. The participation of the former Soviet Union in the Allied Powers itself was a result of mutually calculated temporary marriage amidst the threat of the Axis Powers. Therefore, Korea and her people were sucked, against their will, into the whirlpool of the two superpower rivalry. As Syngman Rhee, the first President of South Korea observed, "the Korean people were divided against their will to which no Korean was a party."[11]

From the beginning, the Soviet occupation forces attempted to implant a pliant pro-Soviet communist regime in the North as the American military administration wanted to establish a palatable pro-American anti-communist government in the South. The abject failure of the Joint U.S.-USSR Commission created to implement the Moscow Agreement and the subsequent pro-and anti-trusteeship schism among Korean political leaders were a foregone conclusion.[12] The verbal arguments of the United States and the former Soviet Union over Korean trusteeship were predictable superficial behaviors indicative of their deep-seated ideological and political differences. In the end, the Soviet occupation forces (1945-1948) achieved the realization of a communist regime in the North as the American military administration (1945-1948) established an anti-communist government in the South.

Thirdly, Korean political leaders themselves were sharply divided ideologically. The communist-nationalist bifurcation among the Korean leaders had existed from the very beginning of their anti-Japanese liberation struggles. Such ideological conflict was downplayed and discouraged under the more pressing task of pannationalist anti-Japanese liberation struggle during the Japanese rule. Antagonism surfaced, however, as soon as Japan withdrew from Korea, and the former Soviet Union and the United States entered the Korean political arenas. This renewed old ideological schism which gained a new momentum with the entrance of the former Soviet Union in the North and the United States in the South, the two archrivals in quest of ideological and political emporium.

The ideological conflict among the Korean political leaders intensified when attempts were made to identify and punish those who had collaborated with the Japanese. The difficulty of formulating a "political sieve" to sort out the pro-Japanese collaborators was complicated by the question of who would pick out the pro-Japanese "traitors" and collaborators. Generally, the political sieve of the Korean leftists (communists) was much finer and more stringent than that of the rightists (nationalists). In the end, the conflict over the definition and identification of the pro-Japanese collaborators resulted in political realignment along the communist and anti-communist lines. The majority of the pro-Japanese collaborators flocked to the rightist or nationalist camp under the anti-communist slogan as though their new association with anti-communism dissociated them from their past collaboration with the Japanese. The nationalists, in fact, made peace with the collaborators in return for the latters' support in the renewed struggle against the communists. The old schism between the communists and nationalists was, thus, soon replaced by a new rivalry—the communists against the anti-communists. Amid the new hostilities between those supporting and those opposing communism, the previous question of pro- and anti-Japanese activity became secondary, if not immaterial.

The end-result of the aforesaid triple incongruities was the emergence of two separate regimes in 1948—the pro-Russian Democratic People's Republic of Korea and the pro-American Republic of Korea. Less than two years later, the Korean War (1950-53), a fratricidal and proxy war, broke out.[13] Sixteen nations defended South Korea under the flag of the United Nations, while the Chinese People's Volunteers and other communist countries sided with North Korea. When the War ended with the

Armistice Agreement, the Korean casualties alone were estimated at over three million—1.3 million South Koreans and 1.5 to 2 million North Koreans. In addition, there were 2.5 million refugees and another 500,000 relief recipients. Since 1945 some five million people have fled to the South from the communist North, not to mention ten to eleven million separated and dispersed families.[14]

Nearly fifty years have elapsed since the Korean partition. Over four decades have passed since the Korean War, but the Korean division continues. Millions of words, proposals, plans, formulae and documents for the realization of Korean reunification have been wasted. Countless Koreans, civilians and soldiers were sacrificed during the Korean War alone. Scores of meetings and conferences have been held intermittently for the North-South dialogue. Still, no immediate prospect for reunification is in sight.

Few areas in the world today are in fact so sharply polarized ideologically, heavily armed militarily and intractably ruptured politically as is divided Korea. Korea is also an area where the interests of four major powers—the United States, Japan, China and Russia—intersect. The ideological, military and political situations besetting North and South Korea today are a microcosm of the current four power relations. North and South Korea's ideological rivalry, arms race, economic competitions and political predicaments reflect in a small scale the conflict, which has existed and is still, to a lesser degree, existing between the United States and the former Soviet Union. Unlike the relations between the U.S. and Russia, both regimes on the Korean peninsula are culturally, historically and linguistically homogeneous and share territorial contiguity. Unlike the United States and the former Soviet Union which had sought mutually incompatible world hegemony, the North and South Korea claim mutually exclusive political legitimacy in the Peninsula. Again, unlike the United States and the former Soviet Union whose arms race has been nuclear-strategic, the military competition between North and South Korea has been essentially non-nuclear, although North Korea's nuclear project has now become the major stumbling block for new changes in this post-nuclear, post-Communist and post-Cold War era. These differences notwithstanding, the similarity in the behavior of the two regimes in Korea and the two superpowers have been striking.

If the Korean division was forced upon the Korean people, simply as a result of the ideological rivalry between the two superpowers and those Koreans who aligned themselves with either of the two ideological camps during the initial occupation period, understanding of political ideology is pivotal in unraveling the current political dynamics on the Korean Peninsula. It was indeed the two competing ideologies which created the two diametrically different political systems in Korea. The continuing political dramas between the North and South and among the four major powers—the United States, Japan, China and Russia—set the new parameters for the contemporary Korean politics. In Chapter Five, therefore, an ideology probe is attempted as an introduction to the politics of division in Korea.

MAP 4-1. Divided Korea in Its Asian Setting

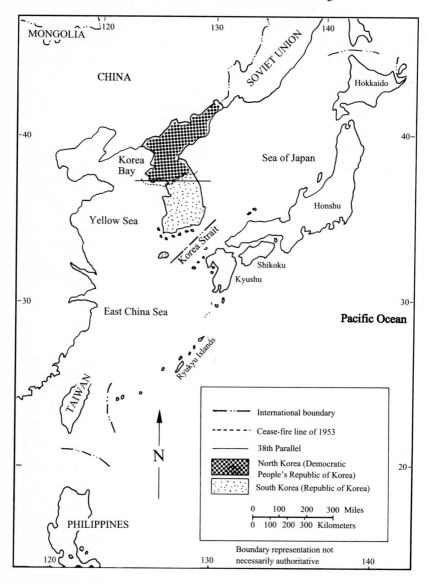

MAP 4-2. *The Administrative Divisions of North Korea*

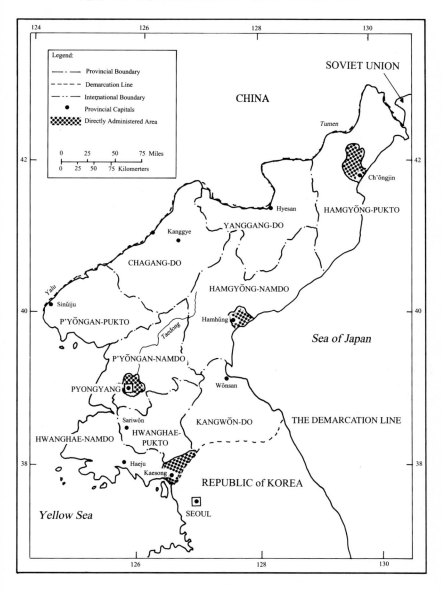

MAP 4-3. Major Cities and Transportation Facilities of North Korea

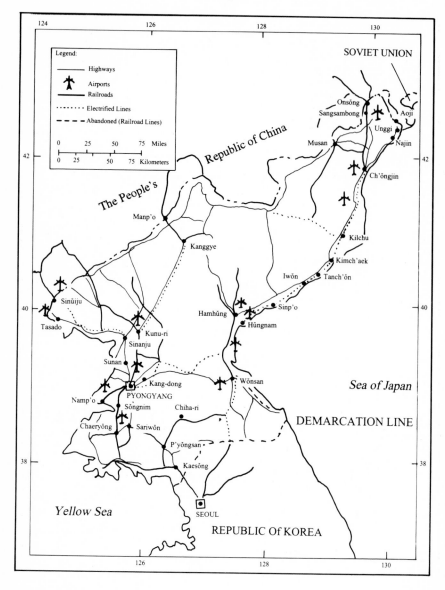

MAP 4-4. Major Resources in North Korea

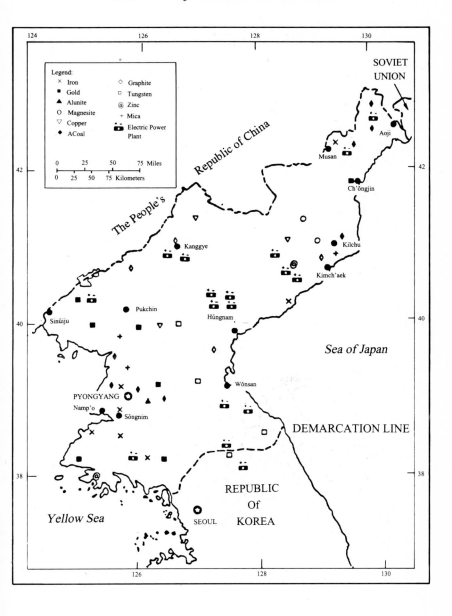

Legend:
× Iron
■ Gold
▲ Alunite
O Magnesite
▽ Copper
◆ ACoal

◇ Graphite
□ Tungsten
@ Zinc
+ Mica
⊡ Electric Power Plant

0   25   50   75 Miles
0   25   50   75 Kilometers

SOVIET UNION

Republic of China

The People's

Aoji

Musan

Ch'ŏngjin

Kanggye

Kilchu

Kimch'aek

Pukchin

Hŭngnam

Sinŭiju

Sea of Japan

Wŏnsan

PYONGYANG

Namp'o

Sŏngnim

DEMARCATION LINE

Yellow Sea

SEOUL

REPUBLIC Of KOREA

MAP 4-5. The Administrative Divisions of South Korea

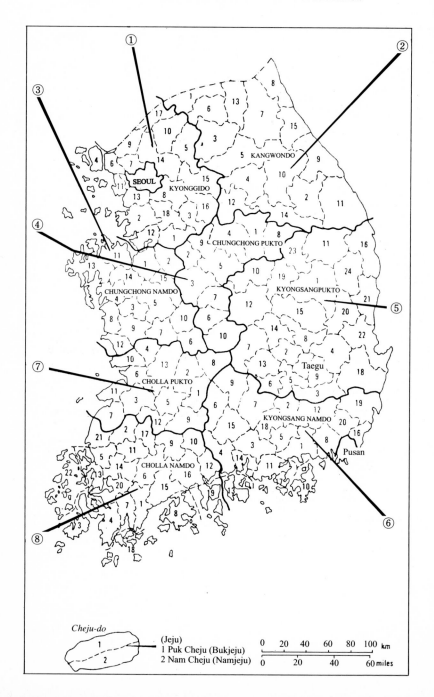

MAP 4-5. Continued

① KYONGGI DO (GYEONGGI DO)
1 Ansong (Anseong)
2 Hwasong (Hwaseong)
3 Ichon (Richeon)
4 Kanghwa (Ganghwa)
5 Kapyong (Gapheong)
6 Kimpo (Gimpo)
7 Koyang (Goyang)
8 Kwangju (Gwangju)
9 Paju
10 Pochon (Pocheon)
11 Puchon (Bucheon)
12 Pyongtaek (Pyeongtaek)
13 Sihung (Siheung)
14 Yangju
15 Yangpyong (Yangpyeong)
16 Yoju (Yeoju)
17 Yonchon (Yeoncheon)
18 Yongin
19 Ongjin

④ CHUNGCHONG PUKTO (CHUNGGHEONGBUG DO)
1 Chechon (Jecheon)
2 Chinchon (Jincheon)
3 Chongwon (Cheorgweon)
4 Chungwon (Jungweon)
5 Koesan (Goesan)
6 Okchon (Okcheon)
7 Poun (Boeun)
8 Tanyang (Danyang)
9 Umsong (Eumseong)
10 Yongdong (Yeongdong)

② KANGWON DO (GANGWEON DO)
1 Chorwon (Cheolweon)
2 Chongson (Jeongseon)
3 Chunsong (Chunseong)
4 Hoengsong (Hoengseong)
5 Hongchon (Hongcheon)
6 Hwachon (Hwacheon)
7 Imje (inje)
8 Kosong (Goseong)
9 Myongju (Myeongju)
10 Pyongchang (Pyeongchang)
11 Samchok (Samcheok)
12 Wonsong (Weonseong)
13 Yanggu
14 Yongwol (Yeongweol)
15 Yangyang

③ CHUNGCHONG NAMDO (CHUNGCHEONGNAM DO)
1 Asan
2 Chonwon (Cheonweon)
3 Chongyang (Cheongyang)
4 Hongsong (Hongseong)
5 Kongju (Gongju)
6 Kumsan (Geumsan)
7 Nonsan (Ronsan)
8 Poryong (Boryeong)
9 Puyo (Buyeo)
10 Taedok (Deadoek)
11 Tangjin (Dangjin)
12 Sochon (Seocheon)
13 Sosan (Seosan)
14 Yesan
15 Yongi (Yeongi)

⑤ KYONGSANG PUKTO
1 Andong
2 Chilgok
3 Chongdo (Cheongdo)
4 Chongsong (Cheongseong)
5 Dalsong (Talseong)
6 Koryong (Goryeong)
7 Kumryung (Geumneung)
8 Kunwi (Gunwi)
9 Kyongsan (Gyeongsan)
10 Mungyong (Mungyeong)
11 Ponghwa (Bonghwa)
12 Sangju
13 Songju (Seongju)
14 Sonsan
15 Uisong (Euiseong)
16 Ulchin (Uljin)
17 Ullung (Ulrung)
18 Wolsong (Weolseong)
19 Yechon (Yecheon)
20 Yongchon (Yeongcheon)
21 Yongdok (Yeongdeok)
22 Yongil (Yeongil)
23 Yongju (Yeongju)
24 Yongyang (Yeongyang)

⑥ KYONGSANG NAMDO (GYEONGSANGNAM DO)
1 Changwon (Changweon)
2 Changyong (Changryeong)
3 Chinyang (Jinyang)
4 Hadong
5 Haman
6 Hamyang
7 Hapchon (Habcheon)
8 Kimhae (Gimhae)
9 Kochang (Geochang)
10 Koje (Geoje)
11 Kosong (Goseong)
12 Milyang (Miryang)
13 Namhae
14 Sachon (Sacheon)
15 Sanchong (Sancheong)
16 Tongnae (Dongrae)
17 Tongyong (Tongyeong)
18 Uiryong (Euinyeong)
19 YUlchu (Ulju)
20 Yangsan

Ullung do

⑧ CHOLLA PUKTO (JEONRABUG DO)
1 Changsu (Jangsu)
2 Chinan (Jinan)
3 Chongup (Jongeub)
4 Iksan
5 Imsil
6 Kimje (Gimje)
7 Kochang (Gochang)
8 Muju
9 Namwon
10 Okku
11 Puan (Buan)
12 Sunchang
13 Wanju

⑦ CHOLLA NAMDO (JEONRANAM DO)
1 Changhung (Jangheung)
2 Changsong (Jangseong)
3 Chindo (Jindo)
4 Haenam
5 Hampyong (Hampyeong)
6 Hwasun
7 Kangjin (Gangjin)
8 Kohung (Goeheung)
9 Koksong (Gokweong)
10 Kurye (Gurye)
11 Kwangsan (Gwansan)
12 Kwangyang (Gwangyang)
13 Muan
14 Naju (Raju)
15 Posong (Boseong)
16 Sungju (Seungju)
17 Tamyang (Damyang)
18 Wando
19 Yochon (Ryecheon)
20 Yongam (Yeongam)
21 Yonggwang
22 Sinan

Notes

1. Quoted in *Korean Unification: Source Materials with an Introduction* (Seoul: Research Center for Peace and Unification, 1973), pp. 83-84.
2. Gregory Henderson, *et al, Divided Nations in a Divided World* (New York: David Mckay, 1974), p. 43.
3. For a recent analysis of Russo-Korean relations, see Andrew C. Nahm, "Korea and Tsarist Russia: Russian Interests, Policy, and Involvement in Korea, 1884-1904," *Korea Journal* (June 1982), pp. 4-19. Nam-hŏn Song, *Hankuk Hyŏndae Chŏngch'isa* [History of Modern Korean Politics] (Seoul: Songmunkak, 1980), Vol. 1, pp. 99-100. Also, William L. Langer, *The Diplomacy of Imperialism* (New York: Knopf, 1934), Vol. 1, p. 406; Andrew Malozemoff, "The Origins of the Russo-Japanese War, 1894-1904" (M.A. thesis, University of California, Berkeley, 1934), p. 112; Soon-sung Cho, *Korea in World Politics: An Evaluation of American Responsibility* (Berkeley: University of California Press, 1967), pp. 13-203.
4. For details, see Sung Chul Yang, *Korea and Two Regimes* (Cambridge: Schenkman, 1981), p. 301 and especially footnote No. 1.
5. Most recently, a Korean scholar in Japan contended that the objectives of the landing of the Soviet forces in Woongki and Najin on August 12 were to prevent the main Japanese forces in Manchuria from fleeing to Japan via Korea and to contain the Japanese forces in Korea from supporting the Japanese forces fighting in Manchuria. For details, see Choong-kun Oh, "Drawing of the 38th Parallel and the Soviet Involvement in the Korean Peninsula" (in Korean), *Singdong-A*, October 1985, pp. 511-527.
6. For details, see Sung Chul Yang, *Korea and Two Regimes*, pp. 123-126. Nam-hŏn Song, *Op. Cit.*, pp. 202-399. A comprehensive and documentary analysis of the background and developments leading to Korean division is found in Sung-chul Yang, *New Approaches to the Study of the Korean Unification* (in Korean) (Seoul: Kyŏngnam University Press, 1989), especially, pp. 19-132.
7. For a detailed study of the KPG's organizations, activities and related documents, see *Chŏngch'i Woekyo Hwaldong* [(Korean Anti-Japanese) Political and Diplomatic Activities], ed. Hŏn-su Ch'u (Seoul: Minjokmunhwa munko kanhaenghoe, 1982), Vol. 3.
8. *Ibid.*, pp. 231-233.
9. *Ibid.* Also, Sung Chul Yang, *Korea and Two Regimes*, p. 174.
10. For details, see Nam-hŏn Song, *Op. Cit.*, pp. 76-84.
11. See, *Foreign Relations of the United States, 1950: Korea* (Washington, D.C.:

United States Government Printing Office, 1976), Vol. 7, p. 429.
12. For a detailed survey of the Joint U.S.-USSR Commission's fruitless efforts to unify Korea, see Nam-hŏn Song, *Op. Cit.*, pp. 202-399.
13. An analysis of the origins of the Korean War is found in Sung Chul Yang, *Korea and Two Regimes*, pp. 133-160.
14. *Ibid.*, pp. 301-303.

CHAPTER 5

IDEOLOGY AND THE KOREAN EXPERIMENTS

It (manufacture) converts the labourer into a crippled monstrosity, by forcing his... dexterity at the expense of a world of productive capabilities and instincts; just as in the States of La Plata they butcher a whole beast for the sake of hide or his tallow. Not only is the detail work distributed to the different individuals, but the individual himself is made the automatic motor of a fractional operation, and the absurd fable of Menenius Agrippa, which makes man a mere fragment of his body, becomes realized.

Karl Marx[1]

These people, who had experienced on their own hides twenty-four years of Communist happiness, knew by 1941 what as yet no one else in the world knew: that nowhere on the planet, nowhere in history, was there a regime more vicious, more bloodthirsty, and at the same time more cunning and ingenious than the Bolshevik, the self-styled Soviet regime. That no other regime on earth could compare with it either in the number of those it had done [put] to death, in hardiness, in the range of its ambitions, in its thoroughgoing and unmitigated totalitarianism—no, not even the regime of its pupil Hitler, which at that time blinded Western eyes to all else.

Aleksandr I. Solzhenitsyn[2]

Introduction

With the possible exception of erstwhile two Germanys and two Vietnams, no country today has displayed the saliency of ideology more than Korea. There are many incidences where differing religions, languages, culture, ethnic and racial origins divide the people within a nation or cause conflicts among nations. But it was the ideology line, more than anything else, along which the Korean people were forced to be separated by the Allied Power's post-War map-makers. It is still the ideology (or more accurately, politics under the ideological garb) that sustains the division. The Korean Peninsula today is indeed a fertile political arena where the meaning and the functions of ideology can be explored in a sharply comparative and realistic manner.

North Korea still proclaims Marxism-Leninism as its official ideology and the *Juche* [self-reliance] idea as its creative application. South Korea rejects such claims. Communism is the ideological foundation of the North Korean political system. Anti-communism is the symbolic pillar of the South Korean political system. At least, on rhetorical and propagandistic planes, communism is a "science" in North Korea. By contrast, it is a subversive idea in South Korea. Nothing separates the North from the South more sharply than the conflicting claims and counter-claims of ideology. A general understanding of ideology may be, thus, one of the first steps toward the understanding of the intricacies and complexities of the current Korean political dynamics. In this chapter, the meaning(s) of ideology and its manipulators (elites and counter-elites) and the manipulated (masses) will be examined. Next, the role of ideology in the North and South Korean political context will be probed in some detail.

Ideology: Its Meaning and Political Implications

No consensus exists as to the meaning of ideology. As Hannah Arendt observed, the word "ideology" implies that an idea can become the subject matter of a science; the suffix in ideology, as in zoology, indicates the logos, the scientific statements.[3] The definitions of ideology abound, and yet practitioners and scholars alike still busy themselves in defining and redefining the term. In a broadest sense, ideology is the symbolic tool of political power. The ruling elites—the holders of power—use ideology to sustain and strengthen their power, whereas, the seekers of power, those elites who are out of or outside power, employ it to replace or overthrow (in an extreme sense) the existing elite.

If ideology represents a symbolic instrument for the establishment power-holders and revolutionary power-seekers, the consensus on its meaning(s)—what it is and what it does—is unattainable as long as both sides are at loggerheads, and until and unless their political strifes and struggles cease. For, they fight over the meaning(s) of ideology as much as for power itself. It can be said, nevertheless, that words precede ideas, and ideas, ideology. As words by themselves do not make ideas, ideas do not become an ideology. As Arendt wrote, an ideology is "the logic of an idea; its subject matter is history, to which the idea is applied; it treats the course of events as if it followed the same "law" as the logical exposition of its "idea." An ideology pretends to know the mysteries of the whole historical process—the secrets of the past, the intricacies of the present, and the uncertainties of the future.[4] To be an ideology, then a set of ideas must be strung together as a coherent explanations, whether they are called theories, thoughts, formula or "laws." A set of explanations does not make a full-fledged ideology. Such explanations must be tied to a set of action plans and programs which directs and shapes an overall political and socio-economic life.

Ideology as a symbolic instrument of politics, is a set of diagnosis of the past, analysis of the present and prognosis of the desirable future polity, economy and society. The ideology of establishment power-holders differs diametrically from counter-ideology of revolutionary power-seekers. The former justifies the current political rules and structures; it defines the values and goals of the state; it harmonizes conflicting interests and claims; and legitimates the power-holders' actions. The latter, on the other hand, defies and attempts to nullify the existing political rules and structures; it provides new alternatives to the existing political values and goals of the states; and it challenges the legitimacy of current political practices to replace ideology of establishment power holders with its own.

A full-fledged ideology appeals to the people with a blue print which details how a "better" polity, economy and society can be realized: power-holders' reform packages and power-seekers' revolutionary formula are the cases in point. Needless to say, between these two extreme ideological spectrums of establishment power-holders and revolutionary power-seekers, exists a wide variety of ideological claims and counter-claims.

Seliger, for instance, distinguishes the inclusive and the restrictive use of ideology. In the former, ideology covers "sets of ideas by which men posit, explain and justify ends and means of organized social action, irrespective of whether such action aims to preserve, amend, uproot or rebuild a given order." In the latter, it is reserved for extremist belief systems and parties.[5] The inclusive conception of ideology is based on the premise that politics is inseparable from ideology. If politics implies the pursuit of policy, no politics can exist without ideology because no policies are conceived and executed without some relation to ideas that embody moral judgments in favor of the justification, emendation or condemnation of a given order.[6] By contrast, the restrictive conception posits that ideology is not a universal belief system, inseparable from politics, but only the extremist belief systems such as Marxism-Leninism and Fascism.

The restrictive conception of ideology can be divided into various types—the Marxian and the non-Marxian, the post-Marxian and the end-of-ideologists. Marx and Engels defined ideology as the reflection of class interest, that is, "false consciousness" or "superstructural" class notions, while Lenin characterized it as a belief system involving mass action and organization.[7] Marx's conception of ideology of false consciousness notwithstanding, the fact that Marxism-Leninism has been the official ideology" of the socialist countries is a historical, political, and theoretical irony par excellence.

Karl Manheim, meanwhile, distinguished ideology from utopia. By utopia he meant those orientations "which... tend to shatter, either partially or wholly, the order of things prevailing at the time," while ideologies are "...effective in the maintenance of the existing order of things."[8] By paraphrasing Manheim's distinction, Lasswell and Kaplan defined utopia as "the political myth designed to supplant, and ideology as the political myth to preserve, the social structure."[9]

From a somewhat different perspective, Hannah Arendt distinguished the full-fledged ideologies of race-thinking (e.g., Nazism) from other ideologies which are based not on a single opinion.[10] Christoph's *Weltanschauung* and attitude structure, King's ideology by purpose and ideology by function, Helenius' manifest ideology and latent ideology, Schurman's pure ideology and practical ideology and Seliger's fundamental ideology and practical ideology are other representative cases of the inclusive view.[11]

The end-of-ideology thesis, once prevalent in the mid-1950s, typifies the restrictive view of ideology. But the advocates of the end-of-ideology have amended their original conception of ideology to extremist political belief systems. In so doing, as Seliger contends, they have de facto blurred their erstwhile restrictive conception of ideology.[12] Shils, for instance, separates "ideological politics," which is concerned with radical change and the totalist orientation, from "civil politics," which tries to maintain and improve society by judging things on their own merits and by respecting tradition. Further, he advocates the "subsidence," not "the end" of the ideological age.[13]

Click's separation of ideological politics from non-ideological politics, Lipset's distinction between extremist and non-extremist systems of integrated concepts and Sartori's differentiation between ideology and pragmatism are essentially analogous to Shils' dichotomy.[14] Lipset contends that what he, Bell and others had meant by the "end" or the "decline" of ideology was not the end of systems of integrated political concepts, of utopian thinking or of class conflict, but the passionate adherence to revolutionary working-class doctrines and the consequent coherent counterrevolutionary doctrines.[15] Similarly, Bell claims that the end of ideology signifies only "the abatement of the dynamism of a creed, and the reduction of ideology as a weapon against external and internal enemies."[16] From this standpoint, Raymond Aaron's distinction of "the end of ideology"—the end of the predominance of ideological systems in politics—from "the end of the age of ideologies"—the disappearance of ideological beliefs and their influence in politics—is pertinent.[17]

The critics of the end or decline of ideology thesis are by no means in short supply. Aiken, for instance, asserts that to declare the end or decline of ideology is tantamount to proclaiming the end of politics itself, and thus the thesis is nothing but an "anti-ideological ideology."[18] Seliger's view is similar. As noted above, ideology is inseparable from politics, and hence, the end of ideology signifies the end of politics itself.[19] LaPalombra, too, criticizes the proponents of the decline of ideology thesis on the ground that their thesis itself is ideological. Further, he avers that the decline theorists treat ideology somewhat pejoratively.[20]

Walter Carlsnaes argued against inclusive conception of ideology because any broad philosophical or normative definition finds no methodological justification in the pages of classics and because such definition is merely notational, devoid of substantive value.[21] Furthermore, he denounced the critics of the decline hypotheses by concurring with Rejai and others that "the most alarming attribute of the antidecline writers is their apparent willingness to disregard the empirical significance of the hypothesis in question and to rely, instead, on semantic justification." Istvan Meszaros' point is also apropos here. He states that the power of ideology cannot be overstated. It affects no less those who wish to deny its existence than those who openly acknowledge the interests and values intrinsic to the various ideologies. He further wrote:

> Ideology is not an illusion or a religious superstition of misdirected individuals, but a specific form of—materially anchored and sustained—social consciousness.... Its stubborn persistence is due to the fact that it happens to be objectively constituted (and constantly reconstituted) as the *inescapable practical consciousness of class societies.*[22]

In the final analysis, then, as is the case with the debate between the decline and anti-decline writers of ideology, the controversy between the restrictive and the inclusive conception of ideology may continue. Depending upon one's *Weltanschauung* and philosophical and scientific orientations, the meaning and types of ideology are bound to vary.

In this chapter, ideology is defined functionally as a set of political symbols such as beliefs, emotions or values, which are employed by political elites primarily to justify, rationalize and legitimize their exercise of political power, in a given polity. The polity consists of elites, who are the manipulators of such symbols, and masses who are the manipulated.[23]

Ideology may consist of three dimensions: cognitive, affective (emotive) and evaluative.[24] The cognitive aspect of ideological elements can be either *closed,* if the elites are not permitted to argue or question certain ideological elements, or *open,* if they are permitted to do so. The affective aspect of the ideological elements can be either felt strongly or weakly, depending on the degree of emotional intensity of the elites toward certain ideological elements. The evaluative status of ideological elements can be viewed either positively or negatively, depending on whether the elites promote or renounce or adopt or reject certain ideological elements.

Finally, the role of ideology may be functional, dysfunctional or nonfunctional. A certain ideology or an ideological element is functional, if it: provides legitimacy for the regime in power, thereby, helping the regime maintain political stability and order (legitimacy function); promotes national unity and/or social solidarity (integration function): and provides a guide to, and sets the goals for, individual and collective action, thereby, helping the members of a given regime attain individual and collective identity and security (identity function). Ideology is dysfunctional if it weakens or jeopardizes legitimacy of the regime in power, or it creates an identity crisis, thereby, increasing individual and/or collective insecurity. It is nonfunctional, if it fails to perform the aforesaid functions, or if it is irrelevant to the polity in question.[25]

The Elites: The Users of Ideology

As the statecrafts of Plato, Acquinas and Machiavelli, for instance, illustrate, ideology, as a set of belief system and political action plan, did not exist prior to the Age of Enlightenment. The term, ideology, may have French origin. It might have originated with the French Enlightenment writers of the 18th century.[26] Marx and Engels are recognized as the first systematic formulators, if not the originators, of ideology as a set of past, present and future explanatory tools of polity, economy and society. Interestingly, Marx and Engels labeled all the early socialist theories of Francois Fourier, Claude Saint-Simon, Louis Blanqui, Robert Owen and Joseph Proudhon "utopian" while they called their own "scientific."[27]

The history, thus far, disputes their "scientific" claims. To begin with, if their socialism were indeed "scientific," why have there been so many hybrid socialist ideologies such as Leninism, Stalinism, Titoism, Maoism and even Kim Il Sungism? How about the existence of the old "renegade" revisionisms of Karl Kautsky and Edward Bernstein?

Is Lenin's theory of political primacy a logical extension of, or a direct and lethal challenge to, Marx's dialectical materialism? More fundamentally, if the state organs in the past and currently remaining socialist countries have expanded vastly in size and power instead of "withering away," and if the "new class" within party, government, army and other professional organizations have merely replaced the old ruling class instead of realizing a "classless" society, the ideology of Marx and Engels is no less "utopian" (unrealistic and unrealizable) than the ideology of those "utopian" socialists they denigrated."[28]

Specifically, have "class antagonisms and all forms of exploitation and oppression of man by man been eliminated forever" in the Democratic People's Republic of Korea, as the Article 6 of North Korea's 1972 Socialist Constitution claims? How realistic is the Chinese Communist Party's assertion that the realization of communism is its "ultimate aim?" Had the former Soviet Union, the precursor and the oldest socialist country, "put an end once and for all to exploitation of man by man, antagonisms between classes, a strife between nationalities" as its 1977 Constitution asserted? Needless to say, all these proclamations are merely rhetorics in North Korea, the former Soviet Union, China and in all present and past socialist countries.

Perhaps, the better answer to the paradoxes of the communist ideological claims and political realities may be found in the elite analyses of Mosca, Bryce, Pareto, Michels and others. Mosca, for one, describes his principle of the ruling class as follows:

In all societies—from societies that are very meagerly developed and have barely attained the dawnings of civilization, down to the most advanced powerful societies—two classes of people appear—a class that rules and a class that is ruled. The first class, always the less numerous, performs all political functions, monopolizes power and enjoys the advantages that power brings, whereas the second, the more numerous class, is directed and controlled by the first, in a manner that is now more or less legal, now more or less arbitrary and violent and supplies the first, in appearance at least, with material means of subsistence and with the instrumentalities that are essential to the vitality of the political organism.[29]

James Bryce's observation is strikingly analogous:

In all assemblies and groups and organized bodies of men, from a nation down to a committee of a club, direction and decisions rest in the hands of a small percentage, less and less in proportion to the larger size of the body, till in a great population it becomes an infinitesimally small proportion of the whole number. This is and always has been true of all forms of government, though in different degree.[30]

Vilfredo Pareto, the advocate of the theory of class-circulation or "circulation of elites," made an essentially similar point:

Ignoring exceptions, which are few in number and of short duration, one finds everywhere a governing class of relatively few individuals that keep itself in power partly by force and partly by the consent of the subject class, which is much more populous. The differences lie principally, as regards substance, in the relative proportions of force and consent; and as regards forms, in the manners in which the force is used and the consent is obtained.[31]

Agreeing basically with Pareto's theory of elite circulation, Robert Michels refined it further by pinpointing that "the circulation of the elites happens less in the form of absolute exchange, than in that of a perennial amalgamation of new elements with the old ones." He emphasized the fusion of the old and new elites rather than the replacement of the old by the new elites.[32]

Similarly, Mosca hinted that the ruling classes can be "continually replenished through the admission of new elements who have in-born talents for leadership and a will to lead."[33] Michels was more categorical on this point. He stated that "the existence of immanent oligarchical tendencies in every kind of human organizations is one of 'the historic necessities.'" He contended that the oligarchic and bureaucratic tendency of party organization is a "matter of technical and practical necessity."[34] He wrote further:

> Society cannot exist without a "dominant" or "political" class, and that the ruling class, whilst its elements are subject to a frequent partial renewal, nevertheless constitutes the only factor of sufficiently durable efficacy in the history of human development. The government, or, the state, cannot be anything other than the organization of a minority. It is the aim of this minority to impose upon the rest of society a "legal order," which is the outcome of the exigencies of dominion and of the exploitation of the masses of helots effected by the ruling minority, and can never be truly representative of the majority. The majority is thus permanently incapable of self-government.[35]

At one point Michels argued that the "iron law of oligarchy" and the Marxian materialist conception of history complement each other. He found no contradiction between the doctrine that history is the record of a continued series of class struggles and the doctrine that class struggles invariably culminate in the creation of new oligarchies which undergo fusion with the old. He further pinpointed that the existence of a political class does not conflict with the essential content of Marxism. He considered Marxism a philosophy of history; for in each particular instance, the dominance of a political class occurs as the concomitant social forces vie for supremacy.[36] What Michels failed to note in this regard is Marx and Engels's insistence that with the abolition of class distinctions all social and political inequality arising from them would disappear. Marx wrote:

> Socialism is the declaration of the permanence of the revolution, the class dictatorship of the proletariat as the necessary transit point to the abolition of class distinctions generally, to the abolition of all the relation of production on which they rest, to the abolition of all the social relations that correspond to these relations of production, to the revolutionizing of all the ideas that result from these social relations.[37]

As it is clear from the above, while Mosca, Bryce, Pareto and Michels saw the existence of the dominant class and of the ruled as the "perennial" and "durable" political phenomenon, Marx envisioned "the class dictatorship of the proletariat" only as the necessary transit point before the realization of a classless society. The claims of Marx and Engels that the class distinctions would disappear (so will the class antagonisms, and the state as the instrument of the ruling class) are utterly unrealistic, as they have been disproved by the practices and realities of the socialist politics today. The ruling class ideas of Mosca, Pareto and Michels, on the other hand, turned out to be too simplistic and broad to describe the forms and functions of the ruling elites in the contemporary politics.

The basic question is no longer the debate on the existence of the ruling elite in any society, but on the relationship between the ruling elite and the ruled. On a generalized and abstract level, the elites are easily distinguishable from the masses, and the leaders from the led. A series of systematic scrutiny and empirical research, however, is required for any one to study the concrete relationships between the ruling group(s) and the ruled in political arenas of a given country.

Suzanne Keller, for one, differentiated the ruling class from what she called the "strategic elites."[38] Contrary to her conceptualization, the ruling class is not always long-lived, not necessarily co-opted because of birth and wealth. The power and authority of the ruling class are rather narrowly concentrated. Likewise, the loss of its power stems more from internal political intrigues, violence, revolution and war than from the loss of wealth. The dubious distinctions between the ruling class and the strategic elites notwithstanding, her identification of four constraints imposed upon the ruling elites in modern society is valuable: (1) increased public control over the leaders and limiting the caprice and arbitrariness of those in power; (2) free and open discussion of timely public issues concerning politics, economics, art, morality and taste; (3) the specialization of authority, constricting the range of power; and (4) the narrowing of the gap between leaders and led with respect to education, standard of living and general well-being. She pointed out that in highly industrialized societies power has become less arbitrary and personal, and it tends to be shared among various groups and institutions.

No single strategic elite has absolute power or priority; none can hold power forever; and none can determine the patterns of selection and recruitment for the rest. For, the varied skills and experiences of the strategic elite result in the formation of a more complex and many-sided social and political core.[39] Thomas Dye's recent findings that the slow and continuous modification of America's institutional elites toward a more specialized, educated and achievement-oriented direction[40] support Keller's thesis.

C. Wright Mills' power elite thesis also deserves attention here. His notion that contrary to America's alleged democratic theory of pluralistic participation in the determination of public policy, the "power elites" —the political directorate, the corporate rich and the higher military— run the country is significant.[41] In his New Haven study, Robert Dahl, however, did not identify such power elite. He found, instead, that different groups are formed for particular decisions and fields of policy, often in spontaneous response to challenges from particular problem areas. Recently, Dahl stated that "theories of minority domination do testify to the extent and pervasiveness of inequality." But he contended that "by asserting the existence of a dominant minority, these theories divert us from a realistic assessment of the time limits and potentialities of democracy in the modern world. Either they offer ill-founded hope for an apocalyptic revolutionary transformation that will lead us into the promised land of perfect freedom, self-realization and full acceptance of the equal worth of all human beings; or else they offer us no hope at all and counsel us, directly or by implication, to give up the ancient vision of a society in which the citizens, possessing all the resources and institutions necessary to democracy, govern themselves as free and equal citizens."[42]

Elite studies by Keller, Mills, Dahl and Dye are directed toward those in highly industrialized countries, especially the United States and other Western democratic systems rather than the "new class" in the industrialized socialist countries. The patron-client and the rational-technical models in the study of the Soviet elite mobility by Philip Stewart and his associates, and the generational model by John Nagle represent elite studies in socialist countries.[43] Nagle asserts, though tentatively, that the claims of the rise of a new exploitative social class in the Soviet system by Djilas and Stojanovic are premature.[44] He contends that the former Soviet elite as bureaucratic stratum monopolized the political process of the Soviet state, but it failed to function as a social class. Hence, it would be more fruitful to examine the points of generational transition within the top leadership than to focus on the rise of the new class.[45]

Welsh, meanwhile, identified three major changes in the political leadership in the socialist systems: (1) the emergence of technocracy as evidenced by the increasing use of "rational-technical" criteria in the selection of political elites, by a decline in the prescriptive importance of ideological considerations in decision-making, by an accompanying change in the role of ideology in the direction of after-the-fact rationalization and by the emergence of a new category of governing elite—the "managerial class"; (2) the decline of personalism and the rise of bureaucratization and routinization; and (3) the replacement of unstructured, intense intraelite conflict by more stable and less disruptive forms of political competition.[46] These observations aside, his general conclusion on political leadership is strikingly similar to that of Mosca, Bryce, Pareto and Michels:

> Regardless of the extension of opportunities for political participation to larger proportion of the population, the actual exercise of political power has remained, in most societies, the prerogative of a small part of the citizenry. In short, the rise of democracy has not signaled the decline of elites.[47]

Similarly, Maurice Duverger's general theoretical statement, though confined to the relationship between leadership stability and oligarchic headship in mass political parties, essentially echoed Robert Michels' oligarchic thesis:

> The leadership of parties tends naturally to assume oligarchic form. A veritable "ruling class" comes into being that is more or less closed; it is an "inner circle" into which it is difficult to penetrate. The phenomenon is just as true of titular leaders as of the real leaders, of autocratic as of democratic rulers. In theory, the principle of election should prevent the formation of an oligarchy; in fact, it seems rather to favour it.[48]

Recently, Field, Higley and Burton classified the states of national elites into four prototypes: disunified elites, imperfectly unified elites, consensually unified elites and ideologically unified elites. They examined the relationship between the states of national elites and stability of political institutions in 81 nations. They, too, discovered, among other things, "the strongly self-perpetuating character of the states of national elites."[49]

It is clear from the foregoing that the ruling elites, whether they are called the strategic elites, the new class, the institutional elites, the national elites or others, do exist in any society; they are the few who rule over the many. As Jean Jacque Rousseau wrote in the *Social Contract,* "it is against the natural order for the many to govern and the few to be governed."[50] And in the *Discourse on Inequality,* he concluded that "it is against the laws of nature, no matter how we define them, that an imbecile lead(s) a wise man."[51] Contrary to the claims of the *Manifesto of the Communist Party,* the past and present communist societies are no exception to this political "law." Marx and Engels declared:

> All historical movements were movements of minorities, or in the interests of minorities. The proletarian movement is the self-conscious, independent movement of the immense majority, in the interests of the immense majority.[52]

What Marx and Engels called "the immense majority" or "in the interest of the immense majority" differs little in real political life from "the minorities"or "in the interests of minorities," for the few still rule whether "in the name of the immense majority" or "in the interests of minorities." Pareto made this point rather unequivocally:

> The term "people" means "the majority." The term "majority" in itself is a new abstraction. In countries where there is no referendum, the will of a small number of individuals is taken as equivalent to the "will of the people" only by a complicated series of abstractions, fictions, inferences.[53]

Lenin's party dictatorship as the "vanguard of the people," and other communist clichés such as "people's democracy," "the leader" or "mass line" can be understood in this light. There are, in short, no countries in the world today, socialist or otherwise, where the ruling elites fade away. The ruling elites in one country differ from those in the other countries in how they are chosen and what mechanism sustains and expands their powers and privileges. A particular ruling elite can be replaced by another, but the demise of the ruling elite per se does not and will not happen. The ruling elites, those who get the most out of politics, be they power, prestige, patronage or privilege, remain and will continue to remain in political arenas.

Needless to say, depending on how one defines the ruling elite, its number, size, longevity and role may vary. Three examples illuminate this point. Townsend estimated the number of political elites and subelites in Chinese communist system to be as high as 83 million, which is considerably larger than one or two million ruling and gentry classes during the Ch'ing Dynasty, although 83 million is still a "minority" in the country of over one billion people.[54] Voslensky identified about 750,000 out of some 271 million as the ruling class (*nomenklatura*) in the former Soviet Union.[55] Thomas Dye and his associates' criteria of the ruling elites in America are even more exclusive. The number of "ruling elites" in the United States does not exceed 5,000.[56]

The Masses: The Manipulated

The ruling elites are the *users* of ideology; they employ it to appeal to, and/or generate support from, the masses, or to mobilize the latter for the goal(s) they set. The masses may find gratification from political lip service, e.g., "for the masses," "for the people," "for the interest of the toiling masses" or "for the benefits of the working classes."

In reality, the masses build the roads, bridges, canals and highrises; they make, mold and manufacture goods and tools; and they plow, plant and produce grains and vegetables. While the ruling elites chant hortatory slogans, "for the masses," the masses are performing back-breaking labors "for the elites."

As Vilfredo Pareto correctly observed, the masses are governed by an elite, by a chosen element in the population. A composition of elite can change with changes in the individuals belonging to it or in their descendants, or even through the infiltration of extraneous elements, which may come from or outside the country.[57] However, the elite, the minority, always governs the masses, the majority. Michels espoused the same idea:

> It is a political postulate of the greatest value that the right to the management of government never does belong to the majority, but to the will of the stronger and to the vitality, more indisputable and indomitable, of an individual or of a conscious group of persons; in sum, of an energetic and compact minority.[58]

He, moreover, contended that as soon as the new ruling elites have attained their ends, as soon as they have succeeded in the name of the "injured rights of the anonymous masses" in overthrowing the tyranny of their predecessors and in attaining power in their turn, they, too, undergo a transformation which renders them similar in every respect to the dethroned tyrants. Hence, the revolutionaries of today become the reactionaries of tomorrow.[59] The masses are, in short, the target of manipulation either by power-holders or power-seekers, or by both. As Michels succinctly stated, "the masses will never rule except *in abstracto*."[60] He wrote:

> History appears to teach us that no popular movement, however powerful and energetic, can effect any lasting changes in the organic structure of social life. The reason is that the most outstanding elements of such movements, the men who originally led them and set them alright, always become gradually detached from the masses and assimilated by the "political class" to whom they contribute few new ideas, maybe, but all the more youthful energy and practical intelligence, and thus through a process of repeated rejuvenation serve to perpetuate their supremacy.... History also teaches us that the government—or, if you like, the state —can only be the organization of minority, whose purpose is to impose on the rest of society a legal order appropriate to the requirements of its own control and exploitation of the masses; it can never have the possibility, nor even the capacity, to govern themselves. A cruel fate of history has predestined them to suffer passively the domination of a small minority risen from their midst, and to serve merely as the pedestal for

the greatness of their rulers.[61]

As Sartori asserted, Michels's iron law by and large still holds, if only as a "bronze law."[62] The masses *cannot* rule because of the oligarchic nature of human organization and *will not* rule because they are politically indifferent and even "grateful" to the ruling elites. The masses *will never rule* as long as they are politically incompetent and immature.

The masses, whether they are the peasants in the countryside or the workers in the urban centers, have frequently revolted throughout history. Revolts and revolutions, if successful, may produce new ruling elites and new masses, but the system is never ruled directly by the masses themselves. Parties, cadres, functionaries and a host of other forms of political "middle man" will represent, link and govern, perhaps *in the name of* the masses, but the masses themselves never rule.

Official claims and ideological assertions notwithstanding, the socialist countries today are no exception to this political axiom. The "pure" democracy such as *ekklesia* in ancient Greek city-state, the public meetings in Swiss cantons or the town meetings in the New England states in America are the rare exceptions. Even in the mob rule or ochlocracy the mob or the masses need the leaders. Like the kings and queens of the constitutional monarchy, the masses in the past and present socialist countries only *rein* and the communist party, state and military elites *rule*. While the former *work,* the latter mince *words.* Unlike the kings and queens, however, the reining powers and privileges of the masses lie more in the realm of the governmental propaganda than in real political life.

In brief, the power-holders and the power-seekers employ ideology as a symbolic guide to manipulate and mobilize the masses. They use it as a form of control mechanism of the masses. Through fusion, replacement or circulation, the ruling elites transform themselves in number, size, role and composition, but at a given moment, there are always the rulers and the ruled, the elites and the masses. Political symbols, abstractions and pretexts may change but the political rule and its corresponding power, prestige and privilege will always remain in the hands of the few, as Orwell proclaimed, "some are more equal than others."

This particular political "truth" in the above may be equally applicable to the current North and South Korean politics. What stands out in the socialist system is, therefore, its unsubstantiated and unsupportable claims made about its polity, economy and society under the banner: "for the masses," "of the masses" and "by the masses." Such claims are not only the fundamental tenets of Marxism-Leninism and all the other variants of communism, but they are still the favorite themes of the governmental propaganda in the remaining socialist countries, including North Korea. In reality, however, the socialist system, whatever its variants in Havana, Hanoi, Beijing or Pyongyang, is more the rule "by the elites," "of the elites" and "for the elites" "in the name of the masses."

In the final analysis, if the rule by a few is an iron law of politics, what matters the most is not the question of the rule by minority or majority, but *who* these few are and *how* they obtain that power and manage it. The questions of *who* and *how* separate elitism from pluralism, oligarchy from polyarchy, democracy from dictatorship and authoritarianism from totalitarianism.[63] Lasswell observed that a democratic social structure depends "on the relations of the elite to the mass—how it is recruited and how it exercises its power."[64] A democratic polity is one in which the ruled shares the minimum of power necessary to hold the rulers accountable.[65] In Sartori's words, no matter how oligarchic the organization of each minority when examined from within, the result of the competition between them is democracy. "An all-encompassing democracy (representative democracy) results from the fact that the power of deciding between the competitors is in the hands of the *demos.*[66]

The Korean Experiences

North Korea

(1) Ideological Elements and their Metamorphoses

North Korea's official ideology still is Marxism-Leninism and the

Juche idea. Its ruling elites are those who occupy the top positions in the party (the Worker's Party of Korea or the WPK), state, military, paramilitary and mass organizations. In Field-Burton-Higley's classification of national elites, the North Korean ruling elites typify the "ideologically unified elites."[67] The condition of ideological and policy conformity resulting in a sharp centralization of elite interaction in a single party (i.e., the WPK), the absence of credible anti-party faction and/or anti-system elements, and a high degree of institutional stability (e.g., an absence of overt seizure of power by force) characterize the present North Korean political system.

The North Korean ruling elites have used various political symbols and policy statements.[68] The *Juche* idea, at least since mid-1950s, has become the leading symbol.[69] Besides the *Juche* idea, anti-Americanism (anti-imperialism), anti-Japanism, anti-Fascism (i.e., "the South Korean Fascist cliques"), unification formula, socialist construction and revolution, and the Kim Il Sung and, increasingly now, Kim Jŏng Il cult phenomena are other prominent political symbols and policy orientations in North Korea.

Several points need to be pointed out here. First, the contents of many aforesaid ideological elements have changed over the years in response to the changing internal and external political milieu. In the 50s and 60s, the *Juche* idea primarily stressed independence from the external powers. Internally, during this period Kim Il Sung began to emerge as the one-man ruler by eliminating his political enemies within the WPK such as the Soviet faction, the South Korean Worker's Party faction and the Yanan faction, which allegedly had foreign ties.[70] Externally, the rift between the former Soviet Union and China began to surface, and Kim adroitly avoided siding with either of the two. Kim's consummate balancing act throughout the years of the slowly changing Sino-Soviet rivalry has, in fact, been one of his political trademarks. Such internal and external conditions propelled Kim to stress "self-identity in thinking, independence in politics, self-support in economy and self-reliance in national defense."[71]

Since the 70s, the focus of *Juche* has become *socialist economic construction*. Although as early as 1962, Kim espoused the so-called three revolution theses—technical, cultural and ideological—he identified "three revolutions" as the primary tasks of the *Juche* idea in the early 70s.[72] His son, Kim Jŏng Il, the official successor-designate, has added a new slogan, "the 70-day Battle Speed," along with the earlier symbols such as *Chŏllima Undong* [Flying Horse Movement] the Chŏngsan-ri spirit and the Daean work system[73] primarily to mobilize the masses for socialist economic construction. The socialist economic construction in the name of *Juche* has also become more militant. It is no longer "movement" or "spirit" but "battles" and "war." The masses are mobilized for economic construction as if to fight a war.[74]

In the 80s and 90s the slogans of "battles"—"200 Day Battles," "creation of speed of the 90s" and "Kangsŏn Speed"—are rampant. Above all, the focus of *Juche* has shifted from the earlier ideas of independence, self-reliant economy or self-defense, to those of unity (trinity) of *Suryŏng* [the great leader], the party (the WPK) and the people. Kim Jŏng Il claims, as noted elsewhere, that human beings have "two bodies"—physical body and socio-political body. Man's physical body is from his (her) parents and socio-political body, from the Great Leader. Further, he argues that as each person has certain blood types, the *Juche* idea must be the only and unique idea running throughout the socio-political body of the North Korean masses. In short, the *Juche* idea in the 80s and 90s are altered again to justify and rationalize the father-son succession scheme.

Likewise, North Korea's anti-Japanism and anti-Americanism have undergone a series of subtle yet significant changes over the years, although its basic antagonistic postures have remained unaltered. In the early phase of the DPRK, anti-Japanism loomed large in a slogan such as "eliminating evil consequences of Japanese imperialist rule." But over the years North Korea and Japan have agreed upon numerous deals and transactions, despite the absence of their formal diplomatic relations amid the South Korean objections. Japan's shipping of its Korean residents to North Korea in 1959 and 1960, and her sports, trade and other formal and informal political contacts and transactions are the cases in point. Their long standing historic ties, territorial propinquity and human linkages (i.e., Korean residents in Japan) have made North

Korea's anti-Japanism merely a slogan with little substance. Particularly in the aftermath of the collapse of Communism, North Korea looks rather desperate in normalizing its relations with Japan, attested to by the intermittently ongoing North Korea-Japan normalization talks.

With the emergence of the two separate regimes in the Korean Peninsula in 1948, America became North Korea's number one "imperialist enemy." First, anti-Americanism focused on the demand for the withdrawal of the U.S. forces from South Korea. With the outbreak of the Korean War, North Korea's anti-Americanism peaked. Its anti-Americanism during the War centered around the question, in Kim Il Sung's words, "How can we defeat the mighty U.S. imperialists?"[75] With the Armistice Agreement in 1953, North Korea's anti-Americanism was once again directed toward the U.S. troop withdrawal from South Korea. Particularly after the Chinese (the Chinese Volunteers Corps) troop withdrew from North Korea in 1958, North Korea's demand for the US troop withdrawal became much more vociferous. Through the Vietnam War years and to the present, North Korea's anti-Americanism remained the same, i.e., the U.S. troop withdrawal from South Korea and the repeal of the 1954 U.S.-ROK Mutual Defense Treaty. Under this facade, however, Pyongyang has frequently shifted its postures toward America in response to the changing political and strategic balances in the Korean Peninsula, the East Asian setting and global arena. Its proposal for a direct bilateral talk with the U.S. to conclude a peace treaty to end the 1953 Armistice Agreement and, a tripartite talk with both the U.S. and South Korea in the early 1980s and the currently on-going North Korea-U.S. diplomatic meetings to improve their relations exemplify such seemingly flexible yet tactical moves and adjustments.[76]

Another political symbol, "Fascism" or "Fascist cliques," is North Korea's code word for the South Korean regime. This symbol, too, has survived all these years except for the personalities to whom such labels are attached. In the forties through early sixties, Syngman Rhee was North Korea's prime target of the Fascist reactionary cliques. With Rhee's downfall and via the Hŏ Chŏng interim administration and the Chang Myŏn government, Park Chung Hee inherited Syngman Rhee's label with a slight modification (i.e., Fascist U.S. military lackeys) from

North Korea in the sixties and seventies. Again, with the fall of Park Chung Hee and via the Choe Kyu Ha interim government, Chun Doo Hwan inherited Park's label from North Korea, then the Roh Tae Woo regime and now Kim Young-sam government have been touted as "the Fascist military clique" by the North Korean propaganda machine.

Similarly, the remaining political symbols, unification formula and the Kim Il Sung-Kim Jŏng Il cult phenomena, have undergone various changes over the years. Since these two questions will be dealt with in detail in the later chapters, it suffices to say here that they, too, like the rest of the symbols and ideological elements, have responded to the changing internal and external political and strategic stimuli.

Secondly, all the above mentioned political symbols and ideological elements in North Korea are "closed" in that they are not subject to questions or debates at any time and under any circumstances. The masses have only the "duty" to follow, obey and chant these symbols, slogans and policies but have no "right" to make input into the formulation, implementation, evaluation and termination of these symbols and policies. All ideological elements in North Korea are "enforceable" but not "debatable." Contrary to the blatant lip services paid to the masses that they are "the masters of the revolution and construction," the masses are "the pupils" of the WPK and its ruling elites are the "teachers."[77] In this regard, the North Korean ideology finds its affinity in Mussolini's "believe, obey and fight" formula or Lenin's "iron discipline."[78]

Thirdly, a Manichaean dualism with a heavy emphasis on negativism prevails in the North Korean ruling elites' use of political symbols. All issues and problems are simplified and reduced to the level of pro-con, good-evil, right-wrong and yin-yang dichotomy. Just about everything is seen in black and white. They are right, good and just, while their internal and external "enemies" are wrong, evil and unjust. They accentuate the negative far more than the positive. The majority of their symbols deal with "antis:" anti-imperialism, anti-feudalism, anti-regionalism, anti-familialism, anti-flunkeyism, anti-dogmatism, anti-revisionism, anti-big power chauvinism, anti-privatism (anti-individualism), anti-passivism, anti-conservatism, anti-factionalism, anti-opportunism, anti-formalism and anti-bureaucratism to mention a few. Evidently, then, the North Korean ideology is not merely "class-antagonistic."[79] It is against certain classes, certain beliefs, certain behaviors and certain nations. Specifically, it is *class*-antagonistic toward landlords and capitalists, *belief*-antagonistic toward feudalists and imperialists, *behavior*-antagonistic toward factionalists and dogmatists and *nation*-antagonistic toward the United States and Japan.[80]

By contrast, the North Korean ruling elites use the positive symbols sparingly, although they never fail to make customary references to "the universal scientific truth" of Marxism-Leninism and the Kim Il Sung's *Juche* idea, and, above all, to the "ultimate and ineluctable triumph of communism over feudalism, capitalism, imperialism and all other "evils" of the world.

Fourthly, a high degree of incongruity and inconsistency exists between Kim Il Sung and his ruling elites' rhetoric and their actual practices. Bluntly put, Max Beloff's characterization of the Soviet government being "capable of bottomless mendacity"[81] is apropos for the present North Korean ruling elites. While anti-imperialism slogans are primarily targeted against America and Japan, North Korea had seldom attacked the former Soviet Union and China despite the fact that both too, have engaged in imperialistic activities (e.g., the Soviet invasion of Afghanistan in 1979 and the Chinese invasion of Tibet in 1954). The South Korean ruling elites are often accused of flunkeyism, big-power chauvinism and dependence on America and Japan, but North Korea, too, has never been totally independent of the former Soviet Union and China. North Korea criticizes dogmatism and revisionism of its fraternal friends, especially the former Soviet Union, but it is silent about its own ideological dogmatism and revisionism.

Kim Il Sung has liquidated anti-party factionalists within the WPK, but he has failed to admit his own partisan factionalist politics. He has attacked the evils of "individual heroism," while permitting his own personality and family cult, which has far surpassed that of Stalin or Mao in magnitude, intensity and duration. He has denounced religion as the opiate of the people, while promoting worship of himself as a "Messiah" in North Korea. He has assailed privatism, nepotism and familialism, while placing his close relatives, former partisan guerrilla comrades and political associates in high strategic positions in the party, state, military and other control apparatus. Above all, he has frequently advocated that the masses are the masters of the revolution and construction, but in reality he has been the master of North Korea for more than forty years.

Finally, the North Korean ruling elites' exercise of political symbols has displayed a high degree of religiosity of the occult variety, which is not uncommon in the communist countries. It is indeed ironic that Marx, who dismissed "sacred" religion as the opium of the people, has become the Messiah of communism. As Russell observed, the layman's faith in Yahweh is equivalent to the communist's faith in dialectical materialism.[82] As Marx represents the communist equivalent of the Christian Messiah, the Communist Party, that of the Church, and the Communist Party elite, that of the Christian elect. The analogy can go on: expulsion from the Communist Party is likened to excommunication from the Church, as the coming of communist utopia corresponds to the second coming of God. As Marx is the Messiah of communism, Lenin, the apostle of the Soviet communism, and Mao, of Chinese communism, so is Kim Il Sung an apostle of North Korean communism. As Mao's Red Book was once read and cited daily like the holy scriptures, so are Kim's remarks and writings in North Korea today. The tragedy is that while in the rest of the world such religious fervor has virtually disappeared with the demise of communism, North Korea has further intensified such frenzy, partly perhaps to mitigate the negative impacts and implications of the death of communism on North Korea and partly to mobilize the mass support for the father-son succession scheme.

In any case the current North Korean ideological fervor surrounding the Kim Il Sung (and Kim Jŏng Il) cult closely resembles religious fanaticism. At the present at least, Kim resembles a corporeal god, ever-victorious and infallible. Again, like religious fanaticism, the cult phenomenon, too, will sooner or later die away. The makers of the icons and their worshippers will and must come to their senses. And normality will and must return. In the final analysis, Kim himself, the chief architect and the object of all these icon-making, is mortal no matter how many icons and idols are dedicated to him. As the cult of Stalin and that of Mao died away with their deaths, so will the cult of Kim. In the end, then, Kim himself will be his own iconoclast, and his death will be icon-oclasm of his cult. Like King Midas, the present idolatry of Kim may end in tragedy. The fact that ideology of Marxism and Leninism has been reduced to nothing but an idolatry of Kim is tragically ironic.

(2) Ideological Elements and their Functions and Dysfunctions

More often than not, ideology is a double-edged sword; it may help or hurt the one who brandishes it. The users of political symbols and other ideological elements in North Korea are no exceptions. From Kim Il Sung and his ruling elites' vantage point, their use of various political symbols and other ideological elements has been, by and large, func-tional. The fact that Kim Il Sung regime is the longest ruling apparatus in the world attests to this point.

The success of the North Korean ruling elites' use of political sym-bols is derived largely from their flexibility amid the seemingly rigid set of ideological matrix. The skeleton of anti-Americanism, anti-Japanism and Fascist cliquism has survived, but its contents have undergone a series of metamorphoses. North Korea's ultimate aim of realizing the victory of Marxism-Leninism remains unchanged, but its strategy, tac-tics and posturing have frequently shifted. The communization of the entire Korean Peninsula has been its immutable objective, but its unifi-cation policies and formula have responded to the changing domestic and international political configuration.

The heightened usage of anti-Japanese and anti-American symbols and slogans, particularly during the formative years in the late 40s, served to provide both the Kim Il Sung regime's legitimacy and the North Korean people's collective national identity. The recognition of external "enemies" had stimulated the North Korean people's national consciousness and identity. In that period of nation-building and Kim's own power-base building, the slogans such as "the liberation of the homeland from the imperialist enemies," "the building of a genuine state of workers and peasants" and "elimination of Japanese collabora-tors" appealed to the masses.[83]

Similarly, the North Korean ruling elites' attack on fascism, which has been directed primarily against the successive South Korean regimes, has served indirectly to legitimize the Kim Il Sung regime itself. By discrediting and nullifying the legitimacy of the South Korean regimes, the North Korean ruling elites hoped to solidify their own rule. Their political logic was that the negation of one regime (the South Korean government) would lead to the affirmation of another (the North Korean regime) in the same area (the Korean Peninsula), where the two regimes vie for their exclusive jurisdiction and legitimacy.

The North Korean ruling elites' incessant invocation of the unification formula, be it the earlier temporary confederal plan, the 1980 permanent confederal plan, the 1984 tripartite talk proposal or the present "one nation-one state-two governments-two systems" formula can be seen in the same light.[84] Their motives for invoking various unification formula and proposals stemmed not so much from their genuine interest in the realization of a united fatherland per se but from their political aim of controlling the North Korean masses. From this standpoint, the North Korean unification policy and formula have been nothing more than another mass control and mobilization device.

In fine, Kim Il Sung and his ruling elites' constant chanting of his revolutionary thought, various unification formulas, and, above all, *Juche,* has been directed at generating the masses' loyalty to him (the Supreme Leader and now his son, the Dear Leader Kim Jŏng Il as well), to the Party and to the fatherland.

It is also evident that some North Korean political symbols and ideological elements have been dysfunctional. Kim Il Sung and his ruling elites have largely succeeded in acquiring and maintaining a complete ideological consensus among elites and between elites and masses. But in the process, all viable ideological and political interplays have been eliminated. Only activities initiated, directed and coordinated by the WPK are permissible. Parties other than the WPK do exist and front organizations perform their appointed tasks. Yet, they function only under the WPK's guidance and ideological framework, neither outside it, nor against it. Parties such as Ch'ŏngudang, the Korean Socialist Democratic Party, and the Revolutionary Party for Reunification are tokenisms, at best, and bogus, at worst.

The control of political symbols and other ideological elements by the WPK make North Korea the typical single party-single ideology regime. Worse still, the frenetic state of the *Juche* and the Kim Il Sung cult has set the possibility, if not probability, of making North Korea's single party-single ideology into single man's ideology. Perhaps, the most dysfunctional of single party-single ideology syndrome is its effects on the masses. In the process of artificially creating a new socialist man of *Juche* revolutionary type, a man of creativity, spontaneity and initiative has been lost. Marx, who aspired to save the workers from becoming a commodity in the labor market, would find it ironic that the masses in North Korea, an avowedly Marxist-Leninist-*Juche* state, have become the victims in the political arena. In rhetoric, the masses are the masters and the motivating forces of revolution and construction, and they will become the masters of the state and society. Until then, they must pledge absolute and unconditional loyalty to the Supreme Leader and the Dear Leader, follow the WPK and work and fight for the fatherland, like a cog in the machine.

South Korea

(1) Ideological Matrix of Seven Regimes

Unlike Kim Il Sung and his ruling elites, whose continuous control of North Korea has been uninterrupted for more than forty years, the South Korean ruling elites have frequently risen and fallen during the same period. There have been seven regimes, two military coups, one major student revolution with a series of off and on student anti-government protests and riots, not to mention almost unceasing number of major and minor political crises. While Kim Il Sung has been the sole head of state during this entire period in North Korea, South Korea has witnessed seven heads of state (presidents)—Syngman Rhee, Yun Bo Sun, Park Chung Hee, Choe Kyu Ha, Chun Doo Hwan, Roh Tae Woo and Kim Young-sam.

Anti-communism has been the master political symbol of South Korea, although its policy content, objectives and instrumentalities have undergone numerous changes over the years. The leaders of both the government and opposition parties, high-level bureaucrats, party functionaries, ex-military officers and the intellectuals, including university students, constitute the South Korean elites. Unlike the North Korean elites, who are by and large monolithic, the South Korean elites are dichotomous, those in power and those out of it. The elite conflicts have not been absent in North Korea, but they have been mostly confined to factional strifes within the WPK, whereas in South Korea the elite strifes have been waged between parties.

The Rhee Government and Political Conservatism

Ideologically, political conservatism characterized the Rhee government (1948-1960). It consisted of five major elements: anti-communism, unification formula, anti-Japanism, pro-Americanism and democracy. On a cognitive level, all elements except democracy were "closed" in that they were not, by and large, open to debate or question. They were "indisputable," and everyone, the elites and the masses alike, had to accept or was coerced to acquiesce.

Rhee and his ruling elites utilized anti-communism as a major device for political manipulation and control. While the threats from North Korea were real and the Rhee government took prudent safeguards against them, Rhee and his ruling elites often misused such threats, real and fabricated, for their own political purposes. They broadened the scope and meaning of communism to such an extent that what would be normally considered acts of political opposition could easily fall under the loose label, *Yonggong* [pro-communism].[85] The Rhee regime, by using *yonggong* label freely, had deliberately blurred the distinction between political opposition and political enemy, between progressive parties and the communist organizations and between personal political foes and the national enemy. Rhee and his ruling elites frequently equated their regime with the state itself and charged any political rivals who oppose them as "the enemies of the state." Two notable cases of Rhee's political rivals who were victimized as the enemies of the state were Shin Ick-hee, then Speaker of the South Korean National Assembly, who was charged with the international conspiracy in 1954 and Cho Bong-am, head of the Korean Progressive Party, who was executed in 1959.[86]

Rhee's unification formula was closely interconnected with the anti-communist political symbol. Although the unification proposal presented at the 1954 Geneva Conference was an official one, he advocated in public the "unification by military force" policy under the slogan of "March North and unify Korea."[87] He created the impression that an attack from North Korea was imminent. Marching North, he contended, would not only preempt such attack, but would be the only solution to unify the nation. Accordingly, all the alternative unification formulas were *closed*. Rhee and his ruling elites, for instance, interpreted a neutralized Korean unification proposal as another version of the communist take-over scheme. In brief, Rhee's anti-communism and unification formula became *kuksi* [the permanent, irrefutable national policy].

Under the Rhee government democracy as a political symbol was debatable. This debate created the primary source of conflicts between the elites in power and those in opposition. The former frequently ignored the principles and procedures of democracy, which gave rise to protests from the latter, including the majority of intellectuals in the university-press nexus.

Both the ruling and the opposition elites were in sharp disagreement over key political issues. The former attempted to strengthen centralization (i.e., the central government control of provincial and local governments), the presidential system, popular election of the president and limited protection of fundamental rights and freedom, while the latter defended or fought for decentralization (i.e., the establishment of local autonomy), the cabinet-responsible system, the election of the president by the National Assembly and the unconditional protection of civil liberties. Rhee's ruling elites won virtually all these key issues over the opposition forces. The 1952 constitutional amendment which authorized the election of the president by direct popular vote, the 1954 constitutional amendment which strengthened the presidential system and the 1958 National Security Law revision which restricted civil rights and civil liberties were the pertinent cases.[88]

On an affective dimension, Rhee's political conservatism revealed a high degree of intensity, especially toward North Korean communism, Japan and America. Considering the fact that the Korean War devastated the country and took millions of lives, the Rhee government's intense aversion to North Korean communism was understandable.

The Korean people's anti-Japanese sentiment or anti-Japanism was even deeper than their anti-communist posture. Rhee once pledged that "if Japan encroaches on Korea again, we will fight back, even with the help of the Communists."[89] He placed an embargo on the flow of Japanese cultural products such as books, records and movies and barred the Japanese from entering Korea. Rhee and his ruling elites attempted to prosecute, though rather unsuccessfully, those Koreans who collaborated with the Japanese during its colonial rule. The Rhee government often attributed its public policy failures to former Japanese colonial exploitations. While the Japanese colonial rule was responsible for some of Korea's ills, blaming Rhee's governmental policy failures entirely on it went too far. The Rhee government's inability to reach an agreement on the Korea-Japan normalization talks for twelve years was also attributable to the Korean people's intense anti-Japanese feelings fanned by the Rhee government. To be sure, the Japanese negotiators' lack of sincerity, arrogant attitudes and occasional derogatory remarks also hindered the negotiation progress. More importantly, some substantive issues—Japan's recognition of the Republic of Korea (South Korea) as the only legitimate and sovereign state, the reparation and return of Korean cultural assets and properties from Japan, the repeal of the Rhee Line in the Sea of Japan and the status of Korean residents in Japan and their reparation—were too complicated and difficult to be settled overnight.[90] Still, the Rhee government policy of *banil* [anti-Japanism] or *bangil* [warding-off Japan] contributed greatly to the failure of the Korea-Japan normalization talks.

As much as Rhee and his ruling elites irrationally adhered to the anti-Japanese postures, they blindly embraced pro-American policy. Doubtless, the reasons for their pro-American orientation were readily understandable since the United States was the "liberator" of Korea from the Japanese colonial rule, the major donor of economic and military aid, an ally who took the initiative and sacrificed countless lives during the Korean War and the partner of the South Korean defense under the 1953 U.S.-ROK Mutual Defence Treaty.

These contributions of the United States to South Korea deserve proper credit, but the Rhee government was too preoccupied with what America did for Korea and often failed to ask why. Why was Korea divided? Why has the United States been helping Korea? Why were the United States' national interests—strategic, political and economic—in the Korean Peninsula vital? The Rhee government's pro-American stance, like its anti-Japanese posture, was more emotional than rational.

On an evaluative dimension, negativism prevailed in Rhee's political conservatism. With the single exception of pro-American posture, the rest were negative, i.e., anti-Japanism and anti-Communism. The Rhee government and its ruling elites even perceived democracy and unification formula in negative light. They were reluctant or even refused to adhere to the principles and procedures of democracy. They were highly suspicious of, perhaps with good reasons, any solution for Korean reunification by peaceful means. They advocated, instead, the unification by military force (i.e., "March North and unify").

The Chang Myŏn Government and Democratism

The fall of the Rhee regime in April 1960 under the pressure from the massive nationwide student uprising precipitated, although only momentarily, a drastic ideological change in South Korean politics. The Hŏ Chŏng interim administration (April-July, 1960) and the Chang Myŏn government (August, 1960-May, 1961) may be credited with the introduction of "democratism." Democratism during this short period was marked by a sudden erosion of the seemingly tight-knit political conservatism of the Rhee regime.

Specifically, on a cognitive dimension, the debate on communism, Japan, the United States and the unification formula were no longer "closed." The elites in power and those in opposition began to reassess or reappraise the government-imposed old formula—anti-communism, anti-Japanism, pro-Americanism and official unification policy—and sought to redefine them. A new ideological element, i.e., modernization or economic development in its embryonic form, too, emerged in this period.[91]

The Chang government abandoned Rhee's "March North and Unify Korea" rhetoric. It no longer considered a neutralized unification formula to be pro-communistic. Its posture toward Japan and the United States became less emotional and more positive than was the case under the Rhee government.

Above all, democracy ceased to be the symbolic bone of contention between the ruling elites and the political opposition, but it became a political reality. With the Chang government, the cabinet-responsible system replaced the presidential system; the president, more a symbol than the real power, was elected once again, not by popular votes but by the members of the National Assembly; fundamental civil rights and civil liberties were fully restored; and local autonomy was implemented. However, the swing toward democracy within such a short time went too far amid the revolutionary fervor. Democracy degenerated into democratism. In Plato's classic term, "extreme democracy" or mob democracy (ochlocracy) emerged.[92] In such fervor the elites and the masses alike confused the ideal of democracy with its method, freedom with self-indulgence or unrestrained rights and revolution with anarchy.

Statistics covering the period from the April 19 Student Revolution of 1960 to the May 16 Military Coup d'etat of 1961, for instance, revealed that university and high school students staged some 170 demonstrations involving 120,000 students. In the same period, there were 35 street demonstrations by various trade unions with more than 20,000 participants. This meant that an average of 150 people demonstrated nearly every day of the eight months-long Chang regime. The press organizations also mushroomed to 1,500. Socialist and progressive parties, whose political activities had been severely curtailed under the Rhee government, also flourished and constituted some 16 of the total 24 political parties.[93] In a nutshell, as one political observer described this period, it was a time in which the Korean people enjoyed "the greatest freedom ever since the advent of Tan-gun," the legendary founder of Korea in 2,333 B.C.[94]

In Sartori's terminology, democracy functioned during this period as an element of "ideological heating."[95] This element was not only open but both elites and masses felt strongly and positively about it. As a direct reaction against the undemocratic practices of the Rhee government, the elites, especially university student leaders, who triggered the downfall of the Rhee regime, conceived of democracy more with passion than with reason, more as an ideal end than as a method. In so doing, they wittingly or unwittingly transformed it into "democratism," marked by passionate revolutionary fervor undermining the orderly democratic process and procedures.

The failure of democracy under the Chang government was attributable mainly to three reasons. Ideologically, Chang's ruling Democratic Party was conservative like Rhee's Liberal Party, and thus, it was incapable of responding to the progressive and reformist demands of the masses triggered by the April Student Revolution. Its conservative character was incompatible with the revolutionary mood of the period. Second, the ruling Democratic Party was preoccupied with its own myopic intra-party factional strifes and, thus, failed to effectively meet the vocal demands of the highly politicized groups, including the labor unions and university students. Worse still, the Old (*kup'a*) and the New (*sinp'a*) factions within the Democratic Party were divided primarily along personal rather than policy lines. Most importantly, the Chang government took the power by default since it was practically "handed" to them by the students in the wake of the April Student Revolution. No doubt, the Chang government emerged through an orderly constitutional process. Strictly speaking, however, the Chang government did not *earned* the power. Students overthrew the Rhee regime but because of the inherent limitations of student political activism (viz, students can overthrow but cannot assume power), Chang and the Democratic Party, the only viable party around then, simply filled the political void. All three ideological and political incongruencies turned out to be fatal for Chang and his Democratic Party.[96]

The Park Chung Hee Government and Pragmatic Conservatism

The forced removal of the Chang Myŏn government by a military coup d'etat in May 1961 brought about another ideological shift in South Korean politics. Two ideological elements—anti-communism and unification formula—became "closed" once again. Besides, several changes in ideological elements and political symbols characterized pragmatic conservatism of the Park regime (1961-1979). Primary policy focus on modernization and economic development, the positive orientation toward Japan, and the creation of political control apparatus were most significant.

First, the new political symbol, modernization, emerged as the prime mover of Park's pragmatic conservatism. Although the Chang government instituted extensive public works project (i.e., National Construction Service) and drafted a Three Year Economic Plan, it was the Park regime which launched a full-fledged modernization program. The symbol, "economic development," surfaced under the Chang regime, but Park Government's slogans, such as "national reconstruction," "national mobilization," "expansion of exports," "economic growth," "modernization of the fatherland" and "miracle of the Han River," gained wide currency and set new national mood.

Specifically, he launched and successfully completed the First Five-Year Economic Plan (1962-1966), the Second Five-Year Economic Plan (1967-1971) and the Third Five-Year Economic Plan (1972-1976) (he was assassinated in the midst of the Fourth Five-Year Economic Plan, 1977-1981), and under the Chun government South Korea completed its Fifth Five-Year Economic Plan (1982-1986). His success in economic development was phenomenal although some negative side-effects had also ensued in the process. The urban-rural gap, regional and sectoral economic disparities and political cleavages, the blind rejection of tradition amid "economy-firstism" and environmental deterioration were some undesirable residual precipitated by the rapid economic development under the Park regime.[97] An important point here is that these negative side-effects were relatively minor in South Korea than in other countries which went through similar economic development stages.[98]

Second, Park and his ruling elites consciously downplayed the Korean people's anti-Japanese sentiments and attempted to redefine it positively and pragmatically, as evidenced by the successful conclusion of the Korea-Japan normalization pact in 1965. This deliberate manipulation of the Park government's so-called "lowly" approach to the Korea-Japan normalization talks aroused violent protests from the opposition parties and college students, and it was largely responsible for many political crises in 1964 and 1965 prior to the signing of the pact.[99] Importantly, under the Park government, *banil* [anti-Japanism] or *bangil* [warding-off Japan] though both were not completely defunct, had never revived to the level under the Rhee government. On the contrary, *ch'inil* [pro-Japanism] or *hyŏpil* [cooperating with Japan] had set the new national mood. Japan was no longer the "enemy" but an economic "partner" of the Park regime. If the Rhee government looked backward and stressed the Japanese past, the Park regime tried to look forward and focused on their present relationship and future economic cooperation. Park's positive and forward-looking orientations toward Japan paid off handsomely. Figuratively speaking, Park had adopted the double-ally (i.e., the United States and Japan) and single-adversary (i.e., North Korea) approach, a major shift from Rhee's single ally (i.e., the United States) and double adversaries (i.e., North Korean and Japan) policy stance.

Thirdly, the Park government strengthened its national security apparatus ostensibly to deal with the threats of communism from the North and exclusively to regulate the unification formula. But in reality he frequently employed the various apparatus for his political purposes. Park toughened the existent Anti-Communist Law and the National Security Law. He added new security and control measures such as the Central Intelligence Act, the Extraordinary Measures for National Reconstruction, the Political Activities Purification Act, and the National Protection Law. The control agencies included the Korean Central Intelligence Agency, the Military Intelligence Agency, the Counter-Espionage Operations Command and the Capital City Military District Command. He also created the new ministry of the National Unification Board, which was designed to, among other things, regulate the flow of both official and unofficial unification proposals and formula. Under the

Park regime, the military, the police forces and other law enforcement agencies also became highly politicized; his ruling Democratic Republican Party was demoted to the status of his hand-maiden; and the judiciary lost even its precarious independence and became pliant to his rule.[100]

The Park government took a decidedly authoritarian step in 1972 with the passage of the so-called *siwŏl yushin* [the October Revitalizing Reforms] and with the subsequent constitutional amendment which rendered him power of the "president-dictator."[101] Two points need to be spelled out at this juncture. Park's pragmatic conservatism occurred from placing a priority on economic development and taking a forward and positive stance on Japan. His politics was from the outset authoritarian, and his authoritarian proclivity in politics reached a climax in the final years of his rule, especially in the wake of the 1972 October Revitalizing Reforms. It is, therefore, more accurate to say that the Park government was economically pragmatic and politically authoritarian. Furthermore, his authoritarian politics had increasingly taken precedence over the pragmatic economic approach in the final phase of his rule. In that sense, his early pragmatic conservatism had turned into an authoritarian conservatism.

The Chun Doo Hwan Government and Progressive Conservatism

With the demise of the Park regime in 1979, the Chun government (1980-1988) via the Choe Kyu Ha interim administration (October 1979-May 1980)came into power. The ideological orientations of the Chun regime may be marked by progressive conservatism. To begin with, the concept "progressive conservatism," which is contradictory in terms, needs clarification. Ordinarily, what is progressive is not conservative, and vice versa. In this study the term "conservatism" is narrowly defined to mean the idea to oppose communism. In that sense, all the South Korean regimes have been "conservative," including the Chang government, although the latter's ideological orientation is characterized here as "democratism." In other words, all the South Korean regimes have commonly opposed communism (i.e., the North Korean communism), and they have been different from each other only in their manner of dealing with it. Rhee's approach to it was antagonistic, closed and negative; Park's was antagonistic and closed yet positive; Chang's was antagonistic but open and positive; and the Chun's was antagonistic, closed but positive, and it turned out to be the most realistic and flexible with the possible exception of the Roh Tae Woo and Kim Young-sam governments. So much for the caveat.

The Chun government's progressive conservatism consisted of the following elements. First, although anti-communism had survived, the emphasis had been to accommodate rather than to antagonize, unlike the Rhee administration. The policy of accommodating communism had begun during the Park regime in the early 70s.[102] But the Chun government had sought aggressively and actively such accommodation with North Korea, China, the former Soviet Union and other socialist countries in trade, sports and other transactions.

Second, the political spill-over of accommodation toward communism was also manifested in the Chun's unification formula,[103] which was more realistic, flexible and open-ended than those of the previous regimes. Third, a series of liberal measures such as lifting the curfew, removing the school uniforms, easing foreign travels, less restrictive guidelines for students studying abroad and immigration, denationalizing the banking institutions, and gradual yet steady lifting of import restrictions, attested to changes in his ideological orientation. In the final years of his rule, however, the Chun government's liberal trends had taken a slight reversal.[104]

Finally, although the aforementioned three elements are far more progressive than those of the previous administrations, the Chun regime, too, was conservative in that a full and unhindered unification debate on ideology in general and on unification question in particular was not possible. Above all, various security apparatuses such as the National Security and Planning Agency (formerly the KCIA), the Defense Security Command, the Counterinfiltration Operation Command (formerly the Counter-Espionage Operations Command) and the Capital Garrison Command were ready to crack down and silence dissident elements and/ or anti-regime political forces.

The Roh Tae Woo Government and Experimental Liberalism

Unlike the previous regimes, the Roh government came into being in February 1988 through a peaceful and constitutional transfer of power process for the first time since the founding of the Republic in 1948. Although it was a within-party, not a between-party political succession, the political transition from Chun to Roh was a significant step forward in South Korea's political development. Having assumed the presidency amid the global cataclysmic ideological transformation, Roh had to meet two challenges. Internally, he had little choice but to create a new domestic political order, as externally he had to accommodate the coming of a new world order with a denuclearized, post-communist, post-Cold War and post-modern vision.

Under such circumstances South Korea's heretofore core ideological elements such as anti-communism, unification formula, posturing toward the United States and Japan and democracy have all been subject to overall scrutiny and new thinking. The Roh regime's ideological orientation in such undertaking had been, by and large, liberal, albeit tentative and experimental. Specifically, under the Roh regime the political symbol, "anti-communism," had been not simply "open," but the wisdom of clinging to such symbol by the political establishments in the midst of metamorphic changes in the former communist states was questioned and challenged. Externally, the Roh government rather aggressively pursued the so-called *Nordpolitik* (though it had often been done in haste) which had made the anti-communism symbol all but obsolete, if not defunct. The passive and defensive strategy of preventing communism from spreading under the anti-communism slogan was being swiftly replaced by active and even offensive strategy of spreading freedom in those countries where communism had failed. The new name, the Freedom League for the former Anti-Communist League, for example, attested to such shift in orientation and operation. Similarly, the matter of legalizing the communist party raised by Chung Ju-yung, the presidential candidate of the United People's Party, was another sign that South Korea's long-held anti-communist ideological orientation was no longer a political sacred cow.

The unification formula, too, had been open to debate under the Roh regime. His 7 July 1988 Special Declaration which, *inter alia,* advocated the North-South Korean partnership and the new unification formula called the *Han* People's Commonwealth Unification Plan (*han minjok kongdongch'e t'ongil pangan*) of September 11, 1988, set the new stage for the North-South dialogue. Meanwhile, significant progress had been achieved by North Korea and South Korea in laying the institutional groundwork for the eventual realization of a united Korea. The North-South Agreement on Reconciliation, Nonaggression, and Exchanges and Cooperation of December 13, 1991, the Joint Declaration on Denuclearization of the Korean Peninsula of December 31, 1991, the creation and on-going operation of the three executive committees and a commission—the Political Subcommittee, the Military Subcommittee, the Exchange and Cooperation Subcommittee and the Joint Nuclear Control Commission represented positive achievements in such direction.

Moreover, the economic costs, political problems and psychological pains of Germany which is presently undergoing post-unity integration process have significantly affected South Korea's symbolic use of unification formula. On the emotive dimension, the South Korean ruling elites and the masses alike have become far less emotional about unification. On the evaluative dimension, they also have "mixed" feelings about the Korean unification since they are now able to assess both its positive and negative implications and impacts.

Likewise, the cut-throat technology and trade competition, the mounting protectionist pressures, especially from the United States, Japan and Europe, and the reluctance of the advanced nations to transfer scientific and technological know-how to the newly industrializing countries have also seriously affected South Korea's relations with, and orientations toward, these countries, especially the United States and Japan. Consequently, bygone are South Korea's erstwhile emotive and highly simplistic anti- or pro-Americanism and anti- or pro-Japanism. South Korea's posturing towards these countries have now become far more pragmatic, realistic and business-like.

Most importantly, although Roh's leadership had often been characterized as being indecisive, his regime's serious efforts to liberalize and democratize the heretofore authoritarian political system had been, by and large, successful. Ideally, a full-fledged democracy must meet three minimal conditions. First, democratic belief systems should be the prevailing political norms of the ruling elites and the masses. To use the political science parlance, the mass public as well as the elite public must be socialized democratically. Second, both the elites and the masses must advocate democratic values and ideas. Third, they must act in accordance with their advocacy for democratic belief systems. Put it simply, one must *believe, preach* and *practice* democracy.

Theoretically, South Korea's democratic development presently lies somewhere between an anti-authoritarian (the "shouting") stage and a de-authoritarian (the "experimental") stage. The first phase of democratization, which is called here an anti-authoritarian or the shouting stage, manifests a political condition in which the ruling elites continue to practice an authoritarian rule which is resisted openly by the opposition groups and the mass public, vociferously advocating democracy. Despite advocating democracy, the opposition groups have not yet firmly embraced democratic belief systems.

The second phase of democratization—deauthoritarian or the experimental stage starts when both the ruling elites and the opposition, as well as the mass public, begin to question their non-democratic belief systems and to recognize the glaring inconsistency in their advocacy of democracy and in their undemocratic belief systems and behaviors. Largely as a result of the Roh regime's liberalizing and democratizing efforts, the political strifes between the ruling elites and the opposition no longer deal with the former's refusal to initiate democratization and the latter's demand for democracy per se. The government and the opposition are still at loggerheads, but they are concerned more about the speed, the scope and the method of attaining liberalization and democratization.

The final stage of democratization or, specifically, South Korea's full-fledged democracy, a desirable but distant goal, will be realized only when the democratic advocacy, action and belief systems become the prevailing political norms and the proper behavior of the politicians and the people. A full-fledged democracy is, as Arend Lijphart correctly pointed out, "a rare and recent phenomenon." He noted that not a single democratic government existed until the first decade of the twentieth century when two countries, Australia and New Zealand, established fully democratic regimes with firm popular control of governmental institutions and universal suffrage. According to his criteria, only twenty-two countries have been continuously democratic since World War II, and among them only Japan is non-Western.[105]

Higley and Burton, too, presented similar findings—"despite dramatic changes in mass conditions and orientations during the modern historical period, the modal pattern of Western politics was one of persistent elite disunity and resulting regime instability." Their findings may equally and easily fit the patterns of non-Western politics of the same period. Higley, Field and Burton further contended that a key feature of stable democracies is substantial consensus and accommodation among elites on rules of the political game and the worth of political institutions. And they identified three historical routes to elites' consensual unity: special colonial legacies where consensus is achieved prior to national independence; elite settlements, where elites negotiate a deliberate compromise; and two-step elite transformations, where first a consensually-oriented bloc gains stable majority electoral support, and at a later stage a radical minority abandons its distinctive ideological position, adhering to the consensus achieved by its adversaries.[106] Interestingly enough, Higley, Burton and Field noted, though rather perfunctorily, that South Korean elites are apparently moving at present in the direction of what they called "elite convergence."[107] In the final analysis, however, only the passage of time will vindicate whether South Korea is presently undergoing some kind of elite settlement or elite convergence. One thing is self-evident, nevertheless. There is no such thing as a fixed and final form of democracy. As Dahl concludes in his recent work, "the democracy of our successors will not and cannot be the democracy of our predecessors.... For the limits and possibilities of democracy in a world we can already dimly foresee are certain to be radically unlike the limits and possibilities of democracy in any previous time or place."[108]

The Kim Young-sam Government and Civilianization

The launching of the current Kim Young-sam government has several political and ideological implications. By virtually ending the 32 year long military rule from Park Chung Hee to Roh Tae Woo, the Kim government is the first civilian rule since the Chang regime which was toppled by the military coup d'etat in May 1961. The Kim regime is, however, by no means a full-fledged democratic government. It is true that unlike his predecessors Park, Chun and Roh, whose governments had been plagued by the political legitimacy crisis, the Kim government is largely devoid of legitimacy crisis. Still, its democratic rule is in an infantile stage.

The following four criteria may illustrate the degree and level of democracy in the Kim Young-sam government. First, the Kim regime has guaranteed individual citizen's basic freedom and civil rights. In other words, there have been no wanton abuses or violations of citizen's civil liberties and rights.

Second, citizen's democratic belief systems, level of civic, communal political activities and participation, relative autonomy of interest groups and other organizations are, however, still inchoate, due primarily to deep-rooted traditional authoritarian political culture, which had been exacerbated by the prolonged military rule. A democratic citizenship and subgroup autonomy are, in brief, still a goal, not yet a political reality.

Third, as far as the realization of democratic representation is concerned, it, too is in a beginning stage. For the second time, Kim Young-sam succeeded in gaining the presidency peacefully and legitimately through a direct popular election. But Kim won the presidency only by abandoning his long opposition political career overnight and joining hands with the ruling party coalition. That is, like the previous political transition from Chun to Roh, Kim's political leadership succession changed hands within the ruling party, not between the party. To put it another way, South Korea has not yet achieved what the former West Germany realized in 1968 when the opposition Social Democratic Party (SDP) coalition government under Billy Brandt replaced the ruling Christian Democratic Union (CDU). More fundamentally, local political autonomy, which is the bedrock of democracy, is still in its infancy. Under the Roh regime, the county, district, city and provincial legislative assembly have been formed and was put into operation. But the direct election of some 160 county and district magistrates, 15 city mayors and provincial governors are yet to be implemented. Worse still, even if they are fully implemented, the local government will be under the close supervision and control of the national government. For, unlike the former West Germany and/or the United States, South Korea's local autonomy is developing in a reverse order. Namely, instead of the local government creating the central government, it is the national government, which is directing the creation of local autonomy. From this standpoint, South Korea's democracy based on an independent viable local government will not be realized soon.

Finally, the Kim's leadership style and decision-making process are still overwhelmingly authoritarian. To begin with, the present constitution empowers the president with virtually unlimited power and authority. Legally, the president can appoint, promote and reassign low ranking public officials (the 5th grade) to the top county magistrates, city mayors, provincial governors and top administrative officials without legislative hearing or consent and approval with the exception of Prime Minister, the Supreme Court judges, the Constitutional Court judges and the Director of Audit. The constitutionally empowered presidential authority coupled with both deep-seated traditional authoritarian political culture and prolonged military praetorianism have made the current Kim regime a far cry from being a full-pledged democratic government.

In sum, the Kim government is presently moving in a right direction toward more civilianization, democratization and liberalization. Nevertheless, its rule is still in an incipient stage as compared with other advanced democratic nations.

Tentative Assessments

It is clear from the foregoing that North Korea's version of communist experiments characterized by one-party and one-man, now increasingly one-party and father-son dictatorship, has proven to be an abject failure. The present dilemmas of North Korean ruling elites lie not in their inability to find the exit from such failure, but in their realization that such exit leads to the extinction of the very system from which their power is derived. Three options are available to the North Korean ruling elites: system-*defensive,* system-*reforming* and system-*replacing.* At the moment, verbally at least, they are still system-defensive, although they are in a frenzy to locate the ideal formula which is both system-defensive and system-reforming. North Korea's present political, economic and social ills require them to adopt system-replacing practices, not system-defensive and/or system-reforming pretensions. Herein lies the North Korean ruling elites' classic avoidance-accommodation dilemma. Avoiding the system-replacing alternative means the continuation of the present comatose political and economic conditions while accommodating it may result in the instant collapse of the system itself.

Meanwhile, South Korea is in the middle of a fragile democratic experimentation. The political tug of war still continues between the democratic forces which demand a speedier liberalization and democratization and the political establishments whose roots are deeply entrenched in a prolonged authoritarian practices. Unlike the Chang Myŏn government's earlier democratism, attempted and failed under a weak economic base and nearly non-existent civic and social pluralism, South Korea's present liberalization and democratization under the Kim Young-sam government are being undertaken in a far better economic and social settings, let alone in the international milieu. South Korea's road to democracy is bumpy and loaded with unpredictability and uncertainty, but still hopeful.

As Michael Burawoy asserts, what we have been witnessing may not be the collapse of Marxism, but the demise of "state socialism" and "the longevity of capitalism guarantees the longevity of Marxism. They are like the Siamese twins where the demise of the one depends on the demise of the other."[109] Still, North Korea's ideological experiments, whatever they are called, have not only been a simple failure but a human tragedy.

In closing, Marxism, Leninism or even Kim Il Sung's *Juche* idea may be debated in the Ivory Tower in years to came. In the daily life of human world however, as Isaiah Berlin pointed out, "we seek warmth rather than cold, truth rather than falsehood, to be recognized by others for what we are rather than to be ignored or misunderstood." He calls these "universal ethical laws."[110] There are less universal, less profound and less crucial canons. He calls them in descending order of importance, customs, conventions, manners, taste and etiquette, and we not only permit but actively expect wide differences among these. He further advocates that "we do not look on variety as being itself disruptive of our basic unity; it is uniformity that we consider to be the product of a lack of imagination, or of philistinism, and in extreme cases a form of slavery."[111] In descending order of importance, where does ideology stand in Berlin's canons? Perhaps, like religion, the tragedy lies in the claims of ideology, be it communism or democracy, being a universal political canon. Then, like religious toleration, the solution to the present ideological predicament must lie in ideological toleration. From this standpoint, both North Korea's forcible imposition of ideological uniformity upon the masses in the name of *Juche* idea and South Korea's hesitant implementation of democracy are shortsighted and misguided. In the end whatever ideology is called or termed, that which promotes and protects human (and natural) diversity must prevail over the one which seeks inhuman (and unnatural) uniformity. In Berlin's words, "we cannot help accepting (the former)... because we are human."[112]

Notes

1. Karl Marx, *Capital* (Moscow: Progress Publishers, 1976), Vol. 1, p. 340.
2. Aleksandr I. Solzhenitsyn, *The Gulag Archipelago, 1918-1956: An Extremism in Literary Investigation,* trans. Harry Villets (New York: Harper and Row, 1976), Vols. 5-7, p. 28.
3. Hannah Arendt, *The Origins of Totalitarianism* (New York: A Harvest Book, 1968), Pt. 3, p. 166.
4. *Ibid.,* p. 167.
5. M. Seliger, *Ideology and Politics* (New York: The Free Press, 1976), pp. 14-26.
6. *Ibid.,* p. 99.
7. A detailed analysis of Marx and Lenin's conceptions of ideology is found in Walter Carlsnaes, *The Concept of Ideology and Political Analysis: A Critical Examination of Its Usage by Marx, Lenin, and Mannheim* (Westport: Greenwood Press, 1981), pp. 23-169. See also, Seliger, *Op. Cit.,* p. 18, p. 85 and p. 146.
8. Quoted in Seliger, *Op. Cit.,* p. 81.
9. The definitions of political myth, political doctrine and political formula, along with the concepts of ideology and utopia, are found in Harold D. Lasswell and Abraham Kaplan, *Power and Society* (New Haven: Yale University Press, 1963), pp. 116-123.
10. Arendt, *Op. Cit., passim.*
11. For a succinct discussion on the topic by Christoph, King, Helenius, Schurman and Seliger, see Seliger, *Op. Cit.,* pp. 180-184 and p. 321.
12. *Ibid.,* pp. 14-30.
13. Quoted in Seliger, *Op. Cit.,* pp. 38-41.
14. *Ibid.*
15. *Ibid.,* p. 44.
16. *Ibid.,* p. 67.
17. *Ibid.,* p. 36.
18. Henry David Aiken, "The Revolt Against Ideology," in C. I. Waxman, ed., *The End of Ideology Debate,* pp. 229ff and 315ff.
19. Seliger, *Op. Cit.,* p. 17, p. 98 and pp. 119-120.
20. J. LaPalombara, "Decline of Ideology: A Dissent and an Interpretation," *American Political Science Review* 60 (1966). Quoted in Waxman, *Op. Cit.,* p. 276.
21. For details, see Carlsnaes, *Op. Cit.,* especially, pp. 235-246.
22. M. Rejai, *et al.,* "Empirical Relevance of the Hypothesis of Decline" in M. Rejai, ed., *Decline of Ideology* (Chicago, 1971), p. 269. Quoted in Carlsnaes,

Op. Cit., p. 238. Istvan Meszaros, *The Power of Ideology* (New York: New York University Press, 1989), p. 10.

23. For details, see Sung Chul Yang, "Political Ideology, Myth and Symbols in Korean Politics," *Asian Forum* (July-September 1972), pp. 30-43.
24. *Ibid.*
25. For details, see Sung Chul Yang, "Ideology in South and North Korea," in Sejin Kim and Chang-hyon Cho, eds., *Korea: A Divided Nation* (Silver Springs: The Research Institute on Korean Affairs, 1976), p. 226.
26. Evidently, Destutt de Tracy (1754-1836), a French scholar, originated the term, ideology. For a discussion of the origin of the term, see Leon P. Baradat, *Political Ideologies: Their Origins and Impact* (Englewood Cliffs: Prentice-Hall, 1976), pp. 30-47.
27. Frederick Engels, *Socialism: Utopian and Scientific* (New York: International Publishers, 1935), p. 53. Also, Karl Marx, *Capital: A Critical Analysis of Capitalist Production* (Moscow: Progress Publishers, 1975), Vol. 1.
28. I have dealt with this subject elsewhere. See the author's article, "Communism and Korean Communism: A Juxtapositional Comparison," paper delivered at the conference on "Accommodation of Communism in Asia," 1986 Seoul, Korea, 16-17 August 1986.
29. Gaetano Mosca, *The Ruling Class*, trans. Hanah Kahn (NewYork: McGraw-Hill, 1939), p. 50.
30. Quoted in Heinz Eulau and Moshe M. Czudnowski, eds., *Elite Recruitment in Democratic Politics: Comparative Studies Across Nations* (New York: Sage Publications, 1976), p. 23.
31. Vilfredo Pareto, *The Mind and Society* (Trattato di Sociologia General), trans. Andrew Bongiorno and Arthur Livingston (New York: Harcourt, Brace and Co., 1935), Vol. 3, p. 1569.
32. Robert Michels, *Political Parties: A Sociological Study of the Oligarchical Tendencies of Modern Democracy*, trans. Cedar Paul (Glencoe: The Free Press, 1915, 1949), p. 63.
33. Mosca, *Op. Cit.*, p. 416.
34. Michels, *Op. Cit.*, p. 142 and p. 35.
35. *Ibid.*, p. 390
36. *Ibid.*, pp. 390-391.
37. *Marx and Engels Reader*, ed. Robert C. Tucker (New York: W. W. Norton, 1972), p. 406.
38. Suzanne Keller, *Beyond the Ruling Class: Strategic Elites in Modern Society* (New York: Random House, 1963), p. 58.
39. *Ibid.*, pp. 276-278.
40. For details, see Thomas Dye, "Identifying Change in Elite Structure," paper delivered at the 1982 Annual Meeting of the American Political Science

Association, 2-5 September 1982. See also his, *Who's Running America* (New York: Prentice-Hall, 1976).

41. C. W. Mills, *The Power Elite* (New York: Oxford University Press, 1956).

42. Robert A. Dahl, *Who Governs* (New Haven: Yale University Press, 1961). See also his, "Critique of the Ruling Elite Model," *American Political Science Review* (June 1958), pp. 463-469. Robert A. Dahl, *Democracy and Its Critics* (New Haven: Yale University Press, 1989), p. 279.

43. Philip Stewart *et al.*, "Political Mobility and the Soviet Political Process," *American Political Science Review* 66 (December 1972): 1269-1290. John D. Nagle, ed., *System and Succession: The Social Bases of Political Elite Recruitment* (Austin: University of Texas Press, 1977). Also, Ronald H. Linden and Bert A. Rockman, *Elite Studies and Communist Politics* (Pittsburgh: University of Pittsburgh Press, 1985).

44. For details, see Nagle, *Op. Cit.*, pp. 183-226. The views of Djilas and Stojanovic are found in Milovan Djilas, "The New Class," in A. Mendel, ed., *Essential Works of Marxism* (New York: Bantam Books, 1961) and Svetozar Stojanovic, *Between Ideals and Reality: A Critique of Socialism and Its Future,* trans. Gerson S. Sher (New York: Oxford University Press, 1973), respectively.

45. Nagle, *Op. Cit.*, p. 226.

46. William A. Welsh, *Leaders and Elites* (New York: Rinehart and Winston, 1979), pp. 122-141.

47. *Ibid.*, p. 1.

48. Maurice Duverger, *Political Parties: Their Organization and Activity in the Modern State* (New York: Wiley, 1963), p. 151. See also, William R. Schonfeld, "Oligarchy and Leadership Stability: The French Communist, Socialist, and Gaullist Parties," *American Journal of Political Science* (May 1981), pp. 215-240.

49. G. Lowell Field and John Higley, "The States of National Elites and the Stability of Political Institutions in 81 Nations, 1950-1982," paper delivered at the 1982 Annual Meeting of the American Political Science Association, Denver, Colorado, 2-5 September 1982. See also, John Higley and M. G. Burton, "The Elite Variable in Democratic Transitions and Breakdowns," *American Sociological Review* 54 (1989): 17-32; J. Higley and G. L. Field, "In Defense of Elite Theory," *American Sociological Review* 55 (1990): 421-426.

50. Quoted in William Ebenstein, ed., *Great Political Thinkers* (New York: Holt, Rinehart & Winston, 1969), p. 468.

51. Quoted in Giovanni Sartori, "Anti-Elitism Revisited" *Government and Opposition* 13 (Winter 1978): 63-64.

52. *Marx and Engels Reader,* p. 344.

53. Pareto, *Op. Cit.*, Vol. 3, p. 973.

54. James R. Townsend, *Politics in China* (Boston: Little, Brown and Co., 1980), pp. 31-52.

55. Quoted in Richard Pipes, *Survival is Not Enough: Soviet Realities and America's Future* (New York: Simon and Schuster, 1984), p. 31. Pipes himself estimated that the number of *nomenklatura* together with their families and other dependents may be 3 million, or less than 1.5 percent of the total population. Medish, meanwhile, estimated that the ruling elites of the Communist Party of the Soviet Union (CPSU) are about a million. They are divided into approximately a quarter of a million party functionaries or *apparatchiks* (e.g., the executives of the party machine) and three-quarters of a million high-ranking party members (e.g., executives within the civil administration, the national economy, the armed forces, police, diplomats, political officers and journalists). For details, see Vadim Medish, *The Soviet Union,* 2nd ed. (Englewood Cliffs: Prentice-Hall, 1984), pp. 88-90.

56. Thomas Dye, *Op. Cit.*

57. Pareto, *Op. Cit.*, Vol. 1, p. 169.

58. Michels, *Op. Cit.*, p. 121.

59. *Ibid.*, p. 184.

60. *Ibid.*, p. 402.

61. Michels, *Archiv fuer Sozialwissenschaft und Sozialpolitik,* Vol. 27, pp. 130-131. Quoted in David Beetham, "From Socialism to Fascism: The Relation Between Theory and Practice in the Works of Robert Michels," *Political Studies* 25 (March 1977): 13.

62. For details, see Sartori, "Anti-Elitism Revisited," pp. 58-79.

63. *Idem.*

64. Quoted in Eulau and Czudnowski, *Op. Cit.*, p. 21.

65. *Idem.*

66. Sartori, *Op. Cit.*, p. 71.

67. Field and Higley, *Op. Cit.*, pp. 11-12.

68. For a discussion of the meaning of political symbols, see S. C. Yang, "Political Ideology, Myth and Symbols in Korean Politics," especially, pp. 31-32.

69. An analysis of the *Juche* idea is found in S. C. Yang, *Korea and Two Regimes,* pp. 197-205.

70. For an overall analysis of Kim's power struggles within the WPK, see Yang, *Korea and Two Regimes,* pp. 183-188.

71. There are virtually dozens of North Korean official publications on Kim's *Juche* idea. To cite just a few: Chang Ha Kim, *The Immortal Juche Idea* (Pyongyang: Foreign Languages Publishing House [FLPH], 1984); *Juche: The Banner of Independence* (Pyongyang: FLPH, 1977); Kim Il Sung, *On Juche In Our Revolution* (Pyongyang: FLPH, 1975), Vol. 1.

72. See, for instance, Kim Il Sung, *On the Juche Idea* (Excerpts) (New York: The Guardian, 1980), pp. 205-231.

73. For a discussion of *Ch'ŏllima Undong* and *Ch'ŏngsan-ri spirit*, see S. C. Yang, *Korea and Two Regimes,* pp. 197-203. Kim Jŏng Il's new slogans are found in In Su Choe, *Kim Jŏng Il* (Pyongyang: FLPH, 1985), pp. 249-254.

74. *Ibid.*

75. Kim Il Sung, *On the Building of the People's Government* (Pyongyang: FLPH, 1978), Vol. 1, p. 275.

76. The so-called tripartite talk proposal was made by a joint meeting of Central People's Committee and Standing Committee of the Supreme People's Assembly of DPRK on January 10, 1984. For details, see the chapter on Korean unification.

77. Kim Il Sung, *On Some Problems of Our Party's Juche Idea and the Government of the Republic's Internal and External Policies,* a pamphlet (Pyongyang: FLPH, 1972). Also, Kim Il Sung, *Revolution and Socialist Construction in Korea: Selected Writings of Kim Il Sung* (New York: International Publishers, 1971), pp. 87-98.

78. Mussolini's formula is found in Ernst Nolte, *Three Faces of Fascism* (New York: Holt, Rinehart and Winston, 1966), p. 421ff. For a discussion of Lenin's "iron discipline," see Carl J. Friedrich, "The Failure of a One-Party System," in Samuel P. Huntington and B. Moore, eds., *Authoritarianism in Modern Society* (New York: Basic Books, 1970) p. 248.

79. Communism as a theory is class-antognistic, and Fascism, class-integrative. For details, see Carl J. Friedrich and Zbigniew K. Brzezinski, *Totalitarian Dictatorship and Autocracy* (New York: Praeger, 1961), p. 2.

80. For a detailed discussion on this topic, see S. C. Yang, "The Politics of Cult in North Korea," *Political Studies Review* 1 (1985): 27-52.

81. Max Beloff, *The Intellectual in Politics and Other Essays* (New York: The Liberty Press, 1971), p. 242.

82. Bertrand Russell, "Dialectical Materialism," in *The Basic Writings of Bertrand Russell,* ed. Robert E. Egner and Lester E. Denonn (New York: Simon and Schuster, 1967), pp. 500-510.

83. For details, see Kim Il Sung, *On the Building of the People's Government* (Pyongyang: FLPH, 1978), Vols. 1 and 2.

84. A full discussion of the North and South Korean unification proposals is found in the chapter on the unification question.

85. Shils, for one, coined the term "opposition mentality" to describe the third world political leaders' inability to distinguish their own political enemies from the enemies of the state. See Edward Shils, "The Intellectuals in Political Development," John H. Kautsky, ed., *Political Change in Underdeveloped Countries: Nationalism and Communism* (New York: John Wiley and

Sons, 1962), p. 229.

86. For details, see *Hapdong Nyŏngam, 1960 (Seoul: Hapdong News Agency, 1960)*, p. 84. Also, Gregory Henderson, *Korea: The Politics of the Vortex* (Cambridge: Harvard University Press, 1968), p. 215.

87. The South Korean official unification proposal is found in *Korean Unification* (Seoul: Ministry of Public Information, 1965). See also, *The 1954 Geneva Conference, Indochina and Korea* (New York: Greenwood Press, 1968), pp. 53-54.

88. For details, see S. C. Yang, *Korea and Two Regimes*, pp. 240-244.

89. Quoted in Byung-ki Min, "Problems in Korean-Japanese Relations," *Koreana Quarterly* 4 (Spring 1964): 44.

90. For a discussion of issues involving the Korea-Japan normalization talks, see David C. Cole and Princeton N. Lyman, *Korean Development: The Interplay of Politics and Economics* (Cambridge: Harvard University Press, 1971), pp. 98-118.

91. For a discussion of the Chang government's economic development planning, see Hahn-been Lee, *Korea: Time, Change and Administration* (Honolulu: East-West Press, 1968), pp. 82-133.

92. Ernst Barker, *The Political Thought of Plato and Aristotle* (New York: Dover Publications, 1959), p. 175.

93. *Korea Annual, 1966* (Seoul: Hapdong News Agency, 1966), p. 113.

94. Sang-cho Shin, "The April Revolution as Democratic Revolution" (in Korean), *Sawŏl Hyŏkmyŏng* (Seoul: Chŏngu-sa, 1965), p. 147.

95. Giovanni Sartori, "Politics, Ideology, and Belief Systems," *The American Political Science Review* 63 (June 1969): 403.

96. For details, see S. C. Yang, *Korea and Two Regimes*, pp. 271-277. Also, Part Three of this book.

97. For details, see Chapter Ten on Developmentalism and Dependency.

98. *Ibid.* See also, S. C. Yang, *Korea and Two Regimes*, pp. 252-256.

99. *Ibid.*, pp. 240-244.

100. *Idem.*

101. *Idem.*

102. President Park Chung Hee's Special Foreign Policy Statement on June 23, 1973, was the prime example. In it he stated that "the Republic of Korea will open its door to all the nations of the world on the basis of the principles of reciprocity and equality. At the same time, we urge those countries whose ideologies and social institutions are different from ours to open their doors likewise to us." For details, see *A White Paper on South-North Dialogue in Korea* (Seoul: The South-North Coordinating Committee, 1979), especially, pp. 362-366.

103. A full text of South Korea's unification proposal is found in the *Hankuk Ilbo*

on January 25, 1982, and the *Korea Herald* carried its English version on
January 23, 1982. South Korea's twenty-point proposal in Korean and
English is found in both *Hankuk Ilbo* and the *Korea Herald,* 3 February
1982. For a comparative analysis of the North Korean Democratic Confederal Republic of Korea plan (1980) and the South Korean Unified Democratic
Republic of Korea plan (1982), see S. C. Yang, "Nationalism and Reunification: The Korean Case," *Journal of East and West Studies* 12 (Fall-Winter
1983): 115-139.

104. A series of decision to reduce the maximum amount of foreign currency that
the Korean travelers can carry overseas, to set new regulations for students
who plan to study abroad, to restore the school uniform to the secondary
school students and to enact (though abortive) a campus regulation act, e.g.,
student reeducation camp, are the examples.

105. Arend Lijphart, *Democracies: Patterns of Majoritarian and Consensus
Government in Twenty-One Countries* (New Haven: Yale University Press,
1984), p. 37.

106. Higley and Burton, *Op. Cit.* (1989), p. 22 and p. 25.

107. Higley, Field and Burton, *Op. Cit.* (1990), p. 425.

108. Robert A. Dahl, *Op. Cit.* (1989), p. 340.

109. Michael Burawoy, "Marxism as Science: Historical Challenges and Theoretical Growth," *American Sociological Review* 55 (December 1990): 792.

110. Isaiah Berlin, *The Crooked Timber of Humanity: Chapters in the History of
Ideas* (New York: Vintage Books, 1992), p. 204.

111. *Ibid.,* p. 205.

112. *Ibid.,* p. 204.

PART III

THE NORTH KOREAN POLITICAL SYSTEM: A TOTALITARIAN POLITICAL ORDER

CHAPTER 6

THE NORTH KOREAN
POLITICAL FRAMEWORK

Utopian socialism differed from "scientific" socialism in degree rather than in kind.

Joseph A. Schumpeter[1]

"When I think about socialism, the image that comes to mind is an abyss between ideology and its implementation," another (Polish high school senior) student wrote.... The imprint on Central-Eastern Europe of 40 years of socialism is nothing like what communism's intellectual founder, Karl Marx, had in mind. His utopian ideology has been virtually obliterated as a motivating force.

Dan Fisher[2]

Approaches to the Study of North Korean Politics

Directly and indirectly, the current North Korean political system is greatly impaired by the collapse or, more accurately, the metamorphoses of communism in Eastern Europe and the former Soviet Union, not to mention the Chinese economic reform, which began more than a decade earlier.

The presently on-going metamorphosis of communism differs fundamentally from the earlier reform initiatives led by Tito and Khrushchev, or Deng Xiaoping, for that matter.[3] If the early reform or revisionist efforts were the political and/or economic measures to correct the wrongs of communist experiments without questioning the basic tenets of orthodox Marxism and Leninism, the present transformation of erstwhile socialist countries in Eastern Europe and the former Soviet Union began with the sober realization that some 70-year old Marxist-Leninist political and economic experiments have abjectly failed. In brief, if the earlier reform or revisionist measures were communist *system-defensive*, the present changes are *system-replacing*. A towering irony is that contrary to the orthodox Marxian materialistic interpretations of history, the current transition is from socialism to capitalism, not the reverse. Whether we distinguish, as Burawoy asserts, Marxism from "Soviet Marxism, its most degenerate form," and further separate "the demise of state socialism" from "the viability of Marxist project,"[4] the direction and the content of political and economic changes in the former Soviet Union and Eastern Europe certainly resemble the embroynic forms of democratic pluralism and free market system.

The four remaining communist countries—China, Vietnam, North Korea and Cuba—are still clinging, officially at least, to the "socialist path," but in reality they, too, have been changing. China since the late 1970s and Vietnam since the late 1980s have cast off their erstwhile militant revolutionary paths, although their one-party political dictatorship still sputters along. Meanwhile, only two founder-rulers, North Korea's Kim Il Sung and Cuba's Fidel Castro, appear more defiant in rhetoric, but they, too, are at a crossroads. The question, then, is will a defiant communist "gang of four" survive or will it sooner or later meet the same fate as the fallen communist stars in Eastern Europe and the former Soviet Union? Ex post facto explanations for the collapse of communism abound, though a priori expositions for the future of these remaining four are scanty.

For example, the October 1991 issue of *World Politics* dealt with the demise of communism in Eastern Europe and the former Soviet Union, but none of the six authors in this issue raised, let alone, explained, the reasons for the apparent durability of the four remaining communist states. Some common features these four share can be illuminated as the partial explanations for their regime durability. First, their communist victory, with the exception of North Korea, was primarily *indigenous*. The communist regime in North Korea, like the former communist states in Eastern Europe came into being under the auspices of the Soviet military occupation authorities. Kim Il Sung was not a simple Soviet puppet, however. All the absurd exaggerations and outright fabrications aside, Kim had some ten years of verifiable anti-Japanese guerrilla activity, which is a respectable credential, necessary, if not sufficient, for his rule. The Comintern and/or the former Soviet Union directly and/or indirectly assisted these four nations to achieve communist triumph, but again with the exception of North Korea, they won the communist victory primarily by the protracted internal struggle.

Second, except for Cuba, all three Asian communist states possess a long tradition of "Oriental despotism." To that extent, Western democratic ideas and political traditions are relatively new and alien to their political history. To put it differently, a lack of traditions in either democratic political experiences and experimentation or in democratic thoughts and movements in these countries, as compared with their Eastern European and the former Soviet counterparts, is glaring.

Thirdly, all three remaining Asian communist states except Cuba have deep-rooted Buddhist and Confucian traditions. Christianity, too, was introduced in these countries but it was, like democratic ideas and thought, a relatively modern addition to their old religious practices and belief systems.

Finally, again with the exception of Cuba, their geographic contiguity, let alone their relatively intimate historical, cultural and ethnic affinity need to be pointed out. The traditional Chinese center-periphery framework -- "middle kingdom-barbarian states" -- has now been replaced by the new claims of the communist patron-client arrangement.[5] The Chinese proclivity to claim her hegemony in the region stems indeed from such deep-rooted historical legacy. The erstwhile Sino-Soviet and Sino-Vietnamese conflicts and military flare-ups can be also understood from this perspective. It further implies that as long as the present Chinese political system persists, so will the Vietnamese and the North Korean system. For, it is unlikely that China will sit idle or do nothing while her two last remaining "fraternal" contiguous socialist states meet with their political extinction. Presently, the "Long Marchers," including Deng, are being replaced by the second and third generation leaders in China, and similar generational leadership changes are occurring in Vietnam and North Korea. Doubtlessly, the uncertainties and unpredictability surrounding these leadership changes and the manner in which the new leadership will ultimately emerge and their policy direction will have enormous implications. For the time being, however, the North Korean political system under the father-son power succession scheme persists rather precariously.

Pro-North Korean propaganda materials, published and disseminated by the North Korean publishing houses, abound. Numerous also are anti-North Korean publications printed in South Korea. Amid the flood of pro-and anti-North Korean propaganda materials and "studies," scholarly and objective analysis of the North Korean political system is meager. Four approaches to the study of North Korean political system are here identified. They are historiographic studies, factionalist models, system analysis and totalitarian approaches.

By far the most numerous are the historiographic studies on the North Korean political system. This approach is basically historical and descriptive. The trailblazing works by Chang-sun Kim, Dae-sook Suh, Chong-sik Lee and others are notable.[6] This approach is, by definition, rich in historical details but lacks explicit analytic framework and/or rigor. Still, the contributions of the historiographic studies are significant in that they serve as the basic materials for more rigorous analytic studies.

Factionalism as an explanatory model of the North Korean politics is nothing new. As noted in the discussion of the Korean political heritage in Part One, it is one of the salient features of Korean politics. Factionalist approaches may vary among scholars in their emphasis and interpretations. Some see factions and factionalism in North Korean politics as the product of peculiar Korean political culture in particular and the Confucian political culture in general.[7] Others view it as a variant of political conflict among power elites.[8] While the former stresses certain cultural and social traits of groups and individuals, the latter focuses on the dynamics of power itself. Still others interpret factionalism as a by-product of communist political culture.[9] These variations notwithstanding, the factionalist approaches are by definition limited in that they may be able to explain the political behavior of the ruling elites in North Korea (and South Korea) but cannot analyze the North Korean political system *in toto.*

The systems approaches denote here the studies on North Korean politics which apply the systems model.[10] Unlike the factionalist model, the systems approaches *can* explain the North Korean political system as a whole in a coherent and comprehensive manner, but they are liable to underestimate both the peculiarities of the North Korean political system and the unique attributes of the communist political system. Still, the studies on the North Korean politics based on the systems approaches, though very few in number, are by far the most analytic and rigorous.[11]

Finally, the totalitarian model is viewed here as one of the two prototypes of contemporary dictatorship. It, along with the authoritarian model, are theoretically explicit but, at the same time, susceptible to *a posteriori* value-judgement by the users. In the closing chapter of the present study, a comprehensive survey of both the totalitarian and authoritarian models is provided. In the present chapter, therefore, only the fundamental features common in contemporary totalitarian dictatorship and some conspicuous elements in the present North Korean political system are probed in some detail.

Totalitarianism as a Model

The North Korean political system represents the prototype of Wiatr's *monoparty* system or Sartori's *totalitarian unipartism* in that only the Workers Party of Korea (WPK) is legally permitted to exist and to control the political process.[12] On paper, there are two other "fraternal parties" in North Korea—the Ch'ŏndoist Ch'ŏng-u Party and the Korean Social Democratic Party—and, thus, the WPK appears to belong to Wiatr's *hegemonic* party category since these two fraternal parties, which do not contest elections, are permitted to exist. In reality, the WPK *is* the only party that governs North Korea and these fraternal "parties" along with other para-political organizations have been nothing more than the WPK's propaganda outfits (See Table 6-1).

In socialist states the opposition parties are either outlawed or eclipsed by the ruling parties. As Rush aptly pointed out, while communist politics does not sanction an *opposition*, a group that stands just outside the portals of power and actively restrains the government, it cannot always prevent the existence of an *alternative* to the government, a group of prestigious individual that stands ready to replace the government and has a basis of support.[13] Since the late 1960s in North Korea, even such an alternative has virtually disappeared. Ever since Kim Il Sung took power in the North, he has purged actual and potential political rivals within the WPK. By the late 1960's, all factions—the Soviet Group, the Yanan Group, the Workers' Party of South Korea Group and the Domestic Group—had been eliminated except for his own Partisan Group within the WPK. From this standpoint, the WPK's 1980 decision to groom Kim Il Sung's eldest son, Kim Jŏng Il (1942-   ), as the official successor to his father can be seen, among other things, as an attempt to fill the political vacuum, which will be created sooner or later by the death of senior Kim (1912-   ).

North Korea shares several basic features with other erstwhile socialist countries. It also possesses unique political characteristics and practices which deviate significantly from its former fraternal socialist countries. First, in this chapter some common elements as well as unique features of the present North Korean political system will be identified and examined in detail. In the following chapter, the key political institutions of the North Korean political system, i.e., the WPK, the Supreme People's Assembly (SPA), the Administration Council, the Central Court and the Central Procurator's Office will be analyzed. In so doing, the present power structures of these institutions as well as their evolutionary changes in the past forty years will be also explicated.

Common Elements: Promise versus Practice

Variations and deviances notwithstanding, the present North Korean political system is inherently a totalitarian socialist state. As in the remaining socialist countries, the governing party, the WPK, is *the official* party and no other parties are permitted to compete in political arena. No other political ideas or ideologies are allowed to circulate except the governing ideology sanctioned by the WPK, i.e., Marxism-Leninism, and the Kim Il Sungism. At the symbolic core of the Kim Il Sungism stands the *Juche* [self-reliance] idea according to the 1992 revised DPRK Socialist Constitution (Article 3).

The WPK's control of the armed forces, public security and intelligence apparatus, mass media and mass communication, education and para-political mass organizations is nearly complete. The state ownership of the means of production and the centralized economic planning, management, production, investment and distribution are the elements that North Korea shares in common with other former socialist fraternal countries. Amid the demise of Communist states, in the former Soviet Union, Eastern Europe, and the reforming China, North Korea, too, has been modifying its rigid totalitarian control, especially in economic area. Still, no concrete reforms, comparable to China's Deng programs, are yet visible and/or feasible.

Specifically, eight features that North Korea shares with other socialist countries are identified below.

1. Marxism-Leninism

All socialist countries past or present have once declared Marxism-Leninism as their all-encompassing official ideology. The seven other features, in fact, delineate Marxism-Leninism. Marxism-Leninism includes, among other things, the dictatorship of the proletariat, the socialist ownership of the means of production, class struggle, the collectivist principle, the leading and guiding role of the communist party, the principle of democratic centralism, the new socialist way of life and the proletarian internationalism.[14] Invariably, all past and present socialist countries, including North Korea, have incorporated Marxism-Leninism into their constitution as the founding and operational ideology of their socialist systems. The former Soviet Union was the prototype. Its 1977 Constitution proclaims that the Communist Party of the former Soviet Union, which is "the leading and guiding force of Soviet society and the nucleus of its political system and of all state organizations and public organizations," is "armed with Marxism-Leninism" (Article 6).

The 1972 DPRK Constitution stated that North Korea "is guided in its activity by the *Juche* (self-reliance) idea of the Workers' Party of Korea, a creative application of Marxism-Leninism to the conditions of our country" (Article 4). This particular declaration serves dual functions. North Korea can cling to the basic tenets of Marxism-Leninism. At the same time, the current Kim Il Sung-Kim Jŏng Il regime can justify (and has justified) any political practices deviant from the orthodox Marxism-Leninism in the name of the *Juche* idea. Similarly, the Preamble to the 1982 Chinese Constitution proclaims that the Chinese people of all nationalities are "under the leadership of the Communist Party of China and the guidance of Marxism-Leninism and Mao Zedong Thought." Like Kim Il Sung's *Juche* idea, the Mao Zedong Thought was utilized as a rationale for political experiments divergent from the orthodox communism, as China had amply demonstrated, particularly during the cultural revolution of the mid-60s to the early 70s. However, as shown below, the so-called *Juche* idea has gradually replaced Marxism-Leninism in North Korean propaganda rhetoric. Marxism-Leninism is now officially abandoned in the revised 1992 Constitution and is no longer uttered in public. In Article 3 of the 1992 Constitution simply states that "The Democratic People's Republic of Korea makes Juche ideology, a revolutionary ideology with a people-centered view of the world...."

2. The Socialist Rules of Conduct

The North Korean Constitution includes a chapter on "Fundamental Rights and Duties of Citizens," which shows a remarkable resemblance to the same chapters in the present Chinese and the former Soviet constitutions. After listing the rights of the citizens—the right to work, the right to rest and leisure, health protection, housing, education and others —all three constitutions include the following rather bone-chilling "duties" of their citizens:

> Citizens must strictly observe the laws of the State and the *socialist norms of life and the socialist rules of conduct* (Article 81 of the 1992 DPRK Constitution).
>
> Work is the glorious duty of every able-bodied citizen. All working people in state enterprises and in urban and rural economic collectives should perform their tasks with an attitude consonant with their status as masters of the country. The state promotes *socialist labour* emulation, and commends and rewards model and advanced workers... (Article 42 of the 1982 PRC Constitution).
>
> Citizens' exercise of their rights and freedoms is inseparable from the performance of their duties and obligations. Citizens of the [former] USSR are obliged to observe the Constitution of the USSR and Soviet laws, comply with the standards of *socialist conduct*, and uphold the honour and dignity of Soviet citizenship (Article 59 of the 1977 USSR Constitution).

The catch in North Korean, Chinese and Soviet citizens' rights and freedom (for that matter, in all past and present socialist countries) lies in this ubiquitous "sponge" phrases—"socialist rules of conduct," "socialist labour" or "socialist norms of life." The state (party) control of the citizens' norms of socialist conduct means, in essence, that the individual citizens have no freedom either in the sense of an absence of external control or in the sense of a capacity to act. The state, i.e., the party, determines and defines what is and should be the proper socialist rules of conduct, not the individual citizens. The North Korean Constitution is far more categorical in this regard: "The State eliminates the way of life left over from the old society and introduces the new socialist way of life in all fields" (Article 42).

In exchange for the state's guarantee of work, housing, education and public health, the citizens have surrendered their power to decide on such intrinsically personal matters as where to work, where to live, what to know and what to learn. In brief, the loss or absence of fundamental human freedoms as a direct result of the state control of the socialist rules of individual conduct stands out as one of the most conspicuous common denominators of all the past and present Communist states.

3. The Socialist Economic System

North Korea is a socialist state (Article 1, the 1992 Socialist Constitution of the DPRK). It is founded upon the socialist relations of production and the self-reliant national economy (Article 19). Thus, the state "defends the socialist system against the subversive activities of hostile elements at home and abroad" (Article 12). The DPRK Constitution is replete with such socialist phraseology as "building of socialism," "accelerates socialist construction," "develops socialist property" and others. These constitutional stipulations of socialism are virtually identical to those of the other socialist fraternal countries. Both the 1977 USSR Constitution and the 1982 Constitution of the People's Republic of China (PRC), for example, declare that their states are founded on socialism (cf. the 1977 USSR Constitution, Article 1 and the 1982 PRC Constitution, Article 1).

In theory, socialism as an economic system in socialist countries parallels capitalism in Western democratic states. In concrete terms, the North Korean economy is planned and managed by the state, i.e., the WPK, and the means of production are owned by the state and cooperative organizations. The state ownership of property is unlimited. All natural resources of the country, major factories and enterprises, ports, banks, transport and communication establishments are owned solely by the state (Article 21). On a limited scale, cooperative organizations still own land, animals, farm implements, fishing boats, buildings, as well as small and medium-sized factories and enterprises. But the state has been developing the socialist cooperative economic system and transforming the property of the cooperative organizations into the property of the state. The right of private ownership, thus, does not exist in North Korea. The personal property is limited to their earnings from work and other benefits such as the small garden plots granted by the state. Since Part Five will examine the North Korean economic system and its performance in greater detail, it suffices to mention here that the North

Korean economic system exemplifies a typical socialist command economy despite some marginal economic changes and reforms since the early 1980's.[15]

4. Dictatorship of the Proletariat

Consistent with Marxism, the North Korean political system has adopted the dictatorship of the proletariat as its symbolic cornerstone. Article 4 of the 1992 DPRK Constitution proclaims that the sovereignty of the DPRK "rests with the workers, peasants, soldiers and working intellectuals." Further, it stipulates that the working people exercise power through their representative organs—the Supreme People's Assembly (SPA) and local People's Assemblies at all levels. In reality, the WPK ruling circles exercise power in the name of the people, and these representative organs are nothing but their rubber stamp. Article 10 is even more direct: the DPRK "exercises the dictatorship of the proletariat and pursues class and mass lines." Similar pronouncements—the "people's democratic dictatorship" (Article 1 of the PRC Constitution) and "the dictatorship of the proletariat" (Preamble to the 1977 USSR Constitution)—in the past and present socialist constitutions are rather commonplace.

In practice, the principle of the proletarian dictatorship has become the dictatorship of the WPK, and the proletariats—workers, peasants, soldiers and working intellectuals—are not the sovereign masters. The proletariats have simply become its (Party's) *human* instruments. In the process of implementing the principle of proletarian dictatorship, *dictatorship* has managed to continue, but not the *proletarian* dictatorship. In North Korea, the proletariats are not the masters of revolution and construction, as its official propaganda constantly declares. Rather, they have become the subjects of one-party-father-son dictatorship.

5. Leadership of the Communist Party

In *What Is To Be Done* (1902), Lenin juxtaposes the spontaneity of the masses and the consciousness of the party members (i.e., the Russian

Social-Democrats) and urges the necessity for the organization of "professional revolutionaries," i.e., the Communist Party. He contends that: (1) no revolutionary movement can endure without a stable organization of leaders maintaining continuity; (2) broader the popular mass drawn spontaneously into the struggle, more urgent the need for such organization because all sorts of demagogues try to sidetrack the more backward sections of the masses; (3) such an organization must consist chiefly of professional revolutionaries; and (4) it should be manned mainly by the working class.[16] Thus, his idea of the communist party as the vanguard of the masses was born.

Article 11 of the DPRK Constitution states that North Korea is guided by the WPK. Similarly, the leading role of the communist party as the vanguard of the people is prefaced in the preambles of both the Chinese and the former Soviet constitutions. Contrary to Lenin's assertion of the spontaneity of the masses, the North Korean people have never been *spontaneously* drawn into the struggle. Rather, they have been *mobilized* by the WPK for its socialist construction and revolution. The WPK is not merely the leader or the vanguard of the masses, but the only party organization in the North Korean political arena. It represents an example of monoparty or unipartism. Paradoxically, therefore, the communist party, which began as the party of "immense majority" to end the exploitation of the masses by the minority, be it the bourgeoisie or the feudal landlords, has become the party of minority only in the name of the majority working class. In essence, the exploitation of the working class has not ended in the remaining socialist countries. Above all, the communist parties in the socialist countries are also the party of tiny minority. What has changed in these countries is only the rhetoric, not the fate of the majority of the working class people. The North Korean working masses have been suffering from the same Orwellian double-talk.

6. The Principle of Democratic Centralism

The WPK has adopted Lenin's idea of democratic centralism[17] as its decision making and organizational principle of government (Article 5). The bylaws of the WPK (Chapter II, Article 11) states that the party is organized on the principle of democratic centralism:

(a) Every leadership organization of the party shall be democratically elected, and the elected leadership organization shall report its work periodically to party organizations.

(b) Party members shall obey the party organizations, the minority shall obey the majority, the lower party organizations shall obey the higher party organizations, and all party organizations shall absolutely obey the Central Committee of the party.

(c) All party organizations should unconditionally support and carry out the party line and policies, and the lower party organizations must execute dutifully the decisions of the higher party organizations. The higher party organizations shall systematically direct and inspect the work of the lower party organizations, and the lower party organizations shall periodically report their work to the higher party organizations.

With some minor variations, virtually all socialist countries have incorporated democratic centralism into their systems as the decision making and organizational guidelines. The Chinese Communist Party (CCP) has upheld the principle of democratic centralism, which is almost identical to the WPK's. The Constitution of the Chinese Communist Party adopted by the 12th National Congress on September 6, 1982, for instance, specifies six rules of the principle of democratic centralism (Chapter II, Article 10):

(a) An individual Party member is subordinate to the Party organizations, the minority is subordinate to the majority, the lower Party organizations are subordinate to the higher Party organizations, and all the constituent organizations and members of the Party are subordinate to the National Congress and the Central Committee of the Party.

(b) The Party's leading bodies at all levels are elected except for the representative organs dispatched by them and the leading Party members' groups in non-Party organizations.

(c) The highest leading body of the Party is the National Congress and the Central Committee elected by it. The leading bodies of local Party organizations are the Party congresses at their respective levels and the Party committees elected by them.

(d) Higher Party organizations shall pay constant attention to the views of the lower organizations and the rank-and-file members. Lower Party organizations shall report their work to higher Party organizations.

Higher and lower Party organizations should exchange information and support and supervise each other.

(e) Party committees at all levels function on the principle of combining collective leadership with individual responsibility based on division of labor. All major issues shall be decided upon by the Party committees after democratic discussion.

(f) The Party forbids all forms of personality cult.

The principle of democratic centralism is also extended to the Chinese National People's Congress (NPC) and the local people's congresses at different levels, which are instituted, at least on paper, through democratic election. They are responsible to the people and subject to the latter's supervision. All administrative, judicial and procuratorial organs of the state are also created by the people's congresses to which they are responsible and under whose supervision they operate.

The division of functions and powers between the central and local state organs is guided by the principle of giving full play to the initiative and enthusiasm of the local authorities under the unified leadership of the central authorities (Article 3 of the PRC Constitution). Similar principle of democratic centralism—the electiveness of all bodies of state authority from the lowest to the highest, their accountability to the people, the obligation of the lower bodies to observe the decisions of the higher ones and combining central leadership with local initiatives and creative activity—has also been included in the former Soviet Constitution and fundamental laws of other socialist countries (e.g., the former USSR Constitution, Article 3).

Two points are particularly noteworthy in North Korea's actual practice of the principle of democratic centralism. First, the principle of democratic centralism has provided the theoretical rationale and device for the Kim Il Sung cult-building (for that matter, the cult building process of Stalin, Mao, Tito and other heads of state in the socialist countries). Although the WPK bylaws stops short of going beyond the rhetoric that "all party organizations shall absolutely obey the Central Committee of the party," the absolute obedience to the higher party organs, in reality, does not end with the WPK Central Committee. The WPK Central Committee, in turn, obeys its Standing Committees, especially, its Political Committee, Secretariat and Central Military Affairs Committee, and these Standing Committees must obey their respective chairmen. In real terms, the entire people and the Party must pledge absolute loyalty to Kim Il Sung and now Kim Jŏng Il. The senior Kim chairs all these key Standing Committees, not to mention the fact that he is concurrently the President of the DPRK, the President of the Supreme People's Assembly Central People's Committee and the Chairman of the WPK Congress.

Herein lies the institutional basis for transforming one-party rule into one-man rule. One-man rule, in turn, tends to generate personality cult. The cult of Kim Il Sung in North Korea, the longest ruling autocrat on the globe today, may be partially explained by the (mis) application of the democratic centralism principle. It is, thus, no accident that the new 1982 Chinese Communist Party (CCP) Constitution has appended a specific provision to the principle of democratic centralism which "forbids all forms of personality cult." Whether or not this particular provision to the principle of democratic centralism will actually prevent the CCP from its cult-building tendency is too early to tell. One thing is quite certain, nevertheless. As the cult of Stalin, Tito, Mao and Ceausescu before and that of Kim Il Sung (Great Leader) and Fidel Castro (Lider Máximo) now have amply demonstrated, to avert the centralizing tendency of power in the central party organizations and ultimately in the hands of the chairman of the party would be extremely difficult, if not impossible.

Second, if "centralism" in the principle of democratic centralism tends to produce a personality cult in socialist systems, its "democratic" process tends to create a political farce. In the virtual absence of basic political freedoms enjoyed by the democratic states in Western Europe, North America, Oceania and Japan, elections in socialist systems are nominal since the voters dutifully elect those candidates who are nominated by the party leadership. An example of recent North Korean local elections illustrates this point rather dramatically. The captions in the front page of the *Pyongyang Times* on March 9, 1983, read: "Demonstration of Our People's United Strength" and "Elections to City and County People's Assemblies: 100% Voter Turnout, 100% Yes Votes."

Under this caption, the following "news story" was printed.

> Elections to the city and county people's assemblies took place from 9 a.m. to 8 p.m. on March 6. The elections were successfully carried out in strict accordance with the Regulations on the Elections of Deputies to the People's Assemblies at all levels of the Democratic People's Republic of Korea. According to the results of the elections totalized at the city and county constituencies, one hundred percent of the electors registered except for those now touring abroad took part in voting and all of them cast their ballots for the candidates registered at all the constituencies. The elections powerfully demonstrated once again the invincible might of our people, united rock-firm around the Central Committee of the Party led by the Great Leader President Kim Il Sung, and the superiority of our genuine socialist system. Elected deputies are representatives of the workers, peasants and working intellectuals, who have worked devotedly with intense loyalty to the Party and the leader for the prosperity of the socialist motherland and the strengthening and development of our people's power. The number of deputies elected to the city and county people's assemblies is 24,562.

On February 25, 1985, the exact same caption—100% Voter Turnout, 100% Yes Votes"—appeared in the front page of the *Pyongyang Times.* The only changes reported in the content of the "news stories" were that the number of deputies have increased from 24,562 in 1983 to 28, 793 in 1985, the WPK's invincible "might" was replaced by the word, "strength," and the "Great Leader President Kim Il Sung" was supplanted by the "Respected Comrade Kim Il Sung."

By contrast, the *Beijing Review* of February 25, 1980, reported, for instance, that the voter turnout in China's Tongxiang County election was not 100% but 98.86%. Even in the election in the former Soviet Union, the "yes" vote was 99.9%![18]

In short, the North Korean-style election of 100% voter turnout and 100% yes vote graphically exhibits North Korea's *democratic* centralism in action. Recently, however, the 26 November 1991 issue of the *Rodong Shinmun* reported... that in the city-county People's Assembly elections, 99.89% (of the) voters casted 100% yes votes. As Table 6-2 on the election results of the Supreme People's Assembly (SPA), "the

highest organ of the state," demonstrates, this *perfect* electoral voting
behavior in North Korea's local elections is nothing but a carbon copy
of its national election. An interesting observation here is that since the
9th Election the 100% voters-100% yes voting pattern developed a
small crack. Now the North Korean media reports that only 99.7% voters took part in the election, although it still claims 100% yes votes. In
sum, despite minor changes, North Korea's malpractice of democratic
centralism still persists.

7. Proletarian Internationalism

Another standard feature of all socialist systems is the idea of proletarian internationalism.The DPRK is to unite with all the socialist countries and with all the people in the world to defeat imperialism and to
actively support and encourage their national liberation and revolutionary struggles. For these efforts, North Korea has incorporated into its
constitution five elements of proletarian internationalism—equality,
independence, mutual respect, noninterference in each other's internal
affairs and mutual benefit (cf. Article 17). These five factors nearly
replicate the Five Principles of Peaceful Coexistence (*Pancha Shila*),
which was originally written into the Indian-Chinese Agreement on
Tibet on April 29, 1954. They are: mutual respect for sovereignty and
territorial integrity, non-aggression, non-interference in each other's
internal affairs, mutual benefit, equality and peaceful coexistence (cf.
Preamble to the PRC Constitution). The former Soviet Union had similar pledges in its constitution—sovereign equality, mutual renunciation
of the use of threat of force, inviolability of frontiers, territorial integrity
of states, peaceful settlement of disputes, non-intervention in internal
affairs, respect for human rights and fundamental freedoms, the equal
rights of peoples and their right to decide their own destiny, co-opera-
tion among states, fulfillment in good faith of obligations arising from
the generally recognized principles and rules of international law and
from the international treaties signed by the USSR (cf. Articles 29 and
30 of the former USSR Constitution). In reality, however, the PRC's
"non-aggression" clauses have not deterred the PRC from its conquest

of Tibet in 1950, intermittent hostilities in the Taiwan straits in the 1950s, Korean intervention (1950-53), brief border wars or skirmishes with India (1962), the former Soviet Union (1969 and 1971) and Vietnam (1978-79), to list a few. Similarly, the aforesaid Soviet pledges have not prevented the former Soviet Union's direct invasion and intervention in Hungary (1956), Czechoslovakia (1968) and Afghanistan (1980-).

Interestingly enough, the "non-aggression" clause is absent in the North Korean Constitution. Since North Korea invaded the South in June 1950, it may be inferred from the absence of the non-aggression clause that North Korea still has not ruled out the option to reunify the country by military means. If this inference is correct, North Korea's constant propaganda rhetoric of reunifying the fatherland by peaceful means is patently false. In the midst of collapsing communism, North Korea now finds herself among a limited number of socialist fraternal countries, so her aim of reunifying the country is increasingly becoming a pipe dream. In all practicality, even preserving and defending her system itself is quickly becoming an impossible task.

8. The Structure of the State

Finally, all present and past socialist states have shared basically the same formal political structures. The national legislative body is the highest organ of the state power. North Korea's Supreme People's Assembly (SPA), China's National People's Congress (NPC), and the former Soviet Union's Supreme Soviet are the cases in point. Both the SPA and the NPC are unicameral, while the Supreme Soviet consisted of the Soviet of the Union and the Soviet of Nationalities. The administrative or executive body, e.g., North Korea's Administration Council, China's State Council, and the former Soviet Union's Council of Ministers, is formed by the national legislative organ. Likewise, the national court and the procurator's office—North Korea's Central Court and Central Procurator's Office, China's Supreme People's Court and Supreme Procuratorate, and the former Soviet Union's Supreme Court and Supreme Procuratorate—are established by the national legislative body. At the local level, local legistrative bodies will form the executive and judicial branches of the government. On paper, therefore, the social- ist political structures are set up on the principle of separation of powers. But in reality, they are run by the party based on the principle of *concentration of powers* in the hands of the party.

Specifically, the communist party guides, leads and controls the above political institutions vertically and horizontally. It does so since its organizations correspond to all governmental apparatus from national (or federal) to local levels, and its organizations at each level control their government counterpart. The crucial point is that the communist party in socialist states is an integral part of the governing structure. Unlike the competitive party systems in Western democracies, where parties *in* power and those *out of* power are in periodic competition with each other, the communist party continues to be *in* power with virtually no challenges from other political forces within. The formal separation of governmental structures notwithstanding, nearly all socialist political systems are founded on the dictatorship of the communist party. As it is clear from the foregoing, the North Korean political system exemplifies the prototype of a communist party dictatorship. The fact that WPK and Kim Il Sung have been in power ever since the establishment of the DPRK graphically illustrates this point.

Deviations: Objective Conditions and Subjective Attributes

Nine salient political features of the North Korean political system are here identified. They are: 1) the ideological posture; 2) the size prin- ciple; 3) the echo policy; 4) the siege mentality; 5) the rationing syn- drome; 6) the personality cult; 7) the *Juche* idea; 8) the succession issue; and 9) the unification formula. Since the *Juche* idea, the succession issue and the unification formula will be examined in other chapters, only the first six variants are discussed below.

1. The Ideological Posture

Marxism-Leninism along with Kim Il Sungism (or the *Juche* idea) are officially stipulated as North Korea's basic ideological tenet, although a gap exists between such symbolic posturing and real political life in North Korea. The mere fact that the present North Korean political system emerged during the period of the Soviet occupation indicates the inordinate influence of the former Soviet Union in North Korean politics. The North Korean political system is, however, not merely a facsimile of the Soviet model, or that of the Maoist formula. As indicated above, all three share a number of fundamental ideological principles in common, but the North Korean system possesses its own unique and peculiar elements to be *sui generis*.

It is interesting to note that the original DPRK Constitution adopted and promulgated by the SPA on September 8, 1948, did not explicitly acknowledge Marxism and Leninism as the "official" ideology. Nor did it stipulate the Worker's Party of Korea as the "official" party, the vanguard of all the people. Again, such basic communist ideological and organizational principles as "the dictatorship of the proletariat," "democratic centralism" and "the building of a classless communist society" were not cited anywhere in the constitution with 104 articles. It failed even to empower the state to own and control the means of production. Rather, the ownership was divided into "state ownership, cooperative ownership and ownership by private natural or private juridical person. Still, except for a garden plot (50 *pyŏng* or 0.04 acre), private ownership of any kind—land, commerce, industry and others—disappeared from North Korea by the end of 1958.[19]

Non-acknowledgment of fundamental ideological principles in the original constitution does not mean that the DPRK had not endorsed and practiced them. To the contrary, Marxism-Leninism has been its "official" ideology; the WPK has been its "official" party since 1948; and the party, state and military organizations have been running largely in accordance with the principles of democratic centralism and of proletarian dictatorship. The state and cooperative ownerships of all means of production in lieu of private ownership have been in operation. The WPK has been controlling the mass media, mass communication and all other literary, artistic, cultural, educational, scientific and social enterprises. The military and other political control apparatus, such as security, public safety and secret intelligence forces, have also been under the WPK control. In short, the North Korean political system shares fundamental features of the totalitarian communist dictatorship.[20]

Non-endorsement of the basic principles and doctrines of communism in the original constitution was only a temporary political camouflage. North Korea explained that between 1948 and 1972 the country had been in a transition from the "anti-feudal, anti-imperialist, democratic revolution" to the socialist revolution. With the 1972 Socialist Constitution, Kim Il Sung contended that North Korea launched its new phase—the consolidation and development of the socialist system.[21] This official explanation notwithstanding, such absence reflected rather unfavorable political settings under which Kim Il Sung's Partisan Group initially had to stage the power struggle against the competing factional forces in the political arena.

At the beginning of the Republic, Kim and his Partisan Group were relatively small in number, as compared with the nationalist organizations and other political forces in North Korea. Within the communist party organizations had existed several competing factions. In addition to the Partisan Group, the returnees from China (the Yanan Group), the Domestic Group and the Worker's Party of South Korea Group had vied for power in the early stages of the North Korean communist politics. Kim's Partisan Group did not even constitute the majority among these rival communist factions. Under such circumstances, Kim and his group chose a broad coalition strategy until they consolidated power and gained strategic positions within the WPK, the state, the military and other political control apparatus.

Herein lies the *evolutionary* character of the North Korean communist system. Kim's power was not absolute from the outset. His power has grown gradually within the WPK. A steady and gradual consolidation of his power meant that other party factions within the WPK had to be eliminated step-by-step. From this standpoint, the formal endorsement of Marxism-Leninism and the *Juche* idea as the fundamental tenets of the North Korean ideology in the 1972 Constitution signified that Kim Il Sung and his group won the power struggles within the WPK, as the absence of the endorsement for such official ideology in the 1948 Constitution indicated his unsettling status as the leader amid inter-party and intra-party factional power struggles. And now the exclusion of Marxism-Leninism and the sole inclusion of his Juche ideology in the 1992 Constitution confirm the further consolidation of his and his son's, ostensibly at least, power.)

2. The Size Principle

Another salient feature of North Korea is here called the size principle. Fraternal northern neighbors, China and the former Soviet Union are two of the largest nations in the world. Compared with North Korea's 23 million people within 47,000 square miles of land area, China has the world's largest population (over 1.2 billion people) and the third largest land area (3.7 million square miles). The former Soviet Union has the world's third largest population (over 290 million) and the largest land area (8.6 million square miles). Compared to North Korea, China is nearly 53 times larger in population and 79 times bigger in size, while the former Soviet Union was 14 times larger in population and nearly 183 times bigger in size. To put it another way, North Korea and its population are much smaller than the average size and population of China's 21 provinces and 5 autonomous regions. It is less than a third of the average size of the former Soviet Union's 53 subgovernmental units [Union Republics (15), Autonomous Republics (2), Autonomous Regions (8) and Autonomous Areas (10)] combined.

North Korea's population and size in relation to its two neighboring giants have had several ideological and political implications. First, being tiny can be tidy, so to speak. Since North Korea's 23 million people are virtually all ethnic Koreans, there are no ethnic and nationality problems. By contrast, China has some 54 minority groups scattered over nearly 60% of its land area, while the Han Chinese constitute 94% of its total population and occupy mostly the fertile coastal areas. Worse still, only about 15% of the Chinese land is arable, with the majority (nearly 85%) of the rural population concentrating on cultivating about sixth of its land mass. As Fairbank noted, a million villages are still generally beyond the reach of easy transportion by road, rail or water and lack marketing networks. Hence, the small-scale industrialization of the country-side is on a do-it-yourself basis and central direction is minimized.[22] Totalitarian control and planning notwithstanding, this illustrates the classic example of what Lucian Pye called the "penetration crisis."[23]

The former Soviet Union's enormous physical and demographic size has created no better, if not worse, situations than those of China. The former Soviet Union contained more than 110 ethnic and national minorities, and the non-Slavic populations have been steadily on the rise, while the so-called "Great Russians" and other Slavic populations have been declining.[24] Before the demise of the Soviet Union the non-Slavic, especially the Soviet Asians, were approaching 50% of the total population. Now, the Baltic States—Estonia, Latvia and Lithuania—have declared independence and other former republics under the loose political arrangement of the Commonwealth of Independent States (CIS) are also claiming similar political independence and autonomy. At present, the future of the CIS is highly uncertain and unpredictable in many ways.

While the size in area and population in China and the former Soviet Union have posed the problem of manageability, penetration and integration, North Korea's size has worked to its advantage. The size principle, as demonstrated above, may explain the different performances in the socialist system. Why have these socialist countries produced different political and economic results when they have been applying basically the same socialist, political and economic principles and programs? Needless to say, the answers, among other things, may be found in differences in their level or stage of economic and societal development, and in culture or in history. Beyond these, however, lies the physical and demographic size which is an important factor that can explain such divergent performances.

Specifically, the socialist agricultural collectivization policy illustrates the classic example of the size principle. In the former Soviet Union, for example, two kinds of collectivized farms existed. There were some 26,000 multi-purpose collective farms, *Kolkhoz*, whose average size was 16,000 acres. A typical collective farm had about 550 households. The state farms, *Sovkhoz*, on the other hand, were more specialized, better mechanized and larger in size. There were about 22,000 state farms whose size averaged 50,000 acres in 1985. The majority of the state farms were specialized in certain agricultural products, such as grain, dairies, fruits or vegetables. An average state farm employed about 550 wage-earning workers.[25] Before the collapse of the Soviet Union the trend had been the gradual increase of the state farms and the declining number of the collective farms.

In North Korea no collective or state farms of comparable Soviet size exist. With the exception of a tiny garden plot allotted to some private households, all farm lands in North Korea are divided into the state-operated farms and the agricultural cooperatives, whose average sizes are far smaller than the Soviet Union's state and collective farms. Like in the former Soviet Union, North Korea's state farms are specialized to grow particular agricultural products. Presently, some 200 such farms which constitute 12% of the total arable land, generate 20% of North Korea's entire agricultural products. When North Korea successfully completed the collectivization of agriculture in 1958, some 3,778 agricultural cooperatives with an average of 476 *Chŏngbo* or 1,155 acres (1 *Chŏngbo* equals 2.45 acres) existed. An average agricultural cooperative has about 300 households.[26] In other words, North Korea's agricultural cooperatives are on the average 14 times and 44 times smaller than their former Soviet counterparts—*Kolkhoz* and *Sovkhoz*.

The arable land in North Korea makes up about 25% of its area, which is mostly of hills and dales, unlike the great plains and prairies of the former Soviet Union. The majority of the farmers live in the scattered villages usually at the foot of the mountains and valleys. A concentration of huge farming population in one particular region or location is rare. The size, topography and demography of North Korea have made, in short, the Soviet-style collectivization inapplicable. Because North Korea's cooperative farms are relatively smaller in size and are usually located in or near the farming villages, they have even managed with much greater efficiency and higher productivity than its former Soviet counterparts.

Even to a casual visitor, many acres of uncultivated farm lands in China and the former Soviet Union were noticeable, but an uncultivated land was very rare to see in North Korea. In brief, North Korea's physical size and resultant cooperative farm sizes have been a positive factor for management and production. Their relatively small sizes have contributed favorably to their centralized economic management in general and political control in particular. Still, North Korea's agriculture has not and cannot overcome the inherent limitations of the collectivized agricultural system. China, after her agricultural reform in the late 1970's, has clearly demonstrated that North Korea's smaller agricultural land size has had some advantages over Chinese and the former Soviet Union's which is, however, nothing compared to the enormous benefits arising from the post-Mao decollectivization of agriculture, i.e., the family unit responsibility system.

Secondly, the size principle has security implications. Unlike the relationship between China and the former Soviet Union, whose respective sizes in territory, population and other human and natural resources are comparable and, thus, make their rivalry inevitable and real, North Korea's relationship with China or with Russia has not created such rivalry. Despite North Korea's steadfast claims of mutual equality and independence, it has been a minor partner of its two giant socialist neighbors. China has challenged the former Soviet Union's ideological orthodoxy and politico-military hegemony, and both sides have clashed militarily over the border issues. And their adversary relationships are not likely to cease in the future.[27] But North Korea alone cannot and will not challenge the ideological orthodoxy and politico-military hegemony of either or both of these two neighboring giants. Nor can it instigate military confrontations with either or both, even on a limited scale. During the era of Sino-Soviet conflict, North Korea had played a political game by balancing one side against the other, without outrightly reneging the relationship with one for the other. The rhetorical claims of independence and equality under the banner of the *Juche* idea aside, herein lies the ultimate parameter of North Korea as a military power and its political leadership role within the socialist camp, let alone in the international community.

Finally, the study by Dahl and Tufte on size and democracy deserves attention in this connection. Among other things, they found that "no single type or size of unit is optimal for achieving the twin goals of citizen effectiveness and system capacity." By citizen effectiveness and system capacity, they meant "citizens acting responsibly and competently to fully control the decisions of the polity," and "the polity has the capacity to respond fully to the collective preferences of its citizens," respectively.[28] Further, they posited that the effectiveness of the citizen may be maximized if the unit is small and homogeneous. At the same time, in such a unit the effectiveness of the dissenting citizen is minimized by the difficulty of finding an ally and by the weakness of political competition. They asserted that the politics of diversity in the larger, more heterogeneous unit may better serve the dissenting citizen. Most importantly, they found that the goal of maximizing citizen effectiveness can and does conflict with the capacity of the system. In the extreme case, a citizen could be maximally effective in a system of minimal capacity for dealing with major issues or minimally effective in a system of maximal capacity for dealing with major issues.[29]

The findings of Dahl and Tufte are relevant to the North Korean political system. To employ their terminology, the socialist political systems in particular are the cases in which citizen effectiveness does not exist except in a nominal sense (e.g., election fanfare of "100% voter turnout and 100% yes votes!") while system capacity is realized in full. North Korea represents the prime example of their "extreme case," i.e., minimal citizen effectiveness and maximal system capacity. Again, North Korea epitomizes a case where the effectiveness of the dissenting citizen is minimized. In the present North Korean political system, a "dissenting citizen" is virtually nonexistent. There have been "enemies of the people" such as "traitors," "the lackeys of Japanese imperialism," "pro-Japanese and pro-American elements," "anti-Party factionalists" and others.[30] The "masses," not the "citizen" and "unity," not "dissent" make up North Korea's standard political vocabulary. To borrow Kim Il Sung's own phraseology, "all Party (WPK) members... breathe the same air, speak the same words and act in unison." Again, in Kim's words, "never before have the whole Party and the entire people been so strongly knit together and united with a single ideology and will as they are now."[31] In short, in North Korea the size principle helped Kim and his ruling elites to maximize system capacity in the virtual absence of "citizen effectiveness."

3. The Echo Effect

Closely related to the size principle is what is here called the echo effect. It represents the phenomenon in which the policy changes (symbolic or substantive) in the political, ideological and security arenas in a socialist country (or, in any other country, for that matter) produce similar changes in other socialist countries. In reality, it is difficult to distinguish between the country which initiates or emulates such changes in line, policy or program because such changes can take place simultaneously or sequentially. The problem of distinction between the initiator and emulator nations aside, the echo effect has been another variable which can explain the peculiarities of the North Korean political system.

On a general plane, for example, North Korea's dialogue with South Korea in the early 70s, 80s and 90s corresponded to the U.S.-USSR and the U.S.-Chinese detente before, and to the demise of communism and the emerging new world order. North Korea, for example, announced that its doors are now open to foreign investment and technology transfer.[32] This volte-face may be regarded as North Korea's new direction in economic strategy, which echoes China's adoption of new economic reform under Deng.

Specific examples, too, abound in this regard. North Korea's *Ch'ŏllima* [Flying Horse] Movement was comparable to China's Great Leap Forward in the late 50's, although the latter ended in abject failure, the former still serves as the official developmental and mobilizational symbol. Kim's *Ch'ŏngsan-ri* in 1960 and Mao's *Dazhai* in 1963 as the ideal models of North Korea's and China's respective cooperative farming methods[33] are another example. Kim Il Sung's *Juche* idea and Mao's doctrine of self-reliance (or, to stretch the comparison further, even Stalin's slogan of "socialism in one country") are literally, if not politically, analogous. Kim's mass line (*gunjung nosŏn*) echoed that of Mao's. North Korea's slogan of three great revolutions—the ideological, technological and cultural—is akin to China's four modernization policy—

modernization of agriculture, industry, national defense and science and technology. North Korea's Children's Guard, the Young Red Guard and the Worker-Peasant Red Guards, too, are not a far cry from Mao's erstwhile Red Guards. Building of the Kim Il Sung cult and grooming of Kim Jŏng Il as the official successor, too, are not so different from the frenetic phase of the Mao cult during the Cultural Revolution and the designation of Lin Piao, the PRC defense minister, as Mao's official successor.

Generally, the success or failure of the initiator's line, policy or program does not necessarily guarantee the same result for the emulator. So many additional factors are at work in each socialist country that the emulator may not obtain a similar result from adopting the initiator's programs. Khrushchev's de-Stalinization campaign, which began in the 1956 Twentieth Congress of the Communist Party of Soviet Union (CPSU), was, at least, temporarily successful. But it eventually ended with Khrushchev's own fall and Brezhnev's rise in 1964. Mao's cult, which peaked during the Cultural Revolution period of 1966-68, died away under the post-Mao leadership in China. Mao's birthplace in the village of Shao Shan, in Hsiang T'an County, Hunan Province, south of Hankow on the Yangtze River was once the mecca for the Chinese and foreign tourists, particularly, during the Cultural Revolution. It is no longer included in the "must list." Mao's pictures and sayings have all disappeared from the public buildings and walls, let alone his Red Books. In Peking, for instance, all his pictures have disappeared from the public places except for the one in the Tiananmen Square. So far, the de-Maoization has been successful under Deng Xiaoping.

By contrast, in North Korea the attacks on Kim Il Sung's personality cult by the Yanan Group within the WPK in the 1956-57 period failed. Such attacks seemed to have intensified the Kim cult.[34] Kim's pictures, statues and monuments are still everywhere; his sayings are displayed in all prominent public places and buildings; and his birthplace Mangyŏngdae, on the outskirts of Pyongyang along the Daedong River is still "the first on the must list" for the North Koreans and foreign visitors. The failure of de-Kimization in the aftermath of de-Stalinization lies principally in the fact that the assault was made while he was alive and well with a firm grip on power. By contrast, Khrushchev attacked

Stalin three years after his death, and Deng, too, downgraded Mao after his death, in a piecemeal and cautious way. If the Soviet and Chinese experiences serve as a guide for North Korea's political future, a possibility of successful de-Kimization after Kim's death is not inconceivable.

Another example is China's so-called "Pingpong Diplomacy" in the early 70's which eventually led to the rapprochement between China and the United States, Japan and other non-Communist countries. But pingpong diplomacy in North Korea, where the World Table Tennis Championship was held in the spring of 1979, did not result in the opening of the DPRK to the West (It may be quite unfair to say, however, that North Korea alone was to blame for the failure to open diplomacy). In the long run, the history of Chinese and Korean relations may reveal that the changes in the former will have a spillover effect on the latter in one form or another.[35] Here again, like the aforementioned size principle, North Korea's resistance to the echo effect has an ultimate limit. North Korea's current efforts to normalize and/or improve relations with Japan and the United States are the cases in point.

To summarize, North Korea has not been and cannot be completely immune from the changes occurring in China, the former Soviet Union, or around the world. Because of North Korea's ideological affinity, physical proximity and security linkage, it is extremely difficult, if not impossible, to avoid or escape from the effects of changes undergoing in China and the former Soviet Union. It is true that North Korea is not, and has not always been, on the receiving end of such changes, and the former Soviet Union and China, on the giving end. The roles of the initiator and the emulator have frequently been reversed as the specific examples in the above demonstrate. It is equally true, however, that North Korea, despite its vociferous claims of *Juche*, has been more an emulator than an initiator.

4. The Siege Mentality

The siege mentality[36] which is intricately intermingled with the size principle and the echo effect, is another peculiar ideological and political trait of North Korea. It refers here to the attitudes, feelings or beliefs held by the top-level party, state, military and para-military leaders that North Korea is besieged by hostile and potentially threatening enemy countries. It is not merely a xenophobia because the ruling elites not only fear the foreign intruders, potential and actual, but feel that North Korea is surrounded and encircled by them. They also exploit such dangers in order to rationalize their power and, in the process, exaggerate foreign threats. A kind of self-fulfilling prophecy has crept in to justify and rationalize their prolonged rule.

The former Soviet Union and China in the northern border have been North Korea's ideological and security allies. At the eleventh hour of the Korean War, China sent its "Volunteers" to rescue North Korea from the UN counter-offensive led by the U.S., which pushed the North Korean troops to the North Korean-Manchurian borders. After the ceasefire in 1953, China and the former Soviet Union offered assistance to North Korea to rebuild the country from the ashes of the war. Since 1961 North Korea has maintained friendship treaties with both; and its economic and military ties with these have been greater than with any other former socialist countries. North Korea has also played an adroit balancing act amid the Sino-Soviet schism in the early 1960s and 1970s.

Despite close and inextricable relationship with China and the former Soviet Union (now the CIS), North Korea has been weary and uneasy about these two northern neighbors. Kim and his ruling elites in Pyongyang have been overly sensitive to the internal political interference by either China or the former Soviet Union or both. Kim's accentuation of the *Juche* idea and his relentless purging of the Soviet faction in the early and mid-50s and pro-Chinese Yanan faction in the late 50s uphold this point.[37] Kim and his ruling circle's irritation, hypersensitivity and apprehension over the Chinese and Soviet interference in North Korea's domestic politics stem basically from the overwhelming inequality in size and power existing between North Korea and its two giant neighbors. In that sense, the siege mentality is a minor partner's subjective feeling toward a major partner in the presence of an overwhelmingly unfavorable objective inequality between the two.

The North Korean ruling elites' siege mentality is abetted by three additional sources—self-imposed, system-imposed and other-imposed isolation. The persistence of division and somewhat diminishing hostility between North and South Korea, the presence of US military forces in the South, a lack of formal relationship with Japan and the physical barriers presented by China and Russia in the northern border make North Korea feel locked in, uneasy and isolated.

The system-imposed encapsulation is even more fundamental. Beyond the fact that all socialist systems create a closed society, the current North Korean political system is indeed watertight. From the basic level work team in the agricultural cooperatives, factories and urban areas to the top level central party, state and military hierarchies, all are vertically and horizontally organized, coordinated and controlled. The regimentation in North Korea today is, in fact, nearly total. And the militarization of its population and the fortification of the entire country are virtually complete. It is a garrison state nonpareil.

The physical movements of the people within the country or abroad are totally controlled.[38] Virtually no room exists for individual initiatives in education, job transfer and training, moving, traveling and other ordinary human transactions. In that sense, the masses in North Korea are *mobilized* and yet *immobile* at the same time. They are mobilized by the WPK, state and military cadres for the socialist construction work and for the fortification and defense of the fatherland, but they are immobile in that they cannot freely travel, choose their place of residence, occupation and the like.

The North Korean siege mentality is also self-imposed. The much propagandized *Juche* idea substantiate this point. The *Juche* idea in the area of foreign and international affairs emphasizes North Korea's political independence and economic autarchy and discourages foreign transactions, trade and investments. A rigid insistence on independence and autarchy in the world of political and economic interdependence has further isolated and encapsulated North Korea. It should be pinpointed that in a time of acute international economic crises such as the Arab Oil Embargo of 1974 and the world-wide recession in the late 70s and the early 80s, North Korea was relatively unaffected by them due to its autarchic economic structures (But unlike resource-rich, especially oil-exporting China and the former Soviet Union, North Korea, too, suffered more than South Korea during the oil crises). Still, an excessive self-reliance leads to self-isolation, which, in turn, breeds ignorance. The North Korean ruling elites' siege mentality is, in fact, comparable to the proverbial "frog in the well." As the frog judged the sky to be as high or as large as what it saw from inside the well, the North Korean ruling elites see the outside world only from their self-imposed, system-imposed and other-imposed perspectives.

The North Korean siege mentality is also other-imposed. The presence of the U.S. troops and arsenals in South Korea, the ROK-U.S.-Japan security arrangement, Japan and the U.S.'s refusal (though some positive movements and bilateral talks are presently ongoing) to recognize the DPRK are the notable cases.[39] The North Korean ruling elites often employ the siege mentality as a tool to control and mobilize the masses. The propaganda that North Korea is besieged by the real and potential enemies, especially the capitalist United States and the militarist Japan, supplies additional ammunition to further regiment, mobilize and militarize the masses for socialist construction and revolution and the defense and reunification of the fatherland. As stated earlier, the use of the siege mentality exemplifies the self-fulfilling prophecy. In the process of alerting the masses of the actual or imagined foreign enemy aggressors and their puppets, the ruling elites convince themselves that North Korea is really surrounded by foreign enemies and their puppets. So the vicious circle of the siege mentality continues.

North Korea's siege mentality is, in essence, a fear, a phobia, an isolation, an encapsulation, an ignorance and even an instrument. The fear of being beleaguered by foreign enemies and their puppets becomes a phobia of all "foreign" elements. Such phobia further secludes the people and the country from the outside world. The isolation from the outside world encourages fortification and militarization, which, in turn, cuts off outside contact and communication. Hence, the encapsulated country remains ignorant about the outside world which is equally in the dark about the former. Worse still, the ruling elites, who initially used fear, phobia, self-isolation, encapsulation and ignorance as an instrument of mass mobilization and control, have themselves become the victims of their own creation. The siege mentality pervades the ruling elites; they have not only tried to convince the masses to believe it but in the process they begin to *believe* in it themselves. The siege mentality has, in short, become a self-fulfilling prophecy for the North Korean ruling elites.

Isolated and impoverished, North Korea's more global minded and moderate ruling elites are now desperately seeking the way out. But whether they will succeed in this new policy change under the Kim Il Sung-Kim Jŏng Il political succession arrangement is more doubtful than hopeful.

5. The Rationing Syndrome

Another conspicuous element in North Korean politics is called here the rationing syndrome. It is an aberration arising from the state control of the means of production and distribution. Under the banner of the socialist principle of equal and fair distribution, the bureaucratic rationing system was born in North Korea. In the process of rationing goods and products to the masses by the state functionaries, these goods and products somehow have metamorphosed into *gifts, perquisites* and *privileges*. These goods and products no longer represent what the masses have manufactured through their own labor and toil. The masses have, instead, become the recipients of these gifts, perquisites and privileges distributed by the state functionaries. Rationing of food items and goods occur in nearly all former socialist countries (non-socialist countries, too, ration items during crises or war). But rationing becomes a syndrome when the masses are led (duped) to believe that rationed items are the largess from the ruling elites, rather than their entitlements.

Perhaps an American farmer giving thanks to God for the food he produced can be likened to a North Korean farmer being grateful to Kim Il Sung, Kim Jŏng Il and the ruling functionaries for the rationed food. However, a fundamental difference separates the two in that while God has no political designs, Kim Il Sung, Kim Jŏng Il and the ruling elites have systematically utilized rationing as a mechanism of mass political control and manipulation.

Although the rationing syndrome is present in all past and present socialist systems, North Korea's variant is conspicuous because it is intertwined with the Kim Il Sung cult and the father-son succession scheme. In North Korea all food and general items are rationed in the name of the "Great Leader" President Kim Il Sung and now increasingly in the name of "Dear Leader" Kim Jŏng Il. Not only general merchandise and food items but also special goods such as children's books, pencils and uniforms are distributed in the name of the "Benevolent Leader" and "Dear Leader." The masses enjoy the benefits and privileges arising from all the new construction—buildings, dams, highways, museums and monuments—and all the new cultural productions— music, movies, plays, operas, paintings and sculptures—which are completed under the direction of "genius" Kim Il Sung and Kim Jŏng Il. The members of the WPK were given wrist watches, television sets, refrigerators, washing machines, and even apartment flats in the name of Kims. These gifts were awarded by the Great Leader and the Dear Leader in their "boundless generosity." In fact, some watches and TV sets are inscribed with the captions, "Gifts of the Great Leader Kim Il Sung or of the Dear Leader Kim Jong Il." The irony is that more often than not, they are made in Japan, Switzerland or some other foreign countries, but foreign manufacters' labels are removed and invariably the senior Kim's or the Junior Kim's inscriptions are attached to the goods as if they were produced in North Korea. On April 15, a national holiday celebrating senior Kim's birthday, the "Great Leader" often appeared at a school playground to personally give away school uniforms, books and other school supplies to students, as if they were his birthday "gifts." Students receive them as the "gifts" from the "Benevolent Great Leader," and often forget that such gifts *are* produced by their own parents' hard work.[40]

The rationing syndrome in North Korea stretches beyond the physical and tangible products such as food, clothes, housing, work, school and domicile. It also extends to the psychological and political domains in the form of rationing information and intelligence in accordance with the hierarchy of power and position held by each recipient. As the goods are rationed according to the workers' grades and skill levels, information and intelligence are apportioned in relation to the party, state and military functionaries' ranks and status. There are, for instance, six grade levels for agricultural workers, ranging from one, the lowest, to six, the highest. The third grade level agricultural worker receives a monthly living allowance (*Saengwhal–bi*) of about 100 *won* ($1.00 equals 1.70 *won*), and 160 *won* is allotted to the sixth grade level worker. The factory workers are divided into eight grade levels whose monthly allowances range from 70 *won* to 120 *won* (These figures were given to me in the summer of 1981 by the cadres in one of the agricultural cooperatives and the factory complex I visited. The actual amount of an average farm and factory worker's allowance may vary).[41]

North Korea is a rigidly stratified society. The workers in North Korea are divided into eight salary grades (China has 24 salary grades in urban areas and 26 salary grades in rural areas, as compared with 18 grades of officialdom under the Qing Dynasty).[42] Interestingly enough, North Korea's grading and stratification is not based on needs, but rather on ability, i.e., both the workers' acquired skills and their capacity to demonstrate and convince the WPK that they are loyal to Kim Il Sung, Kim Jŏng Il and the Party. Accordingly, the socialist principle of "from each according to his ability to each according to his needs" is perverted.

Information and privilege, too, are rationed according to each individual's grade, position and power. As some animals are more equal than others in the Orwell's *Animal Farm*, some ruling elites have more access to intelligence and information than others in North Korea, where mass media and mass communication are tightly controlled and fed by the WPK. Generally, the higher the ranks, more information and intelligence are available to them. By contrast, the masses are fed "information" through the loudspeakers installed (in their homes) by the local party propaganda committees. Similarly, a majority of the rank and file or middle–level cadres and functionaries receives the news at home and around the world through the WPK-controlled TV or radio or through the governmental organs. Like other rationed items, the ruling elites control the news. Thus, a correlation exists between the rank and the amount of information and intelligence available and accessible to a person.

In a way, information allocating is built into any socialist system where all information are party-controlled and where the function of the media is not the dissemination of the news and information to the public but the education, indoctrination and propagandizing of the party rules,

classroom wall. The nursery school children chant stories of Kim's *wunderkind* years; primary school children memorize the activities of his "super-boy" years; secondary school students learn the revolutionary works of his youth; and college students study his anti-Japanese guerrilla struggles. Kim, in short, serves not only as the model for all age groups but is a corporeal god in North Korea. His cult has reached a point of political aberration bordering on absurdity.[47]

Since he took power at age 33 in 1945, he is now the longest ruling autocrat in the world. And his cult has lasted longer than that of any other socialist leaders, including Lenin, Stalin, Mao and Tito. What is more, while Marx, Engels and Lenin received homage posthumously, the idolatry of Kim (and Stalin and Mao) began with his approval. Four points deserve attention in this connection. First, the Kim Il Sung cult is neither an accident nor an overnight phenomenon. It has grown since 1945, if not earlier. Kim rose gradually as the undisputed and unchallenged "supreme leader." His cult-building enterprise has been the *symbolic* facet of his political power struggles (For a detailed analysis of Kim's rise, retention and expansion of power, see Chapter Nine). His cult has served, among other things, as the symbolic weapon against his political rivals and enemies. Hence, his cult can be better understood and explained in the context of his power struggle within the WPK. The last known purging of his "enemies" within the WPK took place from 1968 to 1969. No purge has been reported since then. The Kim cult has also served to promote unity—a rallying point for the ruling apparatus and the masses.[48]

Second, the sources and substance of Kim's cult are not all outright lies and groundless fabrications. Nor is his cult merely the phenomenon of a pseudo-charismatic leader.[49] The problem with his cult is one of *excess* that his personal leadership alone has been responsible for the Korean communist revolution from its early anti-Japanese liberation struggles to the liberation and to the creation and development of the present socialist North Korea. Such exaggerated single-handed feats of Kim Il Sung cannot be substantiated by any historical document on the Korean communist movement, the anti-Japanese armed struggles and on the post-War North Korean politics.

Third, the unprecedented intensity, scope and duration of the Kim Il Sung cult notwithstanding, he has not and, more accurately, cannot *personally* rule North Korea. His cult is so excessive that Kim seems to single-handedly rule North Korea. Quite to the contrary, the Party, the state, the military and para-political and para-military organizational apparatuses have been running the country. He is more of an ultimate mediator than a decision-maker, a legitimator than a formulator and an arbiter than an advocate. He is like the chairman of the board than a chief executive officer. At present, all indications suggest that Kim, an octogenarian, is gradually transferring his power over to his son and other party leaders. He appears to play a nominal role as the symbol of national unity, the head of the state and the ultimate rallying point of the Party and the people.

Finally, if the history of personality cult in socialist countries can serve as a guide, the cult usually dies away with the death of the cult object and the cult may be *imitable* but not *inheritable*. As the de-Stalinization and de-Maoization have amply demonstrated, the intensity of the *de-cultization* is generally proportionate to that of the cult itself. The deification of Kim Il Sung with such symbolic adornments of the "immortal" revolutionary ideas of *Juche* notwithstanding, he himself will become the iconoclast of his own icon. His death will be the iconoclasm of his own cult.[50]

Table 6-1. Parties and Para-political Organizations in North Korea

---

The Workers' Party of Korea

The Korean Social Democratic Party

The Ch'ŏndoist Ch'ŏngu Party

The Central Committee of the Democratic Front for the Unification of
Fatherland

The Committee for the Peaceful Reunification of the Fatherland

The General Federation of Trade Unions of Korea

The League of Socialist Working Youth of Korea

The Union of Agricultural Working People of Korea

The Korean Democratic Women's Union

The Korean General Federation of the Unions of Literature and Arts

The Korean Journalists Union

The Korean General Federation of Industrial Technology

The Central Guidance Committee of the Korean Ch'ŏndoists Association

The Korean Buddhist Federation

The Consultative Council of Former South Korean Politicians in the North for
the Promotion of Peaceful Reunification

The Korean Democratic Lawyers Association

The Korean Students Committee

The Korean Committee for Solidarity with World People

The Korean National Peace Committee

Source: *Pyongyang Times*, 18 January 1983.

Table 6-2. Election Results of the SPA

Term	Date	No. of Seats	Voting (%)	Yes Vote (%)
1st	8/25/48	572(360+212)	99.97	98.49
2nd	8/27/57	215	99.99	99.92
3rd	10/08/62	383	100.00	100.00
4rd	11/26/67	457	100.00	100.00
5th	12/12/72	541	100.00	100.00
6th	11/11/77	579	100.00	100.00
7th	2/28/82	615	100.00	100.00
8th	11/02/86	655	100.00	100.00
9th	4/22/90	687	99.78	100.00

Source: Adapted from *North Korea News*, No. 107 (March 8, 1982); Pukhan Chŏnsŏ (Seoul, 1980), p. 103. Yang Sung Chul, *Bukhan Ch'ŏngch'iron* [*North Korean Politics*] (Seoul: Pak Yŏng-sa, 1991), p. 42.

Notes

1. Joseph A. Schumpeter, *Capitalism, Socialism and Democracy*, 3rd. ed. (New York: Harper Torch Books, 1962), p. 309.
2. *The Los Angeles Times*, 22 July 1984.
3. Political reforms commensurate with a series of economic reforms initiated in 1978 under Deng's leadership have not been launched. Consequently, the Chinese economic reforms have created political dilemmas because the structure of political power remains basically unchanged. David Zwig, "Reforming China's Political Economy," *Harvard International Review* 11 (Spring 1989); Dorothy Salinger, "Economic Reform in China," *Harvard International Review* 11 (Spring 1989). Quoted in Joseph S. Nye, Jr., *Bound to Lead: The Changing Nature of American Power* (New York: Basic Books, 1990), p. 135. An in-depth analysis of the destined failures of reform efforts under the Soviet-type system is found in the January 1990 issue of the *Annals of the American Academy of Political and Social Science*, which focuses on privatizing and marketizing of socialism under special editorship of Jan S. Prybyla.
4. For details, see Michael Burawoy, "Marxism as Science: Historical Challenges

and Theoretical Growth," *American Sociological Review* 55 (December 1990): 792.

5. For a discussion of China's Chou Dynasty as a classic example of historic international systems, see K. J. Holsti, *International Politics: A Framework for Analysis*, 5th ed. (Englewood Cliffs: Prentice-Hall, 1988), pp. 25-36.

6. Chang-sun Kim, *Pukhan Sipŏnyŏnsa* [Fifteen-Year History of North Korea] (Seoul: *Chinmungak*, 1961); Dae-sook Suh, *The Korean Communist Movement*, 1918-1948 (Princeton: Princeton University Press, 1967); Robert A. Scalapino and Chong-sik Lee, *Communism in Korea* (Berkeley: University of California Press, 1972).

7. See for instance, Gregory Henderson, *Korea: The Politics of the Vortex* (Cambridge: Harvard University Press, 1968), pp. 312-333. I have examined Henderson's culturalist approach to the Korean politics in some detail in Chapter Ten. Bruce Cumings, for one, called the North Korean system a "corporatist socialism." For details, see his "Corporatism in North Korea," paper delivered at the 1981 APSA meeting, New York, 3-6 September 1981.

8. A majority of the works on the North Korean politics published in South Korea belongs to this category. To name just a few: *Pukhan Ch'onggam*, 45-68 (Seoul: Kukdongmuncheyŏnkuso, 1980), pp. 157-168; Yong-Pil Rhee, "Characteristics of North Korean Political System," *Unification Policy Quarterly* (Autumn 1978), pp. 16-33; and Keuk-Sung Suh, "Reports on Party Congress and Power Elites in North Korea," *Unification Policy Quarterly* (1980), pp. 11-35. See also, Koon Woo Nam, *The North Korean Communist Leadership 1945-1965* (University: University of Alabama Press, 1974) and Dae-sook Suh and Chae-jin Lee, eds., *Political Leadership in Korea* (Seattle: University of Washington Press, 1977).

9. No systematic works on the North Korean political system based on this model is yet available. But, Chae-wan Yim, for example, urged such approach. See his, "Approach to the North Korean System in terms of Political Culture," *Vantage Point* (September 1984), pp. 1-11. For the works on communist political culture in general, see, for instance, Archi Brown and Jack Gray, *Political Culture and Political Change in Communist States* (New York: Holmes & Meier, 1977); Stephen White, *Political Culture and Soviet Politics* (London: Macmillan, 1979) and his "Political Culture in Communist States: Some Problems of Theory and Method," *Comparative Politics* (April 1984), pp. 351-366; Richard R. Fagan, *The Transformation of Political Culture in Cuba* (Stanford: Stanford University Press, 1969); Andrew J. Nathan, *Peking Politics, 1918-1923: Factionalism and the Failure of Constitutionalism* (Berkeley: University of California Press, 1976). Also, Robert Tucker, "Political Culture and Communist Society," *Political Science Quarterly* (June 1973), pp. 180-185; and Gabriel A. Almond, "Communism and Political Culture

Theory," *Comparative Politics* 15 (January 1983): 127-138. Studies on factionalism in socialist countries are found in Andrew J. Nathan, "A Factionalism Model for CCP Politics," *China Quarterly* 53 (January-March 1973): 34-66; Lucian W. Pye, *The Dynamics of Factions and Consensus in Chinese Politics: A Model and Some Propositions* (Santa Monica: Rand Corporation, 1980).

10. For a full discussion of the systems model, see David Easton, *A System Analysis of Political Life* (New York: John Wiley and Sons, 1965).

11. A notable example is Yong-pil Rhee's edited volume of *Pukhan Chŏngch'i* [North Korean Politics] (Seoul: *Daewang-sa*, 1982). See also, Young Whan Kihl, *Politics and Policies in Divided Korea: Regimes in Contest* (Boulder: Westview Press, 1984). Though theoretically less explicit, some earlier works also attempted to examine the North Korean political system *in toto*. For instance, Dong-wun Park, *Pukhan T'ongch'i Kigulon* [On the North Korean Governing Apparatus] (Seoul: Korea University Asiatic Studies Center, 1964); Glen D. Paige, *The Korean People's Democratic Republic* (Stanford: Hoover Institution on War, Revolution and Peace, 1966). See also, Chun-a Lee, "A Study of Factors Sustaining the North Korean Political System," *Pukhan* (September 1982), pp. 206-221.

12. J. Wiatr, "The Hegemonic Party System in Poland," in S. Rokhan and E. Allardt, eds., *Mass Politics: Studies in Political Sociology* (New York: Free Press, 1970), pp. 281-290 and Giovanni Sartori, *Parties and Party Systems: A Framework for Analysis* (Cambridge: Cambridge University Press, 1979), p. 227.

13. Myron Rush, *How Communist States Change Their Rulers* (Ithaca: Cornell University Press, 1974), p. 85.

14. The theories developed primarily by Marx and Engels are the dialectical materialism, the materialistic interpretation of history and class struggle, the dictatorship of the proletariat and withering away of the state and the theory of surplus value. Lenin's theoretical contributions include the vanguard theory of party and democratic centralism, violent proletarian revolution, the weakest-link-in-the-chain theory of war and the theory of imperialism. A good bibliography on Marx's own writing on these "theories" as well as other scholars' critical analyses of his works are found in Isaiah Berlin, *Karl Marx: His Life and Environment* (London: Oxford University Press, 1973), pp. 285-289. Also, William Ebenstein, *Great Political Thinkers: Plato to the Present* (Hillsdale: Dryden Press, 1969), pp. 977-985 and R. N. Carew Hunt, *The Theory and Practice of Communism* (Middlesex: A Pelican Book, 1971), pp. 293-306. A recent useful anthology of Lenin's works is edited by Robert C. Tucker, *The Lenin Anthology* (New York: W. W. Norton, 1975).

15. For an attempt to classify the various subtypes of communist economic systems, see John M. Montias, "A Classification of Communist Economic

Systems," in Cammelo Mesa-Lago and Carl Beck, eds., *Comparative Socialist Systems: Essays on Politics and Economics* (Pittsburgh: University of Pittsburgh Press, 1975), pp. 39-51.

16. V. I. Lenin, *What Is To Be Done?* (New York: International Publishers, 1929, 1943), pp. 76-77.

17. For Lenin's discussion of democratic centralism, see *The Lenin Anthology*, ed., Robert C. Tucker (New York: W. W. Norton, 1975), pp. 84-96.

18. See Richard F. Starr, "Checklist of Communist Parties in 1983," *Problems of Communism* (March-April, 1984): 41-51.

19. For details, see Part Five.

20. For a detailed discussion of totalitarianism and authoritarianism, see Part Six.

21. See Kim Il Sung, "Let Us Further Strengthen the Socialist System of Our Country," Speech given at the First Session of the Fifth SPA of the DPRK, 25 December 1977.

22. John Fairbank, *The United States and China* (Cambridge: Harvard University Press, 1979), p. 447.

23. The penetration crisis is one of six crises of political development. The other five are: legitimacy, participation, integration, identity and distribution. For details, see the chapter by Lucian Pye in Leonard Binder *et al.*, *Crises and Sequences in Political Development* (Princeton: Princeton University Press, 1971).

24. See, for instance, Richard Pipes, *Survial Is Not Enough: Soviet Realities and American Future* (New York: Simon and Schuster, 1984), pp. 179-186.

25. For details, see Vadim Medish, *The Soviet Union*, 2nd. rev. ed. (Englewood-Cliffs: Prentice-Hall, 1985), pp. 148-151.

26. For an analysis of the North Korean agriculture, see Sŏ-haeng Lee, "Management of North Korean Cooperative Farms, I, II, III" (in Korean), *Pukhan* (September, October, December, 1981): 70-81, 161-171 and 130-143, respectively. A short English version of his article is found in *Vantage Point* 4 (December 1981). Also, Un-gun Kim, "An Estimate of North Korea's Agricultural Output (II)," *Vantage Point* (October 1985): 1-11.

27. See, for instance, Seweryn Bialer, "The Sino-Soviet Conflict: the Soviet Dimension," in Donald S. Zagoria, ed., *Soviet Policy in East Asia* (New Haven: Yale University Press, 1982), pp. 93-120.

28. Robert A. Dahl and Edward R. Tufte, *Size and Democracy* (Stanford: Stanford University Press, 1973), pp. 20-21.

29. *Ibid.*, p. 138.

30. For a detailed analysis of Kim's varying use of "enemies" as a political strategem, see S. C. Yang, *Korea and Two Regimes* (Cambridge: Schenkman, 1981), pp. 177-197.

31. *Ibid.*, p. 187.

32. For details, see Part Five.
33. Kim's *Ch'ŏngsan-ri* method is found in S. C. Yang, *Op. Cit.*, pp. 197-203. For a discussion of Mao's *Dazhai*, see Fox Butterfield, *China: Alive in the Bitter Sea* (New York: Bantam Books), pp. 403-405.
34. See S. C. Yang, "The Kim Il Sung Cult in North Korea," *Korea and World Affairs* (Spring 1981): 161-186 and "The Politics of Cult in North Korea," *Political Studies Review* (1985): 27-52.
35. This theme is found in Chapter Two. For a comparison of North Korean communism with Chinese communism, see Byung-joon Ahn, "North Korean Communism and Chinese Communism," *Pukhan* (January 1980): 120-140.
36. George Kennan describes the Soviet neurotic siege mentality as follows: "it is a state of mind that assumes all forms of authority not under Soviet control to be wicked, hostile and menacing while conjuring up the image of a Soviet regime uniquely endowed with insight, wisdom and benevolence as it stands bravely against misguided and dangerous foreign forces, frustrating their evil designs and protecting its own grateful people. And its public pronouncements are characterized by "preposterous lapses of memory, shameless double-standards, claims of infallibility, cynical misuse of general terms such as 'democracy' and 'progressive' and 'imperialist,' and malicious distortion of the motives of others." George Kennan, *New Yorker*, September 1984. Quoted in *The Bulletin of Atomic Scientists* (January 1985), p. 8. As it is quite clear from the above, Kennan's meaning of the Soviet siege mentality is largely analogous to the siege mentality of the North Korean ruling elites.
37. For details, see Chapter Nine.
38. In 1983, for instance, 1,195,551 foreigners visited South Korea and 493,461 Koreans traveled abroad. A ten-year travel statistics from 1974 to 1983 is found in *Hankuk Ilbo*, 17 February 1984. Also, see *Korea Herald*, 14 February 1984. In 1990, 2,349,693 foreigners visited South Korea and 1,560,923 Koreans traveled abroad in *Korea Statistical Yearbook, 1991* (Seoul: The Korean Statistical Association, 1991), pp. 64-66.
39. The U.S. government's unprecedented act of issuing visas to three North Korean scholars, who took part in a panel sponsored by the Mid-Atlantic Coast Conference of the Association of Asian Studies at the George Washington University on October 26, 1985, is an example.
40. The present author saw a documentary film of this scene while visiting North Korea in the summer of 1981.
41. For details, see Part Five.
42. See, for instance, Fox Butterfield, *China: Alive in the Bitter Sea*, pp. 64-88.
43. *Ibid.*, p. 388. In China, for instance, there are four layers of news. At the bottom comes a four-page tabloid-sized paper called the *reference news*, whose circulation is about 10 million; next is the *reference material*, which is avail-

able only to the party members and cadres through their *danwei* [unit], not to individuals; the *internal reference* is available only to the officials above grade 12 on the ladder of 24 ranks, and finally, there is the *cable news*, which is limited to the members of the Central Committee and the commanders of the large military regions. For details, see Butterfield, pp. 383-405.

44. See, for instance, Philip E. Converse, "The Nature of Belief Systems in Mass Publics," in Norman Luttbeg, ed., *Public Opinion and Public Policy*, rev. ed. (Homewood: Dorsey Press, 1974), pp. 300-344. In his recent article, Converse stated that "state monopoly of information flows is a very central part of the blueprint for governance" in Marxist-Leninist governments, not just in wartime or under duress, but as a routine matter. By contrast, military dictatorships, while keen on monopolizing public information, "tend to come and go in rather short stints." He further lamented about a severe lack of relevant theoretical literature on the relationship between power and information in Marxist-Leninist states. For details, see his "Power and the Monopoly of Information," *APSR* (March 1985): 1-9. Also, Angus Campbell, "The Passive Citizen," in Edward C. Dreyer and Walter A. Rosenbaum, *Political Opinion and Behavior* (North Scituate: Duxbury Press, 1976), pp. 164-184.

45. North Korea's official publications include: *Nodong Sinmun* [Workers' Daily], a daily organ of the Workers' Party of Korea; *Minju Chŏson* [Democratic Korea], an organ of the DPRK government; *Kulloja* [Workers], a theoretical monthly organ of the WPK; *Nodong Ch'ŏngnyon* [Working Youth], a daily organ of the Socialist Working Youth League of Korea; *Nodongja Sinmun* [Worker's News], an organ of the General Federation of Trade Unions published every two days; *Chosŏn Inminkun Sinmun* [Korean People's Army News], a daily organ of the Ministry of People's Armed Forces; *Choguk* [Fatherland], a weekly by the Fatherland United Democratic Front; *Choguk Tongil Sinmun* [Fatherland Unification News], a biweekly by the Committee for the Peaceful Reunification of the Fatherland; *Ch'ŏllima* [Flying Horse], a monthly by *Kunjung Munhwa* [Mass Culture] Publishing House; *Pyongyang Sinmun* [Pyongyang News], a daily organ of the WPK Pyongyang Municipal Committee; and *Pyongyang Times*, an English paper.

46. For details, see S. C. Yang, "The Kim Il Sung Cult in North Korea," and "The Politics of Cult in North Korea."

47. *Ibid.*

48. *Ibid.*

49. The Kim Il Sung pseudo-charisma thesis is developed by Yong-pil Rhee. For details, see his *Pukhan Chŏngch'i* [North Korean Politics] (Seoul: Daewang-sa, 1982), pp. 52-54.

50. For details, see S. C. Yang, "The Politics of Cult in North Korea."

CHAPTER 7

FORMAL POLITICAL STRUCTURES AND THEIR EVOLUTION

The communist party structure is exceedingly strong, and it owes its strength to that very feature that non-communists most dislike—the rigid discipline it imposes.

R. N. Carew Hunt[1]

We take immense pride in summing up the great victories and successes which the Party (WPK) and the people, united firmly as one, have achieved through hard-fought battles.

Kim Il Sung[2]

What politics sets out to accomplish in *form* is sometimes vastly different from its actual outcome in *operation*. Nowhere is such a gap more apparent than it is in North Korea. Kim Il Sung and his key players in the WPK ruling circles dominate politics. The formal political structures are set up to accommodate Kim and his ruling groups rather than the latter following the rules of the former. The North Korean political system is based neither on the principle of *separation* of powers as is the case with the presidential system in the United States, nor on the principle of *diffusion* of powers, as it is practiced under the parliamentary systems. Rather, it is based on *unity* and increasingly on *uniformity* of powers. The North Korean political structure, in short, represents the classic case of the monolithic power.

In the United States, for instance, the three branches of the government—the executive, the legislative, and the judiciary—are independent of each other to a high degree, due to the principles of separation of powers and of checks and balances. The political power is not only separated into various institutions but shared by them. In the United Kingdom, the executive and the legislative powers are diffused in that the party, which controls the majority in the Parliament, is empowered to form the executive cabinet, but without ever losing each other's institutional independence and integrity. By contrast, in North Korea, the executive, the legislative. and the judiciary are institutionally *unified* under the direction and control of the WPK.

Specifically, the WPK leadership determines the nominees of the Supreme People's Assembly (SPA), which, in turn, elects the President of the DPRK and the members of the Central People's Committee (CPC). The President and the CPC control and preside over the Administrative Council, the Central Court and the Central Procurator's Office. The state powers are *concentrated* in one institution, WPK, and, ultimately, in one person, Kim Il Sung (now, increasingly Kim Jŏng Il as well). Kim Il Sung is the General Secretary of the WPK, chairman of the WPK Politburo, chairman of the WPK Central Committee (CC), and chairman of the WPK Central Military Commission. Under the 1972 Constitution he was the President of the DPRK, chairman of the SPA Central People's Committee and chairman of the SPA National Defense Commission. But under the newly revised Constitution enacted on April 9, 1992, the President is no longer the supreme commander of the armed forces, the chairman of the National Defense Commission and is deprived of the power to ratify or annul treaties. Now Kim Jŏng Il, formally at least the designated successor, is de facto "the number one man" in all these key positions. The appointment of the junior Kim as the supreme commander of the armed forces in December 24, 1991, by the WPK 6th Central Committee's 19th Plenum attests to the ongoing father-son succession scheme. Beyond this personalistic predominance, the North Korean political system is marked by the *cross-penetration* of the WPK and the governing organs. For instance, the personnel and their rank in the WPK Central Committee closely overlap those in the

SPA Central People's Committee. Similarly, the WPK Central Military Commission and the SPA National Defense Commission have a virtually identical personnel. In short, North Korea today is ruled by Kim Il Sung-Kim Jŏng Il through the WPK instrumentalities or, conversely, it is ruled by the WPK through the Kim Il Sung-Kim Jŏng Il personality cult. Still, formal structural trappings of the various governing organs are worth studying. What follows is a detailed account of North Korea's formal political organs and instruments.

The Workers' Party of Korea

Origins

The formal origin of the Korean communist movement can be traced back to June 26, 1918, when two Korean expatriates, Yi Dong-hwi (1918-1935) and Kim Rip, founded *Hanin Sahoe-tang* (Korean People's Socialist Party) in Khabarovsk, Soviet Siberia. When Yi Dong-Hwi was named the first Premier of the Korean Provisional Government in Shanghai in the wake of the 1919 March First Movement that year, his Korean People's Socialist Party also moved to Shanghai via Vladivostok. Earlier, on January 22, 1918, a Korean section of the Russian Communist Party was founded in Irkutsk under the leadership of Nam Man Ch'ŏn, a Korean expatriate. Therefore, the Korean communist movement had two origins—the Irkutsk group and the Khabarovsk group (later the Shanghai group). These two groups vied for the hegemony of the Korean communist movement and for the official recognition and support of the Communist International.[3]

In the 1920s, numerous communist and communist-leaning organizations and study groups appeared in Korea, although their secret and underground activities were constantly scrutinized and severely hampered by the Japanese authorities. Kim Yak-su's *Ilwŏl-hoe* [the January Society], Kim Chae Bong and Cho Bong Am's *Hwayo-hoe* [the Tuesday Society], and Yi Yŏng's Seoul Youth Association are noteworthy. The January Society was the offshoot of the earlier Black Wave Society which had been organized in Tokyo by the leftist Korean students in November 1921. When the Black Wave Society moved its base from Tokyo to Seoul in November 1924, its official name was changed to the North Star Society and finally to the January Society in January, 1925.[4]

The Tuesday Society was the outgrowth of the earlier Saturday Society which was organized by Kim Chae-bong and Cho Bong-am on May 20, 1923. The Saturday Society was renamed the New Thought Study Association on July 7, 1923, and then called the Tuesday Society on November 19, 1924.[5]

The Seoul Youth Association, led by Yi Yŏng, Pak Hŏn-yŏng and Kim Sa-guk, was the leftist offshoot of the Federation of Korean Youth, a larger pannational youth organization which was created under the leadership of Chang Dŏk Su on December 20, 1920. The Seoul Youth Association maintained close relations with such communist-leaning organization as the Proletariat Comrade Society which was founded in January 1922. The Proletariat Comrade Society became the Proletariat League on March 31, 1922.

In terms of the Korean communist lineage, the Irkutsk group had an organizational link with the Tuesday Society while the Shanghai group had a close affiliation with the Seoul Youth Association. On April 17, 1925, the three major communist groups in Korea—the Tuesday Society, the January Society and the Seoul Youth Association—agreed to merge and immediately convened their first United Congress of the Korean Communist Party (KCP) in Seoul under the leadership of Kim Chae-bong, who was elected its first secretary. The close Japanese surveillance and constant crackdowns on Korean communist leaders severely impeded the activities and the growth of the Korean communist movement at home. When Kim Chae-bong, the first KCP chairman, was arrested by the Japanese authorities in February, 1926, Kang Dal-yong, another KCP leader succeeded him as the chairman at the second KCP Congress. Kang was captured by the Japanese authorities on July 17, 1926, and the KCP remained for a while without a leader. The Third Party Congress was controlled by the leaders of the executive committee of the Congress, often called the Marxist-Leninist group. They were a coalition of three groups within the KCP, the Seoul group led by Yi

Chong-yun, the Shanghai group led by Kim Ch'ŏl-su, and the January group led by A'n Kwang-ch'ŏn. On February 27, 1928, the Fourth Congress of the KCP was convened under the leadership of Ch'a Gum-bong, who along with other key leaders of the KCP were arrested by the Japanese authorities. Two more attempts were made to reactivate the KCP, first by Kim Ch'ŏl-su, who organized the KCP Reestablishment Preparation Association in June, 1929, and second, by Kwŏn T'ae-hyŏng, who created the KCP Reestablishment Council in February 1931. Both attempts failed without much progress. The KCP remained inactive from 1931 to the end of the Japanese rule in Korea in August 1945.[6]

Founding

North Korea officially celebrates October 10, 1945, as the founding date of the WPK. This is, however, somewhat misleading. On August 20, 1945, Pak Hŏn-yong, formerly a key member of the Tuesday Society and the Kyŏngsŏng Com Club, regrouped the various rival communist organizations in Korea and reactivated the KCP in Seoul. He also drafted his so-called "August Theses."[7] The day after the Korean liberation on August 16, 1945, the Seoul Group (*Changan-p'a*) led by Yi Yŏng, Ch'oe Ik-han and Chŏng Baek had launched its communist activities. But on August 24, four days after the release of Pak's August Theses, which, *inter alia*, attacked factionalism, the Seoul Group decided to dissolve itself and join Pak's KCP Reconstruction Preparatory Committee. On September 8, the two groups held a meeting to merge, and Pak was chosen to lead the unified KCP. On November 23, Pak successfully incorporated his rival Seoul Group of the Irkutsk faction into the KCP. For a while, at least, all rival communist elements in Korea were united under the KCP. One major exception was the New People's Party, whose members consisted of Korean returnees from China, i.e., the Yanan Group.

Pak's leadership did not last long. The *Chŏng-p'an-sa* Incident, among other things, became a political catalyst for the U.S. Military Government to outlaw communist activities within South Korea in May 1946. The police had reportedly found three million *won* in counterfeit currency printed by Chŏng-p'an-sa, the publisher of the *Hae-bang Ilbo* [Liberation Daily], the KCP organ. This bogus money was to help finance the KCP activities. Shortly after this incident, the U.S. Military Government authorities issued a warrant for the arrest of Pak and his associates. Under these excruciating political circumstances, Pak and other communist leaders in the South again went underground.[8]

Meanwhile in Pyongyang, two rival communist groups—the North Korean Branch of the KCP and the New People's Party—held a meeting to merge on October 10-13, 1946, and created the Workers' Party of North Korea (WPNK). In the South, three underground communist groups—the KCP, the New People's Party, and the People's Party—met for a similar purpose on November 23-24, 1946, and established the Workers' Party of South Korea (WPSK). The chairman of the WPNK during its first (August 28-30, 1946) and second congresses (March 27-30, 1948) was Kim Tu-bong, leader of the Yanan group. His counterpart at the WPSK during this period was Hŏ Hŏn (since the *Chŏng-p'an-sa* Incident all communist activities were outlawed in South Korea). Pak Hŏn-yŏng, leader of the WPSK, fled to the North at the end of 1946. From June 30 to July 1, 1949, the Workers' Party of North Korea and South Korea (only those members who fled to the North from the South) merged and, thus, the Workers' Party of Korea (WPK) officially came into being. After this merger, Kim Il Sung took the chairmanship of the WPK. The chairmanship post was replaced by the office of the general secretary at the Fourteenth Plenum of the WPK Fourth Central Committee (CC) on October 12, 1966, and Kim has been the WPK's general secretary ever since.

Organs and Functions

The WPK's party congress is, formally at least, the highest party organization. The bylaws of the first congress stipulated that the party congress meet annually, but this rule was never enforced and the meeting of the party congress was later fixed for every four years. Even this four-year rule has not been observed. The WPK congress has been meeting irregularly. Thus far, the WPK has held six congresses. The first congress convened in August, 1946, the second in March, 1948, the third in April, 1956, the fourth in September, 1961, the fifth in November, 1970, and the sixth in October, 1980.

The second congress was held less than two years after the first but the third congress was not convened until eight years after the second due primarily to the outbreak of the Korean War. As noted above, Kim Tu-bong, served as the chairman of the first and second party congresses, while Hŏ Hŏn, chaired the WPSK congresses. Kim Il Sung was elected the chairman after the North and South Korean branches merged in 1949. Kim Il Sung has chaired the WPK since its inception. Noteworthy also is that Kim Il Sung (1912-   ) and Kim Il (1912-1983), his closest partisan comrade-in-arm, are the only two, who have served in all six congresses as members of the WPK CC.

As the WPK grew, each successive party congress was held for longer durations until the fifth congress. The first congress met for three days, the second for four days, the third for seven days, the fourth for eight days, the fifth for twelve days and the sixth lasted four days (For details, see Table 7-1). Two points deserve attention in this regard.

First, the role of the party congress has been, at best, nominal and ceremonial. As it has been the practice at most socialist countries, the real powers of the WPK are shared by the Central Committee (CC) and its Standing Committees, especially the Secretariat and the Presidium of the Politburo, formerly the Political Committee. Ultimately, the supreme power is in the hands of Kim Il Sung, who is the chairman of these organs: CC, the Secretariat, the Politburo and the Central Military Commission. The delegates listen to the lengthy and mostly self-congratulatory reports of the party work by its chairman and other designated speakers. At these meetings, new economic plans are usually unveiled and the new members of the Central Committee and other committees are elected. According to the 1980 WPK bylaws, the party congress has four major functions: (1) report the work of the Central Committee and the Central Auditing Committee; (2) amend or supplement the platform and bylaws of the party; (3) decide on the party line and policies and of basic problems of strategy and tactics; and (4) elect members of the Central Committee and the Central Auditing Committee of the party.[9]

Second, the party congresses have generally followed the completion of the current economic plan and the launching of the new. The first congress was followed by the first one-year plan in 1947. The second congress coincided with the second one-year plan in 1948. The third congress coincided with the second three-year plan, 1954-1956 (the first three-year plan, 1951-1953, was unfinished due to the Korean War). The fourth congress paralleled the completion of the five-year plan, 1957-1961, completed a year ahead of schedule, and launching of the first seven-year plan, 1961-1967, which was extended to 1970. The second seven year plan, 1978-1984, was, however, launched two years before the 1980 sixth congress. The third seven year plan, 1987-1993, is ongoing but the 7th Congress has not yet convened.

Between party congresses, the Central Committee (CC) directs the work of the Party. It supposedly convenes at least once every six months. The plenary meeting of the CC deliberates and decides on important issues of the party, elects the general secretary, secretaries, and members of the Political Committee, of the Military Affairs Committee and the Inspection Committee and organizes the Secretariat of the party. Other key functions of the CC are to: (1) formulate the monolithic ideological system for the party; (2) organize and direct party policies; (3) direct the organizational life of party members and auxiliary forces; (4) organize the party committees at every level; (5) organize the revolutionary armed forces; (6) represent the party in its external relations with other political parties within and outside of the country; and (7) convene a party conference between party congresses (two party conferences have been held, one in March 1958 between the third and fourth party congresses and another in October 1966 between the fourth and fifth party congresses).[10]

The methods used to elect the CC members and CC candidate members have varied over the years. The first party congress voted on a prepared list of nominees, and it was not disclosed who or how many people served on the nominating committee. The delegates to the second party congress voted for each nominee to the CC separately. Reportedly, all nominees received unanimous approval except O Ki-sŏp, who received five nay votes and was purged in 1958.[11] Article 26 of the revised bylaws of the WPK third party congress stipulated that the election of members to the various party committees and leadership organizations must be by secret ballot, and each nominee must be voted in separately. But at the fourth party congress, a fifty-five member Nominating Council presented a slate of nominees to the various offices, including the CC, and the delegates unanimously approved the slate. Few facts are available about how the fifth and sixth party congresses elected the CC and other party committees. It is speculated that the method similar to the one used by the fourth party congress was adopted at these two congresses.

The number of the CC members elected by the six party congresses and of the delegates to the congresses in parentheses are as follows:

The 1946 First Congress	......	43 (801)
The 1948 Second Congress	......	67 (999)
The 1956 Third Congress	......	71 (916)
The 1961 Fourth Congress	......	85 (1,657)
The 1970 Fifth Congress	......	117 (1,734)
The 1980 Sixth Congress	......	145 (3,220)[12]

The first party CC met twelve times from August 1946 to February 1948. The WPK's first congress bylaws (article 16) stipulated that the CC meet at least once every three months. It met eight times in 1947. The second party CC met seventeen times from March, 1948, to December, 1955. After the merger of the North and South Korean Workers' Party in June 1949, the CC meetings were called joint plenums until after the Korean War. During the War, June, 1950, to July, 1953, only three plenums were held, and from 1954 each plenum was named after the month in which it was held. The third party CC met thirteen times from April 1956 to September 1961. The fourth party CC met twenty times from September 1961 to December 1969. The fifth party CC met twenty times from November 1970 to October 1980. The sixth party CC so far met 20 times as of July 1992.

The agendas for the party congresses and conferences have usually been announced, but the CC agendas are not announced. Most of the CC agendas are later reported in the party organ, but some are kept secret.

The CC secret meetings and agendas often involved intra-party strifes. For instance, at the August plenum of the third CC in 1946, the expulsion of the anti-party reactionaries was discussed. At the fifteenth and the sixteenth plenums of the fourth CC, a large number of generals and party functionaries were expelled from the party.[13]

Day-to-day party activities are coordinated by the WPK Secretariat, one of the two key standing committees of the CC. The Secretariat deals with the problems of cadres, internal and other problems of the party and acts on its decision. The Political Committee, the other powerful standing committee, formulates policies and makes all important policy decisions. It directs and organizes all party work on behalf of the CC between plenary meetings. It meets at least once every month.

In the First WPK Congress in 1946, the central party organs were divided into the Political Committee (5 members), the Standing Committee (13 members) and the Central Inspection Committee (11 members). In the Second Congress in 1948, the Political Committee and the Standing Committee members increased from five to seven and thirteen to seventeen, respectively. The Central Inspection Committee was renamed the Inspection Committee whose members decreased from eleven to six. And a new standing committee, the Organization Committee (5 members), was added. In the Fourth Plenum of the WPK CC on October 12, 1966, the 10-member Secretariat was created while the Standing Committee was abolished. In the Sixth Congress in 1980, the Political Committee was renamed the Politburo.

There are three other standing committees—the Control Commission, the Central Military Affairs Commission and the Central Auditing Commission. The Control Commission, formerly the Inspection Committee, enforces party rules and regulations and supervises party activities. It investigates anti-party, anti-revolutionary factional activities contrary to "the monolithic ideological system of the party." It is noteworthy that only three of forty-three people who served on this committee were reelected and the rate of turnover in membership is the highest among all the CC standing committees. Dae-sook Suh speculates two reasons for this. The committee members take their job too seriously and enforce the rules to the letter and, thus, create too many enemies within the party. Or, their appointment is political and their job is perfunctory.[14] The Central Military Affairs Commission, previously called the Military Committee, is potentially the most potent organ whose chairman is Kim Il Sung. It formulates military policies, operates military industries and commands all armed forces. The Central Auditing Commission, formerly the Central Auditing Committee, deals with the financial affairs of the party.

The WPK CC Political Bureau coordinates and directs provincial, city, county and basic level party organizations. At the provincial level the provincial party conference is the highest party organization. It is convened once every two years by the Provincial Committee (PC). The PC holds a plenary meeting at least once every four months. It elects the general secretary and other secretaries of the standing committees. It organizes the Secretariat and elects members of the Military Committee and the Inspection Committee. The PC Standing Committees meet at least once a month. The PC and its Standing Committees carry out the corresponding functions of the national party CC and CC standing committees at the provincial level.

The city and county party conferences are the highest party organization at that level. They are covened every two years by the City and County Party Committee (CCPC). The CCPC elects its general secretary and secretaries of the CCPC, as well as the members of the Military Committee and the Inspection Committee. The CCPC and its standing committees carry out the corresponding functions of the PC and PC standing committees at the city and county level (see Chart 7-1).

The party cell constitutes the lowest organization of the WPK. It is organized from administration and production units with more than five to fifteen party members. A unit comprising more than sixteen members establishes a primary party committee. A sectional party committee can be set up between the party cell and the primary party committee by an administration or production unit with more than sixteen members. The general meeting represents the highest primary party organizations. The general meeting of the party cell meets once a month; the general meeting of the primary party committee and the sectional party committee is held once every three months. The functions and duties of the primary, the subprimary and the sectional party committees are to carry out the party lines and policies.

Noteworthy also is the fact that the Korean People's Army (KPA) Party Committee and the League of Socialist Working Youth are organized under the direct supervision of the WPK CC. The WPK CC supervises the KPA through the latter's General Political Bureau. The WPK also coordinates activities and programs with other auxiliary organizations, such as the League of Socialist Working Youth, the General Federation of Trade Unions, the League of Agricultural Working People and the Democratic Women's Union of Korea.

Membership

To be a member of the WPK, one must be a revolutionary who "fight [s] for the fatherland, the people and the ultimate victory of socialism and communism," and he or she must be armed with "the monolithic ideological system."[15] The WPK members are recruited from the candidate members who have fulfilled a specified probationary period. The probationary period is a year; it can be extended for another year if a candidate is not fully qualified. For those who failed to qualify for membership at the end of the probationary period, the general meeting of the party cell must decide on expulsion. In special cases, an applicant may be accepted as a member without the probationary period. A person is eligible for admission at age eighteen.

A person must take the following admission procedures: to be a candidate, he or she must submit an application form to the party cell with letters of recommendation from two members of the party; a recommender must have been a party member for more than two years and must know the past and present social and political activities of the candidate; the application form and recommendations are not required for a candidate applying for a membership, unless the party cell deems it necessary; a member of the League of Socialist Working Youth applying to be a candidate may substitute a recommendation from one party member for a recommendation from the city or county committee of the league.

The 1980 WPK bylaws lists ten duties and five rights of its members.

The ten duties are: (1) stand firmly on the monolithic ideological system of the party; "be boundlessly loyal to the Great Leader Comrade Kim Il Sung" (newly added in 1980); unconditionally accept, preserve and carry out the party line and policies; study, preserve and promote the revolutionary tradition of the party; fight against all antiparty and antirevolutionary lines of "capitalism" (newly added instead of "bourgeoisie ideologies"), revisionism, dogmatism, "flunkeyism"(newly added); feudalistic Confucianism, factionalism, provincialism and nepotism; and protect the unity of the party based on the *Juche* idea; (2) participate actively in the organizational life of the party; be trained in the party spirit; revolutionize and "working-classize" oneself; participate actively in party meetings and study groups, carry out the assigned works of the party, review one's party life daily, carry out ideological struggle through self-criticism; and transform himself or herself into a revolutionary; (3) upgrade continuously one's political, ideological, and cultural standards by studying the general principles of Marxism and Leninism; study the party lines, policies, and revolutionary traditions; and analyze current problems based on correct understanding of the party policies; (4) carry out the revolutionary mass line and work with the masses; explain the party line and policies to the masses, educate and transform them, organize them around the party and mobilize them for party work and meet their demands by correctly understanding the masses; (5) set an example for the masses; have a higher standard of political awareness; be a vanguard of revolutionary tasks; should love work and participate actively in the technical revolutionary movement; and increase the level of production, participate in the management of enterprises, preserve and protect social properties of the state; (6) possess lofty communist moral character; sacrifice individual gains for the benefit of the organization; and be frugal, humble, unselfish, humane, cultured, and frank before the party; (7) defend the socialist fatherland; be alert and be ready to be mobilized, and learn about the military; defend the revolutionary gains against enemy intrusions; and be determined to fight in the war of fatherland unification; (8) obey orders of the revolutionary system, maintain vigilance at all times, and keep secrets of the party and state; (9) report problems to appropriate party organizations up to the Central Committee; and (10) pay dues each month.

The WPK members' five rights are: (1) to express "constructive" opinions in the party meetings and in the party publications for the purpose of carrying out party policies; (2) to elect or to be elected to every leading party organization at all levels; (3) to criticize any member in party meetings for cause, and to refuse any order contrary to the monolithic ideological system of the party; (4) to demand participation in any party meeting that deliberates and decides on one's own behavior and work; and (5) to initiate a request or appeal to every party committee including the Central Committee and demand investigation.[16]

The number of party members has grown from about 4,500 in 1945 to 3 million in 1990. Until the fourth party congress, the party statistics dealing with the number of party members, the composition of the delegation to the congresses and the number of basic cell organizations were given at each party congress. But these informations were withheld at the fifth and sixth congresses. The latest figures are the estimate based on Kim Il Sung's speech at the WPK Sixth Congress on October 10, 1980. He remarked that each of those 3,220 delegates attending the congress represents 1,000 members. If this estimate is true, party members, constitute about 17% of the total population, which means that North Korea has the highest ratio of communist party members to the total population in all present and past socialist countries (See Table 7-1).

An Analysis

A personal profile analysis of some 523 WPK CC members from the First Congress through the Sixth Congress reveals a number of interesting characteristics. To begin with, one caveat is in order. The data-gathering for this analysis, let alone in all other areas is severely limited primarily due to the fact that North Korea still remains the prototype of a closed society. Hence, the present profile analysis is heuristic at best and inherently incomplete at worst. Bearing this limitation in mind, the following findings can be spelled out.

First, as Table 7-2 indicates, less than a half of the data for the CC members' place of origin (48.2%) is available. Still, it reveals that among all the regions the Hamgyŏng Provinces, especially North Hamgyŏng has had the largest number of representation in the CC membership. Some 114 CC members out of 523 are identified as being from the North Hamgyŏng Province. Noteworthy also is that the CC members from the former Soviet Union and Manchuria are the third largest, while the identifiable CC members from the South Pyŏngan Province, where Kim Il Sung was born and raised, number only 22 members. Two observations are possible for this. One, the core of the North Korean political leadership was heavily recruited from the anti-Japanese partisan guerrilla groups (For details, see Table 7-6). The Hamgyŏng provinces, particularly the North Hamgyŏng Province, Manchuria and a part of the Soviet Siberia were the main staging areas for anti-Japanese guerrilla activities. Two, deleterious regionalism such as the potential and actual conflict existing between the Kyŏngsang and the Chŏlla provinces in the present South Korean politics is apparently non-existent in North Korea. This further indicates that if in South Korea the *location* where the leader, i.e., the president, was born and raised counts the most in its elite recruitment, in North Korea the "absolute" and "unconditional" *loyalty* to the "Great Leader" and now increasingly to the "Dear Leader" has been the first and foremost criterion for its elite cooptation.

Secondly, the CC member's educational background, although the data for only about a third of its total membership is available (33.5%), is quite interesting. The former Soviet Union represents the country where the largest number of CC members were educated and trained (63 are identified out of 523 CC members). It can be inferred from this that post-Kim Il Sung (and post-Kim Jŏng Il as well) leadership in North Korea is most likely to emerge from some of these Soviet-educated and trained group (For details, see Table 7-3).

Thirdly, Table 7-4 illustrates the CC members' governmental and party positions that they held previously. This category evinces nothing startling except for the reaffirmation that, like in all past and present socialist states the WPK CC members' party, administrative, military and other parapolitical positions clearly demonstrate the overlapping membership characteristics.

Fourthly, the CC members' foreign travel experiences are very interesting. As expected, the two countries to which the CC members traveled most frequently are China and the former Soviet Union. They also traveled to the former socialist countries in Eastern Europe and Afro-Asian and Latin countries. But their travel to Western Europe, the United States and the other so-called non-communist countries has been severely limited. This signifies that they have seen only the communist camp and a part of the Third World, and none of the other parts of the globe at best. Worse still, being a Hermit Kingdom-like society, North Korea has severely limited foreign travel itself to the very select few. This fact alone seriously impairs the North Korean ruling elites' worldview (For details, see Table 7-5).

Finally, the CC members' age and sex characteristics deserve attention. Although only about a third of the age data is available, it is self-evident that the older generations of leadership have been declining in number mostly by natural death and some through purge (See Table 7-7). The Senior Kim, an octogenarian himself and his partisan comrades-in-arms are getting fewer in number. For example, *Rodong Shinmun* carried a front page photograph of Kim Il Sung and his still living anti-Japanese comrades-in-arm on March 14, 1992. According to this picture, those who are still alive number 52, of which 22 are women. The female representation in the CC has been a token symbolism. Only 23 out of the 523 total CC members from the First Congress through the Sixth Congress have been women (See Table 7-8).

The Supreme People's Assembly (SPA)

Origins and Evolution

Like China's National People's Congress (NPC) and the former Soviet Union's Supreme Soviet, the SPA is, nominally at least, the highest legislative body in North Korea (the Supreme Soviet was bicameral, however, consisting of the Soviet of the Union and the Soviet of Nationalities, while the NPC and the SPA are unicameral). Because of the towering presence of Kim Il Sung, the SPA is, perhaps, more nominal than its Chinese and former Soviet counterparts. Prior to the creation of the DPRK in September, 1948, two interim organizations performed similar functions. The North Korean Provisional People's Committee was created in February, 1946, under the auspices of the Soviet occupation authorities. It met three times in 1946 and passed laws on elections, land reforms and administrative redistricting of counties and provinces. It was replaced by the North Korean People's Assembly in February 1947. It performed legislative functions until the SPA formally came into existence in September, 1948. The first SPA lasted nearly ten years from 1948 to 1957 due primarily to the Korean War and its aftermath. The succeeding assemblies were convened every five years: the second assembly, 1957-1962; the third assembly, 1962-1967; the fourth assembly, 1967-1972; the fifth assembly, 1972-1977; the sixth assembly, 1977-1982; the seventh assembly, 1982-1986; the eighth assembly, 1986-1990; and the ninth assembly, 1990 to the present.

Agendas for all sessions are usually reported and known. But in reality, the SPA Standing Committee, a much smaller body of twenty or less members, controls most of the legislative agendas and activities. The SPA Standing Committee agendas are not disclosed.

In 1948 both the North and South Korean government authorities claimed the exclusive sovereignty of the entire Korea. This political atmosphere was reflected in the make-up of both North and South Korean legislative bodies. The First SPA of North Korea proclaimed a fictitious election in the South and filled the seats allocated to the southern half with representatives, in name only in most cases, from the South. Of the 572 representatives, 360 were supposedly elected from the South, while 212 were elected from the North. It was claimed that an incredible 99.97% voters turned out (the National Assembly in the South left almost one-third of its assembly seats vacant for the representatives from the North). In subsequent SPA elections, the North reported a 100 percent voter turnout, but the nominees and those elected were exactly the same in number. An interesting fact is that the WPK, not the people, decides on the nominees to the SPA.

From the Second Assembly, all seats allocated to the representatives from the South were eliminated, and the number of members was reduced from 572 to 215 (the net increase amounted to only 3 since there were 212 representatives from the North in the First Assembly). In the Third Assembly, the membership was increased from 215 to 385, an increase of 68. This increment resulted from a reapportionment of electoral districts from one seat per 50,000 people to one seat per 30,000. The membership was increased from 385 to 457 in the Fourth Assembly, although the ratio of representation remained the same as the Third Assembly.

The Fifth Assembly changed its structure considerably. The center of the SPA powers shifted from the Standing Committee to the Central Peoples Committee (CPC). The Fifth SPA membership rose, once again, from 457 to 541. The Sixth SPA membership increase was modest at 38 from 541 to 579. The membership of both the Standing Committee (eighteen before) and the CPC (twenty-five before) was reduced to fifteen each at the Sixth Assembly. The Seventh SPA membership, again, increased from 579 to 615. The membership of the Eighth and the Ninth Assemblies have been 655 and 687, respectively (For details, see Table 7-9).

The characteristics of the SPA members have changed considerably over the years. In terms of background, the representation of peasants declined significantly from 34% in the First SPA to only 10.2% in the Seventh SPA. Since the Sixth Assembly the category called the "collective farm workers" replaced the "peasant representatives." In the Ninth Assembly the collective farm workers constituted 10.4%. The workers and office workers' representations nearly doubled from 21% in the First Assembly to 37% in the 9th Assembly (For details, see Table 7-10). The SPA delegates are also much older. The 40 to 50 age group has increased, for instance, from 30% in the First SPA to 68.2% in the Ninth SPA. In the Seventh SPA 3.9% were below age 37, 71.2% between ages 36 and 55, and 15.5% above age 55. In educational background, more college graduates are represented; they represented only 40% in the First SPA, but 70% in the Sixth SPA (For details, see Table 7-11).

Organs and Formal Powers

On paper, the SPA is the highest organ of state, and its Central

People's Committee, the highest leadership organ of state in North Korea (Articles 87 and 117 of the 1992 DPRK Constitution). Again, on paper at least, under the new 1992 Constitution the powers of the SPA have been strengthened at the expense of the presidential powers. Likewise, the CPC powers have been weakened and the National Defense Commission powers have been strengthened instead. The SPA deputies are elected for five years on the principle of universal, equal and direct suffrage by a secret ballot. But in reality the SPA election (elections at all level, for that matter) is in name only. The SPA holds regular and extraordinary sessions. The regular session is convened once or twice a year by the SPA Standing Committee. Each session lasts usually two or three days (For details, see Table 7-12). The extraordinary session is held whenever the Standing Committee deems it necessary, or at the request of one-third of the total deputies. The SPA Standing Committee is a permanent body; it consists of the Chairman, Vice-chairmen, Secretary and members. The Chairman and Vice-chairmen of the SPA are concurrently the Chairman and Vice-Chairmen of the Standing Committee. The President of the DPRK is the Chairman of the Central People's Committee (CPC). The CPC includes the President and Vice-Presidents of the DPRK and the Secretary and members of the CPC. The CPC's term of office is four years. In addition, the SPA has Budget Committee, Bills Committee, Unification Policy Committee and Foreign Policy Committee (see Chart 7-2).

The interpretations and implications of reducing the powers of the president which are almost ceremonial under the new 1992 Constitution are as follows:

First, the new Constitution tries to reflect the diminishing ability and the declining health of the aging "great leader" and formally at least, to meet the newly acquired powers of Kim Jŏng Il;

Second, it closely resembles the revised 1982 PRC Constitution (amended again in 1987). The SPA powers are not yet as powerful as those of China's National People's Congress, but they are getting closer to the latter (for details, see Chart 7-2). Likewise, the once powerful presidential powers have become ceremonial, though not yet as ceremonial as those of China's counterpart. Still, the important difference between the 1992 revised Constitution of the DPRK and the 1982 revised Constitution of the PRC lies, among other things, in the fact that the former was revised while Kim Il Sung is still alive and the latter was revamped after Mao's death.

Third, wishfully or not, the framers of the revised Constitution appear to hope that the fading away of the "Great Leader" would not affect the the stability of the nation, especially its military organization and operation. Specifically, unlike the 1972 Constitution under which the President was the *ex-officio* Chairman of the National Defense Commission (NDC), the SPA now elects or recalls the Chairman of the NDC.

What is more, now the Chairman of the NDC, not the president, has full powers of command and control of the military forces. In a way, this is the Constitutional preventive mechanism which, hopefully at least, tries to preempt potential political, military, and/or civil instability arising from the demise of Kim Il Sung and/or the collapse of the current North Korean ruling regimes.

Finally, and most importantly, the framers of the revised Constitution, cleverly anticipating the assumption of the presidency by Kim Jŏng Il in the near future, made the powers and position of the presidency nothing more than a ceremonial duty so that the powers can be exercised by the men who have the real power at the NDC and the SPA.

An Analysis

A personal profile analysis of some 3,438 Supreme People's Assembly members from its First Assembly through its Ninth Assembly reveals basically similar characteristics as those of the WPK CC members. Available data on the SPA members are even more limited than those of the WPK CC members. Still the following observations are discernible.

First, as Table 7-13 indicates, a relatively higher representation from the Hamgyŏng provinces, especially from the North Hamgyŏng Province, is evident as it was the case in the WPK CC members. The reasons for this political phenomenon are virtually the same as the aforementioned explanations for the relatively larger participation of the

Hamgyŏng provinces in the WPK CC.

Secondly, although only 13.6% of the SPA members' educational background data are available, the data differ little from the educational profile of the WPK CC members. Those members who were educated in the former Soviet Union constitute the largest numbers. Note also that a fairly large number of them was educated in Japan. But those who were educated in the former Soviet Union were a relatively younger group who received education mostly after World War II, whereas those who studied in Japan were an older group who received education mostly before the War (For details, see Table 7-14).

Thirdly, like the WPK CC members, the SPA members confirm one of the main characteristics of the Communist totalitarian system, i.e., the overlapping membership (See Table 7-15). Unlike in South Korea or any other non-socialist countries, where the members of the military in active duty, for instance, are legally barred from participating in the legislature, those in uniform or in other governmental and/or party posts, can freely become the SPA members. This feature of overlapping membership pinpoints, albeit indirectly, the political reality in North Korea or, for that matter, in all past and present socialist countries. That is, how nominal, spineless and powerless the SPA is or their so-called legislative outfits had been, respectively. As noted in Table 7-12, the SPA is nothing but a rudderless rubber stamp. Its session is convened rarely and lasts just two or three days. In brief, the overlapping membership dramatically characterizes the principle of the unity (or concentration) of power in a totalitarian communist state in contrast to the principles of the separation of powers and of checks and balances in a democratic polity.

Fourthly, the foreign travel patterns of the SPA members are, again, virtually identical to those of the WPK CC members. Namely, China and the former Soviet Union represent the two most frequented countries in overseas travels (Table 7-16). Again, like the career profile of the WPK CC members, the SPA members' career background reveals no distinguishing features. It is interesting to note once again that like in the WPK CC, the SPA has been represented by relatively higher number of those with anti-Japanese guerrilla background (Table 7-17).

the largest number of cabinet posts with Premier, a first vice-premier, eight vice-premiers, thirty ministers, six commissioners and four additional cabinet-level directors and secretaries. In the fifth cabinet or the first AC (1972-1977), the cabinet posts were reduced to Premier, six vice-premiers, fifteen ministers and seven commissioners. The sixth cabinet or the second AC (1977-1984) had Premier, six vice-premiers, a secretary, twenty-one ministers and seven commissioners. In the seventh cabinet or the third AC (1982-1986), a slight change had occurred in membership with Premier, a first deputy premier, a deputy premier, seventeen ministers, fourteen commissioners and one cabinet level director. The number of the posts for the eighth cabinet or the 4th AC (1986-1990) was the same as the 7th cabinet, but the ninth cabinet or the 5th AC (1990-1992) increased its size to some 51 members (For details, see Table 7-21).

Throughout the nine cabinets from 1948 to 1992, Kim Il Sung had been the premier from 1948 to 1972 and the President of the DPRK from 1972 to the present. Yi Chong-ok (Premier, 1977-1984) is the only one who has served in all seven cabinets, although he was not an original member of the first cabinet (Yi was appointed minister of light industry in December, 1951, three years after the formation of the first cabinet).

For example, Kim Il Sung (1912-) as premier, Nam Il (1914-1976) and Chŏng Chun-t'aek (1902-1973) as vice-premiers, have served in their posts four times. Chŏng Chun-t'aek, Kim Man-gum and Kye Ung-t'ae have been in the same post three times. Some 23 people served in the same cabinet post twice. Chŏng Chun-t'aek and Yi Chong-ok (1905-) have been appointed 12 times; Chŏng Il-yong was appointed 10 times; Nam Il, nine times; Pak Sŏng-ch'ŏl and Yi Chu-yŏn, eight times; Kim Il and Pak Mun-kyu, seven times; Kim Hoe-il and Pak Ui-wan, six times; and Ch'oe Chae-u, Han Sang-du, Hyŏn Mu-gwang, Kim Man-gum, Kim Pyŏng-sik, Kim Tu-sam, Kim Ung-sang and Mun Man-uk, five times. And the rest of the 189 people was appointed four times or less. Yi Chong-ok and Chŏng Il-yong, for example, served in seven different posts during these years. There are three, who worked in five cabinets; six, who served in four cabinets; sixteen, who served in three cabinets; and forty-six who served under two cabinets.

Several points are noteworthy. First, Kim Il Sung's control of the cabinet and later of the AC has been absolute, although the formats of such control have undergone numerous transformations. From 1948 till 1972, Kim had direct cabinet control as Premier. Under the 1972 Constitution, Kim has become the President of the DPRK and the Premier's post was placed under the President of the DPRK and the CPC. Kim Il (1912-1984), one of Kim Il Sung's closest partisan comrades-in-arm, succeeded the latter as the Premier in 1972 and served in the post until 1977. From 1977 till 1984, Yi Chong-ok, another of Kim Il Sung's close associates and a veteran administrator, replaced Kim Il in 1977 until 1984. In 1984 Kang Sŏng-san, first vice-premier under Yi, took over the premiership, while Yi moved up to the post of a vice-president. Kang served the remainder of the 7th AC until the end of 1986. In the 8th cabinet or the fourth AC, Lee Kŭnmo became the premier, but he was replaced by Yŏn Hyŏngmuk in December, 1988. Since then Yŏn had been Premier until 1992 when he was replaced by Kang Sŏng-san. In short, Kim Il Sung's cabinet control formats have changed over the years, from the direct Kim Il Sung rule (1948-1972) to the indirect Kim Il Sung-Kim Il administration (1972-1977), the Kim Il Sung-Yi Chong-ok administration (1977-1984), the Kim Il Sung-Kang Sŏng-san administration (1984-1986), the Kim Il Sung-Lee Kunmo administration (1986-1988), the Kim Il Sung-Yŏn Hyŏngmuk administration (1988-1992) and the Kim Il Sung-Kang Sŏng-san administration (1992-   ) (For details, see Table 7-22).

Second, no radical or abrupt personnel changes had occurred in the cabinet and the Administration Council. The transfer of premiership from Kim Il Sung to Kim Il, from Kim Il to Yi Chong-ok, from Yi Chong-ok to Kang Sŏng-san and the rest appears to have been gradual. All the successors have gone through a period of apprenticeship before taking over the premiership. Kim Il was appointed vice-premier in the second cabinet in 1957, first vice-premier in the third cabinet in 1962 until 1972 when he succeeded Kim Il Sung as the new Premier. Kim Il's successor, Yi Chong-ok, served as the Minister of Light Industry in the first cabinet, became the chairman of the State Planning Commission in the second cabinet, was the vice-premier in the third and the fourth cabinets, and he was appointed chairman of the Heavy Industry Commission in the fifth cabinet in 1972 before becoming the Premier in 1977. Kang Sŏng-san, took a different route from the others, however. Kang ranked 65th in the WPK Fifth Congress CC in November, 1970, but he was catapulted to 17th in the WPK Sixth Congress CC in October, 1980, and became the member of the CC Politburo (18th). In the AC, however, Kang held no cabinet posts until he was appointed as one of the six vice-premiers in the Yi Chong-ok cabinet in 1977. In the seventh cabinet and the second AC in 1982, Kang was appointed the first vice-premier until he replaced Yi as the Premier in 1984.

Finally, the emphasis on industry, technology, science and development has been evident in the expansion of the cabinet and the AC for the past forty years. In the first cabinet, for instance, only one ministry dealt with industry, i.e., the Ministry of Industry. But in the second cabinet, it was subdivided into six: metal industry, machine industry, coal industry, chemical industry, light industry and construction and building materials industry. In addition, the Ministry of Electric Powers and the State Construction Commission were added. In the fourth cabinet, the Ministry of Machine Industry was further divided into the First and Second Ministry and two new ministries—textile and paper industries and foodstuff and daily necessities industries were created. In the fifth cabinet, the Ministry of Ship Machine Building Industry was formed. In the seventh cabinet the Ministry of Natural Resources Development was added. In the 8th and the 9th cabinets, for instance the Electronics and Automation Commission was created.

In sum, the AC (formerly the cabinet) has expanded substantially over the years. Its growth, however, has not been steady and continuous. Rather, it has experienced a cycle of both consolidation and diversification. The majority of its growth and expansion has been in industrial, scientific and technological areas. From this organizational trend, one can infer that the technocrats have gradually yet inevitably replaced the ideologues. But, if the growth patterns of the AC for the past forty years serve as a guide, the task of changing the guards from reds (ideologues) to experts (technocrats) in the forthcoming years may not be either easy or perfect.

An Analysis

A profile analysis of the AC members, too, virtually confirms the essentially similar characteristics of the North Korean ruling elites which we have already examined in the foregoing (For details, see Tables 7-23, 7-24, 7-25 and 7-26).

The Central Court and the Central Procurator's Office

The Central Court (CC) and the Central Procurator's Office (CPO) are not independent of other branches. They are part of the SPA and, ultimately, under the control of the WPK. Like China's Supreme People's Court and the former Soviet Union's Supreme Court, the Central Court and the North Korean judicial system are set up on the basis of the socialist concept of law and justice, viz., law and justice are not anterior or superior to politics, but are rather the ruling party's instruments for achieving political-ideological goals.[17]

Under the 1992 Constitution the court system consists of the Central Court, the court of the province or of municipality, the People's Court and the Special Court. The functions of Central Court are to: hear criminal and civil cases of nation-wide importance; review emergency cases appealed from the provincial courts; and supervise the judicial works of all courts. The SPA elects or recalls the President of the Central Court (Article 91, Section 12). The judges and the people's assessors of the Central Court are elected by the SPA Standing Committee (Article 101, Section 9). The Central Court and the CPO are accountable to the SPA, the DPRK President and the CPC for their activities. Likewise, the activities of the provincial and municipal courts and procurator's offices are accountable to their respective people's assembly. The special courts hear cases involving military personnel and railway and water transportation workers. The special court is comprised of the Military Court and the Traffic and Transportation Court (see Chart 7-4).

The 1948 Constitution designated the Supreme Court as the highest judicial organ. The 1972 Constitution renamed it the Central Court and called its head the "president" rather than "chief justice." The structure and functions of the Central Court have not changed significantly since 1948. The 1992 Constitution has kept the North Korean Court and procurators system virtually intact (For details, see Articles 152-167). The SPA Standing Committee has thus far elected six chief justices and two presidents of the Central Court.

The Supreme People's Assembly (SPA) appoints the procurator-general of the Central Procurator's Office, and the CPO procurator-general, in turn, appoints all other procurator-generals. The procurator-general in the office of the CPO reports to the SPA, the president of the DPRK, and the Central People's Committee, and the provincial, city, county and special procurators' offices are accountable to the CPO. The duties of the procurators include general surveillance, investigation, preliminary examination and prosecution of criminals and offenders. The procurators, also, take appropriate legal sanctions to preserve the laws and implement policies set by the WPK (see Chart 7-4).

Over the years the SPA Standing Committee has elected six chief justices and three presidents of the Central Court. Pang Hak-se, President of the Central Court since the 5th SPA, has been in the office the longest. Kim Il-son has also been intermittently the head for thirteen years from the first through the third SPA. The rest served relatively short periods and many were purged, including Cho Song-mo (in 1958), a member of the Domestic Group, Hwang Se-hwan (in 1957) and Kim Ha-un (in 1957). Since the 4th SPA chief justices have served out their terms. Noteworthy also in this connection is that many chief justices of the Central Court concurrently served in the SPA Legislative Committee.

Like the Central Court presidents (formerly chief justices), many procurator-generals did not complete their terms during the first three SPAs. From the 4th SPA, they have served out their terms. Thus far, ten persons served as the Procurator-General (PG). Many of these PGs were purged, including Pak Se-ch'ang, who had been in the office the longest from 1957 to 1964. He was purged as a member of the Soviet Group in 1967. Until the 6th SPA, no PG concurrently held a membership in the SPA committee. But Yi Chin-su, who was appointed the PG at the 6th

SPA, is also a member of the SPA Legislative Committee.

Two served both as the chief justice and as the PG. For example, Cho Song-mo, the second chief justice of the Central Court from 1955-1956, was the PG from 1956 to 1957, and Yi Kuk-chin, who first served as the PG from 1964 to 1966, was elected chief justice in 1966 (For details, see Table 7-6 below).

Since 1967, both presidents [chief justices] and PGs have served out their terms of office, an indication of the Kim Il Sung regime's political stability.

Table 7-1. *The North Korean Workers Party's Organizational Changes and Evolution*

Time	No. of party	No. of party cells	No. of Assembly representatives		Party member/ population
The 3rd extended executive committee of the North Korean branch of the Korean Communist Party (1) (12/17/45)	4,530				
The Inaugural Assembly of the North Korean Worker's Party (2) (8/28-30/46)	366,000 (366,339)	12,000	801 →	workers: 183 peasants: 157 clerks: 385 others: 76	4%
The 2nd Assembly of the North Korean Worker's Party (3/27-30/48)	725,762	28,000 (29,763)	999 → (absence: 9)	workers: 466 peasants: 451 clerks: 234 others: 29	8%
The 3rd Assembly of the North Korean Worker's Party (4/23-29/56)	1,164,945	58,259	916 → (absence: 2)	workers: 439 peasants: 192 clerks: 246 others: 39	10%
The 4th Assembly of the North Korean Workers's Party (9/11-18/61)	1,311,563	65,000	(1,657 → (absence: 3)	workers: 944 peasants: 451 clerks: 191 others: 71	12.2%
The 5th Assembly of the North Korean Worker's Party (11/2-13/70)	1,600,000	12,000	(1,734) 137*		13%
The 6th Assembly of the North Korean Worker's Party (10/10-14/80)	2,000,000 (3,000,000)	200,000 (300,000)	(3,220) 158*		17%
As of 1988	2,500,000 (3)				

Sources: *Pukhanch'ongram*, p. 188; *Pukhanjŏnso*, p. 87.; Dae-Sook Suh, *Korean Communism, 1945-1980: A Reference Guide to the Political System* (Honolulu: The University Press of Hawaii, 1981), p. 354.

(1) The Korean Communist Party was inaugurated on September 11, 1945. Its North Korean branch was organized on October 13, 1945. Its name was changed to "North Korean Communist Party" at the 3rd extended meeting of the North Korean branch of Korean Communist Party on December 17, 1945.

(2) The New People's Party and the North Korean Communist Party were merged and became the North Korean Worker's Party on August 27, 1946. The North Korean Worker's Party and the South Korean Worker's Party were merged and became the "Worker's Party of Korea" on June 30–July 1, 1949.

(3) From the "Yearbook of Communist Affairs" published by Hoover Institute of Stanford University.

*representatives who have delivered speeches.

Table 7-2. WPK Central Committee Member's Place of Origin

	1st term (No.)	(%)	2nd term (No.)	(%)	3rd term (No.)	(%)	4th term (No.)	(%)	5th term (No.)	(%)	6th term (No.)	(%)	Total (No.)
P'yŏngbuk	–	–	–	–	3	7	1	2	4	7	3	5	11
P'yŏngnam	3	17	3	10	2	4	3	6	5	9	6	11	22
Hambuk	10	55	18	62	20	45	25	52	20	35	21	37	114
Hamnam	3	17	3	10	5	11	6	12	10	17	13	23	40
Hwanghae	–	–	–	–	2	4	–	–	–	–	1	2	3
N. Korea total	16	89	24	83	32	72	35	73	39	68	44	78	190
Kangwŏn	–	–	–	–	1	2	1	2	–	–	1	2	3
Kyŏnggi	–	–	1	3	2	4	1	2	1	2	–	–	5
Kyŏngbuk	–	–	3	10	5	11	5	10	2	3	–	–	15
Kyŏngnam	1	5	1	3	3	7	–	–	2	3	–	–	7
Chŏnbuk	–	–	–	–	–	–	–	–	1	2	–	–	1
Chŏnnam													
Ch'ungch'ŏng													
Seoul													
S. Korea total	1	5	5	17	11	25	7	14	6	10	1	2	31
U.S.S.R. & Manchuria	1	5	–	–	1	2	6	12	12	21	11	20	31
Available data	18	43	29	44	44	63	48	58	57	48	56	39	48.2%
Total	42		66		79		83		118		144		523

Table 7-3. WPK Central Committee Member's Educational Background

	1st term (No.) (%)		2nd term (No.) (%)		3rd term (No.) (%)		4th term (No.) (%)		5th term (No.) (%)		6th term (No.) (%)		Total (No.)
Moscow Univ.	2	11	3	12	3	7	2	8	8	24	7	24	25
Leningrad Univ.	1	5.5	–	–	–	–	–	–	–	–	–	–	1
Tashkent Univ.	1	5.5	1	4	1	2	2	8	2	6	1	3	8
Others	1	5.5	–	–	7	16	6	23	7	21	8	28	29
U.S.S.R. total	5	28	4	16	11	25	10	38	17	52	16	55	63
Tokyo Univ.	–	–	–	–	–	–	1	4	1	3	–	–	2
Meiji Univ.	–	–	1	4	1	2	1	4	1	3	1	3	5
Kyoto Univ.													
Others	2	11	2	8	2	4	2	8	3	9	3	10	14
Japan total	2	11	3	12	3	7	4	15	5	15	4	14	21
Harbin Univ.	–	–	–	–	1	2	1	4	–	–	1	3	3
Econ. Ins.													
Others	2	5.5	1	4	12	27	1	4	–	–	–	–	16
China total	1	5.5	1	4	13	29	2	8	–	–	1	3	19
Kyŏngsŏng Univ.	–	–	–	–	1	2	1	4	1	3	–	–	3
Kimilsŏng Univ.	–	–	–	–	–	–	–	–	–	–	2	7	2
Chungangdang	–	–	–	–	–	–	1	4	3	9	2	7	6
Military school	1	5.5	4	16	5	11	3	12	2	6	–	–	15
Technical school	3	17	5	20	1	2	–	–	1	3	–	–	10
Middle school	2	11	2	8	2	4	4	15	2	6	2	7	14
High school	3	17	4	16	4	9	1	4	1	3	–	–	13
College	–	–	2	8	4	9	–	–	1	3	1	3	8
Available data	18	43	25	38	44	63	26	31	33	28	29	29	33.5%
Total	42		66		70		83		118		144		523

Table 7-4. WPK Central Committee Member's Previous Position

	1st term (No.)	1st term (%)	2nd term (No.)	2nd term (%)	3rd term (No.)	3rd term (%)	4th term (No.)	4th term (%)	5th term (No.)	5th term (%)	6th term (No.)	6th term (%)	Total (No.)
*W.P.K. C.C.	29	100	51	96	62	94	79	100	115	100	143	100	470
Ex-military	3	10	11	21	12	18	23	29	26	23	37	26	112
*A.C.	18	62	29	55	32	48	48	61	54	47	65	45	246
M. P. S.	2	7	7	13	6	9	16	20	12	10	11	8	54
M. P.	1	3	3	6	5	7	7	9	15	13	29	20	60
M. S.	–	–	1	2	–	–	–	–	–	–	–	–	1
P. S. (S. P.)	17	59	20	38	24	36	33	42	40	35	55	38	189
*P.	9	31	20	38	27	41	23	29	45	39	49	34	173
*S.	–	–	2	4	2	3	–	–	–	–	–	–	4
*M.	–	–	1	2	–	–	–	–	–	–	–	–	1
Available data	29	69	53	80	66	94	79	95	115	97	143	99	92.7%
Total	42		66		70		83		118		144		523

* W.P.K. C.C.: The Worker's Party of Korea's Central Committee; M.: Military;
  P.: Party; S.: State; and A.C.: Administration Council

Table 7-5. WPK Central Committee Member's Overseas Travel

	1st term (No.)	1st term (%)	2nd term (No.)	2nd term (%)	3rd term (No.)	3rd term (%)	4th term (No.)	4th term (%)	5th term (No.)	5th term (%)	6th term (No.)	6th term (%)	Total (No.)
U.S.S.R.	11	50	18	46	20	43	23	35	33	42	39	45	144
China	8	36	15	38	20	43	28	43	30	38	26	30	125
Japan	2	9	5	13	5	11	2	3	4	5	4	5	22
Bulgaria	–	–	–	–	–	–	1	2	1	1	–	–	2
Romania	–	–	–	–	1	2	1	2	–	–	4	5	6
E. Germany	–	–	–	–	–	–	4	6	2	2	2	2	10
Yugoslavia											1	1	1
Hungary							1	2			1	1	2
Others	1	4	1	2	1	2	5	8	6	11	10	11	24
Available data	22	52	39	59	47	67	65	78	79	67	87	60	64.8%
Total	42		66		70		83		118		114		523

Table 7-6. WPK Central Committee Member's
Occupational Classification

	1st term (No.)	(%)	2nd term (No.)	(%)	3rd term (No.)	(%)	4th term (No.)	(%)	5th term (No.)	(%)	6th term (No.)	(%)	Total (No.)
Workers	1	5	2	6	3	8	1	2	1	2	–	–	8
Managers	1	5	1	3	1	3	3	5	3	5	9	14	18
Teachers	1	5	5	16	4	11	2	4	–	–	2	3	14
Professors	1	5	–	–	1	3	–	–	4	7	10	15	16
Diplomats	2	9	2	6	3	8	13	24	8	14	19	14	47
Journalists	1	5	2	6	–	–	1	2	1	2	2	3	7
Writers	1	5	1	3	1	3	1	2	1	2	2	3	7
Artists	–	–	–	–	–	–	–	–	1	2	1	2	2
Athletes	–	–	2	–	2	–	1	2	–	–	–	–	5
Leftist movement	–	–	–	–	1	3	1	2	5	9	2	3	9
Independence movement	6	27	6	19	9	26	5	9	1	2	2	3	29
Agrarian movement	2	9	2	6	2	6	–	–	1	2	2	3	29
Labor movement	1	5	1	3	1	3	1	2	–	–	–	–	4
Guerrillas	4	18	7	22	9	26	25	46	30	52	25	33	100
Religionists													
Researchers	–	–	–	–	–	–	–	–	1	2	–	–	1
8th route army	1	5	3	9	–	–	–	–	–	–	–	–	4
Available data	22	52	32	48	35	50	54	65	57	48	66	46	50.9%
Total	42		66		70		83		118		144		523

Table 7-7. WPK Central Committee Member's Birth Year

	1st term (No.)	(%)	2nd term (No.)	(%)	3rd term (No.)	(%)	4th term (No.)	(%)	5th term (No.)	(%)	6th term (No.)	(%)	Total (No.)
1880s	29	76	1	5	1	3	–	–	–	–	–	–	31
1890s	3	8	3	15	7	21	4	10	2	5	–	–	19
1990s	5	13	6	30	13	38	14	34	8	21	6	21	52
1910s	1	3	9	45	13	38	22	54	18	46	14	48	77
1920s	–	–	1	5	–	–	1	2	9	22	7	24	18
1930s	–	–	–	–	–	–	–	–	2	5	1	3	3
1940s	–	–	–	–	–	–	–	–	–	–	1	3	1
Available data	38	90	20	30	34	49	41	49	39	33	29	20	32.9%
Total	42		66		70		83		118		144		523

Table 7-8. The WPK Central Committee Members by Sex

	1st term (No.)	(%)	2nd term (No.)	(%)	3rd term (No.)	(%)	4th term (No.)	(%)	5th term (No.)	(%)	6th term (No.)	(%)	Total (No.)
Male	40	95	63	95	67	96	80	96	110	93	140	97	500
Female	2	5	3	5	3	4	3	4	8	7	4	3	23
Total	42		66		70		83		118		144		523

Table 7-9. An Overview of North Korean Supreme People's Assembly Election

Session	Election date	No. of members	Voting rate	yes votes	Official term (actual duration)	Reference
1	8/25/48	572 (360+212)	99.98/98.49		3 (9.0) years	1 member per 50,000 people including 360 alleged representatives from South Korean districts, Black and White Ballot Box was used
2	8/27/58	215	99.99/99.92		4 (5.2) years	Black and White Ballot Box was used.
3	8/10/62	383	100/100		4 (5.1) years	1 member per 30,000 people. The ballot box allowing only one official candidate.
4	11/25/67	457	100/100		4 (5.1) years	"
5	12/12/67	541	100/100		4 (5.0) years	"
6	11/11/77	579	100/100		4 (4.3) years	"
7	2/28/82	615	100/100		4 (4.3) years	"
8	11/02/86	655	100/100		4 (3.5) years	"
9	4/22/90	687	99.78/100		4 years	"

Source: The author constructed this table based on the information in *Pukhangaeyo* (Seoul: P'yŏnghwat'ongilyŏnguso, 1986), p. 49 and *Pukhangaeyo* (Seoul: Kukt'ot'ongilwon, 1979), p. 35. The data for the 9th session are from *Rodongsinmun*, 20 April 1990 and 24 April 1990.

*Table 7-10. The Supreme People's Assembly Members' Official
Occupational Classification*

		(No.)	Total
1st term	workers	120	
	peasants	194	
	clerks	152	
	others	106	572
2nd	workers	84	
	peasants	68	
	clerical workers	60	
	others	3	215
3rd	workers	215	
	peasants	62	
	clerical workers	101	
	others	5	383
4th	workers	292	
	peasants	70	
	clerical workers	95	457
5th	ex-workers	347	
	ex-peasants	72	
	ex-clerical workers	122	541
6th	workers	248	
	collective farm workers	64	
	others (member of party, government, labor group, People's Army members factory workers, industry and collective farm members, scientific technicians, educational and sanitary workers, artists and so on.)	267	579
7th	workers	213	
	collective farm workers	63	
	others (same with 6th term)	339	615
8th	workers	238	
	collective farm workers	79	
	others (6th term and member of the total commission of North Korea people in Japan)	338	655
9th	workers	254	
	collective farm workers	71	
	others (same with 8th term)	362	687

Source: *Supreme People's Assembly Data Book*, Vol. I-IV.

Table 7-11. The Overall Profile of Supreme People's Assembly Members Based on the Official Data by their Occupation, Education and Age

Term	Number	Occupation	(%)	Education	(%)	Age	(%)
1	572	workers	6.1	college	39.6	under 40	51.8
	(212+360)	peasants	16.2	middle school	25.8	41 – 50	30.4
		*female		*primary school	34.6	over 51	17.8
2	215	workers	39.0	college	27.9	under 40	18.1
		peasants	31.6	technical high	7.9	41 – 50	46.0
		*female	12.5	**mid, tech.	64.1	over 51	35.8
3	383	workers	56.1	college	26.3	under 39	28.9
		peasants	16.1	technical high	6.7	40 – 49	47.2
		*female	9.1	**mid, tech.	66.8	over 50	23.7
4	457	workers	63.8	college	48.3	under 39	14.0
		peasants	15.3	technical high	7.8	40 – 49	48.1
		*female	15.9	**mid, tech.	43.7	over 50	37.8
5	541	workers	64.1	college	50.0	under 40	17.7
		peasants	13.3	technical high	9.6	41 – 50	51.7
		*female	20.8	**mid, tech.	13.1	over 51	30.4
6	579	workers	42.8	college	58.3	under 35	5.6
		peasants	11.0	technical high	11.2	36 – 55	78.9
		*female	20.8	**mid, tech.	30.5	over 55	15.5
7	615	workers	34.6	college	50.4	under 35	3.9
		peasants	10.2	technical high	12.8	36 – 55	71.2
		*female	19.6	**mid, tech.	36.8	over 55	24.9
8	655	workers	36.4	college	56.7	under 35	2.7
		peasants	12.0	technical high	19.1	36 – 55	68.7
		*female	21.1	**mid, tech.	24.2	over 55	28.6
9	687	workers	37.0	college	68.2	under 35	2.9
		peasants	10.4	technical high	—	36 – 55	56.8
		*female	20.1	**mid, tech.	31.8	over 55	40.3

Source: *Supreme People's Assembly Data Book*, Vol. IV (Seoul: Kukt'ot'ongilwŏn, 1988); *Rodongsinmun*, 24 May 1990.
* Female is the percentage of female in the sum total of the Supreme People's Assembly. The author recalculated the average age on the basis of female found in the *Supreme People's Assembly Data Book*, Vol. IV.
** Middle school and technical school

Table 7-12. *An Overview of Supreme People's Assembly Session,*
1948 – 1990

Session (term)	Duration	No. of days	No. of bills passed
1st session (9/2/48 – 9/17/58)			
1st	1948 (9/2 – 9/10)	9	
2nd	1949 (1/28 – 2/1)	5	
3rd	1949 (4/19 – 4/23)	5	
4th	1949 (9/8 – 9/10)	3	
5th	1950 (2/25 – 3/3)	7	
6th	1953 (12/20 –12/22)	3	
7th	1954 (4/20 – 4/23)	4	
8th	1954 (10/28 –10/30)	3	
9th	1955 (3/9 – 3/11)	3	
10th	1955 (12/20 –12/22)	3	
11th	1956 (3/10 – 3/13)	4	
12th	1956 (11/5 – 11/9)	5	
13th	1957 (3/14 – 3/16)	3	
Total: 13		57	29
2nd term (9/18/57 – 10/21/62)			
1st	1957 (9/18 – 9/20)	3	
2nd	1958 (2/17 – 2/19)	3	
3rd	1958 (6/9 – 6/11)	3	
4th	1958 (10/1 – 10/2)	2	
5th	1958 (2/19 – 2/21)	3	
6th	1959 (10/26 – 10/28)	3	
7th	1960 (2/25 – 2/27)	3	
8th	1960 (11/19 – 11/24)	6	
9th	1961 (3/23 – 3/25)	3	
10th	1962 (4/5 – 4/7)	3	
11th	1962 (6/20 – 6/21)	2	
Total: 11		34	16

Table 7-12. Continued

Session (term)	Duration	No. of days	No. of bills passed
3rd term (10/22/62 – 12/13/67)			
1st	1962 (10/22 – 10/23)	2	
2nd	1963 (5/9 – 5/11)	3	
3rd	1964 (3/26 – 3/28)	3	
4th	1965 (5/20 – 5/24)	5	
5th	1966 (4/27 – 4/29)	3	
6th	1966 (11/22 – 11/24)	3	
7th	1967 (4/24 – 4/26)	3	
Total: 7		22	21
4th term (12/14/67 – 12/14/72)			
1st	1967 (12/14 –12/16)	3	
2nd	1968 (4/25 – 4/27)	3	
3rd	1969 (4/24 – 4/26)	3	
4th	1970 (4/20 – 4/23)	4	
5th	1971 (4/12 – 4/14)	3	
6th	1972 (4/29 – 4/30)	2	
Total: 6		18	16
5th term (12/25/72 – 12/14/77)			
1st	1972 (12/25 –12/28)	4	
2nd	1973 (4/5 – 4/10)	6	
5th	1975 (4/8 – 4/10)	3	
6th	1976 (4/27 – 4/29)	3	
7th	1977 (4/26 – 4/29)	4	
Total: 7		30	16
6th term (12/15/77 – 4/4/82)			
1st	1977 (12/15 –12/17)	3	
2nd	1978 (4/18 – 4/20)	3	
3rd	1979 (3/27 – 3/29)	3	
4th	1980 (4/2 – 4/4)	3	
5th	1981 (4/6 – 4/8)	3	
Total: 5		15	9

Table 7-12. Continued

Session (term)	Duration	No. of days	No. of bills passed
7th term (4/5/82 – 12/28/86)			
1st	1982 (4/5)	1	
2nd	1983 (4/5 – 4/7)	3	
3rd	1984 (1/25 – 1/27)	3	
4th	1985 (4/9 – 4/11)	3	
5th	1986 (4/7 – 4/9)	3	
Total: 7		22	11
8th term (12/29/86 – 5/23/90)			
1st	1986 (12/29 –12/30)	2	
2nd	1987 (4/21 – 4/23)	3	
3rd	1988 (4/5 – 4/7)	3	
4th	1988 (12/12)	1	
5th	1989 (4/7 – 4/8)	2	
Total: 5		11	5
9th term (5/24/90)			
1st	1990 (5/24 – 5/26)	3	1

Source: *Pukhanch'oegoinminhoeŭi Charyojip* [Documents of North Korea's Supreme People's Assembly] IV volumes (Seoul: Kukt'ot'ongilwŏn, 1988).

Table 7-13. Leadership Changes in the SPA

	Chairman	Vice-Chairmen
1st Assembly (Sept. 2 1948–Sept. 17, 1957)	Hŏ Hŏn	Kim Tal-hyŏn Yi Yŏng
	Yi Yŏng	Yi Yu-min Hong Ki-hwang (1)
2nd Assembly (Sept. 18, 1957–Oct. 21, 1962)	Ch'oe Wŏn-t'aek	Yi Ki-yŏng Kim Ch'ang-jun
	Ch'oe Wŏn-t'aek	Yi Ki-yŏng Kim Tuk-nan (2)
3rd Assembly (Oct. 22, 1962–Dec. 13, 1967)	Ch'oe Wŏn-t'aek	Yi Ki-yŏng Kim Tuk-nan
4th Assembly (Dec. 14, 1967–Dec. 24, 1972)	Paek Nam-un	Yi Ki-yŏng Hŏ Chŏng-suk
5th Assembly (Dec. 25, 1972–Dec. 14, 1977)	Hwang Chang-yŏp	Hong Ki-mun Hŏ Chŏng-suk
6th Assembly (Dec. 15, 1977–Feb. 27, 1982)	Hwang Chang-yŏp	Hŏ Chŏng-suk Hong Ki-mun
7th Assembly (Feb. 28, 1982–Nov. 1, 1986)	Yang Hyŏng-sŏp	Son Song-p'il Yŏ Yŏn-gu
8th Assembly (Nov. 2, 1986–April 22, 1990)	Yang Hyŏng-sŏp	Yŏ Yŏn-gu Pak In-jun
9th Assembly (April 23, 1990–)	Yang Hyŏng-sŏp	Yŏ Yŏn-gu Pak In-jun

Sources: Adapted from Dae-sook Suh, *Korean Communism, 1945-1980* and *Vantage Point,*
    7 (2) (February, 1982).
  (1) This change was made at the Sixth Session of the First SPA, 20-22 December 1953.
  (2) It took place at the Sixth Session of the Second SPA, 26-28 October 1959.

Table 7-14. North Korean Supreme People's Assembly Members'
*Educational Background**

	1st term		2nd term		3rd term		4th term		5th term		7th term		8th term		Total
	No.	(%)	No.	(%)	No.	(%)	No.	(%)	No.	(%)	No.	(%)	No.	(%)	No.
Moscow U	4	6	4	6	5	6	7	9	8	10	11	18	7	14	46
Leningrad U	–	–	–	–	1	1	1	1	1	1	1	1	1	2	5
Tashkent U	1	1	2	3	2	2	2	2	2	2	1	2	–	–	10
Others	5	8	6	10	11	13	16	21	11	14	12	19	6	12	67
U.S.S.R. Total	10	16	12	20	19	22	26	35	22	29	25	39	14	30	128
Tokyo	3	5	3	5	2	2	1	1	2	2	–	–	–	–	11
Meiji	3	5	1	1	1	1	–	–	–	–	–	–	1	2	6
Kyoto	1	1	2	3	2	2	2	2	–	–	–	–	–	–	7
Others	4	6	4	6	9	10	4	5	8	10	6	10	7	14	42
Japan Total	11	18	10	16	14	16	7	9	10	13	6	10	8	16	66
Harbin U	1	1	1	1	1	1	1	1	1	1	1	2	1	2	7
#Inmin Econ. Ins.	–	–	–	–	1	1	1	1	1	1	–	–	2	4	5
Others	3	5	6	10	3	3	4	5	2	2	3	5	3	6	24
China Total	4	6	7	12	5	6	6	8	4	5	4	6	6	12	36
Kyŏngsŏng	5	8	3	5	3	3	3	4	1	1	2	3	1	2	18
Kimilsŏng U	1	1	–	–	2	2	2	2	5	6	2	3	5	10	17
#Chungang	1	1	1	1	9	10	5	6	8	10	8	13	7	14	39
Military School	3	5	5	8	4	5	5	6	3	4	1	2	1	2	22
Technical School	7	12	7	12	7	8	8	10	9	12	8	13	5	10	51
Middle School	4	6	5	8	7	8	4	5	5	6	1	2	1	2	27
High School	5	8	2	3	–	–	1	1	2	2	1	2	2	4	13
College	9	15	8	13	15	18	8	10	7	9	4	6	–	–	51
Available data	60	10	60	28	22	85	75	16	76	14	62	10	50	8	13.6%
Total	572		215		383		457		541		615		655		3,438

* The information for the 6th SPA Members were not disclosed. So, the data are not available.
# Inmin Econ. Ins.= Inmingyŏngche U; and Chungang=Chungangdang School.

Table 7-15. North Korean Supreme People's Assembly Members'
Position

	1st term No.	(%)	2nd term No.	(%)	3rd term No.	(%)	4th term No.	(%)	5th term No.	(%)	7th term No.	(%)	8th term No.	(%)	Total No.
#WPK	85	82	83	80	147	87	149	84	172	83	202	88	199	98	1,037
#M.	1	10	17	16	32	19	42	24	39	19	40	17	40	20	221
AC.	55	53	59	57	84	49	96	54	95	46	107	47	99	49	595
M. AC. P.	5	5	11	11	17	10	20	11	13	6	11	5	9	4	86
M.P.	1	1	4	4	15	9	16	9	23	11	28	12	25	12	112
M. AC.	2	2	1	1	–	–	1	–	2	1	–	–	–	–	6
P. AC.	33	31	33	32	43	25	54	31	64	31	70	30	76	37	373
#P.	45	43	39	38	72	42	60	34	70	34	91	40	89	44	504
#AC.	14	13	14	13	24	14	21	12	31	15	23	10	14	7	141
M.	3	3	1	1	–	–	5	3	3	1	3	1	6	3	21
Available data	104	18	103	48	171	45	176	39	206	38	228	37	204	31	1,192
Total	572		215		383		457		541		615		655		3,439

WPK: The Worker's Party of Korea; AC: The Administration Council; M: Military; and
P: Party.

Table 7-16. North Korean Supreme People's Assembly Members'
Overseas Travels

	1st term		2nd term		3rd term		4th term		5th term		7th term		8th term		Total
	No.	(%)	No.	(%)	No.	(%)	No.	(%)	No.	(%)	No.	(%)	No.	(%)	No.
U.S.S.R.	35	48	38	51	59	42	67	51	68	47	83	50	73	52	423
China	40	55	41	55	66	48	54	41	76	52	86	51	78	55	441
Japan	7	10	9	12	15	11	9	7	19	13	17	10	17	12	93
Bulgaria	6	8	4	5	10	7	12	9	16	11	22	13	22	16	92
Czecho.	7	10	5	6	10	7	18	14	25	17	25	15	18	13	108
Romania	11	15	6	8	9	6	16	12	31	21	34	20	23	16	130
E. Germany	5	7	7	9	12	9	18	14	20	14	28	17	24	17	114
Yugoslavia	3	4	1	1	5	4	4	3	8	5	12	7	12	9	45
Hungary	4	5	5	7	8	6	16	12	19	13	23	14	19	13	94
Poland	7	10	5	7	9	6	11	8	15	10	15	9	13	9	75
Albania	2	3	5	7	6	4	7	5	4	3	4	2	3	2	31
Asia	14	10	8	11	24	17	25	19	21	14	25	15	21	15	138
Africa	5	7	7	9	21	15	24	18	33	23	37	22	28	20	155
Mid-South America	3	4	1	1	21	15	19	14	24	17	25	15	21	15	114
Europe	9	12	6	8	13	9	11	8	11	7	18	11	16	11	84
Mid-East	4	5	5	7	16	11	9	7	16	11	17	10	13	9	80
Others	5	7	7	9	6	4	5	4	5	3	11	7	8	6	47
Available data	73	13	75	35	138	36	132	29	145	27	167	27	141	22	25.3%
Total	572		215		383		459		542		618		655		3,438

Asia: South-East Asia and South Asia; Mainly Vietnam, Burma, India, Mongolia.
 Africa: Egypt, Guinea, Sudan.
 Mid-South America: Mainly Cuba
 Europe: Finland and Sweden except Eastern bloc nations.
 Mid-East: Mainly Syria, Iraq.
 Others: America, etc.

Table 7-17. North Korean Supreme People's Assembly Members
by Career Background

	1st term		2nd term		3rd term		4th term		5th term		7th term		8th term		Total
	No.	(%)	No.	(%)	No.	(%)	No.	(%)	No.	(%)	No.	(%)	No.	(%)	No.
Workers	2	3	6	7	53	24	43	19	18	7	13	6	11	6	146
Managers	5	8	17	21	52	24	77	25	96	40	86	40	66	25	399
Teachers	7	11	5	6	8	4	7	3	5	2	6	3	4	2	42
Professors	6	9	9	11	21	10	13	6	33	14	25	12	23	12	130
Diplomats	7	11	6	7	21	10	18	8	20	8	18	9	22	12	112
Journalists	2	3	2	2	3	1	2	1	9	4	8	4	7	4	33
Writers	7	11	5	6	4	2	2	1	2	1	3	1	5	3	28
Artists	3	5	2	2	1	–	4	2	3	1	3	1	6	3	22
Athletes	1	2	1	1	–	–	–	–	–	–	1	–	1	–	4
Leftist movement	5	8	3	4	5	2	5	2	4	2	2	1	3	1	27
Independence movement	8	13	5	6	3	1	3	1	2	1	2	1	–	–	23
Agrarian	2	3	1	1	–	–	1	–	2	1	1	2	–	–	7
Labor movement	1	2	2	2	–	–	1	–	1	–	–	–	–	–	5
Guerrillas	6	9	10	12	41	19	40	18	30	12	27	13	22	12	177
Religionists	2	3	5	6	6	3	5	2	8	3	3	1	2	1	31
Available data	64	11	81	38	219	57	223	49	241	45	209	34	191	29	35.7%
Total	5,721		215		383		457		541		615		655		3,438

Table 7-18. North Korean Supreme People's Assembly Members
by Birth Year

	1st term		2nd term		3rd term		4th term		5th term		7th term		8th term		Total
	No.	(%)	No.	(%)	No.	(%)	No.	(%)	No.	(%)	No.	(%)	No.	(%)	No.
1880s	6	14	4	10	1	2	–	–	–	–	–	–	–	–	12
1890s	8	19	7	18	4	7	4	10	2	5	–	–	–	–	25
1900s	17	39	11	28	17	31	12	28	10	25	8	31	7	24	82
1910s	8	19	15	38	27	49	21	50	19	48	11	42	11	38	112
1920s	4	9	2	5	6	11	4	10	8	20	5	19	7	24	36
1930s	–	–	–	–	–	–	–	–	1	2	1	4	1	3	3
1940s	–	–	–	–	–	–	–	–	–	–	1	4	3	10	4
Available data	43	8	39	18	55	14	42	9	40	7	26	4	29	4	7.97%
Total	572		215		383		457		541		615		655		3,438

Table 7-19. The Supreme People's Assembly Members by Sex

	1st term		2nd term		3rd term		4th term		5th term		7th term		8th term		Total
	No.	(%)	No.	(%)	No.	(%)	No.	(%)	No.	(%)	No.	(%)	No.	(%)	No.
Male	503	88	187	87	348	91	384	84	428	79	524	85	578	88	2,952
Female	69	12	28	13	35	9	73	16	113	21	91	15	77	12	486
Total	572		215		383		457		541		615		655		3,438

Total (female): 486 (14.1%)

Table 7-20. The Supreme People's Assembly Members' Overall Data

	Term	1st	2nd	3rd	4th	5th	6th	7th*	8th*	9th*	reference
	Item No. of member	572	215	383	457	541	579	615	655	687	
Previous occupation	worker (1)	120	84	215	292	347	248	213	238	254	
	peasant (2)	194	68	62	70	72	64	63	79	71	
	clerk (3)	152	60	101	95	122	267	339	338	362	
	others	106	3	5	—	—	—	—	—	—	
Age	20 – 30	73	5	12	—	—	—	24	18	20	under 35
	31 – 40	223	34	99	64	96	32	438	450	390	36 – 55
	41 – 50	174	99	181	220	280	457	153	187	277	over 56
	51 – 60	77	54	71	136	126	90				
	61 – 70	21	23	20	37	39					
	over 70	4	—	—	—	—	—	—	—	—	
Education	primary school	198	95	—	—	—	—	226	159	—	mid-level vocational school
										218	
	mid-high school	147	43	256	200	101	176	79	125	—	technical school
	college	227	60	127	257	323	403	310	371	469	
	graduate school	—	17	—	—	117	—	—	—	—	
Sex	male	503	188	348	384	428	459	494	517	549	
	female	69	27	35	73	113	120**	121**	138**	138**	

Source: Dae-Sook Suh, *Op. Cit.*, p. 442; *Pukhanjŏnsŏ 1945-1980* (Seoul: Kŭkdongmunje-yŏnguso, 1980). The 7th
   through the 9th term data are rearranged by the author.

(1) They are called "workers" during the 1st term, "workers representatives" during the 2nd through the 4th term,
   "representatives from workers" during the 5th term, and "workers" from the 6th term to the 9th term.

(2) They are called "peasant representatives" during the 1st through the 4th term, "representatives from peasant"
   during the 5th term, and "collective farm workers" from the 6th term to the 9th term.

(3) They are called "clerks" during the 1st term, "representatives of clerical workers" during the 2nd through the 4th
   term, "representatives from clerical workers" during the 5th term, but from the 6th term no distinction was made.

 * The actual numbers are not available from the 7th to the 9th members. Hence, the numbers are recalculated from the
   percentages given by the North Korean government. The number of members is rounded to the nearest whole number.

** The actual number of female members from the 6th to the 9th SPA are not available. Hence, the numbers are calculated on the basis of the percentages given by the North Korean Government.

Table 7-21. An Overview of Administration Council's (Cabinet)
Structual Changes

Term position	Premier	Vice-premier	Chief (minister)	Chairman	The Chief of Office
1st (9/09/48)	1	3	17	1	–
2nd (9/20/57)	1	6	23	2	–
3rd (10/23/62)	1	8(7+1)	22	5	–
4th (12/16/67)	1	8	30	6	–
5th (12/28/72)	1	6	15	7	–
6th (12/15/77)	1	6	21	7	1
7th (4/05/82)	1	13	19(1)	14	1
8th(12/12/86)	1	9	16(1)	14	1
9th (5/24/90)	1	10	25(1)	14	1

Kim Il Sung was premier from the 1st to the 4th Cabinet and the President from the 5th Cabinet to the present. Kim Il was premier at the 5th and 6th Cabinet, Lee Chongok was premier in 1977. Kang Sŏng-san was the premier of Administration Council on January 1, 1984. Lee Kunmo was the premier of Administration Council on December, 1986. Yŏn Hyŏngmuk is the premier of Administration Council since December, 1988.
(1) Scientific Institute
* The 1st vice-premier position was created on January 20, 1959.

Table 7-22. The Changes in the N.K.'s Presidency, Vice-Presidency, Premiership, Vice-Premiership

	1st term	2nd term	3rd term	4th term	5th term	6th term	7th term	8th term	9th term
President	<Kim Il Sung> (9/48-9/57)	<Kim Il Sung> (9/57-10/62)	<Kim Il Sung> (10/62-12/67)	<Kim Il Sung> (12/67-12/72)	<Kim Il Sung> (12/72-12/77)	<Kim Il Sung> (12/77-4/82)	<Kim Il Sung> (4/82-12/86)	<Kim Il Sung> (12/86-5/90)	<Kim Il Sung> (5/90-)
Vice-President					Choe Yonggŏn (12/72-9/76) Kang Yanguk (12/72-12/77) Kim Tonggyu (11/74-12/77) Kim Il** (4/76-3/84)	Kang Yanuk (12/77-4/82) <Park Sŏngch'ŏl> (12/77-4/82) Kim Il (12/77-4/82)	Kim Il (4/82-3/83) Kang Yanguk (4/82-1/83) <Park Sŏngch'ŏl> (4/82-12/86) <Lee Chongok> (1/84-12/86) <Lim Ch'unch'u> (4/83-4/84)	<Lee Chongok> (12/86-5/90) <Park Sŏngch'ŏl> (12/86-5/90) <Lim Ch'unch'u> (12/86-4/88)	<Lee Chongok> (5/90-) <Park Sŏngch'ŏl> (5/90-)
Premier	<Kim Il Sung> (9/48-9/57)	<Kim Il Sung> (9/57-10/62)	<Kim Il Sung> (10/62-12/67)	<Kim Il Sung> (12/67-12/722)	Kim Il (2/72-4/76) <Park Songchol> (4/76-12/77)	<Lee Chongok> (12/77-4/82)	<Lee Chongok> (4/82-1/84) <Kang Songsan> (1/84-12/86)	<Lee Kŭnmo> (12/86-12/88) <Yŏn Hyŏngmuk> (12/88-5/90)	<Yŏn Hyŏngmuk> (5/90-)
Vice-Premier	Park Hŏnyŏng (9/48-3/53) Hong Myŏnghŭi (9/48-9/57) Hŏ Kai (11/51-3/53) Choe Ch'angik (11/52-9/57) Chŏng Ilyong (11/52-9/57)	Kim Il (9/57-10/62) Park Ŭiwan (9/57-3/58) Hong Myŏnghŭi (9/57-10/62) Chŏng Ilyong (9/57-10/62) Chŏng Chunt'aek (9/57-10/62)	Kim Il* (10/62-12/67) Chŏng Chunt'aek (10/62-12/67) Chŏng Ilyong (10/62-12/67) <Lee Chongok> (10/62-12/67) <Kim Kwanghyŏp> (10/62-12/62)	Kim Il* (12/67-12/72) <Park Sŏngch'ŏl> (12/67-12/72) Chŏng Chunt'aek (12/67-12/72) <Lee Chongok> (12/67-9/69) Kim Kwanghyŏp? (12/67-6/69)	<Park Sŏngch'ŏl> (2/72-4/76) Chŏng Chunt'aek (12/72-1/73) Kim Mangŭm (12/72-9/73) <Choe Chaeu> (12/72-12/77) Nam Il (12/72-3/76)	<Kye Ŭngt'ae> (12/77-4/82) <Hŏ Tam> (12/77-4/82) <Kang Songsan> (12/77-4/82) <Chŏng Chungi> (12/77-4/82) <Kong Chint'ae> (12/77-4/82)	<Kang Sŏngsan> (4/82-1/84) <Kye Ŭngtae> (4/82-1/84) <Hŏ Tam> (4/82-12/86) <Chŏng Chungi> (4/82-12/86) <Choe Chaeu> (4/82-12/86)	<Kim Yŏngnam> (12/86-5/90) <Kim Poksin> (12/86-5/90) <Cho Seung> (12/86-5/90) <Hong Sŏngnam> (12/86-5/90) <Chŏng Chungi> (12/86-5/90)	<Kim Yŏngnam> (5/90-) <Choe Yŏngrim> (5/90-) <Hong Sŏngrim> (5/90-) <Kim Poksin> (5/90-) <Kang Hŭiwŏn> (5/90-)

Table 7-22. Continued

1st term	2nd term	3rd term	4th term	5th term	6th term	7th term	8th term	9th term
Choe Yonggŏn (7/53-9/57)	Nam Il (9/57-10/62)	Nam Il (10/62-12/67)	Nam Il (12/67-12/72)	Hong Wŏngil (12/72-5/76)	<Kim Tuyŏng> (12/72-4/82)	<Kong Chint'ae> (4/82-12/86)	<Kim Ch'angju> (12/86-5/90)	<Kim Yunhyŏk> (5/90-)
Park Ŭiwan (7/53-9/57)	Lee Chuyŏn (3/58-10/62)	Lee Chuyŏn (10/62-12/67)	Lee Chuyŏn (12/67-8/69)	<Lee Kŭnmo> (9/73-12/77)	<Kang Hŭiwŏn> (9/78-4/82)	<Choe Kwang> (4/82-12/86)	<Kim Yunhyŏk> (12/86-5/90)	<Kim Talhyŏn> (5/90-)
Park Ch'angok (3/54-9/57)	<Lee Chongok> (1/60-10/62)	<Choe Yongjin> (7/64-12/67)	Choe Yongjin? (12/67-12/72)	Hŏ Tam (2/73-12/77)	<Choe Chaeu> (6/79-4/82)	<Hong Sihak> (4/82-12/86)	<Kim Hwan> (12/86-5/90)	<Kim Hwan> (5/90-)
Kim Il (3/54-9/57)	Kim Kwanghyŏp (10/60-10/62)	Kim Ch'angman (10/62-5/66)	Kim Changbong? (12/67-12/68)	<Chŏng Chungi> (9/73-12/77)	<Ro T'aesŏk> (8/79-1d/80)	<Hong Sŏngyong> (4/82-12/86)	<Kang Hŭiwŏn> (12/86-5/90)	<Kim Ch'anhgiu> (5/90-)
Chŏng Chunt'aek (3/54-9/57)		Ko Hyŏk? (9/66-3/67)	Sŏk San? (5/68-10/69)	<Hong Sŏngnam> (9/73-9/75)	<Choe Kwang> (3/81-4/82)	<Kim Hoeil> (4/82-12/86)		<Chang Ch'ŏl> (5/90-)
		<Kim Ch'angbok> (10/66-12/67)	Kim Mankŭm (7/69-12/72)	Kim Yŏngju? (6/75-12/77)	<Hong Sihak> (10/80-4/82)	<Kim Tuyŏng>*** (4/82-12/86)		
		<Park Sŏngch'ŏl> (11/66-12/67)	Hong Wŏngil (7/69-12/72)	<Kong Chint'ae> (6/75-12/77)	<Sŏ Kwanhŭi> (10/80-4/82)	<Kim Poksin> (4/82-12/86)		
			<Choe Chaeu> (3/70-12/73)	<Lee Chongok> (12/76-12/77)	<Kim Hoeil> (10/80-4/82)	<Kim Ch'angju> (4/82-12/86)		
				<Kye Ŭngtae> (12/76-12/77)	<Hong Sŏngyong> (10/81-4/82)			
					Kim Kyŏngryŏn? (1/80-4/82)			

* The 1st vice-premier was created on January 20, 1959.

** Kim Il was appointed as the 1st vice-president on March, 1976.

*** Kim Tuyŏng died on September 12, 1985.

< >: survior

?: whereabouts unknown

d: deceased

Table 7-23. The Administration Council Member's Place of Origin

	1		2		3		4		5		6		7		8		Total
	No.	(%)	No.	(%)	No.	(%)	No.	(%)	No.	(%)	No.	(%)	No.	(%)	No.	(%)	
P'yŏngbuk	2	6	–	–	1	3	3	8	2	8	2	9	2	13	2	11	14
P'yŏngnam	4	12	2	6	2	7	3	8	7	27	5	22	3	20	2	11	28
Hambuk	14	42	19	54	13	45	16	44	10	38	11	48	7	47	9	5	99
Hamnam	3	9	4	11	7	24	6	16	2	8	2	9	2	13	3	16	29
Hwanghae																	
North Korea	23	69	25	71	23	79	28	78	21	81	20	87	14	93	16	89	170
Kangwŏn																	
Kyŏnggi	2	6	1	3	1	3	1	3	1	4	–	–					6
Kyŏngbuk	3	9	3	8	2	7	1	3	1	4	–	–					10
Kyŏngnam	1	3	--	–	–	–	1	3	–	–	1	4					3
Chŏngbuk	1	3	–	–	–	–	–	–	–	–	–	–					1
Chŏngnam	1	3	1	3	–	–	–	–	–	–	–	–					2
Ch'ungch'ŏng	2	6	1	3	–	–	–	–	1	4	–	–					4
Seoul																	
South Korea	10	31	6	17	3	10	3	8	3	12	1	4					26
Manchuria	–	–	4	11	3	10	5	14	2	8	2	9	1	6	2	11	19
Available data	33	67	35	63	29	63	36	46	26	56	23	43	15	36	18	35	51.2
Total	49		56		46		78		41	`	53		41		51		420

Total: 420; Available data: 215 (51.2%); North Korean total and South Korean total.

Table 7-24. *The Administration Council Member's Educational Background*

	1		2		3		4		5		6		7		8		Total
	No.	(%)	No.	(%)	No.	(%)	No.	(%)	No.	(%)	No.	(%)	No.	(%)	No.	(%)	
Moscow U Leningrad U	2	7	2	6	–	–	1	5	5	26	5	29	2	20	3	21	20
Tashikent U	1	3	1	3	1	5	1	5	2	10	1	6	1	10	–	–	8
Others	2	7	5	19	5	30	3	21	3	15	2	12	1	10	1	7	22
Total U.S.S.R.	5	17	8	29	6	35	5	31	10	51	8	47	4	40	4	28	50
Tokyo U	1	3	1	3	1	5	–	–	–	–	–	–	–	–	–	–	3
Meiji U	–	–	1	3	1	5	1	5	1	5	–	–	–	–	1	7	5
Others	3	10	3	9	2	10	2	10	4	20	4	23	3	30	2	14	23
Total Japan	4	13	5	15	4	20	3	15	5	26	4	23	3	30	3	21	31
Harbin Univ. Inmin Econ. Ins.	1	3	1	3	1	5	1	5	1	5	1	6	1	10	1	7	8
Others	3	10	2	6	1	5	1	5	–	–	–	–	–	–	–	–	7
Total China	4	3	3	9	2	10	2	10	1	5	1	6	1	10	1	7	15
KyŏngsŏngU	2	7	2	6	1	5	–	–	–	–	–	–	–	–	–	–	5
Kimilsŏng U	–	–	–	–	–	–	–	–	1	5	2	12	–	–	1	7	4
Chungangdang	1	3	–	–	1	5	3	15	–	–	–	–	1	10	1	7	7
Military school	2	7	2	6	1	5	2	10	–	–	–	–	–	–	–	–	7
Technic. school	3	10	5	16	2	10	–	–	–	–	–	–	–	–	–	–	10
Middle school	4	13	3	9	4	20	3	15	1	5	2	12	1	10	1	7	19
High school	2	7	2	6	1	5	1	5	1	5	–	–	–	–	1	7	8
College	4	13	3	9	1	5	2	10	–	–	–	–	–	–	–	–	10
Available data	30	61	31	55	20	43	19	24	19	41	17	32	10	24	14	27	38.1%
Total	49		56		46		78		46		53		41		51		420

Table 7-25. The Administration Council Member's Overseas Travel

	1		2		3		4		5		6		7		8		Total
	No.	(%)	No.	(%)	No.	(%)	No.	(%)	No.	(%)	No.	(%)	No.	(%)	No.	(%)	
U.S.S.R.	24	68	33	77	23	70	35	66	26	60	23	53	18	53	26	62	208
China	24	68	23	53	17	51	29	55	28	72	28	65	26	73	25	59	199
Japan	3	9	5	12	3	9	4	7	4	10	3	7	3	9	4	9	29
Bulgarian	1	3	5	12	6	18	9	17	10	26	11	25	10	29	16	38	68
Czecho.	4	11	5	12	5	15	9	17	6	15	9	21	8	23	9	21	55
Romania	5	14	7	16	5	15	15	28	15	38	13	30	14	41	12	28	86
E. Germany	3	9	3	7	2	6	10	19	10	26	13	30	11	32	9	21	61
Yugoslavia	1	3	1	2	1	3	3	6	4	10	5	12	7	20	5	12	27
Hungary	1	3	3	7	2	6	11	21	7	18	12	28	8	23	7	17	51
Poland	2	6	3	7	3	9	3	6	5	13	9	21	10	29	7	17	42
Albania	2	6	4	9	2	6	4	7	2	5	–	–	2	6	3	7	19
Asia	11	31	17	39	16	49	17	32	11	28	17	39	18	53	16	38	123
Africa	5	14	6	14	4	12	10	19	14	36	15	35	15	44	7	17	76
Mid-South Am.	2	6	4	9	3	9	9	17	3	7	6	14	10	29	8	19	45
Europe	3	9	6	14	6	18	7	13	5	13	2	4	3	9	8	19	40
Middle-East			2	5	3	9	6	11	5	13	10	23	7	20	4	9	37
Others	1	3	–	–	–	–	–	–	3	7	–	–	–	–	–	–	4
Available data	35	71	43	77	33	72	53	68	39	85	43	81	34	83	42	82	76.7%
Total	49		56		46		78		46		53		41		51		420

Table 7-26. The Administration Council Member's Birth Year

	1		2		3		4		5		6		7		8		Total
	No.	(%)	No.	(%)	No.	(%)	No.	(%)	No.	(%)	No.	(%)	No.	(%)	No.	(%)	
1880s	1	5	1	4	–	–	–	–	–	–	–	–	–	–	–	–	2
1890s	5	23	1	4	–	–	–	–	–	–	–	–	–	–	–	–	6
1900s	11	50	8	35	7	32	5	20	3	20	1	10	1	14	–	–	36
1910s	5	23	13	52	14	64	16	67	7	47	6	60	5	72	7	78	73
1920s	–	–	1	4	1	5	3	13	5	33	3	30	1	14	2	22	16
Available data	22	45	24	41	22	48	24	30	15	33	10	19	7	17	9	18	31.7%
Total	49		56		46		78		46		53		41		51		420

<Total No. of Analysis>
The Supreme People's Assmbly: 3,438
The WPK's Central Committee: 523
The Administration Council: 420
Total Numbers: 4,381

Table 7-27. Leadership Changes in the Central Court and
Central Procurator's Office

	Chief Justices	Procurators-General
1st SPA	Kim Ik-son (9/48-3/55) Cho Sung-mo (3/55-3/56) Hwang Se-hwan (3/56-9/57)	Chang Hae-u (9/48-6/53) Yi Song-un (6/53-3/56) Cho Sung-mo (3/56-9/57)
2nd SPA	Kim Ha-un (9/57-10/59) Ho Chong-suk (10/59-11/60) Kim Ik-son (11/60-10/62)	Pak Se-ch'ang (10/62-3/64)
3rd SPA	Kim Ik-son (10/62-9/66) Yi Kuk-chin (9/66-12/67)	Pak Se-ch'ang (10/62-3/64) Yi Kuk-chin (3/64-9/66) Yi Song-un (9/66-12/67)
4th SPA	Yi Yong-gu (12/67-12/72)	Yun T'ae-hong (12/67-12/72)
5th SPA	Pang Hak-se (12/72-12/77)	Chong Tong-ch'ol (12/72-12/77)
6th SPA	Pang Hak-se (12/77-1/84)	Yi Chin-su (12/77-1/84)
7th SPA	Pang Hak-se (1/84-)	Han Sang-gyu (1/84-)
8th SPA	Pang Hak-se (1/84-)	Han Sang-gyu (1/84-)
9th SPA	Pang Hak-se (1/84-7/92)	Han Sang-gyu (1/84-)

Sources: Adapted from *Pukhan Ch'onggam;* Pukhan Chonso; Dae-sook Suh, *Korean Communism, 1945-1980;* and *Vantage Point* 7 (2) (February 1984).Yang Sung Chul, *Pukhan Ch'ong Ch'iron* (Seoul: Pakyong-sa, 1991).

Chart 7-1. WPK Structure

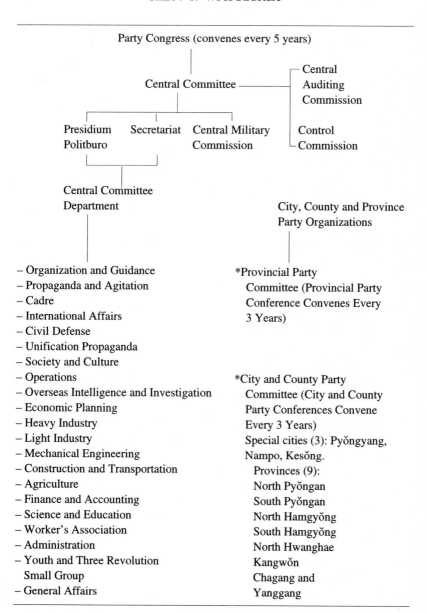

Party Congress (convenes every 5 years)

Central Committee — Central Auditing Commission

Presidium Politburo   Secretariat   Central Military Commission

Control Commission

Central Committee Department

City, County and Province Party Organizations

– Organization and Guidance
– Propaganda and Agitation
– Cadre
– International Affairs
– Civil Defense
– Unification Propaganda
– Society and Culture
– Operations
– Overseas Intelligence and Investigation
– Economic Planning
– Heavy Industry
– Light Industry
– Mechanical Engineering
– Construction and Transportation
– Agriculture
– Finance and Accounting
– Science and Education
– Worker's Association
– Administration
– Youth and Three Revolution
  Small Group
– General Affairs

*Provincial Party
  Committee (Provincial Party
  Conference Convenes Every
  3 Years)

*City and County Party
  Committee (City and County
  Party Conferences Convene
  Every 3 Years)
  Special cities (3): Pyŏngyang,
  Nampo, Kesŏng.
    Provinces (9):
    North Pyŏngan
    South Pyŏngan
    North Hamgyŏng
    South Hamgyŏng
    North Hwanghae
    Kangwŏn
    Chagang and
    Yanggang

Chart 7-2. Supreme People's Assembly (Legislative Organ)

*SPA (deputies elected for a 5-year term)				
Standing Committee				
Credentials Committee	Foreign Relations	Unification Policy	Bills Committee	Budgets Committee

*Provincial, city and county
People's Assembly (A 4-year term for provincial and special city deputies and a 4-year term for city and county deputies)

*Provincial, city and county People's Committee
(exercises the function of the local organ of the state when the People's Assembly is not in session)

*Provincial, city and county Administrative Committee (the administrative and executive body of the local organ of state power)

---

* The Formal Powers of the SPA

- amends the constitution, laws and ordinances
- adopts or amends laws and ordinances
- approves laws adopted by the SPA Standing Committee during the SPA recess
- establishes the basic principles of domestic and foreign policies
- elects the President of the DPRK
- elects or recalls the Vice-Presidents of the DPRK, on the recommendation of the President of the DPRK
- elects or recalls the Secretary and members of the CPC
- elects or recalls members of the Standing Committee of the SPA
- elects or recalls the Premier of the Administrative Council on the recommendation of the President of the DPRK
- elects or recalls the Chairman of the National Defense Commission
- elects or recalls the first Vice-Chairman, Vice-Chairman and members of the NDC on the recommendation of its chairman
- elects or recalls the President of the Central Court and appoint or remove the Procurator-General of the Central Procurator's Office
- approves the State plan for the development of the national economy
- appoints vice premiers, chairmen, ministers and other officials of the AC on the recommendation of the premier
- approves the state budget
- decides on questions of war and peace

Chart 7-3. Administration Council (Executive Organ)

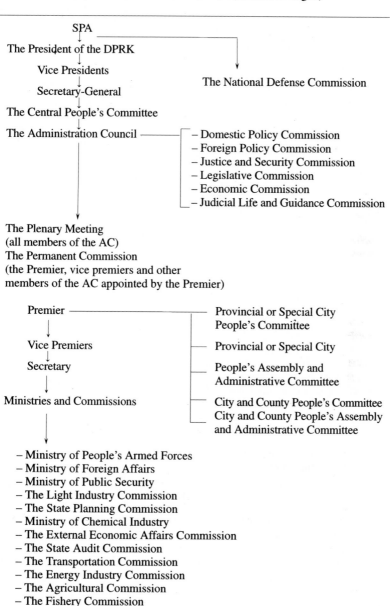

SPA

The President of the DPRK

  Vice Presidents

    Secretary-General

The Central People's Committee

The Administration Council —— ⌐ – Domestic Policy Commission
                             – Foreign Policy Commission
                             – Justice and Security Commission
                             – Legislative Commission
                             – Economic Commission
                            ⌐ – Judicial Life and Guidance Commission

The National Defense Commission

The Plenary Meeting
(all members of the AC)
The Permanent Commission
(the Premier, vice premiers and other
members of the AC appointed by the Premier)

Premier —————————— Provincial or Special City
                              People's Committee

Vice Premiers   Provincial or Special City

Secretary   People's Assembly and
                            Administrative Committee

Ministries and Commissions   City and County People's Committee
                              City and County People's Assembly
                              and Administrative Committee

  – Ministry of People's Armed Forces
  – Ministry of Foreign Affairs
  – Ministry of Public Security
  – The Light Industry Commission
  – The State Planning Commission
  – Ministry of Chemical Industry
  – The External Economic Affairs Commission
  – The State Audit Commission
  – The Transportation Commission
  – The Energy Industry Commission
  – The Agricultural Commission
  – The Fishery Commission

Chart 7-3. Continued

- The State Construction Commission
- The People's Service Commission
- The State Science and Technology Commission
- The Electronic Automation Commission
- Ministry of Metallurgical Engineering
- Ministry of Mechanical Engineering
- Ministry of Mining
- Ministry of Coal Industry
- Ministry of Resource Development
- Ministry of Shipbuilding Industry
- Ministry of Construction
- Ministry of Materials Supply
- Ministry of Forestry
- Ministry of Local Industry
- Ministry of Nuclear Engineering
- Ministry of City Management
- Ministry of Postal Service
- Ministry of Labor Administration
- Ministry of Finance
- The Education Commission
- Ministry of Culture and Arts
- Ministry of Public Health
- Ministry of Railways
- Ministry of Maritime Transportation
- Ministry of Foreign Trade
- Ministry of External Economic Projects
- Ministry of Commerce
- The Academy of Science
- The State Sports Commission

---

*The Powers of the DPRK President

- Is the Head of State (5 years)
- Guides the CPC
- Convenes and presides over meetings of the Administration Council
- Promulgates the laws and ordinances of the SPA, the decrees of CPC and the decisions of the SPA Standing Committees
- Exercises the right of granting special pardon
- Announces the ratification and abrogation of treaties concluded with other countries
- Receives the letters of credence and recall of diplomatic representatives accredited by foreign states
- Announces the appointment or recall of diplomats to foreign countries

---

Table 7-14. North Korean Supreme People's Assembly Members'
Educational Background*

	1st term No.	1st term (%)	2nd term No.	2nd term (%)	3rd term No.	3rd term (%)	4th term No.	4th term (%)	5th term No.	5th term (%)	7th term No.	7th term (%)	8th term No.	8th term (%)	Total No.
Moscow U	4	6	4	6	5	6	7	9	8	10	11	18	7	14	46
Leningrad U	–	–	–	–	1	1	1	1	1	1	1	1	1	2	5
Tashkent U	1	1	2	3	2	2	2	2	2	2	1	2	–	–	10
Others	5	8	6	10	11	13	16	21	11	14	12	19	6	12	67
U.S.S.R. Total	10	16	12	20	19	22	26	35	22	29	25	39	14	30	128
Tokyo	3	5	3	5	2	2	1	1	2	2	–	–	–	–	11
Meiji	3	5	1	1	1	1	–	–	–	–	–	–	1	2	6
Kyoto	1	1	2	3	2	2	2	2	–	–	–	–	–	–	7
Others	4	6	4	6	9	10	4	5	8	10	6	10	7	14	42
Japan Total	11	18	10	16	14	16	7	9	10	13	6	10	8	16	66
Harbin U	1	1	1	1	1	1	1	1	1	1	1	2	1	2	7
# Inmin Econ. Ins.	–	–	–	–	1	1	1	1	1	1	–	–	2	4	5
Others	3	5	6	10	3	3	4	5	2	2	3	5	3	6	24
China Total	4	6	7	12	5	6	6	8	4	5	4	6	6	12	36
Kyŏngsŏng	5	8	3	5	3	3	3	4	1	1	2	3	1	2	18
Kimilsŏng U	1	1	–	–	2	2	2	2	5	6	2	3	5	10	17
# Chungang	1	1	1	1	9	10	5	6	8	10	8	13	7	14	39
Military School	3	5	5	8	4	5	5	6	3	4	1	2	1	2	22
Technical School	7	12	7	12	7	8	8	10	9	12	8	13	5	10	51
Middle School	4	6	5	8	7	8	4	5	5	6	1	2	1	2	27
High School	5	8	2	3	–	–	1	1	2	2	1	2	2	4	13
College	9	15	8	13	15	18	8	10	7	9	4	6	–	–	51
Available data	60	10	60	28	22	85	75	16	76	14	62	10	50	8	13.6%
Total	572		215		383		457		541		615		655		3,438

* The information for the 6th SPA Members were not disclosed. So, the data are not available.
# Inmin Econ. Ins.= Inmingyŏngche U; and Chungang=Chungangdang School.

Table 7-15. North Korean Supreme People's Assembly Members'
Position

	1st term No.	(%)	2nd term No.	(%)	3rd term No.	(%)	4th term No.	(%)	5th term No.	(%)	7th term No.	(%)	8th term No.	(%)	Total No.
#WPK	85	82	83	80	147	87	149	84	172	83	202	88	199	98	1,037
#M.	1	10	17	16	32	19	42	24	39	19	40	17	40	20	221
AC.	55	53	59	57	84	49	96	54	95	46	107	47	99	49	595
M. AC. P.	5	5	11	11	17	10	20	11	13	6	11	5	9	4	86
M.P.	1	1	4	4	15	9	16	9	23	11	28	12	25	12	112
M. AC.	2	2	1	1	–	–	1	–	2	1	–	–	–	–	6
P. AC.	33	31	33	32	43	25	54	31	64	31	70	30	76	37	373
#P.	45	43	39	38	72	42	60	34	70	34	91	40	89	44	504
#AC.	14	13	14	13	24	14	21	12	31	15	23	10	14	7	141
M.	3	3	1	1	–	–	5	3	3	1	3	1	6	3	21
Available data	104	18	103	48	171	45	176	39	206	38	228	37	204	31	1,192
Total	572		215		383		457		541		615		655		3,439

\# WPK: The Worker's Party of Korea; AC: The Administration Council; M: Military; and
  P: Party.

Table 7-16. North Korean Supreme People's Assembly Members'
Overseas Travels

	1st term		2nd term		3rd term		4th term		5th term		7th term		8th term		Total
	No.	(%)	No.	(%)	No.	(%)	No.	(%)	No.	(%)	No.	(%)	No.	(%)	No.
U.S.S.R.	35	48	38	51	59	42	67	51	68	47	83	50	73	52	423
China	40	55	41	55	66	48	54	41	76	52	86	51	78	55	441
Japan	7	10	9	12	15	11	9	7	19	13	17	10	17	12	93
Bulgaria	6	8	4	5	10	7	12	9	16	11	22	13	22	16	92
Czecho.	7	10	5	6	10	7	18	14	25	17	25	15	18	13	108
Romania	11	15	6	8	9	6	16	12	31	21	34	20	23	16	130
E. Germany	5	7	7	9	12	9	18	14	20	14	28	17	24	17	114
Yugoslavia	3	4	1	1	5	4	4	3	8	5	12	7	12	9	45
Hungary	4	5	5	7	8	6	16	12	19	13	23	14	19	13	94
Poland	7	10	5	7	9	6	11	8	15	10	15	9	13	9	75
Albania	2	3	5	7	6	4	7	5	4	3	4	2	3	2	31
Asia	14	10	8	11	24	17	25	19	21	14	25	15	21	15	138
Africa	5	7	7	9	21	15	24	18	33	23	37	22	28	20	155
Mid-South America	3	4	1	1	21	15	19	14	24	17	25	15	21	15	114
Europe	9	12	6	8	13	9	11	8	11	7	18	11	16	11	84
Mid-East	4	5	5	7	16	11	9	7	16	11	17	10	13	9	80
Others	5	7	7	9	6	4	5	4	5	3	11	7	8	6	47
Available data	73	13	75	35	138	36	132	29	145	27	167	27	141	22	25.3%
Total	572		215		383		459		542		618		655		3,438

Asia: South-East Asia and South Asia; Mainly Vietnam, Burma, India, Mongolia.
  Africa: Egypt, Guinea, Sudan.
  Mid-South America: Mainly Cuba
  Europe: Finland and Sweden except Eastern bloc nations.
  Mid-East: Mainly Syria, Iraq.
  Others: America, etc.

Table 7-17. North Korean Supreme People's Assembly Members
by Career Background

	1st term		2nd term		3rd term		4th term		5th term		7th term		8th term		Total
	No.	(%)	No.	(%)	No.	(%)	No.	(%)	No.	(%)	No.	(%)	No.	(%)	No.
Workers	2	3	6	7	53	24	43	19	18	7	13	6	11	6	146
Managers	5	8	17	21	52	24	77	25	96	40	86	40	66	25	399
Teachers	7	11	5	6	8	4	7	3	5	2	6	3	4	2	42
Professors	6	9	9	11	21	10	13	6	33	14	25	12	23	12	130
Diplomats	7	11	6	7	21	10	18	8	20	8	18	9	22	12	112
Journalists	2	3	2	2	3	1	2	1	9	4	8	4	7	4	33
Writers	7	11	5	6	4	2	2	1	2	1	3	1	5	3	28
Artists	3	5	2	2	1	–	4	2	3	1	3	1	6	3	22
Athletes	1	2	1	1	–	–	–	–	–	–	1	–	1	–	4
Leftist movement	5	8	3	4	5	2	5	2	4	2	2	1	3	1	27
Independence movement	8	13	5	6	3	1	3	1	2	1	2	1	–	–	23
Agrarian	2	3	1	1	–	–	1	–	2	1	1	2	–	–	7
Labor movement	1	2	2	2	–	–	1	–	1	–	–	–	–	–	5
Guerrillas	6	9	10	12	41	19	40	18	30	12	27	13	22	12	177
Religionists	2	3	5	6	6	3	5	2	8	3	3	1	2	1	31
Available data	64	11	81	38	219	57	223	49	241	45	209	34	191	29	35.7%
Total	5,721		215		383		457		541		615		655		3,438

Table 7-18. North Korean Supreme People's Assembly Members
by Birth Year

	1st term		2nd term		3rd term		4th term		5th term		7th term		8th term		Total
	No.	(%)	No.	(%)	No.	(%)	No.	(%)	No.	(%)	No.	(%)	No.	(%)	No.
1880s	6	14	4	10	1	2	–	–	–	–	–	–	–	–	12
1890s	8	19	7	18	4	7	4	10	2	5	–	–	–	–	25
1900s	17	39	11	28	17	31	12	28	10	25	8	31	7	24	82
1910s	8	19	15	38	27	49	21	50	19	48	11	42	11	38	112
1920s	4	9	2	5	6	11	4	10	8	20	5	19	7	24	36
1930s	–	–	–	–	–	–	–	–	1	2	1	4	1	3	3
1940s	–	–	–	–	–	–	–	–	–	–	1	4	3	10	4
Available data	43	8	39	18	55	14	42	9	40	7	26	4	29	4	7.97%
Total	572		215		383		457		541		615		655		3,438

Table 7-19. The Supreme People's Assembly Members by Sex

	1st term No.	(%)	2nd term No.	(%)	3rd term No.	(%)	4th term No.	(%)	5th term No.	(%)	7th term No.	(%)	8th term No.	(%)	Total No.
Male	503	88	187	87	348	91	384	84	428	79	524	85	578	88	2,952
Female	69	12	28	13	35	9	73	16	113	21	91	15	77	12	486
Total	572		215		383		457		541		615		655		3,438

Total (female): 486 (14.1%)

Table 7-20. The Supreme People's Assembly Members' Overall Data

Term		1st	2nd	3rd	4th	5th	6th	7th*	8th*	9th*	reference
Item No. of member		572	215	383	457	541	579	615	655	687	
Previous occupation	worker (1)	120	84	215	292	347	248	213	238	254	
	peasant (2)	194	68	62	70	72	64	63	79	71	
	clerk (3)	152	60	101	95	122	267	339	338	362	
	others	106	3	5	—	—	—	—	—	—	
Age	20 – 30	73	5	12	—	—	—	24	18	20	under 35
	31 – 40	223	34	99	64	96	32	438	450	390	36 – 55
	41 – 50	174	99	181	220	280	457	153	187	277	over 56
	51 – 60	77	54	71	136	126	90				
	61 – 70	21	23	20	37	39					
	over 70	4	—	—	—	—	—	—	—	—	
Education	primary school	198	95	—	—	—	—	226	159	—	mid-level
										218	vocational school
	mid-high school	147	43	256	200	101	176	79	125	—	technical school
	college	227	60	127	257	323	403	310	371	469	
	graduate school	—	17	—	—	117	—	—	—	—	
Sex	male	503	188	348	384	428	459	494	517	549	
	female	69	27	35	73	113	120**	121**	138**	138**	

Source: Dae-Sook Suh, *Op. Cit.*, p. 442; *Pukhanjŏnsŏ 1945-1980* (Seoul: Kŭkdongmunje-yŏnguso, 1980). The 7th through the 9th term data are rearranged by the author.

(1) They are called "workers" during the 1st term, "workers representatives" during the 2nd through the 4th term, "representatives from workers" during the 5th term, and "workers" from the 6th term to the 9th term.

(2) They are called "peasant representatives" during the 1st through the 4th term, "representatives from peasant" during the 5th term, and "collective farm workers" from the 6th term to the 9th term.

(3) They are called "clerks" during the 1st term, "representatives of clerical workers" during the 2nd through the 4th term, "representatives from clerical workers" during the 5th term, but from the 6th term no distinction was made.

 * The actual numbers are not available from the 7th to the 9th members. Hence, the numbers are recalculated from the percentages given by the North Korean government. The number of members is rounded to the nearest whole number.
** The actual number of female members from the 6th to the 9th SPA are not available. Hence, the numbers are calculated on the basis of the percentages given by the North Korean Government.

Table 7-21. An Overview of Administration Council's (Cabinet)
Structual Changes

Term position	Premier	Vice-premier	Chief (minister)	Chairman	The Chief of Office
1st (9/09/48)	1	3	17	1	–
2nd (9/20/57)	1	6	23	2	–
3rd (10/23/62)	1	8(7+1)	22	5	–
4th (12/16/67)	1	8	30	6	–
5th (12/28/72)	1	6	15	7	–
6th (12/15/77)	1	6	21	7	1
7th (4/05/82)	1	13	19(1)	14	1
8th(12/12/86)	1	9	16(1)	14	1
9th (5/24/90)	1	10	25(1)	14	1

Kim Il Sung was premier from the 1st to the 4th Cabinet and the President from the 5th Cabinet to the present. Kim Il was premier at the 5th and 6th Cabinet, Lee Chongok was premier in 1977. Kang Sŏng-san was the premier of Administration Council on January 1, 1984. Lee Kunmo was the premier of Administration Council on December, 1986. Yŏn Hyŏngmuk is the premier of Administration Council since December, 1988.
(1) Scientific Institute
* The 1st vice-premier position was created on January 20, 1959.

Table 7-22. The Changes in the N.K.'s Presidency, Vice-Presidency, Premiership, Vice-Premiership

	1st term	2nd term	3rd term	4th term	5th term	6th term	7th term	8th term	9th term
President					\<Kim Il Sung\> (12/72-12/77)	\<Kim Il Sung\> (12/77-4/82)	\<Kim Il Sung\> (4/82-12/86)	\<Kim Il Sung\> (12/86-5/90)	\<Kim Il Sung\> (5/90-)
Vice-President					Choe Yonggŏn (12/72-9/76) Kang Yanguk (12/72-12/77) Kim Tonggyu (11/74-12/77) Kim Il** (4/76-3/84)	Kang Yanuk (12/77-4/82) \<Park Sŏngch'ŏl\> (12/77-4/82) Kim Il (12/77-4/82)	Kim Il (4/82-3/83) Kang Yanguk (4/82-1/83) \<Park Sŏngch'ŏl\> (4/82-12/86) \<Lee Chongok\> (1/84-12/86) \<Lim Ch'unch'u\> (4/83-4/84)	\<Park Sŏngch'ŏl\> (12/86-5/90) \<Lim Ch'unch'u\> (12/86-4/88)	\<Park Sŏngch'ŏl\> (5/90-)
								\<Lee Chongok\> (12/86-5/90)	\<Lee Chongok\> (5/90-)
Premier	\<Kim Il Sung\> (9/48-9/57)	\<Kim Il Sung\> (9/57-10/62)	\<Kim Il Sung\> (10/62-12/67)	\<Kim Il Sung\> (12/67-12/722)	Kim Il (2/72-4/76) \<Park Songchol\> (4/76-12/77)	\<Lee Chongok\> (12/77-4/82)	\<Lee Chongok\> (4/82-1/84) \<Kang Songsan\> (1/84-12/86)	\<Lee Kŭnmo\> (12/86-12/88) \<Yŏn Hyŏngmuk\> (12/88-5/90)	\<Yŏn Hyŏngmuk\> (5/90-)
Vice-Premier	Park Hŏnyŏng (9/48-3/53) Hong Myŏnghŭi (9/48-9/57) Hŏ Kai (11/51-3/53) Choe Ch'angik (11/52-9/57) Chŏng Ilyong (11/52-9/57)	Kim Il (9/57-10/62) Park Ŭiwan (9/57-3/58) Hong Myŏnghŭi (9/57-10/62) Chŏng Ilyong (9/57-10/62) Chŏng Chunt'aek (9/57-10/62)	Kim Il* (10/62-12/67) Chŏng Chunt'aek (10/62-12/67) Chŏng Ilyong (10/62-12/67) \<Lee Chongok\> (10/62-12/67) \<Kim Kwanghyŏp\> (10/62-12/62)	Kim Il* (12/67-12/72) \<Park Sŏngch'ŏl\> (12/67-12/72) Chŏng Chunt'aek (12/67-12/72) \<Lee Chongok\> (12/67-9/69) Kim Kwanghyŏp? (12/67-6/69)	\<Park Sŏngch'ŏl\> (2/72-4/76) Chŏng Chunt'aek (12/72-1/73) Kim Mangŭm (12/72-9/73) \<Choe Chaeu\> (12/72-12/77) Nam Il (12/72-3/76)	\<Kye Ŭngt'ae\> (12/77-4/82) Hŏ Tam\> (12/77-4/82) \<Kang Sŏngsan\> (12/77-4/82) \<Chŏng Chungi\> (12/77-4/82) \<Kong Chint'ae\> (12/77-4/82)	\<Kang Sŏngsan\> (4/82-1/84) \<Kye Ŭngtae\> (4/82-12/86) Hŏ Tam\> (4/82-12/86) \<Chŏng Chungi\> (4/82-12/86) \<Choe Chaeu\> (4/82-12/86)	\<Kim Yŏngnam\> (12/86-5/90) \<Kim Poksin\> (12/86-5/90) \<Cho Seung\> (12/86-5/90) \<Hong Sŏngnam\> (12/86-5/90) \<Chŏng Chungi\> (12/86-5/90)	\<Kim Yŏngnam\> (5/90-) \<Choe Yŏngrim\> (5/90-) \<Hong Sŏngrim\> (5/90-) \<Kim Poksin\> (5/90-) \<Kang Hŭiwŏn\> (5/90-)

Table 7-22. Continued

1st term	2nd term	3rd term	4th term	5th term	6th term	7th term	8th term	9th term
Choe Yonggŏn (7/53-9/57)	Nam Il (9/57-10/62)	Nam Il (10/62-12/67)	Nam Il (12/67-12/72)	Hong Wŏngil (12/72-5/76)	<Kim Tuyŏng> (12/72-4/82)	<Kong Chint'ae> (4/82-12/86)	<Kim Ch'angiu> (12/86-5/90)	<Kim Yunhyŏk> (5/90-)
Park Ŭiwan (7/53-9/57)	Lee Chuyŏn (3/58-10/62)	Lee Chuyŏn (10/62-12/67)	Lee Chuyŏn (12/67-8/69)	<Lee Kŭnmo> (9/73-12/77)	<Kang Hŭiwŏn> (9/78-4/82)	<Choe Kwang> (4/82-12/86)	<Kim Yunhyŏk> (12/86-5/90)	<Kim Talhyŏn> (5/90-)
Park Ch'angok (3/54-9/57)	<Lee Chongok> (1/60-10/62)	<Choe Yongjin> (7/64-12/67)	Choe Yongjin? (12/67-12/72)	Hŏ Tam (2/73-12/77)	<Choe Chaeu> (6/79-4/82)	<Hong Sihak> (4/82-12/86)	<Kim Hwan> (12/86-5/90)	<Kim Hwan> (5/90-)
Kim Il (3/54-9/57)	Kim Kwanghyŏp (10/60-10/62)	Kim Ch'angman (10/62-5/66)	Kim Changbong? (12/67-12/68)	<Chŏng Chungi> (9/73-12/77)	<Ro T'aesŏk> (8/79-1d/80)	<Hong Sŏngyong> (4/82-12/86)	<Kang Hŭiwŏn> (12/86-5/90)	<Kim Ch'anhgiu> (5/90-)
Chŏng Chunt'aek (3/54-9/57)		Ko Hyŏk? (9/66-3/67)	Sŏk San? (5/68-10/69)	<Hong Sŏngnam> (9/73-9/75)	<Choe Kwang> (3/81-4/82)	<Kim Hoeil> (4/82-12/86)		<Chang Ch'ŏl> (5/90-)
		<Kim Ch'angbok> (10/66-12/67)	Kim Mankŭm (7/69-12/72)	Kim Yŏngju? (6/75-12/77)	<Hong Sihak> (10/80-4/82)	<Kim Tuyŏng>*** (4/82-12/86)		
		<Park Sŏngch'ŏl> (11/66-12/67)	Hong Wŏngil (7/69-12/72)	<Kong Chint'ae> (6/75-12/77)	<Sŏ Kwanhŭi> (10/80-4/82)	<Kim Poksin> (4/82-12/86)		
			<Choe Chaeu> (3/70-12/73)	<Lee Chongok> (12/76-12/77)	<Kim Hoeil> (9/81-4/82)	<Kim Ch'angiu> (4/82-12/86)		
				<Kye Ŭngtae> (12/76-12/77)	<Hong Sŏngyong> (10/81-4/82)			
					Kim Kyŏngryŏn? (11/80-4/82)			

* The 1st vice-premier was created on January 20, 1959.

** Kim Il was appointed as the 1st vice-president on March, 1976.

*** Kim Tuyŏng died on September 12, 1985.

< >: survior

?: whereabouts unknown

d: deceased

Table 7-23. The Administration Council Member's Place of Origin

	1 No. (%)		2 No. (%)		3 No. (%)		4 No. (%)		5 No. (%)		6 No. (%)		7 No. (%)		8 No. (%)		Total
P'yŏngbuk	2	6	–	–	1	3	3	8	2	8	2	9	2	13	2	11	14
P'yŏngnam	4	12	2	6	2	7	3	8	7	27	5	22	3	20	2	11	28
Hambuk	14	42	19	54	13	45	16	44	10	38	11	48	7	47	9	5	99
Hamnam	3	9	4	11	7	24	6	16	2	8	2	9	2	13	3	16	29
Hwanghae																	
North Korea	23	69	25	71	23	79	28	78	21	81	20	87	14	93	16	89	170
Kangwŏn																	
Kyŏnggi	2	6	1	3	1	3	1	3	1	4	–	–					6
Kyŏngbuk	3	9	3	8	2	7	1	3	1	4	–	–					10
Kyŏngnam	1	3	--	–	–	–	1	3	–	–	1	4					3
Chŏngbuk	1	3	–	–	–	–	–	–	–	–	–	–					1
Chŏngnam	1	3	1	3	–	–	–	–	–	–	–	–					2
Ch'ungch'ŏng	2	6	1	3	–	–	–	–	1	4	–	–					4
Seoul																	
South Korea	10	31	6	17	3	10	3	8	3	12	1	4					26
Manchuria	–	–	4	11	3	10	5	14	2	8	2	9	1	6	2	11	19
Available data	33	67	35	63	29	63	36	46	26	56	23	43	15	36	18	35	51.2
Total	49		56		46		78		41	`	53		41		51		420

Total: 420; Available data: 215 (51.2%); North Korean total and South Korean total.

Table 7-24. The Administration Council Member's Educational Background

	1 No. (%)		2 No. (%)		3 No. (%)		4 No. (%)		5 No. (%)		6 No. (%)		7 No. (%)		8 No. (%)		Total
Moscow U	2	7	2	6	–	–	1	5	5	26	5	29	2	20	3	21	20
Leningrad U																	
Tashikent U	1	3	1	3	1	5	1	5	2	10	1	6	1	10	–	–	8
Others	2	7	5	19	5	30	3	21	3	15	2	12	1	10	1	7	22
Total U.S.S.R.	5	17	8	29	6	35	5	31	10	51	8	47	4	40	4	28	50
Tokyo U	1	3	1	3	1	5	–	–	–	–	–	–	–	–	–	–	3
Meiji U	–	–	1	3	1	5	1	5	1	5	–	–	–	–	1	7	5
Others	3	10	3	9	2	10	2	10	4	20	4	23	3	30	2	14	23
Total Japan	4	13	5	15	4	20	3	15	5	26	4	23	3	30	3	21	31
Harbin Univ.	1	3	1	3	1	5	1	5	1	5	1	6	1	10	1	7	8
Inmin Econ. Ins.																	
Others	3	10	2	6	1	5	1	5	–	–	–	–	–	–	–	–	7
Total China	4	3	3	9	2	10	2	10	1	5	1	6	1	10	1	7	15
KyŏngsŏngU	2	7	2	6	1	5	–	–	–	–	–	–	–	–	–	–	5
Kimilsŏng U	–	–	–	–	–	–	–	–	1	5	2	12	–	–	1	7	4
Chungangdang	1	3	–	–	1	5	3	15	–	–	–	–	1	10	1	7	7
Military school	2	7	2	6	1	5	2	10	–	–	–	–	–	–	–	–	7
Technic. school	3	10	5	16	2	10	–	–	–	–	–	–	–	–	–	–	10
Middle school	4	13	3	9	4	20	3	15	1	5	2	12	1	10	1	7	19
High school	2	7	2	6	1	5	1	5	1	5	–	–	–	–	1	7	8
College	4	13	3	9	1	5	2	10	–	–	–	–	–	–	–	–	10
Available data	30	61	31	55	20	43	19	24	19	41	17	32	10	24	14	27	38.1%
Total	49		56		46		78		46		53		41		51		420

Table 7-25. The Administration Council Member's Overseas Travel

	1		2		3		4		5		6		7		8		Total
	No.	(%)	No.	(%)	No.	(%)	No.	(%)	No.	(%)	No.	(%)	No.	(%)	No.	(%)	
U.S.S.R.	24	68	33	77	23	70	35	66	26	60	23	53	18	53	26	62	208
China	24	68	23	53	17	51	29	55	28	72	28	65	26	73	25	59	199
Japan	3	9	5	12	3	9	4	7	4	10	3	7	3	9	4	9	29
Bulgarian	1	3	5	12	6	18	9	17	10	26	11	25	10	29	16	38	68
Czecho.	4	11	5	12	5	15	9	17	6	15	9	21	8	23	9	21	55
Romania	5	14	7	16	5	15	15	28	15	38	13	30	14	41	12	28	86
E. Germany	3	9	3	7	2	6	10	19	10	26	13	30	11	32	9	21	61
Yugoslavia	1	3	1	2	1	3	3	6	4	10	5	12	7	20	5	12	27
Hungary	1	3	3	7	2	6	11	21	7	18	12	28	8	23	7	17	51
Poland	2	6	3	7	3	9	3	6	5	13	9	21	10	29	7	17	42
Albania	2	6	4	9	2	6	4	7	2	5	–	–	2	6	3	7	19
Asia	11	31	17	39	16	49	17	32	11	28	17	39	18	53	16	38	123
Africa	5	14	6	14	4	12	10	19	14	36	15	35	15	44	7	17	76
Mid-South Am.	2	6	4	9	3	9	9	17	3	7	6	14	10	29	8	19	45
Europe	3	9	6	14	6	18	7	13	5	13	2	4	3	9	8	19	40
Middle-East			2	5	3	9	6	11	5	13	10	23	7	20	4	9	37
Others	1	3	–	–	–	–	–	–	3	7	–	–	–	–	–	–	4
Available data	35	71	43	77	33	72	53	68	39	85	43	81	34	83	42	82	76.7%
Total	49		56		46		78		46		53		41		51		420

Table 7-26. The Administration Council Member's Birth Year

	1		2		3		4		5		6		7		8		Total
	No.	(%)	No.	(%)	No.	(%)	No.	(%)	No.	(%)	No.	(%)	No.	(%)	No.	(%)	
1880s	1	5	1	4	–	–	–	–	–	–	–	–	–	–	–	–	2
1890s	5	23	1	4	–	–	–	–	–	–	–	–	–	–	–	–	6
1900s	11	50	8	35	7	32	5	20	3	20	1	10	1	14	–	–	36
1910s	5	23	13	52	14	64	16	67	7	47	6	60	5	72	7	78	73
1920s	–	–	1	4	1	5	3	13	5	33	3	30	1	14	2	22	16
Available data	22	45	24	41	22	48	24	30	15	33	10	19	7	17	9	18	31.7%
Total	49		56		46		78		46		53		41		51		420

<Total No. of Analysis>
The Supreme People's Assmbly: 3,438
The WPK's Central Committee: 523
The Administration Council: 420
Total Numbers: 4,381

Table 7-25. The Administration Council Member's Overseas Travel

	1 No.(%)		2 No. (%)		3 No. (%)		4 No. (%)		5 No. (%)		6 No. (%)		7 No. (%)		8 No. (%)		Total
U.S.S.R.	24	68	33	77	23	70	35	66	26	60	23	53	18	53	26	62	208
China	24	68	23	53	17	51	29	55	28	72	28	65	26	73	25	59	199
Japan	3	9	5	12	3	9	4	7	4	10	3	7	3	9	4	9	29
Bulgarian	1	3	5	12	6	18	9	17	10	26	11	25	10	29	16	38	68
Czecho.	4	11	5	12	5	15	9	17	6	15	9	21	8	23	9	21	55
Romania	5	14	7	16	5	15	15	28	15	38	13	30	14	41	12	28	86
E. Germany	3	9	3	7	2	6	10	19	10	26	13	30	11	32	9	21	61
Yugoslavia	1	3	1	2	1	3	3	6	4	10	5	12	7	20	5	12	27
Hungary	1	3	3	7	2	6	11	21	7	18	12	28	8	23	7	17	51
Poland	2	6	3	7	3	9	3	6	5	13	9	21	10	29	7	17	42
Albania	2	6	4	9	2	6	4	7	2	5	-	-	2	6	3	7	19
Asia	11	31	17	39	16	49	17	32	11	28	17	39	18	53	16	38	123
Africa	5	14	6	14	4	12	10	19	14	36	15	35	15	44	7	17	76
Mid-South Am.	2	6	4	9	3	9	9	17	3	7	6	14	10	29	8	19	45
Europe	3	9	6	14	6	18	7	13	5	13	2	4	3	9	8	19	40
Middle-East			2	5	3	9	6	11	5	13	10	23	7	20	4	9	37
Others	1	3	-	-	-	-	-	-	3	7	-	-	-	-	-	-	4
Available data	35	71	43	77	33	72	53	68	39	85	43	81	34	83	42	82	76.7%
Total	49		56		46		78		46		53		41		51		420

Table 7-26. The Administration Council Member's Birth Year

	1 No.(%)		2 No. (%)		3 No. (%)		4 No. (%)		5 No. (%)		6 No. (%)		7 No. (%)		8 No. (%)		Total
1880s	1	5	1	4	-	-	-	-	-	-	-	-	-	-	-	-	2
1890s	5	23	1	4	-	-	-	-	-	-	-	-	-	-	-	-	6
1900s	11	50	8	35	7	32	5	20	3	20	1	10	1	14	-	-	36
1910s	5	23	13	52	14	64	16	67	7	47	6	60	5	72	7	78	73
1920s	-	-	1	4	1	5	3	13	5	33	3	30	1	14	2	22	16
Available data	22	45	24	41	22	48	24	30	15	33	10	19	7	17	9	18	31.7%
Total	49		56		46		78		46		53		41		51		420

<Total No. of Analysis>
The Supreme People's Assmbly: 3,438
The WPK's Central Committee: 523
The Administration Council: 420
Total Numbers: 4,381

Table 7-27. Leadership Changes in the Central Court and
Central Procurator's Office

	Chief Justices	Procurators-General
1st SPA	Kim Ik-son (9/48-3/55) Cho Sung-mo (3/55-3/56) Hwang Se-hwan (3/56-9/57)	Chang Hae-u (9/48-6/53) Yi Song-un (6/53-3/56) Cho Sung-mo (3/56-9/57)
2nd SPA	Kim Ha-un (9/57-10/59) Ho Chong-suk (10/59-11/60) Kim Ik-son (11/60-10/62)	Pak Se-ch'ang (10/62-3/64)
3rd SPA	Kim Ik-son (10/62-9/66) Yi Kuk-chin (9/66-12/67)	Pak Se-ch'ang (10/62-3/64) Yi Kuk-chin (3/64-9/66) Yi Song-un (9/66-12/67)
4th SPA	Yi Yong-gu (12/67-12/72)	Yun T'ae-hong (12/67-12/72)
5th SPA	Pang Hak-se (12/72-12/77)	Chong Tong-ch'ol (12/72-12/77)
6th SPA	Pang Hak-se (12/77-1/84)	Yi Chin-su (12/77-1/84)
7th SPA	Pang Hak-se (1/84-)	Han Sang-gyu (1/84-)
8th SPA	Pang Hak-se (1/84-)	Han Sang-gyu (1/84-)
9th SPA	Pang Hak-se (1/84-7/92)	Han Sang-gyu (1/84-)

Sources: Adapted from *Pukhan Ch'onggam;* Pukhan Chonso; Dae-sook Suh, *Korean Com-munism, 1945-1980;* and *Vantage Point* 7 (2) (February 1984).Yang Sung Chul, *Pukhan Ch'ong Ch'iron* (Seoul: Pakyong-sa, 1991).

Chart 7-1. *WPK Structure*

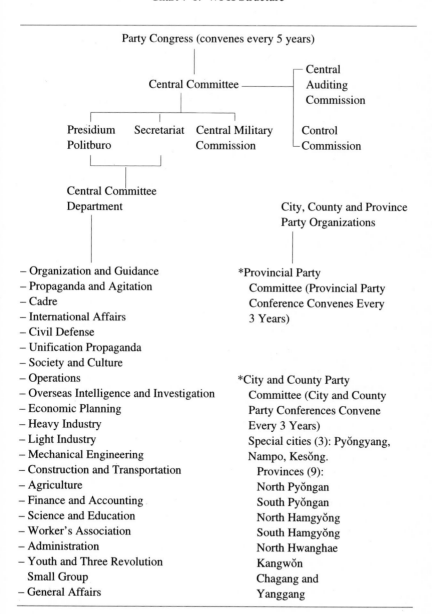

Party Congress (convenes every 5 years)

Central Committee ——— Central Auditing Commission

Presidium   Secretariat   Central Military   Control
Politburo   Commission   Commission

Central Committee Department

City, County and Province Party Organizations

– Organization and Guidance
– Propaganda and Agitation
– Cadre
– International Affairs
– Civil Defense
– Unification Propaganda
– Society and Culture
– Operations
– Overseas Intelligence and Investigation
– Economic Planning
– Heavy Industry
– Light Industry
– Mechanical Engineering
– Construction and Transportation
– Agriculture
– Finance and Accounting
– Science and Education
– Worker's Association
– Administration
– Youth and Three Revolution
  Small Group
– General Affairs

*Provincial Party
  Committee (Provincial Party
  Conference Convenes Every
  3 Years)

*City and County Party
  Committee (City and County
  Party Conferences Convene
  Every 3 Years)
  Special cities (3): Pyŏngyang,
  Nampo, Kesŏng.
  Provinces (9):
  North Pyŏngan
  South Pyŏngan
  North Hamgyŏng
  South Hamgyŏng
  North Hwanghae
  Kangwŏn
  Chagang and
  Yanggang

Chart 7-2. Supreme People's Assembly (Legislative Organ)

*SPA (deputies elected for a 5-year term)				

Standing Committee

Credentials Committee	Foreign Relations	Unification Policy	Bills Committee	Budgets Committee

*Provincial, city and county
People's Assembly (A 4-year term for provincial and special city deputies and a 4-year term for city and county deputies)

*Provincial, city and county People's Committee
(exercises the function of the local organ of the state when the People's Assembly is not in session)

*Provincial, city and county Administrative Committee (the administrative and executive body of the local organ of state power)

* The Formal Powers of the SPA

- amends the constitution, laws and ordinances
- adopts or amends laws and ordinances
- approves laws adopted by the SPA Standing Committee during the SPA recess
- establishes the basic principles of domestic and foreign policies
- elects the President of the DPRK
- elects or recalls the Vice-Presidents of the DPRK, on the recommendation of the President of the DPRK
- elects or recalls the Secretary and members of the CPC
- elects or recalls members of the Standing Committee of the SPA
- elects or recalls the Premier of the Administrative Council on the recommendation of the President of the DPRK
- elects or recalls the Chairman of the National Defense Commission
- elects or recalls the first Vice-Chairman, Vice-Chairman and members of the NDC on the recommendation of its chairman
- elects or recalls the President of the Central Court and appoint or remove the Procurator-General of the Central Procurator's Office
- approves the State plan for the development of the national economy
- appoints vice premiers, chairmen, ministers and other officials of the AC on the recommendation of the premier
- approves the state budget
- decides on questions of war and peace

Chart 7-3. Administration Council (Executive Organ)

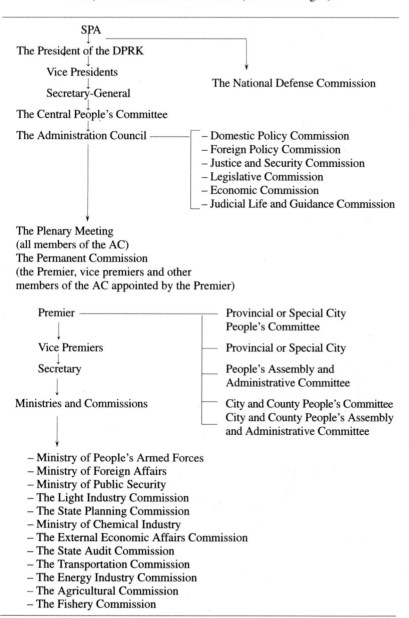

SPA

The President of the DPRK

Vice Presidents

Secretary-General

The Central People's Committee

The National Defense Commission

The Administration Council ──────
- Domestic Policy Commission
- Foreign Policy Commission
- Justice and Security Commission
- Legislative Commission
- Economic Commission
- Judicial Life and Guidance Commission

The Plenary Meeting
(all members of the AC)
The Permanent Commission
(the Premier, vice premiers and other
members of the AC appointed by the Premier)

Premier ────────────────── Provincial or Special City
                            People's Committee

Vice Premiers   Provincial or Special City

Secretary   People's Assembly and
                            Administrative Committee

Ministries and Commissions City and County People's Committee
                            City and County People's Assembly
                            and Administrative Committee

- Ministry of People's Armed Forces
- Ministry of Foreign Affairs
- Ministry of Public Security
- The Light Industry Commission
- The State Planning Commission
- Ministry of Chemical Industry
- The External Economic Affairs Commission
- The State Audit Commission
- The Transportation Commission
- The Energy Industry Commission
- The Agricultural Commission
- The Fishery Commission

Chart 7-3. Continued

- The State Construction Commission
- The People's Service Commission
- The State Science and Technology Commission
- The Electronic Automation Commission
- Ministry of Metallurgical Engineering
- Ministry of Mechanical Engineering
- Ministry of Mining
- Ministry of Coal Industry
- Ministry of Resource Development
- Ministry of Shipbuilding Industry
- Ministry of Construction
- Ministry of Materials Supply
- Ministry of Forestry
- Ministry of Local Industry
- Ministry of Nuclear Engineering
- Ministry of City Management
- Ministry of Postal Service
- Ministry of Labor Administration
- Ministry of Finance
- The Education Commission
- Ministry of Culture and Arts
- Ministry of Public Health
- Ministry of Railways
- Ministry of Maritime Transportation
- Ministry of Foreign Trade
- Ministry of External Economic Projects
- Ministry of Commerce
- The Academy of Science
- The State Sports Commission

---

*The Powers of the DPRK President

- Is the Head of State (5 years)
- Guides the CPC
- Convenes and presides over meetings of the Administration Council
- Promulgates the laws and ordinances of the SPA, the decrees of CPC and the decisions of the SPA Standing Committees
- Exercises the right of granting special pardon
- Announces the ratification and abrogation of treaties concluded with other countries
- Receives the letters of credence and recall of diplomatic representatives accredited by foreign states
- Announces the appointment or recall of diplomats to foreign countries

Chart 7-4. The Court and the Procurator's Office

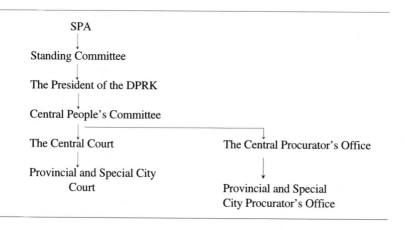

Notes

1. R.N. Carew Hunt, *The Theory and Practice of Communism* (Middlesex: A Pelican Book, 1971), p. 291.
2. Kim Il Sung, *On The Building of the People's Government* (Pyongyang: Foreign Languages Publishing House, 1978), pp. 546-547.
3. Dae-sook Suh examined the relationship between the various Korean communist groups and the Comintern, in "The Korean Communist Movement: Some Basic Characteristics," paper delivered at the Conference on Accommodation of Communism in Asia, Seoul, Korea, 16-17 August 1985.
4. For a discussion of early Korean communist movements, see, Dae-sook Suh, *The Korean Communist Movement, 1918-1948* (Princeton: Princeton University Press, 1967), especially pp. 3-52; Robert A. Scalapino and Chong-sik Lee, *Communism in Korea* (Berkeley: University of California Press, 1971),Vol. 1, especially, pp. 3-65; Chong-sik Lee, *The Korean Worker's Party: A Short History* (Stanford: Hoover Institutions Press, 1978), pp. 1-32; Il-wŏn Pak, *Namno-dang Ch'ongbip'an* [The Criticism of the Workers' Party of South Korea] (Seoul: Kuktongjŏngbo-sa, 1948), Vol. 1, pp. 13-164; and Nam-sik Kim, *Silrok Namno-dang* [The True Account of the Workers' Party of South Korea] (Seoul: Sinhyŏnsil-sa, 1975), especially pp. 1-30. The differences among these authors over dates, names and activities of early communist movements are found in Sung C. Yang, *Korea and Two Regimes* (Schenkman, 1981), Appendix 4.

5. S. C. Yang, *Op. Cit.*, p. 67.

6. A recent account of the decline and demise of the Korean communist movement in the 1930s is found in Dae-Sook Suh, "The Korean Communist Movement: Some Basic Characteristics," especially, pp. 13-15.

7. For a full discussion of Pak Hŏn-yŏng's August Theses, see Il-wŏn Pak, *Op. Cit.*, pp. 30-39; Nam-sik Kim, *Op. Cit.*, pp. 7-16.

8. Che-do O, who dealt with this case as a prosecuting attorney, contended that the KCP was involved in counterfeit money-making scheme, but the KCP denied it. For O's account, see Che-do O, *Pulkŭn Kunsang* [The Mass Image of the Red] (Pusan: Namgyŏng Munhwa-sa, 1951). For the KCP's denial of this charge, see *Chŏson Haebang Nyŏnbo* [The Yearbook of the Korean Liberation] (Seoul, 1946), p. 244. Interestingly enough, N. S. Kim did not link Pak Hŏn-yŏng's misfortune with the *Chŏngp'an-sa* Incident. Instead, he attributed Pak's arrest order issued on September 7 by the U.S. Military Government in Korea to three leftist papers (*Inmin-bo, Hyŏndae Ilbo,* and *Chongang Sinmun*) and to Pak's plan for "general labor strikes." For details, see Nam-sik Kim, *Op. Cit.*, pp. 277-283. In my interview with Kim on August 17, 1985, he too, disagreed with O's claim.

9. An English translation of the 1980 WPK bylaws is found in Tai Sung An, *North Korea: A Political Handbook* (Wilmington: Scholarly Resources Inc., 1983), Appendix 2, pp. 245-268.

10. For details, see Dae-sook Suh, *Korean Communism, 1945-1980: A Reference Guide to the Political System* (Honolulu: University of Hawaii Press, 1981), pp. 273-359.

11. As early as 1946 O Ki-sŏp, leader of the Domestic Group, insisted that the trade unions should play an important role in North Korea, asserting that the workers should be unionized and given the right to strike against the state even if it were a socialist state. O's article on the role of the Korean trade union appeared in *Nodong Sinmun* on September 18, 1946. O's fortune declined from 1946 till 1958 when he was purged and imprisoned. For details, see *Pukhan Ch'onggam* (Seoul, 1968), pp. 170-171.

12. For details, see *Pukhan Chŏnsŏ, 1945-1980* (Seoul, 1980), pp. 82-98 and Dae-sook Suh, *Korean Communism, 1945-1980,* pp. 273-359.

13. Suh, *Korean Communism,* pp. 276-277. Also, *Pukhan Chŏnsŏ,* pp. 76-77.

14. Suh, *Korean Communism,* pp. 273-359.

15. Chapter one, section three of the WPK bylaws.

16. *Ibid.*

17. For a discussion of the Soviet concept of law, see Samuel Hendel (ed.), *The Soviet Crucible: The Soviet System in Theory and Practice,* 5th ed. (North Scituate: Duxbury Press, 1980), Chapter 11, pp. 232-262.

CHAPTER 8

THE RULING ELITES AND
THEIR POLITICAL VICISSITUDES

Only a party that will organize real all-national exposures can become the vanguard of the revolutionary forces in our time.

V. I. Lenin[1]

In the Soviet system, the Communist Party simply provides the framework for the struggle for power. The competitive groups in the Soviet system are factions. The faction is the Soviet bureaucratic equivalent of the American electoral party.

Zbigniew Brzezinski and Samuel P. Huntington[2]

As shown in Chapter Seven, the North Korean formal political structures are not strikingly dissimilar to their Chinese and the former Soviet counterparts. Like in the Chinese and the former Soviet political systems, the party, the Worker's Party of Korea (WPK), *is* the power house. It ultimately directs and controls all the other political, military, economic, social, educational and cultural instrumentalities. In Brzezinski and Huntington's words, both the faction and the party are groups of politicians "bound together by a common interest in acquiring power or in preventing some from getting it. They are the dynamic elements in the political system."[3] Lassalle, in his letter to Marx on June 24, 1852, stressed the same point: party struggles give a party strength and life. And the best proof of the weakness of a party is its diffuseness and its

325

blurring of clear-cut differences. He further pointed out that "a party becomes stronger by purging itself."[4] Within the party, the central committee and its standing committees such as the politburo and the secretariat are the center of such power house. The leadership analysis of the Worker's Party of Korea Central Committee (WPK CC) and especially its Political Committee or the Politburo and Secretariat will, thus, unravel the political vicissitudes of the North Korean ruling strata for the past forty years. The analysis of the North Korean ruling elites in this chapter will be followed by the probe of the Kim Il Sung rule in Chapter Nine.

Factional Configurations

In analyzing the North Korean ruling strata, the following three questions -- one substantive and two technical -- will be answered: (1) Is it fruitful to analyze the North Korean political process as a typical factional strife?; (2) If the answer to the first question is in the affirmative, how do we define the various North Korean factions?; and (3) What is the meaning of the "purges" within the context of the North Korean leadership changes?

If politics by nature involves group conflicts, labeling North Korean politics as "factionalism" may be a simplification, if not an outright misnomer. Whether or not North Korean politics exemplifies "factional strife" is in contention among specialists and observers on this subject. The relative importance of factionalism in North Korean politics varies from one author to another. Scalapino and Lee suggested that placing too much emphasis on the factional affiliations of North Korean political leaders is probably a mistake.[5] Yu Hŏn (and for that matter, Scalapino and Lee) indicates that the anti-Kim Il Sung coalitions of the Soviet-Korean and Yanan groups were a serious challenge to Kim Il Sung leadership in the mid-1950s.[6] While Kim Il Sung and his entourage were traveling in the former Soviet Union and Eastern Europe on the occasion of the Twentieth CPSU Congress in June 1956, the Yanan Group reportedly joined forces with the Soviet Group to form an anti-Kim coalition. After two months of secret planning, the anti-Kim coalition openly attacked Kim's one-man dictatorship at the August Plenum of the 3rd WPK Central Committee. It failed, however, when Kim's Partisan Group counterattacked them, and the leaders of anti-Kim coalition forces were either purged, or forced to flee to China or the Soviet Union.[7] Again, on May 1, 1958, an anti-Kim military coup was reportedly planned by the Yanan Group to seize Pyongyang, with the Fourth Corps of the Korean people's Army under Chang P'yŏng-san, but it, too, was aborted.[8]

Suh, on the other hand, analyzed the same question, and contended that "the Yanan and Soviet-Koreans, as groups, had never been a threat to Kim's Partisan Group. He contended that Kim Il Sung's power was seriously challenged twice, not by the Yanan and the Soviet-Korean anti-Kim coalitions, but by the Domestic Group during the Korean War and later by the members of Kim's own Partisan Group.[9] Another analyst, Nahm, on the other hand, identified three "serious factional strifes" in North Korea: the elimination of northern communists by a coalition of the Soviet-returnees and the Yanan faction, 1945-1948; the elimination of the Workers' Party of South Korea group (WPSK) by the joint forces of the Soviet-returnees and the Yanan faction, 1949-1953; and the factional realignment or a split in the Soviet-returnees into two—the Manchurian partisans and the Soviet-Koreans.[10]

Pukhan Ch'onggam and, more recently, *Pukhan Chŏnsŏ* examined the North Korean politics as a series of Kim's purges and outright elimination of all and any, potential and actual anti-Kim forces. Beginning with the assassination of Hyŏn Chun-hyŏk, the leader of the Domestic Group, and the head of the KCP Pyongan Province in September 1945, and the imprisonment of Cho Man-sik, the leader of the Nationalist Group, in January 1946, Kim's elimination of his political enemies had become a political routine. The ousting of Mu Chŏng, the leader of the Yanan Group in 1951, Pak Hŏn-yŏng, Yi Sung-yŏp and their WPSK Group in 1953, Pak Il-u, Pang Ho-san, Ch'oe Ch'ang-ik, Pak Ch'ang-ok and other leaders of the Yanan Group in 1955 to 1959 and Kim Yŏl and other leaders of the Soviet Group in 1954 to 1958 were notable. Kim Ch'ang-man, leader of the Yanan Group in 1966, Pak Kum-ch'ŏl and Yi Hyo-sun, members of his own ruling circles in 1967 and 1968, respectively, and Kim Ch'ang-bong, Ch'oe Kwang and Hŏ Bong-hak, members of military groups in 1967 were all purged.[11]

The authors seem to differ in degree, if not in kind, over the question of "foreign influences" on North Korean factional strife. Scalapino and Lee seem to suggest that there had been credible foreign pressure or connections. Specifically, though the anti-Kim Il Sung coalition of the Soviet-Koreans and Yanan Group in 1956 failed, it had "contact with both Soviet and Chinese authorities."[12] Suh, on the other hand, contends that "there is no convincing evidence that the Chinese or the Russian Communists made efforts to exert influence in the North through the members of the Yanan or the Soviet groups."[13] At the twentieth anniversary of the WPK on October 10, 1965, Kim Il Sung himself elaborated on this matter:

> Opportunist attacks on our Party became most pronounced around 1956-57. Then a handful of anti-Party factionalists and obstinate dogmatists in our Party challenged it on the basis of revision *with the backing of outside forces.* They not only slandered the lines and policies of our Party but also carried out conspirational maneuvers to overthrow its leadership.[14]

The *Pyongyang Times'* editorial on the WPK's 40th anniversary on October 12, 1985, also, pinpointed the factional strifes within the WPK:

> After its founding the WPK has worked hard to expand and strengthen its ranks organizationally and ideologically. Particularly in the 1950s and 1960s our Party paid deep attention to doing away with flunkeyism and dogmatism and establish *Juche*, and, at the same time, it unfolded a struggle against the anti-Party factionalists and to [sic] root out their ideological venom.

As few examples below indicate, the analysts also disagree in their identification of various North Korean political groups and factions:

1) Soviet-returnees (Kim's Partisan and Soviet-Koreans), Yanan Koreans, northern natives and southern communists (Nahm)
2) Soviet Koreans, Manchurian guerrillas, Kim Il Sung circle, Kapsan, Yanan and Domestic factions (Scalapino and Lee)
3) Domestic, Yanan, Workers' Party of South Korea (WPSK), Soviet

and Kim Il Sung factions (*Pukhan Ch'onggam*)

4) Soviet-Korean, partisan, Yanan, Domestic and new and unknown groups (Suh)

5) Nationalist, Domestic, WPSK, Soviet, Yanan abducted leaders and Kim Il Sung factions (*Pukhan P'yŏnram*)

6) Domestic, WPSK, Yanan, Kim Il Sung factions and military factions (*Pukhan Chuminsaenghwal*)

7) Yanan, Soviet, Kim Il Sung and Domestic factions (*Pukhan Chŏnsŏ, 1974*)

8) Nationalist camp, Soviet faction, Chinese (Yanan) faction, domestic faction and Kim Il Sung faction (*Pukhan Chŏnsŏ, 1980*)[15]

To make matters worse, some analysts identify the various political forces in North Korea simply as political "groups" or "factions."[16]

Two major reasons seem to account for this confusing state of North Korean political elite analysis. One is the failure to clearly define political groups or factions on the basis of explicit criteria. The other is the inability to deal with the North Korean "factions" as a *process* or, an aspect of political dynamics, rather than as a fixed set of individuals. It is evident that the above classifications of the North Korean factions are explicitly or implicitly based on the combination of the following criteria:

1) Geographic affiliations and origins (Soviet, Kapsan, Yanan, Chinese, Domestic, Northern, Southern, Manchurian, etc.)

2) Territorial power bases (Domestic, WPSK, Yanan, Kapsan, Hamgyŏng, Pyŏngan, etc.)

3) Functional power bases (party, military, state bureaucracy, trade unions, peasant origin, technician, etc.)

4) Military and/or political experiences (Partisan, Chinese returnees, Soviet returnees, WPSK, Old Korean communists, etc.)

5) Ideological or attitudinal orientations and affiliations (nationalists, dogmatists, flunkeys, revisionists, formalists, etc.)

6) Foreign connections (the Soviet Union, China, Manchuria, etc.)

For the sake of analysis, four political groups are identified in this study on the basis of these six criteria: the Kim Il Sung (K), the Soviet-Korean (S), the Yanan (Y) and the Domestic (D). The Kim Il Sung Group is subdivided into three—Kim's anti-Japanese comrades-in-arms in Manchuria and northern Korea (the partisan group), his family members, relatives and personal friends and the new group. The number belonging to the Partisan Group ranges from 50 to 150.[17] There are also some members of Kim's ruling circles, who have paternal, maternal or nuptial ties with Kim.[18] The new group constitutes those who joined the WPK *after* the liberation and rose in the party ranks, the state bureaucracy and in the military under Kim's patronage. Kim's Partisan group is his old stalwarts, and the new group is his "born again" adherents, but both have contributed greatly to his bid for one-man supremacy. Now, there is also the Kim Jŏng Il group, consisting mostly of his Mankyŏng Dae Academy and the Kim Il Sung University Alumni.[19]

Unlike Kim's Partisan Group, the Soviet-Korean Group shared no common experiences prior to the liberation except that most were born or lived in the Soviet territory, became her citizens and came to North Korea with the Soviet occupation forces in 1945 or soon thereafter. Thus, they are politically and organizationally far less cohesive than the Partisan Group or the Yanan Group.

The Yanan Group, like the Partisan Group, experienced common political and military bonds, tracing back to the Yanan years with the Chinese communists. Most Yanan Group members belonged either to the North China Korean Independence League or the Korean Volunteers Corps or both. Upon returning to North Korea, the Yanan Group formed the New People's Party and then merged with Kim Il Sung's North Korean Communist Party in 1946. In the beginning, the Yanan Group outnumbered Kim's partisan Group although the latter outmaneuvered the former and gained control of the political initiative almost from the first stage of the North Korean power play with the help of the Soviet occupation forces.

The Domestic Group was a relatively cohesive political force although their regional differences divided them into two wings -- the northern communists and the WPSK Group -- almost from the outset. The membership consisted mostly of the so-called "old Korean communists" who surfaced from underground or were released from the Japanese prison after the liberation.

Gradualism, Tokenism and Purges

A close examination of the top 20 WPK CC members, its Politburo (formerly Political Committee), Secretariat and CC as a whole reveal several interesting points.

First, Kim's road to one-man supremacy is marked by *gradualism*. Although Kim Il Sung appeared from the outset to be "first among equals," his power was by no means secure. Specifically, the top twenty leaders of the First WPK CC were rather evenly divided into three groups. The Yanan Group (Y) perhaps had a slight edge. Five were from the Kim Group (K), six from the Yanan Group, five from the Soviet Group (S), and one from the Domestic Group (the Domestic Group (D) was underrepesented perhaps because the WPSK then had no power base under its direct control). The membership of the powerful Political Committee (PC) and Standing Committee (SC) of the First WPK CC revealed essentially the same political matrix. For the five-member PC of the First WPK CC, one came from each group except for the Yanan which had two representatives: Kim Tu-bong (Y), Kim Il Sung (K), Chu Yŏng-ha (D), Hŏ Ka-i (S), and Ch'oe Ch'ang-ik (Y). In the 13-member SC, the Yanan Group had five, the Kim Group, four, the Soviet Group, three and the Domestic Group, one (For details, see Tables 8-1, 8-2 and 8-3).

The composition of the entire WPK First CC confirmed the same. Of the 43 total CC members, the Yanan, the Kim, the Soviet and the Domestic groups comprised eleven, eight, eight and five, respectively. Eleven other members could not be placed in any of the four groups. Noteworthy also was the fact that Kim Tu-bong, the leader of the Yanan Group, was the chairman of the First CC, and Kim Il Sung and Chu Yŏng-ha, the leader of the Domestic Group, were vice-chairmen.

The composite picture of the ruling elites in North Korea changed slightly in the Second WPK CC in 1948 in favor of the Kim Group. Of the top 20 CC members, the Kim Group occupied six, the Soviet, five, the Yanan, four, the Domestic, four and unidentifiable affiliation, one. In the seven-member PC, the Kim, the Yanan, the Soviet and the Domestic Group, had two, three, one and one, respectively. In the 17-member SC, the Kim Group, the Yanan, the Soviet, and the Domestic, held seven, three, six and one positions, respectively. The composition of the entire 67-member CC revealed a similar trend: the Kim Group (21); the Yanan (11); the Soviet (14); the Domestic (8); and the unidentifiable (12). The political coalition or collusion among the Kim, the Soviet and the Domestic groups during this period to weaken the Yanan Group was evident even in this numerical matrix.

During the Third WPK CC in 1956, the Kim Group emerged supreme. Of the top 20 members of the WPK CC, the Kim Group occupied eleven seats, while the Yanan, the Soviet and the Domestic groups shared only three, five and one seats, respectively. In the eleven-member SC of the WPK CC, the Kim Group held eight out of eleven seats, while the Yanan had two seats and the Soviet had one seat. The picture of the entire WPK CC was basically similar. Of the 71 seats, the Kim Group retained twenty-eight seats, while the Yanan, the Soviet and the Domestic groups held fifteen, ten and sixteen seats, respectively.

By the Fourth WPK CC in 1961, the Kim Group virtually won dominance over all except for a token representation of other groups. Of the top 20 members in the CC, the Kim Group occupied sixteen slots and the Yanan, the Soviet and the Domestic groups, two, one and one seats. The make-up of the PC of the CC revealed the same picture. Out of eleven-member CC, the Kim Group owned nine seats, while the Yanan and the Soviet shared one seat each which was tantamount to a symbolic tokenism. In the 85-member WPK CC, the Kim Group took 71 seats, while the rest divided fourteen seats among themselves: the Yanan (5), the Soviet (1) and the Domestic (8). These figures illustrate that by the 4th WPK Congress, all the factions other than Kim's own group had nearly disappeared from the political arena. The Kim Group's political control has become almost "total" by the Fifth and the Sixth Congresses.

Kim's gradual approach to political control of North Korea has also been evident in the transformation of his ruling elites. For example, the total number of the Kim Il Sung Group, which has served as the WPK CC members in its First Congress in 1946 to its Sixth Congress in 1980, was 329 or 62% of the total 528. Of 329, the Partisan group constituted 153, and the new group, 176. Within Kim's camp, the number of the Partisan Group has declined over the years, while that of the new group has increased in the same period. It is evident that Kim's Partisan Group peaked in the Fourth WPK CC in 1961, but thereafter, the new group assumed the majority in the Kim camp and the gap has been widening.

The CC members who are not easily identifiable to any of the four groups deserve attention. It is very likely that the majority of those "unidentifiables" or "nonaffiliates" may belong to the Kim camp or they are at least "loyal" to Kim and his son, Kim Jŏng Il. Increasingly, the new group and the non-affiliates, who are technocrats or "experts," have comprised the larger proportion of the Kim Group.

Gradualism also characterized the manner in which Kim Il Sung has won the post of the undisputed and unchallengeable *su ryŏng*, "supreme leader." In the First WPK Congress Kim was one of two vice-chairmen, while Kim Tu-bong, leader of the Yanan Group, assumed chairmanship. In the Second WPK Congress, the leadership make-up remained the same except for the replacement of vice-chairman Chu Yong-ha with Hŏ Ka-i, leader of the Soviet Group. Kim Il Sung had become Premier of the DPRK's first cabinet in 1948. His position revealed that he already had a firm political grip (He retained the position until 1972 when the DPRK Constitution was overhauled). At the Third WPK Congress in 1956, Kim Il Sung replaced Kim Tu-bong as its chairman and ranked first in the WPK CC. Interestingly, in the First SPA in 1948, Kim Il Sung ranked first, and Kim Tu-bong, second. Kim's number one rank has not altered from the First SPA through the Ninth Supreme People's Assembly (SPA) in 1990. With the 1972 Constitution, Kim became the President of the DPRK and, concurrently, head of the SPA Central People's Committee since 1972 (in the first to fourth SPA, Kim did not hold official positions in the SPA) and chairman of the SPA National Defense Commission. But, as noted above, in the 1992 Constitution the presidential powers have been drastically curtailed as if it reflects the aging leader's gradual loss of power.

Needless to say, gradualism is a factor in father-to-son succession process from Kim Il Sung to Kim Jong Il. His earlier brother-to-brother succession attempt from Kim Il Sung to Kim Yŏng-ju, though aborted, can be seen in the same light. Relinquishing of his premiership in 1972 could be seen as the beginning of his gradual step-down process although it was to be a step-up since he became the President of the DPRK. Kim's current declining power is marked by gradualism as his earlier rise to power has been (the succession question will be dealt with in fuller detail in Chapter Seventeen).

Secondly, Kim's ruling elites have, thus far, adroitly utilized political tokenism. Although all the contending intraparty factions have been either eliminated or cowed since the 4th WPK Congress in 1961, the Kim Group has carefully retained token representation of rival groups in the WPK's Political Committee or at least in its CC. Kim Ch'ang-man (1907-?) of the Yanan group in the 4th WPK PC and Nam Il (1914-1976) of the Soviet Group in the 4th WPK PC are good examples. In the 5th WPK in 1970 Kim Group filled the entire 11-member PC. But in the WPK CC, Nam Il (S) and Pang Hak-se (S), though demoted, kept their seats. So did Paek Nam-un (D), Ch'oe Wŏn-t'aek (D) and Pak Mun-gyu (D). In the 6th WPK, Hŏ Chŏng-suk (Y) and Pang Hak-se (S) held their seats in the CC, although their ranks dropped further.

The continued existence of the so-called *u-dang* [fraternal parties] in North Korea may also be seen from the standpoint of token symbolism. The so-called Democratic Socialist Party and Ch'ŏndoist Ch'ŏng-u Party which exist in name only and function as another organizational "department" of the WPK, are the notable cases.

The female membership, particularly in the WPK CC and the SPA, has been nominal. It typifies token symbolism. In the 1st WPK Congress, Pak Chŏng-ae was the only female in its 13-member Standing Committee and 43-member CC. In the 2nd WPK Congress, Pak was again the sole female present in its 17-member SC and 67-member CC. She maintained her seat in the 11-member SC and 71-member CC of the 3rd WPK. In the 4th WPK Congress, two women, Pak and Kim Ok-sun, wife of Ch'oe Kwang, represented 85-member CC, and Pak kept her seat in the 11-member SC. In the 5th WPK Congress, no female was represented in its SC, but two women, Chŏng Kyŏng-hui and Kim Sŏng-ae, wife of Kim Il Sung, were represented in the CC. In the Sixth WPK Congress, Kim's wife and Hwang Sun-hui were represented in the CC. Token membership has been evident, too, in the SPA: Kim Tuk-nan, member of the first SPA, and vice-chairman of the second, third and fourth SPA; Hŏ Chŏng-suk, vice-chairman of the fifth and sixth SPA; and Yŏ Yŏn-gu, vice-chairman of the seventh, the eighth and the ninth SPA. Needless to say, severe underrepresentation of women in the key positions in the communist countries and their meagre token presence are well known. Even in the Western democracies, the sexual barriers in the political world have not been completely torn down. South Korea, in this regard, fared no better than North Korea. The complete equality of the sexes both in the East and West is indeed a long way off. Thus, North Korea is by no means conspicuously behind on women's issues. Still, it is rather ironical that one of the first legislation the Korean Provisional People's Committee enacted on July 30, 1946, was the "Law on the Equality of Sexes." In actuality, the Law on the Equality of Sexes meant not so much to give equal status and opportunity for man and woman in all areas of human endeavors in North Korea as to "liberate" women from the traditional household chores and to mobilize them as the new work force of the socialist construction.

Thirdly, like the ruling elites in other past and present communist political systems, North Korean ruling elites have also demonstrated a high degree of overlapping membership in the WPK, the SPA and the Administration Council (AC). This feature was manifested from the founding of the DPRK in 1948, but it has become more conspicuous as the Kim Il Sung regime consolidated its power. Though one year interval separated the 4th WPK Congress in 1961, the 3rd SPA in 1962 and the 3rd Cabinet in 1962, the top leadership in the three organs remained virtually identical. The same leaders occupied the top positions in the 5th WPK Congress in 1970, the 5th SPA in 1972 and the 5th AC in 1972; and the picture was the same in the 6th WPK Congress in 1980, the 6th SPA in 1977 and the 6th AC in 1977. It is true that there have been significant personnel changes in the 7th, 8th and 9th SPA and in the 7th, 8th and 9th AC while the 7th WPK Congress has not been convened to the present. Still, these changes are not sufficient to defy the overlapping nature of North Korean top political leadership per se (For details, see Table 8-4). The intricate and interlocking networks of holding positions concurrently in the WPK, the SPA and the AC are the result of the party-controlled political process. As noted earlier, ultimately the party, the WPK, controls and mans all the other governing apparatus, be they the SPA, the AC or both.

Fourthly, as Tables 8-1, 8-2 and 8-3 below reveal, the transition of political control from the so-called red to experts, from ideologues to pragmatists and from politicians to technocrats has been slow yet steady. In the distribution of the top ruling elites in North Korea in the WPK CC and its PC and SC, the Kim Il Sung Group emerged as the predominant political force by the 3rd WPK Congress in 1956 and by the 4th WPK Congress in 1961, the Kim Group practically obliterated all oppositions within the WPK Congress. As mentioned earlier, Kim's Partisan Group predominated the North Korean ruling hierarchy at the Fourth WPK Congress. From the 5th WPK Congress in 1970, the so-called non-partisan new group within the Kim Group has outnumbered the Partisan Group in the top ruling hierarchy, signaling the gradual replacement of the old guards with the new. As Table 8-3 and 8-4 illustrate, in the Fifth WPK CC the Kim Il Sung's new group outnumbered his Partisan Group by 57 to 42. By the Sixth WPK CC, this gap has widened (79 v. 24) (For details, see Tables 8-1, 8-2 and 8-3).

Again, like in the other socialist countries, from the fate of the former Soviet Union's Old Bolsheviks to that of China's Long Marchers, the transition from the old guards to the new is biologically inevitable. That is, generational change, from the old to new ruling elites is unavoidable. In addition, the political and economic developments in these nations, including North Korea, necessitate the emergence, albeit gradual, of the new elites, who tend to be experts, technocrats or pragmatists. These factors hasten, in short, the rise of the new elites from the wombs of the old elites. North Korea is no exception to this rule. To begin with, the absolute number of Kim's partisan comrades-in-arms never exceeded 200 (Suh Dae Sook identified 177 partisan members). In the meantime many have already died (Ch'oe Yong-gŏn, Ch'oe Hyŏn, O Paek-ryong, Kim Il and Yim Ch'un-ch'u). Some, like Kim Chaek and Kang Kŏn, were killed during the Korean War. A few—Pak Kŭm-chŏl and Yi Hyo-sun—were purged by Kim. Kim Il Sung and his few remaining partisan-comrades-in-arms, Pak Sŏng-ch'ŏl, So Ch'ŏl, Ch'oe Kwang and O Chin-u are now in their late seventies and early eighties. Hence, the shifting of the old guards to the new breed is not only natural and inevitable, but necessary.

Finally, the data analysis of the North Korean ruling elites confirms the gradual yet unmistakable concentration of power in the hands of Kim Il Sung and now Kim Jŏng Il. It also means that no one in North Korea no matter how high his or her position, is politically safe and secure except for the two Kims. Table 8-5, for example, illustrates that Kim Il Sung is the only person who has been elected more than eight consecutive times as the SPA member. Besides Kim Il Sung, only two persons—Kang Yang-uk and Kim Il—had been elected six and seven times, respectively, and only nine persons, including Kim Il Sung, were elected more than five times (For details, see Table 8-5).

Likewise, Table 8-6 indicates the reelection patterns of the WPK CC members. The CC members who were in the First WPK CC (43) and reelected to the Second WPK CC numbered 30 out of 67 people or 69%. In the Third CC 29 out of 71 or 43% were members of the second CC (67). To put it differently, among 43 members of the First CC, only two were in the Sixth CC. They are Kim Il Sung and Hŏ Chŏng-suk, who is now deceased. In the Sixth CC only 6 and 13 are from the Third and Fourth CC, who were reelected, respectively. This reelection pattern, too, graphically demonstrates the fact that it is extremely difficult for a person to become a CC member, and still harder to retain the CC membership.

Similarly, as Table 8-7 shows, only two persons—Kim Il Sung and Kim Il—were elected six times consecutively as the WPK CC members. None was reelected five times as the CC member. Only nine people were reelected four times. They were Choe Hyŏn, Chŏng Ch'un-t'aek, Han Sŏl-ya, Hŏ Chŏng-suk, Kang Chin-gon, Kim Hoe-il, Kim Mang-um, Park Chŏng-ae and Pang Hak-se. Thirty-nine people were reelected more than three times as the CC members.

Meanwhile, Tables 8-8 and 8-9 list the names of the key WPK CC standing committees' members. Again, as it was the case in the SPA membership, Kim Il Sung is the only one who has held a position con-secutively in all six WPK CC standing committees. What is more, the total number of those CC members who have served either in its Polit-buro, Political Committee, Organizational Committee or Standing Committee amounts to 46 people in more than four decades.

A similar pattern is found also in the CC chairmanship, vice-chairmanship and secretary positions. Kim Il Sung, again, is the only person who has served more than six times in these positions. None even served four or five times in any of the above positions in the Party. Choe Yŏnggŏn, having served three times in one of the above positions, came closest to Kim Il Sung. Only five persons—Kim Ch'ang-man, Kim Chung-rin, Kim Il, Kim Tu-bong and Park Kum-ch'ŏl—had served twice in one of the above key posts. It should be noted also that among these five, only Kim Chung-rin is alive. Eighteen persons have served at least once in one of these key posts. It signifies that the total number of persons who have held one of these key posts in the CC amounts only to 25 (For details, see Tables 8-10 and 8-11).

Table 8-12 lists the names of people who have held the presidency, vice-presidency, premiership and vice-premiership of the Administration Council (AC) since 1948 to the present. Table 8-13 covers all the members who have been in the North Korean Cabinet or Administration Council as ministers, commission chairmen or academy presidents. The total number of AC ministers has been 203, of whom only one person (Kim Ŭngsang) had served six times in the cabinet posts. Seven people served five times in the AC. But nearly half of those (96) people have served just once in the AC, however.

In this connection, the term "purge"[20] in dealing with the leadership changes in the socialist countries in general and North Korea in particular needs clarification. The nature of the purge may range from reassignment, simple removal of a person from the party and/or the office, demotion and to death. A purge may be temporary (e.g., temporary reassignment), tactical (e.g., tactical retreat or reassignment) or permanent (e.g., capital punishment and permanent exile). And the purge may also range in magnitude from colossal (e.g., Stalin's purge and Mao's purge during the Cultural Revolution period) to marginal. The purged, if alive, can be later restored or rehabilitated by the purger, or he or she may rise again *after* the purger himself is dead or removed from power. The purge in North Korea has exhibited a unique feature. Namely, unlike the WPSK Group and the Yanan Group (although a few Yanan Group members fled to China), many of the Soviet group returned to the former Soviet Union after they were purged. Whether their return to the former Soviet Union was voluntary or forced upon them as a result of their purge is not clear. What is clear, however, is the pattern of Soviet-Koreans returning to their adopted land in the 1950s and in the early 1960s. With these various meanings of purges in mind, the North Korean purges under the Kim Il Sung regime for the last 40 years can be examined in the next chapter. For, the rise of Kim Il Sung (and Kim Jŏng Il) has been inexorably linked with the downfall of his political enemies. To that extent, the history of purges in North Korea is the chronicle of Kim's political triumph.

Table 8-1. North Korean Top Party Leadership Changes, 1946-1992

First Congress (August 28-30, 1946)	Second Congress (March 27-30, 1948)
(Ranking: KWP Central Committee)	
1. Kim Tu-bong (Y)	Kim Tu-bong (Y)
2. Kim Il Sung (K)	Kim Il Sung (K)
3. Chu Yŏng-ha (D)	Hŏ Ka-i (S)
4. Ch'oe Ch'ang-ik (Y)	Chu Yŏng-ha (D)
5. Hŏ Ka-i (S)	Kim Ch'aek (K)
6. Kim Ch'ang-man (Y)	Ch'oe Ch'ang-ik (Y)
7. Hŏ Chŏng-suk (Y)	Pak Il-u (Y)
8. Kim Yŏng-t'ae (?)	Pak Chŏng-ae (K)[a]
9. Park Ch'ang-sik (S)	Kim Kyo-yŏng (K)[n]
10. Pak Chŏng-ae (K)[a]	Chŏng Chun-t'aek (K)[n]
11. Kim Ch'aek (K)	Pak Ch'ang-ok (S)
12. Mu Chŏng (Y)	Kim Il (K)
13. Yi Ch'un-sam (?)	Kim Chae-uk (S)
14. An Kil (K)	Kim Hwang-il (D)
15. Kim Ye-p'il (?)	Kim Yŏl (S)
16. Kim Il (K)	Ch'oe Kyŏng-dŏk (D)
17. Pak Hyo-sam (Y)	Kim Min-san (Y)
18. Chang Sun-myŏng(S)	Ch'oe Suk-hyang (?)
19. Kim Yŏl (S)	Chin Pan-su (S)
20. Kim Chae-uk (S)	Kang Chin-gŏn (D)

Table 8-1. Continued

Third Congress (April 23-29, 1956)	Fourth Congress (September 11-18, 1961)
(Ranking)	
1. Kim Il Sung (K)	Kim Il Sung (K)
2. Kim Tu-bong (Y)	Ch'oe Yong-gŏn (K)
3. Ch'oe Yong-gŏn (K)	Kim Il (K)
4. Pak Chŏng-ae (K)[a]	Pak Kum-ch'ol (K)
5. Kim Il (K)	Kim Ch'ang-man (Y)
6. Pak Kum-ch'ŏl (K)	Yi Hyo-sun (K)
7. Pak Ch'ang-ok (S)	Pak Chŏng-ae (K)[a]
8. Ch'oe Ch'ang-ik (Y)	Kim Kwang-hyŏp (K)
9. Pak Wi-wan (S)	Chŏng Il-yŏng (K)[n]
10. Chŏng Il-yŏng (K)[n]	Nam Il (S)
11. Han Sang-du (K)[n]	Yi Chŏng-ok (K)[n]
12. Ha Ang-ch'ŏn (Y)	Kim Ik-son (K)
13. Kim Hwang-il (D)	Yi Chu-yŏn (D)
14. Pak Hun-il (Y)	Ha Ang-ch'ŏn (Y)
15. Yi Hyo-sun (K)	Han Sang-du (K)[n]
16. Pak Il-yŏng (S)	Chŏng Chun-taek (K)[n]
17. Yi Il-gyŏng (K)[n]	Sŏ Ch'ŏl (K)
18. Han Sŏl-ya (K)	Ch'oe Hyŏn (K)
19. Sŏ Hui (Y)	Sŏk San (K)
20. Yim Hae (K)	Kim Kyŏng-sŏk (K)

Table 8-1. Continued

Fifth Congress (November 2-12, 1970)	Sixth Congress (October 10-14, 1980)
(Ranking)	
1. Kim Il Sung (K)	Kim Il Sung (K)
2. Ch'oe Yong-gŏn (K)	Kim Il (K)
3. Kim Il (K)	O Chin-u (K)
4. Pak Sŏng-ch'ŏl (K)	Kim Jŏng Il (K)[n]
5. Ch'oe Hyŏn (K)	Yi Chong-ok (K)[n]
6. Kim Yŏng-ju (K)	Pak Sŏng-ch'ŏl (K)
7. O Chin-u (K)	Ch'oe Hyŏn (K)
8. Kim Tong-gyu (K)	Yim Ch'un-ch'u (K)
9. Sŏ Ch'ŏl (K)	Sŏ Ch'ŏl (K)
10. Kim Chung-nin (K)	O Paek-yong (K)
11. Han Ik-su (K)	Kim Chung-nin (K)
12. Hyŏn Mu-gwang (K)	Kim Yŏng-nam (K)[n]
13. Chŏng Chun-t'aek (K)[n]	Chŏn Mun-sŏp (K)
14. Yang Hyŏng-sŏp (K)[n]	Kim Hwan (K)[n]
15. Kim Man-gŭm (K)	O Kuk-yŏl (K)[n]
16. Nam Il (S)	Kye Ung-t'ae (K)
17. Ch'oe Yong-jin (K)	Kang Sŏng-san (K)[n]
18. Hong Wŏn-gil (K)[n]	Hŏ Tam (K)[n]
19. Chŏng Kyŏng-hui (?)	Yŏn Hyŏng-muk (K)[n]
20. Kim Yŏ-jung (K)	Yun Ki-bok (K)[n]

K-Kim Il Sung Group, mostly his partisan guerrilla comrades-in-arms; D-Domestic Group; Y-Yanan Group; and S-Soviet Group.

a: Suh designated Pak Chŏng-ae, wife of Kim Yong-bŏm, as a member of the D Group, while *Pukhan Ch'onggan* and *Pukhan Chŏnsŏ* placed her in the K Group and the S Group, respectively.

n: the member of the Kim group who are not partisan guerrillas.

Adapted from the following sources: *Pukhan ch'onggam, '45-'65* (Seoul: Kong-sankwŏn Munjeyŏnkuso, 1968), pp. 1019-1057; Robert A. Scalapino and Chong-sik Lee, *Communism in Korea* (Berkeley: University of California Press, 1972), Part II, Appendix C; *Pukhan Chŏnsŏ* (Seoul: Kukdongmunjeyŏnkuso, 1980), pp. 871-901; Dae-sook Suh, *Korean Communism, 1945-1980* (Honolulu: The University Press of Hawaii, 1981), pp. 316-336.

Table 8-2. The Top 20 Leaders in the WPK CC and Their Group Affiliations

	1st	2nd	3rd	4th	5th	6th
Kim Il Sung Group	5	6(2)	11(1)	16(3)	18(5)	20(10)
Domestic Group	1	4	5	1	–	–
Yanan Group	6	4	3	2	–	–
Soviet Group	5	5	1	1	1	–
Unidentifiable	3	1	–	–	–	–

The numbers in ( ) are those who were not the members of Kim Il Sung's partisan guerrillas.

Table 8-3. Distribution of All WPK CC Member's Group Affiliations

	1st	2nd	3rd	4th	5th	6th
Kim Group	8(1)	21	28(11)	71(29)	98(56)	103(79)
Domestic Group	5	8	16[8]	8[3]	3[3]	–
Yanan Group	11	11	15@	5	–	1
Soviet Group	8	14	10	1	2	1
Unidentifiable	11	12	2	–	14	40
Total	43	67	71	85	117	145

The number in ( ) are Kim's non-partisan group; the number in [ ] are the Workers' Party of South Korea group. @ Pak Mu, one of the CC members, was identified as the Soviet Group in *Pukhan Ch'onggam*, while Scalapino and Chong-sik Lee placed him in the Yanan Group. The former categorization seems to be correct.

Table 8-4. Overlapping Membership of the Top Leaders and Their Ranking/
Positions in the WPK, the SPA and the AC

4th WPK (Ranking)	3rd SPA (Ranking)	3rd Cabinet or AC (Positions)
1. Kim Il Sung	(1)	premier
2. Ch'oe Yŏng-gŏn	(2)	(chairman, 3rd SPA)
3. Kim Il	(3)	first vice-premier
4. Pak Kum Ch'ŏl	(5)	(vice-chairman, 3rd SPA)
5. Kim Ch'ang-man	(6)	vice-premier
6. Yi Hyo-sun	(7)	(3rd SPA SC)
7. Pak Chŏng-ae	(12)	(3rd SPA vice-chairman)
8. Kim Kwang-hyŏp	(8)	vice-premier
9. Chŏng Il-yong	(9)	vice-premier
10. Nam Il	(10)	vice-premier
11. Yi Chŏng-ŏk	(11)	vice-premier
12. Kim Ik-son	(14)	chief justice
13. Yi Chu-yŏn	(13)	vice-premier
14. Ha Ang-ch'ŏn	(15)	(3rd SPA SC)
15. Han Sang-du	(16)	Minster of Finance
16. Chŏng Chun-t'aek	(17)	vice-premier

5th WPK (Ranking)	5th SPA (Ranking)	5th AC (Positions)
		(Central People's Committee)
1. Kim Il Sung	(1)	president, DPRK
2. Ch'oe Yŏng-gŏn	(2)	
3. Kim Il	(3)	premier
4. Pak Sŏng-ch'ŏl	(5)	vice-premier
5. Ch'oe Hyŏn	(6)	Minister, the PAF
6. Kim Yŏng-ju	(9)	WPK secretary
7. O Chin-u	(7)	SPA National Defense Com.
8. Kim Tong-gyu	(8)	Chair, SPA Credentials Com.
9. Sŏ Ch'ŏl	(4)	in SPA SC.
10. Kim Chung-nin	(10)	
11. Han Ik-su	(15)	in SPA SC
12. Hyŏn Mu-gwang	(11)	Minister of Trans.
13. Chŏng Chun-t'aek	(13)	vice-premier
14. Yang Hyŏng-sŏp	(12)	
15. Kim Man-gum	(14)	vice-premier
16. Nam Il	(21)	vice-premier

Table 8-4. Continued

6th WPK (Ranking)	6th SPA (Ranking)	6th AC (positions)
	(Central People's Committee)	
1. Kim Il Sung	(1)	president
2. Kim Il	(2)	[6th WPK Presidium]
3. O Chin-u	(6)	minister, the PAF
4. Kim Jŏng Il		[6th WPK Presidium]
5. Yi Chŏng-ok	(8)	premier
6. Pak Sŏng-ch'ol	(5)	vice-president
7. Ch'oe Hyŏn	(4)	[6th WPK Politburo]
8. Yim Ch'un-ch'u	(9)	[6th WPK Politburo]
9. Sŏ Ch'ŏl	(7)	[6th WPK Politburo]
10. O Paek-yŏng (d.1984)	(10)	[6th WPK Politburo]
11. Kim Chung-rin		[6th WPK Politburo]
12. Kim Yŏng-nam	(5) SC	[6th WPK Politburo]
13. Chŏn Mun-sŏp		[6th WPK Politburo]
14. Kim Hwan	(12)	[6th WPK Politburo]
15. O Kuk-yŏl		[6th WPK Politburo]
16. Kye Ung-t'ae	(11)	vice-premier

*Table 8-5. Patterns of the Supreme People 's Assembly Members'
Reelection from the 1st Assembly to the 9th Assembly*

1st	2nd	3rd	4th	5th	6th (1)	7th	8th	9th
572	75	23	20	9*	3**	3**	1***	1***
(360 S)#	(13%)							
(212 N)#	(35%)							
	215	71	49	25				
		(33%)	225	101				
			(59%)					
			457	178				
				(39%)				
				541				
					579			
						615	445	
							(72.4%)	
							655	478
								(73%)
								687

*Choe Yong-gŏn, Chong Chun-t'aek, Kang Yang-uk, Kim Il, Kim Il Sung, Kim Tŭk-ran,
Nam Il, Paek Nam-un and Lee Ki-yŏng.
**Kang Yang-uk, Kim Il and Kim Il Sung.
***Kim Il Sung.
Source: 1st-6th term is quoted from Dae-Sook Suh, *Korean Communism, 1945-1980*, p. 429,
Table 3.2; 7th-9th term is analysed and collected by the author.
#S: from South Korea; N: from North Korea.
(1) the names of the 6th Assembly members are not available.

Table 8-6. The WPK's Central Committee Member's Reelection Patterns

Term	1st	2nd	3rd	4th	5th	6th
1st	43	30 (69%)	12 (2)[a]	5 (1)[a]	2	2 (1)[b]
2nd		67	29 (43%)	11 (1)	3 (1)[d]	2
3rd			71	28 (39%)	10	6 (1)[e]
				85	31 (36%)	13 (3)[f]
					117	67 (57%)
						147

Source: Dae-Sook Suh, *Korean Communism, 1945-1980*, p. 347, Table 2.9.
(a) Kim Ch'ang-man and Yun Kong-hŭm were not elected to the 2nd, but reelected to the
3rd. But Kim Ch'ang-man was reelected to the 4th.
(b) Hŏ Chŏng-suk was appointed to the 1st, 2nd, 3rd and 6th.
(c) Lee Puk-myŏng was reelected to the 2nd and 4th, but not to the 3rd.
(d) Pang Hak-se was reelected to the 2nd, 3rd, 5th and 6th, but not to the 4th.
(e) Lee Chong-ok was appointed to the 3rd, 4th and 6th, but not reelected to the 5th.
(f) Choe Kwang, Lee Chae-yun and Lim Kye-ch'ŏl were reelected to the 4th and 6th, but not
to the 5th.

Table 8-7. *The WPK's Central Committee Member's*
C.C. Careers and their Ranking

Times	Name (Ranking)	1st	2nd	3rd	4th	5th	6th
6	Kim Il*	16	12	5	3	3	2
	\<Kim Il Sung\>	2	2	1	1	1	1
4	Choe Hyŏn*			38	18	5	7
	Chŏng Chunt'aek*		10	24	16	13	
	Han Sŏl-ya	24	24	18	27		
	Hŏ Chŏng-suk*	7	29	32			54
	Kang Chin-gŏn*	26	20	58	35		
	Kim Hoe-il			29	64	79	117
	Kim Man-gŭm*			55	46	15	129
	\<Pak Chŏng-ae\>	10	8	4	7		
	Pang Hak-se*		52	26		43	68
3	Choe Ch'ang-ik**	4	6	8			
	\<Choe Wŏn-t'aek\>			60	36	27	
	Choe Yong-gŏn*			3	2	2	
	\<Choe Yong-jin\>				23	17	136
	Chŏn Ch'ang-ch'ŏl*				29	22	53
	\<Chŏn Mun-sŏp\>				26	31	13
	Chŏng Il-yong**		15	10	9		
	Han Il-mu (1)	22	21	40			
	\<Hyŏn Mu-gwang\>				44	12	31
	\<Kang Hŭi-wŏn\>				49	72	75
	Kim Ch'ang-man*	6		27	5		
	\<Kim Chwa-hyŏk\>				70	35	119
	Kim Kwang-hyŏp**		46	37	8		
	Kim Kyŏng-sŏk*		60	44	20		
	Kim Tu-bong*	1	1	2			
	Nam Il*			32	10	16	
	\<O Chin-u\>				25	7	3
	O Ki-sŏp*	31	42	57			
	O Paek-ryong*				54	21	10
	Pak Hun-il (1)	42	22	14			
	Pak Kŭm-ch'ŏl**		66	6	4		
	Pak Mun-gyu*			33	60	41	
	\<Pak Sŏng-ch'ŏl\>				24	4	6
	Pak Yŏng-sun*				51	25	82
	\<Sŏ Ch'ŏl\>				17	9	9
	\<Lee Chong-ok\>			22	11		5
	Lee Song-un (1)		65	53	30		
	Lim Hae**	30	50	20			

Source: Dae-Sook Suh, *Korean Communism, 1945-1980*, pp. 348-349.
#Dae-Sook Suh calculated that those who are reappointed more than twice total 118 and more than one time are 160.
(1): Careers are unclear.
*Those who are deceased; **Those who are purged; \< \>Those who are still alive.

Table 8-8.   The Reelection Patterns of Politburo, Political Committee,
Standing Committee of the WPK's Central Committee

Time	Numbers	Members Reelected
6th	2	Kim Il*, <Kim Il Sung>
5th	0	
4th	1	<Pak Chŏng ae>
3rd	5	Choe Ch'ang-ik**, Choe Yong-gŏn*, Chŏng Il-yong**, Kim Ch'ang-man*, Kim Tu-bong*
2nd	15	Choe Hŏn*, Chu yŏng-ha*, Hŏ Ka-i*, Kim Chae-uk (1), <Kim Chung-rin>, Kim Kwang-hyŏp*, Nam Il*, <O Chin-u>, Pak Il-u**, Pak Kŭm-ch'ŏl**, <Pak Sŏng-ch'ŏl>, <Sŏ Ch'ŏl>, Pak Ch'ang-ok*
1st	23	Chin Pan-su**, Chon Mun-sŏp*, Chŏng Chun-t'aek*, Han Ik-su*, <Kang Sŏng-san>, Ki Sŏk-bok**, <Kim Jong Il>, <Kim Hwan>, Kim Tong-gyu**, Kim Yŏl**, Kim Yŏng-ju**, <Kim Yŏng-nam> <Kye Ŭng-t'ae>, <O Kŭk-ryŏl>, O Paek-ryong*, <Paek Hak-rim>, Pak Ch'ang-sik**, Pak Hyo-sam**, Pak Yong-sŏng*, Lee Hyo-sun**, Lim Ch'un-ch'u*, Lim Hae**, <Yŏn Hyŏng-muk>

** Chin Pansu, purged as Soviet faction in August 1959, sought refuge in the Soviet Union; Ki Sŏk-bok, purged as Soviet faction in August 1956; Kim Yŏng-ju purged; Pak Ch'ang-sik, purged as Soviet faction in 1959, sought refugee in the Soviet Union; Pak Hyo-sam, purged as Yanan faction in 1957; Lee Hyo-sun, purged in 1967; Lim Hae, sought refuge in the Soviet Union in 1962; Kim Kwang-hyŏp, purged in July 1970; Pak Il-u, purged in 1955; Pak Kŭm-ch'ŏl, purged in 1967; Pak Ch'ang-bok, sought refuge in the Soviet Union; Choe Ch'ang-ik, purged in 1957; Kim Tong-gyu, purged in 1978; and Kim Yŏl, dismissed as soviet faction in may 1957.

* Those who are deceased.

(1) : Not identified.

< >: Those who are still alive.

Table 8-9. The Members of Politburo, Political Committee, Organizational Committee and Standing Committee of the WPK Central Committee and their Ranking

Party Meeting	1st		2nd		3rd			4th	5th	6th
	#PB	#SC	PB	SC	#OC	OC	SC	#PC	PC	PB
*Kang Sŏng-san (1931-)									18**	
Ki Sŏk-bok				12						
Kim Tong-gyu (1915-)									8	
Kim Tu-bong (1890-)	1	1	1	1			2			
Kim Kwang-hyŏp (1915-)							10	8		
Kim Il		12	9				5	3	3	2
*Kim Il Sung	2	2	2	2	1	1	1	1	1	1
Kim Yŏl					3					
*Kim Yŏng-nam										12
*Kim Yŏng-ju									6	
Kim Chae-uk		13		10						
*Kim Jŏng Il									10	4
*Kim Chung-rin										11
Kim Ch'aek (1903-1951)		8	4	4						
Kim Ch'ang-man		7				6		5		
*Kim Hwan										14
*Kye Ŭng-t'ae										17
Pak Kŭm-ch'ŏl						4	6	4		
*Pak Sŏng-ch'ŏl									4	6
Pak Yŏng-sŏng				5						
Pak Il-u		6	6	6						
*Pak Chŏng-ae		9	7			3	4	7		
Pak Ch'ang-sik		11								
Pak Ch'ang-ok			8	4						
Pak Hyo-sam		10								
*Paek Hak-rim										19
Nam Il							11	10		
*Sŏ Ch'ŏl									9	9

Table 8-9. Continued

Party Meeting	1st #PB	1st #SC	2nd PB	2nd SC	2nd #OC	3rd OC	3rd SC	4th #PC	5th PC	6th PB
*O Kŭk-ryŏl										**19
O Paek-ryong										10
*O Chin-u									7	3
*Yŏn Hyŏng-muk										15
*Lee Chong-ok								11		5
Lee Hyo-sun								6		
Lim Ch'un-ch'u										8
Lim Hae							7			
*Chŏn Mun-sŏp										13
Chŏng Il-yong				14		5	9	9		
Chŏng Chun-t'aek (1911-73)				13						
Chu Yŏng-ha	3	3	3	15						
Chin Pan-su				11						
Choe Yong-gŏn						2	3	2	2	
Choe Ch'ang-ik	5	5	5	5			8			
Choe Hyŏn (1907-1982)								5	7	
Han Ik-su								11		
Hŏ Ka-i	4	4	3	3	2					

\# PB: Politburo; PC: Political Committee; OC: Organizational Committee; and SC: Standing Committee.

PB was changed to SC at the 3rd meeting, and PC was revived at the 4th meeting and at the CC executive meeting held in October 1966. Standing Committee was created within PC, but it was soon abolished. At the 6th WPK Assembly, PC was revived again and within it the SC of the PC was also established.

* Those who are alive.

** Numbers denote ranking in the various committees.

Table 8-10. The Reelections of Chairmen, Vice-chairmen, Secretaries
of the WPK Central Committee

Time	Numbers Patterns	Members Reelected
6th	1	<Kim Il Sung>
5th	0	
4th	0	
3rd	1	Choe Yong-gŏn*
2nd	5	Kim Ch'ang-man*, <Kim Chung-rin>, Kim Il*, Kim Tu-bong*, Pak Kŭm-ch'ŏl**
1st	18 Total: 25	Chŏng Il-yong**, Chu Nyŏng-ha*, Han Ik-su*, <Hwang Chang-yŏp>, <Hyŏn Mu-gwang>, <Kim Jŏng Il>, <Kim Hwan>, Kim Tong-gyu**, Kim Yŏng-ju**, <Kim Yŏng-nam>, <O Chin-u>, <Pak Chŏng-ae>, <Pak Su-dong>, <Yang Hyŏng-sŏp>, Lee Hyo-sun**, <Yŏn Hyŏng-muk>, <Yun Ki-bok>

**Pak Kŭm-ch'ŏl: dismissed from the Kapsan faction in April 1967.
Chŏng Il-yŏng : rumored to be purged, when he was removed from Minister of Metal-
work Industry.
Kim Tong-gyu : dismissed in 1978 and confirmed to be purged.
Kim Yŏng-ju : rumored to be purged. He remerged as the 7th ranking member of the
WPK Political Committee in 1993.
Lee Hyo-sun : purged at the 15th plenary meeting of the WPK's Central Committee
held in March 1967.
* Those who are deceased (6).
< > Those who are still alive (4).

Table 8-11. The Chairman, Vice-chairman, General Secretary and
Secretary of the WPK Central Committee

Meeting of Party	1st term	2nd term	3rd term	4th term	5th term	6th term
Kim Tong-gyu					** S (5)	
Kim Tu-bong	C	C				
Kim Il				VC (2)	S (2)	
*Kim Il Sung	VC (1)	VC (1)	C	C	GS	GS
*Kim Jŏng Il						S (1)
*Kim Yŏng-nam						S (3)
*Kim Yŏng-ju					S (3)	
*Kim Chung-rin					S (6)	S (2)
Kim Ch'ang-man			VC (5)	VC (4)		
*Kim Hwan						S (4)
Pak Kŭm-ch'ŏl			VC (3)	VC (3)		
*Pak Hyo-dong						S (9)
*Pak Chŏng-ae			VC (2)			
*Yang Hyŏng-sŏp					S (9)	
*Yŏn Hyŏng-muk						S (5)
*O Chin-u					S (4)	
*Yun Ki-bok						S (6)
Lee Hyo-sun				VC (5)		
Chŏng Il-yong			VC (4)			
Chu Yŏng-ha	VC (2)					
Choe Yong-gŏn			VC (1)	VC (1)	S (1)	
Han Ik-su					S (7)	
Hyŏn Mu-gwang					S (8)	
Hong Si-hak						S (7)
*Hwang Chang-yŏp						S (8)

* Those who are still living. Those without * are deceased.
( ) Represents ranking.
** Abbreviations stand for: C, Chairman; VC, Vice-chairman; GS, General Secretary;
and S, Secretary.

*Table 8-12. An Overview of Personnel Changes in the North Korean
Presidency, Vice-Presidency, Premiership and
Vice-Premiership of the Administration Council*

Reappointment	Times (term)	Total
1. President		
<Kim Il Sung>	5 (5, 6, 7, 8, 9)	1
2. Vice-President		
Kim Il	3 (5, 6, 7)	
<Pak Sŏng-ch'ŏl>	4 (6, 7, 8, 9)	
Lee Chong-ok	3 (7, 8, 9)	
Kang Yang-uk	3 (5, 6, 7)	
Kim Tong-gyu	1 (5)	
Lim Ch'un-ch'u	2 (7, 8)	
Choe Yong-gŏn	1 (5)	7
3. Premier		
<Kim Il Sung>	4 (1, 2, 3, 4)	1
4. Vice-Premier		
Kim Il	4 (1, 2, 3, 4)	
Chŏng Chun-t'aek	4 (1, 2, 3, 4)	
Chŏng Il-yong	3 (1, 2, 3)	
<Lee Chong-ok>	3 (2, 3, 4)	
Nam Il	3 (2, 3, 4)	
Lee Chu-yŏn	3 (2, 3, 4)	
Kim Kwang-hyŏp	3 (2, 3, 4)	
6	2 (Pak Sŏng-ch'ŏl, Hong Myŏng-hŭi, Pak Ŭi-wan, Pak Ch'ang-ok, Choe Yong-jin and Kim Ch'ang-bong)	
10	1 (Pak Hŏn-yŏng, Hŏ Ka-i, Choe Ch'ang-ik, Choe Yong-gŏn, Kim Ch'ang-man, Sŏk San, Ko Hyŏk, Kim Man-kŭm, Hong Wŏng-il and Choe Chae-ik)	23
5. Premier of AC.		
<Lee Chong-ok>	2 (6, 7)	
<Yŏn Hyŏng-muk>	2 (8, 9)	
Kim Il	1 (5)	
<Pak Sŏng-ch'ŏl>	1 (5)	
<Kang Sŏng-san	2 (7, 9)	
<Lee Kun-mo>	1 (8)	6

Table 8-12. Continued

Reappointment	Times (term)	Total
6. Vice-Premier of AC.		
<Chŏng Chun-gi>	4 (5, 6, 7, 8)	
<Choe Chae-ik>	3 (5, 6, 7, Vice-premier of the cabinet, 4th)	
Hŏ Tam	3 (5, 6, 7)	
*<Hong Sŏng-nam>	3 (5, 8, 9)	
<Kong Chin-t'ae>	3 (5, 6, 7)	
<Kye Ŭng-t'ae>	3 (5, 6, 7)	
*<Kang Hŭi-wŏn>	3 (6, 8, 9)	
*<Kim Pok-sin>	3 (7, 8, 9)	
*<Kim Ch'ang-ju>	3 (7, 8, 9)	
<Kang Sŏng-san>	2 (6, 7)	
<Kim Tu-yŏng>	2 (6, 7)	
<Choe Kwang>	2 (6, 7)	
<Hong Si-hak>	2 (6, 7)	
<Kim Ho-eil>	2 (6, 7)	
<Hong Sŏng-yong>	2 (6, 7)	
*<Kim Yŏng-nam>	2 (8, 9)	
*<Kim Yun-hyŏk>	2 (8, 9)	
*<Kim Hwan>	2 (8, 9)	
<Pak Sŏng-ch'ŏl>	1 (5, Premier of the cabinet, 3rd, 4th)	
<Lee Chong-ok>	1 (5, Premier of the cabinet, 2nd, 3rd, 4th)	
<Lee Kŭn-mo>	1 (5)	
Chŏng Chun-t'aek	1 (5)	
Nam Il	1 (5)	
Kim Man-kŭm	1 (5)	
<Hong Wŏn-gil>	1 (5)	
Ro T'ae-sŏk	1 (6)	
<Sŏ Kwan-hŭi>	1 (6)	
<Kim Kyŏng-run>	1 (6)	
<Cho Seung>	1 (8)	
*<Kim Tal-hyŏn>	1 (9)	
*<Choe Yŏng-rim>	1 (9)	
*<Chang Ch'ŏl>	1 (9)	32

* They are still in the 9th AC. Those without * and < > are deceased.
< > Those still alive but not in the 9th cabinet.

Table 8-13. An Overview of Personnel Changes in the North Korean
Administration Council Ministers, Commission Chairman
and Academy Presidents

Times	Reappointment (term)	Total
6	*Kim Ŭng-sang (2, 3, 6, 7, 8, 9)	1
5	Kim Hoe-il (1, 2, 3, 4, 7)	
	*Kye Hyŏngsun (4, 6, 7, 8, 9)	
	*O Chin-u (5, 6, 7, 8, 8)	
	*Pak Yong-sŏk (5, 6, 7, 8, 9)	
	*Lee Chi-ch'an (5, 6, 7, 8, 9)	
	*Chŏng Song-nam (5, 6, 7, 8, 9)	
	*Kim Yu-soon (5, 6, 7, 8, 9)	7
4	Chŏng Il-yong (1, 2, 3, 4)	
	Chŏng Chun-t'aek (1, 2, 3, 5)	
	Lee Chong-ok (1, 2, 3, 5)	
	Kim Man-kŭm (2, 3, 4, 5)	
	Hŏ Tam (4, 5, 6, 7)	
	*Kim Pok-sin (4, 7, 8, 9)	
	Kim Tu-sam (1, 2, 3, 4)	
	Kim Yŏng-ch'ae (4, 6, 7, 8)	
	Lee Ch'ang-sŏn (4, 5, 6, 7)	
	Kim Yun-sang (4, 5, 6, 7)	
	*Kong Chin-t'ae (4, 5, 8, 9)	
	*Lee Ch'ŏl-bong (6, 7, 8, 9)	
	*Yun Ki-jŏng (6, 7, 8, 9)	
	*Cho Ch'ŏl-jun (6, 7, 8, 9)	
	*Choe Man-hyŏn (6, 7, 8, 9)	15
3	Lee Chu-yŏn (1, 2, 3)	
	Sŏk San (2, 3, 4)	
	Pak Sŏng-ch'ŏl (3, 4, 5)	
	Hong Sŏng-nam (5, 7, 8)	
	Kye Ŭng-t'ae (4, 5, 6)	

Table 8-13. Continued

Times	Reappointment (term)	Total
	*Kim Kyŏng-un (4, 5, 6)	
	*Kim Yŏng-nam (7, 8, 9)	
	*Kim Hwan (7, 8, 9)	
	Pak Mun-kyu (1, 2, 3)	
	Kim Ik-sŏn (1, 3, 4)	
	Choe Hyŏn (2, 3, 5)	
	Yun Ki-bok (2, 3, 4)	
	Kim Pong-gŭn (2, 3, 4)	
	Kang Chŏm-gu (2, 3, 4)	
	Lee Ryang-suk (2, 3, 4)	
	O Tong-uk (2, 3, 4)	
	Han Sang-du (2, 3, 4)	
	*O Kŭk-ryŏl (4, 8, 9)	
	Pak Lim-t'ae (4, 5, 6)	
	*Lee Chae-yun (4, 8, 9)	
	Lee Chin-su (5, 6, 7)	
	Pak Myŏng-bin (5, 6, 7)	
	Chae Hŭi-jŏng (6, 7, 8)	
	Choe T'ae-bok (6, 7, 8)	
	Choe Chong-gŭn (6, 7, 8)	
	*Kim Chae-yul (7, 8, 9)	
	*Lee Kil-song (7, 8, 9)	
	*Lee Chong-yul (7, 8, 9)	
	Chang Ch'ŏl (7, 8, 9)	
	*Chu Yŏng-hun (7, 8, 9)	
	*Lee Cha-bang (7, 8, 9)	31
2		53
1		96

* They are still in the 9th AC.

Notes

1. V. I. Lenin, *What is To Be Done?* (New York: International Publishers, 1929, 1943), p. 85.
2. Zbigniew Brzezinski and Sameul P. Huntington, *Political Power: USA/USSR* (New York: The Viking Press, 1967), p. 235.
3. *Ibid.*
4. Quoted in V. I. Lenin, *Op. Cit.*
5. Scalapino and Lee stated on the basis of their interview with the defectors from North Korea that the factional divisions in the North Korean politics were neither clear-cut nor meaningful. They further argued that the only viable faction in North Korea has been Kim Il Sung's own group. See Robert A. Scalapino and Chong-sik Lee, *Communism in Korea* (Berkeley: University of California Press, 1972), Vol. 1, pp. 479-480.
6. Hŏn Yu, *Pukhan Isipnyŏnsa* [Twenty-Year History of North Korea] (Seoul: Kwangmyŏng, 1966), pp. 84-88. Also, Scalapino and Lee, *Op. Cit.*, pp. 479-480 and pp. 511-512.
7. *Ibid.*
8. For a recent account of this incident, see Yong-pil Rhee, ed., *Pukhan Chŏngch'i* [North Korean Politics] (Seoul: Daewangsa, 1982), p. 46.
9. According to Suh, during the Korean War, the old Communists attempted to overthrow Kim Il Sung and his regime by military means mobilizing some 3,900 men in early 1953 and led by Yi Sung-yŏp, a top associate of the WPSK leader Pak Hŏn-yŏng, but they failed. Those arrested, purged and executed as a result of this aborted plan were: Yi Sung-yŏp, Cho Il-myŏng, Yim Hwa, Pak Sung-wŏn, Yi Kang-guk, Pae Ch'ŏl, Paek Haeng-bok, Cho Yong-bok, Maeng Chong-ho and Sŏl Chŏng-sik. The second serious challenge against the Kim Il Sung leadership occurred, according to Suh, either in 1964 or 1968, prior to the Fifth WPK Congress in November 1970, in which the intraparty struggle among the Partisan Group members took place. Those "eliminated" in this strife were: Pak Kŭm-ch'ol, Yi Hyo-sun, Kim Kwang-hyŏp, Sŏk San, Kim Ch'ang-bong, Hŏ Bong-hak, Ch'oe Kwang, Yi Yŏng-ho and Yim Ch'un-ch'u (Yim, one of Kim's closest partisan comrade-in-arms, and a vice-president of the DPRK, was temporarily purged and reinstated later). See Dae-sook Suh, "Communist Party Leadership," in Dae-sook Suh and Chae-jin Lee, eds., *Political Leadership in Korea* (Seattle: University of Washington Press, 1976), pp. 181-182 and his paper, "The Korean Communist Movement: Some Basic Characteristics," delivered at the Conference on Accommodation of Communism in Asia, Seoul, Korea, 16-17 August 1985. *Pukhan Ch'onggam* is more specific about the dates of this purge. It began in late April and ended in early May 1967. For details, see *Pukhan Ch'onggam*, p. 82. Also, *Pukhan Chŏnsŏ, 1974*, Vol. I, pp. 254-278. More recently, Rhee and his associates analyzed the

nature of the intraparty conflicts as follows: the preeminence of Kim's partisan and other military elites, such as Kim Kwang-hyŏp, Kim Ch'ang-bong, Ch'oe Hyŏn, Sŏk San, Hŏ Bong-hak, Ch'oe Kwang and O Chin-u in the Kim Il Sung's ruling circle, was apparent in the WPK 14 CC Plenum on October 12, 1966. In 1967 the Soviet economic aid was restored. This aid became the catalyst through which the Kim's ruling elites were divided into the two camps: one led by the party elites such as Pak Kŭm-ch'ol and Yi Hyo-sun, who set the priority on economic development; and the other led by the military elites, who, in turn, were divided into the partisan group such as O Chin-u and Ch'oe Hyŏn and the non-partisan group such as Kim Ch'ang-bong, Ch'oe Kwang and Hŏ Bong-hak (all graduated from the Soviet military colleges). To address this division and subdivision within his ruling circle, Kim first purged Pak Kŭm-ch'ŏl, Yi Hyo-sun and party elites at the 4th WPK 15 CC Plenum in March (the exact dates are May 4-8, 1967) and, next, Kim Ch'ang-bong, Hŏ Bong-hak and Ch'oe Kwang were eliminated in support of his old partisan-comrades-in arms at the 4th WPK 16 CC Plenum from June 28 to July 3, 1967. See Yong-pil Rhee, *Op. Cit.*, pp. 47-48. Also, *Pukhan Chŏnsŏ, 1945-1980*, pp. 75-77.

10. Koon Woo Nahm, *The North Korean Communist Leadership, 1945-1965* (University: University of Alabama Press, 1974), pp. 84-149.

11. See footnote 9. Also, Dae-sook Suh, *Kim Il Sung, The North Korean Leader* (New York: Columbia University Press, 1988), Chapters 7 and 8.

12. Scalapino and Lee are uncertain about "precisely what Mikoyan and Peng Teh-huai told Kim Il Sung" in the wake of the 1956 anti-Kim movement and the purge of the Soviet-Korean and Yanan leaders. See, Scalapino and Lee, *Op. Cit.*, Vol. 1, p. 515. On the basis of Kim Chang-sun's writing, Chung went even further: First Deputy Premier Anastas Mikoyan of the Soviet Union and Marshall Peng Te-huai went to Pyongyang and told Kim Il Sung that the August Incident (August 1956 anti-Kim move) should be treated as "comradely self-criticism of party policy," and the party expulsions should be withdrawn, but Kim ignored their "advice." Chin O Chung, "The Government and Power Structure in North Korea," in Sejin Kim and Chang-hyun Cho, *Government and Politics in Korea* (Silver Springs: Research Center for Korean Studies, 1972), p. 152. Also, Chang-sun Kim, *Pukhan Sipŏnyun-sa* [Fifteen Year History of North Korea] (Seoul: Chimungak, 1961), pp. 57-58.

13. Dae-sook Suh, "Communist Party Leadership," *Op. Cit.*, pp. 181-182.

14. Kim Il Sung, *Selected Works* (Pyongyang: Foreign Languages Publishing House, 1975.)

15. Koon Woo Nahm, *Op. Cit.*, pp. 84-149. Scalapino and Lee, *Op. Cit.*, Vol. 2, Appendix C, pp. 1350-1380. *Pukhan Ch'onggam, '45-'68* (Seoul: Kongsangwŏnmunjeyŏnkuso, 1968), pp. 168-194. Dae-sook Suh, "Communist Party Leadership," *Op. Cit.*, pp. 181-182; *Pukhan P'yŏnram* (Seoul: Kongsangwŏnmunjeyŏnkuso, 1972), pp. 108-140; *Pukhan Chuminsaenghwal* (Seoul: Kong-

sangwŏnmunjeyŏnkuso, 1968), pp. 476-478. *Pukhan Chŏnsŏ* (Seoul: Kukdongmunjeyŏnkuso, 1974), Vol. 1, pp. 103-107. *Pukhan Chŏnsŏ, 1945-1980*
(Seoul: Kukdongmunjeyŏnkuso, 1980), pp. 157-166.

16. Scalapino and Lee seem to prefer the terms "circles" or "groups" to "factions,"
    although they use both interchangeably. See Scalapino and Lee, *Op. Cit.*, Vol.
    II, Appendix C, pp. 1350-1380. The South Korean sources, on the other hand,
    invariably use the term, "factions."

17. According to Suh, "to date there are less than 150 partisans in the North," See
    his, "Communist Party Leadership," p. 188. A South Korean publication listed
    and identified 72 partisan members in North Korea. See *Silrok Kim Il Sung
    gwa Kim Chung Il* (in Korean) (Seoul: Kongsangwŏnmunjeyŏnkuso, 1976),
    pp. 245-249. Scalapino and Lee, although their headcounts are only of those
    who served in the WPK CC during the 1948-1970 period, identified 67 such
    members. See Scalapino and Lee, *Op. Cit.*, Vol. 2, pp. 1350-1379. Recently,
    Dae-sook Suh in his book on Kim Il Sung identified 80 partisans of the United
    Army who have participated in North Korean politics since 1945. He also
    identified 40 partisans (of whom 18 were women) who did not participate in
    North Korean politics. He further listed some 57 partisans who died before the
    liberation of Korea. Among them 14 were Kim Il Sung's superiors or com-
    rades whom North Korea refuses to recognize, 22 whose contributions North
    Korea recognizes, and 21 whom the Chinese Communists recognize. Hence,
    according to Suh's estimate, there were a total of 177 partisan members. For
    detail, see his appendices 1, 2 and 3.

18. For a discussion of Kim's practice of nepotism, see S. C. Yang, *Korea and
    Two Regimes*, pp. 351-363.

19. For an analysis of the Kim Jŏng Il group, see Yang Sung Chul, "An Analysis
    of Post-Kim Il Sung North Korean Leadership" (in Korean) (Seoul: National
    Unification Research Center, 1992).

20. Il-dong Chong, for instance, distinguishes the method of direct terror from that
    of indirect terror in North Korea. The method of direct terror consists of the
    demotion of party rank, demotion, termination of the post, expulsion, arrest,
    labor camp, relocation, sentencing and execution. The method of indirect ter-
    ror includes the surveillance network by the members of the security and intel-
    ligence forces, the Party-member surveillance network by the WPK party
    members and the mass-surveillance network. Chong identified 30 cases of
    purges during the 1945-1970 period. The rhetoric used in these purges
    includes factionalism (e.g., anti-party regionalism, revisionism and military
    groupism), conservatism, formalism, opportunism, spying, anti-Kim and anti-
    revolutionary activities. For details, see his *"Pukhan Chŏngch'i Terror ui Kujo
    wa Kinung"* [The Structure and the Function of the North Korean Political
    Terror] in *Pukhan* (February 1982), pp. 196-209.

CHAPTER 9

KIM IL SUNG'S RISE AND RETENTION OF POWER

*One must be a fox in avoiding traps and a lion in frightening wolves...
a wise leader cannot and should not keep his word when keeping it is
not [sic] to his advantage.... A prince has never lacked legitimate reasons to justify his breach of faith.... Men are so simple and so ready to
follow the needs of the moment that the deceiver will always find someone to deceive.*

Niccolo Machiavelli, *The Prince*[1]

Kim Il Sung is currently the longest ruling autocrat in both the socialist and non-socialist world. His uninterrupted rule in North Korea has
been, however, marked by internecine political strifes and factional
power struggles, although he has remained in firm control since the
founding of the DPRK in 1948. Even before the Republic was launched,
he was already a "national hero" and widely regarded as "first among
equals."[2] What political ingredients and personal attributes did Kim possess that were lacking in other political contenders? How did he defeat
and/or eliminate his political rivals in North Korea? In what ways, did
Hammond's so-called Bolshevik prototypes, i.e., the use of the armed
forces, propaganda, ruthlessness, the party, the planning and camouflage,[3] aid Kim's ascension to power?

In post-liberation North Korean politics, political contenders must
possess several *objective* political ingredients:

1. a record of anti-Japanese struggle;
2. credentials as a member of a communist party organization;
3. blessings of the Soviet occupation forces;
4. public recognition of the power-seeker's reputation;
5. support from the organizational nexus; and
6. youth and physical vigor.

Virtually hundreds of potential political leaders in post-liberation North Korea met some or all of the above criteria, which were *necessary* preconditions but not *sufficient* qualifications. To win power in North Korea, some additional ingredients were necessary. Kim Il Sung has, in fact, demonstrated at least five additional traits which allowed him to gain, retain and expand his power:

1. willingness to form a coalition or a united front with competing political groups;
2. ability to pit one political enemy against another;
3. ability to distinguish long-term political gains from short-term political losses;
4. ability to define and redefine "enemies" and "people" consonant with his own power needs; and,
5. ability to reduce external political, economic and military dependencies and to build his own internal power base.

What follows is a detailed examination of some ingredients and traits which explain Kim's rule in North Korea.[4]

Anti-Japanese Armed Struggle

Although there are disputes about the *magnitude* of Kim's participation in anti-Japanese guerrilla warfare in Manchuria and the North Korean-Manchurian border areas during the 1930s and early 1940s and about his Chinese and Russian connections, no one questions his record of armed anti-Japanese guerrilla activities per se.[5] Besides Kim, hundreds of Korean fighters were engaged in similar anti-Japanese armed struggles in the same areas during the same period. Kim Il Sung is unique in that he was *active* and *alive* at the time of the Korean liberation while most leaders of anti-Japanese armed struggles were dead, old or had to abandon their resistance by then. Moreover, many Korean leaders, nationalists and communists alike, were frequently imprisoned as a result of their anti-Japanese activities, which had been mostly *unarmed* individual gallantry or organizational resistance.

Among the political challengers in North Korea, few could equal the *armed* struggle records of Kim and his partisan comrades-in-arms, the Partisan Group. This factor gave Kim and his Partisan Group a crucial advantage over other contending political groups.

Among the political contenders in North Korea in the wake of the liberation was Mu Chŏng (1905-1951?), who could match Kim's armed struggle record. Mu, a native of Kyŏngsŏng, North Hamgyŏng Province and a graduate of the Whampoa (Chinese) Military Academy, was one of the few Korean "Long Marchers." Before that, he had attended Chungang High School in Seoul but dropped out in 1923 at age eighteen. He then went to Peking (Beijing) via Manchuria. In Peking he reportedly studied at Munhwa College, which he soon left. He enrolled at northern (Chinese) Military (Whampoa?) Academy in 1924. Upon graduation, he was commissioned an artillery officer in the Chinese military. In 1925 he joined the Chinese Communist Party.

In certain respects, Mu appeared to have better credentials than Kim. Mu became a member of the Finance Committee of the Korean Youth League organized in Shanghai in June 1928 (Kim Il Sung's earliest association with communism was in 1926 when he claimed to have led the Kirin Communist Youth League in Kirin, Manchuria).[6] Later Mu Chŏng became a senior officer in the Chinese Eighth Route Army and head of the Korean operations in Yanan. Reportedly, he commanded the artillery corps of the Eighth Route Army and once served as chief-of-staff to the famed Chinese General Peng Teh-huai, Defense Minister of the PRC, who was purged by Mao Tse-tung in 1959.[7]

While in Yanan, Mu Chŏng was regarded by the Chinese communists as the key figure among Korean revolutionaries; he had the distinction of being the only Korean to be given the title "revolutionary leader" in the Chinese communist press at that time. In January 1941, Mu organized the North China Korean Youth Federation at Tungko, Shansi Province, and reactivated the Korean Volunteer Corps in North China.

In August, he established the Korean Revolutionary Youth Cadet School in Tungko to train Korean army officers. On August 15, 1942, when the North China Korean Youth Federation was absorbed by the North China Korean Independence League, Mu Chŏng was elected to a six-member Central Standing Committee.

At first glance, in terms of educational background, official rank, military training, command experience and even political and organizational skills, Mu Chŏng, a senior commander of the Chinese Communist Army (PLA), appeared to be superior to Kim Il Sung, who had never held a position higher than the commander of the Sixth Division of the First Route Army in the Northeast Anti-Japanese United Army. Kim Il Sung (or his partisan comrades-in-arms) had received no formal training at a regular military academy. Nor did Kim have a command experience with a large army. It is no accident, therefore, that Kim Il Sung and his Partisan Group identified Mu Chŏng as the potentially most dangerous political rival.[8]

Notwithstanding the seemingly superior credentials of Mu Chŏng, several substantive factors worked to Kim's advantage. First, Mu Chŏng gained combat and command experiences mainly as a senior officer in the Chinese Communist Army, the PLA, fighting against the Chinese Kuomintang (nationalist) army while Kim Il Sung's armed struggles were directed exclusively against the Japanese forces and their Korean collaborators in Manchuria and the Manchurian-North Korean borders.[9]

Secondly, Mu Chŏng's armed struggle was more "regular" and "co-ordinated" as a part of larger Chinese military operations, while Kim's guerrilla activities were more "irregular" and "random" as small-unit operations against the larger Japanese military establishment. To put it another way, Mu Chŏng's rise in the Chinese communist military hierarchy was credited primarily to his *military intelligence and leadership*, while Kim's survival in the anti-Japanese guerrilla warfare was due to his *tenacity and camaraderie*.

Most important, Mu Chŏng and the Yanan group did not receive the official blessings of the Soviet occupation authorities in North Korea. An attempt by the Yanan group and some 2,000 to 4,000 Korean Volunteer Corps to enter Korea at Antung near the Aprok (Yalu) was initially blocked by the Soviet troops. They were allowed to enter Korea upon disarming themselves. Mu Chŏng and other key Yanan leaders entered North Korea without an army and the Soviet welcome. In the meantime, Kim Il Sung had already seized the opportunity to maneuver the political situation in his favor during the early stages of the power game under Soviet occupation.

Mu Chŏng's political demise was not immediate. He was elected vice-chairman, along with O Ki-sŏp, at the 3rd Enlarged Conference of the North Korean Bureau of the Korean Communist Party on December 17-18, 1945. He ranked 12th in the First WPK CC in 1946 and his rank slipped to 35th in the Second WPK CC in 1948. Thenceforth, his political fortunes began to decline. In July 1946, Mu was assigned to head the artillery corps. As early as March 29, 1948, Kim Il Sung severely criticized key members of the Domestic Group (O Ki-sŏp, Chŏng Tal-hyŏn and Ch'oe Yong-dal) and, at the same time, reprimanded Mu for deviating from the party line.[10] At the beginning of the Korean War, Mu commanded the Second Army of the North Korean People's Army. In October 1950, he was assigned to defend the Pyongyang area but was forced to abandon the mission when the United States-led U.N. forces advanced to the North after successfully landing in Inch'ŏn. Mu was purged at the WPK CC Third Plenum held from December 21 to 23, 1950, ostensibly for his failure to defend Pyongyang and other "crimes."[11]

Thus, Mu Chŏng, a formidable rival, with an impressive *armed* struggle record, became, one of the earliest victims in the North Korean power struggle. Later, the Yanan Group as a whole also fell, faring no better than Mu Chŏng. Scalapino and Lee even speculate that, given the character of the Sino-Soviet relations during that period, Mu Chŏng was feared not only by Kim Il Sung but also by the Russians.[12] In such a manner, one of the major obstacles to Kim's one-man supremacy was removed. The political implications of Mu Chŏng's purge are important. The fact that this action took place during the Korean War, while the Chinese People's Volunteers commanded by Mu's former boss, General Peng Teh-huai, who turned the tide for the retreating North Korean People's Army, unequivocally attests to the degree of Kim's political independence from Chinese influence.

Communist Party Credentials

No one can deny that Kim Il Sung joined a communist party and fought against the Japanese forces under a communist-led guerrilla army. However, no consensus exists as to when, how and with which communist organizations he joined and fought.[13] No one, for that matter, can vouch for the fact that Kim had been the central figure in the annals of the Korean communist movement prior to the liberation despite audacious official North Korean claims.[14] In the pedigree of the Korean communist movement and its leadership configuration, Kim Il Sung's activities, outside of his partisan anti-Japanese armed struggle, remained on the periphery. To be sure, Kim was not an upstart communist, but neither was he *primus inter pares*. Kim's party credentials could not match some of those Korean communist leaders who emerged from the underground, prisons and abroad. To name just a few: Hyŏn Chun-hyŏk, O Ki-sŏp and Chu Yŏng-ha from North Korea; Hŏ Hŏn, Pak Hŏn-yŏng, Yi Sung-yŏp, Yi Yŏng, Kim Ch'ŏl-su, Kim Yak-su and Cho Bong-am from various communist affiliations; and Kim Tu-bong, Ch'oe Ch'ang-ik, Pak Il-u, Mu Chŏng, Kim Ch'ang-man, Yun Kong-hŭm, Han Bin and Hŏ Chŏng-suk of the Yanan Group.[15]

The credentials of Pak Hŏn-yŏng, in particular, illustrate this point. Pak (1900-1955), a native of Yesan, South Ch'ung Ch'ŏng Province, and a graduate of Kyŏnggi High School, was introduced to communism while he was in Shanghai. When the First Congress of the Toilers of the Far East convened in Russia from January 22 to February 2, 1922, Pak was one of fifty-seven Korean delegates.[16] After the Moscow-Petrograd meeting, Pak and his associates attempted to enter Korea via Antung in Manchuria near the Korean border, but they were arrested by the Japanese authorities in April, 1922.

When he was released from prison, Pak and some of his former Shanghai-based Irkutsk faction organized *Hwayo-hoe* [Tuesday Association] in Seoul on November 19, 1923. On April 16, 1925, he played a major role in founding the first Korean Communist Party (KCP) in Seoul and was elected secretary of the Korean Communist Youth League (*Komsomol*). Pak was again arrested by the Japanese authorities in November of that year. He reportedly "feigned mental disorder" and was released from prison in 1928. In August of that year, Pak and his wife broke parole and fled to Vladivostok via Chientao. In June 1929, he enrolled in the preparatory department of the Marx Institute in Moscow and remained there until the summer of 1931. He then returned to Vladivostok and taught in a Korean school for a year. In August 1932, he went to Shanghai, where he was rearrested in July 1933. Upon his release from prison in 1939, Pak went underground. During World War II he reportedly worked as a common laborer at the brick factory in Kwangju, South Chŏlla province.

As noted in Chapter Seven, Pak surfaced from the underground after the Korean liberation and created the KCP Reconstruction Preparatory Committee on August 20, 1945, and drafted the so-called "August Theses."[17] Four days after the release of his August Theses, which, *inter alia*, attacked factionalism, the Seoul Group, which had launched its activities eight days earlier, dissolved itself to join Pak's KCP Reconstruction Preparatory Committee. On September 8, the two groups held a meeting to merge, and Pak was chosen to lead the unified KCP. Thus, he emerged, though for a short time, as the chairman of the newly reactivated KCP in Seoul. For a while, he led both the northern and the southern branches of the KCP.

Pak's leadership was short-lived. After the controversial Chŏng p'ansa Incident (see Chapter 7), the US authorities outlawed communist activities in the South. On October 15, 1946, while underground, Pak reorganized the South Korean branch of the Workers' Party in accordance with the guidelines of the Workers' Party of North Korea. At the end of that year, Pak fled to the North. Thenceforth, Pak's political fortunes began to slide. He was appointed as one of the two vice-premiers as well as foreign minister in the first Kim Il Sung cabinet at the establishment of the DPRK on September 9, 1948. Pak was, also, elected to one of the two vice-chairmanships after the merger of the Workers' Party of North and South Korea in June, 1949. He retained his official position until mid-1953 when key members of the WPSK were purged *en masse* at the Sixth Enlarged Conference of the WPK CC on August 5, 1953. Kim Il Sung's attack on Pak and his WPSK members began, however, as early as December 15, 1952, when Kim criticized the "survival of factionalism":

> ...there also exist elements who care only for high positions, have not the least sense of responsibility for their work, only put on airs for their past revolutionary career, and do not care to take on minor jobs in spite of their inability to tackle big tasks. Phenomena are also observable that people are drawn into political positions without principles because they are relatives, old boys, friends, or because they come from the same native places, localities, South Korea or North Korea....[18]

At a plenary meeting of the WPK CC on April 1, 1955, Kim Il Sung accused "the Pak Hŏn-yŏng-Yi Sung-yŏp gang" for being "the hirelings of U.S. imperialism."[19] Seven months later on December 15, 1955, Pak was secretly tried and executed. On February 8, 1953, Kim recounted Pak's crime as follows:

> Pak Hŏn-yŏng, a spy on the payroll of the American scoundrels, bragged that South Korea had 200,000 (communist) party members and that in Seoul alone there were as many as 60,000. But, in reality, this rascal, in league with the Yankees, totally destroyed our Party in South Korea. Although we advanced as far as the Nakdong River, no revolt broke out in South Korea. Pusan is located a stone's throw from Taegu, and even if a few thousand workers in Pusan had risen to hold a demonstration, the question would have been different. If some people in the South had revolted we would have definitely liberated Pusan and the American scoundrels would not have been able to land.[20]

It is clear from Kim's statement that Pak Hŏn-yŏng was blamed for North Korea's failure to liberate South Korea during the "Fatherland Liberation War" of 1950-1953. Along with Mu Chŏng, Pak was a case of Kim's political scapegoating *par excellence*.

Pak's rise and fall foreshadowed the eventual fate of the old Korean communists in North Korea. What went wrong with the old Korean communists? Why did they fail to capture power in North Korea? Suh, for one, raised a similar but broader question: Why did the old Korean communist leaders fail to carry through the communist movement under the Japanese rule and to assume power in North Korea after the liberation?

Suh supplies a number of important clues. Some major factors which disintegrated the old Korean communists under the Japanese rule were: the premature social and economic conditions in Korea; the weak power base; the intelligentsia-led rather than mass-based organization; factionalism; the lack of basic discipline and ideological training; and the Comintern's withdrawal of support and the lack of tactical and strategic planning. In addition, Suh singled out the old Korean communists' lack of understanding "the permanent nature of the Korean division"[21] as the key reason for their abject political failure in post-liberation politics. To repeat, the old Korean communists misunderstood the true nature of the Korean liberation and totally disregarded the permanence of the "new overlords," i.e., the United States in South Korea and the former Soviet Union in North Korea. Most recently, Suh added another reason to his previous list: the lack of a charismatic or dominant leader who could unite the various segments of the Korean communist movement such as the Yanan Group and the Korean Communists at home.[22]

Above all, Pak and his WPSK Group lost their power base when they fled to the North. Like the Yanan Group, Pak's Group arrived too late in Pyongyang. When Pak and his key WPSK Group joined the WPNK in December 1946, Kim Il Sung and his Partisan Group had already solidified their power base as the "nucleus" of the "Democratic United Front."[23]

Where the old Korean communists failed, Kim Il Sung succeeded. As Yi Sung-man (Syngman Rhee) mastered the objectives of United States politics and policies in South Korea and adapted swiftly to American ways, Kim Il Sung grasped the true meaning and aims of the Soviet presence. In other words, the symbiotic political nexus between Kim Il Sung and the Soviet occupation authorities was developed from the beginning. On the one hand, Kim used the power of the Soviet occupation forces to solidify and expand his power base, while the Soviet occupation forces implemented Soviet policy in the North through Kim. In the initial stages of power game, Kim needed Soviet assistance as much as the latter needed him to "sovietize" North Korea. In that sense, a two-way Kim-Soviet collusion, not a simple one-way Soviet tutelage, existed. In fact, no hard evidence is available to confirm that the former Soviet Union had a design to groom Kim Il Sung as their "man" prior to or immediately after their arrival in North Korea.[24] Contrary to the notion that Kim Il Sung was a Soviet puppet, even from the outset, he was not a mindless clown following the Soviet script. Rather, he was a consummate political actor, who adroitly followed both the Soviet script and his own power scheme.

Soviet Support

Conjecture abounds but no consensus exists as to when and how Kim Il Sung returned to North Korea after the Japanese surrender on August 15, 1945. Kim's mystery goes even further. No conclusive evidence is available to ascertain how and where Kim spent his time from 1941 through 1945. The prevailing assumption is that he and his partisan comrades-in-arms retreated to Soviet Siberia under heavy pressure from Japanese anti-guerrilla campaigns. Although most writers agree that Kim fled to the Soviet Siberia, the dates of his departure vary from late 1940 to 1942. Kim Il Sung's own personal account of his activities, too, is deliberately vague:

> In 1941 or thereabout, during the most difficult period in the anti-Japanese armed struggle, we changed the line of struggle. We trained many cadres in the territory of the Soviet Union in anticipation of the future development of the revolution; with a view to preserving our forces, we switched over from large to small unit operations and intensified the underground struggle.[25]

The explanations for Kim's activities in the former Soviet Union also differ widely. One Japanese intelligence source reported that Kim was in the Okeyanskaya Field School near Vladivostok.[26] An American source conjectured that Kim went to Moscow via Khabarovsk, studied at the Russian Military Academy during World War II, and commanded one of the two Korean units that fought at Stalingrad from 1942 to 1943.[27] The writers, who agree that Kim was a Soviet army officer, disagree over his rank which ranges from colonel to captain.

The North Korean official sources have not clarified the mystery of

Kim's whereabouts during 1940 to 1945 and his rank. Kim's official biography, for instance, stated that his small-unit anti-Japanese campaign was formulated in August 1940 at a meeting of the military and political cadres of the "People's Revolutionary Army" at Hsiaochaerpaling in Tunha County, Manchuria.[28] Kim was in Chiapikou, Wangching County, in June 1941. From spring to early winter, Kim was in Tienpaoshan, Yenchi County, but his guerrilla activities are blank until August 8, 1945, the day the former Soviet Union declared war against Japan. Even at this point, the North Korean sources are unclear about Kim's personal activities. They state that Kim mobilized all units under the Korean People's Revolutionary Army to begin military operations in north, east and south Manchuria and in Korea.[29]

Again, how and when Kim reentered Korea is vague. The date of Kim's reentry into North Korea ranges from early August to mid-September, 1945. Moreover, the North Korean sources allege that Kim and his Korean Revolutionary Army battled to liberate Rajin, Ch'ŏngchin, Ranam and Wŏnsan areas between August 9 to 15, 1945. This claim is particularly interesting in that the dates and the locales of this "liberation battle" correspond to those of the Soviet arrival in North Korea.

Kim's entry with General T. F. Shtykov, the commanding general of the 28th Military Group of the former Soviet Army, which first landed in North Korea, still remains an enigma. How Kim was attired when he entered North Korea is also under dispute (during my visit to North Korea and, especially to Wonsan city, I learned that the official version support the Wonsan harbor as Kim's first entry to North Korea as attested to by the statue of Kim erected at the site to celebrate the event). Many South Korean sources claim that Kim entered North Korea (as major or captain) in a Soviet Army uniform .[30] Suh, for one, dispels the above allegation by pointing out that some writers saw Kim in person on October 14, 1945, at the Pyongyang City Welcoming Rally for "General" Kim Il Sung. On that occasion, Kim appeared in civilian clothes.[31] What is more, except for his pictures during the guerrilla years, no one thus far has been able to recover a picture(s) of Kim in the Soviet military uniform.

The uncertainties about Kim's whereabouts during 1940 to 1945 and his manner of reentry into North Korea notwithstanding, it appears that Kim was not involved in North Korean politics, at least in an official capacity, immediately after the Soviet arrival. When General Ivan Chistiakov's troops arrived in Pyongyang on August 24, 1945, the South Pyongan Branch of the Committee for the Preparation of Korean Independence (CPKI) had been in operation for a week under the leadership of Cho Man-sik, then the leader of the nationalist forces in the North. General Chistiakov demanded the creation of the People's Committee (PC) to replace the existing South Pyongan Branch of the CPKI. He also demanded equal representation of the nationalists and communists in the PC (in the 22-member South Pyongan Branch of the CPKI, 20 were nationalists and only 2, communists). Accordingly, on August 29 the People's Committee was formed, but Kim Il Sung's name was absent from the roster. When the North Korean Branch of the KCP was founded on October 10, 1945, Kim Yong-bŏm was chosen its chairman. Yang Ho-min, a North Koran analyst, speculated that Kim Il Sung did control the KCP North Korean Branch (KCPNKB) at the time of its founding, but he deliberately shunned an official position in order to foster his nonpartisan, united-front image. Yang, further stated that Kim controlled the KCPNKB at the time of its founding and that the Soviet occupational authorities directed its creation.[32]

Kim Il Sung was formally elected chairman at the KCPNKB meeting from December 17 to 18, 1945. At the same meeting, the KCPNKB was renamed the North Korean Communist Party (NKCP). According to Han Chae-dŏk, Kim Il Sung and Cho Man-sik met in Pyongyang in September 1945. Again, in early October, Kim met with Cho and other members of the People's Committee at a Japanese restaurant, *Dayama*, in Pyongyang. General Romanenko, the commanding general of the Soviet occupation forces, introduced Kim Il Sung as "the greatest leader of the anti-Japanese resistance" at the meeting. And Kim spoke in Korean with assistance from the Russian interpreter, Mun Il, a Soviet Korean.[33]

In the earliest stages of the Soviet occupation, the Soviet authorities relied heavily on the Soviet-Koreans or the Sovietized Koreans who came to North Korea with the Soviet troops. The Soviet-Koreans, later called the Soviet Group, were born in the former Soviet territory and held Soviet citizenship. They, not Kim Il Sung and his Partisan Group, received the earliest blessing from Russia. Besides, Kim Il Sung and his Partisan Group were not *directly* involved in North Korean politics during the first three months of the Soviet occupation period.

Significant in this connection is General Ivan Chistiakov's order on October 26, 1945, which *inter alia*, stated that all anti-Japanese parties and democratic organizations in North Korea must register with the Soviet occupation authorities and that all armed units must dissolve and their weapons, ammunitions and other military supplies must be surrendered. The critical Russian support for Kim materialized when the former Soviet Security Command in North Pyongan Province refused to allow some 2,000 (4,000 by the fall of 1945) Korean Volunteer Corps (KVC) and members of the North China Korean Independence League to cross the Aprok River until mid-November, 1945. A special directive was issued by General Bankowsky, the chief of staff of the 25th Soviet Army, to disarm the KVC and prevent them from advancing below Sinuiju. The aim of this Soviet action appeared to be a precautionary measure to head off undue Chinese communist influence in North Korea rather than to extend a helping hand to the rise of Kim Il Sung. From this standpoint, Kim Il Sung was only an indirect beneficiary of the Soviet actions. Whatever the case, at a critical stage of power game in the North the Soviet occupation forces aided Kim in crippling the Yanan Group, his most potent rival political force.

The Soviet-tutelage thesis[34] regarding Kim Il Sung's rise to power deserves attention here. Thomas T. Hammond, for instance, in his typology of communist take-overs, categorized North Korea as "type 2," that is, installation of a communist regime outside the former Soviet Union by the Soviet Army.[35] The Soviet and North Korean sources, on the other hand, stress the spontaneity of the creation of the People's Committee in North Korea.

The political fate of Hǒ Ka-i, leader of the Soviet-Korean Group, documents the case against the prevailing Soviet tutelage-thesis. Hǒ Ka-i, a second generation Soviet-Korean, came with the Soviet occupation forces after the liberation. Prior to the liberation, Hǒ, a graduate of a

Russian university, reportedly served as the secretary of the local Soviet Communist Party, i.e., Maritime District in the former Soviet Siberia. On October 10, 1945, when the North Korean branch of the KCP was formed, Hŏ Ka-i was in charge of its organization department. In December, Hŏ retained the same position in the KCP which was renamed the North Korean Communist Party. When the New People's Party and the North Korean Communist Party merged officially as the Workers' Party of North Korea (WPNK) at a meeting from August 28 to 30, 1946, Hŏ was elected to the five-member political committee (he ranked fourth after Kim Tu-bong, Kim Il Sung and Chu Yŏng-ha). At the Second WPNK meeting from March 27 to 30, 1948, Kim Tu-bong was reelected its chairman and Hŏ Ka-i and Kim Il Sung were elected its vice-chairmen. Hŏ's rank in the Political Committee also rose to third, after Kim Tu-bong and Kim Il Sung. In June and August 1949, when the WPNK and the WPSK merged to become the Workers' Party of Korea (WPK), Kim Il Sung became its chairman, Pak Hŏn-yŏng and Hŏ Ka-i were elected its vice-chairmen. In March 1950, Hŏ Ka-i was at the peak of his political career when he moved up to the position of the WPK's first secretary.

At the Fourth Plenum of the WPK CC on November 2, 1951, Kim Il Sung attacked the "closed door policy" of the party membership which barred peasants and workers from joining the WPK. Hŏ was blamed for the "closed door policy" because it was implemented while he had been the WPK's first secretary. Hŏ was relieved of his party post and reassigned to a vice-premiership in Kim's cabinet for a short time.

Two accounts of Hŏ's demise exist. One, during the Pak Hŏn-yŏng and WPSK Group purge, Hŏ disobeyed Kim's order to repair the Kyŏngyŏng Reservoir located some forty kilometers north of Pyongyang. The reservoir had been destroyed by the UN-U.S. air raid. When Hŏ was ordered to appear before a court of inquiry in April, 1953 for an insubordination charge, he committed suicide. Another version states that Hŏ was ordered to repair the aforesaid reservoir but failed to complete the work because the delivery of materials necessary for its repair was obstructed. Two, he was charged with conspiracy because his name was included in the WPSK list of members who planned to overthrow the Kim Il Sung regime. He was ordered to appear in court for the conspiracy charges, but he requested time to prepare for his defense. He then committed suicide.[36]

One source intimates that Kim purged Hŏ for the latter's close relationship with Pak Hŏn-yŏng. Kim's suspicion intensified when Hŏ admitted far too many WPSK applicants into the party with a token screening process.[37] The official accusation against Hŏ Ka-i was rather insidious. He was charged with having helped the enemy to disrupt the Party from within and to insulate it from the masses. On April 1, 1955, at the WPK CC Plenary Meeting, Kim Il Sung attacked Hŏ Ka-i and other leaders:

> Hŏ Ka-i serves as an example of those from the Soviet Union. He behaved as if he represented those returning home from the Soviet Union.... Those from the Soviet Union, China or the southern half must all bear in mind that they are now members of the Workers' Party of Korea. The selection and allocation of cadres should be decided on Party principles. Those who lack Party spirit and think themselves outstanding figures are of no use to our Party, whether they returned from the Soviet Union, China, or even from Heaven....[38]

In fine, the removal of Hŏ Ka-i by Kim Il Sung amid the "Fatherland Liberation War" when the Soviet military, economic and other assistance was badly needed for war and for post-war reconstruction, illustrates the degree of political independence Kim Il Sung had from the former Soviet Union. Doubtless, in the early stages of the power struggle, the Soviet occupation forces were instrumental in the rise of Kim Il Sung, but their support was not tantamount to one-way Soviet tutelage of Kim. Neither conclusive evidence that the Soviet occupation authorities designated Kim as their puppet nor proof that Kim played according to the Soviet script exist. On the contrary, Kim's political initiative and independence have been amply demonstrated on several occasions, although he acknowledged the former Soviet Union as the "liberator" and Stalin as a "great leader" in his public speeches during the formative period. Kim's independence from the former Soviet Union (and China) did not start after the death of Stalin in 1953 or after the onset of the Sino-Soviet rift in the 1960s but commenced from the very beginning,

albeit in a rudimentary form. In fact, Kim's measure of political freedom from the Soviet political and military power was evident as early as
1948 when the Soviet occupation forces withdrew peacefully from
North Korea, while American troops were "aiding and abetting the Syngman Rhee regime in rigorously putting down the uprising in the South."[39]

Power Game

The political success[40] of Kim Il Sung and his ruling elites has been,
by and large, of their own making. They won with their own strategy
(ies) over other political opponents in post-liberation power games. The
earliest game plan adopted by Kim and his Partisan Group was their version of a united front strategy. Among the communists, the united front
strategy is nothing new as a temporary measure either to buy time or
fight against the greater enemy or both. Such strategy can be seen from
the Chinese united fronts between communists and Kuomintang nationalists in the 1920s and the 1930s.

Kim Il Sung had been absent from Korea since 1925. His fatherland
was as *foreign* to him as Manchurian, Siberian or North Korean border
areas where he had spent his early youth and young adult life as a leader
of anti-Japanese guerrilla forces. When he returned to Korea in 1945, he
received a hero's welcome under the auspices of the Soviet occupation
authorities. Although his followers included some one hundred partisan
comrades-in-arms, he lacked a broad-based organizational infrastructure
in the beginning. When he was elected chairman of the North Korean
Communist Party in December 1945, its membership was still under 5,000.
Not only Kim's Partisan Group but the communists as a whole were,
then, badly outnumbered and outpowered by the nationalists and other
political forces in North Korea.

Under such precarious political dynamics and configurations, Kim
and his Partisan Group championed the united front strategy, which was
followed by several new schemes. Over four decades, Kim's game plans
have, in fact, undergone a series of political metamorphoses, from the
early *united front* appeal to the present *uniformity* approach. At least six

phases of such transformation are discernible. The first phase, the brief period of *national* coalition, was a broad-gauged united front composed of both nationalists and communists. The second phase, the period of *political* coalition, was characterized by a merger of communists and other pro-communist organizations. The third phase, the period of *party unity* was marked by an anti-Party factionalist campaign within the Party. The fourth stage, the period of *intraparty uniformity* stresses purity of ideology, i.e., the *Juche* idea and loyalty to the "Supreme Leader." The fifth stage, the period of cult intensification, led a campaign to glorify both Kim Il Sung's anti-Japanese guerrilla traditions and Kim Jong Il's creative genius in art, culture and other activities. Finally, the sixth stage, the period of formalizing the father-son political succession scheme, focused on rationalizing and justifying the rise of Kim junior (For details, see Table 9-1).

Closely related to Kim's game plans have been his ability to define and redefine his concept of "enemies" and "the people." What he called the "enemies" are his political rivals, potential and actual, or fabricated or genuine. Instead of identifying them as *his* political enemies, he has made them appear as if they were "the enemies of the people." In essence, the gradual consolidation of his power and power base has brought about the narrowing of his definition of the "people" and broadening his definition of the "enemy." His continuing redefinition of the enemy and the people has corresponded to the shifts in his political game plans. Or, more accurately, the former, i.e., the new enemies and the new people, have been the symbolic embodiments of the latter, i.e., the new game plan.

In the formative period (1945-1948), Kim Il Sung and his Partisan Group applied *nationalism* as the principal criterion in identifying and defining the "enemies." The foremost enemies during this period were the "lackeys" of Japanese colonialism and of American imperialism, although *class* enemies -- landlords, comprador capitalists and factional foes -- were also included in their enemy list. Still, the definition of the "people" was broad enough to include not only the workers and peasants but also nationalist groups, patriotic intellectuals, conscientious clergymen and scrupulous capitalists.

Kim's attack on Cho Man-sik and the nationalist group represented the typical cases in this period. As mentioned earlier, Cho led the interim government in Pyongyang and North Korea soon after the liberation. On August 15, 1945, Cho headed the South Pyongan Province Security Maintenace Committee. When the Committee for the Preparation of Korean Independence (CPKI) was organized in Seoul under the leadership of Yŏ Un-hyŏng, Cho renamed his committee the Pyongyang Branch of the CPKI the next day. When the CPKI Pyongyang Branch was dissolved under the direction of the Soviet occupation authorities and the People's Committee (PC) was formed on August 24, Cho assumed the PC's chairmanship. Cho's Democratic Party in particular and the nationalists in the North in general were under frontal attack when the trusteeship issue came to the fore in December. In concert with the nationalists in the South, Cho and his Democratic Party opposed the trusteeship plan,[41] while the former Soviet Union and the communist groups in the North supported it. Kim Il Sung and his group seized this opportunity to smear Cho and his followers as "reactionaries." Due to Cho's anti-trusteeship position, he lost all his formal powers, including the PC chairmanship, and he was under house arrest. In February 1946, Kim emerged as the chairman of the newly created Provisional People's Committee.

As early as August 29, 1946, at the founding of the North Korean Workers' Party, Kim began to narrow the definition of the term, "people," to signify workers, peasants and working intellectuals. With the liquidation of *national* and *class* enemies, Kim soon directed his frontal attacks against *factional* enemies within the WPK. In November 1951, for instance, he criticized the closed-door tendency, the counter-revolutionary elements and all bureaucratic and formalistic styles of work within the Party. These verbal attacks led to the purge of the WPSK Group and the Soviet-Korean Group from 1951 to 1955. From mid to late 1950s, the Yanan Group within the WPK faced a similar fate.

It should be noted here that Kim attacked the pre-*liberation* activities of his national and class enemies, and he assaulted the *post-liberation* behavior of his factional enemies. To put it differently, Kim eliminated his national and class adversaries by resurrecting their past impure *backgrounds*, e.g., lackeys and collaborators of the Japanese colonial-ism, capitalists, compradors and landlords, while purging his factional enemies on the basis of their present undesirable *behaviors*, e.g., bureau-cratism, formalism, dogmatism, factionalism, parochialism, localism, nepotism and revisionism.

As quoted earlier, at the enlarged plenary meeting of the WPK North Hamgyong Provincial Committee on March 23, 1959, Kim urged that "from the Chairman of the Party's Central Committee to the *ri* Party Committee Chairman, and, further, the one million [party] members" should "breathe the same air, speak the same words and act in unison."[42] Two years later, at the Fourth WPK CC on September 11, 1961, Kim reported that "never before have the whole Party and the entire people been strongly knit together and united with a single ideology and will as they are now."[43] His first statement reflected that he was at the last phase of purging the factions within the WPK, while his second remark confirmed their elimination.

Having decimated factional enemies within the Party by the early 1960s, Kim's criticism was directed more toward abstract ideas, signal-ing a new shift in his power struggle, i.e., from interfactional to intrafac-tional strife. Kim acknowledged that factions no longer existed within the Party, only anti-Party factionalists. The liquidation of factions within the WPK does not, however, mean that Kim's "enemies" have all van-ished since the 1960s. Externally, he still faces the same "enemies"—the U.S. imperialists, the Japanese militarists and the South Korean fascists. Internally, his "enemies" persist, but with the exit of the enemies, such as the Yanan Group, the Soviet Group, the Domestic Group and the WPSK Group, his new domestic enemies have become more *abstract* than at any other time. In 1967 Kim prompted the Party to uproot any counter-revolutionary ideological viruses such as the right and left opportunist ideas, flunkeyism toward great powers, capitalist ideas, feu-dalistic Confucian ideas, factionalism, parochialism, nepotism, passivism and conservatism. In 1968 Kim assailed the "hostile" elements within the Party, thereby, hinting at another purge of his political enemies. Labeling them "elements" indicated that factions have been dissolved, and only the hostile elements remained within his own group.

At the Fifth WPK Congress in November 1970, Kim stressed again that the dictatorship should be strengthened over the "hostile elements." In December 1972 at the Fifth SPA, he continued to assault his enemies, though the rhetoric became decidedly more abstract, viz., "smash the insidious maneuvers of hostile classes and do away with the corrosive influence of old ideas once and for all." A similar abstract emphasis was echoed in December 1977. In his report to the Sixth WPK CC in October 1980, Kim remarked that "the whole Party is rallied rock-firm around its CC and [is] knit together in ideology and purpose on the basis of the *Juche* idea." He further stressed that the WPK "has no room for any other idea than the *Juche* idea, and no force can ever break its unity and cohesion based on this idea." Most importantly, he once again pointed a finger at his increasingly more abstract "enemies": "Party organizations should intensify revolutionary, communist education and root out all obsolete ideas remaining in the *minds* of [the] Party members and [the] working people and train them to be true revolutionaries."[44] The *Pyongyang Times'* editorial on the WPK's 40th anniversary on October 12, 1985, made a more positive yet similar note: "our Party has developed into a party of *Juche* led by Comrade Kim Il Sung and which [sic] (the WPK) defends the *Juche* idea and the revolutionary traditions and carries them down through generations, and into a force able to guide the building of an ideal human society." As the Kim Il Sung and Kim Jong Il father-son succession scheme has taken firm root, their political enemies become scarcer, and their political rhetoric, too, become more vague. In recent years the North Korean publications define man as a being who has dual lives: a physical or biological life and socio-political life. His (or her) physical life was given by his own parents, while his socio-political life was given by the "Great Leader" Kim Il Sung, thereby rationalizing and justifying the Kim-Kim succession.

In sum, it is clear from the foregoing that constant redefinition and reidentification of Kim's (and his ruling group's) enemies and people are necessary for his and his son's continuous rule. Kim once stated: "...revolution demands uninterrupted advance[ment]. We cannot be content with the fulfillment of one revolutionary task. We must set forth

and accomplish one new task after another."[45] What is "permanent" or
"uninterrupted" may be, in essence, not the communist revolution per se
but the power struggle, which is in Hobbes' phrases, "a perpetual and
restless desire for power after power, which ceases only in death."[46]
From this standpoint, what Kim meant by "uninterrupted advancement"
is a never-ending search for new enemies—*national, class, factional* and
enemies in the *minds* of the Party members and the people. Having
eliminated all factional and intra-Party enemies and having launched the
new father-to-son succession scheme, his current enemies are those who
have either displayed or felt the slightest doubt about this new strategy.
His "enemies" are ever-present, and only the old ones are always
replaced by the new [For details, see Table 9-1].

Table 9-1. The Metamorphoses of Kim Il Sung's Political Strategy

Period	The characteristics of political coalition	The primary criterion of "political enemy"	"The enemy"
1st stage August 1945- December 1945	national coalition	past pro-Japanese activities and collaboration, anti-nationalistic acts	"national traitors"
2nd stage December 1945- December 1951	political coalition	national reactionaries, landlords and bourgeois class	"reactionaries"
3rd stage December 1951- April 1961	party coalition	anti-Party, factional activities	"anti-Party factionalists"
4th stage April 1961- September 1973	party uniformity	activities of anti-revolutionary tradition, and of Kim Il Sung's revolutionary *Juche* idea	"anti-revolu-tionaries," "anti-*Juche* cliques"
5th stage September 1973- October 1980	cult intensification	activities of anti-Kim Il Sung *Juche* idea and of anti-Kim Il Sung-Kim Jong Il political succession	"anti-revolu-tionary, anti-father-son succession cliques"
6th stage October 1980- present	building of father-son succession scheme	activities of anti-*Juche* idea and of father-son succession movement	"anti-*Juche* cliques" "anti-father-son succession cliques"

Source: Sung Chul Yang, "Two 'Democracies' in Korea," *Korea Journal* 30 (January 1990): 11.

Notes

1. Niccolo Machiavelli, *The Prince*, ed. T. G. Bergin (New York: Appleton-Century-Crofts, 1947), pp. 50-51.
2. For details, see S. C. Yang, *Korea and Two Regimes* (Cambridge: Schenkman, 1981), pp. 161-220.
3. Thomas T. Hammond, ed., *The Anatomy of Communist Takeovers* (New Haven: Yale University Press, 1975), pp. 1-4. See also, pp. 638-648.
4. An extensive analysis of Kim's ascension to political power in North Korea is found in S. C. Yang, *Op. Cit.*, pp. 161-220.
5. For a detailed discussion of his anti-Japanese guerrilla activities, see S. C. Yang, *Op. Cit.*, pp. 75-95. See also, Dae-sook Suh, "The Korean Communist Movement: Some Basic Characterisitics," paper delivered at the Conference on Accommodation of Communism in Asia, Seoul, Korea, 16-17 August 1985. Also his, *Kim Il Sung, The North Korean Leader, Op. Cit.*, especially, pp. 1-57.
6. Most recently, Suh put Kim's claim as follows: "Kim Il Sung never participated in the old Korean communist movement.... Kim Il Sung's guerrilla records are not all manufactured, fabricated tales as some South Koreans claim, and he was responsible for some important victories against the Japanese police as a Communist revolutionary. However, it was in the Chinese Communist guerrilla army that he fought—in the Northeast Anti-Japanese United Army under the Chinese commander Yang Jing-yu, as one of their own... he gained a reputation as a talented guerrilla who fought gallantly against the Japanese under significant odds, but he did not fight for Korea, nor did he ever join any Korean Communist group." For details, See Suh, *Op. Cit.* Suh's statement that Kim "did not fight for Korea" seems too categorical. "The United Army" of which Kim was a member was composed of the united military of both Chinese and Koreans, and he fought against the Japanese, which justifies his claim that he fought against Japan even though he was a part of the Chinese and Korean united army. Hence, he fought for Korea at least indirectly, if not directly. See also, S. C. Yang, *Op. Cit.*, pp. 79-87.
7. Nym Wales and Kim San, *Song of Ariran: A Korean Communist in the Chinese Revolution* (San Francisco: Ramparts Press, 1941), p. 314 and p. 41. A Korean source, however, indicates that Mu was the operational chief of the Chinese Eighth Route Army and later became the commanding general of the Artillery Corps of the Chinese Red Army (PLA). For details, see "Choson Uiyonggun Ch'ongsaryonggwan Mu Chong changgun Ildaegi" [A Biography of General Mu Chŏng, Supreme Commander of the Korean Volunteers Corps] in *Sinch'ŏnji* (March 1946), pp. 238-240.

8. Chae-dok *Han, Kim Il Sung ul kobał handa* [The Indictment of Kim Il Sung] (Seoul: Naeoe Munhwa-sa, 1965), p. 227. Robert A. Scalapino and Chong-sik Lee, *Communism in Korea* (Berkeley: University of California Press, 1972), Vol. 1, p. 354 and p. 394 footnote.

9. Kim Il Sung himself once raised the question:

> Should we become successors to the "independence army" or the "patriotic volunteers corps," which defended the interests of the propertied class, or "volunteers army" or Kim Tu-bong's "independence union" which never engaged in battle with the Japanese scoundrels, and took flight at the mere sight of them?

See Kim Il Sung, *Selected Works* (Pyongyang: Foreign Languages Publishing House, 1965-72), Vol. 2, p. 72.

10. See Kim Il Sung, *Selected Works*, Vol. 1, p. 267.

11. Besides the failure of defending Pyongyang District, Mu Chŏng was charged with the unwarranted killing of his subordinates. See *Kin Nichisei senshu* [Selected works of Kim Il Sung], Japanese ed., Kyoto, 1952, Vol. 2, pp. 105-144. Quoted in Scalapino and Lee, *Op. Cit.*, Vol. 1, p. 406. According to *Pukhan P'yŏnram* (Seoul: Kongsangwŏnmunjeyŏnkuso, 1968), Mu Chŏng's "crimes" were: (1) insubordination; (2) inadequate preparedness for war; and (3) illegal murder during the retreat. According to this source, Mu was executed in July 1951. For details, see *Pukhan P'yŏnram*, pp. 121-122. Note also the difference among the writers concerning the site of the Third Plenum of the WPK. Kim Ch'ang-sun in *Pukhan-P'yŏnram* wrote that it was held in Byulo-ri, Manp'ojin on the Manchurian border. Scalapino and Lee identified it to be Kanggye, a city near the Manchurian border in Chagang Province. For details, see *Pukhan P'yŏnram*, p. 121. Scalapino and Lee, *Op. Cit.*, Vol. 1, p. 405 and footnote 39.

12. Scalapino and Lee, *Op. Cit.*, Vol. 1, p. 405.

13. The North Korean source states that Kim organized the Communist Youth League in Kirin, Manchuria, in 1927. See Bong Baik, *Kim Il Sung Biography* (Tokyo: Miraisha, 1969-70), Vol. 1, p. 580. Chae-dŏk Han maintains that Kim was a member of the Russian Communist Party, see his, *Kim Il Sung ul kobal handa*, p. 138. Suh, on the basis of the Japanese Kirin Consulate Report, wrote that in early May 1929, Kim Il Sung (under the name of Kim Sŏng-ju, a student at Yuwen Middle School) took part in a meeting held by a small group of both Korean nationalists and communists, which was the first recorded meeting that Kim attended. For details, see Dae-sook Suh, *The Korean Communist Movement, 1918-1948* (Princeton: Princeton University Press, 1967), pp. 266-267. See also, Scalapino and Lee, *Op. Cit.*, Vol. 1, pp. 205-206. One South Korean source alleges that Kim had triple communist memberships—the Chinese Communist Party in 1931, the Russian Communist Party in 1941 and the Korean Communist Party in 1945. See *Kim Il Sung gwa Kim Jong Il* (Seoul:

Kongsangwŏnmunjeyŏnkuso, 1976), pp. 157-172. See also, S. C. Yang, *Op. Cit.*, Appendix I.

14. Suh is categorical: "Kim Il Sung never participated in the old Korean Communist movement." See his paper, "The Korean Communist Movement: Some Basic Characteristics," p. 24. Also his, *The Korean Communist Movement* (1967), p. 254. Kim Il Sung himself, nevertheless, argues that his anti-Japanese guerrilla warfare was a continuation of the Korean Communist movement after the failure of the Korean Communist Party in 1928. See Kim Il Sung, *Selected Works*, Vol. 1, p. 3.

15. For a discussion of the demise of these erstwhile old Korean communist leaders, see *Pukhan Ch'onggam* (Seoul: Kongsangwŏnmunjeyŏnkuso, 1968), pp. 59-123; *Pukhan P'yŏnram*, pp. 108-140; *Pukhan Chŏnso* (Seoul: Kukdongmunjeyŏnkuso, 1974), Vol. 1, pp. 254-278. Also, Suh, "the Korean Communist Movement: Some Basic Characteristics."

16. The Korean delegation was the largest in the First Congress of the Toilers of the Far East with fifty-seven of the total 124 delegates, while China had only twenty-seven and Japan, thirteen. The Korean delegates were not all communists. They included many prominent Korean nationalists such as Kim Kyusik, Yŏ, Un-hyŏng, Na Yong-gyun, Chang Kŏn-sang, Kim Wŏn-gyŏng and Wŏn Se-hun. See, *The First Congress of the Toilers of the Far East* (Petrograd, 1922), p. 237. Quoted in Dae-sook Suh, "The Korean Communist Movement: Some Basic Characteristics," pp. 6-7.

17. For a full discussion of Pak Hŏn-yŏng's August Theses, see Il-wŏn Pak, *Namno-dang Ch'ongbip'an* [The Criticism of the Workers' Party of South Korea] (Seoul: Kuktongchŏngbosa, 1948), pp. 30-39; Nam-sik Kim, *Silrok Namno-dang* [The True Account of the Workers' Party of South Korea] (Seoul: Sinhyŏnsil-sa, 1975), pp. 7-16.

18. Kim Il Sung, *Selected Works*, Vol. 1, p. 397.

19. *Ibid.*, p. 523. A secret telegram sent by Langdon, United States Political Adviser in Korea, to the United States Secretary of State on November 14, 1946, is noteworthy:

> The North Korean Democrat Kim Il Sawng [Il Sung] and Kim Doo Bong [Tu-bong] who are said by Lyuh Woon Hyung [Yŏ Un-hyŏng] to be nationalistic-minded and opposed to the subversive anti-American Communist [s] represented by Pak Heun Yung [Hŏn-yŏng] in the south and Kim Moo Chong [Mu Chŏng?] in the north....

See, *Foreign Relations of the United States, 1946: The Far East* (Washington, D. C. : U. S. Government Printing Office, 1971), p. 768. Ironically, however, Pak Hŏn-yŏng was charged with "the hireling sp [ies] of United States imperialism."

20. Kim Il Sung, *Selected Works*, Vol. 3, p. 519.

21. Suh, *The Korean Communist Movement*, pp. 311-338. Scalapino and Lee agree mostly with Suh's assessment of the old Korean communist's failure. See Scalapino and Lee, *Op. Cit.*, Vol. 1, pp. 230-232.

22. Suh, "The Korean Communist Movement: Some Basic Characteristics."

23. For details, see S. C. Yang, *Korea and Two Regimes*, pp. 161-220.

24. Suh assessed Kim's rise in North Korea as follows:

> ...it was not Kim's ability alone that brought him to the leadership; more importantly, it was the failure of the old Communists, plus their miscomprehension, misjudgement and misinterpretation of the political development of liberated Korea, that eventually forced them to give way to Kim and the new Communists. Russian approval of Kim did not necessarily preclude the possibility of the old Communists; there was a definite *evolutionary* element in Kim's advance during the three years between the liberation and his consolidation of power in the North.

Suh (1967), p. 325, and p. 254. Scalapino and Lee appear less certain about the same issue:

> There is no evidence that the Russians had fixed ideas on all of these matters (who would lead the KCP?) when they first arrived as an occupying force in mid-August. We have no firm knowledge as to what type of commitment, if any, had been made to Kim Il Sung, whether Kim had rivals for Soviet affections, or what the Russians may have thought about a man like Pak Hun-yong.

See Scalapino and Lee, *Communism in Korea*, Vol. 1, pp. 317-318. Yang contends that the Soviet authorities "imported" Kim Il Sung to Sovietize North Korea. See Ho-min Yang's article in *Pukhan Ch'onggam*, p. 301. The same line of argument is found also in Wayne S. Kiyosaki, *North Korea's Foreign Relations: The Politics of Accommodation, 1945-75* (New York: Praeger, 1976), p. viii, pp. 4-6 and pp. 33-37.

25. Kim Il Sung, *Selected Works*, Vol. 2, p. 68.

26. "Kin Nichi-sei no katsudo jokyo" [General Conditions of the Activities of Kim Il Sung], *Tokyo gaiji geppo* (November 1944), pp. 76-78. Quoted in Suh (1967), p. 292.

27. *Current Biography* (1951), p. 335.

28. See, for example, *Unhae Ioun Taeyang* [The Benevolent Sun] (Pyongyang: Foreign Languages Publishing House, 1975), Vol. 1, pp. 456-486. Bong Baik, *Kim Il Sung Biography*, Vol. 1, pp. 188-532.

29. Note, however, that Kim himself acknowleged the Soviet army as the "liberator" in his speech on June 20, 1946. See Kim Il Sung, *Selected Works*, Vol. 1, p. 67. Suh contends that Kim "has now changed the name of the United Army (the Northeast Anti-Japanese United Army) to the Korean People's Revolutionary Army, putting himself in the position of supreme commander from the beginning," Suh (1985), p. 25.

30. Chae-dok Han, *Kim Il Sung ul kobal handa*, p. 111. *North Korea: A Case Study in the Techniques of Takeover* (Washington, D. C. : Department of State Publications, 7, 118, Far Eastern Series, 103, 1961), p. 13. Ch'ang-sun Kim, meanwhile, contends that Kim was a "temporary major" in the Soviet army, see his *Pukhan Sipŏnyunsa* (United States Joint Publications and Research Service, 18925), April 26, 1963, p. 29.

31. My conversation with Professor Suh in Honolulu, Hawaii, on June 2, 1978.

32. Ho-min Yang's article in *Pukhan Ch'onggam*, p. 805. Yang's idea that Kim Yong-bŏm was the secretary is based on Ch'ang-sun Kim's *Pukhan Siponyŏnsa*, pp. 95-96. But the same *Pukhan Ch'onggam* which included Yang's article recorded Kim Il Sung as the secretary elsewhere. See, *Pukhan Ch'onggam*, p. 118.

33. Chae-dok Han, *Op. Cit.*, pp. 54-60.

34. John N. Washburn, "Russia Looks at Northern Korea," *Pacific Affairs* (April 1947), p. 153; *Pukhan Ch'onggam*, pp. 803-811; Scalapino and Lee, *Op. Cit.*, Vol. 1, pp. 313-381; Jane P. Shapiro, "Soviet Policy Toward North Korea and Korean Unification, "*Pacific Affairs* (Fall 1975), pp. 335-352; Wayne S. Kiyosaki, *Op. Cit.*, pp. 33-44; *North Korea: A Case Study in the Techniques of Takeover*, Glen D. Paige, *The Korean People's Democratic Republic* (Stanford: The Hoover Institution, 1966), pp. 25-34; Chin O. Chung, *Pyongyang Between Peking and Moscow: North Korea's Involvement in the Sino-Soviet Disputes, 1958-1975* (University: University of Alabama Press, 1978), pp. 11-13.

35. Thomas T. Hammond, *The Anatomy of a Communist Takeover*, pp. 638-640. See also, Dae-sook Suh, "A Preconceived Formula for Sovietization: the Communist Takeover of North Korea," in Hammond, *Op. Cit.*, pp. 475-489. A memo by the U.S. CIA on June 19, 1950, reported that the DPRK is "a firmly controlled Soviet satellite." See *Foreign Relations of the United States, 1950*, Vol. 2, pp. 109-112. For details, see S. C. Yang, *Korea and Two Regimes*, footnote 35, p. 211.

36. For details, see *Pukhan P'yŏnram*, pp. 118-119; *Pukhan Chuminsaenghwal gwa Goesu Kim Il Sung* [The Life of North Korean People and Chieftain Kim Il Sung] (Seoul: Kongsangwonmunjeyŏnkuso, 1968), pp. 464-468. Also, Scalapino and Lee, *Op. Cit.*, Vol. 1, pp. 409-410.

37. Scalapino and Lee, *Op. Cit.*, p. 409 note.

38. Kim Il Sung, *Selected Works*, Vol. 1, pp. 565-567.

39. Note, in this regard, the following comments:

    Mr. Patterson (United States Secretary of Defense) commented that General Hodge had emphasized the political immaturity of the Koreans, characterizing them as very backward and unruly. General Hildring said that the weakness of our (United States) position lies in the fact that the Russians are actually placing

> Koreans in office, however much they may be guided by Russians, and are making political capital out of the situation [but] in our (United States) zone everything is done directly by [US] military government officials.

Foreign Relations of the United States, 1946, p. 682. See also John N. Washburn's commentary of the Soviet press in *Pacific Affairs* (March 1949), pp. 53-58.

40. For a detailed analysis of Kim's rise to power, see S. C. Yang, *Korea and Two Regimes*, pp. 161-220. Also his, "The Kim Il Sung Cult in North Korea," *Korea and World Affairs* (Spring 1981), pp. 161-186 and "The Politics of Cult in North Korea," *Political Studies Review* (1985): 27-52.

41. A detailed account of pros and cons on the Korean trusteeship question is found, for instance, in Nam-sik Kim, *Op. Cit.*, pp. 245-260.

42. Kim Il Sung, *Selected Works*, Vol. 2, p. 392.

43. *Ibid.*, p. 156.

44. Kim Il Sung, *Report to the Sixth Congress of the Workers' Party of Korea on the Works of the Central Committee* (Pyongyang: Foreign Languages Publishing House, 1980), p. 111.

45. Kim Il Sung, *Selected Works*, Vol. 2, p. 262.

46. Thomas Hobbes, *Leviathan* (New York: Dutton, 1950), Chapter II, pp. 79-80.

PART IV

THE SOUTH KOREAN POLITICAL SYSTEM: A DEMOCRATIZING POLITICAL ORDER

CHAPTER 10

THE SOUTH KOREAN POLITICAL FRAMEWORK

\ *Democratic government will work to full advatanage only if all the interests that matter are practically unanimous not only in their allegiance to the country but also in their allegiance to the structural principles of the existing society. Whenever these principles are in question and issues arise that rend a nation into two hostile camps, democracy works at a disadvantage. And it may cease to work at all as soon as interests and ideals are involved on which people refuse to compromise.* \

Joseph A. Schumpeter[1]

Approaches to the Study of South Korean Politics

There are several approaches to, and models of, understanding and analyzing the present South Korean politics. Only four approaches or models are here identified and examined in some detail. For want of adequate terminologies, they are called area-specific studies, culturalism, syncretism and authoritarianism.

By area-specific studies are meant research and analysis of various structural and functional aspects of South Korean politics, be they legislative behavior, electoral behavior, political leadership, foreign policy, unification question, ideology or public administration and decision-making. The area-specific studies on South Korean politics are by far the most numerous. Most of them, are hyper-factual, descriptive or

but impotent; the ruling party predominates while opposition parties exist in constant disarray and moribundity; the military has been greatly politicized; the corporatist government-business-industry-labor nexus has been evident; the political activism of university students, though sporadic and scattered, has been persistent and increasingly radicalized albeit declining in number; and the fundamental individual rights such as freedom of speech, press and assembly have not been fully protected.

In short, South Korea shares some authoritarian features with other so-called newly industrializing countries (NICs). It also manifests several unique political elements. In this chapter, some common factors as well as unique elements besetting the South Koren politics will be identified.

An Authoritarian Political Order: Common Elements

The South Korean political system exhibits a number of authoritarian characteristics: anti-liberalism; anti-parliamentarianism; corporatism; praetorianism; and developmentalism. If the North Korean totalitarianism is a variant of the dictatorship of the left, the South Korean authoritarianism is a form of the dictatorship of the right. In the former the state controls the means of production, distribution and management and denies private ownership or private business enterprise. In the latter, although the state intervention in the private sector of its economy and its collusion with key industries are substantial, it has not reached the point of stifling free market, free enterprise system and private ownership of property. The state control of political process is severe and systematic in an authoritarian polity, but the spill-over effect of such political control into the economic, societal and individual life has never been total. Besides, as Juan Linz aptly pointed out, totalitarian systems possess three fundamental attributes:

1) a monistic but not monolithic center of power;
2) an exclusive, autonomous, and more or less intellectually elaborate ideology that serves to legitimize the leader's power; and
3) citizen participation and active mobilization for political and collective social tasks.[17]

Amos Perlmutter disagreed with Linz. The former asserted that although totalitarian systems possess an exclusive ideology while authoritarian systems lack an "elaborate and guiding ideology," it (ideology) is not the motor that propels the regime, the state and the society "in most, if not all, totalitarian systems."[18] He contended that an examination of political structures, not of ideology, is the most useful tool to explain the political behavior, structural arrangements and political dynamics of modern authoritarian regimes.[19] The survival of all modern authoritarian, totalitarian and autocratic regimes is dependent not so much on their ideological commitment, purity and zealotry, as on their ability to successfully orchestrate the party, the state, the parallel and auxiliary structures and the society in the direction of authoritarianism. Further, he emphasized that only when wedded to political organizations does ideology become an instrument of power and a useful explanatory tool. His concept of authoritarianism, which includes Bolshevism, Fascism and Nazism, is too broad. As he himself acknowledged, even at the height of Hitler's rule in Nazi Germany, the economic system was not entirely state-owned. Neither was it dominated by the party. Rather, it was controlled by the relatively self-autonomous state bureaucracy.[20] Above all, unlike in the former Soviet Union and other socialist countries, Hitler, the Fuehrer, not the Nazi party, held the monopoly of power. Also, unlike in communist states, in fascist, corporatist and praetorian systems, the state and the other political structures are often unstable, inefficient and generally weak. The elite has no cohesion and cannot attain and dominate any hegemonic political structure suitable for establishing its political supremacy.[21]

From a somewhat different angle, Hannah Arendt noted that "proof of the nontotalitarian nature of the Fascist dictatorship is the surprisingly small number and the comparatively mild sentences meted out to political offenders."[22] Mussolini's Fascist Italy (and Hitler's Nazi Germany, for that matter) was not a totalitarian state like other communist states, even though he coined the word. In Bertram Wolfe's words, Italian fascism was "more totalist in aspiration than in realization."[23] Likewise, Hitler's *fuehrerprinzip* (leadership principle) and Kim Il Sung's personality cult, for instance, are different in that in the former Hitler *created* the Nazi Party to guard his leadership, whereas in the latter the WPK *created* the Kim cult as its control mechanism. The Nazi served as Hitler's political instrument as much as the Kim Il Sung cult performed the same role for the WPK.

Perlmutter's concept of authoritarianism is, in short, too broad to distinguish the communist party in the USSR from the Brown Shirts in Nazi Germany (or, for that matter, Black Shirts in Fascist Italy). To him, both are efficient instrument of authoritarianism.[24] But, as noted earlier, it may be more accurate to say that Bolshevism is the prototype of the dictatorship of the left, and Fascism and Nazism represent the dictatorship of the right. To put it differently, one exemplifies totalitarianism and the other, authoritarianism. A clear distinction between totalitarian and authoritarian political orders is useful in understanding and analyzing the North and South Korean political systems. The current North and South Korean political systems provide the living laboratories of totalitarian and authoritarian political orders.

With the above conceptual caveats in mind, five characteristics that the South Korean authortarianism shares with other authoritarian polities[25] are delineated in the following.

1. Anti-liberalism

A shortcut to understanding anti-liberalism is to comprehend the meaning of liberalism. For, anti-liberalism is the antithesis of liberalism. At the core of liberalism lies a fundamental postulate that all values inhere ultimately in satisfactions and realizations of human personality. Liberalism's basic premise is to treat persons as ends rather than as means. Liberalism is a concept of human enlightenment and of unfettered development and self-expression. It attempts to lift the burden of coercion and to proclaim the dignity of human beings and their inalienable rights. In principle, it advocates minimal state intervention under the slogan of *laissez-faire*. The state intervention is justifiable only if it *frees* man from hunger, illiteracy, ill health and squalor.

Specifically, liberal position means: in economics, a commitment to *laissez-faire* ideology, a belief in the vitality of small business, and opposition to strong trade-unions; in politics, a demand for minimal government intervention and regulation; in social life, support of equal opportunity, opposition to artistocracy and redistributive measures; and in culture, anticlericalism and antitraditionalism. In brief, liberalism in European politics, whose ideals were rooted in the Enlightenment and the French Revolution, originally meant the idea of freeing individuals from the domination of both church and state.

Anti-liberalism is the challenge to, and the denial of, the aforesaid ideals and idea of liberalism. Such challenges and denial may come from the left, i.e., Communism or from the right, i.e., Fascism and Nazism. The former denies the ideals and idea of liberalism through the mono-party dictatorship in the name of the proletariat, and the latter, through the mono-party dictatorship in the name of the state. The left "partism" and the right "statism" are graphically illustrated by the Article 6 of the former USSR constitution ("The leading and guiding force of Soviet society and the nucleus of its political system, of all state organizations and public organization, is the Communisty Party of the Soviet Union") and Benito Mussolini's slogan ("all for the State; nothing against the State; nothing outside the State).[26]

As John Stuart Mill declared in *On Liberty*, "over himself, over his own body and mind, the individual is sovereign." Hence, the only purpose for rightfully exercising power over any member of a civilized community is to prevent harm to others. Mill acknowledged and even justified the limitations of freedom, but, at the same time, he distinguished "harm to the interest of others" from "a hurt to themselves." He contended that hurting themselves, however painful, does not sanction interference from society, unless it has an interest in asserting a rule for the benefit of all.[27]

The quintessence of liberalism is to *free* man from all forms of sufferings, suppressions and shackles. Its ideal is to realize man's fullest potential by relieving his or her sufferings resulting from poverty, slavery, war, disease, disasters, dictatorships or other forms of pain. It pursues ideals of civil liberties—freedom of thought, of expression and of association—the security of property and the control of political institutions by an informed public opinion. Hence, the core objective of liberalism is to pursue, protect and promote human freedoms.

Isaiah Berlin, for one, distinguished "negative" from "positive" freedom. The former involves an answer to the question, "What is the area within which the subject—a person or group of persons—is or should be left alone to do or be what he is capable of being or doing without interference from other people?" The latter hinges on the answer to the question, "What, or who, is the source of control or interference that can determine what someone can be or do one thing or the other?"[28] There are some similarities between Aristotle's political liberty and civil liberty and Berlin's positive liberty and negative liberty, respectively.[29] Positive freedom is the process or activity of making one's own choices and acting on one's own initiative. Positive freedom means having control over what are to be those liberties. The wish for positive liberty is tantamount to the wish to be one's own master. If negative liberty is "freedom from" certain activities, then positive freedom is "freedom to" engage in them. Negative freedom is a condition characterized by the absence of constraint or coercion. To have negative freedom is to have liberties, rights, permissions or freedom to act. The wish for negative liberty is synonymous with the desire to be free from other's command, control or interference. Another dimension to freedom is what I call "freedom within." "Freedom within" resembles Mill's moral freedom: "a person feels morally free when he feels that his habits or temptations are not his masters, but theirs." Accordingly, no one is completely free until and unless he or she becomes "a person of confirmed virtue."[30] Freedom within, however, transcends moral freedom. It not only calls for moral self-mastery but also for religious faith, philosophical convictions and conscience. Whether it is called faith, convictions or conscience, it ultimately resides within each individual.

From a somewhat different plane, Bernard Dauenhauer argued that freedom is a relational concept. He defined freedom as the capacity simultaneously to participate in and to maintain oneself as a pole of multiple distinct kinds of relationships involving hegemony, equality or subsumption. Three distinct kinds of relationships which involve freedom are hegemonious, egalitarian and subsumptive. Recently, Rhoda Howard and Jack Donnelly distinguished human rights and human dig-

nity and the latter is culture-bound in that all societies possess conceptions of human dignity but the idea of human dignity underlying international human rights standards requires a particular type of "liberal"
regime.[31]

Carl Friedrich, meanwhile, identified three aspects of freedom: of
independence; of participation; and of creation and innovation. He
defined freedom of independence as natural rights *against* government,
or a personal sphere to which government cannot intrude or invade. The
second freedom concerns civil liberties which involve participation *in*
government. The third freedom is obtained *through* government since
freedom from fear or want (or the right to work) can only be attained
with the help of government. His first two freedoms correspond to
Berlin's negative and positive freedom, respectively, while his third
freedom, that is, freedom of creation and innovation is somewhat new.
Friedrich further pinpointed that between 1787 and 1947 the concept of
freedom shifted from natural rights to civil liberties and to human freedoms.[32] In that sense, the notion of freedom is not simply *dimensional*
but also *developmetal.* Like trees or plants, it goes through a life-cycle.
It may grow, expand and unfold. Or, it may wither away. Jefferson's
often-cited "trees of liberty," which must be refreshed from time to time
with the blood of patriots and tyrants,[33] is not simply provocative. Freedom is never given, it must be acquired, maintained and explored for
further growth and enrichment, lest it shrinks and wilts.

Freedom is not a license to do or to be whatever a person wants without restrictions, constraints or interference. Inciting riots, advocating
crimes or libeling, defaming, slandering and blackmailing cannot be
permitted since they impinge on other's freedom. In principle, a person's
freedom can be curtailed to prevent harm to others, to protect the rights
of others and/or to preserve the liberty of action. As Friedrich rightly
warns, rights and freedom exist only within the context of a political
order wherein they can be enforced. Freedom presupposes an order.[34]
At a first glance, order and freedom appear contradictory, but, in reality,
no freedom can exist without a certain order and vice versa. Some
restrictions on freedom (or, some freedom in a political order) are both
necessary and justified. Aristotle's portrayal of man without a polis,

Hobbes' man in a state of nature, and Locke's and Rousseau's man in a state of nature have one thing in common: man's *natural* liberty in a state of nature aside, man without a civil society has no "real" freedom. Lock's and Rousseau's natural liberty is a pseudo-freedom, at best, since there is no enforcer.

Freedom in a civil society is real because it is not absolute but relative, relational and developmental. Freedom is *relative* to one's own ability to do or not do something or to be or not be someone within external constraints and coercion. Not all external constraints and coercions are legitimate, justifiable and rational. Minimal external constraints and coercion, whether they stem from governmental authority or any other organizations, are prerequisite to freedom. Freedom is *relational* and exists in the context of relationships, be they between persons in relation to others, groups, institutions and governments, and it exists whether such relationships are hegemonial, egalitarian or subsumptive. Freedom is also *developmental* since it grows intensively or extensively. Its intensive growth has been the development from natural rights to civil liberties and to human freedom. Its extensive growth encompasses the expansion of freedom from an autocrat to the privileged few to the masses and ultimately to all humankind.

It is self-evident from the above that the North Korean political system does not merely typify anti-liberalism. Rather, it is *the absence* of liberalism, not simply anti-liberal tendency, that characterizes the current North Korean totalitarian polity.[35] By contrast, not the absence of liberalism but the anti-liberal *tendency* prevails in South Korea's authoritarian political order. Specifically, in South Korea the fundamental civil rights, private property rights and civil liberties are guaranteed by the Constitution. At the same time, however, these rights and liberties have frequently been restricted or suspended under emergency measures and martial law.

For instance, Article 77 in the 1987 Constitution stipulates that in time of natural calamity or a grave financial or economic crisis, or of hostilities threatening the security of the State, the President, may in accordance with the provisions of laws, enact special measures to *restrict* the freedoms and rights of the people prescribed in the Constitution (Section 32). The President also has the power to declare both extraordinary and precautionary martial law under which "special measures" can be taken to curb freedom of speech, press, assembly and association (Article 77, section 1 and 2). The crux of the matter is that only the president can define and decide the existence of such calamity or "grave dangers." Because he alone makes a determination of such conditions, not only the potential for political abuse is ever present but actual misuses of such extraordinary powers have taken place in the South Korean political arena.

In sum, the South Korean Constitution provides the president with "anti-liberal" provisions and extraordinary powers to restrict and limit the *political* process. Such power of the president has infringed upon the exercise of individual rights and liberties. Specifically, from 1948 to 1987 eleven martial laws, which suspended costitutional rule, have been declared. The rule by martial law or the suspension of citizen's fundamental rights and freedom had, in short, been almost a political norm than an exception (For details, see Table 10-1). Nevertheless, with the Roh regime and the present Kim government, serious efforts towards democratization and liberalization have considerably dampened the anti-liberal attributes of the South Korean polity.

2. Anti-parliamentarianism

Anti-parliamentarianism is an idea either to deny or to challenge the independence and efficacy of the legislative body as one of the key governing apparatus. Anti-parliamentarians contend that the legislature is the institution created to produce illusion of human equality. They challenge the notion that democracy is a process in which people make policy and govern themselves. They see the masses as being politically neutral, indifferent and inarticulate.[36] They believe that politicians are corrupt, inefficient and self-seeking and reject the concept of a pluralist democratic state. They charge both "the devilish cleverness on the part of the leaders and childish stupidity on the part of the masses." They also espouse that parliamentary majorities are spurious and do not necessarily represent the realities of the country.[37]

If the legislature means the collection of individuals who are elected as members of the formal parliamentary bodies prescribed by a constitution, it not only exists in the democratic system but also in totalitarian and authoritarian systems. Unlike the legislature in the democratic system, whether a parliamentary system in England or a presidential system in the United States, which plays a pivotal role in the political process, the role of the legislative body in the totalitarian and authoritarian system is ceremonial at best or nominal at worst.

As was the case with anti-liberalism, the challenges to, and the denial of the legislature as the chief agency of the government, the primary democratic institution and as the agent of the sovereign people, come from both the left and the right. The legislature, be it the former Soviet Union's Supreme Soviet, China's National People's Congress or North Korea's Supreme People's Assembly, exists in the totalitarian system only as a nominal handmaiden to the party, and, ultimately, to its central leadership. The totalitarian system *negates* the legislature's independent role. The legislature is impotent yet an integral part of the party dictatorship. Thus, the legislature in the Western democratic sense is virtually non-existent.

The authoritarian system, on the other hand, *challenges* the independent legislature. In so doing, it either regards the legislative body as the source of nuisance or reduces its role to a rubber stamp of the state and of the leader, e.g., Führer, Duce. Thus, the legislature in the Western sense is not extinct but moribund. Needless to say, in the totalitarian system, too, the party dictatorship may lead to the personality cult, e.g., Stalin as *vozhd* and Kim Il Sung as *su-ryŏng*. But, unlike the leadership cult in the authoritarian system which stems primarily from the leader's *personal* charisma, the personality cult in the totalitarian system is often the outgrowth of *party* dictatorship.

To repeat, in the mono-party totalitarian system, the legislature is the tool of the party dictatorship. In the authoritarian system the legislature is criticized, cajoled, used or ignored, depending upon the ruling elites' power needs, their political make-up and the balance between the ruling party members and the opposition. In the totalitarian system, the legislative body is an interdependent part of the mono-party dictatorship. In the authoritarian system, it often poses a roadblock for the ruling party.

In short, the totalitarian system is *non-parliamentarian*, and the authoritarian system, *anti-parliamentarian*. In Arendt's word, only "a sham parliamentary system" exists in the totalitarian system.[38] From this standpoint, the North Korean totalitarian political order is non-parliamentarian, while the South Korean authoritarian political order is essentially anti-parliamentarian. To put it differently, the trials and tribulations of the South Korean National Assembly under the Rhee (1948-60), the Park (1964-1979), the Chun (1981-1988) and the Roh (1988-1993) governments, which will be discussed in some detail in the following chapter, are a classic testimonial to anti-parliamentarianism.

3. Corporatism

A trichotomy of pluralism, partism and corporatism is made here. Pluralism exists when interests represented by various groups are executed in voluntary, competitive and nonhierarchical fashion. And the state control over the interest groups is limited, at best, and the governmental decision-making is a compromise between the competing interests of different groups on varying issues. Pluralism assumes that groups have diverse, frequently contradictory aims, and group conflict is natural and not undesirable nor dangerous, as long as it is staged within the acceptable legal framework.

In a nutshell, pluralism is an alternative to, and a modification of, elitism in democratic systems, an idea that a set of small group of people make key decisions. The basic tenet of pluralism, for example, is that quite contrary to the elitist view of American democracy, the small group that runs urban redevelopment is not the same as those group that run public education, and neither is composed of the two small groups that run the two parties (For details, see Chapter Five).

Partism is a system of interest representation in which the constituent units are created by a single party which, in turn, controls various functional groups such as the trade unions, artist guilds and other professional organizations within the party. Partism exists if the single party or the dominant party controls the state and all the other constituent parts of political, societal and economic systems. Partism *is* an idea of a party-state. Party is neither an instrument of the state nor of the dictator, as in an authoritarian corporatist state. Nor is it an extragovernmental body which competes with other parties to gain control of the government. In a party-state, party *is* the state. More accurately, the state is created by the party as an instrument of political control along with other control mechanisms: the military; trade unions; women's associations; and others.

The role of the military in partism is especially noteworthy in that, as Perlmutter stated, the military is Janus-faced in the communist system, i.e., partism. The military is the guarantor of the civilian party regime and the protector of party hegemony. It may and will intervene in party affairs during hegemonic crises.[39]

Partism is "progressive" and future-oriented in that the violent conflict will end only when the exploiters, i.e., the capitalists, are replaced by the exploited, i.e., the proletariats. It posits that group conflicts are inevitable, and violent group conflicts are even desirable. The Leninist conception of society typifies partism in that the party as the vanguard of the proletariat (the "exploited class") must lead such conflict until a classless communist utopia is realized at home and abroad. Parties in the socialist countries, which seized power in the name of the proletariat, must justify (and have justified) their rule and role by advocating the coming of such utopia at home and abroad. Partism in this study closely resembles, in short, Schmitter's "monist model" or Sartori's "totalitarian unipartism."[40]

The term corporatism may refer to modes of political participation, types of political action, broad cultural traditions or a system of state-group relations. Or, it may mean a specific relationship existing between interest groups and the governing apparatus, i.e., state-group relationships or a particular regime type, e.g., Italian Fascism, a set of belief or an ideology, an explanation or an interpretation or an evolutionary stage.[41]

In this study, the term basically denotes a specific state-group relations. It exists, if interest representation by various groups is compulsory, noncompetitive and hierarchical. In Colliers' words, corporation as a system of state-group relations depends on: (1) state *structuring* of groups that produces a system of officially sanctioned, non-competitive, compulsory interest associations; (2) state *subsidy* of these groups; and (3) state-imposed *constraints* on demand-making, leadership and internal governance.[42] Hence, corporatism is a non-pluralist system of group representation. It is also anti-parliamentarian. It assumes that legislative assemblies based on geographic divisions, representing changing numerical majorities composed of individal citizens, and organized by competitive and potentially divisive political parties, are "artificial." Under corporatism citizens are organized and represented by the hierarchically structured, non-competitive and compulsory groups ("corporations") that are "found in the natural order." These corporations are mostly vocational in nature, such as farming, industry and the professions. The state regulates the relations among them and oversees the selection of leaders within each corporation.[43]

The Fascist Italy represents one of the earliest corporatist models, although corporatism antedates Fascism. Therefore, in Joes' view, all corporatists are not Fascists but all Fascists are corporatists. Under fascism the society is organized into state-controlled syndicates (unions), regional organizations and national corporations. Although the industry is not state-owned, the state controls the price and production through the national corporations and outlaws strikes and boycotts.[44]

Corporatism posits that group conflict is neither inevitable and legitimate nor beneficial. The dominant value of corporatism is "harmony," not "conflict" among groups: each group ("corporations") has its place, its duties and its right to survive in a state-controlled organic whole, i.e., the society. Hence, the struggles and conflicts within the state are unlawful, and different social classes must harmonize their aims in the national interest under the direction of the state. Hence, class cooperation, not class struggle, becomes a norm.

Schmitter, for one, contended that the principal difference between pluralism and corporatism lies in the role of the state vis-a-vis the interest group. The state is basically the compromiser in the former, and the controller, in the latter. Further, he distinguished between "state" and "societal" corporatism. The countries of Latin America, Southern Europe and many Third World, according to him, exemplify state corporatism in that the corporatized groups are "created by and kept as auxiliary and dependent organs of the state which found its legitimacy and effective functioning on other bases." By contrast, he used the term "societal" corporatism to describe systems of post-pluralist interest representation in advanced industrial societies. In such societies, corporative patterns of state-group relations have emerged in which "the legitimacy and functioning of the state [are] primarily and exclusively dependent on the activity" of the corporatized groups. In state corporatism, interest associations are dependent and penetrated, while in societal corporatism, they are autonomous and penetrative.[45] But as Skilling rightly pointed out, Schmitter's distinction between pluralism and corporatism is smudged by his further attempt to subdivide corporatism into "state" and "societal" types.[46] The same can be said about Joes' distinction between "democratic" and "authoritarian" corporatism. If corporatism, by definition, is undemocratic, it is anti-liberal and anti-parliamentarian.[47]

Schmitter, Linz, Stepan, Kaufman-Purcell and others also distinguished "old" from "new" corporatism. By old corporatism they meant an alliance between nonpopulist, military, Catholic, conservative, professional and syndicalist groups. New corporatism is characterized by the active intervention and continuous support of the military, which replaced old oligarchies and liberal politicians who failed to manage the crisis of modernization.[48] Their distinction is, however, confusing because "new" corporatism is basically analogous to praetorianism in the present study.

In recent years, more classification schemes of corporatism have emerged. Schmitter's trichotomy of pluralism, corporatism and syndicalism; Lehmbruch's liberal, statist and traditional corporatisms; Kvavik's competitive, corporate and statist pluralism are the cases in point. In his review essay, Almond characterized new corporatism as the "third wave" of interest group study.[49]

Confining to the politics of Latin America, O'Donnell, for instance, distinguished two subtypes of new corporatism: inclusionary-populist and exclusionary-bureaucratic. In inclusionary-populist corporatism the state's ruling elites attempt to forge a new equilibrium between state and

society through policies that utilize new economic model. They incorporate new political and economic forces, including the working classes,
into the system. They also ally themselves with the national bourgeoisie,
try to derive their legitimacy from populism, and consider the old oligarchy and foreign capital their enemies. By contrast, in exclusionary-
bureaucratic corporatism, the state's ruling elites maintain the state-soci-
ety equilibrium by the use of coercive policies and the restructuring of
the working class groups. They exclude any autonomous organizations
and groups and ally themselves with the international bourgeoisie and
technocracy. They regard populists, radicals and the autonomously organized working classes as their enemies. Their legitimacy is usually
derived from the established order.[50]

Again, on the basis of an analysis of the relationship between the state
and organized labor in Latin America, Colliers distinguished two separate patterns of corporatism. "Inducements," such as registration, monopoly of representation, compulsory membership and subsidy extended
by the state to win the cooperation of groups from "constraints," such as
the state's direct control on collective bargaining and strikes, demand-
making, leadership and internal governance, are the representative cases.[51]

Spalding's findings on the Mexican regime is also worth examination
here. She uncovered many corporatist features in the Mexican regimes --
the presence of a strong and active state, especially its architectural role
in stimulating political organization, molding social structures, providing the semblance of national integration, moderating class confrontations and keeping dissident forces in check. But she also discovered two
important constraints to fully coordinated state action. One, bureaucratic
enclaves exist which are not fully penetrated and controlled by the state
leadership. Two, a business elite has emerged. She contended that
although natural divisions within the business sector, such as foreign vs.
domestic capital, small vs. large scale firms and industrialists vs. agri-
business, can and do reduce its (business elite) strength, enough interests
converge on many key issues to make this elite a potent force in Mexico.[52]

Two crucial differences between partism and corporatism deserve
attention. One is the n: ure and role of the party. In partism, as in North
Korea, China and the former Soviet Union (for that matter, in all past

and present socialist countries), the communist party controls the state and its various interest and functional groups, while in corportism the governing party is only the instrument of the state. The other is the existence and role of private economic sector. In partism the private economic sector is either non-existent, or it is marginal, if it exists at all. In principle and by policy, private property, free enterprise and free market economy are either absent or severely restricted in partism. By contrast, corporatism signifies, by definition, the symbiosis between the state and the private economic sector.

In a corporatist state, the rivalry between the state, the technocracy and the military is purely functional. The dictator, though his rule may be ephemeral, is usually in complete control. Representatives to the legislative assemblies are chosen by the major functional and corporate interests—agriculture, commerce, industry—and by historical and classical corporate institutions—the military, the church and powerful families. The state dominates with the active support of the corporatist groups, such as the military, the technocrats and the church.

Corporatism is not a movement but a state-controlled partnership between government and interest groups. It begins and ends with the state, which is the pillar of such partnership. In a corporate state political mobilization is incidental and is mainly connected with serving the corporatist regime's need for legitimacy. One of the principal aims of corporatism is to modernize the machinery of the society's economic structure. To that extent, corporatism is the right's challenge to the left. It is an economic procedure designed to solve political problems outside of traditional political structures such as parliaments and political parties. Imbued with anti-parliamentary and anti-liberal ideas, consensus is sought, not from the masses but from organized interests through continual bargaining. Organized groups, including the military, participate in national policy making and exercise a political veto because the corporatist regime makes it costly for the government to resist the interests of these groups. It means that political bargaining is conducted usually outside of parliament through government ministries and bureaucracies that are dominated by organized interest groups. And the lines of distinction are blurred between society and state, parliament and the marketplace and class and nation. Power becomes dependent on the state bureaucracy, and ministries that regulate economic and domestic affairs become the nerve centers of the corporatist state.

In the process of securing the loyalty of the military, which is often the best organized and the most powerful institution, a corporate state elevates the military to the status of being the ultimate arbiter of politics. And more often than not, legitimacy is derived from membership in the corporatist hierarchy, where the military is sometimes equal to, and at other times predominant over, the other corporate entities—the church and the guilds. Herein lies a strong praetorian character of a corporatist state.

In fine, as it was clear in Part Three, the North Korean political system is the embodiment of the above-mentioned partism. By contrast, the South Korean political system posseses many features of corporatism, especially the elements of "state" instead of "societal," "old" rather than "new" and more "exclusionary" than "inclusionary" corporatism, although pluralistic features are not entirely absent. Spalding's two constraints on the dominance of the state—the existence of bureaucratic enclave and the emergence of a business elite—are also evident in South Korea. A significant point is that the South Korean governments have never been fully successful in making the intellectual community, especially the university students and some religious organizations "dependent" and compliant. More accurately, the state's assault on, and penetration into the "autonomy" of these communities and organizations, which staged recalcitrant resistance against such attempt, have been the woof and warf of the South Korean politics.

4. Developmentalism and Dependency

As Apter rightly indicated, all societies "develop" in some ways.[53] But developmentalism is not synonymous with development *per se*. It refers here to the idea that the state identifies economic growth as its top priority and acts as the prime mover without fundamentally undermining the market economic system. It refers to the situation in which the ruling elites of the so-called developing countries attempt to accelerate

the growth of their countries by establishing deliberate economic planning and development strategies. In developmentalism, unlike in the
command economic system, the state leads, but not owns and manages,
the economy. To the extent that developmentalism stresses the importance of economic development and the state's role, it is closely related
to state corporatism. To repeat, developmentalism is an economic facet
of state corporatism.

Two models of development are notable. One is the "world-system/
dependency" approach or the "neocolonial" model with its emphasis on
forces external to the nation-state, and the other, is the "modernization/
developmentalist" approach with its emphasis on internal mechanisms.
They differ each other in three main respects: 1) the role of foreign
investment, foreign trade and the multinational corporations (MNCs); 2)
the role of the state or the regime type; and 3) the nature of the relationship between the developed countries (the center) and the underdeveloped countries (the periphery). The dependency model posits that the
non-communist Third-World countries become dependent on an evolv-
ing international economic system dominated by the developed capitalist
powers, including Japan. According to Theotonio Dos Santos, dependency occurs when a number of countries' economy become dependent
on the development and expansion of another, thereby, placing these
countries in a backward position such that they become the target of
exploitation by the dominant countries.[54] The dependency advocates
contended that foreign investment depresses growth; that the core-
periphery or the north-south (the developed countries and the underdeveloped nations) relationship is basically exploitative; that profits are
transferred back to the core rather than reinvested in the periphery; that
economic dependency, thereby, contributes to the periphery's underdevelopment; and the external orientation of periphery economies generates internal distortions and contradictions that retard growth.[55] The
dependency advocates may be broadly divided into exclusive and inclusive schools: the former sees the idea as a phenomenon in capitalist
world. The advocates of this school, like Baran, Veliz, Frank, Dos
Santos, Sunkel, Furtado, Cardoso, Evans and Leys, usually have the
Marxist-Leninist orientations and try to associate the notion of depend-

ency only with international capitalism. [56] The inclusive school represented by Galtung, Walleri and Alschuler views it as a condition existing in both the capitalist and socialist systems.[57]

The dependency proponents may also be divided into the old and the new schools. The old dependency proponents view the political influence wielded by the Multinational Corporations (MNCs) as integral to the perpetuation of center capitalism's economic exploitation of the peripheral countries. The MNCs enlist the political support of domestic compradors, including powerful industrial and trade monopolists and wealthy landowners. This foreign and domestic coalition defends the existing feudal-mercantile order. The new dependency advocates, on the other hand, consider the industrial development of the Third-World countries as merely a new form of economic exploitation by the corporations from center capitalist countries. They regard development as being fostered by an alliance of the state, domestic capitalists and the MNCs, which exclude the masses from the benefits of such development. The new dependency proponents envision the state as an autonomous political actor in contrast to the old dependency advocates who considered it to be a mere handmaiden of foreign capitalists.[58]

The developmentalists or the proponents of the modernization approach, on the other hand, try to overcome underdevelopment and the persistence of tradition either by modernizing social, economic and political institutions or by transforming individuals through their assimilation of modern values. They advocate the rejection of procedures related to traditional institutions and the adoption of new (modern, i.e., Western) ideas, techniques, values and organizations. They try to adopt and adapt to the Western technology to assimilate its values and patterns of action and to import its financial, industrial and educational institutions.[59] Confining themselves to economic development, they assume that foreign investment promotes growth by providing external capital, which either substitutes for or supplements local capital. Their basic premises are that capital, whether it is in the form of direct investment or technology transfer, fosters growth, and its benefits spread throughout the economy.

In brief, as Valenzuelas stated, the modernization approach is be-

Sheahan, meanwhile, contended that if authoritarian rule were needed at all, its aim would be to implement more orthodox, market-oriented policies rather than the "deepening" remedy.[71] Recently, Cohen reported that the Brazilian and the Argentinian bureaucratic-authoritarian regimes are somewhat more effective than the Columbian democratic regime. The formers' annual growth rates have exceeded that of the latter by half a percent. He questioned whether an additional half a percent in annual growth rate of an economy justifies a turn to authoritariarism.[72] Epstein's case study of Argentina, Brazil, Chile and Uruguay is more unsettling. These countries' short term economic success under military regimes in the 60s and 70s notwithstanding, none has been able to do well in the 80s. He cautioned, however, that the economic failure of these regimes do not necessarily presage the disappearance of all authoritarian regimes in the region. Nor does it predict the success or failure of any civilian regime which replaces military rule.[73]

It is clear from the above that no definitive answers are supplied either by the developmentalists or the dependency advocates. At the same time, however, it can be argued that their views are often drawn from a different perspective on the same topic. The developmentalists tend to stress the *positive* effects of the foreign investment, the MNCs, the "hard" state and the economic linkages between the core and the periphery, while the dependency proponents focus on *negative* sides of such factors. At a minimum, as Tony Smith averred, the importance of domestic factors and the critical role of the state in economic development and the genuine gains in economic strength in the developing nations cannot be ignored.[74]

As it will become clear in Part Five, the picture of South Korea within the developmentalist/dependency controversy is, at best, mixed. South Korea has exhibited many features of both developmentalist and dependency models. On the whole, however, there is a general consensus among specialists that the South Korean economy, especially since 1960s, has been a success story. Unlike the case of Brazil and other Latin American countries, which pursued rapid growth through the exclusion of the mass of the population, the basic thrust of the South Korean economic strategy has been to incorporate its population into the

process of growth and sharing of benefits. In Donnelly's words, South
Korea has, by and large, avoided the needs tradeoff and the equality
tradeoff in its pursuance of rapid economic development, although it
certainly has made the liberty tradeoff substantially. In a similar vein,
James Cotton contends that South Korea cannot be seen as an example
of the bureaucratic-authoritarian state type. Neither its position in the
world system nor its industrialization strategy can be used to give a sufficient explanation of its political and social character. Although these
factors have played a part, he further argues, that particular historical,
political and cultural circumstances have permitted the state to enjoy a
degree of autonomy during the period of rapid social and economic
transformation from the 1960s to the 1980s.[75] To that extent, the developmentalist contentions, not the dependency arguments, are more apropos to the South Korean case.

Kohli and his associates, for instance, categorized South Korea as the
case of "moderate inequalities." Adelman and Robinson also pinpointed
that South Korea's export-led, open, labor-and skill-intensive growth
strategy between 1964-73 was a prime example of "hyper-growth" in
Asian economies. They reported that the South Korean economic performance from the mid-50s to the mid-70s has proven that the rapid
growth, needs satisfaction and high level of income equality can be
achieved simultanteously. Kuznets is even more optimistic. Like Japan,
which followed what Akamatsu called a "Wild-Geese Flying" patterns
of growth and industrial development (a sequence beginning with
imports, then import substitution to supply domestic markets, and finally, output for export), South Korea's industrial development, too, has
basically followed a Wild-Geese Flying pattern.[76]

As Donnelly aptly pointed out, there is no single central element to
the South Korean strategy, and no single part can be transplanted to
other countries in isolation with any hope of similar success. Its success
lied in the interconnection of multiple policy goals, strategies and instruments in achieving rapid growth and structural transformation of economy, substantial alleviation of absolute poverty and a relatively egalitarian income distribution. Still, a number of factors for this success are
noteworthy. One, South Korea adopted the strategy of export-oriented,

labor-intensive industrialization in a context of egalitarian rural development. Two, the importance of the active and authoritative role of state (which is similar to Myrdal's "hard state" or what Kuznets called the government's "economic activism") cannot be minimized.[77] The government played a central role in determining the direction and priorities of investment and development in general and restraining the workers' demand for higher wages and better working conditions. Three, abundant, cheap and disciplined labor force has been skillfully utilized in maintaining South Korea's comparative advantage in the new international divison of labor. In addition, the major land reform, the upgrading of skills through rapid educational development and the U.S. aid, advice and pressure, also, contributed significantly to the South Korea's rapid economic growth.[78]

On a somewhat broader plane, Kyŏng-dong Kim and his associates identified twelve factors which have been crucial for the South Korean development for the past 30 years (1954-1984). They are: 1) the bureaucracy and the military and their collaborative efforts toward modernization; 2) the international environment favorable to rapid growth; 3) *chaebŏl* [Korean business congromerates], or the Korean counterpart of Japanese *zaibatsu*, and their export-led economic development; 4) foreign-educated returnees and their leadership in all key areas; 5) working class as the backbone of economic growth; 6) strong desire for education; 7) science and technology as the leading edge of high-tech areas; 8) transportation and communication revolution as the prime mover of structural social changes; 9) urbanization as the base for capitalist industrialization; 10) materialism as the source of mass consumption; 11) opposition forces as the critical impetus; and 12) the rapid increase of religious population and their positive impact on growth.[79]

In fine, the South Korean development has been phenomenal, as compared with the cases of Latin American and other Third-World countries. Still, the South Korean success has been relative. The price of its economic success has been the severe restrictions on civil liberties and civil rights, the outbursts of official corruptions and scandals, and repressive atmosphere in political arena. The other sacrifices involved: the persistence of mass poverty (though extreme material deprivation has largely been alleviated); a gap between city and countryside; between regions, especially Yŏngnam and Honam areas; poor housing conditions; inadequate access to pure water; unsafe and unhealthy industrial working conditions; air, water and soil pollutions; urban traffic congestions; lack of housing; and serious economic and social discrimination of women. In the economic front, the hypergrowth of the 60s and 70s is over. A growing protectionist mood, especially in the developed countries must be overcome, and mounting foreign debts and balance-of-payment deficits must be resolved. On balance, the specter of the dependency syndrome still lurks in the background of the South Korean economic voyage, whose front is nevertheless unfolding with more open and optimistic vista of the developmentalists.

5. Praetorianism

Praetorianism refers to a situation in which military officers play a major or predominant political role by the virtue of their actual or threatened use of force. The Praetorian Guards of the Roman Empire is one of the oldest examples.[80] Praetorian soldiers, old and new, attempt to intrude into a clearly differentiated civilian political arena and to contravene the principles of legality, constitutionalism and civility. The reasons for their intervention in politics vary. There is no single, easily identifiable variable that can be used to explain or to predict the likelihood of their intervention. The causes may be endogenous, exogenous or some combination of the two. The endogenous sources of the military's praetorian proclivity are its unique organizational and professional qualities—a high degree of internal cohesion, a relatively advanced skill and management structure, career lines and a broad-based recruitment practice. The military's need to invervene in politics may also be propelled by such exogenous factors as the defense or enhancement of their own corporate interests—particularly military budgets, organizational autonomy, survival in competition with other government entities such as mass parties—and the failures of poorly institutionalized civilian governments to rule effectively and to promote economic growth, e.g., blatant corruption at all levels of government, the unconstitutional extension of the government's power and longevity, the excessively arbitrary application of the law and a reliance upon coercive measures to keep themselves in power.[81] Johnson and his associates reported that Black African states with relatively dynamic economies whose societies were not very socially mobilized before independence and which have maintained or restored some degree of political participation and political pluralism have experienced fewer military coups, attempted coups, and coup plots than those states with the opposite set of characteristics. Recently, J. Craig Jenkins and Augustine Kposowa analyzed 33 Black African military intervention cases from 1957 to 1984 and found that ethnic diversity and competition, military centrality, debt dependency and political factionalism are the major predictors of coup activity.[82]

In addition to the aforementioned general endogenous and exogenous causes of praetorianism, there are what Klieman called "the immediate circumstances for entry by the armed forces into politics." The application of crisis variants, such as state of siege, martial law or the state of emergency, usually serves as the "trigger event" for military intervention. Klieman identified three crises the professional military faces -- crises of conscience, of identity and of ideology -- in the said "trigger event" situation.[83]

Praetorians share certain common attitudinal attributes and behavioral patterns: bias against mass political activity and civilian politicians; protection of their corporate interests; and creation of authoritarian form of government. They also differ from each other with respect to the level of intervention and the range of objectives. Nordlinger, for one, classified praetorian officers into three prototypes—moderators, guardians and rulers. Praetorian moderators exercise a veto power over a varied range of governmental decisions and political disputes, usually under a civilian government. This situation is created when the civilian rule is pro forma and the real power resides in the military. Praetorian moderators act as highly politicized and powerful pressure groups to the civilian incumbents. Their objectives are usually to preserve the status quo and to maintain the existing balance (or imbalance) of power among contending groups. Such conservative demands are often met by explicit or implicit threats of a coup or by a displacement coup—replacing the existing civilian government with a new civilian government acceptable to them. Over time, praetorian moderators may themselves become guardians or rulers.[84]

Like praetorian moderators, praetorian guardians tend to be conservative in that they, too, attempt to stave off political change to maintain political order. The key difference between the two lies in the fact that the former controls the political process indirectly, while the latter assumes the power themselves. Several additional differences are observable. The guardians may try to effect mild political and economic changes, which include, among other things, the removal of squabbling, corrupt and excessively partisan politicians, the revamping of the governmental and bureaucratic machinery for greater efficiency and the redistribution of power and economic rewards to civilian groups. Praetorian guardians aim to correct the malpractices and deficiencies of the former civilian government such as sluggish economic growth, inflationary spirals, excessive public spending and balance-of-payment deficits.[85]

Praetorian rulers are far less frequent than either moderator or guardian types, constituting about ten percent of all military intervention in politics.[86] Praetorian rulers not only dominate the political process by their direct rule, but they attempt to make a fundamental political and socio-economic changes. Unlike the conservative orientations of praetorian moderators and guardians, praetorian rulers' objective is usually progressive. Praetorian rulers are interested in high-powered investment and modernization programs and more egalitarian redistribution of incomes and occupational opportunities. In doing so, they attempt to enact land and tax reforms, liberal farm loan program, the social security, medical and educational programs and nationalization of key industries. In short, praetorian ruler types are far fewer in number but more authoritarian than the moderator or guardian types, although all three are by definition authoritarian.[87]

From a somewhat different angle, Perlmutter analyzed three forms of the praetorian state or military dictatorship: personal, oligarchical and corporatist.[88] He assumed that the praetorian state draws its major support from the military establishment though the military may not interfere in administration of the state, the economy, the police and the military party. The military is the locus of power in the praetorian state. The personalist praetorian model is a despotic tyranny (Amin's Uganda, Bokassa's Central African Empire and Mobutu's Zaire) or a despotic patrimony (Somoza's Nicaragua, Trujillo's Dominican Republic and Duvalier's Haiti). The system depends heavily on graft and sycophants; it is actually a kleptocracy (government by the ripoff artist), totally dominated by the despot. The tyrant arbitrarily favors loyal regiments, but he does not control all of the military.[89]

The oligarchic praetorian model differs from the personalist in only one respect. In the oligarchic system, the military is autonomous. The military is always in a position to overthrow the military oligarchs, who depend on the military establishment for support.

In the corporatist praetorian model, two structural forms, corporatism and clientalism, converge. The government is the most powerful patron. Composed of military and technocratic groups, it dominates the corporatist social system. The military, the church and the governmental ministries with their bureaucrats and technocrats are autonomous corporatist groups. The corporations are internally and externally clientalistic and depend on the autonomous groups. Although the military, the church and the technocrats serve as the regime's main source of support, the military is the most powerful, which acts as the arbitrator of the corporatist system.[90]

Klieman, meanwhile, identified four basic models of the relationship between the military and civilian elites following the onset of emergency rule. They are nonintervention, direct military rule, indirect military rule and alternative succession.[91]

It is quite clear from the foregoing that neither Nordlinger's trichotomy of praetorian types nor Perlmutter's trichotomy of praetorian states fit the rulers and regime structures of South Korea. Klieman's four models, too, are not readily applicable to the South Korean case. Grossly simplified, the Park regime (1961-1979) and the Chun goverment (1981-1988) and to a far less extent the Roh regime (1988-1993) may be categorized as the praetorian government. Beyond this, however, it is extremely difficult, if not impossible, to categorize the Park, the Chun and the Roh governments into Nordlinger's, Perlmutter's or Klieman's typologies. Their models may be more useful and realistic if each type is seen *sequentially* rather than as a *separate* entity. There is no question that both Park, Chun and even Roh regimes have displayed some features of praetorian ruler-types and praetorian regime-types. Specifically, with the military coup d'etat of May 16, 1961, South Korea first witnessed a semblance of praetorian rule. Formally at least, from 1961 to 1964 may be classified as a period of direct military rule. It was only in 1964 that Park and his coup leaders shed their military uniforms and assumed power under a civilianized government. Similarly, from 1979 to 1981 was a period of *de facto* direct military rule. It was in 1981 that Chun and his mini-coup leaders emerged as the ruling elites of a newly civilianized government. The government under Park (1964-1979) and Chun (1981-1988) may be characterized as *civilianized* regimes rather than *civil* rule. Since the ideological orientations, political and economic objectives and the transformation of the relationship between the ruling civil and military elites of the Park, Chun and Roh regimes are extensively dealt with in Chapter 18, it suffices to point out here that the South Korean government, since the 1961 military coup, possesses several praetorian features.

Variants: Paradoxes and Peculiarities

Eight salient features of the South Korean authoritarian political order are here identified. They are the ideological paradox, the unification formula, the size principle, the inconstancy syndrome, the political symbiosis nexus, the security dilemma, the transfer-of-power issue and the political control apparatus. Since the unification formula, the security dilemma and the transfer-of-power issue are dealt with in separate chapters, only five factors are examined here in some detail.

1. The Ideological Paradox

Since the promulgation of the first ROK Constitution on July 17,

1948, nine constitutional amendments have been made (For details, see Table 10-2). This averages out to one amendment every four years for the past 39 years (1948-1987). Despite frequent constitutional revisions and the rise and fall of leaders, regimes and parties, an undiminished opposition to communism and the communist North Korea has been South Korea's ideological posture since the beginning of its republic. The strategies, policies and approaches to prevent, oppose, counter and ward off communism have varied from one regime to another and from one leader to the next. But all the regimes and leaders who have taken the South Korean political helm have adopted anti-communism as their paramount ideological posture (For details, see Chapter 5).

South Korea's anti-communism is, however, not a water-tight and systematic ideology like North Korea's communism. Aside from the varying strategies, policies and plans to counter communism in general and the North Korean communism in particular, South Korea's anti-communist ideological posture reveals two additional ingredients: the promise of a democracy and a free market economy. In rhetorics, if not in practice, all South Korean regimes have advocated "democracy," whether it is Rhee's and Chang's liberal democracy, Park's national democracy and "Korean democracy," Chun's "creative democracy," Roh's "democratization" or Kim's "civilianization." In sharp contrast to North Korea's socialist economy, South Korea has adopted the capitalist mode of economy with private property, free market and free enterprise system, although the government has often heavy-handedly intruded, intervened and even controlled various sectors and facets of its economy (For details, see Part Five).

Specifically, the constitutional pledge that the Republic of Korea is "a democratic republic" and the ROK's sovereignty "reside[s] in the people" (Article 1) remains unchanged. Even under the so-called *Yushin* [Revitalizing Reform] Constitution in 1972, which made President Park Chung Hee, the *de facto* president-dictator, the claims of "a democratic republic" and popular sovereignty remained intact in the Constitution. Such claims are, however, one thing and the authoritarian practices are quite another. Needless to say, as Myrdal poignantly reported in his seminal *American Dilemma*, a gap may exist between creed and conduct even in the democratic system such as the United States.[92] The ideal claims and the not-so ideal practices are commonplace, and the gap between the two are usually a matter of degree than of kind.

The paradox of Souch Korea's ideological posture is conspicuous in two aspects. First, the magnitude of the gap between the democratic ideal and the authoritarian reality in the South Korean political system is significant enough to warrant a new explanatory model, i.e., authoritarianism. This gap parallels the chasm separating North Korea's communist ideological ideal from its totalitarian reality. Second, closely related to the first is the rhetorical incongruence. The gap between the ideological ideal and the political practice in South Korea is glaring because of the rhetorical incompatibility between the democratic formula and the authoritarian rule. This gap is greatly reduced by the Roh regime's significant efforts for democratization and liberalization. Yet, the remnants of authoritarian practices in governing and authoritarian behaviors of political leaders of the ruling party and of the opposition are still visible and are not likely to be eradicated overnight. By contrast, such rhetoric-reality problem is non-existent in North Korea. Rhetorically, the North Korean ideological claims are *consistent* since dictatorship is proclaimed and practiced. It is true that while the DPRK Constitution vouchsafes "the dictatorship of the proletariat" (the 1972 Constitution, Article 10), or "the people's democratic dictatorship" (The 1992 Constitution, Article 12) in reality the dictatorship is in the hands of the WPK and Kim Il Sung (and now, Kim Jŏng Il). Unlike in South Korea, where democracy is avowed but authoritarianism is practiced, in North Korea *dictatorship* is espoused and practiced, but it is the party dictatorship or one man-one-party dictatorship *in the name of* the proletariat.

South Korean ruling elites have attempted to resolve the ideological paradox emanating from the gap between the democratic ideal and the authoritarian reality and the incongruity between the democratic rhetoric and the authoritarian practices in three ways. One has been the application of terminological devices, namely, adding prefix to "democracy": "national," "Korean," "creative" or others. The South Korean democracy is not simply a democracy but a special case applied to unique Korean

approximately 175 times larger than South Korea's ($2.8 billion). The 1962 GDP figure for Japan was $52.3 billion, which was 18 times larger than that of South Korea.[93] All in all, South Korea has made a substantial gain vis-a-vis the United States and Japan in economic development. Still, the fundamental asymmetry continues. The South Korean economy, considered by some as an "economic miracle," is miniscule compared to that of the United States or Japan.

South Korea's asymmetry in size and power vis-a-vis the United States and Japan and its erstwhile estranged relationship with the former Soviet Union and China has ushered in a kind of "dependency mentality." Dependency mentality refers to the attitudes, feelings and orientations of the ruling elites that South Korea cannot stand alone economically, politically and militarily in defending itself against the threats from North Korea, which is formally allied with the former Soviet Union and China. The logic behind dependency mentality runs thus: North Korea, if pushed from the South, can be driven to the land mass beyond the North Korean border, which happened briefly during the Korean War when the U.S.-led UN forces staged the offensive beyond the Yalu River. South Korea, on the other hand, if attacked from the North, can be driven toward the sea, as such a possibility was created when the capital was moved from Seoul to Pusan in the rapid withdrawal stage of the War in 1950.

Dependency mentality is evident in South Korean ruling elites' postures and policies toward the United States and Japan, which are regarded as the principal political and economic partners and the security insurers. After South Korea normalized its relationship with Japan in 1965, its hitherto unilateral dependency, especially in military and security areas, upon the United States has considerably changed. Currently, no security treaty exists between South Korea and Japan, comparable to the 1953 ROK-U.S. Mutual Defense Treaty. Nevertheless, Japan has not been an idle and indifferent bystander in South Korea's security concerns. To the contrary, beginning with the Nixon-Sato communique in 1969, Japanese prime ministers have all formally linked either South Korea's or the entire Korean Peninsula's security with Japan's.[94] For instance, a survey data indicated that the Korean people continue to regard the United States as the most important security ally and the biggest economic and cultural partner, although such American role has somewhat mitigated in recent years while their dependency on Japan in all these areas is slowly increasing. Still, the U.S. presence in the Korean people's mind is overwhelming (For details, see Table 10-4).

As stated elsewhere, dependency mentality can be compared to an umbilical cord. Severing the umbilical cord is the baby's first act of independence from his/her mother, although his/her mother's care and nurture will continue after the birth.[95] In a similar vein, more self-reliant and independent postures and policies toward the United States and Japan can be likened to severing the umbilical cords, not destroying the relationships *per se*. Security assistance and economic cooperation from the United States and, perhaps, Japan must continue, but without dependency mentality. Several points deserve particular attention on this issue.

The South Korean ruling elites have consciously tried to reduce their dependency mentality over the years, especially since Park Chung Hee's military coup in 1961. From the unilateral dependency on the United States to the bilateral dependency on the United States and Japan to the multi-lateral linkages with the countries in Asia, Africa, Latin America, Western Europe and even Eastern bloc areas have been their formal policy goals. The experiences gained from the Vietnam War and the Arab Oil Crisis of 1973-74 have led to the diversification of South Korea's economic, security and other concerns. Economically, South Korea's lopsided trade dependence on the United States and Japan has been considerably reduced, although they are still the two leading partners. In security area, the U.S. military presence, some 40,000 strong, and the South Korean military's dependence on weapons and other operational concerns still continue, although the U.S. role has become more symbolic than substantive. Nevertheless, the presence of the U.S. forces in South Korea transcends symbolic assurance. At a minimum, the U.S. input into the South Korean military (and, thus, politics) continues to be crucial and critical.

The United States' actions and responses to the circumstances surrounding Park's demise and Chun's rise to power are particularly noteworthy. First, the U.S. government promptly announced that it would "react strongly" to an outside attempt (meaning North Korea) to exploit the uncertainty resulting from Park's assassination on October 26, 1979, by his right-hand man, Kim Chae-kyu, the Director of the KCIA. Two days later, the U.S. gave more specific and concrete signals. One U.S. aircraft carrier and two radar warning planes (AWACS) were dispatched to South Korea to deter "North Korea from taking military advantage of political confusion" in the area.

On December 11, Major General Chun Doo Hwan, the Commander of the Defense Security Command (*Boansa*) staged a military putsch. Chun and his group arrested sixteen military generals, including Gen. Chŏng Sung-hwa, the martial law commander and the army-chief-of-staff. The first stage of Chun's military take-over was, thus, completed, although the Ch'oe Kyu-ha care-taker administration nominally ruled until June 16, 1980. Interestingly, the troops under Chun during his putsch were technically under the joint American-South Korean command, i.e., the Combined Forces Command headed by the U.S. General John A. Wickham.

The second stage of Chun's take-over was prompted by the outbreak of the Kwangju Uprising from May 18 to 27, 1980. A day earlier, martial law was declared throughout the country and the military crackdown of student activists, opposition political leaders and hard-core liberal intellectuals was carried out. Although all the facts surrounding the Chun's maneuver and the Kwangju Uprising are still unknown, it appears the Kwangju Uprising was not the precipitant or the direct cause of Chun's move. It seemed to have been prompted by the Ch'oe Kyu-ha government stalling the speedy political transfer and declaring the nation-wide martial law. In any case, the suppression of Kwangju revolt by the military forces left an indelible political scar. During this uprising, some 230 people were reportedly killed, although the unofficial casualties vary from 600 to 2,000.[96]

The U.S. reacted discretely to this second stage of Chun's move. On May 19, the U.S. government issued the statement that it was "deeply disturbed" by the extension of martial law and reiterated that "progress toward constitutional reform and the election of a broadly based civilian government should be resumed promptly." On May 22, amidst the

Kwangju Revolt, the U.S., again, sent two AWACS planes to Okinawa and an aircraft carrier, *Corral Sea*, was dispatched to the South Korean waters from the Philippines. Two days later, Park's assassin, was executed. Noteworthy was the fact that both for his first putsch and for his suppression of the Kwangju revolt, Chun used the troops, released by Gen. John A. Wickham, commander of the U.S.-ROK Combined Forces Command.

The third and final stage of Chun's take-over was synchronized with the formation of the Special Committee for National Security Measures (*Kukbowi* or SCNSM) on May 31. The SCNSM was created ostensibly to "aid the president in directing and supervising martial law affairs and to examine national policies." In reality it replaced the key government policy making apparatus to play the midwifery role in the creation of the Fifth Republic. The SCNSM was the functional equivalent of the Supreme Council for National Reconstruction (SCNR), which was created in the wake of the May 16 Military Coup D'etat in 1961.

The similarities between Chun's take-over and Park's rise to power do not end here. Like Park, who promoted himself from the rank of major general to general before he retired from the army to assume the presidency in 1964, Chun, too, rose from the rank of major general to general before taking over the presidency. Like Park, who after consolidating his power in November 1961, visited the US to confer with John F. Kennedy, Chun, also, after securing his political power, met with Ronald Reagan in February 1981.

The U.S. government commented when the SCNSM was established: "The U.S. would evaluate the role of the new committee through its actions rather than words in the coming days and weeks." Of particular importance is Gen. Wickham's open endorsement of Gen. Chun for the presidency in his press interview with the *Los Angeles Times* on August 13. Both the U.S. State and Defense departments denied the newspaper story that the U.S. issued a supporting statement for Chun's presidency. The fact that Wickham was the highest ranking U.S. military officer stationed in South Korea and also the fact that his statement was widely publicized at a critical juncture in South Korean political situation speak for themselves. In any case, three days after the Wickham's interview,

Ch'oe Kyu-ha resigned from the presidency. As expected, Chun retired from the military on August 22. On August 27, Chun was elected president by the National Conference of Unification with 2,524 votes out of 2,525. Chun's immediate task, then, was to dismantle Park's so-called Revitalizing Reform Constitution of 1972. A new constitution was drafted on September 29, and it was approved by national referendum on October 22, 1980.

Meanwhile, in the United States the change of command took place in the White House. The Chun's Wasington liaison had contacted the Reagan transition team even before Reagan's inauguration. As early as June 1, Bruce Cumings in his *Newsday* column asserted that "U.S. acquiesced and even backed for the Korean military." Donald L. Ranard contended in his column in the *Los Angeles Times* that three days after his inauguration President Reagan made an "unpalatable deal with the Korean military: Spare Kim Dae Jung and Korea's Gen. Chun Doo Hwan could visit the United States." Alexander M. Haig, Secretary of State, denied that such "deal" was struck at his first press conference. The facts reveal otherwise: Chun visited the White House as one of the first foreign heads of state after Reagan's inauguration. On February 2, 1981, on the eve of South Korea's national election, Chun and Reagan formally reversed Carter's U.S. troop withdrawal plan.

To follow-up the Chun-Reagan meeting, the joint communique of the 13th Annual Security Consultative Meeting between the Republic of Korea and the United States was resumed in San Francisco, California, from April 29 to 30, 1981. This meeting reaffirmed, among other things, that "the security of the Republic of Korea is pivotal to the security of the United States." Specifically, U.S. Secretary of Defense Caspar Weinberger reiterated the United States' firm commitment to render prompt and effective assistance to repel armed invasion against the Republic of Korea in accordance with the Mutual Defense Treaty of 1954. He also pledged the continued presence of the United States' nuclear umbrella, the ROK-U.S. cooperation in the development of South Korea's defense industry, the further enhancement of combined ROK-U.S. defense capability and the Combined Forces Command (CFC), the upgrading of the U.S. Second Infantry Division and the deployment of A10s and F16s to bases in South Korea.[97] Thus, the U.S.-South Korean security relations returned to the familiar track.

In brief, the United States has been the single most influential external actor and partner in shaping South Korea's political, economic and military landscapes since the days of the U.S. military government. The United States was (and still is) "a state within a state" in South Korea. Fairbank called South Korea the model example of the United States' "client state."[98] Reischauer went even further. He likened the American period since World War II in South Korea to the preceding thirty-five years of Japanese colonial rule.[99] Hodgson called President Park Chung Hee the "surrogate" of the U.S.[100] Besides the United States, Japan has emerged as the other major actor and partner in South Korea's economic (implicitly political and military as well) arena since 1965.

Some sources of the dependency mentality are inherent in the Korean geography, history and even culture. The cures for this syndrome are, therefore, not readily available. Recognizing the inherent geopolitical asymmetry is the first step. Severing the mental umbilical cord, attached to the U.S. and Japan is the next step. A gradualist and independent approach in regard to South Korea's relationships with these nations is necessary. Disposing of the small state-weak power mentality and acquiring the middle power orientation is a prerequisite. While South Korea's physical size is unalterable, it can be compensated by her economic and political dynamics, as the gradual changes in relations between Korea and the U.S. and Japan have demonstrated over the past forty years.

3. Inconstancy Syndrome

To begin with, four observations, two on the Korean character and two on the character of the Korean politics, are meaningful. In *East Asia: The Great Tradition*, Reischauer and Fairbank characterized the Chinese, the Koreans and the Japanese as follows:

> All (the Chinese, the Koreans, and the Japanese) appear to have a stronger aesthetic bent than do the peoples of most other parts of the world, but when compared with one another the Koreans seem somewhat

volatile in contrast to the relaxed but persistent Chinese and the more tensely controlled Japanese.[101]

Osgood's study of the Koreans and their culture reached essentially the same conclusion. He described the Koreans as "innately emotional" and "intrinsically the most deeply religious people of the Far East." (Note here that according to Korea Gallup's recent survey, foreign residents in Korea believe that Koreans are very emotional (50.7%) which received the highest ranking in Korean people's traits). By contrast, the Japanese are exquistitely sensitive and esthetic "without equal" and the Chinese are "mature, highly rational, emotionally restrained, and effectively productive."[102] He attributed the peppery character of the Korean people *inter alia* to their natural environment:

> The cycle of the seasons brought its turn of hot summer, with sudden need for an intense spending of energy in the accumulation of food, and afterwards the snow of frozen winter to seal the people into the silence of their valley settlements. First rest, then exuberance, followed by the compression of long nights, the load of pent-up emotions, fears, speculations, and anxiety. This is the aboriginal calendar of cold for northern latitudes. The imagined prototype of the Korean personality is an introverted individual with considerable emotional instability, capable of the sustained quiescence of the hibernating bear and of the fury of the goaded tiger.[103]

His observation on the Korean youth is also very illuminating. The typical Korean youth is "cut off from most of the few sources of manifest affection;" he hates his dominating father; he is deprived of intimacy with the female sex since he cannot even approach the girls who might normally attract and absorb his energy and thus, physical satisfaction and ego gratification are lacking. He wrote further :

> The lack of ego gratifications shows itself in the frequency with which Koreans demonstrate or verbalize their desire to undertake actions of heroic proportions. They will risk the most cruel punishments for the sake of a religious belief or a political cause.... His talk and expectations, irrespective of any evidence of either hard work or genius, set a standard which would be satisfied only by his becoming a Rockefeller or Rachmaninoff... the Korean goal is to be a hero. All this is very frustrat-

ing and rarely results in expression which is adequately satisfying to the ego. The Koreans quarrel interminably without decision, the men will battle physically for hours and in the end one can seldom ascertain who defeated whom. Riots frequently cause no more damage than carnivals. Socially or politically, action is seldom brought to a sharp conclusion.[104]

Henderson, meanwhile, observed the Korean politics as "the politics of the vortex." He wrote:

> In Korea... the imposition of a continuous high degree of centralism on a homogeneous society has resulted in a vortex, a powerful, upward-sucking force active throughout the culture. This force is such as to detach particles from any integrative groups that the society might tend to build—social classes, political parties, and other intermediary groups—thus eroding group consolidation and forming a general atom-ized upward mobility.... The overwhelming problems of power-access that this dynamic creates tend further to the formation of what might be called broad-surface access. The function of broad-surface access is to absorb the maximum number of power aspirants. Because they operate in a homogeneous environment lacking natural cleavages of issues, color, religion, or culture, such needs for access produce artificial fis-sures on the broad surface of government and contention for it via a series of rival aspirant councils (or, under communion, factions) battling over issues generated by contrived hostility and verbal acerbity rather than by belief or vested interest. Rivals compete for the same object in the same way without the possibility of negotiated solution.[105]

Professor Pye makes some very perceptive and penetrating observa-tions on Asia in general and Korea in particular. To cite a few examples, he believes that "in the private calculus of most Asian leaders the gratifi-cation of being thought the supreme figure for the moment outweighs any calculations as to what history may say of them." On Korea he observes that "the ultimate strength of the Korean system lies less in particular institutions or social groupings than in the people's tenacious sense of solidarity and national pride. Koreans are contentious, prone to divisive attacks and self righteous assertions of their individual rights; but they are still deferential and they believe in self-sacrifice. Hence, conflicts which at one moment seem to be taking the community to brink of civil strife can suddenly be contained in favor of the higher imperative of disciplined harmony." He further observes:

> "(Korean) students who have been actively engaged in disseminating
> poisonous rumors that their professors are government agents can, on
> being reminded of their obligations, become suddenly deferential. But it
> is just as likely that reverential students will suddenly assert unorthodox
> views. Similarly, workers can be on the verge of a strike and then
> reverse themselves, even making sacrifices for the interests of the enter-
> prise. They will explain that it is like being a member of a family, that
> the intensity of their criticism is legitimized by their loyalty to the collec-
> tivity. These contradictory characteristics make it hard to anticipate
> developments in Korea, especially since the dominant pattern is to pull
> back into a disciplined mode just before the reckless instinct assumes
> command, although at times the controls are too weak to prevent the
> damaging act from occurring. The basic Confucian concept that authori-
> ty should be omnipotent, which is at the root of the Korean legitimacy
> problem, makes it difficult for any occupant of the Blue House to build
> coalitions in the society and thereby to construct a broad-based establish-
> ment. The Korean view of power makes delegation impossible; indeed,
> the contrary forces prevail in that all decisions must flow up to the Blue
> House, making it the perennial target for criticism."[106]

Korean volatility, extreme emotional instability, the politics of a vortex
and the paradox of self-righteous assertions and of disciplined harmony
observed by Reischauer-Fairbank, Osgood, Henderson and Pye, respectively, resemble what is called here the inconstancy syndrome. All five
refer, more or less, to a high degree of unpredictability, transiency,
evanescence and mutability of the Koreans and their politics. However,
the views expressed by Reischauer and Fairbank and Osgood are broadest in that they refer to the Korean people themselves. Henderson's
vortex model is still broader than the inconstancy syndrome in that he
applies it to the North and South Korean politics. The inconstancy syndrome is much narrower in scope; it deals only with the South Korean
politics. Specifically, it denotes a highly transient and unpredictable
nature of the South Korean politics, the lack of organizational, especially party, durability and the mercurial nature of personalties and loyalty.

As noted earlier, the vortex model is less useful to the power rivalry
between North and South Korea. North Korea's communism and its

variant applications and South Korea's anti-communism and related policy choices are not merely "contrived" and verbally "acerbic," but real and fundamental. Again, his concept is rather irrelevant to the internal North Korean politics. The fact that the Kim Il Sung regime has lasted since the founding of the DPRK annuls Henderson's vortex model. Kim's rule has been, in fact, one of the most durable in the world. There have been factions and factional struggles in North Korea but some, be they Kim's own Partisan Group, the erstwhile Yanan Group, the WPSK Group or the Domestic Group, were formed by a common vested interest and enduring human ties than by "contrived hostility and verbal acerbity."

The inconstancy syndrome is, however, clearly evident in South Korean politics, which has been marked by frequent disruptions and instability. The "true believers" in South Korean politics are, indeed, rare. They are few in number and are the "endangered political species." They are the men of *mannyŏn yadang*, or the enduring opposition core, who stay in opposition despite the regime changes from Rhee to Roh. They criticize, oppose and even attempt to wreck the ruling regime's policies, plans and programs. They are often thrown into jail by the ruling government, but they remain stoic.

The overwhelming majority of the power aspirants lacks party loyalty, personal allegiances and philosophical convictions. As parties stay in and out of power, they, too, switch to parties in power freely and unscrupulously. The men of *mannyŏn yŏdang*, an enduring ruling core, remain in the ruling regimes and parties regardless of the regime and party changes. Frequently, those in the opposition join the party in power. Commonly, those from the defunct old ruling party join the new ruling party. Several ruling parties have risen and fallen, but many from the past ruling parties have joined the present ruling party. Ultimately, the power binds them temporarily; they share neither the vested interests nor the ideological principles. They instinctively support the regime in power; they seldom question its legitimacy and simply go along with it. To the true believers, they appear to be the betrayers, turncoats and even traitors, but to them, their behavior repesents survival instincts, realistic power plays and smart politics.

Needless to say, all politics, democratic or dictatoral, Oriental or Occidental, are by nature highly transcient, unpredictable and even unreliable. From this standpoint, the inconstancy syndrome of the South Korean politics is merely more conspicuous and chronic than that of other nations. South Korea's inconstancy syndrome has been exacerbated by multiple causes. The causes are, among other things, the political instability stemming from frequent regime changes and cabinet reshufflings; the condition of virtually unlimited political aspirants' demand for positions and the acute shortage of such supply; near absence of ethnic, religious, linguistic and cultural heterogeneity, which may form enduring subgroups (except regional, kinship and school ties). In a way, Henderson's vortex model and the inconstancy syndrome are reminiscent of the old Korean saying: when the prime minister's dog dies, throngs of people come and mourn for it, but when the prime minister dies, not even his dog would appear to mourn for him.

4. Political Symbiosis Nexus

Since the May Military Coup d'etat of 1961, a powerful and enduring symbiotic civil-military alliance has become a permanent political fixture in the arena of South Korean politics. This is an alliance formed among high ranking bureaucrats, business executives, industrialists, military officials, civilian politicians and intellectuals in mass media and academia, primarily to protect and promote mutually compatible vested interests and values. This may be the South Korean equivalent of the American military-industrial complex on the South Korean version of praetorianism and corporatism.

The South Korean civil-military fusion did not, however occur overnight. Nor was it created by Gen. Park Chung Hee and his military regime after 1961. Syngman Rhee had already manipulated the war-swollen South Korean military for his political aims as early as 1952, but civilian supremacy was kept intact. It should also be noted that the South Korean military had not been a monolithic group but consisted of many disparate elements infested with factionalism of regional and educational background, although in recent years such divisions have been declining.[107]

Nevertheless, Gen. Park and his military government gave new impetus and momentum to such an alliance and replaced the civilian supremacy principle with the new formula of military dominance. After the initial military rule (1961-64), when Park launched his new civilianized government in 1964, the military infusion into South Korean politics became routine. When Park became a civilian president, many military officers and generals followed his lead. Senior officers and generals were appointed ambassadors, foreign envoys or the heads of the government corporations, government-controlled businesses and corporations and para-governmental agencies and organizations. The Park government also launched a program to place junior level military officers into the mid-level government positions. Graduates of South Korean military academies and military officers were actively recruited for mid-level civil servce jobs through a nominal civil service examination.

Ex-military officials occupying positions in all levels of government, business and industry in South Korea is nothing unusual. Reallocating the skilled personnel from the military into the government and business sector where they are needed is even an economically sound policy. Considering the sheer number of the South Korean military forces and the corresponding retirees from the various branches of the military services, it is also inevitable to a certain extent that a significant number of the ex-military personnels work in the civilian government and business sectors. Park, Chun and Roh's practice was unusual because it was often *politically* motivated. The penetration of the ex-military personnel and active military academy graduates into the civilian government and business sectors had given the Park, Chun and Roh regimes a safety-valve, that is, a significantly militarized pro-government bureaucracy and industry.[108]

The civil-military political symbiosis in South Korea is also backed by its value congruity. Generally speaking, modern bureaucracy and modern army require similar skills and expertise in their respective organizational management and control. Theories advanced by Huntington, Janowitz and Perlmutter illustrate the tendency of fusion between the military and civilian professionals. Huntington contended that the military will become increasingly influential in the making of national security policy and thus fusion between the military and the bureaucracy will be inevitable. Similarly, Janowitz pointed out that the professional officers develop skills and orientation common to civilian administrators and leaders. Perlmutter was more direct: "the relationship between military and state becomes symbiotic." The old virtues of bravery and discipline of the military are replaced by the skills of management and strategy, erasing the antagonisms or differences between the military and civilian bureaucracy. Thus, no gulf separates "civilian" from "military" minds. Huntington and Perlmutter differed, however, in their assessment of military intervention in politics. The former believed that the transition from professionalism, involving a balance in expertise, responsibility and corporateness, to corporatism, leading to military intervention in politics, is a *perversion* of military professionalism. The latter, by contrast, argued that professionalism leading to corporatism, which provides a motive for military intervention in politics, is more or less a *natural outgrowth*, not a perversion. Despite such differences, both agree that common management skills and expertise make military men and bureaucrats *technocrats*, whose values become more congruent than disparate.[109] The value congruity between the military and the bureaucracy can be extended to business executives. Russet, for instance, found in his survey that "in the United States, military and business elites are not measurably different...on domestic issues of civil rights, civil liberties, and income distribution."[110]

A number of studies exploring similar questions on South Korean military and civilian elites support the premise that her military and civilian bureaucrats, business enterpreneurs and politicians share congruent values and expectations. Eugene C. I. Kim's study showed that "party elites in South Korea demonstrate a remarkable degree of political value congruity regardless of their professional, military or nonmilitary background." Both ex-military and nonmilitary elites, for instance had low political participation levels and public trust, and the differences were minimal in their respective orientations on leadership, conflict resolution and national and local orientation issues. Kim further posited that South Korean military and civilian elites are intimately fused in terms of leadership composition and value congruity. Kim wrote:

> The current military (Park) regime is as much civilian as military.... It is a third-world authoritarian system, strongly anchored in the military, but with a large number of civilian politicians and technocrats co-opted into the governing structure."[111]

Although Kim's analysis was confined to the Park regime, it can be easily applied to the Chun and the Roh governments as well.

The study by Bark and Lee on senior South Korean bureaucrats revealed that the bureaucratic elites of both civilian and military backgrounds place a lower priority on democratic norms such as civil liberties and free press than on national security and economic growth. However, slight variations exist among bureaucrats with military backgrounds. Those, for instance, who entered civilian public administration *after* the 1961 Coup tended to agree more on the need for public mindedness, task accomplishment and institutional change than those who had joined it *before* the Coup.[112] Similarly, Chung and Pae's study stated that "a majority of Korean bureaucrats, young and old, have low confidence in the average voter and low support for decentralization and subsystem autonomy.[113] Another study by Kim and Woo revealed that even South Korean legislators in the National Assembly showed a low degree of commitment to the democratic principles of majority rule and minority rights, accountability and adaptability. They found that the legislators elected from single-member districts tended to hold a higher commitment to democratic principles than those of the opposition New Democratic Party. More importantly, they discovered that the higher the educational level, the lower the democratic commitment among the legislators, regardless of party affiliations. The Kim-Woo findings strongly suggested that the party differences are insignificant with regard to commitment to democratic principles. Simply put, Korean legislators showed a low commitment to democracy, irrespective of their party affiliations.[114]

In addition to the various findings in the above that the South Korean civil-military elites lack strong commitment to democracy, one survey on the South Korean population also draws the same conclusion. According to Lee's survey, less than one-half of the adult population exhibited some commitment to fundamental democratic values and beliefs, while a majority still holds authoritarian Confucian values. He discovered that many citizens showed apathy or even antipathy in some cases toward the key democratic principles. He concluded that the Korean citizens show neither a strong support for the fundamental principles of democracy nor a crystallized ideology of democratic government.[115]

It is evident from the above that South Korean political elites with or without military backgrounds, let alone the people, share a high degree of value congruity, i.e., a low commitment to democratic values and principles. If the findings regarding the inverse relation between education and democratic commitment is not confined to South Korean national legislators, then highly educated business and intellectual elites in mass media and academe are also likely to hold an equally low commitment to democratic values and principles. The fact that the majority of these elites, be they legislators, bureaucrats, military, business executives or intellectuals, have been partners, participants and beneficiaries of the Park, Chun and Roh regimes, which have had a low commitment to democratic values and principles, make the question in point more intriguing and disturbing. One thing is quite certain. The power of Chun and Roh, as it was in the case of the Park regime, is not simply founded upon the military's sheer naked force, but upon a symbiotic alliance of the military, civilian, business and intellectual elites in mass media and academe.

5. The Political Control Apparatus

All governments, democratic or dictatorial, possess some form of political control apparatus. To distinguish democratic from dictatorial or liberal from authoritarian government is not the presence or absence of political control apparatus *per se,* but rather in how it is created, and for what purpose it is utilized by the government. From this standpoint, the various political control apparatuses of the present government were created to maintain and strengthen its rule. The control apparatuses include anti-Communist and security laws, measures and decrees, politicized military, police and other enforcement agencies, and political and parapolitical infrastructure. Some laws, such as the Anti-Communist Law and the National Security Law, had existed prior to the Park regime; however, under Park these laws became not only tougher, but new laws have been added. The new laws and measures included Central Intelligence, the Extraordinary Measures for National Reconstruction, the punishment of persons in illicit elections, the Political Activities Purification, the disposition of illicit fortunes, the punishment of special crimes and the National Protection (*Kukabowibŏp*) laws. Under the Chun regime, the KCIA was renamed the Agency for National Security and Planning, and the Social Purification Commission was created.

Like the Supreme Council for National Reconstruction (SCNR), an extraconstitutional governing body created during Park's military coup in May, 1961 till he assumed the civilian presidency in 1964, the Chun government instituted the Special Committee for National Security Measures (SCNSM) until he became president in August, 1980. The SCNSM was created on May 31 in the wake of the May 18 Kwangju Uprising of 1980. Unlike the SCNR, the SCNSM was short-lived. It was replaced by the Legislative Assembly for National Security in late October of the same year.

Under Park the South Korean military and his ruling Democratic Republican Party (DRP), now defunct, were the two principal institutional pillars of his political control. Specifically, Park's institutionalized control apparatuses included, *inter alia*, his Security Service (*Kyunghowŏn*), the CIA, the Military Intelligence Agency (*Boan-sa*), the Counter-Espionage Operations Command (*Bangch'ŏpdae*) and the Capital City Military District Command (*Sudokyŏngbi-sa*). Also included in this category were the highly politicized police force, especially military police (*Chŏngyŏng*), law enforcement agencies with prosecutors in the Ministry of Justice and the pliant judiciary. Other parapolitical and/or paragovernmental infrastructures were also numerous. The National Reconstruction Movement Corps, now defunct, was one of the earliest examples. Still in operation are the New Village Movement (*Saemaul Undong*), the militia (*Minbangwi*), the Home District Military

Reserve (*Hyangt'oyebigun*) and other veteran and anti-Communist organizations such as the Anti-Communist League (*bangongnyŏnmaeng*), which is now called the All Liberty League (*chayu ch'ongyŏnmaeng*). In 1969 Park also institutionalized the unification issue by establishing the National Unification Board, which regulated the flow of private and independent unification ideas and formulae. Also, government propaganda through the Ministry of Culture and Information and the Propaganda Association (*Hongbohyŏphoe*) and the suppression of private press and mass media through censorship, constituted a significant part of Park's political control apparatus. As noted in the above, a few nominal or organizational changes had been made by the Chun and Roh regimes. For example, under the Roh Regime, *Boan-Sa* was renamed *Kimu-sa*, and the Ministry of Culture and Information was divided into two separate ministries—the Ministry of Culture and the Ministry of Public Information. Still, virtually all the political control instruments since the Park regime continue to operate in the present Kim government.

Two main features of the South Korean political control apparatuses under the Park, Chun and Roh governments were the *politicization* of the national security issues and of the military. Doubtless, the division of the country, the legacy of the Korean War, the possibility of renewed military flare-up and the on-going intelligence and espionage warfare between the North and the South had created a unique political situation which made the national security issue one of the chief concerns of the South Korean government. Worse still, incidents of "provocations" between North and South had been numerous although the "provoker" is sometimes difficult to distinguish from the "provoked." Some notable cases are: the North Korean commandoes' infiltration of the Blue House, Park's presidential residence on January 21, 1968; the seizure of the United States intelligence reconnaissance ship, *Pueblo*, on January 23, 1968; the shooting down of a United States Navy EC-121 reconnaissance plane on April 15, 1969; the killing of two United States army officers at the DMZ on August 18, 1976; the discovery of three North Korean underground tunnels, reported in November 1974, March 1975 and October 1978; and, the Rangoon Incident of October 9, 1983, in which four South Korean ministers and twelve other people died in the bomb explosion at Aung San's mausoleum in Rangoon, Burma (Myanmar).

Granted these countless provocations directed against South Korea by North Korea were true, one thing still seems to be self-evident; namely, the *timing* of some of these "incidents" had often been politically calculated or manipulated. The espionage rings, countercoup attempts, revolutionary conspiracies and others had usually appeared during the times of internal political unrest and/or external political uncertainties. To that extent, the claims that the South Korean government had frequently politicized national security issues for their own domestic political needs, are not entirely groundless.

Whenever the South Korean government's routine application of anti-Communist and national security laws and measures got out of hand, and whenever its politicization of national security issues failed to bring forth order and stability, the military, the single largest and the most potent organized force, has often intruded into politics to serve as the ultimate control apparatus. The military intervention in politics had often been justified in the name of "national survival." In reality, what was at stake was not "national survival" per se but the "regime survival." In any case, the politicized military had fulfilled two missions—rescue and rule. The South Korean military intervened in politics either to rescue its leader (Park or Chun) from falling in the midst of rampant political opposition or to execute the plans, programs and proposals that could not be executed otherwise. As a case in point, from 1961 to 1979 Park declared half a dozen national and/or regional martial laws. On each occasion the military intervened and restored order, thereby, enabling Park to control the political opposition and to complete his intended political agenda—necessary constitutional amendments, ratification of the ROK-Japan normalization treaty, the sending of South Korean troops to Vietnam and the creation of the revitalized constitution.[116]

South Korea was under martial law from May 16, 1961, until December 5, 1961, during which Park passed a series of "extraordinary" laws, measures and acts. Again on June 3, 1964, martial law was declared in Seoul to control student demonstrations against the Korea-Japan normalization talks. Martial law was lifted on July 29 but was reinstated in Seoul on August 26 when student protests erupted over the ratification of the Korea-Japan Normalization Pact. The unrest in Pusan and Masan areas led to the declaration of martial law on October 18, 1979, which was Park's last emergency act as the President. Park's assassination on October 26, 1979, produced another martial law on the following day. The martial law was climaxed by the Kwangju Uprising on May 17, 1980. This longest martial law ended on January 24, a month before the inauguration of Chun Doo-hwan as the twelfth president on February 25, 1981.

Above all, the military played a decisive role in a series of constitutional amendments through which Park and Chun had tried to strengthen and/or prolong their rule. Both are not the only South Korean heads of state who had attempted to use the constitutional amendment to perpetuate their rule. Syngman Rhee amended the South Korean constitution twice, on July 7, 1952, and November 29, 1954, to extend his power. Rhee differed, however, from Park and Chun in his use of control mechanisms. Rhee employed the police force as his chief tool, while Park and to a lesser extent Chun, had utilized the military force. Since the inauguration of the Roh regime, the military force had not been used for civil unrest, which was certainly a positive step forward in South Korea's political development.

According to the original South Korean Constitution promulgated on July 17, 1948, the president must be elected by the members of the National Assembly. Rhee, realizing that his prospects for reelection by the members of the Assembly were dim, had attempted to amend the Constitution so that the president can be elected by a direct popular vote. Two abortive attempts were made: in March, 1950 and in January, 1952. He was successful on the third try, on July 7, 1952, although the amendment passed in a questionable police-state atmosphere. Rhee, through questionable means, was able to pass the 1954 constitutional amendment, which removed, *inter alia*, the remnants of the parliamentary or the cabinet-responsible system. The parliamentary system was restored briefly during the Chang Myŏn regime (1960-1961), via two additional constitutional amendments on June 15 and November 29, 1960, but the May coup of 1961 suspended it once and for all.

Park and his military regime reintroducted the presidential system through the fifth constitutional amendment on December 26, 1962. Park's immediate problem after the passage of this amendment was his eligibility for the presidency. He resolved this problem by retiring from the military, and he was elected president in 1964 as a *civilian*. As his presidency was nearing its end, the provision in Article 69 under Section 3 of the 1962 ROK Constitution hindered his continuous rule. Like his predecessor Rhee, Park's attempt to remove the paragraph limiting him to a two-term presidency met with a series of public and political protests. In the end, however, he succeeded in creating Section 3: "No president shall be elected more than *three* terms consecutively" (Section 3, Article 69 of the 1969 Constitution).

As Park approached the end of his third term, this new provision again posed a problem. To solve it, Park again called upon the military for help. First, on October 15, 1972, Park proclaimed a state of emergency in Seoul. On December 6, 1972, a state of emergency was extended to the entire nation; the military swiftly took charge; and all political activities were suspended. This emergency lasted until December 13, 1972, when the October Revitalizing Reforms (*Siwŏlyushin*) were passed. On October 22, 1972, the constitutional amendment called a "national referendum at the point of a bayonet" was successfully executed. The new constitution (*Yushin Hŏnbŏp*) was thus enacted on October 27, 1972.

For all practical purposes, the new October Constitution was a complete departure from the representative form of government. The president's term of office was extended from four to six years, without restrictions on the number of terms. The election of the president was no longer decided by a direct popular vote but by the members of the National Conference for Unification (NCU). More importantly, the president could select one third of the National Assembly members with the consent of the NCU, which was chaired by Park himself. In a way Park's multi-faceted control mechanisms were incorporated into the 1972 October Constitution in a sweeping manner.

To recapitulate, the Constitution itself became Park's major political control apparatus. The Constitution, which was the major roadblock to his power before the 1972 October Revitalizing Reforms, became the *foundation* of his prolonged rule. The October Constitution did not remove the *real* but only the *paper* roadblock for his power, neverthless. Thus, the new foundation of his power turned out to be the *paper* foundation. Political oppositions and protests against the October Constitution and Park's prolonged rule continued despite the sweeping power bestowed upon him by the Constitution. Park enacted a series of emergency measures to crack down political oppositions and domestic unrest. On January 8, 1974, he issued Emergency Decree Numbers 1 and 2, which prohibited criticism of the new constitution and established an emergency military tribunal, respectively. Until his death in 1979, he had issued nine such new decrees. These harsh and repressive edicts and plenipotentiary presidential powers notwithstanding, his presidency ended abruptly when his right-hand man and the KCIA Director, Kim Chae-kyu, assassinated him on October 26, 1979.

It is evident from the above that military intervention in politics had been a rule rather than an exception during the eighteen years of his rule. It is also clear that regardless of the extraordinary political control apparatus a ruler has at his disposal, when power degenerates into a naked force, it may end by the same force.

The South Korean Constitution was overhauled after the demise of Park. The eighth constitutional amendment, which ushered in Chun regime, made some changes but as far as the presidential powers and the mechanisms of the presidential election were concerned, the changes from the *Yushin* to the Chun regime had been nominal and cosmetic. Its single most important change, proclaimed on October 27, 1980, was the 7-year single-term presidency: "the term of office of the President shall be seven years, and the President shall not be reelected" (Article 45). During Chun's tenure, he was forced to revise the Constitution once again on October 29, 1987, which became effective after February 25, 1988. He himself complied with the old provision of the 7-year term and successfully transferred his presidential power to Roh Tae-woo, the first and unprecedented peaceful political change, though it was within the ruling party transfer of power. It was, nonetheless, not a small political achievement in South Korea's fragile democratic development.

The 1987 Constitutional revision eliminated nearly all dictatorial presidential powers under the 1972 October Revitalizing Constitution whose provisions were virtually unaltered in the 1980 Constitution. Only a nominal change was made in the presidential electing body in the 1980 Constitution. Namely, the presidential electoral college replaced the National Conference for Unification, which elected the President through secret balloting under the 1972 October Constitution. But the 1987 Constitution, among other things, stipulates that the president be elected by direct popular vote (Article 67). Above all, it limits the term of the presidency to 5 years and prohibits reelection (Article 70).

One interesting political implication regarding a series of constitutional amendments has been the posturing of the ruling and the opposition parties toward the constitution. From the start of the Republic into the 60s, Rhee's ruling Liberal Party and Park's Democratic Republican Party attempted to *change* the constitution, while the opposition parties tried, though unsuccessfully, to *defend* it. With the passage of the October Revitalizing Constitution, however, the posturing has been reversed. As did Park's ruling DRP, Chun's ruling Democratic Justice Party had tried to *defend* the new constitution, while the opposition parties, especially the New Korea Democratic Party (NKDP) had attempted to overhaul it.

In a nutshell, since 1972, the political control apparatuses, including the Constitution itself, have been the South Korean version of an authoritarian political order, exhibiting anti-liberal, anti-parliamentarian and praetorian features. Since the inauguration of the Roh government in 1988, a series of positive moves and measures to eradicate the authoritarian features of the South Korea political process had been attempted. Still even under the current Kim Young-sam government, the roots of authoritarianism in South Korean politics are deep-seated, while those of democracy are still meagre and fragile.

Table 10-1. History of Martial Law and Emergency Decrees,
1948 to the Present

Cause	Period	Area
Riots at Cheju Province	10/17-12/31/48	Cheju Province
Revolts at Yŏsu & Sunch'ŏn Area	10/21-12/31/48	S. Cholla Province
The Korean War	7/8/50-5/23/53	nation-wide
The April 19th Student Uprising	4/19-6/7/60	nation-wide
The May 16th Military Coup D'etat	5/16-12/5/61	nation-wide
The June 3rd Event	6/3-7/29/64	Seoul Area
The October Revitalizing Reforms	10/7-12/13/72	nation-wide
Unrest in Pusan and Masan Areas	10/19-10/26/79	Pusan and Masan Areas
The Park Assassination	10/27/79-5/17/80	nation-wide except Cheju
The Kwangju	5/17-10/17/80	nation-wide
Uprising	10/17/80-1/24/81	nation-wide except Cheju

Table 10-2. History of Constitutional Amendments: 1948 to the Present

Amendment	Dates	Passed by	Comments
1st.	July 2, 1952	NA*	"Excerpt" Ament.
2nd.	November 29, 1954	NA	"Rounding Off" Ament.
3rd.	June 15, 1960	NA	
4th.	November 29, 1960	NA	
5th.	December 26, 1962	SCNR**	
6th.	October 21, 1969	Referendum	("Third Term" Ament.)
7th.	December 27, 1972	Referendum	("October Revitalizing")
8th.	October 27, 1980	Referendum	
9th.	October 29, 1987	Referendum	

NA*: National Assembly

SCNR**: Supreme Council for National Reconstruction

Table 10-3. History of Presidential Elections

President	Name	Dates	Methods of Election
1st	Syngman Rhee (Yi Sung Man)	7/20/48-8/14/52	NA*
2nd	Syngman Rhee	8/15/52-8/14/56	Direct Popular Vote
3rd	Syngman Rhee	8/15/56-4/27/60	Direct Popular Vote
[4th]	Syngman Rhee	election discredited 3/15/60 (Rhee resigned on 4/26/60)	
Acting	Hŏ Chŏng	4/27-6/16/60	
4th	Yun Bo Sŏn	8/12/60-3/24/62	NA
Acting	Park Chung Hee	3/24/62-12/16/68	
5th	Park Chung Hee	12/17/63-6/30/67	Direct Popular Vote
6th	Park Chung Hee	7/1/67-7/2/71	Direct Popular Vote
7th	Park Chung Hee	7/3/71-12/26/72	Direct Popular Vote
8th	Park Chung Hee	12/27/72-12/26/78	NCU**
9th	Park Chung Hee	12/27/78-10/26/79	NCU
Acting	Ch'oe Kyu Ha	10/26/79-12/5/79	
10th	Ch'oe Kyu Ha	12/6/79-8/16/80	NCU
Acting	Park Ch'ung Hun	8/16-9/1/80	
11th	Chun Doo Hwan	9/1/80-3/5/81	NCU
12th	Chun Doo Hwan	3/5/81-2/24/88	Electoral College
13th	Roh Tae Woo	2/25/88-2/25/93	Direct Popular Vote
14th	Kim Young-sam	2/25/93-	Direct Popular Vote

NA*: National Assembly
NCU*: National Conference for Unification

Table 10-4. *The Korean People's Perceptions of and Attitudes toward
the United States and Other Countries*

Q. 1. Which country do you like the most?

(%)

	(1982)	(1986)	(1985)
United States	43.6	40.5 (1)*	35.1
Switzerland	15.4	10.3 (2)	14.5
W. Germany	5.1	(8)	3.8
France	4.7	2.9 (4)	6.4
England	4.3	2.7 (5)	4.3
Sweden	2.1	(7)	—
Denmark	2.1	(12)	—
Australia	1.9	(6)	4.3
Netherlands	1.8	(11)	—
Canada	1.4	(9)	—
Japan	1.3	3.5 (3)	8.7
Taiwan	1.2	(10)	—
Others	9.3	—	—
No answer	5.7	—	—

Source: Some Results of Social Research in Korea, surveyed by Korea Survey (Gallup)
Polls, Ltd., January 20-January 30, 1982; Korea Survey-Hankuk Ilbo Survey, *Han-
kuk Ilbo,* January 6, 1986. The 1985 data is the *Chungang Ilbo* survey published on
September 27, 1985.
*The figures in the parentheses are the rank order of the countries people liked.

Q. 2. Which country do you dislike the most?

(%)

	(1982)	(1985)
Japan	36.4	36.6
North Korea	34.1	32.0
Soviet Union	12.0	20.5
United States	—	2.7
China	1.8	1.9
All communist nations	1.6	—
Africa	1.1	—
Others	5.0	—
No answer	7.1	—

Table 10-4. Continued

Q. 3. Which country has the greatest cultural impact on Korea?

	(%)
	(1985)
United States	66.2
Japan	24.3
China	4.7
Taiwan	1.8
France	0.7

Q. 4. Which country is the most important for Korea's national security?

	(%)
	(1985)
United States	82.6
Japan	10.8
China	3.0
North Korea	1.7

Q. 5. Which country is the most important for Korea's economy?

	(%)
	(1985)
United States	54.2
Japan	28.1
China	7.5
Saudi Arabia	2.0
North Korea	1.5

Sources: Data for Questions 3, 4 and 5 from the 1985 *Chungang Ilbo* survey.

Notes

1. Joseph A. Schumpeter, *Capitalism, Socialism and Democracy*, 3rd ed. (New York: Harper Torchbooks, 1962), p. 296.

2. For a recent survey of studies on Korean politics, see Young Whan Kihl and Chong Lim Kim, "Studies on Korean Politics in the United States in the 1980s," *Political Studies Review* 1 (1985): 10-26.

3. Gregory Henderson, *Korea: The Politics of the Vortex* (Cambridge: Harvard University Press, 1968), p. 4.

4. *Ibid.*, p. 5.

5. *Ibid.*

6. *Ibid.*

7. See, for instance, William Kornhauser, *The Politics of Mass Society* (New York: Free Press, 1959); Edward Shils, "Daydreams and Nightmares: Reflections on the Criticisms of Mass Culture," *Suwannee Review* 65 (1957): 587-608. For a critical review of the idea of mass society, see Daniel Bell, *The End of Ideology* (Glencoe: Free Press, 1960); Seymour Martin Lipset, *Political Man: The Social Bases of Politics* (New York: A Doubleday Anchor Book, 1963), especially, pp. 439-456; and Leon Bramson, *The Political Context of Sociology* (1961).

8. Henderson, *Op. Cit.*, p. 225

9. See, for instance, David Riesman, *The Lonely Crowd* (New Haven: Yale University Press, 1961), especially, pp. 126-285; Jon M. Shepard, *Automation and Alienation* (Cambridge: MIT Press, 1967).

10. Henderson, *Op. Cit.*, p. 5, p. 194 and p. 363. For a detailed discussion of factionalism in Korean politics, see Part One on the Korean Political Heritage. See also, Byung-joon Ahn, "Political Changes and Institutionalization in South Korea," *Korean Social Science Journal* (1983): 41-65.

11. Henderson, p. 225.

12. For a discussion of *kye*, see Ki-baik Lee, *A New History of Korea*, trans. Edward W. Wagner with Edward J. Shultz (Seoul: Iljokak, 1984), pp. 252-253. Also, Ki-jun Cho, *Hankuk Kyŏngchae-sa* [History of Korean Economy], Rev. ed. (Seoul: Ilsin-sa, 1983).

13. Henderson, p. 367.

14. Doh Chull Shin *et al*, "Cultural Origins of Public Support for Democracy in Korea: An Empirical Test of the Douglas-Wildavsky Theory of Culture," *Comparative Political Studies* 22 (July 1989): 217-238. Also, James Cotton recently identified three approaches or views of the State in the Newly Industralizing Countries of East Asia—the pluralist, the political culture, and the statist or neo-Weberian, for details, see his article "The Limits to Liberalization in Industrializing Asia: Three Views of the State," *Pacific Affairs* 64

(Fall 1991): 311-327.

15. Quoted in Kihl and Kim, *Op. Cit.*, p. 15.

16. For a succinct overview of South Korean political changes and developments since 1945, see Byung-joon Ahn, *Op. Cit.*, pp. 41-65.

17. Juan Linz, "Totalitarian and Authoritarian Regimes," in *Handbook of Political Science*, ed. F. Greenstein and N. Polsby (Reading, Mass.: Addison-Wesley, 1975), Vol. 3, pp. 175-412.

18. Amos Perlmutter, *Modern Authoritarianism* (New Haven: Yale University Press, 1981), p. 67. See also Isaiah Berlin, *The Crooked Timber of Humanity* (New York: Vintage Books, 1992), especially his chapter on "Joseph De Maistre and the Origins of Fascism," pp. 91-174.

19. *Ibid.*, pp. 62-63.

20. *Ibid.*, pp. 144-145.

21. *Ibid.*, pp. 6-7.

22. Hannah Arendt, *Totalitarianism* (New York: A Harvest Book, 1968), Pt. 3, p. 6n.

23. Bertram D. Wolfe, *Communist Totalitarianism: Keys to the Soviet System* (Boulder: A Westview Encore Edition, 1985), p. 276.

24. Perlmutter, *Op. Cit.*, p. 70.

25. Perlmutter postulated that in the ideology of *all* modern authoritarian movements, parties and regimes, five elements converge: radical nationalism; antiliberalism; antiparliamentarianism; an antibourgeois ethos and anti-Semitism and racism. See his, *Op. Cit.*, p. 78. Earlier, Giovanni Gentile (1875-1944) listed seven essential features of Italian fascism. They are: nationalism; anti-parliamentalism; statism; productionism; corporatism; authoritarianism; and elitism. Quoted in Anthony James Joes, *Fascism in the Contemporary World: Ideology, Evolution, Resurgence* (Boulder: Westview Press, 1978), pp. 60-61. Five elements in this chapter are somewhat different from both.

26. The English translation of the 1977 USSR Constitution (Fundamental Law) is found in Vadim Medish, *The Soviet Union*, 2nd rev. ed. (Englewood Cliffs: Prentice-Hall, 1985), pp. 317-340. Mussolini's slogan is quoted in Bertram D. Wolfe, *Op. Cit.*, p. 118.

27. John Stuart Mill, *On Liberty* (New York: Everyman ed., 1931), p. 73.

28. Isaiah Berlin, *Four Essays on Liberty* (London: Oxford University Press, 1969), pp. 121-122. See also, Gerald C. MacCallum, Jr., "Negative and Positive Freedom," in Anthony de Crespigny and Alan Wertheimer, eds., *Contemporary Political Theory* (London: Faber, 1971), p. 175.

29. According to Aristotle, liberty as conceived in democracies is twofold: it is partly political liberty, which means that all have a term of office and the will of all prevails and it is partly civil, and consists in "living as you like." See, *The Politics of Aristotle*, ed. and trans. Ernest Barker (New York:

Oxford University Press, 1962), pp. 257-258.

30. J. S. Mill, *System of Logic*, bks. 4-6, ed. J. M. Robson (London: Routledge and Kegan Paul, 1974), p. 841. Quoted in G. W. Smith, "The Logic of J. S. Mill on Freedom," *Political Studies* 28: 238.

31. Bernard P. Dauenhauer, "Relational Freedom," *Review of Metaphysics* 36 (September 1982): 77-101. Rhoda E. Howard and Jack Donnelly, "Human Dignity, Human Rights and Political Regimes" in *American Political Science Review* 80 (September 1986): 801-817.

32. Carl J. Friedrich, *An Introduction to Political Theory* (New York: Harper and Row, 1967), pp. 1-13.

33. Letters of Thomas Jefferson to James Madison (January 30, 1787) and to Colonel William S. Smith (November 13, 1787). In Bernard Mayo, ed., *Jefferson Himself* (Boston: Houghton Mifflin, 1942), p. 145.

34. Carl J. Friedrich, *Op. Cit.*, pp. 1-13.

35. See, for instance, Gu-jin Kang, "Fiction of Fundamental Rights in North Korean Constitution, I and II," *Vantage Point* (April and May 1982), Nos. 4 and 5.

36. Hannah Arendt, *Op. Cit.*, p. 10. Nazi Primer wrote that "democracies, Jews, Eastern subhumans, or the incurably sick" are not "fit to live." Hitler said that these "dying classes" ought to be "eliminated without much ado." Quoted in Arendt, p. 48.

37. Arendt, *Ibid.*, pp. 39-62.

38. *Ibid.*, p. xx.

39. Perlmutter, *Op. Cit.*, p. 55.

40. Philippe Schmitter, "Still the Century of Corporatism," *Review of Politics*, 36 (January 1974): 93-104; Giovanni Sartori, *Parties and Party Systems: A Framework for Analysis* (Cambridge: Cambridge University Press, 1979), pp. 221-230.

41. For a brief overview of corporatism, see, for instance, Ruth Berins Collier and David Collier, "Disaggregating Corporatism," *American Political Science Review* (December 1979), pp. 967-985; H. Gordon Skilling, "Interest Groups and Communist Politics Revisited," *World Politics* (October 1983), pp. 1-27.

42. Collier and Collier, *Op. Cit.*, p. 968.

43. James Joes, *Op. Cit.*, pp. 215-218.

44. *Ibid.*, pp. 45-74.

45. Schmitter, "Still the Century of Corporatism," pp. 102-103.

46. Skilling, *Op. Cit.*, p. 11.

47. Joes' distinction is found in *Op. Cit.*, p. 217.

48. Juan Linz, "Totalitarian and Authoritarian Regimes," pp. 204-274; P. Schmitter, "The 'Portugalization' of Brazil," in *Authoritarian Brazil*, ed. Alfred Stepan, *The State and Society: Peru in Comparative Perspective*

(Princeton: Princeton University Press, 1978), pp. 127-136; Susan Kaufman Purcell, *The Mexican Profit-Sharing Decision* (Berkeley: University of California Press, 1975), pp. 1-11.

49. P. Schmitter and G. Lehmbruch, *Trends Toward Corporatist Intermediation* (Beverly Hills: Sage, 1979), p. 15ff; Robert Kvavik, *Interest Groups in Norwegian Politics* (Oslo: Universitesforlaget, 1976), p. 20ff. Quoted in Gabriel A. Almond, "Corporatism, Pluralism, and Professional Memory," *World Politics* (January 1983), pp. 245-260. See also, Ross M. Martin, "Pluralism and the New Corporatism," *Political Studies* 31 (1983): 86-102. See also, Gabriel A. Almond "The Return to the State" *American Political Science Review* 82 (September 1988): 874. Also, Bert A. Rockman, "Minding the State or a State of Mind?" *Comparative Political Studies* 23 (April 1990): 25-55.

50. G. O'Donnell, *Modernization and Bureaucratic Authoritarianism* (Berkeley: Institute of International Studies, 1975). Quoted in Perlmutter, *Op. Cit.*, pp. 123-124.

51. Collier and Collier, *Op. Cit.*

52. Rose J. Spalding, "State Power and Its Limits: Corporatism in Mexico," *Comparative Political Studies* 14 (July 1981): 139-161.

53. David E. Apter, *Introduction to Political Analysis* (Cambridge: Winthrop Publishers, 1977), p. 456.

54. Quoted in J. Samuel Valenzuela and Arturo Valenzuela, "Modernization and Dependency: Alternative Perspectives in the Study of Latin American Underdevelopment," *Comparative Politics* (July 1978), p. 544.

55. The advocates of this view are, for instance, Paul Baran, *The Political Economy of Growth* (New York: Monthly Review Press, 1957); Andre G. Frank, *Capitalism and Underdevelopment in Latin America* (New York: Monthly Review Press, 1967); Fernando H. Cardoso and Enzo Faletto, *Dependency and Development in Latin America*, trans. Marjory M. Urguidi (Berkeley: University of California Press, 1978).

56. Some works on the exclusive school are: Paul Baran, *Op. Cit.*; C. Veliz, ed., *Obstacles to Change in Latin America* (New York: Oxford University Press, 1965); A. G. Frank, *Op. Cit.*; Dos Santos, "The Structure of Dependence," *American Economic Review* 60 (May 1970): 231-235; and his, "The Crisis of Contemporary Capitalism," *Latin American Perspectives* 3 (Spring 1976): 84-99; O. Sunkel, "Big Business and Dependencia," *Foreign Affairs* 50 (April 1972): 517-534; C. Furtado, "The Concept of External Dependence in the Study of Underdevelopment," in C. Wilbur, ed., *The Political Economy of Development and Underdevelopment* (New York: Random House, 1973); J. Cardoso, "Associated-dependent Development: Theoretical and Practical Implications," in A. Stephan, ed., *Authoritarian Brazil* (New Haven: Yale University Press, 1973); P. Evans, "Continuities and Contradictions in the

Evolution of Brazilian Dependence," *Latin American Perspectives* 3 (Spring 1976): 30-54.

57. The studies on the inclusive school are: J. Galtung, "A Structural Theory of Imperialism," *Journal of Peace Research* (1971), pp. 81-118; R.D. Walleri, "Trade Dependence and Underdevelopment: A Causal-Chain Analysis," *Comparative Political Studies* (April 1978), pp. 94-126; L. R. Alschuler, "Satellization and Stagnation in Latin America," *International Studies Quarterly* (March 1976), pp. 39-82.

58. The old views are, for instance, held by Paul A. Baran and Andre Gunder Frank. The new views are put forward by F. E. Cardoso, "Associated-dependent Development...;" Peter Evans, *Dependent Development: The Alliance of Multinational, State, and Local Capital in Brazil* (Princeton: Princeton University Press, 1979); and Colin Leys, *Underdevelopment in Kenya: The Political Economy of Neo-Colonialism* (Berkley: University of California Press, 1975). For a critical review of these two views, see H. Jeffrey Leonard, "Multinational Corporations and Politics in Developing Countries," *World Politics* (April 1980), pp. 454-483.

59. The surveys of the developmentalist views are found in J. Sameul Valenzuela and Arturo Valenzuela, "Modernization and Dependency: Alternative Perspectives in the Study of Latin American Underdevelopment," *Comparative Politics* (July 1978), pp. 535-557; Robert W. Jackman, "Dependence on Foreign Investment and Economic Growth in the Third World," *World Politics* (July 1982), pp. 175-196. Tony Smith, "Requiem or New Agenda for Third World Studies?" *World Politics* (1984), pp. 532-561.

60. Valenzuela and Valenzuela, *Op. Cit.*, pp. 550-552.

61. Colin Stoneman, "Foreign Capital and Economic Growth," *World Development* (January 1975), pp. 11-26; Peter B. Evans and Michael Timberlake, "Dependence, Inequality, and the Growth of the Tertiary: A Comparative Analysis of Less-Developed Countries," *American Sociological Review* (August 1980), pp. 531-552; Christopher Chase-Dunn, "The Effects of International Economic Dependence on Development and Inequality: A Cross-national Study," *American Sociological Review* (December 1975), pp. 720-738; David Snyder and Deward L. Kick, "Structural Position in the World System and Economic Growth, 1955-1970: A Multiple-Network Analysis of Transnational Interactions, *American Journal of Sociology* (March 1979), pp. 1096-1226.

62. Alejandro Portes, "On the Sociology of National Development: Theories and Issues," *American Journal of Sociology* (July 1976), pp. 55-85.

63. Robert W. Jackman, "Dependence on Foreign Investment and Economic Growth in the Third World," *World Politics* (July 1982), pp. 175-196.

64. Robert Kaufman and Others, "A Preliminary Test of the Theory of Dependency," *Comparative Politics* (April 1975); David Ray, "The Dependency

Model and Latin America: Three Basic Fallacies," *Journal of Interamerican Affairs and World Studies* (February 1973); Patrick J. McGowan, "Economic Dependency and Economic Performance in Black Africa," *Journal of Modern African Studies, no. 1* (1976); Elliot J. Berg, "Structural Transformation versus Gradualism: Recent Economic Development in Ghana and the Ivory Coast," in Philip Foster and Aristide R. Zolberg, *Ghana and the Ivory Coast: Perspectives on Modernization* (Berkeley: University of California Press, 1971); Patrick J. McGowan and Dale L. Smith, "Economic Dependency in Black Africa: An Analysis of Competing Theories, *International Organization* (Winter 1978). All these citations are quoted in Tony Smith, "The Underdevelopment of Development Literature," *World Politics* (July 1979), pp. 247-288.

65. Atul Kohli et al., "Inequality in the Third World: An Assessment of Competing Explanations," *Comparative Political Studies* (October 1984), pp. 283-318.

66. F. H. Cardoso and E. Faletto, *Dependency and Development in Latin America* (Berkeley: University of California Press, 1978).

67. Peter Evans, *Dependent Development: The Alliance of Multinational, State, and Local Capital in Brazil* (Princeton: Princeton University Press, 1979).

68. R. Dam Walleri, "Trade Dependence and Underdevelopment: A Causal-chain Analysis," *Comparative Political Studies* (April 1978), pp. 94-127. Also, David P. Rapkin, "Modeling Dependence and Underdevelopment: A Comment on Walleri," *Comparative Political Studies* (April 1979), pp. 104-115, and Walleri's rebuttal to Rapkin's critique, pp. 116-120 in the same issue.

69. For details, see Guillermo O'Donnell, "Tensions in the Bureaucratic-Authoritarian State and the Question of Democracy," in D. Collier, ed., *The New Authoritarianism in Latin America* (Princeton: Princeton University Press, 1979), pp. 285-318; also his "Reflections on the Patterns of Change in the Bureaucratic-Authoritarian State," *Latin American Research Review* (1978), pp. 3-38; and his *Modernization and Bureaucratic-Authoritarianism: Studies in South American Politics* (Berkeley: University of California at Berkeley, Institute of International Studies, Politics of Modernization Series No. 9, 1973). See also, Benjamin A. Most, "Authoritarianism and the Growth of the State in Latin America: An Assessment of their Impacts on Argentine Public Policy, 1930-1970," *Comparative Political Studies* (July 1980), pp. 173-203.

70. J. Serra, "Three Mistaken Theses Regarding the Connection between Industrialization and Authoritarian Regimes," in D. Collier, *The New Authoritarianism in Latin America* (Princeton: Princeton University Press, 1979), pp. 99-163.

71. A. Hirschmann, "The Turn to Authoritarianism in Latin America and the Search for its Economic Determinants," in D. Collier, ed., *Op. Cit.*, pp. 61-

98; J. Sheahan, "Market-oriented Economic Policies and Political Repression in Latin America," *Economic Development and Cultural Change* (1980), pp. 267-291.

72. Youssef Cohen, "The Impact of Bureaucratic-Authoritarian Rule on Economic Growth," *Comparative Political Studies* (April 1985), pp. 123-136.

73. Edward C. Epstein, "Legitimacy, Institutionalization, and Opposition in Exclusionary Bureaucratic-Authoritarian Regimes: The Situation of the 1980s," *Comparative Politics* (October 1984), pp. 37-54.

74. Tony Smith, "The Underdevelopment of Development Literature: The Case of Dependency Theory," *World Politics* (January 1979), pp. 247-288. Recently, he characterized developmentalism as being "too fragmented" and dependency, "too holistic" and called for a new synthesis. For details, see his "Requiem or New Agenda for Third World Studies," *Op. Cit.*

75. See, for instance, Jack Donnelly, "Human Rights and Development: Complementary or Competing Concerns?" *World Politics* (January 1984), pp. 255-283. Also, Gary S. Fields, "Growth and Distribution in the Market Economies of East Asia," *World Politics* (October 1982), pp. 150-160. See also, James Cotton, "Understanding the State in South Korea: Bureaucratic Authoritarian or State Autonomy Theory?, *Comparative Political Studies* 24 (January 1992): 512-531.

76. Kohli and others, *Op. Cit.*; Irma Ademan and Sherman Robinson, *Income Distribution Policy in Developing Countries: A Case Study of Korea* (Stanford: Stanford University Press, 1978); Paul W. Kuznets, "Government and Economic Strategy in Contemporary South Korea," *Pacific Affairs* (Spring 1985), pp. 44-67.

77. Kuznets, *Op. Cit.*, and Gunnar Myrdal, *Asian Drama: An Inquiry into the Poverty of Nations* (New York: Twentieth Century Fund, 1968), Vol. I, p. 66 and Vol. II, pp. 895-900.

78. Donnelly, *Op. Cit.* See also, Sung Chul Yang, *Korea and Two Regimes* (Cambridge: Schenkman Publishing Co, 1981), pp. 271-277.

79. Kim and his associates' report was published in *Hankook Ilbo*, 12 June 1984. See also, Kyŏng-Dong Kim "The Distinctive Features of South Korea's Development" in Peter L. Berger and Hsin-Huang Michael Hsiao, eds., *In Search of an East Asian Development Model* (New Brunswick: Transactions Publishers, 1990), pp. 197-219.

80. For a brief overview of praetorianism, see Eric A. Nordlinger, *Soldiers in Politics: Military Coups and Governments* (Englewood Cliffs: Prentice-Hall, 1977), especially, pp. 1-29.

81. *Ibid.*, pp. 63-106.

82. Thomas H. Johnson, Robert O. Slater and Pat McGowan, "Explaining African Military Coup d'Etat, 1960-1982," *American Political Science Review* (September 1984), pp. 622-640. J. Craig Jenkins and Augustine J.

Kposowa, "Explaining Military Coup D'etat: Black Africa, 1957-1984," *American Sociological Review* 55 (December 1990): 861-875.

83. Aaron S. Klieman, "Confined to Barracks: Emergencies and the Military in Developing Countries," *Comparative Politics* (January 1980), pp. 143-163.

84. Nordlinger, *Op. Cit.*, pp. 21-29.

85. *Ibid.*

86. *Ibid.*

87. *Ibid.*, p. 25. Nordlinger stated that all military regimes are authoritarian in that they eliminate or extensively limit political rights, liberties, and competition, at least until the officers are getting ready to return to the barracks.

88. Amos Perlmutter, *Modern Authoritarianism*, pp. 39-62.

89. *Ibid.*

90. *Ibid.*

91. Klieman, *Op. Cit.*

92. Gunnar Myrdal, *An American Dilemma* (New York: Harper & Bros., 1944).

93. The 1962 GDP figures are found in *U.N. Yearbook of National Accounts Statistics*, 1963.

94. For a detailed discussion of South Korea-Japan security question, see Sung Chul Yang, *Op. Cit.*, pp. 252-256; Fuji Kamiya, "The Korean Peninsula after Park Chung Hee," *Asian Survey* (July 1980), pp. 744-753; Jung-suk Youn, "Korea-Japan Relations: 20 Years of Normalization," *Korea and World Affairs* (Fall 1985), pp. 421-440.

95. Sung Chul Yang, *Op. Cit.*, pp. 305-334.

96. Tokyo-based pro-North Korean paper, *The People's Korea*, wrote that during the Kwangju Uprising "more than 2,000 citizens" were killed and 10,000 injured. These figures are highly unlikely to be correct. For details, see *The People's Korea*, 8 June 1985.

97. *The Korea Herald*, 30 April 1981.

98. John K. Fairbank, *The United States and China*, 4th ed. (Cambridge: Harvard University Press, 1979), p. 324.

99. See Reischauer's article in *The Christian Science Monitor*, 26 July 1976.

100. Godfrey Hodgson, *All Things to All Men: The False Promise of the Modern Presidency* (New York: Simon and Schuster, 1980).

101. Edwin O. Reischauer and John K. Fairbank, *East Asia: The Great Tradition* (Boston: Houghton Mifflin, 1960), p. 397.

102. Cornelius Osgood, *The Koreans and Their Culture* (New York: The Ronald Press, 1951), p. 332. One early French missionary described the Koreans as having "an obstinate, diffident, irascible and vindictive character" (1874). For details, see Charles Dallet, *Traditional Korea* (New Haven: Humen Relations Area Files, 1954), p. 153. See Also, Kyŏng-Dong Kim, "The Distinctive Features of South Korea's Development, *Op. Cit.*, p. 201. For details, see *The Gallup Report*, May, June, 1992, pp. 18-24.

103. C. Osgood, *Op. Cit.*, p. 331.
104. *Ibid.*, pp. 331-332. A controlled survey analysis of the Korean people's changing social character is found in Herbert R. Barringer, "Increasing Scale and Changing Social Character in Korea," in Scott Greer et al, eds., *The New Urbanization* (New York: St. Martins Press, 1968), pp. 53-71. In it he contended, among other things, that simplistic models of East and West will not suffice for accurate prediction of behavior.
105. Gregory Henderson, *Korea: The Politics of the Vortex*, pp. 193-194.
106. Lucian W. Pye, *Asian Power and Politics: The Cultural Dimension of Authority* (1985), p. 225, p. 227 and p. 228.
107. Sung Chul Yang, *Korea and Two Regimes*, pp. 223-229.
108. *Ibid.*, pp. 233-244.
109. Samuel P. Huntington, *The Soldier and the State* (Cambridge: Harvard University Press, 1957) and his, *The Common Defense* (New York: Columbia University Press, 1961), especially, pp. 1-25; Morris Janowitz, *The Professional Soldier* (Chicago: Free Press, 1960); Amos Perlmutter, *The Military and Politics in Modern Times* (New Haven: Yale University Press, 1977).
110. Bruce M. Russet, "Political Perspectives of U.S. Military and Business Elites," *Armed Forces and Society* (Fall 1974), p. 88.
111. C. I. Eugene Kim, "The Value Congruity Between ROK Civilian and Former Military Party Elites," *Asian Survey* (August 1978), p. 840.
112. Dong-suh Bark and Chae-jin Lee, "Bureaucratic Elite and Development Orientations," Dae-sook Suh and Chae-jin Lee, eds., *Political Leadership in Korea* (Seattle: University of Washington Press, 1976), pp. 91-133.
113. Joong-gun Chung and Sung-moon Pae, "Orientation of the Korean Bureaucrats Toward Democracy: A Study of Background and Institutional Characteristics," *Korea and World Affairs* (Summer 1977), pp. 219-236.
114. Chong Lim Kim and Byŏng-kyu Woo, "Legislative Leadership and Democratic Development" in Suh and Lee, *Political Leadership in Korea*, pp. 41-66.
115. Nam Young Lee, "The Structure of Democratic Belief System: An Analysis of Political Culture in Korea," *Korea and World Affairs* (Winter 1983), pp. 629-655. Also, Chong Lim Kim, Young Whan Kihl and Seong-Tong Pai, "Modes of Citizen Political Participation," in Chong Lim Kim, ed., *Political Participation in Korea* (Santa Barbara: Clio Books, 1980), pp. 35-55.
116. For a discussion of the South Korean political control apparatus, see Sung Chul Yang, *Korea and Two Regimes*, pp. 240-244.

CHAPTER 11

FORMAL GOVERNMENTAL STRUCTURES
AND POLITICAL PROCESS

In my opinion there are two basic elements in every political system, by virtue of which its true form and quality are either desirable or the opposite. By these I mean its customs and laws. The desirable ones are those which make men's private lives virtuous and well-disciplined and the public character of the state civilized and just; the undesirable are those which have the opposite effect.

Polybius[1]

Unlike North Korea, where one party rule is a norm and electoral process is a ceremony, in South Korea party politics and electoral process do exist, albeit imperfect and distorted. In theory, a semblance of the separation of powers also exists, at least to the extent that the government is *formally* structured in such ways. In reality, however, the single most persistent characteristics of the South Korean politics for the past forty years has been the concentration of power in the presidency. In other words, the *institutional* checks and balances based on the principle of the separation of powers do exist, on paper, but the political dynamics favoring the concentration of power in the executive branch, i.e., the president, have constantly overwhelmed the former. In a nutshell, as noted in Chapter 10, *anti-parliamentarianism* is pervasive. It means that to those in power the term, "liberal democracy" has seldom been more than a political lipservice, while to those in opposition, it has been the symbolic weapon to fight against the authoritarian rule.

In this chapter three formal branches of the South Korean governmental structures and their changes will be briefly reviewed. Next, party politics, legislative process and electoral behavior will be examined in some detail.

Governmental Apparatus and Their Metamorphoses

1. The National Assembly

Minju-eiwŏn [the Democratic Council] created by the U.S. Army Military Government in Korea (USAMGIK) on 14 February 1946 as its Korean advisory board and *Ipbŏp-eiwŏn* [the Legislative Council], created by the USAMGIK on June 3, 1947, which replaced the Democratic Council, were the two precursors of *Kukhoe* [the National Assembly].[2] However, *Chehŏn-eihoe* [the Constituent Assembly], whose members were elected by direct popular votes in the South under the UN supervision on May 10, 1948, was the official beginning of the Republic of Korea's legislative history.

In South Korea's over forty-year history, the National Assembly (NA) has held fourteen separate representative bodies. The average duration of its legislative bodies is about 3 years. With the exception of the 5th NA, the South Korean legislature has been unicameral. But the methods of electing the legislators have changed many times over the years (For details, see Table 12-1).

The formal powers of the NA are: *inter alia*, to ratify treaties, declare war and dispatch armed forces overseas; to inspect the executive branch and request documents and summon officials from the executive branch before the NA or its committees; and to request the Board of Inspection to audit the accounts of revenues and disbursement and to forward its final report from the results of inspection to the NA and the president.

From the Rhee to the Kim regime, however, the NA has never been empowered to increase the expenditures or to create new budget items without the prior consent of the executive branch. Nor has it had the right to confirm the presidential appointment of high-ranking officials except the prime minister (PM) (The Chang government was the only exception). Under the Yushin system, the President handpicked the PM without the NA's consent.

The NA's power of impeachment is also impaired. In the original 1948 Constitution, the NA could make an impeachment motion with no less than 50 members and could pass it with the approval of the two thirds of its members. In the 1952 Constitutional Amendment, the NA's power of impeachment was strengthened: 30 instead of 50 members could initiate the impeachment motion and its passage required a majority rather than the two-thirds of its members. But in the 1969 Amendment, the impeachment motion required 50 plus members rather than 30. In the 1972 revision and the 1980 Constitution, a majority vote, not 50 members plus, is required for the impeachment motion. Worse still, not the NA but the Impeachment Court is entrusted with the final impeachment trial.[3]

In order to pass the impeachment motion against any of the key members of the executive branch, including the prime minister, the current 1987 Constitution requires that more than a third of the NA members must consent. But to impeach the president, more than two-thirds of the NA members must pass the impeachment motion (Article 65). If the motion is passed, *Hŏnbŏpchep'anso* [The Constitutional Court] will deliberate and determine the merits of the impeachment motion. The Impeachment Court was renamed the Impeachment Council under the Park regime. Under the Yushin and the Chun regime, the Constitution Committee replaced the Impeachment Council. The Constitution Committee consists of nine judges—three each appointed by the President, the NA and the Chief Justice of the Supreme Court. During the Roh regime, the Constitutional Court has been in operation and the selection of the court members remained the same as it was under the Chun regime.

Two points are noteworthy in this connection. First, the NA in the Rhee through the Kim regime has never exercised its impeachment power against the president. Second, if the NA should attempt such a motion, the president could have easily counter it by dissolving the NA (the President's power to dissolve the NA is found in Article 86 of 1962, Article 59 of 1972 and Article 57 of 1980 Constitution).[4] The current

Constitution prohibits the presidential power from dissolving the NA.

In short, by design and in practice, the NA has been a powerless body. Especially, from the Park regime, the NA members of the ruling party have been more or less "the errand boy" of the executive branch, while the opposition members have behaved like helpless "crybabies." One example suffices to drive this point home. It took just two minutes and 30 seconds for the NA (without the participation and the knowledge of the opposition party members) to pass the entire 1987 budget, while in the United States it takes a year or more for Congress to deliberate, authorize and appropriate the national budget.

The present National Assembly has a Speaker and two Vice-Speakers, one from the ruling party and the other from the opposition party. The majority party elects its own floor leaders such as the majority leader and the majority whip, as do the minority parties. The NA also has some 16 standing committees. They are:

> House Steering
> Legislature and Judiciary
> Foreign Affairs and National Unification
> Administration
> Home Affairs
> Finance
> Economy and Science
> National Defense
> Education and Information
> Agriculture and Forestry
> Commerce and Industry
> Energy Resources
> Public Health and Social Affairs
> Transportation and Communications
> Construction

In addition, the National Assembly has some two thousand staff members manning its own Secretariat, which consists of the Proceedings Bureau, the Maintenance Bureau, the Public Relations and Interparliamentary Bureau, the Legislative Staff Training Institute, the National Assembly Library, the Legislative Research Bureau, the Reference and Processing Bureau and the Overseas Information Bureau.

2. The Presidency and the State Council

Formally at least, the presidential system has prevailed with the exception of the Chang Myŏn government (1960-1961). During the Rhee regime (1948-1960), the president was the head of the state, the head of the executive branch and the chief legislator. He also exercised judicial powers such as executive clemency, appointment and reappointment of the judges. After the 1954 constitutional amendment, the president was able to run for the office for more than two four-year consecutive terms. Syngman Rhee had, thus, ruled for nearly twelve years consecutively until his regime was toppled by the student revolution of April 1960.

In the Chang Myŏn regime which adopted the cabinet-responsible system, the presidential power became ceremonial. The president was the ceremonial head representing the Republic in foreign relations; he was not allowed to be affiliated with a political party; above all, he was not empowered to exercise veto power. Then, the real powers of the executive branch were vested in the State Council headed by the Prime Minister. But the Chang regime did not last long enough to leave any lasting political imprint or impact. In less than eight months, it was overthrown by the military coup d'etat on May 16, 1961.

Under the Park Chung Hee regime, the presidential system was restored with even more powers in the hands of the president. The State Council became the president's deliberative body rather than a collective decision-making body as it was under the Chang regime. The President had the power to dissolve the NA, but the NA had the power only to "recommend" to the president the removal of the PM and the members of the State Council upon the consent of its majority members. With the so-called Yushin [Revivalizing Reforms] Constitution in 1972, the president became de facto and de jure "the president-dictator." President Park was empowered to take emergency measures in a wide range of state affairs including domestic and foreign affairs, national defense, economic, financial and judicial affairs in the name of national security or public safety.[5] And these measures were not subjected to judicial or NA's review. Worse still, the three-term restrictions on the presidency was abolished; so was the presidential election by a direct popular vote. Thus, he could be elected indefinitely by the newly created National Conference for Unification (NCU), of which he was the chairman. These extraordinary presidential powers notwithstanding, Park's power and terms ended abruptly when he was assassinated by the CIA Director.

During the Chun Doo Hwan Regime (1980-1988), the extraordinary presidential powers under the Park regime have been somewhat curtailed. The presidency was limited to one 7-year term (Articles 45 and 129, 1980). The President also had the obligation to lift the emergency measures if the majority of the NA members consented to the request. The emergency measures were subjected to judicial review, which was not the case under the Park regime. Under the Chun regime, the President could not dissolve the NA within one-year of its formation, while Park could exercise this power at any time. Chun was elected by the presidential electoral college system through secret balloting, not by the NCU.

As noted earlier, the current 1987 Constitution prohibits the president from dissolving the NA. The presidential tenure is limited to one five-year term (Article 70). And the president is now elected by a direct popular vote (Article 67, Section 1). The Roh Tae Woo regime (1988-1993) was, thus, the first government elected by a popular vote since 1971. These marginal curtailing of presidential powers notwithstanding, the president still remains the most powerful, and his authority is unchecked by both the NA and the Judiciary (the powers of the president are listed in Articles 47 through 60). The president's authoritarian proclivity can best be illustrated by the excessive growth and expansion of political control apparatuses and intelligence nextwork at his disposal (For details, see Chapter Ten).

Both the PM and the members of the State Council are appointed by the President but only the appointment of the PM requires the NA's consent. The President is the chairman of the State Council whose members constitute between fifteen to thirty. At present the Executive Branch consists of the President, the PM, two Deputy Prime Ministers (concurrently the minister of the Economic Planning Board and the minister of National Unification Board), some 22 ministers, three agencies, one commission and one board, which are manned by some 600,000 personnels. Various governmental ministries, agencies, commission and board and their dates of establishment are listed below:

Ministry
Agriculture and Fisheries ('73)
Commerce and Industry ('48)
Communications ('48)
Construction ('61)
Culture ('89)
Economic Planning Board ('63)
Education ('48)
Energy and Resources ('77)
Finance ('48)
1st Minister of Political Affairs ('81)
Foreign Affairs ('48)
Government Administration ('63)
Health and Social Affairs ('55)
Home Affairs ('48)
Justice ('48)
Labor ('81)
National Defense ('48)
National Unification Board ('69)
Public Information ('68)
Science and Technology ('67)
2nd Minister of Political Affairs ('81)
Transportation ('48)

Agency
Agency for National Security and Planning ('81)
Legislative Administration Agency ('48)
Veterans Administration Agency ('63)

Commission
Social Purification Commission ('80-'88)

Board
Board of Audit and Inspection ('63)

3. The Judiciary

Like the NA, the Judiciary's powers of checks and balances against the Executive Branch is greatly impaired. Unlike the U.S. Supreme Court, the South Korean Supreme Court does not exercise the power of judicial review except for, under the Park regime; the Supreme Court can only refer a case involving constitutionality of a legislative or a presidential act to the Constitution Court for judicial review. In the 1st Republic only five out of eleven judges of the Supreme Court could be nominated to serve on the Constitution Committee. In the Chang, the Yushin and the Chun regimes only three judges of the Supreme Court were allowed to serve on the Constitution Committee.

Three points are noteworthy in this regard. First, since the members of the Constitution Committee are represented equally by the NA, the Supreme Court and the Executive Branch do not determine the constitutionality of the other two branches as an independent and impartial judiciary, as it is the case in the United States.

Second, in the United States the impeachment procedures and the judicial review are two separate processes entailing two different procedures, the former involving mainly the Congress (i.e., the impeachment proposal initiated by the House of Representatives and the impeachment trial conducted by the Senate, which is headed by the Supreme Court Chief Justice). But in Korea, the Constitution Court has the power to conduct both impeachment trial and judicial review.

Third, while the terms of the U.S. Supreme Court justices and federal judges are indefinite (subject only to impeachment), the term of South Korean Supreme Court justices is limited to ten years (5 years under the Chun regime), and the President may reappoint the Supreme Court justices but the Chief Justice's term of 6 years is not renewable. The possible politicization of the judiciary by the president on its integrity and independence[6] has thus been removed considerably under the 1987 Constitution.

In addition to the above three branches of governmental apparatus, there are three additional seemingly independent government organizations. They are the Constitution Court (Articles 111-113), the Central

Election Management Committee (Articles 114-116) and the local government (Articles 117-118). During the Roh regime, the city, county and the provincial legislative assemblies have been formed, but the direct popular election of the mayors and the governors are not yet instituted which was one of the major bone of contention between the Roh regime and the opposition parties.

In sum, the independent and robust legislature, the impartial judiciary and the viable local governments, the three key institutional safeguards against the abusive and excessive executive in particular and the powerful and pervasive central government in general, are largely missing in South Korea's formal governmental structures by design. The NA's powers are severely curtailed, and the judiciary's independence and integrity are seriously undermined with the substantial increase and expansion of the presidential powers. As noted earlier, the government becomes authoritarian, and governing becomes dictatorial and arbitrary when the NA lacks authority to check the executive branch's anti-parliamentarian tendency, when the judiciary is held back from challenging the executive branch's anti-libertarian proclivity and when the independent local governments are inoperant to counter the central government's centripetal wielding of power. This has been the case for South Korean politics in over 40 years of its history. Until and unless the NA's vitality, the judiciary's integrity and the local governments' autonomy are institutionalized, the presidential proclivity for authoritarianism is likely to prevail.

Political Process and Party Politics

At present, South Korea is a in transition from an authoritarian to a more democratic and pluralistic rule. A number of concrete evidences for democratization is visible. A peaceful transfer of political power, though not *between* the parties but *within* the ruling party was successfully executed for the second time. In February 1988, Chun Doo Hwan handed the power over to Roh Tae Woo and again, from Roh to Kim Young-sam in February 1993. Since then, liberalization of the press, civil liberties and civil rights has taken root, though temporary setbacks are not infrequent. The following *Human Rights Report-Korea* by the U.S. Government (1991) illustrates this point.

> Based on gains made during the watershed years of 1987 and 1988, Korea today is a more tolerant and open society than it was in the mid-1980's. During these 2 years the Korean press became freer, and the judiciary more independent; workers asserted their right to organize unions and bargain collectively. Yet the continuing gap between democratic ideals and actual practice was apparent in the continued arrest of dissidents, students, and workers under the National Security Law, the Law on Assembly and Demonstrations and the Labor Laws.

Freedom in the World Political Rights & Civil Liberties, 1990-1991 also reported that in its 19 years (1973-1991) of surveying freedom, South Korea had been categorized as a country of "partly free" from 1973 until 1987 and "free" from 1987 through 1990, but again "partly free" in 1991.[7] It wrote further in its country report that "(South Korean) people feel free to speak their minds, within some broad limits, and the Agency for National Security is not as pervasive as it once was.... Government influence on radio and television remains strong.... Assemblies that 'undermine the public order' are forbidden, and force was used to break up several demonstrations."[8]

Theoretically, South Korea's democratic development lies somewhere between an anti-authoritarian ("shouting") stage and a de-authoritarian ("experimental") stage. The first phase of democratization, which is called here an anti-authoritarian or the shouting stage, manifests a political condition in which the ruling elites continue to practice authoritarian rule while the opposition groups and the mass public openly resist it and vociferously advocate democracy. Although democracy is advocated by the mass public and the opposition, their democratic belief systems are not firmly ingrained in minds and behaviors.

The second phase of democratization—de-authoritarian or the experimental stage starts when both the ruling elites and the opposition, as well as the mass public, begin to question their non-democratic belief systems and to recognize the glaring gap in advocating democracy and yet clinging to undemocratic behavior and belief systems. In this phase of democratization, virtually everyone advocates democracy. Both the government in power and the opposition, including the extreme left and the extreme right, clamor for democratization, although each use the term, *democracy,* to mean quite different things. More often than not, both the extreme leftists and rightists contradict themselves in advocacy and action. While demanding democracy, the radical left often resorts to physical violence and/or subversive tactics. Contrarily, the radical right frequently displays intolerance under the pretext of defending democracy.

Specifically, since 1988, the Roh Tae-woo government set the democratization in motion. Even before he assumed the presidency, Roh unleashed the so-called eight-point declaration of June 29, 1987, amid the massive anti-government popular uprising. The eight points of the declaration are: (1) assuring the peaceful transfer of power and allowing a direct popular election through the constitutional revision; (2) revising the presidential election laws and guaranteeing a fair election management; (3) releasing and pardoning political prisoners and restoring their civil rights; (4) upholding human dignity and guaranteeing people's basic civil rights; 5) guaranteeing freedom of the press; (6) guaranteeing self-government and autonomy in all aspects of social life; (7) guaranteeing sound political activities of the parties and cultivating the practice of dialogue and compromise; and (8) eradicating crimes threantening the safety and security of our citizens and correcting social corruptions and irregularities.[9]

When Roh became president, he attempted to fulfill his campaign pledges, although there had been some setbacks and retractions. Hence, the government and the opposition had been at loggerheads over their differences in speed, scope and method of democratization. The political issues no longer centered around the non-recognition of the opposition or the demand for democratization *per se.* One of the controversies between the ruling DLP and the opposition parties was the implementation of mayoral and provincial gubernatorial elections as the law required.

The final stage of democratization or, specifically, South Korea's full-fledged democracy, which is still a distant goal, will be realized only when the democratic advocacy, action and belief systems become the prevailing political norm and proper behavior of the politicians and the people. But a full-fledged democracy is, as Arend Lijphart pointed out, "a rare and recent phenomenon."[10] Higley and Burton, too, made similar observation -- "despite dramatic changes in mass conditions and orientations during the modern historical period, the modal pattern of Western politics was one of persistent elite disunity and resulting regime instability."[11] Lijphart noted that not a single democratic government existed until the first decade of the twentieth century when two countries, Australia and New Zealand, established fully democratic regimes with firm popular control of governmental institutions and universal suffrage. According to Lijphart, only twenty-two countries have been continuously democratic since about World War II, and among them only Japan is non-Western.[12]

Meanwhile, Field, Higley and Burton contended that a key feature of stable democracies is substantial consensus and accommodation among elites on rules of the political game and the worth of political institutions. And they identified three historical routes to elites' consensual unity: special colonial legacies where consensus is achieved prior to national independence; elite settlements, where elites negotiate a deliberate compromise; and two-step elite transformations, where first a consensually-oriented bloc gains stable majority electoral support, and at a later stage a radical minority abandons its distinctive ideological position, adhering to the consensus achieved by its adversaries. Interestingly enough, Highley, Burton and Field noticed, though cursorily, that "South Korean elites are apparently moving at present" in that direction.[13] They called it "elite convergence," in which some of the powerful but previously warring factions in a disunified elite form a winning electoral coalition and, through repeated electoral victories, eventually leave dissident elites no alternative but to compete for government executive power under the same rules of the game and other tacit understanding as the winning coalition.

In the final analysis, however, only the passage of time will vindicate whether or not South Korea is presently undergoing any kind of elite settlement or elite convergence. The December, 1992, presidential election has successfully proven once again the viability and resilience of South Korea's democratization efforts.

In this section, the current state of democratization in South Korea will be examined from two different perspectives and observations. First, it will attempt to explain the persisting incongruity between democratic intent and undemocratic "habits of the heart," between democratic advocacy and authoritarian behavior and between democratic form and undemocratic process. Second, it will measure the current state of South Korea's democratization based on the available quantifiable indices.

Persisting Undemocratic Values and Behaviors

South Korea has been one of the fastest growing economies in the world. Positively, whether it is called "the miracle of the Han River" or one of the four dragons or tigers, South Korean economic development has been phenomenal, at least since the mid-1960's. Higher living standards, improved housing, roads, transportation and communication network and other life amenities are some visible signs. In 1949, for example, South Korea's per capita national income was $35, in 1962 it was $110 but in 1990 it was $5,569. As of 1990, South Korea is 77.8% urban; 72.1% of its housing demand is met; 71.5% of its road is paved; 79% of its pipe water demand is supplied; and 31% of its sewage system is in operation. By the year 2001 when the current 3rd development plan (1992-2001) is to be completed, the government is projecting that South Korea will be 86.2% urban and its housing supply and paved road will reach 92.8% and 100%, respectively. By then, the pipe water supply rate and the sewage system will increase to 90% and 70%, respectively.[14]

Few nations can, in fact, match South Korea's rapid economic growth during the same period. Before 1948, Korea was a typical agrarian society. Now it is called one of the fastest growing newly industrializing countries (NICs). *World Development Report 1991* placed South Korea in an "upper-middle-income" nation category.[15] The agricultural sector's contribution to South Korea's gross domestic product (GDP) has declined from 38 percent in 1965 to 10 percent in 1989, while industrial, manufacturing and service sectors have all increased during the same period from 25 to 44 percent, 18 to 26 percent and 37 to 46 percent, respectively.[16] During this rapid economic structural metamorphosis, South Korea has also become, outwardly at least, an urban society. In 1965 South Korea's urban population constituted 32 percent of its total population, but in 1989 it has increased to 71 percent. In 1960 only three cities in South Korea had a population over 500,000, but in 1990 six cities had population over 1,000,000. Again, in 1990 the population of the capital city area was 18 million, which represented 42.7% of the entire South Korean population.[17]

Negatively, however, South Korea's fast economic transformation and urbanization have also created a series of concomitant problems such as urban overcrowding and squalor, traffic congestions, air, water and soil pollution, crimes, labor-management disputes, regional and sectoral disparities, generational conflicts and student radicalism.

The fast transforming South Korea's socio-economic and demographic landscapes notwithstanding, the people's traditional mores, what Tocqueville called "habits of the heart," persist. By "habits of the heart," Tocqueville meant notions, opinions and ideas that "shape mental habits" and "the sum of moral and intellectual dispositions of men in society."[18] As Bellah and his associates pointed out, the habits of the heart deal with the concept of mores, which involve not only ideas and opinions but habitual practices with respect to such things as religion, political participation and economic life.[19]

A reciprocal giving and receiving common in a traditional setting, for example, may lose its original virtue and become the root cause of corrupt practices in urban and industrial life. Corruption, which permeates contemporary Korean society, may also have originated from some transplantation of rural and traditional values and behaviors to the urban and industrial living. Like cancer, it has now spread through the entire community—schools and academe, business, commercial and labor establishments, civil services, mass media and political parties. Few individuals or organizations are, in fact, free of, or immune from, such corruptions—the bribery nexus and network. The recent scandal, called the Susŏ real estate development project irregularities, which led to the imprisonment of several National Assemblymen, real estate developers and high government officials, exemplifies only a conspicuous symptom of a much deeper socio-political disease rooted in agrarian belief systems and traditional behavior in a rapidly urbanizing life. South Korea's newly achieved urban life and industrial economy demand commensurate urban behavior and non-traditional codes of conduct, but traditional and rural *folkways* are diehard.

The more industrialized and urbanized South Korea, the more glaring and outmoded its traditional and rural modes of behavior and transaction appear. Attitudinal and behavioral impediments to South Korean democratization such as political corruption and ritualism, unpredictability and political parochialism, deficient representation and party bossism and ultimate power cultism (*daekwŏn*) are no exception in this regard.

Before these anti- or un-democratic belief systems and behaviors are probed in some detail, five caveats are spelled out. First, these behavioral and belief systems are by no means uniquely and peculiarly Korean. Rather, they are by and large, if not universally, common among the people leading agrarian and rural life styles.

Second, these behaviors and beliefs of rural roots are on the precipitous decline. The outrage at the Susŏ scandal illustrates the public's intolerance for political corruption. The practice of political corruption, which was believed to be the political norm, is now perceived by the mass public as a political aberration, if not outright illegality. To put it another way, this shift seems to pinpoint the development of legal norms in South Korea.

Maine explains that the rise of contract has contributed to the declining role of kinship as the exclusive basis of social organization; Durkheim saw restitutive sanctions replacing repressive ones as a result of the growth of the division of labor and the corresponding shift from mechanical to organic solidarity; Dicey observed the growth of statutory lawmaking from the increased articulateness and power of public opinion; and most notably, Weber viewed the development of formal legal nationality as an expression of, and precondition for, the growth of modern capitalism.[20]

To use Weber's typology, South Korea may be in the process of moving from traditional to charismatic and to rational-legal authority.[21] Korea is, however, still far from becoming the society of rational-legal authority. Examining the number of lawyers in Korea may illuminate this point. According to the Korean Lawyers Association, out of 43 million people 2,754 were lawyers as of February, 1991, and of that number 2,009 are practicing law while 745 remain inactive. By contrast, according to *The United States Statistical Almanac* (1990), out of 239 million people 655,191 were lawyers in the United States in 1985. It translates to one lawyer per 21,403 people in South Korea while the ratio is one lawyer to every 360 people in the United States. To put it another way, South Korea has a long way to go in becoming a rational-legal society, if the United States has perhaps become too legalistic.

As noted in Chapter 2, Korea's non-legal and authoritarian traditions have had much deeper roots. The law was not developed to protect either the individual's political rights or his economic positions. Rather, as Hahm pointed out, it was perceived as an "instrument of chastising the vicious and the depraved" in the Korean political tradition. The law always signified "a norm with physical force as a sanction behind it. It was therefore synonymous with punishment, no more no less."[22] From this standpoint, the current rational-legal orientation of the South Korean political scene is certainly laudable, but it also signifies a long and arduous journey ahead.

Third, as stated at the outset, democratic *format* is easy to establish, but democratic *performance* is more difficult to realize, for the latter requires the interaction of attitude, advocacy and action.

Fourth, what is rational and ideal in one context may be irrational and undesirable in another. For example, *mip'ung yangsok* [venerable behavior and cherished mores] based on Korea's rural and agricultural life may easily become burdensome and outmoded in contemporary urban and industrial environments.

Finally, in a broader context the debates as to whether cultural factors such as Confucianism or Confucian ethic have a causal relationship with economic development can be extended to political development or democracy as well. In explaining a causal relationship between cultural values and economic development, Confucian-derived cultural values such as work ethics, thrift, diligence, respect for educational achievement, avoidance of overt conflict in social relations, loyalty to hierarchy and authority and stress on order and harmony are often identified. A broad consensus exists in fact that Confucianism has been a factor, if not the dominant variable, in explaining the economic dynamics of Japan and the so-called Asian NICs.[23] However, the same case cannot be made between Confucianism and political democracy. On the contrary, Confucianism and/or other traditional value systems such as Buddhism and shamanism, have been more of an impediment than a contributing factor to democratization in Korea. Was Confucianism (Buddhism and shamanism, for that matter) not associated with the millennia-old Korean autocratic and authoritarian monarchical system? Even for the positive causal relationship between Confucianism and economic development, the following questions must be satisfactorily answered before the debate can be settled. One, as Max Weber identified the spirit of capitalism only with the protestant ethic, not Christianity *in toto, which Confucian ethic* has been conducive to economic development of Japan and Asian NICs? For, Confucian values contain both facilitative and detrimental elements to economic growth. The rigid social hierarchy and lack of social mobility, low status of merchant and commercial class, wasteful ceremonial and ritual functions such as wedding, funeral and burial and ancestor worships are the cases in point. What is more, Confucianism has been changing over the years and its practices vary considerably among the Asian nations.

Two, similarities exist between the protestant ethic such as Calvinistic "calling," diligence, thrift, sobriety, prudence[24] and the aforesaid Confucian ethic. Does it mean, then, that the scholars are merely searching for the cultural values which are conducive to economic growth *after* a country is developed? If a phenomenon can be explained through an ex post facto analysis, then an Islamic ethic may be used to explain the fast economic growth of the Arab nations in the future, should they develop rapidly. Weber contends that capitalism is "at least a rational tempering of the irrational impulse—the impulse to acquisition, pursuit of gain, of money, of the greatest possible amount of money." Further, he argues that the "state itself, in the sense of a political association with a rational, written constitution, rationally ordained law, and an administration bound to rational rules or laws, administered by trained officials, is known, in this combination of characteristics, only in the Occident, despite all other approaches to it."[25] In this connection, it is interesting to note that Kyong-dong Kim, for one, attributes Korea's fast economic growth to what he called "adaptability" combined with a motivational force called *hahn* -- a mixture of feelings and emotional states, including a sense of rancor, regret, grief, remorse, revenge, grievances or grudges; these feelings have to do with an accumulated sense of frustration, repeated deprivation of need gratification, or constant suppression of one's own desires. He argues further that if rationality is a requisite for capitalist development, the future of South Korea's capitalist development will largely depend on how successfully Korean people can utilize their adaptability to acquire such rationality.[26]

Setting Weber's rationality argument aside for the moment, if the Protestant ethic and the Confucian ethic (or, the Islamic ethic, for that matter) are merely ex post facto explanatory variables, the causal relations between religious ethic and economic development seem untenable.

Bearing the above-mentioned caveats and limitations in mind, a few key features of political underdevelopment of South Korean politics and political process will be examined below.

1. Political Corruption and Ritualism

It is posited here that the political corruption such as the Susŏ Scandal which outraged the public originated from the deep-seated traditional and rural practices called *reciprocity* or trading of favors or services. It is further assumed that reciprocity in a rural and agricultural community represents a typical *mip'ung yangsok,* which is common in any rural or farming community. A few illustrations suffice to drive this point home. The reciprocity of services and the necessity of group labor for different phases of farm work were observed among the Yako in Southern Nigeria by Forde in his study.[27] Homans reported a variety of common plow teams and common plowing in English villages of the thirteenth century. He further wrote that "in any community where people are poor and the struggle to make a living is hard, mutual help must be a matter of course if the community is to survive. In a community of husband-men, lending tools or animals and working in company with neighbors to get a job done which is beyond the resources of a single family are among the most familiar practices."[28] Similarly, M.C. Yang chronicled the team work of three or more people with an ox and a donkey or an ox and a mule in plowing, sowing and harvesting in a rural Chinese village.[29]

In Korea even today, such practices of reciprocity and mutual help are not uncommon in the rural areas. Seeding, planting and harvesting of rice as well as other crops are labor-intensive tasks. Hence, all work together until the tasks of the entire farming village are completed. All the food, drinks and snacks are provided by the family whose farm is being plowed on a given day. Rapid urbanization and shrinking farming population, introduction of mechanization in farming and of cash pay-ments in farm work have considerably dampened the deep-rooted non-cash reciprocity of mutual assistance. Under rapid urbanization and industrialization, one can now seldom see typical traditional and rural life styles or, for that matter, the prototype of an urban and civic culture. In Moore's phraseology, the Koreans are now witnessing "the depar-tures from traditional norms and canons of behavior and the process whereby adults...become involved in and perhaps emotionally commit-ted to novel social situation." He is also correct to stress that preindustri-al structural and cultural differences may persist because economic sys-tem does not wholly determine other components of social system.[30] As Halpern pointed out, we can no longer speak of a rural-to-urban transi-tion or a rural-urban continuum but can talk only in terms of changing rural and urban contexts. He further writes:

> The dynamics of the situation...are not simply the extension of urban influences into the countryside but the impact of rural migrants and their values upon the city—the peasantization of the town—and the simulta-neous evolution of both types of communities within the larger society. In the process cities are modified but rural society is transformed.[31]

These conspicuous examples of what Halpern called "the peasantiza-
tion of the town" in contemporary urban Korean life may be the practices of one person paying for the group, extravagant wedding ceremonies, prohibitively expensive funeral services and other celebrations
such as the sixtieth birthday, retirement and graduation parties. The person paying the bill for the group is likened here to the host farm family
which supplied all the food, drinks and snacks on the day its farm was
plowed. In traditional rural villages such practices were desirable and
even rational, for everyone knew how much work was involved in completing the tasks in the farm. Above all, reciprocity, though not calculated through exacting mathematical formula, works because all the
farming families will eventually host others in the planting season,
weeding times or harvesting months. In a city, however, one who hosts
a party for a group of people is unsure of reciprocity from the recipients
of free meals, drinks and other favors. City life is too hectic, complex
and unpredictable to expect reciprocity. Noncontractual and unwritten
reciprocity (*p'umasi*), which works in a farming village cannot work in
an urban setting. Worse still, unlike the farmers, the urbanites' wages
and salaries are fixed while their nightly drinking, eating and other
entertainment costs are largely unpredictable. Yet the practice of one
person paying for the group continues. This is the urbanite's dilemma of
adhering to rural habits. It epitomizes a behavioral theorem -- what is
rational and desirable in one spatial and temporal setting may be irrational and undesirable in another context.

The city-dwellers in Seoul or any other city in Korea today have few
options available to overcome or escape this dilemma. One way is simply to stop this practice at the cost of becoming a loner and suffering
ostracism from the fellow workers or other acquaintances as being un-
sociable, selfish or *yamch'ae* [a cad or an egomaniac]. The next option
is to avoid such social ostracism by throwing lavish drinking and entertainment parties to their friends and business associates, and thereby,
incurring a huge debt. A Korean name for such a person is *bong* [a
wastrel]. The cost of entertainment is so prohibitive that finding a middle of the road between avoidance and indulgence and between being a
yamch'ae and a *bong* is impossible. The drinking and entertainment

places range from the expensive and exclusive salon to *p'ochang mach'a* [a makeshift tent bar] alongside the street. Whether one frequents the salons or the *p'ochang mach'a,* the entertainment costs usually far exceed their regular earnings. The third way is to constantly search for other sources of income or money to underwrite the cost of such excessive spending. Herein lies the root cause of irregularities, corruption and bribery. From this context, the one who selects the avoidance approach is not necessarily a *yamch'ae* though the public still perceives the person as such. This option is, in fact, far more rational than self-indulgent living beyond one's means.

Despite the incongruent peasant behavior in the urban setting, one who indulges in lavish drinking and entertainment parties is still admired for being a *sanae daechangbu* [a big man or a macho man]. Also typical Seoulites are stereotyped as being *yaksakpparuda* [shrewd] or [tactful] and the new arrivals from the countryside as being *huhada* [generous] or [unselfish]. If the Seoulites, often pejoratively called *kkakjangi* [a shrewd and stingy person], mean two generations of people -- parents and their children -- who were born and raised in Seoul, they only con-stitute a tiny minority of today's Seoul population. The majority of resi-dents in Seoul today came from the countryside. Thus, peasant behavior still prevails in Seoul. That nearly half of the Seoul residents visit their hometown to meet family members and relatives during the holidays such as *Ch'usŏk* [Autumn Harvest Moon Festival] or *Sŏl* [lunar New Year] illustrates the case. Generally speaking, people over forty still prefer, by and large, the practice of one person paying for the group. Interestingly enough, however, a majority of the younger generation today shares expenses for a group party or recreation. Dutch treat is becoming the social norm of group behavior among the youngsters. From this standpoint, traditional behavior is vanishing from Korean urban life, and will soon be replaced by more sensible behavior in tune with the urban life styles.

Other ramifications of traditional or peasant ritualism in urban life today are found at the scenes of wedding ceremonies, funeral services and other social functions. Traditional wedding rituals are now seldom performed either in the city or in the countryside. Two kinds of wedding scenes are typical today. If the bride or the groom hails from a rich and/or powerful family, the lavishness of the wedding ceremony is beyond description. Rows of expensive floral wreaths and a huge line of people delivering envelopes with money as the wedding present are the usual scenes. The parking lots are full of cars of the guests who came to pay tribute. Similar scenes are repeated at funeral services of the rich or powerful family members. The wedding of the poor family member is rather contrasting: instead of lavishness, there is an almost market-like atmosphere; the ceremony is run like a factory shift; and the ceremony must be completed within an hour since several sets of bridal parties are waiting in line to go through the same ritual in the same room within the given time limit. The wedding hall, usually 4 or 5 story buildings, has two dozen rooms which are run like commercial outfits. Only a few weddings are performed in the churches and temples by the clergy. Most wedding ceremonies are conducted by a celebrity at the commercial wedding halls. Unlike the hustle and bustle of the guests at the funeral services of the rich and/or powerful man, stillness reigns at the poor man's funeral service where only the closest family members and relatives sit and mourn for the dead. Today the wedding and funeral services of the rich or the poor have virtually lost the solemnness and sacredness these rituals demand. In fact, it is not infrequent for a rich or powerful family to receive a large sum of money from the guests at such funeral, wedding and other ceremonial occasions. These scenes represent behaviors which are social misfeasance of the traditional wedding, funeral and other rituals. When *p'umasi* was transplanted from rural to urban life, it became wasteful and excessive, and above all, it has contributed to widespread corruptions in virtually every aspect of society.

National Assemblyman's routine activities serve to illustrate this argument. As Table 11-4 below illustrates, an Assemblyman attends far less National Assembly (NA) sessions than those required by the law. Except for the Ist National Assembly (NA) session, all the rest held less than half of the required session days. When the NA is not in session, the Assemblyman's day usually begins with a breakfast meeting at a hotel or at a restaurant with his or her business or political friends. Then between lunch and dinner, he or she may have to attend a wedding or two on top of visiting one or more funeral services. After dinner or evening reception, he or she usually goes to a drinking party with his political or business associates at one to three bars. Hence, by the time he or she returns home, it is well past midnight, and this hectic and unproductive pace of life is repeated the next day. During the weekends, he or she is often requested by a constituent to preside at a wedding ceremony. During the wedding season, an Assemblyman receives a handful of wedding invitation notices from his or her constituents in a day. These invitations are like a debt which has to be repaid, as are the funeral notices. The Assemblyman must have ten times his or her regular salary to meet such expenses alone. How and from where can he or she obtain the extra money or funds for such expenses? Most of all, when and how can he or she function as a legislator when he or she is expected at these wasteful and unwholesome traditional rituals?

2. Unpredictability and Political Parochialism

Destruction of proper authority in social and political life is a significant feature of authoritarianism. Conversely, therefore, restoration of proper authority to all aspects of social and political life marks the termination of authoritarian politics. An authoritarian regime ignores, undermines and even destroys proper authority at home, school, business and other social and political organizations. Only the authoritarian leader matters, and all the other leaders or authorities are subjected to the former. Under such circumstances, multiple authorities of complex social and political organizations are quickly replaced by the ultimate authority of a dictator. In the process, predictability is sacrificed to the ultimate authority's personal whims. Political unpredictability is most evident in recruitment and promotion practices. If predictability prevails in a democratic polity, unpredictability, especially in elite recruitment, dominates in an authoritarian polity. For example, if a headmaster's job becomes vacant, one should be able to predict with a reasonable amount of certainty as to who would be next in line to assume the post by taking into account seniority and other necessary qualifications. If an expected person is not appointed or promoted, and a totally unexpected person fills the position, the rules of the game are no longer valid. The mark of political development is, then, to minimize such unpredictability and unexpectedness and maximize predictability and rationality. Unpredictability in political recruitment is closely related to nepotic practices and other traditional value systems. It may be true that what is being regarded as a surprise or an unpredictability from a legal rational point of view may not be necessarily so from a traditional perspective. For example, a man with a traditional turn of mind may not be surprised at seeing someone catapulated to a high position overnight because he and the man in power are connected to each other through the same region (*chiyŏn*), the same school (*hakyŏn*) or the same family (*hyŏlyŏn*). But to a man with a rational-legal turn of mind, the same incident may be perceived as being not only unpredictable but even improper, if not illegal.

It is posited here that the South Korean politics is still plagued by surprises, unpredictability and nepotistic practices. The practice of recruiting top political elites and establishing political-business-military elite nexus from a particular region or a school, the TK division (Taegu-Kyŏngbuk High School graduates), for one, comes to mind. The persistence of the TK division reveals not only undemocratic behavior patterns in the present South Korean political arena but also the representative example par excellence of the Korean parochialism and ascriptive elite recruitment practices.[32]

3. Deficient Representation and Party Bossism[33]

The third feature of political underdevelopment or unrepresentativeness, that is, undemocratic political practices in South Korean political arena today, is party bossism. Party bossism is marked by at least two undemocratic political practices. One of the central characteristics of party bossism is manifested in what is called, the "politics of reverse order," in contrast to the "politics of democratic order." The logic for the politics-of-democratic-order runs as follows: contemporary democracy necessitates a representative democracy in which a legislature plays the key role; an election is necessary to create such legislative body; and hence, political parties are organized to find the candidates to run for

legislative offices. Differently put, today's democracy is representation-
al which requires a legislative body, which, in turn, necessitates a
periodic election through open competition among political parties.

By contrast, the logic for the politics-of-reverse-order operates in an
opposite direction: the party boss almost single-handedly creates (or dis-
solves) a political party at will, which, in turn, manages election by controlling almost exclusively the power of nominating the party candidates
of each and every electoral district, and the successfully elected representatives arrive at the National Assembly (NA) and function like a
robot under the strict guidance and leadership of the party boss. The
practice of voting strictly along the party line and of censuring or "disci-
plining" members who defy the party voting at the NA is the prime
example. Hence, unlike the legislature in a working democracy where
party's electoral function virtually ceases after the election, and the legislature, be it the U.S. Congress or the British Parliament, becomes the
center of political and policy process, in South Korean politics today,
not only is the NA not in session most of the time, but even when it is in
session, the party boss' control of his representatives in the NA continues unabated. If the politics of democratic order is that of a bottom-up
organizational and operational structure based firmly on the politics of
grassroots, the politics of reverse order is that of a top-down command
and control hierarchy guided often single-handedly by the party boss.
Hence, cronyism thrives in political arena.

From a citizen's point of view, the true meaning of representation is
undermined by the politics of reverse order and party bossism. Perhaps,
it may be much more accurate or realistic to say that the general publics'
lack of clear understanding of the concept of representation and of
representative democracy has given rise to such undemocratic practices.
Both the citizens and the politicians are at fault in misunderstanding and
even abusing political representation. Still a large number of people
believes that the political candidates, if elected, will amass a large sum
of money. Hence, these voters think that they, too, should have a share
of their representatives' amassed wealth, real or imagined. Consequently,
they often demand money or other support from their representatives for
their private entertainment expenses (one of my politician friends

informed me that some voters had the nerve to ask for a round trip airplane ticket to Cheju Island for their son's and daughter's honeymoon, not to mention their constant requests for floral wreaths and contributions to wedding and funeral expenses).

The politicians, on the other hand, willingly or unwillingly, respond to the absurd demands of their constituents in the hope of winning their support for the next election. Thus, the vicious circle created by the politicians' response to the voters' demands continues as do corruption and bribery. Under such political circumstances, little or no room exists for the survival of either the proper meaning of representation or of the legitimate roles of representatives. This vicious circle will end only when the general public and the voters realize that they are electing their representatives to protect and promote the interests and welfare of their district and the nation. Thus, they must stop portraying their representatives as extortioners or embezzlers of public money or funds.

Two, the party boss acts like a father, who provides security and sustenance to the family members. When the father is gone, the family experiences hardship. Likewise, when the party boss is gone or, is out of power, the party, too, will go out of existence. If the South Korean party is likened to a house on the sand, the party members are the sand and its boss, the house. When President Syngman Rhee, head of the Liberal Party, was removed from power in April 1960, the Liberal Party collapsed; when Prime Minister Chang Myŏn was ousted by the military coup leaders in May 1961, his Democratic Party quickly became defunct; when President Park Chung Hee was assassinated in October, 1979 by Kim Chae Kyu, then the Korean CIA Director, his ruling party, the Democratic Republican Party, too, was dissolved. When President Chun Doo Hwan gave up his power to President Roh Tae Woo, his erstwhile ruling party, the Democratic Justice Party, disappeared. In October 1992, Roh committed an unprecedented political act by leaving his own ruling party, the Democratic Liberal Party (DLP). In so doing, the DLP may continue to survive under the new Kim Young-sam presidency.

One major reason for linking the party boss' fate with the party's life span stems from the practice of the boss usually creating the party instead of the party giving birth to its boss. Hence, when the party boss is gone, the party disappears. Nevertheless, the death of a political party does not necessarily mean the demise of the party boss and his cronies. In reality, the party boss and his cronies continue to survive usually under a different party name. The party frequently changes its names and bosses, and key members continue to survive under a different party name.

Kim Young-sam (1927-), for one, represents one of the best case studies for the game of changing the party name. During the Rhee regime (1948-1960), he began his political career as a member of the ruling party, *Chayudang* [Liberal Party] in 1951 and was elected as a member of the Third National Assembly (NA) in 1954. In 1960 he joined *Minjudang* [the Democratic Party] and became a member of the Fifth NA. When the ruling Democratic Party of the Chang government (1960-1961) was forcibly dissolved by military junta (1961-1963), led by General Park Chung Hee, Kim became a key member of a new party called *Sinmindang* [New Democratic Party] in 1961. But in 1963 he was elected to the NA as a member of *Minjŏngdang* [Democratic Political Party] and two years later he joined *Minjungdang* [Democratic People's Party]. During the Park regime (1964-1972) and the Yushin system (1972-1979), he technically belonged to *Sinmindang* [New Democratic Party] which was created in 1967. During the Chun regime Kim was a leader of *Sinhanminjudang* [New Korea Democratic Party], which came into being in 1985. In 1987 Kim was the leader of the newly created *T'ongilminjudang* [Reunification Democratic Party]. In 1990, he once again joined the newly merged ruling party, *Minjadang* [Democratic Liberal Party]. Thus, he has been a member of nine different parties during some 40 years of his political career.

A number of political saliency characterizes political underdevelopment and undemocratic practices in the aforesaid party boss politics in South Korea. First, as noted above, the South Korean party politics has yet to set the precedent of separating the death or exit of the ruling party leader from the dissolution of the party. The political tradition of the ruling party's survival, irrespective of the exit or demise of its party head, is still absent in South Korean party politics.

Second, the dissolution of the ruling party often means not its permanent extinction, but its reemergence under a new name with the old members. Only the party *name* disappears, but its members continue to survive politically under different party labels.

Third, the opposition party members frequently resort to organizational shuffling and reshuffling among themselves usually just before or immediately after the election. This behavior demonstrates that the party members are more interested in receiving the party nomination and being a successful candidate than in upholding the ideological tenets and political banners of their party.[34]

Fourth, the South Korean political party system is not characterized by the two-party system, the multi-party system, nor the dominant party system. There have always been a dominant ruling party and a handful of weak and fragmented but vociferous opposition parties. Unlike Japan's ruling Liberal Democratic Party (LDP), South Korea's ruling parties, be they Rhee's Liberal Party, Park's Democratic Republican Party, Chun's Democratic Justice Party or Roh's Democratic Liberal Party, have not formally and officially permitted intra-party political competition. To repeat, if Japan's Liberal Party is a typical dominant party under a parliamentary system which allows intra-party competition in the absence of a serious inter-party competition, South Korea's ruling parties have been a dominant party under a presidential system run virtually singlehandedly by the incumbent president in the absence of intra-party competition. If Japan's LDP is a multi-headed dominant party, South Korea's ruling parties have been a single-headed dominant party. Noteworthy is the fact that the current ruling party, the DLP, which was created by the merger of three parties (the Democratic Justice Party, the Reunification Democratic Party and the New Democratic Republican Party), is showing an incipient sign of intra-party rivalry, if not competition.

Several corollaries to these party politics come to mind. The first is the blurring of ideological distinctiveness, that is, party members in power and in opposition are conservative or anti-communistic. As long as the party members profess anti-communism, no other ideological, political or policy differences really matter. What is more, the existence of the two regimes in the Korean Peninsula necessitates the restriction and prohibition of leftist or strong reformist party organizations and activities in the political arena through the legal or institutional sanctions such as the National Security Law, and they are under the close scrutiny and surveillance of intelligence apparatus like the Agency for National Security and Planning.[35] For example, in the 14th National Assembly election on March 24, 1992, no minor socialist or the so-called *minmin wun* [national-democracy movement] candidates won the seat and their combined vote was barely 2.13% of the total national vote. From this standpoint, legal and institutional restrictions and prohibitions also undermine the proper meaning of representation and representative democracy which is being misunderstood and abused by the citizens and the politicians.

The ephemeral nature of the party life is another political corollary. Few parties or, more accurately, few party *names* have in fact survived beyond one regime; no party or party *names* have lasted more than two Korean regimes thus far (See Table 11-2).

The third corollary is that a loyalty to, and identification with, a specific party, its label or organization is absent. Members cannot be loyal to the party because the party names change frequently and the party organization consists usually of a group of key politicians at the central and national level and none at the local or the grassroots level. Hence, unlike in the democratic countries in the West and Japan, where the party *names* have survived for decades and centuries, in understanding South Korean politics another dimension enters into the citizen's so-called party identification and party support. Namely, because of the frequent changes in party's *name*, citizens' attachment to and identification with the name of the party is nearly insignificant. Regardless of the party *name*, they are, thus, prone to identify either with the ruling party of the moment or with the opposition party (parties) at the time of their vote and/or political actions. For, party *names* change frequently, but in a given moment there are always the governing party and the opposition. Besides, the politicians who once served in the previous ruling party are usually coopted into the new ruling party. Similarly, the opposition politicians remain in opposition even after the old opposition party is reshuffled and renamed.

In a study Chan-wook Park and Jung-bin Cho examined the South Korean voters' identification with the ruling party and the opposition parties, without weighing the political significance of the party's name or label itself. Park seems to dismiss the importance of the party *name*. by calling the Democratic Party *chont'ong yadang* [the long-standing opposition party].[36]

Cho discovered that among the opposition-leaning voters who decided on the candidate two weeks before the actual election, the majority tended to support the major opposition party, the Democratic Party (77%), while those who decided to vote for a candidate on the day of the election only 47.5% voted for the DP and the rest voted for the newly-created United People's Party (15.9%) and for the independents (27.3%).[37] This indicates that unlike, for example, in the United States where the party *labels* such as the Democratic Party or the Republican Party have a significant bearing on the voters' party identification, the South Korean voters are primarily divided into either the pro-government-leaning or the opposition-leaning groups, regardless of the party names or labels (See Table 11-3 and Table 11-3a). Ki-sook Cho validated this point rather persuasively. She asserted that the reason the higher rate of Koreans vote for a party rather than for the candidate stemmed from their categorical bifurcation of the parties -- the democratic party versus the anti-democratic party or the anti-dictatorship party versus the dictatorial party.[38]

From a somewhat different plane, Nam Young Lee's research found that 28.9% of the voters decided on the candidate based on the party affiliation. Still, he did not clearly differentiate the party *name* and its political status, i.e., the ruling party or the opposition. In any case he learned that the majority of the non-voters are pro-opposition party rather than pro-ruling party supporters. Specifically, among the non-voters 36% were leaning toward the Democratic Party, 19.5%, to the United People's Party, 8.5%, to the New Political Party and 4.3%, to the People's Party (*Minjung-tang*), while those favoring the ruling party constituted 31.7%. Hence, less the number of voter-turn out, the more advantageous it is for the ruling party.[39]

In brief, the various immature aspects of the Korean party system and its activities graphically testify the degree of South Korean political underdevelopment. The party bossism will not vanish nor will a viable and enduring party system emerge overnight. Until that happens South Korea's representative democracy and party politics will remain in its embryonic stage.

4. Ultimate Power (daekwŏn) Cultism

The ultimate power [*daekwŏn*] denotes the power of the highest office in the South Korean political system, i.e., the presidential power or the presidency. This concept, implicitly, if not explicitly, assumes that political power is ultimately concentrated in one person, the President. Hence, little or no room exists for the concept of power diffusion or power sharing. This concept is used frequently by the South Korean mass media and by the politicians and citizens publicly to refer to the presidential power. Perhaps the prolonged authoritarian politics is responsible for the popular notion that President *can* do or be anything. This view may be unreal or even exaggerated but not utterly groundless or false. There is no question that the presidential powers are truly extraordinary (the presidential powers and authority are found in the 1987 Constitution, especially in articles 66 to 100). The general public and the politicians tend to perceive that the presidential powers and authorities are unlimited and unrestricted. In the process, they overlook the enormous responsibilities and obligations underlying such power. For example, *daet'onryŏng,* an official Korean term for the highest political office and *daekwŏn,* an unofficial term for the office, dramatize one-sided portrayal of the presidency with its uniqueness and concentration of power and authority. *Daet'ongryŏng* refers exclusively to the office-holder of the South Korean presidency. It can only be applied to the incumbent president. But the term, president, in the United States indicates many different persons and positions, ranging from the head of an elementary school student body to corporate officers and to the highest political office, the American Presidency. The word, *daet'ongryŏng,* generates special awe in Korea that the terms like president or prime minister do not. The term, *daekwŏn,* which literally means a "great power," conjures up additional images, meanings and dimensions. In other countries, the term, "great power," is rarely used by the public, the press or the politicians to depict the power of the highest political office, president or prime minister. In international politics the terms, "great powers" or "superpowers," are used to describe economically and/or militarily powerful nations such as the United States and the former Soviet Union. Unlike the internal politics of a nation, the international political arena is often characterized as being a near anarchy or having a very high degree of lawlessness, and, thus, there is a room for the role of the so-called superpowers. The question, then, is why and how has the word *daekwon* become a favorite topic of the South Korean mass media, the general public and the politicians? Does it reflect a relatively high-level of lawlessness and near anarchy of the South Korean internal politics? Whatever the case, one thing seems to be self-evident. The indiscriminate use of the term may stem from the Korean peoples' habits of mind, which became accustomed to a prolonged authoritarian politics. From this standpoint, identifying the presidential power as a "great power" without understanding its commensurate "great responsibility" is not only a linguistic vestige of authoritarianism but another aspect of undemocratic habits of mind.

Some Observable Evidence of Democratization

The Social Science Research Center at Seoul National University conducted a political survey with 2,007 people who were interviewed from October 20 to November 2, 1988. The survey revealed a number of interesting trends. As Table 11-5 indicates, 64.4 percent and 27.5 percent of the participants replied that the South Korean regime five years ago was a dictatorship or a dictatorial authoritarianism, respectively. That is, 91.9 percent of the respondents believed that the regime five years ago was not democratic. But 17.4 percent and 36.9 percent of the same respondents revealed that the South Korean regime at the time of the survey was dictatorial or dictatorial-authoritarian, respectively. And only 14.9 percent of the respondents predicted that the regime will be still undemocratic five years after the survey.[40] Shin and his colleagues found in another study that nearly one in three (31.7%) respondents adhered to authoritarian values while only one in seven (13.7%) respondents held libertarian values.[41] Lee's earlier survey also revealed that Koreans, who are consistent both in democratic attitudes and behavior, constituted less than 10% of the survey respondents.[42] He noted elsewhere that less than one-half of the adult population exhibited some commitment to fundamental democratic values and beliefs, i.e., attitudes toward competition, majority rule and minority rights and self-role perception (political efficacy), while a majority still remained predominantly under the old influence of authoritarian Confucian values.[43]

Meanwhile, Pae's comparative analysis of democratization in 129 countries using longitudinal, dynamic approach presented a rather upbeat assessment of South Korea's democratization. He stated that South Korea, though one of the latest starters of democratization, "has been progressing most rapidly and dynamically." Further, he pointed out that when Gastil's 11 political rights and 14 civil liberties variables are applied to South Korea for 1987 and 1988, there is no doubt that "South Korea has entered [the] threshold of near-full and complete democracy."[44]

On the basis of their survey results which utilized a three-dimensional model of value conflict to estimate the breadth and magnitude of Left-Right conflicts among the South Korean people over political, economic and cultural values, Shin and his associates have concluded somewhat cautiously:

> ... the people in Korea today are deeply divided over the basic values which they hold for themselves and their country. They are divided over "bread and butter" and other economic issues of the Old Politics. They are even more divided over freedom and other noneconomic issues of New Politics. More so than over the issues of the Old and New Politics, Koreans are divided over the question of whether or not their indigenous cultures should be accommodated to those of foreign origin. Korea is no longer a country of homogeneous people; it is a country where a sizable portion of the mass public is in intense conflict over one or more types

of basic values. Korea is also a country where a sizable portion of the mass public is in conflict over the proper roles to be played in the process of democratization. While an overwhelming majority feels that more democracy is needed for their country, only a small minority offers unqualified support for the democratic transformation of authoritarian rule. There is little doubt that the lack of full support among large segments of the mass public for the democratic transformation makes it difficult for Korea to become a state of full and stable democracy within a short span of time.[45]

As Table 11-6 shows, 53 percent of the respondents predicted that the regime change five years later will be more gradual; only 20.8 percent responded that it will be radical. Of the rest, 23.7 percent believed there will be little or no change in the nature of the regime while only 1.7 percent anticipated further deterioration in five years. The same study also revealed elsewhere that more people understood the presidential system (55.5%) than the cabinet-responsible system (16.0%). But more people preferred the cabinet-responsible system (34.8%) to the presidential system (28.3%).[46]

An interesting finding of this survey is that the people's support for the party is extremely low. No party, whether it is in power or in opposition, received more than 22.5 percent of support.[47] Another interesting data presented in this study is the tolerance level of people. While people are very tolerant of the issues concerning North Korea (88.6%), sexual equality (86.4%) and support of the labor union movement (85.3%), they are extremely intolerant of issues dealing with the communist movement (92.2%), the withdrawal of the U.S. forces (68.4%), the confiscation of private properties (60.1%) and with demonstrations (52.7%).[48]

Finally, a recent survey by the Seoul National University's Social Science Research Center is noteworthy. About South Korea's current state of democratization, less than half of the participants (41.7%) replied positively, while 37.2 percent responded that little or no progress has been made in that direction and 16 percent even indicated deterioration in South Korea's democratization efforts (see Table 11-7). The same survey identified the corruptions of the politicians (40.7%), the government's lack of will to democratize (29.4%) and the radicalism of the students and the opposition groups (14.2%) as the three major obstacles to democratization (see Table 11-8). It also revealed that the politicians are considered most corrupt (70.1%), the businessmen were next (10.9%) and the government officials ranked third (9.3%) (see Table 11-9). Despite the persistent corrupt practices and sluggish democratization efforts in South Korea, one index in the survey showed a bright spot. On the factor most crucial to personal success and advancement 10 years later, the overwhelming majority (78%) cited individual effort and ability as the most important ingredient. Factors such as family background and ties, school connections and localism, still considered very crucial in personal career advancement and success, were considered as being insignificant or nearly negligible in the future (Table 11-10).

To summarize, a broad consensus exists that democratization in South Korea is on course, although opinions differ on its speed and the nature of its changes. Most importantly, the future prospect for the South Korean polity is by and large positive and optimistic. From this standpoint, the present political situation, which appears transitional and even traumatic, is only a birth pang of a more democratic and maturer Korean polity.

Concluding Remarks

South Korea is undèrgoing a rapid transformation resulting from accelerated urbanization and industrialization and from conscious efforts to democratize. Interfacing of the traditional and/or agrarian values and belief systems amid predominantly urban and industrial life setting, of the ascriptive elite recruitment practices in an increasingly meritorious society and of the chronic traditional and charismatic authority patterns in a newly emerging rational and legal system continues. South Korea's current problem is not simply the byproduct of a traditional society in transition. Nor is it merely the aftereffects of an old tradition being rapidly replaced by new belief systems. Rather, it is the case of the old habits of the heart being misplaced, misconstrued and misapplied. A desirable polity does not necessarily mean a wholesale removal of the old political tradition; rather, it will occur when the people, elites and the mass public reach a level of sophistication sufficient to distinguish what is or is not viable old tradition in a swiftly transforming urban industrial life. Ideally, a good polity requires the harmonious coexistence of both viable and vital political tradition and modernity. South Korea, a textbook case of the rapidly transforming society and polity of the old tradition and habit, is no exception in this regard.

Table 11-1. The National Assembly (NA) and its Changes

NA	Duration	Type (1)	Methods (2)	Ind.(3)	CR (4)
1th	May 31, 1948 May 30, 1950	U	S D	Yes	
2th	June 19, 1950 April 30, 1954	U	S D	Yes	1st CR (July, 1952)
3rd	June 8, 1954 May 29, 1960	U	S D	Yes	2nd CR (Nov., 1954)
4th	June 7, 1958 July 25, 1960	U	S D	Yes	3rd CR (June, 1960)
5th	August 8, 1960 May 3, 1961	B	S D(HR) N D(HC)	Yes	4th C4 (Nov., 1960)
6th	December 12, 1963 June 30, 1967	U	S D + PR*	No	5th C4 (Dec., 1962)
7th	July 10, 1967 May 25, 1971	U	S D + PR	No	6th C4 (Aug., 1969)
8th	July 26, 1971 October 17, 1972	U U	S D + PR	No	7th C4 (Nov., 1972)
9th	March 12, 1973 March 11, 1979	U	D D + I D	Yes	
10th	May 17, 1979 October 27, 1980	U	D D + I D	Yes	
11th	April 11, 1981 February 15, 1985	U	D D + PR	Yes	8th C4 (Dec., 1980)
12th	February 20, 1985	U	D D + PR	Yes	9th CR (Oct. 1987)
13th	April 26, 1988	U	SD +	Yes	
14th	March 24, 1992	U	SD + PR	Yes	

Sources: Adapted from *Daehanminkuk Sŏnkŏsa, 1985* [History of Election in Korea] (Seoul: Election Management committee, 1985). Also, Hyŏng-sŏp Yun, "National Assembly and its Legislative Process" (in Korean) in Wun-tae Kim, *Hankuk Chŏngch'iron* [On Korean Politics] (Seoul: Pakyong-sa, 1982), pp. 319-393. See also, Chong-Lim Kim et al, "Electoral System and the Dominance of Government Party in Korean Politics," paper delivered at the Second International Conference of the Korean Political Science Association, 25-27 July 1991.
(1) Type is here either unicameral (U) or bicameral (B).
(2) The methods of electing the representatives vary: from 1st through 4th NA, a single-member district by direct popular election (S D) was applied, in the 5th NA, the House of Representatives (HR) used S D, while the member of the House of Councilors (HC) were elected by the nation-wide electorate (N D); in the 6th NA, 2/3 of its members were elected by S D and 1/3 by proportional representation method (PR) on the basis of each party's total national vote tally. In the 9th and the 10th NA, 2/3 of the members were elected by double-member direct election (D D) method and 1/3 were hand-picked by the President. In the 11th and 12th NA, 2/3 were elected by the D D and 1/3 were chosen on the basis of each party's total national vote tally. In the 13th and the 14th NA, the single member district systems were used and 1/3 were chosen on the basis of each party's total national vote tally.
(3) The independent candidates, who have no formal party affiliations, are allowed to run in the election (Yes) or not allowed (No).
(4) There have been 9 constitutional revisions (CR): *inter alia*, in the 1st CR the presidential election method was changed from indirect election by NA to direct popular election; in the 2nd CR the president's terms of office was limited to two terms but the first incumbent president (i.e., Syngman Rhee) was exempt from such requirement; in the 3rd CR the cabinet-responsible system with bicameral legislature was adopted; in the 4th CR special provision was added to punish those who were involved in the 1960 presidential election rigging; in the 5th CR the presidential system and unicameral legislature were restored; in the 6th CR the president's third term was permitted; in the 7th CR, the limit to the president's term of office was abolished; in the 8th CR, the president's term of office is limited to a 7-year one term; and in the 9th CR, the president's term of office is limited to a 5-year one term.

Table 11-2. The National Assembly and the Seats Won by the Political Parties

1st Constituent Assembly (1948-1950)	
Party	No. of Seats
Independents	85
NCEI	55 (G) [24.6]
KDP	29 (0) [12.7]
Others	31
Total	200

NCEI (National Council to Expedite Independence); KDP (Korean Democratic Party); (G) Governing Party; and (0) Major opposition party. The figures in the bracket are % of votes received.

2nd National Assembly (1950-1954)	
Independents	126
KNP	24 (G) [9.7]
DNP	24 (0) [9.8]
NA	14 [6.8]
KYC	10
Others	12
Total	210

KNP (Korean National Party); DNP (Democratic National Party); NA (National Association); and KYC (Korean Youth Corps).

3rd National Assembly (1954-1958)	
LP	114 (G) [36.8]
Independents	67 (0) [7.9]
DNP	15
NA	3
KNP	3
Others	1
Total	203

4th National Assembly (1958-1960)	
LP	126 (G) [42.1]
DP	79 (0) [34.2]
Independents	27
UP	1
Total	233

LP (Liberal Party)
DP (Democratic Party)
UP (Unification Party)

Table 11-2. Continued

5th National Assembly (1960-1961)
[House of Representatives]

DP	175 (G) [41.7]
Independents	49
SMP	4 (0) [5.7]
LP	2 (0) [2.7]
KSP	1
UP	1
Others	1

Total	233

SMP (Social Mass Party); and KSP (Korean Socialist Party).

[House of Councilors]

DP	31 (G)
Independents	20
LP	4 (0)
SMP	1
KSP	1
Others	1

Total	58

6th National Assembly (1963-1967)

DRP	110 (88+22)* (G) [33.5]
DPP	41 (27+14) (0) [20.1]
DP	13 (8+5) [13.6]
LDP	9 (6+3)
Others	1

Total	175

DRP (Democratic Republican Party); DPP (Democratic Politics Party); and LDP (Liberal Democratic Party). * For instance, 88 DRP members were elected by direct election in the single-member districts, while 22 were chosen by the proportional representation method based on the party's total national vote tally.

7th National Assembly (1967-1971)

DRP	129 (102+27) (G) [50.6]
NDP	45 (28+17) (0) [32.7]
Others	1

Total	175

NDP (National Democratic Party)

Table 11-2. Continued

8th National Assembly (1971-1972)

DRP	113 (86+27) (G) [48.8]
NDP	89 (65+24) (0) [44.4]
Others	2
Total	203

9th National Assembly (1974-1979)

YJA	73 (G) [38.7]
DRP	73 (G) [32.5]
NDP	52 (0)
UP	2
Independents	19
Total	219

YJA (Yujŏnghoe, 1/3 of the NA members were handpicked by the president)

10th National Assembly (1979-1980)

YJA	77 (G)
DRP	68 (G) [31.7]
NDP	61 (0) [32.8]
UP	3
Independents	22
Total	231

11th National Assembly (1981-1985)

DJP	151 (90+61) (G) [35.6]
DKP	81 (57+24) (0) [21.6]
KNP	25 (18+7) [13.3]
Independents	11
Others	8
Total	276

DJP (Democratic Justice Party); DKP (Democratic Korea Party); and KNP (Korean National Party).

Table 11-2. Continued

12th National Assembly (1985-1988)

DJP	148 (87+61) (G) [35.25]
NKDP	67 (50+17) (0) [29.25]
DKP	35 (26+9) [19.50]
KNP	20 (15+5)
Independents	4
Others	2
Total	276

NKDP (New Korea Democratic Party)

13th National Assembly (1988-1992)

DJP	125 (6) [34.0]
RDP	59 (0) (23.8]
PPD	70 (0) [19.3]
NDRP	35 [15.6]
Others	1
Total	299

RDP (Reunification Democratic Party); PPD (Party for Peace and Democracy); NDRP (New Democratic Republican Party)

14th National Assembly (1992)

DLP	149 (116+33) (G) [38.5]
DP	97 (75+22) (0) [29.2]
UPP	31 (24+ 7) [17.4]
Independents	21
NPP	1
Total	299

DLP (Democratic Liberal Party); DP (Democratic Party); UPP (United People's Party); NPP (New Politics Party).

Sources: *Idem.* See also Hyun-woo Kim and Soeren Risbjerg Thomsen, "Voter Mobility in the Korean National Assembly Elections, 1985-1988," paper delivered at the Second International Conference of the Korean Political Science Associations, 25-27 July 1991.

The South Korean Political System

Table 11-3. The Percentage of Distribution of Legislative Seats
by Two Major Parties

Republic	Election Yr.	% Seat distribution of two Major Parties	No. of Parties
The Ree regime	1st : '48	27.5 v. 14.5	48 (16)***
	2nd: '50	11.4 v. 11.4	40 (10)
	3rd: '54	56.1 v. 7.4	14 (4)
	4th: '58	54.1 v. 33.9	14 (3)
The Chang regime	5th:'60 [HR][1]	75.1 v. 1.7*	14 (6)
	[HC][2]	53.4 v. 6.9	
The Park regime	6th: '63	62.9 v. 23.4	12 (5)
	7th: '67	73.7 v. 25.7	11 (3)
	8th: '71	55.4 v. 43.6	6 (4)
The Yushin rule	9th: '73	50.0 v. 35.6	3 (3)
	10th: '78	44.2 v. 39.6	3 (3)
The Chun regime	11th: '81	48.9 v. 30.9	12 (8)
		54.7 v. 30.9**	
	12th: '85	47.3 v. 46.2	9 (6)
		52.5 v. 36.2**	
The Roh regime	13th: '88	41.8 v.	14 (5)
	14th: '92	49.8 v. 32.4	6 (4)

Sources: *Daehanminkuk Chŏngdang-sa* [The History of the Political Parties in the Republic
of Korea] (Seoul: the Central Election Management Committee), Vol. 1 (1973) and
Vol. 2 (1981). Also, Sung M. Pae, *Testing Democratic Theories in Korea* (Lanham:
University Press of America, 1986), p. 160 and Byong-man Ahn, *Hankuk Chŏng-
buron* [On Korean Government] (Seoul: Dasanch'ulp'an-sa, 1985), pp. 140-148.
* The Democratic Party was split into two -- the Old and the New factions.
** If the number of the at-large NA members are counted.
***Numbers in the parentheses indicate the parties which actually won the NA seats.
[1] Home of Representatives
[2] House of Councilors

Table 11-3a. The Percentage of Votes Received by the Major Parties
in Parliamentary Elections, 1948-1992

(in percent)

Party	1 1948	2 1950	3 1954	4 1958	5 1960	6 1963	7 1968
Ruling Parties*	24.6% (NCEI)	9.7 (KNP)	36.8 (LP)	42.1 (LP)	41.7 (DP)	33.5 (DRP)	50.6 (DRP)
First Opposition	12.7 (KDP)	9.8 (DNP)	7.9 (DNP)	34.2 (DP)	6.0 (SMP)	20.1 (DPP)	32.7 (NDP)
Second Opposition	9.1 (GYC)	6.8 (NA)	2.6 (NA)	0.6 (UP)	2.7 (LP)	13.6 (DPP)	2.3 (MP)

Party	8 1971	9 1974	10 1978	11 1981	12 1985	13 1988	14 1992
Ruling Parties	48.8% (DRP)	38.7 (DRP)	31.7 (DRP)	35.6 (DJP)	35.3 (DJP)	33.9 (DJP)	38.5 (DLP)
First Opposition	44.4 (NDP)	32.5 (NDP)	32.8 (NDP)	21.6 (DKP)	29.3 (NKDP)	23.8 (RDP)	29.2 (DP)
Second Opposition	4.0 (NP)	10.2 (DUP)	7.4 (DUP)	13.3 (KNP)	19.7 (DKP)	19.2 (PPD)	17.2 (UPP)

* See Table 11-2 for the abbreviation of the major parties.

Table 11-4. The Regular Sessions of the ROK's National Assembly

Assembly	Term	Session days	Session days held (%)	No. of bills passed
1st	2 yrs.	640	399 (62.3)	189
2nd	4 yrs.	1,307	631 (48.3)	322
3rd	4 yrs.	1,270	609 (48.0)	260
4th	2 yrs. 2 mos.	686	212 (30.9)	105
5th	– 10 mos.	258	142 (29.9)	93
6th	3 yrs. 6 mos.	798	345 (43.2)	418
7th	4 yrs.	806	261 (32.4)	479
8th	1 yr. 4 mos.	402	81 (20.1)	70
9th	6 yrs.	615	167 (27.2)	517
10th	1 yr. 7 mos.	118	28 (23.7)	108
11th	4 yrs.	482	144 (29.9)	437
12th	3 yrs. 1 mos.	414	120 (28.9)	300
13th	4 yrs.	–	–	79
			Total	3,377

Source: *Kukjong Shinmun* [Government News], 12 March 1992. Also, Soo Hoon Lee, *Hankuk kwa Chesamsaekye ui Minju Byonhyok* [Democratic Reforms in Korea and the Third World] (Seoul: Kyungnam University Press, 1989), p. 134. Quoted in Sanghyun Ro, "A Comparative Analysis of South Korea's National Assembly and North Korea's Supreme People's Assembly: Structure, Functions, and Process" (MA thesis, the Graduate Institute of Peace Studies, Kyung Hee University, 1990), p. 63.

Table 11-5. The South Korean Regime Types and Regime Changes

Regime Types	5 Years Ago (%)	Now (1988) (%)	5 Years Later (%)
A. Non-democratic			
Dictatorial	64.4	17.4	3.3
Dictatorial-Authoritarian	27.5	36.9	11.6
B. Democratic			
Democratic-Authoritarian	6.6	34.9	32.0
Democratic	1.1	10.6	52.5

Source: Adapted from Doh Chull Shin *et al*, *Hankuk Minjujuiei Mirae* [The Future of Korean Democracy] (Seoul: Seoul National University, 1990), p. 21.

Table 11-6. The Nature of the Regime Change in 5 Years

The Nature of Regime Change	Responses (%)
1. will deteriorate further	1.7
2. will be the same	(23.7)
a. will continue to be dictatorial	2.4
b. will continue to be dictatorial-authoritarian	3.8
c. will continue to be democratic-authoritarian	7.4
d. will continue to be democratic	10.1
3. will change gradually	(53.0)
a. from dictatorship to dictatorial-authoritarianism	7.2
b. from dictatorial-authoritarianism to democratic-authoritarianism	19.2
c. from democratic-authoritarianism to democracy	26.6
4. will change radically	(20.8)
a. from dictatorship to democratic-authoritarianism	5.0
b. from democratic-authoritarianism to democracy	13.2
c. from dictatorship to democracy	2.6

Source: Adapted from Doh Chull Shin *et al, Hankuk Minjujuiei Mirae* [The Future of Korean Democracy] (Seoul: Seoul National University, 1990), p. 28.

Table 11-7. The Degree of Democratization since the Roh Regime

Responses	Percent
Greatly democratized	05.0
Somewhat democratized	41.7
Little change	37.2
Further deteriorated	16.0
No answer	0.2
Total	100.0

Source: Seoul National University Social Science Research Center, *A Survey Report of the Korean People's Belief System in Reference to the Coming 21st Century* (Seoul: Author, 1990), p. 28.

Table 11-8. Obstacles to Democratization

Responses	Percentage
The government's insufficient will to democratize	29.4
Radicalism of students and some opposition forces	14.2
Excessive demands of workers and farmers	7.1
Politicians' corruption	40.7
Military's political intervention	5.6
Others	2.0
Find no Obstacles	0.3
No answer	
Total	100.0

Source: Seoul National University Social Science Research Center, *A Survey Report of the Korean People's Belief System in Reference to the Coming 21st Century* (Seoul: Author, 1990), p. 30.

Table 11-9. Corruption in South Korea by Group or Profession

Responses	No. of Responses	Percent
Politicians	1,071	70.1
Business men	167	10.9
Government officials	141	9.3
Journalists	50	3.3
Military	38	2.5
Educators	31	2.1
Others	20	1.3
No answer	8	0.5
Total	1,527	100.0

Source: Seoul National University Social Science Research Center, *A Survey Report of the Korean People's Belief System in Reference to the Coming 21st Century* (Seoul: Author, 1990), p. 73.

Table 11-10. Important Factors for Success Ten Years Later

Factors	No. of Responses	Percent
Personal efforts and ability	1,192	78.0
Education	204	13.4
Family and parents	86	5.7
Regional or local ties	2	2.1
Others	8	0.5
No answer	5	0.3
Total	1,527	100.0

Source: Seoul National University Social Science Research Center, *A Survey Report of the Korean People's Belief System in Reference to the Coming 21st Century* (Seoul: Author, 1990), p. 76.

Notes

1. Polybius, *The Rise of the Roman Empire* (Harmondsworth: Penguin Classics, 1981), p. 341.
2. For details, see Keun-shik Yun's chapter in Wun-tae Kim, *Hankuk Chŏng-ch'iron* [On Korean Politics] (Seoul: Pakyong-sa, 1982), especially, pp. 231-262.
3. Sung M. Pae dealt with the impeachment issue in detail, see his *Testing Democratic Theories in Korea* (Lanham: University Press of America, 1986), pp. 197-225.
4. *Ibid.*
5. For details, see Sung Chul Yang, *Korea and Two Regimes* (Cambridge: Schenkman, 1981), pp. 260-277.
6. Sung M. Pae, *Op. Cit.*, pp. 210-213.
7. R. Bruce McColm et al., *Freedom in the World: Political Rights and Civil Liberties, 1990-1991* (Lanham: University Press of America, 1991), p. 463.
8. *Ibid.*, p. 234.
9. The English translation is the present author's. Roh's eight-point proposal in Korean is found in *Chugan Kukjŏng News* [Weekly Government News], 29 June 1991.
10. Arend Lijphart, *Democracies: Patterns of Majoritarian and Consensus Government in Twenty-One Countries* (New Haven: Yale University Press, 1984), p. 37.
11. H. Higley and M. G. Burton, "The Elite Variable in Democratic Transitions and Breakdowns," *American Sociological Review* 54 (1989): 22 and 25.
12. Lijphart, *Op. Cit.,* pp. 37-38.
13. Higley and Burton, *Op. Cit.* Also, J. Higley, M. G. Burton and G. L. Field, "In Defense of Elite Theory: A Reply to Cammack," *American Sociological Review* 55 (1990): 421-426.
14. *World Development Report, 1991* (Oxford: Oxford University Press, 1991), p. 209. The 1949 and 1962 data are quoted in Karl Deutsch, *Nationalism and Social Communication* (Cambridge: MIT Press, 1966), appendix. Other data and statistics are from *Chugan Kukjŏng News* [Weekly Government News], 9 September 1991.
15. *World Development Report, 1991*, p. 205.
16. *Ibid.*, p. 209.
17. *Chugan Kukjŏng News, Op. Cit.*
18. Quoted in R. N. Bellah et al., *Habits of the Heart: Invidualism and Commitment in American Life* (New York: Prennial Library, 1985), p. 37 and p. 287.
19. *Ibid.*, p. 37.

20. Quoted in Y. A. Cohen, ed., *Man in Adaptation: The Cultural Present* (Chicago: Aldine. Atherton, 1968), *passim.*

21. Max Weber, *The Theory of Social and Economic Organization*, trans. A. M. Henderson and Talcott Parsons (New York: The Free Press, 1947), pp. 56-57.

22. P. C. Hahm, *The Korean Political Tradition and Law* (Seoul: Hollym Corp., 1967), p. 19. and p. 210. Yoon, too, wrote that in the Yi dynasty law as "an instrument for preserving a social order under Confucian ethics... assumes the form of penal and public law, designed to regulate personal conduct as prescribed by government regulation... individuals represent merely targets of government action, not persons capable of asserting their rights vis-a-vis state. See also, Dae-kyu Yoon, *Law and Political Authority in South Korea* (Boulder and Seoul: Westview Press and Kyungnam University Press, 1990), p. 17.

23. See, for instance, Keith B. Richburg, "Why is Black Africa overwhelmed while East Asia overcomes? *International Herald Tribune*, 14 July 1992.

24. Max Weber, *The Protestant Ethic and the Spirit of Capitalism*, trans. Talcott Parsons (New York: Charles Scribner's Sons, 1958), p. 3.

25. *Ibid.*, p. 17 and p. 16.

26. K. D. Kim, "The Distinctive Features of South Korea's Development," in P. L. Berger and H. H. M. Hsiao, eds., *In Search of An East Asian Development Model* (Oxford: Transactions Books, 1988), pp. 206-207 and p. 217.

27. C. D. Forde, "The Kazak: Horse and Sheep Herders of Central Asia, in Y. A. Cohen, *Op. Cit.*, pp. 168-169.

28. G. C. Homans, "English Villagers of the Thirteenth Century," in Y. A. Cohen, *Op. Cit.*, p. 343.

29. M. C. Yang, *A Chinese Village* (New York: Columbia University Press, 1945), pp. 3-31.

30. W. E. Moore, *The Impact of Industry* (Englewood Cliffs, N. J.: Prentice-Hall, 1965), p. 38 and p. 18.

31. J. M. Halpern, *The Changing Village Community* (Englewood Cliffs: Prentice-Hall, 1967), p. 43 and p. 125.

32. For a comprehensive study of South Korea's ascription-oriented elite recruitment practices, see Sung Chul Yang and Byong Man Ahn, "A Study of North and South Korean Political Elite Recruitment, 1948-1988" (in Korean), a Korean Research Council Study Project, 1990.

33. Weber's description of (American) party boss at the turn of the 20th century is pertinent: "The boss is indispensable to the organization of the party and the organizations is centralized in his hands. He substantially provides the financial means.... The boss, with his judicious discretion in financial matters, is the natural man for those capitalist uncles who finance the election.... He seeks power alone, power as a source of money, but also power for power's

sake. In contrast to the English leader, the American boss works in the dark…. The boss has no firm political 'principles'; he is completely unprincipled in attitude and asks merely: what will capture votes? Frequently he is rather poorly educated man. But as a rule he leads an inoffensive and correct private life. See Max Weber, "Politics as a Vocation," in *From Max Weber: Essays in Sociology*, trans., ed. and with an introduction by H. H. Gerth and C. Wright Mills (New York: A Galaxy Book, 1958), pp. 109-110.

34. Kye Hee Lee, for instance, posits that ideologically, the South Korean opposition parties have metamorphosed from being the party of conservative coalition in the 40s and the 50s, to being the party of anti-dictatorship and democratic struggle in the 50s through the 80s and to being the catchall party in the 80s and beyond. For details, see his "The Prototype of South Korean Opposition Politics" (in Korean), *Sahoekwahak yŏnku* [Social Science Studies] (Suwŏn University Social Science Research Center, 1991), pp. 103-129.

35. Kwangjin You, for instance, listed a number of reasons for the moribund status of the socialist and/or reformist parties in South Korean political arenas, besides the government's legal restrictions. They are: (1) the leaders of these parties were often politically naive and sentimental without having a firm ideological stance; (2) they had had internecine leadership struggles within or between the reformist parties; (3) under the edgy ideological and political atmosphere surrounding the North-South confrontational settings, the mass publics were often suspicious of these reformist parties being pro-communistic; (4) from the launching of the Republic the South Korean government tried to emulate the American-style two-party system and, as a result, the people, too, prefer one powerful opposition party instead of numerous splinter parties; (5) their political slogans and platforms have often been too radical, anti-systemic and extraparliament-oriented. For details, see his "An Analysis of South Korean Socialist Parties' Platforms and Policies" (in Korean), *Social Science Studies* (Suwŏn University Social Science Research Center, 1991), pp. 131-162.

36. Chan-wook Park, "An Analysis of Party Support in the 14th National Assembly Election," paper delivered at the Korean Political Science Association summer seminar, Kyungju, Korea, 2-4 July 1992.

37. Jung Bin Cho, "Pro-government or Opposition-leaning Voters and their Party Support in Relation to their Vote Decision Time" (in Korean), paper delivered at the Korean Political Science Association summer conference, Kyungju, Korea, 2-4 July 1992.

38. See Ki-sook Cho, "The Voters' Rational Choice Model and an Analysis of the Korean Election" (in Korean), paper delivered at the Korean Political Science Association summer seminar, Kyungju, Korea, 2-4 July 1992.

39. For details, see Nam Young Lee, "Voter Participation and Non-voting," paper

delivered at the Korean Political Science Association summer seminar, Kyungju, Korea, 2-4 July 1992.

40. Doh Chull Shin et al., *Hankuk Minjujuiei Mirae* [The Future of Korean Democracy] (Seoul: Seoul National University, 1990), pp. 20-26.

41. D. C. Shin et al., "Left-Right Polarization and Support for Democratization among the Mass Public in Korea," in *Korean National Community and State Development* 1 (1989): 109-154.

42. N. Y. Lee, "The Cultural Basis of Democracy: A Case Study of Public Attitudes and Belief Consistency in Korea" (MA thesis, University of Iowa, 1984).

43. N. Y. Lee, "The Democratic Belief System: A Study of the Political Culture in South Korea," *Korean Social Science Journal* 12 (1985): 46-89.

44. S. M. Pae, "Korea Leading the Third World in Democratization," in *The Korean National Community and State Development* (Seoul: the Korean Political Science Association, 1989), 1, pp. 167-190.

45. D. C. Shin et al., *Op. Cit.* (1989), p. 12.

46. *Ibid.*, p. 60.

47. *Ibid.*, p. 92.

48. *Ibid.*, p. 169.

CHAPTER 12

THE RULING ELITES AND
THEIR MODAL CHARACTERISTICS

The obligation of subjects to the Sovereign, is understood to last as long, and no longer, than the power lasteth, by which he is able to protect them.

Hobbes[1]

Every people is governed by an elite, by a chosen element in the population.

Pareto[2]

In this chapter the findings of the author and Byong-man Ahn's study of the South Korean ruling elites from the Syngman Rhee government through the Roh Tae Woo government will be primarily dealt with.[3] The period covered in this study was from 1948 to 1988. Included in the category of the legislative elites were all the members of the National Assembly (NA) from the 1st through the 13th NA. The administrative elites consist of ministers and vice-ministers of the cabinet, other high-ranking bureaucrats, provincial governors and mayors of Seoul and Pusan in the said period. Only the judges of the Supreme Court were included in the category of the judicial elites. The total number of the personnel under study was 4,560. If, those who were recruited more than twice in these positions were excluded from the figures, the total number in the study would be 2,680.

Five areas were examined—birth date, birth place, education, the previous occupations and the frequency of recruitment. The educational background index was further divided into three areas -- the level of education, the name of colleges attended and the country of education, if a person studied abroad. Incidentally, conspicuously missing in our indices of the South Korean ruling elites' background characteristics is *sex*. This omission was due to the fact that there were only 40 women (or 1.5%) in the sample of 2,680 in this study. Thus, it suggests, though indirectly, the *male* dominance of the South Korean political elites with token and symbolic female representation. In this respect, the North Korean ruling elites are not much different, though better than the South Korean counterparts (For details, see Chapter Eight).

The ruling elites were classified into four categories -- the administrative elites in the executive branch, the legislative elites, the "mixed" elites and the judicial elites. The "mixed" elites denote those who had held positions in two or more branches of the government. The legislative elites were subdivided into those who were elected directly by the constituents in the electoral districts and those who were not. The number of elites in the four classifications were as follows:

Administrative Elites:	677
Judicial Elites:	92
Mixed Elites:	354
Legislative Elites	1,556
Total:	2,680

On the basis of the afore-mentioned criteria and classifications, the following overall profiles of the South Korean ruling elites emerged. A typical political elite is most likely to be a middle-aged, college-educated with a degree from Seoul National University, born in Yongnam and had a high-level bureaucratic experience before he held that covetous position at least once.

Specifically, in terms of age, among 2,680 persons examined, those who were born before 1900 accounted for 299 (or 11.2%), those who were born between 1901 and 1910 totaled 435 (16.2%), between 1911 and 1920, 523 (19.5%), between 1921 and 1930, 713 (26.2%), between 1931 and 1940, 606 (22.6%) and those who were born in 1941 or after amounted to 96 (3.6%). This means that the elites in their 50s through 70s (as of 1990) constituted the majority (68.3%).

In terms of region 858 (32.1%) came from Yŏngnam (the North and South Kyongsang provinces), followed by 556 (20.8%) from Honam (the North and South Cholla and the Cheju provinces). The rest were: 404, (15.1%) from Ch'ungch'ong, 222 (8.3%) from Kyong'ggi, 131 (4.9%) from Kwangwon, 243 (9.1%) from North Korea and 257 (9.6%) from Seoul. A caveat is in order here. Namely, the over-all representation of Honam region appeared relatively high here, primarily because of proportionately higher number of elected legislators from this region. But, as it will become clear in the following, the reverse is true in the case of the administrative, non-elected legislative and mixed elites.

In education, the ruling elites were predominantly college-educated. If those with college degrees (1,475) and those with advanced graduate school degrees (778) were combined, they comprised 84.4% of the total. Those with middle and high school diplomas constituted only 12.5% (333), while only 3.1% (82) had primary school education or less. In terms of the schools they attended, Seoul National University graduates make up 22.9% or 613, the graduates of the military service academies and other military schools 9.7% or 259, Korea University 6.0% or 160 and Yŏnsei University 3.7% or 98. The rest, 35.2% or 943, graduated from schools other than these. The ranking in order of foreign countries where they obtained education were: Japan (66.6% or 474); the United States (22.3% or 159) and the rest (10.3% or 96).

In previous occupations, professional bureaucrats comprised a single largest group at 23.8% (637). They were followed by politicians (14.8% or 397); scholars, those who were college professors or had teaching experiences at the university level (11.8% or 317); businessmen (11.5% or 309); journalists (5.5% or 147); independence movement leaders (2.7% or 73); and others (7.9% or 213).

In frequency of recruitment, those who were recruited only once were the largest (61.7% or 1,654), followed by those who were recruited twice (19.9% or 532), three times (8.9% or 239) and those who were recruited more than four times totaled 8.9% or 112[4] (See Table 12-3).

The breakdown of the South Korean political elites' profile by six regimes should be interesting and meaningful. What follows is the ruling elites' background characteristics of these regimes.

The Syngman Rhee Government

A number of characteristics of the ruling elites stand out in the Rhee regime. First, in age, the number of people born before 1910 constitutes the absolute majority. Among the judicial elites, the people in this age group occupied 80%, among the mixed elites, 78.5%, among the administrative elites, 73% and among the legislative elites, 64.6% (See Tables 12-4, 12-7, 12-10 and 12-13).

Second, in terms of regional distribution, those from Yŏngnam had relatively greater over-all representation, while those from Seoul area had relatively larger representation of the administrative elites and those from North Korea and *Honam* had larger share of the judicial elites.

Thirdly, the judicial elites were the best-educated, namely, they all had college degrees, while the college-educated among the administrative elites and the legislative elites were 70.4% and 60.1%, respectively. As a single school, Seoul National University graduates were the most numerous, but the largest group during this period had foreign education; and, on the whole, those who studied in Japan were predominant. Particularly noteworthy is the fact that all judicial elites during this period were educated in Japan. Despite the fact that Syngman Rhee and his top associates were American-educated, the administrative and mixed elites who studied in the United States constituted mere 22% and 28%, respectively. This meant that the Japanese-educated still maintained a great majority in all elite categories (See Tables 12-5 and 12-14).

Fourthly, for previous occupations, the bureaucrats topped the list, followed by the scholars and lawyers (For details, see Tables 12-6, 12-9, 12-12 and 12-15).

In fine, the majority of the ruling elites in the Rhee regime were born before 1900, hailed from the Yŏngnam region, received education primarily from Japan and came from the bureaucratic backgrounds.

The Chang Myŏn Government

To start with, it is worth noting that the Chang regime was the product of the April Student Revolution of 1960, which led to the downfall of the twelve-year old Rhee regime. The major opposition party (the Democratic Party) under the Rhee regime, whose leaders were heavily recruited from Honam and North Korea, became the new governing party which was soon divided into the Old and the New factions. The general election was held under the freest political atmosphere in the history of the Republic, devoid of any serious political interference or election scandals.

Consequently, the two features of the ruling elites in the Chang regime are quite distinct. First, unlike all the other periods, this was the only time when the regional representation of the ruling elites were balanced. For example, Yŏngnam, Honam and North Korea each had 18%, 21.3% and 21.3% of the administrative elites, respectively. In other periods, the elites from Honam and North Korea had always been underrepresented, particularly among the administrative elites. Second, like in the Rhee regime the Japanese-educated elites predominated, while the American-educated ones declined in number (For details, see Tables 12-4 and 12-5).

The April Student Revolution of 1960 gave birth to the Chang government which was characterized by unprecedented political freedom bordering on chaos at times. While the Japanese-educated were still preponderant, as a result of liberal political atmosphere, the ruling elites from the areas which had consistent underrepresentation previously enjoyed equitable representation.

The Park Chung Hee Government

The Park Chung Hee regime emerged in the wake of the May Military Coup D'Etat of 1961 and the coup leader, then Major General Park Chung Hee, a Japanese Military Academy graduate, was from Yŏngnam, which had significant political implications in elite recruitment in his regime and beyond.

Three salient features of the ruling elites in the Park regime are:

First, the regional imbalances in elite recruitment, especially between Yŏngnam and Honam began to deepen. Among the administrative elites those from Yŏngnam numbered twice as many (26%) as those from Honam (12%). As Figure 12-1 illustrates, as compared with the general population administrative and non-elected legislative elites from Honam areas were underrepresented.

Second, the ruling elites with military background, especially among the administrative and mixed elites, had emerged as a dominant force.

A large influx of military men into the executive branch since the launching of the Park regime is also evident in Kwon's background survey of the administrative elites in the 1950s and the 1960s. According to this study, in the 1950s only 11 (8.8%) out of 138 cabinet appointments, including the prime ministership, went to the military men, while 58 (42.0%) of them were allocated to civilian politicians. By contrast, in the 1960s, 55 (44.0%) out of 125 appointments went to the military men, while only 5 (4.0%) of them were proffered to civilian politicians (For details, see Tables 12-1 and 12-2). Similarly, as Table 12-6 illustrates, the administrative elites with the military background during the Rhee and the Chang governments were only 5.1% and 3.3%, respectively. But during the Park regime the same category rose to 32.7%. To that extent, the Park regime was the beginning of the *militarization* of South Korean politics.

Third, the Japanese-educated elites, especially among the administrative elites, had acquired near absolute majority (81.8%), while the American-educated elites declined further, e.g., only 13.6% of the administrative elites. Note, however, that 85.7% of the Japanese-educated elites had held the key administrative positions since the Chang regime (See Table 12-5).

With the Park regime, ushered in by the May Military Coup of 1961, the composition of the ruling elites shifted to military personnel, became preponderantly Japanese-educated and the imbalance of regional representations in favor of Yŏngnam widened.

The Yushin Government

The Yushin government was the extension of the Park regime except that Park became more of a permanent "dictator-president" under the so-called "Revitalizing Reforms" Constitution of 1972. Accordingly, the features of the ruling elites in the Park regime became more prominent under the Yushin system.

Specifically, the regional imbalances in elite recruitment, especially between Yŏngnam and Honam, worsened. Among the administrative elites, the ratio of those from Yŏngnam to those from Honam was three to one (36% to 12%).

But the elites from the military background in the administrative sector have significantly decreased from 21.2% in the Park regime to 15.3% in the Yushin regime.

A relative decline in the number of elites with foreign educational background was also evident, although the Japanese-educated still maintained a clear majority in all branches (See Tables 12-4 and 12-5).

The Chun Doo Hwan Government

The characteristics of the ruling elites in the Chun Doo Hwan regime differed little from the Yushin regime, at least in its early years. The regional imbalances of administrative elites, especially between Yŏngnam and Honam further widened (41.3% v. 11.7%). As Figure 12-2 indicates, even a rough comparison with the general population in the regions readily shows that Yŏngnam area fared best in all areas of elite recruitment.

Among the administrative elites, the military men rose from 16.2% in the Yushin regime to 21.5% in the Chun regime. Another notable feature is that nearly two-thirds of the elites in all branches were first-timers, indicating a whole-sale replacement of the old ruling elites with new faces (See Table 12-7).

The Roh Tae Woo Government

The coverage of the Roh Tae Woo regime is partial and incomplete. Still, some features can be extrapolated. The administrative elites with the military background has been on the decline, but the Seoul National University graduates have significantly increased. Above all, the regional imbalance in elite recruitment especially the trend of deepening power grips by the Yŏngnam region is still unabated (See Table 12-4).

Preliminary Conclusion

Some political implications of these findings are:

1. The "greening" of the ruling elites over the years is evident. For instance, the elites in their 40s were 38% in the Chang regime, 48% in the Park regime, 52% in the Chun regime and 56% in the Roh regime. To put it differently, each time a new regime emerges, an average age of the new regime elites is about ten years younger than that of the ruling elites in the previous regime. But this does not indicate that the *actual* age of the ruling elites has become younger; it only indicates that the new regime's ruling elites are manned by the new group from the same generation. In short, the average age of the majority of the ruling elites in all republics has been 40-50 years old.

2. The regional imbalances in elite recruitment, especially between Yŏngnam and Honam, have increasingly worsened. This prolonged ascription-oriented recruitment practices may be politically explosive, let alone being morally indefensible, unless some deliberate and firm policy to arrest and reverse this trend is soon put into operation. Several causal factors are responsible for the continuous dominance of the ruling elites from the Kyŏngsang provinces in the South Korean politics. During the Korean War, the Taegu-Pusan region was the only area which escaped the control by the North Korean troops; hence, all foreign aid and other assistance reached

first through this region during and after the war; the relatively heavy concentration of commercial and industrial developments in this region even before the Korean liberation are some factors. The most important element in facilitating and promoting regionalism in South Korea in favor of Kyŏngsang region has to do with President Park Chung Hee's deliberate policy and recruitment practices during his rule. His economic policy in general and industrial development plans in particular were deliberately concentrated in the Kyŏngsang region at the neglect of the Chŏlla and other provinces. One political motive for such discriminatory policy behavior was to strengthen his own power base and to weaken the opposition strongholds. Specifically, Park, a native of the North Kyŏngsang province, recruited his top political associates and lieutenants from his native province and deliberately avoided the recruitment of elites from the Chŏlla provinces, which have been the opposition strongholds since 1945 to the present. The political consequence of such a deliberate regional political gambit is devastating to the point that schism between two regions are deepening rather than narrowing.

3. The steady increase of the elites with bureaucratic backgrounds has both positive and negative implications. Positively, the trend indicates that this particular elite group meets the growing demand for expertise and specialization in governing. Negatively, however, it implies the further entrenchment of bureaucratic dominance and control.

4. Both the steady increase in the number of Seoul National University graduates among the elites (13%, 17%, 23%, 33%, 33%, 23% from the Rhee through the Roh regimes, respectively) and the penetration of the military school graduates into the civilian ruling strata (2%, 3%, 15%, 14%, 12%, 11% from the Rhee through the Roh regimes), too, have negative side effects to the extent that they tend to bar the other educated groups from having a fair share in power. For, these politically alienated group may easily become the prime source of political discontent and instability.

Specifically, the Seoul National University graduates have been consistently and continuously dominating all ruling elite categories (22.9% or 613 out of 2,680 persons). In the judicial elites, the Seoul National University graduates have occupied an absolute majority. It is also interesting to note that the second largest elite groups have been the Korean Military Academy graduates or other military-related professional school graduates. This second largest group (9.7% or 259) reflects what is called here "the politicization of the military." Namely, at least since the successful execution of the 1961 May Military Coup d'etat, the political recruitment of ex-military men had been continuously practiced from the Park regime to the Roh government.

5. Another interesting point is that among the South Korean ruling elites those who studied in Japan (66.6% or 474) constitute the largest and those who studied in the United States (22.3% or 159), the second largest. The trend, however, is that the older the regime, the more Japanese-educated are represented and the newer the regime, the more American-educated are represented. To repeat, the older generation of the South Korean ruling elites were predominantly educated in Japan, while the new generation elites, especially since 1945, have been mostly educated in the United States. Also, in South Korea specialization (e.g., the Higher Civil Service Examination) has been a *sine qua non* in acquiring the elite status from the beginning, especially in the recruitment of administrative elites and judicial elites, although the elected elites such as the National Assembly members have not been subjected to such criterion.

Noteworthy also is the fact that the majority of the South Korean ruling elites had served a key position only once (61.7% or 1,654 out of 2,680 persons). Those who had served twice total only 19.9% or 532 persons. This clearly demonstrates that in South Korea neither a totalitarian leader like Kim Il Sung nor totalitarian elites like the North Korean ruling elites have existed. The political life span of the authoritarian leaders and their followers has been more fleeting than permanent in South Korea. Above all, while Kim Il Sung's totalitarian leadership and his totalitarian elites have never been seriously challenged by other political forces within the WPK and/or within North Korea, the power and authority of South Korea's authoritarian rulers and elites, be it under the Syngman Rhee regime, the Park Chung Hee regime or the Chun Doo-hwan regime, have never been free from protests and challenges of the opposition and dissident elements.

6. This study has confirmed that in South Korea the ascription-oriented elite recruitment rather than achievement-oriented practice has predominated over the years. Perhaps we can project that in the long haul the ascription-oriented elite recruitment practices will be gradually replaced by the achievement-oriented one. But thus far, there is no clear evidence to indicate to the contrary. It is true that to become an administrative elite or a judicial elite one must usually pass the higher civil service examination, which is strictly based on a merit system, i.e., the objective test plus personal interviews. But entering an officialdom is one thing and becoming a top elite in the officialdom *after* entrance are two entirely different matter. The ascription-based practice usually prevails in the promotion process *after* the aspirants successfully enter the administrative or judicial branches. Specifically, the so-called "three connections" -- *hakyŏn* [academic connection or ties], *chiyŏn* [regional connection or ties] and *hyolyŏn* [blood connection or ties] still play a decisive role both in the recruitment of elites per se and their promotion and elevation to the top leadership status. As noted in the above, *hakyŏn* and *chiyŏn* still persist in elite recruitment and promotion, and especially *chiyŏn* is a very serious problem, which divides South Korean politics into an emotion-ridden *Yŏngnam* against *Honam* antagonism. Setting aside the policy or personality which are primarily responsible for this rather anachronistic political phenomenon, the South Korean democratization cannot succeed unless and until the *chiyŏn* factor is successfully resolved and removed not only from the elite recruitment in public sector but in private sector as well.

Table 12-1. The Professional Backgrounds of the South Korean Top
Administrative Elites in the 1950s

(Number of Persons)

Profes-sions	Positions														
	PM	FO	HO	FL	JU	DE	ED	AG	CO	HE	TR	COM	Oth.	Total	(%)
Pol.	1	4	10	2	2	6	1	4	5	2	4	6	6	58	42.0
Bur.	–	2	7	4	–	–	–	9	2	–	2	–	–	26	18.8
Mil.	1	–	2	–	–	4	–	–	1	–	1	2	–	11	8.8
Bus.	1	–	–	4	–	–	–	–	4	–	–	1	–	10	7.2
Law.	–	–	4	–	10	–	–	1	–	–	–	–	–	15	10.9
Edu.	2	1	–	–	–	–	7	1	2	–	–	–	–	13	8.4
Jou.	–	–	–	–	–	–	–	–	1	–	–	–	–	1	0.7
Doc.	–	–	–	–	–	–	–	–	–	4	–	–	–	4	2.9
Rel.	–	–	–	–	–	–	–	–	–	–	–	–	–	–	–
Total	10	7	23	10	12	10	8	15	15	6	7	9	6	138	99.9

Source: Adapted from Il-chun Kwŏn, "A Comparative Study of the North and South Korean
Elite Recruitment" (in Korean) (MA Thesis, Korea University, 1978).
Professions: Pol. (Politicians); Bur. (Bureaucrats); Mil. (Military); Bus. (Businessmen);
Law. (Lawyers); Edu. (Educators); Jou. (Journalists); Doc. (Doctors); and Rel.
(Religious leaders).
Positions: PM (Prime Minister); FO (Minister of Foreign Affairs); HO (Home Affairs); FI
(Finance); JU (Justice) DE (Defense); ED (Education); AG (Agriculture and
Fishery); CO (Commerce); HE (Health and Social Welfare); TR (Transpor-
tation); COM (Communications); and Oth (Others).

Table 12-2. *The Professional Backgrounds of the South Korean Top Administrative Elites in the 1960s*

(Number of Persons)

Positions	Professions										
	Pol.	Bur.	Mil.	Bus.	Law.	Edu.	Jou.	Doc.	Rel.	Oth.	Total
PM		1	3				1				5
DPM*			1	1			1				3
FO	1	2	5								8
HO		3	4								7
FI	1	4	1	6		1					13
JU			3		3						6
DE			6								6
ED			2		2	6					10
AG		4	3			1					8
CO	1	2	3	1							7
ST*		2	5	1		1					9
HE		1	4								5
TR		2	4	1							7
COM		4	4								8
PU*	1	1	2			3			1		8
Oth.	1	7	5			1				1	15
Total	5	33	55	9	6	13	2		1	1	125
(%)	(4.0)	(26.4)	(44.0)	(7.2)	(4.8)	(10.4)	(1.6)		(0.8)	(0.8)	(100)

Source: *Idem.*

Positions: In addition to those listed in Table 12-1, DPM* stands for Deputy Prime Minister; ST*, Science and Technology; PU, Public Information.

Table 12-3. South Korean Government Elites' Overall Profiles

Variable		No.	(Percent)	Variable		No.	(Percent)
Birth	before 1900	299	(11.2%)	College	Seoul N. Univ.	613	(22.9%)
Year	1901 – 1910	435	(16.2)	Attended	Korea Univ.	160	(6.0)
	1911 – 1920	523	(19.5)		Yŏnsei Univ.	98	(3.7)
	1921 – 1930	713	(26.2)		Military Sch.	259	(9.7)
	1931 – 1940	606	(22.6)		Foreign Educ.	605	(22.6)
	1941 – 1950	96	(3.6)		Others	943	(35.2)
Total:		2,672	(99.3)	Total		2,678	(100)
Birth	Seoul	257	(9.6%)	Foreign	Japan	474	(66.6%)
Place	Pusan	69	(2.6)	Education	U.S.A.	159	(22.3%)
	Kyŏnggi	204	(7.6)		Others	96	(10.3)
	Inch'ŏn	18	(0.7)			729	(99.2)
	Kangwŏn	131	(4.9)	Previous	Bureaucrat	637	(23.8%)
	Ch'ungbuk	119	(4.4)	Occupation	Politicians	397	(14.8)
	Ch'ungnam	285	(10.6)		Academician	317	(11.8)
	Chŏnbuk	191	(7.1)		Businessmen	309	(11.5)
	Chŏnnam	329	(12.3)		Lawyers	291	(10.9)
	Cheju	36	(1.3)		Military	290	(10.8)
	Kyŏngbuk	358	(13.4)		Journalist	147	(5.5)
	Taegu	53	(2.0)		Nationalist	73	(2.7)
	Kyŏngnam	378	(14.1)		leaders		
	North Korea	243	(9.1)		Others	213	(7.9)
Total:		2,671	(99.7)	Total:		2,674	(99.7)
Educa-	Primary School	82	(3.1%)	No. of	1st time	1,654	(61.3%)
tion	or Less			Position	2nd time	532	(19.9)
	Middle School	50	(1.9)	Held	3rd time	239	(8.9)
	High School	283	(10.6)		4th	112	(4.2)
	College	1,475	(55.0)		5th	80	(3.0)
	Graduate	778	(29.4)		6th	43	(1.6)
	School or				7th	13	(0.5)
	More				8th	4	(0.1)
					9th	2	(0.1)
Total:		2,688	(100.0)	Total		2,679	(99.6)

Table 12-4. South Korean Administrative Elites' Personal Background

		Administrative Elites					
Personal Background		Rhee Regime	Chang Regime	Park Regime	Yushin Regime	Chun Regime	*Roh Regime
Birth Year	before 1900	32.7%	13.1%	1.2%	—	0.4%	—
	1901–1910	40.3	29.5	7.3	—	—	—
	1911–1920	22.6	37.7	32.7	9.1%	3.6	1.6%
	1921–1930	4.4	19.7	54.7	62.7	33.2	14.1
	1931–1940	—	—	4.1	28.2	62.8	84.4
	1941–1950						
Total:	Percent	100	100	100	100	100	101
	Number	(159)	(61)	(245)	(110)	(223)	(64)
Birth Place	Seoul	21.7%	16.4%	13.1%	6.3%	9.4%	17.2%
	Yŏngnam	21.0	18.0	26.1	36.0	41.3	40.6
	Kyŏnggi & Kangwŏn	9.6	6.6	8.6	13.5	14.3	12.5
	Ch'ungch'ŏng	14.6	16.4	17.6	17.1	12.1	12.5
	Honam	12.1	21.3	12.2	12.6	11.7	10.9
	North Korea	21.0	21.3	22.4	14.4	11.2	6.3
Total:	Percent	100	100	100	99.9	100	100
	Number	(157)	(61)	(245)	(111)	(223)	(64)

* The Roh regime covers only its first administration.
Yŏngnam: Kyŏngbuk & Kyŏngnam; Honam: Chŏnbuk & Chŏnnam.

Table 12-5. South Korean Administrative Elites'
Educational Background

		Administrative Elites					
Personal Background		Rhee Regime	Chang Regime	Park Regime	Yushin Regime	Chun Regime	Roh Regime
Educa-tion	Primary School or Less	1.3%	3.3%	—	0.9%	—	—
	Middle School	1.3	—	—	—	—	—
	High School	13.8	24.6	7.8%	2.7	0.4%	25.0%
	College	70.4	54.1	64.5	50.5	33.6	25.0
	Graduate School or More	13.2	18.0	27.8	45.9	65.9	75.0
Total:	Percent	100	100	101	100	100	100
	Number	(159)	(61)	(245)	(111)	(223)	(64)
	Seoul N. Univ.	17.0%	24.7%	24.9%	43.2%	42.6%	60.9%
College	Korea Univ.	1.9	3.3	4.5	7.2	6.7	7.8
Attended	Yŏnsei Univ.	7.5	4.9	2.9	4.5	2.2	—
	Military*	3.8	3.3	21.2	15.3	19.3	9.4
	Foreign*	47.2	36.1	26.5	9.9	8.1	3.1
	Others	22.6	27.9	20.0	19.8	21.1	18.8
Total:	Percent	100	101	100	100	100	100
	Number	(159)	(61)	(245)	(111)	(223)	(64)
Foreign	U.S.A.	23.3%	14.3%	13.6%	42.9%	69.8%	78.9%
Studies	Japan	65.8	85.7	81.8	42.9	15.1	—
	Others	11.9	—	4.5	14.3	15.1	21.1
Total:	Percent	101	100	100	100	100	100
	Number	(73)	(21)	(66)	(21)	(53)	(19)

* Military: Military School; Foreign: Foreign Education.

Table 12-6. South Korean Administrative Elites' Career Background

Personal Background		Administrative Elites					
		Rhee Regime	Chang Regime	Park Regime	Yushin Regime	Chun Regime	Roh Regime
Previous Occupa-tion	Nationalist leaders	7.0%	—	—	—	—	—
	Academicians	18.4	19.7%	19.2%	9.0%	11.7%	9.5%
	Bureaucrats	43.0	44.3	34.7	62.2	57.8	69.8
	Politicians	1.9	9.8	2.4	—	—	1.6
	Military	5.1	3.3	32.7	16.2	21.5	12.7
	Journalists	1.3	1.6	2.0	1.8	2.2	1.6
	Lawyers	14.6	11.5	5.7	9.0	5.4	3.2
	Businessmen	5.1	8.2	2.9	0.9	0.9	1.6
	Others	3.8	1.6	.04	0.9	0.4	—
Total:	Percent	100	100	100	100	100	100
	Number	(158)	(61)	(245)	(111)	(223)	(63)
No. of Position Held	1st time	63.5%	59.0%	58.0%	53.2%	48.4%	40.6%
	2nd	22.6	21.3	23.7	19.8	31.4	42.2
	3rd	6.3	8.2	10.2	10.8	10.8	9.4
	4th-9th	7.5	11.5	8.2	16.2	9.4	7.8
Total:	Percent	99.9	100	100	100	100	100
	Number	(159)	(61)	(245)	(111)	(223)	(64)

Table 12-7. South Korean Legislative Elites' Personal Background

		Legislative Elites					
Personal Background		Rhee Regime	Chang Regime	Park Regime	Yushin Regime	Chun Regime	Roh Regime
Birth Year	before 1900	27.6%	16.4%	4.5%	0.4%	—	—
	1901–1910	37.0	28.5	14.9	7.4	0.9%	—
	1911–1920	30.1	37.7	28.3	17.6	9.2	1.6%
	1921–1930	5.1	16.0	43.2	56.6	34.9	17.6
	1931–1940	—	1.1	8.9	17.6	46.7	55.6
	1941–1950	0.2	0.4	0.3	0.4	8.3	25.2
Total:	Percent	100	100	100	100	100	100
	Number	(605)	(281)	(382)	(244)	(542)	(250)
Birth Place	Seoul	3.5%	4.6%	6.3%	16.9%	9.2%	17.2%
	Yŏngnam	35.1	31.0	32.2	31.7	33.8	40.6
	Kyŏnggi & Kangwŏn	14.5	17.1	12.0	11.9	12.7	12.5
	Ch'ungch'ŏng	16.2	16.4	16.8	9.1	14.7	12.5
	Honam	28.1	25.6	22.5	23.0	22.4	10.9
	North Korea	2.6	5.3	10.2	7.4	7.2	2.4
Total:	Percent	100	100	100	100	100	100
	Number	(606)	(281)	(382)	(243)	(544)	(250)

Table 12-8. South Korean Legislative Elites' Educational Background

		Legislative Elites					
Personal Background		Rhee Regime	Chang Regime	Park Regime	Yushin Regime	Chun Regime	Roh Regimec
Educa-tion	Primary School or Less	9.4%	5.7%	1.6%	0.8%	0.2%	0.8%
	Middle School	4.1	5.3	0.8	0.4	0.2	0.8
	High School	24.2	20.6	8.9	5.7	1.7	2.8
	College	60.1	63.7	62.6	53.1	49.1	40.2
	Graduate School or More	2.1	4.6	26.2	40.0	48.9	55.4
Total:	Percent	100	100	100	100	100	100
	Number	(607)	(281)	(382)	(245)	(544)	(251)
College Attended	Seoul N. Univ.	8.7%	13.9%	20.6%	26.5%	26.8%	25.5%
	Korea Univ.	4.1	3.6	4.4	10.6	10.1	12.0
	Yŏnsei Univ.	2.0	2.8	4.7	2.9	5.0	6.8
	Military*	2.1	3.6	10.2	14.7	10.1	5.2
	Foreign*	38.9	37.7	24.8	13.1	8.3	4.8
	Others	44.2	38.4	35.2	32.2	39.7	45.8
Total:	Percent	100	100	100	100	100	100
	Number	(607)	(281)	(383)	(245)	(544)	(251)
Foreign Studies	U.S.A.	6.2%	9.3%	9.9%	20.0%	39.4%	72.3%
	Japan	83.1	77.6	74.3	75.0	50.0	19.1
	Others	10.7	13.1	15.8	5.0	10.6	8.5
Total:	Percent	100	100	100	100	100	100
	Number	(242)	(107)	(101)	(40)	(66)	(47)

* Military: Military School; Foreign: Foreign Education.

Table 12-9. South Korean Legislative Elites' Career Background

Legislative Elites						
Personal Background		Rhee Regime	Chang Regime	Park Regime	Yushin Regime	Chun Regime	Roh Regime
Previous Occupation	Nationalist leaders	8.1%	4.3%	1.8%	0.4%	—	—
	Academicians	8.3	10.0	12.5	15.5	13.1%	6.4%
	Bureaucrats	20.1	18.1	15.1	12.2	13.4	4.8
	Politicians	22.4	21.7	20.4	22.9	21.9	30.0
	Military	1.5	4.3	9.1	15.5	10.5	6.4
	Journalists	4.3	5.7	6.8	9.0	9.4	8.4
	Lawyers	5.0	8.5	7.8	5.7	8.5	11.2
	Businessmen	14.5	12.8	17.0	9.4	19.0	19.2
	Others	15.8	14.6	9.4	9.4	4.2	13.6
Total:	Percent	100	100	100	100	100	100
	Number	(606)	(281)	(383)	(245)	(543)	(250)
No. of Position Held	1st time	57.6%	47.0%	37.6%	29.4%	52.0%	62.2%
	2nd	22.6	19.2	20.9	23.3	18.9	18.7
	3rd	8.1	13.9	14.4	16.7	13.6	13.1
	4th-9th	11.7	19.9	27.2	30.6	15.4	6.0
Total:		100	100	100	100	100	100
	Number	(606)	(281)	(383)	(245)	(544)	(251)

Table 12-10. South Korean Judicial Elites' Personal Background

		\multicolumn{6}{c}{Judicial Elites}					
Personal Background		Rhee Regime	Chang Regime	Park Regime	Yushin Regime	Chun Regime	Roh Regime
Birth Year	before 1900	50.0%	16.7%	—	—	—	—
	1901–1910	30.0	50.0	25.0%	—	—	—
	1911–1920	15.0	33.3	68.8	78.6%	18.6%	6.5%
	1921–1930	5.0	—	6.3	21.4	27.1	9.7
	1931–1940	—	—	—	—	54.2	83.9
Total:	Percent	100	100	100	100	100	100
	Number	(20)	(6)	(16)	(14)	(59)	(31)
Birth Place	Seoul	15.0%	33.3%	6.3%	7.7%	3.4%	—
	Yŏngnam	20.0	—	31.3	23.1	36.2	43.3%
	Kyŏnggi & Kangwŏn	—	16.7	—	15.4	13.8	6.7
	Ch'ungch'ŏng	15.0	16.7		23.1	20.7	16.7
	Honam	20.0	33.3	31.3	23.1	20.7	30.0
	North Korea	30.0	—	31.3	7.7	5.2	3.3
Total:	Percent	100	100	100	100	100	100
	Number	(20)	(6)	(16)	(13)	(58)	(30)

Table 12-11. *South Korean Judicial Elites' Educational Background*

		Judicial Elites					
Educational Background		Rhee Regime	Chang Regime	Park Regime	Yushin Regime	Chun Regime	Roh Regime
Educa-tion	Primary School or Less	—	—	—	—	—	—
	Middle School	—	—	—	7.1%	1.7%	—
	High School	—	16.7%	—	—	—	—
	College	100.0%	83.3	93.8%	85.7	98.3	100.0%
	Graduate School or More	—	—	6.3	7.1	—	—
Total:	Percent	100	100	100	100	100	100
	Number	(20)	(6)	(16)	(14)	(59)	(31)
College Attended	Seoul N. Univ.	50.0%	66.7%	60.0%	64.3%	64.4%	61.3%
	Korea Univ.	—	—	—	—	10.2	16.1
	Yŏnsei Univ.	—	—	—	—	—	—
	Military	—	—	—	—	—	—
	Foreign	45.0	16.7	40.0	28.6	8.5	3.2
	Others	5.0	16.7	—	7.1	16.9	19.4
Total:	Percent	100	100	100	100	100	100
	Number	(20)	(6)	(15)	(14)	(59)	(31)
Foreign Educa-tion	U.S.A.	—	—	—	—	—	—
	Japan	100.0	100.0	100.0	100.0	100.0	100.0
	Others	—	—	—	—	—	—
Total:	Percent	100	100	100	100	100	100
	Number	(8)	(1)	(6)	(4)	(5)	(1)

Table 12-12. *South Korean Judicial Elites' Career Background*

		Judicial Elites					
Career Background		Rhee Regime	Chang Regime	Park Regime	Yushin Regime	Chun Regime	Roh Regime
No. of Position Held	1st time	75.0%	33.3%	75.0%	85.7%	81.4%	77.4%
	2nd	25.0	50.0	25.0	—	15.3	19.4
	3rd	—	16.7	—	7.1	3.4	3.2
	4th-9th	—	—	—	7.1	—	—
Total:	Percent	100	100	100	99.9	100	100
	Number	(20)	(6)	(16)	(14)	(59)	(31)

Table 12-13. *South Korean "Mixed Elites'" Personal Background*

		Mixed Elites					
Personal Background		Rhee Regime	Chang Regime	Park Regime	Yushin Regime	Chun Regime	Roh Regime
Birth Year	before 1900	36.7%	16.1%	6.2%	—	—	—
	1901–1910	41.8	35.5	15.4	—	—	—
	1911–1920	19.4	41.9	18.5	38.9%	3.2%	1.9%
	1921–1930	2.0	6.5	55.4	55.6	33.3	30.8
	1931–1940	—	—	4.6	5.6	3.2	1.9
Total:	Percent	100	100	100	100	100	100
	Number	(98)	(31)	(65)	(18)	(63)	(52)
Birth Place	Seoul	5.1%	6.3%	16.4%	—	12.5%	9.6%
	Yŏngnam	15.3	46.9	25.4	16.7	26.6	28.8
	Kyŏnggi & Kangwŏn	27.6	9.4	9.0	16.7	17.2	26.9
	Ch'ungch'ŏng	26.5	12.5	10.4	27.8	20.3	15.4
	Honam	17.3	15.6	20.9	16.7	18.8	9.6
	North Korea	8.2	9.4	17.9	22.2	4.7	9.6
Total:	Percent	100	100	100	100	100	100
	Number	(98)	(32)	(67)	(18)	(64)	(52)

Table 12-14. *South Korean "Mixed Elites'" Educational Background*

		Mixed Elites					
Educational Background		Rhee Regime	Chang Regime	Park Regime	Yushin Regime	Chun Regime	Roh Regime
Educa-tion	Primary School or Less	3.1%	—	—	—	—	—
	Middle School	3.1	—	—	—	—	—
	High School	17.3	6.3%	1.5%	—	3.1%	1.9%
	College	65.3	81.3	68.7	66.7%	37.5	36.5
	Graduate School or More	11.2	12.5	29.9	33.3	59.4	61.5
Total:	Percent	100	100	101	100	100	99.9
	Number	(98)	(32)	(67)	(18)	(64)	(52)
College Attended	Seoul N. Univ.	22.4%	28.1%	29.9%	27.8%	53.1%	40.4%
	Korea Univ.	3.1	9.4	6.0	11.1	7.8	7.7
	Yŏnsei Univ.	7.1	3.1	6.0	—	1.6	1.9
	Military	1.0	6.3	32.8	27.8	21.9	26.9
	Foreign	39.8	40.6	17.9	22.2	1.6	3.8
	Others	26.5	12.5	7.5	11.1	14.1	19.2
Total:	Percent	100	100	101	100	100	99.9
	Number	(98)	(32)	(67)	(18)	(64)	(52)
Foreign Education	Japan	61.0%	83.3%	90.9%	75.0%	15.0%	7.1%
	U.S.A.	22.4	16.7	9.1	25.0	75.0	78.6
	Others	14.6	—	—	—	—	—
Total:	Percent	100	100	100	100	100	100
	Number	(41)	(12)	(11)	(4)	(20)	(14)

Table 12-15. South Korean "Mixed Elites'" Career Background

		Mixed Elites					
Career Background		Rhee Regime	Chang Regime	Park Regime	Yushin Regime	Chun Regime	Roh Regime
Previous Occupation	Nationalist leaders	9.2%	6.3%	3.0%	—	—	—
	Academicians	11.2	21.9	13.4	22.2%	9.4%	3.8%
	Bureaucrats	34.7	28.1	20.9	27.8	40.6	34.6
	Politicians	10.2	15.6	9.0	16.7	12.5	17.3
	Military	1.0	6.3	35.8	27.8	17.2	25.0
	Journalists	6.1	3.1	4.5	—	9.4	9.6
	Lawyers	14.3	9.4	3.0	—	6.3	5.8
	Businessmen	5.1	3.1	6.0	—	4.7	1.9
	Others	8.2	6.3	4.5	5.6	—	1.9
Total:	Percent	100	100	100	100	100	100
	Number	(98)	(32)	(67)	(18)	(64)	(52)
No. of Position Held	1st time	1.0%	3.1%	—	—	1.6%	—
	2nd	29.6	9.4	29.9%	5.6%	23.4	23.1%
	3rd	31.6	12.5	20.9	5.6	23.4	23.1
	4th-9th	37.8	75.0	49.3	88.9	51.6	53.8
Total:	Percent	100	100	101	101	100	100
	Number	(98)	(32)	(67)	(18)	(64)	(52)

Table 12-16. Localism-oriented Ascriptive Recruitment
of South Korean Elites

Career Background		Rhee Regime	Chang Regime	Park Regime	Yushin Regime	Chun Regime	Roh Regime
Admin-istrative Elites	Seoul	21.7%	16.4%	13.1%	6.3%	9.4%	17.2%
	Yŏngnam	21.0	18.0	26.1	36.0	41.3	40.6
	Kyŏnggi & Kangwŏn	9.6	6.6	8.6	13.5	14.3	12.5
	Ch'ungch'ŏng	14.6	16.4	17.6	17.1	12.1	12.5
	Honam	12.1	21.3	12.2	12.6	11.7	10.9
	North Korea	21.0	21.3	22.4	14.4	11.2	6.3
Total:	Percent	100	100	100	100	100	100
	Number	(157)	(61)	(245)	(111)	(223)	(64)
Legislative Elites	Seoul	3.5%	4.6%	6.3%	16.9%	9.2%	9.6%
	Yŏngnam	35.1	31.0	32.2	31.7	33.8	35.2
	Pyŏnggi & Kangwŏn	14.5	17.1	12.0	11.9	12.7	14.0
	Ch'ungch'ŏng	16.2	16.4	16.8	9.1	14.7	13.6
	Honam	28.1	25.6	22.5	23.0	22.4	25.2
	North Korea	2.6	5.3	12.2	7.4	7.2	2.4
Total:	Percent	100	100	100	100	100	100
	Number	(606)	(281)	(382)	(243)	(544)	(250)
Judicial Elites	Seoul	15.0%	33.3%	6.3%	7.7%	3.4%	—
	Yŏngnam	20.0	—	31.3	23.1	36.2	43.3%
	Kyŏnggi & Kangwŏn	—	16.7	—	15.4	13.8	6.7
	Ch'ungch'ŏng	15.0	16.7	—	23.1	20.7	16.7
	Honam	20.0	33.3	31.3	23.1	20.7	30.3
	North Korea	30.0	—	31.3	7.7	5.2	3.3
Total:	Percent	100	100	100	100	100	100
	Number	(20)	(6)	(16)	(13)	(58)	(30)
Mixed Elites	Seoul	5.1%	6.3%	16.4%	—	12.5%	9.6%
	Yŏngnam	15.3	46.9	25.4	16.7%	26.6	28.8
	Kyŏnggi & Kangwŏn	27.6	9.4	9.0	17.2	26.9	—
	Ch'ungch'ŏng	26.5	12.5	10.4	27.8	20.3	15.4
	Honam	17.3	15.6	20.9	16.7	18.8	9.6
	North Korea	8.2	9.4	17.9	22.2	4.7	9.6
Total:	Percent	100	100	100	100	100	100
	Number	(98)	(32)	(67)	(18)	(64)	(52)

Table 12-17. Academic Nexus-oriented Ascriptive Recruitment
of South Korean Elites

Academic Nexux		Rhee Regime	Chang Regime	Park Regime	Yushin Regime	Chun Regime	Roh Regime
Admin-	Seoul N. Univ.	17.0%	24.6%	24.9%	43.2%	42.6%	60.9%
istrative	Korea Univ.	1.9	3.3	4.5	7.2	6.7	7.8
Elites	Yŏnsei Univ.	7.5	4.9	2.9	4.5	2.2	—
	Military	3.8	3.3	21.2	15.3	19.3	9.4
	Foreign	47.2	36.1	26.5	9.9	8.1	3.1
	Others	22.6	27.9	20.0	19.8	21.1	18.8
Total:	Percent	100	100	100	100	100	100
	Number	(159)	(61)	(245)	(111)	(223)	(64)
Legislative	Seoul N. Univ.	8.7%	13.9%	20.6%	26.5%	26.8%	25.5%
Elites	Korea Univ.	4.1	3.6	4.4	10.6	10.1	12.0
	Yŏnsei Univ.	2.0	2.8	4.7	2.9	5.0	6.0
	Military	2.1	3.6	10.2	14.7	10.1	5.2
	Foreign	38.9	37.7	24.8	13.1	8.3	4.8
	Others	44.2	38.4	35.2	32.2	39.7	45.8
Total	Percent	100	100	100	100	100	100
	Number	(607)	(281)	(383)	(245)	(544)	(251)
Judicial	Seoul N. Univ.	50.0%	66.7%	60.0%	64.3%	64.4%	61.3%
Elites	Korea Univ.	—	—	—	—	10.2	16.1
	Yŏnsei Univ.	—	—	—	—	—	—
	Military	—	—	—	—	—	—
	Foreign	45.0	16.7	40.0	28.6	8.5	3.2
	Others	5.0	16.7	—	7.1	16.9	19.4
Total:	Percent	100	100	100	100	100	100
	Number	(20)	(6)	(15)	(14)	(59)	(31)
Mixed	Seoul N. Univ.	22.4%	28.1%	29.9%	27.8%	53.1%	40.0%
Elites	Korea Univ.	3.1	9.4	6.0	11.1	7.8	7.7
	Yŏnsei Univ.	7.1	3.1	6.0	—	1.6	1.9
	Military	1.0	6.3	32.8	27.8	21.9	26.9
	Foreign	39.8	40.6	17.9	22.2	1.6	3.8
	Others	26.5	12.5	7.5	11.1	14.1	19.2
Total:	Percent	100	100	100	100	100	100
	Number	(98)	(32)	(67)	(18)	(64)	(52)

Figure 12-1. The Regional Background of the Ruling Elites in Relation
to the General Population of the Region

Regions	A	LE	LNE	M	J	Population	%
Seoul	13 %	4 %	13 %	15 %	6 %	3,803,000	13
Yŏngnam	26	37	24	27	29	9,085,000	31
Kyŏng'gi & Kangwon	8	12	8	8	0	4,939,000	17
Ch'ungch'ŏng	17	17	13	11	0	4,455,000	15
Honam	12	24	13	23	29	6,910,000	24
North Korea	23	6	30	17	35	—	—
Total:	99	100	101	101	99	29,193,000 *	100

*Based on the 1966 Census.

A: Administrative Elites; LE: Legislative elites who were elected by direct popular votes in
the districts; LNE: legislative elites who were not elected by direct popular vote; M: mixed
elites; and J: judicial elites.

Figure 12-2. The Regional Background of the Ruling Elites in Relation
to the General Population of the Region

Regions	A	LE	LNE	M	J	Population	%
Seoul	12 %	6 %	17 %	33 %	13 %	9,681,296	24.0
Yŏngnam	40	30	39	0	31	12,128,008	30.0
Kyŏng'gi & Kangwŏn	10	18	10	0	13	7,612,512	18.9
Ch'ungch'ŏng	15	17	12	33	25	4,406,052	10.9
Honam	12	23	16	33	19	6,533,976	16.2
North Korea	13	7	7	0	0	—	—
Total:	102	101	101	99	101	40,361,844 *	100.0

*As of December 31, 1984.

Notes

1. Thomas Hobbes, *Leviathan*, ed. C. B. Macpherson (Middlesex: Pelican Classics, 1972), p. 272.
2. Vilfredo Pareto, *The Mind and Society*, ed. Anthor Cingston (NY: Harcourt, Brace, Co. 1935), p. 248.
3. Sung Chul Yang and Byong-man Ahn, "A Comparative Analysis of the North and South Korean Ruling Elites, 1948-1988" (in Korean), May 1991, a research project supported by the Korea Research Foundation. Byong-man Ahn, *Hankuk Chongbu'ron* [On Korean Government] (Seoul: Tasan Ch'ulp'an-sa, 1985), Chapter 3, pp. 161-205. There are several other studies on the South Korean ruling elites. See, for instance, Bae-ho Hahn and Kyu-taik Kim, "Korean Political Leaders, 1952-1962: Their Social Origins and Skills," *Asian Survey* 3 (July 1963): 305-328; Joung-sik Lee, "The Social Origins of Members of the Sixth Assembly," *Korean Affairs* 3 (April 1964): 1-19; Dong-suh Park, "Korean Higher Civil Servants: Their Social Background and Morale," in B. C. Koh, ed., *Aspects of Administrative Development in South Korea* (Kalamazoo: Korean Research and Publications, 1967), pp. 9-29; Chong-lim Kim and Byong-kyu Woo, "Social and Political Background of Korean National Legislator: The Seventh National Assembly," *Asian Forum* 3 (July/September 1971): 123-137; John P. Lovell and C. I. Eugene Kim, *The Governmental Elites of the Republic of Korea (1948-72): Socio-Economic Data*, Unpublished Manuscript; Jang-hyun Lee, "Social Background and Career Development of the Korean Jurists," *Korea Journal* 14 (June 1974): 11-20; and Jang-hyon Lee and George Won, "The Korean Lawyer: A Social Profile," *Journal of Social Sciences and Humanities* (Seoul: Korean Research Center, 1969).
4. For details, see Byong-man Ahn, *Op. Cit.*, pp. 165-168.

CHAPTER 13

LEGITIMACY CRISIS: FROM RHEE TO ROH

Do you know, I said, that governments vary as the dispositions of men vary, and there must be as many of the one as there are of the other?... Yes, he said, the States are as men are; they grow out of human characters.

Plato[1]

Legitimacy is a state of mind and not a condition of legality.

LaPalombara[2]

Introduction

Like a host of countries which have emerged after World War II, Korea, as a new nation, has undergone the crises of nation-building— identity, legitimacy, penetration, participation, distribution and integration.[3] As one of the most culturally homogeneous nations in the world, the Korean people's identity crisis was a relatively minor one. So was the South Korean government's penetration crisis, due to the rapid development of a relatively efficient centralized bureaucracy, not to mention its long tradition of centralized officialdom.

The problems of participation in political arenas and of distribution in economic realms persist. They are, however, as Chapter 16 reveals, relatively less serious in South Korea than in many other developing nations. The creation of two separate states in 1948 has set the built-in integration crisis. The crisis of integration will continue until the Korean people are reunited and the country is reintegrated.

If there is one crisis which had plagued the politics of South Korea most critically and persistently, it is undoubtedly the legitimacy crisis. The legitimacy crisis had been the major source as well as the consequence of South Korea's political instability. Its political instability, which has been more or less a political *norm* than an exception for the past forty or more years, had taken various forms, ranging from palace coups to military coups d'etat, from student protests to mass uprisings and from armed rebellions to war.

In the following a two-part analysis of South Korea's legitimacy crisis is attempted. A brief general discussion of legitimacy and legitimacy crisis will be followed by an overall diagnosis and prognosis of the South Korean experiences of legitimacy crises for more than four decades.

Legitimacy and Legitimacy Crisis

Four aspects of legitimacy—the meaning (s) of legitimacy or illegitimacy, its bases, objects and types—are briefly examined here.

Sternberger defined legitimacy as "the foundation of such governmental power as is exercised both with a consciousness on the government's part that it has a right to govern and with some recognition by the governed of that right."[4] It is interesting to note that he regarded legitimacy as a sort of balance or equilibrium between the ruler's right to govern and the right of the ruled to accept such rule.

Unlike Sternberger, in conceptualizing legitimacy there are those who stress the ruler's right or the polity's capacity to govern and those who put the primary emphasis on the approval of the ruled of such right or capacity. Lichbach's approach, for one, belongs to the former. He and his associate postulated in hypothetical terms that "a polity will have long-lived persistence if and only if it has coherent authority relations (i.e., no structural defects) and noncumulation of performance crises (i.e., no functional difficulties)." Conversely, a polity will have short-lived persistence if and only if it has incoherent authority relations and cumulation of performance crises.[5] To rephrase these two hypotheses in plain terms, if the elements of political instability of government—the illegitimacy and strife manifested by challengers and the inefficacy of the authorities' response to such challenges—occur simultaneously, then the government cannot last.[6]

LaPalombara's concept of legitimacy, meanwhile, stressed the ruled recognizing the ruler's right to govern. According to him, a political system is "legitimate" if those who are affected by political power judge its exercise to be right or appropriate.[7] Further, he distinguished the legitimacy of authority from its legality. For, it is entirely possible that acts of governance that are perfectly acceptable under law may be considered illegitimate by those affected by them. And problems of legitimacy can reach serious crisis level when what has been considered legal and appropriate is "no longer the case."[8] He postulated that generally the more deeply institutionalized political systems are, more flexible and ready they are to handle unusual stresses within the community.[9] The tentative empirical findings by Muller and Williams about a relationship between political performance (i.e., specific support) and attitude about the political system (i.e., diffuse support) are relevant here.[10]

From the standpoint of illegitimacy, Linz emphasized that "in every society, there are those who deny legitimacy to any government and those who believe in alternative legitimacy formulae. Regimes vary widely in the amount and intensity of citizen belief in their legitimacy."[11] Illegitimacy, then to follow a succinct definition by Gurr and McClelland, is "the extent that a polity is regarded by its member as [not] worthy of support."[12]

In brief, the full understanding of legitimacy or illegitimacy issue may not be possible unless the relationships between the ruler and the ruled, the structural problems and the functional difficulties and between political institutionalization and political socialization are adequately dealt with. Recently, Weatherford attempted to integrate both macro perspective on legitimacy emphasing formal system properties (e.g., accountability, efficiency, procedural fairness and distributive fairness) and micro views focusing on citizens' attitudes and actions (e.g., political interest and involvement, beliefs about interpersonal and social relations relevant to collective action and optimism about the responsiveness of the political system). That is, he tried to conceptualize the meaning of legitimacy by incorporating the view from above -- system-level aspects of legitimacy -- and the view from the grass roots -- the relevance of public opinion.[13]

Legitimacy may be based on divine rights, the Mandate of Heaven, popular consent, tradition, ideology, citizen participation, specific policies and others.[14] Or, to paraphrase Weber's concept of leadership, legitimacy may stem from traditional, charismatic or legal-rational foundations. The objects of legitimacy or illegitimacy also vary. Gurr and McClelland, for instance, differentiated three objects of illegitimacy— the political community, the regime and the incumbents.[15] Herz added to Gurr and McClelland's list the international agencies or organizations.[16] Generally, the objects of legitimacy or illegitimacy can be supranational, national or intranational. In short, the targets or objects of legitimacy or illegitimacy are:

> International agencies or organization (e.g., legitimacy of the UN, IMF, NATO, etc.)
> Nation or Nation-state (e.g., Korea)
> Regime (e.g., the Roh Government)
> Incumbents (e.g., Roh Tae Woo)
> Policies or Program (e.g., High-speed Super Train Program)

Closely related to the bases and the objects of legitimacy is its typology. Sternberger, for instance, distinguished two major types of legitimacy: one (numinous) based on divine origin, right or vocation of rulers, and the other (civil) based on consent on the part of a polity's constituents.[17] Herz, on the other hand, differentiated three major types of legitimacy: external (or group), internal (or regime) and global (or international). By external or group legitimacy he referred to the political units as such, in its specific entirety (e.g., the Republic of Korea). Domestic or internal legitimacy meant the internal type of government and societal organizations that characterizes a given unit.[18] He then added the world *system*. He defined the world *system* as not only comprising interstate relations (balance of power, bipolarity, etc.) but also including economic relations which are created by resource or population problems and by environmental deterioration.[19]

In sum, legitimacy is a product of political balance or of an equilibrium between the capacity or the performance level of the governing apparatus on one side and the support/alienation level of the people on the other. The governing apparatus may vary from a particular policy, a particular incumbent, a particular regime, a state and to a world system. The people's support/alienation level ranges from complete approval to total rejection of such governing apparatus. Somewhere between full support and complete alienation may be found what Herz called people's attitude of "sullen toleration."[20]

Legitimacy Crisis in South Korean Politics

Based on the foregoing definitions of legitimacy, the South Korean legitimacy crises are examined here.

During three critical years from its liberation in 1945 until the emergence of two separate regimes in 1948, the Korean legitimacy crisis resembled the problem of what Herz called "external legitimacy." That is, the legitimacy of the political unit, be it the Korean Provisional Government, the Korean People's Republic, a four-power trusteeship, the Republic of Korea or the Democratic People's Republic of Korea, was contested by both the Korean political leaders and masses and the external powers as well.

Specifically, the legitimacy question centered around, first, though briefly, on the status of the Korean Provisional Government (KPG) in exile, which had survived for over a quarter of a century (1919-1945) in China. The U.S. Military Government in Korea refused to recognize the KPG's legitimacy and allowed the leaders of the KPG to enter Korea only as "private individuals." The U.S. Military Government also denied the legal status of the Korean People's Republic, created overnight by Yŏ Wun Hyŏng on 6 September 1945.[21] Next, the legitimacy question arose from the trusteeship plan proposed by the Moscow Agreement of 27 December 1945.[22] The Korean political leaders and masses alike

were sharply divided into two camps -- those in the North under the
Soviet occupation forces supported a four-power trusteeship plan and
those in the South under the American Military Government opposed it.
The crisis worsened and became more complicated because the United
States sided with those who opposed the trusteeship plan, while the for-
mer Soviet Union backed the groups who supported it.

One basic premise of the trusteeship plan was the ultimate creation of
one unified government in the Korean Peninsula. When the trusteeship
plan became unimplementable, due to sharp and irreconcilable division,
not only among the Korean leaders but also between the American and
the Soviet representatives, the idea of creating one unified government
suffered a setback. The focus of legitimacy crisis lied no longer in anti-
or pro-trusteeship plan *per se* but in the establishment of one government or two separate governments in the Korean Peninsula. With the
United States-supported United Nation's resolution (14 November
1947), recommending the occupying forces to "hold elections in their
respective zones no later than March 31, 1948," the original premise of
creating a unified government gave in to the founding of two separate
governments.[23]

In response to this UN resolution, the Korean political leaders and
masses were basically divided into three groups -- one group in the
South led by Syngman Rhee, supporting and formally endorsing the UN
resolution, tried to set up a separate government in the South; the
second group in the North, led by Kim Il Sung, while formally opposing
the UN resolution, but at the same time, created its own separate government (i.e., the People's Committee); and the third group, headed by
Kim Ku and Kim Kyu Sik, while maintaining neutrality and independence from outside forces (i.e., the Soviet and the American influences),
clung to the original idea of establishing one unified government
throughout Korea by steadfastly opposing any attempt to create two
separate governments. In this three-way confrontation, the third group
became the only loser. Its *national* ideal lost to the external and internal
political reality of Korea. For, when its political rhetoric ended, so did
the idea of one unified government. In the end, the Republic of Korea
(ROK) in the South and the Democratic People's Republic of Korea

(DPRK) in the North of the 38th Parallel came into being in August and September 1948, respectively.

With the launching of the two separate regimes in the Korean Peninsula, the focus of legitimacy crisis shifted once again from the disputes over whether there should be one unified government or two separate governments to the two regimes' mutually conflicting claims, of being the only "lawful government." South Korea's claim was based on the UN General Assembly declaration of 12 December 1948:

> that there has been established a *lawful government* (the Government of the Republic of Korea) having effective control and jurisdiction over *that part of Korea* where the United Nations Temporary Commission on Korea was able to observe and consult in which the great majority of the people of Korea reside; that this government is based on elections which were a valid expressions of the free will of the electorate of *that part of Korea* and which were observed by the Temporary Commission; and that this is *the only such government in Korea.*[24]

North Korea, meanwhile, rejected South Korea's claim by denying the legality of the UN resolutions *per se* and proclaimed the legitimacy of its own government. North and South Korea's mutually exclusive claims and counter-claims climaxed with the former's all-out invasion in June 1950, which ended with the ceasefire three years later. Technically, the 1972 North-South Joint Communique terminated each side's claim to exclusive legitimacy. In so doing, both sides granted *de facto*, if not *de jure*, recognition of each other's government (the date of *de facto* recognition may go back farther to the DPRK's participation in the 1953 Military Armistice Agreement as one of the signatories or the participants at the 1954 Geneva Conference by the representatives of both the DPRK and the ROK). The UN resolution of 12 December 1948, declaring the ROK as "the only lawful government" also ceased to be operative with its simultaneous adoption of two draft resolutions—both pro-North Korean and pro-South Korean resolutions in 1975.[25] Above all, the joint entry of the DPRK and the ROK to the United Nations on September 17, 1991, has put, an end not only to the "only lawful government" claims but also to the debate on the existence of one state-two states on the Korean Peninsula.

From the South Korean government's standpoint, the challenges to its legitimacy came from both external and internal political forces. As noted above, North Korea has been the major external challenger to its legitimacy and vice versa. The challenges by various internal political forces against the incumbents have been, however, the most serious source of legitimacy crises confronted by the Rhee regime to the Roh regime. Such challenges have been in most instances the *reaction* against the incumbent's initial political moves, rather than the *intiatives* on the part of the challengers to replace or unseat the incumbents.

During the Rhee regime (1948-1960) his ruling elites had made a series of political moves, and the aim of such moves was transparent: to prolong his rule. Rhee's first major move was initiated in the middle of the Korean War. His proposal for the constitutional revision in July 1952 contained, among other things, a new method of presidential election by direct popular vote. Under the existing Constitution the president was to be elected by the members of the National Assembly (NA). Realizing his slim chance for reelection by the NA,[26] he resorted to an alternative plan. His first proposal of constitutional revision on 18 January 1952 was handily defeated by the vote of 19 to 143. On April 17, 1952, the opposition members in the NA proposed the constitutional amendment to create the cabinet-responsible system. When the signees for this draft reached 123, one more than the two-third votes required for the passage of the constitutional revision, Rhee and his ruling groups were alerted to prevent the passage of this revision proposal. In the meantime, an emergency was declared in both South Kyŏngsang and North and South Chŏlla provinces due to the threats from the Communist partisans. Some ten National Assemblymen were imprisoned for their alleged complicity with the International Communist ring.[27] Many others were placed under house arrest, and a few fled and hid. The police brought many of these frightened assemblymen to the NA often against their own will.

Under this rather terrifying and suppressive political atmosphere, Rhee reintroduced his constitutional revision bill, which was passed with standing vote (163 yes and 3 abstentions) on July 4, 1952. On August 5, Rhee was reelected the president by a "direct popular vote."

It was his first political ploy. He and his ruling elites were frantic and almost desperate in attaining the seeming "legality" of his power and got it ultimately through the constitutional revision at an enormous political price. In the process of obtaining this paper-thin legality, Rhee and his ruling elites' legitimacy was greatly impaired. In Sternberger's definition of legitimacy, Rhee's legality represented only a half of what is required. Rhee had the legality in the sense that "he has the right to govern" but his rule lacked the other half, that is, "some recognition by the governed of that right."[28] So began the first legitimacy crisis of the Rhee government.

The aim of Rhee and his ruling elites' second major political move was the same as the first: to prolong his rule. The primary legal obstacle to this aim was the constitutional provision, restricting the presidency to two consecutive terms. But then, the political balance in the 3rd NA, which was formed through the general election on 20 May 1954, was different. Rhee's own Liberal Party won 114 out of 203 seats, constituting more than a majority, while the main opposition party, the Democratic National Party, had only 15 seats and the Independents, some 67 seats. For the first time since the launching of the Republic, his Liberal Party became a majority party in the NA.

Under this new power balance in the 3rd NA, Rhee's Liberal Party assemblymen set out to acquire the two-thirds majority support needed for the second constitutional revision, which would remove, among other things, the two-term restrictions of the presidency. The constitutional revision draft was put to test on 27 November 1954. The affirmative vote was 135, a vote short of the required two-thirds majority for the passage of the constitutional revision. His second political move was defeated, but two days later on November 29, in the full session of the NA then vice-speaker, Ch'oe Sun-ju, reversed the earlier decision and declared the passage of the constitutional revision by applying the unprecedented mathematical formula of "rounding up" ($203 \times 2/3 = 135.3333...$. The opposition party members protested that 2/3 majority should be more than 135, while the Liberal Party argued that it could be rounded up to 136 since three tenth of a person should be a whole person).[29]

Again, Rhee succeeded in obtaining the necessary legality, i.e., the constitutional revision which permitted him to run for the presidency as many times as he wished. In doing so, he further damaged the legitimacy of his rule.

From then until his downfall by the April Student Revolution of 1960, Rhee and his ruling group had undertaken a series of other *legal* maneuvers. In the process, *legitimacy* crises heightened. The passage of the new National Security Law on 24 February 1958 and the suspended publication of *Kyonghyang Sinmun,* an opposition-leaning daily newspaper on April 30, 1959, were some notable cases. It was the systematic election rigging, planned and executed by the Rhee government during the presidential and vice-presidential elections on March 15, 1960, that led to his rather disgraceful political exit—his forced step-down from the presidency and exile and eventual death in Hawaii.

The political lesson from the Rhee government was simple to learn but too difficult to practice. Any attempt to prolong the rule by concocting some *legal* devices is futile in the long run. Such *legal* devices were bound to intensify the *legitimacy* crisis, which, in turn, would undermine the very *legal* foundation on which such rule depended.

The political problems of the short-lived Chang Myon government (1960-1961) via the Hŏ Chŏng Interim Administration (April-July 1960) were entirely different. The new government, based on the cabinet-responsible system, came into being. For the first time after twelve year-long authoritarian dictatorship of the Rhee regime, the government was democratic and free of political oppression. This government, however, was beset with new kinds of political ailment. The Democratic Party, which had survived as the opposition party under the shadow of the Rhee's Liberal Party, became the ruling party overnight. But it was incapable of "leading" the government as the ruling party. It engaged in intra-party factional strife, which soon split it into two: the Old Faction and the New Faction. The general public was no better in this respect. Especially the students, who led the April Student Revolution and gained "freedom," which they had so desparately yearned and fought for during the Rhee regime, could not "exercise" it with prudence and restraint as required of democratic citizen. They indulged in it, instead.

The political situation under Chang Myŏn government (August 1960-May 1961) was no better. The end-result of the ruling party's lack of unity and direction and the general publics' lack of self-control was obvious—more turmoil, disorder and instability. Positively, it can be said that such turmoil, disorder and instability were "inevitable" for the new democratic government, which could have controlled them in due course. During this turbulent period the military, led by Major General Park Chung Hee, staged a coup on May 16, 1961, and replaced the Chang government with a military junta.

The beginning of the Park regime, therefore, differed sharply from the Rhee and the Chang regimes. Both the Rhee and the Chang regimes came into existence through constitutional and legal procedures. Rhee and his ruling group tried to maintain the seeming *legality* even in their attempts to prolong the rule. The Chang regime's legality and legitimacy were never seriously challenged. But the Park regime started from the *illegal* seizure of power by the military coup. To overcome the illegality, the leaders of the military junta attempted incessantly to gain legitimacy (i.e., popular support) for their rule. To a great extent, their efforts were successful. The measures which contributed to their success were the prompt restoration of public order; the speedy execution of the leaders who mastermined the fraudulent presidential election of March 15, 1960; the enactment of the Political Activities Purification Law; the easing of the debts held by the farmers and fishermen; and the confiscation of illegally amassed wealth and property by corrupt politicians and bureaucrats.

After taking off his military uniform and reversing and revising some of his earlier political remarks and intentions,[30] Park sought the *legality* of his rule for the first time: he ran for the presidency on October 15, 1963. He defeated Yun Bo-sun, the opposition party candidate and the former president. He received 46.6% (4,702,640) and Yun, 45.1% (4,546,614) of the votes.

Despite Park's phenomenal success with modernization policy during his presidency, he, too, faced the same old political dilemma as Rhee. Nearing the end of his second term as president, Park had to overcome the same obstacles that haunted his predecessor Syngman Rhee, i.e., the two-term restrictions for presidency. Like Rhee, Park, too, plotted a constitutional revision, allowing him to run for the third term. On October 17, 1969, the national referendum approved this revision amid violent political protests and political boycotts by the opposition group.

This was another classic example of obtaining the apparent *legality* at the expense of *legitimacy*. Under this new *legality* Park ran for his third term. He won again, with a smaller margin than his previous election (53.2% v. 45.3%, as compared with 51.5% v. 40.9%).

Being unsatisfied with the third term, Park and his ruling groups attempted not only to remove any restriction imposed on the terms of the presidency but to expand the presidential power to the extreme. This was the so-called *Yushin* Constitution of 1972. First, the Park regime declared a martial law in December 1971 and promptly passed the National Defense Act. On November 21 of the following year, the national referendum was conducted under the martial law, which approved the new constitution by a sweeping margin of 91.5% of the vote. So Park and his ruling elites won another *legality* battle. But this *legality* was much like the legendary Emperor's new clothes. To Park and his close ruling associates, the rule had seeming *legality,* but to the rest, like the Emperor's finest clothes, such legality was not real except for the nakedness of power itself. Under the *Yushin* Constitution, Park was *legally* elected by the so-called National Conference for Unification (NCU) by 99.9% of the vote (2,357 out of 2,359 NCU members). Ironically, the legitimacy crisis was at its height. On July 6, 1978, Park was elected President by the NCU members by 99.8% of the vote. The rule by Park, as a virtual president-dictator continued until his violent death in 1979.

Like the beginning of the Park regime, the launching of the Chun regime was devoid of *legality*. It was the so-called 12 December 1979 Military Mini-coup that gave birth to the new regime. The problem of the Chun regime was compounded by the additional burden—the bloody incident in Kwangju in May 1980. From the outset, therefore, the regime's legitimacy question arose, let alone its legality. Like his predecessor Park, Chun, too, sought the legality of his rule. The constitution was again amended, which, among other things, allowed 7-year one-term presidency. He was first elected by the electoral college on August 27, 1980, by 99.9% of the vote. On February 25, 1981, he was reelected as the first full-term president of the new regime by the electoral college votes. The winning margin of the vote was 99.8%. This seeming *legality* of his rule notwithstanding, his regime had been besieged by the aforesaid double legitimacy crisis from the beginning to the end. His usurpation of power in his ultimate bid for power notwithstanding, Chun made one significant contribution to South Korea's political development. His peaceful exit from the presidency and transfer of power to Roh Tae Woo was the first constitutional exercise of its kind.

In sum, it is self-evident from the above that all three regimes— the Rhee, the Park and the Chun—have wrestled with the question of *legality* (the government's right to govern) at the price of *legitimacy* (the people's recognition and support of such right). All three regimes also clearly demonstrated that the prolonging of power by legality without legitimacy has proven to be futile in the long run. In the end, Rhee was forced to stepdown from the presidency and went to exile in Hawaii; Park was assassinated by one of his most trusted political associates, the KCIA director; and Chun was condemned to internal political banishment by his life-long friend and co-plotters. In this continuous vicious circle by the ruling elites to prolong power under various *legal* garbs, be they constitutional revisions, extra-ordinary measures or martial laws, the real political casualty had been the democratic formula for the peaceful transfer of power, which had gone by the wayside until the launching of the Roh government.

The lesson to be learned from these political experiences of the South Korean politics is pure and simple. Those in power must learn to *exit* from power without trying to plot endless "legal" devices to prolong power; and those who are out of power must learn to enter it with less intransigent negativism and obstructionism. In the end, as Plato presaged long ago, *the states are as men are.* The quality of the Korean politics is, then, only the political reflection of the Korean people -- the mass public, the ruling elites and the opposition groups alike.

Notes

1. Plato, *The Republic and Other Works*, trans. B. Jowett (Garden City: Dolphin Books, 1960), p. 235.
2. Joseph LaPalombara, *Politics Within Nations* (Englewood Cliffs: Prentice-Hall, 1974), p. 48.
3. The crises of nation building are discussed in detail in Leonard Binder et al., *Crises and Sequences in Political Development* (Princeton: Princeton University Press, 1971). Also, LaPalombara, *Op. Cit.*, pp. 46-58.
4. See his article, "Legitimacy," in the *International Encyclopedia of the Social Sciences*, Vol. 9, p. 244ff. Quoted in John H. Herz, "Legitimacy: Can We Retrieve it?" *Comparative Politics* 10 (April 1978): 317-343. There are other definitions of legitimacy. For example, Sandara J. Bell-Rokeach defined it as "a collective judgment that attributes the generalities of 'goodness' or 'morality' or 'righteousness' to behavior" (p. 101). It is "a complex of social product which reflects people's subjective states—attitudes, values, needs—as well as their objective states—structural position, rank, etc." (p. 102). For details, see her chapter, "The Legitimation of Violence," in James F. Short, Jr., and Marvin E. Wolfgang, eds., *Collective Violence* (Chicago: Aldine and Atherton, 1970), pp. 100-112. H. L. Nieburg's distinction between legality and legitimacy, though lengthy, is worth quoting here. He defined legality as "an attribute of sovereignty. It is an abstraction which confers the authority of the state upon the acts, records, elections, and so on of those who conduct the offices of state power, and upon the code of law which regulates behavior. Legality is the technicality of formal consistency and adequate authority." He then went on to say that "legitimacy reflects the vitality of the underlying consensus which endows the state and its officers with whatever authority and power they actually possess, not by virtue of legality, but by the reality of support which the citizens pay to the institutions and behavior norms. Legitimacy is earned by the ability of those who conduct the power of the state to represent and reflect a broad consensus. Legitimacy cannot be claimed or granted by mere technicality of law; it must be won by the success of state institutions in cultivating and meeting expectations, in mediating interests and aiding the process by which the values of individuals and groups are allocated in the making, enforcement, adjudication, and general observance of law." See his *Political Violence: The Behavioral Process* (New York: St. Martin Press, 1970), p. 54. Finally, the legitimacy criteria defined by Almond and Powell are: if citizens believe that they ought to obey the laws, then legitimacy is high; if they see no reason to obey, or if they comply only for fear, then, legiti-

macy is low. For details, see G. A. Almond and G. Bingham Powell, Jr., *Comparative Politics Today: A World View* (Boston: Little, Brown, 1980), p. 42.

5. In their definition of authority relations, Lichbach and Culpeper implied, of course, both the ruler's right and capacity and the recognition of the ruled of such right and capacity. They focused on the regime's capacity to survive. In any case, the meaning of authority relations is rather broad and complex, which includes, among other things, the type of executive recruitment, the extent of decisional constraints on the chief executive, executive characteristics, the pattern of political participation, the centralization of power and the scope of governmental control. For details, see Mark Irving Lichbach and Charles E. Culpeper, "Regime Change: A Test of Structuralist and Functionalist Explanations," *Comparative Political Studies* 14 (April 1981): 49-73. Also, Ted R. Gurr, "Persistence and Change in Political Systems, 1800-1971," *American Political Science Review* 68 (December 1974): 1482-1504.

6. Lichbach and Culpeper, *Op. Cit.*, p. 59.

7. LaPalombara, *Op. Cit.*, p. 48.

8. *Ibid.*

9. *Ibid.*, p. 49.

10. Edward N. Muller and Carol J. Williams, "Dynamics of Political Support-Alienation," *Comparative Political Studies* 13 (April 1980): 33-59.

11. J. J. Linz (ed.), *The Breakdown of Democratic Regimes in Europe: Crisis, Breakdown, and Reequilibrium* (Baltimore: Johns Hopkins University Press, 1978), p. 17.

12. T. R. Gurr and M. McClelland, *Political Performance: A Twelve-nation Study* (Beverly Hills: Sage, 1971), p. 30.

13. For a detailed analysis, see M. Stephen Weatherford, "Measuring Political Legitimacy." *American Political Science Review* 86 (March 1992): 149-166.

14. Herz, *Op. Cit.*, pp. 319-321. Also, Almond and Powell, *Op. Cit.*, p. 43.

15. Gurr and McClelland, *Op. Cit.*, p. 30.

16. Herz, *Op. Cit.*, pp. 331-337.

17. Sternberger, *Op. Cit.*

18. Quoted in Herz, p. 318.

19. Herz, p. 318 and p. 331.

20. By an attitude of "sullen toleration" is meant "mere absence of any feeling either for [sic] loyalty or disapproval." Herz, p. 320.

21. See Sung Chul Yang, *Korea and Two Regimes* (Cambridge: Schenkman, 1981), pp. 123-126.

22. *Ibid.* Also, Keun-shik Yun's chapter in Wun-tae Kim, *Hankuk Chŏngch'iron* [On Korean Politics] (Seoul: Pakyŏng-sa, 1982), pp. 231-244.

23. *Ibid.*

24. *Official Records of the General Assembly, Fifth Session,* Supplement No. 16.

25. For a detailed discussion of the United Nations' role on the Korean question, see Sung Chul Yang, "The United Nations on the Korean Question Since 1947," *Korea Journal* (October 1981), pp. 4-10.
26. After 30 May 1950 general election, Shin Ik-hi, the nominee of the major opposition party, Democratic National Party, handily defeated Oh Ha-Yong, the Rhee government's nominee by the vote margin of 96 to 46 as the Speaker of the 2nd NA. This was the first clear signal for Rhee that he could not be re-elected by the member of the NA. For details, see Keun-shik Yun's chapter, pp. 246-262.
27. *Ibid.*
28. See Footnote 4.
29. Keun-shik Yun's chapter, p. 257.
30. For a detailed analysis of Park's reversal of his original pledge that he would not run for the presidency, see Sung Chul Yang, "Revolution and Change: A Comparative Study of the April Student Revolution of 1960 and the May Military Coup D'etat of 1961 in Korea" (Ph.D. dissertation, University of Kentucky, 1970).

PART V

NORTH AND SOUTH KOREAN ECONOMIC ORIENTATION: MOBILIZATION VERSUS MOTIVATION

CHAPTER 14

RESOURCE ENDOWMENTS AND NATURAL CONDITION

Bolshevism... is just a superlative hatred of the thing they call the bourgeois: and what the bourgeois is, isn't quite defined. It is Capitalism, among other things. Feelings and emotions are also decidedly bourgeois that you have to invent a man without them... especially the personal man, is bourgeois: so he must be suppressed. You must submerge yourselves in the greater thing, the Soviet-social thing. Even an organism is bourgeois: so the ideal must be mechanical. The only thing that is unit, non-organic, composed of many different, yet equally essential part, is the machine. Each man is [sic] a machine-part, and the driving power of the machine, hate... hate of the bourgeois. That, to me, is Bolshevism.... Hate's a growing thing like anything else. It's the inevitable outcome of forcing ideas on the life, forcing one's deepest instincts; our deepest feelings we force according to certain ideas. We drive ourselves with a formula like a machine. The logical mind pretends to rule the roost, and the roost turns into pure hate. We're all Bolshevists, only we are hypocrites. The Russians are Bolshevists without hypocrisy.

D. H. Lawrence[1]

Introduction

Ever since 1945 when Korea was partitioned into two halves, the two regimes in the Korean Peninsula have been in rivalry. Their rivalry has not been limited to the areas of their diametrically opposed ideology, politics and economic systems. It encompasses virtually all aspects of individual and national endeavors—war, arms race, diplomacy, sports, economic competition and, ultimately, quality of life.

In the beginning both sides mainly sold their rhetorical "promises"— the North claiming its ideological superiority, political, social and economic egalitarianism and independence, while the South countering them with its own version of democratic ideals and political, social and economic freedom. More than forty years have elapsed since then, a sufficient time for probing and juxtaposing their verbal promises with their actual performances.

The present study focuses only on North and South Korea's economic systems, policies and performances. Generally, comparing the two entirely different economic systems is a hazardous venture. First, it is difficult to isolate and control the effects of an economic system on economic performance from the total environment in which the economic system operates. Second, the two economic systems may have different resource endowments, physical size and starting points, let alone their historical and socio-cultural differences. Third, the needed data, especially of socialist economies, are either severely limited, inaccessible or simply absent. Worse still, those available figures are often unreliable. Fourth, the numerical comparison of the North and South Korean economic performance is bound to be dull, dry, and even misleading. It is misleading because the data may have been exaggerated, if not outrightly falsified. Hence, the numerical comparison of the two regimes is, at best, a measurement, not the totality of their economic conditions. Finally, there are several technical and methodological problems of comparison such as lack of comparable economic concepts, the differences in currency units and foreign exchange rates.[2]

The aforesaid general and methodological difficulties aside, the Korean pair is still an ideal test case for a juxtapositional, if not analytic, comparative study of economic performance because it is relatively easy to control non-economic factors. Until 1945 Korea was a united country with common historical, cultural, ethnic and linguistic heritage. Even today, their mutually incompatible ideological, political and economic systems notwithstanding, the Korean people in the North and the South share relatively high degree of common cultural homogeneity and heritage. Besides, the two are roughly the same in physical size. Initially also, there were no marked differences in both sides either in their level of economic development or natural environments.

In Part Five, five dimensions -- North and South Korea's resource endowments and natural environments, their economic conditions at the time of partition and their respective economic systems, policies and performance -- will be examined in some detail.

Physical Setting

Korea as a whole lies in the temperate zone, although its extreme northern border is closer to the climactic condition of Siberia, and its southern coastal regions are warm and snow-free. Except for mineral deposits, which is almost nine to one in favor of the North, natural conditions and physical settings of North and South Korea do not vary significantly. The Korean division was, in short, a product of politics, not of natural and physical bifurcations.

1. Location

The Korean Peninsula, now divided between North and South Korea, juts out from the Northeast Asian mainland in a southerly direction for about 1,000 kilometers. It is located between continental China and oceanic Japan. The shortest distance between Korea and Japanese territory is 206 km (124 miles), and it is about 190 km (114 miles) to China's Shantung peninsula to the west. The Korean Peninsula is elongated and irregular in shape in north-south direction and divides the Yellow Sea and East Sea (Sea of Japan). The Korean Peninsula with its associated islands lies in longitude 124'11 E-131'53 E and in latitude from 30'07 N to 43'01 N.[3]

North Korea's northern boundary fronts China's two northeastern (formerly Manchurian) provinces for some 1,033 kilometers (640.7 miles) and borders Russia for 17 kilometers (10.4 miles), which is 121 kilometers (75 miles) southeast of Vladivostok. Much of this northern frontier is formed by two large rivers, Aprok (Yalu) and Tuman (Tumen), which flow between China and Korea. The Aprok River rises on the slopes of an extinct volcano, Mt. Paektu, Korea's highest mountain (2,750 meter or 9,022 feet), and flows southwest to the Yellow Sea, while the Tuman River rises in the same area and flows first northeast, then southeast into the East Sea. Viewed as a whole, the configuration of the Peninsula somewhat resembles a rabbit held by its ears.

2. Area

The total area of Korea, North and South, and including offshore islands, is 220,843 square kilometers, about 84,800 square miles. North Korea occupies 122,044 square kilometers (47,639 square miles), or 55 percent of the total area. South Korea is 98,799 square kilometers (38,214 square miles), or 45 percent of the total area. The coastline totals 17,361 kilometers (10,416 miles), with 3,300 off-shore islands, of which about 300 are inhabited. The coastal length of the Peninsula is about 8,600 kilometers and that of the islands about 8,592 kilometers.

The east coast has a relatively simple coastline because mountains run parallel to the coast. Except for the Yŏnghŭng and the Yŏngil bays, the overall coastline is nearly straight with few off-shore islands. The coastal waters of the East Sea are deep, averaging over 1,692 meters (5,509 feet). Beaches can be found where small streams discharge into the sea. By contrast, the south and the west coasts are highly serrated and irregular, with a multitude of small offshore islands, mini peninsulas and bays. The Yellow Sea is shallow, with a mean depth of about 43 meters (140 feet), and the tidal differences range from 6 to 12 meters. The south coast's tidal range is relatively small with 1.3 meters at Pusan on the eastern side and 4.9 meters at Yŏsu, a port city located near the center of the southern coast.

3. Mountains

In North Korea mountains and uplands cover four-fifths of its territory; the proportion is as high as 90 percent in the northern provinces of

Chagang and Yanggang. The major mountain range extends from the vicinity of Mt. Paektu in a southeasterly direction toward the east coast. This range has peaks over 2,000 meters (6,500 feet) in altitude. Running northeasterly from the center of the Mach'ŏllyong Range toward the Tuman River valley is the Hamgyŏng Range, which also has a number of peaks over 2,000 meters, including Mt. Kwanmo, 2,564 meters (8,334 feet), Korea's second highest mountain. The southwest extension of the Hamgyŏng Range is known as the Pujŏllyŏng Range. To the west of the Hamgyŏng Range and Pujŏllyŏng Range lies a relatively low Kaema Plateau (averaging 1,010 meters or 3,280 feet), a heavily forested basaltic tableland. West of the Kaema Plateau is the Nangnim Range, averaging 1,514 meters (4,920 feet), extending to the southeast. To the west of the Nangnim Range are two less prominent ranges, the Chogyurong and the Myohyang, both of which are from 505 (1,640 feet) to 1,010 meters (3,280) in height. The Ch'ŏngch'ŏn River flows in the valley between them.

South of Wŏnsan city rises Korea's other major mountain chain, the T'aebaek, which extends down the eastern side of the Peninsula and is often called the "backbone of Korea." Only a short portion of its length is in North Korea, but this section includes the scenic Mt. Kumgang, 1,650 meters (5,373 feet). The terrain east of the Hamgyŏng and T'aebaek Ranges consists of short, parallel ridges which extend into the East Sea, creating in effect a series of isolated valleys accessible only by rail lines branching off from the main coastal track. West of the T'aeback chain, the terrain of central Korea is characterized by a series of lesser ranges and hills that gradually level off into broad plains along the coast.

Although North Korea's plains regions constitute only one-fifth of the total area, they support most of its farmlands. The plains are alluvial, built up from silt deposited on their banks by rivers in their middle and lower courses. Other plains, such as the Pyŏngyang Peneplain, were formed by eons of erosion from surrounding hills. A number of plains areas exists on the west coast, including the Pyŏngyang Peneplain, Unjŏn, Anju, Chaeryŏng and Yŏnback. Of these, the Chaeyŏng Plain and the Pyŏngyang Peneplain are the most extensive, each covering an area of about 279 square kilometers. They are followed in size by the Yŏnbaek Plain, which is about 166 square kilometers (120 square miles); the rest are about 111 square kilometers (80 square miles) each. The mountains along the east coast drop abruptly to the sea and as a result, few plains are found. The most important are the Hamhŭng, Yŏngch'ŏn, Kilchu, Yŏng-hŭng, and Susŭng Plains, of which Hamhŭng Plain is the largest with 166 square meters.

In South Korea, the highest mountains are mostly in the northeast, roughly paralleling the east coast, with the crests about ten miles inland. This is the T'aebaek Range, extending south for about 256 kilometers (160 miles) from the D.M.Z. to north of Pohang. The T'aeback constitutes the main watershed between drainage to the east and west coasts, the east coast streams being short and small and those flowing west being longer and less straight. Mt. Sŏrak, north of the 38th Parallel, contains the highest peak (1,724 meter or 5,603 feet) in the T'aebaek and the other famous peak, Mt. Kumgang, is in North Korea. West of Kangnung, the crest line of the T'aebaek is remarkably level, only Mt. Odae (1,577 meter or 5,127 feet) stands above the general skyline. This uniformity results from the broad and gentle uplift of a former peneplain in the T'aebaek orogeny. South of Mt. Odae, in the Tanyang-Yŏngwŏl-Chŏngsŏn districts where the Great Limestones of the Palaeozoic era outcrop, there are sinkholes, caves and other features of Karst topography. The streams flow in incised channels and the physiography is very rugged. South of Tanyang, average elevations decline rapidly, with natural basins visible between the mountains.

From this eastern mountain range extend two branches, the Ch'aryong and Sobaek. The Ch'aryong Range, the more northerly of the two, is lower and shorter. Starting from Mt. Odae in Kangwŏn Province, it forms the boundary between Kyŏnggi and North Ch'ungch'ŏng provinces, and continues southwest through South Ch'ung'ch'ŏng to reach the west coast between Taech'ŏn and Piin. The elevation decreases as it winds 1,076 meter (3,500 feet) in North Ch'ungch'ŏng Province to 300-600 meters (1,000-2,000 feet) in South Ch'ungch'ŏng Province, although Mt. Songju rises over 600 meters which is less than 9.6 kilometers (six miles) from the Yellow Sea. The Ch'aryŏng mountains are not high enough to be a real obstacle to transport, nor do they act as a major watershed, but they separate the drainage of the coastal plain south of Seoul from that of the Kŭm River Basin. A small offshoot of the Ch'aryong, extending northwest from Ch'ungju toward Seoul, separates the coastal rivers near Ansŏng from the Han River Basin in which Seoul is located. The Ch'aryong, however, does not extend as far north as Seoul itself, whose surrounding mountains are outliers of the T'aebaek.

Far more important than the Ch'aryong are the Sobaek Mountains, the great interior mountain divide of the country. The Sobaek Mountains also branch westward from the T'aebaek Mountains, but south of the Ch'aryŏng. They form the border between North Ch'ungch'ŏng and North Kyŏngsang provinces, then bend southward to provide the boundary between the two Chŏlla provinces in the west and the Kyŏngsang provinces in the east. These mountains have a general elevation of 1,076 meters (3,500 feet) and present a real obstacle for transportation, which must cross the passes. Of these passes the five principal ones are: Ponghwa, Chukryŏng, Ch'upungnyŏng, Yuksipryŏng and Palryŏng.

The Sobaek terminates in the south in the great Chiri massif, covering parts of three provinces and occupying an area of about 83 square kilometers (60 square miles) between Namwŏn, Sunch'ŏn and Chinju. Here the highest peak rises to 1,933 meters (6,283 feet), the highest on the mainland of South Korea. The Sobaek Mountains separate the northwest, centering on Seoul, from the southeast, centering on Pusan, and also divide the south between the Chŏlla Provinces in the west and the Kyŏngsang provinces in the east (in 1984 a two-lane modern highway called the "Olympic Highway" connecting Kwangju, South Chŏlla Province, and Taegu, North Kyŏngsang Province, was completed). The Sobaek also has an offshoot in the Noryŏng Range, extending southwest along the border between North and South Chŏlla Provinces. These low mountains, rising only to 769 meters (2,500 feet), provide a natural boundary between the two provinces and separate the Honam Plain from the Yŏngsan River Basin.

Mountains occupy roughly 70 percent of the Korean landscape, but the remainders, its lowlands, are the economic core. Here are found the cities and towns and almost all the agricultural areas. As of 1984, 22 percent of South Korea is a cultivated land area, 66.1 percent, mountains and forests and 11.9 percent, other areas of miscellaneous uses. Thus, a total of 33.9 percent can initially be defined as "lowlands." Of the 22 percent cultivated land area, 13.2 percent and 8.8 percent are in paddies and dry lands, respectively, most but not all of which are on the valley floors. Some paddies extend into terraces of upstream headwaters, but 13.2 percent fits the definition of "flat" land. To put it differently, as of 1990, the total area of cultivated land in South Korea amounted to 21 million hectares, of which 13.4 million *ha* (63.8%) were paddy fields and 7.6 million *ha* were upland (36.2%).

South Korea's lowlands are almost exclusively the products of erosion, and few areas are "plains" devoid of hills. The Kyŏnggi Lowlands surrounding Seoul are an excellent example. To the east and north of the city, hills of 600 to 900 meters (2,000-3000 feet) rise between the valleys, and the terrain is a dissected peneplain. Even to the west, in the Kimpo Plain, low rounded hills, left as islands of circumdenudation, abound. In many parts of the country, the granite has weathered more readily than the surrounding harder rocks. The result is a "punch-bowl" with intra-montain basins encircled by harder strata. Kyŏngju, Suwŏn, and Ch'ŏnan lie in such "erosional basin."

Most of the plains are on the west coast, along the lower courses of the rivers. They include the Kimpo Plain along the lower Han, a coastal plain along the Sapkyo Ch'ŏn at Pyŏngt'aek, the Yedang Plain of northern South Ch'ungch'ŏng Province, the Nonsan Plain north of the Kum River, the Honam Plain of North Chŏlla Province, the Yŏngsan Plain of South Chŏlla Province, and the Naktong Plain, in the middle reaches of the Naktong River where the valley broadens to about ten miles. Of these the largest is the Honam Plain, with an area of 139 square kilometers (100 square miles). There is also a narrow coastal plain which fringes the East Sea between Sokch'o and Kangnung.

4. Rivers

The rivers and streams throughout Korea flow strongly during summer, fed by seasonal rainfall and melting snow in the mountains, but their volume drops considerably during the dry winters. In dry months (October through April) the water stage becomes very low, and often much of the river beds are dried up. The rivers serve a threefold economic function: they provide a source of water for irrigation during the dry months; they are utilized as an auxiliary means of transportation to ease the strain on the roads and railroads; and their current is used to generate electricity.

There are some 64 rivers and streams in North Korea. Because its northern and eastern regions are mostly mountains and highlands, and its western region, low hills and plains, major rivers such as Amrok, Taedong, Ch'ŏngch'ŏn, Imjin, and Yesŏng—flow westward into the Yellow Sea. By contrast, rivers and streams on the east coast are short (with the exception of the Tuman and Sŏngch'ŏn) and swift-flowing.

In South Korea there are a total of twelve main river basins and a score of small short streams along the eastern and southern coasts. Provincial boundaries corresponded with the four major river basins: Kyŏnggi and Kangwŏn Provinces with the Han-Imjin complex, North and South Ch'ungch'ŏng Provinces with the Kum, North and South Kyŏngsang Provinces with the Naktong, and the Cholla Provinces with the Sŏmjin and Yŏngsan. In addition to the aforesaid three-fold economic functions of the rivers, valleys and banks along the rivers in both North and South Korea, they have increasingly become the sites for major industrial complexes.

5. Climate

Because Korea is a peninsula, its climate has both marine and continental characteristics. Korea has a relatively short, hot, humid summer and a long, cold and arid winter. Winter temperatures throughout the North show much diversity, mainly because of varying latitude and elevation. Winters are most severe in the northern interior provinces of Chagang and Yanggang, where five winter months have temperatures below freezing and there are only 130 frost-free days a year. The average January temperature at Chunggangjin, on the Aprok River, is –6°F.

The east coast is generally warmer during the winter months because the mountains, especially Hamgyŏng and Pujŏllyŏng Ranges, provide partial shelter from the cold air masses of the Asian hinterland. The average January temperature at Unggi, in the extreme northeast, is 15°F, at Kimch'aek, 21.4°F and at Wŏnsan, farther south, 25°F. The western part of the country, however, receives the full force of the winter wind. Sinuiju, on the mouth of the Aprok has an average January temperature of 15.5°F, Pyongyang, 17.6°F, and the Hwanghae Peninsula, to the south, 22.6°F.

Summer temperatures are much more uniform throughout the north, averaging in the seventies. In the northern interior region, however, summer temperatures prevail for only about two months, so that only fast-maturing crops may be sown. Farther south, the growing season extends for at least 4 months, with an average of about 900 hours of total sunshine from June through September. The southern part of the North has about 175 frost-free days per year.

An average annual precipitation ranges from 13 to 23 centimeters (32 to 60 inches), depending on the locale. Areas with the lightest amount of rainfall include the Tuman River valley, with a range of 7 to 9 centimeters (20 to 25 inches), and the lower parts of the Taedong River, which receives 9 to 11 centimeters (24 to 28 inches) annually. The heaviest rainfall occurs in the upper Ch'ŏngch'ŏn valley, the Wŏnsan area and the Imjin River basin, each recording over 20 centimeters a year. Precipitation is seasonal. From 50 to 60 percent falls during June, July and August, the result of the moisture-laden, summer monsoonal wind from the Pacific. Only 15 percent of the precipitation occurs during the dry months. Snow falls in the northern mountain regions from late October until April; and elsewhere, from early November to March. Typhoons are rare because of the proximity of the continental land mass. Only one or two per year strikes the north, usually in July or August.

In South Korea the prevailing wind direction during the winter months is from the north; a cold, dry air originating over Siberia moves southward across the Korean Peninsula. In the summer months, from June to August, the air masses dominating Korean weather come from the tropical waters of the East China Sea. These air masses are warm and moisture-laden. By August, both the temperature and the relative humidity rise to the nineties. Spring has variable weather, but there is usually a long period of clear crisp days in the autumn, particularly in October.

Rainfall is generally associated with the summer onshore monsoon and occurs principally in June, July and August. The highest rainfall occurs on the southern slopes of Cheju Island where the incoming monsoon first rises across Mt. Halla. Sŏgwipo, a small port and a tourist resort on the southern coast of the island, has an average rain fall of 28 centimeters. But in general, the total precipitation is between 16 to 21 centimeters. Because winter is the dry period of the year, not much precipitation falls in the form of snow. The first fall occurs about November 21 and the last about February 22.

In July, August and early September, typhoons originating in the Pacific, may cross the southern half of the Peninsula having lost some of its strength. The damage caused is due to the intensity of monsoon rains, rather than high winds. September typhoons are particularly feared because the heavy rains flatten the rice plant and burst the dikes in the flooded paddies.

6. Soil

Over 60 percent of the soil in North Korea is derived from gneiss and granite, which produce a brown, infertile soil with a high sand content. A reddish-brown soil, the product of limestone bedrock, exists in the southern parts of South Hamgyŏng and Kangwŏn provinces. Only at the Aprok and Tuman estuaries is a quantity of rich black soil to be found. Most of the soil is alluvial, washed down into the valleys by rivers and streams, and moved about in the coastal lowlands by wind, rain and floods. These movements have minimized weathering, causing the soil to retain the characteristics of the original rock and retarding the chemical processes necessary for fertility.

Most soils in South Korea have been formed in situ. Many mountain soils are thin, with some extensive bare rock surfaces in the high mountains of the T'aebaek and Sobaek. Because so much of the parent rock is granitic, the soils are moderately to strongly acidic and brownish. Small patches along the western and southern coasts have poorly drained clay soils, especially in tidal flats reclaimed from the sea. The predominant soils in the lowland agricultural areas are red-yellow podzolic or lateritic type. When converted to paddies, leaching quickly turns these soils grey.

7. Minerals

On the whole North Korea contains 80 to 90 percent of all known mineral deposits on the Peninsula. It possesses about 300 kinds of minerals, of which approximately 200 have economic values. North Korea ranks among the first 10 nations in the world in both deposits and production of gold, tungsten, graphite, magnetite, barytes, molybdenum, limestone, mica and fluorite. Other important mineral deposits include asbestos, aluminum, chromium, copper, kaolin, lead, nickel, potash, silica, silver and zinc. Iron ore reserves are estimated at 2.4 billion tons, 1 billion in the form of magnetite at the Musan area alone. Coal reserves are estimated at 8 billion tons, 5 billion of which is low-quality anthracite (hard coal). The major anthracite coalfield lies along the Taedong River. There are small amounts of lignite (brown coal) deposit at Anju, Aoji and Kocham coalfields.

By contrast, natural resources in South Korea are meager. The leading resources are coal, iron ore, graphite, gold and silver, tungsten, lead and zinc, comprising more than 60 percent of the total value of mineral resources (See Table 14-1).

Demographic Features

Although North Korea is slightly larger than South Korea in size, the latter has twice more population than the former. As of 1990, populations of North and South Korea were 21.7 million and 43.5 million, respectively. According to *World Development Report, 1984,* North Korea's population is projected to increase to 27 million in 2000 and 42 million in 2050. The figure for South Korea in the same periods are 51 and 67 millions. North Korea's rate of natural increase in population in the year 2000 is projected to be in the range of 1.3 to 1.6, while that of South Korea in the same year is estimated at 1.1.

By the year 2000 both North and South Korean population will be graying. People 65 and over will nearly double from 1980 to 2000, while population growth slows down considerably, and, thus, the increase in the youthful population aged 1-14 will become miniscule. North and South Korea's life expectancy at birth in 1983 was estimated at 65 (63 for male and 67 for female) and 67 years (64 for male and 71 for female), respectively. The 1991 *World Development Report,* however, places South Korea's life expectancy at 70. According to *World Development Report, 1985,* North and South Korean infant mortality and child death rates, too, did not show sharp differences. North Korea's infant mortality rates (aged under 1) declined from 64 (per thousand) in 1965 to 32 (per thousand) in 1983 and its child death rates (aged 1-4) during the said periods from 6 to 2 (per thousand) while South Korea's infant mortality rates in the same period went down from 64 (per thousand) to 29 (per thousand) and its child death rates, from 6 to 2 (per thousand). *World Development Report,* 1991, did not contain the North Korean data, but South Korea's infant mortality rate went down to 23 (per thousand) in 1989.

Urban population in North Korea as percentage of its total population has increased from 45 in 1965 to 62 in 1983; the figures for South Korea in the same periods are 32 and 62. An average annual growth rate of urban population in North Korea has declined slightly from 4.9% (1965-73) to 4.2% (1973-83). A similar trend is shown in South Korea for the same period—from 6.5% to 4.8%. The number of cities with over 500,000 persons in North Korea was two—Pyongyang and Hamhung—in 1990, an increase of one since 1960, whereas in South Korea there were 7 such cities in 1990, four more in the same period.

In sum, some minor variations aside, North and South Korea's physical settings and demographic features are on the whole more comparable than contrasting. The Korean Peninsula is indeed too small to accommodate distinct climatic zones, geologic eras and demographic patterns. It means that if both halves have shown distinct developmental patterns more than forty years after the Korean division, they are man-made rather than the product of nature. As will be clear in the ensuing chapters, the two distinct developmental patterns—the North's state-controlled collectivistic mobilization economy and the South's individual-propelled motivation economy are the main cause of their two contrasting economic life, not their resource endowments and natural conditions.

*Table 14-1. North and South Korea's Resource Endowments
and Physical Settings*

	North Korea	South Korea
Area (Sq. Km)	122,098*	99,022
Population (millions)	22.0	43.2
Major Mountains	Mt. Paektu.........2,750 m	Halla............1,950
	Mt. Kwanmo 2,541	Chiri............1,915
	Mt. Tugu 2,335	Sŏrak..........1,708
	Mt. Kwoesang...2,332	Odae............1,563
	Mt. Pukpote.......2,288	Taebaek.......1,546
Major Rivers	Amrok (Yalu).......821 km	Naktong..........521
(lengths)	Tuman (Tumen) ...520	Han.................514
	Taedong...............439	Kum 401
	Imjin.....................254	Sŏmjin............212
	Ch'ŏngch'ŏn 199	Yŏngsan.........116
Climate [Temperature]	30C in Pyongyang (annual range)	30.3 in Seoul
[frost-free days]	150 to 200	170 to 226
	(70% of the annual precipitation falls in the four months from June to September)	

* The figures vary: (i) the total area of Korea is 220,843 sq. kilometers (84,800 sq. miles), of which North Korea comprises 55% or 122.044 sq. kilometers (46,639 sq. miles), while South Korea occupies 45% or 98,799 sq. kilometers (38,161 sq. miles). Chan Lee, "Geography of Korea: Land and People," paper delivered at Korean Educational Development Institute, October 1982; (ii) the total area of Korea is 220,847 sq. km. (85,269 sq. mi.) and North Korea has an area of 122,370 sq. km. (47,247 sq. mi.) and South Korea, 98,477 sq. km. (38,022 sq. mi.). Patricia M. Bartz, *South Korea*, (Oxford: Clarendon Press, 1972), p. 2; (iii) the total area of Korea is 85,285 sq. mi. and North Korea has an area of 47,071 sq. mi, and South Korea, 38,214 sq. mi., Rinn-Sup Shinn and others, *Area Handbook for North Korea* (Washington, D.C.: U.S. Government Printing House, 1969), p. 11; (iv) *Encyclopaedia Britannica* lists the total area of Korea, of North Korea and of South Korea as 84,822 sq. mi. (219,677 sq. km.), 46,800 sq. mi. (121,200 sq. km.) and 38,022 sq. mi. (98,477 sq. km.), respectively; and (v) *World Development Report 1984* rounded up the areas of North Korea and South Korea to be 121,000 sq. km. and 98,000 sq. km., respectively.

Table 14-1. Continued

Mineral Resources ** (Unit: 1,000 ton)		North Korea	South Korea
Classification	Quality (%)		
Iron Ore	Fe 25 – 50	3,300,000	126,300
Tungsten	Wo3 0.5 – 1	19,123	26,000
Nickel	Ni 0.3 – 1	256	64
Gold	Au 10g/t	2,340	1,180
Silver	Ag 50g/t	15,016	6,948
Lead	Pb 6 – 10	4,790	2,585
Coal	Kcal over 4,500	11,986,000	1,500,000
Copper	Cu 100	2,155	105
Zinc	Zn 100	12,001	738
Limestones	Cao 50	10,000,000,000	14,900,000
Uranium	U308 0.3 – 0.4	26,000	56,000

** The North Korean figures are from the National Unification Board (NUB) data and the South Korean figures are originally from the Mining Bureau, the Ministry of Commerce and Industry, the Republic of Korea. The figures of the National Unification Board's English version differs from its Korean versions. See NUB's *Nampukhan Kyŏngje Pikyo, 1981* and its *A Comparative Study of the South and North Korean Economies.*

Notes

1. D. H. Lawrence, *Lady Chatterley's Lover* (New York: Nelson Doubleday Inc., 1929), pp. 36-37.

2. For a discussion of methodological problems of comparing socialist and capitalist economies see, for instance, Robert C. Campbell *et al.*, "Methodological Problems Comparing the U.S. and USSR Economies," in *Soviet Economic Prospects for the Seventies*, (Washington, D.C.: U.S. Government Printing Office, 1973), pp. 122-146; F. W. Dresch et al., "A Comparison of U.S./ U.S. S.R. Gross National Product, National Security Expenditures and Expenditures for R.D.T. & E," SSC-TN-2010-1, (December 1972) Menlo Park, Cali. SRI, Strategic Studies Center, pp. V-5, VI-6; M. Bornstein, "A Comparison of Soviet and United States National Product," in M. Bornstein and D. R. Fusfeld, eds., *The Soviet Economy, A Book of Readings*, rev. ed. (Homewood: Richard Irwin Press, 1966), pp. 283-293; W. T. Lee, *The Estimation of Soviet Defense Expenditures, 1955-1975* (New York: Praeger, 1977); and W. T. Lee, "The Shift in Soviet National Priorities to Military Forces, 1958-85," *The Annals of the American Academy of Political and Social Science* 457 (1981): 46-66. For discussions on problems of estimating North Korea's economic performance in particular see, for instance, Pong S. Lee, "An Estimate of North Korea's National Income," *Asian Survey* (December 1972), pp. 51-526; Joo-whan Choi, "Estimate of North Korea's GNP," *Vantage Point* (October 1979), pp. 1-16; Poong Lee, "Method of Computing North Korean GNP (I) and (II)" *Vantage Point* (January and February 1982), pp. 1-10 and pp. 1-9. See also, Ha-ch'ong Yŏn and Bong S. Lee, "On the Measurement of the North Korean Economy," Paper presented at the KDI (Fall, 1984) and *Pukhan ei Kukmin Soduk Kaenyŏm gwa GNP Ch'ugyebangbŏp* [The Concept of National Income in North Korea and the Estimating Method of Its GNP] by the Ministry of National Unification Board (April 1986). The 1991 North Korean GNP Estimation (in Korean), The Ministry of National Unification Board (August 1992).

3. The 1991 edition of the *Korea Statistical Yearbook* reports 124'11'0"E 131' 52'42"E and 33'06'40"N-43'00'39"N, instead

CHAPTER 15

ECONOMIC SYSTEMS, POLICIES AND STRATEGIES

That the rich man enjoyed the fruit of the poor man's labour, and the latter were a thousand to one in proportion to the former. That the bulk of our people were forced to live miserably, by labouring every day for small wages to make a few live plentifully.

Jonathan Swift[1]

Economic Conditions at Inception

For 35 years from 1910 to 1945 Korea had been a Japanese colony. Under Japanese colonial rule Korea had undergone substantial economic development and modernization. Japan had developed key industrial bases in Korea, especially in the areas of metal, chemical, mining and textile industries and hydroelectric power facilities. It had built social overhead capital such as communication and railroad networks. It had also introduced modern farming methods such as irrigation, fertilization and mechanization.

Japan developed the Korean industrial base and social infrastructure primarily for its own political, strategic and economic objectives. Politico-strategically, Korea functioned both as a springboard and a principal military and other material supply route for Japan's territorial ambitions to control Manchuria and China proper. Economically, Korea acted as a supplier of important raw materials, semi-finished products, and rice to

Japan, and as a market for the latter's manufactured goods. It was no accident, therefore, that industrial sites in Korea were mostly located in the eastern or western coastal areas near ports so as to connect them efficiently with Japan proper. In agriculture there had been a gradual yet persistent shift in landownership and farm management during the Japanese rule. Many Korean owner-farmers had become tenants and farm laborers, while more Japanese farmers had become landowners. In government and industry few Koreans were hired as officials, managers, engineers and other skilled personnel. The industrial plants that Korea inherited from the Japanese were not in good operational condition due to disinvestment through heavy war-time use and inadequate maintenance.

Long before the partition, Korea's northern and southern regions were often characterized as "industrial north" and "agricultural south." The degree of complementarity, however, between the two regions was much higher and more complex than what this simple characterization suggests. The North led the South in overall gross industrial output, particularly in electricity, fuel industry, mining, metallurgical industry, chemical industry and housing and construction industry, while the latter surpassed the former in machine tool and metal processing industry, textile industry and gross food grain production.

During 1939-40, for instance, the North contributed 58.0 percent of the total manufactured product. The North led in heavy industry while the South was ahead in the consumer goods industries such as textiles. In the chemical and metal industries, the North's output was 4.9 and 8.3 times larger than that of the South, respectively, while the South's textile output was 5 times greater than that of the North. The North led the South in heavy industry while the latter surpassed the former in machine tools and metal processing industry. In electricity the ratio of its generating capacity between the North and the South was nearly 8 or 9 to 1 in the North's favor.[2] For example, on May 14, 1948, the North abruptly discontinued the supply of electrical power to the South in protest of the latter's separate election which was held four days earlier on May 10. It resulted in the sudden lòss of nearly 70% of the south's power source and paralyzed its industries.

The North dominated (still dominates) in mineral reserves. The North's share of known reserves at the time of the partition were: gold ores (72.7 percent); silver ores (99.9 percent); iron ores (100 percent); pig iron (78.5); tungsten and wulfenite ores (71); graphite (99.5); and bituminous and anthracite coal (97.7).[3] In mineral mining and production, too, the North led the South considerably. In 1944, the North produced 79 percent of the coal, 63 percent of the gold, 97 percent of the iron ore, 98 percent of the limestone, 100 percent of the magnetite and apatite, 71 percent of the nickel and 75 percent of the zinc.[4]

In agriculture the North led in the production of wheat, corn and soybeans, while South surpassed the North in rice and barley production, but in overall gross grain production, the latter's output was nearly twice more than the former's (See Table 15-1). The North was also the major producer and supplier of chemical fertilizers for farming at that time. Also, on the whole the North had proportionately more independent, large and medium-sized farmers while the South had smaller farmers (For details, see Table 15-2).

In brief, the two regions in Korea at the time of the partition were highly complementary industrially and agriculturally. The regional differences in the structure of economy and resource endowments existed (and still exist), but they were insignificant in magnitude. The North was slightly ahead in heavy industry, while the South led in light industries. The North produced more corns and soybeans, and the South led in rice and barely production. Relative North-South differentials in pre-partition conditions aside, the Korean economy as a whole was predominantly agricultural then, with more than 70 percent of the labor force engaged in agricultural production, totaling roughly two-thirds of the national output. Korea was (and still is) relatively a resource-poor country. Its arable land space is approximately one-fifth of its total area, and the rest is mostly mountains and rugged uplands.[5]

Systemic Differences

The North and South Korean economies are variants of socialist and capitalist economic systems, respectively. As prototypes or pure forms, both socialist and capitalist economies are in direct contrast (See Table 15-3). The socialist economy is a centralized command economy, whereas the capitalist economy is a highly decentralized competitive market economy. In the socialist economic system, all means of production are owned by the state and/or cooperatives. In the capitalist economy private ownership and free enterprise system prevail. In the socialist economy, the state, i.e., the ruling communist party, sets its economic goals. In the capitalist economy, the goal of the profit-making or profit maximization is determined by individuals and private corporations at their own risks. Economic planning is, thus, essential in the socialist economy, but not in the capitalist system. The incentives and disincentives for the workers in the socialist economic system are either public acclaims and bonuses for overfulfillment or public sanctions and wage reductions for underfulfillment of their work norms defined and determined by the state. By contrast, the primary motivating forces for the workers in the capitalist system are their gains and losses in wages and profits. Hence, the state -- the ruling communist party -- determines the question of labor and management in the socialist economy, while in the capitalist system the same question is left to the choice of each individual and private industry.

The ideal-typical socialist and capitalist economic systems in their purist forms do not exist. What exists in the real world are various "mixed" economic systems in that each country possesses a varying degree of combination of elements from the two systems. Moreover, all economic systems, whether they are socialist or capitalist or any mix of these two, are in flux. They are constantly adjusting and readjusting internally and externally to the changing political, social, economic and strategic environments. The North and South Korean economic systems are no exception to this rule.

As mentioned at the outset, the present North Korean economic system is a variant of command economy (Table 15-4). Still, North Korea is rated as one of the world's most highly centralized, socialized and planned economies, even by communist standards.[6] It has basic features of socialist economic system. Its economy is controlled by the central government, which is, in turn, controlled by the Workers' Party of Korea (WPK). All means of production, distribution and exchange are owned and operated by the state and cooperatives, and private ownership and free enterprise system are virtually nonexistent.

North Korea's socialization of economy began in 1945, but it was interrupted briefly due to the outbreak of the Korean War (1950-53). Its socialization of economy was completed in 1958, and thereby, private ownership of productive means, land, commercial enterprises, transportation and communication facilities was abolished and replaced by state and cooperative ownership and control.

The state, i.e., the WPK, defines and determines the economic needs of the populace. Specifically, the State Planning Commission under the auspices of the WPK drafts economic plans, involving the selection of output, output targets, allocation of inputs, prices, distribution of national income, investment and economic growth. The North Korean economic plan is "imperative" in that all state and cooperative enterprises are required to strictly comply with the planning goals, guidelines and targets. In 1962 North Korea introduced the "unified" and "detailed" planning system in order to further tighten the democratic centralist discipline in overall economic management and to develop its economy in a more planned and balanced way.

North Korea still heavily relies on political and ideological indoctrination, mass movements and exhortations as means to mobilize workers, peasants and managers. The so-called "Three Revolutions (ideological, technical and cultural) Movement," "Three Revolutions Team" or the slogans such as "the speed of the 80s" and "the speed of the 90s" are the pertinent cases. North Korea's central planning of economy with a self-reliant inward-looking economic development strategy has also been relaxing its tight centralized grip on economy by introducing various forms of market mechanism at the micro-level.

North Korea now actively seeks foreign investment and/or joint domestic-foreign economic ventures; it advocates expansion of its "socialist market" and "capitalist market" as well. The "Law of Joint Venture of (North) Korea" announced on September 8, 1984, by North Korea's Supreme People's Assembly's Standing Committee is noteworthy. For this new economic policy orientations, its giant neighbor China's influence and spillover effects have been evident. The constraints on North Korea's new economic orientations are severe, nevertheless. Economically, its new path -- an outward-looking policy orientation and some degree of liberalization and decentralization at micro level similar to China's post-Mao economic policy changes -- may be the only alternative to the present economic strains and limits of its heretofore rigid, self-reliant and centralized economic planning and control. Politically, however, the new economic orientation is inconsistent with North Korea's ideology and present power structure. It is also incompatible with the personality cult of Kim Il Sung and Kim Jŏng Il, the heir presumptive. Economic decentralization and political centralization of power are mutually irreconcilable. Because of such inherent incompatibility, North Korea's new economic policy orientation will be marginal at best or cosmetic at worst, until and unless one presumes some fundamental economic and/or political transformation internally.

By contrast, the South Korean economic system is a mixed economy (Table 15-4). It is basically founded upon the system of private ownership, free enterprise and market economy, although the government involvement in economic decision-making and resource allocation has been quite heavy-handed and extensive at times. The government monopolizes some consumer products such as tobacco, salt, ginseng and others. It also controls various services such as railroads, telephone and telegraphs and postal services. In addition, it owns and operates some 25 key strategic industries and enterprises. The combined revenue of 25 state-run companies in 1984 was $10.5 billion (8,343.6 billion *won*). Their combined net profit in the same year was $551 million (440.9 billion *won*).[7]

The South Korean government is involved in many "private" corporations, including national banks as a major stockholder. In recent years, it has attempted to denationalize financial institutions. In 1972 the Hanil Bank was transferred to private control. Likewise, the Commercial Bank

of Korea, the Korea First Bank, the Bank of Seoul and Trust Company
and the Choheung Bank were denationalized in 1981, 1982 and 1983,
respectively. The government exerts enormous power over the foreign
sector of economy by directly controlling foreign exchange, preferential
tariffs and interest rates and direct and indirect subsidies. It also plays
a guiding role in overall economic decision-making in general and
resource allocation in particular by its manipulation of fiscal and monetary policies.

Since 1962 South Korea has introduced economic planning. Unlike
North Korea's, the South Korean economic plan is an "indicative" planning in that it exerts only indirect pressure on all industries and enterprises through market mechanism with minimal direct government intervention. Enterprises are asked to conform to the basic objectives of the
plan and the government uses fiscal, monetary and other policies to
achieve the planned targets. Again, unlike North Korea, the South
Korean development strategy in relation to other countries has been outward-looking in that it has aggressively been seeking foreign capitals
and inducing foreign investments. Initially, its export-led growth was
headed by light industry and gradually complemented by the injection of
heavy industry.

In sum, the North Korean economic system closely resembles a
socialist prototype—a closed, state-planned economy with state monopoly of all means of production, distribution, exchange and consumption. The South Korean economic system, meanwhile, deviates considerably from a pure capitalist free enterprise market model. The government exerts an enormous influence on the course of the economy
through planning, direct or indirect ownership and control of enterprises
and financial institutions, control of foreign exchange and fiscal and
monetary policies. In that sense, the South Korean system is closer to a
corporate state model than a free enterprise market model. In a corporate state model, the economy is organized in state-controlled associations of capital and labor, all working harmoniously for the common
good, with the aid and guidance of the authoritarian one-party state. The
underlying premise of corporatism is that politics is too complicated and
complex for the mass public to comprehend, and thus, it should be left

to the ruling elites, while the former should be busy with their own work and profession. The facts of corporatism notwithstanding, reliance on the free and open market, private initiative and pecuniary incentives remain the basic tenets of the South Korean economic system.

Grossly simplified, the core concept of North Korean economic system is *mobilization,* and that of South Korean economic system, *motivation.* Mobilization is based on the utility of collectivism; it is state-controlled and, by nature, involuntary. The tasks of "common good" and "common interest" are defined and determined by the state, namely, its ruling obligarchs. Motivation, on the other hand, is premised on the value of individualism; it is individual-centered, and, by nature, voluntary. The fruits of individual interests and initiatives may become the common good for the community, not the reverse. In reality, it may be safer to say that both economic systems are a mixture of collectivistic mobilization and individualistic motivation. But in the North, the former dominates as its guiding principle, while in the South, the latter prevails.

Contrast in Policy and Development Strategy

To begin with, an overall assessment of North and South Korea's respective economic policies and development strategies can be made. Positively, North Korea's economic policy has been consistent and stable. Negatively, it has been rigid, fossilized and doctrinaire. South Korea's economic policy has demonstrated, meanwhile, a high degree of flexibility and resiliency. Negatively, it has shown oscillation and instability.

North Korea

The North Korean economic system is an offshoot of Marxism-Leninism, in rhetoric, if not in reality. Increasingly in recent years, Kimilsungism, especially his *Juche* [Self-reliance] idea, "the creative application of Marxism and Leninism," has become the central ideological underpinning of its economic system. Self-reliance has been the underlying principles of the North Korean economic policy and self-sufficiency or autarchy, its primary policy goal. In achieving this primary goal, North Korea has adopted a variant of balanced growth strategy. It has given priority to the industrial sector without grossly neglecting the agricultural sector. Within the industrial sector it has put high premium on heavy and defense industry over light and consumer industry. It has also adopted basically an inward-looking domestic market strategy, and thereby, minimizing its reliance and dependency on foreign market. The extent of its involvement in foreign market has been determined by its import-substitution strategy based primarily on barter trade.

To put it another way, the North Korean economic system can be analyzed by examining its ideology (spirit of socialism), order and pattern of ownership. The spirit of socialism in North Korea consists of, according to Chŏn, "satisfaction of desire, rationalism and solidarity."[8] The satisfaction of desire is the purpose, rationalism, the method and solidarity, the pattern of interpersonal relations, of economic activity. As a means of satisfying common desires, North Korea adopted a policy of autarchy with "parallel development of light industry and agriculture with top priority given to heavy industry." Heavy industries in the metallurgical, mechanical and power sectors were to be promoted first, followed by mass supply of material means of production to light industry, agriculture and armaments industry sectors, and thereby, accelerating the construction of a self-sufficient economy. Rationalism calls for scientific management and techniques based on the rationality of values, which can be enhanced by ideological, cultural and technical revolution. In the words of Kim Il Sung, labor productivity can be increased by transforming the workers' consciousness through ideological and cultural revolution and by technological innovations.[9] Solidarity is the fabric of proletarian camaraderie which binds the masses into a cohesive community where, at least in rhetoric, no exploiter or exploited exist.

A planned economy is the core of the North Korean economic order. The leading agent of North Korea's planned economy is the government—the WPK, the Administrative Council, and the military and other para-governmental organs. This agent owns and controls all the property in the name of "the entire people" except for personal belongings and daily consumable life necessities. In rhetoric, this agent works for the benefit of the workers, but in reality, the benefactors are the beneficiaries and the beneficiaries, the victims. The primary aim of the planned economy is to satisfy social needs of the masses through continued increase in socialist production under the centralized administrative planning and control.

In the 1960s, North Korea achieved faster economic growth and greater economic equality and stability through its centralized economic planning and control than South Korea. But it began to show the limits and dilemmas of a centralized socialist economic planning and management by the late 1960s. Widening sectoral imbalances resulting from heavy and armaments industry-first policy, worsening quality of products in the absence of competitive decentralized market pricing, and growing dissatisfaction among the masses dependent on state-run rationing of consumer goods are the significant cases. Chon, a specialist on North Korean economy, contends that by 1970 the North Korean economy shifted from its "denotative" growth characteristic of labor-intensive stage of commodity production to the "connotative" growth characteristic of capital-intensive stage of commodity production. The denotative method called for centralized planning, political and ideological stimulation in promoting production and use of production indices in evaluating entrepreneurial performance. North Korea's closed economy during its denotative growth period adopted the method of centralized planning under administrative direction and management. This period was characterized by primacy of politics—strengthened guidance of the WPK, WPK-led mass movements to increase workers' productivity through ideological exhortations and technological revolution. Conversely, the connotative growth formula of an open economic system adopts a decentralized economic planning based primarily on market pricing. Hence, economy prevails over politics in the growth pattern—free and independent enterprise, increased voice of technocrats, and foreign investment and technology transfer.[10]

Specifically, North Korea's economic policy and development strategies can be divided into several distinct phases. First is the socialist nation-building period (1945-1949). It was marked by land reform, nationalization of key industries, restoration of industrial plants and facilities left by the Japanese and preparation for planned economy. The key legislative actions during this period were promulgation of the Land Reform Law (March 5, 1946) and the Labor Law (June 24, 1946), the Law on the Equality of Sexes (July 30, 1946), the Laws on Nationalization of Mineral Resources, Forestry and Fishery Zone (December 22, 1947).

In 1947 and 1948 North Korea launched two One-Year Plans. In this period it restored industrial plants and facilities destroyed and damaged during World War II. In addition, it attempted to solve the shortage problems of food and other life necessities by stressing light industry and agriculture. In 1949 the first Two-Year Plan (1949-1950) was launched. During this period North Korea reached the economic level of 1945, built some key industrial plants, introduced the mechanization method in agriculture and began socialization of commerce, but it stopped short of fulfilling its targets due to the outbreak of the Korean War (1950-1953).

The second phase was interrupted by the outbreak of the Korean War. The War devastated both North and South Korea. During the War North Korea relocated some of its key strategic industrial plants and facilities into northern mountain regions and Manchuria. Still, the North Korean economy plunged precipitously; its productivity in 1953 was less than 64% of its 1949 level. In the third phase, the Three-Year post-Korean War reconstruction period (1954-1956), North Korea received large amounts of reconstruction aids from its socialist fraternal countries such as the former Soviet Union, China and other Eastern European countries. In this period North Korea completed the groundwork for planned economic system, reached pre-Korean War economic productivity level, gave all-out efforts to the development of heavy industry and launched agricultural cooperativism.

The fourth phase, which began with the launching of the First Five-Year Economic Plan (1957-1961) in 1957, was characterized by the full-fledged socialist economic planning with emphasis on heavy industry development. The Plan was completed one year earlier in 1960. The notable accomplishment of this period was the socialization of industry and commerce, and the cooperativization of agriculture in 1958 (a tiny garden plot of 30 to 50 *pyŏng* per household was allowed. Its size was reduced to 20 to 30 *pyŏng* [1 *pyŏng* equals 3.3 square meters] by law in July 1960). In 1959 the Ch'ŏllima [Legendary Flying Horse] Movement was employed as the main symbol of speedy economic development and socialist construction through twin revolutions of ideology and technology. It developed into the Ch'ŏllima Workteam Movement. On February 8, 1960, Kim Il Sung delivered a speech at the general membership meeting of the party organization of Ch'ŏngsan-ri, Kangsŏ County, South Pyŏngan province. In this speech he outlined the Ch'ŏngsan-ri method based on his firsthand experience and on-the-spot-guidance of the Ch'ŏngsan-ri Agricultural Cooperative as the new model of the agricultural management system, with heavy emphasis on the WPK-led ideological education.

During the fifth phase, North Korea emphasized through its First Seven-Year Plan simultaneous development of both defense and heavy industry. In this period the new Daean management system was introduced as the model for the entire industrial management. On December 15, 1961, Kim urged the implementation of this new centralized WPK-led industrial management system extracted from the management experience of Daean Electric Factory. The First Seven-Year Plan (1961-1967) was extended three years in 1966, and thereby, making it a de facto Ten-Year Plan (1961-1970).

In the sixth phase, North Korea continued its heavy emphasis on modernization of industry and agriculture through technological innovations. In its First Six-Year Plan (1971-1976), it attempted, among other things, to narrow the gap between industrial and agricultural workers, and between "light" and "heavy" work schedules and to liberate women from household chores. In accomplishing these new goals, the new slogan "Three Great Revolutions" (ideological, technical and cultural), was coined and the Three Revolutions Teams were organized. It built new oil refinery and petrochemical, steel and cement factories with West European and Japanese technical and economic assistance. Its continuing emphasis on *Juche,* modernization and science in economic development under the banner of "Three Great Revolutions" was reflected even in the Second Seven-Year Plan (1978-1984). Interestingly enough, at the Sixth Congress of the WPK in October 1980, Kim set the so-called ten major production goals, superseding the earlier goals set by the Second Seven-Year Plan. According to one South Korean analysis, North Korea's ten targets were short of the set goal (See Table 15-5).

Finally, the Third Seven-Year Plan (1987-1993) is currently unfolding with a high degree of uncertainty. This latest phase is characterized by some degree of external flexibility and internal relaxation. Externally, there are a few signs of flexibility in North Korea's policy toward capitalist countries, especially in the area of trade, technology transfer and foreign investment. Internally, there is a possibility of relaxing its tightly centralized control of economy, somewhat similar to China's new economic policy under post-Mao leadership. The new changes in economic policy and strategy may include less centralized economic planning, introduction of market-pricing mechanism, more efficiency based on economic and material incentives rather than on solidarity, based on ideological-political agitation and more open economic linkages with the outside world. This new phase provides North Korea with not only new opportunity but new danger as well because its policy of external flexibility and internal relaxation is an anathema to the politico-economic system on which the current ruling elites' power is based.

South Korea

Conversely, interdependence has been the underpinning of the South Korean economic policy and economic growth, its primary policy goal. In realizing this goal, South Korea opted for the sequential unbalanced development strategy. It first adopted the strategy of favoring the industrial and urban sector over the agricultural and rural sector. Unlike North Korea, however, it has given high priority on light and consumer industry over heavy and defense industry. It has shifted its priority from light and consumer industry to heavy and defense industry by early 1970s. With the inauguration of the Saemaul [New Village] Movement of 1971, its earlier unbalanced strategy was replaced by its more balanced strategy in order to stem the deterioration of the agricultural sector and the widening income gap between the rural and urban households, and between the agricultural and industrial workers.[11]

From 1962, when South Korea launched its First Five-Year Plan, to 1981, when the Fourth Five-Year Plan ended, its economy grew at an average annual rate of 8.6 percent. It achieved an average annual growth rate of 7.9% during the First Plan, 9.6 percent in the Second Plan, 9.8% in the Third Plan, 5.7% in the Fourth Plan and 7 to 8% (projected) in the Fifth Plan periods. Before the implementation of the Five-Year Plans, the total value of annual exports was some 30 million US dollars. During the First 5-year Plan period, 1962-66, the annual average export growth rate was 44%; during the Second period, 1967-71, it was 35%, and during the Third period, 1972-76, it was 50%. After that the growth rate of export declined, but the ratio of exports to GNP increased steadily: from 8% in the First Plan period to 40% in the Fifth Plan period. The result is that South Korea has become one of the most trade-dependent economies in the world.

In the First Five-Year Plan (1962-1966), South Korea adopted an outward-looking development strategy emphasizing trade as its basic engine of growth instead of an inward-looking development strategy based on import substitution. In doing so, it stressed the development of social overhead capitals such as electricity, railroads, ports and communication. It promoted labor-intensive manufacturing exports by utilizing basic market principles. It allowed commercial banks to raise interest rates on deposits from 12% to as high as 30% to mobilize domestic savings. It revamped tax administration and eliminated budget deficits in order to reduce chronic inflationary pressures.

In addition, the South Korean government enacted a number of new import-export measures and laws encouraging inflow of foreign capital and investment. In 1964 the multiple exchange rate system of foreign currency was replaced by a unified exchange rate system. The Korean *won* was devalued by nearly 100 percent, and thereby, eliminating a bias against the export sector. The government made available short-term export financing and allowed tax rebates on materials imported for export production. It simplified customs procedures. It liberalized import policy by shifting from its "positive list" system of import controls with a "negative list" system and placed its heretofore policy of self-sufficiency in major grains with that of importation of these grains. In 1966 in order to induce foreign capital and investment, it passed the Foreign Capital Promotion Act, whereby it underwrote the risk borne by foreign investors.

The South Korean government continued its export-propelled outward looking development strategy through the completion of its Second Five-Year Plan period (1967-1971). In the Second Five-Year Plan, it gave high priority to the development of electronic and petrochemical industries. On the eve of launching the Third Five-Year Plan (1972-1976), a number of internal and international developments took place which was highly adverse to South Korea's outward looking economic development strategy. Internally, the growing gap between the urban and the industrial sector and the rural and the agricultural sector led to the launching of the Saemaul Movement. The Saemaul Movement, a comprehensive rural community development program, such as farm road construction, rural electrification, running water drilling and other social and economic projects were implemented jointly by the government supplying the basic equipment and materials, and people in each community providing the required labor. In achieving the twin objectives of improving rural income and insuring self-sufficiency in food grains, the government also adopted a grain price support program. The grain price support program was highly successful initially at least in increasing rice yield per acre and reducing urban-rural income disparity. But this program created a substantial government budget deficit, which, in turn, added fuel to inflation.

Externally, the Nixon administration's decision to reduce the U.S. troop level in Korea by one third, from about 60,000 to 40,000 in 1971, the breakdown of the post-War Bretton Woods System in 1971 (i.e., abandoning the formula of the U.S. dollar as the basic international currency, convertible to gold in value), the imminent collapse of the U.S. backed South Vietnamese government and the rising protectionist trend compelled South Korea to reorient and modify its heretofore outward looking development strategy. Consequently, in the Third Five-Year Plan, it placed priority on both developing heavy and chemical industries along with defense industries and achieving a greater degree of self-sufficiency in major food supplies.

To counter growing protectionism, it was forced to diversify trade and restructure the commodity composition of its exports in favor of more sophisticated, high value-added industrial goods. This reorientation along with the priority development of defense industries accelerated the growth of heavy and chemical industries, including iron and steel, non-ferrous metals, shipbuilding, machinery, electronics and petrochemicals to a degree perhaps unjustified by its factor endowment.

The worldwide commodity boom of 1972-73 and the quadrupling of oil prices in 1973-74 as a direct result of the OPEC embargo and cartel, negatively affected South Korea. The sudden oil price hike deteriorated its balance of payments in an unprecedented fashion. It responded by expanding its exports geographically to Europe and the Middle East beyond Japan and North America and by engaging in the overseas construction works, mostly in the Middle East. These positive readjustments notwithstanding, it confronted new structural imbalances such as over-investment in heavy industries and under-investment in light industries, extensive price distortions and lack of competition due to heavy-handed government control and a rise in real wages exceeding productivity improvement, and thereby, weakening export competitiveness, which, in turn, aggravated foreign debt level.

In the Fourth Five-Year Plan (1977-1981), the priority was given to the development of skilled labor-intensive industries such as machinery, electronics and shipbuilding. In April 1979 in the midst of the Fourth Five-Year Plan, South Korea announced a new economic stabilization program to stem growing inflationary pressures and structural imbalances and to continue its high growth. The new stabilization measures included: lowering the target growth rate of money supply and reforming banking system to control excessive liquidity; suspending temporarily all new projects in heavy and chemical industries and realigning of credit priorities in favor of light industries to narrow the gap between the two sectors; allowing price decontrol of many key commodities to eliminate price distortions; and granting further import liberalization to promote competition.

The new stabilization program was overshadowed by internal and external causes. Another oil price hikes by the OPEC nations following the fall of Shah of Iran in 1979 led to the nearly doubling of South Korea's oil import bill within a year. Above all, the assassination of President Park Chung Hee on October 26, 1979, created a sudden political vacuum, which was followed by a series of political turmoils and instability. Due primarily to these continuing internal crises and external uncertainty, coupled with the worst harvest in 1980, resulting from an unusually cold and damp growing seasons and world-wide recessionary trend, the South Korean economy experienced for the first time a negative growth of 6.2% in 1980, and thereby, breaking the record of more than 20 years of uninterrupted positive growth.

With the emergence of the Chun Doo Hwan government in 1980 (President Chun was formally inaugurated in March 1981), a series of basic institutional reforms had been undertaken to restructure the economy. In so doing, three goals were set: continued high growth; price stability; and improvement in income distribution. First, in order to absorb both the growing new labor force and defense cost, a minimum of 5 to 6% in annual GNP growth was necessary. It was projected that for the next decade the South Korean labor force would grow at 3% per annum, which in absolute terms meant about half a million new workers joining the labor force each year. And because of the Korean division and continuing hostile relations between the two halves, the South Korea spent at least 5 to 6% of its GNP for defense. Second, the need for price stability was essential for continued growth. More government decontrol of prices and less government decision-making in allocation of resources meant less inflation caused by price distortions and more role for free market mechanism in allocation of resources. Third, the need for improvement of income distribution was self-explanatory. For, extreme income differentials either in economic sectors, social classes or geographic regions undermine the fabric of society on which its economic growth and political stability depends.

External Policy Reforms

Specifically, the government import policy in the Fifth Five-Year Plan (1982-86) called for raising the import liberalization ratio from 68.2% in 1980 to 90% by 1986. To do so, import of commodities supplied by monopolistic producers was liberalized first. Concurrently, existing non-tariff protection was gradually replaced by tariff protection, but protective tariffs in all cases were granted for a limited time period only. In its export policy, the government gave priority to exports based on intra-industry specialization rather than inter-industry specialization to stem growing protectionist tendencies. The government had continued its export promotion campaign through market and product diversification. The policy on foreign technology inflow was further liberalized. In areas other than nuclear and defense-related fields, most applications for technology import licenses were automatically approved. In 1983 the requirements for prior approval of technology imports were abolished and importers of technologies were required to report transactions retroactively.

For direct foreign investments, the Chun government enacted a new policy in September 1980. Among other things, this new policy allowed foreign investors to hold a maximum equity share of up to 100% in at least 65 industries defined by the Korean Standard Industrial Classification. In addition, the government did away with prior approval requirements for foreign investment in the course of the Fifth Five-Year Plan.

On July 25, 1983, the Economic Planning Board (EPB) announced the revision of the Fifth Five-Year Plan. The revision was necessary, according to the EPB, for two major reasons: the need to fill the gap between the anticipated and actual external developments; and the earlier completion of key economic objectives in the plan. The revised plan stressed, among other things: consolidation of price stability; export promotion; promotion of industrial productivity through R & D network, master planning of industrial efficiency and effective management of energy demand; renovation of the less-developed sectors of the economy by improving the productivity of small and medium-sized industries, increasing farm household income, stabilizing and improving housing conditions and regional development; invigorating the free market mechanism; and promoting social development. The expansion of market mechanism was also attempted by revising and abolishing administrative measures and laws restricting competition by import liberalization, by liberalizing (government control-free) interest rate. A balanced growth between regions and the measures to prevent the concentration of population in the capital city area were sought by delegating more administrative powers and responsibilities to provincial and local government, by implementing the capital area population dispersion policy and by planning the core growth city projects to absorb population. Finally, the EPB emphasized qualitative improvement of people's standard of living by constructing low-cost housing and rental properties and by providing low-cost health care programs and facilities.[12]

Internal Policy Reforms

The Chun government's internal policy reforms included reforms in business practices, banking system and tax system, policy in agriculture and income distribution.

In 1981 the government enacted the Anti-monopoly Act to eliminate cartel arrangements, price fixing and other monopolistic practices. The government removed interest rate differentials to discontinue the favors given to the customers of policy preference loans. It relinquished its majority equity share in five major commercial banks. It lowered its highest marginal tax rate in both corporate and personal income taxes, from 38% and 60% to 30% and 55%, respectively. It began to phase out the old policy of extending preferential access to credit and preferential treatment in taxation to so-called strategic industries. The ultimate goal was to treat all types of investment in all industries equitably. It took action to phase out the high farm price support programs for major grains. In order to complement this agricultural policy and to provide non-farm income sources, the government took steps to expand credit facilities to support agricultural mechanization and to disperse industrial activities into medium-sized rural towns. Finally, the government believed that the expansion of employment opportunities through rapid growth with minimum inflation, coupled with the educational program designed to increase access to education and training by all groups in society, were the correct strategy for improving income inequity. To this end, it had increased expenditures on education and vocational training, and thereby, providing more skilled and technical manpower in the short run and more equitable income distribution among people in the long run.

Since 1981, South Korea began to recover its earlier pattern of robust growth. In 1981 its annual growth rates was 6.4%. Its inflation in terms of wholesale prices fell to 11% from 42% in 1980, and its inflation in terms of consumer prices was down to 14% from 32% in 1980. In 1982, its GNP growth and export growth rates were 5.4% and 4.8%, respectively. Its inflation rate dropped sharply in 1982; the rise in wholesale and consumer prices was limited to 2.4% and 4.8%, respectively. The Sixth Five-Year Economic and Social Development Plan (1987-1991) was revised to meet the unexpected performance of Korean economy, especially higher growth rate and trade surplus. But under the Roh regime, the trade surplus turned, once again into trade deficit; the sudden wage increase was not matched by labor productivity and the inflationary pressure, coupled with the so-called 2 million Housing Unit Development plan, threatened the hard-earned economic stability. The South Korean economy, which looked sound and strong at the time of his presidential inauguration, turned sour and weak during his rule. Recently, there are a few signs of economic recovery. Under this circumstance, the Seventh Five-Year Plan (1992-1996) is being launched. In the Seventh Socio-Economic Development Plan, R & D is the top priority in the ROK economy. The Plan projects an average GNP growth rate during the period at 7.5%. If the Korean economy grows as planned, its economic structure will be closer to a developed economy. The primary sector will constitute only 6.4%, while the secondary and the tertiary (service) sectors will comprise 33.2% and 61.4%, respectively. The major challenges facing South Korea during the Seventh Five Year Economic and Social Development Plan are: the pursuit of stability in trading relations with the U.S. and Japan, combined with an emphasis on developing regional trading relationships to lessen dependence on these two markets; industrial upgrading in order to develop a comparative advantage in capital and knowledge-intensive industries; deepening integration of the South Korean economy into the world economy and consequent pressures to increase foreign access to the domestic economy; the balancing of social and economic priorities; and a less interventionist approach in industry, incorporating liberalization of the banking sector in particular.[13]

In sum, South Korea's development strategy has been by and large successful. Its success was due to many mutually reinforcing factors, including the merits of an outward-looking development model, the role of the market, the inflow of foreign capital, the capacity to absorb new technology and manpower training, the availability of abundant and relatively cheap labor force, the light industry-led industrial policy, the measures to minimize the negative impacts of protectionism (e.g., diversification of products and markets), the reforms in exchange rate regime, "the managed float system," the constructive government-industry-business-labor partnership and the maintenance of more than a decade-long relative social and political stability.[14] In ensuing years, the government needs to more systematically and forcefully address some of the negative consequences of the country's rapid economic growth, such as labor abuse, downgrading of human rights and freedom, overcrowding, environmental deterioration, pollution, traffic congestions and high rate of crimes.

*Table 15-1. Industrial and Agricultural Facilities and Outputs
in North and South Korea in 1944*

(Unit: %)

	North	South
Gross Industrial Output	60	40
Electric Power Stations	92	8
Fuel Industry	88	12
Mining	78	22
Metallurgical Industry	90	10
Machine Tools and Metal Processing	28	72
Chemical Industry	82	18
Construction Industry	73	27
Textile Industry	33	67
Gross Grain Output	34	66
[Golds]	71	29
[Gold-Silver]	73	27
[Iron]	100	0
[Tungsten]	79	21
[Graphite]	71	29

<Actual Figures>	North	South
Gross Grain Output (unit: sok)	12,232	24,408*
Electricity	1,262,500 (86%)	206,290 (14%)**
(unit: KW)	909,200 (92%)	79,500 (8%)+
Coal (unit: ton)	5,678,855 (79%)	1,438,860 (21%)++

Sources: Adapted from *Chosun Kyŏngjechiri*, Vol. 1, p. 140. Quoted in *A Comparative
    Study of the South and North Korean Economy* (Seoul: National Unification Board,
    1984), p. 49, and *Nampukhan Kyŏngjehyŏnhwang Pigyo* (Seoul: Kukto Tongilwon,
    1981), p. 35. Figures in [ ] are North and South Korean comparison in 1936. For
    details, see *Kyŏngjenyŏngam* (Seoul: Choson Bank, 1949), p. 6.
*figures represent a five-year average output from 1940 to 1944. See *Kyongjenyŏngam
    (1949), p. 13.*
**figures represent the 1944 electric power capacity;
+figures represent the annual average. Both figures are found in *Kyŏngjenyŏngam*, p. 4;
++figures represent North and South Korean comparison in 1944 from *Sanŏp Ch'ongram*
    (Seoul: Bank of Korea, 1954), p. 21. The same figures are found in Ki-chun Cho, *Hankuk
    Kyŏngjesa* [History of Korean Economy] *(Seoul:* Ilsin-sa, 1983), pp. 446-448. See also,
    Man-Ki Lee, *Hankuk Kyŏngje* [On Korean Economy] (Seoul: Ilsin-sa, 1984), p. 466.

Table 15-2. Korea's Farm in 1943

Classification	No. of Farm Household		% of Total Farm	
	All Korea	North	All Korea	North
Independent farmers	536,098	251,261	17.60	25.01
Medium indep. farmers	485,414	164,724	15.98	16.39
Small indep. farmers	499,001	144,419	16.38	14.37
Small farmers	1,481,357	435,868	48.63	43.38
Others	44,231	8,311	1.8	0.85
Total:	3,046,101	1,004,583	100	100

Sources: Adapted from Sŏhaeng Lee, "An Analysis of North Korea's Cooperative Farm Management (I) (in Korean) (September 1981), pp. 70-81. His figures are derived from Japanese data sources.

Table 15-3. Comparison of Capitalist and Socialist Economic Systems:
Ideal Types

Economic Factors	Socialist System	Capitalist system
Economy	centralized; "command"	decentralized; "market"
Ownership of means of production	state; collective; controlled	private; individual; free
Orientation	need oriented; determined by state	profit oriented; decided by individual and/by individual corporations
Economic planning	yes (imperative)	no (indicative, if there is one)
Capital investment fund	state	private
Incentives	work norms plus bonuses for exceeding norms; rewards (public acclaims medals, etc.) or punishment (public sanctions, demotions, etc.)	wages and profits
Competition	prohibited	inherent
Risks and losses	assumed by the people of the entire state	assumed by private investors
Labor	state determines the size, site, kind of labor	the workers' choice
Management	party membership required; highly bureaucratic	selected on merit; must perform to survive
Relation of government to business	no independent business outside of state	mutually independent of each other

Adapted from various sources and books on socialism and capitalism. Among them three are notable: Ferdinand F. Mauser and David J. Schwartz, *American Business: An Introduction,* 4th ed. (New York: Harcourt Brace Jovanovich, 1978), pp. 22-23 and Gert H. Mueller, "Socialism and Capitalism in the Work of Max Weber," *The British Journal of Sociology* (June 1982): 151-171. Richard L. Carson, *Comparative Economic System* (New York: M. E. Sharpe, 1990), parts 1, 2 and 3.

Table 15-4. Comparison of North and South Korean Economic Systems

Economic Factors	North Korea	South Korea
Economy	"command" type; state-control unlimited	"market" type; government intervention limited
Ownership of means of production	state; cooperatives	private; limited public monopoly and corporations
Economic planning	"imperative"	"indicative"
Capital investment fund	state monopoly	private; limited government investment
Incentives	public rewards and (mobilized by state)	wages and profits; limited government rewards (motivated by individuals)
Competition	prohibited	permitted; limited government regulations
Risks and losses	assumed by the entire people	assumed by private investors; limited government subsidies
Labor	state dictates	largely individual choice
Management	party membership required	largely recruited on merit; academic-political-regional-kinship nexus often applied
Relation of government to business	"denotative" control; all pervasive	"connotative" partnership; limited guidance
Development strategy	modified balanced model; import-substitution priority; self-reliance	modified unbalanced model; export-propelled growth; interdependence
Agriculture	cooperative farms	private farming with government-directed cooperative work (New Community Movement)

Adapted from various sources, some of which are: Kwang-su Kim, "North Korea's Recent External Economic Relations" (in Korean), *Pukhan* (September 1980): 48-56; Yŏngkyu Kim, "A Comparison of North and South Korean Economic Developments (in Korean), *Pukhan* (April 1981): 72-92; Myŏng Kim, *A Comparison of North and South Korean Economic Reality* (in Korean) (Seoul: National Unification Board, 1981); Nam-wŏn Suh, "An Approach to the Analysis of North Korean Economy," *Vantage Point* (November 1983): 1-11; *A Comparative Study of the South and North Korean Economies* (Seoul: National Unification Board, 1984); Joseph S. Chung, "Divergent Economic Systems and the Consequences for Economic Performance and Structure: A Small Country Version," paper delivered at the Korea Panel in conjunction with the 1983 American Political Science Association Meeting in Chicago, Illinois, 30 August–2 September 1983; Young Whan Kihl, *Politics and Policies in Divided Korea: Regimes in Contest* (Boulder: Westview, 1984), pp. 130-159.

Table 15-5. North Korea's Ten Major Production Goals

Target Line	Unit	End of 1984 (A)	End of 1989 (B)	B/A	3rd 7-year Plan Target (1987-1993)	Execution	%
Electricity	100 m. kwh	569-600	1,000	1.7-1.8	1,000	277.4	30
Coal	10,000 t	7,000-8,000	12,000	1.5-1.7	12,000	4,300	36
Steel	10,000 t	740-800	1,500	1.9-2.0	1,000	—	—
Nonferrous metal	10,000 t	100	150	1.5	170	—	—
Chemical fertilizer	10,000 t	500	700	1.4	720	—	—
Cement	10,000 t	1,200-1,300	2,000	1.5-1.7	2,200	1,202	54.6
Textile	100 mil. meters	8	15	1.9	15	—	—
Marine products	10,000 t	350	500	1.4	1,100	—	—
Grain	10,000 t	1,000	1,500	1.5	1,500	481.2	32.0
Reclaimed Land	10,000 ha.	10	30	3	30	6	20

Source: The above figures are from Sang-san Lee, "North Korean Economy Faltering in Stagnancy," *Vantage Point* (December 1980), pp. 1-10; Also, Eung-yol Chon, "Ten Major Production Goals and Their Problems" (in Korean), *Pukhan* (December 1980), pp. 96-106; Kwang-su Kim, "[North Korea's] Unbalanced Economic Policy and Sluggish Growth" (in Korean), *Pukhan* (January 1981), pp. 92-101. The figures for the 3rd 7-year plan, is from *Pukhan Kaeyo '91* (Seoul: The Ministry of National Unification Board, 1990), p. 138. Ho-Yol Yu, "North Korea's Economic Policy and the Role of Political Leadership (I)," *Vantage Point* 15 (August 1992).

Notes

1. Jonathan Swift, *Gulliver's Travels* (New York: Signet Classics, 1960), p. 271.
2. For details, see Ki-jun Cho, *Hankuk Kyŏngjesa* [History of Korean Economy] (Seoul: Ilsin-sa, 1983), pp. 415-450. Also, Sang-chul Suh, *Growth and Structural Changes in the Korean Economy, 1910-1940* (Cambridge: Harvard University Press, 1978), p. 141.
3. *Annual Economic Review of Korea, 1948,* pp. 1-101. Also, Ki-jun Cho, *Op. Cit.,* p. 449.
4. George M. McCune, *Korea Today* (Cambridge: Harvard University Press, 1950), p. 58.
5. *Annual Economic Review of Korea, 1948,* pp. 1-51.
6. Joseph S. Chung," Divergent Economic Systems and the Consequences for Economic Performance and Structure: A Small Country Version," paper delivered at the Korea Panel in conjunction with the 1983 American Political Science Association Meeting in Chicago, Illinois, 28 August-1 September 1983, p. 6. Hyun-uk Nam, "A Study of North Korea's Planning System" (in Korean), *Unification Policy Quarterly,* No. 4 (1979): 110-139.
7. South Korea's 25 state-run companies are: Korea Development Bank; Small and Medium Industry Bank; Citizen's National Bank; Korea Housing Bank; Korea Stock Exchange; Government Printing and Mint Agency; Korea Electric Power Corp; Daihan Coal Corp; Korea Mining Promotion Corp; Korea Petroleum Development Corp; Korea General Chemical Industry Corp; Korea Trade Promotion Corp; Korea Highway Corp; Korea National Housing Corp; Industrial Sites and Resources Development Corp; Korea Land Development Corp; Agricultural Development Corp; Agriculture and Fisheries Development Corp; Korea Telecommunications Authority; Korea National Tourisms Corp; Korea Welfare Corp; and Korea Gas Corp. For details, see *Joongang Ilbo,* 16 February 1984. Also, *The Korea Herald,* 31 December 1983.
8. Ung-youl Chŏn, "North Korean Economic System and Prospects for Transformation," *Vantage Point* (May 1978), pp. 1-12.
9. Kim Il Sung, "On Some Theoretical Problems of the Socialist Economy," answers to the questions raised by scientific educational workers, on March 1, 1969, in Kim Il Sung, *Selected Works* (Pyongyang: Foreign Languages Publishing House, 1971-79), Vol. 5, pp. 294-319.
10. Ung-youl Chŏn, *Op. Cit.,* p. 7.
11. For a comprehensive analysis of the New Village Movement's origin, theory and actual performance, see Dae-sun Shin, *Hankuk Jiyŏksahoegaebalron* [On the Korean Regional Society Development] (Seoul: Seyong-sa, 1984).
12. *The Guidelines for the Revision of the Fifth Plan* (in Korean) (Seoul: the Eco-

nomic Planning Board: 1983).

13. An outline of the 7th Five-year plan (1992-1996) is found in *Kukjŏng Sinmun* [Government News], 16 April 1992, p. 16. See also, *Korea year 2000: Prospects and Issues for Long-term Development,* Summary Report (Seoul: Korea Development Institute, 1986). See also, "Entering the 1990s: The Republic of Korea," paper presented at the seminar on Korea to the year 2000, Hoam House, Seoul National University, 7 July 1992. Also, "The Two Koreas: The Status Quo Maintained," paper delivered at the same seminar.

14. For a detailed discussion of favorable factors for South Korea's rapid economic development, see, for instance, Charles R. Frank, Jr. and others, *Foreign Trade Regimes and Economic Development: South Korea* (New York, 1975), pp. 6-24; Parvez Hasan, *Korea: Problems and Issues in a Rapidly Growing Economy* (Baltimore: The Johns Hopkins University Press, 1976), pp. 29-85. Paul W. Kuznets, *Economic Growth and Structure in the Republic of Korea* (New Haven: Yale University Press, 1977), pp. 1-110; and Sung Chul Yang, *Korea and Two Regimes* (Cambridge: Schenkman, 1981), pp. 271-277. Also, Hans W. Singer and Nancy O. Baster, *Young Human Resources in Korea's Social Development: Issues and Strategies* (Seoul: Korea Development Institute, 1980); and Kihwan Kim, "The Korean Economy: Past Performance, Current Reforms, and Future Prospects," unpublished manuscript, March 1983 by Korea Development Institute, especially pp. 30-37.

CHAPTER 16

PERFORMANCE IN COMPARISON

Nothing is great or little otherwise than by comparison.

Jonathan Swift[1]

As mentioned earlier, comparing the two regimes' economic performance on the basis of available and accessible "numbers," some of which are of doubtful quality, is an extremely hazardous venture. This inherent limitation in numerical comparison notwithstanding, strictly from a crude quantitative statistical point of view, both North and South Korea have achieved a high rate of economic development for the past forty years while undergoing fundamental structural changes in their economies. North Korea had an impressive growth in the 1950s and 1960s, but its growth slackened in the 1970s, 1980s and further deteriorated in the 1990s. South Korea, meanwhile, had a sluggish growth in the 1950s and early 1960s, but since the late 1960s its development has been phenomenal, although in the mid-1980s and the early 1990s it has shown signs of slowing down and even those of economic lethargy. Still, North Korea fared relatively better in economic performance among its past and presently remaining socialist fraternal countries, while South Korea has been, at least, since the late 60s, one of the fastest developing nations in the world, and it has become a model for the newly industrializing countries (NICs). What follows is a comparative account of North and South Korean economic performance in terms of their overall national accounts, sectoral growth and quality of life.

Overall Economic Indicators

North Korea has never made public its national output in absolute amounts on a regular and predictable basis. It has enforced a blackout on almost all economic statistics for nearly thirty years. Besides, it uses Net National Material Product (NMP) rather than GNP as its measurement of national income. This, coupled with the task of converting the NMP into GNP and a lack of official exchange rates between North Korean *won* and the South Korean *won* and between the North Korean *won* and the U.S. dollars make comparative analysis extremely difficult, if not impossible. As a result, the figures of national account vary widely from one official data to another, from one analyst to the other (See, for instance, Tables 16-1 and 16-1a).

The North Korean economy has grown at a rapid rate in the post-Korean War years as measured by total and per capita national income. Its veracity aside, North Korea claimed that even during the pre-war period (1947-50) its industrial growth rate was 49.9%. In the post-war 3-year plan (1954-56), it reported 41.7% growth rate. In the following 5-year plan which took four years, the rate was 36.6%. The first 7-year plan (1961-70) was extended three more years, and its growth rate rose to 16.3%. In the second 7-year plan (1978-84), the growth rate was projected at 12.1%.[2] The third 7-year plan (1987-93) is currently under progress. Not just the successful completion of this plan, but its own system survival is, however, in serious jeopardy amid the demise of communism elsewhere and the emergence of new world order.

According to one estimate by Joseph Chung, North Korean national income (NMP) grew from $1.6 billion in 1963 to $13.8 billion in 1979. The GNP equivalent of NMP in 1979 was $15.2 billion. In the same period per capita income (NMP) rose from $140 to $794.[3] The GNP per capita was $873. The 1985 publication of London-based International Institute of Strategic Studies *Military Balance* estimated North Korea's GNP at $14.1 billion in 1981 and $19.6 billion in 1983. Based on this estimate, North Korea's per capita income in 1983 was $1,040. North Korea's official claim was $2,301 in 1983 and $ 2,407 in 1984. According to 1991 *Korea Statistical Yearbook,* North Korea's GNP and per capita GNP in 1990 was $20.6 billion and $980, respectively.[4]

North Korea's growth slowed down considerably during the 1960s. NMP growth declined from phenomenal rate of 30.0% and 21.0%, during the Third-Year Plan (1954-56) and the Five-Year Plan (1957-60), respectively, to 7.5% during the extended Seven-Year Plan (1961-70). Per capita growth rates for the respective periods were 26.0%, 16.6% and 5.5%. In 1966 North Korean industrial output declined by 3 percent for the first time. Slow growth in the first half of the 1960s compelled North Korea to extend its Seven-Year Plan three additional years to the end of 1970. Still, 7.5% actual growth rate of national income (NMP) during the ten year period (1961-70) was far short of its planned growth rate of 18.1%. During the Six Year Plan (1971-76) industrial output grew at 16.3% per annum. About the same rate of growth in industrial output was obtained during the first three years of the Second Seven-Year Plan (1978-84).[5]

South Korea's post-Korean War economic development can be divided into three distinct periods—the reconstruction period (1953-58), the period of economic stagnation and political unrest (1959-62) and the rapid growth period (1963-1978). During the first period, a large scale infusion of economic aid made it possible for the economy to rebuild the war damaged productive facilities. This period was characterized by a moderate economic growth and a high rate of inflation (an annual average rate of 30.1%) in the midst of chronic political unrest. In the second period the rate of inflation slowed down considerably to an annual growth rate of 10.4%, but dwindling foreign aid and import levels, coupled with faster population growth led to the decline of the growth of national output per capita to near zero. Economic stagnation was aggravated further by political unrest. The Syngman Rhee government (1948-1960) was overthrown by the massive nation-wide student uprising in April 1960. The newly launched Chang Myŏn government (1960-1961) was overthrown within eight months of its inception by the military coup on May 16, 1961.

Under the Park Chung Hee government (1961-1979), South Korea underwent a rapid economic growth, beginning in 1963, a year after the implementation of the First Five-Year Plan. It had achieved a high growth of output, income and employment and rapid structural change in the form of rising ratios of investment, saving, export and imports, and industrial output. The GNP (in 1975 constant prices) grew at an annual average of 9.9% during the 16 years between 1963-78. In 1979, the growth rate began to slow down to 6.4% due to a recession. In 1980 South Korea experienced its first negative growth (-6.2%) since its economic take-off in 1963. Since 1981 the South Korean economy had regained its robust economic growth rate, albeit slower than its past growth rate of twenty years. With the single exception of 1980, the South Korean economy in the 80s has been experiencing moderate to high GNP annual growth rate (6 to 8 percent) and low inflation rate of 3 to 5 percent. As noted in the above, under the Roh regime, inflation rate has again risen to a near double digit; trade surplus has turned to trade deficit and the economy in general has shown the signs of recession and relative lethargy.

Still, by any standard, South Korea's economic development, at least, since 1963 has been phenomenal. Its GNP was $2.7 billion in 1963, $13.1 billion in 1973, $65.9 billion in 1983 and $237.9 billion in 1990. Its average annual GNP growth rate for 1962-1982 was 8.53%. Its per capita income in the comparable period, rose from $100 in 1964 to $5,569 in 1990.

In sum, South Korea's GNP in 1990 is more than ten times that of North Korea's $23.1 billion. South Korea's per capita income of $5,569 is five times larger than that of North Korea's $1,064 (approximation).

Governmental Sectors

In comparing North and South Korea's government budgets, several points are noteworthy. First, in North Korea the public sector is overwhelming because the government directs and manages virtually all aspects of the economy through a centralized planning. Hence, the government budget usually comprises nearly three-fourth of its entire GNP. By contrast, the public sector in South Korea is significant, but not ubiquitous. Its government budget makes up about one-fifth of its GNP.

Simply put, the government's often overbearing intervention in the private sector notwithstanding, South Korea's non-governmental private sector is still large and alive. In 1990, for instance, North Korea's budget was 16.6 billion dollars, which is about 71.9% of its GNP of 23.1 billion dollars, while South Korea's 1990 budget was $38.8 billion dollars which is only 16% of its GNP of 242.2 billion dollars (See Table 16-2).

Second, because of uninterrupted continuous hostile relations between the two, the defense outlays in both North and South Korea's budgets have been extremely high. Hidden military expenses and outlays aside, North Korea's officially announced defense outlays alone have consistently been a double digit figure: they were as high as 30.4% of its total budget in 1967, 31.3% in 1970 and 12.1% in 1990 (For details, see Table 16-3). The real figures may run as high as 30 to 40% of its total expenditure. For example, the South Korean government estimated that North Korea's 1990 military budget occupied about 29.9% of its total budget. The figures of South Korea's military expenditures in 1991 and 1992 are respectively 24.7% and 26.3% of its total budget. Since the size of North Korean economy in terms of its GNP is one tenth of South Korea's, the former's defense burden is much heavier than that of the latter. For example, South Korea's defense budget has been increasing from 11.3% in 1989 to 12.5% in 1992. But during the same period its defense budget as a percentage of GNP has decreased from 4.3% in 1989 to 3.8% in 1992.

Third, their budget-making processes, expenditure contents and revenue sources are quite different from each other. In North Korea the state budget is formally drafted by the State Planning Commission on the administrative side and reviewed by the Budget Committee of the Supreme People's Assembly (SPA) and the SPA as a whole. But in reality the budget making process is in strict compliance with the WPK Central Committee's budget guideline, and there is no public scrutiny or input from the opposition parties, which are de facto non-existent. In South Korea the government budget is formally formulated by the Economic Planning Board (EPB) and reviewed and approved by the Budget Committee of the National Assembly (NA) and later by the entire NA. Public scrutiny and inputs from the opposition parties, however limited and nominal, in the budget-making continue to exist.

The contents of North and South Korea's budgets also differ from each other. The typical North Korean expenditure consists of people's economy outlays, social and cultural outlays, military outlays and government maintenance outlays. Of these, at least formally, people's economy outlay comprises 50 to 60%, social and cultural outlay, 10 to 20%, military outlay, 10 to 20%, and government maintenance outlay, 2 to 5% (See Tables 16-3 and 16-4). The typical South Korean expenditure contains general administrative outlays, defense outlays, economic and social development outlays, education outlays, subsidies for local governments and others. Of these, general administrative outlay comprises 10 to 15%, defense outlay, 20 to 30%, development outlay, 40 to 50%, subsidies to local government and others, 10 to 15% (See Table 16-5).

North Korea's revenue is entirely derived from its socialist accounts. Formally at least, various taxes existing in non-socialist countries are "hidden" in their all-embracing socialist accounts. North Korea's socialist accounts consist mainly of wholesale and retail commodity transaction charges, the profits of state enterprises and the incomes of cooperative farms. These sources provide nearly 60% of its revenue. The rest comes from foreign aid, depreciation expenses, fines, fees and the like. Until 1974 North Korea also had income taxes on industrial and agricultural workers and working intellectuals and local autonomy tax. These were abolished in 1975 and since then North Korea acted as if it were "a country without taxes." In reality, it does not mean the disappearance of people's tax burden, but only the omission of the word "tax."

South Korea's revenue is mostly from taxes. The taxes consist of internal taxes which is divided into direct tax—income tax, corporation tax, business tax and others—and indirect tax—value-added tax, special consumption tax, liquor tax, commodity tax and others including carry-over from previous year and stamp revenue and customs duties. Defense surtaxes and education surtax were added in 1975 and 1982, respectively. The rest are from the government's monopoly profits, non-tax revenues, trust-fund and others. In 1982, for instance, the revenue from internal tax and customs duties comprised 82% (70.8% and 11.3% each), from monopoly profits, 8.2%, from non-tax revenues, 4.8%, from trust fund, 0.3%, and from others, 4.7%. In 1990, the revenues from internal taxes, defense surtax, customs duties and others were 61.1%, 14.2%, 8.8% and 15.9%, respectively. The expenditures for the same year consisted of defense (25.0%), economic development (14.1%), general administration (10.2%), social development (8.9%) and others (41.8%).[6]

Agriculture

Background

Korea was a typical agrarian society at the time of its liberation from Japan in 1945. Nearly three-fourths of the Korean people lived on farming. The distribution of land ownership was also highly unequal, primarily due to Japanese colonial land policy and the landowners' exploitation of tenant farmers. For example, landless farm households constituted about 2.7% of all farm households. Worse still, the bottom 81% of all farm households owned only 10% of the total land.[7] With the annexation of Korea in 1910, the Japanese colonial administration initiated the Korea Land Census, through which it conducted the survey of arable land. In this census, landowners were required to identify and re-register their land within a very short time, usually in less than 30 days. Within this period they were compelled to produce documentary evidence of their ownership of land, forestry, fishing grounds and mines. They were also required to install physical landmarks specifying the extent of their landholdings. With little understanding of the real import of the census, many Koreans lost their lands and other ownership by simply failing to produce the required documents within the required duration of time. The lands and other properties unidentified and unregistered during this census were taken away by the Japanese authorities. In that sense, the Land Census was designed to confiscate Korean lands by the Japanese colonial administration.[8]

The end result of this land survey and subsequent colonial rule in Korea was evident in the Japanese land holdings in Korea. According to one study, the Japanese owned approximately 15% of Korea's total farm land and 60% of all forest land. In terms of land value of the holdings of Japanese-owned Korean registered agricultural concerns, 8,000 Japanese owned 68% of the total value of assessed land property while 120,000 Koreans owned 32%. Some 365 Japanese owned the land measuring 100 *chŏngbo* (one *chŏngbo* is equivalent to 2.45 acres or .992 hectare, one hectare is equivalent to 2.471 acres) and more, while only 228 Koreans had land holdings of the same size, at the time of liberation. It meant that 60% of the crops were produced by tenant farming. The number of tenants also increased from 39% of all farm families during 1913-17 to 56% in 1938. The tenanted land area expanded from 1.6 million *chŏngbo* in 1914 to 2.6 million *chŏngbo* in 1938.[9]

In 1945, therefore, any prudent political leaders either in the North or the South had to address the agrarian question. The unequal distribution of land, the disproportionately high percentage of tenant farming, high absentee land ownership and the disposal of land formerly owned by the Japanese were the notable problems awaiting immediate attention of the leaders. The Korean division following liberation led, however, to the two distinctly different approaches to this agrarian question. Both North and South Korea implemented the land reform at the outset to resolve the said questions, but the similarities between the two quickly end there. In the North the land reform was comprehensive, drastic and confiscatory, while in the South it was partial, gradual and compensatory. The former not only redistributed lands from owners to tillers but replaced private ownership through collectivization of agriculture, while the latter simply redistributed lands from large landowners to tillers without abolishing private land ownership or collectivization of the farms.

Specifically, in North Korea the communist-led Five Provinces Administrative Committee (*O-tohaengjŏngkuk*) under the auspices of the Soviet occupation forces announced the decision on September 11, 1945, which called for the expropriation of land without compensation from the Japanese imperialists, the Korean collaborators with the Japanese and the "reactionary" landlords. Other minor landowners were allowed to collect only 30% of the output but they were required to pay taxes in kind. In the following year on March 5, 1946, the Provisional People's Committee promulgated the Law on Agrarian Reform, which was followed by Specific Regulations on Land Reform on March 8. The aims of North Korean land reform were two-fold: (i) confiscation of land owned by the Japanese, by "national traitors," by large land owners of over 5 *ha*, by the absentee owners and by church, temples and other religious organizations (See Table 16-8); and (ii) collectivization of agriculture. From 1946 to 1949 confiscation of land from the aforesaid owners was completed. Collectivization of agriculture took, however, a few more years to implement due to the outbreak of the Korean War and subsequent recovery efforts. It was in 1958 that North Korea completed the collectivization of farm under which the agricultural cooperatives replaced private ownership of land (For details, see Tables 16-9 and 16-10).

In South Korea land reform consisted of two stages. First, in 1948 the United States Military Government in Korea (USMGIK) redistributed lands owned by the Japanese during the period of her colonial rule (1910-1945). The farmlands formerly owned by the Japanese were acquired by the USMGIK and administered by *Shinhan Kongsa*, a public corporation created on February 21, 1946. These farmlands amounted to 282,000 *chŏngbo*, or 13% of South Korea's total farmland. These farms were tilled by some 554,000 farmers as the corporation's tenants. Under USMGIK Governor Ordinance No. 173 on March 22, 1948, these farmlands were sold to Koreans (each tenant was allowed to purchase up to two *chŏngbo*) through the newly established National Land Administration (NLA), which replaced the *Shinhan Kongsa*. The NLA redistributed about 245,000 *chŏngbo* or 87% of the total "enemy-owned" land to 596,000 farm families or 38% of all Korean farmers at the end of 1952. The rest were in the process of being sold or were tied up in legal disputes.[10]

The second stage of land reform was implemented by the South Korean government during the period of 1950-52. First, the Land Reform Act was promulgated in June 1949 in accordance with the 1948 ROK Constitution, Article 86. Under the "land-to-the tiller" principle, the South Korean government redistributed the land owned by absentee landlords and any portion of the lands by owner-farmers in excess of three *chŏngbo* to tenants and landless farmers. The compensation for the farmlands was to be determined by each city, town or township land commission at the rate of 150% of the average annual yield of the farmland. The progressive diminution formula was also applied in determining the amount of compensation, that is, the larger the area owned by one family, the lower the rate of compensation to be paid for the lands. To do so, the South Korean government first conducted a farm household survey from May to December 1949. This survey found that approximately 601,000 *chŏngbo* of farmland, or 29% of the total farmland, were subject to government acquisition for resale to tenants and landless farmers. The number of beneficiaries was estimated at 1,022,000 farm families in South Korea. By 1954 a total of 332,000 *chŏngbo* out of 601,000 *chŏngbo* had been distributed to 915,000 tenant tillers.

To put it differently, the amount of farmlands, including those formerly owned by the Japanese, which was subject to redistribution and resale, was about 834,000 *chŏngbo* or about 40% of the total farmlands in South Korea. But the total land area actually redistributed was only 577,000 *chongbo*, or 69% of the target. In 1945 the total land area available for redistribution was theoretically 1,470,000 *chŏngbo*. It meant that the land reform actually completed only 42% of the total farmland available for redistribution (For details, see Tables 16-2, 16-13, 16-14, 16-15 and 16-6).[11] One additional comment is in order. Unlike North Korea, South Korea paid compensation for the land it took from various landowners, but to a large extent, "compensation" was more illusory than real. Because the government land bonds were partial installment payment to the landowners on a multi-year basis and because of soaring inflation rate as a result of the Korean War, the compensation bonds turned out to be a promissory note of little value. Thus, this extra rural capital quickly evaporated over time and failed to transform it into industrial capital. Even those few landlords who did invest their landbonds into industrial businesses failed from lack of managerial experience.

In sum, superficial and formal semblances notwithstanding, North and South Korean land reforms were fundamentally different. In the

North the land reform paved the road to collectivation of farmlands based on the socialist principles of collectivization and state ownership of land, while in the South it redressed the unequal distribution of farmlands based on the "lands-to-the-tillers" principle without destroying the private ownership of land. Accordingly, the North Korean land reform was comprehensive, drastic and confiscatory, while the South Korean counterpart was, at best, partial, gradual and compensatory.

Both land reforms were successful in removing the centuries-old feudalistic land tenure system. In the North the collectivistic agricultural cooperatives emerged, while in the South basically a small-scale owner-farming system became the primary mode of farming. To the extent that the land reform was the preparatory groundwork for the eventual realization of the agricultural cooperative system, North Korea's land reform was "successful" in its own right in the short run. In the long run, however, a lack of private incentives and self-motivation is lingering problems of the North Korean agriculture.

In the South the effects of its land reform were, in the short run, negative. The further fragmentation of farmlands, the decline of farm productivity and rural savings, the failure to transform rural capitals into industrial capital and the retardation of agricultural modernization were notable examples. The long-term effects of South Korean land reform were, however, positive. Politically, the land reform removed the major source of peasant grievances, which often plagued many agrarian societies when the government failed to or refused to implement similar land reform. Economically, farmers' relatively equalized access to land opened a better opportunity for educating their children, which, in turn, accelerated human capital formation, becoming the primary base of South Korea's economic take-off in the 60s and phenomenal economic growth in the 70s and beyond. Agricultural productivity, too, began to rise in the 60s by the improvement of farming technology and irrigation system. Beginning in the 1970s with the *Saemaul* [New Community] Movement, the rural-urban income differentials, too, began to narrow considerably. In a nutshell, the two diametrically different land reforms executed by the North and South Korean governments in the wake of liberation from Japan laid the groundwork for the two contrasting agricultural performances in the past 40 years and more.

Output Figures

North Korea is a bit larger than South Korea in land area (122,098 vs. 99,092 square kilometers or 55-45% of the total area). But South Korea's arable land is a bit larger than that of North Korea. The North's total arable land is 2.10 million hectares, compared to South's 2.21 million hectares. The composition of the arable land in the two halves also differs. In the North, dry lands constitute 1.47 million hectares or 70% of its total arable land while rice paddies comprise only 630,000 hectares or 30%. By contrast, in the South rice paddies account for 1.31 million hectares or 60% of its total arable land and its dry lands, 900,000 hectares or 40% (For details, see Table 16-6). The North's forest land is nearly 81% of its total area, while the South's is 68%.[12]

The North's farm population was estimated at 7.99 million, while the South's was 7.27 million in 1988. The North's farm household was approximately 1.29 million and the South's, 2 million in 1983.[13] It meant that North's cultivated area per household was a bit larger than that of the South's (1.6 vs. 1.09 *chŏngbo*).

In comparing North and South Korea's grain output figures, two points need to be spelled out. First, the publications of North Korea's grain production figures are irregular, often exaggerated and, thus, un-reliable. Second, the composition of the total grain outputs of the two halves are quite different. Because the North has more dry lands and the South, more rice paddies, in the former non-rice products such as corn and soybeans constitute a significant portion of its grain output, while in the latter, rice occupies its major portion.

Bearing these caveats in mind, the following observations can be made. In 1946, for instance, North and South Korea's total grain outputs were 1.27 million (1.89 million) and 3.03 million tons, respectively. In 1966 North and South Korea's total grain productions, respectively, were 4.40 million and 7.03 million tons. In 1976 the total grain produc-tion for the North and the South were 7.5 million and 8.18 million tons, respectively. In 1980 at the WPK's Sixth Congress North Korea boasted that its total grain production in 1979 reached 9 million tons, which is a quantum jump from its 1978 figure of 7.78 million tons. South Korea estimated North Korea's actual output at 4.79 million tons in 1979 and 5.48 million tons in 1989 (For details, see Table 16-7). Using South Korea's figures, North Korea's total grain production in 1980, 1981 and 1982 were 3.91, 5.36 and 5.45 million tons, respectively. South Korea's figures in the corresponding years were 5.33, 6.92, and 6.81 million tons. Strictly from a numerical point of view, false and exaggerated claims notwithstanding, North Korea's grain production has significantly increased for the past forty years. In 1946 the grain production level between the North and the South was roughly 2 to 1 in favor of the latter. In 1983, it was nearly at the same level in the two halves. In 1990 the percentage of North Korea's 4.81 million tons to South Korea's 6.63 million tons of grain output is 72.5%. That is, the North's production accounts for about two-thirds that of the South's. North Korea's other agricultural output statistics are also generally favorable. According to the South Korean government statistics on livestock, for example, in 1982 the number of North and South Korea's cattle including the milking cows were 810,000 and 1,760,000 heads, respectively; the number of pigs, 1.8 million and 2.19 million; and fowls, 30 million and 47 million, respectively.[14] Considering the fact that the North has less than half of the South's population, the former has fared better in animal husbandry as well.

In conclusion, it is rather ironical that when Korea was divided, the North was characterized, though grossly oversimplied, as "industrial" and the South, "agricultural." Forty years later, however, as it will be clear in the following that the "industrial North" has become "the agricultural North" and the "agricultural South," "the industrial South." In the North the primary sector occupied 26.8% in 1990, while it constituted only 9.1% in the South during the same period. Likewise, the North's secondary and tertiary sectors comprised 56% and 17.2%, respectively, while the South's counterparts made up 44.8% and 46.1%, respectively. Again, grossly over simplified, it is the "rural North" and the "urban South" as well. In 1965 the North was 47.5% urban, the South, 36.6%, but in 1987, the year the data was available the North was 59.6% urban, while in 1990 the South was 74.4% urban.

Behind this new transformation in the two halves, not only their eco-nomic system differences but also their policy differences loom large. As Table 16-11 illustrates, North Korea has basically continued its "bal-anced growth" approach. By contrast, since the early 1960s till the launching of the Saemaul Movement in 1971, South Korea had imple-mented an unbalanced "industrial-development-first" model. It was only in the early 1970s that South Korea attempted to correct the widening gap between the industrial and agrarian sectors. The Saemaul Movement succeeded, initially at least, in improving the agricultural and rural sec-tors in the South.[15]

Industrial Sectors

As mentioned earlier, it is difficult, if not impossible, to compare North and South Korea's performances in various industrial sectors, due to systemic and methodological reasons. Bearing these limits in mind, some gross comparisons of the two halves' industrial performances are possible when comparable data are available.

In energy production, the North's average annual energy growth rate in the 1965-73 period significantly exceeded that of the South's (9.3% vs. 2.6%). But in the 1973-83 period, the growth rate of both North and South Korea tapered off, but at the same time the South not only caught up but surpassed the North (the former, 4.6% vs. the latter, 3.1%).

In energy consumption the South has grown faster than the North. In the 1965-73 period, the North's average annual energy consumption rate was 9.5% as compared with the South's 15.8%. In the 1973-83 peri-od, the North's annual growth rate declined to 3.6%, as compared to that of the South at 8.8%. In terms of per capita energy consumption in 1965, the North surpassed the South overwhelmingly (504 vs. 237). In 1981 the South had significantly improved its ratio, although the North maintained the lead (1,168 vs. 2,093). To put it another way, the South Korean source indicated that in 1983 the North's power generating capacity was 5.74 million kilowatts as compared with the South's 13.1

million kw. In actual output, the North produced 236 million kwh and the South, 488.5 million kwh. In 1990 the North's power generating capacity was 7.14 million kilowatts as compared with the South's 21.10 million kilowatts. The total output for the North was 277.4 million kwh and the South, 1,076.7 million kwh. It is noteworthy that the sources of energy in North and South Korea differ significantly. In the North the sources by percentage are coal (72.9), oil (10.1), hydro-electric power (12.3) and wood for fire (4.7). In the South the energy sources by percentage are oil (56.2), coal (33.2), wood for fire (4.8), atomic power (4.5) and hydro-electric power (1.4). The energy from nuclear power is conspicuously absent in the North. In 1990, for example, North generated, 4.29 million kw from hydroelectric power and 2.85 million kw from thermoelectric power, but none from nuclear power.[16]

Energy resourcewise, the North is rich and the South, poor. It meant that the North was far less dependent upon crude oil import than the South in 1983 (2.5 million vs. 24.6 million tons). In 1990 the North imported 2.52 million tons of oil as compared to the South's 42.63 million tons. The import figures for refined oil showed a general pattern in 1983 (260,000 vs. 2.7 million tons). The North's coal import figures are miniscule as compared to the South's (1.5 to 2 million tons vs. nearly 11 million tons in 1983). As a result, the South's oil refining capacity was far larger and more sophisticated than that of the North. In 1990, for instance, the former had the capacity to refine 840,000 barrels of oil per day, while the latter had only 70,000 barrels per day capacity.[17]

In steel and nonferrous metal industries, the South fared significantly better than the North. The critical boost to South Korea's steel industry was made possible by the completion of the POSCO (Korea Pohang Integrated Steelworks Corp.) in 1973. Using the South Korean statistics, of 1983 North Korea's annual steel, pig iron, and rolled steel productions were 5.08 million, 4.30 million and 3.19 million tons, respectively, as compared to South Korea's 8.83 million, 14.04 million and 18.87 million tons. In 1990 the North's annual steel, pig iron and rolled steel production were 5.94 million, 5.17 million and 4.04 million, respectively. In the same year, the South's pig iron production alone were 15.3 million tons.[18] Three points deserve attention here. First, the North produces most of its basic raw materals for iron and steel works domestically, while the South imports nearly 75% of its iron ore and scrap metals from overseas. Second, the North's steel and iron work plants are mostly obsolete and unautomated, while the South's are technologically and managerially advanced and greatly automated. For instance, the Kim Chaek Steelworks and other steel and iron works produce 4.03 million tons of crude steel annually with some 65,000 workers, while in the South the Pohang Integrated Steel Works alone produces 9.1 million tons of crude steel with only 16,000 employees. Third, at the WPK Sixth Congress in October 1980 North Korea projected an increase in the steel production level by 1984 to 8 million tons and to 15 million tons by 1989, as one of its ten major production goals. Even if North Korea succeeded in achieving the goal, it would have reached South Korea's 1982 annual steel production level.

The South's production figures in other metal industries such as lead, zinc, copper and aluminum are also impressive. In 1984 the North was ahead in the production of lead (30,000 vs. the South's 9,000 tons) and zinc (140,000 vs. 104,000 tons) while the South led in the production of cooper (the North's 48,000 vs. 140,000 tons) and aluminum (0 vs. 18,000 tons).

In machine industry, the North has never succeeded in capturing its momentum from the South. From the beginning, the North was far behind the South in machine tool and metal processing industries as shown in the 1944 production figure of 28% for the North and 72% for the South. Forty years later, the South was far ahead the North in nearly all the categories of major machine industry, not simply in tonnage and production figures but also in the level of technology and in the production scale. Using the South Korean government statistics for 1983, the North's automobile production was only 15,000 units annually, while the comparable figure for the South was 337,000 units (in 1990 the South's passenger car production alone reached 958,035 units). Moreover, the North manufactured only light trucks, jeeps almost exclusively for domestic needs, while the South produced all types of cars and other vehicles for domestic and foreign markets. Other machine industry figures revealed similar patterns: shipbuilding (the North's 210,000 vs.

the South's 4 million tons); machine tools (30,000 vs. 50,000 units); farm machinery (30,000 vs 73,000 tons); TV sets (200,000 vs. 8.8 million); and refrigerators (20,000 vs. 1.7 million units). In 1990 the South's production of color television receivers alone reached 12.8 million units, and household refrigerators increased to 2.8 million units in the same year.[19]

In chemical industry the North surpassed the South initially. In 1944 the North produced 82% of the chemical products while the South's output (200,000 tons) was meagre 18%. Forty years later, as in other industrial sectors, the North lost its edge to the South. In 1983 the North produced 639,000 tons of chemical fertilizers' as compared to the South's 1.4 million tons. In chemical production in general, the South's output (200,000 tons) was nearly ten times greater than that of the North (20,000 tons). The production figures for major synthetic resins and cements showed essentially the same characteristics: resins (North's 92,000 vs. South's 1.04 million tons) and cement (8.6 million vs. 23.4 million tons).[20] In North Korea's target production figures of chemical fertilizers, it projected 5 million tons by 1984 and 7 million tons by 1989. If the South Korean official estimate of the North's 1983 figure is reliable, North Korea's projected goal for 1984 was utterly unrealistic in that the production would have jumped from 600,000 tons to 5 million tons in just two years! In 1990, the North's chemical fertilizer production was estimated at 351.4 million metric tons, as compared with the South's 548.6 million metric tons. In cement production, even if the North Korean target production figures of 12 to 13 million tons were met by 1984, it was comparable to the 1982 production level in the South. In 1989 North Korea projected an annual increase level in cement production which was still less than South Korea's 1982 level of 23.4 millions tons. In 1990 the North's cement production was estimated at 12 million tons as compared to the South's 33.9 million tons. In short, the South overtook the North not only in chemical industry but virtually in all other industrial sectors in forty years.

Like machine tool and metal processing industry, the North was far behind the South in light industry from the outset. In 1944, for instance, of total textile industry output, the North comprised only 33% as compared to the South's 67%. For the past forty years, the North's inferiority in light industry has suffered further deterioration by its deliberate "heavy and defense industry-first policy. Using once again, the South Korean government figures of 1983, the North produced, 128,000 tons of textile and the South, 1.26 million tons. The same pattern emerges in other light industry production figures, e.g., woven goods (North's 600 million vs. South's 5,900 million meters) and shoes (52 million vs. 400 million pairs).[21] Again, like other industrial and manufactured goods, the products from the North are generally of poor quality and are exclusively for domestic consumption, whereas the bulk of the light industrial products from the South are export-bound.

The North is behind the South in transportation and communication areas. As Table 16-17 indicates, the South leads substantially over the North in all major indices of transportation and communication. One example suffices to illustrate this point. In aviation, domestic flights in the North are irregular and international flights are limited to three cities in two countries—Pyongyang-Peking, Pyongyang-Moscow and Pyongyang-Khabarovsk. These international flights were scheduled only once or twice a week on 17 propeller-driven airplanes of the North Korean Air Force with a 40-passenger seating capacity. Foreign visitors are limited to diplomats and government officials, sports teams and official guests, whose numbers may total 100,000 at most annually. By contrast, South Korea operated over 100 airplanes connecting major domestic cities such as Seoul, Pusan, Taegu, Kwangju and Cheju as well as some 30 cities in 20 countries. Foreign visitors to South Korea, reached 100,000 in 1968 while North Korea claimed to have reached the same number of foreign visitors in 1991. In 1982 the number of foreign visitors and tourists to South Korea totaled 1.14 million and in 1990, 2.34 million. The number of South Koreans who traveled abroad has also steadily increased from 1.21 million in 1989 to 1.56 million in 1990.[22]

Foreign Trade

Perhaps the most conspicuous difference between North and South Korea in economic performance can be found in foreign trade and international finance. The contrasting performance by the two halves in trade has been the direct results of the differences in their economic system, policy and strategy. The North Korean economy, like its past and remaining fraternal socialist economies, is a closed autarchic system. This closed economic system was further entrenched by the WPK's deliberate inward-looking, sectorally balanced, self-reliant economic policy. The North had regarded foreign trade as supplementing its basically self-sufficient national economy. Hence, its imports were generally limited to materials which would help in building a self-reliant national economy, and its exports were aimed at earning foreign currency necessary in purchasing the imported goods.

By contrast, the South Korean economic system is by design an open and interdependent part of world economic system. The open system was further strengthened by the Park Chung Hee government's (1961-1979) adoption of the outward-looking, sectorally unbalanced economic strategy. Accordingly, foreign trade has been the major locomotive of South Korea's economic growth.

Beyond the above, there are other differences in the way the both halves handle trade. In the North, foreign trade is still planned, coordinated, and administered exclusively by the government. The Ministry of Foreign Trade is under the DPRK Administrative Council, which is controlled by the WPK Central Committee, and ultimately by the Political Committee and Secretariat chaired by Kim Il Sung. In the South, too, the government intervenes greatly in foreign trade sector in the form of trade information sharing, domestic credit and other banking control, foreign loan guarantee, direct and indirect investment in foreign trade-related technology and research, foreign exchange rate regulations and other laws and regulations in the areas of foreign trade and transactions. No matter how severe the governmental intervention in foreign trade sector in South Korea, private trade sector is and has been still the prime mover of foreign trade. Unlike North Korea where foreign trade is the exclusive domain of the WPK-government control, the South Korean foreign trade system is like a government-private trade industry partnership.

Bearing in mind the above-mentioned differences and contrasts in the foreign trade systems of the two halves, the following observations can be made. First, in overall trade volumes, the North cannot match the South. In 1960 the North's total trade volume was 114 million dollars, as compared to the South's 250 million dollars. In 1970 the North's total trade volume was 801 million dollars, and that of the South, 2.82 billion dollars. In 1980 the North's total trade volume was 3.18 billion dollars, and that of the South, 39.7 billion dollars.[23] Both have also experienced a high degree of growth in trade, although the North, again, cannot be compared to the South with its phenomenal growth. In the 1971-79 period the North's average annual growth rate of exports and imports were 22.0% and 11.1%, respectively. From 1963 to 1982, the South's average annual growth rate of exports and imports were 36.4% and 24.6%, respectively. In 1990 North Korea's total trade volume was 4.77 billion dollars, as compared to South Korea's 134.86 billion dollars (For details, see Tables 16-18 and 16-19).

Second, both experienced trade deficits. From 1970 to 1982, the North imported more than it exported with the exception of 1978 and 1979. The South had trade deficits since 1960 and even earlier, although the relative amount of trade deficit began to taper off in the 1980s.

Thirdly, the North's share of trade occupies less than 25% of its GNP, while the South's portion is more than 70%. The former depends less on trade and is thus, less vulnerable to international trade and business cycles, while the latter depends on world trade and business fluctuations. South Korea depends heavily on world trade volume, and its share has been increasing steadily (0.62% in 1975 to 1.27% in 1982). [24]

Fourthly, in the 1960s the export items from the two sides were usually primary goods, which have been gradually replaced by manufactured goods in the 1970s and the 1980s. In 1982, the North's primary goods and industrial products accounted for 41% and 59%, respectively. The South's exports of primary goods and manufactured goods in the same year were 6% and 94%, respectively. The import items from the two sides are also contrasting. The North's main import items are machines, equipments and appliances, while that of the South are primary products such as raw materials, agricultural products and fuels.[25]

Fifthly, in terms of trade partnerships, until 1954 the North's trade was limited to the former Soviet Union (the formal trade agreement was concluded on March 17, 1949) and China (November 23, 1953). Beginning in 1955 North Korea gradually expanded its trade to all socialist fraternal countries and a few non-aligned and even capitalist countries. Currently the North trades with some 60 countries. Until the late 1960s, its trade with the socialist fraternal countries amounted to nearly 90% of its total trade volume. Notably, the North's trade with the former Soviet Union and China accounted for nearly 80% of its trade with the socialist countries. In the 1970s, North's foreign trade began to change its direction, and it placed its priority primarily on successfully completing its First Six-Year Plan (1971-76) through "technical revolution." For example, in 1971 the North's trade with the communist bloc nations accounted for 85.1% while its trade with the capitalist countries was limited to 14.9% of the total. In 1979, however, its trade with the former dropped to 51.5%, while its trade with the latter rose to 48.4%. Japan has become its top capitalist trade partners, followed by West Germany and France.[26]

Meanwhile, South Korea's two principal trade partners have been the United States and Japan, although it traded virtually with all countries except for the communist countries, at least until the early 1970s.[27] In 1959, Japan accounted for 66% (12.8 million dollars) of South Korea's total export (19.1 million dollars), and the United States, 11%. The United States accounted for 50% (141 million dollars) of South Korea's total imports and Japan, 11%. These two countries accounted for 77% and 61% of South Korea's total exports and imports, respectively. This pattern has not changed significantly for ten years, although South Korea made efforts to expand its import-export markets beyond these two countries. In 1969 the United States and Japan occupied 50.2% and 18.2% of South Korea's total export, and 29.1% and 41.3% of its total imports, respectively. In 1979 the exports and imports with the United States and Japan dropped to 29.1% and 22.3% and 22.6% and 32.7%, respectively. In 1980 South Korea's trade volume with these two countries began to drop below 50%. In 1984, for instance, the South Korea's figures of exports and imports with two countries were 36% and 16% and 22% and 25%, respectively. South Korea now trades with more than 170 countries (For details, see Table 16-19).[28]

Closely related to North and South Korea's trade is their respective foreign debts. Beginning in the early 1970s, the North began to accumulate a relatively higher rate of foreign debts.[29] In 1973 and 1974 the North defaulted in its payment to the creditor countries in the West, including Japan. The amount of this much publicized foreign debt default was about 500 to 600 million dollars. As of 1982 South Korea estimated that the North's foreign debt was around 3.5 billion dollars (1.2 billion dollars to the socialist bloc countries and 2.3 billion dollars to Japan and the West). In 1990, for instance, North Korea's foreign debt was estimated at 85.1 billion dollars, while that of the South was 31.7 billion dollars of which net foreign debts were 4.85 billion dollars.[30]

In summary, the prospect for the future of the North and South Korean economy largely hinges upon the developments of their non-economic factors. At least, four scenarios of their relations are on the drawing board. The worst-case scenario is the sudden collapse of the North Korean regime which would create a havoc in the two halves and fatally wound the economy of the South for years to come. Another scenario is the hastening of the unification process prematurely either by the South or by the North, and the South would thereby have to assume unnecessary burden and expenses. The third scenario is the continuation of the current-style status quo. Namely, the North tries its utmost to keep its socialist system intact, paying verbal lip service and instituting cosmetic changes. The best-case scenario is the gradual, piecemeal transformation of the current North and South Korean system so that the two can be comparable, ideologically, politically and economically. It may take years, if not decades, until such condition can be realized. It also means that the North-South integration process has to be controlled and managed by both sides in the meantime.

Any of the aforesaid scenarios for North Korea's economic future, let alone the future of its system, is in serious trouble. As Table 16-20 indicates, if the current economic trend continues, without cataclysmic changes, the North Korean economy will be on its downward slide. As the Australian research report concluded, North Korea possesses a stagnant economy marked by high foreign debts; few value-added exports; little access to foreign technology or capital; rapidly aging and inefficient plant, machinery and infrastructure; a highly centralized, absolute command system of economic management; and an aging political leadership that continues to emphasize the value of pursuing the very policies that are largely responsible for the current sorry state of affairs.[31] Again, as Table 16-21 indicates, North Korea's international pariah status cannot be ameliorated overnight. Even by the year 2000, its foreign trade will be miniscule, as compared with the South. While in 1990 the North's trade comprised only 20% of its GNP, the South's figure was 57.4%. By the year 2000, the North's trade is projected to constitute only 21.6% of its GNP, whereas the South's trade will comprise 52.1% of its projected GNP ($731 billion dollars) (For details, see Table 16-24).

Therefore, if the North Korean leadership could come to its senses, the best available option open to it is to abandon the useless rhetoric once and for all and to seriously engage in a manageable and controllable inter-Korean economic transactions. As Tables 16-22 and 16-23 illustrate, the inter-Korean trade has been on the rapid rise, since 1989, and the commodity composition of inter-Korean trade is complementary.[32] After all, some simple questions ought to be raised and answered by the ruling elites of the North and the South. Namely, who has benefited the most from the senseless and destructive mutual animosty? Can they escape from the age-old divide and rule trap? Isn't the deadly quarrel of the Koreans against the Koreans as absurd as that of man against man?

The Question of Quality of Life

Unlike the foregoing performance indicators, the quality of life question transcends the economic issue. The quality of life question is an all-encompassing *human* question. It touches on political, economic, social, philosophical and personal questions. It is an ultimate inquiry because the aim of all human activities boils down to the realization of happy life to the most, if not all, people. It is, however, more than a utilitarian question because measuring the greatest happiness of the greatest number can be both quantitative and qualitative and objective and subjective. What makes people happy? It is easy to assert that everyone through all ages yearned for a freer, more just and happier life. But what is freedom, justice and happiness? Who judges, defines and determines them?

The qualitative and quantitative measurements aside, what does the quality of life mean? It means different things to different people. Subjectively, it may mean a sense of well-being, a state of satiation or a state of viability. Objectively, it may mean one's capacity to control his or her resources, and capability to satisfy common needs of a given collectivity.[33]

Maslow, for one, talks about a hierarchy of human needs; Lasswell and Kaplan identified eight base values—power, respect, rectitude, affection, well-being, wealth, skill and enlightenment.[34] But their rank listing is, at best, suggestive, not exhaustive of everything that makes people happy, free and just. It is difficult to define and even identify human needs and values because they vary widely with different people, places and different times. The quality of life involves, in short, the people's overall concerns with life and livelihood.

Beyond the aforementioned problems, North and South Korea's quality of life question is further complicated by their diametrically different ideological, political and economic systems. Any numerical comparison of the two halves' quality of life may indicate, at best, partial, if not superficial, aspects of their total living and livelihood. Bearing this additional caveat in mind, an attempt to compare the two halves' quality of life is made here. In so doing, a modified version of Shin and Synder's ten objective indicators of life quality, though limited and simplistic, are utilized. In their case study of South Korea, they used ten indicators of life quality. They first divided quality of life into three categories— social, physical and personal. Next, they identified various resources for the satisfaction of physiological needs, human relationship needs and self-fulfillment needs. Finally, they identified ten indices of life quality: (1) income; (2) housing; (3) health; (4) safety and security; (5) work; (6) leisure and recreation; (7) love and trust; (8) equality; (9) education; and (10) freedom.[35] By using these criteria and my own yardsticks, the following tentative findings and observations can be made.

The most important question rests with freedom. It is unproductive to present here the unceasing argumentations among scholars and practitioners on the meaning of freedom. For the sake of facility, Pareto's definition of freedom is utilized for this study. To him, freedom is simply "a capacity to act."[36] Two more examples, one abstract and the other concrete, are valuable in this context. J. S. Mill in his classic, *On Liberty*, alluded that freedom means "over himself, over his own body and mind, the individual is sovereign."[37] Much earlier, even in his world of absolute monarchy Thomas Hobbes quite tellingly conceded that "the liberty of subject lies... in only those things which, in regulating their actions, the sovereign has praetermitted: such as is the liberty to buy, and sell; and otherwise contract with one another; to choose their own abode, their own diet, their own trade of life, and institute their children as they themselves think fit; and the like."[38]

The question here, then, is whether or not North Korea today permits its people to exercise such elementary Hobbesian freedom. Unfortunately, the answer is in the negative. As noted earlier, in the North the Hobbesian liberty to buy and sell, that is, in modern parlance, private enterprise, private property and free market system do not exist. Nor are the people free to choose their housing, food, job and their children's education, let alone travel. As Kolakowski pointed out, when Soviet ideologists speak of human rights, they invariably stress that "the chief human right is the right to work," but they failed to add that "this has been achieved by a system of compulsory labor...." Namely, in such a society, every human being becomes "a helpless property of the omnipotent state."[39]

In South Korea, meanwhile, the said Hobbesian freedom does exist, although the government severely controls various aspects of this freedom. In the South many aspects of this basic freedom are still curtailed and controlled, but not absent like in North Korea. Specifically, the Freedom House Survey in 1978, for instance, rated North Korea as "NF" (not a free state) and South Korea as "PF" (a partly free state). In overall ratings of freedom (in terms of political rights, civil liberties, status of freedom and outlook) North and South Korea is ranked 175th and 87th, respectively, out of 211 countries and territories. In 1990-1991 the same survey reported that North Korea has been "not free" while South Korea was rated "free" from 1988 through 1990 but was again rated "partly free" in 1991 (For details, see Tables 16-25).[40]

Next, the economic indicators such as growth rate, per capita income, inflation, unemployment and the like can be used in comparing the two halves' quality of life, although wide variations in numbers exist depending on the sources. Still, South Korea, at least, since the 1960s, has undergone a faster rate of economic growth than that of North Korea. The end result of the South's faster growth is found in their respective per capita income. Although the per capita income level estimates of the two halves range from 5 to 1 in favor of the South, it is safe to conclude that the South edged North Korea in overall growth rate and/or personal income level. North Korea's per capita income ranges from the high of $2,200 claimed by North Korea to $1,040 estimated by International Institute of Strategic Studies and to $736 announced by South Korea in 1982. In 1990 the North's per capita income was $1,064, as compared to the South's $5,569.[41]

No data for North Korea's income distribution is available. But in South Korea only 19.3% of the total income in 1965 belonged to the bottom 40% of the households; in 1976 and 1980 its percentage declined further to 16.8 and 16.1, respectively. In contrast, 41.9% of the total income belong to the top 20% of the households in 1965; the figures have increased to 45.3% in 1976 and 45.4% in 1980. In the same period 38.8%, 37.9% and 38.0%, of the total income belonged to the middle 40% of the households. North and South Korea cannot be compared authoritatively on this account since no data is available for the former. But South Korea, as compared with other third world countries, fared better in this equity account, although it is still far behind countries such as Japan and Taiwan.[42]

The South's substantial edge in economic growth rate notwithstanding, its foreign debt problem had been serious. South Korea's debt service ratio as percentage of GNP has slightly worsened from 3.0 to 5.2, while its debt service ratio as percentage of exports of goods and services has been improving from 19.4 in 1970 to 12.3 in 1983.[43]

In the North unemployment does not, theoretically, exist, while in the South it fluctuates as a part of business cycle. In North Korea an individual worker virtually has no freedom to choose, switch, or relocate his or her job mainly because the government allocates jobs for all the people. People's freedom of choice in jobs suffers as a result. Unemployment exists in the South. The question here is not one of absence or presence of the unemployed, but of degree. In the 1963-1983 period, the South's unemployment rate was as high as 8.2% in 1963 and as low as 3.2% in 1978. In 1982, for instance, the unemployment rate was 4.4%. It meant that out of 26.5 million people of 14 years and older, economically active population were 15 million of which 14.4 million were employed, and 656,000, unemployed. In 1990, of total 30.8 million gainfully employable people of 15 years or older, 18.4 million people were employed and 451,000, unemployed for an unemployment rate of 2.4%.[44]

In North Korea the term "inflation" does not exist, although it may very well be hidden under different names and labels. The government not only controls and manages nearly all means of production, consumption and exchange, but also determines the price of each and every merchandise and commodity. The price in North Korea does not fluctuate with market conditions; it is set by the economic control organs of the government. South Korea, on the other hand, like most countries of free and semi-free market economy, confronts twin and often mutually incompatible economic problems—unemployment and inflation. The South's average annual rate of inflation in the 1965-73 period was 15.5% and in the 1973-83 period it was 19.0%, which was relatively high for a viable economy.[45] Since 1980, the South has been successful in curbing its chronically high inflation rate, which has been under 5% since 1984. In theory, the price of merchandise and other commodities are determined through market mechanism, although the government's price control of land, housing and other commodities has been often heavy-handed and even suffocating. As of December 29, 1984, for instance, the price of some 85 consumer goods items such as soap, sugar, juice, gum, bread, ice cream, piano, telephone, tires, automobiles and the like had been subjected to the government's direct control.[46]

In housing, no data comparable to South Korea exists in North Korea. The fact that the North is slightly larger in size but has less than half the population of the South makes the former's housing problem relatively less serious than the latter. In 1982, for instance, South Korea had a little above 39 million people of 8.4 million households. An average number of persons per household was 4.6, and the total number of housing units were 5.76 million. Thus, each housing unit on the average accommodated 6.8 rather than 4.6 persons. Put it differently, the percentage of homeowners was 63.1 in 1975 which declined slightly to 58.4 in 1980. In the cities, too, the percentage has decreased in the same period from 44.2 to 42.7. Over one million (1,029,000) houses were needed in 1962, if the figures are calculated on the basis of the total number of households minus the total number of housing units, but some 2 million houses were needed to meet the household demands in 1981.[47] Related to housing shortage is the overcrowding (392 persons per square km), air, water, noise pollution, traffic congestions, urban slum areas and shanty settlements. In all these problems related to over-population, ecology and demography, the North fared relatively better than the South which has had faster economic and urban growth rate and greater population size than the former.

In public health, the people in the North receive, again theoretically, a free medical and health care because, like everything else, the government controls all health and medical care. Generally, free medical and health care in the socialist countries suffer from poor quality of service, staff and facilities. North Korea is hardly an exception to this rule. In South Korea, the medical insurance program was introduced in the late 1980s. By 1991 nearly 100% of the people were covered by this national medical insurance program. Specifically these formal and superficial contrasts aside, some facts and figures available deserve attention. In the North there were 430 people per doctor in 1980, while in the South the number for the same year was 1,440. In 1991, the number went down to 1,216 in the South. Thus, if these figures were reliable, the people in the North had easier access to physicians than their Southern counterparts. In the North, the number of nurses for the population is not available. But the South has made a significant progress in this particular area. The population per nursing person was 3,240 in 1960, but it was down to 350 in 1980. The North's daily calorie supply per capita was 3,051 in 1982, which was, as percentage of requirement, 130. The South's daily calorie intake per capita in the same year was 2,936, which was, as percentage of requirement, 125.[48] The life expectancy at birth (years) in 1983, according to the 1984 *World Development Report,* of 65 in the North is slightly lower than 67 in the South. The *UN Statistical Yearbook, 1983,* on the other hand, estimated that North Korea's average life expectancy at birth for male and, female in the 1975-1980 period was 60.5 and 64.6, respectively, while South Korea's in the 1978-1979 period was 62.7 for male and 69.1 for female. The South fared slightly better than the North in life expectancy, despite the latter's "free health and medical care." In 1990 South Korea's average life expectancy was 71.3; 67.4 for male and 75.4 for female.[49]

As of 1983, 62% of the population in the two halves live in urban areas. But the South has a greater number of large cities than the North (7 to 2 cities of over 500,000 people). About 77% of the urban population in the former live in large cities, while in the latter only 19% reside in them.

Also, in other life amenities such as television sets, household appli-ances, cars, telephones, transportation, leisure-related facilities and activities, all available data tend to confirm that the South come out far better than the North (See Table 16-17).

Finally, in education the North has extended its free and compulsory education of 4 years of elementary education in 1949 to 11 years of education in 1972. The extended years of free and compulsory education did not imply better quality of teachers, staffs, facilities, classrooms, textbook contents or methods of teaching.[50] One thing is quite clear. In the midst of the Kim Il Sung cult (his son, Kim Jŏng Il as well), not only education, but mass media, arts, music and literature have all been heavily politicized. What is more, "free" education in the North simply means "cash-free." It does not mean that children and their parents have the freedom of choice in education.

In the South, free and compulsory education covers only 6 years of elementary school (South Korea has extended free and compulsory education for three additional years to the children of remote rural areas and islands). Despite the limited number of years of free education, school-age children's opportunity to education has steadily expanded over the years. The number enrolled in secondary school as percentage of age group was 27 in 1960, but it rose to 89 in 1982. Likewise, the number enrolled in higher education as percentage of population aged 20-24 rose from 5 in 1960 to 24 in 1982.[51] On balance, it is safe to assume that both North and South Korea have made significant progress in education. The North instituted 11-year "cash-free" compulsory education as compared to the South's 6-year. But the North's free education is not really "free" in that the parents de facto underwrite their children's education through work. Nonetheless, the school children in South Korea enjoy relatively more freedom of choice in education, subject only to their scholastic ability and economic means.

Concluding Remarks

Throughout this chapter and others, available and accessible North and South Korean facts and figures have been juxtaposed and compared. In so doing, on a few occasions some value judgments have been made in various juxtapositional comparison of the two halves. But in most instance, an attempt has been made to present objective information.

As stated at the outset, more than forty years of separate developments with two diametrically different economic models, policies and strategies are sufficient to make some interim assessment of North and South Korea's economic performance in particular and their respective management of people's livelihood in general. The interim evaluation, though imperfect and inadequate, was indeed the main objective of this juxtapositional comparison.

Setting aside all those elusive and even misleading facts, figures and numbers for the moment, and focusing, instead on the deeper meaning of human existence and experience in the two halves, we may ask the question, "What makes people happy?" It is quite evident from the foregoing that both North and South Korea have largely succeeded in solving the people's basic bread and circus question. That alone is not a small feat in this world of man-made and/or nature-caused famine, draught, flood and other human miseries and disasters. The Korean people in the two sides, like people in all other parts of the globe, need more than food and diversions. They also need freedom as they do air and water.

Can the people in North Korea use Mill's idea of freedom to declare that, they, not the ubiquitous government and the Party, are sovereign over their body and mind? Do they enjoy, even minimally the Paretoan freedom—the capacity to act? Are they free to choose their own housing, job, education, let alone the freedom to buy, sell or travel. Unfortunately, the answers to these rather *human* questions are in the negative. In the South, meanwhile, the answers to the same questions are by and large in the affirmative, albeit conditionally and with some reservations.

In the final analysis, Confucius' remarks concerning the tasks of government, are noteworthy here. In the *Analects,* he lists three requisites of government: sufficiency of food, sufficiency of military equipment and the confidence of people. Tsze-kung asked Confucius, "if it cannot be helped, and one of three should be foregone first?" "The military equipment," said the Master. Tsze-kung again asked, "if it cannot be helped, and one of the remaining two must be dispensed with, which of them should be foregone?" The Master answered, "Part with the food. From of old, death has been the lot of all men, but if the people have no faith in their rulers, there is no standing for the state."[52] His disciple, Mencius, echoed the same sentiment:

> There is a way to get the empire—get the people, and the empire is got. There is a way to get the people—get their hearts, and the people are got. There is a way to get their hearts:—it is simply to collect for them what they like, and not to lay on them what they dislike.[53]

It appears that the governments and rulers in the two halves have somehow misplaced the priority of governmental tasks in engaging in unceasing mutual hostility and rivalry. They appear to have placed a greater priority on mutual arms race, a modern equivalent of Confucius' "military equipment" than on the people's livelihood. Have the rulers in the both halves sought seriously to win the people's confidence? To be sure, the answers seem mixed and complicated. Perhaps, an answer to these questions may be: the people in the North, have been suffering from virtual absence of freedom although the officials claim that the country is the paradise on earth, while their South Korean brethrens have been struggling to defend their freedom, which have been frequently deprived by the government.

In Korea or elsewhere, what matters for the government and its people are freedom and happiness. Interestingly enough, there is a common thread running through the Occidental philosopher's idea of freedom and Oriental sages' admonitions to the rulers. Both search for, in essence, the happiness of people: Is the government which makes people happy, good government? Are the people happy when they are free and face minimal governmental constraints? In *Politics,* Aristotle asserted that the felicity of the state is the same as that of the individual —political ideals for the state and the individual are the realization of the highest good and of the best and happiest life.[54]

Materialistic gratifications alone cannot make people happy, and even moral and spiritual satiation is necessary. In that sense, the idea of happiness is both rational and emotional, sentimental and spiritual and objective and subjective. Most of all, it is developmental in that both the people and their government (should) constantly strive to achieve higher, better and greater felicity. There is no end to this endeavor. The differences in meaning of happiness among philosophers and practioners aside, what we call "felicity" is, then, the ultimate aim of human existence and of quality of life.

One final comment is in order here. The concept of "economy" in the Chinese character used by Chinese, Japanese and the Korean is *kyŏngje,* which is an abbreviation of *kyŏngkuk jemin,* or *kyŏngse jemin.* It literally means the management of the nation (or world) and the care of its people. If good management of the nation and good care of its people are undertaken by the government what other responsibility is there for the government? Both are the never-ending task of any and all government. Despite their differences in economic systems, policies and strategies, North and South Korean governments must be responsible for good management of governance and good care of their people.

Table 16-1. North and South Korea's GNP Data

(Unit: Million US Dollars)

Year	North Korea			South Korea		
	GNP	GNP per capita	Growth rate(%)	GNP	GNP per capita	Growth rate(%)
1963	—	7.0	27.1	100.0	—	9.1
1964	—	7.6	28.7	103.0	—	9.6
1965	—	–0.6	30.0	125.0	—	5.8
1966	—	–0.6	36.7	142.0	12.7	—
1967	23.9	186	16.9	42.7	142	6.6
1968	25.7	194	13.3	52.2	169	11.3
1969	27.6	203	n.a.	66.2	210	13.8
1970	29.7	213	17.8	78.3	243	7.6
1971	34.7	243	6.7	91.4	278	9.4
1972	40.8	279	5.6	102.5	306	5.8
1973	47.8	319	4.5	131.5	386	14.9
1974	55.8	363	7.4	181.2	523	8.0
1975	64.0	406	7.5	202.3	574	7.1
1976	77.2	478	—	274.2	765	15.1
1977	83.2	502	—	351.6	966	10.3
1978	91.9	541	—	491.5	1,330	10.6
1979	125.1	719	—	580.2	1,546	10.4
1980	135.0	758	—	564.6	1,481	-6.2
1981	[186]	—	—	622.3	1,607	6.4
1982	[205]	—	—	659.8	1,678	5.4
1983	[216]	—	—	[807]	1,914	11.9
1984	—	—	—	870.0	2,044	9.3
1985	151.0	757	—	897.0	2,032	7.0
1986	174.0	853	—	1,028.0	2,505	12.9
1987	194.0	936	—	1,289.0	3,110	13.0
1988	206.0	980	—	1,728.0	4,127	12.4
1989	211.0	987	—	2,112.0	4,994	6.8
1990	231.0	1,064	—	2,379.0	5,569	9.0

Source: South Korean figures are from *Major Statisitics of Korean Economy, 1983* (Seoul: Economic Planning Board, 1983), p. 3. North Korean figures are adapted from *Nampukhan Kyŏngjehyŏnhwang Pikyo* (Seoul: Kuktotongilwŏn, 1981) except for the figures on its GNP annual growth rate, which are adapted from South Korea's Security and Planning Agency's *Pukhan Sahoesang Pyŏngka* (1979), p. 348. Quoted in Sŏhaeng Lee, "An Analysis of North Korea's Agricultural Cooperative's Management" (in Korean), *Pukhan* (December 1981), p. 134. Figures in brackets are from *World Military Expenditures and Arms Transfers, 1985* (Washington, D.C.: ACDA, 1985), p. 69. The figures since 1986 are from *The Social and Cultural Indicators of North and South Korea, Op. Cit.* Also, *A Handbook of Korea* (Seoul: Korea Overseas Information Service, 1990). South Korea's GNP data from 1984-1990 from *Korea Statistical Yearbook, 1991*, 38, p. 467.

Table 16-1a.   *Varying Estimates of North Korea's GNP Growth Rate*

(Unit: %)

Year	NK	Y-L	PL	YKK	JWC	Adj. Rate
1970	31.0	17.2	15.5	27.7	—	19.0
1971	16.0	2.0	10.1	2.8	—	9.8
1972	16.0	2.0	10.1	12.7	—	9.8
1973	19.0	16.6	11.5	25.2	—	11.6
1974	17.2	16.4	14.6	15.9	—	10.5
1975	20.0	15.7	11.3	11.3	11.7	12.3
1976	(11.0)	9.0	7.6	8.9	9.0	(6.7)
1977	(-4.0)	9.2	7.1	9.8	—	(–2.5)
1978	17.0	13.5	11.5	8.3	—	10.4
1979	15.0	11.7	9.6	10.1	—	9.2
1980	1.7	9.5	—	—	—	10.3
1981	—	—	8.1	—	—	—
1982	16.8	9.0	—	—	—	10.2
AAGR*	16.1	11.8	10.9	13.1	—	9.9

NK: North Korea's official reports.

Y-L: Ha-chŏng Yŏn and Bong S. Lee, "An Analysis of Estimating North Korea's Economic Growth" (in Korean), *KDI* Report (Fall 1984), pp. 139-161. Yŏn and Lee estimated North Korea's GNP by a simple formula, i.e., North Korea's budget=60% of its GNP.

PL: Poong Lee, "Method of Computing North Korean GNP (I) and (II), *Vantage Point* (January and February, 1982).

YKK: Y. K. Kim, "Method of Computing North Korean GNP" (in Korean), *Unification Policy* 6 (1980), nos. 3 and 4.

JWC: Joo-whan Choi, "Estimate of North Korea's GNP," *Vantage Point* (October 1979); Adjusted rate is equal to North Korea's official gross industrial growth rate x 0.613.

AAGR* is annual average growth rate. One recent study reported North Korea's GNP growth rate in percentage as follows: 1978 (5.6), 1979 (6.9), 1980 (3.8), 1981 (2.0), 1982 (4.8) and 1983 (4.3). For details, see Young-kyu Kim, "2nd 7-Year Plan of North Korea: Its Performance and Outlook," *Vantage Point* (January 1985).

Table 16-2. North Korea's Budget

Year	Total Revenue (Unit: 10,000 won)	Total Outlays	% Increase over previous year
1963	314,482	302,821	
1964	349,878	341,824	12.9
1965	357,384	347,613	1.7
1966	367,150	357,140	2.7
1967	410,663	394,823	10.6
1968	502,370	481,289	21.9
1969	531,903	504,857	4.9
1970	623,220	600,168	18.9
1971	635,735	630,168	4.7
1972	743,030	738,861	17.2
1973	859,931	831,391	12.5
1974	1,001,525	967,219	16.3
1975	1,158,630	1,136,748	12.5
1976	1,262,583	1,232,550	8.4
1977	1,378,900	1,334,920	8.3
1978	1,565,730	1,474,360	10.4
1979	1,744,780	1,697,260	15.1
1980	1,913,923	1,883,691	11.0
1981	2,068,400	2,033,300	7.9
1982	2,254,600	2,254,600	10.9
1983	2,438,360	2,401,860	10.7
1984	2,655,100	2,615,800	8.9
1985	2,743,887	2,632,883	4.5
1986	2,845,154	2,845,154	4.1
1987	3,037,800	3,037,800	6.8
1988	3,190,580	3,166,090	4.2
1989	3,360,810	3,338,294	5.4
1990	3,565,610	3,565,610	6.8

Source: Adapted from Nam-Kyon Kim, "An Analysis of North Korea's Budget" (in Korean), *Pukhan* (November 1982), pp. 84-94 and Sang-ho Lee, "An Analysis of North Korea's 1982 Budget" (in Korean), *Pukhan* (June 1982), pp. 96-106. The figures for 1983 to 1990 are adapted from *Pukhan Kaeyo '91, Op. Cit.*, p. 155.

Table 16-3. The Composition of North Korea's Outlays

(Unit: % of the Total Budget)

Year	People's Eco. Outlays	Socio-Cultural Outlays	Military Outlays	Management Outlays
1963	74.0	21.5	1.9	2.6
1964	69.5	20.6	5.8	4.1
1965	68.0	19.7	8.0	4.3
1966	68.4 (68.1)	17.3 (17.3)	10.0 (12.5)	4.3 (2.1)
1967	49.9 (50.1)	17.5 (17.5)	30.4 (30.4)	2.2 (2.0)
1968	48.8 (48.9)	17.0 (17.2)	32.4 (32.4)	1.8 (1.5)
1969	47.5 (47.6)	19.7 (19.7)	31.0 (31.0)	1.8 (1.7)
1970	47.0 (49.2)	19.9 (19.7)	31.3 (29.4)	1.8 (1.7)
1971	44.2 (48.0)	22.9 (19.2)	31.1 (31.1)	1.8 (1.7)
1972	55.5 (57.3)	25.4 (23.9)	17.0 (17.0)	2.1 (1.8)
1973	57.2 (59.0)	25.3 (23.8)	15.4 (15.4)	2.1 (1.8)
1974	57.0 (58.6)	24.8 (23.5)	16.1 (16.1)	2.1 (1.8)
1975	57.2 (58.9)	24.3 (23.0)	16.4 (16.4)	2.1 (1.7)
1976	56.2 (58.5)	25.0 (23.7)	16.7 (16.7)	2.1(1.1)
1977	56.8 (58.3)	25.4 (24.1)	15.7 (15.7)	2.1 (1.9)
1978	57.3 (58.4)	24.7 (23.4)	15.9 (15.9)	2.1 (2.3)
1979	59.4 (60.4)	23.6 (22.4)	15.1 (15.1)	1.9 (2.1)
1980	60.5 (60.5)	22.2 (22.2)	14.6 (14.6)	2.7 (2.7)
1981	60.9 (61.3)	21.6 (22.0)	14.7 (14.8)	2.8 (1.9)
1982	61.6 (62.5)	20.8 (20.9)	14.5 (14.6)	3.1 (2.0)
1983	63.1 (62.5)	20.2 (20.2)	14.7 (14.8)	2.0 (2.5)
1984	64.4 (62.3)	19.9 (21.1)	14.6 (14.6)	1.1 (2.0)
1985	62.5 (62.3)	20.7 (21.1)	14.4 (14.6)	2.4 (2.0)
1986	— (63.5)	— (20.3)	— (14.0)	— (2.2)
1987	— (64.3)	— (20.5)	— (13.2)	— (2.0)
1988	67.2 (65.0)	19.0 (20.8)	12.2 (12.2)	1.6 (2.0)
1989	67.4 (67.4)	18.9 (18.9)	12.0 (12.0)	1.7 (1.7)
1990	67.5 (67.2)	18.8 (18.9)	12.1 (12.1)	1.6 (1.8)

Sources: Adapted from *Nampukhan Kyŏngjehyŏnhwang Pikyo*; Also, Sang-ho Lee, *Op. Cit.* The figures from 1983 to 1990 are from *Pukhan Kaeyo '91, Op. Cit.*, p. 157. The figures in the parentheses are from North Korea's Supreme People's Assembly Annual Budget Reports, *Pukhan Kaeyo '91*, p. 424.

Table 16-4. South Korea's Budget

Year	Total Revenues (in million *won*)	Total Outlays (in million *won*)
1963	75,923	72,839
1964	79,387	75,180
1965	105,481	93,534
1966	153,777	140,942
1967	199,018	180,931
1968	275,717	262,064
1969	376,041	370,532
1970	445,856	441,319
1971	551,452	546,271
1972	708,047	701,143
1973	697,585	655,433
1974	1,046,386	1,013,915
1975	1,630,242	1,535,262
1976	2,378,185	2,142,229
1977	2,990,844	2,739,935
1978	4,040,546	3,538,675
1979	5,507,334	5,053,242
1980	6,635,180	6,486,054
1981	8,174,449	7,907,837
1982	9,313,725	9,313,725
1983	11,794.2	11,475.8
1984	13,197.5	12,536.7
1985	14,223.5	13,585.0
1986	16,278.6	15,310.5
1987	19,162.3	17,488.3
1988	24,009.3	22,402.4
1989	28,847.9	28,367.1
1990	34,610.9	34,501.5

Source: Adapted from *Major Statistics of Korean Economy, 1983* (Seoul: Economic Planning Board, 1983), pp. 175-189. The figures from 1983 to 1990 are from *Korea Statistical Yearbook, 1991* (Seoul: the Korea Statistical Association, 1991), p. 499.

Table 16-5. *The Composition of South Korea's Budget Outlays*

(Unit: %)

Year	General Admin.	National Defense	Development	Unallocable Grant to Loc. Govt.	Repayment of Debts & Others
1963	12.1	28.1	53.3	3.0	3.4
1964	12.5	33.1	47.5	2.9	4.0
1965	13.7	32.0	46.9	3.4	4.0
1966	11.9	28.7	50.1	5.9	3.3
1967	13.5	27.4	45.5	10.4	3.0
1968	12.2	24.7	50.2	10.5	2.4
1969	11.6	22.8	52.2	11.4	2.1
1970	11.7	23.2	51.5	12.3	1.3
1971	9.6	26.0	42.2	12.8	9.4
1972	16.4	25.9	36.8	11.9	9.0
1973	12.8	28.0	45.0	11.0	3.3
1974	10.9	29.3	41.0	8.0	10.3
1975	11.3	28.8	46.0	7.7	6.2
1976	10.4	32.9	46.0	7.1	3.7
1977	11.0	34.7	43.9	6.7	3.7
1978	10.2	37.0	42.9	7.0	3.1
1979	9.3	30.8	50.5	6.7	3.7
1980	9.7	35.6	45.7	6.3	2.7
1981	11.4	33.8	43.3	6.6	4.8
1982	10.6	34.8	43.9	7.5	3.2

Year	General Expenses	National Defense	Fixed Capital Formation	Others
1983	53.4	29.3	08.8	08.5
1984	54.4	28.2	07.5	09.7
1985	57.0	27.6	08.6	06.6
1986	56.0	28.3	08.3	07.2
1987	57.2	27.4	07.9	07.4
1988	50.1	24.8	06.8	18.0
1989	51.8	21.6	07.1	19.3
1990	54.9	19.8	06.9	18.1

Sources: Idem. The percentage calculations from 1983 to 1990 are done by the author based on the data from the *Korea Statistical Yearbook 1991*, p. 501.

Table 16-6. North and South Korea's Farm Households, Farm Population and Cultivated Area in 1982 and 1990

	(unit)	North Korea		South Korea	
		1982	1990	1982	1990
Total Area	Square km	122,098		99,092	
Cultivated Area	1,000ha	2,180	2,141	2,130	2,109
Paddies		640 (30%)	64.3	1,310 (60%)	134.5
Dry fields		1,490 (70%)		870 (40%)	
Farm Population	1,000 persons	6,990		9,688	
Farm Households	(1,000)	1,996		1,290	

Sources: Adapted from *Major Statistics of Korean Economy, 1983* and *A Comparative Study of the South and North Korean Economies* (Seoul: National Unification Board, 1983). Also Yŏng-Kyu Kim, "A Comparison of North and South Korean Economic Development" (in Korean), *Pukhan* (April 1981), pp. 72-93. The 1990 data from the ROK government statistics.

Table 16-7. North and South Korea's Agricultural Outputs

(Unit: 10,000 m/t)

Year	Official	North Korea	Growth Rate (%)	South Korea	Growth Rate (%)
1963	—	490 (500)	-2.0	546	8.6
1964	—	450 (500)	-8.1	664	21.6
1965	—	453 (452)	0.6	652	-1.7
1966	—	440 (n.a)	-2.8	703	7.8
1967	—	511 (n.a)	16.1	633	-10.0
1968	—	567 (n.a)	10.9	630	-0.5
1969	—	n.a. (n.a)	n.a.	718	13.9
1970	—	664 (403)	n.a.	694	-3.3
1971	—	675 (433)	0.4	679	-2.2
1972	—	686 (403)	1.5	674	-0.7
1973	—	697 (438)	1.3	675	0.2
1974	—	700 (446)	2.0	690	2.1
1975	770	720 (442)	1.8	766	11.1
1976	—	750 (448)	1.9	818	6.8
1977	—	779 (476)	3.8	797	-2.6
1978	—	778 (456)	-0.12	822	-3.2
1979	—	n.a. (179)	n.a.	811	-1.4
1980	950	764 (391)	-1.75	533	-34.2
1981	—	— (536)	—	692	29.8
1982	—	— (545)	—	681	-1.6
1984	1.000	560 —	—	—	—
1985	—	503 —	—	—	—
1986	—	483 —	—	—	—
1987	—	495 —	—	—	—
1988	—	521 —	—	—	—
1989	—	548 —	—	—	—
1990	—	481.2 —	—	663.5	—

Sources: The North Korean figures are from Won-jun Lee who readusted both FAO publication data and South Korean official data. For details, see his "The Present Situation
of North Korea's Agricultural Policy" (in Korean), *Pukhan* (April 1982), pp. 180-
190. The North Korean figures in parentheses are from *A Comparative Study of
the South and North Korean Economies* (Seoul: National Unification Board, 1983),
p. 44. The South Korean data are from *Major Statistics of Korean Economy, 1983*,
p. 65. The figures from 1984 to 1990 are from *Pukhan Kaeyo, Op. Cit.*

Table 16-8. Land Confiscated under North Korea's Land Reform

Classification	Area (I)		Area (II)		Farm households	
	ha.	%	ha.	%	No.	%
Confiscated land	1,000,325	100.0	1,000,325	100.0	422,646	100.0
Land owned by Japanese	112,632	11.3	100,797	10.1	12,919	3.1
Land owned by national traitors	13,272	1.3	21,718	2.2	1,386	0.3
Land by land-owner (over 5 ha.)	237,746	23.8	285,692	28.6	29.638	7.0
Land by absentee owners	263,436	26.3	338,062	33.8	145,688	34.5
Land owned by absentee owners partially	358,053	35.8	239,650	24.0	223,866	54.1
Land owned by church, temples and other religious organizations	15,193	1.5	14,401	1.4	4,124	1.0

Sources: (I) From *Statistical Returns of National Economy of DPRK* (Pyongyang: Foreign Languages Publishing Co., 1964); (II) from North Korea's 1960 *Chŏson Chungangnyŏngam.* Quoted in *Sekyekongsankyŏnch'ŏnggam* (Seoul, 1972), p. 1003.

Table 16-9. North Korea's Socialization of Industry,
Agriculture and Commerce

(Unit %)

		1946	1949	1953	1956	1957	1958(Jun.)	1958(Dec.)
Ownership*								
Industry	Pu.	73.4	90.7	96.1	98.3	98.7	100	100
	Pr.	26.6	9.3	3.9	1.7	1.3	–	–
Agricul-ture	Pu.	–	3.2	32.0	80.9	95.6	98.6	100
	Pr.	100	96.8	68.0	19.1	4.4	1.4	–
Com-merce	Pu.	3.5	56.5	67.5	84.6	87.9	100	100
	Pr.	96.5	43.5	32.5	15.4	12.1	–	–

*Pu: government or public owned; Pr, privately owned.
Source: ROK Ministry of Unification Board, "A Study of North Korea's Agriculture and
Agricultural Policy (in Korean)" (1972), p. 4. Quoted in Sŏhaeng Lee, "An Analy-
sis of North Korea's Agricultural Cooperative's Management (I)" (in Korean),
Pukhan (September 1981), p. 80.

Table 16-10. North Korea's Collectivization of Agriculture

(Unit: %)

Year	Land under cultivation	Social ownership	Cooperative ownership	Private ownership
1949	100.0	1.9	–	98.1
1953	100.0	4.6	0.6	94.8
1956	100.0	5.3	63.6	31.2
1957	100.0	5.1	80.6	14.3
1958*	100.0	5.8	94.2	–
1959	100.0	8.0	92.0	–
1960	100.0	6.0	94.0	–

Source: *Chosunjungangnyŏngam, 1950-1960.* Quoted in Wŏn-joon Lee, "Changes in North
Korea's Agricultural and Fishery Policies," *Vantage Point* (July 1979), pp. 1-14.
*By 1958 collectivization of farming was completed.

Table 16-11. Changes and Evolution of North Korea's Agricultural Policy

Stage	Period	Agricultural Policy Basic Aims	Specific Measures
1st	1946-49	Removal of feudal patterns of land ownership and management	Land reforms; decree on irrigation; nationalization of forestry and water resources
2nd	1950-53	Increased output for military needs	Wartime mobilization
3rd	1954-59	Cooperative farming	Private farming eliminated;
4th	1960-63	Further refining of collective farming; agricultural control apparatus uniformized	The *Ch'ŏngsan-ri* method introduced; The *Ch'ŏllima* stressed; mechanization and chemicalization of agriculture
5th	1964-70	Technological, cultural, and ideological revolution in rural areas; industry contribution to agriculture stressed	Agricultural Workers Union created; farm work force mobilized; In-kind agricultural tax abolished; agricultural guidance structure reorganized
6th	1971-	Three technological revolutions stressed; farm production intensified	Gap between agricultural and industrial labors to be reduced; freeing women from household chores; gap between hard and light labor to be reduced.

Source: Adapted from Wŏn-Joon Lee, "Changes in North Korea's Agricultural and Fishery Policies," *Vantage Point* (July 1979), p. 3.

Table 6-12. Land Areas and Farm Families under Tenancy
(As end of 1945)

	Land Area[a] (1,000 chŏngbo)	Farm families[b] (1,000 families)
Japanese-owned land under tenancy (A)	230 (10%) (282)[d]	554[c]
Korean-owned land under tenancy (B)	1,240 (53%)	852[e]
Sub-total (A+B)	1,470 (63%)	1,306 (70%)
Total	2,320 (100%)	2,041 (100%)

Sources: a. Bank of Korea, 1948 Chosŏn Kyŏngje Yŏnbo (Annual Report of Korean Economy), pp. 1-29; b. Idem., pp. 1-375; c. As of February 1946, Ministry of Agriculture and Forestry, 1970. Nongji Kaehyŏk-sa [The History of Land Reform], p. 340; d. Including non-farm land, estimated as of February 1946, Idem., p. 352; e. residual number because statistics for 1945 were not available. Quoted in In-Joung Whang, "Administration of Land Reform in Korea, 1949-52" in Korea Journal (October 1984), pp. 4-20.

Table 16-13. Distributions of Farmland Ownership in South Korea,
1944 and 1956

	Pre-reform (1944)			Post-reform (1956)		
% of household	48.6	48.5	2.9	42.8	51.1	6.1
% of Farmland	0.0	0.0	63.4	17.6	64.8	17.6
Area per household (ha)	0.0	0.8	26.0	0.3	1.1	2.6

Sources: Jae-Hong Cho, "Post-1945 Land Reforms and Their Consequences in South Korea" (Ph.D. dissertation, Indiana University, 1964), p. 94; BOK, 1948, Op. Cit., pp. 1-29; and Korea Agricultural Bank, Nongŏp Yŏnbo (Agricultural Yearbook, 1959), p. 63. Readjusted table quoted in Whang, Op. Cit., p. 15.

Table 16-14. Owner-operated vs. Tenant-operated Area in South Korea

(Unit: 1,000 chŏngbo)

Year	Owner-Operated (A)	Tenant-operated (B)	Total (A+B)	% B/A+B
1945	778	1,447	2,225	65
1949	1,240	847	2,087	40
1952	2,044	43	2,087	2

Source: Ki-hyuk Pak,. "Economic Analysis of Land Reform in the Republic of Korea, 1954-55" (Ph. D. dissertation, University of Illinois, 1956), p. 81 Quoted in Whang, *Op. Cit.*, p. 15.

Table 16-15. South Korea's Farm Households by Category of Farm Size Under Cultivation

(Unit: %)

Year	Under 0.5 C* (A)	0.5-0.1 C (B)	1.0-2.0 C (C)	2.0-3.0 C (D)	3.0+ C (E)
1945	72.1% (A and B)		23.8 % (C and D)		4.1
1947	42.2	33.3	18.8	5.3	1.4
1951	42.7	35.8	17.1	4.2	0.1
1953	44.9	34.2	16.5	4.3	0.1
1960	42.9	30.1	20.7	6.0	0.3
1970	31.6	31.7	25.8	5.0	1.5*
1973	32.4	31.5	26.3	4.8	1.5

Sources: Adapted from Ki-hyuk Pak, *Op. Cit.*, p. 82; Ministry of Agriculture and Fisheries, 1974. *Yearbook of Agriculture and Fisheries Statistics*, pp. 28-29.
*C: *Chŏngbo* = 0.992 ha.

Table 16-16. *Number of South Korea's Farm Households by Category of Farm Size under Cultivation*

Year	0.1 h* or less	0.1-0.5	0.5-1.0	1.0-1.5	1.5-2.0	2.0-3.0	3.0 or over
1965 (2,507)**	69.8	831.0	793.9	414.7	228.6	139.6	29.3
1970 (2,483)	36.4	760.4	824.3	446.1	193.3	123.4	37.3
1971 (2,482)	49.7	760.4	786.3	445.6	199.6	120.1	36.2
1972 (2,452)	48.6	752.9	776.8	442.2	194.5	116.5	35.2
1973 (2,450)	52.9	741.9	771.0	443.5	201.1	118.2	37.1
1974 (2,381)	10.1	662.8	808.7	434.7	196.4	118.7	37.3
1975 (2,379)	1.9	689.1	828.2	430.7	187.2	111.7	36.0
1976 (2,336)	4.9	683.8	814.1	415.2	17?.2	104.5	32.9
1977 (2,304)	4.3	681.7	795.3	406.8	170.5	100.5	31.0
1978 (2,224)	1.3	629.9	799.2	412.3	170.5	96.7	30.3
1979 (2,162)	2.4	641.2	764.2	394.2	161.4	89.7	26.8
1980 (2,156)	14.2	597.6	747.6	438.5	190.7	107.6	31.2
1981 (2,030)	8.1	596.6	742.3	388.2	156.3	83.0	23.7
1982 (1,996)	9.3	568.0	724.6	389.4	158.4	82.8	23.0
1983 (2,000)	8.9	562.2	718.6	391.6	160.0	83.4	22.8

Source: ROK Ministry of Agriculture and Fisheries, 1984 *Nongchon Chuyojipyo* [Key Indices of Agricultural Administration], p. 16

* h = hectare.

** The figures (unit: 1,000) in the parentheses are the total farm households.

The total farm households include non-crop farm households. The percentage of non-crop farm households were 72.1 (1970), 84.0 (71), 85.0 (72), 84.6 (73), 112.5 (74), 94.3 (75), 106.0 (76), 113.6 (77), 83.6 (78), 81.9 (79), 27.9 (1980), 30.5 (81), 39.5 (82) and 51.9 (83).

Table 16-17. A Comparison of North and South Korea's Transporation
and Communication (1983, 1990)

Classification	Unit	North		South	
		1983	1990	1983	1990
Total lengths of railroads	km	4,441	5,045	6,129	6,435
(electrified)	km	(2,636)	(3,194)	(1,016)	(524)
Total length of roads	km	21,000	23,000	54,550	56,715
(expressways)	km	(240)	(354)	(1,420)	(1,551)
Automobiles	1,000	189	264	785	3,395
Stevedoring capacity	Million tons	32.8	34,900	96	224,353
Ocean-going vessels	Passenger	—	—	—	—
Airplanes	plane	17	—	101	—
International air routes	countries	3	—	30	—
	(cities)	(2)	—	(20)	—
Telephone circuits	1,000 circuits10 (Pyongyang)	—	1,740 (Seoul)	15,340	

Source: The Republic of Korea National Unification Board, "A Comparative Study of the South and North Korean Economies" (Seoul, 1985), p. 66. The 1990 figures from the Rok Economic Planning Board.

Table 16-18. Shift in North Korea's Trading Patterns by Bloc
and Economic Grouping

(Unit: US. $1,000)

Year	Gross Trade volume	Communist bloc	Non-communist countries [% of adv. + developing]	
1960	114,111	{74,667 (E)* + 39,444 (I)**}		
1962	168,889	{88,222 + 80,667}	—	—
1964	163,556	{80,667 + 82,889}	—	—
1965	178,111	{88,333 + 89,778}	—	—
1971	889,496 (100.0)	759,829 (85.1)	132,667 (14.9)	[12.9+2.0]
1972	1,052,936	809,936 (76.6)	246,000 (23.4)	[21.0+2.4]
1973	1,370,936	902,316 (65.8)	468,620 (34.2)	[27.5+6.7]
1974	1,996,036	945,906 (47.4)	1,050,100 (52.6)	[43.8+8.8]
1975	1,888,927	1,017,787 (53.9)	871,140 (46.1)	[33.6+12.5]
1976	1,632,128	933,778 (57.2)	698,350 (42.8)	[26.2+16.6]
1977	1,643,694	926,274 (56.4)	717,420 (43.6)	[22.1+21.6]
1978	2,294,034	1,256,644 (54.8)	1,037,390 (45.2)	[21.4+23.8]
1979	2,889,764	1,489,114 (51.5)	1,400,650 (48.4)	[24.0+24.4]
1980	3,180,000	—	—	
1981	2,900,000	—	—	
1982	3,300,000	—	—	
1983	2,930,000	—	—	
1984	2,400,000	—	—	
1985	2,846,600	—	—	
1986	3,345,900	—	—	
1987	4,037,000	—	—	
1988	5,021,300	—	—	
1989	4,590,200	—	—	
1990	4,776,800	—	—	

Sources: Adapted from *Bukhanch'onggam, '45-'68* (Seoul: Kongsankwonmunjeyonkuso, 1968), p. 370; IMF, Direction of Trade, Annual, 1980. Quoted in Hong-youn Lee, "Structure and Prospect of North Korean Trade," *Vantage Point*, (September 1981), pp. 1-12. Also his "Muyok kujo wa chŏnmang" *Pukhan* (July 1981), pp. 106-129; Son-keun Pae, "[North Korean] Trade Methods and Its Characteristics" (in Korean), *Pukhan* (July 1981), pp. 92-105; The ROK National Unification Board, "A Comparative Study of the South and North Korean Economies," p. 68. The data from 1984-1990 are from JETRO's quoted in *Pukhan*, 92-20 (Seoul: Korea Trade Promotion Corporation, 1992), p. 113.

*(E) = Export
**(I) = Import

Table 16-19. South Korea's Trade

(Unit: million U.S. dollars)

Year	Gross Trade	Exports		Imports [Non-classifiable]ᵃ			
1960	531.3	180.0		351.3			
1963	647.1	86.8	(58.4)ᵇ	560.3	(32.8)	0.2	8.2
1964	523.5	119.1	(37.2)	404.4	(-27.8)	0.0	2.3
1965	638.5	175.1	(47.1)	463.4	(14.6)	0.0	0.0
1966	966.7	250.3	(43.0)	716.4	(54.6)	0.0	36.7
1967	1316.4	320.2	(27.9)	996.2	(39.1)	0.0	0.8
1968	1918.4	455.4	(42.2)	1462.9	(46.8)	0.1	1.8
1969	2446.1	622.5	(36.7)	1823.6	(24.7)	0.9	0.4
1970	2819.2	835.2	(34.2)	1984.0	(8.8)	0.0	0.1
1971	3461.9	1067.6	(27.8)	2394.3	(20.7)	0.0	1.4
1972	4176.1	1624.1	(52.1)	2552.0	(5.3)	2.1	9.0
1973	7465.3	3225.0	(98.6)	4240.3	68.1)	4.7	8.3
1974	11312.3	4660.4	(38.3)	6851.8	(61.6)	33.2	62.0
1975	12355.4	5081.0	(13.9)	7274.4	(6.2)	22.5	10.9
1976	16488.9	7715.3	(51.8)	8773.6	(20.6)	3.4	20.0
1977	20857.0	10046.5	(30.2)	10810.5	(23.2)	8.3	0.3
1978	27682.5	12710.6	(26.5)	14971.9	(38.5)	214.3	240.1
1979	35394.1	15055.5	(18.4)	20338.6	(35.8)	243.7	617.8
1980	39796.6	17504.9	(16.3)	22291.7	(9.6)	761.4	917.6
1981	47485.2	21253.8	(21.4)	26131.4	(17.2)	943.2	944.8
1982	46104.2	21853.4	(2.8)	24250.8	(-7.2)	979.9	1143.2
1983	50637.3	24445.1		26192.2			
1984	59876.3	29244.9		30631.4			
1985	61418.3	30283.1		31135.7			
1986	66298.4	34714.5		31583.9			
1987	88300.7	47280.9		41019.3			
1988	112507.0	60696.4		51810.6			
1989	123842.0	62377.2		61464.8			
1990	134859.4	65015.7		69843.7			

Source: Adapted from *Major Statistics of Korean Economy 1983* (Seoul: Economic Planning Board, 1983).

a) non-classifiable countries may include the socialist bloc countries with which
South Korea has no formal diplomatic and trade relationships.

b) the figures in parentheses are the annual growth rate. The data from 1983 to 1990
are from *Korea Statistical Yearbook, 1991*, p. 255.

Table 16-20. DPRK: Projection of Major Economic Indicators
(in 1990 prices)

	Unit	1990	1995	2000
Population	Million	21.41	23.38	25.31
(Growth rate)	%	(1.83)	(1.78)	(1.60)
Workforce[a]	million	9.42	10.32	11.30
(Growth rate)	%	(1.62)	(1.84)	(1.83)
Labor Participation[b]	%	66.7	68.0	69.0
GNP	US$ billion	23.1	25.5	28.2
GNP growth rate	%	–3.7[c]	2.0	2.0
Industry structure:				
Agriculture	% in GNP	26.8	25.0	23.0
Mining & Manufacturing[d]	% in GNP	56.0	56.0	54.0
Services	$ in GNP`	17.2	19.0	23.0
GNP per capita	US$	1,064	1,091	1,114

Sources: Korea Development Institute (KDI) and ROK National Unification Board (NUB)
for 1990 figures.
a. Between 16 and 64 years of age
b. Excluding military
c. The average growth rate for 1985-1989 is 2.7%
d. Mining and manufacturing including construction

Table 16-21. Foreign Trade of the DPRK

			(US$ billion)
	1990	1995	2000
Exports	2.02	2.2	3.0
(Percentage of (GNP)	(8.7)	(8.6)	(10.6)
Imports	2.62	2.4	3.1
(Percentage of GNP)	(11.3)	(9.4)	(11.0
Gross External Debt	7.86	8.9	9.5
(Percentage of GNP)	(34.0)	(34.9)	(33.7)

Sources: *Idem.*

Table 16-22. Volume of Inter-Korean Trade

(US$1,000, approval basis)

	1989	1989	1990	Jan.-Aug. 1991
From DPRK	1,037	22,235	20,354	111,472
(% of total DPRK Export)	(0.06)	(1.14)	(1.00)	
From ROK	0	69	4,731	12,570
(% of total DPRK Import)	(0)	(0.00)	(0.18)	
Total	1,037	22,304	25,085	124,042
(%) of the DPRK Total Trade	(0.02)	(0.47)	(0.54)	

Sources: KIEP, KDI.

Table 16-23. Commodity Composition of Inter-Korean Trade

(US$1,000)

	From the DPRK		From the ROK	
1988-90	Steel	9,424	Tetron staple	2,450
	Zinc	9,740	Stocking knitting machines	2,188
	Potatoes	4,021	Cigarette filters	83
	Cement	3,946	Jumpers	69
	Others	17,568	Sugar	10
	Total	41,504	Total	4,880
1991	Farm products	17,505		1,750
	Marine products	25,821		—
	Mineral products	23,152		—
	Non-ferrous metal/steels	91,720		—
	Fabrics	2,342		7,196
	Chemical products	3,141		13,530
	Electric/electronics	—		1,560
	Others	2,315		2,140
	Total	165,996	Total	261,176

Sources: *Idem.*

Table 16-24. Major Economic Indicators of the ROK: Towards 2000

Items	Unit	1985	1990	1995	2000
GNP in current price	trillion won	78	168	317	—
Growth rate of GNP	percent/year	7.0	9.0	7.5	6.0
GNP	US$ billion	103	235	493	731
Per capita GNP	US$ thousand	2.5	5.4	10.9	15.4
Industrial structure:					
Agriculture	percent	12.8	9.1	7.0	5.0
Manufacturing	percent	30.3	29.2	27.0	25.0
SOC* and others	percent	56.9	61.7	66.0	70.0
Total population	million	40.4	43.5	45.4	47.4
Total employment	million	15.0	18.0	20.4	22.2
Unemployment rate	percent	4.0	2.4	2.4	2.4
Employment structure:					
Agriculture	percent	24.9	18.3	14.0	10.0
Manufacturing	percent	24.4	27.3	26.0	25.0
SOC and others	percent	50.7	54.4	60.0	65.0
Exports	US$ billion	30	65	120	193
Imports	US$ billion	31	70	117	188
Inflation rate, CPI	percent/year	1.4	9.5	5.0	5.0
Inflation rate, WPI	percent/year	−2.6	3.0	2.5	2.5
Exchange rate	won/US$	890	716	750	750

Sources: EPB, *The Seventh Five-Year Economic and Social Development Plan*, 1991, and
   The Bank of Korea, *Economic Statistics Yearbook*, 1991.
Notes: Figures for 1995 and 1990 are estimates under the following assumptions:
   1) Figures for 1995 are obtained using the rates of changes used in the Plan.
   2) The growth rate of GNP is assumed to be 6% a year after 1996 to 2000.
   3) The rate of increase of GNP deflator is assumed to be 5% a year after 1996 to
      2000.
   4) The exchange rates in 1995 and 2000 are assumed to be 750 *won* per US$.
   5) Industrial structure and employment structure for 1995 and 2000 are estimated on
      past experiences of the ROK and the other countries, and are a little bit different
      from the presumed assumptions of the Plan.
   6) The growth rate of total population from 1996 to 2000 is assumed to be 0.85% per
      annum.
   7) The unemployment rate is assumed as remaining constant at 2.4%.
   8) Total employment is assumed to be 44% and 47% of the total population in 1995
      and 2000, respectively.
   * SOC = Social overhead capital.

Table 16-25. Freedom House Rating, 1990-1991

	North Korea	South Korea
Political rights	7*	2
Civil liberties	7**	3
Freedom rating	Not free	Free
Human development index	0.789 (medium)***	0.903 (high)
The nineteen-year record of the survey of freedom (1973-1991)	Not free	Partly free (1973-1987) Free (1988-1990) Partly free (1991)

Sources: *Freedom in the World, 1990-1991* by Freedom House Survey Team (New York: Freedom House, 1991).

   * On each scale 1 represents the most free and 7 the least free. States rated 1 come closest to the ideals suggested by the checklist questions, and category 7 includes places where political rights are absent or virtually nonexistent.

  ** States rated 1 in civil liberties come closest to the ideals of freedoms of expression, assembly and demonstration, religion and association. At category 7, countries have virtually no freedom.

 *** The Human Development Index (HDI) from the U.N. Development Program combines life expectancy, literacy and real per capita GDP, and carries the designation "low," "medium" or "high," depending on the country's degree of deprivation of each of these variables.

Notes

1. Jonathan Swift, *Gulliver's Travels* (New York: A Signet Classic, 1960), p. 99.
2. See, for instance, Ha-jong Yŏn, "North Korea's Economic Trends and Policy Decisions (I), *"Vantage Point* (October 1986), pp. 1-13. *The People's Korea*, (March 2, 1985) published by pro-North Korean residents in Japan, reported that North Korea's industrial output had an annual average growth rate of 12.2% during the second 7-Year Plan, and its national income increased 1.8 times over its 1977 figure. The 1970, 1977 and 1984 figures are as follows:

	1970	1977	1984
Electricity (mil. kwh) :	18.5	28.0	53.0
Coal (mil. tons) :	27.5	55.0	80.0
Steel (mil. tons) :	2.2	4.0	7.4
Cement (mil. tons) :	4.0	8.0	14.0
Chemical Fertilizer :	1.5	3.3	5.0
Textiles (mil. meters) :	400.0	580.0	840.0
Aquatic Products (mil. tons) :	1.2	1.6	3.5
Grain :	5.0	8.5	10.0
Shoes : (mil.)	40.0	80.0	120.0
Average Span of Life :	38.0 (pre-'45)	73.0 ('76)	74.0 ('84)
Universities :	129.0 ('70)	155.0 ('76)	216.0 ('84)
Technicians and Specialists: (mil)		1.0 ('76)	1.25.0 ('84)

3. Joseph S. Chung, "Divergent Economic Systems and the Consequences for Economic Performance and Structure: A Small Country Version," unpublished paper (1983).
4. See Yŏng-kyu Kim, "The Second 7-Year Plan of North Korea: Its Performance and Outlook" *Vantage Point* (January 1985), pp. 1-11. *The Social and cultural Indicators of North and South Korea* (in Korean) (Seoul: The Ministry of National Unification Board, 1990), p. 56.
5. South Korean specialists' analyses and North Korean official claims on the actual performance of the second 7-year plan are different. For details, see Footnotes 2 and 4 above.
6. The South Korean data is mostly from *Major Statistics of Korean Economy 1983* (Seoul: Economic Planning Board, 1983). Also, *World Development Report, 1984* (New York: Oxford University Press, 1984). The sources of North Korean data are found in Tables 9-1, 9-2 and 9-3. The 1990 data from

Korea Statistical Yearbook, 1991, p. 498.

7. Sidney Klein, *The Patterns of Land Tenure Reform in East Asia After World War II* (New York: Bookman Associates, 1958), p. 84. Quoted in In-Joung Whang, "Administration of Land Reform in Korea, 1949-52," *Korea Journal* (October 1984), pp. 4-21.

8. In-ho Yu, *Han'guk Nongji Chedo-ui Yŏn'gu* [The Study of Korea's Land System] (Seoul: Pakmun-dang, 1975), pp. 54-64.

9. *Ibid.*, p. 92.

10. Klein, *Op. Cit., pp.* 102-103.

11. Whang, *Op. Cit.*, p. 15.

12. Yŏng-kyu Kim, "A Comparison of North and South Korea's Economic Development" (in Korean) *Pukhan* (April 1981), pp. 83-85. See also, *Northeast Asia and North and South Korea* (in Korean) (Seoul: Pyŏngwha Yŏnkuwŏn, 1990), p. 190.

13. *Ibid.* Also, *Major Indicators of Korean Economy* 1983, p. 64.

14. *A Comparative Study of the South and North Korean Economies* (Seoul: National Unification Board, 1984), p. 45. (The figures for North Korea is estimated by the South Korean government. Hence, the estimates tend to be lower, if they were close to the actual figures at all).

15. For critical studies of the New Village Movement, see, for instance, Mich Moore, "Mobilization and Disillusion in Rural Korea: The Saemaul Movement in Retrospect," *Pacific Affairs* 57 (Winter 84-85): 577-598; David H. Grubbs, "Internationalizing the Saemaul Undong," paper delivered at the 1984 APSA Meeting in Washington, 30 August-2 September 1984. Also, Il Chul Kim and Young-il Chung, "Socio-Economic Study of Small Farmers in Korea" (in Korean) *Social Science Research Report I* (Seoul: Seoul National University, 1977).

16. US CIA's *The World Factbook, 1985*, reported North Korea's electric power, its output and per capita to be 5.9 million kw capacity, 40 billion kwh and 1,992 kwh. South Korea's electric power, its output and per capita in 1985 to be 15.5 million kw, 56.49 billion kwh and 1,325 kwh capacity, respectively. Also, it is interesting to note here that North Korea's 8th Supreme People's Assembly (convened on December 29, 1986) created the new Ministry of Atomic Industry in the Administration Council for the first time. See *The New Korea Times*, 3 January 1987. The 1990 data is from the ROK Government Statistics 141 (September 16, 1991): 41-43.

17. *A Comparative Study of South and North Korean Economies*, p. 52. Also, *Nampukhan Gyŏngje Hyŏnwhang pigyo, 1981* (Seoul: Kukt'ot'ongilwŏn, 1981), p. 36. The 1983 figures from the same source are found in *Joongang Ilbo*, 5 January 1985. The 1990 data from the Rok Government Statistics 141 (September 16, 1991), 41-43.

18. The sources are the same as Note 16 above. the US CIA reported that North Korea's crude steel production in 1984 was 4.0 million metric tons as compared with South Korea's 13.0 million metric tons. The 1990 data is from the *Korea Statistical Yearbook*, 1991, p. 176.
19. *A Comparative Study of the South and North Korean Economies*, p. 59. See also, *the Korea Statistical Yearbook*, 1991, p. 179.
20. *Ibid.*, p. 61.
21. *Ibid.*, p. 62.
22. *Major Statistics of Korean Economy 1983*, p. 141. Also, *The Korea Herald*, 29 December 1984 and 1 January 1987. North Korea's Deputy Director of Tourist Bureau claimed recently that about 100,000 foreign tourists visited North Korea in 1991. For details, see *North Korea News*, No. 646, pp. 5-6. Another way of measuring North Korea's isolation and South Korea's openess is to examine their respective memberships in international organizations. North Korea is a member of some 11 international organizations, while South Korea is a member of some 18 international organizations; both belong to 9 organizations together:

International Organizations	North Korea	South Korea
ADB		+
G-77	+	+
INTELSAT		+
NAM	+	
WFTU	+	
FAO	+	+
GATT		+
IAEA	+	+
IBRD		+
ICAO	+	+
IDA		+
IFAD		+
IFC		+
IMF		+
IMO		+
ITU	+	+
UNESCO	+	+
UPU	+	+
WHO	+	+
WMO	+	+

Sources: Adapted from US CIA's *The World Factbook, 1985*, pp. 286-287.

23. *A Comparative Study of the South and North Korean Economies*, p. 68. Also, Nam-kwŏn Kim, "The Reality of North Korea's Foreign Economic Cooperation" (in Korean) *Pukhan* (July 1982), pp. 116-135. Yŏng-gyu Kim, "An Analysis of North Korea's Foreign Trade Structure," *Unification Policy Quarterly* 161 (1983): 187. UN Conference on Trade and Development's (UNCTAD) *Yearbook of International Commodity Statistics, 1985,* reported similar differences between the North and the South in total value of imports and exports of 18 IPC (integrated program for commodities):

Unit: Millions of US Dollars

Year	North Korea		South Korea	
	Imports	Exports	Imports	Exports
1972	60.9	—	287.5	202.2
1973	79.6	2.9	566.2	324.7
1974	79.4	0.6	766.3	289.8
1975	146.0	1.2	850.7	368.5
1976	91.8	1.5	1008.5	478.7
1977	98.2	0.4	1254.7	572.4
1978	104.5	—	1552.2	649.7
1979	141.0	—	2285.6	765.5
1980	162.0	—	2725.9	859.3
1981	146.7	—	2699.6	861.3
1982	138.6	—	2383.0	489.2
1983	129.2	—	2379.9	412.0

Source: UN Conference on Trade and Development, *Yearbook of International Commodity Statistics, 1985* (New York: United Nations, 1985), pp. 88-89.

24. *The Korea Herald,* 21 October 1983. For instance, South Korea's annual average growth rates of exports (f.o.b) and imports (c.i.f) are:

Period	Exports (%)	Imports (%)
1950-1983	29.7	19.2
1950-1960	1.4	17.2
1960-1970	39.6	21.3
1970-1980	37.2	29.1
1970-1975	49.2	33.7
1975-1983	20.6	18.8
1975-1976	51.8	20.6
1976-1977	30.2	23.2
1977-1978	26.5	38.5
1978-1979	18.4	35.8
1979-1980	16.3	9.6
1980-1981	21.4	17.2
1981-1982	2.8	-7.2
1982-1983	11.0	8.0

Source: UNCTAD's *Handbook of International Trade and Development Statistics, 1985 Supplement* (New York: UN, 1985), pp. 20-21.

25. *A Comparative Study of the South and North Korean Economies*, pp. 69-70. South Korea's export diversification is still slow but steadily increasing. For instance, the number of commodities exported by South Korea in 1970 was 22, but it was 151 in 1982. For details, see UNCTAD's 1985 Supplment, p. 246.

26. *Pukhan Chŏnsŏ, 1945-1980* (Seoul: Keuktong Munje Yŏnkuso, 1980), pp. 398-399. Also, Youn-soo Kim, "Economic Cooperation Between North Korea and Comecon Member Nations," *Vantage Point* (February 1985), pp. 1-11.

27. According to *1981 Yearbook of International Trade Statistics* (New York: United Nations, 1982), South Korea established trade relations, though miniscule, with the former Soviet Union and Eastern European countries since 1976. For details, see p. 565.

28. *Major Statistics of Korean Economy 1983*, pp. 225-234.

29. North Korea's foreign debts are estimated at around 3.5 billion dollars as of 1982. See, for instance, Youn-soo Kim, *Op. Cit.*

30. *Ibid. A Comparative Study of the South and North Korean Economies*, pp. 70-72. The 1990 data from the EPB.

31. See *Korea to the Year 2000: Implications for Australia and Policy Responses*, National Korean Studies Centre, the East Asia Analytical Unit of the Australian Department of Foreign Affairs and Trade, 7 July 1992.

32. *Ibid.*

33. T. F. Juster, "Conceptualizing and Measuring the Generation and Distribution of Well-being," paper presented at the 10th World Congress of Sociology, Mexico City in 1982; L. Winggo, "The Quality of Life: Toward A Micro-economic Definition," *Urban Studies* 10 (1973): 3-18; W. Zapf, "The Policy as a Monitor of the Quality of Life," *American Behavioral Scientist* 20 (May/June 1974): 57-67. These are quoted in Doh C. Shin and Wayne Snyder, "Economic Growth, Quality of Life, and Development Policy: A Case Study of South Korea," *Comparative Political Studies* (July 1983), pp. 195-213.

34. Abraham Maslow, *Motivations and Personality* (New York: Harper, 1954); Harold D. Lasswell and 'Abraham Kaplan, *Power and Society: A Framework for Political Inquiry* (New Haven: Yale University Press, 1963), pp. 83-88.

35. Shin and Snyder, *Op. Cit.*, pp. 199-201.

36. Vilfredo Pareto, *The Mind and Society*, ed. Arthur Livingston, trans. Andrew Bongiorno and Arthur Livingston (New York: Harcourt, Brace, 1935), Vol. 3, p. 1001.

37. John Stuart Mill, *On Liberty* (New York: Everyman edition, 1931), p. 73.

38. Thomas Hobbes, *Leviathan*, ed, C. B. Macpherson (Harmondsworth, Middlesex, England: Pelican Classics), p. 264.

39. Leszek Kolakowski, "Marxism and Human Rights," *Daedalus* (Fall 1983), p. 88 and p. 90.

40. Raymond D. Gastil et al, *Freedom in the World: Political Rights and Civil Liberties 1978* (New York: Freedom House, 1978), pp. 44-45. The Data for South Korean government suppression and deprivation of basic civil and political human rights for 1968 to 1984 were collected by Pae. For details, see Sung M. Pae, *Testing Democratic Theories in Korea* (University Press of America, 1986), pp. 105-107.

41. For details, see *Pukhan ei kukminsoduk Kenyom kwa GNP ch'ukybangbŏp* [North Korean Concept of National Income and the Estimating Methods of GNP] by South Korean Ministry of Unification Board, April 1984. US CIA's *The World Factbook, 1985*, reported that North Korea's GNP per capita in 1984 (in current dollars) was $1,170. The 1990 data from *The Social-cultural Indicators of North and South Korea* (in Korean) (Seoul: National Unification Board, 1990), p. 56.

42. For details, see Man-ki Lee, *Hankuk Kyŏngjeron* [On Korean Economy] (Seoul: Ilsin-sa, 1984), pp. 400-401. Chu, for instance, illustrated that the worsening trend of income distribution in Korea throughout the seventies showed definite signs of reversal by 1982. For details, see Hakchoong Choo, "Estimation of Size Distribution of Income and Its Sources of Change in Korea, 1982," *Korean Social Science* 12 (1985): 90-105.

43. *World Development Report 1984*, p. 249. But UNCTAD's *Trade and Development Report, 1985*, reported otherwise. South Korea's total debt service/exports were 11.6 in 1978 and 14.2 in 1983. For details, see Tables 16-20a.

44. *Major Statistics of Korean Economy 1983*, p. 17. 1990 data from the ROK Statistics Bureau.

45. *World Development Report 1984*, p. 219. UNCTAD reported South Korea's annual average growth rates of consumer price indices as follows:

Period	Rate (%)
1970-1980	16.0
1970-1975	14.3
1976-1977	10.2
1977-1978	14.5
1978-1979	18.3
1979-1980	28.7
1980-1981	21.3
1981-1982	7.3
1982-1983	3.4

Source: UNCTAD's *Handbook of International Trade and Development Statistics 1985 Supplement*, p. 56.

46. For details, see *Joogang Ilbo*, 2 January 1985.

47. Man-ki Lee, *Op. Cit.*, pp. 357-360. *Major Statistics of Korean Economy 1983*, p. 256. As of 1991, for instance, the water supply rate was 80.0% and the

needed sewage system supplied was 33%. *The Weekly Government News* (December 23, 1991), p. 11.

48. *World Development Report 1984,* p. 265. UNCTAD's *Statistical Pocket Book* (1984) reported that in South Korea there were 1,438 people per doctor in 1982, 77% of the people had access to safe water, illiteracy was 12.4% and 7.7 people out of 100 had telephones.

49. *The UN Statistical Yearbook 1983* (New York: United Nations, 1984), p. 454. *World Development Report 1984,* p. 219. According to one study, as of 1984, 48% of the people in South Korea receive some form of medical insurance benefits. For details, see *Hankook Ilbo* (1984). The 1990 data from the ROK Statistics Bureau.

50. For a recent study of North Korea's educational system, see Sung Chul Yang, "Socialist Education in North Korea," in C. I. Eugene Kim and B. C. Koh, eds., *Journey to North Korea: Personal Perceptions* (Berkeley: University of California Press, 1983), pp. 63-83.

51. *World Development Report 1984,* p. 267.

52. *The Four Books,* trans. James Legge (New York: Paragon Book Reprint Corp., 1966), p. 161.

53. *Ibid.,* p. 704.

54. Aristotle, *Politics of Aristotle,* ed. and trans. Ernest Barker (New York: Oxford University Press, 1962), pp. 281-282.

PART VI

CRITICAL ISSUES
AND PROBLEMS

CHAPTER 17

THE SEIZURE OF POWER IN NORTH AND SOUTH KOREAN POLITICS

> *Whoever could make two ears of corn or two blades of grass to grow upon a spot of ground where only one grew before, would deserve better of mankind, and do more essential service to his country than the whole race of politicians put together.*

Jonathan Swift[1]

Introduction

As a divided nation Korea can provide comparativists with one of the most ideal living laboratories. Since the launching of the two separate governments in 1948, two entirely different political systems, economic models, and societal patterns have been in operation in North and South Korea. Because Korea was and still is a nation of cultural and linguistic homogeneity, whatever variations and differences existing in their performances may be attributable primarily to the implementation of two diametrically opposed models now in existence for over forty years. Divided Korea can provide scholars and practitioners with living examples of the on-going debate on the preferences and performances of the totalitarian versus the democratic (or authoritarian) political systems, the command versus the market economic models, and the mobilization versus the motivation (participation) societal patterns. As Paige rightly suggested, one of the great challenges to contemporary social science is to explore the theoretical implications of what has happened in bisected societies such as Korea.[2]

Strategically, few areas in the world today are so ideologically polarized, heavily armed and politically ruptured as is divided Korea. Korea is the area where the interests of the world's four major powers—the United States, Russia, Japan and China—intersect. Divided Korea has been, in short, a microcosm of the divided world, as a unified Korea would be a barometer of new world unity.

Economically, South Korea has been one of the most rapidly developing countries in the world, at least since the mid-60's. Notwithstanding its closed autarchic economic systems and totalitarian political control, North Korea, too, has emerged from the ashes of the Korean War with an economic growth, relatively higher than many of its now demised socialist fraternal countries.[3]

The current politics of North Korea and South Korea is, however, not commensurate with their respective economic performances. North Korea's political problems are created in essence by President Kim Il Sung. The decision by the Worker's Party of Korea (WPK) to groom Kim Jong Il, Kim's eldest son, as his official successor, the excess of Kim's personal and familial cult and North Korea's increasing isolation from the international community are the cases in point. South Korea, meanwhile wrestles with its own political difficulties: the scars of the Kwangju uprising in May 1980 remain; the ruling party and the opposition are at loggerheads over the question of local autonomy election; and large-scale land scandals and the second mobile telephone flipflop plagued the Roh Regime which appeared to be the tip of a much larger societal and governmental corruption.

This chapter will focus only on the seizure of power question in North and South Korean politics. On the surface, at least both North Korea and South Korea have been suffering from similar political symptoms—an irregular political seizure, though its diagnoses and prognoses are miles apart. North Korea's father-son succession issue appears not only irregular, but peculiar. It is unusual even by communist standards; it deviates from the typical patterns of political succession in communist regimes. The absence of peaceful transfer of power in South Korea from 1948 until 1988 had been irregular, but not uncommon, as it frequently occurs among most non-Western nations. At the heart of the North Korean succession question is *sung-gye* [succession],[4] that is, "who succeeds whom?" The crux of the South Korean problem is *gyo-ch'e* [transfer]—how to transfer power from one regime (or party) to the other.

To put it differently, succession is concerned mainly with "the personnel of power," whereas the transfer of power or a regime change focuses on "the mechanism of power."[5] In the former, the primary task of a successor is to maintain continuity. Specifically, the Kim Il Sung-Kim Jong Il succession deals with the change of leadership—from the present "leader" Kim senior to the future leader Kim junior. This leadership change, according to North Korean officials, reflects an extra-legal and extra-constitutional mandate of the "people."[6] In the latter, the predecessor is replaced or removed by the new party (regime) to implement a new set of policies, programs or platforms. In short, North Korea's succession issue centers around the crisis of leadership in a one-party state,[7] while South Korea's transfer of power issue revolves around the crisis of legitimacy in a multi-party political framework, at least, assured on paper by the constitution.

North Korea's Succession Problem

To begin with, one caveat is in order. Although the WPK's Sixth Congress in 1980 formalized Kim Jong Il as his father's successor, the succession question is by no means settled. Not only is it unsettled, but it is most likely to be a potential source of political and military instability on the Korean Peninsula as well as power struggles within the WPK ruling circles. Particularly, South Korea is apprehensive of North Korea's political and military unpredictability, arising from the succession question. Within the WPK's ruling circles, it can serve as a catalyst for renewed power struggles between pro-and anti-Kim Jong Il succession groups. Especially, a generational conflict may ensue between the young party cadres in their 30's and 40's who support the Kim-Kim succession and the old party veterans in their 50's or older who oppose it or vice versa. From this standpoint, the WPK's 1980 decision has generated a new political succession problem rather than resolved it. It simply officialized Kim Jong Il as an "heir-presumptive."[8] It was only the first round of "succession struggle."[9] The father-son succession campaign in North Korea began as early as September 1973 when Kim Jong Il replaced his uncle Kim Yŏng-ju (Kim Il Sung's only surviving younger brother) and took charge of the powerful Organization and Guidance Department of the WPK Secretariat.[10] The succession decision is a political process, not an outcome; it is more a *modus vivendi* than a fait accompli. Too many internal and external political exigencies still exist to lay the succession decision to rest. The Rangoon Incident of October 9, 1983, in which 21 South Korean and Burmese were killed, including the former South Korean President Chun's closest advisers and top cabinet ministers, may be seen from such perspective. The 1986 "news stories" of Kim Il Sung's death, which turned out to be a hoax (the bogus news circulated for at least three days from November 15 till 17), is another such contingency.

Reasons and Rationale

Three official explanations and justifications are provided by the WPK for the 1980 succession decision. One is the need for the continuation and the ultimate completion of revolutionary struggles and socialist construction instituted by Kim Il Sung and the WPK. This task cannot be accomplished in one generation and, thus, must be carried on by the next generation. A new leader must meet three general qualifications to carry out this task: i) he must be absolutely loyal to the Great Leader; ii) he must belong to the new generation (note here that this particular requirement automatically disqualifies Kim Il Sung's brother, Yŏng-ju, once the alleged successor-designate, as well as some of Kim Il Sung's closest associates and comrades-in-arms of the anti-Japanese guerrilla years, such as Pak Sŏng-ch'ŏl, Ch'oe Hyŏn and O Chin-u of the so-called Partisan Group); and iii) he must undergo a rigorous preparation.[11] Further, the North Korean officials insist that Kim Jong Il is the best qualified candidate since he embodies the spirit of the new revolutionary generation (observe here that the current ruling oligarchs, the so-called Partisan Group in North Korea, are fast becoming gerontocrats like their counterparts in the former Soviet Union or the Long Marchers in China). He is and will be absolutely loyal to his father and he is thoroughly familiar with his father's revolutionary ideas and tasks.

Two, a new leader must fill the shoes of the Great Leader. The North Korean official publications shower Kim Jong Il with superlatives and accolades in increasing frequency and intensity, nearly matching those reserved for his father. The phrases—"genius," "brilliant leadership," "uncommon wisdom," "exceptional morality," "Party Center" and "great leader" (*Widae Han Yŏngdoja*) are attributed to Kim junior. Interestingly, the photographs of Kim Jong Il standing next to his father have been appearing in the official North Korean publications, such as *Nodong Sinmun and the Pyongyang Times* with increasing frequency.

A case serves to illustrate the fanaticism involving Kim junior's new cult-building. The thesis he wrote as a student at the Kim Il Sung University was declared so exceptional and extraordinarily profound by his own professor that the latter would become a pupil of Jong Il than his teacher. A list of his extraordinary achievements is indeed long: a revision of the entire curriculum in political economy at the Kim Il Sung University; the formalization of Kim Il Sungism; the introduction of automation into industry; the construction of the Aprok (Yalu) River irrigation system; the construction of the Chang-kwang Street in Pyongyang; the construction of the Mt. Wang-je revolutionary site; the installation of a 4 kilometer long conveyor belt from the Unyul Mine in South Hwanghae Province to the West Sea (the Yellow Sea); the creation of a new revolutionary art form called "p'ibada" [Sea of Blood]; the introduction of "speed battles" in economic construction; and the creation of and the leadership role in the "three revolutions small teams" (thought, technology and culture).[12] In short, the son is as "great" if not greater than his father. A North Korean official spokesman, in fact, reportedly said that "he (Jong Il) is another Kim Il Sung."[13]

In contrast to the North Korean official publications showering adorations on Kim Jong Il, the South Korean and Western assessment of him is mostly negative. He is typically portrayed in the South as a man of "violent, stubborn and adventuresome character." One Western diplomat who has met him remarked that Jong Il lacks "his father's magnetism and seems always (to be) shy."[14] Seen from North Korean documentary films, a few things can be gleaned. Kim junior wears glasses, and he is shorter than his father; he looks unhappy and nervous; and he is glum and less sure of himself, which contrasts sharply with his father, who often smiles, is at ease and self-confident. At a minimum, one objective difference between the father and the son can easily be discerned. When Kim senior at the age of 33 in 1945 emerged in North Korea as the rising political star, he had behind him some ten years of harsh and hardy anti-Japanese guerrilla activities. Since 1945 he built the army (Korean People's Army), the party (WPK), and the state itself (DPRK), in addition to having ruled North Korea for over forty years. By contrast, when Kim junior surfaced as the head of the Organization and Guidance Department of the WPK Secretariat at the age of 33 in 1973, he had led a rather sheltered and privileged life. He had attended the Mangyongdae Revolutionary Academy, an exclusive school for sons, daughters and relatives of revolutionaries. He had graduated from the Kim Il Sung University majoring in political economy, and he had reportedly trained and studied briefly at the East German Air Force Academy. But nothing in his background even remotely resembles his father's revolutionary past and political experiences.[15]

Three, there is a need to take preventive measures, that is, to avoid and preempt political turmoils and power struggles which occur frequently after the death of leaders in the socialist fraternal countries, as they occurred with the demise of Lenin, Stalin and Mao. The notion is to designate a political successor well in advance, while the present leader is still in power, to resolve the thorny succession problem which usually erupts after the leader dies. The Chinese experience, though it was not a father-son succession case, has proven otherwise. Lin Biao, the Defense Minister during the Cultural Revolution period, was designated as the official successor of Mao, and chiefly for that purpose, the Chinese Communist Party Constitution was amended in 1969 to include the following passage, which is not only unprecedented in the annals of the Communist party constitutions but, for that matter, in the history of all constitutional documents as well:

> Comrade Lin Biao has consistently held high the great red banner of Mao Zedong ['s] Thought and has most loyally and resolutely carried out and defended Comrade Mao Zedong's proletarian revolutionary line. Comrade Lin Biao is Comrade Mao Zedong's close comrade-in-arms and successor.[16]

The present post-Mao politics in China has demonstrated that "constitutionalizing" of the official successor designate is a futile exercise. Ironically, Lin was accused of involvement in an abortive coup to overthrow Mao and was reportedly killed somewhere on the Chinese-Soviet border when his single-engine plane failed in his escape flight in 1971.[17] After Mao's death in 1976, the de-Maoization campaign began, and to the present, there is no visible sign of his revolutionary line reviving in Chinese politics. The official rationales provided for Lin to succeed Mao are strikingly similar to those given in support of Kim junior succeeding his father except that the WPK has not yet stated in the preamble of its constitution to accommodate the Kim-Kim succession line and that Lin was not Mao's son. To that extent, the fate of the Mao-Lin succession issue presages the ultimate outcome of the Kim-Kim succession.

Beyond North Korea's official reasons for the succession decision, there are a few other explanations for the father-son succession line, which is not only unprecedented in the history of socialist politics but incompatible with, if not in direct contradiction to, orthodox communist ideology. The first view is what Thomas Hobbes called the "artificial eternity." In *Leviathan,* Hobbes wrote that if the monarch, being mortal, dies without an artificial eternity, that is, the right of succession, man will "return into the condition of war."[18] He asserted that in a democracy, "whole assembly cannot fail, unless the multitude that are to be governed fail." Likewise, "in an aristocracy, when any "member" of the assembly dies, the election of another into his room [place or position] belongs to the assembly, as the sovereign, to whom belongs the choosing of all counsellors and officers." "The greatest difficulty about the right of succession is in monarchy."[19] In modern parlance, one-man rule, whether it is Communist totalitarian political system or an authoritarian political system, needs "artificial eternity" similar to that of the Hobbesian monarchy to prevent the condition of anarchy following the death of a monarch.

Closely related to the Hobbesian thesis is the prevailing view that the father-son succession line in North Korea will lead to dynasty-building or the creation of the "first Communist monarchy" which is analogous to the hereditary succession in the medieval monarchical political tradition.[20] Dong Bok Lee, for instance, contends that the hereditary succession of power in North Korea is "an inevitable consequence of the elder Kim's irrevocable commitment to the dream of founding a dynasty of his own, and of his family, first in the northern half of the divided country and then in the whole of the peninsula.[21] Hence, according to Lee, the North Korean support of the father-son succession for the continuation of the unfinished revolutionary task of socialist construction and reunification amounts to nothing but a pretext to "legitimize the dynastic succession."[22]

The third view, meanwhile, espouses that the North Korean father-son succession decision is not a ploy by Kim to build his dynasty but rather a political aberration arising chiefly from the prolonged one-man-dictatorship which can occur in any Communist, totalitarian or an authoritarian political system. If Franco of Spain, Mao of China or Tito of Yugoslavia had a son like Kim Il Sung, their political coteries could easily have advocated similar father-son succession. If the former President Park Chung Hee of South Korea had had an opportunity to continue his authoritarian rule, would a similar father-son succession issue have arisen? In the 50s when the first Korean President Syngman Rhee, who was childless, adopted a son of his close political associate Yi Ki-bung, similar political speculations concerning the father-son succession arose. The implementation of Taiwan's Chiang Kai-shek—Chiang Ching-kuo line in 1975 (or, India's Nehru-Indira Gandhi—Rajiv Gandhi and Haiti's Francois Duvalier—Jean Claude Duvalier succession in 1971) can, also, be seen in this light. This matter of father-son succession can be construed as an aberrant (not necessarily bad, if the successor is qualified) political by-product of a prolonged autocratic rule where an eligible son (daughter or wife, for that matter) happens to be present to take over the helm.[23]

The fourth interpretation advanced by Chong-sik Lee is closer to the rationale offered by North Korea. Lee asserts that the selection of Jong Il to succeed Kim Il Sung was his (Kim Il Sung's) answer to solving the dual problem of simultaneously modernizing the country and sustaining the revolutionary zeal; it is his attempt to prolong the WPK's role as the mainstay of ideological revolution in the face of the strong currents of modernization that might smother the revolutionary spirit. Kim wishes, according to Lee, that his "revolutionary cause be pushed forward by his son whose loyalty he trusts above all others."[24]

The fifth view by Hannah Arendt is noteworthy, though not readily relevant to the North Korean case. She argues that "the absence of a ruling clique has made the question of a successor to the totalitarian dictator especially baffling and troublesome." She further points out that this problem has plagued all usurpers of power, but "none of the totalitarian dictators ever tried the old method of establishing a dynasty and appointing their sons."[25] (The Kim-Kim case illustrates otherwise; this may not lead to dynasty-building, but certainly in this case the son is appointed.) Her view is based on the premise that under totalitarian conditions, knowledge of the labyrinth of transmission belts equals supreme power, and every appointed successor who actually comes to know what is going on is automatically removed after a certain time. Further, she argues that the succession is not overly important because no special qualities or training are needed for the job; anyone who happens to hold the appointment at the moment of the present ruler's death can rule, because no power-thirsty rivals will dispute his legitimacy.[26] In other words, as techniques of government, she believes, the totalitarian devices appear simple and ingeniously effective; the devices such as the multiplicity of the transmission belts and the confusion of the hierarchy secure the dictator's "complete independence of all his inferiors and make possible the swift and surprising changes in policy." In short, "the body politic of the country is shock-proof because of its shapelessness.[27]

In a similar vein, Friedrich and Brzezinski contend that an adulation for a totalitarian leader and the development of a vacuum around him create a most dangerous hiatus "the moment this mortal god dies." They wrote further that "in the nature of things, the leader has not been able to designate a successor of his choice; even if he had, it would leave such a person without real support after the leader is dead. Indeed, such a designation might well be the kiss of death."[28] Will the younger Kim face the same kind of fate? For Lin Biao, his designation as Mao's successor has indeed turned out to be the "kiss of death." From a somewhat different perspective, Welsh concludes that the absence of regularized elite succession procedures, the relatively great importance of personal patronage and loyalties and the presence of relatively intense interpersonal political competition tend to create a substantial number of "meteoric" political careers—rapid ascendance followed by equally rapid fall.[29] At a minimum, as Rush pointed out, there is no way of ensuring that "a new incumbent will inherit his predecessor's powers."[30]

Two additional interpretations can be made. From Kim Il Sung's point of view, the prospect that his own son will inherit his power may provide an immeasurable source of psychological satisfaction. The older Kim Il Sung (1912-) becomes, the less secure he probably feels; the higher he is elevated outwardly by the WPK-led cult-campaign, the emptier he may feel about his inner life. Under such a state of mind, the prospect of his son continuing his power serves, perhaps, as a security blanket for his inner void.

From the point of view of Kim's potential political rivals, by formalizing the official successor, they are removing themselves from being the target of Kim's suspicion that they are plotting against him, or that they are anxiously waiting in the wing for his death (although some of them undoubtedly are awaiting for that moment). Stalin's so called "Doctors' Plot,"[31] his last suspicion before his death, is a typical case. The formalization of the succession line serves as a safety-valve for those key ruling group, albeit a temporary one, against an actual or a potential paranoia of an aging autocrat.

Scenarios and Schemes

Three possible exit scenarios of Kim Il Sung, the warrior-founder of North Korea and the longest ruling autocrat in the world today, can be hypothesized: The first is what I call the "fade-away" scenario. The earlier rumor that a lump at the back of Kim's head was cancerous turned out to be false. He may, thus, live and stay in power for some time. Instead of dying in illness or by violence, he will fade away, true to his soldierly past. Hence, the piecemeal abdication of his political power will result with the gradual failing of his health. The 1986 hoax about his "death" aside (perhaps this was his "death" act one and more may follow before his actual death), all the indications so far pinpoint this scenario.

The second is the short-term prospect scenario. Kim may stay in power no more than five or six years. Although a wide range of unpredictability accompanies this kind of star-gazing, the second scenario is less likely to occur, for all the reports confirm that he is healthy and alert.

The third exit scenario, the sudden or violent death of Kim seems the least likely since virtually no opposition to Kim's rule exists in North Korea, although a palace coup or a conspiracy is always within the realm of possibilities. Still two examples make this scenario least likely to occur. One was the recent bogus stories of Kim's "death" itself. The other is the reminder that in seventy years after the first emergence of a communist state in Russia, a few heads of state in communist nations died in office; some lost their power or stepped down from office by party purges and/or for other reasons, but no one has, so far at least, been removed from power by violent demise through assassinations or bloody palace coups, unless one presages the demise of communism itself, as we have witnessed in Eastern Europe and the former Soviet Union.

Closely related to Kim's political exit scenarios is the method used for the Kim-Kim succession, which can be bloody or bloodless. Thus far, Kim Il Sung's transfer of power to Jong Il has been gradual, piecemeal and incremental with little or no bloodshed. If, however, the present Kim-Kim succession process is only the initial phase, the nature and the scope of the succession method cannot be known until the succession process is fully finalized one way or the other.

Finally, four possible formats for Kim junior's political take-over may be theorized. Kim Jong Il's assumption of power, if realized, can be nominal. He will become a figurehead, and the real power may rest with one or a number of more seasoned and older political veterans. Under this format, his political life will be short-lived; his figurehead status will last until a strong man or men consolidate the power. The most logical, yet the least likely outcome, would be the emergence of Kim junior as the undisputed autocratic leader like his father. This is what the current Kim-Kim succession-makers are hoping to accomplish, but it is quite unlikely to happen since Kim junior lacks his father's political finesse, acumen and charisma.[32] The third is the formation of a collective leadership, a familiar triumvirate leadership structure represented by party, military and state. Under this plan Kim junior may last as a nominal figurehead until he himself or another strong man, comparable to the present Kim Il Sung emerges. Under this particular format which is the most likely case, intense power struggles within the top party leadership are inevitable; the outcome and the ultimate victor of these struggles are unpredictable. The last possible format is familial.[33] Kim junior's uncle, Kim Yŏng-ju, and his step-mother, Kim Sŏng-ae, (and her own sons and daughters) may collectively gang up against Kim junior in the power struggle. Or, a conspiracy between his uncle or his step-mother with potential political rivals within the WPK to oust him is not an impossibility. A *Dan-jong ae-sa* tragedy, a classic power struggle between the old uncle and the young nephew during the formative years of the Yi Dynasty can be repeated.

In conclusion, the heart of the North Korean political succession question is the personality: Who will succeed Kim Il Sung and how? Who will emerge as the new leader? Will he be as powerful as Kim Il Sung? Will there be changes under his new leadership? The official designation of Kim Junior as the successor notwithstanding, the answers to these questions are not readily available. The death of Kim senior will be only the beginning of the North Korean political succession "act one."

South Korea's Transfer-of-Power Question

For the past forty years and more, if continuity marks North Korean politics, discontinuity characterizes South Korean politics. Kim Il Sung has ruled North Korea ever since the launching of the DPRK in 1948, and the power struggles have been limited to the ruling circles of the WPK. By contrast, six separate regimes and two interim administrations have risen and fallen in South Korea: the Rhee (1948-1960), the Huh (April-July 1960), the Chang (1960-1961), the Park (1961-1979), the Choe (October-December 1979), the Chun (1979-1988), the Roh (1988-1993) and the Kim Young-sam (1993-). Kim Young-sam is the 14th president in forty-five years of its political history.

In North Korea five minor and two major constitutional amendments have been made in the same period.[34] In South Korea six national referenda and nine major constitutional amendments have been attempted.[35] South Korea's constitution was not simply amended, but replaced five times *in toto*. In North Korea the WPK has been the ruling party, while in South Korea the fates of the ruling parties have fared no better than those of the ruling regimes and leadership. With the downfall of the Rhee regime, the ruling Liberal Party faded away; the demise of the short-lived Chang government emasculated the ruling Democratic Party; and the death of Park ended the ruling Democratic-Republican Party. The Democratic Justice Party (DJP) rose with the Chun Doo Hwan government but with Chun's exit, the DJP also became extinct. The Roh Tae Woo regime has also created his own ruling party, the Democratic Liberal Party (DLP) by merging three existing parties—the DJP, the new Democratic Republican Party and the Unification Democratic Party. In North Korea Kim Il Sung has been the only ruler and the WPK, the sole ruling party, while in South Korea eight separate heads of state and five different ruling parties have emerged and disappeared in the past forty years.

To put it differently, in North Korea the continuing one man rule in a one-party dictatorship has meant the absence of transfer of power *per se* for the past four decades, while in South Korea the crux of the political succession problem has been not so much the absence of the transfer of power but the manner through which such transfers have occurred. South Korea's succession problem had been the lack of peaceful or legal transfer of power. The removal of Rhee, and the transfer of power from Chang to Park and from Park to Chun had been carried out by extralegal means. Bullets, not ballots, and bayonets, not bargains had been the catalyst for political change. Why had there not been any peaceful transfer of power in South Korea until the Roh regime? What are the official and unofficial explanations for the lack of peaceful transfer of power? What follows is an analysis of the reasons and rationale for the absence of peaceful transfer of power in South Korea, and a number of possible scenarios available to the former Chun government and the Roh regime in firmly institutionalizing an orderly transfer of political power in South Korea.

Official Explanations and Dilemmas

The North Korean constitution explicitly guarantees one-party proletarian dictatorship; thus, no semantic incongruity exists between the mono-party status of the WPK in theory and in reality. In contrast, South Korea has never resolved the built-in constitutional-political dilemma—the constitutional promise of multi-party competition for power and the political practice of an authoritarian rule. Neither Rhee nor Park (or, for that matter, the Chun regime) had successfully overcome this fundamental constitutional-political paradox. The practice of extralegal and unconstitutional means to gain and retain power had been rationalized by various extraordinary arguments. One common rationale had been ideological—the threats from the Communist North justified the retention of an anti-Communist regime in the South at all costs. Closely related to this ideological reasoning was the security apologia. National security, political stability and public order precede individual rights and political freedom, and thus, individual rights can be suspended and political freedom muzzled, if for the sake of security, stability and order.[36] More often than not, the security apologia was tied to the ruling group's own regime security, which had been a convenient pretext for disregarding the peaceful transfer of power.

The third justification, especially by the military interventionists in politics, had been the corruption-construction nexus. Negatively, the coup leaders in 1961 and 1979 attacked civilian politicians' corruptions and promised to clean up the mess. Positively, they contended that they were better equipped to deal with the rapid modernization and economic construction of the nation. This particular justification is not uncommon in the countries where military intervention in politics is routine.[37]

The fourth is a more sophisticated contention that the peculiarities of the Korean Peninsula—the persistence of division, the potential reinvasion of the South by the Communist North and the geo-political conditions of the Peninsula where the interests of the four major world powers (the United States, Japan, the former Soviet Union and China) overlap—demand a Koreanized version of democracy, different from the Western version. One plausible rationalization for this thesis is the minimization of political costs. The advocates of this thesis contended that South Korea cannot afford the luxury of a Western democracy, and the phenomenal economic growth in the 60's, 70's and 80's is attributable largely to the minimization of political costs by both restricting political activities at the national level and abolishing local and provincial elections.

There is also a familiar yet utterly unpredictable crisis logic. Namely, as were the case of Rhee in 1960 and Park in 1979, the head of the state could be removed by either a popular uprising or a palace coup; political turmoil may ensue; and the regular government machinery would be partially or totally paralyzed. Under such "crisis," the military would be compelled to intervene in politics.[38]

Inherently linked to this crisis logic is what is called here a rescue rationale. The military interventionists in politics asserted that they had the ultimate responsibility to rescue the nation from a brink of collapse. Their primary mission was to rescue the country, not to replace the power, and thus, their task was temporary in nature. Contrary to their professed intentions, however, both the 1961 and the 1979 military interventions in politics turned out to be a permanent political entrenchment of the military core elites by the wholesale replacement and realignment of power groups. The longer this arrangement lasted, the less militarism it exhibited; the gradual recovery and resumption of civilian control of power were synchronized by the equally piecemeal disappearance of the military from the routine political process. Thus, the military, except for those who shed their uniforms for mufti and stayed in key governmental and para-governmental positions, will remain in the political background to await for crisis-rescue mission.

If the military had become the permanent political fixture in South Korean politics since 1961, the explanations must be sought in a much broader and deeper political context. The sheer size of the military and para-military forces—some 650,000 regular armed forces and 4.5 million reserves—makes it extremely difficult, if not impossible, to confine its shadows within the barracks and garrisons.[39] The real culprit for the excessive growth of the armed forces is the division of the nation and the hostile confrontation between the Communist North and the anti-Communist South. Thus, the politicization of the military in South Korean politics comes full circle. Is this vicious circle inevitable? It is no longer theoretically so, although another military intervention cannot be ruled out once and for all. The factors which, in theory, can break such a vicious circle are: the emergence of pluralistic social and political forces with ever increasing and expanding economic horizons especially through the rise of *Chaebŏl* [Korean business conglomerates]; the growing sophistication and enhancement of political understanding and consciousness of the mass public; the gradual professionalization of the military and its growing middle class mentality (e.g. preoccupation with better education for their children, better income and better housing etc.); the increasing neutrality of the bureaucracy, especially the police force and the para-military police (chŏnkyŏng); increasing political tolerance level and, above all, the demise of Communism in the former Soviet Union and Eastern Europe; the end of the Soviet-American strategic rivalry; the virtual extinction of the Cold War; and the subsequent reduction of military tensions between North and South Korea. In real political life, however, the presence of the military either in uniform or in mufti may persist for the time being.

Options and Obstacles

There was a consensus among intellectual circles, if not the general public as a whole, that setting a precedence for the peaceful transfer of political power should be the first order of business on the political agenda for the Chun government. The realization of democracy was, in fact, the first of the Chun government's four governing ideologies.[40] It was no accident, therefore, that one of the "three freedoms" identified as the aim of the Chun administration was the freedom from political oppression and abuses. (The other two were the freedom from war and poverty). Specifically, the new 1980 Constitution stipulated a seven-year, one-term presidency: "the term of office of the President will be seven years, and no one will be allowed to become President for a second term (Article 45)." The 1980 Constitution specified also that any future constitutional amendment enacted to extend the term of office of the President would not be applicable to the President in office at the time of the proposal.

The 1980 Constitution prevented, in short, President Chun from remaining in power beyond seven years. He could have stayed in power only by nullifying the entire constitution itself by extraordinary means. Like his precedessor Park, he could have replaced the existing constitution with a new one and become the president for another term instead of surrendering it to Roh. But he stepped down from the presidency as the Constitution required and as he repeatedly promised.[41] In fact it was impossible for Chun to renege the single-term presidency tenure, because his political legitimacy, unlike his predecessors, was based on such a promise. Following the footsteps of his predecessors, he, too, might have broken the promise, but with much greater political risks and civilian and military repercussions. For Chun, therefore, the old option of his predecessors, namely, to amend the constitution to fit his own political needs, was nearly unthinkable, if not impossible.

One frequently cited succession scenario was, though not adopted, a truncated version of the Mexican format.[42] Like Mexico's PRI (Partido Revolucionario Institucional), the then ruling Democratic Justice Party will remain in power, and only its leader (the president) would be changed. This would mean the change of leadership within the dominant party under an authoritarian political framework, different from such changes within the monoparty system of a totalitarian communist regime like North Korea. This option had merit in that the peaceful transfer of power, though nominal, could be realized, and, at the same time, the ruling party would not vanish when its head steps down. If successful, this formula can accomplish two goals: a precedent will be set for a peaceful transfer of power from one leader to another, and simultaneously, will prevent the ruling political party from collapsing with the downfall of its leader. On the surface, this scenario had an initial appeal, but one must remember the fundamental cultural differences existing between Mexico and Korea in their educational, economic, social and political configurations. In reality, the Mexican format was partially instituted. The orderly transfer of power from Chun to Roh and from Roh to Kim within the ruling party was successfully executed but neither the political reprisals against the predecessor Chun nor the demise of the predecessor's party was prevented by the successor Roh. And Kim Young-sam, Roh's successor, is still under study.

The third alternative is, similar to the Japanese model. The Democratic Liberal Party (DLP), like Japan's Liberal Democratic Party (LDP), will remain a dominant party, and thus the shifts in government (cabinets) and transfer of power will occur at the top by changing hands within the DLP hierarchy. This formula, which was once hotly debated, is now set aside for the time being, although it is not completely abandoned. The difficulty of this option lies in that the dominance of the LDP in Japanese politics had been maintained within the constitutional framework of a parliamentary system, whereas the current South Korean system is presidential or neo-presidential.[42] Within the DLP the Kim Jong Pil faction had advocated this formula, which would require another constitutional revision, while Kim Dae Jung's Democratic Party (DP) was adamantly opposed to such a move.

For chronic political instability and mutual intransigence displayed by both the governing and the opposition parties, Swift in his *Gulliver's Travels* offers a satiric solution:

You take a hundred leaders of each party, you dispose them into cou-
ples of such whose heads are nearest of a size; then let two nice opera-
tors saw off the occiput of each couple at the same time, in such a manner that the brain may be equally divided. Let the occiputs thus cut off be
interchanged, applying each to the head of his opposite party-man....
thus: that the two half brains being left to debate the matter between
themselves within the space of one skull, would soon come to a good
understanding, and produce that moderation, as well as regularity of
thinking....[43]

This satire aside, ideally at least, the Japanese-type cabinet-responsible system is appealing, if a number of provisos is met in advance. A set
of prerequites is: a restoration of a monarch whose role and power is
equivalent to Japanese Emperor (or, for that matter, English King or
Queen) or a creation of symbolic presidency, which is equivalent to the
present German or Indian president; the depoliticization of the military,
the police, the bureaucracy and the various intelligence and/or para-governmental organizations; the institutionalization of electoral systems
guaranteeing fair competition and fair sharing of seats; and, above all,
the full restoration and guarantee of fundamental civil liberties and
rights. But the fact is that fulfilling these prerequisites is even harder
than realizing the Japanese-style cabinet-responsible system.

The worst-case scenario will be the repetition of a format similar to
the 1961 or 1979 military take-over. Considering the long-standing
politicization of the South Korean military, this outcome, however
undesirable, cannot be completely ruled out. The fact that the tension
still exists among military elites deserves attention in this regard. Also, a
parallel, though not direct and identical, can be drawn between the 1974
Independence Day Incident and the 1983 Rangoon Incident. In the former, ex-President Park's wife was assassinated during the ceremony to
celebrate the anniversary of the Korean independence by a young Korean resident from Osaka, Japan. In the latter, 21 people were killed at the
Martyr's Mausoleum in Rangoon, Burma, including President Chun's
closest top advisors by bombs installed by the North Korean terrorist
squads. As Park escaped the assassin's bullets meant for him in August
1974, Chun barely avoided the bomb blast meant for him in October

1983 because his wreath-laying ceremony at the monument was delayed due to a traffic jam in downtown Rangoon. After his wife's death, Park showed paranoic symptoms until his own assassination by his CIA Director in October 1979. Likewise, the tragic and brutal incident in Rangoon must have affected Chun politically and psychologically. In his case, it might have influenced him not to cling to power by all means, legal and extra-legal, as his predecessor Park had done.

Finally, the best-case scenario—an orderly transfer of power from one party to another, no matter how remote its realization—remains an option (or a hope). However desirable this option may seem, the obstacles to its attainment are nearly insurmountable. At a minimum, this alternative requires the existence of a viable opposition party (or parties) and a conducive political environment. But in the present South Korean political setting this minimum condition has not yet been realized satisfactorily.

Concluding Remarks

If one of the convincing indicators of political maturity is a firmly institutionalized transfer of power, both North and South Korean political systems must be labeled as immature. As mentioned previously, North Korea's father-son succession line, if actualized, will be the first of its kind in the annals of Communist history. At the moment the eventual outcome of the father-son succession line as a political campaign is both uncertain and highly unpredictable. Meanwhile in South Korea a regularized transfer of power has been realized twice. But whether or not this tradition will be permanently institutionalized is another question. The leadership transfer from Chun to Roh was the first step in the right direction. The peaceful transfer of presidential power from Roh to Kim Young-sam has met the second test. In the end the successive repetition of the orderly transfer of top leadership will eventually create the political tradition of institutionalized transfer of power.

Notes:

1. Jonathan Swift, *Gulliver's Travels* (New York: A Signet Classic, 1960), p. 151.
2. Glenn D. Paige, "Some Implications for Political Science of the Comparative Politics of Korea," in Fred W. Riggs, ed., *Frontiers of Development Administration* (Durham: Duke University Press, 1970); Bruce R. Sievers, "The Divided Nations: International Integration and National Identity," Jan F. Triska, ed., *Communist Party-States: Comparative and International Studies* (New York: The Bobbs-Merrill Co., 1969); Gregory Henderson at al, *Divided Nations in a Divided World* (New York: David Mckay, 1974); Sung Chul Yang, *Korea and Two Regimes* (Cambridge: Schenkman, 1981); Young-whan Kihl, "Comparative Study of the Political Systems of South and North Korea: A Research Note," *Korea and World Affairs* 5 (1981): 383-402; Han-kyo Kim, "Comparative Studies of Korean Politics," paper delivered at the AKPSNA panel at the 1982 APSA meeting, Denver, Colorado.
3. Roy Hofheinz, Jr. and Kent E. Calder, *The East Asia Edge* (New York: Basic Books, 1982), especially Chapters 1 and 2.
4. For a detailed analysis of the Kim-Kim succession, see Sung Chul Yang, "An Analysis of the North Korean Power Elites and a Prospect for Political Change" (in Korean) (Seoul: The Research Institute for National Unification, 1992).
5. *Ibid.*
6. *Ibid.*
7. *Ibid.*
8. *Ibid.*
9. *Ibid.*
10. *Ibid.*
11. Dong-bok Lee, "Hereditary Succession in North Korea and its Impact on Inter-Korean Relations," paper delivered at the Second National Symposium on Korea at La Trobe University, Melbourne, Australia, November 1980; Ho-min Yang and Il-chŏl Shin, *Kongsanchu-i Bip'an* [Critique of Communism] (Seoul: Kukdongmunje yŏnkuso, 1981); B. C. Koh, "The Cult of Personality and the Succession Issue," in C. I. Eugene Kim and B. C. Koh, eds., *Journey to North Korea: Personal Perceptions* (Berkeley: University of California Press, 1983).
12. Morgan E. Clippinger, "Kim Chŏng-il in the North Korean Media: A Study of Semi-esoteric Communication," *Asian Survey* 21 (1981): 289-309; B. C. Koh, *Op. Cit.*

13. *Far Eastern Economic Review,* 24 April 1981. Quoted in Kwŏn-sang Park, "North Korea under Kim Chŏng-il," *Journal of Northeast Asian Studies* (June 1982), p. 68.

14. For details, see Kwŏn-sang Park, *Op. Cit.*

15. Kim Chŏng Il's publicly known biographical sketch (in South Korea) is as follows:
    He was born on February 16, 1940, in Samarkand in Soviet Asia (his Russian name is Sura). He returned to Korea in October 1945 with his parents. He was admitted to Namsan School in Pyongyang in September 1948. He was briefly enrolled at Kil-rim (Kirin) School in China in June 1950. He was re-enrolled at Namsan School in 1952 and graduating with a high school diploma in August 1958; in the same year he went to study at the Air Force Academy in East Germany. He was admitted to the Department of Political Economy at the Kim Il Sung University as a sophomore in September 1960 and graduated in August 1963. He joined the WPK as a member of its Organization and Guidance Department in 1964. A recent account of Kim Jong Il's biodata is found in *SAPIO,* 21 July–20 August 1992, pp. 16-17.

16. The English text of the CCP Constitution of 1969 is found in James R. Townsend, *Politics in China* (Boston: Little, Brown, 1974).

17. Townsend, *Op. Cit.* (1980 edition), p. 284.

18. Hobbes, *Leviathan,* ed. C.B. Macpherson (Middlesex: Penguin Books, 1972), p. 247.

19. *Ibid.,* p. 248.

20. Chang-sun Kim, *"Kwŏnlyŏk Gye-seung gwa Puja Ch'eje Hwak-lip"* [Power Succession and the Establishment of Father-son System], *Pukhan* (1980): 74-85; Dong-bok Lee, *Op. Cit.,* Yong-pil Rhee et al., *Pukhan Chŏngch'i: Ideologi wa Byonhwa* [North Korean Politics: Ideology and Change] (Seoul: Daewang-sa, 1982); Ho-min Yang and Il-chŏl Shin, *Op. Cit.*; Robert A. Scalapino, "Current Dynamics of the Korean Peninsula," *Problems of Communism* 30 (1981): 16-31; Kwŏn-sang Park, *Op. Cit.*; B. C. Koh, *Op. Cit.*; Yung-hwan Jo, "Succession Politics in North Korea: Implications for Policy and Political Stability," *Asian Survey* (October 1986), pp. 1092-1117; Suk-Ryul Yu, "Political Succession and Policy Change in North Korea," *Korea and World Affairs* (Spring 1986), pp. 31-54.

21. D. B. Lee, *Op. Cit.,* p. 3.

22. *Ibid.,* p. 15.

23. See Sung Chul Yang, "The Problem of Political Succession in North and South Korean Politics," paper delivered at the AKPSNA panel at the 1983 APSA Meeting, Chicago, Illinois.

24. Chong-sik Lee, "Evolution of the Korean Workers' Party and the Rise of Kim Chong-il," *Asian Survey* 22 (1982): 435-447.

25. Hannah Arendt, *Totalitarianism,* Part Three of *The Origins of Totalitarianism* (New York: A Harvest Book, 1968), p. 106.
26. *Ibid.,* pp. 106-107.
27. *Ibid.*
28. Carl J. Friedrich and Zbigniew K. Brzezinsky, *Totalitarian Dictatorship and Autocracy* (New York: Frederick A. Praeger, 1966), p. 71.
29. William A. Welsh, *Leaders and Elites* (New York: Holt, Rinehart and Winston, 1970), pp. 70-71.
30. Myron Rush, "The Problem of Succession in Communist Regimes," *Journal of International Affairs* 32 (1978): 170. See also his *How Communist States Change Their Rulers* (Ithaca: Cornell University Press, 1974).
31. See, for instance, Jerry F. Hough and Merle Fainsod, *How the Soviet Union is Governed* (Cambridge: Harvard University Press, 1979), p. 182.
32. S. C. Yang, *Op. Cit.* (1992), pp. 44-54.
33. *Ibid.*
34. For details, see Dae-Sook Suh, *Korean Communism, 1945-1980* (Honolulu: The University Press of Hawaii, 1981), pp. 499-502.
35. Byŏng-sak Koo, *The Principles of New Constitution* (in Korean) (Seoul: Pakyŏng-sa, 1989), appendix.
36. See Sung Chul Yang, *Korea and Two Regimes,* pp. 240-244.
37. Eric A. Nordlinger, *Soldiers in Politics: Military Coups and Governments* (Englewood Cliffs: Prentice-hall, 1977), especially Chapters one, two and three.
38. Sung Chul Yang, "A Comparative Study of the 1960 April Student Revolution and the 1961 May Military Coup D'etat in Korea" (Ph.D. dissertation, University of Kentucky, 1970).
39. Gregory Henderson, *Korea: The Politics of the Vortex* (Cambridge: Harvard University Press, 1968), p. 357.
40. The governing ideology of South Korea's Fifth Republic are:
   I. Ultimate Aims
       (1) Construction of a Just Democratic Welfare State
       (2) Creation of New Era, New Society, and New History
   II. Principal Tasks
       Political: (1) Realization of Democracy
       Economic: (2) Construction of Welfare Society
       Social: (3) Realization of Just Society
       Educational: (4) Educational Reform
       Cultural: (5) Remolding of National Spirit
   III. Procedural Measures
       (1) New Village Movement
       (2) Society Purification Movement

(3) Policy Consultative Conference for Peaceful Unification.
For details, see President Chun's inaugural address on March 3, 1981.

41. President Chun's pledge for a peaceful transfer of power is found in the following remarks, which were made in his press conference: "I will be in the office not a single day more or less than the term guaranteed by the Constitution," *The Korea Herald*, 4 May 1985."

42. Byŏng-sak Koo, *Op. Cit.*

43. Jonathan Swift, *Gulliver's Travels* (New York: A Signet Classic, 1960), p. 207.

CHAPTER 18

ARMS RACE AND THE TWIN FORTIFICATIONS OF THE KOREAN PENINSULA

Cain attacked his brother Abel and murdered him. Then the Lord said to Cain, "Where is your brother Abel?" Cain answered, "I do not know. Am I my brother's keeper?" Lord said, "What have you done? Hark! Your brother's blood that has been shed is crying out to me from the ground...."

Holy Bible[1]

Hence jarring sectaries may learn
Their real interest to discern;
That brother should not war with brother,
And worry and devour each other.

William Cowper[2]

Introduction

Few areas in the world today are so sharply polarized ideologically, heavily armed militarily and intractably ruptured politically as is divided Korea. The ideological, military and political situations besetting North and South Korea today resemble the erstwhile American and the former Soviet relations. North and South Korea's ideological rivalry, arms race and political predicaments exemplify bipolarity between the two rival regimes within a country, as those of the United States and the former

Soviet Union had been on a global scale. Unlike the relations between the U.S. and the former Soviet Union, however, both regimes on the Korean Peninsula are culturally, historically and linguistically homogeneous and share territorial contiguity. Korea is also a rare area where the interests of four major powers—the United States, Russia, China and Japan—converge. In the 1894-1895 Sino-Japanese War, Japan and China fought over Korea, as Japan and Russia fought over it a few years later in the 1904-1905 Russo-Japanese War. The former Soviet Union and China sided with North Korea, and the United States and other "free" world nations fought on behalf of South Korea directly or indirectly in the Korean War of 1950-53. The Korean War ended with the Armistice Agreement in July 1953, and the fragile cease-fire has lasted for over forty years. To put it differently, the 151-mile demilitarized zone, separating the North from the South, still remains a potential military flash point.

The genesis of the present Korean predicaments lies in the artificial, arbitrary and abnormal division of the country in 1945. For over forty years since its partition, the two Koreas have been in bitter and vicious enmity. After the fratricidal and proxy war of 1950-53, both sides have been under an uneasy peace. An arms race between the two accelerates constantly, skirmishes erupt intermittently, espionage and counter-espionage activities continue, commando raids, shock-troops style attacks of terrorist acts by the North against the South often outrage the world as evinced by the Rangoon Incident of October 8, 1983, and KAL 808 attack in December 1987. The politicization of security issue by the political incumbents in the South notwithstanding, the threats from the North are real. The incidents of such threats abound, although the provoker and the provoked are not always easy to discern. In addition to North Korea's invasion of South Korea in June of 1950, the 1968 North Korean commandos' infiltration of the Blue House, the 1968 seizure of the U.S. intelligence reconnaissance ship, *Pueblo*, the 1969 shooting down of the U.S. Navy EC-121 reconnaissance plane, the 1976 killing of the two U.S. army officers at the DMZ, the discovery of the three North Korean underground tunnels announced in Seoul in November 1974, March 1975 and October 1978 and, above all, the controversy surrounding North Korea's nuclear project are notable. Unlike the earlier incidents, the Rangoon and the KAL incidents were committed in a third country rather than on the Korean Peninsula. These incidents perhaps reveal the degree of desperateness felt by the North Korean ruling circles. The question, then, is why are they so desperate? One of the major reasons may lie in North Korea's inability to compete with South Korea in international diplomacy, arms race, sports or economic development.

In this chapter, the sources and the nature of threats and regime vulnerabilities in North and South Korea will be examined. Next, the arms race between them will be scrutinized. Specifically, North and South Korea's force level, military expenditures and rationale for arms race with its political implications and remedies will be probed.

The Politics of Threats and Regime Vulnerabilities

The Korean Peninsula represents a classic case where the actual source(s) of threats diverges from the perception and exploitation of such threats by the ruling elites in power. The division of Korea in 1945 and the subsequent emergence of two rival regimes on the Korean Peninsula in 1948 commenced mutual tensions and threats, actual or perceived, between North and South Korea. To begin with, the very existence of North and South Korea is a threat to each other's security. To paraphrase Waltz's point that the United States had been the obsessing danger for the former Soviet Union, and the former Soviet Union for the United States,[3] North Korea, too, presents the obsessing danger for South Korea, and vice versa. Each would pose the greatest threat and continue to be the major source of potential damage to the other.

Beyond the aforesaid mutually re-enforcing threats, four additional sources of threats to North Korea can be identified. The first is systemic. North Korea's totalitarian communist system, particularly with its military and para-military organizations, has been in operation under "the premise of threat" and "the promise of liberation." Namely, Kim Il Sung and his Workers' Party of Korea (WPK) have built the North Korean war machines with the premise that the threats from South Korea, aided and instigated by the U.S. imperialists, are "real," and with the promise that the "liberation" of South Korea from the U.S. (and Japanese) imperialism is "imminent." The present North Korean regime justifies its ultimate existence by constantly inculcating the masses with the propaganda that it has the solemn mission to "liberate" the South from the "fascist Kim Young-sam cliques" (or previously from the "Rhee, Park, Chun and Roh cliques") and their "imperialist war-mongers." In recent years, however, the North Korean propaganda machine has become less aggressive in tone toward the United States, Japan and South Korea which signals a necessity to improve relations with them.

The Kim Il Sung-Kim Jŏng Il regime is less vulnerable as long as its premise of threats and promise of liberation can effectively persuade the masses. Conversely, the Kim-Kim regime would be vulnerable if the masses realize that North Korea's propaganda rhetoric of threats and liberation is a ploy to perpetuate its own political and war machinery and the national reunification does not transcend its regime interests. Accordingly, the North Korean regime is most vulnerable to "openness." If the masses in the North are exposed to the news other than those monopolized by the WPK propaganda and agitation machines, and if they are allowed to see South Korea and the outside world as they actually are without the influence of party-controlled propaganda and media and if they are allowed to travel within North Korea and abroad, the Kim Il Sung-Kim Jŏng Il regime may not last in its present form. The current Kim-Kim regime is an extreme variant of a closed communist totalitarian system. An open and free society is an anathema to it.

Second is its size. Although North Korea is slightly larger in area than South Korea, its population is less than half of South Korea's. This, coupled with its relatively smaller economic capacity makes North Korea insecure, if not, threatened. Furthermore, because the present North Korean regime was founded on Marxism-Leninism and Kim Il Sungism, particularly on the *Juche* (self-reliance) idea, which are, as its propaganda constantly asserts, "superior" and "invincible" ideology, North Korea's prospect of losing to South Korea in economic development, arms race, diplomacy and other competitions will be menacing. Because the present North Korean regime was founded upon the premise of the superiority of socialism and communism, the failure to outperform South Korea in these competitions would undermine the very foundation of its system, and, thus, the Kim regime would become vulnerable. It is no accident, therefore, that in recent years North Korea has increasingly become more system-*defensive* than system-*offensive*.

The third is external. North Korea's perception of threats from the South is compounded by the continuing presence of the U.S. troops. The "Team Spirit," the joint annual U.S.-South Korean military exercises began in 1976 as a move to preempt and dissuade military moves against the South by North Korea, though temporarily halted in 1992, has also contributed to the North Korean apprehension. In addition to the 1953 United States and the Republic of Korea Mutual Defense Treaty, the new trilateral—U.S.-Japan-ROK—military "coordination" adds fuel to North Korea's insecurity. South Korea's normalization of relations with Russia and other Commonwealth of Independent States (CIS), her normal relations with China, not to mention her establishment of diplomatic relations with the former Eastern European Countries have compelled North Korea to break away from its self-imposed claustrophobia.

Finally, closely related to North Korea's sources of threats stemming from its size and external forces is its siege mentality. Kim Il Sung and his WPK ruling circles feel that North Korea is besieged by South Korea and by the U.S. forces in the south and Japan in the east, and by China and Russia in the north. Although North Korea's northern neighbors are formally its allies, its only outlet to the outside world on land through China and Russia is limited at best. North Korea is, to repeat, one of the most isolated countries in the world both by choice and by circumstances. The origins of its isolation from the outside world are basically three—self-imposed, other-imposed and geography-imposed. North Korea is sealed off from the outside world, because its communist system sustains itself by depriving its own people's right to travel at home and abroad; South Korea and its allies, especially the United States and Japan, have also tried to contain North Korea, and North Korea is land-locked by two giant neighbors—Russia and China in the north.

Meanwhile, South Korea faces, at least, two additional sources of threats. The first is internal. Unlike North Korea, whose political system is based on a one-party dictatorship of total regimentation and regulation, South Korea has never effectively resolved the political incongruity created since the launching of its republic in 1948, namely, the gulf between the constitutional pledge of a free democratic polity and the practice of an authoritarian rule. In North Korea Kim Il Sung and his WPK ruling elites publicly proclaim, backed by the constitutional stipulation, that the North Korean system is a proletarian dictatorship, and, thus, no semantic incongruity exists between the proclamation of a proletarian dictatorship and the practice of one-man (or, father-son) dictatorship (one-man dictatorship is, theoretically at least, a clear departure from the orthodox Marxist-Leninist principle of the proletarian dictatorship). The South Korean constitution proclaims a free democratic polity, but the actual politics has been authoritarian. Hence, the South Korean governments, had had the burden of explaining, justifying and rationalizing the apparent incongruity. The Roh regime (1988-1993), which initiated the liberalization and democratization campaign and now the Kim Young-sam regime (1993-) have been less threatened by such internal legitimacy dilemma.

South Korea's dilemma, however, will not be resolved until its politics becomes fully liberalized and democratized. In the meantime it must avoid a North Korean style one-man-one-party total regimentation, but in so doing it has to come to grips with the various political oppositions within. The South Korean constitution prohibits, at least, on paper, such totalitarian dictatorship, while the previous regimes in power, had attempted to circumvent the citizens' constitutionally guaranteed rights and liberties in political arena. The ruling elites had tried in two ways, though unsatisfactorily, to resolve this incongruency dilemma. One is by using a semantic device, namely appending different adjectives such as "national," "Korean," "administrative," or "creative," to democracy. The creators of these adjectives had argued that pure or ideal form of democratic system cannot work in Korea because of its unique culture, history, political and military conditions. In so doing, they had somehow sanctioned undemocratic practices. The other method is to trumpet the security alarm. The security alarmists contend that the threats from North Korea is real, which is undoubtedly true, and under such circumstances some curbing of civil rights and liberties is inevitable. The ruling groups have often used one or both of these devices to justify their authoritarian political practices, while those in opposition accused them for such apologia and demanded democracy without excuses. The end-result of this tug of war has been a political trade-off, an emergence of a variant of authoritarian regime, which is half-way between totalitarianism and constitutional democracy. Under the Roh regime a substantial progress in democratization and liberalization had been achieved and further progress has been realized under the new Kim Young-sam regime. Still a political trade-off continues.

Second is external. South Korea feels insecure about North Korea's military build-up, especially its nuclear project. The former Soviet Union's decision to deploy 117 of its 360 new SS-20 missiles in East Asia aimed at China, Japan and South Korea was once another source of South Korea's security allergy. South Korean people's vivid memory, though fading, of the all-out invasion from the North during the Korean War still lingers on. Unlike North Korea, the fact that South Korea has no outlet to the outside world on land also generates additional anxiety. So far, as Goheen pointed out, the assurance of continued protection from the U.S. seems to have been sufficient in checking South Korean moves to develop a nuclear deterrent against the threat from North Korea.[4] South Korea publicly announced that it will abandone its dream of becoming a nuclear power, although it once had held such desire. At present, however, South Korea has modified its perception of erstwhile external threat stemming from the former Soviet Union and China as a result of establishing normal relations with Russia and China.[5]

Ironically, both sides perceive threats from each other's strengths as well as weaknesses. A militarily strong, economically healthy and politically stable North Korea is a threat to South Korea and vice versa, primarily because the weaker side is fearful of the stronger showing off its military strength. North Korea which is militarily weak, economically ailing and politically unstable also poses a threat to South Korea and vice versa since the stronger side is apprehensive of the military move of the weaker to cover up its weakness. In Steven Butler's phraseology, "Is North Korea a self-confident, ferocious bulldog? Or merely a frightened cat, vicious and backed into a corner?"[6] From this standpoint, the vicious circle existing between North and South Korea cannot be broken as long as the two regimes believe in such premises based on half-truth.

Above all, the present political situation on the Korean Peninsula typifies a classic case of what John Herz called a "security dilemma," the condition in which states, unsure of one another's intentions, arm for the sake of security, and in doing so, set a vicious circle in motion. Having armed for the sake of security, states feel less secure and buy more arms because the means to anyone's security poses a threat to someone else, who in turn responds by arming.[7] More arming, therefore, precipitates a new round of arms race. In a similar manner, a vicious spiral of mutual arms race between North and South Korea has continued ever since the creation of the two rival regimes in 1948. The recent tension reduction moves and agreements between North Korea and South notwithstanding, there has been no concrete changes in the two sides over the basic mode of military posturing.

The Paradoxes of Armament and Security

If an arms race is a condition in which two or more parties perceive themselves to be in an adversary relationship, by increasing or improving their armaments and structuring their respective military postures with a general attention to the past, current, and anticipated military and political behavior of other parties,[8] the military build-up in North and South Korea for more than forty years represents the prime example. The Korean Peninsula today is indeed one of the most heavily armed areas in the world. According to the 1991-1992 International Institute for Strategic Studies' *Military Balance,* the combined military forces of North and South Korea exceeds 1,861,000, which make them the fourth largest in the world, trailing only the former Soviet Union (3.4 million), China (3.03 million) and the United States (2.02 million). North Korea's military forces alone (1,111,000) are ranked fifth in the world, while South Korea's armed forces (750,000) are ranked seventh (For details, see Tables 18-1 and 18-2). Considering the fact that those countries— China, Russia, the United States and India—whose military forces exceed North and South Korea are also the world's most populous states, the heavily armed Korean Peninsula is an anomaly. North Korea is even worse. It ranked as the most heavily armed nation in the world (47.7 per 1,000 people), while in South Korea 16.9 per 1,000 people were in the armed services in 1991.

Noteworthy also is that North Korea's armed personnel steadily increased from 30.8 in 1971 to 47.8 in 1991, while in the same period South Korea's declined from 19.9 to 16.9 (See Tables 18-1 and 18-2). Both Koreas are also among the largest military spenders in the world. As it will become clear in the following, North Korea's actual military expenditures are largely shrouded in mystery. Its actual figures (military expenditures as a percentage of gross domestic product) may be two or three times higher than the reported amount, which was, according to *SIPRI 1991 World Armaments and Disarmament,* 10.7% in 1980 but 8.8% in 1989. South Korea's military expenditure as a percentage of GDP was 5.9% in 1980 and 4.4% in 1989.

Military Expenditures and Arms Transfer

In comparing North and South Korea's respective military expenditures, two problems need to be spelled out at the outset. First is systemic. North Korea's military outlays, like those of the former Soviet Union and other socialist countries, are, at best, a rough estimate and an approximation. Not only military expenditure figures but all statistical materials about North Korea are largely inaccessible and unavailable. Even some of these published figures and data cannot be used at face value.[9] The inaccessibility and unreliability of data emanating from North Korea and other former and remaining socialist countries are inherent in all socialist systems, where secrecy prevails. Second, as often manifested when comparing the U.S. and the former Soviet defense expenditures,[10] there are a number of methodological problems.

The problem of measurement—a lack of comparable economic concepts, the differences in currency unit and the question of exchange rate—comes to mind. For example, the concept of aggregate national accounts used in North Korea is similar to GVSP (gross output value of social production, i.e., the sum of gross output value of all separately enumerated production units including the values of inputs from outside each unit), which was used in the former Soviet Union and other East European socialist countries. Converting North Korea's estimated GVSP to GNP or South Korea's GNP to GVSP may, thus, easily distort the actual economic reality of North and South Korea.[11]

Also, computing and converting local currencies is problematic. Technically, North and South Korean defense expenditures could be measured in six different ways: (1) North Korean military expenditures in local currency (North Korean *won*); (2) South Korean military expenditures in local currency (South Korean *won*); (3) North Korean military outlays converted to South Korean *won*; (4) South Korean military outlays converted to North Korean *won*; (5) North Korean military outlays converted to U.S. dollars; and (6) South Korean military outlays converted to U.S. dollars. In conversion of local currencies, the exchange rate poses a problem. The absence of normal relationships between North and South Korea and between North Korea and the United States means the absence of formal exchange rates between these governments, which creates an additional problem of comparison and computation of military outlays.

The end-result of the aforesaid systemic and methodological problems is a wide variation in the military budget figures of North Korea reported by different institutes and analysts. North Korea's military budget estimates by London-based International Institute for Strategic Studies (IISS), Stockholm-based Stockholm International Peace Research Institute (SIPRI), and U.S. Arms Control and Disarmament Agency's World Military Expenditures and Arms Transfer (WMEAT) vary considerably. For instance, the IISS estimate of North Korea's military budget in 1970 was $746 million of its total GNP of $3 billion, whereas the WMEAT figure in the same year was $700 million (current) and $892 million (1979 constant) of its total GNP of $ 4.5 billion (current) and $5.73

billion (1979 constant), respectively. The IISS estimate of South Korea's military budget in 1970 was $333 million of its total GNP of $7.5 billion, and the WMEAT figure in the same year was $344 million (current) and $438 million (constant) of its total GNP of $8.87 billion (current) and $11.3 billion (1979 constant). IISS estimate of North Korea's military budget in 1980 was $1.3 billion of its total GNP of $10.5 billion, which differs considerably from the WMEAT figures of the same period, $1.3 billion of its GNP of $15.9 billion (current) and $1.8 billion of its GNP of $14.4 billion (1979 constant). South Korea's military budget in the same period was $3.45 billion of its total GNP of $46 billion reported by the IISS, and $3.8 billion of its total GNP of $49.9 billion (current) or $3.5 billion of its total GNP of $56.7 billion (1979 constant), calculated by the wheat. In 1990 North Korea's defense budget was $5.2 billion and South Korea's was $10.6 billion in the same year according to the IISS. The SIPRI figures are substantially different from the IISS figures. According to the SIPRI, North Korea's military expenditure in 1990 (at 1988 prices) was $2.0 billion and South Korea's was $7.8 billion.

North and South Korea's military budget figures in local currency also vary widely. As Figures 18-1 below indicates, the estimates of North and South Korean military outlays in 1970 and 1980 by Young Hee Park (YHP), Young Kyu Kim (YKK) and the SIPRI, YKK's North Korean figure in 1970 is, for example, nearly three times larger than the SIPRI estimate. Likewise in 1980, YKK's figure is more than two times larger than YHP's and the SIPRI figures. In 1990, too, as noted in the above, the IISS figures of North Korea's military expenditures are more than twice larger than the SIPRI data. Their South Korean data, too, are significantly different.

Despite the wide variations in military outlay estimates, particularly of North Korea, a few observations can be made concerning North and South Korea's military expenditures and arms transfer.

Figure 18-1

	(North Korea)	(South Korea)
	Unit: million *won*	Unit: 100 million *won*
1970	1,868 (YHP)	1,023 (EPB)
	2,542 (YKK)	
	865 (SIPRI)	1,016 (SIPRI)
1980	2,750 (YHP)	2,257 (EPB)
	6,087 (YKK)	
	3,161 (SIPRI)	3,566 (SIPRI)
1990	5,230 (IISS)	10,950 (IISS)
	2,003 (SIPRI)	7,827 (SIPRI)

First, whether one uses lower or higher military expenditure figures, it is evident that North Korea had higher military expenditure than South Korea until the mid-1970's. South Korea's military expenditure began to surpass North Korea's after 1976. For instance, in 1967, North Korea's military outlays ($460 million) were more than two times larger than South Korea's ($180 million). Roughly the same ratio continued until 1971. Since then, South Korea has been narrowing the gap. A near parity was reached in 1975 (North Korea's $770 million versus South Korea's $ 719 million). Since 1976 according to the SIPRI data, South Korea's military budget has exceeded North Korea's. In 1990, if the IISS data are used, South Korea's defense budget is more than two times greater than North Korea's.

In 1983, for instance, South Korea's military outlays were $4.7 billion, as compared with North Korea's $3.6 billion (estimate). At present, the ratio of the North and South Korean military outlays is the exact reversal of that of the 1960s and the early 1970's (For details, see Table 18-3). As Young Hee Park (YHP) pointed out, the cumulative figures of South Korea's military outlay from 1974 to 1983 are 26.7 billion dollars. Assuming that North Korea's military outlays in the same period were 30% higher than its official figures, its cumulative totals (26.1 billion dollars) are still slightly smaller than those of the South. If the SIPRI data are used, South Korea's military expenditure is a third greater than North Korea's.[12]

Second, wide discrepancies in North Korea's military outlays exist primarily because North Korean specialists use different criteria in their computations of the military budget. For instance, Young Hee Park and Kwang Su Kim use the figures announced by North Korean official publications. By contrast, Young Kyu Kim(YKK) employs his own measurement of North Korea's military expenditures. YKK contends that North Korea's official figures include only the direct or general military expenditures. According to him, North Korea's real military expenditures consist of the direct military expenditures (general), the defense construction expenditures (the munitions industry management) and the defense industry expenditures (the arms manufacturing).

During the peak of the Korean War in 1953, for instance, North Korea's official military expenditure was only 15.2 percent of its total budget, while its military outlay in 1967, the year it supposedly shifted its priority from defense to economic construction, reached 30.4 percent of its total budget. Thus, North Korea's official military outlay figures are disguised and unreliable. North Korea's actual military expenditures from 1961 to 1983 had been two times greater than its published figures. Specifically, its published official figures range from 2.6% of its total budget in 1961 to 14.8% in 1983, while its actual estimated figures were 40.4% and 44.9% in these two years, respectively. Accordingly, YKK places North Korea's real military expenditures at 40% of its total annual budget or 25 percent of its GNP. The U.S. intelligence tends to confirm YKK's estimates: North Korea's military outlays ranged from 15% to 20% in the 1960s and 25% to 30% of its GNP in the 1970's.[13] Interestingly, the North spends much less on personnel and maintenance, but more on arms, than the South.[14]

Third, whatever criteria one uses in comparing North and South Korea's military expenditures, the military outlays on both sides have been steadily on the rise. The single notable exception was the actual decrease of North Korea's military outlays in 1972, the year the North-South mutual dialogue culminated in the proclamation of the July 4th Joint Communique.[15] Whether or not North Korea's published figures are reliable is, however, another matter. It is noteworthy that both

Koreas' military expenditure as a percentage of their respective GDP
has declined over the years, especially in the 1980s (See Table 18-3).

Fourth, one thing is quite certain. More military expenditures may
mean more arms, but more arms may not necessarily mean more security to either side. Quite to the contrary, with all the cumulative military
spending and arms build-up for over forty years, the Korean Peninsula is
not necessarily securer now than before. Both sides fear each other now
no less than before, when they were far less militarily prepared and
armed. More military expenditures in the name of national security may
not necessarily lead to increased collective individual security but it
means less spending on the social, economic and educational sectors.
The current tension surrounding North Korea's nuclear project is another instance of the unbridled arms race that has led to the collective
insecurity of the entire Korean people, let alone the people in the region
and around the world. For instance, Deger and Smith contend that military expenditure has a negative effect on growth and thus retards development.[16] Similarly, Wolpin points out that when military burdens are
high and rapidly increasing, they result in diminished economic growth
rates, unemployment, reduced exports and inflation. North Korea is the
living example of a country which is armed to its teeth with moribund
and stagnant economy.[17]

Fifth, according to the WMEAT figures, North and South Korea had
been primarily importers of arms from the 1960s till the mid-1970s. But
since the mid-1970s, both sides began to export small arms to other
third world countries. It should be pinpointed here that South Korea far
exceeds North Korea in arms imports and exports in sum total, although
North Korea's real arms import figures may be much higher than the
published amount. Specifically, North Korea's total arms imports and
exports between 1973 to 1983 were $1.7 billion dollars and 1.5 billion
dollars (1982 constant), respectively, while South Korea's total arms
imports and exports in the same period were 25.1 billion dollars and 23.
5 billion dollars, respectively. According to the 1991 SIPRI data, North
Korea has been the 15th leading exporters of conventional weapons to
the third world countries. From 1986 to 1990 its exports to the third
world countries amounted to $300 million. During the same period,

North Korea has been the 5th leading importers of major conventional weapons ($4.9 billion), while South Korea has been the 9th leading importer ($3.1 billion) among the 3rd world countries. Among all the countries, North Korea placed 7th and South Korea, 14th during the 1986-90 period in total arms imports (For details, see Tables 18-4 and 18-5).

Why Arms Race?

To paraphrase Anatol Rapoport's seminal work, *Fights, Games, and Debates* (1960), the Korean War typified the *fight* dimension (or mode) of conflict between North and South Korea. The North attempted to sub-jugate the South by force, but the war ended in a draw—*status quo* ante bellum. The continuing exchange of rhetoric on Korean reunification by both sides—most recently the so-called Democratic Confederal Repub-lic of Korea Plan proposed by President Kim Il Sung during the WPK's Sixth Congress in October 1980, his one nation-one state-two systems-two governments formula in the 1990s and the Unified Democratic Republic of Korea Formula announced by President Chun Doo Hwan in January 1982 and the *Han* people commonwealth unification plan by President Roh Tae Woo in 1988 represent the debate dimension of their struggle.[18] Each side has been trying to outwit the other through rhetoric and propaganda rather than to genuinely resolve their mutual differences and to reunify the nation. Rapoport's game dimension is manifested in the arms race between the North and the South, along with their compe-titions in economic development, international diplomacy, sports and others. Arms race is indeed the most severe and fiercest game dimension of the North-South conflict, not to mention the fact that it is the most wasteful and destructive.

The severity and wastefulness of such arms race notwithstanding, why have the two sides continued it? The answers to this question are rather complex. Gray's seven reasons for competitive armament can be a starting point.[19] "Deterrence" -- to prevent the inimical military behav-ior of the other side -- is certainly one motive behind the North and South Korean arms race. It is real to South Korea, which was invaded by North Korea in 1950. Mutual arms build-up in the name of deterrence is not a solution, however, for it increases rather than reduces the probability of another war, which has, so far, deterred another outbreak of war on the Korean Peninsula.

"Defense" -- to attain a more favorable outcome if war should occur -- may be a logically valid reason for the North and South Korean arms race, but hardly a satisfactory solution to the problem. To begin with, another outbreak of war in Korea would be self-destructive and would create the possibility of widening a global conflict. Hence, an arms build-up to attain a more favorable outcome in war is a wishful thinking than a winning strategy.

"Diplomacy" -- to increase its diplomatic weight -- is essentially irrelevant to the Korean case. The military strengths of both Koreas, relative to their size and status in the international community, far exceed their respective diplomatic weight. North Korea's nuclear project, too, seems to be an effective tool to use for political and other purposes at a first glance. But in the long run it will be self-defeating and will backfire.

"The functional threat" -- to enlist or harness the functional hostility of an external rival -- can be applied to the Korean arms race. The ruling elites in North Korea perceive South Korea and her U.S.-Japan security coordination as their external threat, as South Korean counterparts still see North Korea as the primary source of their threat, although they no longer perceive the latter's alliance with Russia and China as menacing as before.

The idea of "vested interests" -- the defense policy is essentially the captive of domestic, industrial, bureaucratic and legislative interests, all of which, therefore, need an external threat -- is also relevant to the continuous Korean military build-up. The so-called military-industrial complex on both sides of the Korean Peninsula have emerged since the Korean War as a result of the mutual arms race for more than forty years.

The "reputation" idea -- to preserve or enhance the measure of dignity and prestige -- can be a factor, albeit minor, behind the Korean arms race. In the North Korean case, Kim Il Sung cult-building and its misguided and self-inflicting military build-up, including its nuclear project, are not unrelated.

Finally, "technology" -- to keep up with a rapid succession of generations of weapons technologies -- is also relevant to the Korean case. If deterrence and defense are the rationale for the two Koreas' arms race, the urge to acquire the latest and best weapons by both sides is rather a natural response. Unlike the arms race between the United States and the former Soviet Union, however, North and South Korea are in competition to acquire rather than develop the latest weaponry.

In addition to the aforementioned standard rationale for arms race, two additional factors have contributed to the Korean arms race. The ideological and political intransigences and the conflicting military strategies are the cases in point. North Korean communism with the one party proletarian dictatorship as its ideological and political doctrine, is not subject to compromise. Conversely, in South Korea anti-communism has served as the pillar of its state policy. The North has attempted to spread its version of communism in the southern half by propaganda, subversion, or even by invasion, as was the case in 1950. The South has countered such attempts with its brand of propaganda, intelligence maneuvering, diplomacy and military readiness. This mutual ideological and political intransigence, in turn, has created what Richard Betts called the syndromes of "the failure in perspective" and "pathologies of communication."[20] The failure in perspective is manifested on the Korean Peninsula in that both sides tend to see each other's negative aspects more than the positive elements and potentials, and that both sides are inclined to be more pessimistic about the possibility of resolving mutual ideological and political reconciliations by peaceful means. It has also created "the pathologies of communication" because the breakdown in communication between the two has been the rule, which, in turn, has been the main source of their misperceptions, miscalculations and misunderstandings. Hence, the current North-South dialogue and the creation of the Political Subcommittee, the Military Subcommittee, the Exchange and Cooperation Subcommittee and the Joint Nuclear Control Commission in accordance with the 1991 North-South Agreement on Reconciliation, Nonaggression, Exchanges and Cooperation and the Joint Declaration on Denuclearization of the Korean Peninsula of December 31, 1991, notwithstanding, as long as both sides cling to their respective ideological and political positions, the military readiness as the ultimate recourse to defend each other's political, ideological and territorial integrity is inevitable. The question here is not the necessity for such readiness per se but its sufficiency and feasibility: How long can such arms race continue? This question cannot be answered until and unless the ultimate objectives of each side's military strategy are probed. What follows is, thus, an account of North and South Korea's respective military strategies.

North Korea's Military Strategy

True to the communist doctrine, the WPK control of the Korean People's Army (KPA) in North Korea is a fact. Beyond that, due to Kim Il Sung's prolonged rule and the intensity of his cult, the KPA seems to be his own "private" army in that the rise and fall of the military leadership within the KPA hierarchy are largely, if not solely, determined by their loyalty to Kim and increasingly now to his son, Jŏng Il. The KPA is also a "revolutionary army" since "the liberation" of the southern half from the "yoke of imperialism" has been its utmost priority in rhetoric, if not in reality. Like its South Korean counterpart, the KPA is a "political army" because it is not politically neutral. The similarity between the two ends here, since the KPA is not directly involved in North Korean politics but simply serves as a military instrument of the WPK and its supreme leader, Kim Il Sung and Kim Jŏng Il.[21]

The development of North Korea's military strategy may be divided into five major periods. The first period (1945-1950) may be characterized as the rapid militarization and war preparation stage under the Soviet auspices and aids. During this period North Korea virtually followed the Soviet military organizational and operational strategy. The Korean War (1950-1953) followed during which North Korea applied both the Soviet and Chinese military operational strategies and tactics. The war experiences led to a review of North Korea's Soviet and Chinese-style military strategies and caused North Korea to seek an independent military line, applicable to the Korean setting. During the third period (1953-1962) North Korea concentrated its efforts in rebuilding and rehabilitating its war-torn military. At the same time Kim Il Sung attempted to establish his own independent military strategy, based primarily on his past experiences of anti-Japanese guerrilla warfares.

The period of the fourth military strategy began in 1962 with the launching of the so-called Four Great Military Lines. At the Fifth Plenum of the Fifth Central Committee of the Fourth WPK on December 10-14, 1962, Kim Il Sung proclaimed the Four Great Military Lines: (1) the militarization of the entire people; (2) the fortification of the entire country; (3) the cadreization of the entire military; and (4) the modernization of the entire military. The militarization of the people meant their military training and readiness. Specifically, the people's militia -- the Workers-Peasant Red Guard originally created in 1959 -- was expanded in October 1966 by lowering the eligibility age from 18 to 45 to 17 to 45 and by training them jointly with the regular KPA. The fortification of the country is essential, according to Kim Il Sung, because today's war can take place anywhere at anytime on land, air or at sea, and, thus, the entire North Korean territory must be fortified. The cadreization of the military involves the training of the officers and the enlisted men so that all the military personnel can lead a military unit one level higher than their present assignment -- the platoon leader can lead the company, the company commander, the battalion, the battalion commander, the regiment, and so on. The modernization of the entire military is self-explanatory as are the modernization of the KPA weaponry and the updating of the military technologies and industries.

In accordance with the above Four Great Military Lines, North Korea had adopted seven key military strategies: (1) emphasizing mountain and night combat training; (2) combining small-unit activities and large-scale operations; (3) combining regular and irregular warfares; (4) fortifying the rear; (5) strengthening soldiers' moral and ideological armaments; (6) improving the quantity and quality of military units; and (7) improving the quality of military leadership. According to a South Korean specialist on North Korean military strategy, North Korea had a specific military plan to re-invade South Korea.[22] Another specialist asserted that North Korea completed its invasion plan by October of 1970.[23] Both Bae and Yun believed that the North Korean military strategy during this period was based on an admixture of regular and irregular warfares, preemptive surprise attacks, speedy execution and completion of war. Specifically, the four-point guidelines based on this military strategy were: (1) destroy South Korea's industrial viability and military retaliatory capacity by surprise attacks; (2) send specially trained commando forces, guerrillas and saboteurs throughout South Korea to disrupt and undermine its rear prior to launching an open frontal offensive; turn the entire territory of South Korea into battle-fields in the initial stage of war by simultaneously executing large-scale surprise attacks, coastal bombardment and naval blockade; (3) occupy Seoul and other metropolitan areas in the South at the earliest possible time; and (4) occupy the entire South Korea as speedily as possible.[24]

The period of the fifth and present military strategy began in the middle of the 1980s when Gorbachev emerged as the new leader of the former Soviet Union. The consequent collapse of the former Soviet Union and Eastern Europe, South Korea's conspicuous success in her Nordpolitik and the US victory in the Gulf War have forced North Korea's military planners to rethink, reorient and reformulate their heretofore military strategy. But the real content of its new strategy is still unknown and undisclosed.

According to a South Korean specialist's analysis, North Korea's recent force deployment postures are "outrightly offensive": more acquisition of locally produced lethal weapons; more formation of mechanized and armored divisions; and more than 65% of the armed forces deployment in the frontline.[25] In fine, it is extremely difficult, if not impossible, to analyze the real picture of North Korea's military strategy (or South Korea's military strategy, for that matter) primarily because the first-hand intelligence data is unobtainable.

South Korea's Military Strategy

The metamorphoses of South Korean military strategy may also be divided into five major periods. Like the sovietization of North Korea's military in the initial period, South Korea's military during the 1945-1950 period was largely the creation of the U.S. Military Government (1945-1948). In this period, South Korean military strategy, if any, was to organize the military constabulary capable of engaging in skirmishes along the 38th parallel and combating such communist or pro-communist riots and mutinies as the Yŏsu-Sunchŏn Rebellion, the Daegu Incident and the Cheju Rebellion within the South.[26] Although the so-called "March North" slogan (i.e., "march to the North and crack down the Kim Il Sung bandits") was often repeated in public by President Syngman Rhee during this period, it was more a political rhetoric than a substantive military strategy.[27]

The North Korean invasion of the South in June 1950 led to changes in South Korean military strategy. With the exception of the so-called roll back policy[28] briefly pursued by both the U.S. and South Korean governments during the euphoric period of the Korean War from September to October of 1950, when the UN forces (virtually all manned by the U.S. forces) successfully landed in Inchon and pushed the North Korean troops to the North Korean-Manchurian border and suddenly confronted the massive Chinese offensive, the South Korean military strategy has been to build a credible military force to prevent another invasion from the North. In that sense, the South Korean military strategy has been essentially defensive and other-reliant. The defensive character of the South Korean military strategy basically has remained unchanged, although its reliance on others has undergone a series of metamorphoses, i.e., from its exclusive reliance on U.S. to its reliance on U.S. and Japan, and to its increasingly more self-reliant defense posture with the coordination of the U.S. and Japan and with the normalization of relations with Russia and China.

During the third period (1953-1960s), South Korea added several new dimensions to its military strategy. First, with the conclusion of the 1954 U.S.-Republic of Korea Mutual Defense Treaty, the joint military strategy between South Korea and the United States was formalized. (Note in this connection that ever since the participation of the United Nations Command in the Korean War, the UN Commander, i.e., the Commander of the U.S. forces in Korea—presently the Commander of the ROK-U.S. Combined Forces Command—has held the military operational power of both South Korean and U.S. forces in the South.) Second, after the successful military coup d'etat in May 1961, the South Korean military has become politicized. The military take-over of political power in 1961 had ended the practice of fragile civilian control of the military during the Rhee (1948-1960) and the Chang (August 1960-May 1961) governments. From then onward, the politicization of the South Korean military has become virtually a semi-permanent political fixture. Thirdly, sending the South Korean troops to South Vietnam and normalizing relationships with Japan in 1965 provided the major catalysts in changes occurring later in its military strategy.

In the fourth period, beginning in the late 1960s, South Korea's more self-reliant defense posture has begun to burgeon. It was more like the South Korean response to Nixon's Guam Doctrine, characterized by "self-help" and "Asia for Asians."[29] Five factors deserve attention in this regard. First was the summit meeting between Nixon and Park on 22 August 1969. Among other things, at this meeting, both agreed that with the U.S. help South Korea was to create the Homeland Reserve Defense Force and to expand the militia. A year later, on 18 November 1970, Nixon announced his plan to reduce the 63,000 United States forces in South Korea. To compensate for this force reduction, South Korea launched a five-year 1.5 billion dollar military modernization plan (FY 1971-1975) in cooperation with the United States. This plan was followed by another five-year Force Improvement Plan (1975-1980), which was extended to 1982.

Second, in 1973 the U.S. grant aid support for the South Korean military operations and maintenance costs was terminated. In 1976 the U.S. grant aid for South Korea's arms purchase also ended. Since 1977 South Korea has been underwriting essentially all of its defense costs, increasingly through commercial purchases and U.S. foreign military sales credits. Third, the failure of the U.S. intervention in the Vietnam War and the fall of South Vietnam in 1974 gave additional impetus to President Park's self-reliant defense posture. South Korea's policy of *ch'ongryŏk anbo* [all-out general mobilization for security], thus, was born. Fourth, the changes in South Korean-Japanese relations deserve attention. Via the period of enmity (1945-1960), the period of normalization (1961-1965) and the period of economic partnership (1965-1969), South Korea and Japan entered a new phase of economic and security partnership in 1969. The often-quoted Nixon-Sato communique on 19-20 November 1969, in which Sato proclaimed that "the security of the Republic of Korea (is) essential to Japan's own security," heralded the new South Korea-Japan-U.S. security links. Since Sato's proclamation, all the Japanese prime ministers during this period had delivered essentially similar reassurances concerning Korea, although their phrases have swung from the security of "the Republic of Korea" to that of "the Korean Peninsula."[30]

Finally, Carter's U.S. troop withdrawal plan, though aborted, compelled Park and his defense planners to reassess South Korea's heavily U.S.-reliant defense policy. With the launching of the Reagan administration, the traditional U.S. commitment to South Korea's security, and the continued presence of 40,000 U.S. forces had been reaffirmed. Still, the traditional bilateral South Korea-U.S. mutual defense strategy has been replaced gradually by the new trilateral South Korea-U.S.-Japan security arrangements. The former Soviet Union's decision to deploy SS-20 missiles in the Soviet Far East and to increase its naval presence in the Sea of Japan and the Pacific had made the closer trilateral coordination paramount.

The fifth and current South Korea's military posturing is characterized by more independence from the U.S. South Korea's assumption of greater military cost-sharing for the U.S. forces in South Korea, its gradual role change as the leading partner in its military alliance with the U.S. playing a "supportive" role and the gradual reduction/withdrawal of the U.S. forces whose presence in the South will be symbolic by the end of this century. Since July 1992, for example, a Korean general heads the UN ground command force although the overall command remains in the U.S. hands. Of course, all these changes are contingent upon North Korea's military behavior including the latter's resolution of nuclear issue.

In sum, South Korea's military strategy has been essentially defensive. It has responded to the changing North Korea's military strategies and to the great power dynamics. Unlike in North Korea, where the Soviet troops and the Chinese Volunteers withdrew in 1948 and 1958, respectively, in South Korea less than 40,000 U.S. troops currently remain as a military and security wedge, i.e., to deter and to dissuade North Korea from contemplating re-invasion of the South. Since the Korean War, the erstwhile bilateral ROK-U.S. mutual defense agreements and the current trilateral ROK-U.S.-Japan security arrangements have been effective in countering the unabating North Korean militancy. The peace on the Korean Peninsula has been fragile, nevertheless. Above all, South Korea's establishment of normal diplomatic relations with Russia and China, due primarily to the Roh government's successful execution of *Nordpolitik*, has initiated the formation of new security order surrounding the Korean Peninsula. Whatever the final form and format of this newly changing security order, South Korea's present three-way defense links with U.S. and Japan remain stronger and more stable than North Korea's security links with Russia and China.

Political Military and Military Politics

The political implications of maintaining and expanding the already swollen military forces in both North and South Korea have been significant. On the surface, the Kim Il Sung-Kim Jŏng Il regime and the Kim Young-sam government are similar in that their respective military machine can serve as the ultimate political control mechanism. In North and South Korea, the military is the single largest organized *political* force although in the South under Roh and now Kim the military's political role, actual and potential, has been dampened considerably. One who controls the military, in turn, controls politics, although the reverse is not always true. The military forces in North and South Korea are, in short, politicized. The similarity between the two regarding the role of the military roughly ends here. The North Korean military is politicized in that the party control (i.e., the WPK, the "Supreme Leader" Kim Il Sung and the Supreme Commander Kim Jong-Il) of the military is firm and complete. The military is an integral part of the WPK's political control mechanism. It serves as the WPK's political instrument. In that sense, the North Korean military is a typical "political military" in a totalitarian communist system.

The North Korean military is controlled by dual political (party) organizations. All the military units of the Korean People's Army, beginning
at the platoon level, contain both the WPK and the League of Socialist
Working Youth organizations. Article 46 of the WPK bylaws (1980)
states that "the Korean People's Army is the revolutionary armed forces
of the Workers' Party of Korea in the glorious tradition of the anti-
Japanese armed struggle." Article 47 is even more specific: "A party
organization shall be organized in every unit of the Korean People's
Army," all party organizations within and the Korean People's Army
function under the direct guidance of the Korean People's Army party
committee. Article 48 stipulates that all the armed forces must be armed
with Kim Il Sung's *Juche* ideology. The WPK Central Committee Secretariat assigns political commissars directly to the regiment level and
up, and political commissars, in turn, dispatch political officers to all the
military units below the regiment levels. The tasks of these political
commissars and their political officers are to organize the party cells
within the military, to implement the Party policy guidelines, to undertake the Party ideology education and to keep all military personnel
under surveillance.

The party control of the military runs as follows: the Supreme Leader
Kim Il Sung and the supreme commander of the people's army, Kim
Jŏng Il are at the top, the next is the WPK Central Committee Secretariat and the Political Committee, followed by Party's Central Military
Committee (Kim Il Sung is its chairman) along with the DPRK National
Defense Commission, the Ministry of People's Armed Forces, the General Political Bureau and the Political Security Bureau and the military
chain of commands from the central headquarters down to the lowest
unit.[31]

The North Korean political military system is different, for instance,
from the civilian control of the military in the United States. In the former, the military is under one-party-one-man dictatorship; it is controlled by a semi-permanent party organization, which is not subject to
replacement by another party organization. In the latter, the civilian
supremacy of the military (i.e., the U.S. President as the Commander-in-
Chief of the armed forces) is guaranteed under the Constitution. But the

civilian control of the military is replaceable by another set of civilians which occurs through periodic electoral process.

The military's politicization began in South Korea since its entry into the political arena in 1961 via a military coup. If North Korea typifies the party control of the military, South Korea had exemplified the military control of politics. Generally, two contrasting arguments exist for the military intervention in politics. At one extreme, it is argued that the defense or enhancement of the military's own corporate interests is the most important interventionist motive.[32] At the other extreme, a military intervention is advocated when a regime is too weak, corrupt or arbitrary to govern and lacks a legitimate political apparatus to assume political power and maintain political stability. The South Korean experience indicates that the truth may lie somewhere between these two poles of argumentations.[33]

Thus far, four patterns of civil-military relations had emerged in the South Korean political arena. They are: (i) the civilian control of the military; (ii) the control of politics by the military in civilian clothes; (iii) the military control of civil politics; and (iv) the civil-military collusion and control of politics. During the Rhee government (1948-1960), the fragile civilian controlled the military. With the successful coup in 1961, the military junta lasted for nearly three years, before it was replaced by another pattern. Namely, Park Chung Hee, as ex-army major-general, set the precedent for the control of politics by the military in mufti in 1964 and had ruled for eighteen years until his assassination.[34]

Generally, the longer the control of the military in mufti, the more likely is the occurrence of the civil-military collusion and control of politics, i.e., the political fusion of the military leaders, top bureaucrats and civilian politicians with the elites in academia, mass media and other social, labor and religious groups. With the exception of the initial military junta during the 1961-1963 period, the direct military control of politics in South Korea under either a martial law or a state of siege had usually taken place during domestic political crises.

The prevailing pattern of civil-military relations in South Korea, beginning in 1961, had been the civil-military political fusion. Like his predecessor Park, President Chun, formerly an army general, had basically followed the same pattern: initially assumed the political power by the military coup; temporarily controlled politics under martial law; exchanged military uniforms for civilian clothes; and gradually fused civil and military political forces. Specifically, Chun overtook power by a successful execution of a mini military putsch on 12 December 1979, after a brief period of power vacuum created by the sudden death of the former President Park. After retiring from the military as a four-star general in 1980, he assumed the South Korean presidency as a civilian on 27 August 1980. During this brief presidential interim amidst domestic political turmoils, most notably, the Kwang-ju uprising in May of that year, Chun was inaugurated as the 12th president of the Republic on 25 February 1981. Since then, the new civil-military fusion had emerged slowly for the second time in South Korean political arena.

Unlike North Korea's political military, South Korea had epitomized military politics from 1961 to 1988 until the popularly elected Roh regime (1988-1993) had emerged, although he, too, initially seized power along with Chun through the military putsch in December 1979. In North Korea the party controls the military as its political instrument, while in South Korea the military entered the political process as the ultimate power broker, as it had demonstrated twice in 1961 and 1979. In North Korea the ultimate political power still flows from the Party to the military. In South Korea it had originated from the military and spilled into the civilian politics especially during the Park and Chun regimes. Specifically, the South Korean power during the Park and Chun regimes (to a certain extent it was also true of the Roh regime) was set into motion as follows:

After a successful execution of the coup, a former army general, became a civilian and gained control of political power through legal and constitutional trappings. He, then, put the military organizations, from the Ministry of Defense to the Armed Forces Headquarters down to the company level under the surveillance through various military and political intelligence officers dispatched from the Agency for National Security and Planning (formerly the KCIA), the Military Intelligence Agency, the Counter-Espionage Operations Command and others (formally, at least, the Commander of the United States and the Republic of Korea Combined Forces Command retains operational power of both the South Korean military and the U.S. forces).

In sum, as long as the military forces in both Koreas continue to remain as the single largest organized forces, and unless and until the ruling elites undertake an overall reassessment and re-direction of their present politico-military policies, North Korea's politicization of its military is most likely to continue. Meanwhile, South Korea's militarization of politics has been challenged and significantly curtailed during the Roh regime and again under the Kim Young-sam regime although it is still too early to pronounce its termination. In the final analysis, it is the artificial, arbitrary and anomalous division of the country that has been the root cause of the maintenance and continual expansion of the two large hostile armed forces in the two sides of the Korean Peninsula. These two sets of swollen armed forces, in turn, have become the source of North Korea's political military and South Korea's military politics.

What Can and Should Be Done

The cost of keeping up with the armaments, the paradox of mutual arms race creating more, not less, tensions and insecurity and the negative political consequences resulting from the already swollen armed forces are the major reasons to reassess and redirect the current military situations on the Korean Peninsula. The search for an arms control and reduction formula acceptable to both North and South Korea would be the answer to the current problem. What can and should be done?

Wilkinson, for one, identified several peace strategies which are often subject to public debate. They are: peace through morality, law, negotiation, political reform, national liberation, disarmament, international organization and power.[35] He further contends that much talk on war and peace amounts to no more than high-handed assertions that my chosen theory is right, and all others are wrong. The debate, according to him, is spiced with epithets: "Your theory is utopian or cynical, rightist or leftist, dovish or amoral, appeasing or militant, capitalistic or socialistic, naive or corrupt." The public debaters usually spend most of their time in "devising new ways of styling each other's views 'rubbish.' "[36] In short, the public discussion of war and peace has been polemical but seldom scientific. The question of peace and war on the Korean Peninsula (or, Korean unification for that matter) is not an exception to this rule.

Bearing Wilkinson's above warnings in mind, a few steps are suggested which can be seen as the new alternative to the present political and military predicaments on the Korean Peninsula.

(1) Continuation of Mutual Dialogue

Talk is infinitely preferable to no talk. A North-South dialogue should proceed in whatever format, preferably with an agreement to end vicious and vitriolic propaganda attacks on each other, let alone the Rangoon Incident-type North Korean terroristic activities. As noted in the above, the North-South dialogue is presently on-going. As an acute foreign observer pointed out, a political and propagandistic "theatrics" or "ritualistic reiteration of basic positions" rather than a move resulting from substantive changes in their "actual modalities" still leads the way, nevertheless.[37] Whatever the case, the continuing dialogue may eventually reduce the mutual tensions, mistrust and misunderstanding. For, the seemingly wasteful dialogue is far preferable to the never-ending mutual arms build-up.

(2) Maintenance of Defensive Capabilities

Although there is a general consensus that defensive capabilities of both the North and the South should be sufficient to deter attacks from the other side, no agreement exists as to what constitutes such sufficiency. Like the Prisoner's Dilemma, the breakdown in mutual communications between the two makes measuring of such sufficiency virtually impossible. The progress in current dialogues will lead to the reduction of mutual distrust and tension, let alone miscalculations of each other's military capabilities. North Korea's Peoples Armed Forces (PAF), presently 1.1 million strong, backed by a 200,000 security force and 3.8 million worker/peasant Red Guards still remain "a credible threat by

reason of its overall size, committment, and its seeming preparedness
and capacity to initiate hostilities." The PAF is, however, handicapped
in various ways, including its primitive transport system, rudimentary
command and control systems and limited exercising possibilities due to
severe fuel shortages.[38] Still, until and unless a radical change in North
Korea's long-standing military strategy occurs, South Korea, too, must
maintain a credible defense system to deter and dissuade the former's
unwarranted military adventurism.

(3) Restraint of Big Powers's Arms Sales and Transfers

Self-restraints in over-all arms sales, especially by the former Soviet
Union and China to North Korea, and by the United States and other
countries to South Korea, respectively, are essential. These allies should
adopt prudent guidelines in selling of offensive weapons and transferring of potentially destabilizing weapons technology. In the short run, it
may be enticing for the arms suppliers to sell arms to both. In the long
run, however, observing self-restraint and adhering to a strict arms sale
guideline would be advantageous to both the arms suppliers and the
recipients. For the accelerated arms race on the Korean Peninsula will
increase military tensions in the area and the probability of an outbreak
for another war, which would be self-destructive to both Koreas and
their respective allies. Needless to mention, the faults may not necessarily lie solely with the venders of such weapons. More often than not,
they rest with the buyers, who, fail to realize the full political, economic
and human consequences of such purchase. Specifically, the 1991 SIPRI
Yearbook reported that in 1990 the value of U.S. arms deliveries
exceeded that of Soviet arms exports. Still, the Soviet-American shares
of the world arms total in 1990 were 29% and 40%, respectively. Note
also that South Korea's exports of major conventional weapons, which
had shown significant growth until the mid-1980s, were virtually eliminated by 1990. North Korea, too, has reduced its arms imports considerably since 1990. Still, North Korea ranked 15th in the 1986-90 aggregate total arms exports, while North Korea and South Korea ranked 5th
and 9th in the total imports of the major conventional arms. What is

more, North Korea's I-Scud, with a maximum range of 500-600km, could be, according to the SIPRI, in a limited operational service after 1991.[39] Above all, because North Korea refused to implement the North-South mutual inspections, nuclear project remains a major obstacle, despite the IAEA inspection of its nuclear facilities (See Tables 18-4, 18-5 and Table 18-6).

(4) Formalization of Political and Military Status Quo

If both sides realize that the military solution is the least desirable and the most self-destructive means to resolve the Korean question, then other strategies must be sought. The prerequisite to search for other means can be the basis for a dialogue, which requires a mutual acceptance of each other's political and military status quo. The so-called four-power (Russia, China, Japan and the United States) guarantee of the political and military status quo in the Korean Peninsula—will help facilitate this process. At present the North-South joint entry into the UN in September 1991, the establishment of Soviet-South Korean diplomatic relations on 30 September 1990, the establishment of the Chinese-South Korean formal diplomatic relations on 24 August 1992, North Korea's off and on meetings with Japan and the United States are all pointing in that direction. Still, the possibility, if not the probability of the present Kim-Kim regime collapsing abruptly, cannot be completely ruled out.

(5) Stabilization of Arms Race and the Peaceful Resolution of the Korean Question

One of the reasons for the failure of the North-South dialogue in the early 1970's was the clash between North Korea's "simultaneous approach" and South Korea's "step-by-step approach." North Korea insisted on the simultaneous resolution of all five areas of the Korean question—the military, economic, political, cultural and humanitarian —while South Korea advocated the resolution of less controversial issues first before tackling the more problematic questions.[40] The current stalemate in the North-South dialogue differs little from the previous

ones. North Korea's earlier simultaneous approach or "package settlement and simultaneous implementation," has proven to be too unrealistic and inflexible. The eventual withdrawal of the U.S. forces from
South Korea, for instance, should be included in all the North-South dialogue agendas, but this point will become relevant later when both sides
have agreed to halt their mutual arms race and to implement the reduction of arms and force levels and have restored their mutual interaction
and communication in the economic, cultural and other non-political
and non-ideological areas.

If an inter-Korean dialogue can lead to less tension and distrust and to
mutual recognition of the political and military status quo in the Korean
Peninsula, guaranteed and cross-recognized by the four powers, then an
opportunity to, first, stabilize the arms build-up and to eventually reduce
the arms and military force level will be ripe. If the present military policy and strategy of North and South Korea lead to further arms race and
more insecurity, then the reduction of their military force levels by
mutual dialogue and understanding becomes a feasible alternative.
Above all, the persistence of the division remains a national problem
requiring a national solution. The continual obsession to resolve the
national question by politico-military means has indeed been its fundamental obstacle. The sooner the ruling elites of the North and the South
separate the national problem from their own politico-military obsession, quicker its resolution. The North-South arms race will continue as
long as the ruling elites on both sides of the Peninsula fail to separate
the two.

In conclusion, rationality seldom prevails in politics. The current
inter-Korean politics, especially the North-South arms race, demonstrates this point. Ideally, the aforementioned alternative approach to the
current arms race in the Korean Peninsula should be implemented at
once, but in reality, it may just remain as one of the numerous alternatives, which have often been swept away by the strong cross-currents of
North Korea's political military and South Korea's military politics. In
the end, then, the persistence of the politico-military dilemma in the
Korean Peninsula is due not to the lack of alternative policies and proposals, but the failure to implement them. For this failure, neither the

North nor the South is blameless, although the former has been far more inflexible and doctrinaire than the latter.

Table 18-1. North Korea's Military Force Level

Year	Population (Million)	Total Armed Forces (1,000)	Armed Froces per 1,000
1991	23.2	1,110	47.8
1990	22.2	1,040	46.8
1987	20.6	840	40.8
1982-83	19.2	784	40.8
1981-82	18.7	782	41.8
1980-81	17.5	678	37.1
1979-80	17.5	632	37.0
1978-79	17.1	512	29.9
1977-78	16.7	500	29.5
1976-77	16.2	495	29.4
1975-76	15.9	467	28.5
1974-75	15.5	467	29.4
1973-74	15.0	470	30.3
1972-73	14.3	402	30.5
1971-72	13.9	401	30.8
1970-71	13.6	413	30.8
1969-70	13.3	384	29.7
1968-69	13.0	384	30.6
1967-68	12.5	368	29.5
1966-67	12.3	368	30.4
1965-67	12.0	353	29.4
1964-65	12.0	325	27.0
1963-64	10.0	280	28.0
1962-63	10.0	338	33.0

Adapted from the International Institute for Strategic Studies (IISS) annual military balance data, 1962-63, 1982-83, 1986-1987, 1989-1990 and 1991-1992 and *The World Military Expenditures and Arms Transfers, 1966-75* (WMEAT) (Washington, D.C.: U.S. Arms Control and Disarmament Agency, 1976), and WMEAT, 1971-80 and 1985.

Table 18-2. South Korea's Military Force Level

Year	Population (million)	Total Armed Forces (1,000)	Armed Forces per 1,000
1991	44.3	750	16.9
1990	43.0	650	15.9
1987	43.0	601	13.9
1983-82	41.4	602	14.5
1981-82	40.7	601	14.8
1980-81	38.2	600	16.1
1979-80	37.7	619	16.3
1978-79	35.9	642	15.6
1977-78	35.2	635	15.8
1976-77	34.6	595	16.4
1975-76	34.4	625	17.5
1974-75	33.7	625(634)	17.8
1973-74	32.6	633	18.2
1972-73	32.0	634	18.7
1971-72	32.7	634	19.2
1970-71	31.8	645	19.9
1669-70	31.0	620	19.5
1968-69	31.0	620	20.0
1967-68	29.0	612	20.2
1966-67	28.7	571	19.3
1965-66	28.0	604	21.5
1964-65	28.0	600	21.4
1963-64	25.0	627	25.0
1962-63	23.0	602	26.1

Adapted from the same sources as Table 18-1.

Table 18-3. North and South Korea's Military Expenditure, 1981-90

Year	North Korea		South Korea	
	Unit: Million *won*	Million US dollars	Million *won*	Million US dollars
1981	3,009 (11.5)	1,349	2,831 (6.0)	5,103
1982	3,242 (11.8)	1,454	3,163 (5.8)	5,318
1983	3,530 (12.3)	1,583	3,406 (5.3)	5,535
1984	3,819 (12.0)	1,713	3,573 (4.9)	5,675
1985	3,935 —	1,765	3,957 (4.9)	6,135
1986	3,976 —	1,783	4,372 (4.7)	6,593
1987	3,971 (9.5)	1,781	4,915 (4.5)	7,195
1988	3,886 (8.7)	1,743	5,753 (4.6)	7,865
1989	4,060 (8.8)	1,821	6,226 (4.4)	8,057
1990	4,466 —	2,003	6,638 —	7,827

Source: *SIPRI Yearbook, 1991*, pp. 164-178. Figures are in million U.S. dollars at 1988 prices and the exchange rate figures in parentheses are North and South Korea's military expenditure as a percentage of their respective gross domestic product.

Table 18-4. The Leading Importers of Major Conventional Weapons,
1986-90

Importers	1986	1987	1988	1989	1990	1986-90
Third World						
1. India	3,729	4,582	3,382	3,754	1,541	16,989
2. Saudi Arabia	2,413	2,400	2,046	1,427	2,553	10,838
3. Iraq	2,484	4,440	2,155	1,177	59	10,314
4. Afghanistan	692	768	1,009	2,183	1,091	5,742
5. Korea, North	1,019	631	1,458	1,276	516	4,900
6. Egypt	1,645	2,379	348	139	206	4,717
7. Syria	1,511	1,172	1,172	336	0	4,191
8. Angola	980	1,140	889	74	508	3,592
9. Korea, South	287	604	987	997	249	3,125
10. Iran	738	704	558	336	578	2,913
11. Israel	446	1,629	507	100	21	2,703
12. Pakistan	609	467	467	760	390	2,693
13. Taiwan	825	575	459	391	178	2,427
14. Thailand	94	644	540	489	558	2,325
15. Libya	1,363	294	78	511	0	2,247
Others	5,279	4,797	3,971	4,306	3,393	21,747
Total	24,114	27,228	20,025	18,256	11,841	101,464
Industrialized World						
1. Japan	1,780	1,768	2,176	3,163	2,083	10,971
2. Spain	1,039	1,513	1,580	794	639	5,565
3. Poland	1,057	1,007	1,147	1,179	330	4,719
4. Czechoslovakia	1,077	964	1,054	1,055	422	4,571
5. Turkey	465	1,028	1,219	1,037	623	4,372
6. Greece	156	93	783	1,367	613	3,012
7. Germany, FR	411	301	298	916	1,043	2,970
8. Australia	699	478	579	714	353	2,822
9. Canada	770	702	443	244	289	2,448
10. German DR	515	359	503	502	412	2,292
11. USSR	473	497	483	359	359	2,172

Table 18-4. Continued

Importers	1986	1987	1988	1989	1990	1986-90
12. Netherlands	702	296	154	761	108	2,021
13. Bulgaria	684	568	187	17	334	1,790
14. Norway	153	395	275	479	348	1,650
15. Yugoslavia	103	234	748	450	14	1,550
Others	2,255	2,345	2,113	2,216	1,914	10,843
Total	12,338	12,549	13,742	15,253	9,885	63,768
All Countries						
1. India	3,729	4,582	3,382	3,754	1,541	16,989
2. Japan	1,780	1,768	2,176	3,163	2,083	10,971
3. Saudi Arabia	2,413	2,400	2,046	1,427	2,553	10,838
4. Iraq	2,484	4,440	2,155	1,177	59	10,314
5. Afghanistan	692	768	1,009	2,183	1,091	5,742
6. Spain	1,039	1,513	1,580	794	639	5,565
7. Korea, North	1,019	631	1,458	1,276	516	4,900
8. Poland	1,057	1,007	1,147	1,1679	330	4,719
9. Egypt	1,645	2,379	348	139	206	4,717
10. Czechoslovakia	1,077	964	1,054	1,055	422	4,571
11. Turkey	465	1,028	1,219	1,037	623	4,372
12. Syria	1,511	1,172	1,172	336	0	4,191
13. Angola	980	1,140	889	74	508	3,592
14. Korea, South	287	604	987	998	249	3,125
15. Greece	156	93	783	1,367	613	3,012
Others	16,119	15,287	12,361	13,552	10,293	67,612
Total	36,453	39,776	33,768	33,509	21,726	165,232

Source: *SIPRI Yearbook, 1991*, p. 199.

*The countries are ranked according to the 1986-90 aggregate exports. The figures are in million US dollars at constant (1985) prices.

Table 18-5. The Leading Exporters of Major Conventional Weapons,
1986-90

Exporters	1986	1987	1988	1989	1990	1986-90
To the Third World						
* 1. USSR	10,440	10,936	8,658	8,862	4,273	43,169
2. USA	4,981	6,328	3,939	3,4675	3,048	21,761
3. France	3,446	2,659	1,413	1,642	1,330	10,490
4. China	1,463	2,553	1,810	817	926	7,569
5. UK	1,091	1,681	1,281	1,187	971	6,210
6. Germany FR	661	254	367	168	496	1,946
7. Netherlands	132	263	402	661	125	1,583
8. Italy	399	320	362	49	39	1,169
9. Brazil	134	491	338	151	22	1,136
10. Israel	261	267	111	241	31	912
11. Sweden	141	298	240	134	1	813
12. Spain	163	139	193	244	62	802
13. Czechoslovakia	124	198	176	178	58	733
14. Egypt	159	194	216	65	33	668
15. Korea, North	48	103	128	11	11	300
Others	471	543	392	383	415	2,203
Total	24,114	27,228	20,025	18,256	11,841	101,464
To the Industrialized World						
1. USA	5,323	6,268	6,564	8,204	5,690	32,050
2. USSR	4,291	3,981	3,901	3,359	2,099	17,631
3. France	650	352	888	936	469	3,293
4. Germany, FR	458	422	903	548	468	2,799
5. Czechoslovakia	373	373	373	259	297	1,674
6. UK	409	135	120	629	249	1,542
7. Sweden	183	191	336	177	114	1,000
8. Canada	278	228	81	51	25	662
9. Poland	92	92	92	92	92	462
10. Italy	58	69	110	119	58	413

Table 18-5. Continued

Exporters	1986	1987	1988	1989	1990	1986-90
11. Switzerland	6	15	19	144	212	394
12. Netherlands	109	2	130	64	27	332
13. Spain	8	0	6	262	12	288
14. Israel	8	73	16	78	8	182
15. Saudi Arabia	39	125	0	0	0	164
Others	54	224	204	332	67	881
Total	12,338	12,549	13,741	15,253	9,885	63,767
To all Countries						
1. USSR	14,731	14,916	12,559	12,220	6,373	60,799
2. USA	10,304	12,596	10,503	11,669	8,738	53,811
3. France	4,096	3,011	2,300	2,577	1,799	13,783
4. UK	1,500	1,817	1,401	1,816	1,220	7,752
5. China	1,463	2,553	1,868	874	926	7,684
6. Germany, FR	1,120	676	1,270	716	963	4,745
7. Czechoslovakia	497	570	548	437	355	2,408
8. Netherlands	240	265	532	725	152	1,915
9. Sweden	324	489	575	311	115	1,813
10. Italy	457	389	471	169	96	1,582
11. Brazil	150	507	356	152	24	1,189
12. Israel	269	340	127	318	39	1,094
13. Spain	172	139	199	506	74	1,090
14. Canada	317	265	106	54	60	802
15. Egypt	159	194	216	65	33	668
Others	656	1,047	735	900	760	4,097
Total	36,453	39,777	33,767	33,509	21,726	165,232

Source: *SIPRI Yearbook, 1991*, p. 198.
* The countries are ranked according to the 1986-90 aggregate exports. The figures are in million US dollars at constant (1985) prices.

Table 18-6. North and South Korea's Major Arms Suppliers
1986-90

Sellers	Recipient	
	North Korea	South Korea
USSR	* 4,406	—
U.S.A.	—	2,887
France	—	62
U.K.	—	104
China	494	—
FRG	—	—
Czechoslovakia	—	—
Netherlands	—	—
Sweden	—	—
Italy	—	65
Others	—	7
Total	4,900	3,125

Sources: *SIPRI Yearbook, 1991*, pp. 208-209.

* Figures are values of major conventional weapon systems transferred in million US dollars
  at 1985 constant prices.

Notes

1. *Genesis*, 4: 9-13.
2. William Cowper, *The Nightingale and Glow-worm*. Quoted in *The Oxford Dictionary of Quotations*, 2nd ed. (London: Oxford University Press, 1966), p. 160.
3. Kenneth N. Waltz, "The International System: Structural Causes and Military Effects," in Douglas J. Murray and Paul R. Viotti, eds., *The Defense Policies of Nations: A Comparative Study* (Baltimore: Johns Hopkins University Press, 1982), p. 13.
4. Robert F. Goheen, "Problems of Proliferation: U.S. Policy and the Third World," *World Politics* 35 (1983): 207-233, especially p. 205. Recent developments in the Korean Peninsula make Goheen's arguments less tenable, nevertheless.
5. The North-South joint declaration of the denuclearization of the Korean Peninsula of December 31, 1991, is the case in point.
6. Steven B. Butler's letter to Institute of Current World Affairs on August 15, 1983 (SBB-3, unpublished).
7. John H. Herz, "Idealist Internationalism and the Security Dilemma," *World Politics* 1 (January 1950): 157-180.
8. Colin S. Gray, "The Urge to Compete: Rationale for Arms Racing," *World Politics* 34 (1974): 207-233.
9. For an analysis of North Korean economic and military data, see *Pukhan ei kukminsodŭk kaenyŏm kwa GNP Ch'ukyebangbŏp* [North Korea's Concept of National Income and its Method of Estimation] by the Ministry of National Unification Board, April, 1986. For details, see Part Five, chapter 16.
10. W. T. Lee, *The Estimation of Soviet Defense Expenditures, 1955-75* (New York: Praeger Publishers, 1977) and his "The Shift in Soviet National Priorities to Military Forces, 1958-1985," *The Annals of the American Academy of Political and Social Science* 457 (1981): 46-66.
11. For a discussion of problems associated with estimating North Korea's GNP and other economic data see, Pong S. Lee, "An Estimate of North Korea's National Income," *Asian Survey* 12 (1972): 518-526; Poong Lee, "An Estimating Method of North Korea's GNP" (in Korean), *Pukhan* (1981), pp. 86-105; Joo-whan Choi, "Estimate of North Korea's GNP," *Vantage Point* (October 1979), pp. 1-16; Poong Lee, "Method of Computing North Korean GNP (I) and (II)," *Vantage Point* (January and February 1982); Ha-chŏng Yŏn and Pong S. Lee, "A Study of Estimating North Korea's Economic Capabilities" (in Korean), Korea Development Institute (Fall 1984), pp. 139-161.
12. Edward T. Fei, "Arms Control in Korea," a paper delivered at the Association

of Asian Studies, 1 April 1978; Young Hee Park, "North Korea's Military Expenditures" (in Korean), a paper delivered at the 5th Joint Korean Political Science Association and the Association of Korean Political Scientists in North America in Seoul, Korea, August 1983. Also, Tong Whan Park, "The Korean Arms Race: Implications in the International Politics of Northeast Asia," *Asian Survey* 20 (1980): 648-660 and his "Political Economy of the Arms Race in Korea: Queries, Evidence, and Insights," *Asian Survey* 26 (August 1986): 839-850; Edward A. Olsen, "The Arms Race on the Korean Peninsula," *Asian Survey* 26 (August 1986): 851-867; Young Ho Lee, "Military Balance and Peace in the Korean Peninsula," *Asian Survey* 21 (1981): 852-864. *The Military Balance, 1989-1990,* pp. 164-165 and *The Military Balance, 1991-1992,* pp. 167-169. Also, *SIPRI Yearbook, 1991,* p. 166.

13. See, for instance, *Korea: The Economic Race between the North and the South,* a Report by National Foreign Assessment Center, U.S. Central Intelligence Agency (Washington, D.C., 1979), p. 6. Evelyn Colbert, "The Military Balance between North and South Korea," a paper delivered at the Association for Asian Studies Meeting, April 1978, p. 8. Also, Norman D. Levin, "Management and Decision-making in the North Korean Economy," A RAND NOTE N-1805/1-NA, February 1982, pp. 26-30. Robert A. Scalapino, "Current Dynamics of the Korean Peninsula," *Problems of Communism* (November-December 1981), pp. 16-31.

14. Young Ho Lee, *Op. Cit.*

15. For a detailed discussion of the North-South dialogue leading up to the 1972 Joint Communique and its subsequent developments, see *A White Paper on South-North Dialogue in Korea* (Seoul: the South-North Coordinating Committee, 1979).

16. Saadit Deger and Ron Smith "Military Expenditure and Growth in the Developed Countries" *Journal of Conflict Resolution* 27 (June 1983): 35.

17. Miles D. Wolpin, "Comparative Perspectives on Militarization, Repression and Social Welfare," *Journal of Peace Research* 20 (1983): 129-155.

18. An analysis of North Korea's so-called DCRK (the Democratic Confederal Republic of Korea) plan is found in Sung Chul Yang, "Twain: Is One Korea Possible?" a paper delivered at the Symposium on Korean Unification sponsored by the College of William and Mary, 20-22 January 1982. For a critical review of South Korea's UDRK (the Unified Democratic Republic of Korea) plan, see Sung Chul Yang, "Korean Reunification: Autism and Realism," *Korea and World Affairs* (Spring 1982), pp. 52-72.

19. C. Gray, *Op. Cit.*

20. Richard Betts, "Analysis, War, and Decision: Why Intelligence Failures are Inevitable?" *World Politics* 31 (1978): 61-89.

21. Yŏng Chul Yŏm, "The Real Picture of Increasing North Korean Military

Power" (in Korean), *Pukhan* (1981), pp. 130-139.

22. Myong Oh Bae, "Development Process of North Korea's Military Strategy," *Vantage Point* 5 (1982): 1-11.

23. Chong-hyŏn Yun, "Kim Il Sung's Concept of War and His Military Strategy" (in Korean), *Pukhan* (1980), pp. 58-72.

24. North Korea's (i.e., Kim Il Sung's) military strategy is found, for instance, in "Let Us Strengthen the Revolutionary Forces in Every Way to Achieve the Cause of Reunification of the Country," a concluding speech by Kim at the eighth plenum of the WPK Central Committee on 27 February 1964. Note-worthy here is the fact that the fifth section of this speech, dealing with the detailed plans of unification policy, was deleted. See *Great Leader Comrade Kim Il Sung's Important Works* (in Korean) (Pyongyang, 1975), pp. 234-249. Kim's revolutionary military strategy is found in *The Principle of Kim Il Sungism* (in Korean) (Pyongyang, 1974), pp. 303-318. The analyses of North Korea's military strategy by South Korean specialists abound: See, for instance, *Pukhan Chŏnsŏ, 1945-1980* (Seoul: East Asian Studies Center, 1980), pp. 411-459; Sang-Woo Rhee, *Security and Unification of Korea* (Seoul: Sogang University Press, 1983); Jun-yŏp Kim, "Structure of North Korea's Strategy Toward South Korea," *Vantage Point* 1 (October 1978): 1-17; Yŏng Chul Yŏm, "The Real Picture of Increasing North Korean Military Power" (in Korean), *Pukhan* (August 1981), pp. 130-139; Myong-oh Bae, "Development Process of North Korea's Military Strategy," *Vantage Point* 5 (May 1982): 1-11; Byŏng-chun Minn, "The Military Alliance System of North Korea," *Vantage Point* 2 (June 1979): 1-12; Hang Ku Lee, "North Korea's War Preparation in the Rear," (in Korean), *Pukhan* (August 1980), pp. 226-235; and Chong Hyŏn Yun, "Kim Il Sung's Concept of War and His Military Strategy" (in Korean), *Pukhan* (August 1980), pp. 58-72.

25. Myong-oh Bae, "An Appraisal of North and South Korean Military Capabilities" (in Korean), *Korean Journal of Unification Affairs* 6 (1986): 79-114. Also, Hwan-gi Paek, "Armament Industry of North Korea, I and II," *Vantage Point* (March and April 1982), pp. 1-11 and pp. 1-11, respectively.

26. For a discussion of South Korea's political problems during this period, see, for instance, Woon Tae Kim et al., *On Korean Politics* (in Korean) (Seoul: Pakyong-sa, 1982), pp. 231-262.

27. *Ibid.* Also, Sung Chul Yang, *Korea and Two Regimes* (Cambridge: Schenkman, 1981), pp. 305-316.

28. The roll back policy was advocated by John Foster Dulles, the U.S. Secretary of State during the Korean War. See, for instance, Sung Chul Yang, *Korea and Two Regimes*, pp. 127-129.

29. The Nixon Doctrine stated: First, the United States will keep all of its treaty commitments; second, the United States will provide a shield if a nuclear

power threatens an allied nation whose survival is vital to the United States securities; third, in cases involving other types of aggression, the United States shall furnish military and economic assistance when requested in accordance with the United States treaty commitments. But the United States shall look to the nation directly threatened to assume the primary responsibilities for providing the manpower for its defense. For details, see Richard M. Nixon, *U.S. Foreign Policy for the 1970s: Shaping a Durable Peace* (Washington, D.C.: U.S. Government Printing Office, 1973), pp. 109-110.

30. For an analysis of Japan's varied security commitments to South Korea and the Korean Peninsula, See Sung Chul Yang, *Korea and Two Regimes*, pp. 252-256.

31. For details, see *Pukhan Chŏnsŏ, 1945-1980*, pp. 425-427. Also, Sung Chul Yang, "North Korea's Military Elites and Politics" (in Korean), *Pukhan Yŏnku* (Spring 1991), pp. 134-156.

32. (1) Those who emphasize the significance of corporate grievances are: e.g., M.C. Needler "Military Motivations in the Seizure of Power," *Latin American Research Review* 10 (Fall 1975): 63-80; Eric A. Nordlinger, *Soldiers in Politics: Military Coups and Governments* (Englewoods Cliffs: Prentice-Hall, 1976); and A. Perlmutter, *The Military and Politics in Modern Times* (New Haven: Yale University Press, 1977). (2) Those who advocate the notions that Third World military organizations represent vanguards of modernization, reform and change are: Guy J. Pauker, "Southeast Asia as Problem Area in the Next Decade," *World Politics* 11 (April 1959): 325-345; Lucian L. Pye, "Armies in the Process of Political Modernization," in J.J. Johnson, ed., *The Role of the Military in Underdeveloped Countries* (Princeton: Princeton University Press, 1962); M. Halpern, *The Politics of Social Change in the Middle East and North Africa* (Princeton: Princeton University Press, 1963); Morris Janowitz, *The Military in the Political Development of New Nations* (Chicago: University of Chicago Press, 1964); and Ernest W. Lefever, *Spear and Scepter: Army, Police and Politics in Tropical Africa* (Washington, D.C.: The Brookings Institution, 1970). There are also those who emphasize the institutional decay: Samuel P. Huntington, *Political Order in Changing Societies* (New Haven: Yale University Press, 1968). (3) Some empirical study results are also available: Thompson (1973), in his enumeration of the apparent grievances of 1946-1970 military coup makers, found that 43% of the cases are related to corporate grievances, and in his 1980 study of some 229 coups he found no statistically significant differences between the relative frequencies of corporate grievances against either civilian or military governments. W. R. Thompson, "Assessing the Impact of Military Rule: Alternative Approaches," in P. C. Schmitter, ed., *Military Rule in Latin America: Function, Consequences, and Perspectives* (Beverly Hills: Sage, 1973) and his

"Corporate Coup-maker Grievances and Types of Regime Targets," *Comparative Political Studies* 12 (January 1980): 485-496 and McKinlay and Cohan found no significant differences between military and nonmilitary regimes in terms of the sizes of military organizations and expenditures. R. D. McKinlay and A. S. Cohan, "Performace and Instability in Military and Nonmilitary Regime Systems," *APSA* 70 (September 1976): 850-64 and their "A Comparative Analysis of the Political and Economic Performance of Military and Civilian Regimes: A Cross-National Aggregate Study," *Comparative Politics* 8 (October 1975): 1-30. Other studies on military regime performances are: Robert W. Jackman, "Politicians in Uniform: Military Governments and Social Change in the Third World," *APSA* 70 (December 1976): 1078-97; E. Nordlinger, "Soldiers in Mufti: The Impact of Military Rule upon Economic and Social Change in the Non-Western States, *APSA* 64 (December 1970): 1131-48; Donald Rothchild, "Military Regime Performance: An Appraisal of the Ghana Experience, 1972-78," *Comparative Politics* 12 (July 1980): 459-479; J. S. Fitch, *The Military Coup D'Etat as a Political Process: Ecuador, 1948-1966* (Baltimore: Johns Hopkins University Press, 1977); Ruth Berins Collier, "Parties, Coups, and Authoritarian Rule: Patterns of Political Change in Tropical Africa," *Comparative Political Studies* 11 (April 1978): 62-93; Henry Bienen, "Military Rule and Political Process," *Comparative Politics 10* (January 1978): 205-225; Thomas H. Johnson et al., "Explaining African Military Coup d'Eat, 1960-1982," *APSA* 78 (September 1984): 622-682.

33. See, for example, Sung Chul Yang, "Revolution and Change: A Comparative Study of the April Student Revolution of 1960 and the May Military Coup d'Etat in 1961 in Korea" (Ph.D. dissertation, University of Kentucky, 1970); Jae Souk Sohn, "The Role of the Military in the Republic of Korea," in Amos Perlmutter and Valerie Plave Bennett, eds., *The Political Influence of the Military: A Comparative Reader* (New Haven: Yale University Press, 1980), pp. 431-439; Jong-Chun Paek, "The Role of the Republic of Korea Armed Forces in National Development: Past and Future," *The Journal of East Asian Affairs* (Fall/Winter 1983), pp. 292-324; C. I. Eugene Kim, "Civil-Military Relations in the Two Koreas," *Armed Forces and Society* 11 (Fall 1984): 11-29; and one recent study identified the military as one of twelve contributing factors to South Korea's rapid modernization and economic development. See *Hankuk Ilbo*, 12 June 1984. This study was conducted by Kyong-tong Kim and his associates at the Social Science Research Institute at Seoul National University.

34. For a detailed analysis of political conditions, which led to Park's death, see Yang, *Korea and Two Regimes.*

35. David Wilkinson, *Deadly Quarrels: Lewis P. Richardson and the Statistical Study of War* (Berkeley: University of California Press, 1980), p. 3.

36. *Ibid.*
37. Adrian Buzo, "The Inter-Korean Talks," paper presented at the seminar "Korea to the Year 2000," Hoam House, Seoul National University, Seoul, Korea, 7 July 1992, p. 6. See also, A. Aron Karp, "Ballistic Missile Proliferation," *SIPRI Yearbook, 1991* (London: Oxford University Press, 1991), p. 319.
38. Adrian Buzo, "Entering the 1990s: The Democratic People's Republic of Korea," paper presented at the "Korea to the Year 2000," Hoam House, Seoul National University, Seoul, Korea, 7 July 1992, p. 6. Also, *The Military Balance, 1991-1992* (London: IISS, 1992), pp. 167-168.
39. *SIPRI, 1991*, pp. 197-227, p. 319.
40. North Korea's simultaneous or all-or-nothing approach and South Korea's step-by-step approach are found in *A White Paper on South-North Dialogue in Korea.*

CHAPTER 19

A SOCIALIST MAN VERSUS
A UNIVERSAL MAN: EDUCATION IN
NORTH AND SOUTH KOREAN POLITICS

> *Is it*
> *the gods who put this fire in our minds,*
> *or is it that each man's relentless longing*
> *becomes a god to him? Long has my heart*
> *been keen for battle or some mighty act;*
> *it cannot be content with peace or rest.*
>
> Virgil[1]

> *Isn't the pathetic grandeur of human existence in some way bound up*
> *with the eternal disproportion in this world, when self-delusion is neces-*
> *sary to life, between the honesty of the striving and the nullity of the*
> *result?*
>
> Hammarskjöld[2]

General Introduction

With the division of the country in 1945, North and South Korea have adopted two diametrically opposed educational systems. After more than forty years of separate educational experimentations, the schools in North and South Korea today, despite their high degree of cultural and linguistic homogeneity, resemble each other very little.

Because North and South Korea are not richly endowed with natural resources, both must develop and utilize their relatively abundant human resources. If there is one thing common in both halves today, it would be the importance of education as the maker and molder of human resources. Education, in fact, has been one of the most effective factors contributing to the phenomenal economic growth of South Korea since the mid-1960's.[3] The same can be said, more or less, about North Korea, which has risen from the ravages of the Korean War with an economic growth that has been rarely matched by any of its past and presently remaining socialist fraternal countries.[4]

Beyond the common policy priority on education, North and South Korea have little in common as far as their respective educational principles, policies and programs are concerned. In a broad sense, North Korea has implemented a truncated variant of socialist pedagogy, while South Korea has followed a modified version of democratic educational philosophy.[5] The fact that these two contrasting educational systems have been applied to one of the most homogeneous people on the globe for more than four decades deserves a serious scholarly attention and analysis.

In North Korea, education serves as the instruments of the ruling party, i.e., the Workers' Party of Korea (WPK). Education is utilized by the WPK as its political mind control device of the young and the mass public. Schools function as a political laboratory for socialist experimentations in creating a new socialist man of the *Juche* (self-reliance) type. Education, which is under the WPK's near total control, is an integral part of the North Korean socialist political system.[6]

In South Korea schools are regarded as the institutions of learning in the society rather than an instrument of the ruling party, although the politicization of education by the government has been frequent. Still, schools provide a learning arena for individual development, that is, for the individual to become, ideally, a universal man or *Hongik Inkan* [a person who benefits all mankind].[7] Education functions as a constitutive element in the South Korean political system, and though the governing elites have frequently attempted to politicize it, it has escaped their total or near total political control.

To the school administrators and students, any interference from and/or control of school systems by the South Korean Ministry of Education is "suffocating" and seriously undermining school autonomy. In fact, one of the key issues raised by the university students in their persistent anti-government protests in recent years has been their vociferous demands for school autonomy.[8] Paradoxically though, the very fact that the South Korean students are able to protest and demonstrate against the government distinguishes them from their brethren in the North. The South Korean government's excessive "control" of the school systems notwithstanding, students find opportunities and freedom to launch anti-government protests, unimaginable in the North.

The differences between the North and South Korean educational systems loom large and clear when the image and the role of students in the both halves are compared. In the North, the ruling party (WPK) deems students as a national asset for socialist construction, as well as its experimental objects. Outside of a few incidents of student anti-Communist demonstrations during the early formative years—the Sin'u-ju Student Revolt of November 11-23, 1945, the Hamhŭng Student Revolt of March 11-13, 1946, and the Pyongyang Student Anti-Trusteeship Demonstration in March 1946—students in the North have been under the WPK's near complete political control.[9]

By contrast, students in the South had frequently become a political liability of, and even a threat to, the government in power, although they, too, have been a national asset for economic development. Politicization of students in the both halves is extensive, but in the North all students are politicized (socialized) by the WPK for the purpose of socialist revolution and construction.[10] In the South, the government in power had politicized education to divert students, especially at the universities and colleges, from their frequent anti-governmental protestations. In the process, a vicious circle had been created. Students had demonstrated against the regime in power demanding, among other things, more school autonomy, and the government, in turn, had imposed heavier control on the school, ostensibly, to prevent such protests. Hence, the more students demonstrated, the heavier the government control and politicization of the school system, and vice versa. Thus, the chronic campus unrest had persisted. In recent years, however, student demonstrations have been lessening primarily from the Roh regime and Kim government's liberalization and democratization efforts at home and the demise of communism and of other radical international movements abroad.

In short, education in North Korea is an integral part of the WPK's political control mechanism. Students are kept under tight surveillance as the vanguard of its socialist construction and revolutionary struggles. In South Korea, education is considered a part, albeit one of the most important, of socio-economic and political systems, and students are often at the forefront of the political arena by opposing the governmental abuses and excessive meddling.

In this chapter, we will focus, first, on the development of the major themes, principles or objectives of education in North and South Korea for the past forty years. Next, we will examine the educational systems and their changes in the both halves. In doing so, a few caveats are in order. First, the present study is more of a juxtapositional comparison than an analytic comparison of the North and South Korean educational systems. Because the two educational systems operate on entirely different pedagogic principles, it is difficult, if not impossible, to find an analytic framework befitting both systems.

Second, since official principles and objectives are utilized, this study is limited to the thematic analysis of North and South Korea's educational principles and objectives. Needless to mention, the government's official pronouncements of educational policy and programs are one thing and their actual implementation, quite another. The gap, in fact, is bound to exist between official policy pronouncements and their implementations. The question is usually raised not on the existence, but on the magnitude, of such gap. This chapter will attempt to probe the political dynamics of the two halves under which the changes in the government educational policy statements have occurred over the said period. The question of how these official policy goals and principles have affected the actual workings of the respective school systems is another important area of study, but it will not be dealt with here since it is not the central concern of the present chapter.

Finally, unlike in South Korea where data and materials on education are relatively plentiful and are easily accessible, in North Korea they are severely limited and virtually unavailable. This situation poses an inherent limitation on any attempt to do comparative study of North and South Korea, including the present study of their official educational policy developments and system changes.

The Metamorphoses of Educational Themes in North Korea

To begin with, socialist pedagogy, like other aspects of North Korean development, has undergone a series of changes over the past four decades (For details, see Table 19-1). Except for a bulk of scattered remarks and reports on education made primarily by Kim Il Sung, no full-fledged charter on socialist education existed until the publication of the "Theses on Socialist Education" at the fourteenth plenary meeting of the Fifth WPK Central Committee on September 5, 1977. The 1977 theses represented the culmination of various heretofore educational pronouncements and programs. Bearing this in mind, four major thematic changes in educational philosophy in North Korea are identified here.[11]

Nation-building (1945-Early 1950's)

A heavy dosage of nationalistic and patriotic slogans and themes in education characterized this period. Thus, this is often called the period of "total mobilization of nation-building thought" or of "introducing communism." The primary emphasis of North Korean pedagogy during these formative years lay in inculcating anti-Japanese and anti-American patriotism, Marxism-Leninism and the party history of the former Soviet Union.

Kim Il Sung's early speeches on education abound in patriotic appeals and communistic ideas: "the independence of the country," "the prosperity of the nation" and "learning for the sake of the country," "being an example to the masses," "rising above one's self-interest" and "fighting in the interests of the people."[12]   For example, five "missions" of university students delineated by Kim Il Sung on the first anniversary of the Kim Il Sung University in 1947 are replete with such nationalistic spirit. They are: (1) to eliminate the remnants of Japanese imperialism; (2) to foster ardent patriotism and democratic ideas for nation-building; (3) to raise political awareness, study internal and international situations and support the policies of the people's government; (4) to equip themselves with Marxism-Leninism while mastering science and technology; and (5) to become cadres of the nation to lead the people with high national pride and revolutionary zeal.[13]

In brief, this was not only the time of nation-building but also that of Kim Il Sung's own power-base building. His power-base, then, being weak and shaky, necessitated the aid of the Soviet occupation forces as well as the temporary united front with its various communist groups to buy time to build his own political infrastructure and to eliminate his immediate political enemies, especially the nationalists.[14] To that extent, the themes of education mirrored such political needs of Kim at the initial stage of his power struggle.[15]

Communist Education (Early 1950's-Late 1950's)

The Korean War (1950–1953) period was marked by the rehabilitation and reconstruction of a war-torn country and the WPK intra-party factional struggles. This was often called the period of "communist class education" or of "modeling communism." The *Juche* (self-reliance) idea was also incubated during this period.[16]

During the Korean War education was interrupted and the students took active part in war efforts. On January 18, 1951, Kim listed eight immediate tasks for the youth: (1) to carry out combat duties; (2) to assist the advancing People's Army behind the enemy lines; (3) to rebuild the ravaged factories, enterprises, cultural establishments, towns and villages; (4) to help strengthen transportation facilities for a smooth flow of goods and supplies; (5) to take the responsibility of hygienic and anti-epidemic work in town and countryside; (6) to intensify propaganda and to increase agitation at the masses; (7) to train five to ten hard-core elements in each village; and (8) to publicize the heroic struggle of the

Korean people.[17]

On December 28, 1955, Kim delivered a speech, "On Eliminating Dogmatism and Formalism and Establishing *Juche* in Ideological Work," to party propagandists and agitators. It contained his first official statement on the now-ubiquitous idea of *Juche*. In it he contended that "...we study the history of the Communist Party of the Soviet Union, the history of the Chinese revolution, or the universal truth of Marxism-Leninism...for the purpose of correctly carrying out our own revolution." Further, he wrote:

> To make revolution in Korea we must know Korean history, geography and customs. Only then can we educate our people and inspire in them an ardent love for their native place and their motherland.[18]

In the late 50's the focus shifted from war and rehabilitation efforts to socialist construction and communist education. On March 19, 1958, Kim outlined four major missions of the youth in the building of socialism: (1) to carry out the assigned works to fulfill the First Five-Year Plan; (2) to master new techniques and advanced technology; (3) to equip themselves with a strong spirit of socialist patriotism; and (4) to play the vanguard role in molding the thinking of all the working people along socialist lines.[19]

In November of the same year, Kim identified six themes of communist education at the meeting of the Agitators of the City and County Party Committees: (1) the superiority of socialism and communism; (2) the ineluctable victory of the new (communism) over the old (capitalism); (3) the resolute resistance against individualism and selfishness; (4) socialistic patriotism and proletarian internationalism; (5) love of labor; and (6) the inculcation of the spirit of uninterrupted revolutionary progress and struggles.[20]

In political terms, Kim virtually eliminated all of his intra-party factional enemies, such as the South Korean Worker's Party faction, the Yanan faction and the Soviet faction during this period. Since only his Partisan group remained, Kim emerged as the unchallengeable supreme leader.[21]

Revolutionary Tradition Education (Early 1960's-Late 1960's)

A heavy emphasis was placed on *Juche* (self-reliance) in education as well as on the revolutionary tradition of anti-Japanese guerrilla struggles. This phase is, thus, called the period of "educating the thought of revolutionary tradition." Externally, Kim maintained more independence from, and equi-distance toward, the two giant socialist neighbors—China and the former Soviet Union. Kim was, in fact, playing the adroit diplomatic maneuvering by utilizing the ever-deepening and irreconcilable Sino-Soviet rift to his advantage. Internally, Kim consolidated his one-man dictatorship.

The shift in focus from education of (universal) communism to that of the (Korean) revolutionary tradition from the mid-50s to the late 60s reflected such changes in domestic and foreign political dynamics. The stress on the revolutionary education also meant, in essence, the integration of communist and *Juche* education. Accordingly, the ultimate aim of socialist education was not merely to create a new socialist, but a new socialist of the *Juche* type. Kim's remarks on April 18, 1963, emphasized this point: "our education should be in accord with the interests of the Korean revolution and the Korean people and should serve (as) the successful fulfillment of our revolution and construction. This is precisely *Juche* in education."[22]

In concrete terms, *Juche* education signaled the further tightening of control over the educational system by the WPK. As Kim asserted, *Juche* education signified that all the educational work should be conducted "in strict conformity with the demands of our Party policy." Specifically, the WPK determines the contents of the textbooks, teaching materials and curricula and directs all educational activities, including scientific research. It is also empowered to recruit and dismiss teachers from preschool to colleges and academies.[23] To put it another way, *Juche* education and education of revolutionary tradition represent nothing more than an intensified indoctrination.[24]

Juche education presents a peculiar mix of time perspectives. Namely, the focus on past anti-Japanese guerrilla activities, often portrayed as the single-handed feat of Kim Il Sung and on North Korea's future communist utopia (the *Juche*ization of the entire society) support this notion. Interestingly enough, in the course of glorifying North Korea's (mainly Kim Il Sung's) past revolutionary achievements and future socialist aspirations, the present state of life in general and educational life in particular are basically (perhaps deliberately) neglected. Youth and adults alike are constantly led to believe that their present hardships and sufferings are not only far less and lighter than those experienced by the anti-Japanese guerrilla fighters, but necessary for the forthcoming communist utopia. In 1961 Kim portrayed the ideal communist utopia in following terms:

> Our ideal is to build a society where everyone is well-fed, well-clothed, and lives a long life, a society where there is no laggard nor idler and all are progressive and work devotedly, a society where all the people live united in harmony as one big family...there is such plenty that people work according to their abilities and receive according to their needs.[25]

Thus, slogans and phrases studded with futuristic visions and the lore and lessons of the past anti-Japanese guerrilla struggles abound. Slogans such as "build socialism in South Korea in the future," "carry the Korean revolution through to its conclusion," "love the future" and "the future belongs to Communism" exemplify the first theme. The second theme can be discerned in such catchphrases as "the only tradition we should carry forward is the revolutionary tradition of the anti-Japanese guerrilla army" and "the work styles of the guerrilla warfare saw the emergence of true Communist revolutionaries and the attainment of firm unity in the revolutionary ranks."[26] This admixture of the past and future provide the justification for the present labor, however harsh and painstaking. In Eric Hoffer's phraseology, North Korean indoctrination epitomizes "an extravagant concept of the prospects and potentialities of the future," let alone an exaggerated view of the past accomplishments and successes.[27]

Monolithic Ideology Education (Late 1960's to the 1980's)

This phase is typified by the intensification of the Kim Il Sung cult and the exclusive emphasis on his revolutionary thought—Kimism or Kim Il Sungism.[28] For instance, on April 13, 1968, Kim declared that "in order to equip ourselves with the Party's monolithic ideology [unitary thought] it is vitally important [for us] to thoroughly oppose flunkeyism, dogmatism, revisionism, and 'left' adventurism."[29] Accordingly, Kim's *Juche* idea had become the centerpiece of North Korea's ideological shibboleths. Article 2 in the 1972 DPRK Socialist Constitution stated that the DPRK "rests on the politico-ideological unity of the entire people based on the worker-peasant alliance led by the working class." Article 4 stipulated that the DPRK is "guided in its activity by the *Juche* idea of the Worker's Party of Korea, a creative application of Marxism-Leninism to the conditions of our country."[30]

With the promulgation of the 1977 Theses on Socialist Education, comprehensive and systematic themes and principles on education were developed for the first time. The 1977 Theses listed four principles of socialist pedagogy: party control and guidance of education; *Juche* education; revolutionary practice; and state guarantee and support of education. Further, it identified political and ideological education, scientific and technical education and physical education as three major content areas of socialist education. In addition, five methods of socialist education were specified: (1) advancing heuristic teaching; (2) combining theoretical education with practical training, as well as, merging education with productive labor; (3) intensifying organized life with social and political activities; (4) combining school and social education; and (5) establishing continuity in preschool, school and adult education.[31]

In 1984, in his thesis, "On Further Developing Educational Work," Kim Jong Il stressed science education and technical training. But at the same time he reaffirmed the party guidance in education:

> Party (WPK) organizations should effectively carry on education in the monolithic ideology of the Party and revolutionary education among the teaching staff and students so that they will arm themselves firmly with our Party's revolutionary idea, think and act upon the Party's idea

and intention anytime and anywhere and be true to the Party to the end.[32]

A North Korean education specialist, for instance, identified eight main themes of North Korea's political indoctrination: loyalty to Kim Il Sung; Juche ideology; revolutionary tradition; class consciousness; anti-imperialism; communist morality; collectivism; and socialist patriotism. The first three themes (the Kim cult, Juche and Kim's revolutionary struggles) are unique, but the rest are quite similar to the main themes of the former East European socialist states.[33]

Politically, the cult of Kim Il Sung and his family during this period had reached such intensity as to elevate him to the status of a demi-god. He is seen as the biggest and brightest star in his illustrious revolutionary family constellation. All practices of the cult and occult variety in North Korea notwithstanding, Kim, an octogenarian, is mortal. His age brought the succession issue to the political forefront. The political seesaw over the succession question between Kim's only surviving younger brother, Kim Yŏng-ju, and his eldest son, Kim Jong Il was once the North Korean watchers' favorite guessing game. Since the 1980 WPK Sixth Congress endorsed Kim Jong Il as the successor, the focus of *who* has shifted to that of *what:* "What will Kim junior be like; what are the real and potential hazards that will make or break his succession? As I witnessed the operation of several schools during my visit to North Korea in the summer of 1981, the emphasis on, and glorification of, the "Dear Leader" Kim junior as the official successor were evident at all levels of schools.[34]

Father-Son Cult Building Education (early 1980s-1990s)

Beginning with the early 1980's, North Korea's school systems from nursery to university, let alone adult education, have been singularly emphasizing and inculcating the righteousness of the father-son succession. To that extent, the North Korean educational themes and principles have further degenerated into father-son cult-building.

The Changes of Official Educational Themes in South Korea

Needless to mention, any attempt to periodize the changes of educational themes in South Korea (all periodization, for that matter) is bound to be arbitrary. At the expense of gross simplification, five major thematic changes in official educational philosophy are identified here (For detail, see Table 19-1).

Introduction of Democratic Education (1945-1948)

South Korea was under the U.S. Army Military Government (USAMG) in this period. Two important educational principles announced by the U.S. military authorities were: (1) to approve private educational institutions; and (2) to prohibit discrimination in education on the basis of nationality and religion. The U.S. authorities and the Korean personnel in the USAMG also attempted to remove all the vestiges of the Japanese colonial education. Anti-Japanese and anti-Communist themes along with the democratic educational principles, proliferated.

Particularly noteworthy in this regard was the creation of the "Council for Korean Education" (CKE) by the USAMG. The CKE, manned mostly by the American trained Korean educators, was created to formulate the educational aims and principles for the Korean people. The CKE identified the realization of *Hongik Inkan* [person who benefits all mankind] through democratic education and the inculcation of national consciousness as the cornerstones of Korean educational philosophy.

In addition, John Dewey's pragmatic educational philosophy such as the emphasis on living in education, on child-centered education and on social reconstruction through education, played an important role in the establishment of the initial Korean democratic education.[35] The CKE recommended the abolishment of the existing European dual ladder system and the adoption of the new American single ladder system of 6-3-3-4 to ensure equality of educational opportunity for all children, the revision of school curricula in order to stimulate student's interest and free activity and the encouragement of group work through living experience, problem solving and self study.

The Period of Democratic National Education (1948-1953)

This period was marked by a series of domestic political violence, which ultimately led to the outbreak of the fratricidal Korean War. With the establishment of the Republic of Korea under the leadership of Syngman Rhee, the initial thrust of democratic education continued, although more emphasis was placed on national than democratic education. On December 31, 1949, the Education Law was promulgated. Its Article 1 stipulated that the purpose of education was to achieve the integration of character, to teach skills for an independent life, to train a citizen for the development of a democratic nation and to contribute toward realization of the ideal co-prosperity in accordance with the concept of *Hongik Inkan* [the greatest service for the benefit of mankind]. In Article 2 seven educational guidelines were identified: (1) development of knowledge and habits necessary for the sound growth and maintenance of the body and cultivation of an indomitable spirit; (2) development of a patriotic spirit for the country and nation in order to preserve and develop national independence and advance the cause of world peace; (3) realization of inheritance and enhancement of our national culture to contribute to the creation and development of the cultures of the world; (4) fostering of a spirit of truth-seeking and an ability to think scientifically for creative activities and a rational life; (5) development of the love of freedom and a high regard for a sense of responsibility in order to participate in community life with the spirit of faithfulness, cooperation and respect; (6) development of an aesthetic sense to appreciate and create sublime fine arts, enjoy the beauty of nature and to utilize leisure time effectively; and (7) encouragement of thriftiness and faithfulness to one's work in order to become a wise consumer and an able producer for a sound economic life. Noteworthy also is section 1 in Article 5, which states that "education shall be carried out in accordance with its original purpose and *shall never be utilized as an instrument of propaganda for any political, partisan, or other personal prejudices*" (emphasis mine).[36]

Two governmental actions during this period were notable. On March 10, 1950, the new 6-3-3-4 single ladder educational system was implemented. In the midst of War on June 4, 1952, the local autonomy in education (The Act Concerning the Establishment of School District) was enforced. This was, in short, the period during which the basic philosophical and institutional frameworks for democratic national education were put into effect.

The Period of furthering Democratic Education (1953-mid-1960's)

In this period the Korean traditional culture was criticized amidst a huge influx of Western democratic thought. Anti-Communism was also heavily stressed along with the idea of democratic citizenship.

During this period the educational aid from international organizations, such as the United Nations Korean Reconstruction Agency (UNKRA) and the International Cooperation Administration (ICA), primarily manned by American teachers, educational consultants and advisors, helped in massive rebuilding and restoring of the war-ravaged schools and school systems. At the time of the Korean Military Armistice Agreement on July 27, 1953, nearly 50% of the classrooms, and close to 80% of equipment and facilities of vocational and higher education were destroyed. To put it another way, a total of 7,544 classrooms were burned down and 15,473 others were partially damaged during the three-year War.[37]

The international aid restored educational facilities and programs. Out of nearly 1.7 billion dollars of the ICA grant, 18,440,000 dollars or 1.1% and out of 121,840,000 dollars of the UNKRA aid, 9,625,000 dollars or 7.9% were spent for educational areas during the 1954-1961 interval. In the six-year period from 1953 to 1958, a total of 16,559 classrooms were newly built.[38] Democratic and modern educational ideas and principles also accompanied the good-will international aid during this period. Democratic and modern school administrative principles, such as scientific management, professionalization, and political neutralization were introduced. In school administration: (1) instead of traditional school inspection system, more discussion and consultation among faculty members and staff were emphasized; (2) various conferences in school decision-making were utilized; and (3) research, planning and evaluation in all educational activities were stressed. Also, democratic citizenship education, extracurricular activities, audio-visual education and teaching aides were put into operation.

This was the period of student political activism, culminating in the overthrow of the Syngman Rhee government in April 1960. Notably, university students in the early to mid-1960's were the first graduates under the new democratic education in South Korea. One source of student political activism rested in their frustrations arising from an acute gap between the ideal democratic polity they learned in school and the real authoritarian polity they witnessed daily in social and political life. They channeled their frustrations arising from this lacuna through political protests against the Rhee government (1948-1960), the Park government (1961-1979), the Chun government (1980-1988) and, to a degree, against the Roh government (1988-1993).

The Period of National Education (the mid-1960s-to the early 1980s)

During this period the educational emphasis further shifted from democratic education to national and ideological (anti-Communistic) education. In 1964 the Park's civilian rule was launched after nearly three years of military rule (1961-1963) following the 1961 May Military Coup d'etat. After two decades of intermittent normalization talks, the Republic of Korea and Japan concluded the Normalization Treaty in 1965.

The principles and objectives of national education were formally instituted in school systems with the promulgation of the new Charter of National Education in 1968. The Charter of National Education identified four major goals of education: (1) the regeneration of the nation ("born into this land, charged with the historic mission of regenerating the nation," and "revitalizing the illustrious spirit of Korean forefathers"); (2) a posture of self-reliance (develop creativity and pioneering spirit in each individual); (3) the new image of the Korean people (cooperative spirit must be combined effectively to enhance the importance of individual services to the cause of national development); and (4) ideological stance and mission (to struggle against communism and to prepare for the eventual reunification of the nation in accordance with democratic principles).[39]

South Korea during this period experienced a phenomenal economic development under Park, whose political power had at the same time become more authoritarian and arbitrary. The passage of the so-called 1972 Revitalizing Constitution, which made, Park at least on paper, a virtual dictator-president, the fall of South Vietnam in 1974 and the increasing political and military instability in Northeast Asia had influenced the intensification of national and ideological education in school systems.

The Park's assassination in October 1979 and the emergence of the Chun regime had brought about a change in the direction of education in South Korea. More emphasis were placed on scientific and technological education in response to the rapidly unfolding electronic and computerized era, and the national and ideological education unleashed by the former president Park had somewhat abated.

The Period of Science Education (the early 1980s-1990s)

An emphasis on science education has continued under the Roh regime. Especially, lifting the ban on foreign travel has greatly changed the south's outlook on life, nation and the world. It has meant that there was less emphasis on ideology, nationalism in education and the expansion of basic science education. These thematic changes and trend are most likely to continue into the 1990s and beyond.

Still, as noted at the outset, the South Korean educational dilemma lies in the inherent incompatibility existing in its twin ideals—democratic education and national/ideological education. The ideals of democratic education demand school autonomy, open and free intellectual intercourse, and de-ideologization. By contrast, the objectives of national/ideological education presuppose the governmental control of school systems in intellectual intercourse and ideology education (anti-Communism). After over forty years of experimentations, there is no easy solution to this intrinsic dilemma, except perhaps to take a more liberalizing and at the same time less nationalizing education with unflappable patience and prudence. The Roh regime and the present Kim government have been, by and large, successful in liberalizing and democratizing education. It is true that an independent teachers' association, Chŏnggyojo [All-nation Teacher's League] which demanded, among other things, educational reform was banned by the government as an illegal organization. To some, however, the South Korean education is still beset with various problems, but, comparatively speaking it is far preferable to North Korea's tidy system under the WPK's near total monopoly and guidance.

In sum, the ultimate goals, priorities and models of education in North and South Korea are diametrically different (See Tables 19-1 and 19-2). In the North, the Party (the WPK) has a prefabricated ideal model—a socialist of *Juche* type—and the purpose of education is to create such men and women. In the South, the final aim of education is to realize a legendary ideal—a universal man. In the former, the emphasis is on creation, the molding and remolding of man so that he or she can fit into the ideal socialist model defined and identified by the Party, while in the latter, the focus is on development, realization and actualization of an individual human potential. A universal man is a person who can fully develop his or her best human potential. To use Richard Wilson's typology, North Korea's morals training is "rigid, closed, moral orientation," namely, indoctrination of group-centered values. Ideally, if not, in reality, South Korea's morals training, on the other hand, is closer to "flexible, open moral orientation," i.e., experimentation and testing of universal values.[40]

In the process of creating a Party-controlled new socialist of the *Juche* type, North Korean children face a fundamental danger of losing their own individuality, spontaneity and creativity.[41] The process of externally molding and creating an ideal person is inherently incompatible with individuality and individual creativity. A socialist of the *Juche* type demands self-denial and self-sacrifice for the good and service of collective will and welfare, whereas a person of creativity and individuality presupposes self-identity, self-autonomy, self-development and self-actualization. Above all, if a human being is an end in itself, the use of education as a mind control instrument of people by the Party is not only unnatural, but intrinsically repugnant.

In South Korea, meanwhile, the primary focus is on individual development and creativity. The state-controlled ideological education has not been absent in the South. The fundamental difference between the North and the South lies, nevertheless, in the fact that while education in the former is an instrument of the WPK, in the latter it is neither the tool of the ruling elites nor of the ruling party. The ideological education in the South is, ideally at least, to withstand and combat the appeals and threats of communism. In reality, however, a balanced picture of North and South Korea has often been sacrificed in the process of capitalizing on the weaknesses and contradictions of communism, especially of North Korean communism (although these faults do by and large exist). The ideological education, which is based on facts and objectivity, has been missing when South Korea tried to emulate North Korea. South Korea's most effective ideological education would be to expose students to the fact that education in North Korea is an instrument of the WPK rather than to introduce its own blend of substitute ideology.

The aim of ideological education in South Korea should not be to create another ideologue—an anti-communist—as opposed to North Korea's communist ideologue, but to develop students' analytical, synthetic and critical skills. As Sabia stated rather succinctly, the best political education is to train students to possess "a sensitivity to the diversity of forms of political life and thought, to the contestability of major political concepts and ideals; an awareness of the complex interrelationships between political thought and political practice; and appreciation for the historical nature of political thought, inquiry and practice."[42]

Several major changes in educational themes and principles in both North and South Korea for the past forty years notwithstanding, the fundamental difference between the two remain unaltered. The party control of education to create a socialist man in the North, despite varying emphases and priorities, continues; as the development of one's best individual and human potential as the goal of education in the South persists despite the excessive meddling of the government in the educational system.

Politicization of Education

In the discussion of evolution and changes of major educational themes, two caveats are in order. First, the aforesaid goals and themes as a set of official "intentions" are one thing, and their actualization is quite another. In North Korea, the said themes were the desirable goals of the WPK, as they were the preferred objectives of the Ministry of Education in South Korea.

As one North Korean specialist asserted, a real communist man in North Korea today may not be the WPK's ideal new communist man.[43] Its ideal communist is the one who abhors exploitation and repression; he is an optimist who believes in people's creativity; he is patriotic and respectful of human rights and dignity; he is for peace and international cooperation; and, above all, he is the one who is highly class-conscious and is willing to overcome any difficulty or hardship in order to achieve the ultimate victory of communism.

By contrast, the actual communist man whom Kim Il Sung himself criticized was a typical bureaucrat who views himself as a privileged individual; clinging only to his own opinions and beliefs, he turns a deaf ear to, or suppresses, other people's constructive suggestions and criticisms, let alone being oblivious to the real conditions of the society; he is an opportunist who is eager for fame and self-promotion while showing little enthusiasm for work; he curries favor with, and becomes blindly obedient to, his superiors while treating his inferiors harshly.[44] According to Park, at least four psychological syndromes of the present North Korean communist man can be identified. They are: (1) anxiety and insecurity—being always busy and worrying about what will happen next; (2) absence of all sense of morality and humanity—as a result of misapplication of the theory of class struggle and of criticism and self-criticism; (3) loss of individuality and obsession with work—little or no time to pay attention to or to respect others; and (4) uniform view of order and distrust of diversity—a by-product of excessive collectivism and of totalitarian politics.[45]

Likewise, an ideal student in South Korea is a healthy person with a well rounded personality and a sound body; a high-minded person of

sensitivity with elevated taste and a love of beauty; a person of competence with a rational mind for solving problems by exercising knowledge and skill; and a person of high morality who respects human
dignity. He is also a man of autonomy responsible for both his personal
and collective way of life.[46] If the typical student in South Korea fit this
ideal portrait, there would be no student demonstrations or protests, let
alone juvenile delinquencies and deviant teenage behaviors. But the
typical student is, in fact, a far cry from such an ideal type.

Secondly, the evolution and changes in major educational themes and
goals in both North and South Korea have been closely linked to their
respective changing political conditions. To put it another way, the
metamorphoses of educational priorities in the both halves have been
highly symptomatic of their respective political developments and
decays. The differences between North and South Korea in this regard
are fundamental. As already mentioned at the outset, education in North
Korea is an integral part of the WPK's political control mechanism, and
hence, its politicization is inherent and inevitable. In South Korea, on
the other hand, education is not an instrument of the governing party or
the government in power, and thus, its politicization is, in principle at
least, neither inevitable nor desirable. With the increasing authoritarian
character of politics under the Park Chung Hee and Chun Doo Hwan
governments, however, the politicization of education had become
prevalent. Unlike in North Korea where the politicization of education
by the WPK is nearly complete, such politicization by the South Korean
government had been, at best, partially undertaken. Above all, South
Korea's politicization of education had been tantamount to the government's response to the students' anti-government political activism.
Since North Korea's near total politicization of education is self-evident,
what follows are some examples of the South Korean government's
politicization of education.

To begin with, the politicization of education means here the use of
education—its policies and programs—for political purposes by the
government. One method of politicization used by the government in
South Korea had been the frequent and abrupt changes in educational
policies and ordinances to divert students from political activism. For

example, on August 12, 1961, less than two months after the Military Coup, the Park regime enforced the state-controlled Entrance Examination System at all school levels. Two weeks later, on September 1, 1961, the government announced the state-controlled College Degree Qualifying Examination. Although to a large extent, both measures were in response to prevalent school irregularities surrounding admissions and the irresponsible graduation standards of many colleges and universities at that time, they were also a political move by the military junta to keep university students from engaging in anti-military government protests. These two measures were abolished on April 11, 1963.

Also, the Full Number Ordinance of College and University was enacted on December 22, 1965, to control the irregular admission practices. This measure, too, further undermined the autonomy of higher education. Considering the fact that violent student demonstrations and protests erupted intermittently in 1964 and 1965 on the questions of normalization treaty with Japan and of sending the South Korean troops to Vietnam, some political implications of this measure were also evident. Another example was the enforcement of the Preliminary College Entrance Examination System on November 15, 1968. This meant that a college aspirant must successfully pass two tests, one conducted by the government and the other by the university of his or her choice. Again, this measure was not completely devoid of political calculations since in the same year the students were protesting the government's move to revise the Constitution which would allow President Park to run for the third consecutive presidential terms. The amendment of school curriculum to include national ethics on February 19, 1971, was more transparently political. The forthcoming presidential election that year and the beginning of a dialogue between North and South Korea were the reasons for enacting the amendment. Park virtually became a dictator-president with the Yushin constitution, and the politicization of education became much more prevalent, as students became one of the most vocal opponents of his new "system." On July 23, 1975, the Education Law was revised to include student guidance responsibility to college and university professors. Worse still, the government revised the Tenure System and Reappointment of College and University Teachers to review, among other things, the reappointment of the tenured faculty members every fifth year which further undermined both the autonomy of the university system and the rights and academic freedom of the professors.

Beginning in 1981 the two-stage college entrance examination system was replaced by a single examination, and each school was required to select students on the basis of the state-run preliminary examination scores and the applicant's high school records. This measure was established to clean up the negative side effects of mushrooming private tutoring institutes and to normalize secondary school system and, above all, to relieve students from undue pressures of preparing for two tests. This may be considered a carrot but the new policy to allow the admission of up to 30% more students than a graduation quota was a stick. This meant that students who were admitted to colleges of their choice must maintain certain grade averages to graduate. One ulterior aim of these moves was to keep the university students on campus and away from anti-government political demonstrations. This new policy had, however, quite the contrary end-results. Students were too pressured by the 30% failure guidelines, and their frustrations were exacerbated by these excessive pressures and tensions, which was one of the major causes of persistent on-campus riots and anti-government rallies. The loss of collegial ambience and the rise of Darwinian mentality from acute competition among fellow students might have been other negative side effects. On September 28, 1983, the Ministry of Education announced further changes in the university admission policy. Schools were allowed to recruit freshmen on the departmental or branch college basis. Also, the 130% rule became flexible in that departments in medical and women's schools were allowed to decide on the percentage of students they will recruit in excess of the graduation quota.[47]

With the Roh regime, further changes in admission and graduation rules and regulations were instituted. On the whole, the university autonomy is being restored and expanded as the university has now more freedom and flexibility in admission and graduation policies. Some universities now also elect their presidents through balloting process.

To conclude, at least since 1960 students in South Korean politics have emerged as a potent political force to be reckoned with. Unlike North Korea, where students are a part of the ruling WPK's political arm, students in South Korea have been one of the most persistent and recalcitrant political foes of the authoritarian regimes. Ironically, more student political activism led to further politicization of education by the government. In concrete terms, the autonomy of university system and academic freedom of students and faculty had been increasingly eroded and underminded, even in some basic civil rights and freedom. Students lost more of these very rights and freedom for which they had been fighting. It is clear, then, who the real winner and the loser had been in this persistent battle between students and the authoritarian government. At least, it can be said that student political activism had been a Pyrrhic victory. This unfortunate vicious circle had continued until the Roh regime chose a different track—an effort to depoliticize academia. This was a beginning in the right direction.

Militarization of Education

The militarization of education refers here to the requirement of military training as an integral part of school instructional program. In North Korea military training begins at the preschool level and becomes more intensive and extensive at higher educational level. Since 1969 instructors from the People's Army have been assigned to middle schools and to all higher educational level schools. At high school levels, for instance, 14 to 15 year-old students are required to join the Young Red Guards and must go through 576 hours of on-campus as well as military camp training (See Table 19-5). At the university level, students must join the Guidance Corps and receive 2,740 hours of military education and training. While high school students are trained for the reserve forces, university students are drilled as the junior reserve officers for national emergency (See Table 19-6).

In South Korea, school military educational programs, such as the student para-military organization called the Student National Defense

Corps (SNDC), founded in 1949 at the middle school, high school and university levels, were implemented during and immediately after the Korean War. But both were phased out as the country recovered from the wounds of the war. After the military coup of 1961, the Reserve Officers' Training Corps (ROTC) program was introduced in colleges but only on voluntary basis. The fall of South Vietnam in 1974 and the subsequent rise of international insecurity, especially in Northeast Asia, led to the revival of the SNDC at the high school and university levels. By the passage of the Law on the Establishment of the SNDC on June 7, 1975, high school students between 15 and 17 years of age were required to join the SNDC and take 216 hours of on-campus military training. Likewise, college students as members of the SNDC must receive 440 hours of military training and exercises for three years except for the seniors (See Tables 19-5 and 19-6).

The degree of student military regimentation in North and South Korea is, however, fundamentally different. With the exception of SNDC requirements, students in South Korea are largely free to pursue their extracurricular activities, while in North Korea students have virtu-ally no free time because of the WPK-controlled extracurricular meet-ings and activities (See Table 19-4).[48] In addition to military education and training, North Korean students are required to participate in "labor education." People's school children through the Juvenile Corps, high middle school and college students through the League of Socialist Working Youth must spend two to twelve weeks a year in helping farm-ing villages, construction works and others, in addition to many more hours of fulfilling the duties and responsibilities as members of these organizations (See Tables 19-3 and 19-4). Like in American schools, South Korean elementary and secondary school students can organize their own self-governments primarily to conduct and coordinate their extra-curricular activities, which are mostly voluntary rather than com-pulsory (See Table 19-4).

In brief, the militarization of education in North Korea is an integral part of its near total regimentation of the society. In that sense, students are not free during or even after school hours. In South Korea the gov-ernments, especially under the Park regime (1961-1979), had tried to implement more regimentation of the society by organizing various security or para-military organizations such as the Central Intelligence Agency (presently the National Security and Planning Agency), the Military Intelligency Agency, the Counter-Espionage Operations Command, the militia, the Home District Military Reserve, and Anti-Communism League and the military police (*chŏnkyŏng*). Although these may be a part of the government's control mechanism and even an indication of more regimentation of the society, the South Korean society as a whole has never been under near total regimentation as it has been in North Korea. To put it another way, the militarization of education in South Korea is much more limited and restrained than its North Korean counterpart.

Evolution and Changes in the Educational System

North Korea asserts that some 2.3 million people in the North were illiterate at the time of the Korean liberation in 1945, and that only 35 percent of school age children attended school. Now, it claims that there is virtually no illiteracy and that all school age children attend school. Then, no universal compulsory education existed. Now, according to the DPRK, an eleven-year universal compulsory education is in effect. In 1945 not a single university existed; but today some 273 universities and colleges, and 576 higher technical and specialized institutions are in operation. As of 1985, according to North Korean official publications, some 3.5 million children are enrolled in more than 60,000 nursery schools and kindergartens (See Tables 19-11, 19-12 and 19-13). Children and students studying in the universal 11-year compulsory education system reached 5 million. And one million students are studying at higher special schools or colleges. Altogether, 8.5 million youngsters, nearly half of the total population, now attend school.[49]

Two points are noteworthy in this connection. First, all of these numbers require qualification, and the issue of the quality of education needs to be addressed. Unfortunately, official figures cannot be checked against the independent sources for veracity. Granting that the official

Critical Issues and Problems

figures are basically correct, the quality of education in terms of school facilities, supplies and teaching staff has been known to be inadequate.[50] Second, these numbers must be viewed against the time in which they appear. More than four decades have elapsed since the liberation, and over four decades since the end of the Korean War. Although much of the credit for these educational advancements should go to the educational policies of the WPK and the "wise leadership" of Kim Il Sung, some are the natural outgrowth of efforts undertaken by a society within a certain span of time, which parallels developments in some other societies, including those having a different socioeconomic system.

The logic of the second point becomes abundantly clear when the statistics of the same matters in South Korea are compared. Like in North Korea, only 30 percent of the school-age children in the South were enrolled in primary schools at the time of the liberation, and only one out of 20 or 30 attended secondary schools, and a very few went to college. The rate of illiteracy, too, was as high as it was in North Korea. By 1960 illiteracy was virtually eliminated. Today, every child of elementary school age is enrolled in school. The percentage of primary school graduates advancing to middle schools rose from 58.4 percent in 1968 to 95.7 percent in 1980. Specifically, the number of elementary schools in the South has increased from 2,884 in 1945 to 6,335 in 1990 (4,790 in North Korea) and the number of elementary students, from 1.3 million to 4.8 million in 1990 (in North Korea 1.9 million is the figure for the same year). The number of middle schools has increased from 97 to 4,157 in the same period (as compared to North Korea's 4,062) and the number of middle school students from 50,340 to 4.5 million (3.0 million in North Korea). In the same period, the number of high schools has increased from 68 to 1,494 and the number of high school students, from 83,514 to 2.01 million. The number of higher educational institutions has grown in the said period from 19 to 405 (as compared with North Korea's 273) and the number of students in these institutions, from 7,819 to 1.12 million (as compared with North Korea's 314,000). South Korea's school population amounts to 12 million, which represents nearly 27 percent of its population (For details, see Tables 19-9 and 19-9a).

These impressive educational successes (expansions) of both North and South Korea aside, both educational systems have little in common. In the following, the changes in the North and South Korean school systems and their respective school curricula and extra-curricular activities will be examined in some detail.

Changes in Educational Systems

One of the earliest pronouncement relating to compulsory education in North Korea was contained in Number 16 of the Twenty-Point Platform of March 2, 1946. It sought to introduce a system of universal compulsory education and to increase the number of primary, secondary, specialized schools and state-run colleges. Earlier the North Korean School Implementation Law was promulgated and in it, among other things, the elementary school was renamed the "people's school on November 21, 1945." On September 10, 1949, the Supreme People's Assembly (SPA) adopted a resolution to implement universal compulsory education at the elementary school level. The resolution was reaffirmed on January 11, 1950, but the outbreak of the Korean War delayed the implementation of universal compulsory education. A four-year compulsory education at the elementary level was finally implemented on September 1, 1956. Two years later on November 1, 1958, the DPRK decided to implement the universal compulsory education at the middle school level. On November 24, 1966, the SPA revised the Education Law in order to implement, *inter alia,* a nine-year (4-year elementary and 5-year secondary) compulsory education. The decision to implement a ten-year (4-year elementary and 6-year secondary) compulsory education was made on July 1, 1972, and this plan was partially implemented on September 1, 1972. Finally, on September 1, 1975, an edict was issued requiring an eleven-year (1-year preschool, 4-year elementary and 6-year secondary) compulsory education.

It is noteworthy that the decrees, decisions, announcements and promulgations relating to compulsory education invariably preceded their actual implementation. The former represented intention, the latter, realization. A caution is necessary in understanding the exact meaning of "implementation." North Korean officials themselves distinguish "partial" from "full" implementation. Thus, the extent of partial implementation remains unclear.

In addition to the changes in compulsory education, some shifts took place in the divisions or categories separating grade levels. From 1946 to 1953, North Korea had a 5-3-3-4 (2) system: five years of people's school, three years each of middle and high school and four years of college. With the promulgation of the DPRK Cabinet Decision Number 111 on July 11, 1953, the people's school was shortened from 5 to 4 years. A 4-3-3-4 system lasted until 1959. On October 26, 1959, the SPA revised the Education Law. Under the new law, a 4-3-4 (2-2)-4 system was implemented: a 4-year people's school and 3-year junior middle school, 2-year vocational school, 2-year higher technical school and 4-year college. On November 24, 1966, the SPA revised, once again, the Education Law to implement a 9-year compulsory education. In so doing, a new 4-5-4 (5) system was implemented on April 1 of the following year: the 3-year secondary school and the 2-year vocational school were merged into a new 5-year middle school. The fifth major revision of the Education Law was enacted on April 9, 1973, and from 1973 to the present, the 4-6 (4-2)-4 (5) system has been in operation. The new feature is the secondary school (*kodŭng chunghakyo*) term, which is now six years, divided into four years of middle school and two years of high school (For details, see Table 19-14).

In South Korea, a six-year compulsory education was guaranteed in principle with the enactment of the Education Law on December 31, 1949 (Article 8). The changes from a compulsory to a compulsory and "free" education at elementary school level have been gradual. Even now various forms of school fees and extracurricular activity expenses except for the textbooks for primary school children are underwritten by the parents. Only the students at "national" and "public" elementary schools are exempted from registration and tuition fees, expenses for experimentation and practical training, but they, too, must pay into some form of school-support fund (endowments for facility expansion plan). The middle school education is still neither compulsory nor free, although virtually all primary school graduates (95.7% in 1990) advance to middle schools. Unlike in North Korea, where no private educational institutions exist, both the public and private schools at all levels exist side by side in South Korea. Specifically, schools are divided into three types—"national" (established and operated by the state), "public" (by province, city or county) and "private" (by private corporations or individuals) (Article 83, the 1949 Education Law). As Table 19-9 below shows, there are more "public" than "private" schools at the elementary and secondary levels and, conversely, there are more "private" than "public" (70%) higher educational institutions, although all schools are considered "public institutions of the Government" and are, thus, subject to the standards provided for by laws and decrees (Article 7). Notably, the educational autonomy system was put into effect on June 4, 1952, but was abolished on January 6, 1962. A year later on November 1, 1963, it was restored. In reality, however, the school autonomy exists only on paper, and the Ministry of Education plays a preponderant role in virtually all aspects of education. After the Roh regime came into being, however, a move to institutionalize educational autonomy was made by creating the provincial education council in 1991. This council is composed of the members who are elected by the country and city assembly and by the provincial assembly. Still, the school autonomy is in its infantile stage.

Two points need examination. First, in South Korea a six-year compulsory education has remained virtually unchanged, although in reality nearly all primary school graduates now go to middle schools and over 89% of the middle school graduates advance to high schools (the plan to gradually implement free and compulsory middle school education was underway in 1985 for implementation in 1990, but there have been setbacks and modifications).[51] Second, as mentioned previously in the discussion of the politicization of education, much changes have occurred in the South Korean educational system in the area of admission and graduation standards, not in the educational system per se. For instance, the single-ladder system of 6-3-3-4 has remained virtually unchanged ever since it replaced the old 6-4-3-4 system on March 10, 1950 (See Table 19-14). Currently, however, the Special Commission on Education Reform appointed by the President is reviewing the 6-3-3-

4 system as well as other areas of the existing educational programs and
procedures.

Politicization of School Curricula

Like in all past and presently remaining socialist countries, where the
party control of education in general and political education in particular
are an integral part of socialist pedagogy, the so-called "culture education" (*gyo'yang gyo'yuk*) has been a major component of North Korea's
school curricula from pre-schools to higher institutions. North Korea
differs from other socialist countries only in its heavy and increasingly
exclusive emphasis on Kim's own revolutionary ideas such as *Juche* and
his anti-Japanese revolutionary tradition in political education (See
Tables 19-7, 19-8 and 19-10). At the National Meeting of the Educational Workers on October 1, 1978, Kim Il Sung remarked that "the
essential feature of Party control over education is to equip teachers and
students firmly with our Party policy."[52] Earlier in the 1977 Theses on
Socialist Education, Kim stressed that the educational administration
should see to it that "teachers thoroughly establish *Juche* in the instruction and base the lessons strictly on the Party policy and impart to the
students a working knowledge useful for the revolution and construction."[53] While other socialist countries attempt to create, at least on
paper, a new socialist man, North Korea has intensified in recent years
its so-called *Juche* education to mold a new socialist man of *Juche* type.

By contrast, education in South Korea had long been, at least, in spirit
and in law, devoid of direct politicization of education. Article 5 of the
1949 Education Law specifically prohibits the use of education as "an
instrument of propaganda or any political, partisan or other personal
prejudices." It also prohibits religious education for any religious
denomination at "national" or "public" schools. With the promulgation
of the Charter of National Education in 1968, "nationalism" in education was accentuated. On February 19, 1971, all school curricula were
revised to incorporate "national ethics" as an integral part of school subjects. One of four general goals of moral education in primary school
was "to alert children to the falsehood and the aggressive policy of

North Korea, and to develop a strong conviction for peaceful unification through understanding the superiority of democracy."

For instance, the objectives and contents of primary school moral education in each grade level with a particular reference to "political" contents are as follows:

Grades 1-2.

Objectives: "the pitiful state of living in North Korea," and "brotherly sympathy for the people in the North."

Contents: (Grade 1) (1) sympathy for the miserable life of children in the North; and (2) awareness of the threat from Communist North Korea.

(Grade 2) (1) sympathy for North Korean people's suffering from compulsory labor; and (2) vigilance against North Korean spies and commandos.

Grades 3-4.

Objectives: "the inhumanity of North Korean Communists" and "the dreadful living conditions of the North Korean people."

Contents: (Grade 3) (1) sympathy for the North Korean people suffering from hard labor; (2) vigilance against North Korean communists' armed provocation; and (3) pride in our freedom and liberty.

(Grade 4) (1) understanding the North Korean people under the conditions of oppressive communist control; (2) precautions against the North Korean communists' war preparation; and (3) mutual loss stemming from the division.

Grades 5-6.

Objectives: "the superiority of democracy."

Contents: (Grade 5) (1) understanding the autocratic nature of the communist North; (2) the inhumanity of North Korean communists; and (3) the North Korean people's yearning for freedom.

(Grade 6) (1) contradictions of a communist society, especially North Korea; (2) awareness of North Korean communists' eradication of national cultural heritage; and (3) efforts toward peaceful unification.[54]

In sum, both primary and middle school children are now required to have moral education two hours a week. At academic high schools, students must take at least 6 units of moral education courses. Students at vocational high schools, too, take 6 units of national ethics courses.

A 3-credit hour national ethics course is also mandatory for all college students (For details, see Tables 19-7 and 19-8).

In all fairness, there are several reasons for South Korea's decision to incorporate moral and national ethics courses into school curricula. Externally, the early 1970s brought a new era of detente. Specifically, the U.S.-Chinese and the U.S.-Soviet relations were undergoing changes in the direction of reducing tensions around the globe as evidenced by the SALT I Treaty and the Nixon-Chou Shanghai communique. Even on the Korean Peninsula, North and South Korea resumed a mutual dialogue. Under such circumstances, the South Korean government felt that, unlike North Korean children who have been all along subject to party-controlled ideological indoctrination, children in the South were not equipped ideologically to withstand the appeals of communist propaganda. This necessitated youngsters to understand the real nature of communism practiced in North Korea and the desirability of democracy.

Two additional problems surrounding the incorporation of moral education in school curricula, however, marred these good intentions. First, this new educational measures roughly corresponded to the implementation of Park's so-called Yushin Constitution. The new educational measures were immediately placed under suspicion as the politicization of education by Park. Second, most importantly, a critical understanding of the true nature of North Korean communism and communism in general required, first and foremost, an objectivity, which was, however, often absent in South Korean moral and national ethics education. In the process of capitalizing on the faults and contradictions of communism, especially North Korean communism, a balanced picture of both North and South Korea has been often remiss. These two factors reinforced each other in undermining the credibility and effectiveness of moral education in South Korea. Herein lies the fundamental difference in ideological education between North and South Korea. By nature and in practice, education in North Korea is an instrument of the ruling WPK. In South Korea an ideological education to combat the appeals and threats of communism is necessary, but such an education needs to be a bi-partisan national policy with popular support, not an instrument of the government in power. As soon as South Korea starts to emulate

North Korea in this regard, its credibility and, hence, effectiveness is lost. For, South Korea's most effective ideological education in regard to North Korea is to reveal that education in North Korea is an instrument of the WPK.

Tentative Findings and Observations

These are some of the tentative findings and observations of the present inquiry:

1. The ultimate goals of education in North and South Korea are diametrically different. In the North, the Party (WPK) has a prefabricated ideal model—a socialist of *Juche* type—and the purpose of education is to "create" such human creature. In the South, the final aim of education is to "realize" a legendary ideal—a universal man. In the former, the emphasis is on creation, molding and remolding of man so that he or she can fit the ideal socialist model that the Party has defined and identified, whereas in the latter, the focus is on development, realization and actualization of an individual human potential. A universal man is, thus, a person who can fully develop his or her potential.

2. The politicization and militarization of education in North Korea are not only thorough but inherent. They are simply political and military aspects of the Party control of education. Education is, to repeat, an integral part of one-party totalitarian dictatorship and control. By contrast, the politicization and militarization of education in South Korea are neither fully successful nor acceptable. Though abating, continuing hostilities on the Korean Peninsula and threats from the North necessitate some form of military education and training at schools. The so-called moral and national ethics education, properly constructed and objectively taught, may also be justified. But in reality, both the Park government and the Chun regime had not been completely immune from the politicization of moral and national ethics education. More fundamentally, if the proper ideological education in South Korea is to criticize North Korea's use of education as a mind control instrument of the WPK, the politicization of education by the South Korean government

is self-defeating. Instead of emulating the North, the government in South Korea should sharply differentiate itself from the former. Ideally, instead of more centralized control of education by the Ministry of Education, more school autonomy is preferable; instead of state-controlled and state-censored ideological education, freer academic environment for objective discussion and analysis of the paradox of communist theory and reality is desirable; and instead of strait-jacketing on-campus student activities, the restoration of campus sanctity is advisable. In reality, however, the government, especially the Park and Chun regimes, because of their inherent weakness and lack of legitimacy, overreacted to on-campus or off-campus student protests and demonstrations. Students had challenged the legitimacy of these governments. More student protests led to more government overreaction and excessive control, which had spiraled the vicious circle.

3. In the process of creating a Party-manufactured new socialist man of *Juche* type, North Korean children face a fundamental danger of losing their own individuality, spontaneity and creativity. The externally imposed molding and creating of an ideal person is inherently incompatible with individuality and individual creativity. A socialist man of *Juche* type demands self-denial and self-sacrifice for the good and service of collective will and welfare, whereas a person of creativity and individuality presupposes self-identity, self-autonomy, self-development and self-actualization. Above all, if human being is an end in itself, the education of human beings as a mind control instrument of the Party is not only unnatural but inherently repugnant. The party control of education is intrinsic in socialist pedagogy, and, thus, as long as the socialist system survives in the North, so will the party control of education.

4. Unlike in North Korea, the politicization of education in South Korea by the government in power is neither necessary nor inevitable. If one of the root causes of the aforesaid vicious circle of student and government confrontations stemmed from the lack of legitimacy of the Park and Chun regimes, the formula to produce a legitimate government can and will resolve it. To a certain extent, the Roh regime and Kim government have been partially successful in this area.

Table 19-1. Evolution of Major Educational Themes
in North and South Korea

North Korea		South Korea	
Period	Major Themes	Period	Major Themes
1945-Early 1950's	Nation-building and Communism	1945-1948	Democratic Education
Early 1950's-Late 1950's	Communist Class Education	1948-1953	National and Democratic Education
Early 1960's-Late 1960's	Education of Revolutionary Tradition	1953-Mid-1960's	Furthering Democratic Education
Late 1960's-1980's	Monolithic *Juche* Education	Mid-1960's-1980's	National Education
Early 1980's-1990's	Father-Son Cult-building Education	Early 1980's-1990's	Science and Technology Education

*Table 19-2. North and South Korean Official Educational Philosophies
and Goals*

North Korea (1945-1960's)	South Korea (1945-1960's)
1. Ultimate Goal (Ideal)	
Creation of a Socialist Man who is equipped with Marxism and Leninism	Development of a Universal Man who can benefit all mankind through self-actualization
2. Priority	
i. communization	i. development of a democratic citizen
ii. specialization	ii. personality development
iii. working classization	iii. development of support skill
3. A Model Man	
i. materialistic value of human beings	i. spiritual value of human beings
ii. person as an instrument of revolution	ii. person as an autonomous citizen
iii. as a builder of socialist construction	iii. as a contributor to democratic nation
iv. working toward the realization of world communism	iv. contributing to the prosperity of mankind
North Korea (Mid 1960's-)	South Korea (Mid 1960's-)
1. Ultimate Goal	
Creation of a communist of *Juche* type	Development of a person with individual creativity and social responsibility and with commitment to national unity and world peace

Table 19-2. *Continued*

2. Priority

i. revolutionalization	i. personality development
ii. working classization	ii. development of nationhood and national identity
iii. communization	iii. development of self-support skills
iv. world communization	iv. contributions to the common prosperity of mankind

3. A Model Man

i. Person who learns revolutionary tradition	i. who inherits and regenerates national identity
ii. who is equipped with *Yuil* [monolithic] ideology	ii. who has an outlook on democratic state with independent nationhood
iii. who is imbued with the Kim Il Sung cult and the *Juche* idea	iii. who is equipped with creative pioneering spirit and cooperative ethos
iv. absolutely and unconditionally support the father-son succession	iv. who is trained to lead the new scientific and globalized world community

Both tables are adapted from the following sources: Kim Il Sung, *On Socialist Pedagogy* (Pyongyang, 1979); also his *The Youth Must Take over the Revolution and Carry it Forward* (Pyongyang, 1976); *Chosŏn Chungang Nyŏngam, 1980* [North Korean Central Year Book] (Pyongyang, 1980); Kim Jong (Chong) Il, *On Further Developing Educational Work* (Pyongyang, 1984); "Education Law No. 87" in *Laws of the Republic of Korea* (Seoul: Korean Legal Center, 1969); *Pukhan Chŏnso 1945-1980* (in Korean) (Seoul, 1980). Also, Park Yong-Hŏn, "Comparative Study on Political Education of South and North Korea," *East Asian Review* (Autumn 1975), pp. 258-282 and his "North Korea's Educational Process and Curricula Content" (in Korean), *Korean Journal of Unification Affairs* 3 (1983): 25-54 and "North Korea's Political Indoctrination Policy and Sense of Values of its Youth," *Vantage Point* (February 1983); *A Comparison of the Present North and South Korean Society and Culture* (in Korean) (Seoul: National Unification Board, 1981); "Schools in North and South Korea" (in Korean) in *Pukhan* (February 1981), pp. 74-91; *The School Curriculum of the Republic of Korea* (I) (Seoul: Korean Educational Development Institute, 1982); *Education in Korea, 1981* (Seoul: Ministry of Education, 1981); *Pukan Kaeyo* [An Outline of North Korea] (Seoul: The Ministry of National Unification Board, 1990); and *Nampukhan Sahoe Munwha Chip'yo* [The Social and Cultural Indicators of North and South Korea] (Seoul: The Ministry of National Unification Board, 1991).

Table19-3. Compulsory Labor Education in North Korea

1. Compulsory Labor Hours

People's School	2 to 4 weeks a year through the Juvenvile Corps.
High Middle School	6 to 8 weeks a year through the League of Socialist Working Youth.
Colleges	12 weeks a year for social sciences and humanities students. 14 weeks a year for natural sciences and engineering majors (practical training substitutable for seniors).

2. Compulsory Work Areas

Helping farming villages	for three to five months a year during the rice planting, weeding and harvesting seasons and irrigation construction by all levels of students.
Economic Construction	for city construction, power plant, railway, machine manufacturing plant construction and mining by high school and college students.
"Good Deed" Movement:	tree planting, rabbit raising, collecting bottles, papers and animal wools by People's and High Middle School students.

Sources: Adapted from "Schools in North and South Korea" (in Korean), *Pukhan* (February 1981), pp. 74-91 and *Comparison of the Present North and South Korean Society and Culture* (in Korean) (Seoul, 1981). Also, Yong-hŏn Park, "North Korea's Political Indoctrination Policy and Sense of Values of its Youth," *Op. Cit.*

Table 19-4. Extracurricular Activities of North and South Korean Youth

A. North Korea

Organization (Eligibility)	Main Activities
The Juvenile Corps (1) (from the 3rd graders of the people's school to the middle school)	cultivate the fighting spirit and participate in rural life.
The League of Socialist Working Youth (2) (from the 3rd year students in the middle school to those in college)	disseminate the WPK policies to the masses; function as the WPK's rear guard or reserve
The Young Red Guards (3) (high-middle school)	self-criticism and thought rectification
One-Thousand *ri* March of Learning (4)	by following Kim Il Sung's childhood travel route on foot, they show their loyalty to him

B. South Korea

Organization (Eligibility)	Main Activities
Children's Council (*uilini hoe*) (all elementary school students)	self-governing body for extra-curricular activity
Korean Boys and Girls' Corps (*Daehan Sonyŏn, Sonyŏ Dan*) (Children's Corps for 4th graders and up; Boy's Corps and Girls' Corps for middle school students; Youth Corps [*nyŏnchang-dae*] for high school students all voluntary)	physical training, character-building and services to the community
Student Government (*Haksaeng-hoe*) (all middle schools)	self-government student activities
Student National Defense Corps (*Hakdo Hoguk-dan*) (all university and high school students)	student military training and education

(1) Founded on June 6, 1946; (2) Founded on January 17, 1967; (3) founded in January 1968; (4) began in March 1973.

Sources: *Idem.*

Table 19-5. Student Military Education in North and South Korea at the High School Level

North Korea	South Korea
1. Objectives	
(i) train the revolutionary fighter for the Great Leader Kim Il Sung	(i) inculcate the mission of national defense
(ii) train them as the reserve forces	(ii) impart the basic military training
2. Organizations The Young Red Guards (*Pul'gun Chŏngnyŏn Kunwi-dae*) of 14-15 year-old high-middle school students' company or battalion formed in each school	Student National Defense Corps of 15-17 year-old high school students' company or battalion in school
3. Training Hours 576 hours for two years –military camp training* 168 hours for two years (336 hours) –on campus training for 120 hours per year for two years (240 hours)	216 hours for three years –only on campus training
4. Courses political science .... 67 hrs. military tactics .... 50 weapons training .... 34 others .... 17 total .... 168 hrs. for 2 years.	general military science .... 74 hrs. military tactics .... 32 weapons training .... 30 others .... 80 total .... 216 hrs. for 3 years
5. Supervision same as college	same as college
6. Number of Forces 790,000 (boys: 410,000 girls: 380,000)	1,650,000 (boys: 960,000 and girls: 690,000)

*Military camp training is usually done during the summer vacation in August.
All students are given AK rifles and Red Guard uniforms. Each group of 400 or 500 students are trained by the military officers at the city or county Red Guard training camp.
Sources: *Idem.*

Table 19-6. Student Military Education in North and South Korea
at the University Level

North Korea	South Korea

1. Objectives

  (i) train the revolutionary guards loyal to Kim Il Sung
  (ii) train the junior reserve officers ready for national emergency

  (i) cultivate the spirit of national self-defense
  (ii) receive the basic military training as soldiers

2. Organizations

Guidance Corps [*Kyodo-dae*]
The Worker-Peasant Red Guard, regiment formation
–all students

Student National Defense Corps
division formation of university regiment for college
–all students except seniors

3. Training Hours

2,740 hrs.
–group training: 445 hrs. for four years (1,780 hrs.)
–on campus training: 240 hrs. per year for four years (960 hrs.)

440 Hrs.
–group training: 80 hrs for one year
–on campus training: 120 hrs per year for three years (360 hrs.)

4. Courses

(hrs.)		
political science	714	
military tactics	534	
weapons training	356	
others	178	
total	1,780 hrs.	

general military studies ... 141
military tactics ... 115
weapons training ... 79
others ... 105
total ... 440

5. Supervision

the WPK Military Affairs Comm. military training jointly by the Administration Council Education Commission and the Ministry of People's Armed Forces

The Ministry of Education military training by the Ministry of National Defense

6. Number of Forces

170,000 (women students included)

350,000 (women students not included)

Sources: *Idem.*

*Table 19-7. A Content Analysis of North and South Korean Elementary
School National (Korean) Language Textbooks**

(Frequency of citations)

North Korea		South Korea	
1. Personality			
focus on living figures		focus on historic figures	
Kim Il Sung	(744)	Admiral Yi Sun Sin	(36)
Anti-Japanese Guerrilla		Great King Sejong	(32)
Fighters	(44)	Lady Sin Saimdang	(17)
		Yi Yul Gok	(10)
2. National Consciousness			
Socialism (Socialist		Our Country	(50)
fatherland	(270)	T'ai'gukgi	(27)
revolution)	(53)	Hangŭl	(24)
		Sa'ram (people)	(17)
		National spirit,	
		Spirit of the March	
		Ist Movement	(17)
3. Enemy Concept			
American Imperialists	(139)	Communist Troops	(22)
Enemy	(85)	Chinese People's Army	(4)
Japanese Imperialists	(52)	Communist Puppet	(1)
		North Korea	(1)

Adapted from "Schools in North and South Korea" (in Korean), *Pukhan* (February 1981), pp. 74-91.
*Based on Korean language texts of the first grade to the sixth grade in South Korea, and on North Korean language texts of Volume 1 of the first grade, Volume 1 of the second grade, Volume 2 of the third grade, Volume 1 of the fifth grade and Volume 2 of the sixth grade.

Table 19-8. *Content of North and South Korean University Curricula*

North Korea (1)	South Korea (2)
(hours)	
I. General Requirement (GR):..1,050	I. GR: 140 Cr.
History of the WPK 280	National Ethics.......................3
World History of the Workers'	National Language.................2
Party Movement.......................140	Composition...........................1
Marxism and Leninism............200	National History.....................2
Political Economy....................110	Physical Education.................4
Russian Language...................320	Military Training...................4
	Others.....................................17
II. Military Science................... 1,200	
III. Major Requirements 3,150	II. Major Requirements............30
to 3,350 (20-23 subjects)	Electives within Major.........33
	General electives..................28

Sources: *Idem.* (1) North Korea's university curriculum is based on the Kim Il Sung University. The Kim Il Sung University requires a total of 5,400 to 6,600 hours. That is, 38 to 40 hours a week for 35 weeks. (2) The South Korean example is based on the 1980 curriculum of the College of Humanities and Social Sciences, Seoul National University. One credit hour means one hour per week for a semester.

Table 19-9. *The Number of South Korean Schools by Level and Types* *(1980, 1990)*

Schools	Total	National	Public	Private
Kindergarten	901 (8,354)*	0	40	861
Primary schools	6,437 (6,335)	15	6,390	32
Middle schools	2,100 (2,474)	4	1,347	749
Academic High Schools	748 (1,096)	6	344	398
Vocational High Schools	605 (587)	5	308	292
Junior Vocational College	128 (117)	20	16	92
Junior Teachers' College	11 (11)	11	0	0
College & University	85 (107)	19	1	65
Graduate School	121 (298)	32	0	89
Special School	57 (104)	4	11	42
Others	12 —	0	0	12

Source: *Education in Korea, 1981* (Seoul: Ministry of Education, 1981), p. 35.

*Numbers in the parentheses are the 1990 figures from *The Social-cultural Indicators of North and South Korea* (in Korean) (Seoul: The Ministry of National Unification Board, 1991). Also, *Korea Statistical Yearbook, 1991* (Seoul: The Korean Statistical Association, 1991), p. 377.

Table 19-9a. The Growth of Education in South Korea

Level	1945	1983	1990
Elementary school			
No. of students	1,366,024	5,257,164	4,868,520
No. of schools	2,884	6,500	6,335
No. of teachers	19,729	124,572	136,800
Middle school			
No. of students	50,340	2,672,307	2,275,751
No. of schools	97	2,254	2,474
No. of teachers	1,810	63,370	89,719
High school			
No. of students	83,5	2,013,116	2,283,806
No. of schools	68	1,494	1,683
No. of teachers	3,214	63,109	92,683
Higher Education Institutions			
No. of students	7,819	1,073,074	1,151,024
No. of schools	19	258	556
No. of teachers	1,490	30,049	41,880

Adapted from *Mun'gyo t'onggye yŏnbo* [Statistical Yearbook of Education, 1985], (Seoul: Ministry of Education, 1985). The 1990 figures are from *Korea Statistical Yearbook, 1991, Op. Cit.*, p. 377.

Table 19-10. North Korea's Politicization of School Curricula

Major themes	Objectives	Content
1. *Juche* idea:	establish independent revolutionary line	emphasis on the self-reliant revolution under the leadership of the WPK
2. Revolutionary tradition:	inculcate loyalty to Kim and the WPK	emphasis on Kim's anti-Japanese guerrilla struggles
3. Communist morality	equip with communist morality and faith	emphasis on the legitimacy of communist revolution, the inevitability of communist victory, revolutionary consciousness of the working class
4. Collectivism:	sacrifice the self for the benefits of all	emphasis on collectivistic principles
5. Work ethic:	love labor and to participate in collective work projects	emphasis on labor and labor productivity
6. Socialist patriotism:	struggle in defense of socialist fatherland	emphasis on the proletarian dictatorship, socialist system, socialist construction
7. Proletarian dictatorship:	lead to the victory of world communism	emphasis on cooperation with other countries struggling for proletarian world revolution
8. Socialist legality:	comply with Communist morality and socialistic mode of life	emphasis on communistic legal order, assault on traditional morality and old-fashioned ways of life

Sources: Adapted from *Theses on Socialist Education* published at the 14th Plenary Meeting of the Fifth Central Committee of the WPK on September 5, 1977. See also, Yong-hŏn Park, "Educational Process and its Contents in North Korea" (in Korean), *Korean Journal of Unification Affairs* 3 (1983): 40 and his "North Korea's Political Indoctrination Policy and Sense of Values of its Youth," *Vantage Point* (February 1983), pp. 1-11.

Table 19-11. North Korean Nursery School System*

Year	No. of Schools	Capacity (No. of Seats)
1946	1	20
1949	12	620
1953	64	2,165
1956	224	6,538
1959	3,404	162,175
1960	7,626	394,489
1961	6,991	457,029
1962	6,638	581,964
1963	6,704	728,258
1964	7,043	787,504
1965	n.a	—

Source: *Chosun Chungang Nyŏngam, 1965,* quoted in Hyŏng-chan Kim, "A Study of Pre-school Education in North Korea" (in Korean), *Pukhan* (September 1982), p. 90.

*The important events concerning the nursery schools are: (1) on June 13, 1946, the North Korean Health Bureau Order No. 5 concerning the nursery school regulations was announced. Among other things, these regulations include the age requirement (one month to three year olds), types of the nursery school, i.e., run by provincial, municipal, county or local people's committees and the list of necessary documents for opening a nursery school; (2) on February 1949, the North Korean Ministry of Health revised the earlier nursery school regulations. Under the new regulations, the nursery school is required to provide 2.5 *pyong* per child indoor space and 4 *pyong* per child building space, to maintain one nurse in each nursery school, one nursery school teacher and one teacher aide per class of 17 to 18; (3) on April 17, 1959, the Ministry of Health Rule No. 21 was announced. This new rule stipulates that the nursery school is divided into three categories—run by various industries and institutes of all government ministries and bureaus, by industries and institutes of the municipal people's committees and by various cooperatives. Three types of the nursery school were also recognized: daily, weekly and monthly; (4) on July 1, 1964, the Cabinet Decision No. 46 concerning the improvement and development of the nursery schools and kindergartens was announced. Among other things, it upgraded the qualifications for the nursery and kindergarten teachers and teacher aides; (5) by the promulgation of the 1976 Law on the Nursing and Upbringing of Children, the universal and free education of children at nursery schools and kindergartens was in principle adopted. For details, see *Pukhan Kwangye Charyo jip* (Seoul, 1973), Hyŏng Chan Kim, *Op. Cit.* and Yong-hŏn Park, "North Korea's Institutionalization of Early Education and Its Underlying Motives" (in Korean), *Pukhan* (September 1982), pp. 74-82. Also, Dong Wun Park, *Education in North Korea* (in Korean) (Seoul, 1977).

Table 19-12. Daily Activities of Nursery School Children in North Korea
(One-month to six-month olds)

Time	Activities
7:00– 8:00	Receiving children and feeding
8:00– 9:00	Sleeping hour
9:00–10:30	Recreational activities and snack
10:30–11:30	Sleeping hour
13:30–14:30	Lunch
14:30–16:30	Recreational and free activities and learning
16:30–17:30	Sleeping hours
17:30–18:30	Meal service
18:30–19:30	Recreation and picked up by parents

Source: Hyon Song Kim, *Methods of Rearing Children* (in Korean) (Pyongyang, 1965), p. 78. Quoted in Hyŏng Chan Kim, *Op. Cit.*, p. 93.

Table 19–13. Daily Activities of Nursery School Children in North Korea
(18-month to 36-month olds)

Time	Activities
7:00– 8:00	Receiving children (meal not served)
8:00– 8:30	Recreation and learning
8:30– 9:00	Snack (after washing hands)
9:00– 9:30	Preparation for walking outdoor
9 :30–11:00	Walking outdoor
11:00–11:30	Wash hands
11:30–12:30	Lunch
12:30–13:00	Get ready for afternoon nap
13:00–15:00	Nap
15:00–15:30	Wash hands
15:30–16:30	Snack
16:30–19:00	Walking, recreation and learning
19:00–19:30	Picked up by parents

Source: *Idem.*

Table 19-14. The Educational System in North and South Korea
(As of 1990)

North Korea	Age	Grade	South Korea
Paksa-won (Ph.D. courses for	Age	Grade	
2 years)	25	20	
Research Institute	24	19	Graduate School
(Yŏngu-wŏn for M.A. or M.S.	23	18	(2-year M.A. or M.S.
for 3 to 4 years)	22	17	and 3-year Ph.D. degrees)
	21	16	
University and College	20	15	University and College
(3-year Teacher's College,	19	14	(2-year Vocational
2 or 3-year Technical College,	18	13	College, 2-4 year
4-year Normal College,			Teacher's College,
and 4 to 6 years for university)			3 years Nursing College,
			4 to 6 years of university)
	17	12	
	(16)	11	High School
	15	10	(3-year high, or
High Middle School			higher trade school)
	14	9	
(4-year middle and 2-year	13	8	Middle School
high school)	12	7	(3 year middle 3 year
			trade, 3 year higher
			schools)
	11	6	
	10	5	Elementary School
	9	4	(6 years)
People's School	8	3	
(4-year)	7	2	
	6	1	
Preschool Education	(5)		Preschool Education
(kindergarten for 2 years,	4		(kindergarten and
nursery schools for those up to	3		nursery schools)
four year olds)	2		
	1		
	0		

Children from 5 year olds to 16 year olds are under 11-year free compulsory education.

Notes

1. *The Aeneid of Virgil,* trans. Allen Mandelbaum (New York: Bantam Books, 1971), p. 221 (Book IX, 245).
2. Quoted in C. P. Snow, *Variety of Men* (New York: Charles Scribner's Sons, 1966), p. 215.
3. For a discussion of education and South Korean economic development in particular, see, for instance, Seung-shik Oh, "Economic Development and Human Resources—With Particular Reference to University Education," *Koreana Quarterly* (Spring 1966), pp. 37-48; Noel F. McGinn et al, *Education and Development in Korea* (Cambridge: Harvard University Press, 1980); Young Chul Kim, "Educational Contribution to Economic Development," *Korean Social Science Journal* 12 (1985): 120-150. For a general analysis of education and economic development, see, e.g., George Psacharopoulos, "Rates of Return to Investment in Education Around the World," *Comparative Education Review* (February 1972), pp. 54-67; Wook Park, "Modernity and Views of Education: A Comparative Study of Three Countries," *Comparative Education Review* (February 1980), pp. 35-47.
4. See, for instance, Roy Hofheinz, Jr. and Kent E. Calder, *The Eastasia Edge* (New York: Basic Books, 1982), pp. 7-8. According to one study, North Korea's average GNP growth rates were: 21.0% (1954-56, three-year plan period), 8.9% (1957-60, 5-year plan period), 8.9% (1961-70, 1st 7-year plan period) and 4% (1978-84, 2nd 7-year plan period). For details, see Hwan-ki Paek, "North Korea's Arms Buildup and Its Economic Dilemma," *Vantage Point* (December 1986), pp. 1-9. For an analysis of Soviet and East European countries' economic performance, see Stephen White, "Economic Performance and Communist Legitimacy," *World Politics* 38 (April 1986): 462-482.
5. There are quite a few studies on North and South Korean educational systems. See, for instance, Gyŏng-su Cha, "Educational Ideology and Basic Policy in North Korea" (in Korean), *Pukhan* (February 1980), pp. 58-68; Kwang-suk Choe, "North Korea's Communist Ideology Education," *Pukhan Chŏngch'i Ch'aekye* (Seoul: Korea University Asiatic Research Center, 1972); Yong-hŏn Chŏn, "Political Socialization in North Korea," I and II, *Vantage Point* (October, November 1984), pp. 1-13 and pp. 1-12; Won-shik Chŏng, "Zeal for Education," *Korea Journal* 26 (October 1986): 45-51; Bum-mo Chung, "Impact of American Culture on Korea Through Educational Exchanges," *Koreana Quarterly* (Winter 1967), pp. 74-87; Ch'ŏn-ki Eun, "A Study of the Reality of Anti-Communism Education and the Better Alternative" (in Korean), *Pukhan* (September 1981), pp. 176-194; Ki-un Hahn, "Study of the Democratization of Education in Korea Based on the History of Education Thought," *Korea*

Observer (April/July 1969); also, his *History of Korean Education* (in Korean) (Seoul: Pakyŏng-sa, 1983); Woong-sun Hong, "Liberal Education in Korean Universities," *Korea Observer* (April/July 1969); Sŏng-mo Hwang, "Mental Structure of North Korean Youth From a Standpoint of Social Psychology," *Vantage Point* (May 1981), pp. 1-10; Chong-chŏl Kim, "The Communist's View on Education" (in Korean), *Pukhan* (June 1981), pp. 74-93; Choong Nam Kim, *Political Socialization and Political Education* (in Korean) (Seoul: Bŏpmun-sa, 1982); also, his "Education As An Independent Variable of (South) Korea's Democratic Development," paper delivered at the 1980 Korean Political Science Association Annual Meeting, Seoul, Korea, and his "Socialization Process and Educational Tasks of North and South Korean Children" (in Korean), *Korean Journal of Unification Affairs* (1983), pp. 7-24; Chŏng-hum Kim, "North and South Korea's Level of Natural Sciences" (in Korean), *Pukhan* (May 1981), pp. 36-45; Ha-hyŏn Kim, "Science and Technology in North Korea: A self-Imposed Dilemma," *Vantage Point* (May 1980), pp. 1-13; Hyung-chan Kim," A Study of North Korean Education Under Communism Since 1945" (Ed.D dissertation, George Peabody College, 1969) and his "Changing Pattern of North Korea's Educational System, 1945-1980," *Vantage Point* (December 1982), pp. 1-10 and "The Changing Process of North Korea's Higher Education (I) and (II)" (in Korean), *Pukhan* (May and June 1980), pp. 174-194 and pp. 199-211; Chong-chŏl Kim, "Higher Education Policies in (South) Korea, 1945-83," *Korea Journal* (October 1983), pp. 4-19; Sin-bok Kim, "Recent Development of Higher Education in (South) Korea," *Korea Journal* (October 1983); Sun-ho Kim, "Higher Education in North Korea," *Vantage Point* (November 1979), pp. 1-10; Sung-wŏn Kim, "North Korea's Education and Family Policy" (in Korean), *Pukhan* (September, October and November 1980); Tong-kyu Kim, "A Study of North Korean Pedagogy" (in Korean), *Korean Journal of Unification Affairs* (1983), No. 1, pp. 55-85; Yong-hyŏn Kim, "North Korea's Strengthening to Thought Education and Its Reality" (in Korean), *Pukhan* (March 1981), pp. 142-151; Young Shik Kim, "The North Korean Educational System and Its Operational Problems" (in Korean), *Pukhan* (February 1980); Joong Lee, "Collectivist Education in North Korea," *Vantage Point* (August and September 1982); Sŏ-haeng Lee, "Ideological Education in North Korea," *Vantage Point* (September 1980), pp. 1-10; *A Study of North Korean Education* (Seoul: North Korean Research Institute, 1977); Kye-hyŏn No, "An Analysis of North Korea's Human Modification (in Korean), *Pukhan* (May 1981), pp. 154-165; Ch'ŏnsok O, *History of New Education in Korea* (in Korean) (Seoul: Hyŏndae Kyoyuk Ch'ulp'an-sa, 1964); In-hak Paek, "The Changing Process of North Korea's Political Thought Education" (in Korean), *Pukhan* (February 1980), pp. 134-155; Tong-wun Park, "Educational Ideology and Ideology Education in North Korea" (in Korean), *Pukhan* (September 1982), pp. 62-72; and Yong-hŏn Park, "Comparative Study on Political Education of South and North Korea," *East Asian Review* (Autumn 1975), pp. 258-282 and his "North Korea's Educational Process and Content" (in Korean), *Korean Journal of Unification Affairs* (1983), pp. 25-54; "Child Education in North Korea," *Vantage Point* (November 1980), pp. 1-10; and "North Korea's Political Indoctrination Policy and Sense of Values of Its Youth," *Vantage Point* (February 1983), pp. 1-11. See also To-song Shin, "Is Anti-Communism or Education?" (in Korean), *Pukhan* (March 1981), pp. 36-46; Byung Soon Song, "Comparative Study of Ideological Influences on Educational Theory and Practice in North and South Korea" (Ph.D. dissertation, Wayne State University, 1975); Ha Wun Sung, "Education and Political Ideology in North Korea: A Critical Analysis of Educational Policy, Aims and Nationalism" (Ph.D. dissertation, George Peabody College, 1976); Hung Yul To, "Comparison of North and South Korean Children's Cognitive Development Process" (in Korean), *Kuktto T'ongilwŏn* (1977) and his "North Korea's Collectivistic Education Model and Its Reality" (in Korean), *Pukhan* (February 1980), pp. 84-93; Sung Chul Yang, "Socialist Education in North Korea" in Eugene C. I. Kim and B. C. Koh, eds., *Journey to North Korea: Personal Perceptions* (Berkeley: University of California Press, 1983), pp. 63-83.

6. An excellent analysis of the party (WPK) control of North Korean educational system is found in Yong-hŏn Park, "Comparative Study on Political Education of South and North Korea," *Op. Cit.*

7. *Hongik Inkan* is the founding philosophy of *Tangun*, the legendary founder of the Korean nation in the year of 2333 B.C. For a detailed discussion of the *Tangun* legend, see Byŏng-do Yi, *A Study of Ancient Korean History* (in Korean) (Seoul: Pakyŏng-sa, 1976), pp. 27-44. Note also that *Hongik Inkan* as Korea's founding philosophy is broad enough to embrace the Western democratic ideal. For a discussion of *Hongik Inkan* and the democratic ideal as the South Korean Educational ethos see, for instance, Ki-un Hahn, *Hankuk Kyoyuk-sa* [History of Korean Education], pp. 536-556.

8. According to one survey, in the spring semester of 1985 alone, there were 443 university student protests in 56 universities and colleges in South Korea. One of the main aims of their grievances was the restoration of school autonomy. For details, see *Hankook Ilbo*, 1 September 1984.

9. For details, see *Pukhan Ch'onggam, '45-'68* (in Korean) (Seoul, 1968), pp. 460-464.

10. See, for instance, Kim Il Sung, *The Youth Must Take Over The Revolution and Carry It Forward* (Pyongyang: Foreign Languages Publishing House, 1976).

11. The dates of educational thematic changes in North Korea differ among

specialists on North Korean education. For example, Gye-hyŏn No identified four stages: the period of total mobilization of the nation-building thought (1946-1954); the period of communist class education (1954-1961); the period of revolutionary tradition education (1961-1967); and the period of monolithic ideology education (1967-). In-hak Paek offers a slightly different version: the period of introducing communism (1945-1950); the period of modelling communism (1950-1959); the period of establishing revolutionary tradition (1959-1967); and the period of establishing monolithic ideology (1968 to the present). Gyŏng-su Cha's four stages are: the period of introducing communism (1945-1950); the period of establishing communist ideology (1950-1959); the period of establishing revolutionary tradition education (1960-1966); and the period of establishing monolithic ideology (1967-). Finally, Young-hŏn Park's four stages are: the period of emulating communism (1945-1950); the period of consolidating class and communist education (1950-1958); the educational establishment of revolutionary tradition (1958-1967) and the established period of unitary thought (1967-). For details, see Gye-hyŏn No, "The Changing Process of North Korean Thought Education" (in Korean), *Pukhan* (May 1981), pp. 154-165; In-hak Paek, "The Changing Process of Political Thought Education in North Korea" (in Korean), *Pukhan* (February 1980), pp. 134-155; Gyŏng-su Cha, "North Korean Educational Ideology and Its Basic Policy" (in Korean), *Pukhan* (February 1980), pp. 58-68; and Yong-hŏn Park, "Comparative Study on Political Education of South and North Korea," *Op. Cit.*

12. Kim Il Sung, *On Socialist Pedagogy* (Pyongyang: Foreign Languages Publishing House, 1979), pp. 5-10.

13. *Ibid.*, pp. 13-14.

14. For an account of Kim's early power struggles, see *Pukhan Chŏnsŏ*, especially, pp. 157-168. Also, Sung Chul Yang, *Korea and Two Regimes* (Cambridge: Schenkman, 1981), pp. 161-220.

15. *Ibid.*

16. Kim Il Sung, *The Youth Must Take Over the Revolution and Carry It Forward,* pp. 38-54.

17. The full text of his speech is found in Kim Il Sung, *On the Building of the Workers' Party of Korea* (Pyongyang: Foreign Languages Publishing House, 1978), Vol. 2, pp. 71-98.

18. Kim Il Sung, *The Youth Must Take Over,* pp. 81-95.

19. Kim Il Sung, *Selected Works* (in Korean) (Pyongyang, 1974), Vol. 4, pp. 129-139.

20. *Ibid.*

21. For a detailed analysis of Kim's elimination of his factional enemies within the WPK, see Sung Chul Yang, "The Politics of Cult in North Korea" *Politi-*

cal Studies Review 1 (1985): 27-52.
22. Kim Il Sung, *Pedagogy*, p. 113.
23. For details, see, for instance, Sung Chul Yang, "Socialist Education in North Korea" *Op. Cit.*, pp. 63-83.
24. I. A. Snook, for one, attempted to explain the differences between indoctrination and education. Simply put, indoctrination occurs when somebody takes advantage of a privileged role (a "teaching" role of some sort) to implant certain beliefs. For details, see his *Indoctrination and Education* (London: Routledge and Kegan Paul, 1972), especially, pp. 99-111.
25. Kim Il Sung, *Pedagogy*, pp. 43-44.
26. Kim Il Sung, *Selected Works*, Vol. 1, p. 72; Vol. 2, p. 343; Vol. 3, p. 373; and Vol. 4, p. 279.
27. Eric Hoffer, *The True Believer* (New York: Perennial Library, 1951), p. 66.
28. For a discussion of the Kim Il Sung cult, see Sung Chul Yang, "The Kim Il Sung Cult in North Korea," in *Korea and World Affairs* (Spring 1980), pp. 161-186 and his "The Politics of Cult in North Korea," *Op. Cit.*
29. Kim Il Sung, *The Youth Must*, p. 160.
30. *On the Socialist Constitution of the Democratic People's Republic of Korea* (Pyongyang, 1975), p. 53.
31. Kim Il Sung, *Pedagogy*, pp. 316-368.
32. Kim Jong (Chong) Il, *On Further Developing Educational Work* (Pyongyang, 1984), p. 29.
33. Yong-hŏn Park, "North Korea's Political Indoctrination Policy and Sense of Value of Its Youth," *Op. Cit.*
34. For details, Sung Chul Yang, "Socialist Education in North Korea," *Op. Cit.* One of the most recent samples of the new cult phenomenon of Kim Jong Il is found in In Su Choe, *Kim Jong Il: The People's Leader* (Pyongyang: Foreign Languages Publishing House, 1985).
35. For a discussion of Dewey's influence on South Korean education, see, for instance, Hyung Jin Yoo, "Centennial History of Korean-American Educational Exchange," paper delivered at the Korean Educational Development Institute, Seoul, Korea, 15 October 1982.
36. *Laws of the Republic of Korea* (Seoul: Korean Legal Center, 1969), pp. 1348-1349.
37. For details, see Hyung Jin Yoo, *Op. Cit.*, pp. 13-22. Also, *Korea: Its People and Culture* (Seoul: Hakwŏn-sa, 1970), pp. 194-195. For information on foreign technical assistance to Korea, see E. C. Wilson, "The Problem of Value in Technical Assistance in Education: The Case of Korea, 1945-1955" (Ed.D. dissertation, University of Maryland, 1959).
38. *Ibid.*
39. For details, see *Education in Korea, 1981* (Seoul: Ministry of Education,

1981), pp. 19-24.

40. See Richard W. Wilson, "Political Socialization and Moral Development," *World Politics* (January 1981), pp. 153-177. But South Korea's "moral" education is quite different from "moral development" education.

41. Sung Chul Yang, "Socialist Education in North Korea," pp. 68-73.

42. Daniel R. Sabia, Jr., "Political Education and the History of Political Thought," *American Political Science Review* 78 (December 1984): 985-999. There are a few, who questioned the effectiveness of South Korea's anti-Communism education policy and programs, e.g., To-sung Shin, *Op. Cit.* and Ch'ŏn-ki Eun, *Op. Cit.*

43. Tong-wun Park, "Educational Ideology and Ideology Education in North Korea" (in Korean), *Op. Cit.* Pyŏn, for one, points out the juvenile delinquency and other youth problems in North Korea today, see Chin-hung Pyŏn, "North Korean Youth and the Reality of Human Modification Campaign" (in Korean), *Pukhan* (June 1982), pp. 120-129.

44. *Ibid.*

45. *Ibid.*

46. See "Education Law" in *Laws of the Republic of Korea* (Seoul: Korean Legal Center, 1969), pp. 1347-1351. For a survey analysis of South Korean secondary school students' cognitive and affective characteristics, see Jong-ha Han et al., *A Study on the Development of Cognitive and Affective Characteristics of Korean Secondary School Students* (in Korean) (Seoul: Korean Educational Development Institute, 1982).

47. The entire educational system is currently under review by the South Korean government.

48. For details, see Yong-hŏn Park, "North Korea's Political Indoctrination Policy and Sense of Values of Its Youth," *Op. Cit.*

49. *The People's Korea*, 13 April 1985.

50. Sung Chul Yang, "Socialist Education in North Korea," *Op. Cit.*

51. The original plan for free and compulsory middle school education by the South Korean government was as follows: all islands and rugged regions by 1985; all schools in *myŏn* [town] by 1986; all schools in *eup* [larger town] area by 1987; all schools in cities except Pusan, Taegu and Inchŏn by 1988; all schools except Seoul by 1989; and all schools in the nation including Seoul by 1990. But this original plan is only partially implemented.

52. Kim Il Sung, *On Socialist Pedagogy*, p. 407.

53. Kim Il Sung, *On the Building of People's Government* (Pyongyang: Foreign Languages Publishing House, 1978), Vol. 2, p. 585.

54. For details, see *A Study on the Moral Development of Korean Students* (Seoul: Korean Educational Development Institute, 1982).

CHAPTER 20

REUNIFICATION AND POLICY MODELS

There are two kinds of falsehood, the one being the result of igno-rance and the other intentional, and that we should pardon those who depart from the truth through ignorance, but unreservedly condemn those who lie deliberately.

Polybius[1]

There is often no more logic in the course of events than there is in the plans of men.

Thucydides[2]

Introduction

The Korean division is real, and its reunification, ideal. During all these years of division, millions of words have been wasted in the form of public speech or private propositions and of formal talks or informal proposals. In a way North Korea and South Korea have been fighting a war of words with the conspicuous exception of the North's unsuccess-ful invasion of the South in 1950s and other continuing espionage and terroristic acts. In North Korea, unification is, territorially at least, tanta-mount to liberation. Kim Il Sung and his ruling elites have rationalized their rule with the promise that the "liberation" of South Korea from the U.S. (and Japanese) imperialism is "imminent," and that they have the solemn mission to "liberate" the South from the "fascist Kim Young-sam cliques" (or previously from the "Rhee, Park, Chun, and Roh cliques") and from their "imperialist war-mongers." Politically, to Kim Il Sung and his ruling elites, unification is synonymous with communization, the application of North Korea's totalitarian political order to South Korea.

In South Korea unification implies no such definitive and absolute goals; it is vague at worst and open-ended at best. In the meantime, a governmental-academic unification complex, resembling a thriving business enterprise, has emerged. A ministry supervising the unification question was created (National Unification Board); scholars and experts specializing on this topic have multiplied; journals, papers, books and pamphlets, let alone conferences and seminars, have flooded the Korean intellectual market. Also, unification research institutes off and on campus and civic organizations at home and abroad, some of which are supported or subsidized by the public sources, have also mushroomed.[3] In this regard, North Korea has been pursuing much the same course, except that all these are more uniformly directed and controlled by the WPK.

Thus far, both sides' approaches to unification have amounted to nothing more than a war of *words*. While they are engaged in this war of words, the reality of division persists, and the ideal of unification remains unrealized. Bearing in mind the increasingly wasteful nature of the unification question, in this chapter two questions will be dealt with in some detail.

First, it will identify some problems and difficulties stemming from the swift realization of united Germany. In so doing, Korea, still a divided land, should maximize the so-called the advantages of the late-comer by learning from the German experiences.

Second, by observing and learning from the German unification experiences, a new approach to the Korean question is proposed here as an alternative to the currently existing official and/or unofficial models and formulas for the Korean unification.

Learning from the German Unification

Contrasts and Similarities

Before the problems and pitfalls of the German unification are identified and examined briefly, a few salient differences between two Germanys and two Koreas are noted here. To begin with, two propositions can be formulated for clarifying the present discussion. First, it is posited that both Kim Il Sung of North Korea and Fidel Castro of Cuba, the last two remaining communist revolutionary dinosaurs[3], will not be an exception to the general trend of communist demise.

Second, South Korea may face both controllable and uncontrollable circumstances like West Germany, if the one-party-father-son regime in North Korea collapses. The question, then, immediately arises: Is South Korea, like West Germany, politically stable and secure, economically strong and sound and socially fair and equitable enough to absorb North Korea? The answer is more likely to be in the negative. South Korea is not West Germany. Nor is North Korea, ex-East Germany. The reality of Korean and German internal political and economic conditions and the complexity of their external relations and alliances are sharply contrasting.

The Federal Republic of Germany (FRG) or West Germany is a decentralized federal government founded originally by *Laenders*. The Federal Republic was created by local governments (*Laender*). What is more, the rise in popularity of federalism over centralism has been impressive.[4] By contrast, the Republic of Korea (ROK) or South Korea is a highly centralized typical unitary government. The ROK's central government is now wrestling with the timetable of when and how to form local administrative governments. Thus far, only the local and provincial legislative assemblies have been formed, and they have been in operation since 1991. In short, West Germany has had (and the current unified Germany has) a firmly rooted local autonomy, while South Korea has just begun its political experiments with local autonomy.[5]

Above all, the FRG has been one of the most stable and efficient democratic nations in the post-War world. Thus far, it has experienced two inter-party transfers of power from the Christian Democratic Union (CDU) coalition to the Social Democratic Party (SPD) coalition in 1969 and from the SPD coalition back to the CDU-CSU (Christian Social Union)-led coalition in 1982. During this period, the FRG had five presidents and thirteen cabinets of which eight were formed by CDU-led coalitions, and five, by SPD-led coalitions.[6]

By contrast, the ROK has been marked by political instability during the same period. It had six republics with nine constitutional revisions, not to mention two military coups (1961 and 1979), three major student and popular uprisings (1960, 1980 and 1986) and some twelve declarations of martial laws and emergency decrees. Since its founding, the ROK has experienced only two peaceful transfer of power in 1988 and in 1993. Even then, the power succession did not occur between parties, but within the ruling party. Thus, South Korea has yet to experience a peaceful transfer of power from the ruling party to an opposition party. All in all, South Korea is in the midst of an early phase of democratization at best, or it is still being plagued by political instability and political infantile paralysis.[7]

Noteworthy also is the fact that West Germany is a typical cabinet-responsible system, while South Korea's current Kim regime is a presidential system. The West German legislature is bicameral, Bundestag and Bundesrat, and that of South Korea is unicameral, the National Assembly. The powers and authority of German *Laender* are strong and growing, but the newly created South Korean local assemblies are inherently weak. They are dependent upon, and subject to, the control of the central government.[8] Worse still, President Roh unilaterally postponed the mayoral and the provincial gubernatorial elections until 1995. In doing so, he has, in fact, violated the local autonomy laws which, among other things, prescribed such elections by June 1992. In protest, opposition parties—the Democratic Party and the United People's Party—boycotted the normal operations of the 14th National Assembly.

The FRG and the ROK's legal or constitutional provisions for unification, too, are in stark contrast. The FRG's Basic Law was "temporary" in nature as its Preamble stipulates, i.e., "desiring to give a new order to political life *for a transitional period*, has enacted, by virtue of its con-

stituent power, this Basic Law of the Federal Republic of Germany...."
Consequently, the German people are yet to enact a new Constitution
(*Verfassung*) for the united Germany. The irony is that the FRG's Basic
Law has remained virtually intact, albeit two revisions during the last
forty years, despite its "transitional" character. By contrast, the ROK's
constitution, its seemingly "permanent" nature notwithstanding, was
revised nine times with six substantial changes.

The FRG's Basic Law had two legal provisions enabling unification
(Articles 23 and 146), while the ROK's current constitution has six provisions dealing with unification. Unlike the West German Basic Law,
however, the South Korean constitution claims the territory covering
both the present South Korea and North Korea (Article 3). Most importantly, the German framers of the Basic Law, let alone its key political
leaders, placed the task of national unity above and before politics.
German politicians of both the ruling and opposition parties seldom
resorted to using the Basic Law or its revision as an instrument for per-
petuating or strengthening their own partisan power. By contrast, the
South Korean politicians have often misused or abused the constitution
or its revision as if it were their personal political tool to rationalize or
perpetuate their own political power.[9]

The glaring differences in international and external dimensions also
exist between Germany and Korea. To begin with, the German people
did not experience the fratricidal proxy war in the early 1950s that victimized the Korean people and others. As a result, the Korean people
both in the North and the South still have a deep-seated and lingering
mutual distrust, while similar feelings are virtually absent from the
minds of the German people.

Germany's centerstage position and Korea's periphery, semi-periph-
ery or, at best, middle-power status are also noteworthy. Germany, the
claimant of the traditional Mittel Europa, the principal actor [culprit] of
both World Wars and the main locomotive of European integration, differs sharply from Korea, the principal victim of both the Sino-Japanese
(1894-1905) and the Russo-Japanese (1904-1905) wars, World War II
and the Korean War, let alone of the Cold War. In this connection,
Gurtov's view that "unlike the German case, where unification was

commonly perceived as a direct contribution to Europe's long-term stability and integration, Korean unification may be perceived as destabilizing, even potentially threatening, to the major powers," is thought-
provoking.[10]

In post-World War alliance and integration frameworks, Germany has
been involved in multilateral arrangements such as the North Atlantic
Treaty Organization (NATO), the European Community (EC) and Conference on Security and Cooperation in Europe (CSCE). The South
Korean security alliance and external relations have been, on the other
hand, primarily bilateral, e.g., the 1954 U.S.-Republic of Korea Mutual
Defense Treaty. In recent years, some multilateral arrangements are in
the offing in Korea and in this region, too, but they are still in their
embryonic stages. The launching of the Asia-Pacific Economic Cooperation (APEC) and the proposal of the Conference on Security and Cooperation in Asia (CSCA), as a counterpart of the CSCE, are the cases in
point.[11]

The economic dimensions of the former FRG vis-a-vis ex-GDR
(German Democratic Republic) and South Korea vis-a-vis North Korea
seem to resemble each other on the surface, but at a closer look their
differences, are more glaring than their similarities. Roughly speaking,
the size of the FRG economy in terms of GNP was about ten times
greater than that of the GDR economy before the unification. After
the unification, the first reliable official economic data was released
recently. According to the Federal Government's Statistical Office, in
the last half of 1990, that is, the first six months *after* the unification, the
East German GNP was estimated at 105.3 billion Deutsch Mark (DM)
or 60.2 billion dollars, while the West German GNP was approximately
1.28 trillion DM. Thus, the East German economic size represents
only 8.3% of West Germany's.[12] Meanwhile, it is reported that the
South Korean GNP ($ 238 billion) in 1990 is roughly nine to ten times
bigger than that of North Korea ($ 23.1 billion).[13]

The similarities between the two nations, however, end quickly here.
Structurally, the Federal Republic of Germany is one of the most
advanced and leading high-tech nations, while South Korea is a mid-
tech newly industrializing country at best, and its per capita income

($5,569 in 1990) is still a third or a fourth the size of the advanced nations. For example, the workers in the FRG have had their political rights to participate and/or organize political parties from its inception. The 1951 Law on Worker Participation stipulated workers' right to equal representation in industrial management, though it was limited to coal and steel industries. A new law on worker participation passed in March 1976 provided equal representation of workers on workers' councils in all large scale companies, although the representation of the share holders remains dominant in the event of a conflict. And, as early as in 1957, the provisions of the Pension Law stipulated that the pension increase was tied to the wage increase, and the 5 days-40 hour work week has now been achieved.[14] In this particular area as well as in other social and economic egalitarian measures, the Federal Republic is substantially ahead of South Korea.

The FRG-GDR Economic, Monetary and Social Union Treaty, which was signed on May 18 and implemented on July 1, 1990, represents a good example. The economic union reaffirmed the Federal Republic's social market economy (*Soziale Markwirtschaft*). Specifically, the private property, free market economic system, the principles of economic competition, the introduction of free commerce and industry, free movement of goods, capital and labor and the introduction of tax, finance and budget system compatible with free market system are the elements of such economy. The monetary union stipulated *inter alia* that the Deutsch Mark (DM) should be the official currency, the Federal Republic's Deutsche Bundesbank, the only official central bank and the differential exchange rates of DM should be applied to *Ost Mark* (OM). For example, one to one ratio was applied to wages, salaries, pension, monthly rent or scholarship. One to one ratio was applied to individual savings up to a certain amount (2,000 OM for the fifteen-year olds or younger, 4,000 OM for the sixteen to sixty-year olds and 6,000 OM for those sixty or older). Two (OM) to one (DM) ratio was used in all other monetary claims except for debts.

Most importantly, the social union, too, meant the wholesale adoption of the Federal Republic's social measures by the GDR. The GDR adopted the Federal Republic's pension, health, unemployment, accident

insurance systems and the low-income people assistance programs. In
addition, the GDR was compelled to adopt the FRG's far superior social
measures and programs for its workers, the autonomy of worker-man-
agement, collective bargaining, the right to organize labor union, the
management of strikes, the practice of co-determination, democracy
within industry and the law to prohibit arbitrary dismissal.[15]

Can South Korea offer North Korea social measures comparable to
that of the FRG which were attractive and sound enough to absorb the
GDR's? Unfortunately, at the present time, the answer cannot be in the
affirmative.

The German Unification: From Euphoria to Dysphoria

On October 3, 1990, which was the 4,323rd anniversary of the founding of the first legendary Korean state, divided German states were united. Of three major divided states in the aftermath of World War II, Vietnam by force and Germany by political settlement, have been unified,
and only Korea still remains divided with much rancor and with little
prospect for immediate reconciliation.

"The German people are the happiest people in the world!" This
remark was made in the mass rally by Mr. Momper, mayor of West
Berlin on November 10, 1989, a day after the Berlin Wall was removed
(open). The German people's euphoria reached its zenith on October 3,
1990, when two Germanys were reunited after some 45 years of other-
imposed partition. In a way, unification is like a marriage. After the
excitement of pre-marital courtship, formal engagement, marriage ceremony and honeymoon, the real life of the newly wed must begin somehow. The real life, however, is unlike the honeymoon period which is
full of honey and happiness. It often requires trials and hardships. In a
similar vein, the pre-unification euphoria could and would not last forever. Before long the German people quickly came to the realization
during the post-unification Germany that in the short run, at least, both
monetary and mental cost of unification far outweighed its benefits. As
Edward Roby pointed out, things are likely to get worse before they get
better. The economies, lifestyles and mentalities of the two regions have

not yet been integrated. The rebuilding of East's decrepit transportation, telecommunications and governmental infrastructure alone will cost more than half a trillion Deutsche marks in coming years.[16] The pre-unification euphoria has, thus, been quickly replaced by the post-unification dysphoria. The political and economic union was relatively quick and easy, but what the German President Richard von Weisaecker called the "human union" will be harder to achieve.[17] Stephen Kinzer reported that when Germans talk of bringing the two sides of their country to economic equality, they speak in terms of years, but when asked how long it will take to achieve "inner unity," they often speak of generations. A Leipzig University professor's lament quoted by Kinzer is memorable in this connection:

> "Not only did their [people in eastern Germany] political system change completely, but so did the material basis of their lives—administrative structures, social relationships, self-image, the meaning of their past, their present and their future, and with it the very point of their existence. Even the familiar smells of their homeland are different, from cleaning fluids to gasoline. With unification came not only a falling away of everything familiar, but also implantation in a completely new world."[18]

Of course, a painless birth of a united state from a long, mutually hostile and separated existence is inconceivable. Still, the costs and pangs of the German unification have turned out to be far more serious than expected. Most recently, Chancellor Helmut Kohl acknowledged that the economic upswing in the former East Germany would take longer and cost more than he originally thought. He stated that "many expectations have been filled in this time, but there have also been disappointments and setbacks.... Some things will take longer than we assumed in the autumn of 1990, and transfer of payments from West to East are higher."[19]

To save space, it suffices to list some of the salient problems that united Germany is currently confronting. They are:

(1) an exorbitant unification cost,[20] including the Federal Republic's subsidy for the withdrawing Soviet troops and their dependents from the

former GDR (some 370,000 in number and 230,000 dependents). For example, outstanding German public-sector debt in 1991 was 1.2 trillion DM, 46% of its GNP. It could soar to 1.8 trillion DM, or over 51% of its GNP by 1995. West German transfer of money to East Germany in 1991 was 170 billion DM, and in 1992 the transfers are estimated at 212 billion with 35 billion DM earmarked for East German taxes. The net shift, thus, is 180 billion DM, which is more than 6% of German GNP, or roughly a quarter of its total public spending[21];

(2) the slow process of privatizing some 45,000 decaying communist factories and faltering businesses in East Germany by Treuhandanstalt, the German state-run privatization agency, in particular, and the problem of transforming a state-planned economy into a market economy, in general[22];

(3) the East German workers' worsening unemployment. For example, unemployment in West Germany rose to 7% in January, 1992, from 6.5% in December of the previous year, while unemployment in East Germany bolted to 17% from 11.8% during the same period.[23]

(4) the treatment of East German secret police (Stasi) and its informants (according to one source, there are 4,000 spies in the NATO member nations and 85,000 former employees and thousands of unknown informants) in particular and the problem of restructuring (dismantling) the ex-East German political systems in general. Regarding Stasi, the remarks of Joachim Lehmann, a Lutheran clergyman in East Germany are apropos here:

> "I have never lived in freedom. Never before have I been allowed to say what I believed. Like all citizens of East Germany, I lived a schizophrenic life. There are certain things you could say only at home, and then very different things you had to say at school or at work. My parents taught me to live that way, and that's what I taught my kids. In East Germany, life consisted mainly of waiting to be told what to do, and then doing it. I'm never going to be able to break away from this conditioning. I will always be an Ossie—an easterner. May be my children will be able to adjust to the new situation. But only the generation of my grandson, who is now one year old, will grow up like normal Germans and Europeans.... Naturally I want to see evil people punished, but why

focus on every Stasi informer and forget the party officials? If we can put the whole politburo and regime on trial, then I'd be for it.... You can't just be a revolutionary for 40 or 50 years. You have to live with the power structure and that means compromising.... People desperately want this moment, unification, to end well. I believe it will. We're disappointed with some things, but at heart we're satisfied, I've never met anyone who wants to go back to the old days.[24]

(5) the deportation question of foreign workers in the former East Germany (estimated at around 100,000, including some 50,000 Vietnamese workers). Worse still, the flow of refugees, including asylum seekers and ethnic Germans, which is currently running at 1,600 a day, poses a serious problem (For details, see Table 20-1);

(6) the over-burdened and under-staffed handling of various property claims, the GDR's national debts and industries' liabilities. There are about 40,000 claims for 16,000 pieces of properties in Leipzig alone;

(7) the efforts to narrow the language differences between two Germanys;

(8) the upward inflationary pressure and the downward economic growth rate. *The Economist* on May 2, 1992, for example, reported that Germany's latest trade deficits for 12 months amounted to 23.3 billion dollars, but the signs of favorable trade balance are evident. So is its GNP after the negative growth rate in 1991. Its unemployment rate is also steady at 6.2%;

(9) the intractable task of narrowing the significant differences in both Germanys' wage, pension and living standards in particular and quality of life in general. In 1991, for example, West Germany's 61 million people enjoyed a GDP per head of 38,000 DM ($ 23,500) a year, while their 17 million eastern brethren had a GDP per head of 13,000 DM.[25] The West German postal workers' average monthly wages were $2,317 as compared with their eastern counterparts' $1,390. West German bus drivers' monthly wages were $2,378, their eastern counterparts', $1,464 and West German white-collar workers' monthly wages were $3,219, as compared with eastern counterparts', $1,290. In other words, a postal worker or bus driver in the east earns just 60 percent of his or her western counterpart. Pensions are also unequal, with retired people in the

east receiving about one-third less than those in the west. The German
government plans to equalize wages and pensions by the end of the
1990s.[26] The West German workers also feel economically pinched. The
public sector strikes that began on April 27th were the first of their kind
in nearly 20 years. Roughly 100,000 workers in transport, postal and
refuse collection services began the action demanding a pay raise of
9.5%;[27]

(10) the so-called "mental disunity" between East and West Germans,
e.g., Ossies' mental depression and feeling of being the second class
citizen in united Germany. As noted above, the political and economic
changes of reunification are insufficient to repair the psychic damage
done by 40 years of socialism. According to one report, nine of every
ten Ossies feel like second-class citizens in the united country[28]; and

(11) the problem of air, water, and soil pollution in East Germany are
serious due primarily to dirty brown coal still providing 70% of its
primary energy needs and 85% of its electricity.[29]

The post-unification elections have in fact evinced the German
people's changing mood. West Germans are angry and weary of their
increasing monetary and social burden, and Ossies are frustrated by
their relative misery and misfortunes. In the all-German election on
December 1, 1990, the CDU-CSU coalition obtained 43.8% of the vote,
which was a slight increase over the results of the 1987 general election
(42.3%). The opposition SPD, on the other hand, received only 33.5%
of the vote, which was a significant loss as compared with the results of
the 1987 election (37.0%) (For details, see Table 20-2).

Since the December general election, however, the CDU-CSU coalition has been losing in the various local elections. The CDU-CSU
lost not only in Schleswig-Holstein, Lower Saxony and Hesse local
elec-tions, but also in such traditionally CDU-CSU strongholds as
Rhineland-Palatinate.[30] As of now, the SPD controls 10 out of 16 *Laenders* and the CDU-CSU coalition holds a majority only in two
Laenders—Bavaria and Baden-Wuertemberg. In Hamburg on June 2,
1991, the SPD took 48% of the vote, a 3% gain over the 1987 election,
while CDU received only 35.1% of the vote, as compared with 40.5%
vote it garnered in the 1987 election. Of the 121 total seats of the Ham-

burg Parliament, the SPD won 61 seats (previously 55), the CDU, 44 (49), FDP, 7 (8) and Greens, 9 (8). Technically, Kohl's chancellorship can last until 1994, but his coalition may collapse sooner, depending on the forthcoming political developments in united Germany. One thing is clear, nevertheless. Like Mikhail Gorbachev, Helmut Kohl has already secured a high place in history as a statesman who successfully led and realized the unification of Germany, but again, like Gorbachev, he, too, can be a victim of his own political success. History is fair in the end, but people are inherently gullible, and politics is, thus, fickle.

A New Approach to the Korean Unification

From the foregoing brief account of German unification experiences, what can the Korean people and the South Korean government do specifically in realizing the united country? A new approach here consists of two components—the conceptualization of Korean unification and the identification and application of policy models pertinent to Korean unification process.

Conceptualization of Key Unification Concepts

To begin with, we need a clear definition of Korean unification. Everybody talks about Korean "unification" but what exactly do we mean by it? Policymakers' attempt to realize Korean unification without having a clear conceptualization is analogous to a traveler wandering without knowing his or her destination. At a closer look, both Koreas' present official unification plans, the North's so-called Democratic Confederal Republic of Koryo (DCRK) unification proposal and the South's *Han* People Commonwealth of Korea (HPCK) unification formula, describe the *form* of a unified state if the Korean unification is realized, including the modes of interaction and the formats of inter-Korean relations in their interim stages. But Korean unification transcends the form of a unified Korea or the formats of inter-Korean relations and the modes of their interaction in pre-unification stages. To that extent, both

Koreas have, thus far, failed to provide a comprehensive conceptualization of Korean "unification." Accordingly, a conceptualization of Korean unification, though by no means definitive, is attempted here. As Table 20-3 illustrates, the meaning of Korean unification is broadly categorized into three dimensions. The first dimension of Korean unification is called the framework of living in a unified state. The framework of living is further subdivided into four components. The united Korea's guiding ideology, its political system, economic system and principal modes of social life. A liberal democracy is identified as the united Korea's guiding ideology. Liberal democracy means an ideology which protects and strengthens Korea's sovereign statehood at the national level and guarantees and promotes political rights and civil liberties at the individual level. From this standpoint, North Korea's present brand of a communist totalitarian *Juche* ideology as well as South Korea's persistent remnants of authoritarian practices must be discarded.

Likewise, the united Korea's political system must supplant the North's one-party-father-son dictatorship and the remnants of South's authoritarian political structures and practices. Specifically, the North needs a multi-party-multi-candidate free election through which a new government must be born. In the South, among other things, a full-fledged local autonomy, though presently postponed, along with an effectively functioning legislature and an impartial and independent judiciary must be implemented.

The economic system for the unified Korea should be basically a market-oriented one. The performance of a planned economy in the socialist states for more than 70 years has amply proven that it cannot be a viable economic system. North Korea's present command economic system must be deconstructed and South Korea's present economic system should be reformed and restructured in a market-friendly direction.

The second dimension of Korean unification is simply the territorial question of *lebensraum* or living space. The Korean Peninsula, originally partitioned into the two halves along the 38th parallel, still remains divided along the demilitarized zones (DMZ) after the Korean War. The Korean unification in this respect means reopening the border and reconnecting the physical split between the two halves. Regarding this, it should be emphasized that until the aforesaid framework of living between the two sides become mutually congruent ideologically, politically, economically and socially, the North-South border should not be opened prematurely. Any hasty opening of the border will create the flood of people and refugees moving most likely in one direction, i.e., from the North to the South, should such condition occur, it will not only be uncontrollable but will create a political and economic havoc on both sides.

The third dimension of Korean unification deals with an ideal portrait of citizenship in a unified state. An ideal person should be a free and ecology-conscious democratic citizen whose political rights and civil liberties are fully guaranteed, and who is fit to live peacefully and cooperatively with the rest of the fellow human beings in a global village (For details, see Table 20-3).

Along with the foregoing conceptualization of Korean unification, the actors who must guide and direct the unification process need to be identified. As Table 20-4 indicates, the principal guide or the primary actors and the secondary actors are distinguished here. The North and South Korean people are the primary actors, and the North and South Korean regimes are the secondary actors in the unification process. The primary actors provide the ultimate legitimacy or legality for the secondary actors, who actually implement the unification process. Plainly speaking, the sovereignty or the ultimate power to create the government(s) lies in the North and South Korean people and the power and resources to implement the unification process rests with the North and the South Korean regimes in power.

The next crucial question, then, is, are the existing North and South Korean regimes in power truly representative of their people? North Korea's present Kim Il Sung-Kim Jong Il regime is devoid of popular representation, let alone the people's will to establish a united fatherland. The current South Korean government, too, is deficient in representing the people's will to realize a united statehood, although it is relatively far more representative than either the Park, Chun and Roh regimes. Ideally then, until and unless both regimes represent the people's will for unification, they are not and cannot be the legitimate secondary actors of unification process. In other words, the emergence of democratic regimes in both halves is *sine qua non* for a genuine progress in unification process. Hence, the present North and South Korean regimes need to be conceptually distinguished from the ideal North and South Korean regimes which are truly representative of their respective people's will for unification (For details, see Table 20-4).

Finally, two sets of unification process concepts—pre-unity integration process and post-unity integration process and the controllable integration process and the uncontrollable integration process need to be distinguished. To start with, if the Korean unification is an integration *process*, it does not end with the realization of unification. For example, in Germany the East-West political reunion on October 3, 1990, was a watershed dividing the pre-unity integration process and post-unity integration process. The legal acts or policy decisions on German political unity as well as its monetary, economic and social unity were accomplished by then, but the process of integrating the two Germany's political, economic and social systems, let alone the mental reunion of the two peoples has been continuing.

Similarly, when the Berlin Wall opened on November 9, 1989, the East-West German integration process was no longer controllable. In fact, the uncontrollable integration process began even earlier than the collapse of the Berlin Wall. The process became already uncontrollable when the people in East Germany began their protest march against the communist regime in power (the Socialist Unity Party), which was crumbling rapidly.

Conceptually, therefore, a conceptual framework for the transformation of a communist system in general and that of a North Korean regime in particular can be formulated as follows. As Table 20-5 illustrates, in understanding and/or analyzing the demise or the transformation of a communist regime, three major policy dimensions need to be separated. They are the removal of the top communist leadership, the destruction of communist political, economic and social systems and the deprogramming of people's communist socialization. The removal of the top communist leadership is relatively easy and quick, although in the initial stages of the communist system transformation, the new lead-

ers replacing the old leadership are usually from the same old communist leadership pool. By contrast, an integration effort to destroy the old
communist system and at the same time to construct and introduce,
instead, the new guiding ideology, political, economic and social systems is a protracted, painful Herculean task. Likewise, as noted earlier
in the German case, realizing the mental unity between the North and
South Korean people will be the most difficult task, and only the passage of time will heal the wounds and narrow the gulf existing between
the two peoples.

Policy Models and Korean Unification

First of all, in dealing with North Korea, the interest-based bargaining
strategy instead of the heretofore used position-based bargaining strategy
needs to be adopted. The interest-based bargaining strategy, predicated
upon four basic objectives, employs a much different set of negotiating
behaviors which are non-adversarial and mutually supportive. Its
elements are: (1) attempts to separate the people involved in the negotiation from the problem which the process is intended to resolve; (2) parties which focus their attention on the interests brought to the negotiation by each side and not on the positions of each player; (3) participants
who work together to devise options which might represent mutually
satisfying solutions; and (4) negotiators who agree to employ objective
criteria in their decision making.[31]
Secondly, in South Korea's foreign policy making as a tool in creating regional and global environments conducive to the ultimate realization of united Korea, both the creative foreign policy model[32] and the
middle power role model[33] can be fully utilized. For example, in their
case analysis of determinants of creativity in foreign policy, Sylvan,
Voss and Beasley found the tendency among the foreign policy scholars
and the psychologists "to attribute creativity to individuals rather than to
groups."[34] One of their findings that only individuals can be creative in
foreign policy is, however, not a new discovery but a reconfirmation.
Their preliminary hypothesis that "the presence of a group leader, open
discussion, contingency planning and the freedom from formally man-

dated group support as a prerequisite for a decision are more likely to foster creativity in foreign policy,"[35] is relevant to the proposal that South Korea should adopt a new approach to North Korea and the four powers in the region.

Likewise, South Korea fits into a middle power leadership concept. For instance, Cooper and Higott conceptualized a three-stage itemized pattern of middle power leadership:

(i) Entrepreneurial leadership, i.e., middle powers may act as a catalyst with respect to a diplomatic effort, providing the intellectual/political energy to trigger an initiative;

(ii) Agenda setting, i.e., the actor (or actors) would be a *facilitator* for some form of associational/collaborative/coalitional activity. The type of work entails the planning and convening and/or hosting of formative meetings, setting priorities for future activities, drawing up declarations/manifestoes; and

(iii) Institution-building, i.e., the actor (or actors) would be a *manager*, creating formal organizations and regimes and developing conventions and norms. Central to institution building is a work program that establishes a division of labor, the development of monitoring activity, and possibly, but not necessarily the establishment of a secretariat or bureaucracy. This managerial stage also requires the development of *confidence-building measures* and facilities for dispute resolution, in which trust and credibility is built up and misunderstandings and misperceptions alleviated through liaison efforts, shuttle diplomacy, the use of alternative formal and informal fora, the creation of transparency and other means to push a given process forward.[36]

From a somewhat different perspective, Stephen Walker conceptualized foreign policy roles, as a conciliationist, a mediator and a recruiter/promoter,[37] which are also pertinent to the new approach proposed here. Namely, South Korea's creative leadership role as a catalyst, a facilitator, a manager, a conciliationist and a promoter in building a common peace and prosperity in the region cannot be overemphasized. Noteworthy in this connection is that the United States' policy makers and Asian specialists have failed to see the potential implications of South Korea assuming such a role, although they have acknowledged the political and economic success story of South Korea and other Asian countries in the region.[38]

Nevertheless, two sets of trilateral alliance system -- North Korea vis-a-vis the former Soviet Union and the People's Republic of China, and South Korea vis-a-vis the United States and Japan, which had been formed and functioning on the Korean Peninsula since World War II -- are in the process of rapid transformation and reformulation. South Korea's *Nordpolitik* has been successful on the whole in this regard, and North Korea, too, though belatedly and reluctantly, began to follow suit under the garb of its own *Sudpolitik*.[39]

Thirdly, as mentioned in the above, the Korean unification process can be divided into three paths: the uncontrollable, the controllable or the mixture of the two. If uncontrollable, deliberate efforts and preparations, including preventive measures, should be taken to respond to and minimize negative consequences resulting from unanticipated political events.

If controllable, two main tasks must be pursued relentlessly. One is the comprehensive research and planning to remove or replace the North Korea's father-son communist totalitarian system. The other is the in-depth study and preparation to deprogram the North Korean people's brainwashed mindset. In doing so, the German unification process should also be intensively and extensively studied to minimize the nega-tive consequences and problems of Korean unification and maximize its comparable benefits and positive outcomes.

Assuming that unification process is under control, three prerequisites must also be satisfied:

(1) the full and uninhibited inspection of North Korean nuclear facili-ties, sites and materials by the International Atomic Energy Agency (IAEA) and the simultaneous mutual inspections, including short-notice challenge inspection, of nuclear sites, facilities and others by North and South Korean inspection teams as agreed upon by the December 1991 denuclearization declaration must be realized. South Korea has pro-posed four regular and twelve special inspections per year for each party. Up to 56 sites on each side would be covered. The inspecting party would unilaterally initiate the special inspections, giving the host

government 24 hours notice and a schedule of sites six hours prior to inspection. South Korea has also called for the installation of sealed surveillance equipment at sites.[40]

In addition, if suspected nuclear reprocessing plants and/or nuclear materials are uncovered, they must be removed, destroyed and/or dismantled.[41] North Korea must also halt the sale of ballistic missiles, especially to Middle Eastern countries and eventually abandon the missile development projects, including the so-called No-Dong 1, a liquid fuel missile, which is believed to have a range of more than 600 miles.[42]

Several points are in order on this issue. Ever since North Korea's nuclear issue became the Korean and the international concerns, Kim Il Sung steadfastly upheld the position that "North Korea has neither intentions nor capabilities of developing nuclear weapons." But in April and May of this year (1992) when the IAEA inspections of North Korean nuclear facilities and sites became inevitable, North Korea, through various official channels, began to acknowledge that "a little bit of plutonium for experimental purposes" has been extracted at a "radiochemical laboratory" at Yŏngbyŏn, the facility cited in the U.S. intelligence estimates as a likely plutonium reprocessing plant. But the news reporting the Yŏngbyŏn facilities is rather conflicting, if not confusing. On the one hand, it is reported that the facilities are "extremely primitive" and "a long way from being finished," which appear to be about 80% complete.[43] Countering Blix's estimate, Gary Milhollin, for example, contended in his recent *New York Times* column that "North Korea now has enough nuclear weapon materials for six to eight atomic bombs."[44] In March 1992, the Russian newspaper, *Arguments and Facts*, reprinted a classified KGB report of February, 1990, for the Soviet Communist Party Central Committee that according to a reliable source "the first North Korean atomic explosive device has been completed... in the city of Yŏngbyŏn."[45] A Russian weekly, *Commersant*, reported that in April, 1992, North Korea had smuggled 56 kilograms of plutonium from the former Soviet Union as well as large amounts of other nuclear materials. A deputy director of the Institute for Oriental Affairs of the Russian Academy of Sciences was quoted by another weekly, *Moscow News*, as giving a similar account of North Korean smuggling plutonium from the former U.S.S.R. According to Nîksch, these Russian news sources are reputable and the KGB reports are relatively reliable.[46]

In summary, it looks as though the IAEA is more concerned about the potential North Korean nuclear disasters like the 1986 Chernobyl Incident, stemming from the mishandling of its rather primitive facilities, while the United States is very suspicious of its crude bomb-making. But the Korean people will be the primary victims of either such nuclear disasters or the bomb. What can be done if North Korea does not fully satisfy either the IAEA investigations or the South Korean, American and Japanese demands? Above all, close coordination and concerted actions of South Korea, the U.S.A. and Japan are vital in persuading and/or coercing North Korea to comply with such demands. An adroit and sophisticated use of both carrots and sticks, rewards and punishments, persuasion and coercion are essential in this matter. The UNDP (the United Nations Development Project) sponsored Tumen River Delta project, North Korea's urgent need for better and new relations with, and economic relief funds, from South Korea, Japan and the United States are some positive enticements. Li Sam-ro, chief of the North Korean delegation to the Pyongyang-Tokyo normalization negotiations, for one, reportedly stated that his government would accept inter-Korean inspection since it had signed a joint declaration. Further, he remarked that "if the United States supports Korean reunification, and if it continues to argue about North Korean threats, its troops may remain in South Korea until it has confirmed the non-existence of those threats."[47] Coincidentally, this rather positive statement by North Korea's senior official resulted in positive U.S. and South Korean military actions. The formal dismantling of the ROK-U.S. Combined Field Army on June 26, 1992, which was activated on March 14, 1980, provides a concrete evidence.[48] Actions through the UN Security Council, the G-7 meeting, other international and/or regional organizations and a resumption of Team Spirit exercises and a reintroduction of U.S. nuclear weapons may be invoked as negative sanctions against North Korean noncompliance.

A point needs to be raised here. Namely, between the peaceful approaches and the military actions in dealing with North Korea exists a host of intermediate options such as trade embargoes (e.g., the enforcement of the trade embargo at sea, the cargo-related air embargo) and financial sanctions, arms embargo, the naval blockade and quarantine, travel restrictions, freezing assets of financial institutions and financial transactions, as the UN Security Council resolutions on the Iraqi invasion of Kuwait had amply demonstrated.[49] Hence, any premature and hasty military action against North Korean nuclear sites and facilities is an absolute taboo. The military option can be justifiable only as the last resort after all means and forms of non-military methods and mechanisms are exhausted and have failed.[50]

Most importantly, if North Korea's nuclear weapon development project is proven to be true, it is against every conceivable interest; against the spirit of the new global current of a denuclearized world; against the genuine interests of the North Korean people, let alone the Korean people as a whole; and against the people in the region.

(2) North Korea and South Korea should remain as two separate states for the time being. During this transitional period, the North should transform itself through political liberalization and democratization process like Eastern Europe and the former Soviet Union, including the launching of its own marketization and privatization, not to mention price, financial, trade reforms and corresponding institution-building. These are indeed a tall order to fulfill but without such self-transformation, any premature unification attempt will bring forth nothing but disasters and misery to the Korean people on both sides of the Demilitarized Zones; and

(3) the North-South Korean control and coordination commission composed of the representatives from both sides must be created to deal with the common external and international affairs and their bilateral questions. Due to the North-South Agreement on Reconciliation, Nonaggression, and Exchanges and Cooperation of December 13, 1991 (went into effect in March 1992), and the Joint Declaration on Denuclearization of the Korean Peninsula of December 31, 1991, four such committees—the Political Subcommittee, the Military Subcommittee, the Exchanges and Cooperation Subcommittee and the Joint Nuclear Control Commission are temporarily stalled. The launching of these commissions notwithstanding, the forty or more years old glacier

between North and South Korea would not and could not melt away overnight. The bitter lessons learned from the 1972 North-South July 4th Joint Communique and the subsequent disappointments of the short-lived North-South Coordinating Committee should be remembered. Only patience, prudence and persistence with the firm goal of mutually beneficial national reunification will remove the glacier bit by bit.

Finally, the format for maintaining the two separate states (for the time being before a fully unified state can be realized) should be a confederation. It is not the North Korean version of the confederation, but the confederation of two independent sovereign states. The American Confederacy under the Articles of Confederation(1776-1787) or the Southern Confederacy (1860-1864) during the American Civil War are closer to the present definition,[51] but it should be a new formulation rather than a replica of historic models. Kim Il Sung's so-called confederation idea(s)[52] is, at best, a Soviet-type central-local political arrangement such as the erstwhile union or autonomous republics, which are now undergoing a rapid transformation or a Chinese-type central-local political structure such as its autonomous regions. The important point to note here is that both the Soviet and Chinese central-local political and governmental arrangements (which are often called the socialist federation)[53] are federal or confederal only in *form* and highly centralized in *actual operation*. The current North Korean political system does follow *form*, and in fact it represents one of the most extreme cases of a centralized totalitarian communist state.[54] From this standpoint, it supports confederation only in name or as a propaganda with little or no feasibility for realization. Worse still, since his initial pronouncement of confederation idea in August, 1960, Kim himself has changed its meaning(s) so many times over the years that a huge discrepancy exists between its earliest version and the latest proposal which is confusing and self-contradictory.[55] In any case, as noted earlier, during the temporary confederate period under the present proposal, the borders between the two should be maintained and controlled, although legitimate travels, mutual investments, joint ventures, and other economic development projects and socio-cultural exchange programs must be encouraged and expanded. During this border control period, democratization and liberalization, particularly decentralization and creation of local autonomy in North Korea should be actively and aggressively pursued. Likewise, South Korea, too, must continue its policy of liberalization, democratization, civilianization and socialization. In addition, it must pursue further decentralization and strengthen local autonomy.

A plain truth is that until and unless the two political and economic systems presently persisting on both sides of the Korean Peninsula become more comparable and compatible, it is not only inconceivable but unwise for government policy-planners or others to contemplate a genuine and bloodless unification in a hasty fashion.

Table 20-1. Migration to Germany, 1981-1992

MIGRATION TO GERMANY (1981 to present)

	Percentage granted refugee status	Asylum seekers	Ethnic Germans	East Germans moving to West
1981	7.7	49,391	69,455	14,504
1982	6.6	37,423	48,170	12,800
1983	22.4	19,737	37,925	10,703
1984	26.6	35,278	36,459	38,655
1985	24.2	73,832	36,968	26,346
1986	15.9	99,650	42,788	26,191
1987	9.4	57,379	8,523	18,961
1988	8.6	103,076	202,673	39,832
1989	5.0	121,318	—	—
1990	4.4	193,063	397,075	238,384
1991	6.9	256,112	221,995	—
1992 (1st qtr)	—	97,397	47,702	—
Total	—	1,143,656	1,596,788	770,230

The total number of asylum seekers and German refugees since 1981 is 3,510,674 (to June 30, 1990, when currency union between the two Germanies meant this category of resettler was abolished. Since then, however, an average of 1,000 east Germans a week has continued to move west).
Source: *The London Times*, April 7, 1992.

Table 20-2. German Party Seat Distribution, as of
2 December 1990 General Election

Party	Seats
CDU	268
CSU	50
FDP	79
Government Coalition	397
SPD	239
Greens (eastern)	8
Ex-communists	17
Independent	1
Total	662

Table 20-3. *A Conceptualization of Korean Unification*

Dimensions	North Korea	South Korea	Unified Korea
<Framework of Living>			
1. Ideoloy			
(ideal)	Communism/*Juche*	Liberal democracy	Liberal democracy
(real)	Jucheization	Democratizing push/authoritarian pull	
2. Political System			
(ideal)	One-party dictatorship	Presidential system	Presidential system; local autonomy
(real)	One-party father-son autocracy	Central government/ executive branch-dominant authoritarian proclivity	
3. Economic System			
(ideal)	Command/planned	Market/free	Market/free
(real)	Virtually defunct	Excessive government intervention	
4. Social life			
(ideal)	Collectivisitic	Individualistic	Community-conscious individualism
(real)	Tension between the ruling elite's collectivistic exhortation and people's individual-istic proclivity	Conflict between community-conscious individualism and self-or in-group-oriented egotism	
<Lebensraum>	Lies to the north of the DMZ	Lies to the south of the DMZ	All physical barriers removed between the two sides
<Portrait>			
(ideal)	Juche-type revolutionary	Democratic citizen	Democratic citizen; peace-minded; ecology-friendly, globally-oriented
(real)	Not fully achieved and unachievable	Not fully achieved but achievable	

Source: Adapted from S.C. Yang, "Why Do We Want Unification?: A Strategy and an Approach toward the North-South Integration Process" (in Korean), *Sahoe Kwahak Chŏngch'aek Yonku* [Social Science Policy Studies Journal] (June 1992).

Table 20-4. *Actors of Korean Unification*

	Primary Actors		Secondary Actors	
<Entity>				
(Real)	DPRK citizen (NK people)	ROK citizen (SK people)	DPRK government in power	ROK government in power
	People's rights and liberties:		Virtually absent	Restricted
	People's will to unification:		Unrepresented	Deficient
(Ideal)	Citizen (NK people)	Citizen (SK people)	A democratic regime	A democratic regime
	People's rights and liberties guaranteed:		Yes	Yes
	People's will to unification represented:		Yes	Yes
<Sources of Authority>	Constitution		North Korean people	South Korean people
<Capability to Implement Unification>	Indirect: forming the government by elections		Direct: using government machinary	Direct: using government machinary

Source: *Idem.*

Table 20-5. A Model of a Communist State's System Transformation

Dimensions	Speed of Change & Mechanism	Changes
<Leadership Change> 1. Initial stage	Relatively fast, irregular	New leadership from the same communist leadership pool; old leaders removed or expelled
2. Interim	Relatively fast, irregular or legitimate in appearance	New leadership from the dissident and/or out group within the communist leadership pool; old communist leadership demoralized and fragmented
3. Final stage	Prolonged and gradual, legitimate and regularized	New non-communist leadership through free election
<System Trans-formation> 1. Initial stage	Relatively fast, through the old system	Introducing multi-party-multi-candidate free election; allowing free press, free speech, free assembly and other freedom
2. Interim stage	Relatively fast, disorderly, through interim leadership	Crumbling of old communist party system; emerging of new non-communist parties; initiating system-*replacing* reforms, i.e., introducing privatizing and marketizing reform
3. Final stage	Prolonged and painful	Old economic, political, military, social and all other systems removed and replaced; privatization and marketiza-tion complete; private ownership, free enterprise system in operation, democracy at work
<Deprograming of people>	Prolonged and painful; nearly generational	Collectivism-oriented political indoctrination to be replaced by individualism-oriented political socializa-tion; state-controlled, mobilization-led passive person to be replaced by individual-initiated, motivation-led active person

Source: *Idem.*

Notes

1. Polybius, *The Rise of the Roman Empire* (Harmondsworth:Penguin Classics, 1979), pp. 432-433.
2. Thucydides, *The Peloponnesian War* (Harmondsworth: Penguin Classics 1954), p. 92.
3. See Sung Chul Yang, "The 'Revolutionary Dinosaur' in the North and the Expanding Relations between Seoul and Moscow," *Sino-Soviet Affairs* 14 (Fall 1990): 77-91.
4. According to a long-running Allenbach survey, in 1952, 60 percent of respondents said they favored "centralism" and only 17 percent "federalism." By 1960, 41 percent of the population called themselves federalists and 25 percent centralists, and by 1988 the percentage favoring federalism has soared to 71 percent, against only 8 percent in favor of centralized government. Quoted in David Marsh, *The New Germany at the Crossroads* (London: Century, 1989), p. 79.
5. The Republic of Korea's 1948 original constitution stipulated the implementation of local autonomy, but it was not realized during the Rhee regime (1948-1960). During the short-lived Chang regime (1960-1961), town, municipal and provincial elections were held but local autonomy was suspended immediately after the military coup in May 1961. During the Park regime the Constitution (Article 7, Section 3) stipulated the local autonomy but it was never implemented. But during the Yushin system (1972-1979) an appendix (Article 10) of the Constitution specified that local autonomy election be held only *after* the realization of Korean unification, thereby de facto abandoning even the constitutional pledge of local autonomy. During the Chun regime (1980-1988), the revised Constitution once again pledged the local autonomy (Articles 118 and 119) and even specified the time tables for local autonomy election (Appendix, Article 10) which was never realized. After the launching of the Roh regime (1988-1993) for the second time in the electoral history of the ROK, both the so-called basic level legislative assembly (*kich'o eihoe*) and the county and city at large (*kwangyŏk eihoe*) elections were held in February and June, 1991, respectively (the pledges for local autonomy are found in the present Constitution, Articles 117 and 118). For details, see Byŏng-sak Koo, *The Principles of New Constitution* (in Korean) (Seoul: Pakyŏng-sa, 1989), pp. 1000-1022.
6. David Marsh, *The New Germany at the Crossroads* (London: Century, 1989), pp. 64-88.
7. See Sung Chul Yang, "The Implications of German Unification for Korea:

Legal, Political, and International Dimensions," *Korea Journal* 31 (Spring 1991): 41-50 and also his "Two 'Democracies' in Korea," *Korea Journal* (January 1990), pp. 4-16.

8. David Marsh, *Op. Cit.*, p. 79.
9. Sung Chul Yang, *Op. Cit.*, p. 43.
10. Mel Gurtov, "The New World Order and U.S. Policy Toward Korea," paper delivered at the Korea-America Workshop, "The Trilateral Relationship among South Korea, North Korea and the United States," by the Korean Association of International Studies, Seoul, Korea, 1-2 June 1992, p. 19.
11. *Ibid.* pp. 43-48.
12. For details, see Sung-jo Park and Sung Chul Yang, *German Unification and Korean Division* (in Korean) (Seoul: Kyungnam University Press, 1991).
13. *Ibid.* See also, *North and South Korean Social and Cultural Indicators* (in Korean) (Seoul: Ministry of Unification Board, 1991), p. 54.
14. For details, see *Questions on German History, Ideas, Forces: Decisions from 1800 to the Present* (Historical Exhibition in the Berlin Reichstag Catalogue, 2nd updated edition, 1984).
15. For a detailed analysis of this subject, see Sung-jo Park and Sung Chul Yang, *Op. Cit.*
16. See Roby's article, "A Painful Healing Process," a special advertising section, *The Asian Wall Street Journal*, 21 November 1991.
17. Quoted in Gunter Hofmann, Interview, "Billy Brandt; Europe is the Future of the New Germany," *Lufthansa Bordbuch* 11/12 (1990): 50.
18. Quoted in *The New York Times*, 18 April 1992.
19. Quoted in *The International Herald Tribune*, 18 June 1992, p. 2.
20. The cost estimates vary greatly among different sources. For details, see Sung-jo Park and Sung Chul Yang, *Op. Cit.* Recently, for example, *Newsweek* (April 1, 1991, p. 9) reported that the German unification will cost one trillion DM over the next decade.
21. For details, see *The Economist*, 23 May 1992, "Germany Survey," p. 5.
22. The weak competitiveness and the dismally low level of productivity of the East German economy stem from a number of reasons: 1) the capital stock in industry is largely obsolete, technology has been outdated, and the quality of commodities is generally low; 2) social overhead capital in transportation and communication is deficient; 3) the market structure is monopolistic or oligopolistic. Kombinates and cooperatives have enjoyed market protection, so that no competition prevails in the whole economy; 4) socialistic central planning system provides no incentives to individuals and management in increasing productivity; 5) autarchical and COMECON-bound trade structure allows no signal function of market price, so that the supply of commodities does not reflect the demand of the consumers. For details, see Doo Soon Ahn,

"Economic Burden of the National Unification, German Unification and the Lessons for Korea," paper delivered at the symposium sponsored by the Institute for Northeast Asian Studies, Kyunghee University, 24 June 1991.

23. *The Asian Wall Street Journal*, 6 February 1992.

24. Stephen Kinzer, "Conversations/Joachim Lehmann," *The New York Times*, 3 May 1992.

25. *The Economist*, 34 May 1992, "Germany Survey," p. 3.

26. *Economist*, 23 May 1992, p. 59.

27. Stephen Kinzer's article in *The New York Times*, 18 April 1992.

28. *The Economist*, 2 May 1992, p. 13.

29. See, for instance, *Newsweek*, 1 April 1991, p. 11. and p. 13. Also, *The Economist*, 23 February 1991, p. 45.

30. *The Economist*, 23 June 1990.

31. For a detailed analysis of the interest-based bargaining strategy, see Max O. Stephenson, Jr., and Gerald M. Pops, "Conflict Resolution Methods and the Policy Process," *Public Administration Review* (September/October 1989), pp. 463-473.

32. For an excellent analysis of determinant of creativity in foreign policy, see Donald A. Sylvan, James G. Voss and Ryan Beasley, "Determinants of Creativity in Foreign Policy," paper delivered at the annual meeting of the International Studies Association, Vancouver, British Columbia, 19-23 March 1991.

33. A most recent discussion of middle power concepts is found in Andrew Fenton Cooper and Richard Higgott, "Middle Power Leadership in the International Order: A Reformulated Theory for the 1990s," paper delivered at the annual meeting of the International Studies Association, Vancouver, British Columbia, 19-23 March 1991.

34. Sylvan, Voss and Beasley, *Op. Cit.*, p. 21.

35. *Ibid.*, p. 22.

36. For details, see Cooper and Higgot, *Op. Cit.*, pp. 4-9.

37. Stephen G. Walker, *Op. Cit.*, especially, pp. 282-289.

38. Chinworth and Cheng, for example, in their recent article emphasized the United States' traditional postwar role as an honest broker in Asia. I am emphasizing here that South Korea, too, can be the best candidate for such a role in the region. For details, see Michael W. Chinworth and Dean Cheng, "The United States and Asia in the Post-Cold War World," *SAIS* (Spring, 1991), pp. 73-91. See also, Bernard K. Gordon, "The Asian-Pacific Rim: Success at a Price," *Foreign Affairs* 70 (Winter 1990/91): 142-155; William J. Crowe, Jr., and Alan D. Romberg, "Rethinking Security in the Pacific," *Foreign Affairs* 70 (Spring 1991): 123-140.

39. For further details, see Yang, "On the Trilateral Relations of North Korea,

South Korea and the Soviet Union," paper delivered at the 4th Conference on "The Current Situation of the Asian-Pacific Region and Soviet-South Korean Relations," co-sponsored by the Institute for Sino-Soviet Studies, Hanyang Academy of Sciences of the USSR, at Kazan, 1-10 June 1991.

40. Chin-kuk Kim, "Contents of the Draft Regulations on South-North Nuclear Inspection," *Chungang Ilbo,* 5 April 1992 p. 2. Quoted in Niksch, *Op. Cit.,* p. 9.

41. Reginald Bartholomew, Undersecretary of State for International Security Affairs, U.S. Department of State, in his recent visit to South Korea stated the three-point policy of the U.S. administration on international inspection of North Korean nuclear facilities: First, North Korea should honor its Nuclear Non-Proliferation Treaty (NPT) without any reservation to the IAEA safe-guards agreement; second, North Korea should faithfully implement the SA agreement after signing it; and third, Pyongyang should also forego nuclear reprocessing capability. See *The Korea Times,* 21 June 1991. Noteworthy in this connection is the report that Kim Yŏng Nam, North Korea's Foreign Min-ister, reportedly demanded two preconditions—a simultaneous inspection of U.S.-possessed nuclear weapons in South Korea [the U.S. government neither confirms nor denies policy on this issue] and the U.S. promise of no nuclear attacks on North Korea—before North Korea will sign the NPT safeguards agreement. The report by the *Washington Post* (21 June 1991) was quoted in *Hankuk Ilbo* on 21 June 1991. The U.S. State Department press officer David Denny rejected Kim's demands, however. See *The Korea Times,* 22 June 1991.

42. For details, see Kenneth R. Timmerman, "North Korea Arms the Mideast," *The Asian Wall Street Journal,* 9 June 1992.

43. Don Oberdorfer, "N. Korea Release[s] Extensive Data on Nuclear Effort," *Washington Post,* 6 May 1992. Quoting David Kyd, information director of the IAEA, Oberdorfer reported recently that the nuclear facilities seen in mid-May of this year by Hans Blix, the IAEA director-general, are about the length of two football fields, but they are "extremely primitive" and which appears a long way from being finished. For details, see his news article, *International Herald Tribune,* 5 June 1992. T. R. Reid, "North Korean Plutonium Plant Cited," *Washington Post,* 17 May 1992 p. A1; Michael Breen, "South Korea Wary after Pyongyang's Nuclear Disclosure," *Washington Times,* 19 May 1992 p. A7. These last two news articles are quoted in Larry A. Niksch, "Beyond the June Nuclear Weapons 'Showdown': The Turn to South Korea," paper delivered at the Korea-American Workshop, "The Trilateral Relation-ship among South Korea, North Korea and the United States," sponsored by the Korean Association of International Studies, Seoul, Korea, 1-2 June 1992.

44. Gary Milhollin, "North Korea's Bomb," *The New York Times,* 4 June 1992.

45. Quoted in Larry Niksch, *Op. Cit.,* p. 6.

46. Niksch, *Op. Cit.*, pp. 6-7.
47. *Ibid*, pp. 70-8.
48. *The Korea Times*, 27 June 1992, p. 3.
49. The UNSC official resolutions are found in *Resolutions and Decisions of the Security Council 1990*, Security Council Official Records: Forty-Fifth Year (New York: United Nations, 1991), pp. 19-28. See also, "The Gulf War: The Law of International Sanctions," *The American Society of International Law*, Proceedings of the 85th Annual Meeting, Washington, D.C., 17-20 April 1991, pp. 169-190 and Young Dahl Oh, "The Legal Role of the United Nations in the Gulf Crisis of 1990-1991" (M.A. thesis the Graduate Institute of Peace Studies, Kyunghee University, May 1992).
50. For example, at the Senate's Subcommittee on East Asian and Pacific Affairs hearing, Joseph Churba, president of the International Security Council, contended that as its ultimate recourse, it would be folly for the U.S. not to consider a contingent policy of "assertive (or preemptive) disarmament" to support its other non-proliferation efforts. At the same hearing, Gary Milhollin, director of the Wisconsin Project on Nuclear Arms Control, stated that if all else fails, one is left with the military option. All indications are that this would be costly. The North Korean army is strong; one cannot expect a replay of Operation Desert Storm. For details, see *The Korea Times*, 27 November 1991.
51. Karl Deutsch, for example, distinguishes a federal government from a confederacy in four main respects: (1) a federal government is relatively strong in regard to organization, personnel, budget, and jurisdiction, while in a confederacy, the common institutions are weak or nearly nonexistent in some or all of these respects; (2) while federal governments act directly upon individuals in all matters within the scope of the national government, the government of confederacy ordinarily deals with individuals only indirectly. A federal government can collect taxes, raise armies, and enforce its own decisions, but a confederacy depends for all these matters on what the states will do for it, or what resources the states will give it; (3) states often may secede from a confederacy, if their governments or voters so desire, whereas such secession is not permitted in a federal union; (4) within the sphere of federal jurisdiction, the laws of a federal union usually prevails over those of the states, and the state governments are expected to obey them and carry them out. In a confederacy, however, a law or decision of the confederal authorities becomes valid in a state only if the state government endorses it, or at least does not exercise its right to veto its application within the state. For details, see his book, *Politics and Government: How People Decide Their Fate* (Boston: Houghton Mifflin, 1974), 2nd ed., pp. 211-212.
52. It is interesting to note that V.P. Tkatchenko, Head of Korean Desk, Central

Committee of the CPSU, and a long time North Korea head, made a casual remark that Kim Il Sung's confederation proposal was Khrushchev's idea and it was the latter who urged the former to propose it in August 1960. According to Tkatchenko, Kim proposed the "confederation" idea without even knowing its meaning(s). My informal conversation with Tkatchenko on June 5, 1991, Kazan, USSR.

53. For a discussion of socialist federation in the USSR, the Czechoslovak Socialist Republic and the Socialist Federal Republic of Yugoslavia, see Boris N. Topornin, "On the Classification of Socialist Political Systems," in Anton Bebler and Jim Seroka, eds., *Contemporary Political Systems: Classifications and Typologies* (Boulder: Lynne Rienner Publishers, 1990), pp. 117-132.

54. Huang Zhong-Liang calls North Korea, along with Romania and Cuba, "individual head (socialist) systems." See his commentary in Bebler and Seroka, *Op. Cit.*, p. 137.

55. North Korea's confederal unification formula has changed over the years. The confederation idea was first proposed by Kim Il Sung on August 14, 1960, to exploit the South Korean political instability in the wake of the April 19th Student Uprising, which led to the downfall of the Syngman Rhee regime. Kim made the following statements: (1) holding of free general elections throughout the North and the South on the basis of democratic principles without any foreign interference for the purpose of peaceful unification of the country; (2) if this should not be acceptable to the South for fear of Communist domination, the North would settle for a North-South Confederation, as a *provisional measure* to iron out different issues; (3) the Confederacy was to be maintained by way of setting up a Supreme National Committee composed of the representatives of the two governments to coordinate the cultural and economic development of the entire Korea, while retaining the two current political systems intact; (4) if the South Korean authorities still could not accept the Confederation, a purely economic commission composed of business representatives of the two governments would be set up to "relieve the South Korean brothers and sisters from hunger and poverty," while setting aside the political questions for the time being; and (5) the mutual reduction of armed forces to a 100,000 man level or less after the withdrawal of U.S. troops from the South. On June 24, 1973, Kim Il Sung countered Park Chung Hee's June 23 proposal by announcing his own five point proposal: (1) remove military confrontation and lessen tension between North and South; (2) realize a many-sided cooperation and interchange between North and South; (3) convene a Great National Congress comprised of representatives of people from all strata, political parties and social organizations in North and South Korea; (4) institute a North-South Confederation under a single nomenclature of Confederal Republic of Koryo; and (5) join the United Nations as a member under

the name of the Confederal Republic of Koryo. It wås, however, at the Sixth Assembly of North Korea's Workers' Party that Kim Il Sung proposed the so-called Democratic Confederal Republic of Koryo (DCRK) plan as a "permanent" form. But in the 1991 New Years's address, Kim stated that two autonomous government under the DCRK plan must have more power for the time being. His statement became more concrete when key North Korean officials such as Yun Ki-bok and Son Song-p'il remarked that two local governments may have diplomatic and military powers. These final statements are inconsistent with its heretofore insistence on a single-seat entry into the UN. North Korea completely reversed its position on UN when its Foreign Ministry announced on May 27, 1991, that it will join the UN separately. See Kim Il Sung, *For the Independent Reunification of the Country* (Pyongyang: Foreign Languages Publishing House, 1976). See also, Sung Chul Yang, "Korean Reunification—Autism and Realism," *Korea and World Affairs* (Spring 1982), pp. 57-72.

CHAPTER 21

NORTH AND SOUTH KOREA AS TWO LIVING POLITICAL LABORATORIES

The human mind craves simple distinctions; Russians, Americans, and Europeans all have their own motives for embracing the "black-and white" approach.

Brzezinski and Huntington[1]

Diversity, in all the glorious disorder of nature, is the best defense of healthy societies.

Kennan[2]

The policy task is to prevent government from swallowing the civic order, or the civic order from creating an anarchic public arena.

Lasswell[3]

A Backward Glance

Despite their separate physical existence and different political experiences for over four decades with virtually no contacts and communications, the homogeneity and affinity of the Korean people in both sides of the Demilitarized Zone continued to be overwhelming. Such affinity notwithstanding, the two diametrically contrasting political systems, emerged in the wake of World War Two, persist, and are likely to remain so in the foreseeable future.

These two systems are like the two bowls molded out of the same clay. The main focus of this study has been to find their *differences* of recent origins rather than their basic *sameness* of long standing. To use the clay-bowl analogy further, the primary interest has been to examine these bowls, their respective shapes (structures), usages (functions), primary users (elites and masses) and things (outputs, performance) that they can hold. In the process, each system's strengths and weaknesses are spelled out, and any judgmental assessments, not based on facts and observations are avoided or minimized.

Few nations in the world today can, in fact, match Korea's high degree of cultural homogeneity and national affinity. Korea's elite political culture and tradition had been unmistakably *authoritarian*, as exhibited in its class-based socio-political culture and tradition, centralized officialdom and dynastic longevity, incessant factionalism and civil-military rivalry, land-based power dynamics, state religion and pacific external linkages. Her mass political culture and tradition, meanwhile, had been marked by periodic and sporadic peasant rebellions and mass uprisings, and nativistic resilience and nationalistic resistance.

It was against this cultural and political background that North and South Korean political systems came into being in 1948. The Korean partition in 1945 was forced upon the Korean people by the external powers. The external liberators of Korea turned out to be the main culprits of her partition. Perhaps, more accurately, the division was the price of her liberation from Japan. In hindsight, such high price was neither necessary nor unavoidable. But the historical clock cannot be rewound or restarted. Forty years and more have passed since the establishment of the two separate regimes, the by-products of the ideological rivalry between the two super powers—the United States and the former Soviet Union, and of the myopic power struggles among Korean political leaders who aligned themselves with either of these two occupation forces.

In this study, the North and South Korean political systems have been examined within the framework of two well-known yet often confusing political systems—totalitarianism and authoritarianism. Conceptually, at least, the present North Korean political system is a variant of communist totalitarianism. The South Korean political system, on the other hand, despite its substantial liberalization and democratization, still exhibits authoritarian tendencies and traits. In lieu of customary conclusion, the final chapter is devoted to the definitional problems of these two models. And these two models will be probed in the light of the North and the South Korean political experiences and performance.

Totalitarianism and Authoritarianism

1. Definitional Problems

To begin with, the meanings and usages of totalitarianism (T) and authoritarianism (A) vary, according to whether T and A refer to certain political movements, regime types, states, political systems, political ideas or belief systems. Even when the concept of T and A is narrowed down to denote certain political systems, as it is the case in this study, the task of defining them is still very difficult, if not impossible. There are some 180 nations in the world today, and classifying even some of them into T or A is not only arbitrary but unrealistic. It does not mean that the students of comparative politics shun the classification of political systems. On the contrary, there are too many such classifications to enumerate here.

One recent example suffices to clarify this point. Berg-Schlosser, for one, classified the existing Third World (whatever it may mean) political systems into ten categories on the basis of some seven criteria: the types of party system; the basis of legitimacy; the recruitment patterns of the chief executives; the vertical and horizontal separation of powers; the nature of real power; the scope of political control; and the ideological orientations. His ten types of political system based on these criteria are: monarchy, oligarchy, semi-competitive, civil-authoritarian, socialist totalitarian-communist, poliarchy, military regimes, and three subtypes of military regimes—personalistic, strong-men (Caudillo) and corporatist.[4]

Ultimately, all classifications are by definition arbitrary. If there are

180 countries in the world, ultimately 180 categories are possible. Since T and A are employed as two broad conceptual models depicting the North and South Korean political systems respectively, the definitional problems of T and A are briefly reviewed here.

The definitional problems and confusions among the users of T and/or A generally fall into five categories. The first group are those who regard authoritarianism as a subtype or a variant of totalitarianism. Hence, they perceive two kinds of totalitarianism—right-wing and left-wing. And right-wing totalitarianism is equal to authoritarianism. The views and the concepts of Merle Fainsod, Roy C. Macridis, N.S. Timasheff, Robert C. Tucker and Carl Friedrich fall into this group.[5]

Conversely, the second group treat totalitarianism as a subtype or a variant of authoritarianism. They, therefore, equate left-wing authoritarianism with communism. Scholars such as Gabriel A. Almond, G. Bingham Powell, Jr., Edward Shils, Talcott Parsons, Herbert McClosky, Dennis Chong, Milton Rokeach and Amos Perlmutter tend to use T and A in this fashion.[6]

The third group are those who sharply distinguish T and A and classify them more or less as *sui generis*. Juan Linz, Ferdinand A. Hermens, Leon P. Baradat, and Jean K. Kirkpatrick[7] belong to this group.

The most numerous are the fourth category. It is rather a collection of scholars, who use T and/or A quite differently from the above three. T. D. Weldon, in his *Vocabulary of Politics,* has an entry only on totalitarianism.[8] John Dewey, meanwhile, defined totalitarianism as the opposite of pluralism.[9] George Sabine, for one, classified nazism and Fascism as totalitarianism and separated them from communism.[10] By contrast, Hannah Arendt, Zbigniew K. Brzezinski and Carl J. Friedrich categorized Nazism, Fascism, and communism as totalitarianism and sought to identify their common elements.[11]

Still others such as Karl Deutsch and Joseph LaPalombara distinguished what they call one-party totalitarianism from one-party authoritarianism. But in the former category they included not only the so-called communist countries such as the former Soviet Union, China and North Korea but also the Nazis Germany and the Fascist Italy, while in the latter group they put Spain under Franco.[12] Irving Louis Horowitz's view is even more puzzling. He characterized the political change in the former Soviet Union, i.e., the downfall of Khrushchev and the rise of Brezhnev, as the transition from totalitarianism to authoritarianism.[13]

Finally, there are those who avoid T and A dichotomy and provide other classificatory schemes. Some representative cases are: Franz Neuman's simple, caesaristic and totalitarian dictatorships; Giovanni Sartori's one-party totalitarian, one-party authoritarian and one-party pragmatic dictatorships; William Welsh's totalitarianism, authoritarianism and pluralism; Jon Devos constitutional polyarchy, authoritarianism and totalitarianism; and Berg-Schlosser's stable polyarchic, stable socialist and stable authoritarian. Robert Dahl uses the term "polyarchy" or democratic institutions as opposed to authoritarian regimes.[14] As noted in the above, Almond and Powell once subdivided an authoritarian political system into radical totalitarian (e.g., the former Soviet Union), conservative totalitarian (e. g., the Nazis Germany), conservative authoritarian (e.g., Spain) and modernizing authoritarian (e.g., Brazil).[15]

To cite another example, Edward S. Malecki recently categorized what he called the authoritarian state and the totalitarian state as two of his six types of capitalist state. He placed all six types on a continuum and ranked their relative susceptibility to radical change. According to him, the types from the most vulnerable to internal radical movements to the least vulnerable, are in the following order: the class warfare state; the transitional state; the partisan state; the liberal state; the authoritarian state; and the totalitarian state.[16]

It is quite evident from the above that the definitions of T and A and other classificatory systems among scholars and other users are very confusing, conflicting and even contradictory. At a closer look, there are, at least, five explanations for these conceptual "messiness."

First, what we generally call totalitarian and authoritarian political systems (ultimately, all political systems for that matter) possess some similar as well as dissimilar elements. Hence, the definitions and meanings of T and/or A vary widely, depending upon the users' focus of the inquiry, i.e., whether they emphasize T and A's mutually similar or dissimilar factors. For instance, the socio-economic bases of support for T and A appear to be quite dissimilar (communism is regarded here as the

prototype of T, and Nazism and Fascism, as that of A). T's focus on
class struggle and association with the lower classes and the A's obsession with race and nationalism and collusion with middle and upper
classes serve as the prime examples. Or, the contrast between Marxist
assertion that Marxism is a "superscience," from which all other scientific truth must be derived, and Nazism's anti-intellectual and anti-ratio-
nalistic tendency is another. Still another difference is that the communist ideology is universalistic, while the Nazi ideology had a restricted
appeal. Above all, communism implies a fundamental economic theory
and it has a specific, if broad, economic purpose. It aims at establishing
a particular type of economy, and one of the objectives of economic
organization is to achieve a pure political responsibility for economic
activity. By contrast, Fascist and Nazi economies are *ad hoc* designed to
achieve limited given objectives in a short period, and the economy
works quasi-independently under a political shield. And the objective of
Fascism and Nazism is the preservation of the economic status quo
against economic revolution. In Lauterbach's own words, the Russians
expropriated, whereas the Nazi system left legal ownership rights virtually untouched, although the latter, too, took a control of economic decision-making.[17]

There are also scholars who base their analyses on the actual workings of communist system. George F. Kennan, for instance, pointed out
certain features of "Russian communism": its reckless injustice; shock-
ing physical cruelty; congenital untruthfulness; cultivation of mass delu-
sions and creation of scapegoats on which to focus mass emotion, the
maintenance of a system of artificial tensions within society, employment of coercion on a vast scale (e.g., the concentration-camp system),
the punishment of those who "might" rebel, rather than those who *do*.[18]

Likewise, Bertram D. Wolfe identified and explored seven distinguishing keys of what he called "communist totalitarianism":

> (1) the struggle for power (e.g., the power levers—the party machine,
> the secret police, and the armed forces; mass organizations, the personal-
> ity cult); (2) the coordination of culture (e.g., "operation rewrite,"
> "history rewrite," history as weapons, the use of science by the Party's
> tool, the mind control and training of the robot); (3) the worker in the

worker's state (e.g., "policing the peasant and the citizen," the new class society, the total militarization of the daily life and labor of an entire people); (4) the Soviet-style election (e.g., "the most democratic election in the world"—100% voter, 100% vote yes; no right of opposition, of real choice, of control from below, of abstention and even of silence); (5) the Kremlin as an ally and a neighbor (e.g., rift with Tito and China); (6) the nature of totalitarianism (e.g., the people for the state, not the state for the people, the demise of voluntary associations, the expropriation of human spirit—"the state is determined to own everything, not only material things but men themselves—to own them body and soul"; the durability of despotism—a closed society, non-transitoriness of total power and transitoriness of collective leadership; undivided and all-embracing power; the structure of the apparatus: an atomized society—the breaking up of all non-state conformations and centers of solidarity; a centralized, monolithic, monopolistic party and its maintenance in a "state of grace"—zeal, doctrinal purity, fanatical devotion, discipline, subordination, total mobilization; a single-party state; a regime of absolute force supplemented by persuasion or by continuous psychological warfare upon its people; a managerial bureaucracy; a centrally managed, totally state owned and state regulated economy; a bare subsistence economy for the bulk of the producers; a completely managed and controlled culture; a monopoly of all the means of expression and communication; a state owned system of "criticism"; an infallible doctrine stemming from infallible authorities, interpreted and applied by an infallible party led by an infallible leader; a method of advance by zigzags toward basically unchanging goals; a system of promotion, demotion, correction of error, modification of strategy and tactics and elimination of differences, by fiat from the summit, implemented by purges of varying scope and intensity—the turnover in the elite, demotion of deadwood and promotion of new forces, the supplying of scapegoats for every error and dramatization of every needed change of line; and a commitment to continuing revolution from the above until the Soviet subject has been remade according to the blueprint of the men in the Kremlin and until communism has won the world); and (7) the Soviet system and foreign policy (e.g., "to remake man and to conquer the world" through "salami tactics" and protracted war).[19]

There are some minor yet significant differences in emphasis and in scope even among those, who consider both T and A as a distinctively twentieth-century mass movement and stress their similar rather than disparate features. Karl Dietrich Bracher, for instance, distinguished what he called "right-wing authoritarian-technocratic state" concepts from "left-wing revolutionary utopianism." But he contended that whatever the different origins and appearances, the aims and promises of Fascism or National Socialism, of Leninism or Stalininism, of communist or nationalist "revolutions," the overriding characteristic was a monopolistic regime which claims, "the total identity of the government with the governed, of the party with the state, of chiliastic ideas with the needs of the citizen, and the complete abolition of civil liberties."[20] Friedrich, Brzezinski, Tucker and others surveyed the basic similarities between T and A in a somewhat narrower sense, that is, to consider the former Soviet Union as a prototype of T, and Nazi Germany and Fascist Italy, as that of A. The dichotomous view of life (e.g., the strong and the weak, the fit and the unfit, winners and losers, the good and the bad, friends and enemies), the premise of conflict-among-unequals (e.g., the minority rule, the one-party state, the leadership principle, the concept of omnipotent elite, the idea of the repulsiveness of all other classes and the untrustworthiness of the working class) and the positive value attached to violence and terror are some values, attitudes, and beliefs both T and A share in common.[21]

There are also organizational (in institutional and structural arrangements) similarities between the two. A single leader at the head of a one-party state, an official ideology, police terror, a monopoly of weapons, a monopoly of communications and mass media, and a controlled economy are the cases in point.[22] Gleichschltung [coordination] and "transmission belt" were the favorite concepts of Hitler and Stalin, respectively, in depicting the said institutional and structural arrangements of political power. To Stalin, party, trade unions, clubs and organizations of all kinds in the former Soviet Union were "transmission belts"— instruments of command and control, by which means the leaders transmitted their will to the masses. Or, in Wolfe's words, mass propaganda, terror, isolation, indoctrination, total organization and total regulation are the weapons that the state uses against its own people.[23] Terror, in Inkeles' words, is "a means for institutionalizing and channeling anxiety. Its purpose is to create in every man a deep sense of insecurity."[24] This insecurity is not merely a fear, a state in which the expectation of harm has a specific referent, but rather is an anxiety in the technical sense.

Noteworthy also in this regard is Erikson's personality profiles of "a totalitarian state": fanatic apostles and the shrewd revolutionaries; lonely leaders and oligarchic cliques; obedient bureaucrats and efficient managers, soldiers, engineers; sincere believers and sadistic exploiters; willing followers, apathetic toilers, and paralyzed opponents; unnerved victims and bewildered would-be and could-be victims.[25] Friedrich, meanwhile, listed five closely linked factors which are shared by all totalitarian societies of our time: an official ideology; a single mass party; a technologically conditioned near-complete monopoly of control of all means of effective armed combat; a similarly technologically conditioned near-complete control of all means of effective mass communication and mass media; a system of terroristic police control.[26]

Second, the conceptual messiness often stems from those scholars and users who employ the terms, T and A, uncritically and indiscriminately without clear and indepth understanding of these two systems. Friedrich's incisive point in this regard is noteworthy:

> Totalitarianism is precisely the opposite of authoritarianism, for it involves the elimination of all stable authority. Those psychologists, who have concentrated on the "authoritarian" personality and have linked "conformity" with authority," must have missed this point. They have fallen into serious error if they tacitly assume that "authoritarian" is either synonymous with "totalitarian" or somehow closely related to it. I believe it is important to realize that every society must be "authoritarian" in some degree, every society must contain "authoritarian" personalities, every society must exact obedience to authority. But totalitarian societies attempt to shatter all traditional types of authority and to replace them with a new kind of social control. In a very real sense, in a totalitarian society true authority is altogether destroyed.[27]

His point is well taken except for the fact that he seems to equate 'authoritarianism' with authority, but the two are different in that the former is only a degenerate form of the latter.

Third, the conceptual confusion is sometimes understandable, if not inevitable, because all political systems including T and A, are subject to change over time and vary by location. Again, to quote Wolfe, "all lands go through a history, and all orders and institutions are subject to continuous modification and ultimate transformation."[28] The great differences between Soviet totalitarianism under Stalin and under Gorbachev, or Yeltsin or between totalitarianism in the former Soviet Union and China are the cases in point.

Fourth, the confusion also arises because some users conceptualize T and/or A primarily as a specific *political order,* a particular *ideology,* or a proto-typical *personality.* When T and/or A designates a specific political order, both may be broadly defined as a society, a political system, a state, a regime, or a set of characteristics of such a society, system, state or regime. N.S. Timasheff, for instance, defined the term "totalitarian society" as a *type* of society characterized by a number of traits such as concentration of power in the hands of a few; the absence of rights ascribed to the individual vs. the collectivity; an unlimited extension of the functions of the state, making the state almost tantamount to society; the ideocratic nature of the state, of imperialism, of the organization of atomized men. A totalitarian society may connote one definite *trait,* namely the unlimited extension of state functions.[29] Waldemar Gurian identified four characteristics of the "totalitarian state": an artificially organized specific ruling group under a leadership and hierarchy; a specific absolute belief in its mission; the existence of political religion connected with the production of public opinion from above; and all direct instruments and means of power in the hands of the state.[30]

Karl Deutsch, on the other hand, identified the three most important performance characteristics that the "totalitarian system" have in common: extreme mobilization of effort, unity of command and effective power of enforcement.[31]

Among those who emphasize psychological traits of T and/or A, some focus on the totalitarian personality or mentality and others examine the authoritarian personality or mentality, and still others employ the two terms interchangeably. Alex Inkeles, for example, defined "the totalitarian, following Ulysses, lashes himself to the mast of his mystique and stops his sailor's ears with wax against the cries of the popular sirens, lest the ship of the revolution be swept up in the current of decadent bourgeois sentimentality and flounder on the rock of compromise."[32] The totalitarian classifies art into two broadly defined groups of the acceptable and the unacceptable; he is the one "who sees the state as an institution with no right to existence in itself, but rather as a mere tool serving the attainment of some higher goal which is above the state." It is, according to Inkeles, essentially the imperative of the higher law which spells the doom of "the rule of law." Hence, the totalitarian is the captive as well as the manipulator of a mystical theory of social development."

Further, Inkeles pointed out that the mystique is a higher law, a universal truth, an incontrovertible truth; hence, assuming one truth, one law, one interest, and one program is the essence of the totalitarian orientation.[33] To Albert Lauterbach, meanwhile, what he called totalitarian mentality basically "reflects the emotional inability of excessively insecure persons to bear criticism."[34]

From a somewhat different perspective, Else Frenkel-Brunswik described the structure and function of individuals who are susceptible to totalitarianism: a more or less pronounced preponderance of mechanization, standardization, self-alienation, stereotype, dehumanization of social contacts, piece-meal functioning, rigidity, intolerance of ambiguity and a need for absolute, lack of individuation and spontaneity, a self-exalted profession of exalted ideals, a combination of over-realism with bizarre and magic thinking as well as of irrationality with manipulative opportunism.[35]

Further, she described the "authoritarian person" as the one who combines within himself "rigid perseverative behavior with an overfluid, haphazard, disintegrated, random approach; compulsive overcaution with the tendency toward impulsive shortcuts to action; chaos and confusion with orderly oversimplification in terms of black-white solutions and stereotype; isolation with fusion; lack of differentiation with the mixing of elements which do not belong together; extreme concreteness with extreme generality; cynicism with gullibility; over-realism with irrationality; self-glorification with self-contempt; submission to powerful authorities with resentment against them; and stress on masculinity with a tendency toward feminine passivity. In short, in her own words, the authoritarian personality may be characterized as "consistently inconsistent, or as consistently self-conflicting."[36]

Finally, the origin of the term, "totalitarianism, "might also have contributed to this disarray in usages. J. L. Talmon, for instance, saw "totalitarian democracy" as the type of society which was being created in France under the Jacobins.[37] The term "totalitarianism" is known to have been coined by Mussolini;[38] perhaps to him, the ultimate goal of Fascism might have been the realization of totalitarianism, but in reality, the political system of the Fascist Italy (or, of Nazi Germany, for that matter) was inclined toward an authoritarian prototype, if the conceptual distinctions between T and A are applied. To put it differently, Italian Fascism was "more totalist in aspiration than in realization."[39] As Gurian pointed out, despite the rejection of the name "totalitarianism," the former USSR had become the purest embodiment of totalitarianism, for in Germany as well as in Italy it did not last long enough.[40]

In this study T and A are conceptually distinguished on the basis of three main criteria—political order, ideology and personality/mentality. From the standpoint of political order, T as an ideal type assumes that political power is absolute, complete, total and/or unlimited, while A presupposes that it is relative, incomplete, partial and limited. In Bertram Wolfe's phraseology, T assumes the state as "coextensive and identical with the whole of society, denying all autonomy to non-state organizations, and to individual conscience, intellect, judgment and will."[41] It means that the totalitarian state, "far from withering away, then swells to totality, embracing every aspect of life in its all-encompassing, steadily more constricting grasp."[42] Under an authoritarian political order, by contrast, the state usually controls political life, while the rest of life is either left uncontrolled or partially interfered with. Leon P. Baradat's point in this regard is pertinent:

> Unlike a totalitarian state, in which ruler controls every aspect of the society, be it cultural, economic, historical, social, or political, an authoritarian dictatorship is less complete. While the authoritarian dictator is in firm control of the political system, he or she has less control over other aspects of the society and is checked by other institutions within the state

such as the church, the military or a property-holding class.[43]

To rephrase it, the key word to identify and describe a totalitarian political order, at least, as an ideal type, is the *absence:* the virtual absence of basic human rights and freedom, of constitutionalism, of political oppositions and/or organizations (except tokenism), of independent and autonomous social organizations and activities, of private space or realm, and of private ownership and enterprises. By contrast, the key word for describing and identifying an authoritarian political order is not the absence, but the *deficiency* of all the aforementioned ingredients. The corollary of such difference between T and A is that there is little or no possibility for T to change into another political order (that is, unless one assumes another cataclysmic political revolution like the Russian Revolution of 1917). In fact, there had never been such historic cases since the launching of the Soviet totalitarian political order, until the metamorphic transformation of the communist states in the former Soviet Union, and Eastern Europe began to unfold since the mid and late 1980s. But there have been numerous historic incidents, in which an authoritarian political order was replaced by another political order of a more democratic type.

From the ideological perspective, under a totalitarian political order ideology is monopolized, sanctified and proselytized by the ruling party or elites primarily to control, manipulate and mobilize the masses. The masses are often mesmerized by mythical, Messianic, eschatological, chiliastic and apocalytical appeal. Arendt's "logocracy," Inkeles's "mystique," Tucker's "pseudo-religious flavor," Lauterbach's "substitute-religion," and Gurian's "ideocracy"[44] typify such ideological dimensions and role. Conversely, under an authoritarian political order the monopoly, sanctification and proselytization of ideology by the ruling party or elites have never been fully achieved; such remain perhaps as their ultimate *goal*, or wishful thinking but not their symbolic *tool* as the way the ruling party and elites in a totalitarian political order have been using.

Finally, the distinction between totalitarian and authoritarian personality or mentality can be drawn. To begin with, there are striking similarities between the two in their political and psychological style, in the treatment of their political opponents and the tactics which they are willing to employ to achieve their ends. McClosky and Chong, for instance, pointed out in a recent study that both left-wing (totalitarian) and right-wing (authoritarian) radicals in America express disdain towards people whom they regard as "soft and idealistic," and show greater preference for unsentimental leadership, which deals strictly, and callously, if necessary, with the people being led. Left and right radicals are also likely to be intolerant of non-conformity, uncertainty and ambiguity; to see things and people in black-and-white, good-and-evil, and right-and-wrong terms; to uphold prerogatives of the majority to ignore the rights and concerns of the minority; and to desire a society which is united behind a single ideology.[45]

To repeat, McClosky and Chong found that both left and right radicals in America are deeply estranged from certain features of their society; are highly critical of what they perceive as the spiritual and moral degeneration of American institutions; and both view American society as dominated by conspiratorial forces that are working to defeat their respective ideological aims. The degree of their alienation is intensified by zealous and unyielding manner in which they uphold their beliefs; both possess an inflexible psychological and political style characterized by the tendency to view social and political affairs in crude, unambiguous, and stereotypic terms. They see political life as a conflict between "us" and "them", a struggle between good and evil played out on a battleground where compromise amounts to capitulation and the goal is total victory. Both are also disposed to: censor their opponents; deal harshly with enemies; sacrifice the well-being even of the innocent in order to serve a "higher purpose;" and to use cruel tactics if necessary to "persuade" society of the wisdom of their goals. Moreover, both tend to support or oppose civil liberties and rights in a highly partisan and self-serving fashion, supporting freedom for themselves and for the groups and causes they favor while seeking to withhold it from enemies and advocates of causes they oppose.[46]

These striking similarities between American left and right radicals notwithstanding, McClosky and Chong also confirmed more or less the conventional view that the far left and the far right stand at opposite ends of the left-right ideological continuum on many issues of public policy, political philosophy and personal belief. Both hold sharply contrasting views on question of law and order, foreign policy, social welfare, economic equality, racial equality, women's rights, sexual freedom, patriotism, social conventions, religion, family values and orientations towards business, labor and private enterprise.[47]

McClosky and Chong's above findings are illuminating but need a few qualifiers. Their surveys are on *American* left-wing and right-wing radicals, and, thus, they as well as their interviewees are subject to American political, social, cultural and economic conditions and environments. Also, what they called left-wing and right-wing radicals are not exactly *identical* to totalitarian and authoritarian personality in this study, although they appear analogous to each other. Most importantly, the aforementioned similarities, they discovered, are only the *personal* beliefs, attitudes and proclivities. Hence, the question as to whether or not these groups have actually achieved such political system or political order is quite another. In this study it is assumed that in a totalitarian political order such "wish list" of radicals are actually achieved and practiced, while in an authoritarian political order they are, at best, partially fulfilled and realized.

One final caveat is in order. The distinction between T and A in this study is only analytic. In real political world, there are political systems closer to T or A, but never the prototypes that are conceptually spelled out here.

2. The North and South Korean Political System: An Overview

Nothing separates North Korea from South Korea more sharply than ideology. Marxism-Leninism, and Kim Il Sungism in the name of *Juche* are North Korea's official ideology. North Korea claims that its ideology is absolute, supreme and unswerving. Ideologically, the North Korean political system is a typical ideocracy. To use Inkeles' terminology, ideology in North Korea is also a mystique. Specifically, Kim Il Sung's *Juche* idea is "the higher goal," which spells the doom of "the rule of law." The *Juche* idea is a higher law, a universal principle, an incontro-vertible truth, and it assumes one truth, one law, one interest and hence only one program.[48]

South Korea rejects North Korea's claims in the name of anti-com-munism. Unlike North Korea's communism, South Korea's anti-com-munism, is largely devoid of specific doctrinal content; it is the master symbol and even a policy in countering the communist threats, but lacks a definite political blue-print and/or an ultimate goal. Anti-communism is not an ideological substitute for communism.

Ironically, North Korea's ideological strengths are South Korea's weaknesses, and vice versa. North Korea's main ideological strengths lie in its strategic firmness with tactical flexibility, and its weaknesses rest in its restrictiveness, which stifles individual spontaneity, creativity and initiative. Conversely, South Korea's major ideological weaknesses lie in its absence of a clear-cut doctrinal content, but its strengths are its amorphousness, which facilitates adjustment and modification to the changing political environments.

One of the key underlying principles of the North Korean political system is the unity of power, a direct opposite to the principle of separa-tion of powers and of checks and balances. The principle of the unity of power here is somewhat analogous to Karl Deutsch's concept of unity of command.[49] In North Korea, power is neither separated nor checked and balanced by mutually independent political units but united in a source, the Workers Party of Korea, and ultimately, its Supreme Leader Kim Il Sung and Dear Leader Kim Jong Il. The principle of the unity of power has degenerated such that the dictatorship of the proletariat has become the dictatorship of the party, which, in turn, has created the dic-tatorship of the dictator. Such political metamorphoses notwithstanding, *dictatorship* itself persists. To that extent, North Korea suffers less from its theoretical and semantic incongruence. To repeat, it is relatively easier for the North Korean ruling elites to justify their dictatorship than their South Korean counterparts, although the masses in the North suffer incomparably more under such "congruent" dictatorship than the cizitens in the South under an "incongruent" dictatorship.

The principle of the South Korean political system comparable to

North Korea's unity of power has been the concentration of powers in the executive, i.e., the presidency. In South Korea power is separated constitutionally but not politically, and a "democratic republic" is assured constitutionally but not actualized fully. Thus, it is far more difficult for the South Korean ruling elites to justify this apparent constitutional and semantic incongruence.

So far, two devices have been used to mitigate this apparent incongruity between pledging for a democratic republic and practicing an authoritarian politics. One stressed the uniqueness of Korean culture and tradition, and thereby contending that a Western-style democracy is not readily applicable to Korean soil. The other emphasized a threat from North Korea. The so-called security alarmists advocate that the threats from North Korea are sufficiently serious to warrant the restrictions and suspension of the citizens' democratic rights and freedom. These two arguments may be necessary, but they are insufficient to resolve this apparent incongruity. A lack of clear-cut and convincing resolution of this incongruity has been the root-cause of South Korea's chronic political instability. The ruling elites have attempted to justify their authoritarian political practices by utilizing these two devices, whose validity and legitimacy have been constantly and continuously challenged by the opposition forces and some segments of the general public, especially university students. Ultimately, there are desirable and undesirable solutions for this political dilemma. Making South Korea's political practices democratic is desirable while making the constitutional pledge more authoritarian is undesirable. The Yushin Constitution represents the prime example of the second. The tragic failure of the Yushin system indicates that there is only one genuine solution for South Korea, that is, an earnest effort to bring about democracy, so that South Korean politics would be in tune with the constitutional promises. The Roh Tae Woo regime has by and large chosen the first option, although it has been adrift without a firm democratic vision and commitment.

Other factors also divide North and South Korea politically. As noted earlier, one of the key words which characterizes a totalitarian political order is *the absence*—the absence of freedom, of individual economic and political autonomy, of political opposition and the like—in contrast to the *deficiency* of these elements in an authoritarian political order. The absence of these elements in North Korea is evident as much as their deficiency is, in South Korea. Putting it another way, if North Korea is *non-liberal* in that there is virtually no room for individual free-doms and basic rights to exist, South Korea is *anti-liberal* in that its rul-ing elites have tried to curb such freedoms and rights, but their attempts have never been completely successful. In the former, the system has successfully eliminated such room itself, while in the latter, the room, though squeezed and suppressed, is still there.

Likewise, the North Korean political system is characterized by its *non-parliamentarianism,* as opposed to the South Korean political sys-tem's *anti-parliamentarianism.* In the former, the legislative organs, the Supreme People's Assembly (SPA) and other regional and local assem-blies, do exist, but they are nothing more than the legislative tool of the Workers' Party of Korea. The legislative powers and functions compa-rable to a parliamentary system in Great Britain or a presidential system in the United States are absent in the SPA. Because the SPA was created as a legislative arm of the WPK, there can be, and is, no political ten-sion between the two. The SPA and other legislative organs are the parts and parcels of the WPK; the former were *not created* to check and bal-ance the powers of the executive and/or the judiciary, let alone the omnipotent and omniscient power of the WPK, and ultimately, of Kim Il Sung and Kim Jong Il.

By contrast, the South Korean political system is anti-parliamentarian as demonstrated by the views of the ruling elites in the executive branch. They perceive the National Assembly (NA) as nothing more than an obstructionist and wasteful debating forum. Hence, the political tensions and strife between the ruling elites, especially the members of the ruling party in the NA, who have often become the handmaiden or the errand boys of the executive, and those small yet recalcitrant and vociferous opposition members never subside. The political strifes con-tinue primarily because the NA was *created* as an independent political unit to check and balance the powers of the executive and the judicial branches. While North Korea's SPA was designed to serve as the WPK's legislative tool, South Korea's NA was created as an independent legislative component of the state, not of the ruling power or party. Hence, the ruling power's effort to reduce the role and status of the NA to the level of the SPA is constantly and consistently challenged and countered by the opposition. Thus far, neither the South Korean ruling elites nor the opposition group have won the battle. One thing is self-evident: if the NA becomes another SPA, it will be a pyrrhic victory to both the ruling power and the opposition.

North Korea's *partism* and South Korea's *corporatism* are another contrasting features. Partism is a system of interest representation in which the constituent units are created by a single party, which controls various functional groups such as the trade unions, artist guilds and all other professional organizations. North Korea is the prime example of partism in that the WPK controls the state and all other constituent parts of political, societal and economic systems. Corporatism exists if interest representation by the groups is compulsory, noncompetitive, and hierarchical. It is a state-controlled partnership between government and interest groups. Unlike in partism, however, the interest groups are not created by the party-state, though heavily controlled by the government in power. South Korea is corporatistic to the extent that it has not eliminated, but only *subordinated* the non-state interest representation to the government in power.

Economically, North Korea's inward-looking self-reliance posture based on the principle of collectivistic mobilization contrasts sharply with South Korea's outward-looking developmental-dependency drive, based on the tenet of individualistic motivation. Amid the metamorphic transformation of the erstwhile communist world, North Korea, too, searches desperately for a new alternative to its heretofore militant revolutionary strategy. Her success in this endeavor is, however, highly doubtful unless her system itself goes through a radical metamorphosis comparable to the former Soviet Union and Eastern Europe.

Militarily, North Korea's "political military" differs fundamentally from South Korea's "military politics" or praetorianism. In North Korea, the armed forces are controlled by the WPK, which is consistent with the principle of Party supremacy. Like all the other functional organizations in North Korea, the armed forces, including para-military forces and militia are nothing more than the WPK's military tool. In South Korea from Park to Chun regimes, the military had been a dominant political force as a result of the breakdown in the principle of civilian supremacy. Grossly simplified, in North Korea the ultimate political power flows from the WPK to the military, while in South Korea it had run from the military to the civilian politics especially since Park Chung Hee's political take-over by the military coup in 1961 to Chun Doo Hwan's similar rise to power in the 1980s. During the Roh regime, demilitarization or civilianization of the South Korean politics had earnestly begun and presently continues under Kim Young-sam government, but its final success is still too early to call.

North and South Korea's approaches to political socialization in general and education in particular, also differ greatly. As is the case with the role and the status of the military, North Korea's "political education" differs inherently from South Korea's "politicization of education." In the North, the chief aim of political socialization and education is to create a new socialist man of *Juche* type. Education, too, is nothing more than the WPK's politicization instrument. Education is an integral part of the WPK's political control mechanism. By definition, school autonomy is thus, non-existent. Meanwhile, in the South, *Hongik Ingan,* a person who benefits all humankind, is the ideal. Education is not the ruling power's political instrument. Nor is school autonomy completely destroyed by the government in power. In short, in North Korea the WPK's use of education as a politicization instrument is built-in, and consistent with its ideal—the creation of a new socialist man of *Juche* type. In South Korea the ruling power's politicization of education is extraneous and inconsistent with its ideal—the realization of a universal person. Herein lies the root cause for chronic campus unrest in the South.

The salient traits of the North and South Korean ruling elites are also noteworthy. Some key features of the North Korean ruling elites are: gradualism in leadership appointment and training; tokenism in sexual, factional, and fraternal parties' representation in elite recruitment; overlapping membership and cross-penetration of the WPK members in party, state, military and mass organizations; the gradual leadership change from "reds" (i.e., Kim Il sung's partisan-comrades-in arms and ideologues) to "experts" (i.e., technocrats) and purges as a means of elite replacement.

By contrast, some distinguishing factors of the South Korean ruling elites are; inconstancy syndrome in elite circulation; political symbiosis of civilian politicians-bureaucrats-military-academicians-mass media specialists; expansion of political control mechanism; and sprawling domestic political surveillance and intelligence networks.

Finally, the contrast in the seizure and transfer of political power in North and South Korea merits a discussion. At the heart of the North Korean succession question is *sŭng-gye* [succession], that is, "who succeeds whom?" The crux of the South Korean problem is *gyo-ch'e* [transfer]—how to transfer power from one regime (or party) to the other. To put it differently, political succession is concerned mainly with "the personnel of power," whereas the transfer of power or a regime change focuses on "the mechanism of power." The one is a within-party take-over and step-down, and the other, a between-regimes transfer. Hence, North Korea's succession question centers around the crisis of leadership: Will Kim Jŏng Il successfully take over his father's power? Will there be a collective leadership immediately after the demise of Kim Il Sung? Who will eventually emerge as a new strong man in North Korea? There also is a set of more fundamental questions. Namely, can the North Korean system itself weather through the storms of the present metamorphic changes in the former communist camp? Can North Korea be an exception to the global onslaught on the communist states? Can the present North Korean system succeed in reform and readjustment without violent popular upheavals and/or without radical departure from the present system and policy?

By contrast, South Korea's transfer of power issue revolves around the crisis of legitimacy: Will the Roh regime and now the Kim Young-sam government further solidify a constitutional and electoral framework, which guarantees fair competitions among the aspirants for the top post? Will the Kim regime succeed for the third time in the constitutional and peaceful transfer of power and lay a firmer foundation for South Korea's incipient democratization?

One thing is clear, in the final analysis. The North Korean political system as a variant of totalitarianism differs substantially from the South Korean political system as a deviant of authoritarianism. The contest of superiority continues between the two systems. Forty years are sufficient to compare these two systems' political and economic performances, but not adequate to declare the winner. The findings of this study serves as an interim report on these systems' performance, not as their final balance sheets.

One final thought is presented here. The persistence of North Korea's totalitarian political order and South Korea's authoritarian political proclivity perhaps demonstrates one of the age-old human paradoxes. As a person is capable of becoming a saint, a satan, a democrat or a dictator at an individual level, depending upon a situation, so are the people who share a high degree of cultural and national affinity at the collective level. That the Koreans, one of the most culturally homogeneous people in the world today, have erected the two most diametrically different political systems and living under them is the proof.

Postscript

As noted in the foregoing, no system, totalitarian, authoritarian or otherwise, is completely immune from change. North Korea, too, struggles to change in its own way. Still, its totalitarian political order is fundamentally intact. Under the Roh regime and now the Kim Young-sam regime South Korea's democratization is making a headway, but it is far from being democratic despite the present efforts in all fronts to shed and replace its deeply entrenched authoritarian garb with a more democratic outfit. South Korea's road toward democracy is and will be indeed long and bumpy. After all, democracy is not a merchandise one can freely and easily pick and discard. Rather, it is like a tree which needs constant nourishment and vigilance. What South Korea needs then is neither an excessive expectation nor an unnecessary despair but patience and prudence.

Notes

1. Zbigniew Brzezinski and Samuel P. Huntingtion, *Political Power: USA/ USSR* (New York: The Viking Press, 1967), p. 7.
2. George F. Kennan, "Totalitarianism in the Modern World" in Carl J. Friedrich, ed., *Totalitarianism* (New York: The Universal Library, 1964), p. 29.
3. Harold D. Lasswell, "The Promise of the World Order Modeling Movement," *World Politics* (April 1977) p. 433.
4. Dirk Berg-Schlosser, "Third World Political Systems: Classification and Evaluation," paper delivered at the 1984 Annual Meeting of the American Political Science Association, Washington, D.C., 30 August-2 September 1984. See also, Anton Bebler and Jim Seroka, eds., *Contemporary Political Systems: Classifications and Typologies* (Boulder: Lynne Rienner, 1990).
5. Merle Fainsod, *How Russia is Ruled,* rev. ed. (Cambridge: Harvard University Press, 1963), pp. 3-4; Roy C. Macridis, *Contemporary Political Ideologies: Movement and Regimes* (Boston: Little, Brown, 1983), pp. 170-231; N.S. Timasheff and Carl Friedrich's views are found in Carl Friedrich,*Op. Cit.*, pp. 39-46 and pp. 47-59, respectively; Robert C. Tucker, *The Soviet Political Mind,* rev. ed. (New York: W.W. Norton, 1971), pp. 3-19.
6. Gabriel A. Almond and G. Bingham Powell, Jr., *Comparative Politics Today: A World View* (Boston: Little, Brown, 1980), pp. 44-45; Edward A. Shils, "Authoritarianism: 'Right' and 'Left,'" in Richard Christie and Marie Jahoda, *Studies in the Scope and Method of the Authoritarian Personality* (Glencoe: Free Press, 1954), pp. 24-29; Talcott Parsons, *The Social Systems* (New York: The Free Press, 1951), p. 194; Herbert McClosky and Dennis Chong, "Similarities and Differences between Left-wing and Right-wing Radicals," *The British Journal of Political Science* 5 (July 1985): 329-363; Milton Rokeach, *The Open and Closed Mind* (New York: Basic Books, 1960); and Amos Perlmutter, *Modern Authoritarianism* (New Haven: Yale University Press, 1981).
7. Juan Linz, "Totalitarian and Authoritarian Regimes," in F. Greenstein and N. Polsby, eds., *Handbook of Political Science* (Reading, Mass.: Addison-Wesley, 1975), Vol. 3, pp. 175-412; Ferdinand A. Hermens, *The Representative Republic* (South Bend: University of Notre Dame Press, 1958), pp. 134-141; Leon P. Baradat, *Political Ideologies: Their Origins and Impact* (Englewood Cliffs: Prentice-Hall, 1979), p. 285; Jeane J. Kirkpatrick, *Dictatorships and Double Standards: Rationalism and Reason in Politics* (New York: Simon and Schuster, 1982).

8. T. D. Weldon, *The Vocabulary of Politics* (New York: A Pelican Book, 1953), pp. 101-138.

9. John Dewey, *The Public and Its Problems* (Chicago: Gateway Books, 1946), pp. 28-73.

10. George H. Sabine, *A History of Political Theory* (New York: Henry Holt, 1959), pp. 897-898.

11. Hannah Arendt, *Origins of Totalitarianism* (New York: Harcourt, Brace, 1951); Carl J. Friedrich and Zbigniew K. Brzezinski, *Totalitarian Dictatorship and Autonomy* (Cambridge: Harvard University Press, 1956).

12. Karl Deutsch, *Politics and Government: How People Decide Their Fate* (Boston: Houghton Mifflin, 1979), p. 66; Joseph LaPalombara and Myron Weiner, *Political Parties and Political Development* (Princeton: Princeton University Press, 1966), pp. 37-40.

13. Irving Louis Horowitz, *Three Worlds of Development: The Theory and Practice of International Stratification* (New York: Oxford University Press, 1966), pp. 155-163.

14. Franz Newman, *The Authoritarian and the Democratic State* (New York: New York: Free Press, 1957), pp. 233-247; Giovanni Sartori, *Parties and Party Systems* (Cambridge: Cambridge University Press, 1976), p. 222; William A. Welsh, *Studying Politics* (New York: Praeger, 1973), p. 101; Jon Devos, *Introduction to Politics* (Cambridge: Winthrop Publishers, 1975), pp. 99-123; and Dirk Berg-Schlosser, "African Political Systems: Typology and Performance," *Comparative Political Studies* 17 (April 1984): pp. 121-151. Robert A. Dahl, *Democracy and Its Critics* (New Haven: Yale University Press, 1989), pp. 314-315.

15. Gabriel A. Almond and G. Bingham Powell, Jr., *Comparative Politics: A Developmental Approach* (Boston: Little, Brown, 1966), p. 217.

16. Edward S. Malecki, "The Capitalist State: Structural Variation and Its Implications for Radical Change," *Western Political Quarterly* 34 (June 1981): pp. 246-269.

17. Albert Lauterbach, "Totalitarian Appeal and Economic Reform," in Carl Friedrich, *Op. Cit.*, pp. 281-296.

18. George F. Kennan, *Op. Cit.*, p. 18 and p. 22.

19. Bertram D. Wolfe, *Communist Totalitarianism: Keys to the Soviet System* (Boulder: A Westview Encore Edition, 1985), *passim*.

20. Karl Dietrich Bracher, "Experience and Concepts-Between Democracy and Dictatorship," *Government and Opposition* 15 (Summer/Autumn 1980): 289-296.

21. Friedrich and Brzezinski, *Op. Cit.*, and Tucker, *Op. Cit.*

22. Tucker, especially Chapter 2, pp. 36-59.

23. Wolfe, *Op. Cit.*, p. 268.

24. Alex Inkeles, "The Totalitarian Mystique: Some Impressions of the Dynamics of Totalitarian Society," in Friedrich, *Op. Cit.*, p. 106.
25. Erik H. Erikson, "Wholeness and Totality—A Psychiatric Contribution," in Friedrich, *Op. Cit.*, p. 159.
26. Friedrich, *Op. Cit.*, pp. 52-53.
27. *Ibid.*, p. 274.
28. Wolfe, *Op. Cit.*, p. 270.
29. N. S. Timasheff, *Op. Cit.*, p. 39.
30. Waldemar Gurian, "The Totalitarian State," *The Review of Politics* 40 (October 1978): 514-527.
31. Karl Deutsch, "Cracks in the Monolith: Possibilities and Patterns of Disintegration in Totalitarian Systems," in Friedrich, *Op. Cit.*, pp. 308-332.
32. Inkeles, *Op. Cit.*, p. 97.
33. *Ibid.*, p. 100.
34. Lauterbach, *Op. Cit.*, p. 286.
35. Else Frenkel-Brunswik, "Environmental Controls and the Impoverishment of Thought," in Friedrich, *Op. Cit.*, p. 175.
36. *Ibid.*, p. 188.
37. J. L. Talmon, *The Origins of Totalitarian Democracy* (New York: Fredrick A. Praeger, 1960).
38. Quoted in Robert Tucker, *Op. Cit.*, p. 4.
39. Wolfe, *Op. Cit.*, p. 276.
40. Gurian, "Totalitarianism as Political Religion," in Friedrich, *Op. Cit.*, p. 121.
41. Wolfe, *Op. Cit.*, p. 161, and p. 261.
42. *Ibid.*, p. 126.
43. Leon P. Baradat, *Op. Cit.*, p. 285.
44. Arendt, Inkeles, Lauterbach and Gurian's concepts are found in Friedrich, ed., *Op. Cit.*, pp. 88-100, p. 121 and p. 134. Also, Tucker, *Op. Cit.*, p. 39.
45. McClosky and Chong, *Op. Cit.*
46. *Ibid.*
47. *Ibid.*
48. Inkeles, *Op. Cit.*, p. 100.
49. Karl Deutsch, *Op. Cit.*, p. 309.

APPENDICES

APPENDIX 1

A CHRONOLOGY OF HISTORIC EVENTS

CHINA	KOREA	JAPAN
Early Han, 206 B.C.–A.D. 8 Later Han, A.D. 25–220 Colonies at Lolang and Taifang, northern Korea, expelled by Koguryŏ	4th century B.C.–3rd century A.D.: Chinese Han colonies in the north, Tribal Leagues (Mahan, Chinhan, Pyŏnhan) in the south. c. A.D. 350 end of Chinese colonies	
Sui Dynasty, 518–618	Three Kingdoms Period: Koguryŏ, 37 B.C.–A.D. 668 Paekche, 18 B.C.–A.D. 663 (Kaya, A.D. 42–A.D. 562) Old Silla, 57 B.C.–A.D. 668	Wang In of Paekche trans- mits Analects of Confucius, A.D. 375 Buddhism imported from Paekche, 552.
T'ang Dynasty 618–906		Taika-Nara-Heian Period, 645–847
Sung Dynasty, 960–1279	Silla Dynasty, 668–935 Later Paekche, 892–936 Later Koguryŏ, 901–918	
Chin Dynasty, 1155–1234	Koryŏ Dynasty, 918–1392	
Yuan (Mongol), 1206–1368	Yi dynasty, 1392–1910	Ashikaga (Muromachi)
Ming Dynasty, 1368–1644	1592, Hideyoshi Invasion	Period, 1336-1573 Nobunaga, 1534–1582
Chinese defeated Japanese in Korea, 1592	1636, Mongol Conquest Ports opened to Japan, 1876;	Invasions of Korea, 1592, 1597
Ch'ing Dynasty, 1644–1912	U.S., 1882; France, 1886	Tokugawa Era, 1660–1867 Meiji Era, 1867–1912
Sino-Japanese War, 1894–5	Sino-Japanese War, 1894–5 Japanese Protectorate, 1905 Annexation by Japan, 1910	Sino-Japanese War, 1894–5 Russo-Japanese War, 1904–5 Annexation of Korea, 1910
Republic of China, 1912–1949	Japanese Government General 1910–1945	Taisho Era, 1912–1926
Korean Provisional Govt. established at Shanghai, 1919	March 1 –Uprising, 1919	Showa Era, 1926–1990 Conquest of Manchuria, 1932 Attack on Peking, 1937 Attack on Pearl Harbor, 1941
	Liberation of Korea, 1945 Military Government, 1945–8, Soviet in the North, U.S. in the South 1948	15 Aug. 1945: surrender, end of Second World War

Appendix 1. Continued

CHINA	KOREA	JAPAN
1949, People's Republic of China established in Peking. Nationalist government moves to Taiwan.	Republic of Korea, (South Korea); Democratic People's Republic of Korea (North Korea).	
1950, Chinese Communist Army enters Korean War 1953, Armistice signed at Panmunjom. Mainland China signs Mutual Defense Pact with North Korea	*Korean War*, 1950–53 Armistice signed by U.N. Command, 1953, with People's Republic of China and Democratic People's Republic of Korea (North Korea) 1953, R.O.K.-U.S. Mutual Defense Pact 1960, President Syngman Rhee government ousted 1961, Chang Myŏn government overthrown by military coup	
		1965, Normalization of R.O.K.-Japanese relations

APPENDIX 2
DYNASTIC LINEAGES*

Old Chosŏn
古朝鮮

Tan'gun Wanggŏm ··· Pu Wang ─────────── Chun Wang
檀君王儉 (2333 B.C.-?)   否王   準王 (?-194 B.C.)

Wiman Chosŏn
衛滿朝鮮

Wiman Wang ──────────── ○ ─────────── Ugŏ Wang
衛滿王 (194 B.C.-?)   右渠王 (?-108 B.C.)

Puyŏ (Hae)
夫餘(解)

············ Si Wang ─────────── Wigut'ae ············ Put'ae Wang ·········
  始王   尉仇台 (fl. 121) 夫台王

·· Wigut'ae Wang ─── Kanwigŏ Wang ── Mayŏ Wang ─── Ŭiryŏ Wang ····
尉仇台王 (?-ca.200) 簡位居王 摩余王   依慮王 (?-285)

            ·· Ŭira Wang ············ Hyŏn Wang
            依羅王 (286-?) 玄王(?-346)

Pon Kaya (Kim)
本加耶
(42-532)

1. Suro Wang ── 2. Kŏdŭng Wang── 3. Map'um Wang ── 4. Kŏjilmi Wang ──
首露王 (42-199) 居登王 (199-259) 麻品王 (259-291) 居叱彌王(291-346)

└ 5. I(si)p'um Wang ─────── 6. Chwaji Wang ──────── 7. Ch'wihŭi Wang ──
伊(尸)品王 (346-407) 坐知王 (407-421) 吹希王 (421-451)

└ 8. Chilchi Wang ─────── 9. Kamji Wang ─────── 10. Kuhyŏng Wang
銍知王 (451-492) 鉗知王 (492-521) 仇衡王 (521-532)

Tae Kaya
大加耶

1. Ijinasi Wang 9. Inoe Wang ── Wŏlgwang T'aeja 16. Tosŏlchi Wang
伊珍阿豉王   王異腦王 月光太子   道設智王
(ca. 42-?)   (fl. 522)   (?-562)

---

*For the ancient period, including the Three Kingdoms and Parhae, records giving the surname of a royal house (in the parentheses following the name of the kingdom), the names and titles of the kings, and the dates of their reigns (in the parentheses under the king's name) in many cases are at variance or are problematic. Foundation dates and the reign dates of the founding kings of these early dynasties are regarded as mostly unreliable but are provided here in Korean historiographic tradition.

Koguryŏ (Ko)
高 句 麗 (高)
(27 B.C.-668)

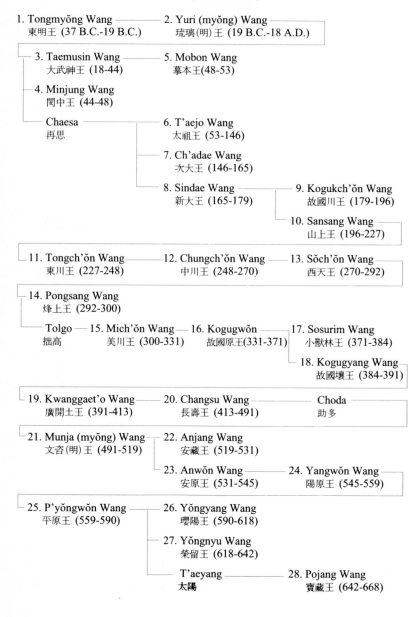

1. Tongmyŏng Wang — 2. Yuri (myŏng) Wang
   東明王 (37 B.C.-19 B.C.) 琉璃(明)王 (19 B.C.-18 A.D.)

3. Taemusin Wang — 5. Mobon Wang
   大武神王 (18-44) 慕本王(48-53)

4. Minjung Wang
   閔中王 (44-48)

   Chaesa — 6. T'aejo Wang
   再思 太祖王 (53-146)

   7. Ch'adae Wang
      次大王 (146-165)

   8. Sindae Wang — 9. Kogukch'ŏn Wang
      新大王 (165-179) 故國川王 (179-196)

   10. Sansang Wang
       山上王 (196-227)

11. Tongch'ŏn Wang — 12. Chungch'ŏn Wang — 13. Sŏch'ŏn Wang
    東川王 (227-248) 中川王 (248-270) 西川王 (270-292)

14. Pongsang Wang
    烽上王 (292-300)

    Tolgo — 15. Mich'ŏn Wang — 16. Kogugwŏn — 17. Sosurim Wang
    拙高 美川王 (300-331) 故國原王(331-371) 小獸林王 (371-384)

    18. Kogugyang Wang
        故國壤王 (384-391)

19. Kwanggaet'o Wang — 20. Changsu Wang — Choda
    廣開土王 (391-413) 長壽王 (413-491) 助多

21. Munja (myŏng) Wang — 22. Anjang Wang
    文咨(明)王 (491-519) 安藏王 (519-531)

    23. Anwŏn Wang — 24. Yangwŏn Wang
        安原王 (531-545) 陽原王 (545-559)

25. P'yŏngwŏn Wang — 26. Yŏngyang Wang
    平原王 (559-590) 瓔陽王 (590-618)

    27. Yŏngnyu Wang
        榮留王 (618-642)

    T'aeyang — 28. Pojang Wang
    太陽 寶藏王 (642-668)

Paekche (Puyŏ)
百濟(扶餘)
(18 B.C.-660)

1. Onjo Wang — 2. Taru Wang — 3. Kiru Wang
溫祚王 (18 B.C.-28 A.D.)   多婁王 (28-77)   己婁王 (77-128)

4. Kaeru Wang — 5. Ch'ogo Wang — 6. Kusu Wang — 7. Saban Wang
大武神王 (128-166)   肖古王(166-214)   仇首王 (214-234)   沙伴王 (234)

11. Piryu Wang
比流王 (304-344)

8. Koi Wang — 9. Ch'aekkye Wang — 10. Punsŏ Wang
古爾王(234-286)   責稽王(286-298)   汾西王 (298-304)

12. Kye Wang
契王(344-346)

13. Kŭn Ch'ogo Wang — 14. Kŭn Kusu Wang — 15. Ch'imnyu Wang
近肖古王 (346-375)   近仇首王 (375-384)   枕流王 (384-385)

16. Chinsa Wang
辰斯王(385-392)

17. Asin (Ahwa) Wang — 18. Chŏnji Wang — 19. Kuisin Wang
阿莘(華)王 (392-405)   전支王 (405-420)   久爾莘王 (420-427)

20. Piyu Wang — 21. Kaero Wang — 22. Munju Wang — 23. Samgŭn Wang
毗有王 (427-455)   蓋鹵王 (455-475)   文周王 (475-477)   三斤王 (477-479)

Konji — 24. Tongsŏng Wang
昆支   東城王 (479-501)

25. Muryŏng Wang — 26. Sŏng Wang — 27. Widŏk Wang
武寧王 (501-523)   聖王 (523-554)   威德王 (554-598)

28. Hye Wang
惠王 (598-599)

29. Pŏp Wang — 30. Mu Wang — 31. Ŭija Wang
法王 (599-600)   武王 (600-641)   義慈王 (641-660)

Silla (Pak, Sŏk, Kim)
新研 (朴, 昔, 金)
(57 B.C.-935)

(Pak) 1. Hyŏkkŏse Kŏsŏgan ———— 2. Namhae Ch'ach'aung
          赫居世居西干(57 B.C.-4 A.D.)   南解次次雄(4-24)

       3. Yuri Isagŭm ————   7. Ilsŏng Isagŭm ————   8. Adalla Isagŭm
          儒理泥師今(24-57)   逸聖履師今(134-154)   阿達羅履師今(154-184)
       Lady Aro   5. P'asa Isagŭm ————   6. Chima Isagŭm
          阿老夫人   婆娑履師今(80-112)   祇摩履師今(112-134)
(Sŏk) 4. Tarhae Isagŭm ————   Kuch'u   9. Pŏrhyu Isagŭm
          脫解履師今(57-80)   仇鄒   伐休履師今(184-196)

       Kolchŏng   11. Chobun Isagŭm   14. Yurye Isagŭm
          骨正   助賁履師今(230-247)   儒禮履師今(284-298)
                                12. Ch'ŏmhae Isagŭm   Kŏlsuk   15. Kirim Isagŭm
                                    点解履師今(247-261)   乞淑   基臨履師今(298-310)

       Imae ————   10. Naehae Isagŭm ————   Uro ———— 16. Hŭrhae Isagŭm
          伊買   奈解履師今(196-230)   于老   許解履師今(310-356)

                                                            Lady Kwangmyong
                                                            光明夫人

(Kim)   Alchi ············· Kudo ————   13. Mich'u Isagŭm
          關智   仇道   味鄒履師今(262-284)
                                                        Malgu
                                                            末仇
                                                        Taesŏji —— 18. Silsŏng Maripkan
                                                            大西知   實聖麻立干(402-417)

       17. Naemul Maripkan ————   19. Nulchi Maripkan ————   20. Chabi Maripkan
           奈勿麻立干(356-402)   訥祇麻立干(417-458)   慈悲麻立干(458-479)

                                                                21. Soji Maripkan
                                                                    炤知麻立干(479-500)
                                                                Lady Chosaeng
                                                                    鳥生夫人
                                            ◯ ————————————   Sŭppo
                                                                    習寶

       22. Chijŭng Wang ————   23. Pŏphŭng Wang
           智證王(500-514)   法興王(514-540)
                                   Ipchong ————   24. Chingŭng Wang
                                       立宗   眞興王(540-576)
       Tongnyun ————   26. Chinp'yŏng Wang   27. Sŏndŏk Yŏwang(Queen)
           銅輪   眞平王(579-632)   善德女王(632-647)
                                   Kukpan ————   28. Chindŏk Yŏwang(Queen)
                                       國飯   眞德女王(647-654)
       25. Chinji Wang ————   Yongch'un ————   29. (T'aejong)MuyŏlWang
           眞智王(576-579)   龍春   太宗武烈王(654-661)

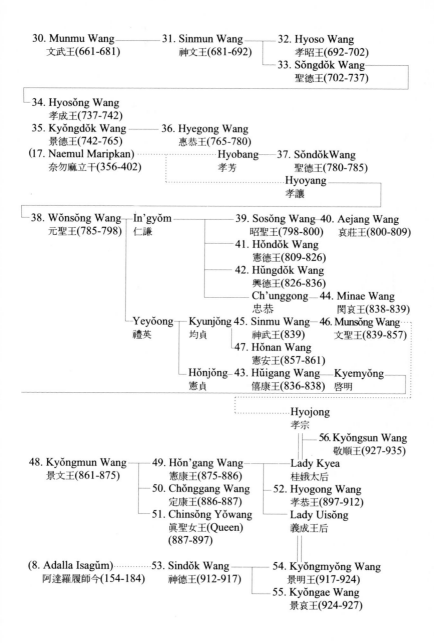

30. Munmu Wang———31. Sinmun Wang———32. Hyoso Wang
　　文武王(661-681)　　　　神文王(681-692)　　　孝昭王(692-702)
　　　　　　　　　　　　　　　　　　　　　　　33. Sŏngdŏk Wang———
　　　　　　　　　　　　　　　　　　　　　　　　　聖德王(702-737)

34. Hyosŏng Wang
　　孝成王(737-742)
35. Kyŏngdŏk Wang———36. Hyegong Wang
　　景德王(742-765)　　　惠恭王(765-780)
(17. Naemul Maripkan)·············　　　　Hyobang———37. SŏndŏkWang
　　奈勿麻立干(356-402)　　　　　　　孝芳　　　　聖德王(780-785)
　　　　　　　　　　　　　　　　　　　　　Hyoyang———
　　　　　　　　　　　　　　　　　　　　　孝讓

38. Wŏnsŏng Wang┬In'gyŏm—————————39. Sosŏng Wang–40. Aejang Wang
　　元聖王(785-798)│仁謙　　　　　　　　　　昭聖王(798-800)　哀莊王(800-809)
　　　　　　　　　　│　　　　　　　　　　41. Hŏndŏk Wang
　　　　　　　　　　│　　　　　　　　　　　憲德王(809-826)
　　　　　　　　　　│　　　　　　　　　　42. Hŭngdŏk Wang
　　　　　　　　　　│　　　　　　　　　　　興德王(826-836)
　　　　　　　　　　│　　　　　　　　　Ch'unggong—44. Minae Wang
　　　　　　　　　　│　　　　　　　　　　忠恭　　　閔哀王(838-839)
　　　　　　　　　　└Yeyŏong┬Kyunjŏng 45. Sinmu Wang–46. Munsŏng Wang·······
　　　　　　　　　　　禮英　│均貞　　　　神武王(839)　　文聖王(839-857)
　　　　　　　　　　　　　　│　　　　47. Hŏnan Wang
　　　　　　　　　　　　　　│　　　　　憲安王(857-861)
　　　　　　　　　　　　　　└Hŏnjŏng–43. Hŭigang Wang—Kyemyŏng———
　　　　　　　　　　　　　　　憲貞　　僖康王(836-838)　啓明
　　　　　　　　　　　　　　　　　　········Hyojong
　　　　　　　　　　　　　　　　　　　　孝宗
　　　　　　　　　　　　　　　　　　　　　├— 56. Kyŏngsun Wang
　　　　　　　　　　　　　　　　　　　　　│　敬順王(927-935)
48. Kyŏngmun Wang┬49. Hŏn'gang Wang————┬Lady Kyea
　　景文王(861-875)│　憲康王(875-886)　　│桂娥太后
　　　　　　　　　　├50. Chŏnggang Wang　├52. Hyogong Wang
　　　　　　　　　　│　定康王(886-887)　│　孝恭王(897-912)
　　　　　　　　　　└51. Chinsŏng Yŏwang └Lady Uisŏng
　　　　　　　　　　　　眞聖女王(Queen)　　義成王后
　　　　　　　　　　　　(887-897)

(8. Adalla Isagŭm)··········53. Sindŏk Wang———┬54. Kyŏngmyŏng Wang
　　阿達羅履師今(154-184)　　神德王(912-917)　│　景明王(917-924)
　　　　　　　　　　　　　　　　　　　　　　└55. Kyŏngae Wang
　　　　　　　　　　　　　　　　　　　　　　　景哀王(924-927)

Parhae (Tae)
渤海 (大)
(698-926)

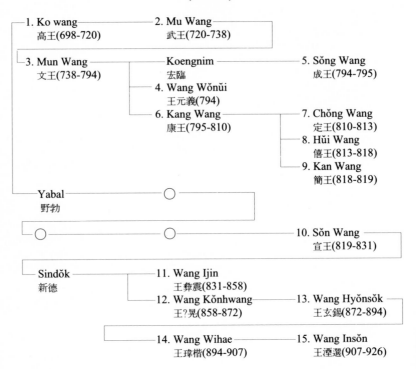

1. Ko wang
高王(698-720)

2. Mu Wang
武王(720-738)

3. Mun Wang
文王(738-794)

Koengnim
宏臨

4. Wang Wŏnŭi
王元義(794)

6. Kang Wang
康王(795-810)

5. Sŏng Wang
成王(794-795)

7. Chŏng Wang
定王(810-813)

8. Hŭi Wang
僖王(813-818)

9. Kan Wang
簡王(818-819)

Yabal
野勃

10. Sŏn Wang
宣王(819-831)

Sindŏk
新德

11. Wang Ijin
王彝震(831-858)

12. Wang Kŏnhwang
王?晃(858-872)

13. Wang Hyŏnsŏk
王玄錫(872-894)

14. Wang Wihae
王瑋瑎(894-907)

15. Wang Insŏn
王諲譔(907-926)

Koryŏ (Wang)
高麗(王)
(918-1392)

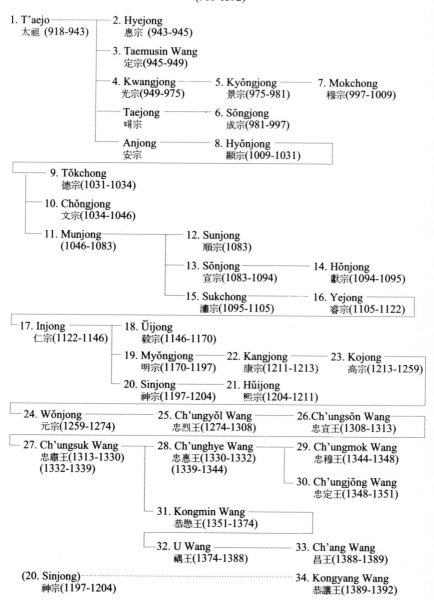

1. T'aejo — 2. Hyejong
太祖 (918-943)　惠宗 (943-945)

3. Taemusin Wang
定宗(945-949)

4. Kwangjong — 5. Kyŏngjong — 7. Mokchong
光宗(949-975)　景宗(975-981)　穆宗(997-1009)

Taejong — 6. Sŏngjong
태宗　成宗(981-997)

Anjong — 8. Hyŏnjong
安宗　顯宗(1009-1031)

9. Tŏkchong
德宗(1031-1034)

10. Chŏngjong
文宗(1034-1046)

11. Munjong — 12. Sunjong
(1046-1083)　順宗(1083)

13. Sŏnjong — 14. Hŏnjong
宣宗(1083-1094)　獻宗(1094-1095)

15. Sukchong — 16. Yejong
肅宗(1095-1105)　睿宗(1105-1122)

17. Injong — 18. Ŭijong
仁宗(1122-1146)　毅宗(1146-1170)

19. Myŏngjong — 22. Kangjong — 23. Kojong
明宗(1170-1197)　康宗(1211-1213)　高宗(1213-1259)

20. Sinjong — 21. Hŭijong
神宗(1197-1204)　熙宗(1204-1211)

24. Wŏnjong — 25. Ch'ungyŏl Wang — 26. Ch'ungsŏn Wang
元宗(1259-1274)　忠烈王(1274-1308)　忠宣王(1308-1313)

27. Ch'ungsuk Wang — 28. Ch'unghye Wang — 29. Ch'ungmok Wang
忠肅王(1313-1330)　忠惠王(1330-1332)　忠穆王(1344-1348)
(1332-1339)　(1339-1344)

30. Ch'ungjŏng Wang
忠定王(1348-1351)

31. Kongmin Wang
恭愍王(1351-1374)

32. U Wang — 33. Ch'ang Wang
禑王(1374-1388)　昌王(1388-1389)

(20. Sinjong) .... 34. Kongyang Wang
神宗(1197-1204)　恭讓王(1389-1392)

Chosŏn (Yi)
朝鮮 (李)
(1392-1910)

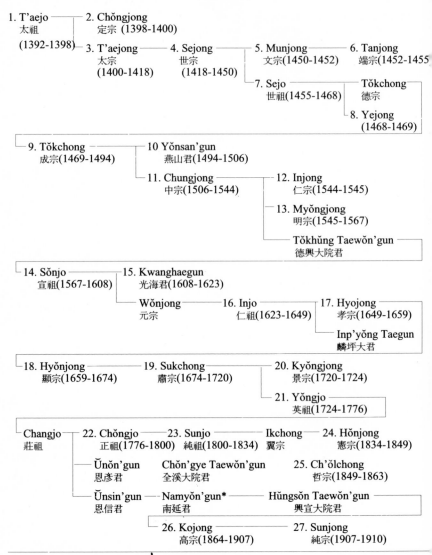

1. T'aejo ──────── 2. Chŏngjong
   太祖   定宗 (1398-1400)
   (1392-1398)── 3. T'aejong ──── 4. Sejong ──── 5. Munjong ──────── 6. Tanjong
                    太宗   世宗   文宗(1450-1452)   端宗(1452-1455
                    (1400-1418)   (1418-1450)
                                                 └─ 7. Sejo ──────────── Tŏkchong ──
                                                      世祖(1455-1468)   德宗
                                                                       └─ 8. Yejong
                                                                          (1468-1469)

── 9. Tŏkchong ──────────── 10 Yŏnsan'gun
     成宗(1469-1494)   燕山君(1494-1506)
                          └── 11. Chungjong ──────── 12. Injong
                                中宗(1506-1544)   仁宗(1544-1545)
                                                    ── 13. Myŏngjong
                                                       明宗(1545-1567)
                                                    └──── Tŏkhŭng Taewŏn'gun ──
                                                          德興大院君

── 14. Sŏnjo ────────── 15. Kwanghaegun
     宣祖(1567-1608)   光海君(1608-1623)
                      └── Wŏnjong ──────── 16. Injo ──────── 17. Hyojong ──
                          元宗   仁祖(1623-1649)   孝宗(1649-1659)
                                                           └── Inp'yŏng Taegun
                                                               麟坪大君

── 18. Hyŏnjong ──────── 19. Sukchong ──────────── 20. Kyŏngjong
     顯宗(1659-1674)   肅宗(1674-1720)   景宗(1720-1724)
                                                   └── 21. Yŏngjo
                                                       英祖(1724-1776)

── Changjo ── 22. Chŏngjo ──── 23. Sunjo ──────── Ikchong ── 24. Hŏnjong
   莊祖   正祖(1776-1800) 純祖(1800-1834)   翼宗   憲宗(1834-1849)
            ── Ŭnŏn'gun   Chŏn'gye Taewŏn'gun   25. Ch'ŏlchong
               恩彦君   全溪大院君   哲宗(1849-1863)
            └── Ŭnsin'gun ── Namyŏn'gun* ──────── Hŭngsŏn Taewŏn'gun ──
                恩信君   南延君   興宣大院君
                          └── 26. Kojong ──────── 27. Sunjong
                              高宗(1864-1907)   純宗(1907-1910)

*A sixth generation descendant of the Inp'yŏng Taegun, the third son of Injo; adopt to contin
the lineage of the already deceased Ŭnsin'gun in 1815.

Source: Ki-baik Lee, *A New History of Korea,* trans. Edward W. Wagner with Edward J.
Shultz (Seoul: Iljokak, 1984), pp. 387-94.

APPENDIX 3

CONSTITUTION OF THE DEMOCRATIC PEOPLE'S REPUBLIC OF KOREA*
April 9, 1992
(officially published on November 26, 1992)

CHAPTER 1. POLITICS

Article 1

The Democratic People's Republic of Korea is an independent social-ist state that represents the interests of all the Korean people.

Article 2

The Democratic People's Republic of Korea is a glorious revolution-ary power that opposes the imperialist aggressors and seeks the realiza-tion of national liberation and the freedom and happiness of the people.

Article 3

The Democratic People's Republic of Korea makes chuche ideology, a revolutionary ideology with a people-centered view of the world that aims towards the realization of the independence of the masses, the guiding principle of its actions.

Article 4

The sovereignty of the Democratic People's Republic of Korea rests with the workers, peasants, working intelligentsia, and all working people.

The working people exercise their sovereignty through their represen-tative organs—the Supreme People's Assembly and the local People's Committees at various levels.

Article 5

All state organs within the Democratic People's Republic of Korea are organized and operated on the principle of democratic centralism.

Article 6

From the County People's Committees up to the Supreme People's Assembly, each organ of power is elected on the principle of universal, equal and direct suffrage by secret ballot.

Article 7

Deputies for each organ of power have a close connection with the voters and are accountable to the electors for their activities.

Article 8

The Democratic People's Republic of Korea's socialist society is a people-centered social system in which the working masses are the masters of everything, and everything within society is geared to the working masses.

The state protects and defends the interests of the workers, peasants, and working intellectuals who, having been liberated from exploitation and oppression, have become masters of society and the state.

Article 9

The Democratic People's Republic of Korea strengthens the people's government and brings about the complete victory of socialism in the northern half through the execution of the three revolutions of ideology, technology and culture, while struggling for the realization of unification of the fatherland on the principles of independence, peaceful unification and grand national unity.

Article 10

The Democratic People's Republic of Korea is based upon the political-ideological unity of all the people which derives from the worker's league that guides the working class.

The state revolutionizes all members of society and imbues them with working class spirit by strengthening the ideological revolution, making the entire society into a single, unified group in a comradely way.

Article 11

The Democratic People's Republic of Korea carries out all its activities under the leadership of the Korean Workers Party.

Article 12

The state strongly defends the people's sovereignty and the socialist system from the destructive maneuvering of both internal and external hostile elements by maintaining the class line and by strengthening the people's democratic dictatorship.

Article 13

The state embodies the mass line and, in all its work, thoroughly implements the Chongsan-ri spirit and Chongsan-ri method in which the upper echelon assists the lower echelon, a means is sought by which to go within the masses and solve problems, and self-conscious enthusiasm is aroused by giving priority to work with the people.

Article 14

The state expedites the construction of socialism to the greatest degree possible by the energetic conduct of mass movements, such as the Movement to Win the Three Revolutions Red Flag.

Article 15

The Democratic People's Republic of Korea defends the democratic, national rights of overseas Koreans and their legitimate rights under international law.

Article 16

The Democratic People's Republic of Korea guarantees the legitimate rights and interests of foreigners within its territory.

Article 17

Independence, peace and friendship form the basic ideology of the DPRK's foreign policy and are the principles of its foreign activities.

The state establishes diplomatic as well as political, economic and cultural relations with all friendly countries on the principles of complete equality, independence, mutual respect, noninterference in each other's internal affairs and mutual benefit.

The state actively supports and encourages the struggles of people in countries that unite with all the peoples of the world that defend independence, oppose all forms of aggression and internal interference and work towards realizing independent sovereignty along with nationalist and class liberation.

Article 18

Laws of the Democratic People's Republic of Korea reflect the will and interests of the working people and are the basic weapon of state administration.

Respect for and strict abidance and enforcement of the law is mandatory for organizations, enterprises, groups and citizens at all levels.

CHAPTER 2. ECONOMY

Article 19

In the Democratic People's Republic of Korea, socialist production relations are based upon the foundation of an independent, national economy.

Article 20

In the Democratic People's Republic of Korea, the means of production are owned solely by the state and cooperative organizations.

Article 21

State property belongs to the whole people. There is no limit to the properties that the state may own.

All natural resources of the country, major factories and enterprises, ports, banks, transportation and telecommunications establishments are owned solely by the state.

The state places priority on protecting and expanding state property that plays a leading role in the economic development of the country.

Article 22

Property of collectively owned organizations is collectively owned by the working people involved in the cooperative economy.

Land, draft animals, farm implements, fishing boats and buildings, as well as small and medium factories and enterprises may be owned by cooperative organizations.

Article 23

The state raises the ideological consciousness and technology culture level of the peasants, increasing the guiding role played by property of the whole people as concerns cooperative property aimed at an organic synthesis of the two types of property. The state strengthens and develops the socialist cooperative economic system and gradually transforms the property of collective organizations into the property of all the people on the basis of the voluntary will of the entire membership.

Article 24

Personal property is property for personal use by the working people for the purpose of consumption.

The personal property of the working people derives from the socialist distribution according to work done and from additional benefits granted by the state and society.

Article 25

The Democratic People's Republic of Korea sets as its supreme principle of activities the unceasing improvement of the people's material and cultural life.

In our country, where taxes have disappeared, the endlessly increasing material wealth of society is returned in full to promoting the welfare of the working people.

The state provides the working people with all conditions necessary so that they may eat, dress and live.

Article 26

The independent national economy that has been created in the Democratic People's Republic of Korea forms a solid basis for a happy socialist life and for the independent development of the fatherland.

The state seizes the socialist self-dependent national economy construction line by expediting the development of chuche, modernization, and scientification of the people's economy to create a chuche economy in which the people's economy is developed to a high degree, while struggling to amass a material technical basis suitable for a complete socialist economy.

Article 27

The technological revolution is the basic link in developing the socialist economy.

The state always gives priority to issues of technological development in carrying out economic activities. It expedites science and technology development as well as the technological reconstruction of the people economy, strongly carrying out the technological innovation movement to free the working people from difficult and arduous labor and narrow the difference between physical and mental labor.

Article 28

The state, in order to eliminate the differences between urban and rural areas as well as class distinctions between the working class and peasants, expedites the technological revolution in the countryside to industrialize agriculture, enhances the role of the country and strengthens its guidance and assistance to the countryside.

Article 29

Socialism and communism are constructed according to the creative labor of the working masses.

Labor within the Democratic People's Republic of Korea is the independent and creative labor of the working people who have been freed from exploitation and oppression.

The state works to make the labor of our working people, who are ignorant of unemployment, more enjoyable, so as to make it worthwhile labor in which the workers work with conscious enthusiasm and creativity for society, the group and themselves.

Article 30

The working day is eight hours long.

The state may reduce the length of the working day depending upon the degree of difficulty and the special conditions for work.

The state works to ensure that working hours are fully utilized through the proper organization of labor and the strengthening of labor discipline.

Article 31

In the Democratic People's Republic of Korea, the minimum working age for citizens is 16 years old. The state prohibits work by children under the working age.

Article 32

The state, in its guidance and management of the socialist economy, firmly maintains the principle of properly integrating political and economic-technical guidance, the integrated guidance of the state and the creativity found at every unit level, unitary leadership and democracy, and political-moral and material incentives.

Article 33

The state directs and manages the nation's economy through the Taean work system, a form of socialist economic management whereby the economy is managed and operated scientifically and rationally on the basis of the collective strength of the producer masses, as well as through the agricultural guidance system whereby agricultural management is guided by industrial methods.

Article 34

The national economy of the Democratic People's Republic of Korea is a planned economy.

In accordance with the laws of economic development of socialism, the state develops and implements plans for the development of the national economy so that economic construction is expedited with a proper balance between accumulation and consumption, the people's living standards is steadily raised, and the nation's defense potential may be strengthened.

The state ensures a high rate of growth in production and a balanced development of the national economy by implementing a policy of unified and detailed planning.

Article 35

The Democratic People's Republic of Korea compiles and implements the state budget according to the national economic development plan.

Appendices

The state shall strengthen the struggle for increased production and economization in all sectors and shall enforce strict financial control so that the state can systematically increase state accumulation and expand and develop socialist property.

Article 36

External trade in the DPRK shall be conducted by the state or under the supervision of the state.

The state shall develop external trade under the principles of complete equality and reciprocity.

Article 37

The state shall encourage joint operation and joint venture enterprise between our country's agencies, enterprises and organizations and other countries' juridical persons or individuals.

Article 38

The state shall enforce tariff policy in order to protect the self-reliant national economy.

CHAPTER 3. CULTURE

Article 39

The socialist culture which is coming into bloom and developing in the DPRK shall contribute to enhancing the working people's creative ability and to meeting their sound cultural and mental demands.

Article 40

The DPRK shall thoroughly carry out the cultural revolution, lead all the people to become socialist and communist builders with deep knowledge of nature and society and of a high cultural, technological level and assimilate society into intelligentsia.

Article 41

The DPRK shall construct genuinely people-oriented, revolutionary culture which serves the socialist working people.

The state shall oppose the imperialists' cultural infiltration and restorationist tendency in constructing socialist national culture and shall preserve national cultural inheritances and inherit and develop them in conformity with socialist realities.

Article 42

The state eliminates the way of life that is a remnant of the old society and establishes the new socialist way of life in all fields.

Article 43

The state implements the principles of socialist pedagogy and brings up the rising generation to be steadfast revolutionaries who fight for society and the people, to be new communist men who are knowledgeable, virtuous and healthy.

Article 44

The state gives top priority to public education and the training of national cadres above all other tasks, closely blending general education with technical education and education with productive labor.

Article 45

The state develops a mandatory 11-year education system, including one year of preschool education, with high standards commensurate with trends in the development of modern science and technology and meeting the realistic demands of socialist construction.

Article 46

The state develops the education system for the regular system of education as well as various forms of education for those who study part-time while working, fostering capable technicians and experts by raising the scientific and theoretical levels of technical, social science and basic science education.

Article 47

The state educates all students at no cost and provides scholarships to students of colleges and professional schools.

Article 48

The state strengthens social education, guaranteeing all conditions necessary to allow the working people to study.

Article 49

The state brings up all children of preschool age in nurseries and kindergartens at the state's and society's expense.

Article 50

The state raises the nation's science and technology to international standards by establishing chuche in scientific research, actively accepting advanced science and technology and pioneering new fields of science and technology.

Article 51

The state properly establishes a science and technology development plan, establishes rules for its absolute execution, and promotes science and technology development of the country by strengthening the creative cooperation between scientists, technicians and producers.

Article 52

The state develops chuche-oriented and revolutionary literature and art, national in form and socialist in content.

The state creates conditions allowing writers and artists to create many works with high degrees of ideological and artistic qualities, as well as conditions under which a wide-spectrum of the masses may participate in literary and artistic activities.

Article 53

All workers are allowed by the state to enjoy a cultural and spiritual socialist life, providing them with adequate modern cultural facilities to meet the demands of people who continuously strive to develop themselves spiritually and physically.

Article 54

The state protects our language from all forms of stratagem aimed at destroying our national language, while also developing the language to meet modern needs.

Article 55

The state pursues a plan for making physical fitness available to the masses and part of everyone's daily lives so as to prepare all people for work and national defense and develops physical fitness technology commensurate with our nation's conditions and trends in modern physical fitness technology development.

Article 56

The state consolidates and develops the universal free medical service system, strengthens the district-doctor system, and promotes a policy of preventive medical care so as to protect lives and promote the health of the working people.

Article 57

The state sets environmental protection measures ahead of production, preserves and creates the natural environment, and creates a cultural and sanitary living environment and work conditions for the people by preventing environmental pollution.

CHAPTER 4. NATIONAL DEFENSE

Article 58

The Democratic People's Republic of Korea depends upon a nation-wide and state-wide defense system.

Article 59

The mission of the Armed Forces in the Democratic People's Republic of Korea is to defend the interests of the working people, defend the socialist system and the gains of the revolution from external invasion, and protect the freedom, independence and peace of the fatherland.

Article 60

The state pursues a self-reliant national defense line, built upon the foundation of arming all the military and all the people politically and ideologically, with arming all the populace, turning the entire country into a fortress, converting the entire Army into a cadre arm, and modernizing the entire army as its basic contents.

Article 61

The state will work to strengthen military discipline within the military as well as discipline of the masses, enhancing the traditional lofty virtue of unity between officer and enlisted and unity between the military and civilian populace.

CHAPTER 5. FUNDAMENTAL RIGHTS AND
DUTIES OF CITIZENS

Article 62

The Democratic People's Republic of Korea stipulates by law the condition to become a citizen according to citizenship.

Regardless of the residence of a citizen, he receives the protection of the Democratic People's Republic of Korea.

Article 63

In the Democratic People's Republic of Korea, the rights and duties of citizens are based on the collectivist principle of "One for all and all for one."

Article 64

The state effectively guarantees genuine democratic rights and liberties as well as the material and cultural well-being of all citizens.

In the Democratic People's Republic of Korea, the rights and freedoms of citizens increase with the consolidation and development of the socialist system.

Article 65

Citizens all enjoy the same rights in all spheres of state social life.

Article 66

All citizens who have reached the age of 17 have the right to elect and be elected irrespective of sex, race, occupation, length of residence, property status, education, party affiliation, political views and religion.

Citizens serving in the Armed Forces also have the right to elect and be elected.

Insane persons and those deprived by court decision of the right to vote are denied the right to elect and be elected.

Article 67

Citizens have freedom of speech, publishing, assembly, demonstration and association.

The state guarantees conditions for the free activities of democratic political parties and social organizations.

Article 68

Citizens have freedom of religious belief. This right also guarantees the right to building buildings for religious use, as well as religious ceremonies.

No one may use religion as a means by which to drag in foreign powers or to destroy the state or social order.

Article 69

Citizens are entitled to make appeals and submit petitions. Appeals and petitions must be looked into and dealt with by procedures and institutions stipulated by law.

Article 70

Citizens have the right to work.

All able citizens capable of working may choose occupations according to their desire and skills, and are guaranteed stable jobs and working conditions.

Citizens work according to their ability and receive remuneration in accordance with the quantity and quality of work done.

Article 71

Citizens have the right to rest.

This right is ensured by a system of working hours, a holiday system, paid leave system, sanitoriums and rest homes funded at state expense, and by an ever-expanding network of cultural facilities.

Article 72

Citizens are entitled to free medical care, and persons who have lost the ability to work because of old age, sickness or deformity, and old people and children with no guardians to watch after them have the right to material assistance.

This right is ensured by free medical care, a growing network of hospitals, sanatoria and other medical institutions and the state social insurance and security system.

Article 73

Citizens have the right to be educated.

The state guarantees this right through the advanced educational system and national education policy of the state.

Article 74

Citizens have freedom of scientific, literary and artistic activities.

The state grants benefits to inventors and innovators. Copyright and patent rights are protected by law.

Article 75

Revolutionary fighters, families of revolutionary and patriotic martyrs, dependents of People's Army personnel and disabled veterans enjoy the special protection of state and society.

Article 76

Woman are accorded equal social status and rights as men.

The state provides special protection to mothers and children through maternity leave, shortened working hours for mothers of large families, increasing the network of maternity hospitals, preschools, and kindergartens and other measures.

The state creates various conditions for the advancement of women in society.

Article 77

Marriage and the family are protected by the state.

The state pays great consideration to preserving the family, the most basic and underlying unit of society.

Article 78

Citizens are guaranteed the inviolability of the person and the home, as well as privacy of correspondence.

Citizens cannot be detained or placed under arrest and the home cannot be searched without any legal basis.

Article 79

The Democratic People's Republic of Korea protects citizens from other countries who have sought asylum after fighting for peace and democracy, national independence and socialism, or for the freedom of scientific and cultural pursuits.

Article 80

Citizens must defend political-ideological unity and cohesion.

Article 81

Citizens must obey the laws of the state and the socialist norms of life and must guard the honor and dignity of being a citizen of the Democratic People's Republic of Korea.

Article 82

Collectivism is the basis of social living within socialism.

Citizens must cherish their organization and collective and must demonstrate a character of devoting themselves to society and the populace.

Article 83

Work is the sacred duty and honor of the people.

Citizens must voluntarily and honestly participate in work and strictly observe labor discipline and working hours.

Article 84

Citizens must take good care of state and communal property, combat all forms of misappropriation and waste and run the nation's economy assiduously as befitting a master.

Article 85

Citizens must always raise their revolutionary vigilance and must struggle with all their efforts for the security of the state.

Article 86

National defense is a supreme duty and honor for citizens.

Citizens must defend the fatherland and serve in the military as stipulated by law.

Treason against the fatherland and its people is the most heinous of crimes, and those who betray the fatherland and its people will be punished severely in accordance with the law.

CHAPTER 6. STATE INSTITUTIONS

Section 1. The Supreme People's Assembly

Article 87

The Supreme People's Assembly is the highest organ of power in the Democratic People's Republic of Korea.

The permanent body when the Supreme People's Assembly is not in session is the Standing Committee of the Supreme People's Assembly.

Article 88

Legislative power is exercised by the Supreme People's Assembly and the Standing Committee of the Supreme People's Assembly.

Article 89

The Supreme People's Assembly is composed of deputies elected on the principle of universal, equal and direct suffrage by secret ballot.

Article 90

The term of office for the Supreme People's Assembly is five years.

Elections for the new Supreme People's Assembly are held in accordance with a decision of the Standing Committee of the Supreme People's Assembly prior to the expiration of the term of the current Supreme People's Assembly.

Article 91

The Supreme People's Assembly has the authority to:
1. Amend the constitution.
2. Enact or amend law and ordinances.
3. Approve laws adopted by the Standing Committee of the Supreme People's Assembly while the Supreme People's Assembly is not in session.
4. Establish the basic principles of domestic and foreign policies of the state.
5. Elect or recall the president of the Democratic People's Republic of Korea.
6. Elect or recall the vice president of the Democratic People's Republic of Korea on the recommendation of the president of the Democratic People's Republic of Korea.
7. Elect or recall the chairman of the National Defense Commission of the Democratic People's Republic of Korea on the recommendation of the president of the Democratic People's Republic of Korea.
8. Elect or recall the first vice chairman, the vice chairman, and members of the Democratic People's Republic of Korea's National Defense Commission on the recommendation of the chairman of the National Defense Commission.
9. Elect or recall the secretary and members of the Central People's Committee.
10. Elect or recall the secretary and members of the Standing Committee of the Supreme People's Assembly.
11. Elect or recall the committee chairmen, vice chairmen, and members of the specialized committees within the Supreme People's Assembly.
12. Elect or recall the president of the central court.
13. Appoint or remove the Procurator-General of the Central Prosecutor's Office.
14. Elect or recall the premier of the State Administration Council on the recommendation of the president of the Democratic People's Republic of Korea.
15. Appoint the vice premier, committee chairmen, vice chairmen, and

other members of the State Administrative Council on the recommendation of the premier of the State Administrative Council.

16. Approve the state plan for the development of the national economy and deliberate and approve reports on its implementation.
17. Approve the state budget and deliberate and approve reports on its implementation.
18. As necessary, receive project reports from the central state organs organized by the Supreme People's Assembly and establish counter-measures.
19. Decide whether to ratify or abrogate treaties presented to the Supreme People's Assembly.
20. Decide on questions concerning war and peace.

Article 92

The Supreme People's Assembly holds regular and extraordinary sessions.

The regular session is convened one or two times a year by the Standing Committee of the Supreme People's Assembly.

Extraordinary sessions are convened when the Standing Committee of the Supreme People's Assembly deems necessary, or at the request of over one-third of the total number of deputies.

Article 93

The Supreme People's Assembly needs more than two-thirds the total number of delegates to meet.

Article 94

The Supreme People's Assembly elects both its chairman and vice chairmen.

The Chairman presides over the session, and also represents the Supreme People's Assembly in international relations.

Article 95

Items to be discussed at the assembly are those submitted by the president of the Democratic People's Republic of Korea, the National Defense Commission of the Democratic people's Republic of Korea, the Standing Committee of the Supreme People's Assembly, the Central

People's Committee, the State Administrative Council and the commit- tees of the Supreme People's Assembly.

Deputies may also present items.

Article 96

The first session of the Supreme People's Assembly elects a Creden- tials Committee and based upon the report submitted by that committee, adopts a decision confirming the credentials of the deputies.

Article 97

The Supreme People's Assembly makes laws, ordinances, and deci- sions. Laws, ordinances, and decisions of the Supreme People's Assem- bly are adopted when over half of the deputies present give approval through a show of hands.

Article 98

The Supreme People's Assembly establishes necessary committees such as a Legislative Committee, Budget Committee, Foreign Affairs Committee, and a Unification Policy Committee.

Committees of the Supreme People's Assembly consist of chairmen, vice chairmen, and committee members.

Committees of the Supreme People's Assembly assist in the work of the Supreme People's Assembly by either drafting or deliberating policy and laws of the State and establishing measures for their implemen- tation.

Committees of the Supreme People's Assembly operate under the guidance of the Standing Committee of the Supreme people's Assembly when the Supreme People's Assembly is not in session.

Article 99

Deputies to the Supreme People's Assembly are guaranteed inviola- bility as such.

No deputy to the Supreme People's Assembly can be arrested without the consent of the Supreme People's Assembly or, when it is not in ses- sion, without the consent of the Standing Committee of the Supreme People's Assembly.

Article 100

The Standing Committee of the Supreme People's Assembly consists of the chairman, vice chairmen, secretary, and members.

The chairman and vice chairmen of the Supreme People's Assembly serve concurrently as the chairman and vice chairmen of its Standing Committee.

The term of office for the Standing Committee of the Supreme People's Assembly is similar to that of the Supreme People's Assembly.

Article 101

The Standing Committee of the Supreme People's Assembly has the following duties and authorities:

1. Examine and adopt bills and amendments to existing laws and ordinances that are presented when the Supreme people's Assembly is not in session, obtaining approval for these bills and amendments at the following Supreme People's Assembly.
2. In cases where new laws or amendments to existing laws are adopted, abolishes laws that may conflict with these.
3. Interpret current laws and ordinances.
4. Convene the session of the Supreme People's Assembly.
5. Conduct the election of deputies to the Supreme People's Assembly.
6. Work with the deputies to the Supreme People's Assembly.
7. Work with the Committees of the Supreme People's Assembly.
8. Organize the elections of deputies to the local people's assemblies.
9. Elect or recall the judges and people's assessors of the Central Court.
10. Conduct external work, to include work with Assemblies from other nations and with international parliamentary organizations.

Article 102

The Standing Committee of the Supreme People's Assembly adopts decisions and issues directives.

Article 103

The Standing Committee of the Supreme People's Assembly continues to carry out its mission until a new Standing Committee has been elected even when the term of the Supreme People's Assembly has expired.

Article 104

The Standing Committee of the Supreme People's Assembly is accountable to the Supreme People's Assembly for its activities.

Section 2. The President of the Democratic People's Republic of Korea

Article 105

The president of the Democratic People's Republic of Korea is the head of state and represents the Democratic People's Republic of Korea.

Article 106

The term of the president of the Democratic People's Republic of Korea is the same as that of the Supreme People's Assembly.

Article 107

The president of the Democratic People's Republic of Korea has the following duties and authorities:

1. Guide the Central People's Committee in its work.
2. Convene and guide the State Administrative Council as necessary.
3. Promulgate the laws and ordinances of the Supreme People's Assembly, the decisions of the Standing Committee of the Supreme People's Assembly, and important laws, ordinances, and decisions of the Central People's Committee.
4. Exercise the right of granting special pardon.
5. Promulgate the ratification or abrogation of treaties made with other countries.
6. Announce the appointment or recall of diplomatic representatives stationed in other countries.
7. Receive the letters of credence and recall of envoys from other countries.

Article 108

The president of the Democratic People's Republic of Korea issues orders.

Article 109

The president of the Democratic People's Republic of Korea is accountable to the Supreme People's Assembly for his activities.

Article 110

The vice presidents of the Democratic People's Republic of Korea assist the president in his work.

Section 3. The DPRK National Defense Committee

Article 111

The DPRK National Defense Committee is the supreme military guidance organ of the DPRK sovereign power.

Article 112

The DPRK National Defense Committee is composed of the chairman, first vice chairmen, vice chairmen, and members.

The National Defense Committee's term is the same as that of the Supreme People's Assembly.

Article 113

The chairman of the DPRK National Defense Committee commands and controls all the Armed Forces.

Article 114

The DPRK National Defense Committee has the following duties and rights:

1. Guide all Armed Forces of the state and Army building work.
2. Appoint and dismiss major military cadres.
3. Enact military titles and give military titles to military officials above the rank of general.
4. Declare a state of war and issue mobilization orders in an emergency.

Article 115

The DPRK National Defense Committee issues decisions and orders.

Article 116

The DPRK National Defense Committee takes responsibility for their work before the Supreme People's Assembly.

Section 4. The Central People's Committee

Article 117

The Central People's Committee is the DPRK president's supreme guiding organ.

Article 118

The head of the Central People's Committee is the DPRK president.

Article 119

The Central People's Committee is composed of the DPRK president, vice presidents, Central People's Committee secretary, and members.

The term of the Central People's Committee is the same as that of the Supreme People's Assembly.

Article 120

The Central People's Committee has the following duties and rights:
1. Map out state policies and devise measures to implement them.
2. Guide the work of the Administration Council, regional people's assemblies, and people's committees.
3. Guide the work of judiciary and prosecution institutions.
4. Guide state institutions' observance and application of laws and handles problems in executing laws.
5. Supervise the execution of the Constitution, decrees and decisions of the Supreme People's Assembly, decisions and instructions of the Supreme People's Assembly Standing Committee, orders of the DPRK president, and decrees, decisions, and instructions of the Central People's Committee; suspend the execution of regional people's committee decisions that contradict the aforementioned Constitution, decrees, decisions, and instructions; and abolish decisions and instructions of state institutions.
6. Establish or abolish committees and ministries of the Administra-

tion Council which are administrative executive institutions for different fields.

7. Appoint or dismiss vice premiers, committee chairmen, ministers, and other Administration Council members on the recommendation of the premier of the Administration Council when the Supreme People's Assembly is in recess.

8. Appoint or dismiss members of various committees under the Central People's Committee.

9. Ratify or abolish treaties signed with foreign countries.

10. Decide to appoint or recall diplomacy representatives based in foreign countries.

11. Institute orders and medals, titles of honor, and diplomatic positions and award orders, medals, and titles of honor.

12. Exercise the right to grant clemency.

13. Newly establish or change administrative districts.

Article 121

The Central People's Committee issues decrees, decisions, and instructions.

Article 122

The Central People's Committee can have under it necessary committees that help its work.

Article 123

The Central People's Committee takes responsibility for its work before the Supreme People's Assembly.

Section 5. The Administration Council

Article 124

The Administration Council is the supreme sovereign power's administrative executive organ.

The Administration Council works under the guidance of the DPRK president and the Central People's Committee.

Article 125

The Administration Council is composed of the premier, vice premiers, committee chairmen, ministers, and other necessary members.

The term of the Administration Council is the same as that of the Supreme People's Assembly.

Article 126

The State Administrative Council has the following duties and authorities:

1. Direct the work of each committee, ministry, and organization directly subordinate to the State Administrative Council, and local administrative and economic committee.
2. Establish or abolish organs directly under its authority.
3. Draft the state plan for the development of the national economy and adopt measures to put it into effect.
4. Compile the state budget and adopt measures to implement it.
5. Organize and carry out work in industry, agriculture, construction, transport, communications, commerce, trade, land management, city management, education, science, culture, health, environmental protection, tourism and other various fields.
6. Adopt measures to strengthen the monetary and banking system.
7. Conclude treaties with foreign countries and conduct external affairs.
8. Adopt measures to maintain social order, to protect the property and interests of the state and cooperative organizations, and to safeguard the rights of citizens.
9. Annul the decisions and directives of administrative and economic organs that run counter to the decisions and directives of the State Administrative Council.

Article 127

The State Administrative Council convenes both a plenary meeting and a permanent commission.

Article 128

The plenary meeting of the State Administrative Council discusses and decides on new and important problems arising in the state administration.

The permanent commission of the State Administrative Council discusses and decides on matters entrusted to it by the plenary meeting of the State Administrative Council.

Article 129

The State Administrative Council adopts decisions and issues directives.

Article 130

The State Administrative Council is accountable for its activities to the Supreme People's Assembly, the president of the Democratic People's Republic of Korea, and the Central People's Committee.

Article 131

The newly elected premier of the State Administrative Council, representing the members of the State Administrative Council, takes his oath before the president of the Democratic People's Republic of Korea at the Supreme People's Assembly.

Article 132

State Administrative Council committees and ministries are departmental executive bodies of the State Administrative Council. State Administrative Council committees and ministries issue directives.

Section 6. Local People's Assemblies and People's Committees

Article 133

The People's Assembly at the province (or directly administrated city), city (or district) and county is the local organ of power.

Article 134

The local People's Assembly consists of deputies elected on the principle of universal, equal, and direct suffrage by secret ballot.

Article 135

The term of office for local People's Assemblies at the provincial (or directly administered city), city (or district), or county level is four years.

Article 136

The local People's Assembly has the following duties and authorities:
1. Deliberate and approve the local plan for the development of the national economy and report on its implementation.
2. Deliberate and approve the local budget and report on its implementation.
3. Develop measures by which to enforce the laws of the state within the assembly's area if jurisdiction.
4. Elect or recall the chairman, vice chairmen, secretary, and members of the corresponding People's Assembly.
5. Elect or recall the chairman of the corresponding administrative and economic committee.
6. Appoint or dismiss the vice chairmen, secretary, and members of the corresponding administrative and economic committee.
7. Elect or recall the judges and people's assessors of the corresponding-level court.
8. Annul inappropriate decisions and directives of the People's Committee at the corresponding level and of the People's Assemblies and People's Committees at lower levels.

Article 137

The local People's Assembly convenes regular and extraordinary sessions.

The regular session is convened once or twice a year by the People's Committee at the corresponding level.

The extraordinary session is convened when the People's Committee at the corresponding level deems it necessary or at the request of a minimum of one-third the total number of deputies.

Article 138

Two-thirds or more of the total deputies must be in attendance for the People's Assembly to be held.

Article 139

The local People's Assembly elects its chairman. The chairman presides over the session.

Article 140

The local People's Assembly adopts decisions. Decisions of the local People's Assembly are announced by the corresponding People's Committee.

Article 141

The People's Committee of the province (or directly administered city), city (or district) or county is the local organ of power when the corresponding People's Assembly is out of session.

Article 142

The local People's Committee consists of the chairman, vice chairmen, secretary, and members.

Article 143

The local People's Committee has the following duties and authorities:
1. Convene the session of the People's Assembly.
2. Organize work for the election of deputies to the People's Assembly.
3. Work with the deputies of the People's Assembly.
4. Adopt measures to implement the decisions of the corresponding People's Assembly and higher-level People's Assemblies and People's Committees.
5. Direct the work of corresponding administrative and economic committees.
6. Direct the work of the People's Committees at lower levels.
7. Direct the work of organs, enterprises, and organizations within their corresponding area.
8. Annul inappropriate decisions and directives of corresponding administrative and economic committee and lower-level People's Assemblies and administrative and economic committees; suspend the implementation of inappropriate decisions of lower-level People's Assemblies.

9. Appoint or dismiss the chairman, vice chairmen, secretary, and members of the administrative and economic committee when the People's Assembly is not in session.

Article 144

The local People's Committee adopts decisions and issues directives.

Article 145

The local People's Committee continues to conduct its own duties even after the term of the corresponding People's Assembly has expired until a new People's Assembly is elected.

Article 146

The local People's Committee receives guidance from and is accountable for its activities to the corresponding People's Assembly as well as higher-level People's Assemblies and People's Committees.

Section 7. Local Administrative and Economic Committees

Article 147

The local administrative and economic committee of the province (or directly administered city), city (or district) and county is the administrative and executive body of the local organ of state power.

Article 148

The local administrative and economic committee consists of the chairman, vice chairmen, secretary, and members.

The term of office for the local administrative and economic committee is similar to that of the corresponding People's Assembly.

Article 149

The local administrative and economic committee has the following duties and authorities:

1. Organize and carry out all administrative and economic work within its given area.
2. Carry out the decisions and directives of the corresponding People's Assembly and People's Committee, as well as those of

higher-level People's Assemblies, People's Committees, and administrative and economic committees.

3. Draft the local plan for the development of the national economy and establish measures to implement it.

4. Compile the local budget and establish measures for its implementation.

5. Establish measures to maintain social order, to protect the property and interests of the state and cooperative organizations, and to safeguard the rights of the citizens in its given area.

6. Guide the work of the local administrative and economic committees at lower levels.

7. Annul inappropriate decisions and directives of the local administrative and economic committees at lower levels.

Article 150

The local Administrative and Economic Committee adopts decisions and issues directives.

Article 151

The local Administrative and Economic Committee is subordinate to higher Administrative and Economic Committees and the State Administrative Council.

Section 8. The Court and the Procurator's Office

Article 152

Justice is administered by the Central Court, the Court of the province (or directly administered city), the People's Court, and the Special Court.

Article 153

The term of office for the chairman of the Central Court is the same as the term for the Supreme People's Assembly.

Article 154

The chairman and judges of the Special Court are appointed or dismissed by the Central Court.

The People's Assessors of the Special Court are elected by the corresponding Servicemen and Employees Meetings.

Article 155

The Court performs the following duties:

1. Protect the sovereignty and socialist system of the Democratic People's Republic of Korea, the assets of the state and social cooperative organizations, and the constitutional rights, life and property of the citizens through judicial activities.
2. Ensure that all institutions, enterprises, organizations, and citizens strictly observe the laws of the state, opposing and actively struggling against all class enemies and law-breakers.
3. Render judgements and findings with regard to property and conduct notarial work.

Article 156

Justice is administered by courts consisting of one judge and two people's assessors. In special cases there may be three judges.

Article 157

Court cases are conducted publicly, and the accused is guaranteed the right of defense.

Hearings may be closed to the public as stipulated by law.

Article 158

Judicial proceedings are conducted in the Korean language.

Foreigners may use their own languages during court proceedings.

Article 159

In administering justice, the Court is independent, and judicial proceedings are carried out in accordance with the law.

Article 160

The Central Court is the highest judicial organ of the Democratic People's Republic of Korea.

The Central Court supervises the judicial activities of all courts.

The Central Court receives guidance from the Central People's Committee.

Article 161

The Central Court is accountable for its activities to the Supreme People's Assembly, the president of the Democratic People's Republic of Korea, and the Central People's Committee.

Provincial (or directly administered city) Courts and the People's Court are accountable for their activities to the appropriate People's Assembly.

Article 162

Investigation and prosecution are conducted by the Central Procurator's Office, the Procurator's Offices of the province (or directly administered city), city (or district) and county, and the Special Procurator's Office.

Article 163

The term of the Procurator-General of the Central Prosecutor's Office is the same as that of the Supreme People's Assembly.

Article 164

Procurators are appointed or removed by the Central Procurator's Office.

Article 165

The Procurator's Office exercises the following duties:
1. Ensure the strict observance of state laws by institutions, enterprises, organizations, and citizens.
2. Ensure that decisions and directives of state organs do not contravene: the Constitution; the laws and ordinances of the Supreme People's Assembly; the decisions and directives of the Standing Committee of the Supreme People's Assembly; the edicts of the president of Democratic People's Republic of Korea; the decisions and edicts of the Democratic People's Republic of Korea National Defense Commission; the decrees, decisions, and directives of the Central People's Committee; and the decisions and

directives of the State Administrative Council.

3. Defend the sovereignty and socialist system of the Democratic People's Republic of Korea, the assets of the state and social collective organizations, and the constitutional rights, life, and property of the people by exposing offenders of the law to include criminals and make them legally accountable for their actions.

Article 166

Investigation and prosecution are conducted under the coordinated leadership of the Central Procurator's Office. All procurator's offices are subordinated to their higher procurator's office and to the Central Procurator's Office.

The Central Procurator's Office receives guidance from the Central People's Committee.

Article 167

The Central Procurator's Office is accountable for its activities to the Supreme People's Assembly, the president of the Democratic People's Republic of Korea, and the Central People's Committee.

CHAPTER 7. NATIONAL EMBLEM, FLAG, AND CAPITAL

Article 168

The national emblem of the Democratic People's Republic of Korea has the design of a grand hydroelectric power plant under the sacred mountain of the revolution, Mt. Paektu, and a brightly beaming light of a five-pointed red star, ovally framed with ears of rice bound with a red band bearing the inscription "The Democratic People's Republic of Korea."

Article 169

The national flag of the Democratic People's Republic of Korea has a wide red panel across the middle of the banner, bordered above and below in sequence by a thin white stripe and a thick blue stripe. On the red panel near the staff is depicted a five-pointed red star within a white circle.

The ratio of width to length is 1:2.

Article 170

The state song of the Democratic People's Republic of Korea is the "aegukka" [national anthem].

Article 171

The capital of the Democratic People's Republic of Korea is Pyong-yang.

---

* This English text is from *On the Socialist Constitution of The Democratic People's Republic of Korea* (Pyongyang: Foreign Languages Publishing House, 1975) with minor editing by the present author.

APPENDIX 4

CHARTER (OR RULES) OF THE WORKERS' PARTY OF KOREA

The original charter of the Workers' Party of Korea (WPK) was adopted on 30 August 1946. For its full text in Korean, see *Pukchosŏn Nodong-dang Ch'angnip Taehoe* [Founding Congress of the North Korean Workers's Party] (Pyongyang: Pukchosŏn Nodong-dang Chungang Ponpu, n.d.), pp. 47-56.

The first revision of the charter was made on 30 March 1948 at the 2nd WPK Congress. For the complete Korean text, see *Pukchosŏn Nodong-dang Cheiech'a Chŏndang Taehoe Heuerok* [Proceedings of the Second Congress of the North Korean Workers' Party] (Pyongyang: Pukchosŏn Nodong-dang Chungang Ponpu, n.d.), pp. 191-213.

The second revision of the charter was made during 4-6 August 1953 at the sixth plenum of the 2nd WPK Congress. This revision was never made public.

The third, and very extensive, revision was made on 28 April 1956 at the 3rd WPK Congress. For the Korean and English texts, see Democratic People's Republic of Korea, *The Third Congress of the Workers' Party of Korea: Documents and Materials, April 23-29, 1956* (Pyongyang: Foreign Languages Publishing House, 1956), pp. 387-405; and Pak Chong-ae, "*Chosŏn Nodong-dang Kyuyak Kaechŏng e Kwanhan Poko*" ["Report on the revision of the Charter of the Workers' Party of Korea"] in *Chosŏn Nodong-dang Ch'ulpansa* [The Workers' Party of Korea Publishing House], *Chosŏn Nodong-dang Chesamch'a Taehoe Monhŏnjip* [Materials on the Third Congress of the Workers' Party of Korea] (Pyongyang: 1956), pp. 405-38.

The fourth revision of the charter was made on 18 September 1961 at the 4th WPK Congress. For the Korean and English texts, see *Pukhan Ch'onggam, 1945-1968* [General Survey of North Korea, 1945-68] (Seoul: Kongsankwŏn Munje Yŏnguso, 1968), pp. 672-768; and Robert A. Scalapino and Chong-sik Lee, *Communism in Korea* (Berkeley and

Los Angeles: University of California Press, 1972), 2:1331-49.

A fifth revision was made on 13 November 1970 at the 5th WPK, whose English text is found in Dae-sook Suh, *Korean Communism, 1945-1980* (Honolulu: University Press of Hawaii, 1981), pp. 524-44.

On 13 October 1980 at the 6th WPK Congress, the sixth revision was made, the full text of which is printed below. The English translation, with the present author's minor editing, is that of Tai-Sung An.

PREAMBLE

The Workers' Party of Korea is the *Juche*-type, revolutionary Marxist-Leninist party created by the great leader Comrade Kim Il Sung.

The great leader Comrade Kim Il Sung, who organized in 1926 the first anti-imperialist alliance within the framework of the Communist revolutionary organization, established the WPK on the organizational and ideological foundation for party building which was forged during his long anti-Japanese revolutionary struggle.

The WPK is the vanguard organization of the working class and the entire working masses of the Democratic People's Republic of Korea, and it is the highest form of revolutionary body among all organizations of the working masses.

The WPK represents the interests of both the Democratic People's Republic of Korea and the Korean people.

The WPK is organized with vanguard fighters from among the workers, peasants and working intellectuals who fight devotedly for the interests of the working masses and the victory of the great revolutionary tasks of socialism and communism.

The WPK is guided in its activities solely by the great leader Comrade Kim Il Sung's *Juche* ideology.

The WPK inherits and develops the glorious revolutionary tradition established by the great leader Comrade Kim Il Sung's anti-Japanese revolutionary struggle.

The WPK firmly opposes revisionism, dogmatism, and all kinds of opportunism and bourgeois ideologies that have been manifested in the history of the international Communist movement and labor movement.

The present task of the WPK is to ensure the complete victory of socialism in the Democratic People's Republic of Korea and the accomplishment of the revolutionary goals of national liberation and the people's democracy in the entire area of the country.

Its ultimate task is to imbue the entire society with the *Juche* ideology while, at the same time, establishing a Communist society throughout the country.

The WPK upholds its unitary ideological system as the basic principle, both in its daily work and in carrying out revolutionary tasks in the country.

The WPK strives to strengthen the ideological unity of its entire body on the basis of the *Juche* ideology.

The WPK strengthens the dictatorship of the proletariat and implements fully the *Ch'ŏllima* movement and the triple revolutions of ideology, technology and culture which constitute the general line of the party for the construction of socialism and communism.

The WPK heightens the leadership role of the working class and fights for the consolidation of the united front of all segments of patriotic, democratic forces behind the banner of worker-peasant alliance.

The WPK holds as its highest task to implement constantly the material and cultural life of the people.

The fundamental task of the WPK is to work with the people.

Upholding both the class line and the mass line is also the basic task of the WPK.

The WPK thoroughly upholds the *Ch'ŏngsan-ri* spirit and *Ch'ŏngsan-ri* method which derive from the glorious tradition of anti-Japanese revolutionary struggle in the pre-1945 era.

The WPK continuously implements the tasks of revolutionizing, communizing and intellectualizing the entire society and actively carries out the triple revolutions of ideology, technology and culture for the purposes of firmly building the material and technical foundations of socialism, strengthening the socialist system and ultimately achieving the final victory of socialism in the country.

The WPK develops the struggles for both expelling American imperialist forces from South Korea and frustrating the return of Japanese militarism to the Korean Peninsula; ardently supports the struggle of the

South Korean people for social democracy and independent national existence; and fights for a self-reliant, peaceful reunification of the fatherland in order to develop the unified development of the entire Korean people in every aspect.

The WPK cooperates with all socialist [Communist] countries of the world for the purpose of strengthening the international Communist movement based upon the principles of independence and proletarian internationalism; develops amicable relations with the newly developing countries of the world and their peoples; supports the anti-imperialist, national-liberation movements of the people of Asia, Africa, and Latin America and the revolutionary struggles of the working class and other people of capitalist countries against monopoly capitalism; opposes international capitalism and dominationism under the leadership of the United States by forming the broad anti-imperialist and anti-American front; and fights for peace, democracy, national independence, and victory for common struggles of socialist countries.

CHAPTER 1. PARTY MEMBERS

1. Members of the WPK are *Juche*-type, Communist revolutionaries who fight singlemindedly for the great leader Comrade Kim Il Sung, the fatherland, the people and the ultimate victory of socialism and communism.

2. Members of the WPK are composed of Korean citizens and workers who are armed with the party's unitary ideological system, defend the party line and decisions, fight for the realization of them and obey party rules.

3. Members of the WPK are recruited from among alternate members who have passed through the specified probationary term.

Under special circumstances, however, one may join the party as a regular member without going through the probationary term.

One may join the party on reaching the age of eighteen.

The admissions procedure is as follows:

a) One who is desirous of joining the party as an alternate member must submit to the party cell concerned a written application and the recommendations of two party members.

In case of the admission of a member of the Socialist Working Youth League of Korea, the recommendation of the city or county committee of the league can stand for the recommendation of a party member.

When an alternate member is admitted to the party, he (she) does not need to submit a formal application and recommendation to the party cell concerned.

When the party cell deems it necessary, however, it may demand a new recommendation.

b) The recommender must have a party standing of more than two years and know well the applicant's past and present social and political activities.

The recommender bears full responsibility to the party for the credibility of his (her) recommendation.

c) Admission to the party shall be conducted by individual enrollment. The admission to the party shall be discussed and decided upon at the general meeting of the party cell with the participation of the applicant, and the decision becomes effective when it is endorsed by the city or county party committee.

The presence of the recommender at the discussion of admission is not essential.

The city or county party committee must consider and act on the admission within a month after the decision of the party cell.

d) An application for admission from those who work under special circumstances is considered under special procedures and rules of the party Central Committee.

e) Admission to the party of a person who seceded, or was expelled, from another party requires the recommendations of three party members who have a party standing of more than three years.

Admission to the party of an ordinary member of another party shall be finally endorsed by the city or county party committee; that of one who was a member or a cadre of a city or county committee of another party by a provincial party committee; and that of one who was a member or a cadre of the central or provincial-level committee of another party by the party Central Committee.

f) The term of alternate membership is fixed for one year. The party cell shall concretely guide and assist the alternate member in becoming qualified for regular membership within the fixed term. Upon the expiration of the probationary term of an alternate member, the party cell shall consider and decide upon his (her) admission at a general meeting.

In special cases, admission to membership may be considered and decided before the alternate member's probationary term has expired.

When it is established that an alternate member is not fully prepared for admission, the general meeting can prolong the probationary term for another year.

When it is established that an alternate member having gone through the probationary term, is not fit for admission to the party owing to his (her) personal qualities, the general meeting of the party cell shall consider and decide upon his (her) expulsion.

g) Admission of an alternate member to regular membership or direct admission without a probationary term dates from the day when the general meeting of the party cell decides thereupon.

4. The duties of a party member are as follows:

a) A party member should stand firmly on the unitary ideological system of the party.

A party member should be boundlessly loyal to the great leader Comrade Kim Il Sung and the party and unconditionally accept, thoroughly defend and accurately implement party line and policies.

A party member should constantly study, preserve and defend the revolutionary tradition of the party by applying it to his (her) daily work and life.

A party member should fight against all antiparty and anti-revolutionary lines of capitalism, feudalistic Confucianism, revisionism, dogmatism, flunkeyism, factionalism, provincialism and nepotism that are prejudicial to the unitary ideological system of the party and should uphold the unity of the party based on the *Juche* ideology.

b) A party member should actively participate in the organizational life of the party, be trained in the party spirit, and revolutionize himself (herself) to become an active proletarian revolutionary among the working class.

A party member should actively participate in party meetings, study sessions, and the organizational and ideological lives of the party; carry out party decisions and assigned work of the party correctly; review his (her) party life daily; actively carry out ideological struggle through self-criticism; and transform himself (herself) into a revolutionary vanguard.

A party member should strictly observe the party charter that applies to all members, irrespective of rank and accomplishments and fight against violators of the party charter.

c) A party member should have revolutionary study habits and continuously raise his (her) political, ideological and cultural standards.

A party member should accurately grasp the *Juche* ideology and the party line, policies and tradition on revolution; keep abreast of contemporary situations; and make efforts to raise his (her) cultural standards by studying the problems of socialist economic management and advanced science and technology.

d) A party member should carry out the revolutionary mass line and must always work with the toiling masses. He (She) should constantly explain party line and policies to the masses, educate and organize them, unite them around the party and mobilize them for party work and meet their demands in time by correctly understanding them.

e) A party member should set an example for the masses in his (her) daily work and life and play the role of a vanguard in all works of the country.

A party member should have a higher standard of political awareness for himself (herself) and his (her) family, to set an example for the masses in carrying out the tasks of revolution.

A party member should love to work, voluntarily observe regulations, and set an example by taking on difficult work as well as assigned work.

A party member should fight against conservatism and negativism, actively participate in the technical revolutionary movement, raise the level of production, participate in the management of enterprises, actively endeavor to protect and multiply state and cooperative property and be frugal.

f) A party member should possess lofty Communist moral character, love his (her) organization and groups and sacrifice individual gains for the benefit of the organization.

A party member should bravely tackle all sorts of difficulties by displaying the lofty revolutionary spirit of self-reliance.

A party member should always be thrifty, humble, unselfish, frank before the party, humane and cultured and he (she) should set an example in observing national laws, social order and social morality.

g) A party member should defend the socialist fatherland.

A party member should always be alert and ready to be mobilized, learn about military affairs, defend revolutionary gains against enemy intrusions and be determined to participate actively in the great revolutionary task of reunifying the fatherland.

h) A party member should uphold orders of the revolutionary system, fight against indolence, hold high political vigilance at all times and strictly keep secrets of the party and state.

i) A party member should report problems arising from party work and party life to the party.

A party member should fight against shortcomings and negative tendencies not only in the phenomena prejudicial to the unitary ideological system of the party but also in general work and life, and should report them in time to party bodies of all levels up to the party Central Committee.

j) A party member should pay a determined amount of dues each month.

5. The rights of a party member are as follows:

a) A party member has the right to express constructive opinions in party meetings and in party publications for the purpose of achieving better results in carrying out party policies and doing party work.

b) A party member has the right to elect and to be elected to every leading party body at all levels.

c) A party member has the right to criticize any member in party meetings, when there are due reasons and grounds, and has the right to refuse any order prejudicial to the unitary ideological system of the party.

d) A party member has the right to demand personal participation in party meetings, at which discussions are held and decisions regarding his (her) activities and work are deliberated.

e) A party member has the right to request party bodies at all levels up to the party Central Committee to consider the petition he (she) has presented on any question.

f) An alternate member has the same duties and rights as those of a regular member, except the right to elect and be elected and the right to vote.

g) A party member who violates the party charter shall be punished by the party.

(i) A party member who acts prejudicial to the unitary ideological system of the party, forms factions in opposition to party line and policies, cooperates with enemies and seriously harms the party shall be expelled from the party.

(ii) A party member who has not committed an offense serious enough to warrant expulsion from the party may receive, depending on the gravity of the offense, a reprimand, warning or temporary suspension of rights in the party.

(iii) The aim of a reprimand lies in educating the party member who has committed the offense. In making decisions on the application of punishment, maximum caution and comradely consideration shall be exercised and the prime motive and cause of the offense shall be thoroughly investigated.

(iv) Appropriate punishment to be applied to a party member shall in principle be discussed and decided upon, with his (her) participation, at the general meeting of the party cell to which he (she) belongs. In special cases, the punishment can be decided upon without the participation of the member.

The party Central Committee and the provincial, city or county party committees can directly punish party members for violation of the party charter.

The decision of the party cell to punish a party member should be approved by the city or county party committee, and the decision of the party cell to deprive a party member of his (her) membership should be approved by the provincial party committee.

Except for special cases, a party member should be allowed to participate in party activities and the member's party card should not be withdrawn until the decision of the party cell is approved.

(v) The penalty for both regular and alternate members of the party Central Committee should be decided upon in the plenary meeting of the party Central Committee, and the penalty for both regular and alternate members of the provincial, city or county party committees should be decided upon in plenary meetings of the respective committees.

The party cell may submit its own views on the application of punishment to the higher party committees when members and candidate members of the party Central Committee, provincial, city or county party committees violate the party charter.

However, when the offenses committed by both regular and alternate members of the provincial, city, or county party committees have no direct relevance to the work of the respective committee, the party cell may decide on the penalty, up to a warning and such decision must be approved by the respective committee.

6. Investigation of party disciplinary problems of party members who participate in factions and other factional activities should be as follows:

The provincial party committee shall investigate members and officers of the city or county party committee, and the party Central Committee shall investigate members and officers of the provincial committee or the central party organs.

7. The party Central Committee and the provincial, city or county party committees should promptly investigate and solve problems related to party discipline requested by a member.

8. The party cell should always help punished members, and when such members recant and correct errors and reform themselves, the party cells should decide on the removal of the punishment at the general meeting.

The decision of the party cell to remove the punishment must be approved by the city or county party committee.

The removal of the punishment of both regular and alternate members must be approved by the respective committee that made the final decision.

9. For a party member who fails to participate in party activities for more than six months without such decision must be approved by the city or county party committee.

10. The registration and transfer of party members should follow the rules and procedures set by the party Central Committee.

CHAPTER 9. THE PARTY'S ORGANIZATIONAL PRINCIPLES AND STRUCTURE

11. The party is organized on the principle of democratic centralism.

a) All leading party bodies from the lowest to the highest shall be democratically elected, and the elected leading party bodies at all levels shall report their work periodically to the party organizations by which they were elected.

b) Party members are subordinate to the party organization, the minority to the majority, a lower party body to the higher party body, and all party organizations absolutely to the party Central Committee.

c) All party organizations should unconditionally support and carry out party line and policies, and the lower party organizations must execute dutifully the decisions of higher party organizations.

The higher party organizations shall systematically direct and supervise the work of lower party organizations, and the lower party organizations shall periodically report their work to higher party organization.

12. Every party organization is organized in accordance with regional or production units.

The regional party organization is the highest organization of all party organizations of the region, and the party organization in charge of party affairs that affect the entire region is the highest party organization in party work.

13. Every party committee is the supreme leadership organ and political general staff of each region.

Collective leadership is the guiding principle for each party committee's activity.

Each party committee must make decisions on the basis of collective discussion and decision and must execute the decisions effectively and efficiently by combining initiatives and responsibility.

Each party committee is autonomous in discussing and deciding its own local affairs. However, autonomous decisions upon local affairs should not be in conflict with party line and policies.

14. The supreme leadership organ of each party organization is as follows:

a) For the entire party, it is the congress; and between party congresses, it is the Central Committee elected by the party congress.

For the provincial, city or county party organizations, it is the party conference; and between party conferences, it is the respective party committees elected by the party conferences.

For the primary party organizations, it is the general meeting of the party cell or the party conference; and between general meetings of the cells or party conferences, it is the respective party committee elected by the general meeting of the party cell or the party conference.

b) Representatives to the party congress or the party conference shall be elected by the party congress or the party conferences of lower party organizations.

The ratio of elected representatives to the provincial, city or county party organizations is determined by the respective committee in accordance with the ratio established by the party Central Committee.

The number of both regular and alternate members of the party Central Committee is determined by the party congress.

The number of both regular and alternate members of the provincial, city or county party committees and the number of executive committee members of the primary party committees are determined by the respective party conferences or the general meetings of the party cells in accordance with the standards set by the party Central Committee.

Both regular and alternate members of the party Central Committee and the provincial, city or county party committees are elected from core members who directly engage in production work.

The election in each leading party organ is conducted in accordance with election rules set by the party Central Committee.

15. By-election or expulsion of both regular and alternate members of the party Central Committee and provincial, city or county party committees are conducted by plenary meetings of the respective party committees.

Vacancies in the membership of the party Central Committee and the provincial, city or county party committees shall be filled from alternate members of the respective party committees.

In special cases, vacancies in the membership of the party Central Committee and the provincial, city or county party committees may be filled by party members who are not alternate members of the respective party committees.

By-election or expulsion of members of leadership organs of the primary party organizations are conducted by the respective general meeting or conference of the party cell.

In case of the impossibility of convening the general meeting or conference of the party cell partly because the structure of the organs below the primary party organization is big and dispersed geographically or partly because of the special nature of their activities, the appropriate primary party committee may institute a by-election to fill in vacancies in members of leadership organs of the primary party organizations.

When there is a vacancy in the higher party organizations, the lower party committees may send their secretary to fill this vacancy.

Alternate members of every party organization may participate in the plenary meeting but may not vote.

16. The quorum for any party meeting is two-thirds of the regular and alternate members of the individual party organization, and the decision of the meeting is made by a simple majority of the members participating in the meeting.

17. Necessary departments may be set up in the party Central Committee and the provincial, city or county party committees.

The right to establish or dissolve such departments is vested in the party Central Committee.

18. The establishment and dissolution of any provincial, city or county party committees on the same level performing similar functions should be approved by the party Central Committee: The establishment and dissolution of primary party committees or sectional primary party committees should be approved by the provincial party committee. The establishment and dissolution of a primary party committee with a small number of members, a sectional party committee, and party cells should be approved by the city or county party committee.

The provincial, city or county party committees should report such establishments and dissolutions to the party Central Committee.

19. The party Central Committee may adopt decisions to dissolve any party organization that violates the party platform and the party charter or fails to carry out party policies, investigate members of such an organization individually or reorganize them under a new organizational setup.

20. For important regions under special political, economic, and military considerations, the party Central Committee may establish a separate organization, prescribe operational methods and decide on other problems of the party.

CHAPTER 3. CENTRAL ORGANS OF THE PARTY

21. The highest organ of the party is the party congress.

The party congress is convened once every five years by the party Central Committee.

The party Central Committee, when necessary, may convene earlier or later than the prescribed five-year period.

The party Central Committee shall announce the date and agenda of the party congress three months prior to the congress.

22. The functions of the party congress are as follows:
   a) To hear, discuss and approve the reports of the party Central Committee and the Central Auditing Committee;
   b) To amend or supplement the party platform and the party charter;
   c) To adopt party line and policies and the strategy and tactics of implementing them;
   d) To elect members of the party Central Committee and the Central Auditing Committee.

23. The party Central Committee directs the work of the party between party congresses.

The party Central Committee firmly establishes the unitary ideological system for the entire party, organizes and directs the party to carry out party policies, strengthens the rank and file of the party, directs and supervises the administrative and economic work of the party committees at every level, organizes revolutionary armed forces and enhances their fighting capabilities, represents the party in its external relations with other political parties within and outside the country and manages the finances of the party.

24. The party Central Committee shall convene a plenary meeting of its own at least once every six months.

The plenary meeting of the party Central Committee discusses and decides important issues of the party; elects the general secretary, secretaries and members of the Political Bureau and its Presidium; organizes the Secretariat of the Party; and elects members of the Military and Control committees.

25. The Political Bureau and its Presidium of the party Central Committee organize and direct all party work on behalf of the party Central Committee between plenary meetings.

The Political Bureau of the party Central Committee shall meet at least once every month.

26. The Secretariat of the party Central Committee periodically discusses and decides on the problems of cadres, internal problems of the party, and other tasks of the party, and supervises the execution of party decisions.

27. The Military Committee of the party Central Committee discusses and decides on the party's military policy and methods of its execution; organizes work to strengthen military industries, the people's militia, and all armed forces; and directs the military establishment of the country.

28. The Control Committee of the party Central Committee investigates members who commit antiparty, antirevolutionary factional activities and other activities prejudicial to the unitary ideological system of the party and who fail to observe the party platform and the party charter or violate other rules of the party. It also examines and settles cases appealed by individual party members and proposals from the provincial

party committees related to problems of party discipline.

29. The Central Auditing Committee shall audit the finances and accounting work of the party.

30. The party Central Committee may convene a party conference between party congresses.

The election procedures and ratio of representatives to the party conference are decided by the party Central Committee.

The party conference shall discuss and decide on urgent problems of policies, strategies and tactics of the party and shall expel those regular and alternate members of the party Central Committee who fail to perform their duties and elect new regular and alternate members.

CHAPTER 4. PARTY ORGANIZATION OF THE PROVINCES

31. The highest organization of the provincial party organization is the provincial party conference.

The provincial party conference is convened every three years by the provincial party committee.

When necessary, the provincial party conference may be convened earlier or later than the three-year period.

The provincial party committee must notify its subordinate organizations of the date and agenda of the party conference two months in advance.

32. The functions of the provincial party conference are as follows:

a) To review the work of the provincial party committee and the provincial control committee;

b) To elect members of the provincial party committee and the provincial control committee;

c) To elect representatives to the party congress.

33. The functions of the provincial party committee are as follows:

a) To organize and direct work to bring about the enthusiastic support of the unitary ideological system of the party by party members and the working masses.

b) To arm party members and the working masses with the unitary ideological system of the party; motivate them to support and carry out party line and policies thoroughly; fight against capitalism, feudalistic Confucianism, revisionism, dogmatism, flunkeyism, nationalism, provincialism and nepotism prejudicial to the unitary ideological system of the party; and protect the unity and consolidation of the party based upon the *Juche* ideology.

c) To strengthen the rank and file and auxiliaries, organize the forces of the party, assign rationally revolutionary tasks to the members, direct their party life and strengthen the organizational structure of its subordinate party organizations by supervising their activities.

d) To promote and strengthen the educational program for party members and the working masses, whose main subjects deal with the *Juche* ideology, the party charter, the glorious anti-Japanese revolutionary tradition and the class struggle. The main purposes of this educational program are to instill the virtues of communism and socialist patriotism in the minds of party members and the working masses and to consolidate their strength around the party by forging them into the revolution-conscious working class.

e) To strengthen the social organizations of workers and direct and supervise their work so that they can successfully carry out assigned work on their own and it performs a leadership role in administrative and economic works to assure successful completion of revolutionary tasks.

f) To strengthen the Worker-Peasant Red Guards, assure military mobilization and upgrade their strategic forces.

g) To manage the finances of the provincial party organizations and periodically report the financial situation to the party Central Committee.

34. The provincial party committee shall convene a plenary meeting at least once every four months.

The provincial party committee discusses and decides on the methods of implementing party line and policies, elects the general secretary and secretaries of the standing committee of the provincial party committee, organizes the secretariat and elects members of the military committee and the control committee of the provincial party committee.

Between plenary meetings of the provincial party committee, the standing committee of the provincial party committee supervises party works and other administrative, economic organizations' activities on behalf of the provincial party conference.

The standing committee of the provincial party committee shall meet at least twice per month.

The secretariat of the provincial party committee discusses internal party problems and cadre work and organizes and directs the implementation of decisions.

The military committee of the provincial party committee discusses and decides on military policy and organizes and directs its implementation.

35. The control committee of the provincial party committee investigates members who commit antiparty or antirevolutionary factionalist activities or other activities prejudicial to the unitary ideological system of the party and those who violate the party charter. It also approves decisions related to party discipline and expulsion of members submitted by the city and county party committees and resolves appeals from members on problems related to party discipline.

CHAPTER 5. PARTY ORGANIZATION OF THE CITY/COUNTY

36. The highest organization of the city/county party organization is the city/county party conference.

The city/county party conference is convened every three years by the city/county party committee. When necessary, the city/county party conference may be convened earlier or later than the three-year period.

The city/county committee must notify its subordinate organizations of the date and agenda of the conference two months in advance.

37. The functions of the city/county party conference are as follows:

   a) To hear, discuss and approve reports on the work of the city/county auditing committee;

   b) To elect members of the city/county party committee and the city/county control committee;

   c) To elect representatives to be sent to the provincial party committee.

38. The functions of the city/county party committee are as follows:

   a) To organize and direct work to bring about the enthusiastic support of the unitary ideological system of the party by party members and the working masses.

b) To arm party members and the working masses with the unitary ideological system of the party; motivate them to uphold the party line and policies thoroughly; fight against capitalism, feudalistic Confucianism, revisionism, dogmatism, flunkeyism, factionalism, provincialism and nepotism prejudicial to the unitary ideological system of the party; and protect the unity and consolidation of the party based upon the *Juche* ideology.

c) To strengthen the rank and file and auxiliaries by training and educating them systematically.

d) To direct the party life of the party members, strengthen and expand core members of the party, solidify the rank and file, constantly organize and direct recruitment of party members and educate both regular and alternate members of the party.

e) To promote and strengthen the educational program for party members and the working masses whose main subjects deal with the *Juche* ideology, the party charter, the glorious anti-Japanese revolutionary tradition and the class struggle. The main purposes of this educational program are to instill the virtues of communism and socialist patriotism in the minds of party members and the working masses and to consolidate their strength around the party by forging them into the revolution-conscious working class.

f) To strengthen the organizational structure of the lower party organizations and their core committees and make constant efforts to improve the functions and tasks of these lower party organizations.

g) To strengthen the social organizations of the workers and direct and supervise their work so that they can successfully carry out assigned work on their own.

h) To perform a leadership role in administrative and economic works to assure the successful completion of revolutionary tasks.

i) To strengthen the Worker-Peasant Red Guards, assure military mobilization and upgrade their strategic forces.

j) To manage the finances of the city/county party committee and periodically report the financial situation to the higher party Committee.

39. The city/county party committee shall convene a plenary meeting

at least once every three months.

The city/county party committee discusses and decides on the methods of implementing the party line and policies, elects the general secretary and secretaries of the standing committee of the city/county party committee, organizes the secretariat and elects members of the military committee and the control committee of the city/county party committee.

Between sessions of the party conference of the city/county party committee, the standing committee of the city/county party committee directs the organizational, administrative, and economic tasks on behalf of the city/county party conference.

The standing committee of the city/county party committee shall meet at least twice per month.

The secretariat of the city/county party committee discusses internal party problems and cadre work and organizes and directs implementation of its decisions.

The military committee of the city/county party committee discusses and decides on military policy and organizes and directs its implementation.

40. The control committee of the city/county party committee investigates members who commit antiparty or antirevolutionary factionalist activities or other activities prejudicial to the unitary ideological system of the party and those who violate the party charter. It also approves decisions related to party discipline and expulsion of members submitted by the party cells and resolves appeals from members on problems related to party discipline.

CHAPTER 6. BASIC PARTY ORGANIZATION

41. The basic organization of the party is a party cell. The party cell is the starting point of party life, and it is a fighting unit that carries out party line and policies by uniting the working masses around the party.

42. The methods of organizing the basic party units are as follows:

a) A unit with five to thirty party members organizes the party cell.

A unit with fewer than five regular and alternate party members may belong to the party cell of a neighboring unit, or two such units may form one party cell by taking into account the nature of their activities and geographical propinquity.

In special cases, a unit with fewer than five members or more than thirty members may organize a party cell.

A unit with fewer than three members may organize a small party unit with a chairman appointed by the city or county party committee.

b) A unit with more than thirty-one members shall organize a primary party committee.

c) A production or other functional unit with more than thirty-one members may organize a sectional party committee between the party cell and the primary party committee.

d) When it is not possible to organize a production or other functional unit with the organizational formula for a primary party committee, a sectional party committee or a party cell, such a unit may be organized as a subprimary party committee.

In case of extreme difficulty in following the above-mentioned methods of organizing basic party units, other appropriate types of basic party units may be established with the approval of the party Central Committee.

43. The highest organization of the primary party organization is the general meeting.

a) A general meeting of the party cell shall be convened at least once per month.

b) General meetings of the primary, sectional and subprimary party committees shall be convened at least once in three months.

A primary party organization that has more than 500 members, or whose units are widely dispersed, may convene a party general meeting once per year.

44. The primary party organization shall elect members of an executive organization with one-year terms.

a) The general meeting of the party cell shall elect a secretary and a deputy secretary.

b) Members of the primary party committee, the subprimary party committee, and the sectional party committee shall be elected by the respective general meeting, and the secretary and deputy secretary shall be elected by the respective party committee.

The primary, sectional and subprimary party committees, if necessary, may organize an executive committee.

The primary party committee shall convene its meetings at least three times per month; the subprimary and sectional party committees shall convene their meetings at least once per month; and the executive committees of the primary, subprimary and sectional party committees shall convene their meetings at least twice per month.

c) A party leadership committee may be organized in the primary party organization as one of its central organizations.

45. The duties of the primary party organization are as follow:

a) To make party members and the working class uphold firmly the unitary ideological system of the party, have them accept the system unconditionally and help them to carry out party line and policies correctly; to fight against capitalism, feudalistic Confucianism, revisionism, dogmatism, flunkeyism, factionalism, provincialism and nepotism prejudicial to the unitary ideological system of the party; and to arm party members and the working masses with the *Juche* ideology of the party to maintain and strengthen the solidarity of the party;

b) To systematically solidify the rank and file of the lower party organizations, build and train core members of the party and steadily strengthen and expand them;

c) To strengthen the party life of members and uplift their party spirit; to set up regular study sessions of the party charter, make them always conscious about the revolutionary tasks, assign them party work so as to play a vanguard role, conduct party meetings on a high level of political consciousness, understand fully the party life of members, forge them as revolutionaries, develop ideological struggle through self-criticism, investigate the mistakes of members and help them to correct their mistakes;

d) To find prospective party members, scrutinize and train them systematically and help newly recruited members and candidate members of the party;

e) To strengthen the ideological training work of party members and the working masses; to promote and strengthen the educational program for party members and the working masses whose main subjects deal with the *Juche* ideology, the party charter, the glorious anti-Japanese revolutionary tradition and the class struggle; and in so doing, to instill the virtues of communism and socialist patriotism in the minds of party members and the working masses and to consolidate their strength around the party by forging them into the revolution-conscious working class;

f) To accept humbly the opinions and demands of the working masses, solve their problems in time, improve the level of their material and cultural life, establish order and system in all administrative and production units and strengthen the fight against antirevolutionary elements;

g) To strengthen social organizations of the workers, point out the direction of their work; and lead them to carry out their duties correctly;

h) To apply the anti-Japanese guerrilla-warfare methods and the *Ch'ŏllima* movement and spirit to all party activities, put political work ahead of all other works and accomplish revolutionary tasks effectively by showing correct leadership in administrative and economic work; to direct party members and the working masses to carry out their revolutionary tasks faithfully, continuously revitalize production and construction, actively participate in the Three-Revolution Red Flag Movement and the competitive socialist movement, strengthen the technical revolution, increase labor production capabilities, strengthen labor regulations, uphold state laws and be thrifty with social and state properties;

i) To thoroughly strengthen the Worker-Peasant Red Guards; upgrade their ideological, political and military education; and prepare them for the call of the party;

j) To educate both regular and alternate members of the party, collect dues and regularly report activities to higher party committees.

CHAPTER 7. PARTY ORGANIZATION IN THE KOREAN PEOPLE'S ARMY

46. The Korean People's Army is the revolutionary armed forces of the WPK in the glorious tradition of the anti-Japanese armed struggle.

47. A party organization is organized in every unit of the Korean People's Army, and all party organizations within the Korean People's Army function under the direct guidance of the Korean People's Army party committee.

The Korean People's Army party committee's functions are similar to those of the provincial party committee.

The Korean People's Army party committee shall function directly under the party Central Committee, work under its direction and regularly report its activities to the party Central Committee.

48. The functions of every party committee within the Korean People's Army are as follows:

a) To educate and train the entire armed forces with the *Juche* ideology;

b) To make party members and soldiers of the Korean People's Army firmly uphold the unitary ideological system of the party and train and strengthen them as genuine revolutionary fighters who are willing to sacrifice their lives for the party, the great leader Comrade Kim Il Sung, the fatherland and the Korean people;

c) To strengthen party cadres among military officers, educate officers of military auxiliaries, organize and direct the party life of those members, preserve their link with the party and strengthen and enlarge party ranks;

d) To promote and strengthen the educational program for party members of the Korean People's Army, officers and soldiers whose main subjects deal with the *Juche* ideology, the party charter, the glorious anti-Japanese revolutionary tradition and the class struggle; and, in the process, to instill the virtues of communism and socialist patriotism in the minds of party members of the Korean People's Army, officers and soldiers and also consolidate their strength around the party by forging them into the revolution-conscious working class;

e) To strengthen the organization of the Socialist Working Youth

League of Korea in the Korean People's Army and direct members of the league to improve their fighting and revolutionary capabilities;

f) To strengthen party leadership in military works; to carry out military policy of the party and the *Juche*-oriented military strategy and tactics, arm the military with the revolutionary spirit of one against one hundred enemies, and further develop the Three-Revolution Red Flag Movement and the Red Flag Company Movement;

g) To maintain constantly a state of full alertness among party members of the Korean People's Army, officers and soldiers, as well as the invincible fighting capabilities among them;

h) To promote and preserve the noble revolutionary comradeship and the traditional spirit of unity among party members of the Korean People's Army, officers and soldiers.

49. Each party committee in the Korean People's Army operates in accordance with the directives and approved principles of the party Central Committee and the party charter.

50. Each party committee in the Korean People's Army should maintain a close working relationship with local party organizations.

With the approval of the party Central Committee, the Korean People's Army party committee may recommend political and military cadres to become members of the provincial, city or county party committees or the primary party committees where they are stationed.

CHAPTER 8. POLITICAL BUREAUS

51. The party Central Committee, when necessary, shall organize political bureaus in important sectors of the political, economic and military fields.

The Political bureaus organized in the central party organizations and other political bureaus direct the political and educational work of members and perform the function of an executive group of party committees in that unit.

The General Political Bureau of the Korean People's Army and its subordinate organs exercise the functions of a political unit of the appropriate party committee and direct the political work of party organizations within the Korean People's Army.

52. The General Political Bureau of the Korean People's Army and the political bureaus at each level belonging to the central party organizations work directly under the leadership of the party Central Committee and periodically submit reports on their activities to the party Central Committee.

53. The political bureaus of the central party organizations shall maintain close working relationships with local party committees when directing the work of the lower-level party organizations.

54. The political bureaus may convene party activists' conferences for the purpose of mobilizing members and the working masses to carry out party line and policies.

55. The political bureaus operate under the principles and directions approved by the party Central Committee and the party charter.

CHAPTER 9. THE PARTY AND ORGANIZATIONS
OF THE WORKING MASSES

56. The organizations of the working masses are political and supporting organizations of the party that inherit the glorious revolutionary tradition of the anti-Japanese guerrilla struggles.

The organizations of the working masses are ideological training organizations of the masses and the party's faithful helpers that tie the party to the masses.

The Socialist Working Youth League of Korea is the revolutionary organization of young people that directly inherits revolutionary tasks and is the party's fighting rearguard unit.

The organizations of the working masses operate under the direction of the party.

57. The organizations of the working masses consolidate the strength of their members around the unitary ideological system of the party, strengthen their members' party life and ideological work, unite their members around the party by revolutionizing them as the revolution-conscious working class, actively participate in the Three-Revolution

Red Flag Movement and the competitive socialist movement and direct-ly mobilize their members to the revolution and construction.

58. Each party organization must strengthen the rank and file of the working masses, establish the working system of the masses through organizations of the working masses, correctly devise methods for their activities in accordance with special characteristics of the masses and lead them to voluntarily participate in completing their duties.

CHAPTER 10. PARTY FINANCES

59. Party finances consist of dues from the members of the party, income from party organizations and party enterprises and other income.

60. Party dues of both regular and alternate members of the party are two percent of their monthly income.

APPENDIX 5

THE CONSTITUTION
OF THE REPUBLIC OF KOREA

Established on July 12, 1948
Promulgated on July 17, 1948
Amended on July 7, 1952
Amended on November 29, 1954
Amended on June 15, 1960
Amended on November 29, 1960
Wholly Amended on December 26, 1962
Amended on October 21, 1969
Wholly Amended on December 27, 1972
Wholly Amended on October 27, 1980
Wholly Amended on October 29, 1987

PREAMBLE

We, the people of Korea, proud of a glorious history and traditions from time immemorial, succeeding the orthodoxy of the Provisional Republic of Korea Government founded throughout March First Independence Movement of 1919 and the democratic ideal of April Nineteenth Noble Uprising of 1960 having protested against injustice, being based on the mission of democratic reformation and peaceful unification of homeland, have pledged:

To consolidate national unity with justice, humanity and brotherhood; to destroy all social evils and injustice;

To afford equal opportunities to every person and provide the fullest development of the capabilities of each individual in all fields, including political, economic, social and cultural life by further strengthening the basic order of free democracy with the autonomy and consonance;

To help each person discharge those duties and responsibilities concomitant to freedoms and rights; and

To promote the welfare of the people, strive for a lasting world peace, promote international prosperity and, thereby to ensure security, liberty and happiness for ourselves and our descendants forever.

We do hereby amend, through referendum after passing in the National Assembly, the Constitution, ordained and established on the Twelfth Day of July in the year of Nineteenth Hundred and Forty-Eight A.D., and amended eight times.

Oct. 29, 1987

CHAPTER 1. GENERAL PROVISIONS

Article 1

(1) The Republic of Korea shall be a democratic republic.

(2) The sovereignty of the Republic of Korea shall reside in the people, and all state authority shall emanate from the people.

Article 2

(1) The citizenship of the Republic of Korea shall be determined by law.

(2) The State shall have the duty to protect citizens residing abroad in accordance with the provisions of law.

Article 3

The territory of the Republic of Korea shall consist of the Korean Peninsula and its adjacent islands.

Article 4

The Republic of Korea shall seek unification and shall formulate and carry out a policy of peaceful unification based on the basic order of free democracy.

Article 5

(1) The Republic of Korea shall endeavor to maintain international peace and shall renounce all aggressive wars.

(2) the Armed Forces shall be charged with the sacred mission of national security and the defense of the land, and their political neutrality shall be observed.

Article 6

(1) Treaties duly concluded and promulgated in accordance with the Constitution and the generally recognized rules of international law shall have the same effect as that of the domestic laws of the Republic of Korea.

(2) The status of aliens shall be guaranteed in accordance with international law and treaties.

Article 7

(1) All public officials shall be servants of the whole people and shall be responsible to the people.

(2) The status and political impartiality of public officials shall be guaranteed in accordance with the provisions of law.

Article 8

(1) The establishment of political parties shall be free and the plural party system shall be guaranteed.

(2) Political parties shall be democratic in their purposes, organization and activities, and shall have the necessary organizational arrangements for the people to participate in the formation of the political will.

(3) Political parties shall enjoy the protection of the State and may be provided with operational funds by the State in accordance with the provisions of law.

(4) If the purposes or activities of a political party are contrary to the basic democratic order, the Government may bring action against it in the Constitution Court for its dissolution, and the political party shall be dissolved in accordance with the adjudication of the Constitution Court.

Article 9

The State shall strive to sustain and develop the cultural heritage and to enhance national culture.

CHAPTER 2. RIGHTS AND DUTIES OF CITIZENS

Article 10

All citizens shall be assured dignity and value of human beings and have the right to pursue happiness. It shall be the duty of the State to confirm and guarantee the fundamental and inviolable human rights of individuals.

Article 11

(1) All citizens shall be equal before the law, and there shall be no discrimination in all fields of political, economic, social or cultural life on account of sex, religion or social status.

(2) No privileged caste shall be recognized or ever established in any form.

(3) The awarding of decorations or distinctions of honor in any form shall be effective only for recipients, and no privileged status shall be created thereby.

Article 12

(1) All citizens shall enjoy personal liberty. No person shall be arrested, detained, seized, searched, interrogated except as provided by law, and be subject to punishment, preventive restriction and involuntary labor except by law and due process of law.

(2) No citizen shall be tortured or to be compelled to testify against himself in criminal cases.

(3) Warrants issued by a judge upon the request of a prosecutor in accordance with the due process of law shall be presented in case of arrest, detention, seizure or search. However, in case a criminal suspect is apprehended *flagrante delicto*, or where there is danger that a person suspected of committing a crime punishable by imprisonment of three years or more may escape or destroy evidence, investigating authorities may request an *ex post facto* warrant.

(4) All persons who are arrested or detained shall have the right to prompt assistance of counsel. When a criminal defendant is unable to secure counsel by his own efforts, the State shall assign counsel for the defendant as provided by law.

(5) No one shall be arrested or detained without given a notice about the reason therefor and the right to be assisted by a counsel. The reason for and time and place of arrest or detention shall be given without delay to the family, etc., as designated by law, of a person arrested or detained.

(6) All persons who are arrested or detained shall have the right to request the court to review the legality of the arrest or detention.

(7) In case a confession is determined to have been made against a defendant's will by means of torture, violence, intimidation, unduly prolonged arrest, deceit, etc., or in case a confession is the only evidence against a defendant, such a confession shall not be admitted as evidence toward a conviction nor shall punishment be meted out on the basis of such a confession.

Article 13

(1) No citizen shall be prosecuted for an act which does not constitute a crime under the law effective at the time it was committed, nor shall he be twice put in jeopardy of punishment for the same crime.

(2) No restrictions shall be imposed upon the political rights of any citizen, nor shall any person be deprived of property rights by means of retroactive legislation.

(3) No citizen shall suffer unfavorable treatment on account of an act not of his own doing but committed by a relative.

Article 14

All citizens shall enjoy freedom of residence and moving.

Article 15

All citizens shall enjoy freedom of choice of occupation.

Article 16

No citizen shall be subject to violation of freedom of residence. In case of seizure or search in a residence, a warrant issued by a judge upon request of a prosecutor shall be presented.

Article 17

No citizen shall be subject to violation of the secrecy and freedom of privacy.

Article 18

No citizen shall be subject to violation of the secrecy of any means of communication.

Article 19

All citizens shall enjoy freedom of conscience.

Article 20

(1) All citizens shall enjoy freedom of religion.

(2) No State religion shall be recognized, and religion and politics shall be separated.

Article 21

(1) All citizens shall enjoy freedom of speech and the press, and freedom of assembly and association.

(2) Licensing or censorship of speech and the press, and licensing of assembly and association shall not be allowed.

(3) The equipment standard of communication and broadcasting and the necessary matters for the guarantee of the function of newspapers shall be provided by law.

(4) Neither speech nor the press shall violate the honor or rights of other persons, or undermine public morals or social ethics. Should speech or the press violate the honor or rights of the other persons, claims may be made for the damage resulting therefrom.

Article 22

(1) All citizens shall enjoy freedom of learning and the arts.

(2) The rights of authors, inventors, scientists, technical experts and artists shall be protected by law.

Article 23

(1) The right of property of all citizens shall be guaranteed. The contents and limitations thereof shall be determined by law.

(2) The exercise of property rights shall conform to the public welfare.

(3) Expropriation, use or restriction of private property for public necessity and the compensation thereof shall fit the law, and the just compensation shall be paid.

Article 24

All citizens shall have the right to vote in accordance with the provisions of law.

Article 25

All citizens shall have the right to hold public office in accordance with the provisions of law.

Article 26

(1) All citizens shall have the right to petition in writing any State organization in accordance with the provisions of law.

(2) The State shall be obligated to examine all such petitions.

Article 27

(1) All citizens shall have the right to be tried in conformity with the law by judges qualified under the Constitution and the law.

(2) Citizens who are not on active military service or employees of the military forces shall not be tried by a court martial in the territory of the Republic of Korea, except in the case of crimes involving important classified military information, sentinels, sentry-ports, the supply of harmful food, prisoners of war, and military articles as defined by law; and except when extraordinary martial law has been declared.

(3) All citizens shall have the right to a speedy trial. A criminal defendant shall have the right to a public trial without delay in the absence of justifiable reasons to the contrary.

(4) The criminal defendant shall be presumed innocent until a determination of guilt has been confirmed.

(5) The criminal victim shall be entitled to defense in the trial process for the concerned case in accordance with the provisions of law.

Article 28

In case the criminal suspect or defendant under detention is nonprosecuted or acquitted as provided by law, he shall be entitled to claim against the State for just compensation in accordance with the provisions of law.

Article 29

(1) In case a person has sustained damages by unlawful acts of public officials done in the course of their official duties, he may make a claim against the State or public agency for just compensation in accordance with the provisions of law. In this case, the public officials concerned shall not be immune from liabilities.

(2) In case a person on active military service, an employee of the military forces, a police official or others as defined by law sustains damages in connection with the performance of official duties such as combat action, drill and so forth, he shall not be entitled to a claim against the State or public agency on the grounds of unlawful acts of public officials done in the course of official duties, except for compensation as provided by law.

Article 30

Any person aggrieved in life or body by others' criminal act may be relieved by State in accordance with the provisions of law.

Article 31

(1) All citizens shall have the right to receive an equal education corresponding to their abilities.

(2) All citizens who have children to support shall be responsible at least for their elementary education and other education as provided by law.

(3) Compulsory education shall be free.

(4) Independence, professionalism or political impartiality of education and academic autonomy shall be guaranteed in accorded with the provisions of law.

(5) The State shall promote lifelong education.

(6) Fundamental matters pertaining to the educational system, including in-school and lifelong education, administration, finance, and the status of teachers shall be determined by law.

Article 32

(1) All citizens shall have the right to work. The State shall endeavor to promote the employment of workers and to guarantee optimum wages

through social and economic means, and put in force the minimum wage system in accordance with the provisions of law.

(2) All citizens shall have the duty to work. The State shall determine the contents and conditions of the duty to work by law in conformity with democratic principles.

(3) Standards of working conditions shall be determined by law in such a way as to guarantee human dignity.

(4) Special protection shall be given to labor of women, and women shall not be discriminated in employment, wage and labor conditions.

(5) Labor of youth shall be specially protected.

(6) The opportunity to work shall be accorded preferentially to members of the bereaved families of those who have given distinguished service to the State, wounded veterans and policemen, and military servicemen and policemen killed in action in accordance with the provisions of law.

Article 33

(1) To enhance working conditions, workers shall have the right to independent association, collective bargaining and collective action.

(2) Workers, who are public officials, shall have the right to association, collective bargaining and collective action only when designated by law.

(3) The right to collective action of the workers who are engaged in important defense industry designated by law may be restricted or denied as provided by law.

Article 34

(1) All citizens shall have the right to a life worthy of human beings.

(2) The State shall have the duty to endeavor at promotion of social security and social welfare.

(3) The State shall endeavor to promote the welfare and rights of women.

(4) The State shall have duty to put in force the policy for promotion of welfare for the youth and the old.

(5) The disabled and citizens who are incapable of earning a livelihood for illness or old age shall be protected by the State as provided by law.

(6) The State shall endeavor to prevent calamities and to protect citizens from the danger thereof.

Article 35

(1) All citizens shall have the right to live in a healthy and comfortable environment, and both the State and citizens shall endeavor to preserve the environment.

(2) Contents and exercise of the environmental right shall be provided by law.

(3) The State shall endeavor to provide citizens a comfortable residence through housing projects, etc.

Article 36

(1) Marriage and family life shall be entered into and sustained on the basis of individual dignity and equality of the sexes, and the State shall guarantee it.

(2) The State shall endeavor to protect maternity.

(3) The health of all citizens shall be protected by the State.

Article 37

(1) Freedoms and rights of citizens shall not be neglected on the grounds that they are not enumerated in the Constitution.

(2) The freedoms and rights of citizens may be restricted by law only when necessary for national security, the maintenance of public order or public welfare. Even when such restriction is imposed, no essentials of the freedom or right shall be violated.

Article 38

All citizens shall have the duty to pay taxes in accordance with the provisions of law.

Article 39

(1) All citizens have the duty to defend the nation in accordance with the provisions of law.

(2) No citizen shall be discriminated against on account of fulfilling his obligation of military service.

CHAPTER 3. THE NATIONAL ASSEMBLY

Article 40

Legislative power shall be vested in the National Assembly.

Article 41

(1) The National Assembly shall be composed of members elected by universal, equal, direct and secret ballot by the citizens.

(2) The number of members of the National Assembly shall be determined by law, but the number shall be more than 200.

(3) The electoral districts of members of the National Assembly, proportional representation and other matters pertaining to National Assembly elections shall be determined by law.

Article 42

The term of office for members of the National Assembly shall be four years.

Article 43

Members of the National Assembly shall not concurrently hold any other office prescribed by law.

Article 44

(1) During the sessions of the National Assembly, no member of the National Assembly shall be arrested or detained without the consent of the National Assembly except in case of *flagrante delicto.*

(2) In case of apprehension or detention of a member of the National Assembly prior to the opening of a session, such member shall be released during the session upon the request of the National Assembly, except in case of *flagrante delicto.*

Article 45

No member of the National Assembly shall be held responsible outside the National Assembly for opinions officially expressed or votes cast in the Assembly.

Article 46

(1) Members of the National Assembly shall maintain high standards of integrity.

(2) Members of the National Assembly shall give preference to national interests and shall perform their duties in accordance with conscience.

(3) Members of the National Assembly shall not, through abuse of their positions, acquire rights and interests in property or position, or cause other persons to acquire the same, by means of contracts with or dispositions by the State, public agencies or industries.

Article 47

(1) A regular session of the National Assembly shall be convened once every year in accordance with the provisions of law, and extraordinary sessions of the National Assembly shall be convened upon the request of the President or one-fourth or more of the members on the register.

(2) The period of regular sessions shall not exceed one hundred days and of extraordinary sessions thirty days.

(3) If the President requests the convening of an extraordinary session, the period of the session and the reasons for the request shall be clearly specified.

Article 48

The National Assembly shall elect one Speaker and two Vice-Speakers.

Article 49

Unless otherwise provided for in the Constitution or in law, the attendance of a majority of the members on the register, and the concurrence of a majority of the members present, shall be necessary for decisions of the National Assembly. In case of a tie vote, the matter shall be regarded as rejected by the National Assembly.

Article 50

(1) Sessions of the National Assembly shall be open to the public. However, they may be closed to the public when so decided by a majority of the members present, or when the Speaker deems it necessary to do so for the sake of national security.

(2) Publication of contents of sessions which are not open to the public shall follow the provisions of law.

Article 51

Bills and other matters submitted to the National Assembly for deliberation shall not be abandoned on the ground that they were not acted upon during the session in which they were introduced. However, it shall be otherwise in case the term of the members of the National Assembly has expired.

Article 52

Bills may be introduced by members of the National Assembly or by the Executive.

Article 53

(1) Each bill passed by the National Assembly shall be sent to the Executive and the President shall promulgate it within fifteen days.

(2) In case of objection to the bill, the President may, within the period referred to in Paragraph 1, return it to the National Assembly with written explanation of his objection, and request it be reconsidered. The President may do the same during adjournment of the National Assembly.

(3) The President shall not request the National Assembly to reconsider the bill in part, or with proposed amendments.

(4) In case there is a request for reconsideration of a bill, the National Assembly shall reconsider it, and if the National Assembly repasses the bill in the original form with the attendance of more than one-half of the members on the register, and with concurrence of two-thirds or more of the members present, the bill shall become law.

(5) If the President does not promulgate the bill, or does not request the National Assembly to reconsider it within the period referred to in Paragraph 1, the bill shall become law.

(6) The President shall without delay promulgate the law as determined in accordance with the foregoing Paragraphs 4 and 5. If the President does not promulgate a law within five days after the law has been determined under Paragraph 5, or after the law determined has been returned to the Executive under Paragraph 4, the Speaker shall promulgate it.

(7) A law shall take effect twenty days after the date of promulgation unless otherwise provided.

Article 54

(1) The National Assembly shall deliberate and decide upon the national budget bill.

(2) The Executive shall formulate the budget bill for each fiscal year and submit it to the National Assembly within ninety days before the beginning of a fiscal year. The National Assembly shall decide upon it within thirty days before the beginning of the fiscal year.

(3) If the budget bill is not passed by the beginning of the new fiscal year, the Executive may, in conformity with the budget of the previous fiscal year, disburse funds for the following purposes until the budget bill is passed by the National Assembly:

1. The maintenance and operation of agencies and institutions established by the Constitution or law;
2. Execution of the obligatory expenditures provided by law; and
3. Continuation of projects previously approved in the budget.

Article 55

(1) In case it shall be necessary to make continuing disbursements for a period longer than one fiscal year, the Executive shall determine the length of the period for such continuing disbursements and obtain the approval of the National Assembly for the continuing disbursements.

(2) A reserve fund shall be approved by the National Assembly in total. The disbursement of the reserve fund shall be approved during the subsequent session of the National Assembly.

Article 56

When it is necessary to amend the budget, the Executive may formulate a supplementary revised budget bill and submit it to the National Assembly.

Article 57

The National Assembly shall, without the consent of the Executive, neither increase the sum of any item of expenditure nor create any new items in the budget submitted by the Executive.

Article 58

When the Executive plans to issue national bonds or to conclude contracts which may incur financial obligations on the State outside the budget, it shall have the prior concurrence of the National Assembly.

Article 59

Items and rates of taxes shall be determined by law.

Article 60

(1) The National Assembly shall have power to consent to the conclusion and ratification of treaties pertaining to mutual assistance or mutual security; treaties concerning important international organizations; treaties of friendship, trade and navigation; treaties pertaining to any restriction in sovereignty; peace treaties; treaties which will burden the State or people with an important financial obligation; or treaties related to legislative affairs.

(2) The National Assembly shall have power to consent to the declaration of war, the dispatch of armed forces to foreign states, or the stationing of alien forces in the territory of the Republic of Korea.

Article 61

(1) The National Assembly may inspect affairs of state or investigate specific matters of state affairs, and may demand the production of documents, the attendance of a witness and the statement of testimony or opinions necessary thereto.

(2) The procedure and other necessary matters for the parliamentary inspection and investigation shall be provided by law.

Article 62

(1) The Prime Minister, members of the State Council or government delegates may attend meetings of the National Assembly or its committees and report on the state of administration or deliver opinions and answer questions.

(2) When requested by the National Assembly or its committees, the Prime Minister, members of the State Council or government delegates shall attend any meeting of the National Assembly and answer questions. If the Prime Minister or State Council members are requested to

attend, the Prime Minister or State Council members may have State Council members or government delegates attend any meeting of the National Assembly and answer questions.

Article 63

(1) The National Assembly may recommend to the President the removal of the Prime Minister or a State Council member.

(2) A recommendation for removal prescribed in Paragraph 1 may be proposed by one-third or more of the members on the register of the National Assembly, and shall be passed with the concurrence of a majority of the members on the register of the National Assembly.

Article 64

(1) The National Assembly may establish the rules of its proceedings and internal regulations, provided that they are not in conflict with law.

(2) The National Assembly may review the qualifications of its members and may take disciplinary actions against its members.

(3) The concurrence of two-thirds or more of the members on the register of the National Assembly shall be required for the expulsion of any member.

(4) No action shall be brought to court with regard to decisions taken under Paragraphs 2 and 3.

Article 65

(1) In case the President, the Prime Minister, members of the State Council, Heads of Executive Ministries, judges of the Constitution Court, judges, members of the Central Election Management Committee, The Chairman and commissioners of the Board of Audit and Inspection, and other public officials designated by law have violated the Constitution or other laws in the performance of their duties, the National Assembly may pass motions for their impeachment.

(2) A motion for impeachment prescribed in Paragraph 1 shall be proposed by one-third or more of the members on the register of the National Assembly, and shall require concurrence of a majority of the members on the register of the National Assembly for passage. However, a motion for the impeachment of the President shall be proposed by a majority of the members on the register of the National Assembly,

and shall require the concurrence of two-thirds or more of the members on the register of the National Assembly.

(3) Any person against whom a motion for impeachment has been passed shall be suspended from exercising his power until the impeachment has been adjudicated.

(4) A decision on impeachment shall not extend further than removal from office. However, it shall not exempt the person impeached from civil or criminal liability.

CHAPTER 3. THE EXECUTIVE

Section 1. The President

Article 66

(1) The President shall be the head of State and represent the State in relations with foreign states.

(2) The President shall have the responsibility and duty to safeguard the independence, territorial integrity and continuity of the State and the Constitution.

(3) The President shall have the duty to pursue sincerely the peaceful unification of the homeland.

(4) The executive power shall be vested in the Executive Branch headed by the President.

Article 67

(1) The President shall be elected by universal, equal, direct and secret ballot by the citizens.

(2) In case the candidates who have gained the largest numbers of votes in the ballot prescribed in Paragraph 1 are two or more, the person who polls a majority in the open session attended by more than half of the members on the register of the National Assembly shall be elected.

(3) In case the candidate for the President is single, he shall not be elected as President unless he obtains one-third or more of the votes of the whole electorates.

(4) Citizens who are eligible for election to the National Assembly and

who, as of the day of the presidential election, shall have reached the age of forty years or more, shall be eligible to be elected to the presidency.

(5) Matters pertaining to presidential election shall be determined by law.

Article 68

(1) At the expiration of the term of office of the President, a successor shall be elected between forty and seventy days before the term of office of the incumbent President expires.

(2) In case of vacancy in the office of the President, death of the elected or disqualification due to judgement and other causes, a successor shall be elected within sixty days.

Article 69

The President, at the time of his inauguration, shall take the following oath: "I do solemnly swear before the people that, by observing the Constitution, defending the State, and endeavoring to unify the homeland peacefully and to promote the freedom and welfare of the people, and national culture, I will faithfully execute the duties of the President."

Article 70

The term of office of the President shall be five years, and no person shall be elected to the office of the President more than once.

Article 71

In case of a vacancy in the office of the President, or of his inability to discharge the powers and duties of the presidency, the Prime Minister or the members of the State Council in the order of priority as determined by law shall act as the President.

Article 72

The President may submit important policies relating to diplomacy, national defense, unification and other matters relating to the national destiny to a national referendum if he deems it necessary.

Article 73

The President shall conclude and ratify treaties; accredit, receive or dispatch diplomatic envoys; and declare war and conclude peace.

Article 74

(1) The President shall be Commander-in-Chief of the National Armed Forces in accordance with the provisions of the Constitution and law.

(2) The organization and formation of the National Armed Forces shall be provided by law.

Article 75

The President may issue presidential decrees concerning matters which are within the scope specially delegated by law and which are deemed necessary to enforce the law.

Article 76

(1) In case that prompt measures are needed for national security or maintenance of public order in troubles both at home and abroad, natural calamities or financial and economic crises, and there is no time to convene the National Assembly, the President may take necessary financial or economic measures within the minimum extent or issue decrees thereon having the full force and effect of a law.

(2) In case that prompt measures are needed for national defense in serious state of war relating to the destiny of the State, and the convening of the National Assembly is impossible, the President may issue decrees having the full force and effect of a law.

(3) In case the decrees are issued or the measures taken as prescribed by Paragraphs 1 and 2, the President shall notify the National Assembly thereof without delay and shall obtain the consent of the National Assembly.

(4) In case the decree and measure fail to obtain the consent of the National Assembly, as prescribed by Paragraph 3, the decrees and measures shall lose effect forthwith. In this case, the law amended or abrogated by the decree shall recover the effect naturally from the time the decree fails to obtain the consent.

(5) The President shall publish the reason for Paragraphs 3 and 4 without delay.

Article 77

(1) When there is a military necessity or a necessity to maintain the public safety and order by mobilization of the military forces in time of war, armed conflict or similar national emergency, the President may proclaim martial law in accordance with the provisions of law.

(2) Martial law shall be of two types, extraordinary martial law and precautionary martial law.

(3) Under extraordinary martial law, special measures may be taken, as provided by law, with respect to the warrant system, freedom of speech, press, assembly and association and with respect to the powers of the Executive and the Judiciary.

(4) When martial law is proclaimed, the President shall notify the National Assembly thereof without delay.

(5) The President shall lift martial law when the National Assembly so requests with the consent of a majority of the members on the register of the National Assembly.

Article 78

The President shall appoint and remove public officials in accordance with the provisions of the Constitution and law.

Article 79

(1) The President may grant amnesty, commutation and restoration of rights in accordance with the provisions of law.

(2) The President shall receive the consent of the National Assembly in granting a general amnesty.

(3) Matters pertaining to amnesty, commutation and restoration of rights shall be determined by law.

Article 80

The President shall award decorations and other honors in accordance with the provisions of law.

Article 81

The President may attend and address the National Assembly or express his views by written message.

Article 82

The acts of the President performed in accordance with law shall be executed by written document, and such documents shall be countersigned by the Prime Minister and the members of the State Council concerned. The same shall apply to military affairs.

Article 83

The President shall not concurrently hold the office of Prime Minister, a member of the State Council, the head of any Executive Ministry, or other public or private posts prescribed by law.

Article 84

The President shall not be charged with a criminal offense during his tenure of office except for insurrection or treason.

Article 85

Matters pertaining to the status and courteous treatment of former Presidents shall be determined by law.

Section 2. The Executive Branch

Sub-Section 1. The Prime Minister and Members of the State Council

Article 86

(1) The Prime Minister shall be appointed by the President with the consent of the National Assembly.

(2) The Prime Minister shall assist the President and shall supervise, under order of the President, the Executive Ministries in their administration.

(3) No military personnel shall be appointed as Prime Minister unless he is retired from active service.

Article 87

(1) The members of the State Council shall be appointed by the President on the recommendation of the Prime Minister.

(2) The members of the State Council shall assist the President in the

conduct of State affairs and, as constituents of the State Council, shall deliberate on State affairs.

(3) The Prime Minister may recommend to the President the removal of a member of the State Council from office.

(4) No military personnel shall be appointed as a member of the State Council unless he is retired from active service.

Sub-Section 2. The State Council

Article 88

(1) The State Council shall deliberate on important policies that fall within the power of the Executive.

(2) The State Council shall be composed of the President, the Prime Minister, and members of the State Council, whose number shall be no more than thirty and no less than fifteen.

(3) The President shall be the chairman of the State Council, and the Prime Minister shall be the vice-chairman.

Article 89

The following matters shall be referred to the State Council for deliberation:

1. Basic plans for State affairs, and general policies of the Executive;
2. Declaration of war, conclusion of peace and other important matters pertaining to foreign policy;
3. Draft amendments to the Constitution, proposals for national referendums, proposed treaties, legislative bills, and proposed Presidential decrees;
4. Proposed budgets, closing of accounts, basic plan for disposal of State properties, contracts incurring financial obligation on the State, and other important financial matters;
5. Prompt decree, prompt financial or economic decree or measure, and proclaim and lift martial law of President;
6. Important military matters;
7. Requests for convening an extraordinary session of the National Assembly;
8. Awarding of honors;

9. Granting of amnesty, commutation and restoration of rights;
10. Matters pertaining to the determination of jurisdiction between Executive Ministries;
11. Basic plans concerning delegation or allocation of powers within the Executive;
12. Evaluation and analysis of the administration of State affairs;
13. Formulation and coordination of important policies of each Executive Ministry;
14. Action for the dissolution of a political party;
15. Examination of petitions pertaining to executive policies submitted or referred to the Executive;
16. Appointment of the Prosecutor General, the Chairman of the Joint Chiefs of Staff, the Chief of Staff of each armed service, the presidents of national universities, ambassadors, and such other public officials and managers of important state-run enterprises as designated by law; and
17. Other matters presented by the President, the Prime Minister or a member of the State Council.

Article 90

(1) A National Senior Advisory Council composed of elder statesmen, may be established to advise the President on important affairs of State.

(2) The immediate former President shall become the Chairman of the National Senior Advisory Council. In the absence of an immediate former President, the President shall appoint the Chairman.

(3) The organization, scope of function and other necessary matters pertaining to the National Senior Advisory Council shall be determined by law.

Article 92

(1) An Advisory Council on Democratic and Peaceful Unification may be established to advise the President on the formulation of peaceful unification policy.

(2) The organization, scope of function and other necessary matters pertaining to the Advisory Council on Democratic and Peaceful Unification shall be determined by law.

Article 93

(1) A National Economy Advisory Council may be established to advice the President on the formulation of important policy for the national economic development.

(2) The organization, scope of function and other necessary matters pertaining to the National Economy Advisory Council shall be determined by law.

Sub-Section 3. The Executive Ministries

Article 94

Heads of Executive Ministries shall be appointed by the President from among members of the State Council on the recommendation of the Prime Minister.

Article 95

The Prime Minister or the head of each Executive Ministry may, under the powers delegated by law or Presidential Decree, or *ex officio*, issue ordinances of the Prime Minister or the Executive Ministry concerning matters that are within their jurisdiction.

Article 96

The establishment, organization and the scope of function of each Executive Ministry shall be determined by law.

Sub-Section 4. The Board of Audit and Inspection

Article 97

The Board of Audit and Inspection shall be established under the President to audit the closing of accounts of revenues and expenditures, the accounts of the State and such organizations as prescribed by law, and to inspect the administrative functions of the executive agencies and public officials.

Article 98

(1) The Board of Audit and Inspection shall be composed of no less than five and no more than eleven commissioners, including the Chairman.

(2) The Chairman of the Board shall be appointed by the President with the consent of the National Assembly. The term of office of the Chairman shall be four years, and he may be reappointed only once.

(3) The commissioners of the Board shall be appointed by the President on the recommendation of the Chairman. The term of office of the commissioners shall be four years, and they may be reappointed only once.

Article 99

The Board of Audit and Inspection shall audit the closing of accounts of revenues and expenditures every year, and report the results to the President and the National Assembly in the following year.

Article 100

The organization and scope of functions of the Board, the qualifications of the commissioners of the Board, the range of the public officials subject to inspection and other necessary matters shall be determined by law.

CHAPTER 5. THE COURTS

Article 101

(1) Judicial power shall be vested in courts composed of judges.

(2) The courts shall consist of the Supreme Court, which is the highest court of the State, and other courts at specified levels.

(3) Qualifications for judges shall be determined by law.

Article 102

(1) Departments may be established in the Supreme Court.

(2) There shall be Supreme Court Justices at the Supreme Court. However, judges other than Supreme Court Justices may be assigned to the Supreme Court in accordance with the provisions of law.

(3) The organization of the Supreme Court and lower courts shall be determined by law.

Article 103

Judges shall judge independently according to their conscience and in conformity with the Constitution and law.

Article 104

(1) The Chief Justice of the Supreme Court shall be appointed by the President with the consent of the National Assembly.

(2) The Supreme Court Justices shall be appointed by the President on the recommendation of the Chief Justice with the consent of the National Assembly.

(3) Judges other than the Chief Justice and the Supreme Court Justice shall be appointed by the Chief Justice with the consent of the Conference of the Supreme Court Justices.

Article 105

(1) The term of office of the Chief Justice shall be six years and he shall not be reappointed.

(2) The term of office of the Supreme Court Justices shall be six years and they may be reappointed in accordance with the provisions of law.

(3) The term of office of judges other than the Chief Justice and the Supreme Court Justices shall be ten years and they may be reappointed in accordance with the provisions of law.

(4) The retirement age of judges shall be determined by law.

Article 106

(1) No judge shall be removed from office except by impeachment or sentence of imprisonment or more severe criminal punishment, nor shall he be suspended from office, have his salary reduced or suffer any other unfavorable treatment except by disciplinary action.

(2) In the event a judge is unable to discharge his official duties because of mental or physical impairment he may be removed from office in accordance with provisions of law.

Article 107

(1) When the constitutionality of a law is a prerequisite to a trial, the court shall request a decision of the Constitution Court, and shall judge according to the decision thereof.

(2) The Supreme Court shall have the power to make a final review of the constitutionality or legality of administrative decrees, regulations or dispositions, when their constitutionality or legality is a prerequisite to a trial.

(3) Administrative adjudication may be established as a procedure prior to a judicial trial. The procedure of administrative adjudication shall be determined by law and shall be in conformity with the principles of judicial procedures.

Article 108

The Supreme Court may establish, within the scope of law, regulations pertaining to judicial proceedings and internal rules and regulations on administrative matters of the court.

Article 109

Trials and decisions of the courts shall be open to the public. However, trials may be closed to the public by court decision when there is a danger that such trials may undermine the national security or disturb public safety and order, or be harmful to public morals.

Article 110

(1) Military court may be established as special courts to exercise jurisdiction over military trials.

(2) The Supreme Court shall have the final appellate jurisdiction over military court.

(3) The organization and authority of military court, and the qualifications of their judges shall be determined by law.

(4) Military trials under an extraordinary martial law may not be appealed in case of crimes of soldiers and employees of the military; military espionage; and crimes as defined by law in regard to sentinels, sentry-posts, supply of harmful food, and prisoners of war unless a capital punishment is sentenced.

CHAPTER 6. THE CONSTITUTION COURT

Article 111

(1) The Constitution Court shall have adjudications about the follow ing matters in charge:

1. The constitutionality of a law upon the request of the courts;

2. Impeachment;
3. Dissolution of a political party;
4. Conflict of jurisdiction between State organs, between State organ and local government, or between local governments;
5. Constitutional petition provided by law.

(2) The Constitution Court shall be composed of 9 adjudicators with qualification for a judge, and they shall be appointed by the President.

(3) Among the members referred to in Paragraph 2, three shall be appointed from persons selected by the National Assembly, and three appointed from persons nominated by the Chief Justice.

(4) The Chairman of the Constitution Court shall be appointed by the President from among the members with the consent of the National Assembly.

Article 112

(1) The term of office of the judges of the Constitution Court shall be six years and they may be reappointed in accordance with the provisions of law.

(2) The judges of the Constitution Court shall not join any political party, nor shall they participate in political activities.

(3) No judge of the Constitution Court shall be expelled from office except by impeachment or sentence of imprisonment or more severe criminal punishment.

Article 113

(1) When the Constitution Court makes a decision on the unconstitutionality of a law, impeachment, dissolution of political party or admission of constitutional petition, the concurrence of six members or more shall be required.

(2) The Constitution Court may establish, within the scope of law, regulations pertaining to adjudicational proceedings and internal rules and regulations on administrative matters of it.

(3) The organization, operation and other necessary matters of the Constitution Court shall be determined by law.

CHAPTER 7. ELECTION MANAGEMENT

Article 114

(1) Election Management Committees shall be established for the purpose of fair management of elections and national referendums, and dealing with affairs concerning political parties.

(2) The Central Election Management Committee shall be composed of three members appointed by the President, three members selected by the National Assembly, and three members nominated by the Chief Justice of the Supreme Court. The Chairman of the Committee shall be elected from among the members.

(3) The term of office of the members of the Committee shall be six years.

(4) The members of the Committee shall not join political parties, nor shall they participate in political activities.

(5) No member of the Committee shall be expelled from office except by impeachment or sentence of imprisonment and more severe punishment.

(6) The Central Election Management Committee may, within the limit of laws and decrees, establish regulations pertaining to the management of elections, national referendums, and matters concerning political parties, internal rules.

(7) The organization, scope of function and other necessary matters of the Election Management Committees at each level shall be determined by law.

Article 115

(1) Election Management Committees at each level may issue necessary instructions to administrative agencies concerned with respect to matters pertaining to elections such as the preparation of the voters and matters pertaining to national referendum.

(2) Administrative agencies concerned, upon receipt of such instructions, shall comply.

Article 116

(1) Election campaign should be conducted under the guidance of

each unit election maintenance committee as prescribed by the law and equal opportunity must be guaranteed.

(2) The expenses incurred in the preparation of the election should not be charged to the political parties or the candidates except as prescribed by the law.

CHAPTER 8. LOCAL AUTONOMY

Article 117

(1) Local governments shall deal with matters pertaining to the welfare of local residents, manage properties, and may establish,within the limit of laws and decrees, rules and regulations regarding local autonomy.

(2) The kinds of local government shall be determined by law.

Article 118

(1) A local government shall have a council.

(2) The organization and powers of local councils, and the election of members; the methods of election for heads of local government bodies; and other matters pertaining to the organization and operation of local government bodies shall be determined by law.

CHAPTER 9. THE ECONOMY

Article 119

(1) The economic order of the Republic of Korea shall be based on the principle of respect for freedom and creative ideas of the individual and enterprise in economic affairs.

(2) The State may regulate and coordinate economic affairs for the balanced growth and stabilization of national economy, maintenance of fair distribution of income, prevention of market domination and abuse of economic power, and the democratization of economy through the coordination between economic bodies.

Article 120

(1) Licenses to exploit, develop or utilize mines and all other important underground resources, marine resources, water power, and natural powers available for economic use may be granted for limited periods of time in accordance with the provisions of law.

(2) The land and natural resources shall be protected by the State, and the State shall establish a plan necessary for their balanced development and utilization.

Article 121

(1) The State shall endeavor to realize the land-to-the-tillers principle with respect to agricultural land. Tenant farming shall be prohibited.

(2) Leasing of farmland and the management of farmland on consignment to increase agricultural productivity or to be originated from unavoidable circumstances, shall be recognized in accordance with the provisions of law.

Article 122

In accordance with the provisions of law, the State may impose restrictions or obligations necessary for the efficient and balanced utilization, development and preservation of the land which is the basis of production and life of all citizens.

Article 123

(1) The State shall establish and put in force such necessary plans as comprehensive development of fishing and agrarian villages and support etc. to protect and upbring agriculture and fishery.

(2) The State shall have duty to foster local economy for balanced development of all regions.

(3) The State shall protect and foster the small and medium industries.

(4) The State shall protect the interest of farmers and fishermen by seeking price stabilization by endeavoring to achieve equilibrium of supply, demand and improvement of distribution structure.

(5) The State shall foster organization founded on the spirit of self-help among farmers, fishermen and businessmen engaged in small and medium industry and shall guarantee their autonomy and development.

Article 124

The State shall, in accordance with the provisions of law, guarantee the consumer protection movement intended to encourage sound consumption activities and to urge improvement in the quality of products.

Article 125

The State shall foster foreign trade, and may regulate and coordinate it.

Article 126

Private enterprises shall not be nationalized or transferred to public ownership, nor shall their management be controlled or administered by the State, except in cases determined by law to meet urgent necessities of national defense or national economy.

Article 127

(1) The State shall endeavor to develop national economy through the innovation of scientific technology and the development of information and human resources.

(2) The State shall establish a national standard.

(3) The President may establish an advisory body for the purpose referred to in Paragraph 1.

CHAPTER 10. AMENDMENTS TO THE CONSTITUTION

Article 128

(1) A proposal to amend the Constitution shall be made either by the President or by a majority of the members on the register of the National Assembly.

(2) Amendments to the Constitution for the extension of the term of office of the President or for a change allowing for the reelection of the President shall not be effective for the President in office at the time of the proposal for such amendment to the Constitution.

Article 129

Proposed amendments to the Constitution shall be put before the public by the President for twenty days or more.

Article 130

(1) The National Assembly shall decide upon the proposed amendments within sixty days of the public announcement, and passage by the National Assembly shall require the consent of two-thirds or more of the members on the register of the National Assembly.

(2) The proposed amendments to the Constitution shall be submitted to a national referendum not later than thirty days after passage by the National Assembly, and shall be determined by more than one-half of all votes cast by over one-half of the eligible votes in elections for members of the National Assembly.

(3) When the proposed amendments to the Constitution receive the consent prescribed in Paragraph 2, the amendments to the Constitution shall be finalized, and the President shall promulgate it without delay.

SUPPLEMENTARY PROVISIONS

Article 1

This Constitution shall enter into force from February 25, 1988. However, the preliminary arrangements such as the enactment or amendment of laws necessary for the enforcement of this Constitution, and the election of the President and the members of the National Assembly under this Constitution, may be allowed before the enforcement of this Constitution.

Article 2

(1) The first Presidential election under this Constitution shall be held forty days before the enforcement date of this Constitution.

(2) The term of office of the first President under this Constitution shall commence on the enforcement date of this Constitution.

Article 3

(1) The first National Assembly elections under this Constitution shall be held within six months from the promulgation date of this Constitution. The term of office of the members of the first National Assembly elected under this Constitution shall commence on the date of its first convening under this Constitution after the election.

(2) The term of office of the members of the National Assembly incumbent at the time this Constitution enters into force shall terminate on the previous day of the first convening date referred to in Paragraph 1.

Article 4

(1) Public officials and staffs of enterprise appointed by the Government incumbent at the time this Constitution enters into force shall be regarded as appointed under this Constitution. However, public officials whose election methods or appointing authorities are changed by this Constitution, the Chief Justice of the Supreme Court and the Chairman of the Board of Audit and Inspection, shall remain in office until such time as their successors are chosen under this Constitution, and their terms of office shall terminate the day before the installation of their successors.

(2) Judges attached to the Supreme Court who are not the Chief Justice or Justices of the Supreme Court and who are in office at the time of the enforcement of this Constitution shall be considered as having been appointed under this Constitution notwithstanding the proviso of Paragraph 1.

(3) Those provisions of this Constitution which prescribe the terms of office of public officials or which restrict the number of terms that public officials may serve take effect upon the dates of the first elections or the first appointments of such public officials under this Constitution.

Article 5

Laws, decrees, ordinances and treaties in force at the time this Constitution enters into force shall remain valid unless they contradict this Constitution.

Article 6

Organs incumbent at the time this Constitution enters into force, taking charge of the function which will belong to newly established one under this Constitution, shall continue to exist and carry out their function until the new organ will have been established under this Constitution.

INDEX

Subject Index

The Act Concerning the Establishment of School District, 756
Administration Council, 224, 286, 289, 338
administrative elites, 516-525
Agency for National Security and Planning, 201, 491, 443
Agitators of the City and County Party Committees, 749
Agreement on Reconciliation, Non-aggression, Exchanges and Cooperation, 713
agricultural south, 582
All Liberty League, 444
Allied Powers, 150-152
anti-communism, 153, 192, 193, 201-202, 424, 437, 490, 848
Anti-Communist Law, 443
Anti-Communist League, 444
anti-liberal, 402-404, 408, 410, 449, 850
anti-liberalism, 396, 398
Anti-monopoly Act, 599
anti-parliamentarian, 405-406, 449
anti-parliamentarianism, 396, 403, 463, 850
April Student Revolution of 1960, 197, 519
Aprok, 3, 5, 29, 45, 109, 371, 571
armed revolts, 55-59
Armistice Agreement, 698

arms race, 704, 711
Articles of Confederation, 819
artificial eternity, 679
ascription-oriented elite recruitment, 525
Asia-Pacific Economic Cooperation (APEC), 802
August Theses, 269, 365
autarchy, 588
authoritarian, 365, 834
authoritarian person, 843
authoritarian system, 404
authoritarian values, 495
authoritarianism, 394-398, 485, 834-847
avoidance-accommodation dilemma, 208

bangil [warding-off Japan], 199
banil [anti-Japanism], 199
Basic Law, 801
Berlin Wall, 812
Black Wave Society, 267-268
Bolshevism, 397, 563
bong, 482
bribery nexus, 476
Buddhism, 36, 479
bureaucratic authoritarianism, 415

Cabinet Decision Number, 770
cabinet-responsible system, 496
Capital City Military District Command, 443

Name Index